T0181115

Lecture Notes in Computer Science   12059

More information about this series at http://www.springer.com/series/7410

Joseph Bonneau · Nadia Heninger (Eds.)

Financial Cryptography and Data Security

24th International Conference, FC 2020
Kota Kinabalu, Malaysia, February 10–14, 2020
Revised Selected Papers

 Springer

Editors
Joseph Bonneau
New York University
New York City, NY, USA

Nadia Heninger
University of California
La Jolla, CA, USA

ISSN 0302-9743   ISSN 1611-3349   (electronic)
Lecture Notes in Computer Science
ISBN 978-3-030-51279-8   ISBN 978-3-030-51280-4   (eBook)
https://doi.org/10.1007/978-3-030-51280-4

LNCS Sublibrary: SL4 – Security and Cryptology

This Springer imprint is published by the registered company Springer Nature Switzerland AG
The registered company address is: Gewerbestrasse 11, 6330 Cham, Switzerland

Preface

The 24th International Conference on Financial Cryptography and Data Security (FC 2020), was held February 10–14, 2020, at the Shangri-La Tanjung Aru Resort in Kota Kinabalu, Sabah, Malaysia.

We received 162 paper submissions. Of these, 34 full papers and 2 short papers were accepted, a 22.2% acceptance rate. Revised papers appear in these proceedings.

We are grateful for the contributions of the 76 members of the Program Committee. The review process took place over approximately seven weeks in October and November 2019. An extensive online discussion phase was utilized to guide decisions. The review process was double-blind and carried out entirely online via the HotCRP review platform. All accepted submissions received at least three reviews. A total of 554 reviews were completed, an average of 3.6 per submitted paper. The Program Committee members provided thoughtful and constructive feedback on all papers, which considerably strengthened the quality of the final program. We are especially thankful to Program Committee members who served as shepherds for 11 of the 36 accepted papers which were accepted conditionally on specific improvements being completed. We also appreciate the reviews contributed by 27 external reviewers.

The community's interest in blockchain-based cryptocurrencies continued to grow and for the first year represented the majority of the program. As was done for the 2019 program, papers were submitted into one of two self-selected "tracks": traditional financial cryptography and blockchains. The Program Committee was composed of approximately equal proportions of reviewers for the two tracks. The final program contained 31 papers submitted as blockchain papers and only 5 submitted primarily as papers on traditional topics. Analysis completed after the peer review process found that this was partially a result of more papers being submitted on blockchain topics (over 75% of submissions) and these papers also receiving more positive reviews. However, the resulting program led to some controversy within the community. Discussion at the conference during the general meeting affirmed that nearly all members of the community would like to continue to see a balance of areas represented in the program. Several ideas were proposed for continuing to attract a scientifically diverse program on all areas of financial cryptography.

The program ran over four days. In addition to 20-minute presentations of all accepted papers, the program began with a keynote address from Allison Nixon, Chief Research Officer at Unit221B entitled "Fraudsters Taught Us that Identity is Broken." The keynote featured many interesting examples from industry on challenges with fraud in online payments and other systems. The program concluded with a panel discussion "Crypto engineering for the real world" organized by Ross Anderson and featuring Jean Camp, Peter Landrock, Allison Nixon, and Alex van Someren as panelists. A rump session was held on Tuesday evening featuring humorous talks and recent results.

The program was noticeably affected by the emerging Covid-19 pandemic (known simply as the novel coronavirus at the time of the conference). While there were no known cases in Bornean Malaysia at the time of the event, travel restrictions on China and Hong Kong went into effect before the conference began, which prevented a number of members of the community from attending in person. Attendance was estimated to be reduced by 10–20% as a result and seven presentations were conducted remotely via pre-recorded video with authors available by video conference to answer questions. The general consensus at the conference was that remote presentations went smoothly and there was enthusiasm for increasing opportunities for virtual attendance and presentation in future years. Fortunately, we are unaware of any attendees contracting the virus as a result of attending the conference.

Overall, feedback at the conference was overwhelmingly positive despite the pandemic and the location being far from the traditional Carribean region. We would like to thank Rafael Hirschfeld and Patrick McCorry for their service as conference general chairs, without whom the event would not have been possible especially in a logistically challenging year. We also thank the IFCA directors and Steering Committee for their service.

Finally, we would like to thank the sponsors of the conference for their generous support: our Platinum sponsors the Ethereum Foundation, Protocol Labs, and Tezos; our Gold sponsor Chainalysis; our Silver sponsors Calibra and IOHK; our sponsors in kind Blockstream, Indiana University, and Worldpay; as well as generous help and support from the Ministry of Tourism, Arts and Culture Malaysia and the Malaysia Convention and Exhibition Bureau.

May 2019   Joseph Bonneau
                                                                Nadia Heninger

Organization

General Chairs

Rafael Hirshfeld   Unipay Technologies, The Netherlands
Patrick McCorry   PISA Research, UK

Program Committee Chairs

Joseph Bonneau   New York University, USA
Nadia Heninger   University of California, Santa Cruz, USA

Steering Committee

Joseph Bonneau   New York University, USA
Rafael Hirshfeld   Unipay Technologies, The Netherlands
Andrew Miller   University of Illinois at Urbana-Champaign, USA
Monica Quaintance   Kadena, USA
Burton Rosenberg   University of Miami, USA

Program Committee

Ittai Abraham   VMware, Israel
Ross Anderson   University of Cambridge, UK
Elli Androulaki   IBM Research, Switzerland
Diego F. Aranha   Aarhus University, Denmark
Frederik Armknecht   University of Mannheim, Germany
Foteini Baldimtsi   George Mason University, USA
Shehar Bano   Calibra, UK
Iddo Bentov   Cornell Tech, USA
Alex Biryukov   University of Luxembourg, Luxembourg
Rainer Böhme   Universität Innsbruck, Austria
Nikita Borisov   University of Illinois at Urbana-Champaign, USA
Xavier Boyen   Queensland University of Technology, Australia
Benedikt Bunz   Stanford University, USA
Christian Cachin   University of Bern, Switzerland
Alvaro A. Cardenas   University of California, Santa Cruz, USA
Pern Hui Chia   Google, USA
Jeremy Clark   Concordia University, Canada
Shaanan Cohney   University of Pennsylvania, USA
George Danezis   Calibra, University College London, UK
Matteo Dell'Amico   Symantec Research Labs, USA
Benjamin Edwards   Cyentia Institute, USA

Vanessa Teague	University of Melbourne, Australia
Luke Valenta	Cloudflare, Inc., USA
Marie Vasek	University College London, UK
Madars Virza	MIT Media Lab, USA
Marko Vukolic	IBM Research, Switzerland
Nick Weaver	International Computer Science Institute, University of California, Berkeley, USA
Pieter Wuille	Blockstream, USA
Eric Wustrow	University of Colorado Boulder, USA
Aviv Zohar	The Hebrew University of Jerusalem, Israel

Additional Reviewers

Ambrona, Miguel
Bernau, Daniel
Boehler, Jonas
Bootle, Jonathan
Campanelli, Matteo
Dryja, Thaddeus
Eaton, Ted
Ersoy, Oguzhan
Fauzi, Prastudy
Fischer, Andreas
Fraser, Ashley
Fuhry, Benny
Kelkar, Mahimna

Krips, Toomas
Krupp, Johannes
Nizzardo, Luca
Prabhu Kumble, Satwik
Schanck, John
Siim, Janno
Slamanig, Daniel
Szepieniec, Alan
Tran, Muoi
Tueno, Anselme
Vesely, Noah
Weggenmann, Benjamin
Zajac, Michal

Contents

Smart Contracts

Attacks

Leveraging Bitcoin Testnet for Bidirectional Botnet Command and Control Systems

Federico Franzoni$^{(\boxtimes)}$ iD, Ivan Abellan iD, and Vanesa Daza iD

Universitat Pompeu Fabra, Barcelona, Spain
{federico.franzoni,vanesa.daza}@upf.edu, iabellan@pm.me

Abstract. Over the past twenty years, the number of devices connected to the Internet grew exponentially. Botnets benefited from this rise to increase their size and the magnitude of their attacks. However, they still have a weak point in their Command & Control (C&C) system, which is often based on centralized services or require a complex infrastructure to keep operating without being taken down by authorities. The recent spread of blockchain technologies may give botnets a powerful tool to make them very hard to disrupt. Recent research showed how it is possible to embed C&C messages in Bitcoin transactions, making them nearly impossible to block. Nevertheless, transactions have a cost and allow very limited amounts of data to be transmitted. Because of that, only messages from the botmaster to the bots are sent via Bitcoin, while bots are assumed to communicate through external channels. Furthermore, for the same reason, Bitcoin-based messages are sent in clear. In this paper we show how, using Bitcoin Testnet, it is possible to overcome these limitations and implement a cost-free, bidirectional, and encrypted C&C channel between the botmaster and the bots. We propose a communication protocol and analyze its viability in real life. Our results show that this approach would enable a botmaster to build a robust and hard-to-disrupt C&C system at virtually no cost, thus representing a realistic threat for which countermeasures should be devised.

Keywords: Blockchain · Bitcoin · Security · Botnets · C&C

1 Introduction

A botnets is a network of infected devices, called *bots*, collectively controlled by a single actor, called the *botmaster*. Botnets have been a major threat on the Internet for a long time, being used for a variety of malicious activities,

F. Franzoni—The work of this author is partly supported by the Spanish Ministry of Economy and Competitiveness under the Maria de Maeztu Units of Excellence Programme (MDM-2015-0502).

V. Daza—This author was supported by Project RTI2018-102112-B-I00 (AEI/FEDER, UE).

© International Financial Cryptography Association 2020
J. Bonneau and N. Heninger (Eds.): FC 2020, LNCS 12059, pp. 3–19, 2020.
https://doi.org/10.1007/978-3-030-51280-4_1

like spamming, credentials stealing, and Distributed Denial of Service (DDoS) attacks [17]. A lot of research has been done to help detect and disrupt such activities on the web [12]. However, the frequency and magnitude of botnet attacks drastically increased in the past few years, due to the massive adoption of computing devices and the advent of the Internet of Things (IoT), which is connecting millions of insecure devices to the web [7]. Recent attacks from the infamous Mirai botnet [4], showed the potential of this threat, with DDoS attacks of up to 1.1 Tbps [15].

Meanwhile, blockchain is also becoming increasingly adopted as a tool for building distributed systems where different parties are able to exchange assets and data in a trustworthy manner [24]. Recent research showed how blockchains can be leveraged to implement the command and control (C&C) system of a botnet [2,13]. In fact, using public blockchains, like Bitcoin, as the communication channel has several advantages for a botnet. First of all, they come with the strengths of all distributed networks, such as robustness and efficiency. Secondly, they are not regulated by any authority, making them censorship-resistant, meaning that no specific content or user can be banned. Furthermore, they privilege privacy, by making use of pseudonyms and hindering the association between a transaction and the device that generated it. As such, although possible [9,16], it is not trivial to identify nodes participating in a botnet, and even more importantly, to identify the botmaster. All such properties are ideal for a botnet [27], as they allow to operate, protected, over a long period of time, with virtually no risk of having communications disrupted.

Most state-of-the-art research proposes Bitcoin transactions as the main C&C vector, following different strategies to embed commands from the botmaster. However, these proposals have important limitations. First of all, they only cover communications from the botmaster, delegating replies form the bots to external channels, typically employing a web server. Furthermore, messages are very limited in size and are sent in clear, as cryptography is only implemented on the external channel. Finally, messages have a cost, since they are sent via transactions. All these limitations make this approach seem impractical or inconvenient for a real-world botnet implementation.

In this paper, we show it is possible to overcome such limitations by leveraging the Testnet network, instead of Mainnet. We propose a bidirectional communication protocol that implements encryption and allows bigger amounts of data to be exchanged. To the best of our knowledge, this is the first paper to study bidirectional C&C communications on top of Bitcoin. Our approach makes a fully-blockchain-based botnet implementation both practical and economical.

Organization of the Paper. The rest of the paper is organized as follows. Section 2 describes the necessary background topics, that is Botnet C&C and Bitcoin. Section 3 covers previous research work and discuss its limitations. In Sect. 4, we show the advantages of using Testnet as the C&C channel. In Sect. 5, we describe our communication protocol design and in Sect. 6 we show our experimental results. Section 7 analyzes the viability and robustness of our proposal. Section 8 concludes the paper and discuss future work.

2 Background

2.1 Botnet C&C Communication

In order for a botnet to operate, a communication channel is needed between botmaster and bots. The infrastructure used for that purpose is known as the Command & Control (C&C) system. This is a crucial component for a botnet, as it is the only means to keep control over the bots. As such, it is has to be designed carefully, in order to avoid being disrupted. In other words, the C&C system should allow controlling the botnet as long as possible, providing stealthy and efficient communication between botmaster and bots.

Strategies to implement C&C changed over the years, following the evolution of available technologies and the ability of authorities to counter existing approaches [20]. First-generation botnets leverage hardcoded Internet Relay Chat (IRC) channels, where bots connect to receive instructions from the botmaster. This system is simple and cheap but is also easy to detect and take down [1,8]. Second-generation botnets make use of HTTP, with hardcoded web domains, periodically contacted by the bots to download instructions. This approach allows to effectively blend messages into legitimate Internet traffic. Nonetheless, effective techniques exist to detect botnet communications [14,18], allowing to quickly shutdown malicious domains [29].

Early botnets relied on a client-server model, thus having a central point of failure, which can always be detected and shut down by the authorities. Last generation botnets overcome this issue by adopting a P2P model. Bots and C&C server connect as peers to the same network, making it difficult to distinguish the source of the commands [28]. This architecture makes the botnet much more robust and hard to shut down. Nonetheless, it is still possible to detect P2P-botnet traffic using advanced techniques [22,25]. Moreover, to join the network, bots need hardcoded addresses, which can be easily blocked by authorities if detected. Modern botnets tend to use a mix of techniques, such as P2P network with HTTP C&C server, or leverage cloud-based services and social media as rendezvous points [20]. Although these services are easy to setup and access, providers can promptly block any detected malicious account.

2.2 Bitcoin

Bitcoin is a digital payment system released in 2009. Participating actors are identified by alphanumeric strings called *addresses*. Each address represents the public part of an (asymmetric) cryptographic key pair, whose private part is used by the owner to sign transactions. When a coin is sent to a specific address, only the owner of the corresponding private key can spend it. Transactions are validated by nodes of a P2P network that cooperate to maintain a distributed ledger, structured as a chain of blocks (or *blockchain*). Each block contains a set of valid transactions and is linked to the previous one by including its hash. Blocks are concurrently created by special nodes called *miners*, which compute the solution of a cryptographic puzzle over the transactions of the new block.

This solution is known as *Proof of Work* (PoW) and is included in the block itself. Transactions and blocks are validated and distributed by all the peers of the network. To decide on conflicting versions of the ledger, peers always choose the longest chain they know, that is the one with the biggest PoW. By following this scheme, the ledger is considered to be immutable and able to avoid *double spending* the same coin [23].

OP_RETURN. Since 2014, it is possible to embed a small amount of data inside a transaction, using the OP_RETURN opcode [30]. This possibility was introduced to discourage other wasteful methods of embedding data, such as using non-existing transaction output addresses. The new opcode allows adding a non-spendable output, which carries up to 80 bytes of arbitrary data. OP_RETURN is often used to implement asset exchange protocols on top of Bitcoin or to add valuable data in the blockchain [6].

Testnet. As other public blockchains, Bitcoin provides a separate network for developers to test their applications, known as Testnet [31]. While running the same protocol as the main network (Mainnet), Testnet has some important differences. First of all, Testnet coins (tBTC) have no real value, and can be easily obtained via online services called *faucets*. Secondly, the mining difficulty is also set to a lower value than Mainnet, making the blockchain grow faster. Finally, some restrictions are ignored to allow developers to test edge cases. In particular, non-standard transactions are allowed, thus being relayed and mined by the network. We will see how these and other characteristics significantly help implementing a botnet C&C.

Bitcoin Nodes. There are two main options to access the Bitcoin blockchain: full nodes and Simple Payment Verification (SPV) nodes. Full nodes are the building blocks of the P2P network. They validate all transactions and blocks, and relaying them to their peers. This is the most secure way to use Bitcoin, but requires to download the whole blockchain, which can be very resource-consuming. SPV nodes, like full nodes, receive and relay all transactions, but do not download the whole blockchain. Instead, they only download block headers and rely on other peers to retrieve the blocks they need to validate transactions of interest. This make the node suitable for resource-constrained devices at the expense of a certain level of trust into other peers. Thanks to their better performances, SPV nodes are today the most popular choice on Bitcoin [26].

3   Related Work

ZombieCoin [2] was the first paper to propose Bitcoin as a means for C&C communications. Bots embed the botmaster public key and decode transactions coming from the corresponding address. To embed commands, the OP_RETURN opcode is used, which allows to carry up to 80 bytes of data. In [3] the same authors propose enhancements such as *transaction-chaining* to embed longer messages and external upstream communication by means of periodical *rendezvous-point* announcements. The main limitations of this proposal are the server-based upstream communication and the cost of messages sent on the blockchain. The authors claim that it would be impractical and economically prohibitive to implement upstream communication on top of the blockchain. We show that this is not true when leveraging Testnet.

ChainChannels [13] proposes a more generic approach, which can be used on different blockchains as it does not leverage Bitcoin-specific features. The authors describe a method to insert hidden data into transaction signature, which can be later decoded with the private key used for the signature. For this purpose, the authors propose a key-leakage scheme that allows bots to decipher messages at a later time. This is a very portable approach, since virtually all blockchains employ digitally-signed transactions with a compatible signature scheme. Nonetheless, this approach suffers from the same limitations as ZombieCoin: messages are costly and limited in size; communication is unidirectional and unencrypted. Furthermore, bots can only decrypt messages in a second moment, assuming they execute commands altogether after these have been issued, something that might not be realistic.

In [5], the authors propose an approach based on *Whisper*, a communication protocol that runs on top of the Ethereum network. This approach does not use transactions and thus has no cost. It also provides a good level of privacy and allows for two-way communication. Moreover, as messages are not in transactions, they are not added to the blockchain, making their backward analysis harder. However, Whisper, which is still in a PoC stage, it is not enabled by default on the standard Ethereum client (geth) and there are no known statistics about how many nodes currently run the protocol. Consequently, its reliability is unknown, making it unlikely to be actually used by a botnet as of today.

4 Leveraging the Testnet Network

As explained in Sect. 2, Bitcoin Testnet follows the same protocol as the Mainnet but has some important differences. In particular:

- Testnet coins have no value in real life. For this reason, they can be easily obtained for free through online services called *faucets* [31].
- Mining is much easier, since the PoW difficulty is set to a lower value. As a consequence, unlike Mainnet, it is feasible to run a solo miner [19] to earn coins.
- The Testnet network and blockchain are about ten times smaller than Mainnet [11]. This makes clients synchronize faster and consume less resources.
- Non-standard transactions are validated and relayed by the network. This feature enables the following characteristics:
  - OP_RETURN can be bigger than 80 bytes. In fact, there is no explicit limit to the amount of data that can be actually embedded;
  - Transactions can have multiple outputs with the same address as well as multiple OP_RETURNs;

- Transaction outputs can be below the dust limit[1];
- Transaction size can be greater than the maximum (which is around 100 kB).

All these properties give numerous benefits for the implementation of a botnet. First of all, the botmaster can easily obtain the necessary amount of coins to run its botnet, either by using faucets or running a miner. Secondly, the reduced size of Testnet blockchain and network make bots less resource-demanding, allowing them to hinder detection and even to run on low-resource devices. Finally, non-standard transactions give the ability to send bigger and more complex messages.

These features allow overcoming all the main drawbacks of previous Bitcoin-based proposals: botnet communications have no cost thanks to the fact that Testnet coins have no real value; bidirectional communication can be implemented thanks to the great number of coins that can be obtained for free; encryption can be implemented thanks to the larger amount of data that can be embedded in each transaction.

5   Botnet Design

In this section, we propose a viable communication protocol for Testnet, based on non-standard transactions, that provides a bidirectional and encrypted C&C channel at zero cost.

As in previous works, we assume there exist an infection mechanism that takes control of devices and downloads the bot client. The botnet is composed by a C&C server node, directly controlled by the botmaster, and a number of bot nodes. We assume the C&C server is not resource-constrained and runs a full node. On the other side, bots run an SPV node to consume less resources and hinder detection.

In the rest of this section, we explain how the communication works (transactions, fees and encryption) and describe the different phases of the protocol (registration, commands and responses).

5.1   Communication

All communications between the botmaster and the bots happen through transactions.

Data Embedding and Fees. We use OP_RETURN outputs to embed messages inside transactions. As previously mentioned, this operator has no explicit limits of size on Testnet. As such, the amount of data that can be embedded is only limited by the maximum size of a transaction, which, again, is not explicitly

---

[1] On Bitcoin, it is considered *dust* any output smaller than the amount needed to spend that output. Hence its value actually depends on the transaction size, but its minimum is usually considered to be 546 satoshis.

limited on Testnet. This makes the theoretical size limit bound by the size of a block (around 1 MB). However, a practical limit to this amount is given by the minimum fee needed to have the transaction relayed by other peers. This value is known as the *minimum relay fee* (MRF). MRF does not differ between Mainnet and Testnet and is proportional to the size of the transaction itself. This means that, although sending very large messages is possible, this can be excessively expensive in terms of fees. We will see more details about MRF later in Sects. 6 and 7.

In our protocol, all transactions spend a fee equivalent to the corresponding MRF. To this respect, it is important to notice that using low fees might make the transaction mined later. However, from the botnet perspective, it is not important if and when messages are added to the blockchain, but only if they travel across the network and reach the C&C server.

Encryption and Authentication. In order to protect communications, we use encryption in both directions. To obtain the best compromise between security and efficiency, we make use of an hybrid approach.

We assume the botmaster creates an asymmetric key pair, called *botmaster keys* before the creation of the botnet and hardcode bots with the public key. This key pair is completely unrelated to the address used to send commands, which in fact, can change at every message. Additionally, a symmetric key is also embedded in the bots, called *botnet key*.

For the sake of clarity, we distinguish between *downlink* encryption, used from the botmaster to the bots, and *uplink* encryption, used by the bots to communicate with the botmaster.

Downlink encryption works this way: when the botmaster wants to send a command, it encrypts it with the botnet key and signs it with its private key; when bots receive a transaction with an OP_RETURN, they check the signature using the botmaster public key. If the signature is valid, they decrypt the message with the botnet key and execute the command. This scheme allows the bots to recognize transactions from the botmaster even without knowing its address. Moreover, thanks to the signature, bots are assured about the authenticity of the source.

For uplink encryption, each bot creates a private symmetric key, called the *bot key*, which is sent to the botmaster at the time of registration, encrypted with the botmaster public key. When sending messages, bots encrypt data with their bot key. Furthermore, bots use a new address for each message, which corresponds to the change address of the previous transaction. In order to recognize and decrypt bots messages, the botmaster keeps track of the current address of each bot and the corresponding encryption key.

Transactions. We have the following types of transactions: *quotas, registrations, fundings,* and *messages*. Quotas have one input and several outputs (the quotas), which are used as input for the registration transactions. Registration transactions have one input (a quota) and one OP_RETURN output. The quota equals the MRF for the registration message, so no change output is required. Funding transactions have one input and one output, which equals the input value minus the MRF. Messages (commands and responses) always have two outputs, one with the OP_RETURN carrying the message and the other sending the change (minus the MRF) to another address belonging to the sender (i.e. the *change address*).

5.2 Bot Registration

When a new bot joins the network, the first thing it needs is to get some funds to send transactions. As the bot cannot obtain funds autonomously (like the botmaster does), it needs to ask the botmaster to provide some. However, at the same time, the botmaster needs to know the address of the bot in order to send such funds.

We solve this problem by having all bots sharing a common private key, that gives access to all transactions of an address called the *shared account*. The botmaster periodically puts funds on the account, while new bots use such funds to register to the botnet. They do so by sending a *registration message* which contains their own address and encryption key. Since SPV clients do not store the UTXO set (the set of unspent transactions), they ask their peers about any available fund on the account. The botmaster monitors transactions sent from the shared account and when it detects one, it stores the information about the new bot and sends it some funds. After the registration, bots will only receive funds directly from the botmaster.

If more bots try to register at the same time, there might be a conflict between their transactions (i.e. a double spend). In order to minimize this risk, the botmaster puts on the account several transactions, called *quotas*, containing just the right amount of coins needed to send the registration message. Furthermore, to reduce concurrency, it always sends multiple quotas at the same time. When a new bot wants to register, it picks a random quota and tries to send the message. It then sets a timeout for receiving the funding from the botmaster. If the timeout expires, the bot picks another quota and repeats the process. The same happens if its transaction gets rejected by peers or if another transaction spending the same quota is detected. At any time, the botmaster makes sure there are enough quotas on the shared account, according to the rate at which new bots are joining.

Since the registration transaction comes from a shared account and only has an OP_RETURN output, neither the botmaster address nor the bot one are revealed.

It is worth noting that creating quotas would not be possible on Mainnet, as they would be considered as dust outputs and rejected by the network.

5.3 Commands and Responses

We distinguish between commands, that are messages sent by the botmaster, and responses, that bots send after executing a command. Bots can execute three types of commands: *hardcoded, shell* and *script*.

Hardcoded commands are functions that are already implemented by the bot code. They can be executed once or repeated over a period of time. Examples of hardcoded commands include a DoS function to attack a target or a keylogger to steal credentials. The botmaster can send parameters such as interval and number of iterations, or make the function run indefinitely until it sends a stop command.

Shell commands are command-line instructions that the bot directly execute on the infected machine. When the bot receives such command, it runs it and converts the output into a hexadecimal string to be sent as a response.

Script commands work similarly, but they use code stored on the blockchain. In particular, the code to execute is embedded by the botmaster in a previous transaction, called *script transaction*, and encrypted with a symmetric key, which is unknown to the bots. The command includes the transaction ID of the script transaction and the key to decrypt. When bots receive these commands, they retrieve the data, decrypt the payload and execute the code. They then convert the output into a hexadecimal string and send it the botmaster. In order to ensure all bots can send their response, the botmaster checks current funds of each bot before sending the command. If any bot does not have sufficient funds, the botmaster sends them more coins.

This approach takes advantage of the larger storage capacity of transactions on Testnet, which allow storing kilobytes of code on the blockchain. Additionally, this technique enables the botmaster to reuse the same code several times, saving coins and reducing its traffic. By using shell and script commands, bots are not limited to the functions their code implements, but are able to perform a variety of attacks, making it harder to estimate their real capacity.

6 Experimental Results

We created a PoC botnet that implements our protocol, and then, we simulated its basic activities. In particular, we verified the ability to send, receive, execute and reply to commands. We then calculated the necessary amounts of coins needed for each type of transaction we use. Our results show that the proposed protocol is both viable and sustainable.

6.1 Non-standard Transactions and Fees

As a preliminary step, we verified the ability to send non-standard transactions on the network. We also tested the limits we could reach while still having transactions relayed.

As stated in Sect. 4, non-standard transactions allow us to do the following:

- send OP_RETURN outputs that are larger than 80 bytes,
- send repeated outputs, both OP_RETURN and addresses,
- send dust outputs,
- send transactions larger than 100 kB.

We used Bitcoin Core v0.18.0 to perform our tests. We had to patch its code to allow creating transactions with repeated outputs (OP_RETURN or address). All other tests were possible without any modification.

For what concerns OP_RETURN size, we successfully sent transactions carrying as much as 50 kB of data. All transactions got immediately relayed and, after some time, mined. Although theoretically possible to send more, we were not able to send transactions carrying more data due to a limitation on the size of the argument that can be passed through the Linux command line[2]. As such we were not able to verify the ability to send transactions bigger than 100 kB. However, we are confident this is actually possible, as this limit is not enforced for non-standard transactions.

Transactions with repeated outputs, both addresses and OP_RETURN, were also accepted and relayed by all peers.

For what concerns dust outputs, we successfully sent transactions with as little as 0 satoshis, having them relayed and mined.

6.2   PoC

We implemented the C&C server with our patched version of Bitcoin Core, while bots run an SPV node using `bitcoinj`, which did not need any modification to use our protocol. Both bots and the C&C server run on a Linux operating system.

Encryption. For asymmetric encryption and digital signature, we use RSA with a 2048-bit key and OAEP padding, which generates outputs of 256 bytes. This allows bots to send up to 214 bytes of encrypted data to the botmaster.

For symmetric encryption we use AES with 256-bit keys, using CRC block mode and PKCS5 padding. This encryption mode requires a random 128-bit IV (Initialization Vector), which is also needed for decryption. As the IV does not need to be secret, we send it in clear along with the cyphertext.

Fees. The default MRF value on Bitcoin Core clients is set to a value of 1000 satoshis (sats) per kB. However, with the introduction of the so-called Segregated Witness (BIP141), transaction fees became dependent on what is known as virtual size, which is a function of the actual transaction size[3]. More specifically, the current MRF is calculated as 1 sat/vB, where vB stands for *virtual Byte*.

In our implementation, we make use of the embedded functions of the clients to calculate this value for each transaction.

---

[2] This is a known limitation of the Linux kernel; the actual argument size limit depends on the stack size of the system [21].

[3] The virtual size v is computed as $v=(w+3*s)/4$, where w is the size of the transaction and s is the size of the corresponding base transaction (without the witness). In case of non-SegWit transaction, the virtual size is the actual size.

Transactions. As stated in Sect. 5, we have the following types of transaction: quotas, registration, fundings, commands and responses. All transactions in our protocol have only one input.

Quotas transactions have 11 outputs, corresponding to batches of 10 quotas plus the change address. Each quota corresponds to the MRF of a registration message.

Registration messages have a quota as the input and 1 OP-RETURN output containing the payload. The payload contains a 36-byte-long Testnet address and a 32-byte-long AES key, encrypted with the public RSA key of the botmaster, which generates an output of 256 bytes.

Fundings contain two outputs: the bot address, receiving the funds, and the change address of the botmaster.

Commands and responses have 1 OP-RETURN output, plus the change address of the sender. Hardcoded commands have 3 bytes for the command plus the arguments (e.g. a target). The payload is encrypted with AES, so their output size corresponds to the size of the payload, padded to fit the block size (16 bytes), plus the IV (16 bytes). So, for example, an instruction like dos www.domain.com, which is 19-byte long, will have a data output of 32 bytes. Adding the IV we have 48 bytes. The script command has the following format: scr TXID KEY, where TXID is a 32-byte-long transaction ID and the key is a 32-byte AES key. The corresponding IV is stored alongside the script itself.

Commands. We implemented the following commands: *dos* and *stop* as hardcoded commands, *lshw* as shell command, and one script command called *screenshot*. After executing shell and script commands, bots convert the output to a hex string and send it as a response message. To convert outputs into hex they use the following command: $(CMD) | tr -d '\n' | xxd -r -p, where CMD stands for the command they are executing. The dos command makes the bot attack a specific target, which is sent as a parameter. The DoS attack is performed using hping3 and can be interrupted by a stop command. This command has no output. The lshw shell instruction makes the bot gather information about the hardware of the infected machine. On our bot machine, this command generates approximately 12 kB of data. The *screenshot* script is shown in Listing 1.1.

This script takes a screenshot in PNG format, which is around 500 kB, then compress it to JPEG format, reducing its quality to fit into 50 kB of data. The cat command dumps the content of the file to produce the output to send as a response.

```
import −window root screenshot.png
convert −quality 5 screenshot.png screenshot.jpg
cat screenshot.jpg
```

Listing 1.1. The *screenshot* script

7 Discussion

In this section, we analyze the sustainability of our protocol in terms of the amount of coins needed to run a botnet, as well as the robustness of its architecture and the security of its design.

7.1 Cost Analysis

Funding the Botnet. At the time of writing, we were able to find six active faucets on the web. The amount of coins obtained per request varies from 0.0001 to 0.089 tBTC, with an average of 0.05 tBTC per request. By making a single request per faucet, we obtained approximately 0.12 tBTC. Requests are usually limited by faucets to one per day, for each given IP address. However, it is not hard to bypass the limit by using VPNs or proxy services. Furthermore, as previously discussed, a botmaster could run a miner to obtain a much greater amount of coins, without any restriction.

As such, we consider the estimate of 0.1 tBTC per day as a conservative lower bound of the funds that a botmaster can obtain to operate its botnet. In a real-life context, it is likely feasible to obtain ten to hundred times more than such an amount.

Protocol Messages Cost. As discussed in Sect. 5, all messages sent by the botnet spend the minimum relay fee (MRF), which is directly proportional to the size of the message and calculated as 1 satoshi per virtual byte.

In our protocol, transactions can have a fixed size, like quotas, registrations, and fundings, or variable size, like commands, responses, and scripts. Table 1 shows the MRFs for all transactions used in our protocol. For a quota batch transaction, which has 11 outputs, a MRF of 454 sats is needed. Registration transactions have a payload of 256-byte long, corresponding to a MRF of 373 sats. Fundings, which have 2 outputs, can be sent with 166 sats. Commands payload size is the smallest multiple of the AES block size (16 bytes), plus the IV (16 bytes). To simplify things, we assume hardcoded commands are short enough to fit into 2 blocks (32 bytes), which adds up to 48 bytes, with the addition of the IV. To send such a transaction, a fee of 161 sats is needed. We also assume shell commands are smaller than 100 bytes, with bigger instruction sent as scripts. Since the minimum size is 17 bytes (1-byte command plus the IV), the MRF varies from 133 to 230 sats. Script commands have a 3-byte command plus a 32-byte transaction ID, a 32-byte script encryption key and the IV. This sums up to 83 bytes, requiring a MRF of 197 sat. We assume the maximum size of script transactions and responses is 50 kB. For what concerns our non-hardcoded commands, we have the following values. The encrypted screenshot script, along with the IV, is 128-byte long, corresponding to a MRF of 242 sats. To send the response (50 kB), 51349 sats were needed. To send the output of lswh (12 kB), 12860 sats were needed.

Table 1. Minimum relay fees for our protocol transactions

Message	OP_RETURN (Bytes)	Fee (Satoshis)
Quotas Batch	N/A	454
Registration (quota)	256	373
Funding	N/A	166
Hardcoded Command	48	161
Shell Command	17–116	133–230
Script Command	83	197
Script (Transaction)	117–51200	231–51349
Response	17–51200	133–51349

Running the Botnet. To have 1000 bots registered, 100 quota batches are needed, corresponding to 373000 sats. Considering the fees for the batch transactions (45400 sats), this sums up to 418400 sats (0.004184 tBTC), which is then the amount required to register 1000 bots. To fund the same number of bots, assuming an initial funding of 0.0001 tBTC each, and considering fees for the funding transactions (166000 sats), we have a total of 0.10166 tBTC. This means that 0.1 tBTC (our estimated lower bound) are enough to register and fund 1000 bots per day.

For what concerns daily operations, assuming a specific behaviour is hard, as C&C communications for real botnets can be very diverse. As such we will focus on the number of bytes that can be sent per day by a 1000-bot botnet, assuming it is funded with 0.1 tBTC per day. To simplify things, we assume 1 sat is needed to send 1 byte of data. This way, 0.1 tBTC is enough to send around 10MB per day, which translates to 10 kB per bot in our example, which is likely to be insufficient for a modern botnet, according to available statistics [10].

However, by analyzing the Testnet blockchain, it is easy to see that a solo miner could obtain an average budget of as much as 4 tBTC per day, which would allow the botmaster to run, for instance, a spamming botnet, or to use this channel as a component of a larger hybrid botnet.

7.2   Architecture Analysis

Testnet. Despite being a testing network, Testnet is a very solid blockchain, as it constitutes a fundamental component of the Bitcoin ecosystem. In fact, it allows developers to test changes to the protocol and new applications without wasting money or messing the real chain. Specifically, being released in 2012, the current version of the network (Testnet3) is one of the longest-running blockchains in the wild. Although a new version might be introduced, this would affect a lot of ongoing projects and protocol improvements development, making it unlikely to happen soon. As such, Testnet is a very stable backbone for a botnet C&C system.

A possible drawback of leveraging Testnet for a botnet might be its reduced network size, as fewer nodes might ease detection. However, the botmaster could mitigate this by deploying more nodes.

Faucets. Faucets are a vital service for Testnet, as they allow developers to easily obtain the coins they need tu run their tests. In their absence, developers would need to run a miner, making their job both harder and more expensive. As such, it is unlikely that such services will cease to work.

Bandwidth. Despite the use of non-standard transactions in our protocol allows transmitting bigger amounts of data, message size is still limited compared to the traditional client-server model. However, this system gains in terms of robustness, as communications are very hard to disrupt.

Given the above, it is possible that a real botnet would adopt a hybrid approach, with commands and responses happening on the blockchain, and larger data transmission being sent to a server, whose address changes periodically and gets updated via transactions.

7.3 Security

Stealthiness. As communications happen via transactions, botnet messages will be permanently stored on the blockchain, creating an accessible evidence of past botnet activities and facilitating their analysis. Furthermore, the use of non-standard transactions makes it easier to recognize botnet messages. To mitigate this risk, the botmaster can limit their usage to only a part of the communications, trying to make other messages more similar to regular transactions.

Encryption. All communications in our protocol are encrypted. However, if a bot is compromised, the adversary can learn both the botmaster public key and the botnet key, enabling the monitoring of all the messages coming from the botmaster. While this can help fighting the botnet activities, it does not prevent other bots from receiving and executing commands, thus being irrelevant to their operation.

To prevent this risk, the botmaster could encrypt and send messages individually for each bot. This would make the protocol more expensive and less scalable but it might still be feasible if the botmaster were able to obtain coins at a fast rate.

Shared Account. In case a bot is compromised an adversary can also learn the private key of the shared account and try to drain all the funds, preventing new bots from registering.

A possible solution for the botmaster would be to employ a backup registration system, such as an external channel where new bots can post their encrypted registration message. To avoid disruption, the botmaster can regularly change it and communicate the updated info via transaction[4].

---

[4] Note that bots are able to receive messages from the botmaster regardless of their registration status.

Another way the adversary can steal funds is to register fake bots to get the corresponding coins sent by the botmaster. This would increase the cost of the botnet and possibly make it infeasible to sustain. The botmaster, however, can monitor and test bots to detect and ban misbehaving ones. As an additional precaution, the botmaster could initially send a smaller amount of coins, and only send more if the bot behaves as expected.

Another issue, related to the shared account, is that it allows to compute the size of the botnet in terms of spent quotas. To mitigate this risk, the botmaster could periodically spend quotas at a random rate. Although this would make the system slightly more expensive, it would effectively conceal the real number of bot registrations.

Countermeasures. As mentioned above, the non-standard nature of the transactions used in our protocol allows to detect many of the botnet messages. Additionally, if a bot is compromised, it is possible to monitor and decrypt all messages from the botmaster. Furthermore, new bots can be prevented (or at least hindered) from registering.

Nonetheless, blocking botnet communications is hard as they are embedded into valid transactions. If a botnet is detected, messages coming from the botmaster could be prevented from spreading. However, this would be in sheer contrast with the anti-censorship principle at the base of the Bitcoin blockchain.

The most effective way to limit botnet communications would be to disallow non-standard transactions. However, it is unclear how this would affect the regular operations of Bitcoin developers.

8   Conclusion and Future Work

In this paper, we showed how it is possible to implement a bidirectional encrypted C&C communication system on top of Bitcoin Testnet, which is both practical and economically affordable. We described a viable protocol that allows to register, fund, and control bots. Communications between bots and botmaster are encrypted and allow exchanging large amounts of data, enabling advanced functionalities, such as outsourcing bots code to the blockchain. According to our estimates and experimental results, this system could be used in real life to run a small spamming botnet or as a component for larger hybrid botnet architectures.

This should call for an effort in either limiting the possibility of misusing Bitcoin Testnet for malicious purposes or devising appropriate countermeasures.

Future work includes a characterization of the communication patterns should be done to help designing effective detection mechanisms, as well as an analysis of strengths and weaknesses of this kind of botnet protocols, along with a study of valid alternatives. Finally, an estimation of the impact that such malicious activities might have on the network could help to evaluate undesired side effects.

References

1. Abu Rajab, M., Zarfoss, J., Monrose, F., Terzis, A.: A multifaceted approach to understanding the botnet phenomenon. In: Proceedings of the 6th ACM SIGCOMM Conference on Internet Measurement, IMC 2006, pp. 41–52. ACM, New York (2006). https://doi.org/10.1145/1177080.1177086. http://doi.acm.org/10.1145/1177080.1177086
2. Ali, S.T., McCorry, P., Lee, P.H.-J., Hao, F.: ZombieCoin: powering next-generation botnets with bitcoin. In: Brenner, M., Christin, N., Johnson, B., Rohloff, K. (eds.) FC 2015. LNCS, vol. 8976, pp. 34–48. Springer, Heidelberg (2015). https://doi.org/10.1007/978-3-662-48051-9_3
3. Ali, S.T., McCorry, P., Lee, P.H.-J., Hao, F.: ZombieCoin 2.0: managing next-generation botnets using Bitcoin. Int. J. Inf. Secur. **17**(4), 411–422 (2017). https://doi.org/10.1007/s10207-017-0379-8
4. Antonakakis, M., et al.: Understanding the Mirai botnet. In: 26th USENIX Security Symposium (USENIX Security 2017), pp. 1093–1110. USENIX Association, Vancouver, BC, August 2017. https://www.usenix.org/conference/usenixsecurity17/technical-sessions/presentation/antonakakis
5. Baden, M., Ferreira Torres, C., Fiz Pontiveros, B.B., State, R.: Whispering botnet command and control instructions. In: 2019 Crypto Valley Conference on Blockchain Technology (CVCBT), pp. 77–81, June 2019. https://doi.org/10.1109/CVCBT.2019.00014
6. Bartoletti, M., Pompianu, L.: An analysis of bitcoin OP_RETURN metadata. In: Brenner, M., et al. (eds.) FC 2017. LNCS, vol. 10323, pp. 218–230. Springer, Cham (2017). https://doi.org/10.1007/978-3-319-70278-0_14
7. Bertino, E., Islam, N.: Botnets and internet of things security. Computer **50**(02), 76–79 (2017). https://doi.org/10.1109/MC.2017.62
8. Binkley, J.R., Singh, S.: An algorithm for anomaly-based botnet detection. SRUTI **6**, 7 (2006)
9. Biryukov, A., Khovratovich, D., Pustogarov, I.: Deanonymisation of clients in bitcoin P2P network. In: Proceedings of the 2014 ACM SIGSAC Conference on Computer and Communications Security, CCS 2014, pp. 15–29. ACM, New York (2014). https://doi.org/10.1145/2660267.2660379. http://doi.acm.org/10.1145/2660267.2660379
10. Correia, P., Rocha, E., Nogueira, A., Salvador, P.: Statistical characterization of the botnets C&C traffic. Procedia Technol. **1**, 158–166 (2012)
11. Delgado-Segura, S., et al.: TxProbe: discovering bitcoin's network topology using orphan transactions. CoRR abs/1812.00942 (2018)
12. Feily, M., Shahrestani, A., Ramadass, S.: A survey of botnet and botnet detection. In: 2009 Third International Conference on Emerging Security Information, Systems and Technologies, pp. 268–273, June 2009. https://doi.org/10.1109/SECURWARE.2009.48
13. Frkat, D., Annessi, R., Zseby, T.: Chainchannels: private botnet communication over public blockchains. In: 2018 IEEE International Conference on Internet of Things (iThings) and IEEE Green Computing and Communications (Green-Com) and IEEE Cyber, Physical and Social Computing (CPSCom) and IEEE Smart Data (SmartData), pp. 1244–1252, July 2018. https://doi.org/10.1109/Cybermatics_2018.2018.00219
14. Gu, G., Zhang, J., Lee, W.: BotSniffer: detecting botnet command and control channels in network traffic (2008)

15. Kolias, C., Kambourakis, G., Stavrou, A., Voas, J.: DDoS in the IoT: mirai and other botnets. Computer **50**(7), 80–84 (2017)

16. Koshy, P., Koshy, D., McDaniel, P.: An analysis of anonymity in bitcoin using P2P network traffic. In: Christin, N., Safavi-Naini, R. (eds.) FC 2014. LNCS, vol. 8437, pp. 469–485. Springer, Heidelberg (2014). https://doi.org/10.1007/978-3-662-45472-5_30

17. Liu, J., Xiao, Y., Ghaboosi, K., Deng, H., Zhang, J.: Botnet: classification, attacks, detection, tracing, and preventive measures. EURASIP J. Wirel. Commun. Netw. **2009**(1), 692654 (2009). https://doi.org/10.1155/2009/692654

18. Livadas, C., Walsh, R., Lapsley, D., Strayer, W.T.: Using machine learning techniques to identify botnet traffic. In: Proceedings of the 2006 31st IEEE Conference on Local Computer Networks, pp. 967–974, November 2006. https://doi.org/10.1109/LCN.2006.322210

19. Lopp, J.: How to solo mine on bitcoin's testnet (2015). https://blog.lopp.net/how-to-solo-mine-on-bitcoin-s-testnet

20. Mahmoud, M., Nir, M., Matrawy, A., et al.: A survey on botnet architectures, detection and defences. IJ Netw. Secur. **17**(3), 264–281 (2015)

21. Mascheck, S.: Arg_max, maximum length of arguments for a new process (2016). https://www.in-ulm.de/~mascheck/various/argmax

22. Nagaraja, S., Mittal, P., Hong, C.Y., Caesar, M., Borisov, N.: BotGrep: finding P2P bots with structured graph analysis. In: Proceedings of the 19th USENIX Conference on Security, USENIX Security 2010, p. 7. USENIX Association, Berkeley (2010). http://dl.acm.org/citation.cfm?id=1929820.1929830

23. Nakamoto, S., et al.: Bitcoin: a peer-to-peer electronic cash system (2008)

24. Nofer, M., Gomber, P., Hinz, O., Schiereck, D.: Blockchain. Bus. Inf. Syst. Eng. **59**(3), 183–187 (2017). https://doi.org/10.1007/s12599-017-0467-3

25. Saad, S., et al.: Detecting P2P botnets through network behavior analysis and machine learning. In: 2011 Ninth Annual International Conference on Privacy, Security and Trust, pp. 174–180, July 2011. https://doi.org/10.1109/PST.2011.5971980

26. Sheinix: The bitcoin network (2018). https://medium.com/coinmonks/the-bitcoin-network-6713cb8713d

27. Silva, S.S., Silva, R.M., Pinto, R.C., Salles, R.M.: Botnets: a survey. Comput. Netw. **57**(2), 378–403 (2013)

28. Wang, P., Wu, L., Aslam, B., Zou, C.C.: A systematic study on peer-to-peer botnets. In: 2009 Proceedings of 18th International Conference on Computer Communications and Networks, pp. 1–8, August 2009. https://doi.org/10.1109/ICCCN.2009.5235360

29. Westervelt, R.: Botnet masters turn to google, social networks to avoid detection (2009)

30. Bitcoin Wiki: Op_return (2018). https://en.bitcoin.it/wiki/OP_RETURN

31. Bitcoin Wiki: Testnet (2019). https://en.bitcoin.it/wiki/Testnet

Security Analysis on dBFT Protocol of NEO

Qin Wang[1], Jiangshan Yu[2(✉)], Zhiniang Peng[3], Van Cuong Bui[1],
Shiping Chen[4], Yong Ding[5], and Yang Xiang[1]

[1] Swinburne University of Technology, Melbourne, Australia
{qinwang,vancuongbui,yxiang}@swin.edu.au
[2] Monash University, Melbourne, Australia
jiangshan.yu@monash.edu
[3] Qihoo 360 Core Security, Beijing, China
pengzhiniang@360.cn
[4] Csiro, Data61, Sydney, Australia
Shiping.Chen@data61.csiro.au
[5] Cyberspace Security Research Center, Shenzhen, China
stone_dingy@guet.edu.cn

Abstract. NEO is ranked as one of the top blockchains by market capitalization. We provide a security analysis on its backbone consensus protocol, called delegated Byzantine Fault Tolerance (dBFT). The dBFT protocol has been employed by NEO and other blockchains like ONT. dBFT claims to guarantee safety when no more than $f = \lfloor \frac{n}{3} \rfloor$ nodes are Byzantine, where n is the total number of consensus participants. However, we identify attacks to break the safety with no more than f Byzantine nodes. This paper provides the following contributions. First, we evaluate NEO's source code and present the procedures of dBFT. Then, we present two attacks to break the safety of dBFT protocol with no more than f nodes. Therefore, the system cannot guarantee the claimed safety. We also provide recommendations on how to fix the system against the identified attacks.

Keywords: Blockchain · NEO · dBFT · Safety

1 Introduction

NEO has been one of the top-ranked blockchain platforms by its market capitalization. Rebranding from the Antshares in June 2017, NEO becomes the earliest and the longest-running public chain in China. From about 0.1 USD at the beginning of 2017, NEO reached a value of 160 USD at the end of 2017. At the time of writing, it's market capitalization is about 0.67 billion USD[1]. The thousandfold return on the investment placed NEO in the ranks of top blockchains within China and abroad. NEO has successfully established a matured ecosystem with decentralized applications (DApps), including games,

---

[1] https://coinmarketcap.com/currencies/neo/. Data fetched on 21st Sept. 2019.

© International Financial Cryptography Association 2020
J. Bonneau and N. Heninger (Eds.): FC 2020, LNCS 12059, pp. 20–31, 2020.
https://doi.org/10.1007/978-3-030-51280-4_2

lotteries, wallets, and exchanges. Furthermore, NEO has developed a complete architecture covering the consensus mechanism and components including NeoX, NeoFS, NeoQS [20,29]. As the core protocol, dBFT was later adopted by the Ontology platform as one of the pluggable consensus mechanisms [23].

Consensus protocols make distributed participants collectively reach an agreement, which enables the immutability and prevents the forks within blockchain systems. Byzantine fault tolerance (BFT) consensus and its variants (together denoted as BFT-style consensus) tolerate a certain number of Byzantine participants who can misbehave. BFT-style mechanisms are permissioned, and provide a deterministic consensus guarantee [25,26]. Various projects [18] employ the BFT-style consensus for their special needs. In particular, Practical Byzantine Fault Tolerance (PBFT) [9] is used as the foundation of many variants, as it enables the system to efficiently (with polynomial complexity) tolerate participants with arbitrary faults. For example, a variant of PBFT has been implemented for Hyperledger Fabric v0.5 and v0.6 [3] and Hyperledger Sawtooth v1.0 [4,7].

dBFT is also a variant of PBFT, with the modifications on network model (from Client/Server to P2P), rule of permission (from fixed to dynamic) and procedure of commit (from 3-phase to 2-phase). dBFT focuses on the performance and scalability, however, the security has not been seriously analyzed. A comprehensive security analysis is absent from the official documents, including its whitepaper [20], documentation [29], and GitHub documents [19]. In fact, after examining the source code, we find that the implemented protocol is slightly different from what has been presented in the whitepaper. For example, in the official presentation of the protocol, not all messages transferred are signed, while in the actual implementation they are all signed and should provide a better security guarantee.

To evaluate the security of NEO, we first analyze the source code and provide a formal and accurate presentation of dBFT with the security goals. Then, we proposed two attacks against dBFT. Both attacks are on the safety of dBFT, making conflict decisions possible. This violates the agreement property where all honest replicas should agree on the same decision. Both identified attacks need to require a view change to happen. The first attack assumes a malicious primary to trigger the view change and the second attack requires a timeout (when the network asynchrony makes a quorum unavailable) to trigger the view change. Both attacks only require no more than $f = \lfloor \frac{n}{3} \rfloor$ malicious replica, where n is the total number of consensus participants and f is the number of Byzantine nodes that the system is supposed to tolerate. We also provide recommendations on fixing the identified vulnerabilities. Our contributions are summarized as follows:

- We provide the first clear presentation of the widely adopted dBFT consensus mechanism, based on its source code [5]
  `git commit 5df6c2f05220e57f4e3180dd23e58bb2f675457d.`
- We identify two attacks on dBFT. Both attacks are feasible with no more than $\lfloor \frac{n}{3} \rfloor$ nodes, where the first attack requires the primary to be Byzantine, and the second attack requires a timeout of the current view.
- We provide recommendations to fix the identified problems.

The rest of our paper is structured as follows: Sect. 2 provides an overview of PBFT. Section 3 defines the network assumption and the security properties, and Sect. 4 provides the detailed dBFT protocol, with a comparison with PBFT protocol. Our identified attacks are presented in Sect. 5. We provide the recommended fix in Sect. 6, and the related work in Sect. 7. Finally, Sect. 8 concludes the paper.

Communication with NEO. We have fully disclosed our results, including both identified vulnerabilities and the recommended fixes, to the NEO team. They acknowledge that our attacks are valid on their system, and have applied the fixes [1,2].

2   Overview of PBFT

Practical Byzantine Fault Tolerance (PBFT), proposed by Castrol [9], is the most prevailing BFT consensus mechanism employed by current permissoned blockchain systems. It enables a system to efficiently (with polynomial complexity) tolerate $f = \lfloor \frac{n}{3} \rfloor$ malicious nodes out of the total n nodes. PBFT is designed in the partially synchronized network model, and proceeds in rounds denoted as *view*. There are three entities contained in PBFT: *Client*, *Primary* and *Replica* and three phases involved in the protocol: *Pre-Prepare*, *Prepare* and *Commit*. We follow the descriptions of [9] and [22], and the communication pattern of PBFT protocol is shown in Fig. 1.

In the *Pre-prepare* phase, upon receiving a REQUEST message from a client, the primary node creates and broadcasts the PRE-PREPARE message to all the replicas. In the *Prepare* phase, each replica checks the validation of the received PRE-PREPARE message. If the message is valid, the replica creates and sends a PREPARE message to all nodes. In the *Commit* phase, upon receiving validated PREPARE messages from a quorum (i.e., $2f + 1$ replicas), this node creates and broadcasts a COMMIT message to all nodes. The last step is to reply to the client about the result. If a node receives a quorum COMMIT messages from $2f + 1$ different nodes, then it executes the client request, creates and sends the reply to the client. A client accepts the reply if it receives a reply from at least $f + 1$ nodes. The *Pre-prepare* phase is a one-to-all communication, while the *Prepare* and *Commit* phases are all-to-all communications.

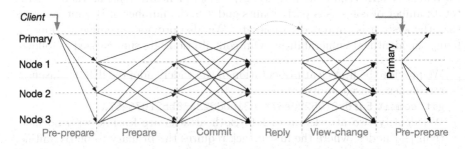

Fig. 1. PBFT protocol

The primary is changed through a *View-change* protocol, if only if the primary is faulty or if network asynchrony breaks the availability of a quorum. In this case, the current round (view) is terminated and nodes initiate a view-change to update the primary. *View-change* makes a new primary node select from other nodes, and requires it to propose and send NEW-VIEW message containing the changed request under the same sequence number. After that, it enters the new view and continues the protocol.

3   Security Property

Safety and liveness are the main properties of a BFT protocol. The safety property requires that a "bad" event in the system will never happen, and the liveness property states that a "good" event will eventually happen. For example, PBFT guarantees safety when no more than $f = \lfloor \frac{n}{3} \rfloor$ are malicious, where n is the total number of nodes running PBFT. PBFT guarantees liveness when no more than f nods are malicious and the network is partial synchrony.

Network Assumption. Similar to PBFT, dBFT assumes a partially synchronous network [11], where a message sent from an honest node will eventually arrive within a fixed time-bound, but the bounded is unknown.

Security and Liveness. While safety guarantees that the system behaves like a centralized implementation to maintain a total order sequence of decisions, liveness guarantees that clients eventually receive replies to their requests [9]. As a variant of PBFT, dBFT aims at providing the same guarantee under the same assumption – the safety is guaranteed when no more than f nodes are malicious, and the liveness is guaranteed with an additional assumption of a partially synchronous network.

4   dBFT Protocol

This section presents how dBFT works and its comparison with PBFT. Our presentation is based on the NEO official source code [19] and its technical reports [20,29]. We summarize the detailed procedures and provide the call function workflow in the Appendix. Note that, to make it easier to understand, we adapt the terms used in PBFT to present dBFT.

4.1   Overview of dBFT

Entities in dBFT. dBFT has three types of nodes, called "speaker", "delegates" and "common nodes", and these types of nodes can be considered as the *Primary*, *Replica* and *Client* in the PBFT protocol, respectively. In dBFT, the primary node is randomly selected from the replicas to generate and send messages (proposals/blocks). The replicas are required to vote for the received messages and maintain the globally ordered sequence of decisions (ledgers/blocks). They are selected from clients according to their reputation as defined by NEO. The client helps to disseminate messages through the underlying peer-to-peer network. They provide various end-user services including payment, exchange, and smart contracts.

State Transition in dBFT. There are three phases in the dBFT protocol, namely "Prepare", "Response" and "Publish". The former two phases serve for the consensus decision where the "publish" is used to broadcast the replies to a request. In particular, the "Prepare" and "Response" phases are similar to the "Pre-prepare" and "Prepare" phases in PBFT, respectively. The "Publish" is similar to the "Reply" step of the PBFT. For simplicity, we will use the terms defined in the PBFT to present the dBFT protocol, as they have been well accepted for decades.

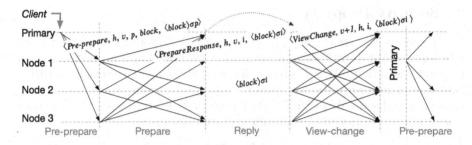

Fig. 2. dBFT protocol

As shown in Fig. 2, upon receiving the requests from a client, the primary starts the *Pre-prepare* phase by sending the PRE-PREPARE message to all replicas. Each replica verifies the validity of the received message. If valid, then it broadcasts a PREPARE message as its response. If a node receives PREPARE messages from a quorum ($2f+1$ nodes), then it executes the request and broadcasts its reply as its final decision. If the primary fails, dBFT runs its *View-change* protocol to reset the parameters and rotate the primary node.

4.2   Detailed Procedures of dBFT

Each execution of the dBFT protocol is initiated by its committee selection algorithm and leader election algorithm to form a consensus group and to select a primary from the group. When a primary and a consensus group is defined, the actual consensus execution protocol contains two main phases, namely *Pre-prepare* and *Prepare*. It also contains a *View-change* protocol when the primary is faulty or when the network asynchrony breaks the availability of a quorum.

Let h be the current block height (i.e., the length of the blockchain). Each replica is labeled by an index number i where $i \in [0, n-1]$ and n is the size of the consensus group. At the beginning of each round, the primary p is selected from the consensus group following the rules of $p = (h - v) \mod n$. To reach an agreement on a block proposed by the primary node, each replica collects $2f$ signatures on the proposed block from other replicas, where $f = \lfloor \frac{n-1}{3} \rfloor$ is the assumed maximum number of Byzantine nodes. Once the agreement is reached, a new round of consensus begins, and the view is reset to $v = 0$. The block signed by replica i is defined as $block_{\sigma_i}$. Here we give the detailed procedures of each step, and the corresponding call function chart of each step can be found in the Appendix.

- *Committee selection:* The replicas (i.e., consensus committee members) are selected from the clients by the NEO foundation according to their reputation. Therefore, we omit the exact process here and put our focus only on the consensus algorithm.
- *Leader election:* The primary is determined by $(h - v) \mod n$, based on the current block height h, current view v and the size n of the consensus group. The leader rotates in the committee due to increased h.
- *Pre-prepare:* The primary creates a block containing valid transactions collected from the network, and sends a signed pre-prepare message $<\texttt{PRE-PREPARE}, h, v, p, block, <block>_{\sigma_p}>$ to all replicas.
- *Prepare:* After receiving the pre-prepare message, replica i checks the correctness of the message, including the validity of signatures, the correctness of h, v, p, block and the contained transactions. If the received proposal is valid, then it broadcasts a signed prepare message $<\texttt{PREPARE}, h, v, p, i, block, <block>_{\sigma_i}>$ to all replicas.
- *Reply:* After collecting signed and validated $\texttt{PREPARE}$ messages from a quorum, the replica i is convinced that consensus is reached, and executes the request and broadcasts its reply $<\texttt{REPLY}, h, v, m, i, <block>_{\sigma_i}>$.
- *View-change:* When detecting a faulty primary or when a quorum is not available, the replica i sends a $\texttt{VIEWCHANGE}$ message $<\texttt{VIEWCHANGE}, h, v + 1, p, i, block, <block>_{\sigma_i}>$ to other nodes. *View-change* is triggered when valid messages are received from a quorum.

4.3   Comparison with PBFT

dBFT is a variant of PBFT protocol with several modifications, as follows. In terms of protocol phases, dBFT removes several sub-protocols of PBFT. In particular, it removes the core *Commit* phase from the PBFT, and also removes the auxiliary protocols including *GarbegeCollection* and *Checkpoint*. In terms of the communication model, dBFT employs a peer-to-peer network topology to disseminate messages, rather than the previous client-server communication model. In terms of the message authentication, dBFT uses digital signatures to authenticate messages rather than using MAC as in PBFT. In terms of consensus committee, there are several changes. First, dBFT does not have a fixed consensus group as in PBFT. Rather, it implements a mechanism to enable dynamic joining/leaving of nodes to offer flexibility. Second, for leader election, dBFT enforces the change of primary for each round of consensus. In particular, at the beginning of each consensus round, the new primary p is determined by $p = (h - v) \mod n$. So, whenever a new block is accepted in the blockchain, the primary will be changed.

5   Identified Attacks

This section presents two identified attacks on the safety of dBFT. Both attacks need to enforce a view change. The first attack requires a malicious primary to trigger the view change and the second attack requires a timeout (when the network asynchrony makes a quorum unavailable) to trigger the view change. Both attacks only require no more than f malicious replica, which is the case the dBFT is supposed to tolerate. We make use of a simple scenario with four nodes to demonstrate our attacks. Let $n = 4$, so $f = 1$. Let A_i be the identity of the i-th replica, where $i \in [0, n-1]$.

5.1 Attack Case 1

Let A_0 be the Byzantine node, and it is selected as primary. The detailed attack process is shown as follows.

- *step 1:* The Byzantine primary A_0 creates two blocks, *block1* and *block2*, such that they contain conflict transactions for e.g. spending a coin multiple times. A_0 then sends <Pre-prepare> on *block1* to A_1 and A_2, and sends <Pre-prepare> on *block2* to A_3.
- *step 2:* As both blocks are valid, A_1 and A_2 will create and broadcast a <Prepare> message on the *block1*, and A_3 will broadcast a <Prepare> message on *block2*.
- *step 3:* Since no replica receives enough valid <Prepare> message $(2f + 1)$ from a quorum, the current round will timeout, and it triggers the view change protocol.
- *step 4:* Run view change protocol honestly. Since in the previous view $(v = 0)$, $(h - 0) \mod 4 = 1$, so in this view $v = 1$, A_3 will be elected as the primary, i.e. $(h - 1) \mod 4 = 3$.
- *step 5:* Run the consensus on *block2* with $v = 1$. When a decision is reached, A_0 can create a conflict decision by releasing $2f + 1 = 3$ valid <Prepare> messages on *block1* of view $v = 0$. This breaks the consensus safety.

5.2 Attack Case 2

Attack case 2 considers the scenario where the Byzantine replica is not primary for the current view, and it relies on the view change triggered by network asynchrony. (Note that unlike liveness, the safety should hold under network asynchrony.)

- *step 1:* Select the leader according to $p = (h - v) \mod n$.
- *step 2:* The honest leader sends a valid proposal <Pre-prepare> on *block1*.
- *step 3:* the Byzantine replica performs the following strategy. If it receives $2f + 1 = 3$ signed <Prepare> messages from others, it runs the protocol honestly. If it only receives two signed messages, then it does not react. This can happen due to network asynchrony. In the second case, there is a possibility that replicas timeout the current view, and request a new view.
- *step 4:* If a view change is triggered, then the Byzantine replica runs it honestly.
- *step 5:* If the Byzantine replica is selected as primary, then it proposes a valid proposal <Pre-prepare> on *block2*, which contains transactions conflict with the ones contained in *block1*.

– *step 6:* all nodes run the consensus protocol, and reach a decision on *block2* with the current view number. When the decision is reached, the Byzantine replica releases the two signed `<Prepare>` messages on *block1* collected in the previous view, together with its signed `<Prepare>` message also on *block1*. This creates a conflict decision and breaks the consensus safety.

6 Recommended Fix

As shown in the previous section, the safety of dBFT cannot be guaranteed even when no more than f replicas are malicious, as conflict agreements can be reached. Our identified attacks are in fact not new. It is known that it is possible to have a secure two-phase protocol for crash fault tolerance (CFT) protocols, but a two-phase PBFT is vulnerable against Byzantine replicas. Thus, the *Commit* phase becomes necessary [9,13]. The fix then becomes straight forward – the *Commit* phase is necessary to guarantee the safety, and dBFT needs to add this phase back to make the protocol secure against the two identified attacks.

The *Commit* phase plays a role to check if at least $2f + 1$ replicas have responded to the request. If a node has collected $2f + 1$ signed responses in the *Prepare* phase, then it commits the block by signing it together with state information, and sends it to all replicas. If at least $2f + 1$ valid commits messages are collected, then the replica updates the local state of the blockchain by including the block into it, and broadcasts the result to the network. As this is a standard construction in the classic BFT protocol, and is proved to be secure [21], we omit the formal proofs in this paper.

7 Related Work

The consensus problem can be traced back in early 1975, when the Two Generals Problem with its insolubility proof was proposed [6]. The problem was formally proved to be unsolvable, providing a base of realistic expectations for any distributed consistency protocols. The *FLP* impossibility result [13] placed an upper bound on what it is possible to achieve with distributed processes in an asynchronous environment. The *CAP* [14] theorem states that distributed systems cannot satisfy all three conditions, namely consistency, availability, and partition tolerance. BFT protocols can tolerate at most $f \leq \lfloor \frac{3}{n} \rfloor$ Byzantine nodes, unless a trusted component is used [24].

Bitcoin. Bitcoin [17] is a cryptocurrency introduced in 2008. It aims at tolerating <50% malicious power in the system. Unlike traditional consensus protocols, it does not require a pre-fixed consensus group. Instead, it allows any node to join and leave the system. It makes use of a public ledger (a.k.a. a blockchain) to record all transactions in the system. The public ledger is a chain of blocks, where each block contains a sequence of transactions that have not been recorded in previous blocks. Everyone can read the ledger from the Bitcoin network, and can write on it by finding a block such that the hash value of the block is small enough. The process of finding a valid block is called *"proof of work"*. This concept defeats Sybil attacks, where an attacker can create many fake nodes at a low cost. Different participants may create conflicting blocks. To provide consensus on the conflicting blocks, participants only accept the longest chain. However, this way of agreeing about blocks only provides a probabilistic guarantee, as it is possible for malicious participants to work on a short chain to race with a longer one, until the shorter one beats the longer chain. This leads to attacks such as double spending attacks [30] and selfish mining attacks [12]. In addition, the block size is currently limited to 1 MB. This limits its transaction throughput to 7 transactions per second, whereas other existing payment systems handle way more. For example, Visa confirms a transaction within seconds, and processes 2k TPS on average, with a maximum rate of 56k TPS. For more detail, we refer readers to a detailed comparison [25] between Bitcoin and BFT protocols.

Adapting BFT Protocols in Blockchain. Classic BFT protocols provide a better throughout and security guarantee. PBFT [9] proposes the first practical Byzantine fault-tolerant algorithm with acceptable performance. Zyzzyva [16] is a speculation-based BFT protocol that reduces cryptographic over-heads and increases peak throughput for demanding workloads compared to traditional state machine replication. However, an attack [15] on the safety of Zyzzyva has been identified. MinBFT/MinZyzzyva [24] proposes to use a trusted component to improve the performance and security of PBFT and Zyzzyva.

However, these systems cannot be adapted directly in the blockchain, as they require a pre-fixed consensus group. Many systems (e.g. [22,27,28]) have been proposed to adapt BFT protocols to address the shortcomings of Bitcoin blockchain. PeerCensus [10] was the first blockchain to propose using proof-of-work for selecting consensus committees, and use a BFT-style protocol for reaching consensus. dBFT takes a different approach, where the consensus committee is defined by NEO based on the social reputation of nodes. We refer readers to existing comprehensive surveys [8,18,26] on the membership selection algorithms, blockchain consensus, and identified attacks.

8 Conclusion

NEO, as the pioneer of public blockchain projects around the world, confronts severe security threats. Our security analysis is focusing on the core component of NEO, i.e., its dBFT consensus. As a variant derivative of PBFT, the dBFT consensus removes the important *Commit* processes compared to the original ones, resulting in deterministic forks under the specific conditions. In fact, it is known that removing the commit phase would lead to insecurity. This paper provides a study to revisit this issue, as a lesson learned from the already deployed and widely adapted consensus algorithm.

A dBFT Flow Chart

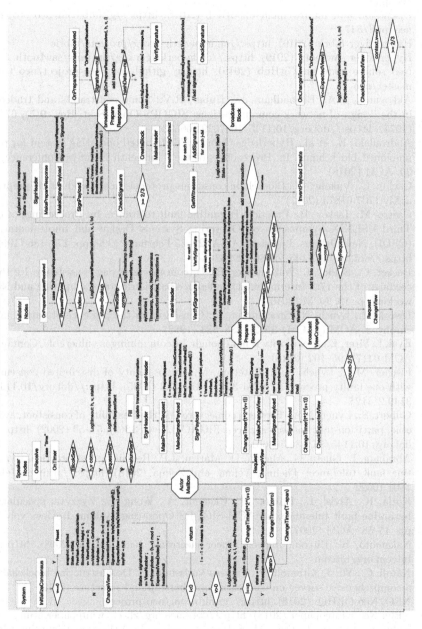

NEO DBFT Consensust Flow Chart with call functuin

References

1. Discussion and improvement on dBFT (2019). https://github.com/neo-project/neo/pull/320
2. Discussion and improvement on dBFT (2019). https://github.com/neo-project/neo/pull/547
3. Hyperledger fabric (2019). https://cn.hyperledger.org/projects/fabric
4. Hyperledger sawtooth (2019). https://cn.hyperledger.org/projects/sawtooth
5. Neo source code on GitHub (2019). https://github.com/neo-project/neo/tree/master/neo
6. Akkoyunlu, E.A., Ekanadham, K., Huber, R.V.: Some constraints and tradeoffs in the design of network communications. SIGOPS Oper. Syst. Rev. 9(5), 67–74 (1975). https://doi.org/10.1145/1067629.806523
7. Androulaki, E., et al.: Hyperledger fabric: a distributed operating system for permissioned blockchains. In: Proceedings of the Thirteenth EuroSys Conference, p. 30. ACM (2018)
8. Cachin, C., Vukolić, M.: Blockchain consensus protocols in the wild. arXiv preprint arXiv:1707.01873 (2017)
9. Castro, M., Liskov, B.: Practical Byzantine fault tolerance. In: Proceedings of the Third USENIX Symposium on Operating Systems Design and Implementation (OSDI), New Orleans, Louisiana, USA, 22–25 February 1999, pp. 173–186 (1999). https://doi.org/10.1145/296806.296824
10. Decker, C., Seidel, J., Wattenhofer, R.: Bitcoin meets strong consistency. In: Proceedings of the 17th International Conference on Distributed Computing and Networking, p. 13. ACM (2016)
11. Dwork, C., Lynch, N., Stockmeyer, L.: Consensus in the presence of partial synchrony. J. ACM (JACM) 35(2), 288–323 (1988)
12. Eyal, I., Sirer, E.G.: Majority is not enough: bitcoin mining is vulnerable. Commun. ACM 61(7), 95–102 (2018)
13. Fischer, M.J., Lynch, N.A., Paterson, M.: Impossibility of distributed consensus with one faulty process. J. ACM 32(2), 374–382 (1985). https://doi.org/10.1145/3149.214121
14. Gilbert, S., Lynch, N.A.: Brewer's conjecture and the feasibility of consistent, available, partition-tolerant web services. SIGACT News 33(2), 51–59 (2002). https://doi.org/10.1145/564585.564601
15. Abraham, I., Gueta, G., Malkhi, D., Martin, J.P.: Revisiting fast practical Byzantine fault tolerance: Thelma, Velma, and Zelma (2018). https://arxiv.org/abs/1801.10022
16. Kotla, R., Alvisi, L., Dahlin, M., Clement, A., Wong, E.: Zyzzyva: speculative byzantine fault tolerance. In: ACM SIGOPS Operating Systems Review, vol. 41, pp. 45–58. ACM (2007)
17. Nakamoto, S.: Bitcoin: a peer-to-peer electronic cash system (2008). https://bitcoin.org/bitcoin
18. Natoli, C., Yu, J., Gramoli, V., Esteves-Verissimo, P.: Deconstructing blockchains: a comprehensive survey on consensus, membership and structure (2019)
19. NEO: Neo GitHub (2018). https://github.com/neo-project
20. NEO: Neo whiteopaper (2018). http://docs.neo.org/zh-cn/whitepaper.html
21. Rahli, V., Vukotic, I., Völp, M., Esteves-Verissimo, P.: Velisarios: Byzantine fault-tolerant protocols powered by coq. In: Ahmed, A. (ed.) ESOP 2018. LNCS, vol. 10801, pp. 619–650. Springer, Cham (2018). https://doi.org/10.1007/978-3-319-89884-1_22

22. Stathakopoulou, C., David, T., Vukolić, M.: Mir-BFT: high-throughput BFT for blockchains. arXiv preprint arXiv:1906.05552 (2019)
23. Ontology Team: Ont consensus (2018). https://github.com/ontio/ontology/tree/master/consensus/dbft
24. Veronese, G.S., Correia, M., Bessani, A.N., Lung, L.C., Verissimo, P.: Efficient Byzantine fault-tolerance. IEEE Trans. Comput. **62**(1), 16–30 (2011)
25. Vukolić, M.: The quest for scalable blockchain fabric: proof-of-work vs. BFT replication. In: Camenisch, J., Kesdoğan, D. (eds.) iNetSec 2015. LNCS, vol. 9591, pp. 112–125. Springer, Cham (2016). https://doi.org/10.1007/978-3-319-39028-4_9
26. Vukolić, M.: Rethinking permissioned blockchains. In: Proceedings of the ACM Workshop on Blockchain, Cryptocurrencies and Contracts, pp. 3–7. ACM (2017)
27. Yin, M., Malkhi, D., Reiter, M.K., Gueta, G.G., Abraham, I.: HotStuff: BFT consensus with linearity and responsiveness. In: Proceedings of the 2019 ACM Symposium on Principles of Distributed Computing, pp. 347–356. ACM (2019)
28. Yu, J., Kozhaya, D., Decouchant, J., Veríssimo, P.J.E.: Repucoin: your reputation is your power. IEEE Trans. Comput. **68**(8), 1225–1237 (2019)
29. Zhang, E.: Neo consensus (2018). http://docs.neo.org/en-us/basic/consensus/consensus.html
30. Zhang, R., Preneel, B.: Lay down the common metrics: evaluating proof-of-work consensus protocols' security. In: 2019 IEEE Symposium on Security and Privacy (SP). IEEE (2019)

Breaking the Encryption Scheme of the Moscow Internet Voting System

Pierrick Gaudry[1(✉)] and Alexander Golovnev[2]

[1] CNRS, Inria, Université de Lorraine, Nancy, France
pierrick.gaudry@loria.fr
[2] Harvard University, Cambridge, USA

Abstract. In September 2019, voters for the election at the Parliament of the city of Moscow were allowed to use an Internet voting system. The source code of it had been made available for public testing. In this paper we show two successful attacks on the encryption scheme implemented in the voting system. Both attacks were sent to the developers of the system, and both issues had been fixed after that.

The encryption used in this system is a variant of ElGamal over finite fields. In the first attack we show that the used key sizes are too small. We explain how to retrieve the private keys from the public keys in a matter of minutes with easily available resources.

When this issue had been fixed and the new system had become available for testing, we discovered that the new implementation was not semantically secure. We demonstrate how this newly found security vulnerability can be used for counting the number of votes cast for a candidate.

1 Introduction

Electronic voting is more and more widely used for low-stakes elections, with systems of various qualities. The situation for important politically binding elections is more contrasted. Some countries have completely banned the use of e-voting in that case (for instance, Germany in 2009, the Netherlands in 2008, or Norway [11] in 2013), while other countries use it on a regular basis or organize experiments with higher and higher stakes elections (Switzerland [9,15,26], Estonia [16], Canada [12]).

The term electronic voting can cover different situations, and in this work, we are interested in Internet voting, not machine-assisted voting that takes place in polling stations. This increases the difficulty to guarantee properties like authentication or coercion-resistance that are easier to obtain at a polling station, where an officer can check classical identity cards and where the voters can go to a polling booth to isolate themselves and choose freely.

But even more basic properties like vote secrecy and verifiability are not easy to obtain if one wants to keep things simple and without advanced cryptographic tools like zero-knowledge proofs, proof of equivalence of plaintexts, oblivious transfer, etc.

© International Financial Cryptography Association 2020
J. Bonneau and N. Heninger (Eds.): FC 2020, LNCS 12059, pp. 32–49, 2020.
https://doi.org/10.1007/978-3-030-51280-4_3

For high-stakes elections, a bad practice that tends to become less accepted by the population is to have some designated experts that study the security of the product, but how it really works remains secret to voters. Therefore, in more and more cases, the organization will ask for a product that can be audited by independent experts, and as an incentive to have more feedback, public testing with an associated bug bounty program can be organized. For instance, this has been recently the case in Switzerland, which is a country with a long history of experiments with Internet voting. A security problem was actually discovered at this occasion [14, 22].

In Russia, September 8, 2019 was a day of local elections, where governors and representatives for local parliaments must be elected. In Moscow, at the occasion of this election for the City Parliament (Moscow Duma), it was decided to test the use of Internet voting. Voters from 3 electoral districts (among a total of 45 districts) were allowed to register for using Internet voting instead of using classical paper voting at polling stations.

A voting system was designed specifically for this election. For lack of a proper name, we will call it the Moscow Internet voting system. Its deployment is the responsibility of a service of the City called the Department of Information Technology. In July, the system was opened for public testing.

Description of the Public Challenge

On July 17, 2019, some of the system's code was posted online [10], and the organizers asked the public to test several attack scenarios [24]. A bounty program of up to 2 millions rubles (approx. $30,000) was associated to it. We believed that the fact that most of the information is in Russian and that almost no description of the system (in any language) is available apart from the source code was a reason for having a low advertisement of this challenge at the international level, even among the e-voting community.

The system is poorly documented, but from the source code and brief descriptions of the system [20], we know that it uses the Ethereum blockchain [3] and ElGamal encryption. No advanced cryptographic tools are present in the source code (no verifiable mixnets [13], for instance, while they are quite frequent in modern systems).

In one of the attack scenarios, the organizers publish a challenge consisting of the public key and some encrypted messages. The attack was considered successful if the messages got decrypted within 12 h (the duration of the future, real election), before the organizers reveal the private key and the original messages. All of these cryptographic challenges (keys and encrypted data) were put in the public repository of the source code, in a special sub-directory called `encryption-keys`.

Contributions

In this paper, we describe two attacks that we mounted on the system, following this attack scenario. The first attack uses the fact that the key sizes are so small that, with specialized software, it is possible to compute discrete logarithms and deduce the private keys in far less than the 12 h allowed for this task. After this, the source code was modified. Our second attack is against this new version and relies on a subgroup attack that reveals one bit of information related to the original message. In an e-voting context, this can be enough to get a lot of information about the voter's choice, and indeed, in the Moscow system, the leakage was really strong. During August, several public tests were done, with volunteers, after the system was patched against our attacks. In this work, after describing our attacks, we will discuss the general protocol, which is some kind of moving target, since there is no proper specification, no clear security claims and on top of that, deep changes were made until very late before the real election.

For this work, we used the following different sources of information about the Moscow Internet voting system:

- The public source code, of course. This includes Javascript code to be run on the client side, PHP code for the server side, and Solidity code to be run as smart contracts in an Ethereum blockchain.
- The articles published in the press, sometimes quoting the designers of the system. This includes various sources, with different opinions about the use of Internet voting in this context. We considered some of these sources as non-reliable.
- Private discussions with the designers and with journalists investigating the current situation.

In the following, we will refer to different versions of the source code. In order to make our terminology precise, we give the exact revision numbers of these versions, corresponding to `git` commits in the public repository [10]:

- The "original" version, i.e. the one that was published and used for the first public test: revision d70986b2c4da.
- The "modified" version, that took into account our first attack: revision 1d4f348681e9.
- The "final" version that was used for the election: revision 51aa4300aceb.

2   Attacks on the Encryption Scheme

2.1   Attack on the Original Implementation

In the original version of the source code (rev d70986b2c4da), the encryption scheme can be found in the files `elGamal.js` and `multiLevelEncryptor.js` of the `smart-contracts/packages/crypto-lib/src/` subdirectory. The first file contains a textbook version of the ElGamal encryption algorithm, while the second one builds on top of it a "multilevel" variant that we are going to describe here since this is a non-standard construction.

Let us first fix the notations for the textbook ElGamal encryption. Let G be a cyclic group generated by g of order q. An ElGamal keypair is obtained by choosing a (secret) decryption key sk as a random integer in $\mathbb{Z}_q$, and the corresponding (public) encryption key pk is given by $\text{pk} = g^{\text{sk}}$. Let us denote by $\text{Enc}_{g,\text{pk}}(m) = (a, b)$ the ElGamal encryption of the message $m \in G$ with a public key pk and a generator g. This is a randomized encryption: an integer r is picked uniformly at random in $\mathbb{Z}_q$, and then the encryption is obtained as

$$\mathsf{Enc}_{g,\mathrm{pk}}(m) = (a, b) = (g^r, \mathrm{pk}^r \cdot m).$$

The corresponding decryption function $\mathsf{Dec}_{g,\mathrm{sk}}(a, b)$, that uses the secret key sk corresponding to pk is then given by

$$\mathsf{Dec}_{g,\mathrm{sk}}(a, b) = b \cdot a^{-\mathrm{sk}} = m.$$

The multilevel variant is obtained by successively applying the ElGamal encryption, with three different parameter sets, first on the message m, and then on the a-part of the successive ElGamal ciphertexts. In the Moscow system, there are 3 levels. Each level uses a group G_i which is the multiplicative group of a finite field $\mathbb{F}_{p_i}$, where p_i is a safe prime. An important remark, here, is that the p_i's being different, there is no algebraic map from one group to the other. It is necessary to lift an element of $\mathbb{F}_{p_1}^*$ to an integer in $[1, p_1 - 1]$ before mapping it to $\mathbb{F}_{p_2}^*$. This mapping will be without loss of information only if p_2 is larger than p_1; and similarly we need p_3 bigger than p_2. These conditions are indeed enforced in the source code.

Let us denote by g_1, g_2, g_3 the generators of the 3 groups G_1, G_2, G_3. There are 3 ElGamal key pairs $(\mathrm{sk}_1, \mathrm{pk}_1)$, $(\mathrm{sk}_2, \mathrm{pk}_2)$, $(\mathrm{sk}_3, \mathrm{pk}_3)$ used for the encryption and decryption of the ballots. In order to encrypt a message $m \in G_1$, we compute the following successive ElGamal encryptions:

$$\begin{aligned}(a_1, b_1) &:= \mathsf{Enc}_{g_1,\mathrm{pk}_1}(m); &&\text{map } a_1 \text{ to } G_2; \\ (a_2, b_2) &:= \mathsf{Enc}_{g_2,\mathrm{pk}_2}(a_1); &&\text{map } a_2 \text{ to } G_3; \\ (a_3, b_3) &:= \mathsf{Enc}_{g_3,\mathrm{pk}_3}(a_2),\end{aligned}$$

and then the ciphertext is the quadruple in $G_1 \times G_2 \times G_3^2$ given by

$$\mathsf{MultiEnc}(m) = (b_1, b_2, a_3, b_3).$$

The values a_1 and a_2 are forgotten, but someone knowing the private keys sk_1, sk_2, sk_3 corresponding to pk_1, pk_2, pk_3, will be able to recover m from the ciphertext with the following decryption procedure:

$$\begin{aligned}a_2 &:= \mathsf{Dec}_{g_3,\mathrm{sk}_3}(a_3, b_3); &&\text{map } a_2 \text{ to } G_2; \\ a_1 &:= \mathsf{Dec}_{g_2,\mathrm{sk}_2}(a_2, b_2); &&\text{map } a_1 \text{ to } G_1; \\ m &:= \mathsf{Dec}_{g_1,\mathrm{sk}_1}(a_1, b_1).\end{aligned}$$

The purpose of this multilevel encryption is not known to us. We will speculate on this in Sect. 3. An obvious observation, however, is that if the discrete logarithm problem is not hard in G_1, G_2 and G_3, then it is possible to deduce the secret keys sk_i's from the public keys pk_i's and an attacker can then decrypt encrypted messages as quickly as the legitimate possessor of the secret keys.

In the published source code, the primes p_i's have less than 256 bits. Discrete logarithms in finite fields defined by such small primes have been computed for the first time in the middle of the 90's: Weber, Denny and Zayer did a series of computation in 1995–1996, starting from 215 to 281 bits [33]. At that time, the computing resources required for the computations were rather high, and solving the 3 discrete logarithm problems to get the private keys would not have been easily feasible in less than 12 h as required by the challenge.

More than 2 decades later, computers are much faster and have much more memory. Furthermore, the Number Field Sieve algorithm [21], which is the fastest known method asymptotically was still a very new algorithm in the mid-90's, and many theoretical and practical optimizations have been developed since then [7,18,25,30]. The current record is a computation modulo a 768-bit prime [19].

We have tried the following software products that contain a full implementation of discrete logarithm computations in prime fields:

Software	SageMath [29]	Magma [4]	CADO-NFS [27]
Version	8.8	2.24-2	rev. 6b3746a2e

Note that Magma is proprietary software, while the others are free software.

The experiments were first made on a typical personal computer equipped with a 4-core Intel i5-4590 processor at 3.3 GHz and 16 GB of RAM. It is running a standard Debian distribution. SageMath uses GP/Pari [28] internally for computing discrete logarithms. On this machine, the computation took more than 12 h, and actually we had to stop it after 4 days while it was still running. According to GP/Pari documentation, the algorithm used is a linear sieve index calculus method. As for Magma, the handbook tells us that depending on arithmetic properties of the prime, the algorithm used can be the Gaussian integer sieve or a fallback linear sieve. The prime we tested was compatible with the Gaussian integer sieve. But during the linear algebra step, the memory requirement was much larger than the available 16 GB. We started the computation again, on a 64-core server node with 192 GB of RAM. On this machine, Magma computed the discrete logarithm in a bit less than 24 h with 130 GB of peak memory usage. It should be noted that both Magma and SageMath use only one of the available computing cores, so that there does not seem to be an easy way to go below the 12 h limit with them, even with an access to a powerful machine.

CADO-NFS is an implementation of the Number Field Sieve for integer factorization and discrete logarithms in prime fields (and some experimental support for small degree extensions of prime fields). The last stable release 2.3.0 is two years old, so we used the development version, available on the public git repository. With CADO-NFS, on the standard personal machine, the running times to retrieve the private keys of August 18 were as follows:

Key number	Time
1	7 min 5 s
2	8 min 27 s
3	5 min 14 s

Note that the variation in the running time from one key to the other is not unusual for computations with moderately small primes. Also, we should mention that when doing this work, we realized that the development version was not robust for numbers of this size: it sometimes failed in the final step called "individual logarithm" or "descent". The revision number we gave above corresponds to a version where we have fixed these problems, so that CADO-NFS can reliably compute discrete logarithms in finite fields of about 256 bits.

Due to mathematical obstructions, the Number Field Sieve is an algorithm that can compute discrete logarithms only in a sub-group of prime (or prime-power) order. In the present situation where the order of the generator is twice a prime, a small Pohlig-Hellman step must be added. This part is not included in CADO-NFS and must be done by hand. Similarly, peculiarities of the Number Field Sieve imply that the base for the discrete logarithm computed by CADO-NFS is arbitrary. Therefore, in order to compute one of the sk_i, the program must be run twice, once for the generator and once for the public key. Fortunately, in the Number Field Sieve algorithm, many parts of the computation can be shared between the two executions modulo the same prime (this is the basis of the LogJam attack [2]), and CADO-NFS indeed shares them automatically. The running times given above include those 2 runs for each key. For completeness and reproducibility, we provide in Appendix A a script to obtain the keys; this includes the few additional modular operations to be done apart from the calls to CADO-NFS.

Of course, for a real attack, the three private keys can be computed simultaneously on 3 machines in parallel. Indeed, the chaining involved in the multilevel ElGamal is not relevant for the keys, it occurs only during the encryption/decryption of messages.

Additionally to this immediate 3-fold parallelism for the attack, CADO-NFS also has some parallelism capabilities so that machines with more cores can reduce the time for a single key. However, there is some limit to it with the current implementation. For instance, the private key number 1 still required 160 s of wall clock time on the same 64-core machine that we used for testing Magma.

2.2 Attack on the Modified Version

After the first attack was sent to the developers of the system and made public a few days later, the public source code has been modified. The key size has been increased to 1024 bits, and the multilevel ElGamal has been removed and replaced by a single ElGamal encryption.

In the original version, the generators in all the involved groups were generators for the full multiplicative group of the finite fields, thus their orders were twice a prime numbers. This exposed the danger of leakage of one bit of information on the message, with a subgroup attack. This is an old technique [23], but there are still frequent attacks, in particular when an implementation forgets the key validation step [31]. Although we did not push in this direction in the first attack, it was explicitly mentioned as a weakness. Therefore in the modified version, the generator was chosen to be a quadratic residue, thus having prime order.

We discovered however that the other parts of the implementation were not changed accordingly, so that an attack was still possible.

Let $p = 2q + 1$ be the 1024-bit safe prime used to define the group, where q is also a prime. Let Q_p be the group of quadratic residues modulo p; it has order $|Q_p| = (p-1)/2 = q$. The chosen generator g belongs to Q_p, and therefore, so is the public key pk, since it is computed as before as pk $= g^{\text{sk}}$, where sk is randomly chosen in $\mathbb{Z}_q$.

The problem with the modified implementation is that the message m is allowed to be any integer from $[1, q-1]$ which is naturally mapped to an element of $\mathbb{F}_p^*$. For semantic security (under the Decisional Diffie-Hellman assumption), the message m should instead be encoded as one of the q elements of the group Q_p generated by g. In the case where m is not necessarily picked from the group of quadratic residues, the Decisional Diffie-Hellman assumption does not hold and indeed it is possible to build an efficient distinguisher, thus showing that the encryption scheme in the modified version is not semantically secure.

Let us make this explicit. If the message m becomes a quadratic residue after being mapped to $\mathbb{F}_p^*$, then for *every* choice of randomness of the encryption algorithm, in the resulting ciphertext $\text{Enc}_{g,\text{pk}}(m) = (a, b)$, the second component b is also a quadratic residue. Indeed, if g and m belong to Q_p, then there exist x and y in $\mathbb{F}_p^*$ such that $g = x^2$ and $m = y^2$ Then

$$b = \text{pk}^r \cdot m = g^{r \cdot \text{sk}} \cdot y^2 = (x^{r \cdot \text{sk}} y)^2 \in Q_p.$$

Similarly, if m is not a quadratic residue, then $b = \text{pk}^r \cdot m$ is not a quadratic residue either.

Testing the quadratic residuosity of b can be done by computing the Legendre symbol of b and p. Thanks to the law of quadratic reciprocity, a very efficient algorithm similar to the Euclidean algorithm is available [32]. Therefore from just the knowledge of a ciphertext, it is possible to immediately deduce if the corresponding cleartext m belongs or not to Q_p. Roughly half of the messages are mapped to Q_p. Hence, one bit of information is leaked.

In order to test the validity of this attack, we checked whether the b-parts of the published encrypted messages belonged or not to Q_p. It turned out that exactly five out of the ten were quadratic residues modulo p. This shows that indeed, some of the cleartexts were in Q_p and some were not. Details for reproducing these computations are given in Appendix B.

2.3 On the Role of Encryption in the Protocol – What Did We Break?

As in many e-voting protocols, the encryption scheme is used to encrypt the choice of the voter to form an encrypted ballot. From the Javascript source code (under a sub-directory called `voting-form`) that is supposed to be run on the voting device of the voter, we deduce that the encrypted data consists solely of this choice (with no additional nonce or meta-data). It takes the form of a 32-bit unsigned integer called "deputy id" that looks random.

The link between the deputy ids and the real names of the candidates is public, since the Javascript source code that must present the choices to the voters has to include it.

In the original version of the encryption scheme, as soon as the election starts, the 3 public keys of the multilevel ElGamal must become public, and from them, in a matter of minutes the decryption keys can be deduced. Then, this is as if the choices of the voters were in cleartext all along the process. Even if there is a strong trust assumption on the server that receives these votes, and even if it is honest and forgets the link between the voters and the ballots, there is still the issue of putting them in the blockchain for verifiability. Since the ballots are (essentially) in cleartext, the partial results become public all along the day of the election, which can have a strong influence on the result. Actually, it is illegal in Russia to announce any preliminary result while the election is still running.

Our second attack will not give full information about a ballot. Just one bit of information is leaked from an encrypted ballot, namely whether or not the chosen candidate has a deputy id which is a quadratic residue. As the deputy ids seem to be chosen at random with no specific arithmetic property, there is a one-half probability that they belong to Q_p, as for any element of $\mathbb{F}_p^*$. There could be some bias if the deputy ids had only a few bits, but with 32-bit integers, according to standard number theoretic heuristics this will not be the case. A plausible scenario for the attack is then a district where two candidates concentrate most of the votes, one of them having a deputy id in Q_p and the other not. Then, from an encrypted ballot, by computing a Legendre symbol, one can deduce the voter's choice unless she voted for a less popular candidate.

Therefore, as for the first attack, this second attack means that vote secrecy relies on a very strong trust assumption in the voting server, and that the partial results are leaked all along the process.

At first, it seems that the designers were skeptical about the feasibility of this second attack, and they denied that it was a threat. However on August 28, 2019, they organized a last public testing, with only two deputy ids. It would have been fully vulnerable to the described attack, since one of the ids was in Q_p and the other not. Even though the public source code was not yet modified, the (minified) Javascript served to the volunteers during the test included a patch against our second attack.

3 Discussion

3.1 The Role of the Blockchain in the Protocol

Blockchain as a Distributed Ledger. In the protocol, the encrypted ballots are sent to an Ethereum blockchain and stored as transactions, one transaction per ballot. The argument for doing so is a typical one used in e-voting, namely offering the possibility for the voters to check that their vote is indeed taken into account. At the end of the election, again via the blockchain, the voters are also given a way to relate each encrypted ballot to the corresponding vote in cleartext. The goal is to provide the cast-as-intended property: if the voting client were to silently modify the choice of the voter, this would be detected.

In the above quick description, we implicitly assumed that once the voter has done the check that her ballot is present in the blockchain it will stay there and be counted in the tally. This also assumes that the voters are given enough information and tools to record the link between their vote and the corresponding entry in the blockchain, so that the check can be done in the few days (and maybe weeks or months) after the election.

In the Moscow election, a specific, permissioned Ethereum blockchain was used. The impossibility for the nodes running this blockchain to rewrite the history of the ledger in order to remove a ballot after the voter has checked it, relies therefore on the assumption that enough nodes are honest. Furthermore, the access to this specific blockchain was not guaranteed to stay for long, and actually was cut by the organizers quickly after the election.

Without access to the specifications of the protocol it is difficult to draw strong conclusions, but we consider that the verifiability properties were not as strong as what could be hoped for from a blockchain-based ledger.

More generally, using a public bulletin board is a well-known strategy in e-voting, and a distributed blockchain is not the only and probably not the best way of trying to achieve it. This is still a topic of active research [6,17].

To Use or Not to Use a Smart Contract for Decryption. In the original implementation, at the end of the election, the 3 private keys of the multilevel ElGamal were used to publicly decrypt all the ballots. This decryption was implemented in the Solidity programming language, to be run as part of a smart-contract by the nodes of the blockchain. The security properties that were sought by doing so are unclear. There are many ways to guarantee that a decryption has been correctly done, the most obvious in an ElGamal encryption setting is to include a simple zero-knowledge proof (as done for instance in Helios [1]).

In the version that was modified after our first attack, the protocol was changed, so that the decryption was done outside the smart-contract. The decryption results, namely the votes in clear, were uploaded to the blockchain as simple transactions with no computation. This operation occurs of course at the end of the election, in order to compute the tally. And additionally, the private key was also stored in the blockchain. This indeed allows the voters to verify that the decryption is correct.

Doing such a big change in the protocol just a couple of weeks before a real use in a real and high-stakes election is definitely not a good practice. However, again, without a proper specification, it is hard to deduce all the consequences. Did the trust assumptions change in the process? This also leaves open speculations about the possibility that programming the decryption in a smart contract was nothing but a peculiarity of the original design.

Is It the Origin of the Small Key Sizes? The original code included many checks ensuring that the primes used to defined groups for the multilevel ElGamal encryption had a size small enough so that they would fit in 256 bits. This was taking the form of comparisons to a constant called SOLIDITY_MAX_INT defined as $2^{256} - 1$. It indeed corresponds to the largest (unsigned) integer type natively supported by the Solidity programming language of the Ethereum smart contracts. A private communication with the designers confirmed that the reason for removing the ballot decryption of the smart-contract code and changing the protocol accordingly was due to the lack of time to implement a multi-precision library in Solidity, that became necessary after increasing the key size to 1024 bits.

Although the coincidence of the originally chosen bit size for the primes and the largest integer size natively supported in Solidity is striking, it is hard to be sure that this is the reason for the mistake. We can however speculate and consider that the purpose of the multilevel variant of ElGamal was to compensate for this admittedly small key size. Maybe the designers hoped for a much better security by using the three successive encryptions, just like Triple-DES is much stronger than DES. Unfortunately, things are quite different for asymmetric cryptography.

Another cause of using 256-bit keys could be the confusion between the security brought by elliptic curve cryptography and the one offered by using finite fields.

3.2   What Occurred on D-Day

The public source code repository was updated on September 6 (two days before the election) in order to take into account our second attack. In the final version the message m to be encrypted is now squared before being passed to the ElGamal encryption, so that, indeed, the data that is encrypted is a quadratic residue.

The prime chosen to define the group is congruent to 3 modulo 4. This has the following consequence: (-1) is a quadratic non-residue in $\mathbb{F}_p^*$, and the Tonelli-Shanks modular square root algorithm [32] takes its simplest form, namely raising to the power $(p + 1)/4$.

In order to recover the original message after the decryption, this square root by modular exponentiation is performed, and the sign choice is based on the relative size of $p - m$ and m as integers between 1 and $p - 1$. Indeed, all the deputy identities that are encrypted as integers that are much smaller than p.

This is close to a fix we proposed when publishing our second attack, but instead of doing an additional exponentiation during encryption and having a cheap decryption, here the encryption is cheap and the decryption includes the additional exponentiation. This makes sense, since the decryption can be done on high-end servers, while the encryption is done on the voter's device which might be a smartphone.

Therefore, on September 8, the election took place with an encryption procedure which was not easy to break. Even though 1024 bits are not enough for even a medium-term security, it is certainly hard (not to say infeasible) to solve a discrete logarithm problem of that size in less than 12 h of wall clock time. With the current public algorithmic knowledge (and extrapolations based on existing record computations [2, 19]), billions of computing cores would have to be mobilized and made to cooperate, which sounds unlikely, even with the resources of a major company or governmental agency.

According to the organizers, more than 10 thousands of Muscovites used the Internet voting system, in the 3 districts. In one of the districts, the difference between the first and the second candidates was less than 100 votes in total. This proves in retrospect the really high stakes of this experiment, since a risk of fraud in the system directly implies a risk of getting a wrong final result.

During the election, it was possible to access the blockchain data with a web interface, and the encrypted ballots were present in it. At the end of the day, the private key was also sent to the blockchain for verifiability purposes. But a few hours later, the access to the blockchain was cut. Fortunately, analysts of the Meduza online newspaper recorded everything and made the data available[1]. They also used the private key to decrypt the 9810 encrypted ballots they found in the blockchain and published them. The statistics they observed from this data raises questions about the fairness of the election, but it is impossible to draw conclusions from just the published data.

This cutting of the access to the blockchain just after revealing the decryption key looks like an attempt to mitigate the risk of leaking the votes, while still having some kind of verifiability. This seems not to have been convincing: Soon after the election, the head of the Central Election Commission of the Russian Federation, Ella Pamfilova, made a public declaration[2] clearly expressing concern about the results of this experiment and that in the coming years this should not be extended to the whole territory.

3.3 On the Absence of Specification

In our opinion, the main problems with the Moscow Internet voting system are:

– the absence of a public specification;
– the modifications made in a rush, just before the election.

In a clear specification, we expect to find much more details about the task of each entity playing a role in the system. From just the source code it is not always clear who is supposed to run some part of the code. What is also needed is clear statements about the security claims and the trust assumptions.

While the designers obviously had some verifiability properties in mind, hence used a blockchain, they certainly also wanted to maintain vote secrecy, as it is always a requirement in such a political context. It seems however, that vote secrecy with respect to the web server that received the (encrypted) ballots was

---

[1] https://meduza.io/slides/meriya-sluchayno...chto-strannoe.
[2] https://www.kommersant.ru/doc/4095101.

not a goal. Furthermore, as far as we can see, coercion-resistance was not at all a concern, at least initially.

We do not claim that having coercion-resistance and privacy with respect to the voting server is necessary for any voting system. But this should be clearly stated, so that the officials who validate the use of the system can take the decision, while knowing the risks.

This ideal process of having a clear specification, with well-stated trust assumptions and security claims is deeply incompatible with the way this election was organized. Indeed, while making a slight modification to a protocol to fix a problem is certainly feasible without having to do again the security analysis from scratch, the changes made by the designers just a few weeks or even a few days before the election were so important that they would have required to revise pages and pages of documentation if this documentation was public. And in fact, it seems that the decision to cut the access to the blockchain shortly after the end of the election was made as a quick response to some bad press about the risks on privacy and coercion. Somehow, they decided to reduce the verifiability to try to save other properties.

4   Lessons Learned and Conclusion

The first lesson learned from this story is, not surprisingly, that designers should be very careful when using cryptography. The authors of the Moscow system made many mistakes with the encryption scheme they decided to use. And in fact, even now, technically the encryption is still weak for two reasons. First, the 1024-bit key is too small for medium term security, and if the protocol changes so that vote privacy relies on it, this will not be enough. Furthermore, as far as we could see, the way the prime was chosen is not public, so that it could include a trapdoor making discrete logarithms easy to compute for the designers [8]. Second, textbook ElGamal, which is what is implemented now, is not IND-CCA2. Depending on the protocol, this might lead to minor or devastating attacks. As an example of the latter, in a protocol that would include a decryption oracle that allows to decrypt any ciphertext that is not in the ballot box (for instance, for audit purpose), it would be easy to use the homomorphic properties of ElGamal to get all the ballots decrypted.

The second lesson is that using a blockchain is not enough to guarantee full transparency. There are various notions of verifiability in the e-voting literature [5], and the designers must clearly say which property they have, under precise trust assumptions. These trust assumptions must be made even more carefully when using a permissioned blockchain, where the nodes running the blockchain are probably specifically chosen for the election, and where the access to the blockchain can be cut at any time.

Even more specific to e-voting, the Moscow system is a good example of the difficulty for an Internet voting system to make the vote secrecy rely uniquely on cutting the link between the voters and their encrypted ballots when they arrive on a server that should also authenticate the voters. What is really required is to cut the link with the vote in clear, and, for this, classical methods exist like homomorphic decryption or verifiable mixnets. In such a high-stakes election, many seemingly incompatible security properties must be satisfied (secrecy vs transparency), and advanced cryptographic tools are almost impossible to avoid.

Finally, as a conclusion, although our attacks led to the system using a better encryption scheme, it is clear that the system as a whole is still far from being perfect. We consider it likely that if the specification were becoming public in the future, other attacks would be revealed. Therefore, we believe that the main impact of our work was to draw the attention to the system as something that was maybe not as secure as what was claimed. The bad publicity in the press hopefully influenced some potential voters who decided not to take the risk of using this still really problematic system and went for paper ballots instead.

Acknowledgements. Thanks to Iuliia Krivonosova and Robert Krimmer, for sharing some information about the Moscow Internet voting. In particular Iuliia's blog post [20] was quite useful. We also thank Noah Stephens-Davidowitz for his comments on an earlier version of this note. We thank Mikhail Zelenskiy and Denis Dmitriev for sharing some data and information about the voting scheme.

A   A Shell Script for the First Attack

```
## These are commands to be run on a Linux machine (Debian or Ubuntu).
## The main tool for the discrete logarithm computations is CADO-NFS,
## and we use GP-Pari as a 'pocket calculator' for modular arithmetic.
# install some packages
sudo apt install pari-gp jq
sudo apt install libgmp3-dev gcc g++ cmake libhwloc-dev
alias gpnoc="gp -q --default colors=\"no\""
# download and compile cado-nfs
cd /tmp
git clone https://scm.gforge.inria.fr/anonscm/git/cado-nfs/cado-nfs.git
cd cado-nfs
git checkout 6b3746a2ec27  # version of 16/08
make cmake
make -j 4

# download blockchain-voting and extract public keys
cd /tmp
git clone https://github.com/moscow-technologies/blockchain-voting.git
cd blockchain-voting
git checkout d70986b2c4da  # most recent version at the time of writing
cd /tmp

# loop on the 3 public keys; could be done in parallel on 3 machines.
for i in {0,1,2}; do
    start=`date +%s`
    # extract the public key information
    keyfile="/tmp/blockchain-voting/encryption-keys/keys/public-key.json"
```

```
p='jq .modulos[$i] $keyfile | tr -d \"'
g='jq .generators[$i] $keyfile | tr -d \"'
h='jq .publicKeys[$i] $keyfile | tr -d \"'
ell='echo "($p-1)/2" | gpnoc'
# run cado-nfs to get log of h (takes a few minutes)
wdir='mktemp -d /tmp/cadorunXXXXXX'
log_h='/tmp/cado-nfs/cado-nfs.py -dlp -ell $ell \
      workdir=$wdir target=$h $p'
# run again to get log of generator
# (faster, since it reuses precomputed data)
log_g='/tmp/cado-nfs/cado-nfs.py $wdir/p75.parameters_snapshot.0 \
      target=$g'
# deduce private key
x='gpnoc <<EOF
xell=lift(Mod($log_h,$ell)/Mod($log_g,$ell)); half=lift(1/Mod(2,$ell));
x0=lift(Mod(2*half*xell, 2*$ell)); h0=lift(Mod($g,$p)^x0);
if (h0 != $h, x0=lift(Mod(2*half*xell+$ell, 2*$ell)));
x0
EOF'
  stop='date +%s'
  echo "Private key number $((i+1)) is $x, computed in \
      $((stop-start)) seconds."
done
```

B Encrypted Messages Are Not Quadratic Residues

In this Appendix we use the provided public key and encrypted messages in the modified version of the public repository [10] (revision 1d4f348681e9) to show that not all messages are quadratic residues in $\mathbb{F}_p^*$. Here b is the set of the second components of the encrypted messages (that is, each element of the set is $\text{pk}^r \cdot m$ where m is some plain message, pk is the public key, and r is a random number). The following Python code shows that only five out of ten elements are quadratic residues. For simplicity, we compute the Legendre symbol by modular exponentiation: the quadratic residues give 1 when raised to the power $(p-1)/2$.

```
p =
10062759081450625618037903678618826196600591242500860802791085970455088
29615914188038720723057459046019130152450978128758867982127126946624453
23678201384359740027439588690880234391145675099291004487668846511981135
30933109486902142540395785614572268133031351548262091859360232929939444
13790774277488668822254003

q = (p-1)//2

b = [
86911001506497462251782638567319361833688978813664946437333829354738909
40443974481927929263283486987233406326466505025027434679060583881689706
23263052860581382950555984777741255550170498945067604675549635835663141
2
74356550963994173797345489306417174072514309856175754908122436241421564
```

```
    8591783263203132049456 49,
    3299457871584631562533428246538912811301519308444499447158313577 2127926
    4495189216142745357056676629897986418517052061640312479742701073 0707520
    1610948340405359817499941661787769955180551913736127546566546769 1230764
    4437522488935754148894266768571418820380541697208586367468659980 3137288
    02786163926222734481398 0,
    2560545139910662067665287310202196464136245462414840931145977295 8496440
    6701684357831590854518407777279459383097915161681981096625570956 7920814
    1307781970980669472368996913795738392317034953045148344118833747 7065322
    8715183899750959829920614795647938102256321597876410019562966371 2388182
    647511089787862332483202,
    3093619755156726968584704235224083428717175654186238229585885251 6666762
    1175580597972987902300728528688073267489198900774102263333080055 0368742
    5634694123708900938179463238979856207845679644295864478950135707 6108208
    7796254747070326877377617473361742706781012217551529249331750729 52910690
    305403946708512011344065,
    9018922765936569735506350094170653683647853755146175994563182331 9091683
    1313053994704341622298458027052615259375645755548559901874024322 9324226
    8496056123926044272963767175613487057669605358427303185798116851 8983390
    5386408492905570624005530715191873695245660821070093795336320833 6695605
    30841450436378971478235 5,
    9176471491583444531026571713619544684591502051085470863482880774 1642908
    6508880523401650934200991380942879591972292661384753907905599781 6788187
    9917052624500221133644203420782690236378637668193427162338885285 7592304
    1327840153384626088839825387791598125452056287269861768570597961 2448346
    470413913994244174120780,
    5318013354169192087730339310662287621388055747016360479359765563 4027675
    1336068511676837675830033887865196195563319184412558762005750052 4945640
    2393227799616594227461148863031287440218730437548530377230727786 7299568
    0523214261366131217146138614042957662153084546941080912320427351 8058446
    9752663616941869119402 44,
    9638911028764875850934477338665759448813254970258956501202882352 2666392
    6032317432687128953469019011782725423525194203741918181682678104 5590593
    2937115562363365747923634081141969330929808282300805577394037992 8788914
    6124369763018306865512065168549924876309245900093030687143136619 8968873
    6095553019415993930349 47,
    6886851896871840196194756588328695767849685951608120864539139405 1517430
    6015408956986801439660007868571874231097634963676188431246376221 4119090
    1701436781411116307892372626892480783711873063933988540884639378 93954685
    3097965701800706584840528069727689283919454214761611987409749455 7367533
    44803639667081357573332,
    5904933193593240919170352198144917803389783373936393880337478049 6048381
    0816785264911600953745938638603259926718273185522180400354596301 6545542
    4123146739280023651401037057755563599858583753397421886557753387 4244033
    4500313336568587824556213052011164907718663215720509585133491214 1011894
    784614717824328145876601
]

for i in range(len(b)):
    print(pow(b[i], q, p))
```

C   Parameters from the Public Testing Held on August 28

In this Appendix we show the encryption parameters used for the last public testing held on August 28, 2019. These were not included in the GitHub public repository but were extracted from the Javascript code sent to the voters. There were two candidates, one option corresponded to a quadratic residue, while the other one corresponded to a quadratic non-residue. Therefore, the second attack described in Sect. 2.2 would have decoded all votes.

```
p =
12270848251665690851841155105748670756648053237913900516699359405362771
39717263095726449865110213728719981659033550058365258369834144969686617
29191112587333253191262755602784412922675331893614019119979108938727080
35007007749458130783976450013979645236359373116042676595576310035726012
4300619948890487736216143
q = (p-1) // 2
m1 = 3247602110
m2 = 667396531
print(pow(m1, q, p))
print(pow(m2, q, p))
```

References

1. Adida, B., De Marneffe, O., Pereira, O., Quisquater, J.J.: Electing a university president using open-audit voting: analysis of real-world use of Helios. In: Proceedings of the 2009 Conference on Electronic Voting Technology/Workshop on Trustworthy Elections, EVT/WOTE 2009, p. 10. USENIX (2009)
2. Adrian, D., et al.: Imperfect forward secrecy: how Diffie-Hellman fails in practice. In: 22nd Conference on Computer and Communications Security, ACM CCS 2015, pp. 5–17. ACM Press (2015)
3. Buterin, V.: Ethereum white paper (2013). GitHub repository. https://github.com/ethereum/wiki/wiki/White-Paper
4. Cannon, J., Bosma, W., Fieker, C., Steel, A.: Handbook of MAGMA functions (2006). http://magma.maths.usyd.edu.au/magma/handbook/
5. Cortier, V., Galindo, D., Küsters, R., Mueller, J., Truderung, T.: SoK: verifiability notions for e-voting protocols. In: IEEE Symposium on Security and Privacy (S&P 2016), pp. 779–798. IEEE (2016)
6. Culnane, C., Schneider, S.: A peered bulletin board for robust use in verifiable voting systems. In: 2014 IEEE 27th Computer Security Foundations Symposium, pp. 169–183 (2014)
7. Franke, J., Kleinjung, T.: Continued fractions and lattice sieving. In: Special-Purpose Hardware for Attacking Cryptographic Systems-SHARCS, p. 40 (2005)
8. Fried, J., Gaudry, P., Heninger, N., Thomé, E.: A kilobit hidden SNFS discrete logarithm computation. In: Coron, J.-S., Nielsen, J.B. (eds.) EUROCRYPT 2017. LNCS, vol. 10210, pp. 202–231. Springer, Cham (2017). https://doi.org/10.1007/978-3-319-56620-7_8

9. Galindo, D., Guasch, S., Puiggali, J.: 2015 Neuchâtel's cast-as-intended verification mechanism. In: 5th International Conference on E-Voting and Identity, (VoteID 2015), pp. 3–18 (2015)
10. Public source code of the Moscow internet voting system (2019). https://github. com/moscow-technologies/blockchain-voting
11. Gjøsteen, K.: The Norwegian internet voting protocol. In: Kiayias, A., Lipmaa, H. (eds.) Vote-ID 2011. LNCS, vol. 7187, pp. 1–18. Springer, Heidelberg (2012). https://doi.org/10.1007/978-3-642-32747-6_1
12. Goodman, N.J.: Internet voting in a local election in Canada. In: Grofman, B., Trechsel, A.H., Franklin, M. (eds.) The Internet and Democracy in Global Perspective. SPC, vol. 31, pp. 7–24. Springer, Cham (2014). https://doi.org/10.1007/978-3-319-04352-4_2
13. Groth, J.: A verifiable secret shuffle of homomorphic encryptions. J. Cryptol. **23**(4), 546–579 (2010)
14. Haenni, R.: Swiss Post public intrusion test - generating random group elements (2019). https://e-voting.bfh.ch/publications/2019/
15. Haenni, R., Koenig, R.E., Locher, P., Dubuis, E.: CHVote system specification. Cryptology ePrint Archive, Report 2017/325 (2017). https://eprint.iacr.org/2017/325
16. Heiberg, S., Willemson, J.: Verifiable internet voting in Estonia. In: 2014 6th International Conference on Electronic Voting: Verifying the Vote (EVOTE), pp. 1–8. IEEE (2014)
17. Hirschi, L., Schmid, L., Basin, D.: Fixing the Achilles heel of e-voting: the bulletin board. Cryptology ePrint Archive, Report 2020/109 (2020). https://eprint.iacr.org/2020/109
18. Joux, A., Lercier, R.: Improvements to the general number field sieve for discrete logarithms in prime fields. A comparison with the gaussian integer method. Math. Comput. **72**(242), 953–967 (2003)
19. Kleinjung, T., Diem, C., Lenstra, A.K., Priplata, C., Stahlke, C.: Computation of a 768-bit prime field discrete logarithm. In: Coron, J.-S., Nielsen, J.B. (eds.) EUROCRYPT 2017. LNCS, vol. 10210, pp. 185–201. Springer, Cham (2017). https://doi.org/10.1007/978-3-319-56620-7_7
20. Krivonosova, J.: Internet voting in Russia: how? (2019). https://medium.com/@juliakrivonosova/internet-voting-in-russia-how-9382db4da71f
21. Lenstra, A.K., Lenstra, H.W. (eds.): The Development of the Number Field Sieve. LNM, vol. 1554. Springer, Heidelberg (1993). https://doi.org/10.1007/BFb0091534
22. Lewis, S.J., Pereira, O., Teague, V.: Trapdoor commitments in the Swiss-Post e-voting shuffle proof (2019). Blog note: https://people.eng.unimelb.edu.au/vjteague/SwissVote.html
23. Lim, C.H., Lee, P.J.: A key recovery attack on discrete log-based schemes using a prime order subgroup. In: Kaliski, B.S. (ed.) CRYPTO 1997. LNCS, vol. 1294, pp. 249–263. Springer, Heidelberg (1997). https://doi.org/10.1007/BFb0052240
24. Public testing of the Internet voting system (2019). https://www.mos.ru/upload/documents/files/5381/Formal_Offer.pdf. (in Russian)
25. Schirokauer, O.: Discrete logarithms and local units. Philos. Trans. R. Soc. London Ser. A **345**(1676), 409–423 (1993)
26. Scytl: Swiss On-line Voting Protocol (2016, manuscript)
27. The CADO-NFS Development Team: CADO-NFS, an implementation of the number field sieve algorithm (2019). Development version fdae0f9f382c: http://cado-nfs.gforge.inria.fr/

28. The PARI Group: PARI/GP version 2.11.0 (2018). http://pari.math.u-bordeaux.fr/
29. The Sage Developers: Sagemath, the Sage Mathematics Software System (Version 8.8) (2019). https://www.sagemath.org
30. Thomé, E.: Subquadratic computation of vector generating polynomials and improvement of the block Wiedemann algorithm. J. Symb. Comput. **33**(5), 757–775 (2002)
31. Valenta, L., et al.: Measuring small subgroup attacks against Diffie-Hellman. In: NDSS (2017)
32. Von Zur Gathen, J., Gerhard, J.: Modern Computer Algebra, 3rd edn. Cambridge University Press, Cambridge (2013)
33. Weber, D., Denny, T., Zayer, J.: Discrete logarithms mod p: 215, 248 and 281 bit computation announcements on the NMBRTHRY mailing list (1995). https://listserv.nodak.edu/cgi-bin/wa.exe?A0=NMBRTHRY

Short Paper: XOR Arbiter PUFs Have Systematic Response Bias

Nils Wisiol$^{(\boxtimes)}$ (iD) and Niklas Pirnay

Chair for Security in Telecommunications, Technische Universität Berlin,
Berlin, Germany
nils.wisiol@tu-berlin.de, niklas.pirnay@campus.tu-berlin.de

Abstract. We demonstrate that XOR Arbiter PUFs with an even number of arbiter chains have inherently biased responses, even if all arbiter chains are perfectly unbiased. This rebukes the believe that XOR Arbiter PUFs are, like Arbiter PUFs, unbiased when ideally implemented and proves that independently manufactured Arbiter PUFs are not statistically independent.

As an immediate result of this work, we suggest to use XOR Arbiter PUFs with odd numbers of arbiter chains whenever possible. Furthermore, our analysis technique can be applied to future types of PUF designs and can hence be used to identify design weaknesses, in particular when using Arbiter PUFs as building blocks and when developing designs with challenge pre-processing. We support our theoretical findings through simulations of prominent PUF designs. Finally, we discuss consequences for the parameter recommendations of the Interpose PUF.

Investigating the reason of the systematic bias of XOR Arbiter PUF, we exhibit that Arbiter PUFs suffer from a systematic uniqueness weakness.

Keywords: Physically Unclonable Function · Bias · Arbiter PUF · Interpose PUF

1 Introduction and Related Work

Physically Unclonable Functions (PUFs) are "biometrics" for integrated circuits. Like fingerprints for humans, PUFs should expose (somewhat) unique characteristics of a circuit instance that can be used to identify or even authenticate a particular circuit. The specific characteristics of a circuit are usually formalized as input-output ("challenge-response") behavior. *Strong* PUFs have the additional requirement that each circuit has such a large number of features (input-output pairs) that it is infeasible for an attacker to copy and imitate all features.

Research in strong PUFs has spent much attention on Arbiter PUFs, which were introduced by Gassend et al. [3], and its countless variations. While the Arbiter PUF does have an exponentially large challenge-space, Gassend et al. noted that its behavior can be characterized by a hyperplane and is thus an easy

© International Financial Cryptography Association 2020
J. Bonneau and N. Heninger (Eds.): FC 2020, LNCS 12059, pp. 50–57, 2020.
https://doi.org/10.1007/978-3-030-51280-4_4

target for prediction algorithms trained with machine learning on observed examples. This raises legitimate concern, as in many usage scenarios, such training data could be easily obtained by a man-in-the-middle attacker. Sölter and Rührmair et al. [8,13] demonstrated that prediction is even possible when multiple Arbiter PUFs are used and only the XOR of the responses is returned. Their attack on the *XOR Arbiter PUF* demonstrated that training of a model is feasible, even though the PUF behavior cannot be characterized by a single hyperplane anymore. This also holds true for the Lightweight Secure PUF by Majzoobi et al. [6] that modifies a given challenge before passing it to an underlying XOR Arbiter PUF. Most recently, Nguyen et al. [7] proposed the Interpose PUF, essentially consisting of two XOR Arbiter PUFs. However, using deep neural networks, successful attacks on XOR Arbiter PUF and Interpose PUF have been claimed [11].

Side-channel-based attacks on XOR Arbiter PUFs have also been successfully mounted. In 2013, Delvaux and Verbauwhede [2] modeled a single Arbiter PUF based on the response reliability. In 2014, Tajik et al. [14] were able to extract physical features of the Arbiter PUF circuit using photonic emission analysis, allowing them to deduce a mathematical model and prediction algorithm for the PUF. In 2015, Becker [1] demonstrated an attack against the "4-way" XOR Arbiter PUF, where four variations of the same challenge are fed in the same Arbiter PUF and the parity of the four responses is output to the user. The attack trains a model using an evolution-strategy algorithm based on the reliability of responses rather than their bit-value.

Hardware implementations of Arbiter PUFs have been extensively studied. Katzenbeisser et al. [4] conducted an analysis of Arbiter PUFs implemented in ASIC, evaluating the reliability of responses and sensitivity to temperature change. In a similar study, Maes et al. [5] studied the uniqueness and reliability of Arbiter PUFs in ASIC under the influence of ageing. Sahoo et al. [10] studied the bias inherent to the *implementation* of a PUF design, considering FPGA implementations of the Arbiter PUF.

This paper is organized as follows. Sect. 2 introduces the additive delay model and contains the theoretical analysis of XOR Arbiter PUF bias. In Sect. 3, we present simulation results to support our analysis and discuss the results and consequences. We conclude the paper in Sect. 4.

2 Bias Analysis

2.1 Background: Additive Delay Model

An Arbiter PUF consists of two symmetric signal paths going through n *stages* before reaching the *arbiter*. At each stage, the signals may be interchanged, depending on the challenge bit that is assigned to this particular stage. The arbiter will output whether there is a signal first on the top or bottom line of its input. An XOR Arbiter PUF consists of k parallel Arbiter PUFs, but only the parity (XOR) of their responses is output to the user. A schematic representation of a 2-XOR Arbiter PUF can be found in Fig. 1.

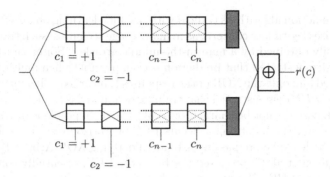

Fig. 1. Schematic representation of an XOR Arbiter PUF with $k = 2$ parallel arbiter chains.

To model the behavior of XOR Arbiter PUFs, the additive delay model is widely and successfully used [3,6,8,13]; Delvaux and Verbauwhede [2] give a physical motivation. Modeling results above 99% accuracy, as obtained by the modeling attacks mentioned above, show that the additive delay model can model physical Arbiter PUFs with very high accuracy.

Written using -1 and 1 to represent bit values, the additive delay model states that any instance of the Arbiter PUF with n stages can be modeled as an affine hyperplane,[1]

$$r(c) = \mathrm{sgn}\left[\langle w, x \rangle + w_0\right] = \mathrm{sgn}\left[\left(\sum_{i=1}^{n} w_i x_i\right) + w_0\right],\qquad(1)$$

where $w \in \mathbb{R}^n$ and $w_0 \in \mathbb{R}$ model the physical properties of the particular instance and x is a function of the given challenge bits c defined by $x_i = c_i \cdot c_{i+1} \cdots c_n$. Note that while the *threshold* w_0 relates to the bias $\mathbb{E}_c\left[r(c)\right]$ of the Arbiter PUF, the relation of these two values is not linear, as small perturbation of the threshold does not change the bias. We approximate the relation of threshold and bias below.

Building on the Arbiter PUF model, a k-XOR Arbiter PUF can be modeled by the product[2] of k Arbiter PUF models,

$$r(c) = \mathrm{sgn}\prod_{l=1}^{k}\sum_{i=1}^{n} w_{l,i} x_i + w_{l,0}.\qquad(2)$$

In the additive delay model, the $k \cdot n$ parameters $w_{l,i}$ and the $w_{l,0}$ are assumed to be normally distributed[3]. XOR Arbiter PUF variants that transform the input

[1] The *sgn* function returns the sign of the argument. In our setting, sgn 0 will only occur with probability zero; for completeness we define sgn 0 = 1.
[2] Notice that when using -1 and 1 to represent bit values, the standard product of bit values corresponds to the logical XOR operation.
[3] In fact, some parameters have different variances [2], but this is immaterial to the discussion in this paper.

challenge before processing it with the arbiter chains, e.g. the Lightweight Secure PUF [6], can be modeled by appropriately augmenting the definition of x.

2.2 Analysis

XOR Arbiter PUF bias can be analyzed by expanding the product of the additive delay model (see (2)) to observe the resulting threshold term. In order to focus on the *systematic* bias of XOR Arbiter PUF designs, we assume each Arbiter PUF to be independently chosen and *unbiased*.

The term $\prod_{l=1}^{k} \sum_{i=1}^{n} w_{l,i} x_i$ in (2) is a polynomial of degree k over variables x_i that take values in $\{-1, 1\}$. Hence, $r(c)$ is a polynomial threshold function of degree at most k, including some monomials of the form $x_i^k \cdot \prod_{l=1}^{k} w_{l,i}$. If (and only if) k is even, these monomials contribute to the threshold term. When k is odd, no product will degenerate into a constant term, i.e. perfectly unbiased Arbiter PUFs will yield a perfectly unbiased XOR Arbiter PUF. As an example, a 2-XOR Arbiter PUF can then be modeled as

$$
r(c) = r_1(c) \cdot r_2(c) = \text{sgn} \left[\sum_{\substack{i,j \\ i \neq j}} w_{1,i} w_{2,j} x_i x_j + \sum_{\substack{i,j \\ i=j}} w_{1,i} w_{2,j} \right]. \tag{3}
$$

It can be seen that even assuming unbiased building blocks, we obtain a non-zero threshold term of $\sum_{i=1}^{n} w_{1,i} w_{2,i}$. While the expectation of this value in the manufacturing process is zero, a high variance causes the 2-XOR Arbiter PUF to likely have significant bias. In other words, any 2-XOR Arbiter PUF consisting of two *unbiased* arbiter chains is biased with probability 1.

Theorem 1. *The responses of independently chosen unbiased Arbiter PUFs queried on the same challenge are not statistically independent.*

Proof. Let r_1, r_2 be models of unbiased Arbiter PUFs with parameters $w_i^{(1)}$ and $w_i^{(2)}$ for $1 \leq i \leq n$ chosen independently at random and $w_0^{(1)} = w_0^{(2)} = 0$ as defined in (1). As demonstrated in (3), the threshold of $r_1(c) \cdot r_2(c)$ is non-zero and hence[4] $\Pr[r_1(c) \cdot r_2(c) = 1] \neq 1/2$. However, assuming statistical independence we have $\Pr[r_1(c) \cdot r_2(c) = 1] = \Pr[r_1(c) = r_2(c)] = 1/2$.   □

---

[4] An approximation of the bias $E_c[r(c)]$ in dependence of the threshold value can be obtained using the Berry-Esseen-Theorem to approximate $\sum_{i,j} w_{1,i} w_{2,j} x_1 x_2$ for $i \neq j$ as a Gaussian random variable with variance σ^2 over uniformly chosen random challenges, resulting in $E_c[r(c)] \approx \text{erf}\left(\frac{\sum_{i=1}^{n} w_{1,i} w_{2,i}}{\sigma \sqrt{2}}\right)$; the value $\sum_{i=1}^{n} w_{1,i} w_{2,i}$ in turn follows (in the manufacturing random process) a distribution composed of the sum of product-normal distributions, which has increasing variance for increasing n. Extending the setting, for higher (but even) k the distribution narrows as the variance of the product-normal distribution narrows. The later effect can be observed in our simulations, cf. Fig. 2.

These results are relevant for novel designs based on several XOR Arbiter PUFs, like the Interpose PUF, as well as for designs based on a single XOR Arbiter PUF, but with novel transformation of the challenge. As an example, Theorem 1 can easily be extended to cover all input transformations that result in the same challenge for each arbiter chain.

Finally, we emphasize again that the analytical results hold regardless of any implementation weakness and thus are a systematic weakness of the Arbiter PUF design.

3   Discussion

3.1   Simulation Results

We confirmed the systematic XOR Arbiter PUF bias in simulations[5] for different XOR Arbiter PUF sizes and input transformations, including the Interpose PUF. All simulations are based on the additive delay model with standard Gaussian weights and were conducted using *unbiased* arbiter chains. The distribution of the systematic bias is based on sampling 100 instances each; the bias of each instance is estimated using 1,000,000 responses to uniformly random challenges.

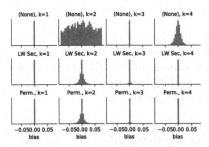

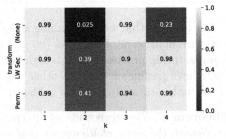

(a) Histogram of bias estimates. A bias value of zero represents perfectly unbiased responses.

(b) Proportion of instances that passed the NIST frequency test at significance level 1%.

Fig. 2. Analysis results for simulated 64-bit k-XOR Arbiter PUFs, k-Lightweight Secure PUFs and k-Permutation XOR Arbiter PUFs build from unbiased Arbiter PUFs. For each type and size, 5000 instances were sampled and queried with one million uniformly random challenges each.

In Fig. 2 we show the estimated bias distribution for XOR Arbiter PUFs and Lightweight Secure PUFs, which confirm our theoretical findings. As expected, the systematic bias is only present for PUFs with an even number of arbiter chains, while PUFs with an odd number of arbiter chains remain (systematically) unbiased. The bias variance becomes smaller as k increases. The statistical

---

[5] The software used for simulation and analysis publicly available as free software at https://github.com/nils-wisiol/pypuf/tree/2020-systematic-bias.

significance of these findings can be confirmed by applying a bias test like the one specified in NIST's SP-800-22 test suite [9]: while our simulation passes the tests on 99% of XOR Arbiter PUF instances whenever k is odd; it fails for almost all instances when $k = 2$, and fails for the majority of instances when $k = 4$ (see Fig. 2). This is also in line with our theoretical findings and simulation results, as we expect the effect to become smaller as k increases.

We hence recommend using an odd number of arbiter chains to avoid potential additional attack surface and especially discourage the use of two or four parallel chains. These recommendations also apply whenever (XOR) Arbiter PUFs are used as building blocks for larger PUFs, such as is the case in the Interpose PUF, as bias in intermediate values can result in increased predictability.

The bias distribution also suggests that the input transformation as done by the Lightweight Secure PUF [6] compensates the systematic bias to some extend, which may be a contributing factor to the increased machine learning resistance [8,15] of the Lightweight Secure PUF. On the other hand, the Lightweight Secure PUF and Permutation XOR Arbiter PUF [15] seems to introduce bias for the case $k = 3$. Such effects should be considered when designing novel input transformations.

Our findings also extend to the recently proposed Interpose PUF [7], which is a combination of two XOR Arbiter PUFs and was designed to be resilient against all state-of-the-art modeling attacks, while being CMOS-compatible. Consisting of two interposed XOR Arbiter PUFs, our simulation shows that the "down" XOR Arbiter PUF plays an important role for the systematic bias, while the "up" XOR Arbiter PUF only has minor influence on it (see Fig. 3).

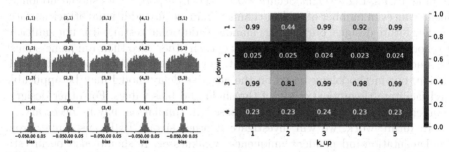

(a) Histogram of bias estimates. A bias value of zero represents perfectly unbiased responses.

(b) Proportion of instances that passed the NIST frequency test at significance level 1%.

Fig. 3. Analysis results for simulated 64 bit (k_{up}, k_{down})-iPUF instances build from unbiased Arbiter PUFs. For each size, 5000 instances were sampled and queried with one million uniformly random challenges each.

Given these findings, we provide additional evidence for the original author's advice to use the Interpose PUFs with an odd number of arbiter chains in the lower layer. Furthermore, as our findings are applicable any XOR Arbiter PUF, we extend the parameter recommendation to include the upper layer as well.

3.2 XOR Arbiter PUF Bias and Arbiter PUF Uniqueness

Our results above, stated in terms of the bias of XOR Arbiter PUFs, are closely related to the uniqueness of Arbiter PUFs. The theoretical and simulation results show that any 64 bit 2-XOR Arbiter PUF has significant bias with high probability, even when implemented ideally (i.e., composed of unbiased Arbiter PUFs). In terms of uniqueness this means that any independently chosen pair of (ideal) Arbiter PUFs has, with high probability, low uniqueness, as perfectly unique Arbiter PUFs are statistically independent and hence their XOR Arbiter PUF would not have any bias. It must be noted though, that, as per the properties of the parity, the uniqueness will only play out in a systematic bias whenever k is even, hence our recommendation to use XOR Arbiter PUFs with odd k.

The inherent low uniqueness of Arbiter PUFs, independent of their implementation, may relate to findings by Schaub et al. [12] that claim an upper bound to the entropy of Arbiter PUFs at $O(n^2)$.

4   Conclusion

In this paper, we exhibited that XOR Arbiter PUFs with an even number of arbiter chains have systematic bias, independently of implementation issues. As bias is an inherent weakness to any PUF, parameter recommendations for XOR Arbiter PUFs, Lightweight Secure PUFs, and Interpose PUFs should no longer include an even number of arbiter chains to remove any additional attack surface.

For future designs, our findings mandate additional testing: it is not sufficient to choose building blocks independently of each other; also their uniqueness must be studied implementation-independent. For designs based on the Arbiter PUF design, our methodology based on the additive delay model may be applicable and facilitate theoretical study of threshold and bias values. For other designs, a different model or empirical testing based on simulation may be necessary.

In future work, we will investigate if other strong PUFs also suffer from implementation-independent uniqueness weaknesses. It should also be investigated if the bias of an XOR Arbiter PUF can assist a modeling attack.

References

1. Becker, G.T.: The gap between promise and reality: on the insecurity of XOR arbiter PUFs. In: Güneysu, T., Handschuh, H. (eds.) CHES 2015. LNCS, vol. 9293, pp. 535–555. Springer, Heidelberg (2015). https://doi.org/10.1007/978-3-662-48324-4_27
2. Delvaux, J., Verbauwhede, I.: Side channel modeling attacks on 65 nm arbiter PUFs exploiting CMOS device noise. In: 2013 IEEE International Symposium on Hardware-Oriented Security and Trust (HOST), pp. 137–142. IEEE (2013)

3. Gassend, B., Lim, D., Clarke, D., van Dijk, M., Devadas, S.: Identification and authentication of integrated circuits. Concurr. Comput. Pract. Exp. **16**(11), 1077–1098 (2004). https://onlinelibrary.wiley.com/doi/abs/10.1002/cpe.805
4. Katzenbeisser, S., Kocabaş, Ü., Rožić, V., Sadeghi, A.-R., Verbauwhede, I., Wachsmann, C.: PUFs: myth, fact or busted? A security evaluation of physically unclonable functions (PUFs) cast in silicon. In: Prouff, E., Schaumont, P. (eds.) CHES 2012. LNCS, vol. 7428, pp. 283–301. Springer, Heidelberg (2012). https://doi.org/10.1007/978-3-642-33027-8_17
5. Maes, R., Rozic, V., Verbauwhede, I., Koeberl, P., van der Sluis, E., van der Leest, V.: Experimental evaluation of physically unclonable functions in 65 nm CMOS. In: 2012 Proceedings of the ESSCIRC (ESSCIRC), pp. 486–489. IEEE, Bordeaux, September 2012. http://ieeexplore.ieee.org/document/6341361/
6. Majzoobi, M., Koushanfar, F., Potkonjak, M.: Lightweight secure PUFs. In: Proceedings of the 2008 IEEE/ACM International Conference on Computer-Aided Design, ICCAD 2008, pp. 670–673. IEEE Press, Piscataway (2008). http://dl.acm.org/citation.cfm?id=1509456.1509603
7. Nguyen, P.H., Sahoo, D.P., Jin, C., Mahmood, K., Rührmair, U.: The Interpose PUF: Secure PUF Design against State-of-the-art Machine Learning Attacks, p. 48 (2018)
8. Rührmair, U., Busch, H., Katzenbeisser, S.: Strong PUFs: models, constructions, and security proofs. In: Sadeghi, A.R., Naccache, D. (eds.) Towards Hardware-Intrinsic Security. ISC, pp. 79–96. Springer, Heidelberg (2010). https://doi.org/10.1007/978-3-642-14452-3_4
9. Rukhin, A., et al.: A Statistical Test Suite for Random and Pseudorandom Number Generators for Cryptographic Applications. NIST Special Publication 800-22, p. 131 (2010)
10. Sahoo, D.P., Nguyen, P.H., Chakraborty, R.S., Mukhopadhyay, D.: Architectural Bias: A Novel Statistical Metric to Evaluate Arbiter PUF Variants, p. 14 (2016). https://eprint.iacr.org/2016/057
11. Santikellur, P., Bhattacharyay, A., Chakraborty, R.S.: Deep Learning based Model Building Attacks on Arbiter PUF Compositions, p. 10 (2019)
12. Schaub, A., Rioul, O., Joseph, Boutros, J.J.: Entropy Estimation of Physically Unclonable Functions via Chow Parameters. arXiv:1907.05494 [cs, math], July 2019
13. Sölter, J.: Cryptanalysis of electrical PUFs via machine learning algorithms, p. 52 (2009)
14. Tajik, S., et al.: Physical characterization of arbiter PUFs. In: Batina, L., Robshaw, M. (eds.) CHES 2014. LNCS, vol. 8731, pp. 493–509. Springer, Heidelberg (2014). https://doi.org/10.1007/978-3-662-44709-3_27
15. Wisiol, N., Becker, G.T., Margraf, M., Soroceanu, T.A.A., Tobisch, J., Zengin, B.: Breaking the Lightweight Secure PUF: Understanding the Relation of Input Transformations and Machine Learning Resistance, p. 9 (2019). https://eprint.iacr.org/2019/799

Consensus

Selfish Mining Re-Examined

Kevin Alarcón Negy[1($\boxtimes$)], Peter R. Rizun[2], and Emin Gün Sirer[1]

[1] Computer Science Department, Cornell University, Ithaca, USA
kevinnegy@cs.cornell.edu
[2] Bitcoin Unlimited, Vancouver, Canada

Abstract. Six years after the introduction of selfish mining, its counterintuitive findings continue to create confusion. In this paper, we comprehensively address one particular source of misunderstandings, related to difficulty adjustments. We first present a novel, modified selfish mining strategy, called *intermittent selfish mining*, that, perplexingly, is more profitable than honest mining even when the attacker performs no selfish mining after a difficulty adjustment. Simulations show that even in the most conservative scenario ($\gamma = 0$), an intermittent selfish miner above 37% hash power earns more coins per time unit than their fair share. We then broadly examine the profitability of selfish mining under several difficulty adjustment algorithms (DAAs) used in popular cryptocurrencies. We present a taxonomy of popular difficulty adjustment algorithms, quantify the effects of algorithmic choices on hash fluctuations, and show how resistant different DAA families are to selfish mining.

1 Introduction

Twelve years ago, the Bitcoin (BTC) white paper [26] introduced a novel consensus protocol that kicked off an era of permissionless blockchains. In describing this protocol, Nakamoto asserted that the system was secure as long as a majority of miners were honest [25]. To encourage honest participation, Bitcoin offers financial incentives in the form of newly minted bitcoins as well as transaction fees. These incentives, Nakamoto argued, would be more profitable than defying the protocol. Tantamount to an incentive compatibility claim for the protocol, these assertions were adopted widely and became folk theorems, and even garnered justification from formal modeling [18].

Nonetheless, these assertions were proven false. In a counterintuitive result, Eyal and Sirer showed that there existed an alternative strategy, known as selfish mining, whose financial incentive surpassed that of mining honestly [11]. Selfish mining involves withholding mined blocks and releasing them only after honest miners have wasted resources mining alternative blocks. Until a difficulty adjustment, wasting competitors' blocks confers no benefit to the selfish miner (SM). Following a difficulty adjustment, however, the selfish miner can collect much more than its fair share of block rewards, depending on its percentage of total network hash power (α) and what proportion of honest miners mine on a SM's block during a fork in the network (γ). Counterintuitively, the selfish mining

© International Financial Cryptography Association 2020
J. Bonneau and N. Heninger (Eds.): FC 2020, LNCS 12059, pp. 61–78, 2020.
https://doi.org/10.1007/978-3-030-51280-4_5

strategy returns excess profits for any miner or pool with more than $1/3$rd of the global hash power ($\alpha > 33\%$), even with the assumption that no honest miner mines on a selfish block in a fork ($\gamma = 0$). As $\alpha \rightarrow 50\%$, a selfish miner collects close to 100% of rewards in the network, a doubling of its honest income.

Ever since its introduction, the selfish mining paper has attracted a cult of denialism [8,16,35]. Leaving aside claims that stem from an inaccurate model of how the Bitcoin protocol and pooling work [12], the resulting arguments revolve around the issues of difficulty adjustments.

First, critics have asserted that selfish mining is unprofitable because time spent forking blocks only serves to reduce the speed at which the main chain grows. Hence, the argument goes, an increase in relative revenue is meaningless because profit per time-unit decreases. Second, critics have claimed that selfish mining must necessarily involve long-duration attacks that persist past a difficulty adjustment in order to be profitable.

In this paper, we show both of these claims to be false. We illustrate a surprising selfish mining variant where the attacker ceases to act selfishly immediately after a difficulty adjustment, yet, paradoxically, still earns more than an honest miner. We call this strategy *intermittent selfish mining*. We then investigate the profitability of selfish mining under different difficulty adjustment algorithms. In particular, we quantify the benefits of selfish mining on Bitcoin Cash, Bitcoin SV, Ethereum, and Monero, and show the conditions under which profit per time-unit exceeds honest mining.

Overall, this paper introduces intermittent selfish mining (Sect. 3) and quantifies its benefits when applied to the Bitcoin protocol (Sect. 3.2). This protocol is, even more counterintuitively than the original selfish mining strategy, profitable even without performing any attack past the difficulty adjustment. Second, this work provides a taxonomy of difficulty adjustment algorithms (DAAs) (Sect. 4.1). Finally, it examines selfish mining profitability under the DAAs of Bitcoin Cash, Bitcoin SV, Ethereum, and Monero (Sect. 4.3). Overall, the paper provides a more complete picture of selfish mining's implications, and can inform the design of future proof-of-work (PoW) systems.

2 Background

This work describes an adversary employing selfish mining in proof-of-work cryptocurrencies. In this section, we first describe the PoW mining process and then outline the selfish mining algorithm.

2.1 Mining in PoW Cryptocurrencies

At their core, cryptocurrencies allow clients to publish transactions which are collated and placed into blocks by miners. In PoW cryptocurrencies, these blocks are mined by hashing the block data with a nonce until the resulting hash value is below a target value. The target value is determined by a coin's difficulty adjustment algorithm (DAA). *Difficulty* describes how difficult it is to generate a hash below this target value. Once a miner obtains a valid hash, it broadcasts the block to receive newly minted coins and collect transaction fees. Once a block resides on the longest chain, it is considered accepted. *Orphans* are blocks that do not reside on the longest chain. Accepted blocks must then be buried under a sufficiently long suffix of the blockchain for their transactions to be considered finalized.

2.2 Selfish Mining Strategy

In selfish mining, the selfish miner with a hash rate of α withholds newly-mined blocks instead of immediately publishing them. As a result, honest miners are unaware of these blocks and, unknowingly, are coerced into wasting hash power mining blocks that are likely to be replaced in the chain. In this way, a selfish miner probabilistically earns more block rewards than honest miners.

There are three scenarios in which a selfish miner publishes a block.

First, if the SM has a private chain of length two and the next block is found by an honest miner, the new chain height difference is one. At this point, the SM publishes its entire private chain to ensure a fork win.

Second, if the SM has a private chain of length greater than two and the next block is found by an honest miner, the SM publishes only one block, the oldest block in its private chain, while keeping the rest of its private chain hidden.

Third, if the SM has found a single block and the next block is found by the honest miner, the SM will publish its block immediately. At this point, the network is in a forked state. The SM will try to mine on its own block, while the honest miners choose whether to mine on the honest or selfish block. The proportion of honest miners that mine on the selfish block is referred to as γ. Zero represents the most pessimistic γ value; it cannot be negative.

3   Intermittent Selfish Mining

We now introduce the *intermittent selfish mining* strategy. Intermittent selfish mining is a modification of selfish mining in which a miner alternates between selfish and honest mining at every difficulty adjustment in Bitcoin. The Bitcoin DAA targets a block time of ten minutes and adjusts after every 2016 blocks on the main chain. We assume the worst-case scenario for the attacker and omit transaction fees and mining costs from our analysis.

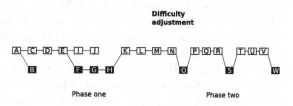

Fig. 1. Intermittent selfish mining timeline. Black indicates ISM-mined blocks. An ISM engages in selfish mining pre-difficulty adjustment, sometimes losing blocks (e.g. block B), but causes difficulty to drop by excluding blocks (e.g. I and J). The ISM mines honestly post-difficulty adjustment and collects more rewards per unit time than it would normally.

Intermittent selfish mining is comprised of two phases. In phase one, an intermittent selfish miner (ISM) employs selfish mining. The goal of phase one is to knock out the honest miners' blocks and set up the attacker to profit in the epoch directly following the attack. As pointed out by critics of selfish mining, although this results in an increase in the number of blocks won relative to the honest miner, this by itself does not lead to increased profit for the selfish miner, not taking into account transaction fees. Phase one merely extends the time it takes to reach 2016 blocks on the main chain; it does not increase the number of blocks per minute produced by the selfish miner. In fact, the profit of the attacker slightly decreases in this phase because at every fork of equal height, the selfish miner risks losing its forked block if the honest miners are able to mine on the honest block before the selfish miner can extend its chain, when $\gamma < 1$. Nonetheless, it will force the network to lower the mining difficulty to make up for slower block times and what it perceives as a lower hash rate.

In phase two, following the difficulty adjustment, the ISM switches to honest mining. With the new lower difficulty, honest mining results in a faster mining rate than normal for all miners. Though this increased rate of minting profits all miners equally in phase two, over the two phases, the ISM profits more relative to the honest miner and per time unit. Surprisingly, this is sufficient for the attacker to gain an advantage over honest miners. This lays to rest the claim that a selfish mining attack must be launched and remain active past a difficulty adjustment. Even though no selfish mining activity takes place after a difficulty adjustment, the attacker still gains an economic advantage. Further, this change in strategy also lowers the likelihood that the honest community will detect selfish mining. An ISM could repeat this strategy over multiple periods and profit more than honest mining in each iteration.

Figure 1 shows an example of intermittent selfish mining over the length of a single iteration. The example involves an ISM with about 30% hash power. In the diagram, blocks are mined in alphabetical order. White blocks represent non-ISM, honest blocks and black blocks are ISM-mined blocks. Selfish mining is employed only in phase one. The ISM mines block B, withholds it, and then is forced to publish it to compete with honest block C. The honest miners mine block D faster than any block is mined on B and therefore B is orphaned. Later, the ISM succeeds in knocking out blocks I and J by withholding its private chain of blocks F, G, and H until the latest possible moment to guarantee a win. Once the difficulty adjustment is reached, selfish mining results in a lower difficulty to compensate for the slower build of the public chain. After this adjustment, in phase two, the ISM mines honestly. Although it wins blocks at its expected rate, the lower difficulty results in more blocks per time unit.

Intermittent selfish mining dispels a misconception about the profitability of selfish mining. Selfish mining is often argued to be impractical because the attack, it is erroneously claimed, must be maintained for several difficulty periods in order for the attacker to earn a profit. The crux of the argument is that because the selfish miner earns less revenue per unit time during the first difficulty period due to its elevated orphan rate, it must maintain the attack for several additional difficulty periods to compensate. Grunspan & Perez-Marco [16] formalized such a time-based revenue model for selfish mining and calculated that an attacker with 10% of the network hash rate and with a γ parameter of 0.9 must maintain the attack for ~10 weeks. Their calculation is incorrect because they fail to account for the profit earned by the attacker in the difficulty period following the attack. Their revenue calculation stops one difficulty period too early, when selfish mining ends. Initiating the attack results in less revenue per unit time during the first difficulty period, but this should be considered a loan rather than a loss: the attacker gets paid back at the conclusion of the attack.

It is easy to show that the selfish miner in the previous example ($\alpha = 10\%$, $\gamma = 0.9$) will earn a profit even if conducting the attack for only a single, 2016-block difficulty period and then switching to honest mining, exactly as would an intermittent selfish miner, using the state probabilities and state transitions from [11]. The presence of an ISM in phase one drives up the orphan rate for the honest miners to 8.61% and its own to 6.74%. We can use the equation

$$2016 = (n * (1 - i) * \alpha) + (n * (1 - h) * (1 - \alpha))$$

to calculate expected, non-orphaned block wins, where i and h are the ISM and honest orphan rate, respectively, and n is the number of blocks that need to be found to complete a difficulty period. In expectation, the ISM will have won 205 blocks, which is 3 blocks more than if employing honest mining, and the honest miners will have won 1811 blocks. The expected time until the difficulty adjustment stretches from 14 days to 15.29 days. Although the ISM earns more than its fair share of block rewards, its revenue per day falls from 14.40 blocks/day to 13.43 blocks/day during phase one. The following difficulty period makes up for this temporary dip.

To compensate for the fact that the last set of 2016 blocks took 15.29 days to find rather than 14 days, the Bitcoin network adjusts the difficulty parameter downwards, making the next 2016 blocks come faster. At this point, the intermittent selfish miner returns to mining honestly in phase two, thereby reducing the network orphan rate back to normal. Because of the lower difficulty, the next 2016 blocks take 12.82 days in expectation. Although the intermittent selfish miner, now mining honestly, earns only 202 blocks in expectation, its expected revenue per day increases to 15.72 blocks/day during phase two.

During these two phases, the equivalent of two difficulty periods, the intermittent selfish miner wins in expectation $205 + 202 = 407$ blocks over the course of $15.29 + 12.82 = 28.11$ days, for an average revenue rate of 14.47 blocks per day. Since its expected revenue per unit time is greater than if it were mining honestly (14.40 blocks per day), intermittent selfish mining is profitable for attack durations significantly shorter than the 70 days computed in [16].

3.1   Intermittent Selfish Mining Evaluation

We examine the intermittent selfish mining strategy using a Monte Carlo simulation to generate a chain of 8064 blocks excluding orphaned blocks, the equivalent

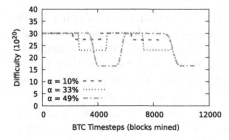
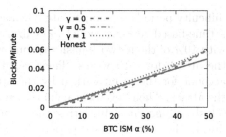

Fig. 2. An ISM causes the difficulty to lower after selfish phases and rise after honest phases ($\gamma = 0$).

Fig. 3. ISM block-win rate.

of two intermittent selfish iterations. At each simulated second, each miner has a random chance of finding a block, set to the miner's hash rate divided by the difficulty of its most recent block.

We design our experiments to answer the following questions. (1) How does intermittent selfish mining affect difficulty? (2) What is the ISM's block-win rate (blocks/minute) and how does it fluctuate in each phase of intermittent selfish mining? (3) Does the overall chain-growth rate (i.e. number of blocks added to the longest chain per minute) change in the presence of an ISM?

To answer these questions, we analyze difficulty, block-win rate, and chain-growth rate as each block is generated in a given run under various α and γ levels. We simulate each combination of parameters 100 times and then calculate averages and standard deviations for the data points.

3.2 Results

First, Fig. 2 shows how an ISM with $\gamma = 0$ affects difficulty throughout two periods. We only show data for $\alpha = 10\%$, 33%, and 49%, which in the original selfish mining paper were minority rates that incurred losses, broke-even, and profited, respectively. As α increases, the number of blocks necessary to reach the end of the two iterations increases. Additionally, the effects of an ISM are more apparent when $\alpha = 49\%$. Selfish mining in phase one requires almost double the normal 2016 blocks to reach a difficulty adjustment. Once the difficulty lowers, honest mining in phase-two occurs for about 2016 blocks, then the period ends.

Next, Fig. 3 shows the intermittent selfish miner's block-win rate for three γ levels: 0, 0.5, and 1. In comparison with the original selfish mining strategy, the potential rewards of intermittent selfish mining are more modest. Nonetheless, expected profits for an ISM surpass the profits of honest mining above certain hash rates depending on the γ value. Even in the most conservative estimation, when $\gamma = 0$, the ISM profits if its hash rate is above 37%. The block-win rates at each γ level converge at around 0.06 as α reaches 50%, which surpasses its expected 0.05 block-win rate.

The corresponding cumulative block-win rate (blocks/minute) by the ISM is shown in Fig. 4. Due to the way the ISM alternates strategies, the win rate fluctuates between phases. In phase one, which includes timesteps 0 to about 4000 for $\alpha = 49\%$, selfish mining has a win rate of about 0.047, which is lower than the expected 0.049 win rate. In phase two, the win rate increases to about 0.057 at its peak, before the next phase shift. Of course, the difficulty adjustment rising back to a higher level combined with resuming selfish mining brings the cumulative block-win rate to 0.053. The win rate will continue to fluctuate, but it will converge to about 0.0568. Figure 4 shows that a miner only has to engage in intermittent selfish mining for a little over one difficulty period to immediately win more blocks per minute than it would under honest mining.

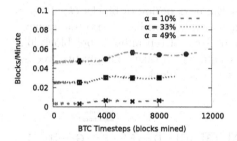

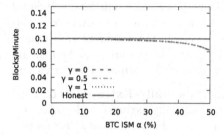

Fig. 4. ISM block-win rate after some number of timesteps ($\gamma = 0$).

Fig. 5. Chain-growth rate in the presence of an ISM. The three γ curves are superimposed since γ values do not affect growth rate.

Finally, Fig. 5 shows the chain-growth rate in the presence of an ISM. In BTC, the expected chain-growth rate is 0.1 blocks/minute. Initially, one might predict that intermittent selfish mining causes deflation by using difficulty to increase the chain-growth rate and, therefore, the supply of bitcoins. Yet, this figure shows that increasing an ISM's α rate lowers the chain-growth rate. Intermittent selfish mining, surprisingly, slows the coin mint rate. Each slow phase-one outweighs the rapid phase-two, which, as an unintended side-effect, leads to a lower chain-growth rate overall, despite increasing profits for the ISM.

4   Difficulty Adjustment Algorithms

We now focus our analysis on difficulty adjustment algorithms (DAAs). Given that there now exist various PoW coins with diverse protocols, an analysis of several current DAAs and their impact on selfish mining was necessary.

The main goal of a difficulty adjustment algorithm is to set a difficulty that causes blocks to be mined at regular target time intervals. A responsive DAA allows a cryptocurrency to quickly adjust difficulty to prevent blocks from being mined at levels too high or low compared to the target rate. On the other hand, being too responsive would allow difficulty levels to be easily manipulated by large miners entering and exiting whenever it benefits them.

In this section we classify various DAAs and evaluate their responsiveness to increases in hash power, both from an honest miner and a selfish miner.

4.1 DAA Taxonomy

Existing approaches to DAA can be classified into three categories:

Period-Based. Period-based DAAs are algorithms in which difficulty is adjusted only at the end of a typically fixed period. A period is defined as the amount of time it takes to generate w blocks on the main chain. The period width, w, can be chosen to be large enough to minimize extreme difficulty fluctuations, but must be small enough to adjust to major hash rate changes.

Figure 6a shows a period-based DAA with $w = 3$. After block F is mined, the period ends and the difficulty is recalculated based on the block times of blocks D - F. The difficulty is then set for the next period of blocks G - I.

Our evaluation of DAAs uses Bitcoin as the period-based cryptocurrency. The Bitcoin DAA targets an average mining time of ten minutes per block [6]. After 2016 blocks are mined on the main chain, which takes roughly two weeks, the difficulty is adjusted to get closer to the target block time.

Incrementally-Extrapolated. The incrementally-extrapolated DAA is one in which difficulty is incremented/decremented depending on how far outside of the block timing bounds a new block is. In contrast to Bitcoin, where a proportion can be used to calculate a new difficulty, incrementally-extrapolated difficulties increase/decrease the current difficulty by a fractional amount. This DAA limits the responsiveness of the cryptocurrency to hash rate changes.

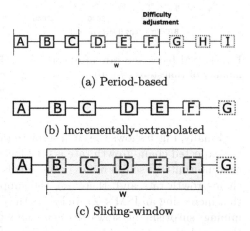

(a) Period-based

(b) Incrementally-extrapolated

(c) Sliding-window

Fig. 6. DAA Taxonomy. Blue blocks are used in the difficulty calculation. Red blocks are mined using the new difficulty. (Color figure online)

Figure 6b shows an example of an incrementally-extrapolated DAA. To mine block G, the DAA only looks at the elapsed time since the parent block F was generated and then adds or subtracts from the parent difficulty depending on how close the elapsed time was to the target block time.

Ethereum (ETH), as of Byzantium, uses an incrementally-extrapolated DAA that adjusts at every new block [9]. Each new block difficulty is calculated by measuring the time difference between the current timestamp and that of its parent, then incrementing or decrementing the parent difficulty depending on whether the time difference is outside of the desired bounds of 9–17 s. As will be shown in the results, a sudden doubling of the hash rate in the network will cause a slow difficulty change compared to a DAA which uses proportion calculations and can adjust difficulty completely within one block.

Sliding-Window. The sliding-window DAA is similar to period-based except its difficulty recalculation occurs at every new block. To calculate the current difficulty, a block-window of width w consisting of ancestor blocks is used. A new difficulty is calculated based on the amount of time it took to generate the blocks in the block-window compared to the expected time.

Figure 6c shows a sliding-window DAA with $w = 5$. To mine block G, the DAA slides its window over blocks B - F and recalculates the difficulty based on how long it took to generate the blocks within the window compared to a target value. Once G is mined, it will be included in the next window.

Cryptocurrencies that use sliding-window DAAs are Bitcoin Cash (BCH), Bitcoin SV (BSV), and Monero (XMR). Given that BSV branched off BCH [1], both share the same DAA and for this paper we refer to them collectively as BCH/BSV. BCH/BSV targets ten minutes per block [3], while Monero targets two minutes per block [23]. The sliding window widths are ~144 and 600 blocks for BCH/BSV and XMR, respectively. To avoid timestamp-based attacks, BCH/BSV chooses the median of the three most recent blocks and the median of the blocks 144–146 behind the current block based on timestamp to use as the beginning and end of the window, respectively [4]. XMR, on the other hand, orders the last 745 blocks, excludes the most recent 15, then omits the outer 120 blocks (i.e. 60 recent and 60 oldest) leaving 600 blocks in its window [24].

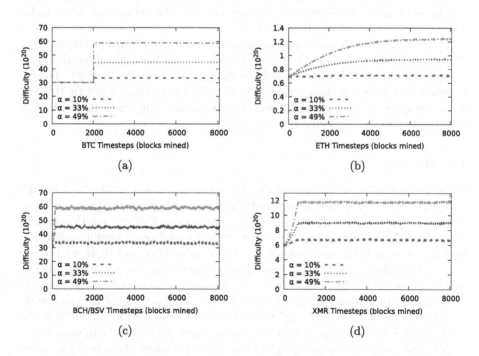

Fig. 7. Difficulty once a new honest miner enters the system ($\gamma = 0$).

4.2   DAA Evaluation

To evaluate these difficulty adjustment algorithms, we examine attacks launched by renting extraneous hash power and ask the following questions. (1) How effective are DAAs at adjusting difficulty if a substantial amount of hash power is introduced to the network? (2) How much can a new miner profit in terms of block-win rate upon entering a new cryptocurrency?

First, we analyze how the various DAAs of Bitcoin, ETH, BCH/BSV, and Monero alter difficulty once a new honest miner enters the system. We also evaluate the block-win rate of the new miner while it takes advantage of the old difficulty. Second, we compare the profitability of a new selfish miner under the different DAA schemes. As before, each experiment simulates the generation of 8064 blocks on each blockchain, not including orphans.

Thus, our simulations start with a network of a given hash power, and then add additional mining power belonging to the adversary. For instance, to introduce a miner with a 30% hash rate, we give the miner enough hash power, S, such that $S/(S + H) = 0.3$, where H is the initial hash power in the network.

We disregard timestamp manipulation attacks by miners because they are an orthogonal concern and their full treatment is beyond the scope of this paper. So, when choosing median BCH/BSV outer blocks, the middle block is always the outer block since the three blocks are guaranteed to be in timestamp order. Recent data from these systems indicate that the timestamp in new blocks matches global time to within seconds.

Our simulations also take into account the difficulty clamps of Bitcoin and BCH/BSV. If the blocks used in a difficulty adjustment were mined too slowly or too quickly, the difficulty adjusts only to the limits set by the difficulty clamps. Bitcoin has a difficulty clamp of $4\times$ or $0.25\times$ the target time, while BCH/BSV has a clamp of $2\times$ and $0.5\times$. As Sect. 4.3 will show, selfish miners under 50% hash power will be unaffected by these clamps.

4.3   Results

We first examine how difficulty adjusts if a new honest miner enters the network, shown in Fig. 7. With the exception of ETH, period/window width is the most significant determining factor in the adjustment period. This width is the amount of blocks necessary to completely adjust difficulty and reach equilibrium when hash power is added to the network. For this reason, BSV and BCH, with their 144 block-window, are the fastest to adjust. Monero takes longer at 675 blocks, which come from the 600 block-window width and the 75 newest blocks that are omitted from the sliding-window. Finally, Bitcoin takes longest of the three with a period width of 2016. ETH differs in that there is no concept of width in its DAA. Since it is incremental, difficulty takes about 10,000 blocks to stabilize.

We omit showing difficulty graphs when a new SM enters the network because difficulty does not adjust much, if at all, for any of the schemes analyzed. A new selfish miner spends time trying to create forks in the network instead of using its hash power to help grow the longest chain. As such, DAAs will not adjust in

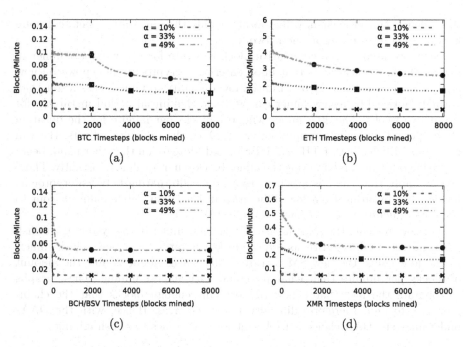

Fig. 8. Cumulative block-win rate of an new honest miner after some number of timesteps ($\gamma = 0$).

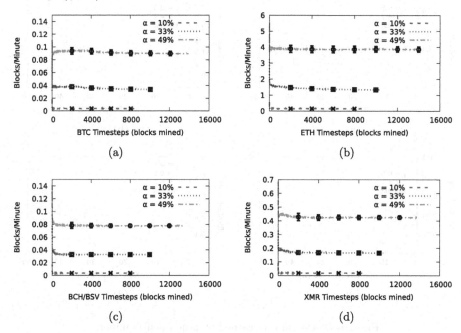

Fig. 9. Cumulative block-win rate of a new selfish miner after some number of timesteps ($\gamma = 0$).

this scenario since the chain will grow at roughly the same rate as before despite having extra hash power in the network.

Next, we analyze the cumulative block-win rate for a new honest miner in Fig. 8. The key takeaway is that upon entering a cryptocurrency, powerful new miners can take advantage of an initial low difficulty to mine blocks faster than normal. Noticeably, a new miner can leverage this initial period in Bitcoin for about two weeks. The 49% miner wins 0.1 blocks per minute for the duration of the period immediately upon entering. Once the difficulty adjusts, the win rate gradually declines. ETH, BCH/BSV, and Monero, on the other hand, begin adjusting difficulty and lowering the miner block-win rate almost instantly. These graphs imply that there is a benefit to a miner alternating between cryptocurrencies and profiting from low difficulties in each, only abandoning a coin to allow its difficulty to revert back to profitable levels.

We now evaluate the same measure if the new miner in the system is a selfish miner. Figure 9 shows corresponding block-win rates for a new selfish miner. In the four coins, the new SM with $\alpha = 49\%$ earns about double the amount of blocks per minute than what it should with honest mining. These graphs corroborate the fact that a new SM orphans enough blocks that the chain-growth rate and, therefore, difficulty barely changes. Hence, with the DAAs under analysis, DAA choice is irrelevant when it comes to selfish mining.

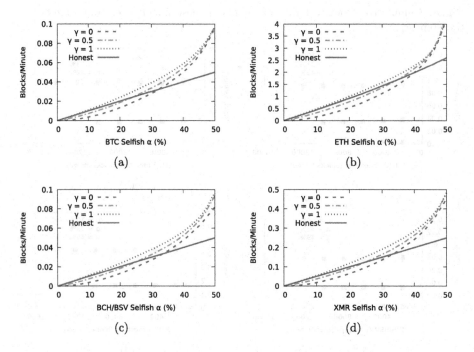

Fig. 10. Block-win rate earned by a new selfish miner.

The next graphs in Fig. 10 show the block-win rate at the end of the simulation. As expected, higher γ leads to higher win rate. It also lowers the threshold of hash power needed to break even. $\gamma = 1$ allows a new selfish miner with any amount of hash power to enter any coin and at the very least make what it was expected to make if it had employed honest mining. A more reasonable low γ rate would require about 33% of the global hash rate to break even.

As shown in Fig. 11, suppose the SM takes an initial hidden lead of 3 blocks (S_1, S_2, and S_3). The honest miner (HM) then spends time mining on the original parent and creates its own chain with block H_1. The SM publishes block S_1 to compete with H_1. In $\gamma = 0$, the HM will try to mine on its own H_1 block while it thinks it is a winnable chain. Assume the SM mines a fourth block, S_4, in its private chain and

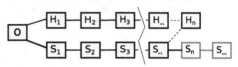

Fig. 11. After a lengthy chain-race, the honest miner chooses whether to build on H_{n-1} or S_{n-1}. In this scenario, the honest chain will have a lower difficulty than the selfish chain, since it took longer to produce. Blocks S_n and S_{n+1} are unpublished.

then the HM mines on its own block H_2, and both alternate some number of blocks. When mining block H_n, the HM has a choice: in $\gamma = 0$, it chooses to mine on its own block, H_{n-1}; in $\gamma = 1$, it chooses to mine on the selfish block, S_{n-1}. This choice has a significant effect on difficulty. Since S_{n-1} was mined long before H_{n-1} was mined, mining on S_{n-1} should have a higher difficulty than mining on H_{n-1}. Therefore, choosing to mine on the selfish block is the same as choosing to mine on a more difficult chain.

If n is on the order of hundreds, as can happen when α is close to 50%, the honest chain could have a significantly lower difficulty than the selfish chain. Since the HM will inevitably lose, the decision of which chain to mine on determines how fast an HM can force the SM to release all private blocks. In $\gamma = 0$, honest miners can catch up to the SM much faster by taking advantage of a lower difficulty. When $\gamma = 1$, however, honest miners choose to mine on the harder chain and will more slowly catch up to the selfish miner. In the long run, honest miners choosing the more difficult chain means more honest blocks are orphaned and the SM is able to extend its winning chain for longer than if $\gamma = 0$. Thus, the selfish block-win rate and the proportion it earns in $\gamma = 0$ is significantly less than in $\gamma = 1$ for high hash rates.

The gap seen in Fig. 10c between $\gamma = 0$ and 1 will be more or less pronounced depending on the length n the two chains reach before merging and the DAA block width, w. In our experiments, we observed n to be on the order of hundreds. If $n < w$, the difference in difficulties between the two chains will be less significant as with Bitcoin, whose block width is 2016. For this reason, the original selfish mining analysis did not exhibit a gap at higher α values. BCH/BSV, on the other hand, has a block width of 144. When the value of n is on the order of hundreds it significantly impacts the difficulty in BCH/BSV. Finally, Monero exhibits a gap that is greater than Bitcoin but smaller than BCH/BSV since its block width of about 675 falls in the middle of the other two widths.

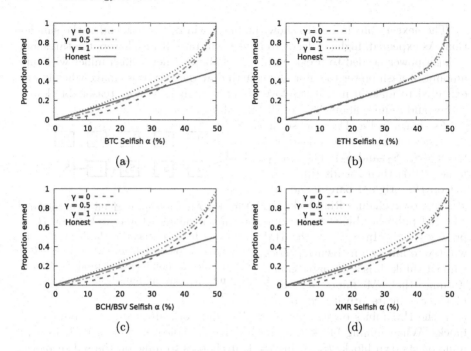

Fig. 12. The proportion of profit earned by a new SM. Uncle rewards in ETH practically nullifies any penalties an SM would pay from creating forks.

Although ETH should have the widest gap, since it only looks at the difficulty of the parent, it does not exhibit this gap due to its incremental nature that causes difficulty to adjust gradually as seen in Fig. 7b.

Finally, the graphs in Fig. 12 show the proportion earned by the selfish miner relative to the honest miner. For BTC, BCH/BSV, and XMR, the results are similar to the results from the original selfish mining results, with the exception of the BSV γ gap, mentioned above. ETH, on the other hand, shows that a new selfish miner with any hash rate and any γ value can at least break-even. This finding is entirely due to the uncle block reward system that exists in ETH, which is described in more detail in Appendix A.

5   Related Work

This work covers two areas of research: difficulty adjustment algorithms and deviant mining behavior. We discuss related work below.

Difficulty Adjustment Algorithms. Prior work in DAAs focuses on the relationship between hash power and difficulty. Kraft [17] analyzed the Bitcoin DAA in the presence of exponentially-increasing hash rate and found that it resulted in lower average block times than desired. Noda et al. [28] compared several DAAs and concluded that Bitcoin's DAA could not stabilize block times in the face of fluctuating hash power. Neither work considers how difficulty adjusts in the presence of deviant mining behavior.

A few recent studies have looked into leveraging DAAs to increase profits. Fiat et al. [13] examined equilibria when miners are allowed to throttle their hash power to bring down the difficulty level. Smart mining [15] is similar to intermittent selfish mining in that it also employs alternating strategies. It alternates between honest mining and remaining idle at every difficulty adjustment. Our work differs from both studies in that our adversary exerts its full hash power and it actively attempts to harm the profits of other miners by employing selfish mining. We leave quantitative comparisons between intermittent selfish and smart mining as future work.

Deviant Mining Behavior. Since its introduction, selfish mining researchers have looked at various contexts and strategy modifications to see how its profitability is affected [14,27,31,32]. Sapirshtein et al. [31] and Nayak et al. [27] showed that small modifications to selfish mining lead to higher profits depending on the α and γ rates. Göbel et al. [14] analyzed selfish mining using a propagation-delay model. These studies all assume a constant difficulty level.

The selfish mining strategy is one of several attacks that creates forks in the blockchain. Liao and Katz [21] present a strategy where so-called whale transactions with large fees are used to convince miners to fork the network. Kwon et al. [19] introduce the fork-after-withholding attack where a mining pool participant only tries to fork blocks from miners in competing pools.

Most previous work falls under the larger umbrella of mining attacks and deviant strategies. For example, research has looked at unintended mining behavior once Bitcoin no longer confers block rewards [7,34], strategies employed by mining pool participants [10,20,22,30], and coin-hopping strategies [2,5,33].

6   Conclusion

This paper examined the controversy around selfish mining and evaluated its application to a range of popular cryptocurrencies. Specifically, it introduced intermittent selfish mining and examined several difficulty adjustment algorithms with selfish mining in action. With intermittent selfish mining, this paper showed that selfish mining under the Bitcoin DAA can be profitable without extending the attack past a difficulty adjustment. Separately, this work quantified the envelope within which selfish mining is a feasible strategy against the various DAAs present in BTC, ETH, BCH, BSV, and XMR.

Selfish mining is an instance of game-theoretic attacks that take advantage of information asymmetry in distributed systems. Such attacks tend to be subtle, unexpected, and at times, counterintuitive. We caution laypeople against accepting folk theorems at face value.

Acknowledgements. We thank Soumya Basu, Ittay Eyal, Kai Mast, and the anonymous reviewers for their insightful suggestions. We also thank Vitalik Buterin for providing inspiration for intermittent selfish mining. This work is supported by Alfred P. Sloan Foundation Grant 2016-20166039.

A   Uncle Blocks and Selfish Mining

An *uncle block* is an orphaned block whose parent resides on the main chain.
Uncle blocks in ETH can be referenced by later blocks on the main chain and are
rewarded according to the equation $(8-h)*b/8$, where b is the block reward and
h is the height difference, up to 6, between the uncle block and the referencing
block. Additionally, the creator of the referencing block is rewarded with an
extra $b/32$ per uncle that is included, up to two uncles. Note that if a losing
fork is longer than one block long, only the first block in the losing chain will be
rewarded as an uncle. This system incentivizes miners to reference uncle blocks
to gain extra rewards, while disincentivizing small miners from joining mining
pools by rewarding, albeit minimally, these losing blocks.

This reward structure has the unintended consequence of nullifying the risks
and penalties of selfish mining. As has been
noted before [29], uncle block rewards allow
selfish miners to fork without suffering a
massive loss if the fork loses. As shown in
Fig. 12b, uncle block rewards in ETH allow
selfish miners to at minimum break even,
no matter what amount of hash power they
possess.

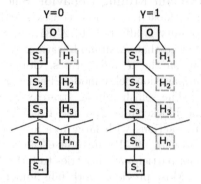

Fig. 13. In ETH, $\gamma = 0$ results in only
one honest uncle block, H_1, whereas
$\gamma = 1$ results in n possible uncles.

Interestingly, the graph shows unexpected behavior when α is around 45%.
Around this hash rate, a selfish miner earns
less relative to the honest miner under $\gamma = 1$ than if $\gamma = 0$. Normally, $\gamma = 1$ allows an
SM to win all forks and earn more than if
$\gamma = 0$ and the SM has to compete to win a fork. Yet, here we find the reverse
to be true. This counter-intuitive finding stems directly from the uncle reward
structure.

Figure 13 shows an example that provides the intuition behind this finding.
Suppose an SM has mined a private chain of length 3 (S_1, S_2, S_3) on block o,
the origin block. By not publishing any block, the SM allows the honest miner
to waste resources mining on block o. If the honest miner is able to mine a block,
H_1, then the SM releases S_1 to create an artificial fork. Assume the SM then
mines a block, S_4, to maintain a chain length difference of 3. Then the honest
and selfish miner begin alternating mining blocks. In $\gamma = 0$, the honest miner
chooses to mine on its own blocks. No matter how long the two chains become,
the honest miner will lose all its blocks, but H_1 will be eligible to be rewarded
as an uncle block since its parent o is on the winning chain. However, when
$\gamma = 1$, once the artificial fork of S_1 and H_1 is created, the honest miner will
abandon H_1 and mine on S_1. As the two miners alternate finding blocks, the
honest miner will always abandon its own block and mine on the selfish block.
The key is that now all honest blocks from H_1 to H_n can be included as uncle
blocks. Since the selfish miner was ahead throughout the entire chain buildup,

most of the uncle blocks will be included by the selfish miner if following a greedy inclusion strategy. Although both uncle creator and including miner are mutually rewarded for the uncle block, the inclusion of each additional uncle block gives a relatively higher reward to the creator than the including miner. Thus, in the best case scenario for the selfish miner, where b is the block reward, the honest miner would receive $2/8 * b$ and the selfish miner that has included the uncle block receives $1/32 * b$, if the height difference is 6. Normally, the honest miner would be rewarded even more since the uncle block would likely be included within a few block generations. In the example above, if H_1 is included in the block S_4, which is the earliest that the selfish miner could know about H_1, the height difference between the uncle and the new block would be three and the honest miner would then receive $5/8 * b$. Ritz and Zugenmaier [29] discuss other uncle inclusion strategies for the selfish miner.

References

1. Bitcoin SV Version 0.1 Goes Live. https://bitcoinsv.io/2018/10/21/bitcoin-sv-version-0-1-goes-live/. Accessed 7 Nov 2018
2. Altman, E., et al.: Mining competition in a multi-cryptocurrency ecosystem at the network edge: a congestion game approach (2019)
3. Bitcoin-ABC Community: Bitcoin-ABC Source Chainparams. https://github.com/Bitcoin-ABC/bitcoin-abc/blob/master/src/chainparams.cpp. Accessed 02 Nov 2018
4. Bitcoin-ABC Community: Difficulty Adjustment Algorithm Update. https://www.bitcoinabc.org/2017-11-01-DAA/. Accessed 5 Nov 2018
5. Bonneau, J.: Why buy when you can rent? In: Clark, J., Meiklejohn, S., Ryan, P.Y.A., Wallach, D., Brenner, M., Rohloff, K. (eds.) FC 2016. LNCS, vol. 9604, pp. 19–26. Springer, Heidelberg (2016). https://doi.org/10.1007/978-3-662-53357-4_2
6. Bonneau, J., Miller, A., Clark, J., Narayanan, A., Kroll, J.A., Felten, E.W.: SoK: research perspectives and challenges for bitcoin and cryptocurrencies. In: 2015 IEEE Symposium on Security and Privacy (SP) (2015)
7. Carlsten, M., Kalodner, H., Weinberg, S.M., Narayanan, A.: On the instability of bitcoin without the block reward. In: Proceedings of the 2016 ACM SIGSAC Conference on Computer and Communications Security (2016)
8. Courtois, N.T., Bahack, L.: On subversive miner strategies and block withholding attack in bitcoin digital currency. arXiv preprint arXiv:1402.1718 (2014)
9. Ethereum Community: Byzantium Hard Fork changes. https://github.com/ethereum/wiki/wiki/Byzantium-Hard-Fork-changes. Accessed 2 Feb 2019
10. Eyal, I.: The miner's dilemma. In: 2015 IEEE Symposium on Security and Privacy (2015)
11. Eyal, I., Sirer, E.G.: Majority is not Enough: Bitcoin Mining is Vulnerable. CoRR abs/1311.0243 (2013). http://arxiv.org/abs/1311.0243
12. Felten, E.: Bitcoin isn't so broken after all. https://freedom-to-tinker.com/2013/11/07/bitcoin-isnt-so-broken-after-all/. Accessed 10 Apr 2019
13. Fiat, A., Karlin, A., Koutsoupias, E., Papadimitriou, C.: Energy equilibria in proof-of-work mining. In: Proceedings of the 2019 ACM Conference on Economics and Computation (2019)
14. Göbel, J., Keeler, H.P., Krzesinski, A.E., Taylor, P.G.: Bitcoin blockchain dynamics: the selfish-mine strategy in the presence of propagation delay. Perform. Eval. **104**, 23–41 (2016)

15. Goren, G., Spiegelman, A.: Mind the mining. In: Proceedings of the 2019 ACM Conference on Economics and Computation (2019)
16. Grunspan, C., Pérez-Marco, R.: On profitability of selfish mining. arXiv preprint arXiv:1805.08281 (2018)
17. Kraft, D.: Difficulty control for blockchain-based consensus systems. Peer-to-Peer Netw. Appl. **9**(2), 397–413 (2015). https://doi.org/10.1007/s12083-015-0347-x
18. Kroll, J.A., Davey, I., Felten, E.W.: The Economics of Bitcoin Mining, or Bitcoin in the Presence of Adversaries (2013)
19. Kwon, Y., Kim, D., Son, Y., Vasserman, E., Kim, Y.: Be selfish and avoid dilemmas: fork after withholding (FAW) attacks on bitcoin. In: Proceedings of the 2017 ACM SIGSAC Conference on Computer and Communications Security (2017)
20. Lewenberg, Y., Bachrach, Y., Sompolinsky, Y., Zohar, A., Rosenschein, J.S.: Bitcoin mining pools: a cooperative game theoretic analysis. In: Proceedings of the 2015 International Conference on Autonomous Agents and Multiagent Systems (2015)
21. Liao, K., Katz, J.: Incentivizing blockchain forks via whale transactions. In: Brenner, M., et al. (eds.) FC 2017. LNCS, vol. 10323, pp. 264–279. Springer, Cham (2017). https://doi.org/10.1007/978-3-319-70278-0_17
22. Luu, L., Saha, R., Parameshwaran, I., Saxena, P., Hobor, A.: On power splitting games in distributed computation: the case of bitcoin pooled mining. In: 2015 IEEE 28th Computer Security Foundations Symposium (2015)
23. Monero Community: Monero Source Cryptonote-Config. https://github.com/monero-project/monero/blob/master/src/cryptonote_config.h. Accessed 02 Nov 2018
24. Monero Community: Monero Source Difficulty. https://github.com/monero-project/monero/blob/master/src/cryptonote_basic/difficulty.cpp. Accessed 7 Dec 2018
25. Nakamoto, S.: Bitcoin P2P e-cash paper. https://satoshi.nakamotoinstitute.org/emails/cryptography/threads/1/?view=satoshi#014849. Accessed 11 Apr 2019
26. Nakamoto, S.: Bitcoin: A Peer-to-Peer Electronic Cash System (2008)
27. Nayak, K., Kumar, S., Miller, A., Shi, E.: Stubborn mining: generalizing selfish mining and combining with an eclipse attack. In: 2016 IEEE European Symposium on Security and Privacy (EuroS&P) (2016)
28. Noda, S., Okumura, K., Hashimoto, Y.: A Lucas Critique to the Difficulty Adjustment Algorithm of the Bitcoin System. SSRN (2019). https://ssrn.com/abstract=3410460. Accessed 15 Sept 2019
29. Ritz, F., Zugenmaier, A.: The impact of uncle rewards on selfish mining in Ethereum. In: 2018 IEEE European Symposium on Security and Privacy Workshops (EuroS&PW) (2018)
30. Rosenfeld, M.: Analysis of bitcoin pooled mining reward systems. arXiv preprint arXiv:1112.4980 (2011)
31. Sapirshtein, A., Sompolinsky, Y., Zohar, A.: Optimal selfish mining strategies in bitcoin. In: Grossklags, J., Preneel, B. (eds.) FC 2016. LNCS, vol. 9603, pp. 515–532. Springer, Heidelberg (2017). https://doi.org/10.1007/978-3-662-54970-4_30
32. Shomer, A.: On the phase space of block-hiding strategies. IACR Cryptology ePrint Archive (2014)
33. Spiegelman, A., Keidar, I., Tennenholtz, M.: Game of coins. arXiv preprint arXiv:1805.08979 (2018)
34. Tsabary, I., Eyal, I.: The gap game. In: Proceedings of the 2018 ACM SIGSAC Conference on Computer and Communications Security (2018)
35. Wright, C.S.: The Fallacy of the Selfish Miner (1): Economic Argument Critiqued (2017)

Fairness and Efficiency in DAG-Based Cryptocurrencies

Georgios Birmpas[1], Elias Koutsoupias[1], Philip Lazos[2],
and Francisco J. Marmolejo-Cossío[1(✉)]

[1] University of Oxford, Oxford, UK
{georgios.birmpas,elias.koutsoupias,francisco.marmolejo}@cs.ox.ac.uk
[2] Sapienza University of Rome, Rome, Italy
lazos@diag.uniroma1.it

Abstract. Bitcoin is a decentralised digital currency that serves as an alternative to existing transaction systems based on an external central authority for security. Although Bitcoin has many desirable properties, one of its fundamental shortcomings is its inability to process transactions at high rates. To address this challenge, many subsequent protocols either modify the rules of block acceptance (longest chain rule) and reward, or alter the graphical structure of the public ledger from a tree to a directed acyclic graph (DAG).

Motivated by these approaches, we introduce a new general framework that captures ledger growth for a large class of DAG-based implementations. With this in hand, and by assuming *honest* miner behaviour, we (experimentally) explore how different DAG-based protocols perform in terms of *fairness*, as well as *efficiency*. To do so, we isolate different parameters of the network (such as k, the number of pointers to previous blocks) and study their effect on those performance metrics.

Our results demonstrate how the DAG-based ledger protocols described by our framework cope with a high transaction load. More specifically, we show that even in a scenario where every miner on the system is honest in terms of when they publish blocks, what they point to, and what transactions each block contains, fairness and efficiency of this kind of ledgers can break down at specific hash rates if miners have differing levels of connectivity to the P2P network sustaining the protocol. (The full version of this paper can be found in [2]).

1 Introduction

Bitcoin and many other decentralised digital currencies maintain a public ledger via distributed consensus algorithms implemented using blockchain data struc-

Georgios Birmpas was supported by the ERC Advanced Grants 321171 (ALGAME) and 639945 (ACCORD). Philip Lazos is supported by the ERC Advanced Grant 788893 (AMDROMA) and the MIUR PRIN project ALGADIMAR. Francisco J. Marmolejo-Cossío was supported by the Mexican National Council of Science and Technology (CONACyT). We would also like to thank Elizabeth Smith for fruitful discussions during the preparation of this work.

© International Financial Cryptography Association 2020
J. Bonneau and N. Heninger (Eds.): FC 2020, LNCS 12059, pp. 79–96, 2020.
https://doi.org/10.1007/978-3-030-51280-4_6

tures. End users of the currency post transactions to the P2P network sustaining the protocol and said transactions are bundled into blocks by *miners*: agents tasked with the upkeep of the ledger. With respect to Bitcoin, the prescribed *longest chain rule* dictates that miners must bundle pending transactions into a block that also includes a single hash pointer to the end of the longest chain seen by the miner in their local view of the ledger. Furthermore, in order for a block to be valid, its hash must lie below a dynamically adjusted threshold. Hence, miners must expend computational resources to find valid blocks. Due to this *Proof-of-Work* structure, if all miners follow the protocol, the number of blocks they contribute to the blockchain is proportional to the computational resources they dedicate to the protocol, i.e. their hash power. In addition, miners are incentivised to follow the protocol via judicious incentive engineering through block rewards. This latter point also implies that miners earn block reward proportional to their hash power, thus making Bitcoin a *fair* protocol.

As mentioned before, Bitcoin dynamically adjusts its target hash for valid blocks so that the totality of all miners active in the protocol find a block every ten minutes on average. This feature of the protocol makes consensus more robust, as this time-scale is much larger than the time it takes for a block to propagate on the P2P network supporting Bitcoin. However, since the size of blocks is limited, Bitcoin inherently suffers from a scalability problem. Thus in spite of Bitcoin being strategy-proof and fair, it suffers in its *efficiency*: which we define as the expected ratio of the number of valid transactions in the ledger to the number of all transactions posted in the P2P network. On the other hand, simply decreasing confirmation times and demanding higher transaction throughput by either increasing the overall block creation rate or block size can also affect these very properties of the protocol. For instance, delays in the P2P network may cause miners to have different views of the ledger, which can in turn directly make achieving a consensus more difficult, or lead miners to be strategic when they would have otherwise acted honestly. Ultimately, it seems that Bitcoin fundamentally strikes a delicate balance between being strategy-proof and fair at the cost of efficiency.

There have been many attempts to cope with Bitcoin's inherent throughput limitations, with [16,21–23] being some notable examples. All of these papers focus on how security can be maintained when the throughput is increased and follow the common direction of either modifying Bitcoin's longest chain rule or implementing a different graphical structure underlying the ledger.

In GHOST [22] an alternative consensus rule is proposed to the longest chain of Bitcoin, focusing on creating a new protocol that maintains security guarantees even when faced with high transaction loads. In this setting, GHOST takes into account the fact that forks are more likely to be produced when the underlying ledger still takes the form of a tree, as with Bitcoin. More specifically, when deciding what a newly mined block should point to, GHOST no longer myopically points to the head of the longest chain, but rather starts from the genesis block and at each fork, chooses the branch of the fork that leads to the heaviest subtree in the ledger until reaching a leaf to point to. In this way, blocks that are off the main chain can still contribute to the final consensus, which arguably maintains a degree of robustness to strategic mining while coping with high throughput better than Bitcoin.

In [21,23] protocols SPECTRE and PHANTOM are proposed, with ledger structures in the form of directed acyclic graphs (DAG). The protocols in both of these implementations suggest that every newly created block has to point to every available (visible) leaf in the ledger. In that way every created block will eventually become part of the consensus, and the security of the system remains unaffected by forks that will be produced due to high throughput, since they will in turn be part of the ledger. A possible advantage is that the system can become more resilient to attacks that focus on increasing the block rewards of a miner. On the other hand, ordering the transactions and preventing other types of strategic behaviour becomes more complicated.

Motivated by these ideas, we design a new theoretical framework that captures a large family of DAG-based ledger implementations (including those mentioned in previous paragraphs). We achieve this by introducing a parametric model which lets us adjust the number of blocks each newly created block can point to, the block attributes a miner takes into account when choosing what blocks to point to, and the number of transactions a block can store. Finally, we describe a theoretical framework for ledger growth in these DAG-based models, along with a novel simplification for extrapolating valid transactions from a ledger under the assumption that all miners are honest. With this in hand, we are able to answer how our family of DAG-based ledgers copes with the high transaction loads they are intended to tackle. Indeed, our results are structural in nature, for we show how fairness and efficiency suffer from high transaction rates in spite of all agents behaving honestly in a given DAG-based ledger.

We want to mention at this point that we are mostly interested on parameter k, the number of pointers to previous blocks. In contrast to the existing literature regarding DAG-based protocols which assumes that k is conditioned to other parameters of the system (i.e. informational parameters q in our model), something crucial for the security of this kind of protocols, we choose to study this parameter unconditioned for reasons that we will explain shortly.

1.1 Our Results

We provide a parametric model that tries to capture a large family of DAG-based ledgers and we make an attempt to quantify what is the effect of adjusting the different parameters of our model on *fairness* and *efficiency*. As we already mentioned, an important parameter for our model is k, for which we assume that is specified by the protocol, fixed and independent of the other parameters (i.e *informational* parameters) that we will eventually introduce in our model. Although this comes in contrast with most of the existing literature where k depends on the informational parameters of the system, the reason behind this choice is twofold: We want to study the contribution of parameter k to the protocol in terms of *fairness* and *efficiency*, while in addition we desire to explore what would happen in a situation where the optimal value of k, the value that does not produce orphaned blocks and thus makes the protocol inherently fair, cannot be selected (i.e. when it is huge). Although this approach may lead to loss of *security* for the protocol (since the chosen k may not be the optimal one), we want to explore how this parameter affects *fairness* and *efficiency* under the assumption of *honest* mining.

In this line of thought, our simulations allow us to show how specific transaction load regimes affect the efficiency of different protocols in our class of DAG-based ledgers. Furthermore, we show that in almost all transaction load regimes *fairness* is affected and exhibits a complicated relationship with respect to agent connectivity in the underlying P2P network. Our results are exploratory in nature, fixing most aspects of the network (assuming a simple, or worse case, setting if possible) and modulating specific parameters to study their effect on fairness and efficiency.

We are interested in exploring the behaviour of the protocol under several value choices of k and q. Some highlights of our results, that we consider both interesting and surprising, are the following: 1) Although we assume honest behaviour from the miners, it is interesting to explore the performance for choices of k and q that increase the security of the system (i.e. choices of values where both the number of the pointers as well as the information that the miners have for the network is high). In our simulations the safest such zone is for $k \geq 2$ and $q = 0.2$. In particular, for smaller values of k we observe that fairness is compromised leading to interesting mining behaviour: the gains of small miners are generally increasing in their q_i, whereas for larger miners they *decrease*: this is because small miners care more about making sure their few blocks are retained, while large miners appear to act 'selfishly' by mining in parallel to the others' blocks, not by malice but by ignorance. 2) Leaving the security of the system aside, another region that we find interesting is the one where q can vary from 0.0001 up to 1 and for which we observe that there is a huge increase in the efficiency of the system as k increases from 1 to 2. On the other hand, something that seems surprising is that by increasing the value of parameter k to 3 or even to ∞ seems that does not provide a significant added benefit to the efficiency of the system. This quite interestingly implies that we can achieve efficiency guarantees even if we do not choose the optimal value for k (since this behaviour is the same for a variety of values of q).

1.2   Related Work

Bitcoin was introduced in Nakamoto's landmark white paper [18] as a decentralised digital currency. Since its inception many researchers have studied several aspects of the protocol, i.e. its security and susceptibility to different types of attacks [1,7,9,10,17,19], how it behaves under a game-theoretic perspective [4,13,15] and how its scalability and inherent transaction throughput issues can be improved. Since the latter is the most related to our work, we give a more detailed exposition in the paragraphs that follow. Before we proceed, we also want to refer the reader to [3,24] for some extensive surveys which provide a good view of the research and challenges that exist in the area.

Sompolinsky and Zohar [22], study the scalability of Bitcoin, analysing at the same time the security of the protocol when the delays in the network are not negligible. More specifically, they build on the results of Decker and Wattenhofer [5] and explore the limits of the amount of transactions that can be processed under the protocol, while also studying how transaction waiting times can be optimised when there is also a security constraint. In the same work, the Greedy Heaviest-Observed Sub-Tree chain (GHOST) is also presented as a modified version of the Bitcoin protocol selection rule, and as a way of obtaining a more scalable system with higher security guarantees. It is interesting to mention that many existing cryptocurrencies currently use variations of the GHOST rule, with Ethereum [6] and Bitcoin-NG [8] being some notable examples. The authors argue that under this rule, the possible delays of the network cannot affect the security of the protocol even if the designer allows high creation rates of large-sized blocks and thus a high transaction throughput.

Subsequently, Kiayias and Panagiotakos [14] further study the GHOST protocol and provide a general framework for security analysis that focuses on protocols with a tree structure. They expand upon the analysis of [22] and follow a direction similar to the one presented in the work of Garay et al. [10], which only studies chain structures and cannot be directly implemented in the setting of GHOST. We would like to point out that in [10] Garay et al. also provide an extended analysis of their framework for the partially synchronous model under the existence of bounded delays in the underlying P2P network of the protocol.

Lewenberg et al. [16] propose the structure of a DAG, instead of a tree, as a way of dealing with high block creation rates and blocks of large size. Building on this idea, the same authors in [21] present SPECTRE, a new PoW-based protocol that follows the DAG-structure, and is both, scalable and secure. More specifically, they argue that SPECTRE can cope with high throughput of transactions while also maintaining fast confirmation times. They also analyse its security by studying several types of attacks. Part of the contribution of the paper is also introducing a way to (partially) order created blocks via a voting rule among existing blocks, which also contributes to the security of the protocol. SPECTRE has drawn the attention of many researchers after its introduction and we refer the reader to [11,12,20,23] for some indicative related works.

2   DAG-Based Ledgers

In this section we will describe a family of decentralised consensus algorithms for public ledgers that generalise Bitcoin and SPECTRE. In what follows, we assume that there are n strategic miners $m_1, ..., m_n$ with hash powers $h_1, ..., h_n$ respectively. When a given block is found globally by the protocol, h_i represents the probability that this block belongs to m_i. We will be studying DAG-based ledger implementations. Formally, these ledgers are such that blocks and their pointers induce a directed acyclic graph with blocks as nodes and pointers as edges. The maximum out-degree of a block, k is specified by the protocol and is in the range $1 \leq k \leq \infty$. Thus it is straightforward to see that Bitcoin for example, is a DAG-based ledger where the DAG is in fact a tree (with $k = 1$). Finally, since blocks have bounded size, we define $1 \leq \eta < \infty$ to be the maximum number of transactions a block can store.

As mentioned in the introduction, we are primarily interested in studying issues of fairness and ledger efficiency in DAG-based protocols catered to a high throughput regime. We recall that a protocol is fair if a miner can expect to see a block reward proportional to their hash power, and that a protocol efficiency is the ratio of all valid transactions to all transactions broadcast over the P2P network. In this setting, and under the assumption of a discrete time horizon, transactions and blocks that are propagated by users in the P2P network may take multiple *turns* (the time it takes for the entire system to find a block) before they are seen by certain agents within the system. For this reason, miners only see a portion of the entire block DAG produced by a decentralised protocol as well as a portion of all transactions propagated by all end users of the ledger.

In actuality, transactions that are posted to the P2P network of digital currencies directly depend on other transactions. For this reason, we also model the set of transactions that end users generate as a DAG. Furthermore, the structure of the transaction DAG itself has important implications for how transactions are packed in blocks for any DAG-based ledger. For example, if the transaction DAG is a path, and we are considering SPECTRE as our DAG-based protocol, it is easy to see that transactions will only be packed proportional to the deepest node of the block DAG, which in the high throughput regime can grow at a much slower rate than that at which transactions are generated. At the other extreme, if the transaction DAG only consists of isolated nodes, then any block can contain any transaction, and the efficiency of SPECTRE is thus constrained by what transactions miners see rather than the structure of the block DAG.

Ultimately, in addition to having computational power, a miner also has informational power, which encapsulates how connected they are to the P2P network and consequently, how much of each of the aforementioned DAGs they see at a given time. We model the informational parameter of an arbitrary miner m_i as a parameter $q_i \in [0, 1]$. As q_i approaches 1, m_i is likely to see the entirety of both DAGs, whereas as q_i approaches 0, m_i is likely to only see the blocks he mines and transactions he creates.

2.1   Ledger Growth Preliminaries

We begin by setting some preliminary notation about graphs that it will be used in several parts as we define the model. Let $\mathcal{G}$ be the set of all finite directed graphs. For $G \in \mathcal{G}$, $V(G)$ and $E(G) \subseteq V(G)^2$ are the set of vertices and directed edges of G respectively. Furthermore, for a tuple $x = (x_i)_{i=1}^n$, we let $\pi_i(x) = x_i$ be the projection onto the i-th coordinate. Finally, we define the *closure* of a subset $X \subseteq V(G)$ of vertices, which will be needed in order to describe how a miner perceives the current state of the network.

Definition 1 (Closure). *Suppose that $G \in \mathcal{G}$, and let $X \subseteq V(G)$ be a subset of vertices. We denote the closure of X in G by $\Gamma(X \mid G)$ and define it as the subgraph induced by all vertices reachable from X via directed paths.*

We now proceed by formally describing and exploring the stochastic growth of a DAG-based ledger given $m_1, ..., m_n$ strategic miners in a step-by-step fashion. As we already mentioned, we assume that the ledger grows over a finite discrete time horizon: $t = 1, ..., T$. Each turn will consist of four phases: a *block revelation phase*, in which nature picks a miner to initialise a block, an *information update phase*, where miners update their views of the block and transaction graphs, an *action phase*, in which miners employ their strategies depending on their local information, and a *natural transaction generation phase*, in which non-miners stochastically publish transactions to the P2P network.

At the end of the action phase of each turn t, we maintain a global block-DAG and transaction directed graph, denoted by G_t^{glob} and T_t^{glob} respectively. We say that the vertices of G_t^{glob} are blocks and we have that G_t^{glob} contains every block (public or private) that has been created up to turn t. Similarly, for T_t^{glob} we have that it consists of every transaction present in the network up to point t. We denote $V(G_t^{glob}) = \{B_1, ..., B_t\}$, where the i-th block was created at the i-th turn and $V(T_t^{glob}) = T_t^* \cup \bar{T}_t$, where $T_t^* = \{tx_1^*, ..., tx_t^*\}$ (enumerated) represents the set of the respective block rewards and $\bar{T}_t$ the set of the transactions.

Each block B_t, has out-degree of at most k and carries at most $\eta + 1$ transactions denoted by $Tx(B_t) \subseteq V(T_{t-1}^{glob})$ such that $tx_t^* \in Tx(B_t)$. On the other hand, the out degree of every transaction in T_t^* is 0 and the out degree of every vertex in $\bar{T}_t$ is at least 1. The reason for the aforementioned constraints on the vertices of G^{glob} and T^{glob} is that when a block is found, block reward is created "out of thin air", and can hence be a designated as a transaction with no dependencies on which future transactions can depend. In addition, if $A \subseteq G^{glob}$, we let $Tx(A) = \cup_{B_j \in V(A)} Tx(B_j)$ be the set of all induced transactions from the subgraph A. Finally, these time-evolving graphs will have the property that if $t_1 < t_2$, then $G_{t_1}^{glob} \subseteq G_{t_2}^{glob}$ and $T_{t_1}^{glob} \subseteq T_{t_2}^{glob}$.

Let us now explore both the block and the transaction directed graphs from the perspective of a miner. We suppose that each miner m_i has the following information at the end of turn t:

- $G_{i,t}^{pub}$: The DAG consisting of all blocks m_i has inferred from G_t^{glob} via the P2P network.
- $PB_{i,t} \subseteq V(G_t^{glob})$: A set of private blocks m_i has not yet shared to the P2P network.
- $T_{i,t}^{pub}$: The directed graph consisting of all transactions m_i has inferred from T_t^{glob} via the P2P network.
- $PT_{i,t} \subseteq V(T_t^{glob})$: A set of private transactions m_i has not yet shared to the P2P network.

Finally, we let G_t^{pub} and T_t^{pub} be the set of all blocks and transactions that have been shared to the P2P network respectively.

Definition 2 (Local Information). *For a given miner m_i, we let $L_{i,t} = (G_{i,t}^{pub}, PB_{i,t}, T_{i,t}^{pub}, PT_{i,t})$ and say this is the local information available to miner at the end of round t. We also say that $L_t = (L_{i,t})_{i=1}^t$ is the local information of all miners at the end of round t.*

We conclude by defining what we mean by a single-step P2P information update for a miner, as well as what the strategy space available to a miner is.

Definition 3 (Information Update). *Suppose that $H \subseteq G$ are graphs. Furthermore, suppose that the vertex set $A \in V(G) \setminus V(H)$. We define the distribution $U((H, G), A, q)$ as a single P2P information update via a specific sampling procedure. To sample $G' \sim U((H, G), A, q)$ we do the following:*

- *Let $X = \emptyset$*
- *Independently, for each $v \in A$, with probability q, add v to X.*
- *Let $G' = \Gamma(V(H) \cup X \mid G)$.*

Definition 4 (Memoryless Miner Strategies). *A miner strategy for m_j is denoted by $S_j = (S_j^I, S_j^P, S_j^T)$ and consists of an initialisation strategy S_j^I, a publishing strategy S_j^P, and a transaction creation strategy S_j^T. Each of these functions takes as input $L_{j,t} = (G_{j,t}^{pub}, PB_{j,t}, T_{j,t}^{pub}, PT_{j,t})$ at any given round t.*

- Initialisation strategy: $S_j^I(L_{j,t}) = (X^I, Y^I)$ where $X^I \subseteq V(T_{j,t-1}^{pub}) \cup PT_{j,t-1}$ and $Y^I \subseteq V(G_{j,t-1}^{pub}) \cup PB_{j,t-1}$. Furthermore, $|X^I| \leq \eta$ and $1 \leq |Y^I| \leq k$.
- Publishing strategy: $S_j^P(L_{j,t}) = (X^P, Y^P)$ where $X^P \subseteq PB_{j,t}$ and $Y^P \subseteq PT_{j,t}$. with the property that if $B_i \in X^P \Rightarrow tx_i^* \in Y^P$.
- Transaction creation strategy: $S_j^T(L_{j,t}) = (\{x_1, ..., x_k\}, \{\Gamma^1(x_1), ..., \Gamma^1(x_k)\}, W)$, where each $x_i \notin V(T_{t-1}^{priv})$, each set $\Gamma^1(x_i) \subseteq V(T_{t-1}^{priv})$ is non-empty, and $W \subseteq \{x_1, ..., x_k\}$.

To make sense of Definition 4, it suffices to note that S_j^I is invoked when m_j is chosen to mine a block. Set X^I represents the set of the transactions that the block will contain. The number of these transactions can be at most η and each block forcibly contains tx_t^*. On the other hand, set Y^I describes the set of the blocks that the newly created block will point to. The number of these blocks can be at least 1 and at most k. Moving to S_j^P, this is invoked when m_j wishes to publish hidden blocks/transactions to the P2P network. Finally, S_j^T is invoked when m_j wishes to create an arbitrary (finite) amount of new transactions $x_1, .., x_k$ that depend on transactions in $T_{j,t-1}^{priv}$ (each x_i has a non-empty set $\Gamma^1(x_i)$ of dependencies). Notice that since $\Gamma^1(x_i) \neq \emptyset$, that forcibly each x_i can not be of the form tx_r^* for some r. Finally, $W \subseteq \{x_1, ..., x_k\}$ represents which of the newly created transactions will be broadcast to the P2P network.

3 $\mathcal{P}_{f,k}$ Ledger Models and Honest Behaviour

The main purpose of this section is twofold: first we introduce a family of honest strategies that generalise honest mining in Bitcoin and SPECTRE called $\mathcal{P}_{f,k}$ mining, and second we introduce constraints on $\mathcal{D}$ that represent honest transaction generation by end-use agents in a DAG-based ledger (this includes Bitcoin and SPECTRE as well).

Definition 5 (Depth and Weight of a Block). *Suppose that $G \in \mathcal{G}$ is a block-DAG. In other words, G is connected and has a genesis block B_0. For a given $B_t \in G$, we let $w(B_t) = |\Gamma(\{B_t\} \mid G))| - 1$ be the weight of B_t. This is the number of predecessors B_t has in G. We also define $D(B_t) = d_G(B_t, B_0)$ as the depth of B_t. This is the graphical distance between B_t and B_0, i.e. the length of the (unique) shortest path between B_t and B_0 in G.*

In Bitcoin, miners resolve ambiguity in ledger consensus by initialising found blocks to point to the longest chain in the DAG. One reason for this is that agents have provably used significant computational power to grow said chain, and re-writing this history is thus computationally infeasible. In DAG-based ledgers, agents may point to multiple blocks. Thus, following this same thought process, they should point to blocks with a provably significant amount of computation in their histories. The issue, however, is that measuring how much computation exists in the past of a leaf is ambiguous in DAGs: a block could have either large weight or large depth (unlike in Bitcoin where these quantities are always the same), and it is unclear to decide which to give precedence to. In order to completely rank the importance of leaves in a block DAG, we simply use a family of score functions that expresses convex combinations of depth and weight.

Definition 6 (Score Function). *Suppose that $\alpha \in [0,1]$ and $\beta = 1 - \alpha$. We say that f is an (α, β) block-DAG score function if for a given block-DAG, $G \in \mathcal{G}$, $f(B_t) = \alpha D(B_t) + \beta w(B_t)$.*

In a nutshell, honest block-DAG growth in $\mathcal{P}_{f,k}$ protocols with parameter α and β prescribes that miners prepare blocks with at most k pointers that point the locally visible blocks in the block-DAG that with highest score under f.

3.1 Valid Blocks and Transactions

In ledgers employing decentralised consensus protocols, there is an explicit consensus mechanism whereby agents are able to look at their local view of the ledger and extrapolate valid blocks and subsequently valid transactions within the local view of the ledger. In Bitcoin for example, valid blocks consist of the longest chain in the ledger, and valid transactions consist of transactions within said longest chain. SPECTRE, on the other hand, has any seen block as valid, but the valid transaction extraction process is a complicated voting procedure that extracts a subset of transactions within the local view of the DAG as valid. We proceed by providing a definition of valid block and transaction extractors in $\mathcal{P}_{f,k}$ models that generalises both of these examples.

Definition 7 (Valid Block Extractors and Valid Transaction Extractors). *Suppose that G is a block-DAG and that $\ell_1, .., \ell_k$ are the k leaves in G that have the highest score under f. Then we say that $VB(G) = \Gamma(\{\ell_1, ..., \ell_k\} \mid G)$ is the DAG of valid blocks in G under $\mathcal{P}_{f,k}$. In addition, we let $VT(G) \subseteq Tx(VB(G))$ be the set of valid transactions for a specified transaction extractor function VT. We say that VT is in addition monotonic if it holds that if $VB(H) \subseteq VB(G)$, then $VT(H) \subseteq VT(G)$.*

In what follows we define a special type of monotonic valid transaction selection rule called *present transaction selection*. The reason we outline this simple selection rule is that in Sect. 3.4 we will show that if all miners employ monotonic valid transaction selection and the honest strategies presented in Sect. 3.2, then we can assume without loss of generality that they employ present transaction selection as a valid transaction selection rule.

Definition 8 (Present Transaction Selection). *Suppose that G is a block-DAG and that $\ell_1, .., \ell_k$ are the leaves in G that have the highest score under f. Then we say that $VB(G) = \Gamma(\{\ell_1, ..., \ell_k\} \mid G)$ is the DAG of valid blocks in G under $\mathcal{P}_{f,k}$. In addition we say that $PVT(G) = Tx(VB(G))$ is the set of present valid transactions in G under $\mathcal{P}_{f,k}$.*

3.2   Defining S^I, S^P, and S^T for Honest Mining in $\mathcal{P}_{f,k}$

We define $H_j = (H_j^I, H_j^P, H_j^T)$ as the honest strategy employed by m_j in $\mathcal{P}_{f,k}$, and describe each component below.

- H_j^I: Compute $A = VB(G_{j,t}^{pub})$ and $B = VT(G_{j,t}^{pub})$. Let $H_j^I(L_{j,t}) = (X, Y)$. X is the set of at most η oldest non-block-reward (i.e. not of the form tx_r^*) transactions in $T_{j,t}^{pub} \setminus B$ (ties are broken arbitrarily) with a graphical closure in B. $Y = \{\ell_1, ... \ell_k\}$ is the set of k highest-score leaves in $G_{j,t}^{pub}$ under f.
- H^P: Publish all private blocks and transactions immediately
- H^T: Create no new transactions (the assumption is that transactions created by pools are negligible with respect to the total transaction load of the ledger)

Before continuing, we note that in the $\mathcal{P}_{f,k}$ model, H^T ensures that honest miners do not create and broadcast any transactions themselves. This, of course, is not the case in practice, but it is an accurate approximation to a regime in which the fraction of transactions created by miners is a negligible fraction of all transactions created by end-users of the ledger.

Also notice that H_j^I dictates that the oldest transactions will be included to agents' j block. We make this choice for simplicity reasons, however we want to point out that a more sophisticated selection strategy may be more beneficial for the protocol, especially in terms of *efficiency* (as we will see in Sect. 4).

3.3   Implementation of Bitcoin and SPECTRE as $\mathcal{P}_{f,k}$ Protocols

With the previous machinery in place, we can see that block-DAG and transaction-DAG growth in Bitcoin and SPECTRE are special cases of $\mathcal{P}_{f,k}$ ledgers. For Bitcoin, we let $k = 1$, and any parameter setting, (α, β) for f results in Bitcoin growth. As for SPECTRE, we let $k = \infty$ and once more any parameter setting (α, β) for f suffices to implement honest SPECTRE ledger growth.

3.4   Honest Transaction Consistency and Generation

As mentioned in Sect. 3.1, we can show that amongst monotonic transaction extractors, present transaction extractors are all we need for honest ledger growth in the $\mathcal{P}_{f,k}$ model.

Theorem 1. *If the valid transaction extractor, VT, is monotonic and all miners employ $H = (H^I, H^P, H^T)$, then VT is a present transaction extractor.*

Proof. Suppose that $L_{i,t} = (G_{i,t}^{pub}, PB_{i,t}, T_{i,t}^{pub}, PT_{i,t})$ is the local information available to m_i at turn t. Since m_i is honest, one can easily see that $G_{i,t}^{pub} = G_{i,t}^{priv} = G_{i,t}$ and $T_{i,t}^{pub} = T_{i,t}^{priv} = T_{i,t}$. Clearly $VT(G_{i,t}) \subseteq PVT(G_{i,t})$. Now suppose that $x \in PVT(G_{i,t})$. This means that $x \in Tx(B_r)$ for some block B_r found by say m_j. This means that in turn r, m_j invoked H^I to create B_r, which means that since $x \in Tx(B_r)$, all dependencies of x are in $VT(\Gamma(B_r \mid G_{i,t}))$, the valid transactions from the DAG consisting of the closure of B_r in the block DAG. However $VT(\Gamma(B_r \mid G_{i,t})) \subseteq VT(G_{i,t})$ since VT is monotonic. Therefore x has its dependencies met in $VT(G_{i,t})$ so that $x \in VT(G_{i,t})$. This implies $VT(G_{i,t}) = PVT(G_{i,t})$ as desired.   □

In light of this theorem, we focus on monotonic valid transaction extractors given their generality. Hence, from now on we assume that when we invoke VT, we in fact mean that VT is a present transaction extractor.

Regarding the honest transaction generation, H^T dictates that each m_i does not produce or propagate transactions created by themselves. Hence, it is crucial that we properly define $\mathcal{D}$ in the $\mathcal{P}_{f,k}$ model. At first one may be tempted to simply treat the random growth of T_t^{glob} as independent of G_t^{glob}, but this is a grave mistake. To see why, imagine that G_t^{glob} contains some block B_r that is orphaned by each m_i (note that this can only happen if $k < \infty$). If the growth of T_t^{glob} is independent of that of G_t^{glob}, then it could be the case that many (if not infinitely many) future transactions depend on t_r^*. However, if B_r is orphaned by all miners, tx_r^* is not valid, hence none of these future transactions will be added to the ledger via close inspection of how H^I is defined.

A compelling fact is that if all miners have orphaned B_r, then chances are that whatever local view of G_t^{pub} an end-user has, they too will have orphaned B_r, and thus will not have tx_r^* as a valid transaction. In more direct terms, any money created via the block reward of B_r is not actually in the system for an end-user, so if this end-user is honest, there is no reason why they would produce transactions that would depend on this illegitimate source of currency.

Definition 9 (Honest Transaction Distributions). *Let G_t^{glob} be a global block DAG at turn t with k highest leaves are $\ell_1, ..., \ell_k$. In an honest setting, $VB(G_t^{glob}) = \Gamma(\{\ell_1, ..., \ell_l\} \mid G_t^{glob})$ and $VT(G_t^{glob}) = Tx(VB(G_t^{glob}))$. We say that $\mathcal{D}(G_t^{glob}, T_t^{glob})$ is an honest transaction distribution if $x \sim \mathcal{D}(G_t^{glob}, T_t^{glob})$ is such that $x \notin T_t^{glob}$ and its dependencies lie strictly in $VT(G_t^{glob})$.*

3.5   Assumptions: Non-atomic Miners, Payoffs and Transaction Generation Rate

Non-atomic Miners. For our simulations we assume that a set of honest miners, each of whom has small enough hash power, can be modelled as one larger miner who re-samples their view of both DAGs each time they are chosen for a block initialisation. This is reasonable if, for example, each miner in said collection finds at most one block in time horizon $t = 1, ..., T$ with high probability. We call these miners *non-atomic*.

Block Rewards and Transaction Fees. We suppose that at time-step T, miners get a normalised block reward of 1 per block that they have in $VB(G_T^{glob})$. As for transaction fees, the full generality of $P_{f,k}$ protocols only specifies how to extrapolate valid transactions conditional upon everyone being honest, and not who receives transaction fees (this is subsumed in the details of VT in the general setting). For this reason we further assume that transaction fees are negligible in comparison to block rewards over the time horizon $t = 1, ..., T$.

Transaction Generation Rate. Although in full generality there is no restriction on how many transactions nature may create in a given turn, we impose a fixed constraint on this quantity: λ. As such, each turn introduces $\{x_{t,1}, ..., x_{t,\lambda}\}$ transactions sampled from a specified honest transaction distribution $\mathcal{D}$. Furthermore, in our simulations we let $\lambda = \eta$, so that the ledger infrastructure can, in theory, cope with the transaction load if all miners have full information, and thus we can see specifically it falls short of this objective in the partial information setting.

4   Results

4.1   Fairness

We recall that one of the key properties of Bitcoin is that it is fair: miners earn block reward proportional to the computational resources they expend on extending the ledger. One of the most significant observations from our simulations is that $\mathcal{P}_{f,k}$ ledgers are not necessarily fair as soon as the agents begin having informational parameters, $q < 1$, as is the case in a high throughput setting. To illustrate this phenomenon, we study a two-miner scenario with agents m_0 and m_1 of hash power $(1 - h_1, h_1)$ and informational parameters (q_0, q_1). m_0 is modelled as a non-atomic miner and we empirically compute the surplus average block reward of m_1 relative to the baseline h_1 they would receive in a fair protocol. Our results are visualised in Fig. 1. Each row of the figure represents $k = 1, 2, 3$ respectively and each column represents $q_0 = 0.005, 0.05, 0.2$. Each individual heatmap fixes k and q_0 and plots average block reward surplus for m_1 as $q_1 \in [0, 1]$ and $h_1 \in (0, 0.5]$ are allowed to vary. Finally, each pixel contains the average block reward surplus for $T = 50$ and averaged over 50 trials. We notice that an added strength to our fairness result is that they hold, irrespective of the underlying honest transaction distribution $\mathcal{D}$ used in practice.

The most jarring observation is that, depending on the parameters, m_1 earns a vastly different average block reward than their fair share h_1. In fact, for fixed k and q_0, there seem to be three regions of the hash space $h_1 \in (0, 0.5]$ with qualitatively distinct properties:

- If h_1 is large enough, m_1 strictly benefits from having lower q_1 values. This is due to the fact that an honest miner with small q_0 necessarily sees his own blocks and is inadvertently acting somewhat "selfishly". Hence if their hash rate is high enough, their persistent mining upon their own blocks may end up orphaning other blocks and give them a higher share of valid blocks in the final DAG.
- If h_1 is small enough, m_1 strictly benefits from having higher q_1 values. Contrary to the previous point, at small hash values, m_1 only finds a few blocks, and hence they risk losing their entire share of blocks if these blocks aren't well positioned in the block DAG, since they are in no position to inadvertently overtake the entire DAG via pseudo-selfish behaviour resulting from low q_1 values.
- Finally, for intermediate h_1 values, m_1 no longer has a monotonic surplus with respect to q_1 but rather a concave dependency. This can be seen as an interpolation of the previous two points.

We notice that where these qualitative regions of h_1 values lie within $(0, 0.5]$ depends entirely on k and q_0. In general, for fixed k (i.e specific rows within Fig. 1), as q_0 increases, the transitions between these regions shift rightwards, and for fixed q_0 (i.e. specific columns in Fig. 1) as k increases, also shifts rightwards, as increasing k can be seen to informally have the same effect as uniformly increasing q_0 and q_1 as agents are more likely to see blocks due to multiple pointers. Of course, for $k = \infty$ the protocol becomes fair, as every block eventually joins the DAG. As a final observation, roughly speaking, "small" miners benefit from increasing their connectivity to the P2P network, rather than investing in extra hash power, while for large miners it is the opposite.

Remark 1. In practice, the parameter k would depend on the q_i's as well as many other aspects of the network. We present a variety of results, with the throughput ranging from relatively tame to pushed beyond what the network can handle, where rampant strategic mining becomes an issue more important than fairness. This is by design: assuming honest behaviour and fixing k for different q_i's allows us to measure the worst-case improvement in fairness, even for cases that would rarely appear in reality. Moreover, our results only cover *block reward* fairness. When transaction fee rewards are included the resulting setting is far more complicated, as a limited view of the network means that even though no blocks are orphaned (for large enough k) there is no guarantee transaction rewards are fairly distributed.

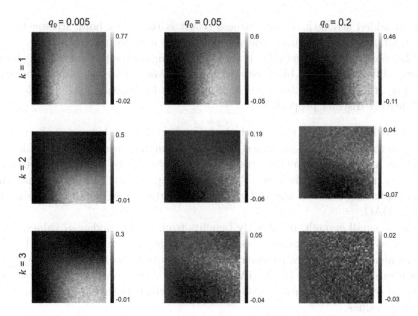

Fig. 1. Surpluses for $k = 1, 2, 3$ at $q_0 \in \{0.005, 0.05, 0.2\}$

4.2   Efficiency

DAG-based ledgers have been created with the aim of tackling a higher transaction load in cryptocurrencies. Given that we have a way of modelling honest transaction growth, there are three different metrics we use to precisely quantify how well DAG-based ledgers deal with a higher throughput of transactions. The first and most important is the *Proof of Work Efficiency*. More specifically, for a given DAG-based Ledger, we say that the PoW efficiency is the fraction of globally valid transactions that are present within the valid sub DAG of the block DAG, over all published transactions.

This is the most important metric, since the goal of a ledger is to maximise the rate at which new transactions are processed. We also compare ledgers in terms of the average fraction of orphaned blocks they create and their transaction *lag*, which is defined as the time difference between the issue and successful inclusion of the DAG's most recent transaction and the final turn of the time horizon.

For our experiments, we compared $\mathcal{P}_{f,k}$ performance for $k \in \{1, 2, 3, \infty\}$ and $n = 4$ atomic miners each with $h_i = 1/4$ and varying q_i's (Fig. 2). For all graphs, we have $\eta = 6, T = 100$ and the results have been averaged over 50 trials.

First of all, we notice that for all parameter settings of $\mathcal{P}_{f,k}$, there exist information regimes where if each q_i is low enough, the ledger suffers in its efficiency–even in the case where $k = \infty$. We also observe that increasing k improves all metrics except lag, but not dramatically. For reasonable values of q_i, before fairness becomes an issue, there is a significant performance increase between $k = 1$ and $k \geq 2$. However, $k > 2$ is only really necessary for extremely small q_i.

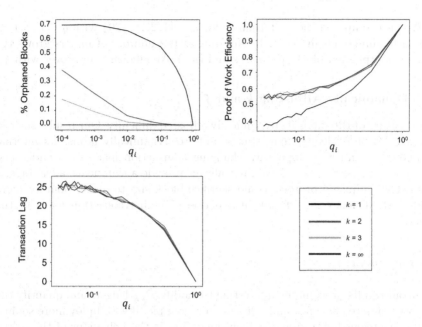

Fig. 2. Performance Metrics for $n = 4$ miners and $k \in \{1, 2, 3, \infty\}$

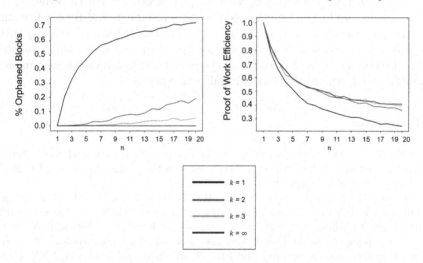

Fig. 3. Performance Metrics for $n \in \{1, 2, \ldots, 20\}$ and $k \in \{1, 2, 3, \infty\}$

Remark 2. This result depends on the assumption that miners add the *oldest* transactions they can, every time they mine a block. A more sophisticated strategy, such as greedily adding the more valuable transactions or a mix from different branches (as in [16]) could improve efficiency for higher k.

We also compared the performance for $n \in \{1, 2, \ldots, 20\}$ with $q = h = 1/n$, leading to similar results (Fig. 3). Notably, as the number of miners grows the number of orphaned blocks decreases and the PoW efficiency improves with k.

4.3 Dynamically Adjusting k and f

A key feature of Bitcoin is its dynamically adjusted difficulty. Our results suggest that a DAG-based ledger may also be able to dynamically adjust its internal parameters k and f to cope with changing transaction loads from end users. Even though larger values of k do not always provide a significant advantage, a dynamically adjusted protocol could sacrifice block size to make room for more pointers if efficiency is suffering in a period of high transaction loads to the ledger.

5 Discussion

Given our results, it would be interesting to modify $\mathcal{P}_{f,k}$ ledgers and quantify the improvements to efficiency and fairness. For example, if we employ more sophisticated strategies for transaction inclusion, what is the behaviour of the ledger in terms of efficiency? In addition, what happens if we augment the ledger space with a different and more complicated class of score functions? By conditioning k to the informational parameters q_i, capturing the essence of existing DAG protocols more concretely, how fairness is affected in case we no longer assume negligible transaction fees? It would also be interesting to drop the honest mining assumption and explore this model in full generality.

References

1. Babaioff, M., Dobzinski, S., Oren, S., Zohar, A.: On bitcoin and red balloons. In: Proceedings of the 13th ACM Conference on Electronic Commerce, EC 2012, Valencia, Spain, 4–8 June 2012, pp. 56–73 (2012)
2. Birmpas, G., Koutsoupias, E., Lazos, P., Marmolejo-Cossío, F.J.: Fairness and efficiency in DAG-based cryptocurrencies. arXiv preprint arXiv:1910.02059 (2019)
3. Bonneau, J., Miller, A., Clark, J., Narayanan, A., Kroll, J.A., Felten, E.W.: SoK: research perspectives and challenges for bitcoin and cryptocurrencies. In: 2015 IEEE Symposium on Security and Privacy, SP 2015, San Jose, CA, USA, 17–21 May 2015, pp. 104–121 (2015)
4. Carlsten, M., Kalodner, H., Weinberg, S.M., Narayanan, A.: On the instability of bitcoin without the block reward. In: Proceedings of the 2016 ACM SIGSAC Conference on Computer and Communications Security, pp. 154–167. ACM (2016)
5. Decker, C., Wattenhofer, R.: Information propagation in the bitcoin network. In: 13th IEEE International Conference on Peer-to-Peer Computing, IEEE P2P 2013, Trento, Italy, 9–11 September 2013, pp. 1–10 (2013)
6. Ethereum/wiki: A next-generation smart contract and decentralized application platform, October 2015. https://github.com/ethereum/wiki/wiki/WhitePaper/

7. Eyal, I.: The miner's dilemma. In: 2015 IEEE Symposium on Security and Privacy, SP 2015, San Jose, CA, USA, 17–21 May 2015, pp. 89–103 (2015)
8. Eyal, I., Gencer, A.E., Sirer, E.G., van Renesse, R.: Bitcoin-NG: a scalable blockchain protocol. In: 13th USENIX Symposium on Networked Systems Design and Implementation, NSDI 2016, Santa Clara, CA, USA, 16–18 March 2016, pp. 45–59 (2016)
9. Eyal, I., Sirer, E.G.: Majority is not enough: bitcoin mining is vulnerable. In: Christin, N., Safavi-Naini, R. (eds.) FC 2014. LNCS, vol. 8437, pp. 436–454. Springer, Heidelberg (2014). https://doi.org/10.1007/978-3-662-45472-5_28
10. Garay, J., Kiayias, A., Leonardos, N.: The bitcoin backbone protocol: analysis and applications. In: Oswald, E., Fischlin, M. (eds.) EUROCRYPT 2015. LNCS, vol. 9057, pp. 281–310. Springer, Heidelberg (2015). https://doi.org/10.1007/978-3-662-46803-6_10
11. Gilad, Y., Hemo, R., Micali, S., Vlachos, G., Zeldovich, N.: Algorand: scaling byzantine agreements for cryptocurrencies. In: Proceedings of the 26th Symposium on Operating Systems Principles, Shanghai, China, 28–31 October 2017, pp. 51–68 (2017)
12. Karlsson, K., et al.: Vegvisir: a partition-tolerant blockchain for the internet-of-things. In: 38th IEEE International Conference on Distributed Computing Systems, ICDCS 2018, Vienna, Austria, 2–6 July 2018, pp. 1150–1158 (2018)
13. Kiayias, A., Koutsoupias, E., Kyropoulou, M., Tselekounis, Y.: Blockchain mining games. In: Proceedings of the 2016 ACM Conference on Economics and Computation, pp. 365–382. ACM (2016)
14. Kiayias, A., Panagiotakos, G.: On trees, chains and fast transactions in the blockchain. In: Lange, T., Dunkelman, O. (eds.) LATINCRYPT 2017. LNCS, vol. 11368, pp. 327–351. Springer, Cham (2019). https://doi.org/10.1007/978-3-030-25283-0_18
15. Koutsoupias, E., Lazos, P., Ogunlana, F., Serafino, P.: Blockchain mining games with pay forward. In: The World Wide Web Conference, WWW 2019, San Francisco, CA, USA, 13–17 May 2019, pp. 917–927 (2019)
16. Lewenberg, Y., Sompolinsky, Y., Zohar, A.: Inclusive block chain protocols. In: Böhme, R., Okamoto, T. (eds.) FC 2015. LNCS, vol. 8975, pp. 528–547. Springer, Heidelberg (2015). https://doi.org/10.1007/978-3-662-47854-7_33
17. Liu, H., Ruan, N., Du, R., Jia, W.: On the strategy and behavior of bitcoin mining with N-attackers. In: Proceedings of the 2018 on Asia Conference on Computer and Communications Security, pp. 357–368. ACM (2018)
18. Nakamoto, S.: Bitcoin: a peer-to-peer electronic cash system (2008)
19. Nayak, K., Kumar, S., Miller, A., Shi, E.: Stubborn mining: generalizing selfish mining and combining with an eclipse attack. In: IEEE European Symposium on Security and Privacy, EuroS&P 2016, Saarbrücken, Germany, 21–24 March 2016, pp. 305–320 (2016)
20. Pass, R., Shi, E.: Hybrid consensus: efficient consensus in the permissionless model. In: 31st International Symposium on Distributed Computing, DISC 2017, Vienna, Austria, 16–20 October 2017, pp. 39:1–39:16 (2017)
21. Sompolinsky, Y., Lewenberg, Y., Zohar, A.: SPECTRE: a fast and scalable cryptocurrency protocol. Cryptology ePrint Archive, Report 2016/1159 (2016). https://eprint.iacr.org/2016/1159

22. Sompolinsky, Y., Zohar, A.: Accelerating bitcoin's transaction processing. Fast money grows on trees, not chains. Cryptology ePrint Archive, Report 2013/881 (2013). https://eprint.iacr.org/2013/881
23. Sompolinsky, Y., Zohar, A.: PHANTOM: a scalable blockDAG protocol. Cryptology ePrint Archive, Report 2018/104 (2018). https://eprint.iacr.org/2018/104
24. Tschorsch, F., Scheuermann, B.: Bitcoin and beyond: a technical survey on decentralized digital currencies. IEEE Commun. Surv. Tutor. **18**(3), 2084–2123 (2016)

Stake Shift in Major Cryptocurrencies:
An Empirical Study

Rainer Stütz[1]([✉]) [iD], Peter Gaži[2], Bernhard Haslhofer[1] [iD], and Jacob Illum[3]

[1] AIT Austrian Institute of Technology, Vienna, Austria
Rainer.Stuetz@ait.ac.at
[2] IOHK, Hong Kong, China
[3] Chainalysis, New York, USA

Abstract. In the proof-of-stake (PoS) paradigm for maintaining decentralized, permissionless cryptocurrencies, Sybil attacks are prevented by basing the distribution of roles in the protocol execution on the stake distribution recorded in the ledger itself. However, for various reasons this distribution cannot be completely up-to-date, introducing a gap between the present stake distribution, which determines the parties' current incentives, and the one used by the protocol.

In this paper, we investigate this issue, and empirically quantify its effects. We survey existing provably secure PoS proposals to observe that the above time gap between the two stake distributions, which we call *stake distribution lag*, amounts to several days for each of these protocols. Based on this, we investigate the ledgers of four major cryptocurrencies (Bitcoin, Bitcoin Cash, Litecoin and Zcash) and compute the average *stake shift* (the statistical distance of the two distributions) for each value of stake distribution lag between 1 and 14 days, as well as related statistics. We also empirically quantify the sublinear growth of stake shift with the length of the considered lag interval.

Finally, we turn our attention to unusual stake-shift spikes in these currencies: we observe that hard forks trigger major stake shifts and that single real-world actors, mostly exchanges, account for major stake shifts in established cryptocurrency ecosystems.

Keywords: Cryptocurrencies · Blockchain · Stake shift · Proof of stake

1 Introduction

The introduction of Bitcoin [1] represented the first practically viable design of a cryptocurrency capable of operating in the so-called permissionless setting, without succumbing to the inherently threatening Sybil attacks. In the decade following Bitcoin's appearance, cryptocurrencies have arguably become the main use case of the underlying blockchain technology. Most deployed cryptocurrencies such as Bitcoin are relying on *proofs of work (PoW)* to prevent Sybil attacks

J. Bonneau and N. Heninger (Eds.): FC 2020, LNCS 12059, pp. 97–113, 2020.
https://doi.org/10.1007/978-3-030-51280-4_7

and provide a robust transaction ledger. However, the PoW approach, also has
its downsides, most importantly the associated energy waste (see e.g. [2]).

A promising alternative approach to maintaining a ledger in a permissionless
environment is based on so-called *proof of stake (PoS)*, where Sybil attacks are
prevented by, roughly speaking, attributing to each participant in the consensus
protocol a weight that is proportional to his stake as recorded in the ledger itself.
Several PoS protocols embracing this idea have been shown to achieve provable
security guarantees in various models [3–8].

More concretely, in all these PoS schemes, whenever a protocol participant
needs to be selected for a certain role in the protocol, he is chosen with a probability that is proportional to his stake share in some *stake distribution SD*, by
which we mean a record of ownership of all the assets maintained on the ledger
at a given time, allowing to determine what proportion of this stake is in control
by any given party. In other words, the stake distribution is a snapshot of the
ownership of the ledger-based asset at a given time (for simplicity of exposition,
we assume only a single-asset ledger in this discussion).

Ideally, the selection of a party for any security-relevant role in the protocol
at time t should be based on a stake distribution SD that is as up-to-date as
possible. However, for various security-related reasons that we detail in Sect. 2.1,
the protocols cannot use the "current" distribution of assets SD_t and are forced
to use $SD_{t-\Lambda}$ that is recorded in the ledger up to the point in time $t-\Lambda$ for some
time interval Λ that we call the *stake distribution lag* of the protocol. However,
roughly speaking, the security of the protocol is determined by—and relies on
a honest-majority assumption about—the present stake distribution SD_t. To
account for this difference, existing protocols assume that not too much money
has changed hands during the past time interval of length Λ, and hence the
distributions $SD_{t-\Lambda}$ and SD_t are close. Their distance, called *stake shift* in [4],
is the focus of our present investigation.

OUR CONTRIBUTIONS. Up until now, the notion of stake shift has only been discussed on a theoretical level and not yet quantified based on real-world data; we
set up to fill this gap. We conjecture that the stake shift statistics of a cryptocurrency are mostly influenced by its proliferation, market cap and daily trading
volumes, rather than its underlying consensus algorithm. Therefore, in an effort
to understand the stake shift characteristics of a mature cryptocurrency, we focus
our analysis on PoW ledgers with a strong market dominance such as Bitcoin.[1]
We perform a systematic, empirical study of the stake shift phenomenon. More
concretely, our contributions can be summarized as follows:

1. We adjust the formal definition of stake shift given in [4] to be applicable
   to studying the execution of the protocol in retrospect, based only on the
   stabilized ledger produced, without access to the states held by the parties
   during its execution.

---

[1] As of September 13, 2019, about 68% of the total market capitalization of cryptocurrencies is stored in Bitcoin (cf. https://coinmarketcap.com).

2. We provide a scalable algorithmic method for computing stabilized stake shift over the entire history of PoW ledgers following the UTXO model. We computed it in ledgers of four major cryptocurrencies (Bitcoin, Bitcoin Cash, Litecoin, and Zcash) from their inception until July 31st, 2019.
3. We study the evolution of stabilized stake shift in all ledgers and found that hard forks may trigger major stake shifts. We also fitted a simple quadratic polynomial model that mimics the real-world sublinear growth of stake shift with respect to the considered stake distribution lag.
4. We pick top spikes occurring within the last two years, and determine the likely real-world identities behind them. We can observe that exchanges are behind those spikes, at least in established cryptocurrencies such as Bitcoin or Bitcoin Cash.

Our results show that the stake-shift phenomenon has a noticeable impact on the provable-security guarantees provided by PoS protocols from the literature. We argue in Sect. 2.1 that the stake shift over the stake distribution lag period of a PoS protocol counts directly against the threshold of adversarial stake it can tolerate (typically $1/2$ or $1/3$), and the values of stake shift that we observe are clearly significant on this scale, as we detail in Sect. 6.

While our initial intention was to inform the design of PoS protocols, we believe that our results can be interesting to a wider community and shed some light on the real-life use of the studied cryptocurrencies as tools for value transfer. Therefore, we make our research reproducible by releasing the implementation of our stake shift computation method. It can be used for computing stabilized stake shifts with configurable lag for any other cryptocurrency that follows Bitcoin's UTXO model.

Finally, note that all measurements were performed on UTXO-based currencies and some of the mentioned PoS protocols envision an account-based ledger. This aspect, however, is completely irrelevant to our investigation. Also, while our motivation comes from PoS protocols, we believe that most robust and useful data can be obtained from mature blockchains and hence we focus our measurements on PoW ledgers. To reemphasize, it seems reasonable to believe that the maturity (age, market cap, trading volume, etc.) of a blockchain are more determining for its stake shift behavior than the underlying consensus mechanism, hence justifying our choice.

We start by providing more details on the relevance of stake shift for PoS security, and survey the stake distribution lags in existing proof-of-stake protocols in Sect. 2. Then we provide a formal definition of stabilized stake shift in Sect. 3 and describe our datasets and computation methods in Sect. 4. We present our findings in Sect. 5 and discuss them in Sect. 6.

2   Background

In this section we provide a more detailed discussion of the relevance of stake shift for PoS protocols, and survey stake distribution lags of several known PoS proposals.

2.1 Importance of Stake Shift for Security of PoS-Based Blockchains

As mentioned in Sect. 1, the selection of a party for any security-relevant role in a PoS protocol should ideally be based on a stake distribution $\mathcal{SD}$ that is as up-to-date as possible. However, this is often difficult, as we detail next.

First, in the eventual-consensus PoS protocols such as [4–8], there is no consensus about the inclusion of the most recently created blocks into the stable ledger, such a consensus is only achieved gradually by adding more and more blocks on top of them. Consequently, during the protocol execution, the view of the current stake distribution $\mathcal{SD}_t$ at time t by different honest parties might actually differ and hence $\mathcal{SD}_t$ cannot be used for electing protocol actors.

On the other hand, in PoS protocols based on Byzantine Agreement such as [3], where the consensus about a block is achieved before proceeding to further blocks, the most recent stake distribution still cannot be used for sampling protocol participants. The reason is that the security of the protocol requires the stake distribution to be old enough so that it was fully determined *before* the adversary could have any information about the bits of randomness used to sample from this distribution (which are also produced by the protocol).

Therefore, in all these protocols, participants that are allowed to act at some time t are sampled according to a distribution $\mathcal{SD}_{t-\Lambda}$ recorded in the ledger up to the point in time $t - \Lambda$ for some stake distribution lag Λ. This is done with the intention that $\mathcal{SD}_{t-\Lambda}$ is both

- stable (in the case of eventual-consensus protocols), and
- recent enough so that it can be assumed that it does not differ too much from the current distribution $\mathcal{SD}_t$.

However, the incentives of the participants are, of course, shaped by the current distribution of the stake: For example, a party P that used to own a significant portion of the stake, but has just transferred (e.g., sold) all of it in time t_1, has no longer any stake in the system and hence no direct motivation to contribute to its maintenance. Nonetheless, at any time t during the time interval $(t_1, t_1 + \Lambda)$, the stake distribution $\mathcal{SD}_{t-\Lambda}$ will still attribute some stake to P and hence P will be allowed (and expected) to act accordingly in the protocol. This discrepancy is present in all PoS protocols listed above, and in fact in all provably-secure PoS protocols in the literature.

The security of these PoS protocols is typically argued based on the assumption that at any point during the execution, less than a fraction T of the total stake in the system is controlled by adversarial parties (for $T = 1/2$ in [4–8] and $T = 1/3$ in [3]). To formally account for the above mismatch, one has to choose between the following two approaches:

(i) Directly assume that, at every point t during the execution, less than a T-fraction of stake in the *old* distribution $\mathcal{SD}_{t-\Lambda}$ is controlled by parties that are adversarial *at time* t.

(ii) Make an additional assumption that, at any point t during the execution, some (normalized) "difference" between $\mathcal{SD}_{t-\Lambda}$ and the current factual distribution of stake $\mathcal{SD}_t$ in the system is bounded by a constant $\sigma \in (0,1)$;

i.e., that not too much money has changed hands between $t - \Lambda$ and t. This assumption allows to conclude security as long as the *current* adversarial stake ratio $\alpha \in [0,1]$ in $\mathcal{SD}_t$ satisfies

$$\alpha \leq (1 - \varepsilon) \cdot T - \sigma \qquad (1)$$

for some $\varepsilon \geq 0$ (see e.g. [4, Theorem 6], respectively Theorem 5.3 in the full version of [4]).

All of the provably secure PoS protocols adopt one of these two approaches. While the assumption in approach (i) is formally sufficient, it is arguably cumbersome and counter-intuitive, making the reasoning (ii) preferable. As evidenced by Eq. (1), in the approach (ii) the quantity σ, called stake shift, plays a significant role for the protocols' security.

Let us clarify that our primary motivation for investigating stake shift pertains to the distributions $\mathcal{SD}_t$ and $SD_{t-\Lambda}$ as described above and defined by individual PoS protocols, and does not aim at addressing the dangers of long-range attacks (see e.g. [9] for an overview of those). In a typical long-range attack setting, the considered time interval would be much longer and one could hardly expect a limited stake shift over it.

Finally, following the above motivation, below we focus on provably secure PoS proposals. All these protocols use all existing coins for staking, not distinguishing between "staked" and "unstaked" coins, and so we don't consider this distinction below. It is worth mentioning that practical implementations of these protocols, as well as other PoS blockchains such as EOS[2] and Tezos[3], often deviate from this approach and allow for coins that do not participate in staking.

2.2   Stake Distribution Lag in Existing PoS Protocols

Here we survey the value of stake distribution lag in several provably secure PoS protocol proposals.

OUROBOROS. The Ouroboros PoS protocol [4] divides its execution into so-called *epochs*, where each epoch is a sequence of $10k$ slots for a parameter k (this structure is dictated by the inner workings of the protocol). The stake distribution used for sampling slot leaders in epoch ep_j is the one reflected in the current chain up to slot $4k$ of the preceding epoch ep_{j-1}. Therefore, the stake distribution lag amounts to at most $14k$ slots.

In the deployment of the Ouroboros protocol in the Cardano project[4], each slot takes $20\,$s and k is chosen to be 2160. Therefore, the above upper bound on the stake distribution lag corresponds to exactly 7 days.

OUROBOROS PRAOS AND OUROBOROS GENESIS. These protocols, which are defined in [6,7], also divide their execution into epochs. However, the stake distribution used for sampling slot leaders in epoch ep_j is the one reflected in the

---

[2]   https://eos.io.

[3]   https://tezos.com.

[4]   https://www.cardano.org.

current chain up to the last slot of the epoch ep_{j-2}. Hence the stake distribution lag amounts to at most 2 epochs. Assuming the same epoch length as above, this would result in a stake distribution lag of exactly 10 days.

ALGORAND AND VAULT. For the protocols Algorand [3,10,11] and Vault [12] we consider the parametrization given in [12], where the authors suggest to consider a stake distribution lag of 1 day for Algorand and hence 2 days for Vault.

SNOW WHITE. The Snow White protocol employs a "look-back" of 2ω blocks for a parameter ω that is sufficient to invoke the common-prefix and chain-quality properties (see [5]). The authors do not propose a concrete value of ω, however, given that the requirements put on ω are similar to other protocols (common prefix, chain quality), it is safe to assume that an implementation of Snow White would also lead to a stake distribution lag between 1 and 10 days.

3   Stabilized Stake Shift Definition

We are interested in executions of blockchain ledger protocols, and will be assuming a model in the spirit of [13] to formalize such executions. In particular, we assume there is an *environment* orchestrating the execution, a set of *parties* $\mathcal{P}$ executing the protocol, and an *adversary* $\mathcal{A}$ allowed to corrupt the parties upon approval from the environment; parties yet uncorrupted are called *honest*. We assume that the protocol execution is divided into a sequence of disjoint, consecutive time intervals called *slots*, indexed by natural numbers (starting with 1). The set of honest parties at each slot sl is denoted by $\mathcal{H}[sl]$. Finally, we denote by $\mathsf{C}^{\mathsf{P}}[sl]$ the chain held by an honest party P at the beginning of slot sl.

Finally, let $\mathcal{SD}^{\mathsf{P}}[sl]$ denote the stake distribution recorded in the chain $\mathsf{C}^{\mathsf{P}}[sl]$ up to slot sl, seen as a probability distribution (i.e., normalized to sum to 1). As a notational convenience, let $\mathcal{SD}^{\mathsf{P}}[0]$ denote the initial stake distribution recorded in the genesis block.

To define stake shift, we use the standard notion of statistical distance of two discrete probability distributions.

Definition 1 (Statistical distance). *For two discrete probability distributions $\mathcal{X}$ and $\mathcal{Y}$ with support $\mathcal{S}_{\mathcal{X}}$ and $\mathcal{S}_{\mathcal{Y}}$ respectively, the* statistical distance *(sometimes also called the* total variation distance*) of $\mathcal{X}$ and $\mathcal{Y}$ is defined as*

$$\delta(\mathcal{X}, \mathcal{Y}) \triangleq \tfrac{1}{2} \sum_{s \in \mathcal{S}_{\mathcal{X}} \cup \mathcal{S}_{\mathcal{Y}}} \left| \Pr_{\mathcal{X}}[s] - \Pr_{\mathcal{Y}}[s] \right|.$$

Seeing stake distributions as probability distributions allows for the following definition inspired by [4, Definition 5.1].

Definition 2 (Stake shift). *Consider an execution $\mathcal{E}$ of a blockchain protocol Π for L slots, and let $sl \in \{\Lambda, \ldots, L\}$. The Λ-stake shift in slot sl is the maximum, over all parties P_1 honest in slot $sl - \Lambda$ and all parties P_2 honest in slot* *sl, of the statistical distance between the stake distributions in slots sl − Λ and sl as perceived by* P_1 *and* P_2, *respectively. Formally,*

$$SS_\Lambda(\mathcal{E}, sl) \triangleq \max_{\substack{P_1 \in \mathcal{H}[sl-\Lambda] \\ P_2 \in \mathcal{H}[sl]}} \delta\left(\mathcal{SD}^{P_1}[sl - \Lambda], \mathcal{SD}^{P_2}[sl]\right).$$

Naturally, we extend this notion over the whole execution and define the Λ*-stake shift of* $\mathcal{E}$ *to be*

$$SS_\Lambda(\mathcal{E}) \triangleq \max_{\Lambda \leq sl \leq L} SS_\Lambda(\mathcal{E}, sl).$$

Finally, note that the quantity $SS_\Lambda(\mathcal{E}, sl)$, and consequently also $SS_\Lambda(\mathcal{E})$, cannot be determined based solely on the final stabilized ledger **L** that was created by the protocol, as it does not contain the views of the participants during the protocol execution. For this reason, any long-term empirical study that is only based on the preserved stabilized ledger **L** (e.g. the Bitcoin blockchain) has to aim for an analogous quantity capturing stake shift in **L**, as defined next.

For a stable ledger **L**, we denote by $\mathcal{SD}^{\mathbf{L}}[sl]$ the stake distribution as recorded in **L** up to slot *sl*.

Definition 3 (Stabilized stake shift). *Consider an execution* $\mathcal{E}$ *of a blockchain protocol* Π *for L slots, let* **L** *denote the resulting stable ledger produced by* Π *during* $\mathcal{E}$, *and let sl* ∈ {Λ,...,L}. *The stabilized* Λ*-stake shift in slot sl is defined as*

$$\hat{SS}_\Lambda(\mathcal{E}, sl) \triangleq \delta\left(\mathcal{SD}^{\mathbf{L}}[sl - \Lambda], \mathcal{SD}^{\mathbf{L}}[sl]\right),$$

and similarly, the stabilized Λ*-stake shift of* $\mathcal{E}$ *is*

$$\hat{SS}_\Lambda(\mathcal{E}) \triangleq \max_{\Lambda \leq sl \leq L} \hat{SS}_\Lambda(\mathcal{E}, sl).$$

For the reasons noted above, we will focus on *stabilized* stake shift in our empirical analysis; whenever we use the term *stake shift* below, we refer to its stabilized variant as per Definition 3.

4   Data and Methods

Before we can empirically investigate stake shifts in deployed cryptocurrencies, we first need to translate the definition of *stake shift* into a scalable algorithmic procedure that can compute stake shift with configurable lags over a currency's entire history, which in the case of Bitcoin spans more than 440M transactions and 0.5B addresses. In this section, we describe how we prepare the required datasets from the underlying blockchains and the technical details of our stabilized stake shift computation method.

4.1   Dataset Preparation and Structure

We consider datasets from four different cryptocurrency ledgers: first, we take *Bitcoin (BTC)*, which is still the cryptocurrency with the strongest market dominance. Additionally, we take three alternatives derived from the Bitcoin Core code base: *Bitcoin Cash (BCH)*, which is a hard fork from the Bitcoin blockchain to increase the block size limit, which took effect in August 2017; *Litecoin (LTC)*, which was an early altcoin, starting in October 2011, and is very similar to Bitcoin. The key differences to Bitcoin are its choice of the proof-of-work algorithm (*scrypt*) and the network's average block creation time, which is roughly 2.5 min. Finally, we also consider *Zcash (ZEC)*, which is a cryptocurrency with enhanced privacy features, initially released in October 2016. Zcash coins are either in a transparent or a shielded pool. The transparent (unshielded) pool contains ZEC in transparent addresses (so-called *t-addresses*). Due to the anonymity features in Zcash, our analysis is limited to the transparent transactions in the unshielded pool. However, as observed in [14], a large proportion of the activity on Zcash does not use the shielded pools. A summary of the used datasets is provided in Table 1.

Table 1. Summary of considered cryptocurrency datasets.

Currency	# Blocks	Last timestamp	# Txs	# Addresses	# Clusters	# Entities
BTC	588,007	2019-07-31 23:55:05Z	440,487,974	540,942,127	50,162,316	260,182,367
BCH	593,795	2019-07-31 23:54:09Z	275,765,798	302,098,643	31,173,961	142,884,996
LTC	1,677,479	2019-07-31 23:57:21Z	36,009,400	44,256,812	3,052,978	23,304,076
ZEC	577,390	2019-07-31 23:59:54Z	5,052,970	3,488,294	206,506	1,680,481

For each cryptocurrency ledger, we partition these addresses into maximal subsets (clusters) that are likely to be controlled by the same entity using the well-known and efficient multiple-input clustering heuristics [15]. The underlying intuition is that if two addresses (e.g., A_1 and A_2) are used as inputs in the same transaction while one of these addresses along with another address (e.g., A_2 and A_3) are used as inputs in another transaction, then the three addresses (A_1, A_2 and A_3) must somehow be controlled by the same entity, who conducted both transactions and therefore possesses the private keys corresponding to all three addresses. Being aware that this heuristic fails when CoinJoin transactions [16] are involved, we filtered those transactions before applying the multiple-input heuristics.

Before describing our stake shift computation method in more detail, we introduce the following notation for key entities in our dataset: we consider a blockchain $B_{t_{\mathrm{end}}} = (A, T)$ with its associated set of addresses A and set of transactions T at time t_{end}.

The multiple-input heuristics algorithm is applied to the complete transaction dataset at time t_{end} to obtain a set of clusters $C = \{C_1, \ldots, C_{n_c}\}$. Each cluster C_i is represented by a set of addresses, where $|C_i| \geq 2, \forall i \in \{1, \ldots, n_c\}$.

The set of entities E is represented by the union of C with the remaining single address clusters, i.e., $E = C \cup \{\{a\} \mid a \in A \wedge \forall C \in C : a \notin C\}$. The (cumulative) balance for entity $e \in E$ at time t is denoted by b_e^t, and the total balance over all entities at time t is given by $b_{\text{total}}^t = \sum_{e \in E} b_e^t$.

The last three columns in Table 1 show the number of addresses in each ledger, the number of computed clusters, as well as the number of entities holding the corresponding private keys of one or more addresses.

For further inspecting the real-world identities behind entities causing major stake shifts, we rely on Chainalysis[5], which is a proprietary online tool that facilitates the tracking of Bitcoin transactions by annotating Bitcoin addresses with potential owners.

4.2   Stake Shift Computation

Given the dimensionality of our dataset, the challenge lies in finding a method that follows Definition 3 and can compute the distances δ in a scalable, distributed and memory-efficient manner.

In a naïve approach one would calculate the cumulative balance for each entity at every time period (e.g., days). The stake distribution is represented by the relative frequencies, which are the result of dividing the cumulative balances at time t_p by the total balance $b_{\text{total}}^{t_p}$. This approach would result in huge temporary datasets that must be persisted in memory for subsequent computation steps. For instance, for the computation of the stabilized stake shift in Bitcoin, a grid of $3{,}862 \times 260{,}182{,}367$ (number of days $\times$ number of entities) data points needs to be cached, which is computationally inefficient and hardly feasible in practice given today's hardware limitations.

Therefore, we propose an iterator-based approach coupled with a custom aggregation method, which can be executed on a distributed, horizontally scalable data processing architecture: First, we join the transaction data with the relevant entity information, and use the entity IDs for partitioning. Then, for calculating the cumulative balances, we sort every partition by time period. The iterator represents basically a loop over the grid of predefined time periods for a given entity. Internally, we build up a data structure that holds the following information in each iteration step: (i) entity ID e, (ii) time period t_p, (iii) the cumulative balance $b_e^{t_p}$, (iv) the contribution of the current entity to the stake distribution $R_e^{t_p} = b_e^{t_p}/b_{\text{total}}^{t_p}$ at time t_p; and (v) the absolute difference of the stake distribution contributions at time t_p and $t_{p-\ell}$: $\delta_e^{t_p} = |R_e^{t_p} - R_e^{t_{p-\ell}}|$.

To compute the stake shift for arbitrary lag values ℓ, a FIFO (first in, first out) structure is needed to hold at most ℓ instances of the above data structure for the last ℓ periods. That data structure can efficiently be partitioned across computation nodes and requires zero communication costs. An aggregation method then collects all partial results to obtain the stake shift value $\hat{SS}_\ell^{t_p}$ at time period t_p.

---

[5] https://www.chainalysis.com/.

We implemented our stake shift computation method as single Apache Spark[6] job operating directly on a pre-computed dataset provisioned by the GraphSense Cryptocurrency Analytics Platform[7]. For further technical details, we refer to the source code, which will be released with this paper.

5   Analysis and Results

In the following, we first report results on the longitudinal evolution of stake shifts in all considered cryptocurrencies (BTC, BCH, LTC, ZEC). Then we hand-pick past stake shift spikes and analyze them in more detail, in order to gain a better understanding on the factors causing those shifts. We also elaborate on cross-ledger similarities and differences.

5.1   Evolution of Stabilized Stake Shifts

Figure 1 depicts the evolution of **Bitcoin** stake shifts over the observation period for three different lag settings Λ: 1 day, 7 days, and 14 days. We can observe huge spikes (0.933 for $\Lambda = 1$) right after the generation of the genesis block and another major spike occurring on June 19th, 2011. That spike is most likely related to a security breach on Mt. Gox, at this time one of the dominating Bitcoin exchanges. After an attacker illegally transferred a large amount of Bit-coins, 424,242 BTC were moved from a *cold storage* to a Mt. Gox address on June 23rd 2011[8]. We can also observe that hard forks trigger major stake shifts: Bitcoin Cash, for instance, hard forked on August 1, 2017.

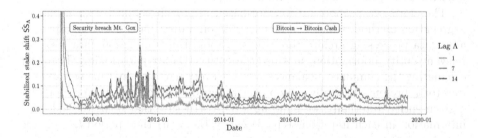

Fig. 1. Stake shift for BTC (stake distribution lag Λ: 1, 7, and 14 days). (Color figure online)

Due to the lack of space, we will in the following refrain from depicting stake evolutions for the other investigated currencies and focus on reporting key observations and findings instead. For further visual inspection, we refer the interested

---

[6] https://spark.apache.org/.

[7] https://graphsense.info.

[8] https://en.wikipedia.org/wiki/Mt._Gox.

reader to the Appendix of this paper. We also restrict subsequent discussions to $\Lambda = 1$ because we can observe that stake shifts evolve synchronously and differ only in lag amplitudes.

Bitcoin Cash shows similar behavior to Bitcoin: since it is a hard fork of Bitcoin, stake shifts run synchronous to Bitcoin until the hard fork date. Stake shift values in Bitcoin Cash also show a higher variability after November 15, 2018. On this date a hard fork was activated by *Bitcoin ABC*[9] (at the time the largest software client for Bitcoin Cash) and *Bitcoin SV*[10] (Satoshi's Vision).

In general, the variability of stake shifts in **Litecoin** (\$4.7B market capitalization) appears to be higher than the one in Bitcoin. The biggest spikes appear on the following dates: 2014-02-05, 2015-03-08, and 2018-11-30. The first two spikes are represented by a couple of dominating entities. We observed either a direct currency flow between them, or a indirect flow via some intermediary cluster or address. One exception is the spike on November 30th, 2018: on that day, approximately 35.4M LTC were transferred within a 24 h period, with a total value of \$1.1B at that time. This is extraordinary, because the Litecoin network has recorded approximately \$100M of trading volume per day, on average. After investigating involved transactions, we noted that a significant portion of the transaction volume appears to originate from a single entity, which was not captured by the multiple-input clustering heuristic. At least 40 new wallets have entered the list of the richest Litecoin addresses, each with a balance of 300,000 LTC (~\$10M). In total, the addresses account for 12.9M LTC (approximately \$372M). The reason for the movement is still unclear, but, as we will discuss later in Sect. 5.3, we can observe that the entities involved in those stake shifts were controlled by Coinbase, which is a major cryptocurrency exchange.

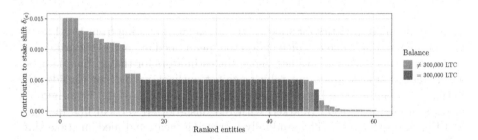

Fig. 2. Ranked contributions (top 60) to stabilized stake shift for $\Lambda = 1$ (LTC on November 30th, 2018).

Figure 2 provides a more detailed view on that single Litecoin spike. It shows the top 60 contributions to the stake shift for Litecoin on November 30th, 2018. A block of consecutive addresses sharing a certain transaction behavior becomes visible between rank 16 to 46. They share the following common characteristics:

---

[9] https://www.bitcoinabc.org/.
[10] https://bitcoinsv.io/.

(i) the number of incoming transaction is either 40 or 41; (ii) transactions are executed in chunks of 7,500 LTC; and (iii) the total balance is 300,000 LTC.

The remaining 11 addresses of this entity appear in the tail of the distribution. The reason is that the transactions already started on the day before (2018-11-29 21:18:59Z). Therefore, these 11 addresses do not (fully) account to the stabilized stake shift of November 30th, 2018.

When regarding the stake shift evolution of **Zcash** ($366M market capitalization), we can, as in Litecoin, observe higher variability than in Bitcoin or Bitcoin Cash. This could be explained by the differences in market capitalization ($5.5B BCH vs. $177B BTC) in these two currencies[11].

Table 2. Summary statistics of stabilized stake shift for different lag values.

Lag (in days)	BTC			BCH			LTC			ZEC		
	Mean	Median	Std Dev	Mean	Median	Std Dev	Mean	Median	Std Dev	Mean	Median	Std Dev
1	0.013	0.010	0.0098	0.013	0.011	0.0102	0.014	0.011	0.0123	0.014	0.012	0.0102
2	0.020	0.017	0.0129	0.020	0.017	0.0134	0.022	0.017	0.0177	0.023	0.020	0.0146
3	0.026	0.022	0.0155	0.026	0.023	0.0161	0.030	0.023	0.0219	0.031	0.027	0.0181
4	0.031	0.027	0.0177	0.032	0.027	0.0183	0.036	0.029	0.0255	0.038	0.034	0.0211
5	0.036	0.031	0.0196	0.037	0.032	0.0203	0.042	0.034	0.0289	0.045	0.040	0.0238
6	0.040	0.035	0.0213	0.041	0.036	0.0221	0.048	0.039	0.0319	0.051	0.047	0.0262
7	0.045	0.039	0.0229	0.045	0.039	0.0238	0.053	0.044	0.0347	0.058	0.053	0.0286
8	0.049	0.042	0.0244	0.050	0.043	0.0253	0.058	0.048	0.0374	0.063	0.059	0.0308
9	0.053	0.045	0.0257	0.053	0.046	0.0267	0.063	0.052	0.0399	0.069	0.065	0.0328
10	0.056	0.049	0.0270	0.057	0.050	0.0281	0.068	0.057	0.0423	0.074	0.070	0.0346
11	0.060	0.052	0.0282	0.061	0.053	0.0293	0.073	0.060	0.0446	0.079	0.075	0.0364
12	0.063	0.055	0.0294	0.064	0.056	0.0305	0.077	0.064	0.0469	0.084	0.081	0.0380
13	0.067	0.058	0.0305	0.068	0.059	0.0317	0.082	0.068	0.0490	0.089	0.085	0.0395
14	0.070	0.061	0.0316	0.071	0.062	0.0329	0.086	0.072	0.0510	0.094	0.090	0.0410

More detailed statistics for stake distribution lag Λ ranging from 1 to 14 days are summarized in Table 2, which shows the mean, median, and standard deviation of resulting stake shift values. Since the estimators for the arithmetic mean and standard deviation are not robust against outliers, we did not consider the initial parts of the time line and disregarded the first 6% of the total number of days in our estimation (marked with red dash-dotted vertical line in Fig. 1 and Fig. 5, respectively). The gradually increasing mean and median stake shift values confirm our previous observation of growing amplitudes.

5.2 Modeling Stake Shift

Having observed that stake shifts for different lags evolve synchronously and vary in amplitudes, we next fitted regression models to the computed mean, median, and standard deviations (Fig. 3). We can observe that estimated values show a clear, strictly monotonic increasing trend with growing lag. More specifically, we found that quadratic polynomials capture well the relation between the location/scale estimators and lag Λ (coefficient of determination $R^2 \geq 0.99$).

---

[11] https://coinmarketcap.com/all/views/all/, retrieved on 2019-09-19.

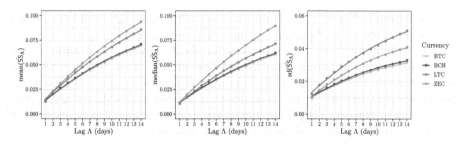

Fig. 3. Fitted trends for mean, median, and standard deviation of stake shift.

5.3 Attributing Selected Stake Shift Spikes

In order to shed some more light on the real-world actors behind observable stake shift spikes, we selected the top five $\Lambda = 1$ spikes in each currency and attributed them to real-world identities using the Chainalysis API. Due to the limited availability of attribution tags, we focus only on the period between August 1, 2017 and July 31, 2019. Before continuing, we note that a fully fledged systematic analysis of real-world entities and their motivation for transferring large amounts is out of scope in this paper.

Figure 4 shows the distribution of stake shift contributions at the spike that occurred during the Bitcoin Cash hard fork (cf. Sect. 5.1). We can clearly see that known exchanges such as Bitfinex, Kraken, Coinbase, and Korbit were the major entities behind those stake shifts. The largest stake shift was caused by a transfer from a Bitfinex operated address to some multisig wallet, which is not a public deposit address but known to be operated by Bitfinex as well. This suggest that this spike represents a major hot-to-cold wallet transfer. However, it remains unclear why this co-occurs with the Bitcoin Cash hard-fork date.

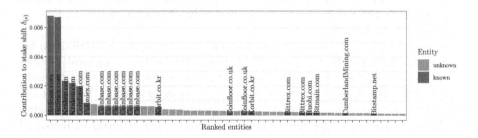

Fig. 4. Attributed BTC stake shift spike triggered by Bitcoin Cash fork (2017-08-01)

We also attributed the top five Bitcoin Cash and Litecoin spikes and see that exchanges play a major role in stake shifts, however to a lesser extent than in Bitcoin. In the selected Litecoin spike the identity of involved entities is unknown. However, we note that only limited attribution tags are available for that currency. For further details on intra-spike stake shift distributions, we refer to the plots in the Appendix of the arXiv version of this paper[12].

The underlying cause and motivation for being involved in a major stake shift is not always apparent. Possible reasons are migration of funds between hot and/or cold wallets, or institutional investors taking a serious long position. Summarizing the results, we can conclude that, at least in established cryptocurrencies such as Bitcoin, a small number of real-world entities – usually exchanges – may account for major stake shifts in cryptocurrency ecosystems.

6   Discussion

KEY FINDINGS. Our analysis of stabilized stake shift presented in Sects. 5.1 and 5.2 leads us to the following conclusions:

- The two main observable reasons for extreme stake-shift spikes are hacks and migration of funds to different wallets. Large stake shifts resulting from hacks are clearly problematic for a proof-of-stake based cryptocurrency, as the entity getting control of these funds can be reasonably considered adversarial, with unpredictable future actions.
- When considering the levels of adversarial stake ratio that a proof-of-stake protocol can provably tolerate, one needs to be aware that this threshold is affected by the assumed maximal stake shift σ as per Eq. (1). Our measurements, summarized in Table 2, show that depending on the protocol's stake distribution lag, this effect may decrease the guaranteed resilience bound by several percent even for lag intervals where the stake shift achieves average values (as the most extreme example, consider the average stabilized stake shift for a (hypothetical) two-week lag interval in ZEC, which amounts to 9.4%). Note that, as captured in Fig. 1 and the standard deviation values in Fig. 2, the stake shift value can deviate considerably from this average. This is particularly noteworthy for protocols that only aim for the threshold $T = 1/3$ in Eq. (1) such as [3].
- Unsurprisingly, our data confirms that with increasing stake distribution lag also the corresponding stake shift increases, the precise (empirical) sublinear dependence is captured in Fig. 3. This advocates for the need to make the stake distribution lag as small as possible in any future PoS protocol design. More importantly, knowing the exact slope of this function (and hence the price being paid for longer stake distribution lag in terms of increased expected stake shift) allows the designers of existing and future proof-of-stake protocols to weigh these costs against the benefits of longer lag intervals, leading to more informed design decisions.
- Our results empirically support the natural assumption that high stake shift mostly appears at the beginning of the lifetime of a cryptocurrency, and hence older, more established cryptocurrencies experience lower average and

---

[12] https://arxiv.org/abs/2001.04187.

median stake shift for a given lag interval, as well as less occurrences of extreme stake shift spikes. This observation allows for some optimism on the side of PoS-protocol designers, as the role of stake-shift-related weakening of the proven security guarantees should diminish during the lifetime of the system. On the other hand, the initial vulnerability of a new, bootstrapping PoS cryptocurrency could be prevented for example by the "merged staking" mechanism discussed in [17].

Additionally, our investigation of the extremal stake-shift spikes conducted in Sect. 5.3 results in the following observations:

– The spikes motivated by migration of funds can be assumed to be often triggered by a single entity, we conjecture that the main reason of these transfers was moving the considerable funds to a more secure, multisig-protected wallet. In such cases, it is natural to assume that the funds are controlled by the same party after the transfer, making these spikes benign from the perspective of our considered PoS scenario.

LIMITATIONS. The main limitation of our results with respect to the question motivating our investigation lies in the imperfections of clustering techniques and incompleteness of attribution tags linking entities to real-world identities (despite using the best currently known). Having a better understanding of which keys are controlled by the same real-world entity would give us a more precise picture of the experienced stake shift. However, it appears likely that more realistic clustering would lead to more keys being clustered, and hence lower stake-shift estimates. One can thus see our results as reasonable upper bounds of these quantities.

FUTURE WORK. One clear area of future work is to devise new and better address-clustering and attribution data sharing techniques. On top of that, it might be interesting to expand our investigation in time and considered cryptoassets. After more data is available, future studies should also include assets or currencies built on top of PoS protocols. Such studies should also investigate the role of exchanges, which typically hold major stakes and might become important players in a PoS-based consensus. This is particularly interesting for PoS protocols where coins must be explicitly "staked" to participate in the consensus, and hence the total participating stake is typically much smaller than the overall stake. Finally, it would be interesting to perform a more careful and detailed investigation of the activity behind the five considered major stake shift spikes, as well as other unusually large spikes uncovered by our work.

Acknowledgments. We thank Patrick McCorry for reviewing and commenting on the final draft, and our AIT colleagues Hannes Koller and Melitta Dragaschnig for insightful discussions regarding the Apache Spark implementation. Work on this topic is supported inter alia by the European Union's Horizon 2020 research and innovation programme under grant agreement No. 740558 (TITANIUM) and the Austrian FFG's KIRAS programme under project VIRTCRIME (No. 860672).

A   Additional Figures

In this section, we provide additional plots for visual inspection of our findings reported in Sect. 5. Figure 5 depicts the evolution of stake shifts for Bitcoin (BTC), Bitcoin (BCH), Litecoin (LTC), and Zcash (ZEC).

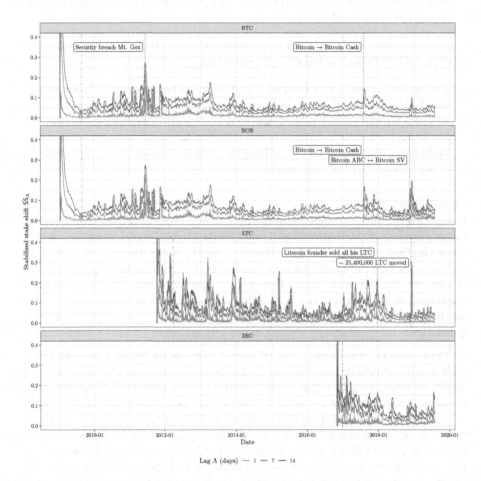

Fig. 5. Stake shift for all analyzed cryptocurrencies (stake distribution lag Λ: 1, 7, and 14 days). (Color figure online)

References

1. Nakamoto, S.: Bitcoin: a peer-to-peer electronic cash system (2009)
2. Digiconomist: Bitcoin energy consumption index. https://digiconomist.net/bitcoin-energy-consumption. Accessed 15 Sept 2019

3. Chen, J., Micali, S.: ALGORAND. arXiv e-prints. arXiv:1607.01341 (2016)
4. Kiayias, A., Russell, A., David, B., Oliynykov, R.: Ouroboros: a provably secure proof-of-stake blockchain protocol. In: Katz, J., Shacham, H. (eds.) CRYPTO 2017. LNCS, vol. 10401, pp. 357–388. Springer, Cham (2017). https://doi.org/10.1007/978-3-319-63688-7_12
5. Bentov, I., Pass, R., Shi, E.: Snow white: provably secure proofs of stake. Cryptology ePrint Archive, Report 2016/919 (2016). http://eprint.iacr.org/2016/919
6. David, B., Gaži, P., Kiayias, A., Russell, A.: Ouroboros praos: an adaptively-secure, semi-synchronous proof-of-stake blockchain. In: Nielsen, J.B., Rijmen, V. (eds.) EUROCRYPT 2018. LNCS, vol. 10821, pp. 66–98. Springer, Cham (2018). https://doi.org/10.1007/978-3-319-78375-8_3
7. Badertscher, C., Gazi, P., Kiayias, A., Russell, A., Zikas, V.: Ouroboros genesis: composable proof-of-stake blockchains with dynamic availability. In: Lie, D., Mannan, M., Backes, M., Wang, X. (eds.) ACM CCS, pp. 913–930. ACM Press (2018)
8. Badertscher, C., Gaži, P., Kiayias, A., Russell, A., Zikas, V.: Ouroboros chronos: permissionless clock synchronization via proof-of-stake. Cryptology ePrint Archieve, Report 2019/838 (2019). https://eprint.iacr.org/2019/838
9. Gaži, P., Kiayias, A., Russell, A.: Stake-bleeding attacks on proof-of-stake blockchains. Cryptology ePrint Archive, Report 2018/248 (2018). https://eprint.iacr.org/2018/248
10. Gilad, Y., Hemo, R., Micali, S., Vlachos, G., Zeldovich, N.: Algorand: scaling Byzantine agreements for cryptocurrencies. Cryptology ePrint Archive, Report 2017/454 (2017). http://eprint.iacr.org/2017/454
11. Chen, J., Gorbunov, S., Micali, S., Vlachos, G.: ALGORAND AGREEMENT: super fast and partition resilient byzantine agreement. Cryptology ePrint Archive, Report 2018/377 (2018). https://eprint.iacr.org/2018/377
12. Leung, D., Suhl, A., Gilad, Y., Zeldovich, N.: Vault: fast bootstrapping for cryptocurrencies. Cryptology ePrint Archive, Report 2018/269 (2018). https://eprint.iacr.org/2018/269
13. Garay, J.A., Kiayias, A., Leonardos, N.: The Bitcoin backbone protocol: analysis and applications. In: Oswald, E., Fischlin, M. (eds.) EUROCRYPT 2015. LNCS, vol. 9057, pp. 281–310. Springer, Heidelberg (2015). https://doi.org/10.1007/978-3-662-46803-6_10
14. Kappos, G., Yousaf, H., Maller, M., Meiklejohn, S.: An empirical analysis of anonymity in Zcash. In: 27th USENIX Security Symposium (USENIX Security 2018), Baltimore, MD, pp. 463–477. USENIX Association (2018)
15. Meiklejohn, S., Pomarole, M., Jordan, G., Levchenko, K., McCoy, D., Voelker, G.M., Savage, S.: A fistful of Bitcoins: characterizing payments among men with no names. In: Proceedings of the 2013 Conference on Internet Measurement Conference, pp. 127–140. ACM (2013)
16. Möser, M., Böhme, R.: Join me on a market for anonymity. In: Proceedings of the Workshop on the Economics of Information Security (WEIS). University of California at Berkeley (2016)
17. Gaži, P., Kiayias, A., Zindros, D.: Proof-of-stake sidechains. In: 2019 IEEE Symposium on Security and Privacy (SP), Los Alamitos, USA, pp. 677–694. IEEE Computer Society (2019)

Coded Merkle Tree: Solving Data Availability Attacks in Blockchains

Mingchao Yu[1(✉)], Saeid Sahraei[1], Songze Li[2], Salman Avestimehr[1],
Sreeram Kannan[2,3], and Pramod Viswanath[2,4]

[1] University of Southern California, Los Angeles, USA
fishermanymc@gmail.com, ss_805@usc.edu, avestimehr@ee.usc.edu
[2] Trifecta Blockchain, Palo Alto, USA
songzeli8824@gmail.com
[3] University of Washington Seattle, Seattle, USA
ksreeram@uw.edu
[4] University of Illinois at Urbana-Champaign, Champaign, USA
pramodv@illinois.edu

Abstract. In this paper, we propose coded Merkle tree (CMT), a novel
hash accumulator that offers a constant-cost protection against data
availability attacks in blockchains, even if the majority of the network
nodes are malicious. A CMT is constructed using a family of sparse
erasure codes on each layer, and is recovered by iteratively applying a
peeling-decoding technique that enables a compact proof for data availability attack on any layer. Our algorithm enables any node to verify
the full availability of any data block generated by the system by just
downloading a $\Theta(1)$ byte block hash commitment and randomly sampling $\Theta(\log b)$ bytes, where b is the size of the data block. With the help
of only one connected honest node in the system, our method also allows
any node to verify any tampering of the coded Merkle tree by just downloading $\Theta(\log b)$ bytes. We provide a modular library for CMT in Rust
and Python and demonstrate its efficacy inside the Parity Bitcoin client.

1 Introduction

Blockchains (e.g., Bitcoin [26] and Ethereum [35]) maintain a ledger of ordered
transactions, organized into a chain of blocks. Starting from the genesis block,
network nodes extend the ledger by creating and appending more blocks, following specific block generation rules (e.g., the longest-chain rule is used in Bitcoin
[26]). The transactions in the received blocks are validated by *full nodes* which
download the entire block tree. However, for better scalability, it is imperative
for a blockchain to allow *light nodes*, which may only be interested in verifying
some specific transactions.

In Bitcoin [1,26], light nodes are implemented using the Simple Payment
Verification (SPV) technique: a Merkle tree is constructed for each block using
the transactions as the leaf nodes, and the Merkle root is stored in the block
header. Utilizing the Merkle root, a light node can verify the inclusion of any

© International Financial Cryptography Association 2020
J. Bonneau and N. Heninger (Eds.): FC 2020, LNCS 12059, pp. 114–134, 2020.
https://doi.org/10.1007/978-3-030-51280-4_8

transaction in a block through a Merkle proof. Light nodes and SPV have been leveraged extensively to scale computation and storage of blockchain systems over resource-limited nodes (e.g., smartphones) [3–5,7,16,18,19,25,36].

Besides inclusion, what is more important for a light node is to validate the transaction based on the ledger state. Due to limited resources, a light node cannot download the entire ledger. Instead, it could use the depth of the block that contains this transaction as a proxy. That is, the deeper this block is buried into the chain, the more confident the light node is about the validity of the transaction. However, for it to work, a majority (in terms of hashing power, stakes, etc.) of full nodes must be honest and must follow protocol. Further, there is a significant *tradeoff* between confirmation latency (due to the depth) and the security about transaction validity.

Therefore, efforts to study 1) the scenario of a light node being connected to *dishonest majority of full nodes*, and 2) how to achieve faster confirmation at light nodes are becoming a major research direction [9,10,17,26]. The overall idea is to design new block structures that allow full nodes to generate and broadcast *succinct fraud proofs* of individual transactions. This way, a light node will be able to timely verify fraud transactions and blocks as long as it is connect to *at least one* honest full node. One efficient construction that utilizes the roots of the intermediate state Merkle trees after executing a subset of transactions is proposed in [9]. However, it is vulnerable to the so-called "data availability attack" described in [9], for which [9] proposed an erasure code based solution. Stating the data availability attack formally and solving it comprehensively is the main goal of this paper.

Data Availability Attack. A malicious block producer 1) publishes a block header, so that light nodes can check transaction inclusion; but 2) withholds a portion of the block (e.g., invalid transactions), so that it is impossible for honest full nodes to validate the block and generate the fraud proof.

Although the honest full nodes are aware of the data unavailability, there is no good way to prove it. The best they can do is to raise an alarm without a proof. However, this is problematic because the malicious block producer can release the hidden parts *after* hearing the alarm. Due to network latency, other nodes may receive the missing part before receiving the alarm and, thus, cannot distinguish who is prevaricating. Due to this, there is no reward and punishment mechanism that can properly reward honest full nodes while also deterring false alarms and denial-of-service attacks.

Therefore, for fraud proofs to work, light nodes must determine data availability by themselves. This leads to the following key question: *when a light node receives the header of some block, how can it verify that the content of that block is available to the network by downloading the least possible portion of the block?*

Need to Encode the Block. Since a transaction is much smaller than a block, a malicious block producer only needs to hide a very small portion of a block. Such hiding can hardly be detected by light nodes unless the entire block is down-loaded. However, by adding redundancy to the data through appropriate erasure codes [22], any small hiding on the origin block will be equivalent to making a significant portion of the coded block unavailable, which can be detected by light nodes through randomly sampling the coded block with exponentially increasing probability. As a counter measure, a malicious block producer could instead conduct coding incorrectly to prevent correct decoding. Light nodes rely on honest full nodes to detect such attacks and prove it through an incorrect-coding proof.

For example, an (n, k) Reed-Solomon (1D-RS) code [32] encodes k data symbols into n coded symbols, and any k out of these n coded symbols can be used to decode the k data symbols. Thus, to prevent decoding, a malicious block producer will have to make at least $n-k+1$ coded symbols unavailable, which yields a detection probability of $1 - (1 - k/n)^s$ after sampling s distinct coded symbols uniformly at random. But an incorrect-coding proof will consist of k coded symbols, which is of the same size as the original block and thus is too large. This cost is alleviated to $\sqrt{k}$ in [9] by using two-dimensional RS codes (2D-RS), at the costs of reduced sampling efficiency, and increased block hash commitments of $2\sqrt{n}$ Merkle roots to verify the coding correctness within each dimension. In addition, 1D-RS and 2D-RS codes have a high decoding complexity of $O(k^2)$ and $O(k^{1.5})$, respectively.

In summary, with erasure coding, a light node pays 3 download costs for data availability, including block hash commitments, symbol sampling, and incorrect-coding proofs. Among them, the incorrect-coding proof cost must be minimized to defend fake proofs, for which both 1D-RS and 2D-RS are sub-optimal.

Our Contributions. In this paper, we propose SPAR (SParse frAud pRotection), the first data availability solution that promises order-optimal performance on *all* the metrics, including 1) a constant block hash commitment size; 2) a constant sampling cost for a given confidence level on data availability; 3) a constant incorrectly-coding proof size; and 4) linear decoding complexity (Table 1).

Table 1. Light node download costs and full node decoding complexity (b: block size in bytes).

	Hash commitment size (bytes)	# of samples to gain certain confidence about data availability	Incorrect-coding proof size (bytes)	Decoding complexity
Uncoded	$O(1)$	$O(b)$	-	-
1D-RS	$O(1)$	$O(1)$	$O(b \log b)$	$O(b^2)$
2D-RS [9]	$O(\sqrt{b})$	$O(1)$	$O(\sqrt{b} \log k)$	$O(b^{1.5})$
SPAR	$O(1)$	$O(1)$	$O(\log b)$	$O(b)$

At the core of SPAR is a novel cryptographic hash accumulator called coded Merkle tree (CMT). Starting from the bottom, CMT iteratively encodes layers of the tree and uses the hashes of the coded layer as the data for the next layer. A light node can detect the availability of the *entire tree* through the Merkle proofs of bottom layer leaves. With the entire tree available, SPAR uses a novel hash-aware peeling decoder and a special ensemble of random LDPC (low-density

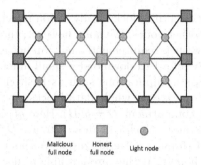

Fig. 1. The connections between full nodes and light nodes. Every honest (green) node is connected to at least one honest full (square) node. A light (circle) node may connect to more malicious (red) full nodes than honest full nodes. (Color figure online)

parity-check) codes to maximize sampling efficiency, minimize incorrect-coding proof to one parity equation, and achieves linear decoding complexity.

SPAR and CMT Implementation. We have developed a complete and modular CMT library in Rust and Python [2]. We have also implemented SPAR in the `Bitcoin Parity` client [28], which outperforms state of the art [9] by more than 10-fold in hash commitments, incorrect coding proof, and decoding speed.

Related Works. This work was inspired by pioneering research in [9], which proposes succinct fraud proofs and 2D-RS based data availability solution. Besides this work, coding also improves scalability of blockchains in other areas: [29] studies the coding efficiency of distributed storage systems [8,14,15,31]. In a related vein, [30] uses a combination of Shamir's secret sharing [33] (for storing the headers and the encryption keys) and private distributed storage (for the blocks) to reduce the storage overhead while guaranteeing data integrity and confidentiality. [21] uses Lagrange coding to simultaneously scale storage, computation, and security in a sharded blockchain [20,24], via cross-shard coding.

2   Security Model

The core functionality of a blockchain is to produce, verify, and accept/store valid data blocks in a consistent but decentralized manner. A data block, denoted by B, is a byte string of length b that carries a batch of transactions. B is valid for acceptance if and only if *every* single transaction in it is valid (e.g., enough balance, no double spending). Thus *incomplete* data blocks are tantamount to being unacceptable. Data incompleteness is not a threat to a node that fully downloads the block. However, state-of-the-art blockchain systems also run light nodes which do not download the blocks in entirety. We next describe these two types of nodes formally (see Fig. 1).

Full nodes are able to produce blocks (e.g., by batching submitted transactions), and to download and verify blocks produced by other full nodes. Upon acceptance, they store the entire block locally. Upon rejection, they broadcast a fraud proof to alert the other nodes. We note, however, that malicious full nodes do not necessarily follow such requirements, and can act arbitrarily.

Light nodes can only afford to download a small amount of data from each block and perform simple computations such as hash checks and fraud proof verification, but not to operate on whole data blocks. By accepting a block B, they only store its hash commitment $D = g(B)$. Here $g()$ is a hash accumulator such as Merkle tree generator, which will allow it to use D to verify the inclusion of any transaction in B through a Merkle proof. Without loss of generality, we assume light nodes are honest, as they are not able to deceive full nodes.

We assume the following network model:

1. Reliable communication: Two directly connected nodes can reliably communicate via both unicast and broadcast without message loss or corruption.
2. Connectivity: Every honest (full and light) node is directly connected to at least one honest full node. In other words, we assume a connected sub-graph of honest full nodes, and all the light nodes are connected to it.
3. The network is synchronous. These three assumptions together means that a valid message sent by an honest node can be received by all appropriate honest nodes (e.g. blocks for honest full nodes, block headers and fraud proofs for light node) within a fixed delay if every honest node re-broadcasts it.
4. The network allows nodes to send messages anonymously.

Importantly, our network model allows *dishonest majority*, i.e., each light node can be directly connected to more malicious full nodes than honest ones. Due to this, a light node cannot determine the completeness of a block through its connected full nodes, via a majority vote for instance.

A malicious block producer is thus motivated to conduct a *data availability attack*, where it 1) does not fully disclose B, so that honest full nodes are not able to verify B; and 2) broadcasts D, so that itself and its colluding full nodes can forward D to their connected light nodes and deceive them that the B that satisfies $g(B) = D$ is valid for accepting. Thus, the key for a light node to protect itself from accepting a fraudulent block is to make sure that B is fully available. This gives rise to the main problem we try to address in this paper:

Data availability problem: *Upon receiving a hash commitment D, how can a light node efficiently verify that a data block B that satisfies $g(B) = D$ is fully available to the system?*

A simple strategy for a light node is to randomly sample portions of B, and determine that it is unavailable if it does not receive all requested portions. Since the size of a transaction is usually much smaller than the block, a malicious block producer only needs to hide a very small portion (say, e.g., a few hundred bytes) of a fraudulent block, which can hardly be detected through random sampling.

A malicious block producer could also conduct *selective disclosure*: when requested by light nodes, the malicious block producer may select a subset of the light nodes and fully disclose their requested portions, as long as the total disclosed portions do not reveal B. These light nodes will be deceived about the availability of B and will accept it, as no fraud proof of B can be produced.

Thus, as similarly done in [9], we characterize the security of the above described system using the following measures:

Soundness: If a light node has determined that a data block is fully available, then at least one honest full node will be able to fully recover this data block within a constant delay.

Agreement: If a light node has determined that a data block is fully available, then all the other light nodes in the system will determine that the data block is fully available within a constant delay.

Recently, an erasure coding-assisted approach was proposed in [9] to improve sampling efficiency and suppress the data availability attack. In the next section, we will motivate this approach and overview the challenges it faces.

3 Overview of Erasure Coding Assisted Approach

An (n, k) erasure code evenly partitions a block B of b bytes into k data symbols of $\frac{b}{k}$ bytes each as $B = [m_1, \cdots, m_k]$, and linearly combines them to generate a coded block with $n > k$ coded symbols, $C = [c_1, \cdots, c_n]$. The ratio $r = k/n$ is called the coding rate. The n hashes of these coded symbols are accumulated to obtain the hash commitment D of C, which is published with C. With a good erasure code, a block producer's hiding of one data symbol is equivalent to making the value of many coded symbols unavailable to the system. In general, a pair of good erasure code and decoding algorithm yields a large **undecodable ratio** α, which is the minimum fraction of coded symbols a malicious block producer needs to make unavailable to prevent full decoding. Such hiding can be caught by a light node with an exponentially increasing probability of $1 - (1-\alpha)^s$ through randomly sample s coded symbols when n is large, indicating that $O(1)$ samples are sufficient. Below is an example.

Example 1. **Uncoded v.s. coded sampling efficiency.** *Given a block of 4 data symbols $[m_0, \cdots, m_3]$, a block producer generates 8 coded symbols as follows:*

$$\begin{cases} c_0 = m_0, \ c_1 = m_1, \ c_2 = m_2, \ c_3 = m_3, \\ c_4 = c_0 + c_1, \ c_5 = c_1 + c_2, \ c_6 = c_2 + c_3, \ c_7 = c_3 + c_0. \end{cases} \tag{1}$$

To prevent decoding through hiding, a malicious block producer must either publish no more than 3 data symbols or no more than 5 coded symbols. Both will make at least 3 coded symbols unavailable to the system ($\alpha = \frac{3}{8}$). Such unavailability can be caught with a probability of $1 - \frac{5}{8} \cdot \frac{4}{7} = 64.3\%$ after randomly sampling 2 distinct coded symbols. In contrast, without coding, the hiding of one data symbol can be caught with a probability of only $1 - \frac{3}{4} \cdot \frac{2}{3} = 50\%$.

To counter erasure coding assisted random sampling, a malicious block producer could conduct an ***incorrect-coding attack***: It generates coded symbols that fail the parity equations (the equations describing the linear relations between coded symbols in Example 1) specified by the erasure code, and generates D using these invalid coded symbols. This way, it can pass light node random sampling through hiding only one data symbol and publishing most of the coded symbols, which will not allow honest full nodes to correctly decode B.

Fortunately, this attack can be detected by honest full nodes by comparing the decoded block with the commitment D. Upon detection, an honest full node can generate an ***incorrect-coding proof***, which consists of the coded symbols of failed parity equation(s) and appropriate hash commitments, so that light nodes can verify them and reject the block. Using Example 1, an incorrect coding proof about $c_4 = c_0 + c_1$ could be c_0 and c_1 with matching Merkle proofs, plus the Merkle proof of c_4, which, however, does not match the value of $c_0 + c_1$.

To keep incorrect coding proofs small, [9] applies 2D-RS (2-dimensional Reed-Solomon) code. The k data symbols are placed as a $\sqrt{k} \times \sqrt{k}$ square, then a $(\sqrt{n}, \sqrt{k})$ RS code is applied to every row/column. The resulted $2\sqrt{n}$ rows/columns yield $2\sqrt{n}$ Merkle roots, which are downloaded by light nodes as block header. Each root allows a light node to verify the associated row/column by decoding it using any $\sqrt{k}$ coded symbols of it (from incorrect-coding proof) and reproducing the root. Thus, 2D-RS offers light nodes 1) a header cost of $O(\sqrt{b})$, 2) a sampling cost of $O(\log b)$, and 3) an incorrect-coding proof size of $O(\sqrt{b} \log b)$. Here $\log b$ is due to logarithmic growth of Merkle proof size with b.

In this paper, we propose SPAR (SParse frAud pRotection), the first solution to the data-availability problem that is order-optimal in all the above three metrics: a header cost of $O(1)$, a sampling cost of $O(\log b)$, and an incorrect-coding proof size of $O(\log b)$. To this end, SPAR leverages four core components:

1. a novel hash accumulator named coded Merkle tree (CMT), which encodes every layer of the tree to protect the availability of the entire tree. This way, the Merkle proof of every coded symbol will be available, which will enable every parity equation to be committed and verified *alone*;
2. a dedicated sampling mechanism that enables a light node to check the availability of the entire CMT by sampling $O(\log b)$ bytes plus one Merkle root;
3. a hash-aware decoding algorithm that is able to detect and prove any single failed parity equation, provided the Merkle proofs of all the coded symbols;
4. a special ensemble of random LDPC (low-density parity check) codes with a constant parity equation size and a constant undecodable ratio under the above hash-aware decoding algorithm, which protects all CMT layers equally.

4   Detailed Description of SPAR

In this section, we describe the four core components of SPAR: the construction of the coded Merkle tree by the (honest) block producer, the sampling mechanism of the light nodes, the decoding and alerting operations of the honest full nodes, and the erasure codes used by SPAR. At the end of this section, we will summarize the action space of each node in the network.

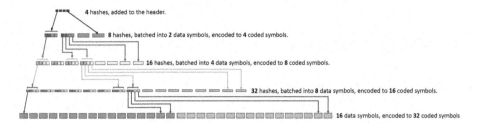

Fig. 2. Coded Merkle tree for $k = 16$ data symbols using rate $r = \frac{1}{2}$ erasure codes. Each data symbol of a higher layer is constructed by batching the hashes of $qr = 2$ data symbols and $q(1-r) = 2$ parity symbols of its child layer.

4.1   Construction of Coded Merkle Tree

In SPAR, an honest full node detects and proves incorrect-coding using the membership proofs of *all* the d coded symbols in one parity equation and the values of at least $d - 1$ of these coded symbols. Since any parity equation can be compromised, a light node needs to make sure the membership proofs of *all* the n coded symbols are available at honest full nodes. In other words, it needs to make sure the entire Merkle tree is available.

To this end, we propose CMT. At a high level, CMT applies erasure coding to every layer of the tree, where the data symbols of a layer are generated using the hashes of the coded symbols of its child layer. This way, a light node can check the availability of every layer through random samplings, whilst an honest full node can detect and prove the incorrect coding at any layer, with the help of the hashes of this layer provided at its parent layer.

More specifically, given a block of k data symbols, a rate-r ($r \leq 1$) erasure code with an undecodable ratio of α is applied to generate $n = k/r$ coded symbols, where the first k are the original data symbols and the remaining $n - k$ are called parity symbols (hence the name systematic). Then the hashes of every q coded symbols are batched as one data symbol for the next (parent) layer. This yields a total of n/q data symbols for the next layer, which will be encoded using a smaller (in terms of k) rate-r systematic code with the same undecodable ratio. This iterative encoding and batching process stops once there are only t ($t \geqslant 1$) hashes in a layer. These t hashes are the root of the CMT, and will be included in the block header and published with the original data block.

CMT layer size reduces at a rate of qr. Thus, $qr > 1$ for CMT to converge. In addition, to enable efficient sampling of both data and parity symbols (will discuss next), batching is interleaved, namely, the q coded symbols whose hashes are batched together consist of qr data symbols and $q(1-r)$ parity symbols. An example of CMT with $k = 16$, $r = \frac{1}{2}$, $q = 4$, and $t = 4$ is illustrated in Fig. 2. Indeed, a classic Merkle tree is a special CMT with $r = 1$ and $q = 2$.

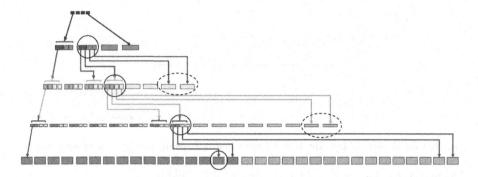

Fig. 3. Merkle proof in CMT, and probabilistic sampling of parity symbols in intermediate layers. The solidly circled symbols constitute a base layer coded symbol and its Merkle proof. For the 2 dash-circled yellow parity symbols, with a probability of $1 - r = 0.5$, one of them (with equal chance) will be included in the proof for sampling purpose. So will the 2 dash-circled blue parity symbols. (Color figure online)

4.2   Sampling Mechanism of Light Nodes

In SPAR, a light node randomly samples the base layer coded symbols with their Merkle proofs to decide the availability of the base layer. The special structure of CMT allows them to further utilize these proofs to efficiently sample higher layer symbols to decide the availability of higher layers.

Similar to a classic Merkle tree, the Merkle proof of a base layer symbol in CMT consists of all the sibling hashes between this symbol and the root. The only difference is that the number of sibling hashes per layer is now $q - 1$ instead of 1, which effectively provides the light node one data symbol from every intermediate layer. Thus, when a light node randomly samples s distinct base layer coded symbols, the associated Merkle proofs will automatically sample, at *no* extra cost, s distinct data symbols from every intermediate layer w.h.p.

To properly check the availability of an intermediate layer, a light node should also randomly sample about $(1 - r)s$ parity symbols from this layer. To avoid downloading extra Merkle proofs for these parity symbols and to minimize the correlation between the samplings[1], SPAR samples parity symbols of intermediate layers probabilistically: For every pair of parent and child intermediate layer, if a parent layer data symbol is sampled, then with probability $1 - r$, one of its $q(1 - r)$ child parity symbols (thanks to interleaved batching) will be sampled uniformly at random. Thus, the response size of one sampling request will be:

$$\frac{b}{k} + [y(q - 1) + yq(1 - r)] \log_{qr} \frac{k}{rt}, \tag{2}$$

where $\frac{b}{k}$ is the base layer symbol size, y is the hash size (e.g., 32 bytes), $y(q-1)$ is the size of the partial data symbol from an intermediate layer for Merkle proof,

---

[1] Otherwise, the malicious block producer can hide the highly correlated symbols of the same layer together to reduce light nodes' detection probability.

$yq(1 - r)$ is the average size of probabilistically sampled parity symbol from an intermediate layer, and $\log_{qr} \frac{k}{rt}$ is the number of layers. See Fig. 3 for sampling response of a coded symbol on the based layer of the CMT in Fig. 2.

Finally, to counter selective disclosure conducted by the malicious block producer, a light node will make the s requests separately, anonymously, with replacement, and with some delay between every two requests. This will prevent the malicious block producer from selectively deceiving any particular light node, or deceiving the set of light nodes that make requests at the beginning. Therefore, every light node will have the same chance to catch data availability attack.

4.3   Hash-Aware Peeling Decoder and Incorrect-Coding Proof

A hash-aware peeling decoder is similar to conventional LDPC peeling decoder. Given the hashes of all the n coded symbols and $(1 - \alpha)n$ coded symbols of a layer, it iteratively solves degree-1 parity equations and check each decoded symbol against its hash and associated parity equations (Algorithm 1). This way, the detection and proof of incorrect-coding is minimized to one parity equation.

The key condition for the peeling decoder to work is that the hashes of all the coded symbols are available. This is assured by CMT: By first downloading the root, the decoder will have all the hashes needed to decode the previous layer. Once this layer is successfully decoded, the decoded data symbols will provide all the hashes needed to decode its child layer. This top-down decoding continues until the data block is decoded, or incorrect-coding is detected at one of the layers. To prove a failed parity equation that consists of d coded symbols, the decoder only needs to provide the Merkle proofs of these coded symbols, and the value of $d - 1$ coded symbols. Note that the higher the failed layer, the shorter the Merkle proof of each symbol in the incorrect-coding proof.

In addition, the peeling decoder only works if 1) there are $(1 - \alpha)n$ coded symbols available, and 2) that these coded symbols allow the recovery of all the k data symbols. While the first condition is checked by light nodes through random sampling, the second condition requires us to find, for every layer, a erasure code whose undecodable ratio is α under peeling decoding. The best performance is achieved if the codes are extremely sparse (with a small d) and have a large α. We now present such an ensemble of LDPC codes.

4.4   Construction of Erasure Code

An (n, k) erasure code can be described by an $n \times (n - k)$ parity check matrix H, where each column of H describes a parity equation, such that $CH = \overrightarrow{0}$ for any valid codeword C. In addition, every *stopping set* of H corresponds to a set of coded symbols whose hiding will prevent the full recovery of data symbols using peeling decoder. For an $n \times (n - k)$ parity check matrix H, a set of rows $\tau \subset [n]$ is called a *stopping set* if no column in H_τ has one non-zero element. Here H_τ is the submatrix of H that only consists of the rows in τ.

Algorithm 1: Hash-aware peeling decoding algorithm

---

1 **Inputs:** the hashes of all n coded symbols and $(1 - \alpha)n$ coded symbols;
2 **Initial check:** checks all the degree-0 parity equations (i.e., those whose coded symbols are all known). If any parity equation is failed, report an incorrect-coding proof and exit;
3 **while** *not all the k data symbols are recovered* **do**
4   Find a degree-1 parity equation, which only has one unknown coded symbol;
5   Recover this coded symbol and verify it with its hash. If failed, report an incorrect-coding proof and exit;
6   Check all the associated degree-0 parity equations. If any parity equation is failed, report an incorrect-coding proof and exit.
7 **end**

Correspondingly, there is no parity equation that includes exactly one coded symbol among those indexed by τ. Thus, if this set of coded symbols are hidden, there is no degree-1 parity equation to recover them. Since the peeling decoder is essential for us to construct small incorrect-coding proof, the undecodable ratio α of a block is equivalent to the *stopping ratio* of $\boldsymbol{H}$, which is the size of the smallest stopping set divided by n.

While CMT admits any erasure codes, SPAR uses the method introduced in [12,23] and analyzed in [27] for its proved ability to create, with high probability, parity matrices with a large stopping ratio. Given two integers c and d that satisfies $nc = (n - k)d$, we first generate an $nc \times (n - k)d$ permutation matrix $\boldsymbol{J}$ (a random row permutation of an $nc \times (n - k)d$ identity matrix). We then partition $\boldsymbol{J}$ into $n \times (n - k)$ slices, where each slice is a $c \times d$ sub-matrix. Then $\boldsymbol{H}_{i,j} = 1$ if and only if slice-(i,j) contains an odd number of 1s, for $i \in [1 : n]$ and $j \in [1 : n - k]$. Such a random $\boldsymbol{H}$ has the following three critical properties:

1. It has a maximum row weight of c, and a maximum column weight of d;
2. It has a non-zero probability to have a stopping ratio of at least α^*, where α^* is a critical stopping ratio inherent to this method and is independent of k;
3. It is NP-hard to find the minimum stopping set and determine the stopping ratio of $\boldsymbol{H}$.

Property 1 implies that the corresponding LDPC code has a maximum parity equation size of d. Property 2 implies that we could provide the same undecodable ratio (thus same sampling requirements) for all layers. Both are desirable.

Nevertheless, Property 2 and 3 together imply that we, as the developers, are not able to determine whether the LDPC codes we generate are good ($\alpha \geqslant \alpha^*$) or not, for any reasonably large k (e.g., $k = 1024$).

Fortunately, this problem can be easily solved through a **bad-code proof**. If an honest full node cannot fully decode the k data symbols after receiving $(1 - \alpha^*)n$ coded symbols, then this code is bad, and its small undecodable set has been found and hidden by a (very strong) malicious block producer. In this case, the honest full node can prove this code bad by broadcasting the indices of the α^*n coded symbols it is missing. Upon receiving and verify this bad-code proof, all the nodes in the system reject the associated block, and regenerate a code for the failed layer using an agreed random seed. This seed can be drawn from a pre-defined number sequence or the block header of a previous block, so that no consensus protocol is needed. Alternatively, distributed random number generation algorithms such as [34] and [11] can also be used for strictly unbiased randomness and consensus.

In other words, we solve the NP-hard problem of finding good codes by exploiting the computational resources of malicious party. Once it finds a small undecodable set and hides it, the system can easily detect this, reject the block, and update the code. This way, the system will settle at a good code for every layer eventually. As we will show in the next section, the probability of generating good codes is extremely high, so that SPAR can settle at good codes very quickly without having light nodes accept any fraud blocks. In addition, since bad code is a rare event, a heavy incentive/punishment scheme can be applied to deter false bad-code proof. Thus, the download and verification cost of bad-code proof is amortized to negligible throughout the course of the system.

4.5 Summary of the Actions of Different Node Types

- **Block producer (full node):** (a) It generates CMT and broadcasts the CMT root to all nodes, as well as broadcasts the entire original block (not CMT, as it can be retrieved using the original) to the full nodes only. (b) On receiving sample requests from the light nodes, respond to them.
- **Light node:** (a) On receiving a new CMT root (or a CMT root of a pending block from a new full node), it makes separate, anonymous, and intermittent sampling requests with replacement to full nodes who claim that the block is available, as described in Sect. 4.2. (b) On receiving a sample, it broadcasts it to all connected full nodes. (c) If a node receives all requested samples, it assumes the block is available. (d) If a node does not receive all requested samples within a fixed time, it "pends" the block (i.e., keeps it in pending status). (e) If a node receives an incorrect-coding proof or bad-code proof, it rejects the block. In case of bad-code proof, it will also update the erasure code of the failed layer.
- **Other full node.** (a) On receiving valid samples, it tries to recover the data block through both downloading the original data block from the other full nodes and collecting coded symbols forwarded by the light nodes. It will decode the tree from top to bottom using a hash-aware peeling decoder. (b) It rebroadcasts the received valid samples. (c) If an incorrect coding or a bad code has been detected, it will send the corresponding proof and reject this block. (d) If it has received/fully decoded a data block and verified it, it will declare the availability of this block to all other nodes and respond to sample requests from light nodes.

5   Performance Analysis

5.1   Security

Theorem 1. *In SPAR, a block producer cannot cause the soundness and agreement to fail with a probability lower than*

$$P_f \leq \max \left\{ (1 - \alpha_{\min})^s, \quad 2^{\max_i \left[H(\alpha_i) n_i - ms \log \frac{1}{1-\alpha_i} \right]} \right\}.$$

Here n_i and α_i are the number of symbols and undecodable ratio of layer-i of CMT, $\alpha_{\min} \triangleq \min_i \alpha_i$, and s is the number of base layer coded symbols a light node samples.

Theorem 1, proved in Appendix A, implies that the security of SPAR increases exponentially with the number of samples each light node takes (s), when the number of light nodes (m) is linear with the block size.

5.2   Costs and Complexity

A light node has three download costs: 1) the header, which is the CMT root of size t; 2) the random sampling, and 3) the incorrect-coding proof. In CMT, the header is the CMT root of size t. The sampling cost can be computed using the average parity-symbol-sampled Merkle proof size given in (2) to be:

$$s \left(\frac{b}{k} + y \left(2q - 1 - qr \right) \log_{qr} \frac{k}{rt} \right) = O(\log k) = O(\log b), \qquad (3)$$

where b is the size of a block, and the equations hold due to that 1) s is a constant; and 2) b/k is the base layer symbol size, which is a constant. The incorrect-coding proof size can be similarly computed as

$$\frac{(d-1)b}{k} + dy(q-1) \log_{qr} \frac{k}{rt} = O(\log b), \qquad (4)$$

where the first term is the size of $d-1$ coded symbols, and the second term is the size of d Merkle proofs. Finally, since the hash-aware peeling decoder decodes one coded symbol using $d-1$ coded symbols in one parity equation, the decoding complexity is $O(1)$ per symbol and, thus, is $O(b)$ in total.

5.3   Choice of Parameters

Our first key parameter is the coding rate r. A smaller r means more parity symbols and thus a potentially larger undecodable ratio and less sampling. But it will also increase the height of CMT, the Merkle proof size, and the decoding complexity. For a reasonable tradeoff, we choose $r = 0.25$.

Given r, the next two parameters we should decide are a pair (c, d) that satisfies $c/d = 1 - r = 0.75$ for the random LDPC code generator, where d is

Table 2. The critical undecodable ratio α^* as a function of d

d	4	8	12	16	20
α^*	0.0795	0.124	0.111	0.0981	0.0877

the maximum parity equation size. This gives us $c = 0.75d$ and requires us to find the critical undecodable ratio of the ensemble as a function of d, which is provided in Table 2 based on the analysis in [27].

Evidently, $d = 8$ maximizes the critical undecodable ratio. In addition, it also admits a small incorrect coding proof that only requires only 7 coded symbols and 8 Merkle proofs. As a result, we choose $(c, d) = (6, 8)$.

5.4 How Quickly Does SPAR Settle at a Good Erasure Code?

Due to random code generation, each layer of SPAR eventually settles at a good code (with an undecodable ratio of at least α^*) after a few bad codes have been deployed by the system and potentially utilized by malicious block producer to hide the data. We study the number of such attacks (note that they will never succeed) and updates before SPAR can settle: intuitively, this number can be computed as $(1 - P(\alpha < \alpha^*))^{-1} - 1$, where $P(\alpha < \alpha^*)$ is the probability that a randomly generated code has an undecodable ratio smaller than $\alpha^* = 0.124$. Using an upper bound on $P(\alpha < \alpha^*)$ characterized in [27] we can derive the settlement speed of SPAR as below. We note that most of the layers of CMT will immediately settle at a good code upon launching. The only exception is the layer with $n = 256$, which will settle after 7.7 bad codes, but without any fraudulent blocks been accepted. The proof is in Appendix B.

Theorem 2. *Using the random $(6, 8)$-LDPC code in Sect. 4.4, the expected number of bad erasure codes ($\alpha < \alpha^* = 0.124$) a CMT layer with n coded symbols will use before it settles at a good code ($\alpha \geq 0.124$) is approximated in Table 3.*

Table 3. Number of bad code before settlement.

n	256	512	1024	2048	4096	> 4096
$P(\alpha < \alpha^*)$	0.886	5.3e-2	2.0e-3	1.3e-3	3.2e-4	<3.2e-4
# bad codes	7.7	0.06	0.002	0.001	0.0003	< 0.0003

6 Implementation for Bitcoin and Experiments

We developed in Rust a Coded Merkle Tree library [2] for Parity Bitcoin [28] clients (see Appendix C for more details). Our library integrates seamlessly into the current mainnet implementation, and requires minimal change on the block data structure (only need to add CMT root to the block header). Note, however, that this change is incompatible with existing Bitcoin clients. Developing a SPAR-protected Bitcoin testnet and a Bitcoin Improvements proposal (for Bitcoin Core) are ongoing research activities outside the scope of this paper.

We combine the CMT library with the performance analysis in Sect. 5, and numerically evaluate SPAR's light node download costs (header, sampling, and incorrect-coding proof) and full node decoding speed, for a wide range of block sizes (Table 4), and compare them with the 2D-RS based solution proposed in [9] using its C++/Python implementation [6,13].

Table 4. Experiment Parameter Configuration

Parameter	Value	Notes
Symbol size (B)	256	
Base layer k	2^{12} to 2^{22}	Block size is thus 1 to 1024 MB
Coding rate r	0.25	Thus $n = 4k$
Hash size (B)	32	SHA256 is used
Target confidence	99%	Each light node keeps sampling until it is 99% confident
SPAR specific parameters		
LDPC sparsity	(6, 8)	Each parity equation has at most 8 coded symbols
Stopping ratio β	0.124	$0.124n$ symbols must be hidden to prevent decoding
Batching factor q	8	CMT layer size reduction rate is $qr = 2$ as ordinary trees
CMT root size t	256 hashes	The same as 2D-RS header size for 1MB blocks

Header (Fig. 4(a)): A SPAR light node only downloads fixed $t = 256$ hashes in header, whilst 2D-RS requires $1 + 2\sqrt{n}$. Thus, the header download cost of SPAR becomes much smaller than 2D-RS with growing block size. For a 64MB block, the cost is only 0.01% of the block size in SPAR, but is 0.1% in 2D-RS.

Incorrect-Coding Proof (Fig. 4(b)): A SPAR incorrect-coding proof only involves $d - 1 = 7$ coded symbols and their Merkle proofs, whilst 2D-RS requires $\sqrt{k}$. Thus, the incorrect-coding proof download cost of SPAR becomes much smaller than 2D-RS with growing block size. For a 64MB block, the cost is only 0.051% of the block size in SPAR, but is 0.48% in 2D-RS.

Sampling Cost (Fig. 4(c)): 2D-RS has a higher undecodable ratio of 25% compared to SPAR's 12.4%. Thus, for 99% confidence, $s = 17$ distinctive samples are enough in 2D-RS, whilst SPAR requires $s = 35$ if the adversary is strong enough to find, with NP-hardness, the size-$0.124n$ stopping set. But under a realistically weak adversary that randomly selects CMT symbols to hide, SPAR only requires $s = 8$ because our LDPC ensemble can tolerate an average of 47% missing symbols. On the other hand, the over-sampling of each layer increases SPAR's sampling cost. Thus, although both techniques offer $O(\log k)$ sampling costs that quickly reduces with growing block size, the cost of SPAR is about 10~16 (resp. 2.5~4) times of 2D-RS under strong (resp. weak) adversaries. However, in practice, one can further reduce SPAR sampling cost by increasing the header size t, thus reducing the size of the Merkle proof of each symbol.

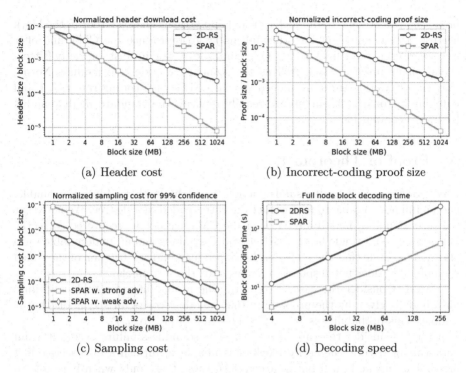

Fig. 4. Communication costs and decoding speed of SPAR and 2D-RS.

Decoding Speed (Fig. 4(d))**:** SPAR's sparse and binary encoding, at its current implementation level is already over 10 times faster than 2D-RS for all the tested block sizes.

7   Conclusion and Discussions

By iteratively applying a special ensemble of LDPC codes to every layer of a Merkle tree and batching the hashes of each coded layer into the data symbols of the next layer, we invented a novel hash accumulator called coded Merkle tree (CMT). Built upon CMT, we proposed a novel data availability verification system called SPAR, which allows the availability and integrity of the entire tree to be checked at constant costs.

SPAR can play a key role in scaling blockchain systems that incorporate light nodes because it empowers these nodes with real-time verification of data availability and integrity at small and constant costs. SPAR can also be used to scale the communication of sharded blockchain systems (e.g., [20, 21, 24]), where full nodes of one shard operate as light nodes of other shards, as SPAR allows them to efficiently check the availability and integrity of blocks in other shards.

Integrating SPAR into existing blockchain systems requires minimum changes and no extra bandwidth consumption. An honest block producer only needs to broadcast the original data block as usual and attach the CMT root in the block header. This is sufficient for other full nodes to reproduce the CMT and offer sampling services for light nodes. Our library for CMT in Rust for Parity Bitcoin clients maintains the same API as the standard Merkle tree module. Noting that classic Merkle trees are indeed special CMTs with coding rate $r = 1$ and batching factor $q = 2$, our library readily replaces the standard module and is backward compatible.

A   Proof of Theorem 1

Proof. Soundness: Soundness fails if a light node thinks that a block is available, and no full node is able to reconstruct the entire coded Merkle tree. We note that the reconstruction fails if any layer of the CMT cannot be recovered correctly. Let us focus on a single layer i with n_i coded symbols and an undecodable ratio of α_i, and assume that the malicious block producer hides α fraction of the coded symbols (and does not respond to requests for those symbols).

Case-1: Consider the case of $\alpha \geq \alpha_i$. The probability of soundness failure for a node is given by the probability that a node receives all s symbols that it samples, this probability is $(1 - \alpha)^s \leq (1 - \alpha_i)^s \leq (1 - \alpha_{\min})^s$.

Case-2: Consider the case of $\alpha < \alpha_i$. The soundness failure occurs if a full node cannot decode the entire block or is unable to furnish a incorrect-coding proof. The full node will fail to accomplish these tasks only when it is able to receive fewer than $1 - \alpha_i$ fraction of symbols. Define Z_i to be the total number of distinct symbols collected by the honest full node ($Z_i \in \{0, 1, .., n_i\}$). Let m be the total number of light nodes, then $m \cdot s$ is the total number of i.i.d. samples. Now we have

$$P(Z_i \leq (1 - \alpha_i)n_i) \leq \binom{n_i}{\alpha_i n_i} \frac{(n_i - \alpha_i n_i)^{ms}}{n^{ms}}, \tag{5}$$

$$\leq 2^{H(\alpha_i)n_i} (1 - \alpha_i)^{ms}, \tag{6}$$

$$= 2^{H(\alpha_i)n_i - ms \log \frac{1}{1-\alpha_i}} \leq 2^{\max_i \left[H(\alpha_i)n_i - ms \log \frac{1}{1-\alpha_i} \right]}. \tag{7}$$

Here (5) is by counting the number of sampling instances that provide less then $(1 - \alpha_i)n_i$ distinct symbols. $H(p) = p \log \frac{1}{p} + (1 - p) \log \frac{1}{1-p}$ is the binary entropy function. It is apparent that we would need m large to make the above bound vanish exponentially with s.

The probability of soundness failure is smaller than the maximum probability of the two cases.

Agreement: We will argue here that soundness implies agreement for our protocol. As defined, soundness ensures that a honest full node is able to decode the block. Once a honest full node decodes the block, it will let all light nodes know that it has that block. The light nodes have either already accepted the block or have "pend"-ed the block (the light nodes could not have rejected the block since it is a valid block). The light nodes that pended the block will query with the honest full node and eventually accept the block. Thus soundness implies agreement (since now every light node agrees on the availability of the block). ∎

∎

B Proof of Theorem 2

Based on the proof of Theorem 8 of [27], we know that for an (n, k) LDPC code that is randomly chosen from a (c, d) ensemble, described in Sect. 4.4, the probability that the stopping distance of the code is smaller than $\alpha^* n$ is upper-bounded by

$$P(\alpha n < \alpha^* n) \leq \min\left\{\inf_{0<\delta<\alpha^*}\left(n(\alpha^* - \delta)e^{n\max_{\theta\in[\delta,\alpha^*]}\gamma(\theta)} + \sum_{i=1}^{\delta n-1} I_i\right), 1\right\} \quad (8)$$

where for $c = d(1-r)$, $h(\theta) = -\theta\log\theta - (1-\theta)\log(1-\theta)$, and x_0 as the only positive solution to $\frac{x(1+x)^{d-1}-x}{(1+x)^d-dx} = \theta$,

$$\gamma(\theta) \triangleq \frac{c}{d}\log\left(\frac{(1+x_0)^d - dx_0}{x_0^{\theta d}}\right) - (c-1)h(\theta),$$

$$I_i \triangleq \binom{n}{i}\frac{\binom{n(\frac{c}{d}+\frac{\delta c}{2}-\frac{\delta c}{d})}{\lfloor\frac{ic}{2}\rfloor}(2d-3)^{ic}}{\binom{nc}{ic}}.$$

For $\alpha^* = 0.124$, the above upper bound for small n (e.g., $n = 256$) becomes degenerated (i.e., reduces to the trivial bound of 1). In order to obtain a good approximation for all the values of n, we approximate the upper bounds on $P(\alpha < 0.124)$ using a slightly smaller undecodable ratio of 0.116. Then, we evaluate the upper bounds on $P(\alpha n < 0.116n)$ in (8), for all the considered values of n in Theorem 2 to obtain the probabilities in the second row of Table 3.

We note that since 0.116 is very close to 0.124, SPAR's inherent oversampling of intermediate layers will provide sufficient protection for data availability on these layers, so that the light node sampling cost will not increase.

C Coded Merkle Tree Library

We developed in Rust a Coded Merkle Tree library [2] for Parity Bitcoin [28] clients. We modify the data structure of the block header to add a new field coded_merkle_roots_hashes, which are the hashes of the coded symbols on the last level of the coded Merkle tree constructed from this block.

To use the Coded Merkle Tree library on a block, we require the following input parameters from the users:

- BASE_SYMBOL_SIZE: size of a symbol on the base level, and hence the number of systematic symbols on the base level.

- AGGREGATE: number of hashes to aggregate into a symbol on the next level.
- HEADER_SIZE: number of hashes stored in the block header. This also decides the total number of levels in the coded Merkle tree.
- Codes for all levels of coded Merkle tree, in forms of sparse representations of their parity-check matrices.

Given the above parameters, Coded Merkle Tree implements the following key functionalities:

- coded_merkle_roots: construction of the coded Merkle tree from the block content.
- merkle_proof: generating the Merkle proof for any symbol on any level of coded Merkle tree. By design, this returns a set of symbols on the higher level.
- sampling_to_decode: sampling symbols on the base level, together with their Merkle proofs.
- run_tree_decoder: decode the entire coded Merkle tree level by level from the roots. Each level is decoded by running a hash-aware peeling decoder, using the decoded symbols on the previous level as the hash commitments.
- generate_incorrect_coding_proof: 1) when a coding error is detected, this function returns $d - 1$ symbols in a parity equation, and Merkle proofs for all d symbols in that equation; 2) when the peeling process gets stuck before all symbols are decoded, this function returns the indices of the missing symbols as a stopping set.

References

1. Bitcoin operating modes. https://bitcoin.org/en/operating-modes-guide#introd uction. Accessed 12 May 2019
2. Coded Merkle tree library. https://github.com/songzLi/coded_merkle_tree
3. Cryptonite. http://cryptonite.info/. Accessed 24 June 2019
4. Electrum bitcoin wallet. https://electrum.org/#home. Accessed 24 June 2019
5. Light ethereum subprotocol. https://wiki.parity.io/Light-Ethereum-Subprotocol-(LES). Accessed 24 June 2019
6. Sample Reed-Solomon code implementation. https://github.com/ethereum/research/tree/master/erasure_code/ec65536. Accessed 21 Sept 2019
7. Connection bloom filtering (2012). https://github.com/bitcoin/bips/blob/master/bip-0037.mediawiki
8. Aguilera, M.K., Janakiraman, R., Xu, L.: Using erasure codes efficiently for storage in a distributed system. In: 2005 International Conference on Dependable Systems and Networks (DSN 2005), pp. 336–345. IEEE (2005)
9. Al-Bassam, M., Sonnino, A., Buterin, V.: Fraud and data availability proofs: maximising light client security and scaling blockchains with dishonest majorities. e-print arXiv:1809.09044 (2018)
10. Bano, S., Al-Bassam, M., Danezis, G.: The road to scalable blockchain designs. USENIX; login: magazine (2017)
11. Bonneau, J., Clark, J., Goldfeder, S.: On bitcoin as a public randomness source. IACR Cryptology ePrint Archive. https://eprint.iacr.org/2015/1015.pdf

12. Burshtein, D., Miller, G.: Asymptotic enumeration methods for analyzing LDPC codes. IEEE Trans. Inf. Theory **50**(6), 1115–1131 (2004)
13. Buterin, V.: A note on data availability and erasure coding. https://github.co m/ethereum/research/wiki/A-note-on-data-availability-and-erasure-coding. Accessed 21 Sept 2019
14. Dimakis, A.G., Godfrey, P.B., Wu, Y., Wainwright, M.J., Ramchandran, K.: Network coding for distributed storage systems. IEEE Trans. Inf. Theory **56**(9), 4539–4551 (2010)
15. Dimakis, A.G., Ramchandran, K., Wu, Y., Suh, C.: A survey on network codes for distributed storage. Proc. IEEE **99**(3), 476–489 (2011)
16. Dorri, A., Kanhere, S.S., Jurdak, R., Gauravaram, P.: LSB: a lightweight scalable blockchain for IoT security and privacy. e-print arXiv:1712.02969 (2017)
17. Eyal, I., Gencer, A.E., Sirer, E.G., Van Renesse, R.: Bitcoin-NG: a scalable blockchain protocol. In: 13th USENIX Symposium on Networked Systems Design and Implementation (NSDI 2016), pp. 45–59 (2016)
18. Frey, D., Makkes, M.X., Roman, P.L., Taïani, F., Voulgaris, S.: Bringing secure bitcoin transactions to your smartphone. In: Proceedings of the 15th International Workshop on Adaptive and Reflective Middleware (ARM 2016), pp. 1–6. ACM (2016)
19. Gervais, A., Capkun, S., Karame, G.O., Gruber, D.: On the privacy provisions of bloom filters in lightweight bitcoin clients. In: Proceedings of the 30th Annual Computer Security Applications Conference, pp. 326–335. ACM (2014)
20. Kokoris-Kogias, E., Jovanovic, P., Gasser, L., Gailly, N., Syta, E., Ford, B.: Omniledger: a secure, scale-out, decentralized ledger via sharding. In: 2018 IEEE Symposium on Security and Privacy (SP), pp. 583–598. IEEE (2018)
21. Li, S., Yu, M., Avestimehr, S., Kannan, S., Viswanath, P.: Polyshard: coded sharding achieves linearly scaling efficiency and security simultaneously. e-print arXiv:1809.10361 (2018)
22. Lin, S., Costello, D.J.: Error Control Coding. Pearson, New York (2004)
23. Luby, M.G., Mitzenmacher, M., Shokrollahi, M.A., Spielman, D.A.: Efficient erasure correcting codes. IEEE Trans. Inf. Theory **47**(2), 569–584 (2001)
24. Luu, L., Narayanan, V., Zheng, C., Baweja, K., Gilbert, S., Saxena, P.: A secure sharding protocol for open blockchains. In: Proceedings of the 2016 ACM SIGSAC Conference on Computer and Communications Security, pp. 17–30. ACM (2016)
25. McConaghy, T., et al.: BigchainDB: a scalable blockchain database. White paper, BigchainDB (2016)
26. Nakamoto, S., et al.: Bitcoin: a peer-to-peer electronic cash system (2008)
27. Orlitsky, A., Viswanathan, K., Zhang, J.: Stopping set distribution of LDPC code ensembles. IEEE Trans. Inf. Theory **51**(3), 929–953 (2005)
28. Parity-Technologies: The parity bitcoin client. https://github.com/paritytech/parity-bitcoin. Accessed 21 Sept 2019
29. Perard, D., Lacan, J., Bachy, Y., Detchart, J.: Erasure code-based low storage blockchain node. e-print arXiv:1805.00860 (2018)
30. Raman, R.K., Varshney, L.R.: Dynamic distributed storage for scaling blockchains. arXiv preprint arXiv:1711.07617 (2017)
31. Rashmi, K.V., Shah, N.B., Kumar, P.V.: Optimal exact-regenerating codes for distributed storage at the MSR and MBR points via a product-matrix construction. IEEE Trans. Inf. Theory **57**(8), 5227–5239 (2011)
32. Reed, I.S., Solomon, G.: Polynomial codes over certain finite fields. J. Soc. Ind. Appl. Math. **8**(2), 300–304 (1960)

33. Shamir, A.: How to share a secret. Commun. ACM **22**(11), 612–613 (1979)
34. Syta, E., et al.: Scalable bias-resistant distributed randomness. In: 2017 IEEE Symposium on Security and Privacy (SP), pp. 444–460. IEEE (2017)
35. Wood, G., et al.: Ethereum: a secure decentralised generalised transaction ledger. Ethereum Project Yellow Paper **151**, 1–32 (2014)
36. Xu, L., Chen, L., Gao, Z., Xu, S., Shi, W.: EPBC: efficient public blockchain client for lightweight users. In: Proceedings of the 1st Workshop on Scalable and Resilient Infrastructures for Distributed Ledgers, p. 1. ACM (2017)

Cryptoeconomics

Decentralized Privacy-Preserving Netting Protocol on Blockchain for Payment Systems

Shengjiao Cao[1], Yuan Yuan[1(✉)], Angelo De Caro[2], Karthik Nandakumar[3], Kaoutar Elkhiyaoui[2], and Yanyan Hu[3]

[1] Ant Financial Services Group, Hangzhou, China
{s.cao,ida.yuan}@antfin.com
[2] IBM Research Zurich, Rüschlikon, Switzerland
{adc,kao}@zurich.ibm.com
[3] IBM Research Singapore, Singapore, Singapore
{nkarthik,yanyanhu}@sg.ibm.com

Abstract. This paper proposes a decentralized netting protocol that guarantees the privacy of the participants. Namely, it leverages the blockchain and its security properties to relax the trust assumptions and get rid of trusted central parties. We prove the protocol to be optimal and we analyze its performance using a proof-of-concept implemented on top of Hyperledger Fabric.

Keywords: Decentralized netting · Payment systems · Blockchain · Zero-knowledge proofs

1 Introduction

Currently, banks settle their liabilities to each other through *inter-bank payment systems* generally managed by their country's central bank. The central bank opens an account for the local banks in its jurisdiction and enforces that each account maintains a certain level of liquidity to accommodate future settlements. Upon receiving a payment instruction, say bank A transfers x home-currency to bank B, the central bank deducts x from A's account while adding x to B's account.

Historically, inter-bank payments were settled via (end of day) netting systems, but as the volume and the value of transactions increased central banks became wary of the risks involved in deferred net settlement systems. Now, central banks favor real-time gross settlement (RTGS) systems. In RTGS, payment instructions are settled individually and immediately at their full amount. However, the benefit of immediate finality incurs high liquidity costs on the banks. The liquidity demands in RTGS systems are enormous; in fact, the daily transfer volume in typical inter-bank payment systems could be as large as a substantial fraction of the annual GDP [1]. Figure 1 on the left illustrates a simple scenario

© International Financial Cryptography Association 2020
J. Bonneau and N. Heninger (Eds.): FC 2020, LNCS 12059, pp. 137–155, 2020.
https://doi.org/10.1007/978-3-030-51280-4_9

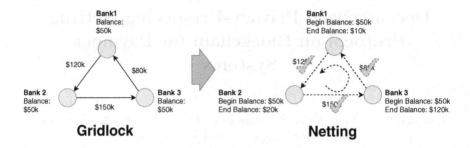

Fig. 1. Illustration of a gridlock scenario and netting procedure

in which participating banks are not able to settle their payments individually due to insufficient liquidity, bringing the system to a halt known as *gridlock*. To resolve gridlocks, banks combine RTGS with liquidity saving mechanisms (LSM), of which *netting* is the most effective one. Figure 1 on the right illustrates how triple-lateral netting helps resolve system gridlock.

Traditionally, central banks are in charge of resolving gridlocks and guaranteeing that the system runs smoothly without interruptions. Essentially, they operate a centralized payment queue to which every participating bank submits its payment instructions, and perform *multilateral netting*. That is, the process of offsetting the value of multiple payments due to be exchanged between the banks. After netting, the central banks settle the net liability of the participants without overdraft. In addition to performing netting correctly, central banks are trusted to preserve the confidentiality of payment instructions coming from each bank. While placing such trust in central banks may be justified, it comes with great liability risk for them. Furthermore, in the case of cross-border multi-currency transfer, it is challenging to find a *trusted mediator* to settle payments. This is why central banks are actively looking for alternatives to centralized netting and settlement.

Thanks to the emergence of Bitcoin [2] and the ensuing interest in blockchain technology, financial institutions have been investigating avenues to make *decentralized inter-bank payment systems* a reality, e.g., Project Jasper [3], Project Ubin [4]. However, while these two projects succeed in removing the single point of failure and achieving immediate and final settlement without the need for transaction reconciliation, their prototype systems are missing the crucial functionality of decentralized multilateral netting, making them less practical.

We recall here that a multilateral netting process is viable, if it is correct and fair. Correctness ensures that (i) when the sender's account is debited x dollars, the receiver's account is credited x dollars; and (ii) participants will not pay more than their current balance plus their allowed credit. These two properties guarantee that the total liquidity in the system remains the same before and after settlement. Fairness on the other hand, captures the requirement that netting should not favor any participant in terms of payment settlement priority, rather it should reach an overall optimal netting strategy, i.e. either the maximum number of instructions settled, or the maximum amount of payments settled.

In the case of centralized netting [5–7], correctness and fairness are easy to satisfy as the central party sees all payment instructions and can perform the netting and update the banks' accounts accordingly. In contrast, meeting these requirements in a decentralized payment system is a real challenge. Without a trusted central party, participants might be reluctant to advertise their payment instructions for everyone to see. This means that in a decentralized netting protocol, participants should see only their own payment instructions and based on those decide which payments to settle first. An ill-designed protocol however could allow a malicious participant to choose to settle only the payments that increase her current liquidity balance to the detriment of others'. Therefore, the best approach to design decentralized netting solutions is to enable each participant to solve their own net settlement locally, and have in place a mechanism to verify that the local settlements are both fair and correct.

In this paper, we propose a solution that leverages the blockchain to implement decentralized netting without sacrificing the privacy of the participants. It should be noted that we are not the first to propose leveraging the blockchain for netting. Recently, Wang et al. [8] introduced a blockchain-based netting solution for gridlock, but it differs from ours in two aspects: (i) it relies on a central party to check the netting result and make sure that the total liquidity is preserved; and (ii) while it hides the individual payment amount of the involved banks, it reveals the net amounts that should be paid.

Contributions. The contributions of this paper are two-fold:

- A first-of-its-kind decentralized netting protocol that does not require any central party but still guarantees correctness and fairness. The proposed protocol collects the local settlements of the participants and feeds them to a smart contract running on the blockchain to reach a *globally optimal, correct* and *fair* settlement.
- An enhanced privacy-preserving extension that further protects the confidentiality of the payment amounts. In this extension, payment amounts are encoded as *homomorphic Pedersen commitments* and *zero-knowledge proofs* are provided to the smart contract to verify the correctness of the local settlement in a privacy-preserving manner.

The remainder of the paper is organized as follows. In Sect. 2, we formulate our problem followed by the proposed decentralized netting protocol without privacy. In Sect. 3, we give a detailed description of how to enhance our protocol with privacy. In Sect. 4, we construct a blockchain-based payment system and analyze its security properties. In Sect. 5, we present an implementation of the protocol on Hyperledger Fabric and discuss our evaluation results. We conclude our paper in Sect. 6 with possible future work.

2   Decentralized Netting Protocol

The general netting problem is NP complete and can be solved only approximately using the algorithms in [6,7]. These algorithms often yield multiple possible solutions instead of the optimal one, hence *sacrificing fairness*. In practice, central banks sort payments according to an order determined either by settlement deadlines or by priorities defined by the participants themselves. Payments with high priority are settled before payments with low priority. These allow central banks to find the optimal solution and achieve fairness.

In the remainder of the paper, we restrict ourselves to the problem formulation in [5] that focuses on netting for payments with priority constraints.

Notation. For $n \in \mathbb{N}$, let $[n] = \{1, \ldots, n\}$. For $\mathbf{x} = [x_1, \ldots, x_n], \mathbf{y} = [y_1, \ldots, y_n]$, let $\mathbf{x} \geq \mathbf{y}$ denote $x_k \geq y_k, \forall k \in [n]$. Let $I(\cdot)$ denote the indicator function, i.e., $I(b) = 1$ if b is true, otherwise $I(b) = 0$.

2.1   The Netting Problem

Let n be the number of participants in the payment ecosystem and P_i refer to the ith participant. Let d_i denote the credit limit of (or the amount of cover money deposited by) P_i. Let $\mathbf{PayOutQ}_i$ denote the queue containing the outgoing payment instructions of P_i (i.e., outstanding payments where P_i is the sender):

$$\mathbf{PayOutQ}_i = [\text{PayOut}_{i,1}, \ldots, \text{PayOut}_{i,m_i}] \tag{1}$$

$$\text{PayOut}_{i,k} = (\text{Rec}_{i,k}, \text{Amt}_{i,k}) \tag{2}$$

$$\text{Rec}_{i,k} \in \{P_j\}_{j=1, j \neq i}^n \tag{3}$$

$$\text{Amt}_{i,k} > 0 \tag{4}$$

where m_i is the number of payment instructions in $\mathbf{PayOutQ}_i$, $\text{Rec}_{i,k}$ and $\text{Amt}_{i,k}$ are the receiver and amount in payment instruction $\text{PayOut}_{i,k}$, respectively. Let $x_{i,k} \in \{0,1\}$ be the indicator of whether $\text{PayOut}_{i,k}$ will be settled after netting:

$$x_{i,k} = \begin{cases} 1 \text{ if} & \text{PayOut}_{i,k} \text{ will be settled} \\ 0 \text{ o/w} \end{cases} \tag{5}$$

Let $\mathbf{x}_i \overset{\text{def}}{=} [x_{i,1}, \ldots x_{i,m_i}]$ and $\mathbf{x} \overset{\text{def}}{=} [\mathbf{x}_1, \ldots \mathbf{x}_n]$. Given $\mathbf{x}$, we define:

$$T_i(\mathbf{x}) = \sum_{k=1}^{m_i} x_{i,k} \tag{6}$$

$$S_i(\mathbf{x}) = \sum_{k=1}^{m_i} x_{i,k} \text{Amt}_{i,k} \tag{7}$$

$$R_i(\mathbf{x}) = \sum_{j=1}^{n} \sum_{k=1}^{m_j} x_{j,k} \text{Amt}_{j,k} I(\text{Rec}_{j,k} = P_i) \tag{8}$$

$T_i(\mathbf{x})$ denotes the number of outgoing payment instructions from P_i that will be settled after netting, $S_i(\mathbf{x})$ denotes the total outgoing amount from P_i and $R_i(\mathbf{x})$ denotes the total incoming amount to P_i. Let $\hat{B}_i$ and $\tilde{B}_i$ be the ex-ante (before netting) and ex-post (after netting) balances of P_i, respectively. The relationship between $\hat{B}_i$ and $\tilde{B}_i$ is given by:

$$\tilde{B}_i = \hat{B}_i - S_i(\mathbf{x}) + R_i(\mathbf{x}) \tag{9}$$

The **netting problem** corresponds to finding the optimal solution that satisfies the following equations:

$$\max_{\mathbf{x}} \sum_{i=1}^{n} f_i(\mathbf{x}) \tag{10}$$

$$\text{s.t. } \tilde{B}_i \geq -d_i, \forall i \in [n] \tag{11}$$

where the **liquidity constraint** (11) stipulates that if the payments are simultaneously settled according to $\mathbf{x}$ then the ex-post balances plus credit limit of each bank has to be non-negative. Here $f_i(\mathbf{x})$ can be either $T_i(\mathbf{x})$ for the number of payments, or $S_i(\mathbf{x})$ for the total monetary value settled. We impose the constraint that the payment instructions in the outgoing queue can only be settled in the given priority order:

$$x_{i,k+1} \leq x_{i,k}, \forall i \in [n], \forall k \in [m_i - 1] \tag{12}$$

For example, for any $j > k$, $\text{PayOut}_{i,j}$ can not be settled if $\text{PayOut}_{i,k}$ is not settled, implying that $x_{i,j}$ must be 0 if $x_{i,k} = 0$. Under these constraints, either choice of $f_i(\mathbf{x})$ leads to the same optimal solution, as proved in [5].

Let $h(\mathbf{x}_i)$ denote the index of the lowest priority instruction in **PayOutQ**$_i$ that can be settled:

$$h(\mathbf{x}_i) = \begin{cases} 0 & \text{if } x_{i,k} = 0, \forall k \in [m_i] \\ \max_k kI(x_{i,k} = 1) & \text{o/w} \end{cases} \tag{13}$$

2.2 Blockchain-Based Decentralized Netting

In the following, we describe our solution for blockchain-based decentralized netting without privacy.

Each participant is endowed with a system-wide public key and an account associated with that public key. Each payment instruction submitted to the blockchain comes with a signature of its sender and a priority order. The payment smart contract verifies the signature and settles the payment instruction immediately if there is enough balance in the sender's account and no other higher priority payment instruction in the outgoing queue. Otherwise, the payment instruction is added to the sender's outgoing queue to be settled later.

Netting of payment instructions is triggered either periodically or the moment the total queue size reaches a certain threshold defined by the system administrator. The netting process iterates through multiple rounds until convergence. Each round consists of two operations:

Algorithm 1. Blockchain-based Decentralized Netting

1: **Inputs**: $\hat{B}_i, d_i, \mathbf{PayOutQ}_i, \forall i \in [n]$ // $\hat{B}_i$ is ex-ante balance
2: **Outputs**: x   // Indicator of payments that can be settled
3: **Initialization**: $t \leftarrow 1, x_{i,k}^0 \leftarrow 1, \forall i \in [n], k \in [m_i], l^0 = \sum_{i=1}^n m_i$
4: **repeat**
5:      At each P_i: calculate the local proposal $\mathbf{x}^t$ for round t:
6:          Set $\mathbf{x}^t \leftarrow \mathbf{x}^{t-1}, z_i \leftarrow h(\mathbf{x}_i^t)$ // Include all payments from last round
7:          **While** $z_i \geq 0$ // Iterate until liquidity constraint is satisfied
8:              $\tilde{B}_i^* = \hat{B}_i - S_i(\mathbf{x}^t) + R_i(\mathbf{x}^t)$ // Calculate ex-post balance
9:              **If** $\tilde{B}_i^* \geq -d_i$ // Liquidity constraint is satisfied
10:                  **break**
11:              **Else**
12:                  $x_{i,z_i}^t \leftarrow 0, z_i \leftarrow z_i - 1$ // Remove lowest priority payment
13:          **If** $z_i = m_i$
14:              Submit the proposal $\{\mathbf{x}_i^t, \tilde{B}_i^*, \emptyset\}$ to the ledger
15:          **Else**
16:              $\tilde{B}_i' \leftarrow \tilde{B}_i^* - \text{Amt}_{i,z_i+1}$ // Calculate hypothetical balance
17:              Submit the proposal $\{\mathbf{x}_i^t, \tilde{B}_i^*, \tilde{B}_i'\}$ to the ledger
18:      **Smart Contract**: Upon receiving proposals from N participants for round t
19:          **for** i=1,...,n
20:              **Verify Priority Constraint**: $x_{i,k+1}^t \leq x_{i,k}^t, \forall k \in [m_i - 1]$
21:              **Verify Convergence Constraint**: $x_{i,k}^t \leq x_{i,k}^{t-1}, \forall k \in [m_i]$
22:              **Verify Liquidity Constraint**: $\tilde{B}_i^* \equiv \hat{B}_i - S_i(\mathbf{x}^t) + R_i(\mathbf{x}^t)$ and $\tilde{B}_i^* \geq -d_i$
23:              **If** $z_i < m_i$
24:                  **Verify Optimality**: $\tilde{B}_i' \equiv \tilde{B}_i^* - \text{Amt}_{i,z_i+1}$ where $z_i = h(\mathbf{x}_i^t)$ and $\tilde{B}_i' < -d_i$
25:          **end**
26:          Calculate $l^t = \sum_{i=1}^n \sum_{k=1}^{m_i} x_{i,k}^t$ // total number of payments to be settled
27:          **If** $l^t \equiv l^{t-1}$,
28:              Exit $\mathbf{x} \leftarrow \mathbf{x}^t$
29:          **Else**
30:              $t \leftarrow t + 1$, continue to next round.
31: **until** converged
32: return x

---

1) **Participant Proposal:** Each participant P_i calculates her nettable set, which corresponds to the maximum number of payments that can be settled from P_i's outgoing queue without violating the liquidity and the priority constraints, see Algorithm 1 lines 5 to 12. The calculation also takes into consideration the incoming payments from the aggregate nettable set of the previous round. Note that in the first round, all incoming payments are included. P_i then submits her nettable set and to-be-post-balance (i.e. new balance once the payments in the nettable set are finalized). Furthermore, P_i proves the *optimality* of her nettable set by including the highest priority payment that cannot be resolved in the current proposal and showing that the corresponding hypothetical to-be-post-balance is less than $-d_i$, cf. line 16.

2) **Smart Contract Verification and Net Payment Aggregation:** Upon receiving proposals from all participants, the smart contract verifies whether each proposal **(i)** satisfies the **priority and liquidity constraints** and **(ii)** is optimal, check lines 20 to 24. If the verification succeeds, then the individual

nettable sets of all participants are aggregated to obtain the *aggregate nettable set* for this round.

The smart contract next checks whether the new aggregate nettable set is the same as the one in the previous round. If so, then netting process has converged and the smart contract concludes its execution by returning the aggregate nettable set, cf. lines 27 and 28. If the aggregate nettable set is empty, we call it a DEADLOCK as no payments can be settled on a net basis. In the case of a DEADLOCK, the participants are unable to settle any of the queued payments unless new liquidity is injected into the system.

If all participants are honest, then this decentralized netting protocol achieves the global optimal solution for the netting problem.

Theorem 1. *Algorithm 1 always finds a unique and optimal solution for problem defined by Eqs. (10) to (12). In addition, the solution is independent of the choice of the objective function as either maximum total value settled or maximum number of payments settled.*

The proof of Theorem 1 is deferred to Appendix A.

3   Decentralized Privacy-Preserving Netting

Although Algorithm 1 is optimal, it does not protect the privacy of system participants. All payment instructions are posted to the ledger in the clear. To preserve the privacy of the participants, we enhance our decentralized netting protocol with Pedersen commitments [11] and zero-knowledge range proofs [12].

3.1   Pedersen Commitments for Privacy-Preserving Ledger

Instead of posting account balances and payment amounts to the ledger in the clear, we obfuscate them using Pedersen commitments. These commitments are *hiding* and *binding*: meaning that they do not reveal any information about the committed values and that they cannot be opened to different values later.

Let $\mathbb{G}$ be a cyclic group of large prime order p and let g and h be two random generators of $\mathbb{G}$. A Pedersen commitment to a value $v \in \mathbb{F}_p$ is computed as $\mathsf{com}(v, r) = g^v h^r$, where $r \in \mathbb{F}_p$ is a randomly-chosen blinding factor. By construction, Pedersen commitments are *additively homomorphic*:

$$\mathsf{com}(v_1, r_1)\mathsf{com}(v_2, r_2) = \mathsf{com}(v_1 + v_2, r_1 + r_2)$$

On the ledger, the account balance $\hat{B}_i$ of P_i is stored as $\mathsf{com}(\hat{B}_i, \hat{r}_i)$ while the amount $\mathrm{Amt}_{i,k}$ of the k-th payment message in P_i's outgoing queue is stored as $\mathsf{com}(\mathrm{Amt}_{i,k}, r_{i,k})$, where $\hat{r}_i$ and $r_{i,k}, \forall i \in [n], k \in [m_i]$ are randomly-sampled in $\mathbb{F}_p$. We assume that the sender transmits the payment amount ($\mathrm{Amt}_{i,k}$) and

---

Algorithm 2. Decentralized Privacy-Preserving Netting

1: **Public Inputs:** $\mathsf{com}(\hat{B}_i, \hat{r}_i), d_i, \mathbf{PayOutQ}_i, \forall i \in [n]$
2: **Outputs: x**   // Indicator of payments that can be settled
3: **Initialization:** $t \leftarrow 1, x_{i,k}^0 \leftarrow 1, \forall i \in [n], k \in [m_i], l^0 = \sum_{i=1}^n m_i$
4: **repeat**
5:     **At each P_i:** calculate the local proposal $\mathbf{x}^t$ for round t:
6:         $\mathbf{x}^t \leftarrow \mathbf{x}^{t-1}, z_i \leftarrow h(\mathbf{x}_i^t)$ // Include all payments from last round
7:         **While** $z_i \geq 0$ // Iterate until liquidity constraint is satisfied
8:             $\tilde{B}_i^* = \hat{B}_i - S_i(\mathbf{x}^t) + R_i(\mathbf{x}^t)$ // Calculate ex-post balance
9:             **If** $\tilde{B}_i^* \geq -d_i$ // Liquidity constraint is satisfied
10:                 **break**
11:             **Else**
12:                 $x_{i,z_i}^t \leftarrow 0, z_i \leftarrow z_i - 1$ // Remove lowest priority payment
13:         Calculate $\mathsf{com}(\tilde{B}_i^*, \tilde{r}_i^*) \leftarrow \mathsf{com}(\hat{B}_i, \hat{r}_i)\mathsf{com}(S_i(\mathbf{x}^t), r_i')^{-1}\mathsf{com}(R_i(\mathbf{x}^t), r_i'')$
14:         Construct zkrp$_{\text{II}}$ proof $\pi(\tilde{B}_i^*)$ // zero-knowledge range proof
15:         **If** $z_i = m_i$
16:             Submit proposal $\{\mathbf{x}_i^t, \mathsf{com}(\tilde{B}_i^*, \tilde{r}_i^*), \pi(\tilde{B}_i^*), \emptyset, \emptyset\}$ to ledger
17:         **Else**
18:             $\mathsf{com}(\tilde{B}_i', \tilde{r}_i') \leftarrow \mathsf{com}(\tilde{B}_i^*, \tilde{r}_i^*)\mathsf{com}(\mathrm{Amt}_{i,z_i+1}, r_{i,z_i+1})^{-1}$
19:             Construct zkrp$_{\text{III}}$ proof $\pi(\tilde{B}_i')$ // zero-knowledge range proof
20:             Submit proposal $\{\mathbf{x}_i^t, \mathsf{com}(\tilde{B}_i^*, \tilde{r}_i^*), \pi(\tilde{B}_i^*), \mathsf{com}(\tilde{B}_i', \tilde{r}_i'), \pi(\tilde{B}_i')\}$ to ledger
21:     **Smart Contract:** Upon receiving proposals from N participants for round t
22:     **for** i=1,...,n
23:         **Verify Priority Constraint:** $x_{i,k+1}^t \leq x_{i,k}^t, \forall k \in [m_i - 1]$
24:         **Verify Convergence Constraint:** $x_{i,k}^t \leq x_{i,k}^{t-1}, \forall k \in [m_i]$
25:         **Verify Liquidity Constraint:**
26:             $\mathsf{com}(\tilde{B}_i^*, \tilde{r}_i^*) \equiv \mathsf{com}(\hat{B}_i, \hat{r}_i)\mathsf{com}(S_i(\mathbf{x}^t), r_i')^{-1}\mathsf{com}(R_i(\mathbf{x}^t), r_i'')$
27:             and $\mathsf{Verify}_{\text{II}}(\pi(\tilde{B}_i^*), \mathsf{com}(\tilde{B}_i^*, \tilde{r}_i^*)) \equiv 1$
28:         **If** $z_i < m_i$
29:             **Verify Optimality:**
30:                 $\mathsf{com}(\tilde{B}_i', \tilde{r}_i') \equiv \mathsf{com}(\tilde{B}_i^*, \tilde{r}_i^*)\mathsf{com}(\mathrm{Amt}_{i,z_i+1}, r_{i,z_i+1})^{-1}$ where $z_i = h(\mathbf{x}_i^t)$
31:                 and $\mathsf{Verify}_{\text{III}}(\pi(\tilde{B}_i'), \mathsf{com}(\tilde{B}_i', \tilde{r}_i')) \equiv 1$
32:         Calculate $l^t = \sum_{i=1}^n \sum_{k=1}^{m_i} x_{i,k}^t$ // Total number of payments to be settled
33:         **If** $l^t \equiv l^{t-1}$,
34:             Exit $\mathbf{x} \leftarrow \mathbf{x}^t$
35:         **Else**
36:             $t = t + 1$, continue to next round.
37: **until** converged
38: **return x**

---

randomness $(r_{i,k})$ to the receiver privately. Thanks to the homomorphic property of Pedersen commitments, we are able to translate the plain-text balance calculation in Eq. (7) to (9) into an obfuscated calculation as follows:

$$\mathsf{com}(S_i(\mathbf{x}), r_i') \overset{\mathrm{def}}{=} \prod_{k=1}^{m_i} \mathsf{com}(\mathrm{Amt}_{i,k}, r_{i,k})^{x_{i,k}} \qquad (14)$$

$$\mathsf{com}(R_i(\mathbf{x}), r_i'') \stackrel{\mathrm{def}}{=} \prod_{j=1}^{n} \prod_{k=1}^{m_j} \mathsf{com}(\mathrm{Amt}_{j,k}, r_{j,k})^{x_{j,k} I(\mathrm{Rec}_{j,k} = P_i)} \tag{15}$$

$$\mathsf{com}(\tilde{B}_i, \tilde{r}_i) \stackrel{\mathrm{def}}{=} \mathsf{com}(\hat{B}_i, \hat{r}_i)\mathsf{com}(S_i(\mathbf{x}), r_i')^{-1}\mathsf{com}(R_i(\mathbf{x}), r_i'') \tag{16}$$

Note that Pedersen commitments support positive integers only. However, account balances in our solution may become negative in the case of an overdraft. If we assume that the total liquidity in the system is less than some integer U and that $2U < p$, then Pedersen commitments can be used to handle all integers in $(-U, U)$ by simply mapping negative numbers $w \in (-U, 0)$ to $w + p > p/2$. With this mapping, we ensure that for all $v \in (0, U)$, $\mathsf{com}(v, r_1)\mathsf{com}(-v, r_2) = \mathsf{com}(v, r_1)\mathsf{com}(p - v, r_2) = \mathsf{com}(0, r_1 + r_2)$. For ease of notation, we just write negative integers as they are, i.e., $w \in (-U, 0)$ instead of $w + p$.

3.2 Zero Knowledge Range Proofs

Since both balances and payment amounts are hidden, smart contracts cannot rely only on the information in the ledger to verify the correctness and optimality of the participant proposals. We therefore require that each payment instruction comes with a zero knowledge proof that the payment amount is less than U and the participant proposals carry zero knowledge proofs that shows that the liquidity and optimality constraints are not violated. More precisely, participants are asked to produce three types of zero-knowledge range proofs (zkrp for short).

Definition 1. *A type I zero knowledge range proof* zkrp_I *is defined as* $\pi(\mathrm{Amt}_{i,k})$, *with verification function* $\mathsf{Verify}_I\big(\pi(\mathrm{Amt}_{i,k}), \mathsf{com}(\mathrm{Amt}_{i,k}, r_{i,k})\big) = 1$ *if* $0 \leq \mathrm{Amt}_{i,k} < U$; $\mathsf{Verify}_I\big(\pi(\mathrm{Amt}_{i,k}), \mathsf{com}(\mathrm{Amt}_{i,k}, r_{i,k})\big) = 0$ *otherwise.*

This proof ensures that the amount in each payment instruction is non-negative and less than the total liquidity U. This circumvents attacks in which a participant submits a payment instruction with a negative amount in the aim of stealing liquidity from the prospective receiver. Any payment with negative amount should be rejected and considered an attack.

Definition 2. *Let* $\tilde{B}_i^*$ *denotes* P_i's *to-be-post-balance in her proposal, at the* t^{th} *iteration, defined in Eq. (9). A type II zero knowledge range proof* zkrp_{II} *is defined as* $\pi(\tilde{B}_i^*)$, *with verification function* $\mathsf{Verify}_{II}\big(\pi(\tilde{B}_i^*), \mathsf{com}(\tilde{B}_i^*, \tilde{r}_i^*)\big) = 1$ *if* $-d_i \leq \tilde{B}_i^* < U$; $\mathsf{Verify}_{II}\big(\pi(\tilde{B}_i^*), \mathsf{com}(\tilde{B}_i^*, \tilde{r}_i^*)\big) = 0$ *otherwise.*

This proof allows anyone to check that the P_i's proposal does not violate the liquidity constraint.

Definition 3. *Let* $\tilde{B}_i'$ *denotes* P_i's *hypothetical to-be-post-balance in her proposal, at tth iteration, defined in line 16 of Algorithm 1. A type III zero knowledge range proof* zkrp_{III} *is defined as* $\pi(\tilde{B}_i')$, *with verification function* $\mathsf{Verify}_{III}\big(\pi(\tilde{B}_i'), \mathsf{com}(\tilde{B}_i', \tilde{r}_i')\big) = 1$ *if* $-U < \tilde{B}_i' < -d_i$; $\mathsf{Verify}_{III}\big(\pi(\tilde{B}_i'), \mathsf{com}(\tilde{B}_i', \tilde{r}_i')\big) = 0$ *otherwise.*

This proof essentially checks whether P_i's proposal in round t is optimal; i.e. P_i is not holding back payments that can be settled.

We note that all of these zero-knowledge range proofs can be implemented using the schemes in either [12] or [13]. For space limitations, details are omitted.

3.3   Solution Description

Algorithm 2 describes our privacy-preserving decentralized netting.

A payment transaction in Algorithm 2 includes the priority of the payment and the identity of the receiver in the clear, the amount however is obfuscated using a Pedersen commitment. The transaction also contains a zero-knowledge range proof that shows that the amount in Pedersen commitment does not exceed the total liquidity U. The sender of a payment signs her transaction revealing thus, her identity and submits it to the ledger. Moreover, the sender transmits the opening of the Pedersen commitment to the intended recipient through a secure channel.

Before the netting session starts, each participant P_i constructs her outgoing payment message queue $\mathbf{PayOutQ}_i = [\mathrm{PayOut}_{i,1}, ..., \mathrm{PayOut}_{i,m_i}]$ with $\mathrm{PayOut}_{i,k} = (\mathrm{Rec}_{i,k}, \mathrm{com}(\mathrm{Amt}_{i,k}, r_{i,k})), \forall k \in [m_i]$. We assume that P_i is associated with an ex-ante balance stored in the ledger as $\mathrm{com}(\hat{B}_i, \hat{r}_i)$.

In each round t, P_i submits a nettable set $\mathbf{x}_i^t$ to the network. She also provides a zero-knowledge range proof that her to-be-post-balance $\tilde{B}_i^*$ encoded in commitment $\mathrm{com}(\tilde{B}_i^*, \tilde{r}_i^*)$ is in the range $[-d_i, U)$. Additionally, P_i provides a zero-knowledge range proof that the hypothetical to-be-post-balance $\tilde{B}_i'$ hidden in commitment $\mathrm{com}(\tilde{B}_i', \tilde{r}_i')$ is less than $-d_i$. The hypothetical to-be-post-balance is calculated by including the payment message with the highest priority that cannot be settled (i.e. message with index $h(x_i^t) + 1$ in $\mathbf{PayOutQ}_i$).

It is easy to see that this protocol hides the payment amounts and account balances and guarantees the correctness of nettable set selection. Furthermore, according to Theorem 1, the proposed protocol also achieves fairness.

3.4   Hiding Senders and Receivers

In the current design, only the account balances and payment amounts are hidden using commitments, while the identities of senders and receivers are disclosed. One way to hide these is to express a payment instruction as an n-sized commitment vector, which commits to the payment amount (positive number) for the receiver, and the negative of payment amount for the sender and zero for other participants. This is the approach adopted by [9]. Although this approach successfully hides the identities of sender and receiver, it is not scalable: the transaction size, zero-knowledge proof generation and verification times are all proportional to the size of the commitment vector (i.e. the number of participants). Alternatively, participants can inject zero-valued payment instructions to random receivers in the network. These fake payment instructions help disguise the actual instructions. The frequency of these fake payments can be decided based on a trade-off between performance and the desired privacy level.

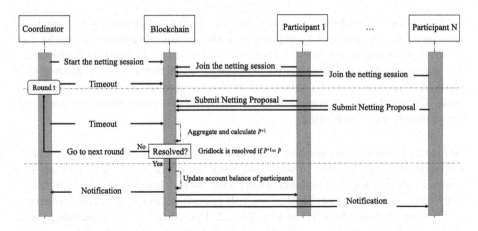

Fig. 2. The detailed decentralized netting protocol illustration

4   Payment System Construction and Security Analysis

4.1   Blockchain-Based Payment System

System Participants. We assume that all n participants $P_1, ..., P_n$ have peers running on the blockchain network. We conflate the participants with their peers. We also assume that there is a *system administrator* that initializes the participants' accounts at setup time.

Participant Accounts. Each participant has an account stored in the ledger. The account is addressed with the participant's public key and its balance is encoded in a Pedersen commitment. When the system is first bootstrapped, the administrator initializes each account by computing a Pedersen commitment reflecting the current balance. The administrator communicates the opening of each Pedersen commitment to the corresponding participant, so that the latter can submit payment instructions. To counter *front-running attacks*[1], the account of each participant is locked the moment she joins the netting session and then unlocked once the netting session ends.

Payment Instructions and Gross Settlement. Each payment instruction identifies the sender and the receiver and includes a Pedersen commitment to the payment amount and a zero-knowledge proof that the amount is non-negative. If the sender has enough liquidity to settle the payment, then she finalizes her transaction (via gross settlement) immediately by submitting to the network a zero-knowledge range proof that her updated account balance, by deducting the payment amount from the current account balance, is non-negative. The network

---

[1] These attacks send a payment instruction to change account balances while netting is taking place to invalidate the range proofs computed prior to the update.

verifies the zero-knowledge proof, updates the sender and receiver's account balance using the homomorphic property of Pedersen commitments and marks the payment instruction as settled. Otherwise, the payment instruction is stored in the sender's outgoing queue based on priority (and time). We recall that the sender is required to send to the receiver the opening of the Pedersen commitment. Our protocol assumes that the participants leverage secure channels to communicate with each other.

Gridlock Resolution and Net Settlement. Gridlock [5] is a situation where no participant can proceed to settle her outgoing queue using gross settlement, however, all participants collaboratively may settle their payments simultaneously using net settlement. To that end, all participants engage in the decentralized netting protocol depicted in Algorithm 2. To facilitate netting, our algorithm uses a *coordinator* that acts as a timing service, which initiates netting sessions and keeps track of timeouts in each round, see Fig. 2.

At first, the coordinator submits a request to the network to start a netting session. Interested participants respond by sending a request to join the netting session. A timeout transaction triggered by the coordinator starts the first round of the netting protocol. In each round, the participants submit proposals as defined in Algorithm 2 line 16 or 20. At the end of each round (triggered by the coordinator's timeout), the blockchain verifies the proposals and aggregates them to calculate the nettable set for the current round. If the nettable set does not change from the previous round, then the algorithm *has converged*. In the absence of a DEADLOCK, net settlement takes place automatically. Namely, the blockchain updates all the involved accounts by adding payment amounts to the receivers' accounts and subtracting the same payment amounts from the senders' accounts. After settlement, the network marks the payment instructions as settled by removing them from the outgoing queue. If the algorithm has not converged yet, a new round starts automatically.

4.2   Trust Model

Participants. We assume malicious participants. They may attempt to steal liquidity from other participants, hide liquidity, manipulate liquidity balances, provide false proofs and break the privacy of other participants. However, we assume that if a participant sends a valid payment instruction, then she would provide the corresponding recipient with the correct Pedersen decommitment.

Shared Ledger. We assume the ledger to be **live**: *valid* payment transactions will eventually be stored in the ledger. It is also assumed to be **immutable**: once a transaction is stored in the ledger it cannot be removed or modified. These two properties ensure that the ledger will always reflect an up-to-date version of the account balances of the participants. The ledger is available at all times to all participants in the system to submit their transactions and can be constructed on a platform using either a crash-tolerant consensus protocol like Hyperledger Fabric [14], or Nakamoto-like consensus protocol [2] like Ethereum.

Robustness. The network waits for all participants to submit a proposal in each round. If the proposal of some participant suffers delays, then our solution simply times out and excludes all incoming and outgoing payment instructions of that party. This guarantees that the efforts of honest parties are not wasted.

Security. The security of the underlying blockchain consensus algorithm guarantees that the smart contract verifying the payment instructions and the proposals be executed correctly. We recall that the smart contract logic consists of checking a set of zero-knowledge range proofs that ensure that the system predefined rules and invariant are not violated. Thanks to the soundness property of zero-knowledge proofs, no participant can make the smart contract accept an *invalid* payment transaction or proposal.

5   Implementation

5.1   Proof of Concept Implementation

For evaluation purposes, we implemented an experimental decentralized blockchain payment system on Hyperledger Fabric 1.2. Our zero-knowledge range proofs are based on Boneh-Boyen signature [12]. We use the Go's official BN256 curve [15], a bilinear group with 128-bit security level, to compute Pedersen commitments and range proofs. Our implementation consists of a number of Fabric chaincode (smart contract) interfaces that combined deliver the functionalities of payment, netting and settlement. Appendix B lists the main functions we have implemented and the code could be found at [16]. We set the credit limit to 0 for all participants and we enforce the priority constraint as defined in Eq. (12). We ran our experiments on an Ubuntu 16.04 with Linux kernel version of 4.4.0-133 virtual machine, with 32 VCPUs of 2.0 GHZ and 48 GB memory.

5.2   Protocol Evaluation

In our evaluation, a payment message is settled immediately if the sender has sufficient funds and no other higher priority payment messages are in her outgoing queue. Otherwise, the payment message is added to the outgoing queue according to its priority. Once a participant receives an incoming payment, she tries to locally settle as many outgoing payments as possible while respecting their priorities. At some predefined time, all participants engage in the decentralized netting protocol and conduct a multi-lateral net settlement based on the netting result. We note that periodical netting improves the settlement ratio of the payment system, which is defined as the ratio of the settled payment messages to the total number of messages. In our experiment, we randomly pick a sender and a receiver for each payment message and we draw the value of the payment from a Pareto distribution. We call a *window* the time between the start of two consecutive netting sessions.

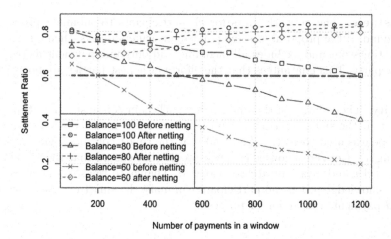

Fig. 3. The settlement ratio before and after netting versus number of payment messages in a window for different initial account balances = 80, 60, 100. Pareto parameter: $X_m = 20, \alpha = 2$

Our experiment involves 10 participants and injects different number of payment messages per window into the system. Figure 3 plots the settlement ratio before and after running the netting protocol against the number of payment messages, for different initial account balances. The more payment messages we inject, the more netting improves the settlement ratio. It is intuitive that as the account balance increases, the probability of a gridlock decreases and the settlement ratio before netting improves. In a practical setting, e.g. we want to keep the settlement ratio always above 60% (horizontal line), netting must take place for every 200, 500 and 1200 messages for initial account balance of 60, 80 and 100 respectively. As the initial account balance decreases, netting must take place more frequently to keep the settlement ratio high. Figure 4 shows the average number of rounds to reach convergence versus the number of payment messages for different initial account balances. As the number of payment messages increases in a window, it takes more rounds to reach convergence (the longer is the window); as the account balance decreases, it takes slightly longer to reach convergence. However, the total number of rounds increases only logarithmically.

Besides the Boneh-Boyen signature (BBS) based range proof, we also implemented another variety: Borromean ring signature (BRS) based proof [10] and compared their performances. We used the elliptic curve secp256k1 [18] for BRS-based range proof. Table 1 compares the time to generate and verify the zero-knowledge range proofs for different ranges using different proof methods. Table 1 also compares the size of various proofs, which is proportional to $\log(L)$, with L being the size of the range. Our implementation shows that BRS-based range proofs have better performances and slightly smaller proof size than BBS-based range proofs.

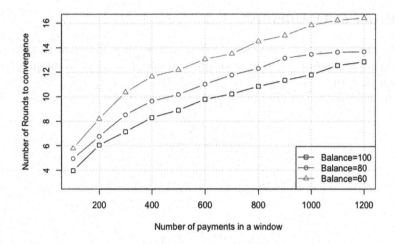

Fig. 4. The total number of rounds to reach convergence versus number of payment messages per window for different initial account balances = 80, 60, 100. Pareto parameter: $X_m = 20, \alpha = 2$

Table 1. Creation and verification time and proof size of various components

Component	Prove	Verify	Size
BBS $[0, 10^4]$	249 ms	363 ms	2624B
BBS $[0, 10^8]$	485 ms	724 ms	4928B
BBS $[0, 10^{16}]$	963 ms	1420 ms	9536B
BRS $[0, 10^4]$	17 ms	22 ms	1664B
BRS $[0, 10^8]$	30 ms	40 ms	3360B
BRS $[0, 10^{16}]$	58 ms	83 ms	6688B

6   Conclusion

This paper presents a possible approach to design a truly-decentralized netting algorithm without compromising any security or privacy requirement. The proposed solution is optimal while still being relatively efficient as the evaluation results show. As a future work, we plan to 1) evaluate our protocol using more efficient zero-knowledge range proofs e.g. Bulletproofs [13] and 2) explore decentralized solutions for more general netting problems.

A   Proof of Optimality

We first prove for $f_i = T_i(\mathbf{x})$, then we show the result is invariant to the choice of f_i. Without loss of generality, we also assume $d_i = 0, \forall i$ to simplify proof notation. Let $\mathbf{m} = [m_1, m_2, \ldots, m_n]^\top$ and $\mathbf{T} = [T_1, T_2, \ldots, T_n]^\top \in \mathbb{R}^n$. The problem defined by Eqs. (7) to (12) can be rewritten as

$$\max_{0 \leq \mathbf{T} \leq \mathbf{m}} \sum_{i=1}^{n} T_i \tag{17}$$

$$\text{s.t. } \tilde{B}_i \overset{\text{def}}{=} \hat{B}_i - S_i(T_i) + R_i(\mathbf{T}) \geq 0, \ \forall i \in [n] \tag{18}$$

$$S_i(T_i) \overset{\text{def}}{=} \sum_{k=1}^{T_i} \text{Amt}_{i,k} \tag{19}$$

$$R_i(\mathbf{T}) \overset{\text{def}}{=} \sum_{j=1}^{n} \sum_{k=1}^{T_i} \text{Amt}_{j,k} I(\text{Rec}_{j,k} = i) \tag{20}$$

where $0 \leq \mathbf{T} \leq \mathbf{m}$ stands for $0 \leq T_i \leq m_i, \forall 1 \leq i \leq n$. Note that the definitions of $S_i(T_i)$ and $R_i(\mathbf{T})$ above implicitly model the constraints defined in (12) for each participant i. In other words, if there are T_i payments settled for participant i, $S_i(T_i)$ imply that they must be the first T_i payments in $\mathcal{Q}_i$. Let $\mathbf{T}^t$ denote the value of $\mathbf{T}$ at the tth iteration of Algorithm 1. In addition, $\mathbf{T}^0$ is set to $\mathbf{m}$ for initialization. Then Algorithm 1 essentially becomes

- Initialization: $\mathbf{T}^0 \overset{\text{def}}{=} \mathbf{m}$
- Repeat following steps
  - Calculate $R_i(\mathbf{T}^t), \forall i \in [n]$
  - $\forall i \in [n]$ find

$$T_i^{t+1} = \text{argmax}_T \left\{ T \in [m_i] \right\} \tag{21}$$

such that

$$\hat{B}_i - S_i(T_i^{t+1}) + R_i(\mathbf{T}^t) \geq 0 \tag{22}$$

$$x_{i,k+1} \leq x_{i,k}, \forall k \in [m_i - 1] \tag{23}$$

  - If $\mathbf{T}^{t+1} = \mathbf{T}^t$, stop. Otherwise, continue the loop.

The decentralized netting protocol is guaranteed to find the optimal solution. To prove this, we first prove that line 6–12 in Algorithm 1 is equivalent to Eqs. 21–23 above.

By the exit condition, we have $\tilde{B}_i^{t+1} \geq 0$. Therefore we could construct the following case, where

$$\tilde{B}_i^{t+1} = 0 \implies \hat{B}_i - S_i(T_i^{t+1}) + R_i(\mathbf{T}^t) = 0 \tag{24}$$

Suppose there exists another optimal solution $T_i > T_i^{t+1}$ and

$$\tilde{B}_i^T = \hat{B}_i - S_i(T_i) + R_i(\mathbf{T}^t) \tag{25}$$

Since

$$S_i(T_i) = \sum_{k=1}^{T_i} \text{Amt}_{i,k} > S_i(T_i^{t+1}) = \sum_{k=1}^{T_i^{t+1}} \text{Amt}_{i,k} \tag{26}$$

it implies that

$$\tilde{B}_i^T < \tilde{B}_i^{t+1} = 0 \tag{27}$$

Equation 27 clearly violates the non-overdraft condition. Therefore such T does not exist and T_i^{t+1} is the maximum value that can be achieved at $t+1$th iteration. Furthermore, we have

$$h(\mathbf{x}_i^{t+1}) = \max_k(I(x_{i,k}^{t+1}) = 1) \tag{28}$$

$$h(\mathbf{x}_i^t) = \max_k(I(x_{i,k}^t) = 1) \tag{29}$$

In view of line 12 in Algorithm 1, the above two equations imply that

$$h(\mathbf{x}_i^{t+1}) < h(\mathbf{x}_i^t) \implies x_{i,k}^{t+1} < x_{i,k}^t \tag{30}$$

$$\implies T_i^{t+1} < T_i^t \tag{31}$$

We note that the decentralized netting protocol starts with all the payment in queue and removes current invalid payments for each deficient participant. The optimality of T_i at each iteration plus the monotonicity of T_i over iterations guarantee that the first feasible solution will also be the optimal solution and it is unique.

Next, we show its invariance. If there is only one feasible solution, then it also achieves the maximum total value and number of payments. If there are two or more feasible solutions, the monotone decreasing of T_i imply that any other feasible solution after the first one contains same or fewer payments for each participant and thus less value. This completes the proof.

B Functions of the Smart Contract

In Table 2, we describe the detailed functions of our implemented smart contract.

Table 2. Functions and logic of smart contract

Functions	Logics
mintAccount	Smart contract initializes each participant's account with commitments ($cm_b = g^b h^r$) to their balances (b) and verifying zkrp ($U > b \geq 0$)
addMessage	Smart contract adds a payment message to the system with commitment ($cm_a = g^a h^r$) to payment amount (a) and verifying zkrp ($U > a \geq 0$)
grossSettlement	Smart contract settle the first payment in the outgoing queue, update account balance ($cm_b' = cm_b - cm_a$) and verify zkrp ($U > b' = b - a \geq 0$)
proposeNettableSet	Smart contract update a participant's gridlock proposal, verifying two zkrps (refer to the protocol)
tallyGridlockProposal	Smart contract calculate and check the new global nettable set. If it is the same as previous round, the gridlock resolution protocol converges
netSettlement	Smart contract settle all payment messages in the nettable set and update all parties' account balances for a successful gridlock resolution

References

1. Furgal, A., Garratt, R., Guo, Z., Hudson, D.: A proposal for a decentralized liquidity savings mechanism with side payments. R3 Report 2018
2. Bitcoin: A Peer-to-Peer Electronic Cash System. https://bitcoin.org/bitcoin.pdf
3. Chapman, J., Garratt, R., Hendry, S., MacCormack, A., McMahon, W.: Project Jasper: are distributed wholesale payment systems feasible yet. https://www.bankofcanada.ca/wp-content/uploads/2017/05/fsr-june-2017-chapman.pdf
4. Project Ubin Phase 2. https://www.mas.gov.sg/schemes-and-initiatives/Project-Ubin
5. Bech, M., Soramäki, K.: Gridlock resolution in interbank payment systems. Discussion Paper 9/2001, Bank of Finland
6. Güntzer, M., Jungnickel, D., Leclerc, M.: Efficient algorithms for the clearing of interbank payments. Eur. J. Oper. Res. **106**(1), 212–219 (1998)
7. Shafransky, Y., Doudkin, A.: An optimization algorithm for the clearing of interbank payments. Eur. J. Oper. Res. **171**(3), 743–749 (2006)
8. Wang, X., Xu, X., Feagan, L., Huang, S., Jiao, L., Zhao, W.: Inter-bank payment system on enterprise blockchain platform. In: IEEE CLOUD 2018 Cloud and Blockchain Workshop (2018)
9. Narula, N., Vasquez, W., Virza, M.: zkLedger: privacy-preserving auditing for distributed ledgers. In: 15th USENIX Symposium on Networked Systems Design and Implementation (NSDI 2018). USENIX Association (2018)
10. Poelstra, A., Back, A., Friedenbach, M., Maxwell, G., Wuille, P.: Confidential assets. In: Financial Cryptography Bitcoin Workshop. https://blockstream.com/bitcoin17-final41.pdf

11. Pedersen, T.P.: Non-interactive and information-theoretic secure verifiable secret sharing. In: Feigenbaum, J. (ed.) CRYPTO 1991. LNCS, vol. 576, pp. 129–140. Springer, Heidelberg (1992). https://doi.org/10.1007/3-540-46766-1_9
12. Camenisch, J., Chaabouni, R., Shelat, A.: Efficient protocols for set membership and range proofs. In: Pieprzyk, J. (ed.) ASIACRYPT 2008. LNCS, vol. 5350, pp. 234–252. Springer, Heidelberg (2008). https://doi.org/10.1007/978-3-540-89255-7_15
13. Bunz, B., Bootle, J., Boneh, D., Peolstra, A., Wuille, P., Maxwell, G.: Bulletproofs: short proofs for confidential transactions and more. In: 2018 IEEE Symposium on Security and Privacy (SP). IEEE (2018)
14. Hyperledger Fabric 1.2. https://hyperledger-fabric.readthedocs.io/en/release-1.2/whatis.html
15. bn256. https://golang.org/x/crypto/bn256
16. Blockchain based payment system and netting protocol implementation. http://github.com/blockchain-research/gridlock
17. Borromean Ring signature based zero-knowledge range proof implementation. http://github.com/blockchain-research/crypto
18. Package btcec implements support for the elliptic curves needed for Bitcoin, July 2017. https://godoc.org/github.com/btcsuite/btcd/btcec

The Arwen Trading Protocols

Ethan Heilman[(⊠)], Sebastien Lipmann, and Sharon Goldberg

Arwen, Boston, USA
ethan@arwen.io
http://arwen.io/

Abstract. The Arwen Trading Protocols are layer-two blockchain protocols for traders to securely trade cryptocurrencies at a centralized exchange, without ceding custody of their coins to the exchange. Before trading begins, traders deposit their coins in an on-blockchain escrow where the agent of escrow is the blockchain itself. Each trade is backed by the coins locked in escrow. Each trade is fast, because it happens off-blockchain, and secure, because atomic swaps prevent even a hacked exchange from taking custody of a trader's coins. Arwen is designed to work even with the "lowest common denominator" of blockchains—namely Bitcoin-derived coins without SegWit support. As a result, Arwen supports essentially all "Bitcoin-derived" coins *e.g.,* BTC, LTC, BCH, ZEC, as well as Ethereum. Our protocols support Limit and RFQ order types, we implemented our RFQ protocol and it is available for use at arwen.io.

1 Introduction

The promise of blockchain-backed cryptocurrencies is the ability to transact without relying on a single trusted party. Blockchains therefore present a breakthrough that circumvents a long-standing result in cryptography: namely, that *atomic swaps* are impossible without the help of a trusted third party [31]. In an atomic swap, two parties that do not trust each other swap items, such that either (1) the swap occurs, OR (2) each party reclaims their item. Atomic swaps of digital assets are possible when the blockchain acts as the trusted third party [8].

The Arwen Trading Protocols seek to deliver on this promise by bringing atomic swaps to the mainstream use case of cryptocurrency trading. With Arwen, traders benefit from the liquidity at centralized cryptocurrency exchanges without trusting the exchange with custody of their coins. Arwen traders maintain custody of their cryptographic keys and their coins. Each coin's native blockchain acts as the agent of escrow. Arwen trades are fast because they happen off blockchain, and secure, because they are atomic swaps. We have implemented and deployed the Arwen trading RFQ protocol. It is currently enabling

Major contributions to the design of these protocols were made by James Dalessandro, Ezequiel Gomes Perez, Haydn Kennedy, Yuval Marcus, Chet Powers, Omar Sagga, Aleksander Skjolsvik and Scott Sigel.

J. Bonneau and N. Heninger (Eds.): FC 2020, LNCS 12059, pp. 156–173, 2020.
https://doi.org/10.1007/978-3-030-51280-4_10

atomic swaps between Bitcoin (BTC), Bitcoin-cash (BCH), Litecoin (LTC) and Ethereum (ETH) on one of the largest global cryptocurrency exchanges, Kucoin [2].

Our protocols are specifically designed for the trading use case and supports trading instruments from traditional finance such as RFQs (Request For Quote) and limit orders. RFQs are a valuable trading instrument for atomic trades as they allow traders to swap coins immediately at current market prices. We use RFQs instead of market orders because in an RFQ, the trader learns the price the order will execute at before agreeing to execute the order, whereas in a market order the trader has no recourse if the exchange sets an absurdly low price. Limit orders are a basic and critical tool since they let a trader set their own price on an exchange's order book.

In Sect. 2 we discuss issues hampering mainstream atomic swap adoption and how Arwen overcomes them. Section 3 provides an overview of Arwen followed by our protocol for RFQs (Sect. 4) and limit orders (Sect. 5). Finally we compare Arwen to related work (Sect. 6).

2   Whither Atomic Swaps?

Cross-blockchain atomic swaps seek to supplant today's dominant form of cryptocurrency trading: *custodial trading* at centralized exchanges. With custodial trading, when users wish to trade they must first deposit their coins at the exchange; this is done using an on-blockchain transfer of coins from the user to the exchange. Trading occurs within the databases of the centralized exchange, and is not recorded on the blockchain. Finally, users can take custody of their coins by withdrawing from the exchange; that is, the exchange uses an on-blockchain transaction to send coins from the exchange back to the user. Custodial trading at a centralized exchange exposes users to serious counterparty risk—the exchange may be unable to transfer coin back to the user's wallet. This risk has been realized, starting with the hack of MtGox [42] and continuing to the present [7, 9, 10, 12, 18–20, 27, 36, 37, 44].

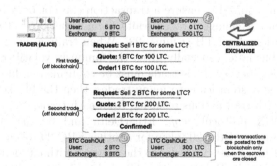

Fig. 1. Arwen Trading Protocol for two RFQ trades between the user and exchange.

The Bitcoin TierNolan Protocol. The TierNolan protocol [40] is the original Bitcoin-compatible atomic swap; it can also be used for cross-blockchain atomic swaps for "Bitcoin-like" blockchains (*e.g.,* BCH, LTC, ZEC, *etc.*). TierNolan uses *Hashed Time-Locked Contract (HTLC)* smart contracts as follows.

Bob chooses a random *solution* x and computes a *puzzle* y, where $y = H(x)$ and H is a cryptographic hash function. Bob reveals the puzzle y to Alice and keeps x secret. Next, Bob locks up 100 LTC in an HTLC smart contract on the Litecoin blockchain which stipulates: "before time tw_B, 100 LTC can be claimed by a transaction signed by Alice containing the solution to puzzle y". Alice similarly locks up 1 BTC on the Bitcoin blockchain in an HTLC, which stipulates: "before time tw_A, the 1 BTC can be claimed by a transaction signed by Bob containing the solution to the puzzle y". The atomic swap executes when Bob claims 1 BTC by posting a transaction to the Bitcoin blockchain containing x. Thus, Alice learns x and can post her solve transaction to the Litecoin blockchain and claim 100 LTC. Security follows from the fact that Bob must reveal x in order to claim his coins.

There are number of subtle issues that prevent current non-custodial trading solutions from seeing widespread adoption for cryptocurrency trading. Below we highlight several of these issues, and explain how Arwen overcomes them.

The challenge of providing liquidity. Most decentralized exchange (DEX) protocols, including EtherDelta [1], 0x [41], and SparkSwap [5], are peer-to-peer trading systems; Each trade involves a transfer of funds directly from trader Alice's wallet to trader Bob's wallet. The peer-to-peer approach limits liquidity, because Alice can only trade with traders that use that same peer-to-peer trading system. If a system has too few users, it will not be able to provide good liquidity.

Arwen eschews the peer-to-peer approach because, today, the best liquidity for cryptocurrency trading is found at centralized exchanges. With Arwen, Alice can benefit from the liquidity at a centralized exchange even if she is the only Arwen user at the exchange.

The pitfalls of on-blockchain protocols. On-blockchain protocols such as TierNolan, EtherDelta [1] and 0x [41] suffer from slow trade execution because they are bound by the speed at which blockchains confirms blocks. Many confirmations are often required to ensure a transaction can not be reversed [14] *e.g.,* the cryptocurrency exchange Kraken waits 6 confirmations (60 min) for BTC and 30 confirmations for ETH (6 min) [22]. When trading, even a few seconds of latency is problematic, especially given the famously volatile cryptocurrency prices. Even worse, if every single trade must be confirmed on-blockchain, and a healthy trading ecosystem leads to many trades, then the blockchains involved will be clogged with transactions resulting from each trade.

Ethereum DEX protocols *e.g.,* EtherDelta and 0x, use the Ethereum blockchain to trade one ERC-20 token for another ERC-20 token. In EtherDelta and 0x Alice first broadcasts an order to the network without identifying a counterparty. A counterparty Bob then sees Alice's broadcast, decides to trade with Alice, and adds his information to the order. Bob then posts the order to the blockchain. Anyone can learn the details of Alice's trade with Bob, and attempt to profit from it by front-running Bob's trade [13,41].

Arwen avoids these speed, scalability and frontrunning pitfalls, because trades execute off-blockchain.

Dealing with lockup griefing. Lockup griefing affects any protocol that requires users to lock coins in a smart contract. In TierNolan, Alice and Bob's coins are locked in smart contracts until the trade executes or the timelock on the smart contracts expires. To ensure the security of the swap, timelocks are generally a few hours long. These long expiry times creates a "lock-up griefing" problem where one party (Alice or Bob) tricks the other into pointlessly locking coins in the smart contract.

In Arwen the exchange has no incentive to launch a lockup griefing attack; such an attack harms the exchange's reputation, and prevents Alice from trading, which is the exchange's main source of revenue. The exchange, however, must protect itself from Alice who might ask the exchange to lock up coins without the intention to trade. Arwen introduces a novel escrow fee mechanism (see Sect. 3.2) that compensates the exchange for locking up coins while rewarding Alice for unlocking the exchange's coins in a timely manner.

Atomic swaps as trading instruments. To use atomic swaps to provide traditional trading instruments Arwen must avoid a misalignment of incentives. We've already discussed how Arwen aligns incentives of opening escrows; we now focus on trading incentives. Let's revisit the TierNolan protocol.

The TierNolan Protocol is asymmetric as only Bob knows the secret solution x. This means that Bob has the unilateral ability to decide whether to execute the atomic swap by revealing x (or not). Because the timelocks tw_A, tw_B on the smart contracts must at least be as long as the time it takes to confirm transactions on the blockchain, Bob has minutes or hours to decide whether market conditions justify the execution of the swap (or not). This means that the TierNolan Protocol is actually an *American call option*: namely, Bob has the right, but not the obligation, to buy 1 BTC from Alice at a strike price of 100 LTC, any time before the expiry time tw_A. Typically, the asymmetry in an option is handled by requiring Bob to pay a premium to Alice before the option is set up. However, in TierNolan Bob gets the option for free, resulting in a misalignment of incentives.

Arwen is explicitly designed to support additional trading instruments beyond the American call option. For example in Arwen's RFQ trade, the exchange commits to a price, called the *quote*, before Alice decides whether or not to place an order for the trade. (Quote: "You can buy 40 BCH, quote open for 1 second"). Importantly, RFQs are inherently asymmetric, because Alice gets to decide whether the trade executes. Therefore, to align incentives, the exchange's quote includes a spread around the current price compensating the exchange for price movements after the quote is given. If the exchange is unable to execute a trade against a quote it provided, the exchange can abort the trade. While no coins are lost, this is sufficiently harmful to the exchange's reputation that we would expect an exchange to avoid aborting if possible.

3   Arwen Overview

The Arwen Trading Protocol is a blockchain-backed two-party cryptographic
protocol between a user Alice and a centralized exchange. Alice first locks her
coins in an on-blockchain *user escrow*. Next, Alice asks the exchange to lock
its coins in an on-blockchain *exchange escrow*. To compensate the exchange
for locking up its coins, Alice pays an *escrow fee* to the exchange from Alice's
user escrow. Each trade is an off-blockchain atomic swap. From these we build
non-custodial unidirectional trading instruments for RFQs (Sect. 4) and limit
orders (Sect. 5). Our full version [17] extends our protocols from unidirectional
to bidirectional payment channels.

3.1   On-Blockchain Escrows

Escrows are opened and closed by confirming a transaction on the coin's native
blockchain. Opening and closing escrows takes the same amount of time it would
take to deposit or withdraw coins from a custodial centralized exchange.

Lets look at an example. Alice wishes to trade bitcoins for litecoins as shown
in Fig. 1. Alice funds the on-blockchain *user escrow*. The user escrow locks *e.g.,* 5
BTC from the user's wallet on the Bitcoin blockchain until the pre-agreed-upon
expiry time tw_A. The initial balance in this escrow is 5 BTC owned by the user,
and 0 BTC owned by the exchange. The exchange funds the *exchange escrow*. To
open the exchange escrow, Alice pays the exchange an escrow fee, as described
in Sect. 3.2. The exchange escrow locks 500 LTC from the exchange's wallet on
Litecoin's blockchain until some pre-agreed-upon expiry time tw_B. The initial
balance in this escrow is 0 LTC owned by the user, and 500 LTC owned by the
exchange.

Escrow smart contracts. The Arwen escrow is a timelocked two-of-two multisig smart contract that stipulates the following:

"spending requires joint signatures of the user and the exchange, OR
after time tw only the signature of the party that funded this escrow."

Escrows come with an expiry time that protect each party against a malicious
counterparty. Escrow expiry times can vary, but must be longer than the time
needed to reliably confirm a transaction on blockchain.

If the exchange and user are cooperative then escrows can be closed at any
time, even before they expire. Each escrow is closed via a jointly signed *cashout
transaction*, posted to the blockchain, that reflects the balance of the escrow.
If either counterparty is malicious the other party can unilaterally recover their
funds. These unilateral recovery procedures are specific to each of Arwen's trading instruments.

Arwen smart contracts are written in *Bitcoin-script* allowing support for
BTC, BCH, LTC, ZEC, *etc.*. The Ethereum implementation of Arwen leverages
the functionality of Ethereum smart contracts to replicate the Bitcoin-script
smart contracts. For more details see our full version [17] or our git repos[1].

---

[1] github.com/cwcrypto/arwen-eth-contracts github.com/cwcrypto/arwen-btc-scripts.

3.2   Arwen's Escrow Fee Mechanism

When an exchange funds an exchange escrow for the user the exchange locks coins in an escrow. To compensate the exchange for locking up its funds the user first pays an *escrow fee*. Arwen's escrow fees are an in-band mechanism that avoids the introduction of out-of-band payments or superfluous fee tokens. Instead the user pays the escrow fee via a fast off-blockchain transfer out of the coins locked in one of her user escrows. The escrow fee is proportional to the amount of coin locked in the exchange escrow, and to the expiry time of the exchange escrow. If the user cooperatively closes the exchange escrow early she receives a rebate of a portion of the escrow fee. This rebate is paid from the exchange escrow when it closes. See [17] for more details.

3.3   Security Model

Arwen assumes the exchange is almost always online, while the user is usually not online. Atomic swap security for users of Arwen assumes (1). The traded coins' native blockchain is secure *i.e.*, when selling or buying bitcoins we assume Bitcoin's blockchain is secure. (2). The user comes online in order to recover coins from frozen escrows during their coin-recovery time period, and to close escrows in a "timely manner". Each Arwen protocol has a specific definition of what it means to close escrows in "timely manner".

4   Unidirectional RFQs

The following protocol is *unidirectional* [38] because it only allows Alice to sell coins from her user escrow, and buy coins to her exchange escrow. See our full version [17] for details on how we port this protocol to ETH or a description of our more complex *bidirectional* RFQ protocol.

Each off-blockchain RFQ trade is backed by a user escrow (with expiry time $tw_\mathcal{A}$) and an exchange escrow (with expiry time $tw_\mathcal{B}$). The protocol for opening these escrows is in Sect. 3.1. Each trade generates a pair of *puzzle transactions* for puzzle $y = H(x)$ and solution chosen by the exchange x. One puzzle transaction spends the user escrow and has timelock $\tau_\mathcal{A}$, and the other spends the exchange escrow and has timelock $\tau_\mathcal{B}$. Each pair of puzzle transactions reflects the new balance of coins in the escrows after the trade, and "overwrites" the transactions from previous trades. This protocol enables each party to *unilaterally* close escrows with the correct balance even if the other party is malicious.

4.1   Security Assumptions

Timelocks. Security of this protocol follows from setting the timelocks to be

$$\tau_\mathcal{A} = tw_\mathcal{A} \qquad \tau_\mathcal{B} = \max(tw_\mathcal{B}, \tau_\mathcal{A} + 2\varrho) \qquad (1)$$

where ϱ is the time required for a transaction be reliably confirmed on the blockchain. There is no relationship between the escrow expiry times $(tw_{\mathcal{A}}, tw_B)$. We can pair any user escrow and exchange escrow regardless of expiry time.

Closing escrows in a timely manner. To withstand attacks by a malicious exchange the user must close her exchange escrow before it expires at time tw_B. If the user forgets to do this, an honest exchange will close the escrow on the user's behalf, but a malicious exchange may be able to steal coins from the escrow. This requirement is for exchange escrows only; there is no requirement that the user close her user escrows in a timely manner. Similarly, to withstand attacks by a compromised or malicious user the exchange must close its user escrow before it expires at time $tw_{\mathcal{A}}$. Finally, the time period in which the user can unilaterally recover coins from frozen escrows is $(tw_{\mathcal{A}}, \tau_B)$.

4.2   Off-Blockchain RFQ Trades

As shown in Fig. 1 we suppose that Alice wants to do a trade, selling 2 bitcoins for 200 litecoins. We also assume that, in all previous successfully-completed trades, Alice has sold at total 1 BTC from the user escrow and 100 LTC from the exchange escrow that are backing the current trade. Each RFQ is an off-blockchain four-message protocol comprising the following four messages.

Request. Alice requests a quote to sell 2 BTC in order to buy LTC.

Quote. The exchange responds with the quote—"2 BTC can be sold for 200 LTC, open for time δ". The exchange has now committed to executing the trade should Alice choose to place an order before the quote expires at time δ.

To commit to the quote, the exchange chooses a secret x and computes a puzzle $y = H(x)$. The exchange sends Alice a Litecoin *puzzle transaction* signed by the exchange's key, spending the output of the exchange escrow, and reflecting the current balance in the LTC exchange escrow, except that 200 LTC is locked in an HTLC smart contract stipulating

"spending requires the user's signature and the solution to puzzle y, OR after time τ_B only exchange's signature"

Order. If the user decides not to place the order, then the escrows remain open and can be used for other trades.

To place an order, Alice signs and sends the exchange a new Bitcoin *puzzle transaction* using the same puzzle y chosen by the exchange. The puzzle transaction spends the output of the user escrow and reflects the current balance in the user escrow, except that 2 BTC is locked in an HTLC smart contract stipulating

"spending requires exchange's signature and the solution to puzzle y OR after time $\tau_{\mathcal{A}}$ only user's signature"

At this point the exchange can now unilaterally decide whether or not the trade executes. (This follows because the exchange can use this puzzle transaction, and the solution x, to unilaterally close the user escrow).

Execute. If the user placed the order before time δ, then the exchange is expected to execute the trade by releasing x. After which both Alice and the exchange hold transactions that allow them to unilaterally close their escrows, reflecting the new balance after the trade. (the user can unilaterally close the exchange escrow; the exchange can unilaterally close the user escrow.) In most situations the user will prefer to keep trading against her open escrows. In this case, no transactions are posted to the blockchain and both escrows remain open.

If the exchange does not properly execute the trade by releasing x Alice will *freeze* the user escrow and exchange escrow that backed the aborted trade and launch a procedure for recovering her coins, as described in Sect. 4.5.

4.3 The Magic of Unidirectionality

The security of our protocol follows, in part, from an observation made by Spilman [38]. This is a unidirectional protocol, which means that the user can only use the exchange escrow to buy coins from the exchange. Thus, each subsequent trade changes the balance of coins in the exchange escrow such that the user holds more litecoins and the exchange holds less litecoins. For this reason, the user will always prefer to post the transactions resulting from the most recent trade to the Litecoin blockchain. This is why the Litecoin transactions resulting from a new trade will "overwrite" the Litecoin transactions of the previous trade. Both parties are incentivized to close the escrow they funded before it expires using transactions from the most recent trade. If a party goes rogue and closes the escrow they funded using transactions from a prior trade they only hurt themselves (they get fewer coins, their counter party gets more coins)!

Paying escrow fees. Unidirectionality makes it easy for the Alice to pay escrow fees out of her user escrow. Suppose that, after the second trade in Fig. 1, Alice wishes to pay an 0.02 BTC escrow fee to open a new exchange escrow. To do this, Alice signs and sends the exchange a *cashout transaction* that reflects the current balance of the user escrow, with an additional 0.02 BTC allocated to the exchange. The same unidirectional argument means that the exchange is incentivized to have this cashout transaction "overwrite" the puzzle transaction received from the previous trade.

4.4 Cooperative Close

If neither the user or the exchange are unresponsive or malicious, escrows can be closed prior to their expiry using the cooperative close. Both parties jointly sign and post *cashout transactions* spending and reflecting the final balance of each escrow. Cooperatively closing is in the interest of both parties. It reduces mining fees by closing an escrow with a single transaction rather than two (*i.e.,* the puzzle and solve transactions) and a cooperative close of the exchange escrow rebates the user some escrow fees.

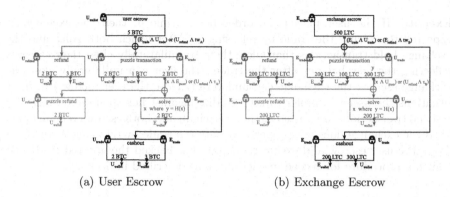

(a) User Escrow   (b) Exchange Escrow

Fig. 2. Unidirectional RFQ protocol transaction diagram. Balances are per Fig. 1. Green and blue transactions unilaterally close the escrow if a counterparty is uncooperative. Purple transactions refund the escrow after it expires at time tw_A or tw_B. Magenta transactions refund the puzzle transactions after the expiry time τ_A or τ_B. The $\oplus$ symbol is an XOR: only one of the transactions from the $\oplus$ can be posted to the blockchain. The lock symbol represents a signature. (Color figure online)

4.5   Unilaterally Closing an Open Escrow

What happens if the user and exchange fail to cooperatively close an escrow?

First we consider the case where all trades against the escrow have properly completed. If the exchange refuses to close an exchange escrow before time tw_B Alice signs and posts the latest puzzle and solve transactions releasing the final balance to both parties. If Alice does not close the exchange escrow before time tw_B the exchange can unilaterally close the exchange escrow after it expires at time tw_B using a *refund transaction* (Fig. 2(b)). If the user Alice forgets to close the user escrow before time tw_A, then the exchange signs and posts the latest puzzle and solve transactions unilaterally closing the user escrow. If the exchange refuses to close the user escrow, the user waits until the user escrow expires at tw_A, and unilaterally closes the user escrow via a *refund transaction.*

Next we consider the case where Alice places an order against a quote provided by the exchange, but the exchange does not release the preimage x. Alice asks the exchange to cooperatively close the user escrow backing this trade. If the exchange refuses Alice unilaterally closes the exchange escrow by posting the puzzle transaction from the aborted trade. The coins from the aborted trade are now locked in the puzzle transaction's smart contract until time τ_B. We call these coins the *outstanding coins*. If the exchange executes the aborted trade the outstanding coins belong to Alice; otherwise, the outstanding coins belong to the exchange. To claim the outstanding coins whenever they are rightfully hers, Alice comes online during time window (tw_A, τ_B) and performs the correct action for each case:

User escrow closed using a successful trade. The exchange closed the user escrow on the Bitcoin blockchain via a puzzle transaction for any trade *prior to* the aborted trade. No further action is needed from Alice. The outstanding coins rightfully belong to the exchange. The exchange uses a puzzle-refund transaction to unilaterally claim the coins once the timelock τ_B expires.

User escrow closed using the aborted trade. The exchange closed the user escrow on the Bitcoin blockchain via a puzzle transaction for the aborted trade, as well as its corresponding solve transaction. Alice learns the solution x from the Bitcoin solve transaction and uses x to claim her coins on the Litecoin blockchain via a solve transaction. She must complete this action before τ_B as the outstanding coins can be unilaterally claimed by the exchange after τ_B.

User escrow partially closed. The exchange posted the puzzle transaction for the aborted trade, but the coins locked in this puzzle transaction on the *Bitcoin blockchain* are unspent. Alice recovers the coins locked in the puzzle output from the *user escrow* by unilaterally posting a puzzle-refund transaction to the Bitcoin blockchain after the timelock expires at time τ_A.

User escrow not closed. The exchange did not execute the aborted trade. To recover her coins in the user escrow Alice posts the refund transaction. This must be done after the user escrow expires at tw_A and before τ_B.

4.6 Deployment Status

We implemented the unidirectional RFQ protocol described in this section. A release of our trading software is currently available for download enabling users to atomically trade on the orderbook of the centralized exchange kucoin. We support BTC, BCH, LTC and ETH on their respect mainnets. Our client is composed of a daemon written in C# which acts as the user's agent in the protocol and a graphical interface written in typescript. The other protocols described in this paper *e.g.,* limit orders, have not yet been implemented.

5   Limit Orders

In this section we introduce off-blockchain atomic trading protocols for *All-or-None (AoN) limit orders* and *partial-fill limit orders*. Our limit order protocols allow the user Alice to place a order for a specified amount and limit price against a (user escrow, exchange escrow) pair. For example, Alice might say "I will sell 3.1 BTC at the price of 1 BTC for 100 LTC". In our *All-or-None limit order*, this order would remain open until the limit price is met for the entire amount, then the exchange would execute the entire order (*e.g.,* Alice sells 3.1 BTC and buys 310 LTC). In our partial-fill limit order the exchange can execute or fill the order in increments *e.g.,* the exchange could execute the trade 0.3 BTC for 30 LTC. Then later when the price is met again, the exchange could fill (*aka,* execute) an additional trade of 0.8 BTC for 80 LTC. Unlike RFQs, limit orders can remain open for long periods of time. The user can cancel her limit order at any time. When the user cancels a partial-fill limit order, she only cancels the unfilled part of the order (*e.g.,* if Alice's order has already filled for 110 LTC,

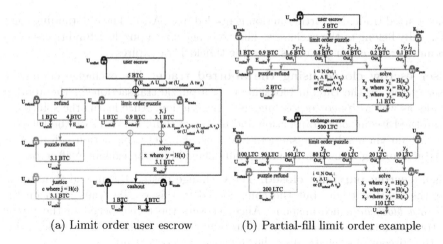

(a) Limit order user escrow   (b) Partial-fill limit order example

Fig. 3. (a). User Escrow modified for limit orders by adding a cancel condition on the puzzle output (b). Unilaterally closed partial-fill limit order with $N = 5$ puzzle outputs

the remaining 200 LTC of the order is canceled, with result being that Alice sold 1.1 BTC to buy 110 LTC).

Technically speaking, our limit orders protocols and transactions are very similar to our RFQ protocol (Sect. 4) with one exception. We add the ability for the exchange to "cancel" a limit order after the user places it. To ensure the exchange can not steal the user's funds by posting canceled orders, our cancel functionality must be cryptographically enforceable by the user. This change is necessary because limit orders, unlike RFQs, are not designed to execute immediately and can stay open indefinitely. Users often cancel and reissue limit orders depending on market conditions.

Canceling user escrow puzzles
We modify the user escrow puzzle transaction so the puzzle output stimulates:

"spending requires the user's signature and the cancel value c
OR after time τ_C the exchanges signature and the solution to puzzle y
OR after time τ_A the user's signature."

Figure 3(a) shows our modified user escrow. For each user escrow puzzle transaction the exchange randomly chooses a secret cancel value c, hashes it to generate $\jmath = H(c)$, and uses $\jmath$ as the cancel condition in the puzzle transaction puzzle output. When the exchange wishes to cancel the puzzle output, it sends c to the user. We say the output is "canceled" because, if the exchange misbehaves by posting the transaction that contains that output, the then user can retaliate and claim all coins in the canceled output at anytime before time τ_C.

5.1 Security Assumptions

Timelocks. Security of this protocol follows from setting the timelocks to be

$$tw_{\mathcal{A}} + 2\varrho < \tau_C \qquad \tau_C + 2\varrho < \tau_{\mathcal{A}} \qquad \tau_{\mathcal{B}} = \max(tw_{\mathcal{B}}, \tau_{\mathcal{A}} + 2\varrho) \qquad (2)$$

where ϱ is the time required for a transaction be reliably confirmed on the blockchain. There is no enforced relationship between the escrow expiry times $(tw_{\mathcal{A}}, tw_{\mathcal{B}})$. Escrows can be paired regardless of expiry time.

Closing escrows in a timely manner. As in Sect. 4.1 the user must close her exchange escrow before it expires at time $tw_{\mathcal{B}}$. Similarly, to withstand attacks by a malicious user, the exchange must close its user escrow before it expires at time $tw_{\mathcal{A}}$. However in limit orders, the user must now come online between $tw_{\mathcal{A}}$ and τ_C to either post her user escrow refund or if a malicious exchange has posted a canceled puzzle output the user must then use the cancel value c to claim the coins from that output. Finally, the time period in which the user can unilaterally recover coins from frozen escrows is $(tw_{\mathcal{A}}, \tau_{\mathcal{B}})$.

Prior to opening a limit order on an escrow pair, the user and the exchange must cancel any currently open limit orders on that escrow pair using the *Cancel Limit Order* procedure.

5.2 All-or-None (AoN) Limit Orders

This protocol allows the user to place a limit order for a specified amount and price against a (user escrow, exchange escrow) pair. The order remains open until the limit price is met for the entire amount. Once the limit price is met, the exchange executes the order.

Limit Order. To place the limit order, the user specifies the amount and the limit price *e.g.*, "I will sell 3.1 BTC at the price of 1 BTC per 100 LTC". To place the limit order, the user and exchange perform the "Request", "Quote" and "Order" steps of the RFQ protocol in Sect. 4.2 for the price that the user requested. The exchange now has the ability to execute or fill the limit order by posting the user escrow solve and puzzle transactions thereby releasing x.

Execute Limit Order. To execute the order, the exchange performs the "Execute" step of the unidirectional RFQ protocol in Sect. 4.2. This fills the order at the limit price for the specified amount.

Cancel Limit Order. The user can cancel her order at any time after placing it and prior to it being filled. She can't force the exchange to participate in the cancel protocol, but if the exchange does complete the protocol, even a malicious exchange can't execute the order. To do this the user requests the order be canceled. In reply the exchange releases the cancel value c for the user escrow puzzle transaction used to place the limit order. This cancels the limit order since if the exchange misbehaves and posts the canceled puzzle transaction the user can reclaim the coins the exchange would be buying in the trade.

5.3   Partial-Fill Limit Orders

We now show how to use our All-or-None Limit Order Protocol from Sect. 5.2 to construct a partial-fill limit order *i.e.*, an order that can be incrementally filled/executed at the limit price. Partial fill limit orders are important for trading as they are the default order type supported by all centralized exchanges. In fact, partial-fill limit orders are so basic that the term *limit orders* typically refers to partial-fill limit orders. Our partial-fill limit order is composed of N All-or-None limit orders (Sect. 5.2), which we call *sub-orders*. By selectively executing some of these sub-orders and not-executing others, the exchange is able to control how much of the limit order fills.

Our partial fill limit order will use puzzle transactions with N puzzle outputs rather than a single puzzle output as done in our other protocols. These N puzzle outputs $Out_1, \ldots Out_N$ place N different All-or-None limit *sub-orders*. We denote the amount of coin the i-th sub-order locks in out_i as a_i. The amounts $a_1, \ldots a_N$ locked in the N outputs are chosen such that each amount decreases by one half from the previous amount, $a_i = \frac{1}{2} \times a_{i+1}$ and that they sum to the total amount $A = \sum_{i=1}^{N} a_i$ which the user is selling in partial-fill limit order. Thus, for any N and A we determine the amount a_i to lock in a puzzle output out_i as

$$a_i = \frac{A(2^{N-i})}{(2^N - 1)} \tag{3}$$

Using this sub-orders the exchange can execute as limit order trade for any amount between 0 to A in increments of $a_N = A/(2^N - 1)$.

Lets look at the example in Fig. 3(b), Alice placed a limit order selling $A = 3.1$ BTC for $A = 310$ LTC. Thus if we set $N = 5$ Alice's user escrow puzzle output amounts would be $a_1 = 1.6, a_2 = 0.8, a_3 = 0.4, a_4 = 0.2, a_5 = 0.1$ (BTC) and using the price she set her exchange escrow puzzle output amounts are $a_1 = 160, a_2 = 80, a_3 = 40, a_4 = 20, a_5 = 10$ (LTC). By selectively executing only the All-or-None sub-orders in Out_2, Out_4, Out_5 the exchange fills the order so that Alice sells $0.8 + 0.2 + 0.1 = 1.1$ BTC and buys $80 + 20 + 10 = 110$ LTC.

Once a user opens a partial-fill limit order it stays open until (a). the user cancels it, (b). it fills completely, or (c). one of the parties unilaterally closes the user or exchange escrows. To determine how much of her limit order has filled the user runs the *Update Limit Order* protocol with the exchange.

Limit Order. To place the limit order, the user specifies the amount A and the limit price *e.g.*, "I will sell 3.1 BTC at price of 1 BTC per 100 LTC". The user and exchange then perform the Limit Order step of our all-or-nothing protocol N-times. Creating one puzzle transaction per escrow, with each puzzle transaction having N puzzle outputs. Since the exchange knows the solutions $x_0 \ldots x_N$ the exchange can release a subset of these puzzles to fill the order by amount it fills on the exchange's order book.

Update Limit Order. If the user is online, she can query the exchange to learn how much of the limit order she placed has been filled. To do this, the exchange signs and sends the user a new exchange escrow puzzle transaction reflecting the balance of the coins which have been bought and sold as part of the fill. This new exchange escrow puzzle transaction contains a new set of puzzle outputs holding the smaller yet to be filled remainder of the order. In reply, the user signs and sends the exchange a new user escrow puzzle transaction with puzzle outputs mirroring those in the new exchange escrow puzzle transaction. The exchange then releases all the cancel values $c_1, \ldots c_N$ for the previous user escrow puzzle transaction. If the order filled completely, then the order is moved to closed, and cashout transactions are used in place of puzzle transactions.

Cancel Limit Order. The user can ask the exchange to cancel her order at any time after she places the order. This is exactly like our Update Limit Order but both parties exchange cashouts rather than puzzle transactions.

5.4   Closing Limit Orders

We will describe the process for closing escrows whose last trade was a partial-fill limit order. All-or-None limit orders can be treated as a specific case of the partial-fill protocol where $N = 1$. The limit order cooperative close is the same as used by our RFQs protocol in Sect. 4.4.

Our unilateral close is very similar to the unilateral close and aborts given in unidirectional RFQ protocol given in Sect. 4.5. However the addition of a cancel on the user escrow puzzle transaction places new requirements on the user and the exchange. The magic of unidirectionality (Sect. 4.3) protects both the user and the exchange from the other party posting old cashout transactions.

To unilaterally close an exchange escrow the user Alice posts the latest exchange escrow cashout or puzzle transaction. She must come online after $tw_{\mathcal{A}}$ and before τ_C to check if the exchange has unilaterally closed the associated user escrow. If the user escrow has not been spent she signs and posts the refund transaction and is done. If on the other hand it has been spent there are three cases. The user escrow was spent with: (1) the most recent cashout transaction in which case the user is done, (2) a canceled puzzle transaction in which case she claims the coins in the puzzle outputs, or (3) the latest puzzle transaction in which case she then waits until $\tau_{\mathcal{A}}$ after which she claims the unspent puzzle outputs with a refund transaction and uses the solutions in the spent puzzle outputs to claim her coins from the exchange escrow.

The exchange must come online before $tw_{\mathcal{A}}$ to post the latest user escrow cashout or puzzle transaction. If the exchange posted a puzzle transaction it must wait until τ_C to spend the puzzle outputs by posting a solve transaction containing some of the $x_1, \ldots x_N$ solutions reflecting the how much of the limit order filled. After τ_B the exchange must come online and may post an escrow refund transaction or a puzzle refund transaction refunding the unsolved and unspent puzzle outputs closing the exchange escrow.

6 Related Work

Atomic swap protocols. The first description of an atomic swap is commonly attributed to TierNolan's 2013 forum post [40]. Many works have since explored atomic swaps [4,23,32,34], including cross-chain auctions [35], improved fungibility [16,24], trading across blockchains [5,6] and forks [26] or between tokens on Ethereum's blockchain [33]. An alternative approach to cross-chain atomic swaps is the trustless issuance of pegged tokens [30,43].

Layer-two or Off-blockchain protocols. A layer-two blockchain protocol [29] binds off-blockchain transfers of funds to an on-blockchain smart contract. Typically they do not require the addition of a trusted third party, trusted oracle, or trusted gateway. There has been a variety of work on layer-two protocols for Bitcoin [11,16,23,32,34,38], where transfers of funds are accomplished via atomic swaps. In 2013, Spilman's unidirectional payment channel was the first to use the "magic of unidirectionality" that Arwen uses in Sect. 4.3. Meanwhile, bidirectional payment channels for Bitcoin payments were first proposed by [11,34], and significant progress has been made on the Lightning Network [3]. Today's Lightning Network requires SegWit, and thus only supports Bitcoin and Litecoin, while Arwen does not require SegWit and thus supports more Bitcoin-derived coins, including BCH, ZEC. [23,32] build layer-two protocols "scriptlessly", without smart contracts, by cleverly leveraging digital signatures. BOLT [15] is a layer two payments protocol with very strong privacy guarantees designed for Zcash. Sparkswap [5] is a peer-to-peer trading platform for BTC and LTC built on top of Lightning. Bitcoin covenants [28] proposes a change to Bitcoin allowing coins to carry scripts even after they are spent.

Smart contracts on Ethereum are Turing-complete, and thus support a dramatically richer set of operations than smart contacts written in Bitcoin Script. Thus, it is no surprise that Ethereum supports layer two protocols including "state channels" [4,25]. Plasma [33] is a proposal for a layer-two decentralized exchange protocol on Ethereum. Similar to Plasma is NOCUST [21] which uses zkSNARKs to ensure correctness of state updates and employs collateral-based protocols for faster transaction finality. Truebit is a fascinating approach, where computations (rather than payments) are moved off the Ethereum blockchain via a layer-two protocol [39]. Generally speaking [4,21,25,33,39] are for Ethereum and ERC-20s only, and so they leverage the richness of Ethereum smart contracts.

Fees. Payment focused protocols typically structure incentives around transaction fees, *i.e.,* fees earned when payments are made. This does not solve the problem of lockup griefing because no fees are earned if no payments are made. Arwen addresses this via escrow fees and reputation. Komodo [6] also aims to solve the lockup griefing problem for on-blockchain atomic swaps using fees.

7 Conclusion

Arwen is a layer-two blockchain trading protocol allowing traders to benefit from liquidity at centralized exchanges without trusting exchanges with custody of their coins. Instead, Arwen trades are backed by on-blockchain escrows, and executed via fast off-blockchain atomic swaps. Arwen's RFQ protocol has been implemented and is currently deployed offering secure RFQ trades. Arwen solves many of the incentive issues that emerge when payment protocols are repurposed for cryptocurrency trading. Arwen supports a wide range of coins including Bitcoin, "Bitcoin fork" coins (BCH, LTC *etc.*), and Ethereum.

Acknowledgments. The authors would like to thank Underscore VC, Digital Garage, Notation, United Bitcoiners, Highland Capital Partners, and the Cybersecurity Factory for their support of Arwen. We also acknowledge Patrick McCorry, Ben Jones, David Vorick and our anonymous reviewers for their valuable feedback.

References

1. Etherdelta. https://etherdelta.com/
2. KuCoin: Download arwen to trade on KuCoin directly from your wallet. https://www.kucoin.com/page/arwen
3. Lightning daemon (LND). https://github.com/lightningnetwork/lnd
4. Raiden network. https://raiden.network/
5. Sparkswap. https://sparkswap.com/
6. Komodo. White paper, 3 June 2018
7. Baldwin, C.: Bitcoin worth $72 million stolen from Bitfinex exchange in Hong Kong. Reuters, 3 August 2016
8. Barber, S., Boyen, X., Shi, E., Uzun, E.: Bitter to better—how to make bitcoin a better currency. In: Keromytis, A.D. (ed.) FC 2012. LNCS, vol. 7397, pp. 399–414. Springer, Heidelberg (2012). https://doi.org/10.1007/978-3-642-32946-3_29
9. Bloomberg. CoincheckHack: How to Steal $500 Million in Cryptocurrency. Fortune, 31 January 2018
10. Buterin, V.: Bitfloor Hacked, $250,000 Missing. Bitcoin Magazine, 5 September 2012
11. Decker, C., Wattenhofer, R.: A fast and scalable payment network with bitcoin duplex micropayment channels. In: Pelc, A., Schwarzmann, A.A. (eds.) SSS 2015. LNCS, vol. 9212, pp. 3–18. Springer, Cham (2015). https://doi.org/10.1007/978-3-319-21741-3_1
12. DeMartino, I.: Mintpal hacked 'considerable amount' of vericoin stolen. Cointelegraph, 13 July 2014
13. Eskandari, S., Moosavi, S., Clark, J.: SoK: transparent dishonesty: front-running attacks on blockchain. In: Bracciali, A., Clark, J., Pintore, F., Rønne, P.B., Sala, M. (eds.) FC 2019. LNCS, vol. 11599, pp. 170–189. Springer, Cham (2020). https://doi.org/10.1007/978-3-030-43725-1_13
14. Gervais, A., Karame, G.O., Wüst, K., Glykantzis, V., Ritzdorf, H., Capkun, S.: On the security and performance of proof of work blockchains. In: Proceedings of the 2016 ACM SIGSAC Conference on Computer and Communications Security, pp 3–16. ACM (2016)

15. Green, M., Miers, I.: Bolt: anonymous payment channels for decentralized currencies. In: Proceedings of the 2017 ACM SIGSAC Conference on Computer and Communications Security, pp. 473–489. ACM (2017)
16. Heilman, E., Alshenibr, L., Baldimtsi, F., Scafuro, A., Goldberg, S.: Tumblebit: an untrusted bitcoin-compatible anonymous payment hub. In: Network and Distributed System Security Symposium (2017)
17. Heilman, E., Lipmann, S., Goldberg, S.: The arwen trade protocols (full version). IACR Cryptology ePrint Archive (2020)
18. Higgins, S.: Details of 5 Million Bitstamp Hack Revealed. Coindesk, 1 July 2015
19. Higgins, S.: Cryptsy threatens bankruptcy, claims millions lost in bitcoin heist. Coindesk, 15 January 2016
20. Higgins, S.: Bitcoin exchange youbit to declare bankruptcy after hack. Coindesk, 19 December 2017
21. Khalil, R., Gervais, A.: NOCUST-A Non-Custodial 2nd-Layer Financial Intermediary. IACR Cryptology ePrint Archive (2018)
22. Kraken. How long do digital assets/cryptocurrency deposits take?
23. Malavolta, G., Moreno-Sanchez, P., Schneidewind, C., Kate, A., Maffei, M.: Anonymous Multi-Hop Locks for Blockchain Scalability and Interoperability. In: Network and Distributed System Security Symposium (NDSS) (2019)
24. Maxwell, G.: CoinSwap:Transaction graph disjoint trustless trading. Bitcoin-talk (2013)
25. McCorry, P., Bakshi, S., Bentov, I., Miller, A., Meiklejohn, S.: Pisa: arbitration outsourcing for state channels. IACR Cryptology ePrint Archive (2018)
26. McCorry, P., Heilman, E., Miller, A.: Atomically trading with roger: gambling on the success of a hardfork. In: Garcia-Alfaro, J., Navarro-Arribas, G., Hartenstein, H., Herrera-Joancomartí, J. (eds.) ESORICS/DPM/CBT -2017. LNCS, vol. 10436, pp. 334–353. Springer, Cham (2017). https://doi.org/10.1007/978-3-319-67816-0_19
27. Morris, D.Z.: BitGrailCryptocurrency Exchange Claims $195 Million Lost to Hac kers. Coindesk, 11 February 2018
28. Möser, M., Eyal, I., Gün Sirer, E.: Bitcoin covenants. In: Clark, J., Meiklejohn, S., Ryan, P.Y.A., Wallach, D., Brenner, M., Rohloff, K. (eds.) FC 2016. LNCS, vol. 9604, pp. 126–141. Springer, Heidelberg (2016). https://doi.org/10.1007/978-3-662-53357-4_9
29. Narula, N.: The Importance of Layer 2, 27 May 2018
30. Keep Network. tBTC A Decentralized Redeemable BTC-backed ERC-20 Token (2019)
31. Pagnia, H., Gärtner, F.C.: On the impossibility of fair exchange without a trusted third party. Technical report, TTUD-BS-1999-02, Darmstadt University of Technology (1999)
32. Poelstra, A.: Scriptless Scripts (2018)
33. Poon, J., Buterin, V.: Plasma: scalable autonomous smart contracts (2017)
34. Poon, J., Dryja, T.: The bitcoin lightning network (2016)
35. Prestwich,   J.:   Summa.One: Cross-chain Auctions via Bitcoin Double Spends (2018)
36. Rizzo, P.: Poloniex Loses 12.3% of its Bitcoins in Latest Bitcoin Exchange Hack. Coindesk, 5 March 2014
37. Russell, J.: Korean crypto exchange coinrail loses over $40m in tokens following a hack. Techcrunch, 10 June 2018
38. Spilman, J.: [bitcoin-development] anti dos for tx replacement, 20 April 2013

39. Teutsch, J., Reitwießner, C.: A scalable verification solution for blockchains (2017)
40. TierNolan. Re: Alt chains and atomic transfers. Bitcoin-talk, 21 May 2013
41. Warren, W.: Front-running, Griefing and the Perils of Virtual Settlement (2017)
42. Wikipedia. Mt. Gox
43. Zamyatin, A., Harz, D., Lind, J., Panayiotou, P., Gervais, A., Knottenbelt, W.: XCLAIM: trustless, interoperable, cryptocurrency-backed assets. In: IEEE Security and Privacy. IEEE (2019)
44. Zhao, W.: Crypto exchange zaif hacked in $60 million bitcoin theft. Coindesk, 20 September 2018

SoK: A Classification Framework for Stablecoin Designs

Amani Moin[1,2(✉)], Kevin Sekniqi[1,2], and Emin Gun Sirer[1,2]

[1] Cornell University, Ithaca, NY 14853, USA
{amani,kevin,egs}@avalabs.org
[2] AVA Labs, Brooklyn, NY 11232, USA

Abstract. Stablecoins promise to bridge fiat currencies with the world of cryptocurrencies. They provide a way for users to take advantage of the benefits of digital currencies, such as ability to transfer assets over the internet, credibly commit to minting schedules, and enable new asset classes, while also partially mitigating their volatility risks. In this paper, we systematically discuss general design, decompose existing stablecoins into various component design elements, explore their strengths and drawbacks, and identify future directions.

Keywords: Stablecoins · Stable payments

1 Introduction

Cryptoasset prices are famous for their volatility. Though many cryptoassets aspire to become world currencies, most are frequently dismissed as no more than speculative assets due to their wild price swings.

Money is supposed to have three functions: a store of value, a unit of account, and a medium of exchange. Stability is key to all these functions. Store of value is the most salient; if people store their wealth in an asset that constantly fluctuates in value, their wealth will fluctuate accordingly. A volatile asset is also a poor unit of account, because it is inconvenient to denominate prices in something which constantly changes in value. Every time the value of the unit of account changes, all prices must be adjusted accordingly. Finally, and most crucially, a currency needs to be stable to function as a medium of exchange; this allows people to be fairly and predictably compensated for goods and services without changes in value during the payment process.

Stablecoins are a class of cryptoassets created to provide the stability money needs to function. As the name implies, they are designed to be price stable with respect to some reference point, such as USD. There has recently been an explosion in the number of stablecoin projects announced, especially following the crash in Bitcoin prices in early 2018. There are over a hundred stablecoins in existence or in progress, with the top three projects now representing a market capitalization of $4.6B [22]. Although the sheer number of projects seems overwhelming, they can all be decomposed into a few key features.

© International Financial Cryptography Association 2020
J. Bonneau and N. Heninger (Eds.): FC 2020, LNCS 12059, pp. 174–197, 2020.
https://doi.org/10.1007/978-3-030-51280-4_11

Roadmap. We briefly review related works in Sect. 2. In Sect. 3, we break down the taxonomy of stablecoins based on the first three constituent axes: the peg type, the collateral type, and the collateral amount. In Sect. 4, we expand on additional axes by discussing the stabilization mechanism chosen by various stablecoin families. In Sect. 5 we discuss methods to measure prices. In Sect. 6, we discuss some design features relevant to digital currencies in general, but especially important for stablecoins. Finally, we discuss future directions for stablecoins in Sect. 7.

2   Related Work

One of the first stablecoin taxonomies classified stablecoin projects by collateral type and discussed pros and cons of each category [55]. Several papers and reports have followed a similar taxonomy, adding more detail on individual projects [47,56,57]. A paper by Pernice et al. takes a different approach, categorizing stablecoins by monetary and exchange rate regimes [53]. Our contribution is extending the existing taxonomies with a discussion of other important stablecoin design aspects, namely price stabilizing mechanisms and price measurement methods. We also categorize many of the existing stablecoin projects according to our extended taxonomy (Fig. 1).

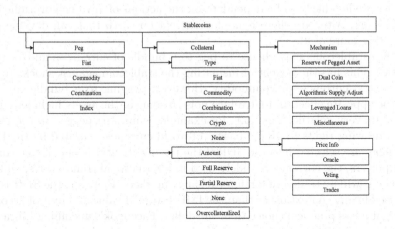

Fig. 1. Stablecoin taxonomy, decomposed into four main axes: peg, collateral, mechanism, and price information.

3   Peg and Collateral

3.1   Peg

The most salient choice for stablecoin design is the peg, or what the stablecoin is meant to stay stable relative to. This choice is so significant that it is often included in the name of the stablecoin.[1] USD is a popular choice, likely due to USD being typically considered a stable store of value around the world. In fact, it is not uncommon for foreign citizens, especially those in emerging and developing economies, to store their wealth in USD rather than their national currency. The other benefit of using USD is that price comparison is easy. A singular fiat currency peg allows one to check whether the peg holds by simply comparing the dollar price of an object to the pegged coin price of the same object. However, this feature can also be a drawback, since it becomes very obvious if the price stabilization mechanism is not working. Other stable fiat currencies, such as the Euro, the Japanese Yen, and the Swiss Franc, are also popular choices for similar reasons. The largest drawback to pegging a stablecoin to a fiat currency is that it is often more convenient to simply hold the fiat currency itself. Cash can be used for transactions that are arguably more instant and anonymous, and electronic transfers of fiat are usually easy, fast, and cheap.

Besides fiat, there are also stablecoins pegged to commodities, most commonly gold. Some examples include Digix [27] and HelloGold [31]. It is interesting to note that, in general, there are fewer commodity-pegged coins than fiat-pegged coins. A possible explanation is that commodity prices fluctuate in value more than fiat currencies, although typically less severely than most digital currencies. This makes commodity pegged stablecoins a less viable form of money than a fiat pegged one. On the other hand, stablecoins pegged to commodities are less likely to be dependent on the actions of any one government or central bank. After all, there is no government on earth that can devalue gold by printing more of it.

Other stablecoins may choose to peg to a bundle of currencies and/or commodities. This has the benefit of insulating the stablecoin against shocks to any one country, currency, or commodity. However, pegging to a bundle can also have the opposite effect and introduce noise if some of the assets included in the bundle are very volatile. Saga [59], for example, is initially pegged to the IMF's special drawing rights (SDR), a basket of world currencies curated by the IMF. Currencies are selected into the SDR if the issuing country is one of the world's top exporters, the currency is widely used in international transactions, and the currency is widely traded in foreign exchange markets. However, the SDR is seldom used in any context other than the IMF's store of value and unit of account, making it a less practical choice than the dollar. Facebook's upcoming Libra also plans to peg its currency to an as of yet undetermined basket of currencies and assets.

Saga plans to later peg their currency to the consumer price index (CPI) if they outgrow the SDR, i.e. if they become a dominant world currency. The CPI is a unitless index which tracks the inflation of the price of a basket of consumer goods. No stablecoin is currently pegged to the CPI, so it is unclear how this would be executed. It is possible, for example, that the stablecoin supply would be adjusted so the nominal price level remains constant. Pegging to a

---

[1] Examples include TrueUSD [68], USDC [20], USDX [54], USDVault [70], A-Eurs [60], and many others.

fiat currency or commodity with finite supply can eventually lead to problems of scale, and pegging to an index can circumvent this problem.[2] However, the choice of CPI as a peg is not ideal for a variety of reasons. It is typically measured monthly or even less frequently, due to logistical challenges in determining what should be in the basket and how much each component should be weighted. There are also regional differences in consumption, so it is unclear how to construct a basket that reflects global spending patterns.

3.2 Collateral

Emergent currencies often make use of collateral to ensure that the circulating currency has redemption value. This provides a lower bound on the price, thereby mitigating some of the risk of holding, using, and denominating debts in the currency. Since the goal of collateralizing is to bound the redemption value, it is easiest and most effective, but not necessary,[3] to use whatever the stablecoin is pegged to. Assuming that the stablecoin initially trades at the pegged price and users can redeem one unit of the stablecoin for one dollar, arbitrageurs should ensure that there are no persistent long term deviations from the target price.

Unfortunately, collateralizing a coin creates the problem of securely storing large quantities of the collateral. Traditionally, the best place to store large quantities of cash is in a bank because it is secure, relatively easy to audit, and often comes with deposit insurance. However, this is also centralized, thus making it prone to deceptive practices. For example, Tether [65] recently admitted it was only 74% collateralized [64], despite initially claiming full collateralization [65]. Moreover, there are often limits to how much deposit insurance covers, potentially leaving the majority of the reserve uninsured.[4] Some stablecoins avoid this problem by storing their collateral in a network of banks instead of a single one (USDC) or as physical cash in a vault instead of a bank (Rockz). For example, Rockz [58] stores 90% of its collateral in the form of physical fiat currency in an underground vault in the Swiss Alps.

Commodity backed stablecoins also suffer from the problem of where to store their collateral, since there are fewer institutions which accept and insure deposits in the form of commodities than ones that accept cash. This, in turn, leads to a high degree of centralization. One possible alternative, currently not in use, would be to collateralize using assets that track the price of these commodities rather than the commodities themselves. For example, it would be logistically simpler to collateralize using gold futures rather than gold bars. However, this design choice could lead to different types of legal issues.

One way to avoid having to store large amounts of fiat is to collateralize with another cryptocurrency. This has the advantage of potentially decentralized operation, and allows for easier diversification across backing assets. The problem

---

[2] This is one of the reasons the US went off of the gold standard.

[3] USDVault for example is pegged to USD but collateralized with gold.

[4] There has thus far been no regulatory precedent establishing how much protection end users of stablecoins receive from deposit insurance.

with this approach is that digital collateral can itself be very volatile, making it hard to use as a guarantee of value. Any stablecoin backed by cryptocurrencies must have some mechanism built in to safely handle large swings in the value of the underlying collateral. We discuss these mechanisms in Sect. 4.

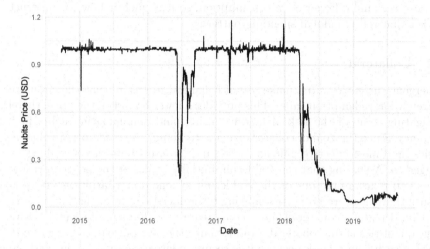

Fig. 2. NuBits price collapse

Other stablecoins do away with the problem of volatile collateral by simply not collateralizing the currency at all. This has many advantages. First, not having any collateral to store or transfer simplifies many logistical challenges. Second, it is also cheap to operate, since it does not require the issuer to keep real or cryptoassets on hand. Third, stablecoins that are not collateralized can not limited in scale by the circulating amount of the underlying collateral. Unfortunately, this ease of operation comes with drawbacks. Algorithms are usually gameable. The value of the currency in this case stems purely from the reliability of the issuing mechanism and/or people's beliefs. Once users' expectations of the coin's stability change, whether due to a flaw in design or idiosyncratic changes in sentiment, there may be little to keep the price afloat because there is no inherent redemption value. Consequently, when these stablecoins fail, they tend to do so swiftly and catastrophically. One example is NuBits [44], which dropped from its pegged price of $1 to less than $0.30 over the course of 2 weeks in early 2018. It never recovered its peg, and has been trading below $0.10 for the past six months[5] (Fig. 2).

---

[5] Note that USD is not collateralized, and yet it remains stable. However, when the dollar was a fledgling currency it was backed by gold. It was only after extensive global adoption that the backing was gradually eased-off. Additionally, the US government has the infrastructure to support this type of regime. US federal law makes it so that businesses are required to accept US issued currency as legal tender. There are also regulatory and executive agencies that enforce compliance.

3.3   Collateral Amount

Hand in hand with the decision of collateral type comes the decision of collateral amount. Since collateral serves to support the price by creating a reliable redemption value, the best choice seems to be a fully collateralized stablecoin. However, one to one collateralization is sometimes excessive, and sometimes insufficient.

Having a full reserve, where the value of the collateral is exactly the value of the circulating currency, makes it hard for a currency to scale. As the stablecoin becomes more widely used, the issuers have to keep buying more collateral in order to keep up with demand. Nevertheless, this stablecoin design has been successfully utilized by Hong Kong's currency board; the Hong Kong Dollar is fully collateralized by USD and has maintained a roughly 7.8 to 1 peg to the US dollar since the early 1980s. It is currently the 13th most traded currency in the world [35].

Instead of staying fully collateralized, some currencies, like Saga, try to mimic the historical trajectory taken by the US Dollar. Such currencies initially fully collateralize their stablecoin, then slowly reduce their collateral ratio and ease off the peg once the money supply has exceeded some threshold. Although Tether eventually admitted they were not fully collateralized as they initially claimed, there was no ostensible detriment to the price. Full collateral is not necessary as long as people do not believe that more than the entire reserve amount will ever be cashed out at once. However this could potentially be an issue if something, for example a bad news event, triggered a run on Tether reserves.

It is also worth noting that almost any supposedly fully collateralized fiat backed stablecoin whose collateral is being held in a bank, such as USDC, is functionally a partial reserve currency. All commercial banks keep only some of their deposits on hand and use the rest for investments or to issue loans. However, in order for this to be an issue for USDC, the bank itself and possibly federal deposit insurers would have to catastrophically fail.

Other coins, especially algorithmic ones such as Basis [2], do not keep any collateral at all. Instead, value is preserved purely by expanding supply when the price is too high and contracting it when the price is too low. On the other end of the spectrum, many currencies collateralized by crypto-currencies keep more than the value of the circulating currency in reserve to guard against price swings in the collateral. This way, even if the collateral asset depreciates, there is still enough for each unit of the stablecoin to be redeemed for an equivalent amount or more of the underlying asset.

4   Mechanics

All stablecoins require some mechanism to adjust the price when it deviates from the peg. Usually, this is done by expanding supply when the price is too high and contracting it when the price is too low. This means that there often needs to be some way of measuring the price (covered further in the next section) and knowing how much to expand or contract the supply. Most stablecoins are designed such that rational, self interested users will act to restore the peg when the price deviates. For example, this could be achieved by allowing users to redeem stablecoins for collateral when the price of the stablecoin is too low. Other stablecoins issue a secondary token designed to absorb the volatility of the first, resulting in a stablecoin/volatilecoin pair. Still others depend on an algorithmic market making mechanism or central-bank contract to manage the supply. Each have different merits but also suffer from different challenges to scale.

Reserve of Pegged Asset. Many stablecoins utilize a mechanism where users will be incentivized to expand or contract the supply until the price returns to the peg. The simplest and most common way to achieve this is in a fully collateralized system backed by the pegged asset, and allow users to expand supply when the price is too high and redeem when the price is too low. Arbitrageurs earn money while helping maintain the peg. For example, if a stablecoin initially pegged to USD trades at less than $1, stablecoin holders should redeem the coin for the underlying collateral, thereby buying a dollar for less than a dollar. This will contract the supply until the price returns to the peg and the arbitrage opportunity disappears, or until the reserve runs out.

On the other hand, if the market price of the stablecoin is above $1, many systems will allow users to expand the supply by wiring funds to the account where the rest of the collateral is being held. This allows the user to buy something worth more than $1 by paying only $1 for it. The simplicity and autonomy of this system makes it extremely appealing, which is why a majority of stablecoins in circulation today use this method, or a very similar one. However, it is not foolproof. On October 15, 2018, the price of Tether briefly dropped below $0.93 due to a large selloff. The price recovered to above $0.98 within the day and appears to have suffered no lasting effects [22]. Because each Tether is hypothetically redeemable for a dollar, people quickly bid the price back to the vicinity of the pegged price.[6] Other notable examples of this design include USDC, TrueUSD, Carbon [18], Paxos [19], Gemini Dollars [23], and many others.

As stated previously, the main problem with allowing users to always redeem for collateral is storing large amounts of collateral at some physical location. The other problem with this type of system is the ability to scale. The maximum value of such a currency is tied to the value of whatever is used as collateral. This makes it difficult, though not impossible, to become a global currency. This inconvenience is one of the reasons USD outgrew the gold standard.

A common variation on this design requires a central authority to mint the coins, but allows people to redeem the stablecoin for the underlying collateral. This creates a lower bound on the price of the stablecoin but not an upper bound, since users can redeem when the stablecoin price is too low but cannot mint when the price is too high. This is common in cases where the collateral is not necessarily dollars, such as Digix. Since it would be inconvenient to accept

---

[6] Note that the user does not necessarily have to redeem the Tether themselves for this reasoning to hold-it is enough to believe that they can sell it to someone else for more than what they paid for it.

and verify gold deposits from individual users, users are not allowed to mint Digix by contributing capital to the collateral pool. They can, however, still redeem their Digix for physical gold, thereby creating a lower bound on the value of Digix.

Another variation being employed by Facebook's Libra [45] is to allow only the set of validators to mint or redeem coins, instead of all users. This reduces overhead since larger amounts are transacted each time, and at a lower frequency. This may come at the cost of a lower speed of adjustment, since the set of potential arbitrageurs who can correct the price is restricted.

Dual Coin. Another way to maintain stability is to pair the pegged coin with a secondary coin designed to absorb the volatility of the first. The best known example of this is the seigniorage shares model employed by the original formulation of Carbon. When the price of the stablecoin falls below the peg, a secondary coin is auctioned in exchange for the stablecoin. The proceeds from the auction are then burned to contract the supply. When the price of the stablecoin is above the peg, additional coins are minted to holders of the secondary token. Holders of the secondary token prop up the price when the stablecoin inflates and are rewarded during deflationary periods.

Although this design benefits from the advantage of not having to store collateral, there are three big drawbacks. One is that the secondary coin often meets the SEC's definition of a security. Regulatory complications stemming from this designation were enough to keep Basis from launching [1]. Carbon also changed from a dual coin system to holding a reserve of USD for undisclosed reasons, possibly due to regulatory hurdles. The second concern is that if holders of the primary token do not believe that the stablecoin will appreciate in the future, there is no incentive to buy or hold the secondary token. In other words, one needs a strong contingent of users who, even during a downturn, believe that the stablecoin will eventually appreciate in value. Additionally, since cryptocurrency markets are often subject to long downturns, people may be reluctant to wait for extended, indeterminate amounts of time for their investment to pay off. When there is no collateral backing this system, if people are not willing to buy the secondary coin, there will be no force propping up the value of the stablecoin. Third, it is difficult to scale such a system. As the circulation of the stablecoin grows, larger amounts have to be burned to correct for the deflation in the currency. It would be unwieldy to coordinate such an auction on the scale required for a national currency, and difficult to find enough people to take on the risk of investing in the volatility absorbing token.

Variations on this design use concepts from dual coin systems and redemption based systems to keep their stablecoins pegged. USDX is a stablecoin collateralized with Lighthouse (LHT), a unpegged digital currency designed to absorb volatility in USDX. Users can always trade one USDX for $1 worth of LHT held in a reserve, incentivizing a contraction of USDX when USDX trades for less than $1. Celo, a stablecoin collateralized with CeloGold, BTC, and ETH uses a design similar to USDX, but with an additional algorithmic market maker which buys and sells Celo and CeloGold to stabilize the price. Using a redemption based system instead of an auction one eases the scaling issue mentioned previously. However, the scale of the stablecoin is still limited by the desirability of the secondary token. Allowing users to exchange for a secondary token is an effective way to maintain the peg only if people want the secondary token.

Therefore, a necessary condition for the original seigniorage shares and above mechanisms to work is that the secondary coin has to have value. A few potential solutions to this issue have been proposed. StatiCoin/RiskCoin [61] is a stablecoin/volatilecoin pair where the secondary coin has more explicit value. Users send ETH to the contract as collateral and mint either StatiCoin or RiskCoin. StatiCoin is always redeemable for $1, while each RiskCoin can be redeemed for $\frac{(total\ value\ of\ ETH\ in\ the\ contract) - (total\ value\ of\ StatiCoin\ outstanding)}{total\ number\ of\ RiskCoin\ outstanding}$. StatiCoin is unique because it is crypto-collateralized but does not require overcollateralization, an inefficient mechanism for absorbing volatility. However, if the value of the collateral falls below the number of StatiCoin minted, the price of RiskCoin will drop to 0. Moreover, StatiCoin may become unpegged because not all holders of StatiCoin will be able to redeem for the underlying collateral. StatiCoin will become an unreliable store of value precisely when Ethereum is losing value and a stable valued asset is most needed.

Another solution comes in the form of Luna, which absorbs volatility from stablecoin Terra [39]. Luna is bought and sold to adjust the price of Terra, but also serves as the staking token of the system. As long as people are using the Terra/Luna blockchain, Terra should retain some value. Fees and rewards, also paid in Luna, are additionally adjusted to entice users to buy and hold Luna even during downturns.

In the previous examples, one coin absorbs all of the volatility in the system. However, "dual coin" systems are not necessarily limited to only two coins. The volatility absorbing coin can be tranched, as exemplified in the three coin design of Basis. Basis bonds are sold to contract the supply when the price of Basis falls below $1 and are redeemable for Basis when the price is above $1. If all of the Basis Bonds have been redeemed and the price of Basis is still above $1, additional Basis is minted to holders of Basis Shares. There are infinite ways to split the volatility absorbing coin; in theory there could be systems with four or more coins distributing the stablecoin volatility across several parties. This allows for the volatility of the stablecoin to be absorbed by people with different expectations and risk preferences.

Algorithmic Supply Adjustments. Other currencies use a fully algorithmic approach to adjust the supply of the stablecoin in response to price fluctuations. This can be used in systems with no, full, or partial collateral. These types of systems are tricky to implement because it is difficult to know how much to adjust the supply to effect the desired price change in the stablecoin. As the supply is adjusted, the market cap of the stablecoin might also change in unpredictable ways. This is why most central banks do not depend on algorithmic supply adjustments and instead will gradually adjust reserve ratios and open market operations until the desired price level is attained.

One example of a coin that uses fully algorithmic supply adjustments is Ampleforth, previously named Fragments [41]. Whenever the value of Ampleforth changes, token holders have their balances adjusted proportionally to preserve the value of a single token. For example, if Ampleforth is originally worth $1, then, after an increase of 10% to $1.10, all balances will automatically be inflated by 10%. This makes Ampleforth a stable unit of account, since by design, the ratio of Ampleforth's market cap to the number of Ampleforth tokens is periodically adjusted to be $1. Unfortunately, this is not a good store of value. Holding Ampleforth is no different than holding a non-pegged coin: if the market cap of Ampleforth declines, users' balances and outstanding payments will decline proportionally. Moreover, the market cap of the currency may adjust as the supply of the currency is adjusted; an algorithm as straightforward as Ampleforth's may never converge on a stable equilibrium price.

A different algorithmic approach is employed by Saga. Although Saga does not peg the long run value of its coin, it uses an algorithmic path-independent market maker inspired by Bancor [34] to provide liquidity and dampen sudden price fluctuations. The market maker sets the price and bid ask spread for Saga based on how much collateral it has in its reserve. For example, since Saga recently launched and its reserve is small, the price is set at 1 SDR, and the market maker will sell a Saga at a price of 1.0015 SDR worth of fiat and buy for 0.9985 SDR worth of fiat.[7] This makes it so that users should not sell Saga on secondary markets for a value of less than 0.9985 SDR or buy for more than 1.0015 SDR, which limits how suddenly the price can change. As the reserve grows and shrinks, the price and spread are gradually adjusted in response. Like Ampleforth, Saga does not guarantee that the value of Saga holdings will be stable over time. However, the market maker does guard against sudden price movements, and thus provides short-term stability. Although Saga does not necessarily fulfil all the functions of money, it does have the potential to scale. When people's confidence in Saga grows and the market cap of Saga increases, Saga decreases the fraction of collateral held in reserve until Saga can act as a standalone currency.

Leveraged Loans. Leveraged loans are loans issued to borrower with low or unknown credit rating which demand a high cost of capital to compensate for risk. Leveraged loans are used in a system of overcollateralized stablecoins which utilize components from all the previously discussed stabilization mechanisms. Dai [46] is the most successful example of such a system, and most leveraged loans type stablecoins use the same format with different nomenclature. Collateralized debt positions (CDPs) are contracts where users lock up collateral, such as Ethereum and other cryptoassets. They can then borrow against this collateral to mint Dai, a stablecoin pegged to $1, up to 2/3 the value of the collateral in the CDP. Users can then unlock their collateral by paying back the borrowed Dai, plus a stability fee that accrues over time. Dai is destroyed once it is paid back. In addition to Dai's use case as a stablecoin, the leveraged

---

[7] Saga prices are quoted in terms of SDR, but users can buy using fiat such as USD.

loans mechanism also allows users to hold a leveraged position in ETH or other cryptoassets. This can be achieved by using the minted Dai to purchase more ETH.

If the value of the collateral in a CDP drops below 1.5× the Dai borrowed, the debt position is automatically liquidated, and the collateral is used to purchase the amount of Dai borrowed against it. Any remaining collateral, minus a liquidation fee, is returned to the original CDP owner. If the value of the collateral depreciates quickly and drops below the value of the Dai borrowed, a secondary coin is minted to cover the difference. The secondary coin, MKR, also serves as the governance token for the Dai system. Since MKR holders are diluted when CDPs are underwater, there is an incentive for the holders of the governance token to set parameters such that users are not defaulting on their loans. However, we note that the probability of the value of the collateral declining to less than the Dai borrowed is low since the price of the collateral would have to suddenly drop by over 33%.

Users are incentivized to buy Dai and unlock their collateral when the price of Dai decreases, because a decrease in the price of Dai makes it cheaper for them to unlock their collateral. This contracts the supply and restores the peg. If Dai continues to trade at a price lower than its intended peg, MKR holders can vote to raise the stability fee charged to CDP holders. This serves as further incentive for CDP holders to liquidate their positions and contract supply.

Dai received a lot of attention in March 2019 for consistently trading around $0.98 instead of $1 as it was supposed to. Since then, it underwent a series of stability fee increases, some of which quixotically lowered the price of Dai instead of raising it as intended. Despite this puzzling market reaction and a ~90% decrease in the price of ETH since Dai launched, Dai has managed to remain within ~2% of its pegged value (Fig. 3).

However, this stabilization mechanism still has several drawbacks. One is that Dai and similar stablecoins can never have a market cap larger than whatever cryptoassets are used as collateral. In fact, since locking up collateral in a CDP functionally takes it out of circulation, Dai can be detrimentally disruptive to the cryptoassets used as collateral. The overcollateralization necessitated by this design is also an inefficient and risky use of capital. If someone is not vigilant about their CDP balance and the value of their collateral falls to 1.49x the Dai they withdrew, they are penalized with a steep 13% liquidation fee. As of Dec 2019, over 40M of Dai had been liquidated, which means over 5.2M of stability fees charged. To put this value into perspective, the current amount of Dai outstanding is approximately 41M [48]. Finally, it is not clear why Dai has traded at such a consistent price. Due to the overcollateralization, when Dai is paid back, it unlocks an amount of collateral far in excess of the amount of Dai paid.

Miscellaneous. There are a few other designs that do not neatly fit into any of the above categories. For example, Steem [62] props up the price of its stablecoin, Steem Dollars, by paying interest on Steem Dollars. However, since they don't set negative interest rates, this mechanism may not work if the price of Steem

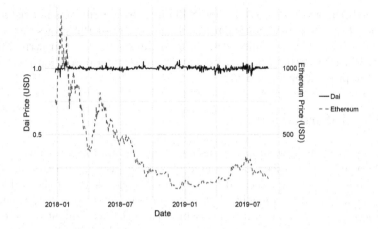

Fig. 3. DAI remains relatively price stable despite decline in ETH price.

is too high and the interest rate is already low. Steem Dollars traded for more than its $1 peg for months despite an interest rate of 0%, demonstrating the ineffectiveness of this stabilization method.

Another design is employed by NuBits (now defunct), a stablecoin which is minted when holders of a secondary coin (NuShares) vote to create more. Users are also paid interest if they temporarily remove their NuBits from circulation. Voting on supply changes is a slow process, thus forcing adjustments in price to lag by several days or more. Additionally, if holders of NuShares also hold NuBits, they may be reluctant to dilute the value of NuBits by printing more.

Kowala [4] keeps the price stable by adjusting its mining rewards. When the price of the stablecoin is too high, rewards increase to dilute the supply; when the price of the stablecoin is too low, transaction fees are burned to contract the supply. Unfortunately, a decline in the price of the stablecoin might be correlated with fewer transactions occurring, since a break from the peg would diminish users' confidence in the stablecoin. Since price adjustments are effected through mining and transactions, recovering from a decrease in price would take a long time. Furthermore, since mining rewards decrease during contractionary periods, miners have less incentive to provide security which may further diminish the value of Kowala. This could lead to a feedback loop where Kowala never recovers from a price decrease.

Finally, Phi [30] offers people the opportunity to issue loans denominated in Phi, a stablecoin. The loan issuer has to put up collateral, which is used to pay the loan if the borrower defaults. Although the issuer does collect interest on the loan, the issuer has no way to recover their capital if the borrower defaults. Moreover, because there is no connection to real world identities, there is no ostensible consequence to defaulting, so borrowers will likely abscond with the loan. If the borrower does pay back the loan, they are supposed to pay it with interest denominated in Phi. Since, for every loan originated in Phi, the amount paid exceeds the amount created, there will only be enough coins in existence to pay back all existing loans with interest if the supply of Phi grows faster than the interest rate. This is unlikely to be a sustainable rate of growth. Finally, although Phi is needed to pay back loans, there is no stabilization mechanism keeping the price at or around $1.

5   Price Information

A crucial step in making supply adjustments at the appropriate times is accurately measuring the price. Most stablecoins make use of an external oracle, an independent price feed deemed trustworthy by the issuers of the stablecoin. This leaves a crucial component of the system completely out of the hands of the stablecoin issuer. The entities publishing the price feed might deviate from their standard practice in how they calculate prices and trigger disastrous downturns or upturns for the stablecoin. This is not unheard of, since, for example, CoinMarketCap suddenly and abruptly decided to stop including prices from exchanges in South Korea, resulting in a sudden drop in reported prices [21]. If a stablecoin was formerly using this price feed and desired no change in how prices are calculated, the system would be left with few options other than to accept the new price feed, find a different oracle, or adjust oracle prices to correct for the new calculation method. Short term pricing errors can arise from using an oracle too, as was the case with Synthetix. In June 2019, a commercial API used by Synthetix suffered a glitch and began to report incorrect exchange rates, resulting in a bot making over $1B during this period [9]. Although the bot owner chose to reverse the trades during this episode, there is no guarantee that the next profiteer will be as generous. Note that these are examples which arose even with no malicious adversaries in the system.

Opting for an internal oracle can mitigate these surprises, but introduces the problem of an additional layer of centralization, and can lead to a conflict of interest. For example, if the issuing body loses money from price changes in the stablecoin, there is incentive to update prices slowly or smooth the prices reported.

If there is a malicious actor intent on sabotaging the stability, a price oracle can serve as a potential target. Increasing the number of price feeds might be a potential solution to this issue. However using the median makes price updating slow, since the system must wait for sufficient majority of price feed reports. As a result, even some of the most active and popular stablecoins, including MakerDao, use only a few price oracles, making them a potential source of attack vectors [48]. There are only 14 price oracles for MakerDao, so hijacking of any 8 would corrupt the median-price rule. Moreover, these oracles may not be fully independent, as they might have overlap in where they obtain their price information or in their deployment platform.

Nonetheless, the use of external oracles persists because the alternatives are generally worse. Prices for most assets are generated based on the prices at which the assets are transacted on exchanges. However, many crypto exchanges, both centralized and decentralized, suffer from poor liquidity. This leads to stale prices and/or inflation of trade volumes [7]. If trades are being inflated by the exchange or other parties, it is possible that exchanges might just be taking prices from some external feed and adding noise. Unless the initial exchanges are chosen wisely and with near perfect foresight, a non-noisy price feed is just as good or better.

Alternately, Schelling point mechanisms [16], a.k.a. crowd oracles, can also be used to set the price. The justification for this method is that it is hard for voters to coordinate on a deceptive answer. However, with a pegged coin, there exists a natural alternate coordination point: the pegged price. If this is a more advantageous equilibrium for voters, then information obtained in this manner is not going to be trustworthy. Many of these schemes use rewards for being close to the median and slashing for voters far from the median to incentivize truth telling. However, this may incentivize people to answer how they think others will answer, commonly known in economics as the beauty pageant problem. Take for example Basis, a variant of the dual coin example discussed earlier, whose original design mentioned the possibility of using a crowd oracle. If users correctly express that the stablecoin has appreciated and is trading above its peg, more of the stablecoin will be minted, and users who only hold the stablecoin and not the secondary coin will be diluted. This makes it such that the payoff for holders of the stablecoin is higher if they lie and claim that the stablecoin is trading at its intended price rather than its true price. Even if a user wants to tell the truth, when enough people are incentivized to divert, the rest of the honest users will have to lie, abstain from voting, or be penalized.

Terra tries to address the problem of dishonest voting by sampling only a subset of voters to make collusion difficult. However, if there is a non truthful equilibrium that is beneficial for a majority of voters, then the subsampling may not help. Celo also uses a crowd oracle and acknowledges that there is potential for price manipulation. The designers of Celo trust that holders of the voting token will prioritize long term growth over short term profit, which may be an incorrect assumption.

Some stablecoins are designed so that no external oracle is needed for the stablecoin to remain stable. In systems where users can always trade in for the underlying collateral, such as USDC or TrueUSD, there is no need for a price feed. Instead, prices are measured using users' trades. Individual users decide how to value the token and then cash in or out accordingly. However, as previously discussed, the convenience of not having to measure the price usually comes at the cost of having to store collateral. Others require an oracle but not for the stablecoin or any other cryptoassets. Saga uses information on the prices of SDR and the component currencies to set the bid and ask for Saga. Though this still requires a price feed, this information is easier to get than crypto prices because SDR currencies have liquid markets and easily available price information.

6 Other Considerations

Fees. Fees can be built into a variety of the designs discussed previously. They can be used to incentivize good behavior, such as how Dai's liquidation fee penalizes low levels of collateral. The presence of this fee rewards MKR holders who are supposed to police the CDPs and penalizes CDP owners who are negligent with their balances. Fees can also be used to adjust the supply of a currency in order to return it to its pegged price, as is the case with Terra.

However, fees such as those employed by TrueUSD can also introduce a friction which prevents arbitrageurs from taking advantage of and correcting price discrepancies. Suppose that a coin which is supposed to trade for $1 is instead trading for $0.99. If there is a cashing out fee of $70 (as with TrueUSD), someone would have to buy $6930 worth of TrueUSD and cash it in at $7000 just to break even. To make a profit, they would have to invest even more money into this strategy. This is can be capital intensive for the arbitrageur. Moreover, the cashing out process is not instantaneous since wire transfers take time to process. This introduces an opportunity cost as this strategy can tie up capital for a day or more each time it is used.

Governance. Flexible governance is the ability to change system parameters and operation dynamically in response to changes in the environment, allowing a coin to scale or overcome unforeseen obstacles. This is an emerging choice for digital currencies, first popularized by Tezos. It has since been adopted by others, including several stablecoins. The extent to which governance matters varies widely by stablecoin design. Stablecoins that depend on a reserve of the pegged asset have few governable parameters aside from fees. Others, such as Dai have numerous parameters that might need to be adjusted, and several possible design features that can be added.

Although the idea of crowd-sourcing system parameters caters to a democratic ideal consistent with crypto's ethos of decentralization, in actuality, participation may be low. This may leave important decisions in the hands of a motivated minority. For example, the March 7, 2019 stability fee increase in Dai was approved with less than 1% of MKR holders voting and a single address contributing more than 50% of the stake [49]. Besides low turnout, voting may suffer from high latency. If specific governance changes require human participation, then the process becomes highly contentious and complicated. On the other hand, if there is no way to amend the governance, the founding team must foresee every problem or potentially hard fork every time a change has to be made. This can lead to systems which are inflexible and react poorly to changing global environments.

Regulatory Compliance. Another aspect some coins are grappling with is the degree of regulatory compliance. Although Know Your Customer (KYC) and Anti Money Laundering (AML) compliance avoids the possibility of regulatory problems down the road, it also alienates some potential users. Some people may demand absolute privacy, be concerned about secure consumer data storage, or be unbanked because they lack the paperwork necessary to go through the KYC process. These people may opt to use cash instead of stablecoins. Other regulatory costs, such as the time, effort, and lawyers required to file with the relevant regulatory agencies, make it prohibitively expensive to launch a coin, as was the case with Basis [1]. And finally, being KYC/AML compliant in one country does not protect the issuer from liability if the coin is being used in another country, as KYC and AML laws often differ widely across countries.

It is especially crucial for coins that are fiat backed with collateral stored in banks to not break any laws because banks can freeze accounts if they suspect suspicious or illegal activity. For example, if the stablecoin is being abused for money laundering or other similar purposes, depository banks can stop money from being withdrawn or deposited in the account. This would prevent users from creating or redeeming tokens and hinder quantity adjustments necessary to keep the price stable. This is not a purely hypothetical problem. In April 2017, Tether found themselves unable to accept international wire transfers into their Singapore bank accounts and were denied outgoing wire transfers by Wells Fargo [71].

Other types of coins suffer from regulatory risk as well. Crypto regulation is currently a work in progress, and because most cryptoassets are so new there is very little helpful judicial precedent. This makes it difficult to know which new designs might run into legal problems later on, or which current laws they might be violating.

7   Future Directions

7.1   Stable Pay

One alternative to stabilizing an entire currency supply is to only stabilize the portion of the currency that has been used for payments. This type of currency is not a good unit of account or store of value, but it can be a reliable medium of exchange. The only currency currently incorporating this strategy is Xank [40]. Payments on the Xank network have the option of being stabilized by the algorithmic central bank. If person A sends a stabilized Xank transaction to person B, the bank subtracts Xank tokens from person B's balance when the price of Xank increases and adds Xank when it declines. This keeps the dollar value of what A sent to B constant. The central bank continues to make these adjustments until the tokens are used in another transaction or the user exits their Xank position. Crypto markets tend to have fairly long run ups and declines, so there is a high degree of serial correlation in returns. If users expect prices to increase, they should unpeg their transactions. If users expect prices to decrease, they will keep their payments stabilized. In a prolonged downturn, this can lead to the central bank running out of money and being unable to continue to stabilize payments. The largest problem with this design is that the central bank is essentially providing a free put option, and providing a valuable service for free is a difficult business model to sustain long term.

7.2   Peg to Other Assets

Another area for stablecoin expansion is assets pegged to financial assets other than currencies, such as real estate or stock or bond indices. This would make it easier for people to diversify their holdings across digital currencies and real assets without the inconvenience of cashing out of crypto in order to do so. The traditional finance sector is slowly becoming more interested in crypto markets. Bitcoin futures have been listed on the Chicago Mercantile exchange since the end of 2017; NASDAQ lists several blockchain companies and is exploring uses for blockchain technology. This may indicate an openness to an integration between the traditional financial sector and crypto. Although there are several regulatory hurdles in the way, it is possible that a broader range of financial assets might eventually be available on crypto markets.

8 Conclusion

Stablecoins, that is, low-volatility, programmable, and auditable currencies, promise to bridge the chasm between fiat currencies and digital currencies. Their importance in on-ramping the trillions of assets into digital form is evident in the sheer number of stablecoins issued over the last few years. In this paper, we provided a systematic overview of all the different types of stablecoins developed, and divided the various proposals into constituent design elements, based on peg, collateral type and amount, stabilizing mechanism, and price information. Although there are over a hundred projects in existence, most are variations of the same few components. There is still much potential for growth in this area. Although there are many promising designs, none are without their flaws. Further innovation will be necessary before cryptocurrencies adequately fulfill the functions of money well enough to be adopted by mainstream users.

9   Appendix A: Illustration of Stablecoin Mechanisms

(See Figs. 4, 5, 6 and 7).

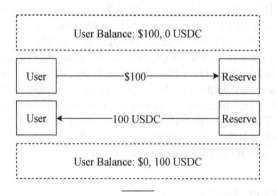

Fig. 4. Reserve of Pegged Asset (ex. USDC)

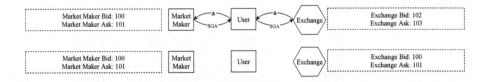

Fig. 5. Algorithmic (ex. Saga)

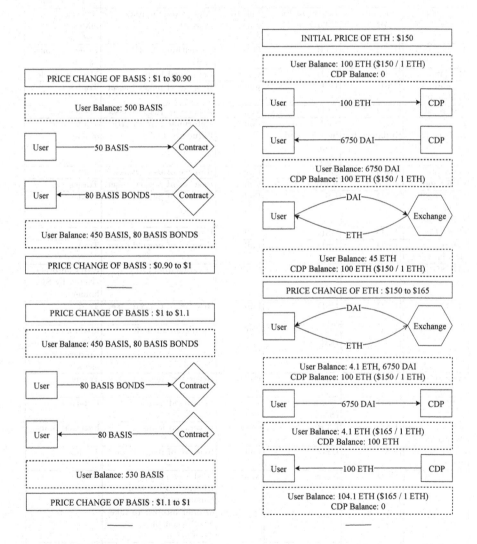

Fig. 6. Dual Coin (ex. Basis)   **Fig. 7.** Leveraged Loans (ex. Dai)

Appendix B: Classification of Existing Stablecoins

Name	Peg	Collateral	Collateral Amount	Price & Supply Adjustments	Price Information
Carbon	USD	USD	Full	Reserve of pegged asset	Trades
Tether [65]	USD	USD/Euro	Partial	Reserve of pegged asset	Trades
TrueUSD [68]	USD	USD	Full	Reserve of pegged asset	Trades
Basis	USD	None	None	Two coin	Oracle
BitUSD [12]	USD	BTS	Full or over	leveraged loans	Elected delegates input exchange prices
Saga [59]	initially SDR, later CPI or none	Basket of Fiat (SDR)	Full to partial	Algorithmic market maker	Based on amount of reserve
Bancor [34]	ETH	ETH	Over	Algorithmic market maker	Based on token balances
Dai [46]	USD	ETH	Over	Leveraged loans	Median oracle
Gemini Dollar [23]	USD	USD	Full	Reserve of pegged asset	Trades
USDC [20]	USD	USD	Full	Reserve of pegged asset	Trades
AAA Reserve [29]	Avg inflation for G-10 countries	Fiat, fixed income, and loan investments	Full	Determined by by Arc Fiduciary Ltd	Trades and oracle
DGX [27]	Gold	Gold	Full	Reserve of pegged asset	Trades
EURS [60]	Euro	Euro	Full	Reserve of pegged asset	Trades
StableUSD/ Stably/ USDS [36]	USD	USD	Full	Reserve of pegged asset	Trades
PAX [19]	USD	USD	Full	Reserve of pegged asset	Trades
White standard [24]	USD	USD	Full	Reserve of pegged asset	Trades
SDUSD [3]	USD	NEO	Over	Leveraged loans	External oracle elected by SDS holders
JPM Coin [37]	USD	USD	Full	Reserve of pegged asset	Trades
USDX [54]	USD	Lighthouse (LHT)	200%+	Dual coin variant	Median of exchange prices, validated by users
Stronghold USD [63]	USD	USD	Full	Reserve of pegged asset	Trades
sUSD [14]	USD	Synthetix (SNX)	5x	Leveraged loans	External oracle
eUSD (Havven) [15]	USD	ETH	Over	Leveraged loans	External oracle
eUSD by Epay [28]	USD	USD	Full	Reserve of pegged asset	Trades
NuBits [44]	USD	None	None	Nushareholders vote whether to list more NuBits on an exchange, or offer interest to take NuBits out of circulation	Voting
Token [67]	USD	USD	Full	Reserve of pegged asset	Trades

Monerium [69]	One for each major currency	Same as peg	Full	Reserve of pegged asset	Trades
Reserve [13]	initially USD	initially USD, later other assets	Initially full	Reserve of pegged asset	Trades
Terra [39]	SDR	None	None	Dual coin	Randomly sample users who vote on price
Ampleforth [4]	USD	None	None	Supply is expanded or contracted proportional to market cap	Whitelist of trusted oracles
Augmint [6]	Euro	ETH	2x	Leveraged loans	Exchanges
Bridgecoin [25]	USD	ETH	2x	Leveraged loans +algorithmic market maker	Oracle
HelloGold [31]	Gold	Gold	Full	Reserve of pegged asset	Trades
Kowala [4]	USD	None	None	Block rewards increase when price is high and are burned when price is low	Large holders of mUSD(staking token) act as oracles
x8c [72]	None	Gold, USD, Euro, GBP, JPY, AUD, CAD, NZD, CHF	Full	AI shifts funds across currencies to keep value constant	External oracle
NOS [50]	USD	USD	Full	Reserve of pegged asset	Trades
Phi [30]	USD	TBD	Over	Phi is minted when validators issue a loan and burned when the loan is paid back	TBD
Celo [38]	USD	Celo Gold, BTC, ETH	Variable	Dual coin + algorithmic central bank	Crowd oracle
Aurora Boreal [42]	USD	ETH and other reserves	Partial	Supply expands when Decentralized Capital issues loans denominated in Boreal and contracts when loans are repaid, users will also receive grants to act as market makers	Unknown
Stableunit [43]	USD	Cryptoassets	Initially over	Algorithmic market maker	Median oracle
Rockz [58]	CHF	CHF	Full	Reserve of pegged asset	Trades
Steem Dollars [62]	USD	None	None	Interest accrues to Steem Dollar holders	Steem Power holders elect oracles
USDVault [70]	USD	Gold	Full	Reserve of pegged asset, "sophisticated gold hedging process" to maintain peg	Trades
Globcoin.io [33]	Gold and currency basket	Gold and 15 largest currencies	Full	Reserve of pegged assets, can cash out to any one currency in basket	Oracle
JCash [8]	USD, KRW and other assets	USD, KRW and other assets	Full	Reserve of Pegged asset	Trades

Staticoin [61]	USD	Eth	Full	Dual coin variant	24h exchange price
Unum [66]	USD	Cryptoassets	Under to over depending on prices	Algorithmic market maker: users sell crypto or Unum to smart contract	External oracle
Poly [32]	None	Tokenized commodities	Full	Reserve of pegged asset	Trades
BitBay [10]	None	None	None	Freeze and unfreeze tokens based on transaction and staking history. Users receive interest on frozen coins	Dynamic Peg oracle
BitCNY [12]	Chinese Yuan	BTS	Full or over	leveraged loans	Elected delegates input exchange prices
EOSDT [26]	USD	EOS	Over	Leveraged loans	Oracle
Neutral [51]	USD	Other stablecoins (PAX, TUSD, DAI, and USDC)	Full	Reserve of pegged asset	Trades
Candy [11]	Mongolian Tugrik	Mongolian Tugrik	Full	Reserve of pegged asset	Trades
Onegram [52]	Gold	Gold	Full	Reserve of pegged asset	Trades
Carats.io [17]	Diamonds	Diamonds	Full	Reserve of pegged asset	Trades
Libra [45]	Collateral basket	Bank deposits and short-term government securities	Full	Reserve of pegged asset	Trades and oracle
Anchor [5]	Monetary measurement unit	None	None	Dual coin	Oracle

References

1. Basis: A stable, algorithmic cryptocurrency protocol (2018). https://www.basis.io
2. Al-Naji, N., Chen, J., Diao, L.: Basis: a price-stable cryptocurrency with an algorithmic central bank (2017). https://www.basis.io/basis_whitepaper_en.pdf
3. Alchemint: Alchemint (2018). https://tinyurl.com/yy4vbn7o
4. Ancheta, A.: For a few dollars less: Kowala stablecoin backed by math and code (2018). https://cryptobriefing.com/for-a-few-dollars-less-kowala-stablecoin-backed-by-math-and-code/
5. Anchored by the global economy (2019). https://theanchor.io/
6. Augment: Stable cryptocurrencies as a medium of exchange (2017). https://bit.ly/2LhMeXm
7. https://www.sec.gov/comments/sr-nysearca-2019-01/srnysearca201901-5164833-183434.pdf
8. Barghuthi, Y., Mezrin, V.: Jibrel network (2018). https://github.com/jibrelnetwork/
9. Biggs, J.: https://www.coindesk.com/synthetix-trader-rolls-back-broken-trades-that-netted-1-billion-profit

10. Bitbay: Bitbay: Decentralized peg (David Zimbeck). https://bitbay.market/downloads/whitepapers/bitbay-dynamic-peg.pdf?utm_source=medium&utm_medium=blog&utm_campaign=dynamic-peg-whitepaper
11. Bitcoin.com: Mongolian central bank authorizes a digital coin (2018). https://news.bitcoin.com/new-stablecoins-from-cryptopound-and-metal-backed-swiss-coin-to-mongolian-candy/
12. Price-stable cryptocurrencies. https://bitshares.org/technology/price-stable-cryptocurrencies/
13. Brent, T., et al.: Reserve stabilization protocol (2019). https://reserve.org/whitepaper.pdf
14. Brooks, S., Jurisevic, A., Spain, M., Warwick, K.: Havven: a decentralised payment network and stablecoin (2018). https://www.synthetix.io/uploads/havvenwhitepaper.pdf
15. Brooks, S., Jurisevic, A., Spain, M., Warwick, K.: Havven: a decentralised payment network and stablecoin (2018). https://www.synthetix.io/uploads/havven_whitepaper.pdf
16. Buterin, V.: Schellingcoin: a minimal-trust universal data feed. https://blog.ethereum.org/2014/03/28/schellingcoin-a-minimal-trust-universal-data-feed/
17. Carats.io: Whitepaper (2018). https://www.carats.io/whitepaper.pdf
18. Carbon money. https://www.carbon.money/
19. Cascarilla, C.: Paxos standard (2018). https://account.paxos.com/whitepaper.pdf
20. Centre: Centre whitepaper (2018). https://www.centre.io/pdfs/centre-whitepaper.pdf
21. https://cointelegraph.com/news/coinmarketcap-removes-south-korea-exchanges-ripple-market-cap-drops-20-billion
22. https://coinmarketcap.com/
23. Company, G.T.: The Gemini dollar: a regulated stable value coin. https://bit.ly/2oVLfkI
24. Eisele, S.: The white company launches 'white standard' $usd-backed stablecoin, bringing long-awaited liquidity, transparency, and stability to cryptocurrency holders (2018). https://tinyurl.com/y3ngachk
25. English, J.: Bridging the gap to a stable token (2018). https://blog.sweetbridge.com/bridging-the-gap-to-a-stable-token-c4fdbd70e9c3
26. EOSDT: Technical specification (2019). https://eosdt.com/specification
27. Eufemio, A., Chng, K., Djie, S.: Digix's whitepaper (2016). https://digix.global/whitepaper.pdf
28. Epay USD: A compliant, stable value currency (2019). https://www.epay.com/en/eusd_white_paper_en.pdf
29. Findlay, S.W.: Q&A introduction to AAA reserve currency (2017). https://medium.com/arc-blog/q-a-introduction-to-arc-reserve-currency-in-1-000-words-49bea91c22eb
30. Finlay, D.: Phi: Decentralized lending and stable currency might not actually be stable (2016), https://medium.com/@danfinlay/phi-decentralized-lending-and-stable-currency-might-not-actually-be-stable-36f472948591
31. Foundation, H.: Technical whitepaper (2017). https://static.coinpaprika.com/storage/cdn/whitepapers/763.pdf
32. Georgen, C.: Topl: empowering growth by enabling investment (2017). https://tinyurl.com/y4suph2r
33. Globcoin: https://globcoin.io/howitworks.html

34. Hertzog, E., Benartzi, G., Benartzi, G.: Bancor protocol (2018). https://storage.googleapis.com/website-bancor/2018/04/01ba8253-bancor_protocol_whitepaper_en.pdf

35. Triennial Central Bank Survey: Foreign exchange turnover in April 2016. https://www.bis.org/publ/rpfx16fx.pdf

36. Hoang, K., Zhang, D., Diwan, A., Guy, B.: Stably: transparent reserve-backed stablecoins for multiple blockchain protocols (2018). https://www.stably.io/static/whitepaper.pdf

37. J.P. Morgan creates digital coin for payments (2019). https://www.jpmorgan.com/global/news/digital-coin-payments

38. Kamvar, S., Olszewski, M., Reinsberg, R.: Celo: a multi-asset cryptographic protocol for decentralized social payments. https://bit.ly/2HyGvLK

39. Kereiakes, E., Kwon, D., Maggio, M.D., Platias, N.: Terra money: stability and adoption (2019). https://s3.ap-northeast-2.amazonaws.com/terra.money.home/static/Terra_White_paper.pdf?201904

40. Kim, R., Choi, B.: Xank: a treasury-backed stability-guaranteed cryptocurrency (2018). http://paper.xank.io

41. Kuo, E., Iles, B., Cruz, M.R.: Ampleforth - a new synthetic commodity (2019). https://www.ampleforth.org/paper/

42. Labs, A.: Aurora: a decentralized financial institution utilizing distributed computing and the ethereum network (2019). https://auroradao.com/whitepaper/Aurora-Labs-Whitepaper-V0.9.7.pdf

43. Lebed, A.: Stableunit: a low-volatility p2p electronic cash system (2018). https://stableunit.org/StableUnit-whitepaper.pdf

44. Lee, J.: Nu (2014). https://nubits.com/NuWhitepaper.pdf

45. Libra white paper (2019). https://libra.org/en-US/white-paper/#introducing-libra

46. Maker: The dai stablecoin system (2017). https://bit.ly/2DwX21S

47. Mita, M., Ito, K., Ohsawa, S., Tanaka, H.: What is stablecoin?: A survey on price stabilization mechanisms for decentralized payment systems. https://arxiv.org/abs/1906.06037

48. https://mkr.tools/system/feeds

49. https://finance.yahoo.com/news/makerdao-governance-risk-call-march-191947369.html

50. Neetzel, D., Konopka, R., Jeger, F., Trobe, B.L., Heyden, H.: Instant, feeless and green p2p value transfer with fiat stablecoins (2018). https://docsend.com/view/k9hyw3f

51. Neutral: FAQ (2019). https://blog.neutralproject.com/posts/2019/05/14/what-is-neutral.html

52. OneGram: Whitepaper (2018). https://onegram.org/whitepaper

53. Pernice, I.G., Henningsen, S., Proskalovich, R., Florian, M., Elendner, H., Scheuermann, B.: Monetary stabilization in cryptocurrencies - design approaches and open questions. In: Crypto Valley Conference on Blockchain Technology (CVCBT) (2019)

54. Peshkov, A., Sapunov, E., Zhuravlenko, D.: Usdx whitepaper (2018). https://drive.google.com/file/d/10Ph2AhPHDXsgqXwD1CglRFTVCvxW0SSC/view

55. Qureshi, H.: Stablecoins: designing a price-stable cryptocurrency (2018). https://hackernoon.com/stablecoins-designing-a-price-stable-cryptocurrency-6bf24e2689e5

56. https://www.blockchain.com/ru/static/pdf/StablecoinsReportFinal.pdf

57. https://bit.ly/2v9pZuM
58. Rockz: Whitepaper.   https://s3.eu-central-1.amazonaws.com/alprockz-docs/RockzWhitePaperEnglish_v7.pdf
59. Saga: Saga. https://www.saga.org/static/files/saga-whitepaper.pdf
60. Stasis: Eurs (2019). https://eurs.stasis.net/
61. Staticoin: Whitepaper (2017). http://staticoin.com/whitepaper/
62. Steem: An incentivized, blockchain-based, public content platform (2018). https://steem.com/steem-whitepaper.pdf
63. Stronghold: Stronghold. https://docsend.com/view/gg3p9ce
64. Stuart Hoegner Affidavit 4–30
65. https://tether.to/wp-content/uploads/2016/06/TetherWhitePaper.pdf
66. Titus, J.: From many, Unum (2017). https://medium.com/unum/from-many-unum-8c8493a8db9d
67. Stablecoin for instant payments and for use on exchanges—token (2019). https://token.io/x-consumers
68. TrustToken: Trusttoken - trueusd. https://tether.to/wp-content/uploads/2016/06/TetherWhitePaper.pdf
69. Valfells, S.: Why Monerium e-money is unlike Facebook's Libra cryptocurrency (2019).   https://monerium.com/monerium/2019/08/12/why-monerium-e-money-is-unlike-facebook-libra-cryptocurrency.html
70. Vault: USDVault stablecoin. http://vault.ch/usdvault-stablecoin-gold-standard/
71. https://tether.to/tether-update/
72. X8Currency: Faq (2018). https://www.x8currency.com/faq/

Layer 2

Layer 2

SoK: Layer-Two Blockchain Protocols

Lewis Gudgeon[1]([✉]), Pedro Moreno-Sanchez[2], Stefanie Roos[3],
Patrick McCorry[4], and Arthur Gervais[1,5,6]

[1] Imperial College London, London, UK
`l.gudgeon18@imperial.ac.uk`
[2] TU Wien, Vienna, Austria
`pedro.sanchez@tuwien.ac.at`
[3] TU Delft, Delft, The Netherlands
`s.roos@tudelft.nl`
[4] PISA Research, London, UK
`stonecoldpat@gmail.com`
[5] Lucerne University of Applied Sciences and Arts, Lucerne, Switzerland
[6] Liquidity Network, Zurich, Switzerland
`arthur@gervais.cc`

Abstract. Blockchains have the potential to revolutionize markets and services. However, they currently exhibit high latencies and fail to handle transaction loads comparable to those managed by traditional financial systems. *Layer-two* protocols, built on top of (*layer-one*) blockchains, avoid disseminating every transaction to the whole network by exchanging authenticated transactions *off-chain*. Instead, they utilize the expensive and low-rate blockchain only as a recourse for disputes. The promise of layer-two protocols is to complete off-chain transactions in sub-seconds rather than minutes or hours while retaining asset security, reducing fees and allowing blockchains to scale.

We systematize the evolution of layer-two protocols over the period from the inception of cryptocurrencies in 2009 until today, structuring the multifaceted body of research on layer-two transactions. Categorizing the research into payment and state channels, commit-chains and protocols for refereed delegation, we provide a comparison of the protocols and their properties. We provide a systematization of the associated synchronization and routing protocols along with their privacy and security aspects. This Systematization of Knowledge (SoK) clears the layer-two fog, highlights the potential of layer-two solutions and identifies their unsolved challenges, indicating propitious avenues of future work.

Keywords: Applied cryptography · Blockchain applications · Layer-two blockchain protocols · Blockchain scaling · Cryptocurrency adoption

The full version of this paper available at https://eprint.iacr.org/2019/360.pdf.

© International Financial Cryptography Association 2020
J. Bonneau and N. Heninger (Eds.): FC 2020, LNCS 12059, pp. 201–226, 2020.
https://doi.org/10.1007/978-3-030-51280-4_12

1 Introductions

Blockchains offer a mechanism through which mutually mistrusting entities can cooperate in the absence of a trusted third party. However, the permissionless nature of their consensus algorithms (i.e. where no third party is entrusted with the safekeeping of funds) limits their scalability to about ten transactions-per-second (tps) [1,2], far fewer than custodian payment systems offering thousands of tps [3]. These scaling issues have led to a rich literature corpus exploring different blockchain scaling solutions: (i) alternative blockchain consensus architectures [4–13], (ii) sharding [14–18] and (iii) side-chains [19], some of which were systematized in related work [20]. However, modifying a consensus mechanism implies changing one of the key elements of a blockchain system while already in-use, which creates crucial issues such as a lack of backward compatibility, clearly hindering their implementation in practice. Additionally, consensus changes might even lead to different, forked systems [21].

Layer-two protocols are an orthogonal scaling solution. Contrary to the aforementioned solutions, layer-two protocols scale blockchains *without* changing the layer-one trust assumptions and they do not extend or replace the consensus mechanism. Layer-two protocols enable users to perform so-called *off-chain* transactions through private and authenticated communication, rather than broadcasting every single transaction on the (parent) blockchain. This optimization reduces the transaction load on the underlying blockchain and is fully backward compatible. The theoretical transaction throughput is only bounded by the communication bandwidth and latency of the involved parties. Off-chain transaction security can be guaranteed via allocated collateral, e.g. in payment channel designs [22–25] or by offering delayed transaction finality in commit-chain proposals [26].

A rich body of literature has emerged on off-chain protocols, proposing payment [22–25,27], state [28] and virtual [29] channels, payment channel networks (PCNs) [25,27] and related routing protocols [30–35], channel rebalancing [36] and channel factories [37] constructions, commit-chains [26,38], channel hubs [39,40], privacy-enhancing channels [39,41–43] and protocols for refereed delegation [44,45]. However, the sources of information about layer-two protocols are highly disparate. Moreover, in part due to the rapid pace of advancement in the blockchain field, we observe, mostly outside academia, a frequent underspecification of constructions and their adversarial assumptions. This makes it exceedingly difficult to discern thought-through concepts from marketing activities. We aim to clear the fog surrounding layer-two protocols, equipping newcomers to this inaccessible field with a concise reference, and inform the directions of future work. This Systematization of Knowledge (SoK) provides a systematic overview of layer-two systems since the inception of cryptocurrencies in 2009 and identifies the complete set of proposed layer-two protocol types.

This SoK is structured as follows. Section 2 outlines the necessary background followed by different layer-two design classes, *channels* in Sect. 3, *commit-chains* in Sect. 4 and *protocols for refereed delegation* in Sect. 5. For completeness, Sect. 6 presents two sets of complementary approaches to layer-two protocols. Section 7 considers the anonymity and privacy aspects of layer-two protocols, Sect. 8 covers security properties and we conclude the paper in Sect. 9.

2   Blockchains and Off-Chain Transactions

This section establishes the necessary background and isolates the blockchain components relevant to layer-two. The background presented here is necessarily not a complete overview of blockchain-related concepts, which have been surveyed in other SoKs [20, 46]. We distinguish between four different layers within a blockchain system: the *hardware, layer-zero, layer-one* and *layer-two* (cf. Fig. 1).

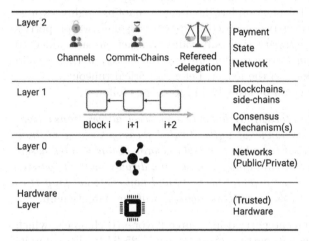

Fig. 1. Suggested blockchain layers. Layer-two channels and commit-chains operate without additional consensus mechanism and transact payments, state, and spawn networks.

Hardware Layer. Trusted Execution Environments (TEE) substitute the need for a blockchain clock with a trusted hardware assumption, thus enabling efficient protocols at other layers such as off-chain payments [47, 48], the removal of dispute processes and backward compatibility [49]. TEE (e.g. Intel SGX) execute sensitive or security-critical application code within *enclaves* [50, 51], tamper-proof from the operating system or other higher-privileged software.

The Network Layer. The network layer, or layer-zero, is typically a peer-to-peer layer on which blockchain nodes exchange information asynchronously [52]. The network layer is of utmost importance to the scalability [53, 54], security [1] and privacy [55] of a blockchain. An efficient layer-zero enables higher transaction throughput and stronger resilience against malicious actors [1]. Blockchain miners, who write transactions to the blockchain, are connected through dedicated *miner* P2P networks (e.g. Fibre [56]), in addition to the public blockchain P2P network. Note that the network layer encompasses the complete network stack of the traditional network architecture rather than only the classical network layer, which focuses Internet routing. More concretely, the network layer should provide reliable communication between two participants in a blockchain.

The Blockchain Layer. Layer-one hosts an immutable append-only chain of blocks that accumulates transactions from parties in a network for public verifiability [46]. Each transaction encodes an update of the state of the blockchain.

A transaction can exchange digital assets between parties or invoke an application (i.e. smart contract). The integrity of the blockchain is ensured by means of a consensus algorithm executed across participants. Consensus algorithms rely on e.g. the computationally expensive Proof-of-Work (PoW) [13,57–60] or a large number of alternatives [8,9,61–65]. Blockchains can be permissionless or permissioned depending on whether participation is open or restricted. We focus on permissionless blockchains as permissioned blockchains lack the non-custodial property, but layer-two concepts apply equally to permissioned blockchains. Crucial for the design of layer-two protocols is the scripting language of the underlying blockchain. Bitcoin-like blockchains are based on a restricted Script language [57] and operate via a set of Unspent Transaction Outputs (UTXO), while other blockchains support Turing-complete languages enabling highly expressive smart contracts [66]. Layer-two protocols typically assume two properties from the blockchain layer: *integrity* (i.e. only valid transactions are added to the ledger) and *eventual synchronicity with an upper time-bound* (i.e. a valid transaction is eventually added to the ledger, before a critical timeout).

We informally define off-chain or layer-two protocols as follows.

Definition 1. *(Layer-two protocols). A layer-two protocol allows transactions between users through the exchange of authenticated messages via a medium which is outside of, but tethered to, a layer-one blockchain. Authenticated assertions are submitted to the parent-chain only in cases of a dispute, with the parent-chain deciding the outcome of the dispute. Security and non-custodial properties of a layer-two protocol rely on the consensus algorithm of the* parent-chain.

Off-chain protocols can be categorized into three flavors: (i) channels, which are formed between n coequal parties (Sect. 3, e.g., [25,27]); (ii) commit-chains, which rely on one central intermediary, trusted regarding availability but untrusted regarding funds. (Section 4, e.g. [26,67]); and (iii) protocols for refereed delegation (Sect. 5, e.g. [44,45]). While side-chains [19] let parties transact on a distinct blockchain, they are not layer-two as they have their own consensus algorithm.

3   Channels

In this section we first provide an account of the evolution of channel constructions (Sects. 3.1 to 3.4), including the requirement for new watching services (Sect. 3.3), before considering how multiple single channels can be synchronized (Sect. 3.5); the routing challenges that synchronized channels present (Sect. 3.6); and finally the construction of payment channel hubs (Sect. 3.7).

3.1   Channel Overview

A channel establishes a private peer-to-peer medium, governed by pre-set rules, e.g. a smart contract, allowing the involved parties to consent to state updates unanimously by exchanging authenticated state transitions off-chain.

Payment channels emerged [22] to support rapid one-way payments, then transitioned towards bi-directional channel designs [25], where both parties can issue and receive payments. *State channels* [28] generalize the concept to support the execution of arbitrary state transitions. A state channel allows n parties to agree, via *unanimous* consent, to a new state of a previously agreed smart contract. A channel's lifetime consists of three phases: *(i)* channel establishment, *(ii)* transition and *(iii)* channel closure or disputes[1].

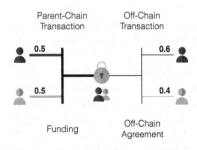

Fig. 2. Payment channel funding (UTXO model) and off-chain transaction.

Channel Establishment. All parties cooperatively *open* a channel by locking collateral on the blockchain (cf. Fig. 2). The funds can only be released by unanimous agreement or through a pre-defined refund condition.

Channel Transitions. Once the channel is open, all parties can *update* the channel's state in a two-step process. First, one party proposes a new state transition by sending a signed command and the new $state_i$ to all other parties. Each party computes the state transition as $state_i \leftarrow T_\alpha(state_{i-1}, cmd_\alpha)$, where T_α denotes the transition function for application α and cmd_α denotes a given command relevant to application α. Second, all other parties re-compute the state transition to verify the proposed state before signing it and sending their signature to all other parties.

Channel Disputes/Closure. If an honest party does not receive n signatures before a local timeout, it assumes that there has been a disagreement about the proposed state. The honest party may trigger a layer-one *dispute* and enforce a new state transition without the cooperation of the other parties.

We generalize [28,29] the properties and security guarantees for responsive parties offered by channels:

Unanimous Establishment: A channel is only considered open if all n parties agree to its establishment.
Unanimous Transition: A transition on layer-two, i.e. without an on-chain dispute, requires all n parties to agree.
Balance Security: An honest party can always withdraw the agreed balance from the channel with an on-chain dispute.
State Progression: A party can always enforce an off-chain state transition on-chain, the state machine thus always reaches a terminal state.

---

[1] While the earliest channel protocols differ slightly from the above three-part *state replacement* technique, they nonetheless fit within the framework of unanimous consent coupled with the local verification of state transitions.

3.2   State Replacement Overview

Channel constructions are inherently based on state replacement techniques (cf. Fig. 3). These techniques assume that participants in a channel are rational and follow the strategy with the highest payoff (e.g. a user publishes an older state if it represents a payment of higher value for this user). To be applicable for the wide range of protocols used to realize channels, the following section discusses generic state transitions. We distinguish four state replacement techniques:

– *Replace by Incentive (RbI)*. A sender shares newly authorized states with a receiver. A rational receiver only signs and publishes the state that pays the highest amount.
– *Replace by Time Lock (RbT)*. Every state is associated with a time lock[2], which decrements every time the state changes. The state with the lowest time lock is considered the latest state, as it can be accepted into the blockchain before all previously authorized states. Once a channel closes, the state that is included in the blockchain deprecates all other states.
– *Replace by Revocation (RbR)*. All parties collectively authorize a new state before revoking the previous state. Upon dispute, the blockchain provides a time period for parties to prove that the published state is a revoked state.
– *Replace by Version (RbV)*. States have a monotonic increasing counter representing the state version. Upon dispute, the authorized state with the highest state version is considered the latest state. A new state replaces a previous state if it has a larger version number.

For *RbI* and *RbT*, the latest state can only be written to the blockchain once. *RbR* and *RbV* introduce a dispute process where the counter-party can provide evidence that a state submitted to the blockchain is invalid. After the dispute, the off-chain contract can either be redeployed to the blockchain (i.e. *closure dispute*) or a set of commands can be executed via the blockchain (i.e. *command dispute*). The introduction of a dispute process introduces a new assumption critical to the channel's security; the *always online assumption* [68] (cf. Sect. 8). Watching services mitigate the assumption by allowing users to delegate their responsibility of raising disputes to a third party.

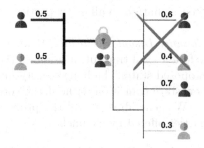

Fig. 3. Payment channel update (UTXO model), invalidate outdated state.

---

[2] Time locks define either *absolute* time expressed as a blockchain block height, or *relative* time expressed as the number of blocks that must elapse after a transaction is included in the blockchain.

3.3 Watching Services

To alleviate the online assumption for channel users, related work proposes to outsource the responsibility of issuing challenges to third-party watching services [68–70]. Users outsource their latest state to the watching service before parting offline. Watching services then act on behalf of the users to secure their funds. Users can still verify the correct behavior of watching services and punish them (e.g. by keeping pre-allocated collateral) in case of non-compliance. Monitor [69] provides watching services within the Lightning Network. Watch-Tower [70] is designed for Eltoo and requires $O(1)$ storage but is currently not compatible with Bitcoin's consensus rules. PISA [68] provides watching services for state channels and requires $O(1)$ storage. PISA instances provide receipts to offline users; the users can burn an instance's security deposit if it misbehaves.

DCWC [71] enables users to engage with multiple watching services, increasing the probability of at least one honest watcher protecting the offline user's interests. On the other hand, Brick [72] proposes an additional proactive role for a watching service. Watchtower committees are formed to manage dispute resolution on behalf of channel participants (i.e. as opposed to executing the dispute process on the blockchain). This approach ensures channel participants are protected against blockchain latency and high transaction fees as the committee will decide the final agreed state for the channel and post it to the blockchain at a later time, but like PISA, its security relies on financial incentives and collateral lockup by members of the watchtower committee.

Outpost [73] achieves O(1) storage for a watchtower in Bitcoin without the need to change any consensus rules. Instead of sending an encrypted justice transaction to the watchtower for every update in the channel, the encrypted justice transaction is stored in the corresponding channel state (as an OP_RETURN). When there is a dispute in the channel, the encrypted justice transaction is recorded in the blockchain. Thus an observer with the decryption key can simply decrypt the justice transaction and relay it to the network. Cerberus [74] considers how to build financially accountable watchtowers in Bitcoin (as PISA accomplished in Ethereum). It requires the watchtower to lock up collateral for each channel it is watching and to participate in every channel update. If the watchtower fails to protect the channel participants, then the participants can force the watchtower to forfeit its deposit.

3.4 Channel Hierarchy

Aiming to reduce the number of required on-chain transactions, there have been proposals to increase the flexibility of channels with regard to applications and participants.

Multiple Applications. Dziembowski et al. [75] and Counterfactual [76] explore the possibility of installing and uninstalling applications off-chain (i.e. without on-chain fee). This allows parties to execute multiple concurrent applications (e.g. tic-tac-toe, poker and bi-directional payments). Such modular channels maintain a set of application instances and each instance operates on an individually allocated collateral. Application instances are isolated from each other (even in case of disputes) and based on *RbV*. Collateral is unanimously assigned to one application and cannot be used simultaneously for other applications due to security reasons.

Channel Factories. Burchert *et al.* [37] propose the concept of a channel factory for Bitcoin, whereby n parties lock coins into a n-party deposit that is then re-allocated to a set of pair-wise payment channels. Each party may maintain one or more pair-wise channels to facilitate transactions. Whenever two parties want to establish a direct channel, all parties cooperatively agree to create a new re-allocation of pair-wise payment channels by jointly updating the n-party deposit. This re-allocation of pair-wise channels can be built using DMC [37], while Ranchal-Pedrosa *et al.* [77] replace DMC with Lightning channels.

3.5 Channel Synchronization

The channel designs discussed in the previous section are limited to the direct interaction among connected parties. This brings forth a new question of whether it is possible for two (or more parties) to avoid setting up a new direct channel on the parent blockchain (and thus avoid prohibitive fees) by finding a path of separate existing channels that indirectly connects them on the network. For instance, if Alice has a channel with Bob, and Bob has a channel with Caroline, then Alice could transact with Caroline via Bob. Such a network of channels is known as a Payment Channel Network (PCN). To facilitate synchronizing a payment (or executing a smart contract) across a path of channels, we present *conditional transfers*. Those allow the sender to lock coins into a transfer such that the receiver can only claim the funds if a condition is satisfied before an expiry time [78–81]. Channel synchronization requires every hop along the path to set up conditional transfers with their counterparty. Two security properties are crucial for channel synchronization. First, *no counterparty risk* is required to ensure that no party defaults on its obligation to execute a transaction in the prescribed manner. Second, *atomicity* ensures that a transaction either succeeds or fails in its entirety. Atomicity is particularly important if one transaction is split over multiple payments or paths.

Virtual Channels. In all constructions discussed previously, intermediate users are required to remain online and explicitly confirm all mediated transactions to successfully synchronize their channels. Dziembowski et al. [29,75] address these shortcomings with the introduction of virtual channels that support payment and state transitions. All intermediaries along the route can lock coins for a fixed period of time and both parties can treat the path as a new *virtual channel* connecting them directly. In this manner, A and B can transact without interacting with intermediaries along the path, thus reducing the transaction latency. Virtual channels are limited by the need to recursively set up a new virtual channel for every intermediary along the path. It is the intermediary's responsibility to ensure the channels close appropriately. Dziembowski et al. [82] extended virtual channels to support more than two parties such that any number of parties can set up a virtual channel without blockchain interaction.

3.6 Routing

If A wants to pay B using a set of intermediate channels, it is necessary to first find one or several paths of open channels from A to B. If the payment only utilizes a single path, all channels need to have sufficient collateral to conduct the payment. If the payment is split over multiple paths, it is necessary to divide the payment in such a manner that channels on each path can handle the partial payment. In this section, we introduce *routing algorithms*, i.e. algorithms for finding paths in a network of payment or state channels. For simplicity, we use the example of payment channels throughout the section. The protocols, however, do apply to state channels.

Existing network routing algorithms for data transmission experience unique challenges when applied to PCNs. The goal of data routing algorithms is the transfer of data from one node to another, i.e. routing changes the state of nodes by transferring information. Node links and bandwidth capacities in data networks moreover are not considered private information. Retransmission of data is an inherent feature of e.g. TCP, and typically doesn't induce significant economic losses to either sender or receiver.

In contrast, the goal of a payment channel routing algorithm is to change the state of the traversed channels to secure the asset delivery from sender to receiver. Depending on the transaction amount, certain channels may not be suitable to route a payment, and channel balances are thus an obstacle that routing algorithms have to account for. An executed channel transaction permanently alters the state of all channels along the path. Further parameters, such as bandwidth and network latencies moreover influence channel path delay characteristics. To protect user privacy, only the total capacity of a channel is disclosed, not the distribution of funds among the two channel participants. Channel transactions might therefore fail and the routing algorithms attempt different execution paths until one succeeds. PCN routing algorithms, therefore, have to account for the unique characteristic of channels to provide satisfactory path recommendations[3]. We summarize five crucial properties routing algorithms for payment channels should satisfy [30–32].

Effectiveness: Given a PCN snapshot and the channel balances, the algorithm should find paths which maximize the success probability of a payment. The algorithm should remain effective when channel balances change.

Efficiency: The overhead of path discovery should be low in latency, communication and computation. Changes of the PCN topology should entail a low update overhead cost.

---

[3] Note that Tor-like routing is inappropriate, as Tor assumes a random relay selection, which wouldn't account for channel capacities.

Scalability: The routing algorithm should remain effective and efficient for large-scale PCNs and high transaction rates.

Cost-Effectiveness: The algorithm should find paths with low transaction fees. The fees of a layer-two transaction should be lower than a layer-one transaction.

Privacy: Routing paths between two parties should be found without disclosing transaction values (i.e. value privacy) and the involved parties (i.e. sender and receiver privacy).

We distinguish between two classes of routing algorithms: global routing and local routing. In global, or source routing, each node maintains a local snapshot of the complete PCN topology. In local routing, the algorithm operates on local information, i.e. is only aware of the node neighbors with which it established channels with.

3.7 Payment Channel Hubs

Related work [83] observes that layer-two systems benefit from centralized (but non-custodial) star-topologies to reduce *(i)* collateral lockup costs and to *(ii)* simplify routing complexities. A payment channel hub (PCH) is essentially a node in a PCN that maintains many channels with different peers. Having a network with multiple interconnected PCHs should result in a lower average path length. A reduced path length implies a reduction in collateral cost and route discovery complexity. Still PCHs face significant locked capital requirements for each channel. For example, a PCN node with $1M$ channels, each channel sending on average \$1000 of transaction volume, requires the hub to lock up a total of \$$1B$. Rebalancing operations are only possible via costly and slow parent-chain transactions. Moreover, user-onboarding is a costly process, a PCN node with $1M$ users would require $1M$ parent-chain setup transactions (costing more than \$$100k$ on Ethereum).

3.8 Summary

In this section we have presented the evolution of channel constructions from *Replace by Incentive* through to *Replace by Version*. Given a network of channels, we have considered the role of conditional transfers to let parties synchronize payments (or construct new virtual channels) across a path of channels. With respect to routing and finding a path that connects two parties in a channel-based network, we discussed the limitations of deployed routing algorithms due to their reliance on source routing. Alternative algorithms that rely only on local knowledge offer some promise, but require further work to achieve effectiveness comparable to that of source routing. Finally a significant consequence of channel networks is the requirement for users to remain online and synchronized with the network to watch for malice disputes. To alleviate the online assumption, there are several proposals for third party watching services who can respond to a dispute on the user's behalf. All proposals tend to focus on building highly available watching networks and using on-chain collateral to ensure the watching services can be held financially accountable.

The aforementioned results suggest that blockchains can scale further by leveraging layer-two technologies and thus without changes to the underlying layer one. However, PCNs experience limitations and their scalability properties have not yet been quantified appropriately. While layer-one transaction costs are quantified by their *size* (on UTXO blockchains), or computational complexity (on smart contract blockchains), the transaction costs on layer-two are primarily correlated to the transaction value (in \$). The higher a layer-two transaction value, the more on-chain collateral needs to be reserved, locking up potentially considerable amounts of funds *in advance*. Analysis of the economic consequences of channel constructions, (e.g. as conducted in [84]), is an open and important area for future work, particularly in relation to the economic incentives for channel watching services [85] and the fee structures for channel payments [86].

4   Commit-Chains

4.1   Commit-Chain Overview

In contrast to channels, commit-chains are maintained by one single party that acts as an untrusted intermediary for managing transactions between users. Hence, commit-chains serve a similar purpose as payment channel hubs but with protocols specifically optimized for this scenario. The operator is responsible for collecting commit-chain transactions from the users and periodically submits a commitment to all collected transactions to the parent-blockchain. Unlike channels, commit-chains do not rely on a three-state model (opening, transitions, dispute/closure phase), but rather on an *always ongoing state* once launched. After an operator has launched a commit-chain, users can join by contacting the operator. They can then conduct transactions that are recorded on the commit-chain. Users can anytime withdraw or move their assets to the parent chain.

Periodic Checkpoint Commitments. Commit-chain users may need to periodically return online to observe the on-chain checkpoint commitment, which can be instantiated as a Merkle tree root or a Zero Knowledge Proof (ZKP) [26,87]. Merkle root commitments do not self-enforce valid state transitions and therefore require users to participate in challenge-response protocols if a commitment is invalid. In contrast, ZKPs enforce consistent state transitions on-chain, thus reducing potential operator misbehavior. A challenge response mechanism is still required to ensure the completeness of the checkpoint (i.e., that it summarizes the latest state of all user accounts). Currently, there exists no efficient method to instantiate commit-chains on blockchains without highly expressive scripting languages.

Data Availability. As commit-chain data is not broadcast for efficiency reasons, users must retrieve/maintain data required to (partially) exit a commit-chain, commonly referred to as the data availability requirement. Data availability challenges may challenge a commit-chain operator to provide the necessary data or halt the operator upon misbehavior [26], allowing users to exit with their last confirmed balance.

Centralized but Untrusted Intermediary. The centralized operator may become a point of availability failure, but it does not hold custody of funds. The operator may thus censor commit-chain transactions, encouraging mistreated users to exit anytime and move towards another commit-chain.

Eventual Transaction Finality. Unlike previously discussed layer-two protocols, the intermediary commit-chain operator does not require on-chain collateral to securely route a payment between two commit-chain users. In this setting, commit-chain transactions do not offer instant transaction finality (as in channels), but eventual finality after commit-chain transactions are recorded securely in an on-chain checkpoint.

Reduced Routing Requirements. Because a commit-chain can potentially host millions of users, few statically connected commit-chains are envisioned to spawn stable networks with low routing complexity. However, we are not aware of any proposals for atomic cross commit-chain transactions.

We generalize the security properties for users as follows:

Free Establishment: Users join a commit-chain without an on-chain transaction by requesting an operator signature [26].

Agreed Transition: A commit-chain transaction is agreed upon by at least the sender and the commit-chain operator.

Balance Security: Honest users can always withdraw agreed balances from the commit-chain with an on-chain dispute.

State Progression: User can enforce an off-chain state transition on-chain.

Commitment Integrity: Users can verify the integrity of commitments and force the commit-chain operator to seize operation (and rollback to the latest commitment)[4].

Unlike with channels, *state progression* is not a default security property for commit-chains, because they only offer *eventual finality*, unless off-chain transactions are secured by additional collateral [26]. In the worst case, transactions remain unconfirmed if the next commitment is invalid or not provided.

4.2   Summary

Unlike channels, commit-chains allow transaction recipients to remain offline at the time of payment, approaching similar usability properties to layer-one transactions. Conditional on using smart contract enabled blockchains, commit-chains also allow for a reduction in the required layer-two collateral.

Commit-chains have been shown to scale PoW blockchains by several orders of magnitude [26], trading-off decentralization for a more centralized (but non-custodial) architecture. Due to periodic checkpoints in commit-chains, delayed

---

[4] To mitigate the possibility of a false accusation attack by a user against the operator, the operator may require the user to subsidize the cost of a response to such a challenge. Note that this in turn may introduce a user grieving vector. To date, no appropriate parameterization or more elegant solution has been proposed.

transaction finality is secure without collateral of the intermediate operator [26]. Operator collateral is "re-usable" [26] after each checkpoint, potentially reducing the locked capital and on-chain costs of PCHs.

Table 1 provides an overview and comparison of channel, channel-hub and commit-chain constructions.

5   Protocols for Refereed Delegation

In this section, we overview the protocols that focus on solving disputes among participants differently to how they are handled in channels and commit-chains[5].

So far we have assumed that all state transitions in an off-chain protocol can be executed on a layer-one blockchain. Such transitions range from the execution of conditional transfers to the execution of an application for a state channel. Yet while the layer-two approaches we have considered so far allow us to significantly increase the number of state updates performed among two or more parties, they are restricted to those whose dispute resolution mechanism builds upon a mechanism that can be *fully* executed on-chain. We now present two approaches which seek to reduce the on-chain requirements for the dispute resolution, thereby enlarging the set of feasible layer-two applications.

Table 1. Comparison of layer-two transaction designs[a].

	Channel	Channel Hub	Commit-Chain
Topology	Mesh	Star	Star
Lifecycle	3-phase	3-phase	Periodic commit
Compatibility	Any chain	Any chain	Smart Contract chain
Privacy	value privacy, relationship anonymity	payment anonymity, ✗ unlinkability	✗
Offline TX Reception	✗	✗	✓
Mass-Exit Security	✗	✗	✓(payments)
TX Finality	Instant	Instant	Delayed or Instant
Instant TX Collateral	Full	Full	Reusable [26]
Delayed TX Collateral	NA	NA	0
Collateral Allocation	$O(n)$ on-chain	$O(n)$ on-chain	$O(1)$ on-chain [26]
User On-Boarding	On-chain TX	On-chain TX	Off-chain [26]

[a] Protocols for refereed delegation, distinct in nature with less focus on payments, are presented in Section 5.

5.1   Bi-section Protocols

Instead of forcing conflicting users to post their (partial) state on-chain, a bisection protocol works in two stages: (i) users look for the minimal verification

---

[5] In contrast to channels, commit-chains have not yet been specified to support arbitrary state transitions.

step required to convince a third party (e.g., miner) of the validity of their statement; (ii) miners verify the (simplified) state from conflicting users to determine who is right. Truebit [45] and Arbitrum [44] are two approaches in this paradigm.

Truebit [45], inspired by verifiable computation, proposed the use of bisection protocols to extend the computational capacity of a layer-one blockchain by taking the computation off-chain. At a high level, for a given computational task, a *solver* will post the solution alongside a commitment to a list of sub-tasks that led to the solution. The blockchain enforces a challenge period to let challengers verify the solution's correctness off-chain and issue a challenge if they disagree. If there is a disagreement, the blockchain enforces a verification game that performs a binary-search for the list of sub-tasks. When it finds the task that led to the disagreement, it will simply execute it on-chain and verify the claim. While the above approach permits scalable off-chain computation, every verification game requires a logarithmic number of transactions depending on the size of the computation.

Arbitrum [44] takes this approach further by introducing a new virtual machine and a state channel. This lets a distributed set of parties execute a program in a custom virtual machine and unanimously agree to a commitment (i.e. state assertion) of the program's new state. If co-operation in the state channel breaks down, then any party in the channel can compute a state transition and post a commitment to the new state to the blockchain (i.e. a disputable assertion). This triggers a similar dispute process to that used in Truebit, where any other party can challenge the assertion and participate in a bi-section protocol.

6 Complementary Approaches for Layer-Two Protocols

In this section we present two sets of approaches which are complementary to layer-two protocols: (i) trusted execution environments and (ii) side-chains. In contrast to layer-two protocols, these approaches invoke additional and differentiated trust assumptions. Trusted execution environments require a shifted trust assumption towards the CPU manufacturer. Side-chains require trust in the independent consensus algorithm of the side-chain.

6.1 Trusted Execution Environments

The trusted execution environment (TEE), e.g. Intel SGX [88], approach constitutes an orthogonal approach to that of existing layer-two protocols and can provide a high level of efficiency while requiring a benign hardware manufacturer.

Trusting a TEE to provide integrity naturally overcomes many obstacles of non-TEE protocols:

No collateral lockup: TEEs absorb the trust requirements, otherwise guaranteed via on-chain collateral.

Interoperability: The computation at the TEE can encode the logic and transaction format required for any blockchain.

Parallelized Disputes: TEEs can emulate the logic of global preimage manager to enable parallel disputes.

Ensured fees: TEEs follow the protocol definitions and pay honest users for their synchronization service.

Note that besides the shifted trust assumptions towards the CPU manufacturer, TEEs suffer from their own security concerns such as rollback [51] and side-channel attacks [89].

Teechain [47] and Teechan [48] synchronize payments across channels using TEEs. TEE enable expressive and off-chain smart contracts on restricted Bitcoin-based blockchain [49]. Tesseract [90] proposes to construct a scalable TEE based real-time cross-chain cryptocurrency exchange. In relation to light clients in Bitcoin, BITE [91] leverages TEEs to enable full nodes to serve privacy-preserving requests from light clients, when used in combination with other private information retrieval and side-channel protection techniques. ZLiTE [92] also leverages TEEs to provide privacy-preserving light clients for Zcash, whereby light clients operate in conjunction with a TEE-enabled server (e.g., running Intel SGX [88]).

6.2   Side-Chains

A second complementary approach is that of side-chains [19]. A side-chain is a distinct blockchain with a separate consensus algorithm attached to a parent-chain. Side-chains validate transactions and hence take over some of the parent-chain's load. Side-chains enable digital assets to be moved between a parent-chain and a side-chain, such that alternative blockchains can be developed without necessitating the creation of an alternative digital asset or coin: the parent-chain asset can be used directly on the side-chain.

The central innovation for side-chains is that of a two-way peg. A two-way peg is the mechanism permitting the transfer of digital assets at a certain exchange rate between a parent-chain and a side-chain. A two-way peg allows digital assets to be transferred from a parent-chain to a side-chain by sending parent-chain coins an output on the parent-chain that is locked by a Simplified Payment Verification (SPV) proof [19], which can then be unlocked by an SPV proof on the side-chain. For the period in which digital assets are locked on the parent-chain, the assets can be moved freely around on the side-chain. To transfer assets back to the parent-chain, funds are sent to an SPV locked output on the side-chain and an SPV proof on the parent-chain unlocks previously locked funds on the parent-chain. The varieties of a two-way peg are as follows.

Symmetric: SPV security is required to transfer funds between the side-chain and the parent-chain, independently of the direction.

Asymmetric: where users of the side-chain are fully aware of the state of the parent-chain, such that an SPV proofs are not required to transfer funds from a parent-chain to a side-chain, but are required to transfer funds back.

Side-chain constructions treat assets from different parent-chains as different asset types, which are not interchangeable but which can be explicitly traded.

Potential limitations to the use of side-chains [19] include, for instance, an increase in complexity at both the network and asset level, the creation of new attack vectors, and an increase in the risks associated with centralized mining.

7 Anonymity and Privacy

In this section we set out the relevant privacy concepts for layer-two (Sect. 7.1).

Layer-one transaction anonymity and privacy is extensively studied [93–96], uncovering that blockchain pseudonymity does not entail strong privacy guarantees. A public blockchain allows an adversary to link a sender and receiver of payments as well as trace back the origin of coins, breaking the *unlinkability* and *untraceability* properties. Privacy-focused blockchains [97–100] build upon cryptographic techniques [101–103] to obfuscate on-chain information. Unfortunately, side-channel information (e.g. usage patterns) enable linkability and traceability attacks [97,104–107]. As off-chain transactions only have a minimal blockchain footprint, one might believe they provide privacy-by-design.

However, achieving privacy and unlinkability of layer-two transactions is not trivial [41,78,108]. The creation of a channel associates a permanent pseudonym (e.g. public keys), while synchronization among channels (cf. Sect. 3.6) may reveal the pseudonym of the cooperating parties. In Lightning, the a node ID is linked with an IP address and this information is broadcast across the network. Furthermore, naive route discovery among two channels with a disjoint set of participants might require the knowledge of the (partial) topology for the channel network. In HTLC payments (cf. Sect. 3.5), the intermediate channels on the path use the same cryptographic condition $y = H(R)$. An adversary on the path can observe the channel updates (i.e. share the same condition y) and can deduce who is paying to whom.

7.1 Layer-Two Privacy Notions

We differentiate between *(i)* an *off-path* adversary, which only has access to the blockchain; and *(ii)* an *on-path* adversary, which additionally participates in the layer-two protocol.

Payment Hub Privacy. A PCH (cf. Sect. 3.7) or commit-chain (cf. Sect. 4) operator may have access to mediated transaction amounts and sender or receiver pseudonyms. In this setting, we consider the following privacy notions.

Payment Anonymity [41]: In the absence of side channels, the receiver of a payment, possibly in collusion with a set of malicious senders, learns nothing about an honest sender's spending pattern.

Unlinkability [39]: The operator cannot link the sender and the receiver of a given payment among the set of all feasible sender-receiver pairs.

Multi-hop Privacy. We consider the following privacy properties for routed payments (cf. Sect. 3.6).

(Off-path) Value Privacy [78]: An adversary not involved in a payment does not learn the transacted value. If the adversary is part of the payment path it trivially learns the transacted value while forwarding it.

(On-path) Relationship Anonymity [78]: Given two payments between two pairs of honest sender and receiver, the adversary (who might control some of the intermediate channels) cannot tell which sender paid to which receiver with a probability higher than 50%. Off-path adversaries are not considered here since transaction data is shared only among involved participants.

Unlike other payment networks such as credit networks [30, 109–111], existing privacy notions in PCNs do not consider link privacy (e.g. whether an adversary can determine the existence of a payment channel between two users) or whether it is possible to infer the (partial) topology of a PCN. Channels may be unannounced (e.g. private Lightning channels), such that an adversary may be unaware of the link between users.

7.2 Summary

We have seen that while the default transaction privacy on layer-two is likely better than on layer-one, layer-two transactions cannot by default be considered private. TumbleBit and A2L achieve unlinkability but not payment anonymity. BOLT does not support Bitcoin but offers stronger privacy guarantees. Even in the simplified PCH setting, it seems that tradeoffs between privacy and compatibility are required. Multi-hop payment protocols do not enforce single hop privacy guarantees (e.g a user learns predecessor and successor in a payment path) at the gain of global privacy guarantees such as value privacy and relationship anonymity. As demonstrated in AMHL, it is possible to achieve privacy guarantees and backwards compatibility with most existing blockchains. State channels and commit-chains demonstrate interesting functionalities based on the expressiveness of rich scripting languages. These protocols, however, to date do not aim at providing anonymity and privacy guarantees from the commit-chain operator. Instead, privacy is considered an orthogonal research problem. Recent work [44, 45] demonstrates that including additional verification functionality to the consensus layer opens the door for hiding contract activity in state channels.

8 Security

This section provides an overview of layer-two security concepts.

The consensus [1, 112] and network [113] security of blockchains has been extensively investigated. Security is fundamental to distributed ledgers, as the shift of trust assumptions from a single custodian to a decentralized non-custodial network only prevents the loss of funds if the system's security properties are sound. Layer-two research benefits from this body of literature, but necessitates the introduction of new requirements, trust assumptions and adversarial models.

8.1 Layer-Two Security Notions

While experimental studies so far focus on the connectivity of PCNs [114], formal security studies focus on the notion of *balance security*, both in the payment hub [39,41] and multi-hop payment [78] settings, as well as provably secure off-chain protocols for multi-party computation [115]. Balance security intuitively defines that layer-two protocols must achieve two properties: (i) the adversary cannot extract more funds than previously allocated in the channel's funding; (ii) honest users do not lose funds even when other parties collude. As with privacy, this security concept has been formalized in both paradigms: cryptographic games and the UC framework. BOLT, A2L and TumbleBit are the payment hub systems with formal security guarantees, while Rayo & Fulgor, AMHL and Perun provide formal security guarantees in the multi-hop setting. While previous work assumes a somewhat ideal model for the underlying blockchain to highlight the security and privacy properties at layer-two, recent work [116] shows a security analysis of the Lighting Network, tracing how its security properties build upon a blockchain model that faithfully represents Bitcoin at present. However, the work [116] does not model aspects such as fees, privacy, or cooperative channel closure. NOCUST provides a thorough study of *balance security* for commit-chains.

Consistency Proofs. Many layer-two protocols rely on challenge-response protocols to detect and prove misbehavior using the blockchain as a recourse for disputes. An alternative strategy to enforce consistency of an off-chain protocol is to let the blockchain verify a succinct proof attesting to consistency of the second layer's state. While ZKPs [117] suffer from expensive on-chain verification costs (approximately 650k gas on Ethereum) per proof [118], they can attest to potentially large state transitions which otherwise would require significant on-chain resources. For commit-chains, zkSNARKS were shown to enforce consistent checkpoints [26], leaving data availability of the external ledger as the remaining challenge vector.

8.2 Layer-Two Security Threats

There are security threats idiosyncratic to layer-two, as follows.

Hot Wallets: Channels' requirement of unanimous agreement for state updates, and therefore that all involved parties need to be online with access to their signing keys, makes it critical to keep keys online in a *hot wallet*. These wallets make parties prime targets for adversaries.
Online Assumption: Parties are required to remain online and fully synchronized with the PCN and blockchain. Therefore if a party goes offline, they become vulnerable to an adversary.
Blockchain Reliability and Mass Exits: Layer-two designs assume that the underlying blockchain accepts transactions eventually; however, under congestion, parties may fail to meet deadlines to settle disputes.

Security of Synchronizing Protocols: such as the *wormhole attack* [79], where transaction fees can be stolen, and the *American Call Option Attack* [119], where an adversary sets up a multi-hop payment but does not release the trigger to finalize the payment.

8.3 Summary

The security guarantees of layer-two transactions rely not only on the parent chain's consensus guarantees and on-chain security collateral data availability concerns and blockchain congestion threats introduce a new dimension of game-theoretic challenges that are not considered by current formal definitions. For instance, current UC definitions consider the blockchain as ideal components, which disregards the mass-exit concern.

9   Conclusion

This SoK systematizes the rich literature that has emerged on layer-two transactions since the inception of cryptocurrencies in 2009, categorizing the work into three main approaches: payment and state channels, commit-chains and protocols for refereed delegation. In addition to presenting the central aspect of the protocols in these three categories, we review in detail their anonymity, privacy and security aspects. Our over-arching aim in this paper is to lower the *barrier to entry* to the study of layer-two protocols.

We observe, overall, that layer-two protocols enable blockchains to scale without modification on the base layer but that the performance improvement results in different security guarantees for off-chain payments than on-chain transactions. We also observe a likely inherent trade-off between collateral and transaction finality at layer-two. In the context of channel constructions, instant finality requires full collateralization. For commit-chains, the requirements for full on-chain collateralization is reduced but in exchange for eventual finality. Notably, commit-chains enable secure off-chain transactions without collateralizing the full off-chain transaction volume.

Both payment channels and commit-chains face privacy challenges. Our discussion highlights clearly that not publishing transactions on a public blockchain is not sufficient for solving the privacy issues experienced in blockchain systems. Privacy in off-chain transactions requires common definitions and new protocols.

We explicitly lay out the shift in transaction costs from transaction size (in bytes) to transaction value. It stands to reason that such a shift entails economic consequences. In particular, the relation between on-chain and off-chain fees raises interesting game-theoretical questions for a rational actor aiming to minimize the fees they pay or maximize the fees they gain.

Acknowledgments. The authors would like to thank Alexei Zamyatin and Sam Werner for their valuable feedback on earlier paper versions. This work has been partially supported by EPSRC Standard Research Studentship (DTP) (EP/R513052/1);

220   L. Gudgeon et al.

by Chaincode Labs; by the Austrian Science Fund (FWF) through the Lisa Meitner program; by the Ethereum Foundation, Ethereum Community Fund and Research Institute.

References

1. Gervais, A., Karame, G.O., Wüst, K., Glykantzis, V., Ritzdorf, H., Čapkun, S.: On the security and performance of proof of work blockchains. In: Conference on Computer and Communications Security, pp. 3–16. ACM (2016)
2. Croman, K., et al.: On scaling decentralized blockchains. In: Clark, J., Meiklejohn, S., Ryan, P.Y.A., Wallach, D., Brenner, M., Rohloff, K. (eds.) FC 2016. LNCS, vol. 9604, pp. 106–125. Springer, Heidelberg (2016). https://doi.org/10.1007/978-3-662-53357-4_8
3. VISA: Visa inc. at a glance (2015). https://usa.visa.com/dam/VCOM/download/corporate/media/visa-fact-sheet-Jun2015.pdf
4. Kiayias, A., Russell, A., David, B., Oliynykov, R.: Ouroboros: a provably secure proof-of-stake blockchain protocol. In: Katz, J., Shacham, H. (eds.) CRYPTO 2017. LNCS, vol. 10401, pp. 357–388. Springer, Cham (2017). https://doi.org/10.1007/978-3-319-63688-7_12
5. Buterin, V.: Slasher: A punitive proof-of-stake algorithm (2014). https://blog.ethereum.org/2014/01/15/slasher-a-punitive-proof-of-stake-algorithm/
6. Anon: Casper (2018). https://github.com/ethereum/casper
7. Miller, A., Juels, A., Shi, E., Parno, B., Katz, J.: PermaCoin: repurposing bitcoin work for data preservation. In: Symposium on Security and Privacy, pp. 475–490 (2014)
8. Hønsi, T.: Spacemint-a cryptocurrency based on proofs of space. IACR Cryptology ePrint Archive (2017)
9. Sawtooth (2019). https://intelledger.github.io/introduction.html
10. Kogias, E.K., Jovanovic, P., Gailly, N., Khoffi, I., Gasser, L., Ford, B.: Enhancing bitcoin security and performance with strong consistency via collective signing. In: USENIX Security Symposium, pp. 279–296 (2016)
11. Luu, L., Narayanan, V., Baweja, K., Zheng, C., Gilbert, S., Saxena, P.: SCP: a computationally-scalable byzantine consensus protocol for blockchains. IACR Cryptology ePrint Archive 2015/1168 (2015)
12. Pass, R., Shi, E.: Hybrid consensus: efficient consensus in the permissionless model. In: 31 International Symposium on Distributed Computing, p. 6 (2017)
13. Eyal, I., Gencer, A.E., Sirer, E.G., Van Renesse, R.: Bitcoin-NG: a scalable blockchain protocol. In: Symposium on Networked Systems Design and Implementation, pp. 45–59 (2016)
14. Anon.: Sharding roadmap (2019). https://github.com/ethereum/wiki/wiki/Sharding-roadmap
15. Luu, L., Narayanan, V., Zheng, C., Baweja, K., Gilbert, S., Saxena, P.: A secure sharding protocol for open blockchains. In: Conference on Computer and Communications Security, pp. 17–30. ACM (2016)
16. Gencer, A.E., van Renesse, R., Sirer, E.G.: Service-oriented sharding with aspen. arXiv preprint arXiv:1611.06816 (2016)
17. Zamani, M., Movahedi, M., Raykova, M.: Rapidchain: scaling blockchain via full sharding. In: Proceedings of the 2018 ACM SIGSAC Conference on Computer and Communications Security, pp. 931–948. ACM (2018)

18. Kokoris-Kogias, E., Jovanovic, P., Gasser, L., Gailly, N., Syta, E., Ford, B.: OmniLedger: a secure, scale-out, decentralized ledger via sharding. In: Symposium on Security and Privacy, pp. 583–598 (2018)
19. Back, A., et al.: Enabling blockchain innovations with pegged sidechains (2014). http://www.opensciencereview.com/papers/123/enablingblockchain-innovations-with-pegged-sidechains
20. Bano, S., et al.: Consensus in the age of blockchains. arXiv preprint arXiv:1711.03936 (2017)
21. Bitcoin cash (2008). https://www.bitcoincash.org
22. Hearn, M.: Micro-payment channels implementation now in bitcoinj (2013). https://bitcointalk.org/index.php?topic=244656.0
23. Anon: bitcoinj (2019). https://bitcoinj.github.io/
24. Decker, C., Wattenhofer, R.: A fast and scalable payment network with bitcoin duplex micropayment channels. In: Pelc, A., Schwarzmann, A.A. (eds.) SSS 2015. LNCS, vol. 9212, pp. 3–18. Springer, Cham (2015). https://doi.org/10.1007/978-3-319-21741-3_1
25. Poon, J., Dryja, T.: The bitcoin lightning network: scalable off-chain instant payments (2016). https://lightning.network/lightning-network-paper.pdf
26. Khalil, R., Gervais, A., Felley, G.: NOCUST-a securely scalable commit-chain (2018). https://eprint.iacr.org/2018/642.pdf
27. AG, B.T.: Raiden network (2019). https://raiden.network/
28. Miller, A., Bentov, I., Kumaresan, R., McCorry, P.: Sprites: payment channels that go faster than lightning. arXiv preprint arXiv:1702.05812 (2017)
29. Dziembowski, S., Eckey, L., Faust, S., Malinowski, D.: PERUN: virtual payment channels over cryptographic currencies. In: Symposium on Security and Privacy (2019)
30. Malavolta, G., Moreno-Sanchez, P., Kate, A., Maffei, M.: SilentWhispers: enforcing security and privacy in credit networks. In: Network and Distributed System Security Symposium (2017)
31. Roos, S., Moreno-Sanchez, P., Kate, A., Goldberg, I.: Settling payments fast and private: efficient decentralized routing for path-based transactions (2018)
32. Sivaraman, V., Venkatakrishnan, S.B., Alizadeh, M., Fanti, G., Viswanath, P.: Routing cryptocurrency with the spider network. arXiv preprint arXiv:1809.05088 (2018)
33. Sunshine, C.A.: Source routing in computer networks. SIGCOMM Comput. Commun. Rev. **7**(1), 29–33 (1977)
34. Anon: Lightning-onion (2018). https://github.com/lightningnetwork/lightning-onion
35. Prihodko, P., Zhigulin, S., Sahno, M., Ostrovskiy, A., Osuntokun, O.: Flare: an approach to routing in lightning network (2016). https://bitfury.com/content/downloads/whitepaper_flare_an_approach_to_routing_in_lightning_network_7_7_2016.pdf
36. Khalil, R., Gervais, A.: Revive: rebalancing off-blockchain payment networks. In: Conference on Computer and Communications Security, pp. 439–453. ACM (2017)
37. Burchert, C., Decker, C., Wattenhofer, R.: Scalable funding of bitcoin micropayment channel networks. R. Soc. Open Sci. **5**(8), 180089 (2018)
38. Poon, J., Buterin, V.: Plasma: scalable autonomous smart contracts (2017). https://plasma.io/plasma.pdf
39. Heilman, E., Alshenibr, L., Baldimtsi, F., Scafuro, A., Goldberg, S.: TumbleBit: an untrusted bitcoin-compatible anonymous payment hub (2017)

40. Heilman, E., Lipmann, S., Goldberg, S.: The Arwen trading protocols (2019)
41. Green, M., Miers, I.: Bolt: anonymous payment channels for decentralized currencies. In: Conference on Computer and Communications Security, pp. 473–489. ACM (2017)
42. Heilman, E., Baldimtsi, F., Goldberg, S.: Blindly signed contracts: anonymous on-blockchain and off-blockchain bitcoin transactions. In: Clark, J., Meiklejohn, S., Ryan, P.Y.A., Wallach, D., Brenner, M., Rohloff, K. (eds.) FC 2016. LNCS, vol. 9604, pp. 43–60. Springer, Heidelberg (2016). https://doi.org/10.1007/978-3-662-53357-4_4
43. Atlas, K.: The inevitability of privacy in lightning networks (2017). https://www.kristovatlas.com/the-inevitability-of-privacy-in-lightning-networks/
44. Kalodner, H., Goldfeder, S., Chen, X., Weinberg, S.M., Felten, E.W.: Arbitrum: scalable, private smart contracts. In: USENIX Security Symposium, pp. 1353–1370 (2018)
45. Teutsch, J., Reitwiessner, C.: A scalable verification solution for blockchains. https://people.cs.uchicago.edu/~teutsch/papers/truebit.pdf
46. Bonneau, J., Miller, A., Clark, J., Narayanan, A., Kroll, J.A., Felten, E.W.: SoK: research perspectives and challenges for bitcoin and cryptocurrencies. In: Symposium on Security and Privacy, pp. 104–121. IEEE (2015)
47. Lind, J., Eyal, I., Kelbert, F., Naor, O., Pietzuch, P., Sirer, E.G.: Teechain: scalable blockchain payments using trusted execution environments. arXiv preprint arXiv:1707.05454 (2017)
48. Lind, J., Eyal, I., Pietzuch, P., Sirer, E.G.: Teechan: payment channels using trusted execution environments. arXiv preprint arXiv:1612.07766 (2016)
49. Das, P., et al.: FastKitten: practical smart contracts on bitcoin (2019)
50. Costan, V., Devadas, S.: Intel SGX explained. IACR Cryptology ePrint Archive 2016(086), 1–118 (2016)
51. Matetic, S., et al.: ROTE: rollback protection for trusted execution. In: USENIX Security Symposium, pp. 1289–1306 (2017)
52. Neudecker, T., Hartenstein, H.: Network layer aspects of permissionless blockchains. IEEE Commun. Surv. Tutor. 21, 838–857 (2018)
53. Decker, C., Wattenhofer, R.: Information propagation in the bitcoin network. In: Conference on Peer-to-Peer Computing, pp. 1–10 (2013)
54. Klarman, U., Basu, S., Kuzmanovic, A., Sirer, E.G.: bloXroute: a scalable trustless blockchain distribution network (2018). https://bloxroute.com/wp-content/uploads/2018/03/bloXroute-whitepaper.pdf
55. Gervais, A., Čapkun, S., Karame, G.O., Gruber, D.: On the privacy provisions of bloom filters in lightweight bitcoin clients. In: Computer Security Applications Conference, pp. 326–335 (2014)
56. Bitcoin fibre (2019). http://www.bitcoinfibre.org/
57. Nakamoto, S.: Bitcoin: a peer-to-peer electronic cash system (2008). https://bitcoin.org/bitcoin.pdf
58. Sompolinsky, Y., Zohar, A.: Accelerating bitcoin's transaction processing. fast money grows on trees, not chains. IACR Cryptology ePrint Archive 2013/881 (2013)
59. Lerner, S.D.: Decor+ hop: a scalable blockchain protocol. https://scalingbitcoin.org/papers/DECOR-HOP.pdf
60. Sompolinsky, Y., Lewenberg, Y., Zohar, A.: SPECTRE: a fast and scalable cryptocurrency protocol. IACR Cryptology ePrint Archive 2016/1159 (2016)
61. Zhang, F., Eyal, I., Escriva, R., Juels, A., Van Renesse, R.: REM: resource-efficient mining for blockchains. In: USENIX Security Symposium, pp. 1427–1444 (2017)

62. David, B., Gaži, P., Kiayias, A., Russell, A.: Ouroboros Praos: an adaptively-secure, semi-synchronous proof-of-stake blockchain. In: Nielsen, J.B., Rijmen, V. (eds.) EUROCRYPT 2018. LNCS, vol. 10821, pp. 66–98. Springer, Cham (2018). https://doi.org/10.1007/978-3-319-78375-8_3

63. Bentov, I., Pass, R., Shi, E.: Snow white: provably secure proofs of stake. IACR Cryptology ePrint Archive 2016/919 (2016)

64. Milutinovic, M., He, W., Wu, H., Kanwal, M.: Proof of luck: an efficient blockchain consensus protocol. In: Proceedings of the 1st Workshop on System Software for Trusted Execution, p. 2. ACM (2016)

65. Borge, M., Kokoris-Kogias, E., Jovanovic, P., Gasser, L., Gailly, N., Ford, B.: Proof-of-personhood: redemocratizing permissionless cryptocurrencies. In: 2017 IEEE European Symposium on Security and Privacy Workshops (EuroS&PW), pp. 23–26. IEEE (2017)

66. Wood, G.: Ethereum: a secure decentralised generalised transaction ledger. Ethereum Proj. Yellow Paper 151, 1–32 (2014)

67. Plasma cash: Plasma with much less per-user data checking (2018). https://ethresear.ch/t/plasma-cash-plasma-with-much-less-per-user-data-checking/1298

68. McCorry, P., Bakshi, S., Bentov, I., Miller, A., Meiklejohn, S.: Pisa: arbitration outsourcing for state channels. IACR Cryptology ePrint Archive 2018/582 (2018)

69. Dryja, T.: Unlinkable outsourced channel monitoring (2016). https://scalingbitcoin.org/transcript/milan2016/unlinkable-outsourced-channel-monitoring

70. Osuntokun, O.: Hardening lightning, harder, better, faster stronger (2015). https://cyber.stanford.edu/sites/g/files/sbiybj9936/f/hardening_lightning_updated.pdf

71. Avarikioti, G., Laufenberg, F., Sliwinski, J., Wang, Y., Wattenhofer, R.: Towards secure and efficient payment channels. arXiv preprint arXiv:1811.12740 (2018)

72. Avarikioti, G., Kogias, E.K., Wattenhofer, R.: Brick: asynchronous state channels. arXiv preprint arXiv:1905.11360 (2019)

73. Khabbazian, M., Nadahalli, T., Wattenhofer, R.: Outpost: a responsive lightweight watchtower. In: Proceedings of the 1st ACM Conference on Advances in Financial Technologies, pp. 31–40. ACM (2019)

74. Avarikioti, G., Litos, O.S.T., Wattenhofer, R.: Cerberus channels: incentivizing watchtowers for bitcoin. Financial Cryptography and Data Security (FC) (2020)

75. Dziembowski, S., Faust, S., Hostáková, K.: General state channel networks. In: Conference on Computer and Communications Security, pp. 949–966. ACM (2018)

76. Joleman, J., Horne, L., Xuanji, L.: Counterfactual: generalized state channels (2018). https://l4.ventures/papers/statechannels.pdf

77. Pedrosa, A.R., Potop-Butucaru, M., Tucci-Piergiovanni, S.: Lightning factories (2019)

78. Malavolta, G., Moreno-Sanchez, P., Kate, A., Maffei, M., Ravi, S.: Concurrency and privacy with payment-channel networks. In: Conference on Computer and Communications Security, CCS 2017, pp. 455–471. ACM, New York (2017). https://doi.org/10.1145/3133956.3134096

79. Malavolta, G., Moreno-Sanchez, P., Schneidewind, C., Kate, A., Maffei, M.: Anonymous multi-hop locks for blockchain scalability and interoperability. In: Network and Distributed System Security Symposium (2019)

80. Egger, C., Moreno-Sanchez, P., Maffei, M.: Atomic multi-channel updates with constant collateral in bitcoin-compatible payment-channel networks. In: CCS (2019)
81. Tairi, E., Moreno-Sanchez, P., Maffei, M.: A^2l: anonymous atomic locks for scalability and interoperability in payment channel hubs. IACR Cryptology ePrint Archive 2019/589 (2019). https://eprint.iacr.org/2019/589
82. Dziembowski, S., Eckey, L., Faust, S., Hesse, J., Hostáková, K.: Multi-party virtual state channels. In: Ishai, Y., Rijmen, V. (eds.) EUROCRYPT 2019. LNCS, vol. 11476, pp. 625–656. Springer, Cham (2019). https://doi.org/10.1007/978-3-030-17653-2_21
83. Avarikioti, G., Janssen, G., Wang, Y., Wattenhofer, R.: Payment network design with fees. In: Garcia-Alfaro, J., Herrera-Joancomartí, J., Livraga, G., Rios, R. (eds.) DPM/CBT -2018. LNCS, vol. 11025, pp. 76–84. Springer, Cham (2018). https://doi.org/10.1007/978-3-030-00305-0_6
84. Brânzei, S., Segal-Halevi, E., Zohar, A.: How to charge lightning. arXiv preprint arXiv:1712.10222 (2017)
85. Avarikioti, G., Laufenberg, F., Sliwinski, J., Wang, Y., Wattenhofer, R.: Incentivizing payment channel watchtowers (2018). https://scalingbitcoin.org/transcript/tokyo2018/incentivizing-payment-channel-watchtowers
86. Di Stasi, G., Avallone, S., Canonico, R., Ventre, G.: Routing payments on the lightning network. In: 2018 IEEE International Conference on Internet of Things (iThings) and IEEE Green Computing and Communications (GreenCom) and IEEE Cyber, Physical and Social Computing (CPSCom) and IEEE Smart Data (SmartData), pp. 1161–1170. IEEE (2018)
87. Merkle, R.C.: A digital signature based on a conventional encryption function. In: Pomerance, C. (ed.) CRYPTO 1987. LNCS, vol. 293, pp. 369–378. Springer, Heidelberg (1988). https://doi.org/10.1007/3-540-48184-2_32
88. Intel: Intel software guard extensions (Intel SGX) (2019). https://software.intel.com/en-us/sgx
89. Brasser, F., Müller, U., Dmitrienko, A., Kostiainen, K., Čapkun, S., Sadeghi, A.R.: Software grand exposure:SGX cache attacks are practical. In: 11th USENIX Workshop on Offensive Technologies (WOOT 2017) (2017)
90. Bentov, I., et al.: Tesseract: Real-time cryptocurrency exchange using trusted hardware. IACR Cryptology ePrint Archive 2017/1153 (2017)
91. Matetic, S., Wüst, K., Schneider, M., Kostiainen, K., Karame, G., Čapkun, S.: Bite: bitcoin lightweight client privacy using trusted execution. IACR Cryptology ePrint Archive 2018/803 (2018)
92. Wüst, K., Matetic, S., Schneider, M., Miers, I., Kostiainen, K., Čapkun, S.: ZLiTE: lightweight clients for shielded Zcash transactions using trusted execution. In: Goldberg, I., Moore, T. (eds.) FC 2019. LNCS, vol. 11598, pp. 179–198. Springer, Cham (2019). https://doi.org/10.1007/978-3-030-32101-7_12
93. Karame, G.O., Androulaki, E., Roeschlin, M., Gervais, A., Čapkun, S.: Misbehavior in bitcoin: a study of double-spending and accountability. ACM Trans. Inf. Syst. Secur. (TISSEC) 18(1), 2 (2015)
94. Androulaki, E., Karame, G.O., Roeschlin, M., Scherer, T., Capkun, S.: Evaluating user privacy in bitcoin. In: Sadeghi, A.-R. (ed.) FC 2013. LNCS, vol. 7859, pp. 34–51. Springer, Heidelberg (2013). https://doi.org/10.1007/978-3-642-39884-1_4
95. Meiklejohn, S., et al.: A fistful of bitcoins: characterizing payments among men with no names. In: Proceedings of the 2013 Conference on Internet Measurement Conference, pp. 127–140. ACM (2013)

96. Böhme, R., Christin, N., Edelman, B., Moore, T.: Bitcoin: economics, technology, and governance. J. Econ. Perspect. **29**(2), 213–38 (2015)
97. Möser, M., et al.: An empirical analysis of traceability in the Monero blockchain. Proc. Priv. Enhancing Technol. **2018**(3), 143–163 (2018)
98. Sasson, E.B., et al.: Zerocash: decentralized anonymous payments from bitcoin. In: Symposium on Security and Privacy, pp. 459–474. IEEE (2014)
99. Grin: minimal implementation of the mimblewimble protocol (2019). https://github.com/mimblewimble/grin
100. Beam: Scalable confidential cryptocurrency. A mimblewimble implementation (2019). https://github.com/BeamMW/beam
101. Courtois, N.T., Mercer, R.: Stealth address and key management techniques in blockchain systems. In: ICISSP, pp. 559–566 (2017)
102. Bender, A., Katz, J., Morselli, R.: Ring signatures: stronger definitions, and constructions without random Oracles. In: Halevi, S., Rabin, T. (eds.) TCC 2006. LNCS, vol. 3876, pp. 60–79. Springer, Heidelberg (2006). https://doi.org/10.1007/11681878_4
103. Feige, U., Fiat, A., Shamir, A.: Zero-knowledge proofs of identity. J. Cryptol. **1**(2), 77–94 (1988)
104. Kappos, G., Yousaf, H., Maller, M., Meiklejohn, S.: An empirical analysis of anonymity in Zcash. In: USENIX Security Symposium, pp. 463–477 (2018)
105. Hinteregger, A., Haslhofer, B.: An empirical analysis of Monero cross-chain traceability. CoRR abs/1812.02808 (2018). http://arxiv.org/abs/1812.02808
106. Kumar, A., Fischer, C., Tople, S., Saxena, P.: A traceability analysis of Monero's blockchain. In: ESORICS, pp. 153–173 (2017)
107. Biryukov, A., Feher, D.: Privacy and linkability of mining in Zcash. In: 2019 IEEE Conference on Communications and Network Security (CNS), pp. 118–123. IEEE (2019)
108. Herrera-Joancomartí, J., Navarro-Arribas, G., Ranchal-Pedrosa, A., Pérez-Solà, C., Garcia-Alfaro, J.: On the difficulty of hiding the balance of lightning network channels. Cryptology ePrint Archive, Report 2019/328 (2019). https://eprint.iacr.org/2019/328
109. Moreno-Sanchez, P., Kate, A., Maffei, M., Pecina, K.: Privacy preserving payments in credit networks. In: Network and Distributed Security Symposium (2015)
110. Moreno-Sanchez, P., Zafar, M.B., Kate, A.: Listening to whispers of ripple: linking wallets and deanonymizing transactions in the ripple network. PoPETs **2016**(4), 436–453 (2016). https://doi.org/10.1515/popets-2016-0049
111. Moreno-Sanchez, P., Modi, N., Songhela, R., Kate, A., Fahmy, S.: Mind your credit: assessing the health of the ripple credit network. WWW 2018, pp. 329–338 (2018)
112. Wüst, K., Gervais, A.: Ethereum eclipse attacks. Technical report, ETH Zurich (2016)
113. Gervais, A., Ritzdorf, H., Karame, G.O., Čapkun, S.: Tampering with the delivery of blocks and transactions in bitcoin. In: Conference on Computer and Communications Security, pp. 692–705. ACM (2015)
114. Rohrer, E., Malliaris, J., Tschorsch, F.: Discharged payment channels: quantifying the lightning network's resilience to topology-based attacks. CoRR abs/1904.10253 (2019). http://arxiv.org/abs/1904.10253
115. Kumaresan, R., Bentov, I.: Amortizing secure computation with penalties. In: Proceedings of the 2016 ACM SIGSAC Conference on Computer and Communications Security, CCS 2016, pp. 418–429. Association for Computing Machinery, New York (2016). https://doi.org/10.1145/2976749.2978424

116. Kiayias, A., Litos, O.S.T.: A composable security treatment of the lightning network. Cryptology ePrint Archive, Report 2019/778 (2019). https://eprint.iacr.org/2019/778
117. Ben-Sasson, E., Chiesa, A., Tromer, E., Virza, M.: Succinct non-interactive zero knowledge for a Von Neumann architecture. In: 23rd USENIX Security Symposium (USENIX Security 2014), pp. 781–796 (2014)
118. Buterin, V.: On-chain scaling to potentially 500 tx/sec through mass tx validation (2018). https://ethresear.ch/t/on-chain-scaling-to-potentially-500-tx-sec-through-mass-tx-validation/3477
119. ZmnSCPxj: (lightning-dev) an argument for single-asset lightning network (2018). https://lists.linuxfoundation.org/pipermail/lightning-dev/2018-December/001752.html

MicroCash: Practical Concurrent Processing of Micropayments

Ghada Almashaqbeh[1($\boxtimes$)], Allison Bishop[2,3], and Justin Cappos[4]

[1] CacheCash Development Company, New York, NY, USA
ghada@cs.columbia.edu
[2] Columbia University, New York, NY, USA
allison@cs.columbia.edu
[3] Proof Trading, New York, NY, USA
[4] New York University, New York, NY, USA
jcappos@nyu.edu

Abstract. Micropayments have a large number of potential applications. However, processing these small payments individually can be expensive, with transaction fees often exceeding the payment value itself. By aggregating the small transactions into a few larger ones, and using cryptocurrencies, today's decentralized probabilistic micropayment schemes can reduce these fees. Unfortunately, existing solutions force micropayments to be issued sequentially, thus to support fast issuance rates a customer needs a large number of escrows, which bloats the blockchain. Moreover, these schemes incur a large computation and bandwidth overhead, limiting their applicability in large-scale systems.

In this paper, we propose MicroCash, the first decentralized probabilistic framework that supports concurrent micropayments. MicroCash introduces a novel escrow setup that enables a customer to concurrently issue payment tickets at a fast rate using a *single* escrow. MicroCash is also cost effective because it allows for ticket exchange using only one round of communication, and it aggregates the micropayments using a non-interactive lottery protocol that requires only secure hashing and supports fixed winning rates. Our experiments show that MicroCash can process thousands of tickets per second, which is around 1.7–4.2× times the rate of a state-of-the-art sequential micropayment system. Moreover, MicroCash supports any ticket issue rate over any period using only one escrow, while the sequential scheme would need more than 1000 escrows per second to permit high rates. This enables our system to further reduce transaction fees and data on the blockchain by ~50%.

1 Introduction

Micropayments, or payments in pennies or factions of pennies, have a large a number of potential applications as diverse as ad-free web surfing, online gaming,

G. Almashaqbeh—Most work done while at Columbia supported by NSF CCF-1423306.

A. Bishop—Supported by NSF CCF-1423306 and NSF CNS-1552932.

© International Financial Cryptography Association 2020
J. Bonneau and N. Heninger (Eds.): FC 2020, LNCS 12059, pp. 227–244, 2020.
https://doi.org/10.1007/978-3-030-51280-4_13

and peer-assisted service networks [19]. This paradigm allows participants to exchange monetary incentives at a small scale, e.g., pay per minute in online games. Such a fine-grained payment process has several advantages, including a great deal of flexibility for customers who may stop a service at any time. In addition, it reduces the financial risks between mutually-distrusted participants, where there is no guarantee that a client will pay after being served, or that a server will deliver service when paid in advance.

However, processing these small payments individually can incur high transaction fees that exceed the payment value itself. For example, the average base cost of a debit or credit card transaction in the US is around 21 to 24 cents, and 23 to 42 cents [5,6], respectively. In cryptocurrencies such a fee could be even higher, e.g., above $1 in Bitcoin [3]. Beside this financial drawback, handling micropayments individually can impose a huge workload on the system, and may make the logs needed for accountability purposes unwieldy. Thus, there is a need for a payment aggregation mechanism that records fewer transactions while still compensating properly for the small payments received to date.

Probabilistic micropayment schemes have emerged as a solution that fits the criteria outlined above [18,21–23]. In these models, the total payment value is locked in an escrow and micropayments are issued as lottery tickets. Each ticket has a probability p of winning a lottery, and when it wins, produces a transaction of β currency units. This means that, on average, only one transaction is processed out of a batch of $1/p$ tickets. Unfortunately, these early proposals rely on a trusted party to audit the lottery and manage payments. Such a centralized approach may increase the deployment cost and limit the use of the payment service to systems with fully authenticated participants [14].

As cryptocurrencies evolved, a number of initiatives attempted to convert these schemes to distributed ones [14,19]. This was done by replacing the trusted party with the miners, and utilizing the blockchain to provide public verifiability of system operation. Yet, these approaches have several drawbacks that may hinder their usage in large-scale systems. First, they force a customer to issue micropayments sequentially using the same escrow. This is because in these schemes an escrow is only funded to pay only one winning lottery ticket. Hence, a new ticket cannot be issued until the merchant reports the lottery outcome and confirms that the previous one did not win. To issue tickets at a fast rate under this restriction, the customer needs to create a large number of escrows, which increases the amount of data on the blockchain and transaction fees. Second, these schemes rely on computationally-heavy cryptographic primitives [14,19], and several rounds of communication to exchange payments [14]. Such performance issues reduce the potential benefits of micropayments.

To address these issues, this paper introduces MicroCash, the first decentralized probabilistic framework that supports *concurrent* micropayments. MicroCash features a novel escrow setup that allows a customer to issue micropayments in parallel and at a fast rate using a *single* escrow that can pay many winning tickets. This is achieved by having the customer specify the total number of tickets it may issue, and provide an escrow balance that covers all winning tickets under its payment setup.

MicroCash is also cost effective because it introduces a lightweight non-interactive lottery protocol. This protocol requires only secure hashing and allows a payment exchange using only one round of communication without demanding the merchant to report anything to the customer. Furthermore, this protocol is the first to eliminate the possibility that all lottery tickets may win or lose the lottery. Although the probability of these events is very small, the fear of paying much more than expected may discourage customers from using the system [18]. Moreover, accounting for the worst case when almost all tickets win requires a large escrow balance, which increases the collateral cost. Our protocol alleviates this concern by selecting an *exact* number of winning tickets each round (where a round is the time needed to mine a block on the blockchain). In particular, all tickets issued in the same round are tied to a *lottery draw* value in a future block on the blockchain. This value is used to determine the fixed-size set of winning tickets through an iterative hashing process. Lastly, the security of the system is enforced using both cryptographic and financial techniques. The latter requires a customer to create a penalty escrow that is revoked upon cheating, with a lower bound derived using a game theoretic modeling of the system.

To evaluate the efficiency of MicroCash, we test its performance against MICROPAY [19], a state-of-the-art sequential micropayment scheme. Our results show that a modest merchant machine in MicroCash is able to process 2,240–10,500 ticket/sec, which is around 1.7–4.2× times the rate in MICROPAY, with 60% reduction in the aggregated payment size. Furthermore, a modest customer machine in MicroCash is able to concurrently issue more than 33,000 ticket/sec using *one* escrow over any period, while MICROPAY requires the creation of more than 1000 escrows per second to support a comparable issue rate. This allows MicroCash to reduce transaction fees and amount of data on the blockchain in a video delivery and online gaming applications by ∼50%.

2 Related Work

To orient readers to the current state-of-the-art in probabilistic micropayments, in this section we review prior work done in this area. In addition, we review an alternative payment aggregation mechanism, called payment networks [15,20], focusing on its limitations when used to handle micropayments.

Probabilistic Micropayments. The idea of probabilistic micropayments dates back to the seminal works of Wheeler [23] and Rivest [21,22]. In these schemes, a customer and a merchant run the lottery (on each ticket independently) by using a simple coin tossing protocol, with a chance of more, or less, winning tickets than expected. All of these schemes rely on a centralized bank to track and authorize payments. This imposes additional overhead on the users who have to establish business relationships with this bank. It also limits the use of the service to only fully authenticated users. Although they allow for concurrent micropayments [22], this centralization issue is viewed as one of the main reasons for the limited adoption of such solutions [14].

Cryptocurrency-based probabilistic micropayments can potentially overcome both the cost and efficiency problems inherent in earlier schemes. To the best of our knowledge, only two such schemes have been proposed to date in the literature, MICROPAY [19] and DAM [14].

MICROPAY translates what Rivest [21] proposed into an implementation on top of a cryptocurrency system. Instead of using an authorized bank account, any customer creates an escrow on the blockchain to issue lottery tickets. MICRO-PAY implements a similar interactive coin tossing protocol for the lottery, and adds an alternative non-interactive version that reduces the communication complexity (a merchant still has to report the lottery result back to the customer). However, the latter is computationally-heavy since it requires public key cryptography-based operations and a non-interactive zero knowledge (NIZK) proof system. Moreover, MICROPAY only supports sequential micropayments as mentioned earlier. DAM shares similar constraints, but unlike the public MICROPAY it preserves user privacy by implementing anonymous micropayments.

We believe that the added blockchain transactions due to sequential payments, coupled with the high computation cost, point to the need for optimized approaches that support concurrent micropayments at a lower overhead. This need is the motivation behind building MicroCash.

Payment Channels and Networks. Payment channels were originally developed to handle micropayments in Bitcoin [2], where they rely on a similar concept of processing small payments locally. Later on, this paradigm was utilized to improve the scalability of cryptocurrencies [15,17,20], where off-chain processing is utilized to reduce on-chain traffic, and hence, increase the transaction throughput of the system.

In general, payment channels and networks require an escrow to be created between each pair of parties along the payment path. This may result in a higher collateral cost than probabilistic micropayments, since in the latter the same escrow can be used to pay several parties directly. These costs may indirectly push the network towards centralization [7] since only wealthy parties can afford multiple escrows to create payment paths. Thus, most users will rely on these parties, or hubs, to relay the off-chain transactions. In addition, each hub on the path charges a fee to relay payments. With micropayments, such a setup would be infeasible because these fees could be much larger than the payments themselves. Probabilistic approaches, on the other hand, eliminate any fees when exchanging lottery tickets. As a result, distributed probabilistic micropayments provide a better solution for handling small payments in cryptocurrency systems.

3   Threat Model

Processing off-chain transactions in distributed probabilistic micropayments creates the potential for various types of attacks. In this section, we outline a threat model capturing these attacks, which guided the design of MicroCash. In developing this model, we make the following assumptions:

- No trust is placed in any (insider or outsider) party.
- Participants are rational, meaning that they choose to follow the protocol, or deviate from it, based on what will maximize their utility gain.
- The underlying cryptocurrency scheme is secure in the sense that the majority of the mining power is honest. This means that the confirmed state of the blockchain contains only valid transactions, and that an attacker who tries to mutate or fork the blockchain will fail with overwhelming probability.
- Hash functions are modeled as random oracles, and the hash values of the blocks on the blockchain are modeled as a uniform distribution.
- Efficient adversaries cannot break the basic cryptographic building blocks (SHA256, digital signatures, etc.) with non-negligible probability.
- Communication between customers and merchants takes place over a channel that provides integrity, confidentiality, and authenticity, such as TLS/SSL.

We used the ABC framework [10] to build a comprehensive threat model for distributed probabilistic micropayment schemes[1]. During this process, we identified the assets to be protected in such systems, which include the escrows, the lottery tickets, and the lottery protocol. Then, by analyzing the security requirements of these assets, and examining more than 120 threat cases, we produced the following list of broad threat categories endemic to distributed probabilistic micropayments:

- **Escrow overdraft:** A customer creates a payment escrow insufficient for honoring the winning lottery tickets, or creates a penalty deposit that does not cover the cheating punishment imposed by the miners. Such a threat could stem from creating small balance escrows, or from front running attacks in which a customer withdraws the escrows before paying.
- **Unused-escrow withholding:** An attacker prevents or delays a customer from withdrawing its unused escrows. For example, merchants may delay claiming their winning lottery tickets to keep the payment escrow on hold.
- **Lottery manipulation:** An attacker attempts to influence the outcome of the lottery draw, and hence, bias the payment process.
- **Denial of service (DoS):** This is a large threat category that threatens any distributed system. This work focuses on attacks related to the payment process, like preventing a customer from creating escrows.
- **Duplicate ticket issuance:** A customer uses the same sequence number to issue several lottery tickets to different merchants. As this means creating more tickets than the escrow can cover, the customer obtains more service than it can pay for.
- **Invalid payments:** A malicious customer issues lottery tickets that do not comply with its payment setup or with the system specifications. Because these tickets will be rejected by the miners if they win the lottery, the customer can avoid paying merchants.

---

[1] A detailed documentation of this process is available online [8] and is based on the generic description of probabilistic micropayments as described in the introduction.

Note that dealing with malicious merchants who collect lottery tickets and do not deliver a service is outside the scope of MicroCash. The same is true for dealing with malicious customers who may obtain the service without paying. In this work, we are concerned with the payment scheme design, rather than how to exchange service for a payment, which is part of the application design.

In addition, MicroCash does not address payment anonymity (as in [14]). Addressing this issue securely, while preserving the low overhead of MicroCash, is a direction for our future work.

4   MicroCash Design

Having outlined the security threats to probabilistic micropayments, and the limitations of existing solutions, this section presents the design of MicroCash, a concurrent micropayment system that addresses these issues. We start with an overview of the system, followed by a more detailed technical description.

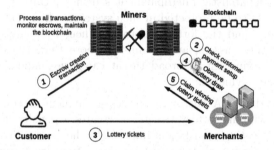

Fig. 1. Flow of operations in MicroCash.

A high level illustration of MicroCash, that also captures the remainder of this section's organization, is found in Fig. 1. As shown, during the payment setup (**Step 1**, Sect. 4.1), each customer issues a transaction creating two escrows: payment and penalty. The customer uses the former to pay merchants in the form of lottery tickets, while the miners use the latter to financially punish this customer if it cheats. Merchants can check the escrow setup before transacting with the customer when the escrow transaction is confirmed on the blockchain (**Step 2**). In exchange for the delivered service, the customer issues lottery tickets according to a schedule that limits the number of tickets over a set period (**Step 3**, Sect. 4.2). To claim payments, a merchant holds a ticket until its lottery draw time, and determines if this ticket won based on a value derived from the block mined at that time (**Step 4**, Sect. 4.3). If it is a winning ticket, the merchant can claim currency from the customer's escrow during the ticket redemption period (**Step 5**, Sect. 4.4). This interaction continues until the end of the escrow lifetime. At that time, and after all issued tickets expire, the customer can spend any remaining funds.

4.1 Escrow Setup

MicroCash introduces a novel escrow setup that allows multiple winning tickets to be redeemed. This enables both concurrent ticket issuance and reduces the amount of escrow-related data. This setup also provides techniques to determine the escrow balance needed to cover all concurrent tickets, and to track the issuance of these tickets in a distributed way.

Escrow Creation. As an off-chain payment scheme, MicroCash must ensure that customers can and will pay. This includes honoring winning tickets, and, if caught cheating, complying with a stipulated financial punishment. To satisfy these requirements, each customer must create payment and penalty escrows with sufficient funds to cover both eventualities.

Given that each payment escrow must be tied to a penalty escrow, a customer sets up both using one creation transaction. This transaction provides funds to be locked under each escrow balance, which we refer to as B_{escrow} (payment) and $B_{penalty}$ (penalty). It also configures a set of parameters that influence how these balances are computed, and how they are to be spent. These parameters, whose values are specified by the customer possibly after negotiating with the merchants, include the following:

- The lottery winning probability p.
- The currency value of a winning lottery ticket β.
- The ticket issue rate tkt_{rate}, which is the maximum number of tickets a customer is allowed to hand out per round. This is used to calculate which *ticket sequence numbers* are valid within each ticket issuing round.
- A lottery draw round length, denoted as $draw_{len}$, such that $draw_{len} \in \{1, \ldots, c\}$ for some small system parameter c. The customer has to configure $draw_{len}$, p, and tkt_{rate} in a way that makes $p\, tkt_{rate} draw_{len}$ of an integer value (this is the number of winning tickets in a lottery draw).
- The set of beneficiary merchants that can be paid using the escrow, where the size of this set is denoted as m.

Computing B_{escrow} and $B_{penalty}$ based on the above parameters proceeds as follows. To permit concurrent micropayments, B_{escrow} must be large enough to pay all winning tickets tied to an escrow. Given that each winning ticket has a value of β currency units, and that there are $p\, tkt_{rate} draw_{len}$ winning tickets per $draw_{len}$ rounds, B_{escrow} can be simply computed as follows (where l_{esc} is the escrow lifetime in rounds, and there are $l_{esc}/draw_{len}$ lottery draws)[2]:

$$B_{escrow} = \beta\, p\, tkt_{rate} l_{esc} \tag{1}$$

For $B_{penalty}$, we compute a lower bound for this deposit by using an economic analysis that quantifies the additional utility gain, or profit, a customer obtains

---

[2] Compared to previous schemes [14,19], this is the same expected payment amount needed to cover the same number of winning tickets. However, since these works are sequential, they distribute this amount among multiple escrows instead of one.

by cheating. The profit is the monetary value of the service exchanged for invalid or duplicated tickets to merchants before cheating is detected, i.e., before any of these tickets wins the lottery and is claimed through the miners (assuming that merchants do not exchange any information about the received tickets). Thus, to make cheating unprofitable, and hence, unappealing to rational customers, $B_{penalty}$ is set to be at least equal to this additional utility as given by the following equation[3]:

$$B_{penalty} > (m-1)p\,\beta\,tkt_{rate}draw_{len}\left(\frac{1-p}{1-\rho^{-1}} + draw_{len}\Big((1-p)(d_{draw}-1)+d_{redeem}\Big)\right) \tag{2}$$

where d_{draw} is the lottery draw period in rounds, d_{redeem} is the ticket redemption period in rounds (more about these parameters in Sect. 4.3), and $\rho = \binom{a}{b}$ such that $a = tkt_{rate}draw_{len}$ and $b = (1-p)a$. The full details of deriving this bound are found in Sect. 5 in the full version of the paper [11].

Upon receiving the escrow creation transaction, the miners verify the correctness of a payment setup as follows. First, they check that the customer owns the input funds. Then, the miners use B_{escrow} to compute the escrow lifetime as $l_{esc} = \frac{B_{escrow}}{\beta\,p\,tkt_{rate}}$. After that, they check that both l_{esc} and $p\,tkt_{rate}draw_{len}$ are of integer values, $draw_{len}$ is within the allowed range, and that l_{esc} is multiples of $draw_{len}$. Lastly, the miners verify that $B_{penalty}$ satisfies the bound given above. If all these checks pass, the miners add the escrow transaction to the blockchain. Otherwise, they reject the escrow by dropping its transaction.

Escrow Management. In MicroCash, the escrow funds can be spent only for a restricted set of transactions. These include claiming winning tickets, presenting proofs-of-cheating, and enabling a customer to spend its unused escrow funds.

To track the locked funds, miners maintain a state for each escrow in the system. This state includes the following:

- The ID of the escrow, which is a random value generated by the miner who adds the escrow creation transaction to the blockchain.
- The balances of both the payment and penalty escrows.
- The public key of the owner customer, which is used to verify all signed tickets that are issued using this escrow.
- The values of p, β, l_{esc}, tkt_{rate}, $draw_{len}$, and the set of beneficiary merchants (both the public key of each merchant and a corresponding index).
- An escrow refund time, denoted as t_{refund}, at which the customer can spend any remaining funds. Miners set this time to be equal to the expiry time of the tickets issued in the last round of an escrow lifetime.

---

[3] Compared to DAM [14], MicroCash's penalty escrow will be larger. This is because the cheating detection period in MicroCash is longer (several rounds until the lottery is run and a winning ticket is claimed). In DAM, the lottery is run over a ticket immediately when it is received, and a claim, if any, can be issued at the same time. Thus, assuming identical payment setup, $B_{penalty}$ in MicroCash is approximately $T_{MicroCash}/T_{DAM}$ times the one in DAM, where T is the cheating detection period.

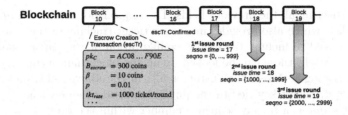

Fig. 2. An example of a ticket issuing schedule.

Ticket issuance using an escrow must follow a schedule based upon the tickets' sequence numbers. That is, if an escrow supports a rate of tkt_{rate} tickets per round, then in the first round tickets with sequence numbers 0 to tkt_{rate}-1 may be issued. In the second round tickets with sequence numbers tkt_{rate} to $2tkt_{rate}$-1 can be issued, and so on until the last round of an escrow lifetime. Merchants will accept tickets in the current round with sequence numbers that follow this assignment schedule. As customers and merchants may have inconsistent views of the blockchain, and hence, may not agree on what is the current round, i.e., height of the blockchain, merchants will also accept tickets from the prior and next round, as long as these tickets use the correct sequence number range.

An example of a ticket issuing schedule is found in Fig. 2. As shown, the escrow creation transaction is published at round 10 and confirmed at round 16. This escrow has $l_{esc} = 3$ rounds, and allows a ticket issue rate of 1000 tickets per round. Thus, the customer has 3 ticket issuing rounds, starting at round 17, with the sequence number ranges shown in the figure.

The miners update the escrow state based on the escrow related transactions (mentioned earlier) they process. For example, redeeming a winning ticket reduces B_{escrow} by β coins, and receiving a valid proof-of-cheating against the customer causes the miners to revoke the funds in $B_{penalty}$. All these transactions are logged on the blockchain, which permits anyone to validate the state.

The miners discard an escrow state once all tickets tied to this escrow expire. This happens at time t_{refund}, or when an escrow is broken after receiving a valid proof-of-cheating (discussed in Sect. 4.5). At that time, the customer may spend any remaining funds in its escrows.

4.2 Paying with Lottery Tickets

After the escrow is confirmed on the blockchain, a customer can start paying for service by giving merchants lottery tickets. A lottery ticket tkt_L is a structure containing several fields as follows:

$$tkt_L = index_M||id_{esc}||seqno||\sigma_C \tag{3}$$

where $index_M$ is the recipient merchant index as listed in the escrow state, id_{esc} is the escrow ID, $seqno$ is the ticket sequence number, and σ_C is the customer's signature covering all the previous fields. The *seqno* field, along with id_{esc}, identifies a ticket, which also provides means for ticket tracking in the system. Note there is no need to include the escrow configuration or the parties' public keys in the ticket itself, these can be looked up on the blockchain using id_{esc}.

When issuing a ticket, the customer fills in the above fields and signs the ticket using its secret key tied to the public key used when creating the escrow. The ticket *seqno* can be any sequence number within the range assigned to the current ticket issue round. The customer can continue issuing lottery tickets, without waiting for the lottery results of previously issued ones, until it finishes all sequence numbers in this range. After that, it must wait the next round to generate more tickets.

Upon receiving a ticket, a merchant verifies it as follows:

- Check that the escrow is not broken.
- Check that its index $index_M$, that appears in the ticket, is identical to the one listed in the escrow state.
- Check the freshness of *seqno* (i.e., that no earlier ticket, associated to the same escrow, carries the same *seqno*).
- Verify that *seqno* is within the valid range based on the ticket issuing schedule. (As mentioned before, to handle inconsistencies in the blockchain view, tickets from the previous or next issuance round can be accepted.)
- Verify σ_C over the ticket using the customer's public key.

If any of the above checks, except the fourth one, fails, the merchant drops the ticket. On the other hand, if the ticket has an out-of-range sequence number (i.e., larger than the maximum sequence number allowed by the escrow), the recipient merchant can issue a proof-of-cheating that will cost the customer its penalty deposit. Otherwise, if all the above checks pass, the merchant accepts the ticket and keeps it until its lottery draw time.

4.3   The Lottery Protocol

MicroCash introduces a lightweight lottery protocol that relies solely on secure hashing. This protocol does not require any interaction between the customer and the merchant. Instead, it utilizes only the state of the blockchain, where the lottery draw outcome is determined by a value derived from the block mined at the lottery draw time.

To specify the lottery draw time, MicroCash defines two system parameters, d_{draw} and $draw_{len}$. d_{draw} represents the least number of rounds a ticket has to wait after its issue round (which we call t_{issue}) until it enters the lottery. $draw_{len}$ determines the number of consecutive ticket issuing rounds that all their lottery tickets enter the same lottery draw. Hence, if $draw_{len} = 1$, then the draw time t_{draw} of a ticket is computed as $t_{draw} = t_{issue} + d_{draw}$. On the other hand, if $draw_{len} > 1$, then t_{draw} of a ticket is t_{draw} of the last ticket issuing round in the contiguous set of rounds[4].

---

[4] Since $draw_{len}$ affects t_{draw} of a ticket, MicroCash specifies a small interval for its possible values to prevent a customer from excessively delaying paying merchants.

A clarifying example of determining the lottery draw time is found in Fig. 3. As shown, starting with round 28, which the first ticket issuing round, each set of contiguous $draw_{len}$ rounds enter the lottery together. For example, all tickets issued in rounds 28, 29, and 30 enter the lottery at round 40, which is 10 rounds after the last ticket issue round in this set.

Whether a ticket wins or loses depends on a lottery draw value tied to the block mined at time t_{draw}. This value is computed using a simple verifiable delay function (VDF) [13] that is evaluated over this block. This evaluation takes a period of time, hence the name delay function, where this period is a system parameter. Consequently, when a miner mines the block at index t_{draw}, it cannot tell immediately which ticket will win or lose. This miner has to compute the VDF over this block to know the lottery draw outcome.

We instantiate this VDF using iterative hashing, where the number of iterations is set to a value that delays producing the output by the period specified in the system. In addition, we let the miners compute this function as part of the mining process. That is, when a miner mines a new block, it evaluates the VDF over the previous block. Therefore, the VDF value of the block at index t_{draw} appears on the blockchain when the block at index $t_{draw} + 1$ is mined.

Accordingly, in our protocol a merchant holds a ticket tkt_L until its lottery draw time t_{draw}. Then, after observing the VDF value of the block mined at that time, the miners, and any party, can compute the set of winning sequence numbers for that round as follows. First, the hash of the VDF value along with the escrow ID is computed, which we call h_1, and then h_1 is mapped to a sequence number within the assigned range of the ticket issuing rounds tied to t_{draw}. To obtain the second winning sequence number, the hash of h_1 is computed to obtain h_2, and then h_2 is mapped to a sequence number in the given range. If a collision occurs, i.e., a previously seen number is produced, it is discarded and the process proceeds with hashing h_2 to obtain h_3, and so on. This continues until a set of distinct $p\ tkt_{rate}draw_{len}$ winning sequence numbers is drawn[5].

The previous process is clarified by the example depicted in Fig. 3. As shown, tkt_L was issued in round 28, the first ticket issuing round, and hence, it entered the lottery at round 40. The VDF value of the block with index 40 appears inside block 41. By using this value, a set of winning sequence numbers has been chosen, based on which the ticket in the figure is a winning one because its sequence number is within this set.

Note that the lottery draw involves only values that are part of the escrow state. In other words, it relies on parameters that the issuing customer cannot manipulate, which do not include the merchant recipient address. This means that a ticket's chance of winning the lottery is not affected by who owns it. As such, if a customer issues tickets with duplicated sequence numbers to multiple merchants, all these tickets will win or lose together. If the tickets win, detecting

---

[5] We design a version of this lottery protocol with independent ticket winning events in Appendix A in the full version [11]. This can be used in case it is infeasible in some applications to configure $p\ tkt_{rate}draw_{len}$ to be an integer.

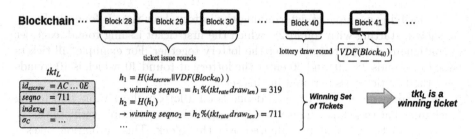

Fig. 3. Lottery draw example ($draw_{len} = 3$, $p = \frac{1}{300}$, $tkt_{rate} = 10^3$, and $d_{draw} = 10$).

cheating is trivial because merchants will publish their winning tickets to the blockchain to redeem the tickets.

4.4   Claiming Winning Tickets

After the lottery draw, a merchant can collect currency from the customer's escrow by redeeming its winning tickets (if any). This is done by issuing a redeem transaction that has the winning ticket as input, and has β coins directed to the merchant's address as output.

To allow the miners to resolve tickets and release escrow funds back to the customer in a reasonable timeframe, MicroCash specifies a redeem period for each ticket. This is done by defining a system parameter called d_{redeem} that determines the number of rounds during which a ticket can be redeemed. A ticket expires at time $t_{expire} = t_{draw} + d_{redeem}$. Thus, d_{redeem} must be set to a value that allows merchants to redeem their winning tickets.

After receiving a redeem transaction, the miners process it as follows:

- Check that the transaction complies with the system specifications.
- Verify the redeemed ticket as outlined in Sect. 4.2.
- Verify that the ticket is a winning one by checking that its sequence number is among the winning set drawn at time t_{draw} of this ticket.
- Check that the ticket has not expired.
- Verify the merchant's signature over the redeem transaction using the public key corresponding to $index_M$ found in the escrow state.
- Check that no other ticket with the same sequence number and tied to the same escrow has already been redeemed. If it is, this is a proof of duplicate ticket issuance and is used as a proof-of-cheating against the customer.

If all these checks pass, miners approve the redeem transaction and update the escrow state accordingly. Otherwise, they drop an invalid transaction and, if a proof-of-cheating is produced, revoke the customer's penalty deposit.

4.5   Processing Proof-of-Cheating

A proof-of-cheating is a transaction any party who witnesses a cheating incident can present to the miners. In MicroCash, such an incident could be issuing tickets with out-of-range sequence numbers or issuing duplicated tickets. A signed ticket with an out-of-range sequence number or signed tickets with duplicated sequence numbers are publicly verifiable proofs against the issuing customer.

If cheating is verified, miners revoke the customer's penalty escrow tied to its payment escrow referenced in the ticket as follows. In case of ticket duplication, the miners first pay all duplicated winning tickets from the payment escrow, and then from the penalty deposit. Next, they publish an escrow break transaction containing the proof-of-cheating on the blockchain. This transaction burns the revoked penalty deposit rather than providing them to another party to eliminate the chance that this party may collude with the customer to receive those funds. Respecting the lower bound of $B_{penalty}$, as specified before, ensures that all the above cheating behaviors are less profitable than acting in an honest way. Hence, it makes such behaviors unappealing to rational customers.

5   Security and Game Theory Analysis

In this section, we analyze the resilience of MicroCash to the threats outlined in Sect. 3. To defend against these threats, our scheme utilizes cryptographic and financial approaches. Due to space constraints, this section presents a brief version of this analysis, but a more complete and detailed one can be found in Sect. 6 in the full version of the paper [11].

MicroCash addresses the *escrow overdraft* threat by using its escrow setup. The miners will reject any escrow with payment or penalty balances that do not satisfy the bounds defined earlier. Furthermore, no customer can perform a front running attack by withdrawing escrows before paying. This is because escrow fund release is triggered only by the receipt of a valid winning lottery ticket (for a payment escrow) or a valid proof-of-cheating (for a penalty escrow). In addition, a customer who tries to perform an indirect withdrawal by issuing winning tickets to itself after observing the lottery draw outcome will also fail. As the ticket issue schedule specifies both issue and lottery draw time for each round, it will be too late to select only winning sequence numbers after t_{draw}. By that time, merchants have already received their tickets, and any unissued winning ticket that a customer may try to claim is covered by the escrow balance.

The *unused-escrow withholding* threat is also handled by MicroCash's escrow setup. When all tickets tied to an escrow expire, i.e., at time t_{refund}, the miners will allow the customer to spend the residual balance. This prevents locking unused escrow funds indefinitely on the blockchain.

The *lottery manipulation* threat is addressed by MicroCash's lottery draw mechanism. The draw outcome depends only on values that a customer cannot manipulate. These include a ticket sequence number, which must be within a predetermined range, the escrow ID that appears in the escrow state, and the VDF value of the block mined at time t_{draw}. The probability of predicting the latter is negligible (in the random oracle model and under the assumption that block hashes on the blockchain are modeled as a uniform distribution). Hence, a customer cannot know which ticket will win or lose in advance. Also, given

that the VDF takes time to be computed, a miner who may perform selective
mining (possibly in collusion with the customer) by evaluating the VDF first,
and then announcing a favorable block, will have a low chance of publishing this
block on the blockchain. This is because other miners will announce their newly
mined blocks immediately, which will have higher probability of being adopted.
As such, any lottery ticket has a fair chances of winning the lottery.

For *DoS*, which is a large threat category to any system, we limit our focus
to cases related to the design of MicroCash. These include preventing customers
from creating escrows, preventing merchants from claiming their winning tickets,
or selectively relaying blocks based on their content. The case of miners disregarding specific transactions/blocks may take place when an attacker controls
a substantial portion of the mining power, or when the attacker controls the
network links and tries to isolate participants. Under the assumption that the
majority of the mining power is honest, and by having each participant connect
to a large number of miners, the impact of this threat can be reduced. To protect
against selective relaying, techniques that allow propagating messages without
disclosing their content can be employed, e.g., BloXroute [4]. Such mechanisms
are independent of the design of MicroCash, and so it is up to the parties themselves to adopt suitable solutions.

MicroCash uses a detect-and-punish approach to financially mitigate the
duplicate and invalid ticket issuance threats. Any party that detects any of these
events can produce a proof-of-cheating against the issuing customer containing
the duplicated or invalid tickets as a proof. Once such an incident is verified,
miners burn the customer's penalty escrow as a punishment.

We compute the value of $B_{penalty}$ by using a game theoretic analysis in which
we model the setup of MicroCash as a repeated game over the escrow lifetime[6].
Then we quantify the the monetary value of the additional service a customer
can obtain in exchange for the duplicated, or invalid, tickets during the cheating
detection period. That is, cheating is detected when any of the duplicated tickets
wins the lottery and is claimed through the miners, which happens in $d_{draw} +
d_{expire}$ rounds after the ticket issue time. Thus, we set $B_{penalty}$ to be at least
equal to service monetary value obtained during this period. Here, we only state
our result while the full modeling and proof can be found in Sect. 5 in the full
version [11].

Theorem 1. *For the game setup defined in Sect. 5 in the full version [11], issuing invalid or duplicated lottery tickets is less profitable in expectation than acting
in an honest way if (where $\rho = \left(\frac{tkt_{\text{rate}}}{(1-p)tkt_{\text{rate}}}\right)$):*

$$B_{\text{penalty}} > (m-1)p\,\beta\,tkt_{\text{rate}}\text{draw}_{\text{len}}\left(\frac{1-p}{1-1/\rho} + \text{draw}_{\text{len}}\left((1-p)(d_{\text{draw}}-1)+d_{\text{redeem}}\right)\right)$$

---

[6] Although Chiesa et al. [14] present an economic analysis for the DAM penalty escrow,
the derived bound cannot be used with MicroCash. This is due to the differences in
the system setup and the lottery timing, which affects the cheating detection period
and the duplication decisions a customer can make.

6   Performance Evaluation

To understand the performance benefit of concurrent probabilistic micropayments, in this section we evaluate the computation, bandwidth, and payment setup costs of MicroCash. We implemented benchmarks for the functions used for generating tickets, verifying these tickets, and performing a lottery draw[7]. We used SHA256 for hashing, and for digital signatures, we tested the most widely used schemes: ECDSA over secp256k1, ECDSA over P-256, and EdDSA over Ed25519 [12]. To put our results in context, we compare our scheme with MICROPAY [19], particularly its fully decentralized version MICROPAY1 with its non-interactive lottery protocol. In implementing this protocol, we used the verifiable random function (VRF) construction introduced by Goldberg et al. [16].

For each of the tested schemes, we computed the rate at which customers, merchants, and miners can process lottery tickets. Also, we calculated the bandwidth overhead by reporting on the size of tickets when exchanged between the various parties. To evaluate the effect of micropayment concurrency, we computed the number of escrows a customer would need to support the ticket issue rate in each of the tested schemes. Lastly, we studied two real life applications, online content delivery and online gaming, to derive workload numbers and used them to quantify the overhead of processing micropayments in such applications.

Our experiments were implemented in C on an Intel Core i7-4600U CPU @ 2.1 GHz, with 4 MB cache and 8 GB RAM. Each of the payment processing functions was called 10^6 times. Due to space constraints, this section provides only a brief discussion, while a complete report can be found in the full version [11].

Lottery Ticket Processing Rate. Table 1 shows the ticket processing rates. Customers in both schemes generate tickets at comparable rates because the operations performed are almost identical in MicroCash and MICROPAY. Given that the heaviest operation in this process is signing a ticket, the generation rates improve by using an efficient digital signature scheme, where performance is boosted by around 17x and 14x when ECDSA (secp256k1) is replaced with ECDSA (P-256) and EdDSA (Ed25519), respectively.

The trend is different for merchants and miners. These parties in MicroCash are 1.7×, 4.2×, and 3.2× faster than in MICROPAY for the three digital signature schemes. This is because of the operations that miners and merchants need to perform when running and verifying the lottery draw outcome in each system. In MicroCash, this process involves only lightweight hash operations, while the lottery in MICROPAY requires evaluating a computationally-heavy VRF.

Furthermore, the table shows that merchants and miners in MicroCash benefit more from the efficiency of the digital signature scheme. This is because the

---

[7] It should be noted that due to requiring a VDF evaluation and the new transaction types, MicroCash is not compatible with Bitcoin-like systems. For smart contract-based systems, if a periodic unbiased source of randomness exists to replace the VDF, then MicroCash can be implemented as a smart contract that uses this source for the lottery.

Table 1. Ticket processing rate (ticket/sec).

	MICROPAY			MicroCash		
	ECDSA (secp256k1)	ECDSA (P-256)	EdDSA (Ed25519)	ECDSA (secp256k1)	ECDSA (P-256)	EdDSA (Ed25519)
Customer	1,859	32,471	26,238	1,868	33,006	26,749
Merchant	1,328	2,399	2,561	2,249	10,505	8,473
Miner	1,340	2,448	2,617	2,241	10,345	8,368

heaviest operation these parties perform in MicroCash is verifying a customer's signature. However, in MICROPAY the bottleneck is evaluating a VRF and producing a correctness proof of the output the merchant side, and verifying this proof on the miner side. As shown in the table, MICROPAY obtains only around 1.9x improvement when replacing ECDSA (secp256k1) with any of the other two schemes. In contrast, MicroCash achieves around 4.7x and 3.8x improvement when replacing ECDSA (secp256k1) with ECDSA (P-256) or EdDSA (Ed25519), respectively.

Lottery Ticket Bandwidth Overhead. In terms of bandwidth, MicroCash incurs less overhead than MICROPAY because its lottery tickets are smaller. A ticket sent from a customer to a merchant is 110 bytes in MicroCash, while it is 274 bytes in MICROPAY. A winning ticket sent from merchants to miners is also 110 bytes in MicroCash, while it is 355 bytes for MICROPAY because this ticket must be accompanied with a NIZK proof. This means that MicroCash incurs only 40% of the bandwidth overhead of MICROPAY between customers and merchants, and only 31% of the overhead between merchants and miners.

To put these numbers in context, we report on the transaction sizes in Bitcoin. The average size is around 500 bytes, where a transaction with one or two inputs is about 250 bytes [9]. Adding a winning ticket as one of these inputs produces a claim transaction with a size of 360 bytes in MicroCash, which is less than the average Bitcoin transaction size. On the other hand, in MICROPAY the size of a claim transaction will be 605 bytes, exceeding the average size.

Size of Escrows on the Blockchain. One major difference between concurrent and sequential micropayment schemes is that a customer in the latter needs a new escrow after each winning ticket, and to issue tickets in parallel at a fast rate, this customer has to create a large number of escrows. This dramatically increases the overhead since each of these escrows requires an individual creation transaction, paying a transaction fee, and logging on the blockchain.

For example, to support the ticket issue rates reported in Table 1, a MICRO-PAY customer would need a number of escrows that depends on the network latency and a merchant's ticket processing rate. Using the average US RTT of 31 ms [1], in the best case an escrow in MICROPAY can be used to issue 32 tickets per second (if none of these ticket win or only the last one wins). Therefore, a customer in MICROPAY would need 60, 1019, or 653 escrows per second to support the generation rates for signature schemes ECDSA (secp256k1), ECDSA

(P-256), or EdDSA (Ed25519), respectively, as found in Table 1. On the other hand, a customer in MicroCash would need only *one* escrow with the proper balance to pay at any given ticket rate. As such, MicroCash dramatically reduces the amount of data logged on the blockchain.

Micropayments in Real World Applications. To ground our results in real world numbers, we examined two applications; online gaming and peer-assisted content delivery networks (CDNs). We computed the overhead of processing micropayments with parameter values derived from the service price and the application workload. This is done for three cases: Bitcoin with no micropayment scheme, Bitcoin with MICROPAY, and Bitcoin with MicroCash.

Our results confirm that MicroCash is cost efficient enough to be used in online gaming and content distribution. Since it is a concurrent scheme that allows issuing payments in parallel using a single escrow, MicroCash decreases the total data added to the blockchain by around 50% as compared to MICROPAY. The full details of this evaluation can be found in Sect. 7.3 in the full version [11].

7 Conclusions

In this paper, we introduce MicroCash, the first decentralized probabilistic framework that supports concurrent micropayments. The design of MicroCash features an escrow setup and ticket tracking mechanism that permit a customer to rapidly issue tickets in parallel using only *one* escrow. Moreover, MicroCash is cost effective, as it implements a non-interactive lottery protocol for micropayment aggregation that requires only secure hashing. When compared to the sequential scheme MICROPAY, MicroCash has substantially higher payment processing rates and much lower bandwidth and on-chain traffic. This demonstrates the viability of employing our scheme in large-scale micropayment applications.

References

1. AT&T Network Averages. https://ipnetwork.bgtmo.ip.att.net/pws/averages.html
2. Bitcoinj. https://bitcoinj.github.io/working-with-micropayments
3. BitInfoCharts, Bitcoin avg. transaction fee. https://bitinfocharts.com/comparison/bitcoin-transactionfees.html
4. BloXroute: A Scalable Trustless Blockchain Distribution Network. https://bloxroute.com/wp-content/uploads/2018/03/bloXroute-whitepaper.pdf
5. Board of Governers of the Federal Reserve System, press release June 2011. https://www.federalreserve.gov/newsevents/pressreleases/bcreg20110629a.htm
6. Board of Governers of the Federal Reserve System, Regulation II. https://www.federalreserve.gov/paymentsystems/regii-about.htm
7. Lightning network will be highly centralized. https://cointelegraph.com/news/lightning-network-will-be-highly-centralized-gavin-andresen
8. Supplemental Material. https://www.dropbox.com/s/799j92dnyz2bskk/microcashThreatModel.pdf?dl=0
9. TradeBlock: Analysis of Bitcoin Transaction Size Trends. https://tradeblock.com/blog/analysis-of-bitcoin-transaction-size-trends

10. Almashaqbeh, G., Bishop, A., Cappos, J.: ABC: a threat modeling framework for cryptocurrencies. In: IEEE INFOCOM Workshop on Cryptocurrencies and Blockchains for Distributed Systems (CryBlock) (2019)
11. Almashaqbeh, G., Bishop, A., Cappos, J.: MicroCash: practical concurrent processing of micropayments. arXiv preprint arXiv:1911.08520 (2019). https://arxiv.org/abs/1911.08520
12. Bernstein, D.J., Duif, N., Lange, T., Schwabe, P., Yang, B.-Y.: High-speed high-security signatures. J. Cryptograph. Eng. **2**, 2 (2012)
13. Boneh, D., Bonneau, J., Bünz, B., Fisch, B.: Verifiable delay functions. In: Shacham, H., Boldyreva, A. (eds.) CRYPTO 2018. LNCS, vol. 10991, pp. 757–788. Springer, Cham (2018). https://doi.org/10.1007/978-3-319-96884-1_25
14. Chiesa, A., Green, M., Liu, J., Miao, P., Miers, I., Mishra, P.: Decentralized anonymous micropayments. In: Coron, J.-S., Nielsen, J.B. (eds.) EUROCRYPT 2017. LNCS, vol. 10211, pp. 609–642. Springer, Cham (2017). https://doi.org/10.1007/978-3-319-56614-6_21
15. Decker, C., Wattenhofer, R.: A fast and scalable payment network with bitcoin duplex micropayment channels. In: Pelc, A., Schwarzmann, A.A. (eds.) SSS 2015. LNCS, vol. 9212, pp. 3–18. Springer, Cham (2015). https://doi.org/10.1007/978-3-319-21741-3_1
16. Goldberg, S., Naor, M., Papadopoulos, D., Reyzin, L.: NSEC5 from elliptic curves: provably preventing DNSSEC zone enumeration with shorter responses. IACR Cryptology ePrint Archive 2016/83 (2016)
17. Heran, M., Spilman, J.: Bitcoin contracts (2012). https://en.bitcoin.it/wiki/Contract
18. Micali, S., Rivest, R.L.: Micropayments revisited. In: Preneel, B. (ed.) CT-RSA 2002. LNCS, vol. 2271, pp. 149–163. Springer, Heidelberg (2002). https://doi.org/10.1007/3-540-45760-7_11
19. Pass, R., Shelat, A.: Micropayments for decentralized currencies. In: CCS, pp. 207–218. ACM (2015)
20. Poon, J., Dryja, T.: The Bitcoin lightning network: scalable off-chain instant payments. Technical report (draft) (2015)
21. Rivest, R.L.: Electronic lottery tickets as micropayments. In: Hirschfeld, R. (ed.) FC 1997. LNCS, vol. 1318, pp. 307–314. Springer, Heidelberg (1997). https://doi.org/10.1007/3-540-63594-7_87
22. Rivest, R.L.: Peppercoin micropayments. In: Juels, A. (ed.) FC 2004. LNCS, vol. 3110, pp. 2–8. Springer, Heidelberg (2004). https://doi.org/10.1007/978-3-540-27809-2_2
23. Wheeler, D.: Transactions using bets. In: Lomas, M. (ed.) Security Protocols 1996. LNCS, vol. 1189, pp. 89–92. Springer, Heidelberg (1997). https://doi.org/10.1007/3-540-62494-5_7

LockDown: Balance Availability Attack Against Lightning Network Channels

Cristina Pérez-Solà[1,4], Alejandro Ranchal-Pedrosa[2],
Jordi Herrera-Joancomartí[3,4], Guillermo Navarro-Arribas[3,4],
and Joaquin Garcia-Alfaro[5(✉)]

[1] Universitat Oberta de Catalunya, Barcelona, Spain
[2] University of Sydney, Sydney, Australia
[3] Universitat Autònoma de Barcelona, Bellaterra, Spain
[4] CYBERCAT-Center for Cybersecurity Research of Catalonia, Tarragona, Spain
[5] Institut Polytechnique de Paris, Télécom SudParis, Évry, France
jgalfaro@ieee.org

Abstract. The Lightning Network (LN) is a payment network running as a second layer on top of Bitcoin and other Blockchains. This paper presents the possibility of performing a balance lockdown in the LN due to misbehaving nodes associated to a given channel. We formalize and introduce a practical attack, minimizing the economic cost of the attack. We present results that validate our claims, and provide experimental results and potential countermeasures to handle the problem.

Keywords: Bitcoin · Blockchain · Network security · Off-chain payments channels · Lightning Network (LN) · Denial of service

1 Introduction

The Lightning Network (LN) is a peer-to-peer (P2P) payment network running as a second layer on top of Bitcoin and other Blockchains. Two nodes in the network can create a payment channel with a fixed capacity and use it to exchange payments between them with low fees. Nodes can route payments through other nodes when no direct channel exists between a payer and a payee. To preserve some degree of privacy, the LN uses an onion-routing protocol for multihop payments. Nodes only publish the minimum information needed to establish the payment routes. Besides the capacity of a channel, its *balance* determines how this capacity is balanced between two nodes (i.e., the bandwidth of the channel in each direction). A node with 0 balance is not able to perform a payment in the channel, since all the capacity is held by the other node.

In this paper, we uncover the possibility of balance lockdown due to misbehaving nodes associated with a given channel. The attack affects the payment channels of the LN nodes. More specifically, in a balance lockdown attack an adversary can block LN middle nodes in multipath payments. If successful, the attack gives the adversary a dominant position in the LN, which can be later

© International Financial Cryptography Association 2020
J. Bonneau and N. Heninger (Eds.): FC 2020, LNCS 12059, pp. 245–263, 2020.
https://doi.org/10.1007/978-3-030-51280-4_14

exploited either for data gathering information or for increasing the benefits of particular LN gateway nodes. We formalize and elaborate some practical evidence of our attack while minimizing the economic cost of the adversary. We present experimental results that validate our claims and discuss potential countermeasures.

Section 2 introduces the necessary background to understand the proposed attack. Section 3 describes the threat model and the attack. Section 4 provides the experimental results. Section 5 discusses countermeasures. Finally, Sect. 6 surveys related work and Sect. 7 concludes the paper.

2   Lightning Network Background

The LN is a separated P2P network, connected to the main Bitcoin P2P network with nodes that run a LN software client [3,4,15]. Each client maintains a P2P connection with other nodes of the LN and also a connection with a node in the Bitcoin main P2P network. When nodes establish connections with other peers in the Lightning P2P Network, they can open a payment channel in which they exchange Bitcoin transactions without the need for such transactions to be set down in the blockchain. Such payment channels are the core elements of the LN. Details of the LN specification can be found in [14]. High level introductions about the LN exist in the literature [2,9,10]. The background key point for our proposal is the multihop approach. Payments in the LN between nodes that do not share a payment channel have to be routed through a multihop path through a payment route. In all current LN implementations, such route is constructed by the source node that performs the payment. To allow such construction, nodes in de LN maintain a topology structure of the LN network that is used for route discovery. LN implementations, given a target node, return the more suitable route based on the number of hops and the fees each hop charges for routing the payment. However, being a P2P environment, there is no deterrent for a source node to compute the payment route at his choice with the information he has available.

In the multihop approach, payments at each individual payment channel cannot be performed exactly in the same way that with a single hop. An intermediate user has to enforce he would receive the payment from the preceding node once he has performed the payment to the next one, otherwise he would lose the amount of the payment. The enforcement of this type of atomic exchange between all the nodes of the path (i.e., all simple one-hop payments have to be completed or none can be processed) is performed using Hashed Timelock Contracts (HTLCs) [1]. In an HTLC between the sender A and the receiver B, A can deposit Bitcoins that can be redeemed by B if B can perform a digital signature and provide a preimage of a hash value. Furthermore, the deposit performed by A has an expiration date after which A can retrieve the deposit providing a digital signature. For a two-hop payment, $A \leftrightarrow B \leftrightarrow C$, the idea is that C generates a random value x and sends $h(x)$ to A. A performs the single hop payment to B with an HTLC based on $h(x)$ and B also performs the single hop payment to C with an HTLC based on the same value $h(x)$. In that way, since C knows x, he can redeem the transaction from B, but redeeming the transaction implies revealing the value of x. This implies that B may also redeem the payment from A.

When node B_1 performs a payment to node B_m in the LN using the route $B_1 \to B_2 \to \cdots \to B_m$, the atomicity needed in such operation implies that all route payments cannot be executed until the last node of the route, B_m, provides the corresponding preimage x of the $h(x)$ included in the HTLC. In a normal scenario, B_m reveals this preimage as soon as he receives the payment in his channel since he wants to collect the payment. However, in case that the payment gets stuck for any reason in node B_i, all payments from node B_1 to node B_i will be locked. To bound the locking time, B_1 sets a total timelock. Such time frame for the payment, determined as an absolute blockheight value, and known as its expiration blockheight, θ, limits the time that money will be locked in case the payment does not succeed. Then, when the payment is being routed every node of the route also decreases such value θ. Each node of the LN advertises for each of its channels, the value δ that will be used for decreasing θ at each hop. With such public information, the payer creates the route with an initial θ ensuring that after subtracting each δ of each intermediate node, the last node will obtain a not expired time, that is $(\theta - \sum_{i=2}^{m} \delta_i) > 0$. Notice that this mechanism allows the payer to bound the time a payment will be locked but, without any other mechanism, a malicious payer could lock the funds of intermediate nodes by setting a large initial value θ. To avoid such situation, each node sets his own T_{max} value that bounds the locking time of a payment. Then, when a node receives a payment as an intermediate node route, if $\theta > T_{max}$ the node will refuse to route the payment and the payer will have to choose another route.

3   LockDown Attack

The proposed attack is focused on a target victim A, a node of the LN. The goal of the adversary is to block the victim A as a middle node in multipath payments. By achieving such goal, an adversary may obtain a dominant position in the LN since blocking some selected nodes may let the adversary be the main gateway to route payments allowing him to have a dominant position that can be exploited either for data gathering information or just for increasing the benefits as a LN gateway node.

To simplify the description of the attack, we omit some of the maximum values that LN implementations introduce. However, we discus how such values impact the cost of real attacks in Sect. 4. Regarding the notation, and for the rest of the paper, we assume that the victim node is A, the adversary is M and A has open channels with a list of n different nodes, denoted by B_i for $i = 1, \cdots, n$. Furthermore, we denote by C_{AB_i} the capacity of the channel that A and B_i have open and by $balance_{AB_i}$ (resp. $balance_{B_iA}$) the balance that A (resp. B_i) has in this channel. We denote C_{attack} the capacity that M has to hold in channels in the LN to perform the attack.

3.1   Attack Design

The atomicity needed in a multihop payment enforces that the intermediate payments in a multihop route should be held until the complete route is constructed and all payments can be performed together. During the time the route is being constructed, nodes in the route lock the balance of the payment until such payment takes place. With such underlying mechanism, a malicious user can lock a total amount of p balance in a channel AB_i, during the time a payment is being constructed, by sending a payment of value p through that channel AB_i. However, such action, that we label as a naive attack, has two main drawbacks from an adversarial point of view. The first one is related to the cost of the attack and the second one is related to the time the balance is locked.

Regarding the cost, in a naive attack, to block p balance in channel AB_i, the adversary needs to perform a payment of value p so the adversary needs to hold the same capacity that the attack is locking. In that sense, we can define the Attack Effort Ratio.

Definition 1. *The **Attack Effort Ratio** (AER) is the ratio between the capacity needed to perform the attack and the capacity that the attack blocks, i.e.,*

$$AER = \frac{C_{attack}}{C_{blocked}}$$

The naive attack achieves $AER = 1$ and such attack can be considered a brute force attack since it always can be performed by design of multihop payments. Notice that AER measures the profitability of the attack, and in case an adversary can reduce the AER then, more efficient is the attack, in economic terms, and higher can be the incentive for the adversary to perform such attack.

Regarding the time during which the balance is locked, in a naive attack the adversary only locks the balance during the time the whole payment is being constructed and, in regular conditions, such period is often very short since the final receiver of the payment in a multihop route "executes" the payment as soon as the payment arrives. For more powerful attacks we can define the Δ function.

Definition 2. *The $\Delta(b)$ **function** is a time based decreasing function that measures the total capacity blocked w.r.t. the time during which the attack has been conducted. The block generation time, b, is used as the time unit for this function.*

For instance, $\Delta(0) = C_{blocked}$ since it provides the total capacity blocked at the initial time of the attack. Eventually, $\Delta(b) = 0$ for a large b since the blocking effectiveness of the attack decreases over the time. In a naive attack, $\Delta(1) = 0$ since the capacity is unblocked almost instantly after the payment, long before the appearance of the first block ($b = 1$) after the attack execution.

As we will detail later, an attack is performed through multiple payments. For that reason, the $\Delta(b)$ function is computed taking into account the expiration values of each payment that forms the attack. If we define $\Delta_i(b)$ as the capacity blocked by payment i during b blocks, then $\Delta(b) = \sum_i \Delta_i(b), \forall i \in attack$.

For comparison purposes, we define two single value metrics that compress the $\Delta(b)$ function: the Total Blocked Time and the Normalized Total Blocked Time.

The **Total Blocked Time**, TBT, of the attack is the sum of the $\Delta(b)$ values:

$$TBT = \sum_{b=0}^{\infty} \Delta(b)$$

The **normalized** TBT, $\widetilde{TBT}$, is defined as:

$$\widetilde{TBT} = \frac{TBT}{C_{blocked} \cdot \max\{T_{max}\}},$$

where $\max\{T_{max}\}$ is the maximum default value of T_{max} seen in any implementation. Therefore, $0 < \widetilde{TBT} \leq 1$, and the ideal attack with $\widetilde{TBT} = 1$ would be blocking $C_{blocked}$ capacity during 5000 blocks, that is, more than 34 days.

Once we have described how to perform a naive attack to a single channel, we now describe how to improve the efficiency of the attack, both minimizing the AER and maximizing TBT. We focus the attack goal to block the victim A as a middle node in multipath payments. In that case, the value $C_{blocked}$ is the total capacity of node A in the LN, that is $C_{blocked} = C_A = \sum_{i=1}^{n} C_{AB_i}$. Notice that regarding the attack goal, for blocking a middle node in a payment route it is sufficient to block all incoming balances to A or all outgoing balances from A. In any of both situations, A cannot route any payment. Then, the naive attack over a single node A achieves $C_{attack} = \min\{\sum_{i=1}^{n} balance_{AB_i}, \sum_{i=1}^{n} balance_{B_iA}\}$. Clearly, $C_{attack} \leq C_A$. The AER for such an attack is reduced with respect to the naive attack of a single channel. Notice that, with this approach, the AER reduction cannot be determined by the adversary, i.e., the adversary cannot directly control the balances. However, the AER can be also reduced when the same payment is used more than once to block different channels. In fact, in a multihop payment, a single payment p blocks up to $m \cdot p$ capacity being m the number of hops of the payment route. Another strategy to reduce AER is to construct the largest possible route. However, if the attack is focused on a victim A, not only the length of the route has to be computed but also the route should be kept close to A to ensure all blocking capacity obtained for that route is able to block incoming or outgoing channels of A. As we will see, the best strategy to keep the payment route close to the victim is to perform routes through A with loops as short as possible that return to A. Such possibility will depend on the topology of the payment network in which A is connected.

The improvement of the attack can also be measured regarding the time during which the attack takes place. The objective is to maximize the TBT value. To that end, the adversary can be placed at the end of the route, to hold the payment as much time as possible before the funds of the route are unlocked. As we will see in detail in the next section, this strategy increases the value C_{attack} needed for the adversary.

3.2   Adversarial Knowledge

To implement the ideas described in the previous section, the adversary needs precise knowledge of the network. To construct payments routes which pass through victim A, the adversary needs to know the topology of the network to construct such paths. This information is available using any LN implementation, since it is needed to perform standard payments. Additionally to the topology of the network, the detailed information about balances of every channel are needed to perform the attack. This information can be derived from existing attacks in the literature [5].

Furthermore, to minimize AER, the number of hops of a payment route has to be maximized. Although payment routes in the LN are bounded to 20 hops [16], the exact number of hops that a route may contain is also limited by values T_{max} and δ of each node of that route. Notice that a node does not accept a payment that locks its funds more than T_{max} time and such time is fixed by the adversary but decreased in each hop by the δ of each node. Then depending on the values T_{max} and δ of each node of the route, the total number of hops in a route could be lower than 20. For that reason, the adversary also needs to know the values T_{max} and δ of each node of the network.

3.3   Attack Description

To describe our attack we use a simple scenario where the victim A is a hub between two users, B_1 and B_2, as depicted in Fig. 1. Capacity values are $C_{AB_1} = p_1 + p_4$ and $C_{AB_2} = p_2 + p_3$ being p_i the balances in each direction for each channel. The objective of the adversary Mallory, M, is to disrupt the availability of A, by either blocking the availability of incoming links or outgoing links, that is rendering $p_1 = 0$ and $p_3 = 0$ or either $p_2 = 0$ and $p_4 = 0$.

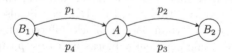

Fig. 1. Simple scenario

To perform the attack, M opens a channel with A as depicted in Fig. 2(a). The attack complexity depends on the balances between A and B_i and we can distinguish the two following cases:

Shorter Loop – The first case is when $p_1 \leq p_4$ and $p_3 \leq p_2$. Notice that with this conditions, $p_1 + p_3 \leq p_2 + p_4$ so M would prefer to block incoming paths to A since C_{attack} is lower than blocking outgoing connections. Then, M can block all incoming path by performing two single payments with a short loop. The first payment will follow the route $M \rightarrow A \rightarrow B_1 \rightarrow A \rightarrow M$ with value p_1 and the second payment will follow the route $M \rightarrow A \rightarrow B_2 \rightarrow A \rightarrow M$ with value p_3. With these payments $balance_{B_1A} = balance_{B_2A} = 0$. Notice that with this scenario the channel that M has to open with A to perform the attack needs a capacity[1] $C_{attack} = C_{MA} = 2(p_1 + p_3)$.

---

[1] The capacity that M has to open with A is the double of the payment value since the payment is performed by M but also has to return to M to extend the time that the payment is blocked.

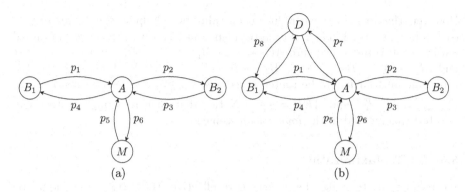

Fig. 2. (a) Simple scenario with adversary. (b) Simple scenario with external node

Longer Loop – In case either $p_1 > p_4$ or $p_3 > p_2$, then the adversary needs to proceed in a different way.[2] Without lost of generality, assume that $p_1 > p_4$ and $p_3 \leq p_2$ and also that $p_1 + p_3 \leq p_2 + p_4$ so M would prefer to block incoming paths to A. With this balance distribution, M can perform a short loop as before to block the incoming path from B_2 by performing the payment of value p_3 following the route $M \rightarrow A \rightarrow B_2 \rightarrow A \rightarrow M$. However, since $p_1 > p_4$, M cannot perform a payment route $M \rightarrow A \rightarrow B_1 \rightarrow A \rightarrow M$ with value p_1 since the channel AB_1 has $balance_{AB_1} = p_4 < p_1$. At most, M can perform a payment with value p_4 through the path $M \rightarrow A \rightarrow B_1 \rightarrow A \rightarrow M$. Such payment locks p_4 but some balance is still available in the channel, precisely $p_4 - p_1$. For M to lock that capacity of the channel, since the path $A \rightarrow B_1$ is already exhausted, M needs another path from A to B_1 with capacity $p_4 - p_1$ with such exact direction. Figure 2(b) shows a simple example in which there exists a node D with opened channels with A and B_1 and such that $balance_{AD} = p_7 \geq p_4 - p_1$ and $balance_{DB_1} = p_8 \geq p_4 - p_1$. In that case, M can perform a second payment with value $p_4 - p_1$ with route $M \rightarrow A \rightarrow D \rightarrow B_1 \rightarrow A \rightarrow M$. This payment will lock the remaining funds of $B_1 \rightarrow A$.

The hard assumption of the existence of node D can be relaxed with the existence of multiple possible paths that all together can route the total $p_4 - p_1$ value. Notice, however, that the payment graph topology hardly determines the existence of such paths.

3.4   AER Minimization

The attack described in the previous section can be improved in terms of AER. For instance, regarding the *shorter loop* case example, the AER value depends on the difference between $p_1 + p_3$ and $p_2 + p_4$. In the extreme case in which, $p_1 + p_3 = p_2 + p_4$, such attack has the worst possible AER since $C_A = (p_1 + p_3) + (p_2 + p_4) = 2(p_1 + p_3)$ and $C_{attack} = C_{MA} = 2 \cdot (p_1 + p_3)$, so $AER = 1$.

---

[2] Notice that if both inequations hold, then $p_1 + p_3 > p_2 + p_4$ and M would prefer to block outgoing paths as in the "Shorter loop" case.

However, the adversary can reduce such value by relooping the nearer part of each route next to A. Then, if each payment route can be m hops, each original path can be transformed into $M \rightarrow A \rightarrow B_1 \rightarrow A \rightarrow B_1 \rightarrow A \rightarrow \cdots \rightarrow M$ and $M \rightarrow A \rightarrow B_2 \rightarrow A \rightarrow B_2 \rightarrow A \rightarrow \cdots \rightarrow M$. With those loops, the total amount that has to be routed is reduced to $\frac{2p_1}{m-2}$ and $\frac{2p_3}{m-2}$ respectively, so $C_{attack} = \frac{4(p_1+p_3)}{m-2}$ and $AER = \frac{2}{m-2}$. Notice that such relooping strategy can also be implemented in the *longer loop* scenario.

3.5 TBT Maximization

We recall that, to make the attack more effective, the TBT value should be maximized. To that end, the adversary takes the advantage of being at the beginning and end of each payment.

As a first node, the adversary can determine the maximum Δ_i for a particular payment i since such value depends on values δ and T_{max} of each node and the node position in the route. The first one, T_{max}, is the maximum amount that a node allows an outgoing payment in a channel to be locked. And the second one indicates the difference, in blocks, that each hop in the route requires. When a node receives a payment, he sets an expiration time[3], θ, for the payment, and subtracts his δ. In case that the resulting value is lower than his T_{max}, then he will keep forwarding the payment, in other case, the node will refuse the payment, the route will be discarded and the payer will need to find another route. Then, the best strategy for an adversary to maximize Δ_i is to simulate the route assuming that each node, instead of discarding the payment, will set the new θ as his T_{max} (see Appendix A for a detailed example).

As a last node of the payment, the adversary can hold the payment during the received $\theta = \Delta_i$ value, being sure that the previous node does not cancel the payment before that time—since it fits the proper waiting values of the implementation.

4 Experimental Results

To analyze the feasibility of the proposed attack and provide a proof-of-concept, we need to ensure that nodes in the LN behave in a particular way. Firstly, to minimize AER we need to test if the type of routes with cycles used in our attack can be routed through the nodes of the LN. Secondly, to maximize TBT, we need to verify if the payee of a multihop route is able to retain a payment during a certain period of time before the payment is finally processed locking channels involved in the payment route. Furthermore, we are also interested to implement a mechanism for which the payee can cancel the payment without paying any fee to the routing nodes.

We perform a test in a simnet controlled environment to validate that our claims are correct and that the routes generated in our attack containing loops

---

[3] For simplicity, we assume θ as a relative block height value.

can effectively been deployed in the three most relevant available implementations of the Bitcoin LN, namely LND (lnd), C-lightning (c-lightning) and Eclair (eclair). Results can be found in Appendix A.

Once the feasibility of the attack has been proved from an implementation point of view, we have performed some attack simulations for the LN of the Bitcoin mainnet in order to measure the AER of the attack, the function $\Delta(b)$, and its economic cost. Notice that there is no technical reason that stops us from effectively executing the simulated attacks in the Bitcoin mainnet. However, for ethical reasons, we have not performed the attack on the Mainnet and, instead, we have performed a responsible disclosure to the developers of the LN implementations.

Our simulations will assess the effectiveness of the attack given the actual topology of the network. We base our simulations on the attack algorithm described in Sect. 3, but in order to provide accurate results, we have taken into account different restrictions that actual LN implementations take over their parameters.

Firstly, we bound to 20 the maximum hops that a payment route may have in the LN as described in [14]. Regarding the length of routes, we assume that the expiration time for a route θ at each hop cannot be lower than zero.

Secondly, all existing LN implementations fix the maximum value of a channel at 16777215 satoshis[4]. Such value may impact the channel that M has to open with the victim A. Since such payment channel needs to have a total capacity of C_{attack}, in case $C_{attack} > 16777215$ then M needs to open more than one channel with A.

Once such values have been taken into account, to perform our simulations, we take a snapshot of the topology of the LN[5] of the bitcoin mainet on January, 20th, 2020 at 20:00.

4.1 Simulation Assumptions

To execute the attack algorithm described in Sect. 3, the adversary needs to complement the information of the network graph with further data. The information needed is: the balance of each channel and the values T_{max} for each node of the network.

Regarding the balances, they can be obtained executing the attack described in [5]. However, instead of performing such attack, we have assigned the balances of each channel using different statistical distributions, trying to reproduce the different scenarios that could be found in the network. In order to assign balances to channels, we proceed in the following way: for each channel, first the balance of

---

[4] This bound is just an implementation parameter. There are already channels in the LN with larger values. The availability of larger channels reduces the number of channels for the attack, as well as total fees to pay for every open channel and the total cost of the attack.

[5] Such information can be obtained, for instance, with the instruction `describegraph` of the lnd implementation.

one of the nodes is randomly selected using one of the selected distributions, and taking the capacity of the channel as the maximum possible value to generate. Then, the balance of the other node in the channel is set as the remaining balance (that is, the capacity minus the balance). Five different distributions are used to assign balances to channels: *deterministic*, *uniform*, *normal*, *exponential*, and *beta*. The *deterministic* distribution always assigns half of the capacity of the channel to each of the nodes; the *normal* distribution is used with $\mu = 0.5$ and $\sigma = 0.2$; the *exponential* distribution uses $\lambda = 1$; and the *beta* distribution $\alpha = \beta = 0.25$.

The value T_{max} is a network node parameter that is not publicly available since it is not advertised by the nodes. However, such value is implementation dependent[6] Hence, by inferring the LN implementation of each node, we can obtain the values of T_{max} for that node. To infer the LN client implementation run by each node, we take into account the fee rate, the fee base rate, and the δ values announced in the nodes' channels policies. As shown in Table 1, default values for the fee rate and δ parameters allow to uniquely identify the LN implementation. We use those values to infer node implementation. Moreover, the default value for the fee base rate is always 1000. We use this third value to further validate that the node is using default values in its policies.

Table 1. Values that help infer the implementation a node is running.

	lnd (old)	lnd (new)	c-lightning	eclair
Fee rate	1	1	10	100
Fee base rate	1000	1000	1000	1000
δ	144	40	14	144

However, users may indeed change channel policies, or even use different policies for different channels. On the one hand, if a node is not announcing any policy with the fee rate, fee base rate, and delta values corresponding to any of the described implementations, we assume the implementation of that node is unknown. On the other hand, whenever a node announces different policies in its channels but only one of them corresponds to a default behavior, the node is tagged with this implementation. Finally, if multiple policies are announced and multiple default policies are identified, then again the node is tagged as unknown.

Taking this approach, using the selected snapshot of the network, we end up with a small percentage of unknown nodes (12.03%), for which we are not able to properly infer the implementation. In that case, we randomly tag those nodes with one of the three main implementations, with the same percentage distribution than those nodes already tagged. Using such approach, network nodes for the analyzed graph have been classified as shown in Table 2.

---

[6] One may assume users changing some LN implementation parameters. However, the T_{max} value is not expected to be one of those easily modifiable parameters.

Table 2. Number of nodes, with at least one channel, classified in one of the main implementations for the snapshot graph used in our analysis.

	nodes (number)	(percentage)
lnd	2294	92.65 %
c-lightning	154	6.22%
eclair	28	1.13%
Total	2476	100%

4.2   Attack Simulation Results

To perform the simulation, we focus the attack on one of the most relevant nodes in the network. Such node has 516 opened active channels with a total capacity slightly above 40 BTC. Then, we test the effectiveness of the attack in case such node runs one of the three main implementations, lnd, c-lightning or eclair. For each implementation we also test each of the balance distributions. In order to present more representative results, being the balance distribution a probability distribution, we execute the experiments 10 times and take the mean values.

For each implementation and for each balance distribution, we have performed the attack and measured the AER value of the attack, the percentage of the capacity of the victim that has been blocked, the total channels needed to perform the attack, and the normalized Total Blocked Time, $\widetilde{TBT}$ (cf. Table 3). Furthermore, we also have analyzed the Δ function of the attack (see Fig. 3).

Table 3. Attack results for the different balance distributions.

Distibution	Implementation	EAR	Blocked capacity	Channels needed	$\widetilde{TBT}$
	lnd	0.232	86.47 %	60.5	0.32
beta	c-lightning	0.179	83.80 %	48.3	0.07
	eclair	0.524	86.10 %	128.6	0.05
	lnd	0.176	100.00 %	43.0	0.47
Deterministic	c-lightning	0.109	86.80 %	27.0	0.14
	eclair	0.500	100.00 %	121.0	0.09
	lnd	0.192	92.74 %	52.9	0.38
Exponential	c-lightning	0.143	86.41 %	39.7	0.10
	eclair	0.498	92.43 %	125.0	0.07
	lnd	0.216	96.16 %	49.8	0.42
Normal	c-lightning	0.187	87.60 %	38.1	0.11
	eclair	0.526	96.13 %	125.6	0.08
	lnd	0.234	93.04 %	55.8	0.38
Uniform	c-lightning	0.180	87.02 %	43.9	0.10
	eclair	0.548	92.80 %	128.7	0.07

Table 3 shows that the attack is effective in all scenarios (implementations and balance distribution) since the AER is lower than 2 which was the value for a naive attack. Notice that in the worst attack, for a Uniform distribution in which the node runs an eclair implementation, the AER is 0.548, which is half of the capacity of the victim to block its 92.80% capacity. In fact, the percentage of the victim capacity blocked is high for all the scenarios, never below the 83%. Moreover, the $\widetilde{TBT}$ also shows that lnd implementations are the ones allowing the adversary to block more capacity over time (as can also be observed in Fig. 3).

Figure 3 plots the Δ function which shows which is the amount of time locking the funds. As expected, graphics show that the value of T_{max} of each implementation determines the length of the time. When the victim runs an lnd implementation, 80% of the capacity of the victim can be locked during 287 blocks (almost two days) in any balance distribution tested. But if we look at the 50%, such value is increased to 2407 blocks (more than 16 days). Even for the eclair implementation which has the lowest T_{max} value of all three implementations ($T_{max} = 1008$), 50% of the capacity can be blocked during 287 blocks (almost two days) for all tested balance distributions.

Besides the effectiveness of the attack showed so far, we also measure the economic cost of the attack. For such measure, we take the same methodology than in [5] in which the total cost of the attack can be divided between the entrance barrier cost and the economic cost. On the one hand, the entrance barrier cost takes into account the economic resources that the adversary has to control to be able to perform the attack. Such resources will be completely recovered after the attack has been finished. On the other hand, the economic cost of the attack is the amount of money that the adversary will lose due to the execution of the attack.

Regarding **the entrance barrier cost**, the proposed attack needs to fund one or multiple LN channels with the capacity C_{attack}. Such amount is represented by the channels needed value of Table 3. For instance, the attack for the uniform distribution over c-lightning has an entrance barrier cost of 44 channels (or 7.38197460 BTC) to block 87.02% of the capacity of the node.

With regard to **the economic cost of the attack**, two values have to be taken into account: (i) the fee corresponding to the funding transaction of the channel; (ii) the fee corresponding to the transaction that closes the channel. Regarding the fees of the funding transactions, such cost depends on the number of channels needed to perform the attacks. The cost in fees for each channel depends on the size in bytes of the funding transaction. However, such size mostly depends on its inputs that will vary for each particular transaction, but a funding transaction with a single input can cost as low as 0.00000154 BTC[7]. Secondly, and regarding the closing transaction, it is also difficult to estimate the exact fee for a generic closing transaction, since again multiple parameters

---

[7] See, for instance, transaction:
f42012119a50afda6717a29957fba043d8afba9b0ff9a0f11 32670232eb61feb It is the funding transaction corresponding to the Channel Id 67509 5741575593984 opened on January 22, 2020, by node
031a02081118bcbd899756f8cd d9feaf5dbf3f1014a1d811e33e8f5a4d8079e2fe.

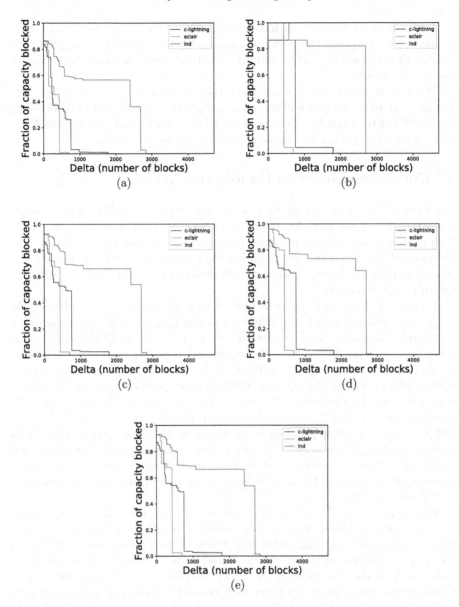

Fig. 3. $\Delta(p)$ function results for every tested distribution: (a) Beta, (b) Deterministic, (c) Exponential, (d) Normal, (e) Uniform.

may affect such a value. A cost rounding 0.00000460 BTC can be achieved, as can be seen in different existing closing transactions[8].

---

[8] For instance, Channel Id 671792808627666945 with total capacity 0.0005 BTC has been closed with the following close transaction d2f676a3085f46d6636f1197ab3fec 2855bc7c8fffb3cb48b83396220ad1dc0a.

Notice that we have not included the Lightning fees as a cost because they are never applied (since the payments never succeed). For that reason, the total number of payments needed to perform the attack does not affect the economic cost of the attack.

With such values, we can estimate the economic cost of an attack. For instance, an attack based on a normal distribution assuming an lnd node blocks the 96.16% of the capacity of the node with 50 channels, that means 0.00030700 BTC in fees for opening and closing the channels, around 2 Eur.

5 Countermeasures to Handle the Attack

The main countermeasures are focused on increasing the AER in order to make the attack less profitable. As discussed in Sect. 3, AER is reduced thanks to the possibility that a single payment performs a route with multiple hops. Furthermore, if the adversary may maintain the route near the victim, the AER is even more reduced. So to not allow the adversary perform such strategy different measures can be adopted.

First of all, loops in a payment route should be minimized or forbidden. In particular, cycles of length two (the ones of the form $A \rightarrow B \rightarrow A$) should be completely forbidden since are the ones that most reduce AER and keep the route close to a possible victim. We argue that imposing such restriction does not damage any possible functionality of the LN. Notice that lightning payments, even those in a multihop route, are designed to be performed atomically in the sense that they are executed completely or not executed at all. A payment with a subpath of the form $A \rightarrow B \rightarrow A$, once executed it lefts the state between A and B exactly as it was previous to the payment. The implementation of such measure is straightforward even assuming that routing in the LN is performed through onion routing. Notice that in the onion routing approach, every node is aware of the previous and next node in the route so he can reject a route in case both nodes are the same.

Regarding cycles of length larger than two, it is clear that its restriction also increases AER and hinders the attack. Again, although the LN currently routes using onion packets and nodes are only aware of the previous and next hop in the route, additional information transferred between routes and shared by all nodes, such as the hash used in the HTLC can be used to detect that a cycle is passing through a node and reject such possibility. However, in contrast with cycles of length two, longer cycles do not keep the same state of the channel and it can be used for legitimate purposes, like spontaneous payments[9], whose restrictions could impact future LN features.

Besides cycles, increasing the length of a payment route also reduces AER so a possible countermeasure for the proposed attack is the reduction of the maximum length of a route. Such value is set to 20 in the LN specification and it could be reduced to increase the AER of an attack. However, such value

---

[9] SPSP, Simple Protocol for Spontaneous Payments, https://lists.linuxfoundation.org/pipermail/lightning-dev/2018-June/001327.html.

directly impacts in the performance of the network since its reduction could potentially discard possible routes for legitimate payments. More testing should be performed before implementing this type of countermeasure.

Another straightforward countermeasure that can be performed to reduce the effectiveness of the attack is the fine tuning of some lightning parameters that, until that moment, are not properly addressed. Such parameters are T_{max} and δ, which have two different implications for our attack. On one hand, despite the maximum hop value (set to 20) T_{max} and δ can effectively determine a lower bound for the number of hops in a route.[10] Since reducing the maximum number of loops increases AER, setting the proper values could potentially prevent the attack. On the other hand, the time value during which a channel or victim can be blocked without the adversary needing to perform any action is also dependent on those two parameters. So reducing the actual values of T_{max} and δ is a countermeasure for our attack since it reduces the time during which the adversary may lock the funds. However, assessing the correct values for T_{max} and δ deserves a detailed and exhaustive analysis and test.

6   Related Work

Recent literature on the security of LN and payment channels mentions *channel exhaustion* and *payments griefing* attacks [6,11]. Rohrer *et al.* [12] suggest an adversarial combination of both techniques, to build an attack that resembles the *naive attack* reported in Sect. 3.1. Rohrer *et al.* refer to the combination of channel exhaustion and payments griefing as an attack which '*requires E to first open a channel with a capacity that is equal or greater than the total balance of A's outbound channels*'. This is equivalent to the *naive* scenario reported in our work (cf. Section 3.1, *naive attack*). While Rohrer *et al.*'s attack has always an AER higher than one (i.e., $AER = 2$ if we consider that their attack requires an outbound channel), our work builds upon optimization techniques to obtain attacks with lower AER (cf. Sect. 4, reduction from $AER = 2$ to $AER = 0.1$). Recall that attacks with an AER higher than one must be considered as brute forcing, with marginal adversarial incentives, in economic terms.

Other differences with Rohrer *et al.*'s work include the experimental setup reported in [12]. Instead of five independent lnd instances, we report in Sect. 4 experimental work using three different implementations, including lnd, c-lightning or eclair. Some other improvements included in our work is the use of extended network measurements. Previous work (cf. [12], Section II.B and citations thereof) only uses the properties of the topology edges, without taking into account the balance of every node associated to the edges. This is impor-tant, since without processing this information, an adversary can estimate the use of routes that may not be used, in the end (i.e., the estimated diameter is wrong).

---

[10] For instance, a payment route in which all nodes run an eclair implementation can be at most 7 hops.

Privacy issues are also reported in recent literature of payment channels. Tang *et al.* address in [17] the impact of using payment channels w.r.t. privacy preservation. Since users need to route their transactions using other nodes, they must find paths through the payment network, and with enough pre-allocated funds to route their transactions. This poses the problem of hiding the balance of each payment channel node. Joancomarti *et al.* show in [5] the difficulty of hiding such balances. Their work uncovers a balance discovery attack that can be used to deanonymize the precise balance of each network payment node, hence leading to the de-anonymization of the network transactions, in the end. Tang *et al.* and Malavolta *et al.* assume in [8,17] that the adversary is passive, i.e., the adversary observes only the public information released in the network, whereas prior work by Malavolta *et al.* and Ross *et al.* [7,13] considers active adversaries acting as corrupt relay nodes, trying to learn the destination of other nodes transactions.

7   Conclusion

We have addressed the possibility of availability attacks affecting the bandwidth of payment channels of the Lightning Network (LN). We show that an adversary can take advantage of misbehaving nodes associated with a given victim in order to block its ability to act as an intermediate node in multihop payments. The attack can achieve a lockdown during a reasonable time with a low economic cost. We have formalized the attack and provided a practical implementation showing its performance in the LN from the Bitcoin mainnet. The results validate our claims showing the relatively low cost required to lock down an important percentage of the total capacity of a victim. We have discussed potential countermeasures to handle the problem by making the attack less profitable, or less cost-effective attractive for adversaries.

The presented attack is focused towards locking the balance of the channels of a given node, the victim. That is, the goal is to lock down the ability of a specific node to act as intermediary node in payment routes. A similar approach can be used to affect not a single node but the whole network or a subset of nodes. Further research can be carried on whether such attacks are economically and technically feasible and provide interesting metrics such as the locking percentage of overall network capacity (in similar terms as the proposed AER and TBT metrics).

Acknowledgments. Work partially supported by the BART (Blockchain Advanced Research & Technologies) initiative (cf. https://www.bart-blockchain.fr/en/), the European Commission under grant agreement 830892 (H2020 SPARTA project), and the Spanish Government under Grant RTI2018-095094-B-C22 "CONSENT".

A   Simnet Network

To perform our experiments, we create a Lightning simnet network with eleven nodes, $M, A, B_1, \cdots, B_9$. Node M will be the adversary and A the victim. Nodes $B_1, \cdots, B_9$ will represent victim's neighbors. To test all implementations in our simnet, we run different implementations for different nodes. More precisely, the following configuration has been taken. Nodes M, A, B_1, B_2, B_3 run the LND implementation with version 0.5.2-99-beta, nodes B_4, B_5, B_6 the c-lightning with version v0.7.0 and nodes B_7, B_8, B_9 run eclair with version *version=0.2-SNAPSHOT*. Over this configuration, we have created 10 payment channels, as shown in Fig. 4(a).

With this settlement, M performs a payment to himself, following the route $M \rightarrow A \rightarrow B_1 \rightarrow A \rightarrow B_2 \rightarrow A \rightarrow B_3 \rightarrow A \rightarrow B_4 \rightarrow A \rightarrow B_5 \rightarrow A \rightarrow B_6 \rightarrow A \rightarrow B_7 \rightarrow A \rightarrow B_7 \rightarrow A \rightarrow B_9 \rightarrow A \rightarrow M$.

The correct execution of such experiment proves that the payment has been processed by all nodes and that routes can effectively contain loops. Notice that the loops tested in this experiment are the shortest possible which validates the *shorter loop* case of our attack (see Sect. 3). Notice that the implementation selected for each node ensures that such behavior is equivalent in all implementations.

Figure 4(b) shows a new scenario where we have added a payment channel between nodes B_6 and B_9. With this scenario, M performs a payment to himself, following the route $M - A - B_6 - B_9 - A - B_6 - B_9 - A - M$.

Again, the test shows that the payment is correctly processed by all nodes and it proves that all implementations can also accept the *longer loop* case, since we have chosen A, B_6 and B_9 all with different implementations.

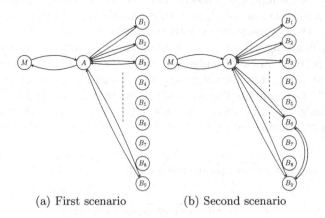

(a) First scenario   (b) Second scenario

Fig. 4. Simnet scenarios

Once we have ensured that routes with cycles are possible to execute in any implementation, we would like to study how to maximize Δ_p, the time that a payee can lock a payment p. Such value can be estimated using information of the nodes that are included in a route. More precisely, values δ and T_{max} of each node and the node position in the route determines the maximum time a payment can be blocked.

In our scenario, the adversary controls both the first and the last node of the route. We first describe how, as a first node, the adversary can determine the maximum Δ_p for a particular route. Then, we will detail how the adversary, as the last node of the route, may block the payment during Δ_p and how, after that time, he can cancel the payment without paying any fee to the routing nodes and, furthermore, leaving all the channels in the same setting than the initial phase of the attack being able to reexecute the attack without any cost.

As pointed out in Sect. 2, the parameters that determine the actions of each node of the route are T_{max} and δ. The first one, T_{max}, is the maximum amount that a node allows an outgoing payment in a channel to be locked. And the second one indicates the difference, in blocks, that each hop in the route requires. Such parameters are different for every lightning implementation as Table 4 shows. When a node receives a payment, he sets an expiration time[11], θ, for the payment, and subtracts his δ. In case that the resulting value is lower than his T_{max}, then he will keep forward the payment, in other case, the node will refuse the payment, the route will be discarded and the payer will need to find another route. Then, the best strategy for an adversary to maximize Δ_p is to simulate the route assuming that each node, instead of discarding the payment, will set the new θ as his T_{max}. For instance, suppose the following route $M - B_i - B_j - B_k - M$ and assume that B_i is a lnd implementation, B_j is an eclair implementation and B_k is a c-lightning implementation. Assuming the default values of Table 4, the simulation performed by M will start with $\theta = \infty$. When processing the first hop, B_i has a lnd implementation which means $T_{max} = 5000$ and $\delta = 144$ so for that hop, we can compute $\theta = 5000 - 144 = 4856$. In the next hop, B_j runs an eclair implementation, hence $T_{max} = 1008$ and $\delta = 144$. In that case, since the received $\theta = 4856$ is greater than 1008 we will set $\theta = 1008 - 144 = 864$. Then B_k runs a c-lightning with $T_{max} = 2016$ and $\delta = 14$ and the received $\theta = 864$ is lower than 2016, we can calculate $\theta = 864 - 14 = 850$. Since this is the last hop, $\theta = 850$ is the time during which the channel can be blocked. With this procedure, M can compute the optimal θ value that he will include in the first hop to maximize Δ_p. In that case $\theta = 850 + 14 + 144 + 144 = 1152$ will provide a maximum Δ_p, in that case 850

Table 4. Default parameters for different implementations.

	lnd	c-lightning	eclair
δ	144	14	144
T_{max}	5000	2016	1008

---

[11] Although the θ is an absolute block height value, here we will refer as a relative value to simplify the explanation.

References

1. Decker, C., Wattenhofer, R.: A fast and scalable payment network with bitcoin duplex micropayment channels. In: Pelc, A., Schwarzmann, A.A. (eds.) SSS 2015. LNCS, vol. 9212, pp. 3–18. Springer, Cham (2015). https://doi.org/10.1007/978-3-319-21741-3_1
2. Di Stasi, G., Avallone, S., Canonico, R., Ventre, G.: Routing payments on the lightning network. In: 2018 IEEE International Conference on Internet of Things (iThings) and IEEE Green Computing and Communications (GreenCom) and IEEE Cyber, Physical and Social Computing (CPSCom) and IEEE Smart Data (SmartData), pp. 1161–1170. IEEE (2018)
3. Donet Donet, J.A., Pérez-Solà, C., Herrera-Joancomartí, J.: The bitcoin P2P network. In: Böhme, R., Brenner, M., Moore, T., Smith, M. (eds.) FC 2014. LNCS, vol. 8438, pp. 87–102. Springer, Heidelberg (2014). https://doi.org/10.1007/978-3-662-44774-1_7
4. Elements Project. c-lightning - a lightning network implementation in C (2019). https://github.com/ElementsProject/lightning
5. Herrera-Joancomartí, J., Navarro-Arribas, G., Ranchal-Pedrosa, A., Pérez-Solà, C., Garcia-Alfaro, J.: On the difficulty of hiding the balance of lightning network channels. In: Proceedings of the 2019 ACM Asia Conference on Computer and Communications Security, CCS 2019, Asia, pp. 602–612. ACM, New York (2019)
6. Khosla, A., Schwartz, E., Hope-Bailie, A.: Interledger RFCs, 0018 DRAFT 3, Connector Risk Mitigations. Github (2019). http://j.mp/2m2OvfP
7. Malavolta, G., Moreno-Sanchez, P., Kate, A., Maffei, M.: Enforcing security and privacy in decentralized credit networks. In: NDSS, Silentwhispers (2017)
8. Malavolta, G., Moreno-Sanchez, P., Kate, A., Maffei, M., Ravi, S.: Concurrency and privacy with payment-channel networks. In: Proceedings of the 2017 ACM SIGSAC Conference on Computer and Communications Security, pp. 455–471. ACM (2017)
9. McCorry, P., Möser, M., Shahandasti, S.F., Hao, F.: Towards bitcoin payment networks. In: Liu, J.K.K., Steinfeld, R. (eds.) ACISP 2016. LNCS, vol. 9722, pp. 57–76. Springer, Cham (2016). https://doi.org/10.1007/978-3-319-40253-6_4
10. Poon, J., Dryja, T.: The bitcoin lightning network: scalable off-chain instant payments (2016)
11. Robinson, D.: HTLCS-considered-harmful. In: Stanford Blockchain Conference, Stanford, CA, USA, January 2019. http://j.mp/2m7BsKf
12. Rohrer, E., Malliaris, J., Tschorsch, F.: Discharged payment channels: quantifying the lightning network's resilience to topology-based attacks. CoRR, abs/1904.10253 (2019)
13. Roos, S., Moreno-Sanchez, P., Kate, A., Goldberg, I.: Settling payments fast and private: efficient decentralized routing for path-based transactions (2017). arXiv preprint arXiv:1709.05748
14. Samokhvalov, A., Poon, J., Osuntokun, O.: Basis of lightning technology (BOLTs) (2018)
15. Samokhvalov, A., Poon, J., Osuntokun, O.: The lightning network Daemon (2018)
16. Samokhvalov, A., Poon, J., Osuntokun, O.: Lightning network in-progress specifications. Bolt 4: onion routing protocol (2018)
17. Tang, W., Wang, W., Fanti, G., Oh, S.: Privacy-utility tradeoffs in routing cryptocurrency over payment channel networks. CoRR, abs/1909.02717 (2019)

Ride the Lightning: The Game Theory of Payment Channels

Zeta Avarikioti$^{(\boxtimes)}$, Lioba Heimbach, Yuyi Wang, and Roger Wattenhofer

ETH Zürich, Zürich, Switzerland
{zetavar,hlioba,yuwang,wattenhofer}@ethz.ch

Abstract. Payment channels were introduced to solve various eminent cryptocurrency scalability issues. Multiple payment channels build a network on top of a blockchain, the so-called layer 2. In this work, we analyze payment networks through the lens of network creation games. We identify betweenness and closeness centrality as central concepts regarding payment networks. We study the topologies that emerge when players act selfishly and determine the parameter space in which they constitute a Nash equilibrium. Moreover, we determine the social optima depending on the correlation of betweenness and closeness centrality. When possible, we bound the price of anarchy. We also briefly discuss the price of stability.

Keywords: Blockchain · Payment channels · Layer 2 · Creation game · Network design · Nash equilibrium · Price of anarchy · Price of stability

1 Introduction

1.1 Motivation

Bitcoin [31] and other cryptocurrencies [25,34,35] are electrifying the world. Thanks to a distributed data structure known as the blockchain, cryptocurrencies can execute financial transactions without a trusted central authority. However, every computer participating in a blockchain must exchange, store and verify each and every transaction, and as such the transaction throughput of blockchains is embarrassingly low. The Bitcoin blockchain for instance does not process more than seven transactions per second.

With seven transactions per second, Bitcoin cannot rival established payment systems such as Visa, WeChatPay, or PayPal. Consequently, various research groups have proposed a blockchain paradigm shift – *payment channels* [17,32, 33]. All payment channels follow the same basic principle: Instead of sending every transaction to the blockchain, transactions are only exchanged between the involved parties. If Alice and Bob expect to exchange multiple payments, they can establish a payment channel. The channel is set up with a blockchain funding transaction. Once the channel is available, Alice and Bob exchange all

© International Financial Cryptography Association 2020
J. Bonneau and N. Heninger (Eds.): FC 2020, LNCS 12059, pp. 264–283, 2020.
https://doi.org/10.1007/978-3-030-51280-4_15

payments directly, by sending each other digitally signed payment messages. If Bob tries to cheat Alice, Alice can show the signed payment messages as a proof to the blockchain, using the original funding transaction as security.

Instead of establishing a payment channel to every other person and company in the world, thanks to a technique called Hash Time Locked Contracts (HTLCs) [1,17,32], payments can also be sent atomically through a path of payment channels. More precisely, each payment channel is now an edge in a *payment network*, and payments will be routed along a path of payment channels in the payment network. Such a payment network is called the layer 2 of the blockchain, the blockchain itself being the layer 1.

The payment channels/networks have many significant advantages over vanilla blockchains: With payment channels, the transaction throughput becomes unlimited, as each transaction is only seen by the nodes on the path between sender and receiver of a payment. This is like sending a packet in the internet instead of sending every packet to a central server. Solving the throughput problem will also drastically decrease transaction fees. In addition, payments will be instantaneous, as one does not have to wait multiple minutes before the blockchain verifies a transaction. Payment networks also allow for more privacy as transactions are only seen by the parties involved. On the negative side, to set up a channel, the channel owner(s) must lock some capital. However, whenever a payment channel routes a transaction on behalf of other parties, the channel owner(s) can collect a transaction fee.

Payment networks are currently a hot topic in blockchain research. In practice, the first payment networks have been deployed, and are being actively used. Prominent examples are Bitcoin's Lightning network [16,32] with more than 30,000 active channels, or Ethereum's Raiden network [3].

As Bitcoin's Lightning network is growing quickly, we need to understand these newly forming payment networks. Which channels will be created, and what will the network topology eventually look like? Network creation games [21] are a perfect tool to understand these questions, since they capture the degradation of the network's efficiency when participants act selfishly.

In a network creation game, the incentive of a player is to minimize her cost by choosing to whom she connects. In our model, players weigh the benefits they receive from using payment channels against the channels' creation cost, and selfishly initiate connections to minimize their cost. There are two types of benefits for each player: (i) the forwarding fees she receives for the transactions she routed through her channels, (ii) the reduced cost for routing her transactions through the payment network in comparison to publishing the transactions on the blockchain (blockchain fee). On the other hand, establishing a channel costs the blockchain fee. Thus, a player has to balance all these factors to decide which channels to establish to minimize her cost. Our goal is to gain a meaningful insight on the network structures that will emerge and evaluate their efficiency, in comparison to centralized structures designed by a central authority that previous work has shown to be almost optimal.

1.2 Our Contributions

In this work, we provide a game-theoretic approach to analyze the creation of blockchain payment networks. Specifically, we adopt betweenness centrality, a natural measure for fees a player is expected to receive by forwarding others' transactions on a path of payment channels. On the other hand, we employ closeness centrality as an intuitive proxy for the transaction fees encountered when executing transactions through other players in the network. We reflect the cost of payment channel creation by associating a price with link creation. Therefore, we also generalize previous work on network creation games as our model combines both betweenness and closeness centralities.

Under this model, we study the topologies that emerge when players act selfishly. A specific network structure is considered a Nash equilibrium when no player can decrease her cost by unilaterally changing her connections. We examine various such structures and determine the parameter space in which they constitute a Nash equilibrium. Moreover, we determine the social optima depending on the correlation of betweenness and closeness centrality. When possible, we bound the price of anarchy, the ratio of the social costs of the worst Nash equilibrium and the social optimum [26], to obtain insight into the effects of lack of coordination in payment networks when players act selfishly. Furthermore, we briefly discuss the price of stability, the ratio of the social costs of the best Nash equilibrium and the social optimum [6], specifically concerning the parameter values that most accurately represent blockchain payment networks.

The omitted proofs can be found in the full version [11].

1.3 Related Work

Various payment channel protocols have been proposed in literature [8,9,17,24, 27,28,32,33], all presenting different solutions on how to create payment channels. However, our work is independent of the channel construction specifications and thus applies to all such solutions.

Payment networks have been studied from an algorithmic (not game theoretic) viewpoint by Avarikioti et al. [7,10]. In [7], they examined the optimal graph structure and fee assignment to maximize the profit of a central authority that creates the payment network and bears the relevant costs and benefits. Furthermore, in [10], they investigated the online and offline computation of a capital-efficient payment network for a central authority. In contrast, our work studies the decentralized payment network design, where the network is created by multiple participants and not a single authority. This model reflects more accurately the currently operating payment networks, which are indeed created by thousands of users rather than a single company, following the decentralized philosophy of cryptocurrencies like Bitcoin.

Network creation games were originally introduced by Fabrikant et al. [21]. In their game, referred to as sum network creation game, a player unilaterally creates links to minimize the sum of distances to other players in the network (closeness centrality). Later, Albers et al. [4] improved the upper bound for the price of anarchy and also examined a weighted network creation game. While these works solely focus on a player's closeness centrality, our model is more complex and additionally includes another metric, the players' betweenness centrality that represents the importance of a player in the network.

In parallel, network creation games were expanded to various settings. The idea of bilateral link creation was introduced by Corbo and Parkes [15]. Demaine et al. [18] devise the max game, where players try to minimize their maximum distance to any other player in the game. Intrinsic properties of peer-to-peer networks are taken into account in the network creation variation conceived by Moscibroda et al. [29,30]. Nodes strive to minimize their stretch, the ratio between the distance of two nodes in a graph, and their direct distance. The idea of bounded budget network creation games was proposed by Ehsani et al. [19]. In bounded budget network creation games, players have a fixed budget to establish links. Moreover, Àlvarez et al. [5] introduced the celebrity game, where players try to keep influential nodes within a fixed distance. However, the objectives in all these games give little insight to the control a player has over a network. This control is desired by players in blockchain payment networks to maximize the fees received for routing transactions, in essence their betweenness centrality.

A bounded budget betweenness centrality game was introduced by Bei et al. [12]. Given a budget to create links, players attempt to maximize their betweenness centrality. Due to their complexity, betweenness network creation games yield limited theoretical results, in comparison to those of the sum network creation game, for instance. In contrast to our work, a players closeness centrality is not taken into account in [12]. Thus, this model is insufficient for our purpose since it does not consider how strategically connected is a player that wants to route many transactions through the payment network.

Buechel and Buskens [14] compare betweenness and closeness centralities; however, not in a network creation game setting, as their notion of stability does not lead to Nash equilibria. We, on the other hand, study the combination of betweenness and closeness incentives in a network creation game setting.

2   Preliminaries and Model

In this section, we first introduce the essential background and assumptions for our payment network creation game, and then we introduce the necessary notation and the game-theoretic model.

2.1   Payment Networks

Payment channels operate on top of the blockchain (Layer 2) and allow instant off-chain transactions. Generally, a channel is set up by two parties that deposit capital in a joint account on the blockchain. The channel can then be used to make arbitrarily many transactions without committing each transaction to the blockchain. When opening a channel, the parties pay a blockchain fee and place capital in the channel. The blockchain fee is the transaction fee to the miner, paid to have the transaction included in a block and thereby published on the blockchain. The deposited capital funds future channel transactions and is not available for other transactions on the blockchain during the channel's lifetime.

In our model, we assume a player single-handedly initiates a channel to a subset of other players. Incoming channels are always accepted and once installed, the channels can be used to send money in both directions (from sender to receiver, and vice versa). While any player can typically choose the amount to lock in a channel, we assume that the locked capital placed in all channels is high enough to be modeled as unlimited. In particular, we assume that all players are major (large companies, financial institutions etc.) that have thus access to large amounts of temporary capital. It is natural to assume only major players to participate in the network creation game. Typically, a market is created when there is demand for a service. Thus eventually, the payment network will be dominated by service providers that will individually connect with clients and act as intermediaries for all transactions. In this work, we only consider the flow of transactions through these service providers. Therefore, the cost of opening a channel in our model solely reflects the permanent cost, i.e. the blockchain fee, and is set to 1 (wlog). Furthermore, since we assume major players only, the transactions between the players can be considered uniform.

In addition to enabling parties connected by a channel to exchange funds off-chain, payment channels can also be used to route off-chain transactions between a sender and receiver pair not directly connected by a channel. Transactions between the sender and receiver can be routed securely through a path of channels. Since we assume that all channels are funded with unlimited capital, the channel funds cannot deplete, and so any path in the payment network between sender and receiver is viable.

Together, the payment channels form a payment network. In the network, players receive a payment when transactions are routed through their channels. This payment is a transaction fee, which is typically proportional to the value of the routed transaction, to compensate the intermediate node for the loss of her channel's capital capacity. However, we consider a fixed fee for all nodes, independent of the routed value, since we assume unlimited channel capital.

2.2 Formal Model

A payment network can be formally expressed by an unweighted undirected graph consisting of V nodes, representing the set of players, and E edges, representing the set of payment channel between the players.

A payment network game consists of n players $V = \{0, 1, \ldots, n-1\}$, denoted by $[n]$. The strategy of player u expresses the channels she chooses to open and is denoted by s_u, and the set $S_u = 2^{[n]-\{u\}}$ defines u's strategy space. We denote by $G[s]$ the underlying undirected graph of $G_0[s] = \left([n], \bigcup_{u \in [n]} \{u\} \times s_u\right)$, where $s = (s_0, \ldots, s_{n-1}) \in S_0 \times \cdots \times S_{n-1}$ is a strategy combination. Note that while a channel can possibly be created by both endpoints, this will never be the case in a Nash equilibrium.

Betweenness Centrality. The fees received by a player for providing gateway services to other players' transactions are modeled by her betweenness centrality. Betweenness centrality was first introduced as a measure of a player's importance in a social network by Freeman et al. [22]. According to [22], the betweenness centrality of a player u in a graph $G(V,E)$ is $\sum\limits_{\substack{s,r\in V \\ s\neq r\neq u, m(s,r)>0}} \dfrac{m_u(s,r)}{m(s,r)}$, where $m_u(s,r)$ is the number of shortest paths between sender s and receiver r that route through player u and $m(s,r)$ is the total number of shortest paths between s and r. Additionally, $s\neq r\neq u$ indicates that $s\neq r$, $s\neq u$ and $r\neq u$. Intuitively, the betweenness centrality of player u is a measure of the expected number of sender and receiver pairs that would choose to route their transactions through her in a payment network. Providing an insight into the transaction fees a player is expected to receive, the betweenness centrality lends itself to reflect the motivation of a player in a payment network to maximize the payments secured through providing transaction gateway services.

However, in our model, the betweenness of player u is measured as follows:

$$\text{betweenness}_u(s) = (n-1)(n-2) - \sum_{\substack{s,r\in[n]: \\ s\neq r\neq u, m(s,r)>0}} \frac{m_u(s,r)}{m(s,r)}.$$

We subtract u's betweenness centrality, as defined by Freeman et al. [22], from her maximum possible betweenness centrality to ensure that the social cost is always positive - avoiding cases where price of anarchy is undefined.

Closeness Centrality. Furthermore, we model the fees encountered by a player when having her transactions routed through the network with her closeness centrality. Closeness centrality measures the sum of distances of player u to all other players and is given by

$$\text{closeness}_u(s) = \sum_{r\in[n]-u} \left(d_{G[s]}(u,r) - 1\right),$$

for a player u, where $d_{G[s]}(u,r)$ is the distance between u and r in the graph $G[s]$. With the transaction fees fixed per edge in our model, the distance to a player r estimates the costs encountered by player u when sending a transaction to player r. Therefore, the sum of distances to all other players is a natural proxy for the fees u faces for making transactions when assuming uniform transactions.

Thus, the combination of betweenness and closeness centralities accurately encapsulates the incentives inherent to players in a blockchain payment network.

Cost. The cost of player u under the strategy combination s is $\text{cost}_u(s) = |s_u| + b \cdot \text{betweenness}_u(s) + c \cdot \text{closeness}_u(s)$, where $b \geq 0$ is the betweenness weight and $c > 0$ the closeness weight. Letting $c > 0$ ensures that the graph is always connected, as a player's cost is infinite in a disconnected graph. Additionally, the model assumes the same price for all nodes and embeds this into coefficients b and c. While this does not exactly encapsulate reality, it is a reasonable assumption. Different paths offer similar services to payers. In such a setting, Bertrand competition [13] suggests that competition will drive the prices from different players to be within a close region of each other.

Social Optimum. The objective of player u is to minimize her cost, $\min_{s_u} \text{cost}_u(s)$. The social cost is the sum off all players' costs, $\text{cost}(s) = \sum_{u \in [n]} \text{cost}_u(s)$. Thus, the social optimum is $\min_s \text{cost}(s)$.

3   Payment Network Creation Game

To gain an insight into the efficiency of emerging topologies when players act selfishly, we will first analyze the social optimum for our model. After studying if and when prominent graphs are Nash equilibria, we conclude by bounding the price of anarchy and the price of stability.

3.1   Social Optimum

By the definition of the cost function, the social cost is

$$\text{cost}(s) = \sum_{u \in [n]} \text{cost}_u(s) = |E(G)| + b \sum_{u \in [n]} \text{betweenness}_u(s) + c \sum_{u \in [n]} \text{closeness}_u(s),$$

for any graph where no channel is paid by both endpoints. This condition is met for all Nash equilibria. To lower bound the social cost, we will first simplify the social cost expression. Lemma 1 is proven in [23] and relates the average betweenness and distance in a connected graph.

Lemma 1 (Theorem 1 [23]). *The average betweenness $\overline{B}(G)$ in a connected graph G can be expressed as: $\overline{B}(G) = (n-1)(\overline{l}(G)-1)$, where $\overline{l}(G)$ is the average distance in G.*

We take advantage of Lemma 1 to simplify the social cost expression. With this we show in Lemma 2 how the social cost can be expressed directly in terms of the number of edges and the sum of the players' closeness centrality costs, facilitating further analysis.

Lemma 2. *The social cost in G is given by $\text{cost}(s) = |E(G)| + b \cdot n \cdot (n-1)(n-2) + (c-b) \cdot \sum_{u \in [n]} \text{closeness}_u(s)$.*

Proof. According to Lemma 1 the social cost can be expressed as follows for all $b \geq 0$ and $c > 0$.

$$\mathrm{cost}(s) = |E(G)| + b \sum_{u \in [n]} \mathrm{betweenness}(u) + c \sum_{u \in [n]} \mathrm{closeness}(u)$$

$$= |E(G)| + b \sum_{u \in [n]} \left((n-1)(n-2) - \sum_{\substack{s,r \in [n]: \\ s \neq r \neq u, \\ m(s,r) > 0}} \frac{m_u(s,r)}{m(s,r)} \right)$$

$$+ c \sum_{u \in [n]} \sum_{r \in [n]-u} \left(d_{G[s]}(u,r) - 1 \right)$$

$$= |E(G)| + b \cdot n \cdot (n-1)(n-2) - b \cdot n \cdot \overline{B}(G) + c \cdot n \cdot (n-1)(\overline{l}(G) - 1)$$

$$= |E(G)| + b \cdot n \cdot (n-1)(n-2) + (c-b) \cdot n \cdot (n-1)(\overline{l}(G) - 1)$$

$$= |E(G)| + b \cdot n \cdot (n-1)(n-2) + (c-b) \cdot \sum_{u \in [n]} \sum_{r \in [n]-u} \left(d_{G[s]}(u,r) - 1 \right) \quad \square$$

The distance of a vertex v of a connected graph G is $d(v) := \sum_{u \in [n]-v} d_G(v,u)$. The distance of a connected graph G is $d(G) := \sum_{v \in [n]} d(v)/2$. If G is not connected, then $d(v) = \infty$ for any v, and $d(G) = \infty$.

Lemma 3 (Theorem 2.3 [20]). *If G is a connected graph with n vertices and k edges then* $n \cdot (n-1) \leq d(G) + k \leq \frac{1}{6} \cdot (n^3 - 5 \cdot n - 6)$.

Lemma 3 provides bounds for the distance of a graph G,

$$d(G) = \frac{1}{2} \sum_{u \in [n]} \sum_{r \in [n]-u} d_G(u,r)$$

which is useful for finding the social optimum for our game.

In [20] Lemma 3 is proven and stated that the path graph achieves the upper bound; maximizes the distance term. This can be used to find the social optimum. Dependent on the weights b and c, the social optimum for our payment network creation game is given in Theorem 1, and illustrated in Fig. 1.

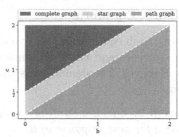

Fig. 1. Parameter map for social optimum.

Theorem 1. *The social optimum is a complete graph for $c > \frac{1}{2} + b$, a star graph for $b \leq c \leq \frac{1}{2} + b$ and a path graph for $c < b$.*

Proof. Using Lemma 2 we can lower bound the social cost for $c \geq b$ as follows:

$$\text{cost}(s) = |E(G)| + b \cdot n \cdot (n-1)(n-2) + \underbrace{(c-b)}_{\geq 0} \sum_{u\in[n]} \sum_{r\in[n]-u} \left(d_{G[s]}(u,r) - 1\right)$$

$$\geq |E(G)| + b \cdot n \cdot (n-1)(n-2) + (c-b)(n \cdot (n-1) - 2|E(G)|)$$

$$= (1 - 2 \cdot (c-b)) \cdot |E(G)| + b \cdot n \cdot (n-1)(n-2) + (c-b)(n \cdot (n-1))$$

since every pair of nodes that is not connected by an edge is at least distance 2 apart [21]. This lower bound is achieved by any graph with diameter at most 2. It follows that for $c > \frac{1}{2} + b$ the social optimum is a complete graph, maximizing $|E|$, and for $b \leq c \leq \frac{1}{2} + b$ the social optimum is a star, minimizing $|E|$.

To find the social optimum for $c < b$, we rewrite the social cost as

$$\text{cost}(s) = |E(G)| + b \cdot n \cdot (n-1)(n-2) - (b-c) \cdot \sum_{u\in[n]} \sum_{r\in[n]-u} \left(d_{G[s]}(u,r) - 1\right)$$

$$= |E(G)| - 2 \cdot (b-c) \cdot d(G) + b \cdot n \cdot (n-1)(n-2) + (b-c) \cdot n \cdot (n-1)$$

For a connected graph the social cost is then minimized for a tree, as $|E(H)| - a \cdot d(H) > |E(G)| - a \cdot d(G)$ if G is a subgraph of H and $a > 0$. For any tree, the number of edges is $n - 1$. Using Lemma 3, we get that

$$\text{cost}(s) = |E(G)| + b \cdot n \cdot (n-1)(n-2) - (b-c) \sum_{u\in[n]} \sum_{r\in[n]-u} \left(d_{G[s]}(u,r) - 1\right)$$

$$\geq \left(1 + \left(\frac{2}{3}b + \frac{1}{3}c\right) n \cdot (n-2)\right)(n-1)$$

is a lower bound for the social cost which is achieved by a path graph.   □

In areas most accurately describing payment networks, we expect the weights b and c to be smaller than the cost of channel creation and close to each other. For these cases, we observe the star graph is the social optimum.

3.2   Nash Equilibria

To find a Nash equilibrium, one could follow a naive approach: start with a fixed graph structure and then continuously compute a player's best response in the game. However, Theorem 2 shows that it is NP-hard to calculate a player's best response.

Theorem 2. *Given a strategy $s \in S_0 \times \cdots \times S_{n-1}$ and $u \in [n]$, it is NP-hard to computed the best response of u.*

Therefore, with this in mind, we analyze prominent graph topologies theoretically, to see if and when they are Nash equilibria in our game. The results are illustrated in Fig. 2. However, complementary to the theoretical analysis we also run a simulation to get insights into emerging graph topologies for a small number of players.

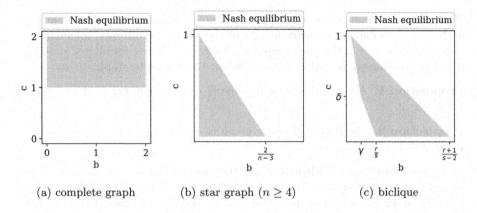

(a) complete graph   (b) star graph ($n \geq 4$)   (c) biclique

Fig. 2. Parameter map for prominent graphs. In Fig. 2c, r and s are the subset sizes ($3 \leq r \leq s$). With $\alpha = \frac{s \cdot (s-1)}{r \cdot (s-2)}$ and $\beta = \frac{1}{s-r+1} \left(\frac{s \cdot (s-1)}{r} - \frac{(r-2)(r-1)}{s+1} \right)$, (γ, δ) is the intersection between $1 = \frac{s}{r}b + \frac{s+r-3}{s-1}c$ and $1 = \min\{\alpha, \beta\} \cdot b + c$.

Complete Graph. For large values of c the complete graph is the only Nash equilibrium as stated in Theorem 3. Additionally, the complete graph is also a Nash equilibrium for $c = 1$, but it is not necessarily the only one. However, for small values of c, which are the values we expect to encounter in a payment network creation game, the complete graph is not a Nash equilibrium, as stated in Theorem 4.

Theorem 3. *For $c > 1$, the only Nash equilibrium is the complete graph.*

Proof. The addition of an edge by a player never increases her betweenness cost. Thus, by the definition of the cost function any Nash equilibrium cannot be missing any edges whose addition would reduce a players closeness by more than 1, the cost of building an edge. As $c > 1$, no edge can be missing in the graph and the only Nash equilibrium is the complete graph.   □

Theorem 4. *For $c < 1$ and $n \geq 3$, the complete graph is never a Nash equilibrium.*

Proof. In a complete graph the removal of an edge by a player does not change her betweenness cost and her closeness cost is increased by c. Thus, the cost of a player would decrease when removing one edge. Therefore, the complete graph is not a Nash equilibrium for $c < 1$.   □

Figure 2a visualizes the combination of these results, i.e., when the complete graph is a Nash equilibrium in our game. We observe that for some weight combinations the complete graph is both the social optimum and a Nash equilibrium. However, most payment networks are not expected to fall into this area of the parameter space.

Path Graph. While the path graph is the social optimum for a significant area of the parameter space, we show it can only be a Nash equilibrium for small sets of players. For $n = 3$, the path graph is a Nash equilibrium for all $c \leq 1$, as it is the only possible connected graph that is not the complete graph.

Proposition 1. *For $n = 4$, the path graph is a Nash equilibrium if and only if $1 \leq b + 2 \cdot c$.*

Proposition 2. *For $n = 5$, the path graph is a Nash equilibrium if and only if $1 \leq 2 \cdot b + 4 \cdot c$.*

Propositions 1 and 2 identify when the path graph is a Nash equilibrium for networks with four and five players respectively. These bounds partly overlap with areas in which the path graph is the social optimum. While this partial correspondence between the Nash equilibrium and social optimum appears promising for the coordination of our game, Theorem 5 suggests to the contrary.

Theorem 5. *For $n \geq 6$, the path graph is never a Nash equilibrium.*

Proof. To show that the path graph is never a Nash equilibrium for $n \geq 6$, we will show that at least one player in a path graph consisting of more than six players can always reduce her cost by changing strategy.

In a path graph with at least six players, at least one player u has an outgoing edge to a player v at least two steps from the end of the path on the opposite side of player u. This is illustrated in Fig. 3a and we consider this to be strategy s. In this case it is always more beneficial for player u to connect to player w instead of player v. Let's refer to this strategy as strategy $\tilde{s}$ (Fig. 3b).

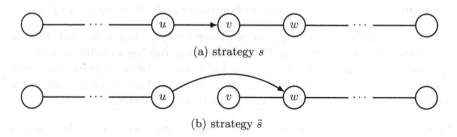

(a) strategy s

(b) strategy $\tilde{s}$

Fig. 3. Strategy deviation of player 1.

The change in cost for this strategy is given as

$$\Delta \text{cost}_u(s \text{ to } \tilde{s}) = -c \cdot (m - 2),$$

where m is the number of edges player v is away from the endpoint on the opposite side u. Thus, the change in cost is negative and the path graph cannot be a Nash equilibrium for $n \geq 6$. $\square$

Hence, the path graph is not expected to be a Nash equilibrium for payment networks that typically consist of many nodes.

Circle Graph. The results we find for the circle graph are similar to those for the path graph. For small values of n, the circle graph can be a Nash equilibrium depending on the weights b and c. The circle graph and the complete graph are the same for $n = 3$. Thus, for $n = 3$ the circle graph is a Nash equilibrium if and only if $c \geq 1$.

Proposition 3. *For $n = 4$, the circle graph is a Nash equilibrium if and only if $c \leq 1 \leq b + 2 \cdot c$.*

Proposition 4. *For $n = 5$, the circle graph is a Nash equilibrium if and only if $b + c \leq 1 \leq 2 \cdot b + 4 \cdot c$.*

Propositions 3 and 4 show that for small n, the circle graph can be a Nash equilibrium depending on the weights b and c. However, for large n the circle graph is never a Nash equilibrium, as stated in Theorem 6.

Theorem 6. *There exists a $N > 0$, such that for all $n \geq N$ the circle graph is never a Nash equilibrium.*

We note that simulations suggest that for $n \geq 6$ the circle graph is never a Nash equilibrium. Parameter sweeps indicating that $N = 6$ can be found in the full version [11].

Star Graph. The star graph is the social optimum for a significant part of our parameter space. In a star graph the player in the center has minimal closeness and betweenness costs; all other players have maximal betweenness cost. While this does not directly appear to be a stable network, Theorem 7 suggests that the star graph is a Nash equilibrium for smaller values of b and c. These results are depicted in Fig. 2b.

Theorem 7. *For $n \geq 4$, the star graph is always a Nash equilibrium if and only if $0 \leq 1 - \frac{n-3}{2}b - c$.*

Proof. To show that the star is always a Nash equilibrium for $n \geq 4$ and $0 \leq 1 - \frac{n-3}{2}b - c$, we will consider a star graph consisting of n players $V = \{0, 1, \ldots, n - 1\}$. Without loss of generality we assume that player 0 is the center of the star.

No player in the star graph has an incentive to remove an edge, as this would lead to infinite cost. Thus, player 0 has no incentive to change strategy, as she is connected to everyone.

Next we consider star graphs where all links are initiated by player 0 and star graphs where at least one link is initiated by another player separately.

If all links are initiated by player 0, players 1, 2, ..., $n - 1$ are all in an equivalent position and it is therefore sufficient to solely consider player 1. Player 1 would only add links, if this leads to a decrease in her cost. Initiating an edge to player 0 would only increase her cost. Additionally, for the remaining $n - 2$ players, it only matters to how many player 1 connects. The change in cost when adding m, where $1 \leq m \leq n - 2$, edges is given by $\Delta\mathrm{cost}_1(\text{add } m \text{ links}) = m -$

$\dfrac{m \cdot (m-1)}{2} b - m \cdot c$. Thus, player 1 will change strategy if $\Delta \text{cost}_1(\text{add } m \text{ links}) <$ 0. The change in cost is minimized for $m = n - 2$.

In star graphs where at least one player other than 0 initiates a link, players that have no outgoing links are in the same position as those analyzed previously. Thus, it suffices to consider player i, where $i \neq 0$, that has one outgoing link. In addition to only initiating new links, player i can remove the link to player 0 and initiates l, where $1 \leq l \leq n - 2$, new links. The change in cost is then given as $\Delta \text{cost}_i(\text{add } l \text{ links}) = (l - 1) - \dfrac{l \cdot (l-1)}{2} b - (l - 1) \cdot c$. However, this leads to more restrictive bounds and there is no need for players other than player 0 to have outgoing links.

Thus, the star is a Nash equilibrium if and only if $0 \leq 1 - \frac{n-3}{2} b - c$.   □

We note that the areas where the star is both a Nash equilibrium and the social optimum overlap partially.

Complete Bipartite Graph. The star graph is a complete bipartite graph where one group has size one. In this section, we analyze more general complete bipartite graphs or bicliques $K_{r,s}$, where r is the size of the smaller subset and s is the size of the larger subset. In a complete bipartite graph, every node from one subset is connected to all nodes from the other subset.

Theorem 8. *The complete bipartite graph $K_{r,s}$ with $3 \leq r \leq s$ is stable if and only if $\frac{s-2}{r+1} b + c \leq 1 \leq \min \left\{ \frac{s}{r} b + \frac{s+r-3}{s-1} c, \min\{\alpha, \beta\} \cdot b + c \right\}$, where $\alpha = \frac{s \cdot (s-1)}{r \cdot (s-2)}$ and $\beta = \frac{1}{s-r+1} \left(\frac{s \cdot (s-1)}{r} - \frac{(r-2)(r-1)}{s+1} \right)$.*

Proof. Additional links can only be created within a subset in a complete bipartite graph. Similarly to adding links in a star graph, the change in cost when adding m links is given by $\Delta \text{cost}_u(\text{add } m \text{ links}) = m - \dfrac{m \cdot (m-1)}{l+1} b - m \cdot c$, where $l \in \{r, s\}$ is the size of the subset not including the player.

A player changes strategy when $\Delta \text{cost}_u(\text{add } m \text{ links}) < 0$. The change in cost is minimized when m is maximized and $l = r$. m can therefore be $s - 1$ at most. Thus, the upper bound for $K_{r,s}$ being a Nash equilibrium is $1 \geq \dfrac{s-2}{r+1} b + c$.

Players in the subset of size r, benefit more from a link to the other subset, as their betweenness cost is smaller. Thus, players from the larger subset with outgoing links would change strategy sooner. In the case where the subsets are of equal size, the link direction does not matter. Hence, to find a lower bound for b and c we only consider complete bipartite graphs, in which all links are established from the smaller subset, as seen in Fig. 4a. Without loss of generality we will only consider player u in the following analysis. It is not reasonable for player u to remove all her links without adding any new links, as her cost would become infinite. Depending on the other parameters, it might be more optimal to remove all her previous links and only connect to one player in her subset (Fig. 4b), connect to one player in her subset and one player from the other subset (Fig. 4c), or to remove all her previous links and instead connect to all other players in her subset (Fig. 4d). When player u changes to strategy $\tilde{s}_1$, seen in Fig. 4b the change in cost is as follows:

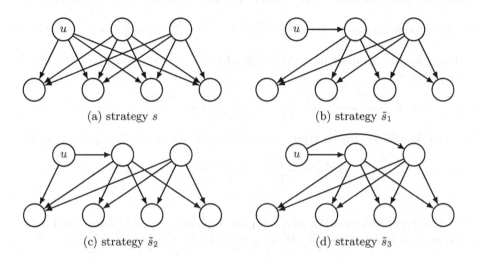

(a) strategy s

(b) strategy $\tilde{s}_1$

(c) strategy $\tilde{s}_2$

(d) strategy $\tilde{s}_3$

Fig. 4. Strategy deviations of player u.

$$\Delta \text{cost}_u(s \text{ to } \tilde{s}_1) = -(s-1) + \frac{s \cdot (s-1)}{r} b + (s+r-3) \cdot c$$

as player u initiates $s-1$ less links than before - losing all her previous betweenness. Additionally, she is one edge further away from all other players except for the one she connects to directly. Thus, the above strategy is less preferable than the complete bipartite graph for player u, if

$$1 \leq \frac{s}{r} b + \frac{s+r-3}{s-1} c.$$

Player u's change to strategy $\tilde{s}_2$ (Fig. 4c) leads to $s-2$ less links initiated by her. The player is further away from $s-1$ players from the other subset and closer to one in her own. All transaction-routing potential is lost. Therefore, the change in cost is given by

$$\Delta \text{cost}_u(s \text{ to } \tilde{s}_2) = 2 - s + \left(\frac{s \cdot (s-1)}{r} \right) b + (s-2) \cdot c.$$

Hence, for this strategy to be less preferable than the complete bipartite graph,

$$1 \leq \left(\frac{s \cdot (s-1)}{r \cdot (s-2)} \right) b + c = \alpha \cdot b + c.$$

When severing all previous links and connecting to all players in her subset instead, strategy $\tilde{s}_3$ (Fig. 4d), player u builds $s-r+1$ less links than before.

Furthermore, she is closer to players previously in her own subset and further away from the rest. While player u can now transmit transactions of players previously in her own subset, she is no longer a preferable intermediary for players previously in the other subset. Therefore, the change in cost is given by

$$\Delta\text{cost}_u(s \text{ to } \tilde{s}_3) = r - s + 1 + \left(\frac{s \cdot (s-1)}{r} - \frac{(r-1)(r-2)}{s+1}\right) b + (s - r + 1) \cdot c.$$

Hence, for this strategy to be less preferable than the complete bipartite graph for player u,

$$1 \leq \frac{1}{(s-r+1)} \left(\frac{s \cdot (s-1)}{r} - \frac{(r-1)(r-2)}{s+1}\right) b + c = \beta \cdot b + c.$$

To summarize, the complete bipartite graph $K_{r,s}$ is a Nash equilibrium for

$$\frac{s-2}{r+1} b + c \leq 1 \leq \min\left\{\frac{s}{r} b + \frac{s+r-3}{s-1} c, \min\{\alpha, \beta\} \cdot b + c\right\}.$$

□

The parameter map for the complete bipartite graph is drawn in Fig. 2c. There (γ, δ) is the intersection between $1 = \frac{s}{r}b + \frac{s+r-3}{s-1}c$ and $1 = \min\{\alpha, \beta\} \cdot b + c$.

Simulation. To better understand the behaviour of a player in our payment network creation game, we implement a simulation of the game [2]. Our simulation enumerates all Nash equilibria for a given number of players n, as well as the weights for the betweenness and closeness costs. However, this is only feasible for small n. Parameter sweeps for the weights b and c can also be performed to see when a given topology is a Nash equilibrium. Some parameter sweeps for topologies previously analyzed can be found in [11]. Finally, starting from an initial graph the progression of the game can be simulated.

3.3   Price of Anarchy

The ratio between the social optimum and the worst Nash equilibrium is the price of anarchy (PoA), formally,

$$\text{PoA} = \frac{\max_{s \in N} \text{cost}(s)}{\min_{s \in S} \text{cost}(s)},$$

here S is the set of all strategies and N is the set of strategies that are Nash equilibria.

The price of anarchy provides an insight to the effects of lack of coordination, i.e. measures the performance degradation of the system when players act selfishly in comparison to central coordination. When the price of anarchy is low, selfish actors do not heavily degrade network efficiency. In contrast, a high price of anarchy indicates that network formation by a central authority would significantly increase efficiency.

For $c > 1$, we can determine the price of anarchy exactly, as we established both the social optimum and the (unique) Nash equilibria for $c > 1$.

Corollary 1. *For $c > 1$ and $c > \frac{1}{2} + b$, the price of anarchy is $PoA = 1$.*

Corollary 2. *For $c > 1$ and $b \leq c \leq \frac{1}{2} + b$, the price of anarchy is*

$$PoA = \frac{\left(\frac{1}{2} + (n-2) \cdot b\right) \cdot n}{1 + (c + b \cdot (n-1))(n-2)}.$$

Corollary 3. *For $1 < c < b$, the price of anarchy is*

$$PoA = \frac{\left(\frac{1}{2} + (n-2) \cdot b\right) \cdot n}{1 + \left(\frac{2}{3}b + \frac{1}{3}c\right) \cdot n \cdot (n-2)}.$$

Combining the results of Corollary 1, 2 and 3 allows us to upper bound the price of anarchy to a constant for $c > 1$, as stated in in Corollary 4. This upper bound is asymptotically tight, as the price of anarchy is always greater or equal to one (hence at least constant) by definition.

Corollary 4. *For $c > 1$, the price of anarchy is $PoA = \mathcal{O}(1)$.*

Proof. For $c > 1$ and $c > \frac{1}{2} + b$, the price of anarchy is one and therefore it is also $\mathcal{O}(1)$.

We have that for $c > 1$ and $b \leq c \leq \frac{1}{2} + b$,

$$PoA = \frac{\left(\frac{1}{2} + (n-2) \cdot b\right) \cdot n}{1 + (c + b \cdot (n-1))(n-2)} = \mathcal{O}\left(\frac{b \cdot n^2}{b \cdot n^2}\right) = \mathcal{O}(1),$$

and for $1 < c < b$,

$$PoA = \frac{\left(\frac{1}{2} + (n-2) \cdot b\right) \cdot n}{1 + \left(\frac{2}{3}b + \frac{1}{3}c\right) \cdot n \cdot (n-2)} = \mathcal{O}\left(\frac{b \cdot n^2}{b \cdot n^2}\right) = \mathcal{O}(1).$$

Thus, for $c > 1$ we have $PoA = \mathcal{O}(1)$. $\qquad\square$

For small b and c we can also upper bound the price of anarchy as follows:

Theorem 9. *For $c + b < \frac{1}{n^2}$, the price of anarchy is $PoA = \mathcal{O}(1)$.*

Proof. For $c + b < \frac{1}{n^2}$, all Nash equilibria are trees. Unless the distance to a player is infinite, no player in the network will have an incentive to build an edge.

As both the maximum possible change in betweenness$_u(s)$ and closeness$_u(s)$ for a node u in a connected graph is less than n^2 and all Nash equilibria are connected, $\Delta \text{cost}_u(s) > -n^2 \cdot c - n^2 \cdot b + 1$. We require $\Delta \text{cost}_u(s) \geq 0$ such that u does not benefit from initiating an additional channel. Thus, for $c + b \leq \frac{1}{n^2}$ all Nash equilibria are spanning trees.

For $c + b \leq \frac{1}{n^2}$ the social optimum is also a spanning tree, as it is either the star or path graph. It easily follows that for $c + b \leq \frac{1}{n^2}$ and all spanning trees $\text{cost}(s) = \Theta(n)$ and therefore the price of anarchy is $\mathcal{O}(1)$.

Finally, for $c+b \geq \frac{1}{n^2}$ and $c < 1$, we show an $\mathcal{O}(n)$ upper bound for the price of anarchy.

Theorem 10. *For $c+b \geq \frac{1}{n^2}$ and $c < 1$, the price of anarchy is $PoA = \mathcal{O}(n)$.*

Proof. The price of anarchy is

$$PoA = \mathcal{O} \left(\frac{|E(G)| + n^3 \cdot b + (c-b) \cdot \sum_{u \in [n]} \sum_{r \in [n]-u} (d_G(u,r) - 1)}{n^3 \cdot b + n} \right).$$

We can say that $d_G(u,r) < \mathcal{O} \left(\frac{2}{\sqrt{c+b}} \right)$, as player u would connect to player r otherwise. Player u would become closer to half the nodes on the path otherwise and reduce her betweenness cost through the routing potential gained by the link addition. Therefore we have,

$$PoA = \mathcal{O} \left(\frac{|E(G)| + n^3 \cdot b + n^2 \frac{c-b}{\sqrt{b+c}}}{b \cdot n^3 + n} \right).$$

It follows that

$$\mathcal{O} \left(\frac{n^3 \cdot b}{n^3 \cdot b + n} \right) = \mathcal{O}(1), \quad \text{and} \quad \mathcal{O} \left(\frac{n^2 \frac{c-b}{\sqrt{b+c}}}{n^3 \cdot b + n} \right) = \mathcal{O} \left(\frac{c-b}{n^2 \cdot b + 1} \right) = \mathcal{O}(1),$$

as $c+b \geq \frac{1}{n^2}$ and $c < 1$. Thus, it only remains to consider $\mathcal{O} \left(\frac{|E(G)|}{b \cdot n^3 + n} \right)$.

As $|E(G)| = \mathcal{O}(n^2)$ for any Nash equilibrium, we have $PoA = \mathcal{O}(n)$.   □

3.4   Price of Stability

The price of stability (PoS), a close notion to price of anarchy, is defined as the ratio between the social optimum and the best Nash equilibrium,

$$PoS = \frac{\min_{s \in N} \text{cost}(s)}{\min_{s \in S} \text{cost}(s)},$$

where S is the set of all strategies and N is the set of strategies that are Nash equilibria. The price of stability expresses the loss in network performance in stable systems in comparison to those designed by a central performance. Corollary 5 gives insight into the price of stability in regions of the parameter space previously discussed in the context of the price of anarchy.

Corollary 5. *For $c > 1$ and $b + c < \frac{1}{n^2}$, the price of stability $PoS = \mathcal{O}(1)$.*

Proof. As the price of stability is smaller than or equal to the price of anarchy, we can follow from Corollary 4, that the price of stability is $\mathcal{O}(1)$ for $c > 1$. Additionally, Theorem 9 indicates that $PoS = \mathcal{O}(1)$ for $b + c < \frac{1}{n^2}$.   □

However, we expect blockchain payment networks to fall into the remaining area, where $c + b \geq \frac{1}{n^2}$ and $c < 1$. In particular, considering the underlying uniform transaction scenario and the fixed blockchain fee equal to one (wlog), a competitive transaction fee would be $\frac{1}{n}$. Thus, an appropriate allocation for the weights is $b = \frac{1}{2n}$ and $c = \frac{1}{n}$, as the betweenness term counts each sender and receiver pair twice. For these weights the star is the social optimum (Theorem 1), as well as a Nash equilibrium (Theorem 7). Hence, the price of stability for payment networks is one; indicating that an optimal payment network is stable in a game with selfish players. Thus, payment networks can be stable and efficient.

4   Conclusion

We introduced a game-theoretic model to encapsulate the creation of payment networks. To this end, we generalized previous work, as our model is more complex and demands a combination of betweenness and closeness centralities that have thus far only been studied independently in network creation games.

First, we identified the social optimum for the entire parameter space of our game. Depending on the weights placed on the betweenness and closeness centralities either the complete graph, the star graph or the path graph is the social optimum. In the area of the parameter space that most accurately reflects payment networks, we found the star graph to be the social optimum.

Next, we examined the space of possible Nash equilibria. After establishing that finding the best response of a player is NP-hard, we analyzed prominent graphs and determined if and when they constitute a Nash equilibrium. We showed that the complete graph is the only Nash equilibrium if players place a large weight on their closeness centrality; reflecting payment channels in which players execute many transactions or value privacy highly. On the other hand, both the path and circle graph are Nash equilibria only for small number of players and thus are not expected to emerge as stable structures in payment networks. On the contrary, the star graph emerges as a Nash equilibrium for the areas of our parameter space most accurately representing payment networks. In addition, we observed that depending on the size of the subsets, the complete bipartite graph is also a Nash equilibrium in similar regions of the parameter space as the star graph.

Last, combining our results, we bounded the price of anarchy for a large part of the parameter space. In particular, we proved that when the closeness centrality weight is high, meaning that the players execute transactions frequently or demand privacy, the price of anarchy is constant; indicating little loss in network performance for selfish players. On the other hand, for small weight on the closeness centrality, we showed an $\mathcal{O}(n)$ upper bound on the price of anarchy. Nevertheless, the price of stability in payment networks is equal to one, since the star is both the social optimum and a Nash equilibrium for suitable parameters; demonstrating that blockchain payment networks can indeed be both stable and efficient, when forming more centralized network structures.

References

1. Hash time locked contracts. https://en.bitcoin.it/wiki/Hash_Time_Locked_Contra cts. Accessed 25 June 2019
2. Micropayment channels network creation game simulation. https://gitlab.ethz.ch/ hlioba/micropayment-channels-network-creation-game-simulation. Accessed 19 June 2019
3. Raiden network (2017). http://raiden.network/
4. Albers, S., Eilts, S., Even-Dar, E., Mansour, Y., Roditty, L.: On Nash equilibria for a network creation game. ACM Trans. Econ. Comput. **2**(1), 2:1–2:27 (2014)
5. Àlvarez, C., Blesa, M.J., Duch, A., Messegué, A., Serna, M.: Celebrity games. Theor. Comput. Sci. **648**, 56–71 (2016)
6. Anshelevich, E., Dasgupta, A., Kleinberg, J., Tardos, E., Wexler, T., Roughgarden, T.: The price of stability for network design with fair cost allocation. SIAM J. Comput. **38**(4), 1602–1623 (2008)
7. Avarikioti, G., Janssen, G., Wang, Y., Wattenhofer, R.: Payment network design with fees. In: Garcia-Alfaro, J., Herrera-Joancomartí, J., Livraga, G., Rios, R. (eds.) DPM/CBT -2018. LNCS, vol. 11025, pp. 76–84. Springer, Cham (2018). https://doi.org/10.1007/978-3-030-00305-0_6
8. Avarikioti, G., Kogias, E.K., Wattenhofer, R.: Brick: asynchronous state channels. arXiv preprint: arXiv:1905.11360 (2019)
9. Avarikioti, G., Litos, O.S.T., Wattenhofer, R.: Cerberus channels: incentivizing watchtowers for bitcoin. In: Bonneau, J. (ed.) Financial Cryptography and Data Security, FC 2020. LNCS, vol. 12059, pp. 346–366. Springer, Cham (2020)
10. Avarikioti, G., Wang, Y., Wattenhofer, R.: Algorithmic channel design. In: 29th International Symposium on Algorithms and Computation (ISAAC), pp. 16:1–16:12 (2018)
11. Avarikioti, Z., Heimbach, L., Wang, Y., Wattenhofer, R.: Ride the lightning: the game theory of payment channels (2019)
12. Bei, X., Chen, W., Teng, S.H., Zhang, J., Zhu, J.: Bounded budget betweenness centrality game for strategic network formations. Theor. Comput. Sci. **412**(52), 7147–7168 (2011)
13. Bertrand, J.: Book review of theorie mathematique de la richesse social and of recherches sur les principes mathematiques de la theorie des richesses. Journal des Savants (1883)
14. Buechel, B., Buskens, V.: The dynamics of closeness and betweenness. J. Math. Sociol. **37**(3), 159–191 (2013)
15. Corbo, J., Parkes, D.C.: The price of selfish behavior in bilateral network formation. In: Proceedings of the Twenty-Fourth Annual ACM Symposium on Principles of Distributed Computing, PODC, pp. 99–107 (2005)
16. Decker, C., Russell, R., Osuntokun, O.: Eltoo: a simple layer 2 protocol for bitcoin. https://blockstream.com/eltoo.pdf
17. Decker, C., Wattenhofer, R.: A fast and scalable payment network with bitcoin duplex micropayment channels. In: Pelc, A., Schwarzmann, A.A. (eds.) SSS 2015. LNCS, vol. 9212, pp. 3–18. Springer, Cham (2015). https://doi.org/10.1007/978-3-319-21741-3_1
18. Demaine, E.D., Hajiaghayi, M.T., Mahini, H., Zadimoghaddam, M.: The price of anarchy in network creation games, vol. 8, pp. 13:1–13:13 (2012)
19. Ehsani, S., et al.: A bounded budget network creation game. ACM Trans. Algorithms (TALG) **11**(4), 34 (2015)

20. Entringer, R.C., Jackson, D.E., Snyder, D.: Distance in graphs. Czechoslovak Math. J. **26**(2), 283–296 (1976)
21. Fabrikant, A., Luthra, A., Maneva, E.N., Papadimitriou, C.H., Shenker, S.: On a network creation game. In: Proceedings of the Twenty-Second ACM Symposium on Principles of Distributed Computing, PODC, pp. 347–351 (2003)
22. Freeman, L.C.: Centrality in social networks conceptual clarification. Soc. Netw. **1**(3), 215–239 (1978)
23. Gago Álvarez, S.: The betweenness centrality of a graph (2007). https://pdfs. semanticscholar.org/5673/a1a7229855a3b5a4bbfb69cf3571bcf73379.pdf
24. Green, M., Miers, I.: Bolt: anonymous payment channels for decentralized currencies. In: Proceedings of the 2017 ACM SIGSAC Conference on Computer and Communications Security, pp. 473–489. ACM (2017)
25. Hopwood, D., Bowe, S., Hornby, T., Wilcox, N.: Zcash protocol specification. Technical report, 2016–1.10. Zerocoin Electric Coin Company, Technical Report (2016)
26. Koutsoupias, E., Papadimitriou, C.: Worst-case equilibria. In: Meinel, C., Tison, S. (eds.) STACS 1999. LNCS, vol. 1563, pp. 404–413. Springer, Heidelberg (1999). https://doi.org/10.1007/3-540-49116-3_38
27. Lind, J., Naor, O., Eyal, I., Kelbert, F., Sirer, E.G., Pietzuch, P.R.: Teechain: a secure payment network with asynchronous blockchain access. In: Proceedings of the 27th ACM Symposium on Operating Systems Principles, SOSP, pp. 63–79 (2019)
28. Miller, A., Bentov, I., Bakshi, S., Kumaresan, R., McCorry, P.: Sprites and state channels: payment networks that go faster than lightning. In: Goldberg, I., Moore, T. (eds.) FC 2019. LNCS, vol. 11598, pp. 508–526. Springer, Cham (2019). https://doi.org/10.1007/978-3-030-32101-7_30
29. Moscibroda, T., Schmid, S., Wattenhofer, R.: On the topologies formed by selfish peers. In: Proceedings of the Twenty-Fifth Annual ACM Symposium on Principles of Distributed Computing, PODC, pp. 133–142 (2006)
30. Moscibroda, T., Schmid, S., Wattenhofer, R.: Topological implications of selfish neighbor selection in unstructured peer-to-peer networks. Algorithmica **61**(2), 419–446 (2011)
31. Nakamoto, S.: Bitcoin: a peer-to-peer electronic cash system (2008)
32. Poon, J., Dryja, T.: The bitcoin lightning network: scalable off-chain instant payments (2015)
33. Spilman, J.: Anti dos for TX replacement. https://lists.linuxfoundation.org/ pipermail/bitcoin-dev/2013-April/002433.html. Accessed 17 Apr 2019
34. Van Saberhagen, N.: Cryptonote v 2.0 (2013)
35. Wood, G., et al.: Ethereum: a secure decentralised generalised transaction ledger (2014)

How to Profit from Payments Channels

Oğuzhan Ersoy[✉], Stefanie Roos, and Zekeriya Erkin

Delft University of Technology, Delft, The Netherlands
{o.ersoy,s.roos,z.erkin}@tudelft.nl

Abstract. Payment channel networks like Bitcoin's Lightning network
are an auspicious approach for realizing high transaction throughput
and almost-instant confirmations in blockchain networks. However, the
ability to successfully conduct payments in such networks relies on the
willingness of participants to lock collateral in the network. In Lightning, the key financial incentive to lock collateral are low fees for routing
payments of other participants. While users can choose these fees, real-
world data indicates that they mainly stick to default fees. By providing
insights on beneficial choices for fees, we aim to incentivize users to lock
more collateral and improve the effectiveness of the network.

In this paper, we consider a node **A** that given the network topology
and the channel details establishes channels and chooses fees to maximize
its financial gain. Our contributions are i) formalization of the optimization problem, ii) proving that the problem is NP-hard, and iii) designing
and evaluating a greedy algorithm to approximate the optimal solution.
In each step, our greedy algorithm establishes a channel that maximizes
the increase to **A**'s total reward, which corresponds to maximizing the
number of shortest paths passing through **A**. Our simulation study leveraged real-world data sets to quantify the impact of our gain optimization
and indicates that our strategy is at least a factor two better than other
strategies.

1 Introduction

Payment channel networks [14] overcome the need to globally agree on every
transaction in a blockchain. Instead, nodes can open and close *channels* that
they can use to transfer coins directly. In the absence of disputes, transactions
only require local communication between the parties involved in a transaction.
Nodes without a direct payment channel can route payments via intermediaries
to avoid the transaction fees and delays of channel opening. Thus, by moving transactions off-chain, payment channels have the potential to drastically
increase the transaction throughput while reducing the confirmation times from
tens of minutes to sub-seconds. The most notable examples of payment channel
networks are Bitcoin's Lightning [19] and Ethereum's Raiden [2].

When opening a payment channel, nodes need to lock coins that they cannot
use outside of the channel during the lifetime of the channel. This opportunity cost makes it unattractive to maintain payment channels. However, routing

© International Financial Cryptography Association 2020
J. Bonneau and N. Heninger (Eds.): FC 2020, LNCS 12059, pp. 284–303, 2020.
https://doi.org/10.1007/978-3-030-51280-4_16

payments in a network requires that the network has well-funded channels [14]. The key incentives for locking collateral in a channel are i) frequent transaction with the other party [7] and ii) financial gain through routing fees [11], i.e., fees that nodes charge for routing payments as intermediaries. Our analysis of the Lightning network shows that the fees charged for routing are currently low and mainly equal to the default value [21]. We conjecture that the current payment channel networks primarily rely on the first incentive. However, research on the Lightning network suggests that this incentive entails networks of a low resilience with a few central hubs [22]. Analyzing the second incentives and show-casing that payment channels can entail financial profit is the most promising avenue of research to incentivize the participation in payment channel networks and fully leverage the potential of this promising blockchain scalability approach.

In this paper, we adapt a payment channel network (PCN) model based on Lightning. We assume a known topology and fees. Nodes select the cheapest path to conduct a payment. A node **A** aims to maximize its profit through routing fees by choosing both its payment channels and fees. The problem is challenging as higher fees indicate a higher profit if the node routes the payment but also a lower probability to be chosen for routing due to the transactions taking the cheapest path.

Despite the importance of fees in payment channel networks, the issue has been mainly ignored in past research. The majority of papers deal with cryptographic protocols for channel establishment and multi-hop payments (e.g., [6,7,10,15,17]) as well as algorithms for routing payments (e.g., [16,20,23]). There is some work on comparing routing fees to the on-chain fees of blockchains and presenting an economical analysis of the relation between the two fee types [5,11]. It is interesting to note that routing fees are related to the payment value whereas on-chain blockchain fees usually relate to the size of the transactions. In contrast, Di Stasi et al. [24] evaluated the impact of routing fees on keeping channels balanced, i.e., ensuring that a channel is not used exclusively in one direction. The authors suggest a novel linear fee policy for each channel to improve channel balances. Most similar to our work, Avarikioti et al. [3] studied the optimal fee assignment of channels from the point of view of a payment service provider (PSP). The authors analyzed optimal channel fees of the whole network that maximizes the total reward of the PSP instead of focusing on a node, which defines our problem. However, the authors can only solve for tree-structured networks, which does not make the approach useful in practice.

We are hence the first to cover the aspect of maximizing fees in payment channel networks. More precisely, we formalize the problem of maximizing fees in a Lightning-inspired system model. We present an algorithm for solving the defined optimization problem heuristically. Our greedy algorithm iteratively i) adds channels and ii) selects fees such that each added channel increases the profit maximally for the previously selected channels. For this purpose, we leverage the concept of (edge) betweenness centrality, i.e., the fraction of cheapest paths a vertex or edge is contained in. We evaluate our algorithm for real-world data sets of the Lightning network. Our evaluation strongly indicates that our approach does not only greatly improve the profit in comparison to default fees but also that leveraging betweenness centrality for selecting channels offers considerably better results than other network centrality measures. More preciously, our algorithm increases the profit by a factor 4 in comparison to default fee values and is at least a factor 2 better than other strategies. Our evaluation further demonstrates that nodes with already established channels can increase their profit by utilizing only our fee selection algorithm without establishing new channels.

2 Background

This section summarizes key concepts from the field of payment channels. Furthermore, as our algorithm relies on graph centrality metrics, this section defines these metrics and gives some intuition on their role.

2.1 Payment Channel Networks

Payment channel networks are one key approaches to scaling blockchains by moving transactions off-chain [14]. Two parties open a payment channel through an initial funding transaction on the blockchain that locks coins such that they can only be used for transactions between the two parties. After this initial funding transaction, the two parties can conduct payments without directly interacting with the blockchain. They commit to the latest balance of the channel, i.e., the distribution of the total number of locked coins over the two parties. For instance, let nodes u and v open a payment channel such that u locks x coins and v locks y coins. The initial *balance* of the channel is (x, y) and its total *capacity* is $x + y$. If u sends one coin to v, the balance changes to $(x - 1, y + 1)$.

In case of a dispute about the channel balance, the signed commitments documenting the state changes are published on the blockchain. The blockchain consensus then assigns the coins according to the latest valid channel state. Once the two parties decide to close their channel, they have to conduct a closing transaction on the blockchain. Afterward, they receive the coins locked in the channel with the number of coins per party corresponding to the channel balance at the time of the closure. In the absence of disputes, the intermediary transactions are almost instant and the number of transaction is merely bound locally by the bandwidth and latency of nodes.

Establishing a payment channel does not make sense if parties do not trade with each other regularly due to i) the on-chain fees for establishing the channel and ii) the opportunity cost caused by locking coins to the channel. Thus, most nodes will only establish a few channels with frequent trading partners. Routing payments via a path consisting of multiple channels nevertheless allows nodes to trade without having a direct channel. For instance, a node s can make a payment to a node r via two intermediary nodes u and v, meaning that the payment is routed via three payment channels: s to u, u to v, and v to r. The balances along all these channels change according to the transaction value.

The intermediary nodes charge fees for the use of their channels. For a channel Ch_i from u to v, these fees consist of a basic fee BF_{Ch_i} for using the channel and fee rate FR_{Ch_i} per transferred unit. The overall fee of a transaction tx for the channel is hence

$$\mathbf{f}(Ch_i, tx) = BF_{Ch_i} + FR_{Ch_i} \cdot |tx|, \qquad (1)$$

where $|tx|$ denotes the transaction amount. The fees are determined by and paid to u. The sender s has to pay the fees. Note that the fee calculation formula given in Eq. 1 is specific to the Lightning network [1]. Still, the other payment or state channel networks have a similar structure.

2.2 Graph Centrality Metrics

In this work, we model a PCN network as a directed graph. In this manner, each node in the payment channel represents a vertex in the graph and each channel is represented by two directional edges between the nodes (one for each direction). The channel fees correspond to the weights of the edges.

As a consequence, we can make use of graph metrics that characterize the importance of certain nodes in a weighted directed graph. Our key metrics are (vertex) betweenness centrality and edge betweenness centrality.

Definition 1 (Betweenness Centrality). *The betweenness centrality of a vertex [12] v is proportional to the total number of shortest paths that pass through that vertex, i.e.,*

$$\mathbf{bc}(v) = \sum_{\substack{s \neq t \neq v \\ \sigma_{st} \neq 0}} \frac{\sigma_{stv}}{\sigma_{st}},$$

where σ_{st} denotes the number of shortest paths between s and t and σ_{stv} is the number of such shortest paths containing the vertex v.

Similarly, the edge betweenness centrality [13] of an edge relates to the total number of shortest paths that pass through that edge, i.e.,

$$\mathbf{e}([v_1 v_2]) = \sum_{\substack{s \neq t \\ \sigma_{st} \neq 0}} \frac{\sigma_{st[v_1 v_2]}}{\sigma_{st}},$$

where $\sigma_{st[v_1 v_2]}$ is the number of shortest paths passing through the edge $[v_1 v_2]$.

The analysis of this paper makes use of the following result about vertex betweenness centrality to assess the suitability of our greedy heuristic for selecting channel fees.

Theorem 1 ([4]). *For each vertex v, betweenness centrality function $\mathbf{bc}(v)$ is a monotone function for the set of edges incident to v.*

An important problem concerning the betweenness centrality is the *maximum betweenness improvement* (MBI) problem.

Definition 2 (MBI problem [4]**).** Maximum Betweenness Improvement *problem: Given a directed graph G and a vertex v, find k edges incident to node v such that* **bc**(v) *is maximal.*

With the help of the following theorem concerning the MBI problem, we prove that our problem of maximizing the reward (MRI) is NP-hard.

Theorem 2 ([4]**).** *MBI problem cannot be approximated in polynomial time within a factor greater than* $1 - \frac{1}{2e}$, *unless* $P = NP$.

3   Our PCN Model

There are a number of PCNs with Lightning [19], Raiden [2], Perun [9] and Celer [8] being key examples. All of them use slightly different assumptions and properties. We base our system model on Bitcoin's Lightning network.

In the following, we first describe our PCN model **LN**. In this model, we then define the problem of an individual participant aiming to maximize their gain. We summarize the notation used in the paper in Table 1.

Table 1. Notation and Abbreviation Table

Symbol	Explanation
CSF	The channel selection function
CFF	The channel fee function
LN	The payment channel network
c(X)	The total amount of coins of X
f(Ch, tx)[1]	The charging fee of the channel Ch for a transaction of value tx
bc(n, **N**) (See footnote 1)	The betweenness centrality of the node n in a network **N**
e(Ch, **N**) (See footnote 1)	The edge betweenness centrality of the channel Ch in a network **N**
s(Ch_i), **r**(Ch_i)	The source and destination nodes of the channel Ch_i
ChCost	The channel opening and closing on-chain cost

3.1   Network Topology, Fees, and Routing

Nodes open and close payment channels through blockchain transactions. For simplicity, we assume that the cost *ChCost* of opening and closing remains constant over time.

In Lightning, the complete topology of the network is known to every node. Nodes publicly announce on the blockchain that they establish or close a channel. Furthermore, nodes willing to route payments announce their channels and fees

---

[1] For brevity in the notation, tx and **N** can be omitted unless they alter with time.

to the complete network. Thus, we assume in our model that both the topology and the fees of all nodes are publicly known. For simplicity, we assume that the topology and routing fees of the nodes that do not strategically change them remain fixed over time. Otherwise, our fee selection strategy would require a model to anticipate the expected changes. Current research on payment channel networks does not provide such a model. Our analysis of the Lightning network data from $1ml.com$ indicates that fees are indeed usually the default value. As topology changes require on-chain transactions, which are costly in both time and on-chain fees, the topology also should not change considerably. Moreover, we assume that nodes apply source routing to find one cheapest path from source to destination, as is the case in the current implementation of Lightning.

3.2   Problem Definition

We represent a network **LN** as a graph $G = (V, E)$ of vertices V and edges E. A node **A** aims to maximize its revenue in running a node in a payment channel network. For this purpose, **A** opens channels with other nodes in the network, each channel having a total cost of $ChCost$ for opening and closing. We assume that **A** can strategically select the nodes it establishes channels with from all nodes in the network. After all, these nodes do not need to invest anything into the channel as **A** completely funds them and they will likely receive additional monetary gains through routing fees. Furthermore, **A** has a budget of $\mathbf{c(A)}$ coins to use as collateral for the channels in total.

Formally, let C be the set of channels established by **A**. For each channel $Ch_i \in C$, we have the coins allocated to the channel $\mathbf{c}(Ch_i)$ and the channel fee $\mathbf{f}(Ch_i, tx)$ for a transaction value tx. Wlog, transaction values are integers between 1 and $\mathbf{T}_{max}$ following a distribution T. Let $X_i(tx, S, R)$ be the event that a transaction of value tx going from a node S to a node R passes through the channel Ch_i. Then the expected fee from that transaction is $\mathbf{f}(Ch_i, tx)Pr[X_i(tx, S, R)]$. Last, we require the distribution M that returns a sender-receiver pair. **A**'s objective is to find C, f, and $\mathbf{c}()$ such that the overall expected gain of one transaction

$$\sum_{\substack{\forall S, R \in V \\ S \neq R \neq \mathbf{A}}} Pr(M = (S, R)) \sum_{j=1}^{\mathbf{T}_{max}} Pr(T = j) \sum_{Ch_i \in C} \mathbf{f}(Ch_i, j) \cdot Pr[X_i(j, S, R)] \quad (2)$$

is maximized while adhering to the constraint that $\sum_{Ch_i \in C} \mathbf{c}(Ch_i) \leq \mathbf{c(A)}$. Equation 2 computes the expected gain over the involved variables T and M. If the capacity of the channel $\mathbf{c}(Ch_i)$ is less than the transaction amount tx, $Pr[X_i(tx, S, R)] = 0$. Similarly, if there does not exist a shortest path from S to R that passes through Ch_i, $Pr[X_i(tx, S, R)] = 0$. Otherwise, $Pr[X_i(tx, S, R)]$ is equal to the number of shortest paths from S to R passing through Ch_i divided by the total number of shortest paths from S to R.

Note that Eq. 2 ignores the cost of opening C channels, $|C| \cdot ChCost$. The impact of this cost depends on the number of transactions K that occur during the lifetime of a channel. Let max be the maximal value for Eq. 2. The overall gain of the node is then the difference: $K \cdot max - |C| \cdot ChCost$. By increasing the lifetime of the channel arbitrarily, the impact of $|C| \cdot ChCost$ diminishes, which is why we disregard it for Eq. 2. Our model furthermore disregards the opportunity cost caused by locking coins due to the absence of suitable models for such a cost.

4   Our Fee Strategy

We start by showing that maximizing the objective function given in Eq. 2 is NP-hard. Afterwards, we present our greedy algorithm for approximating a solution. As our algorithm contains an equation for choosing channel fees without a closed-form solution, the last part of the section demonstrates a method for solving the equation numerically.

Our proof and algorithm act on a version of Eq. 2 for specific distributions T and M. In the absence of real-world data for these distributions, we utilize two straight-forward distributions. Concretely, our work considers a fixed transaction value, i.e., the random variable T only takes one value tx. For the distribution M, which characterizes the likelihood of two nodes to trade, assuming that all nodes are equally likely to trade with each other is the most natural choice in the absence of a concrete alternative model. Thus, M is a uniform distribution over all pairs of nodes in the following.

For the design of our algorithm, we furthermore bound the maximal channel fee by f_{max}. Assuming a maximal channel fee does not reduce the generality of our approach. As nodes send payments along the path with the lowest fee, any channel fee that entails the channel is not contained in any such path can be disregarded.

4.1   NP-Hardness of the Problem

Before presenting the actual proof, we rephrase Eq. 2 to relate it to the concept of (edge) betweenness centrality.

Choosing M to be a uniform distribution implies that $Pr(M = (S, R)) = \frac{1}{(|V|-1)(|V|-2)}$ [2] is a constant, which can disregarded for the optimization. Furthermore, choosing a constant transaction value tx removes the second sum in Eq. 2. Hence our modified objective function is

$$\sum_{Ch_i \in C} \mathbf{f}(Ch_i, tx) \cdot Pr[X_i(tx, S, R)]. \tag{3}$$

The next step relates $Pr[X_i(\text{tx}, S, R)]$ in Eq. 3 to the betweenness centrality. There are two important quantities to consider: the number of shortest paths

---

[2] $(|V| - 1)(|V| - 2)$ is the number of pairs of nodes when not including $\mathbf{A}$.

including the channel and total fee reward gained from these paths. Maximizing the number of shortest paths passing through a channel or node corresponds to the edge or vertex betweenness centrality (BC), respectively, as defined in Sect. 2. However, maximizing the BC does not necessarily imply maximal revenue. As fees represent edge weights, the shortest path here is a path whose edges have the minimal sum of weights. Choosing low fees hence increases the probability to be contained in the shortest path but low fees also indicate a low gain from each transaction.

Rather, the expected reward of a channel Ch_i is equal to the probability of the transaction passing through that channel times the fee. Note that each channel needs to have a capacity of at least tx for the payment to choose this path. Thus, an optimal solution for Eq. 3 will only create channels of sufficient capacity and we can exclude the capacity aspect from $Pr[X_i(tx, S, R)]$. With $\mathbf{e}(Ch_i)$ denoting the edge betweenness centrality of a channel Ch_i with fees $\mathbf{f}(Ch_i)^3$, the formal expression for the expected reward of Ch_i is

$$\mathsf{ER}(Ch_i) = \mathbf{f}(Ch_i) \cdot \mathbf{e}(Ch_i). \tag{4}$$

As a consequence, the total expected reward of $\mathbf{A}$ from Eq. 3 is

$$\mathsf{ER}(\mathbf{A}) = \sum_{Ch_i \in C} \mathsf{ER}(Ch_i). \tag{5}$$

Now, we can formally define the problem from Eq. 2 as the *maximum reward improvement* (MRI) problem.

Definition 3 (MRI Problem). Maximum Reward Improvement *problem: For a payment channel network $\mathcal{LN}$ and a node n, find k channels incident to node n such that* $\mathsf{ER}(n)$ *is maximized.*

The following theorem states that it is not possible to design an algorithm CSF that finds the optimum solution within polynomial time, unless $P = NP$.

Theorem 3 (MRI Approximation Theorem). MRI *problem cannot be approximated in polynomial time within a factor greater than* $1 - \frac{1}{2\epsilon}$, *unless* $P = NP$.

Proof. To prove this theorem, we reduce our MRI problem to the MBI problem presented in Definition 2. Using Eq. 5, we can formulate the MRI problem as follows:

$$\mathsf{MRI}(\mathbf{LN}, n, k) \to \mathcal{CH}_M = \operatorname*{argmax}_{\substack{|\mathcal{CH}| \leq k \\ \mathbf{s}(Ch_i) = n \\ \mathbf{f}(Ch_i) \in [1, f_{max}]}} \left(\mathsf{ER}(n) = \sum_{Ch_i \in \mathcal{CH}} \mathsf{ER}(Ch_i) \right).$$

---

[3] For the rest of section, we drop the transaction amount tx from the channel fee formula $\mathbf{f}(Ch_i)$ as it is fixed.

We introduce a subproblem, namely MRI_FF, where the upper limit of the fee f_{max} is equal to 1, which means that all the channel fee are equal to 1. Using the Eq. 4, MRI_FF can be formulated as:

$$\text{MRI\_FF}(\mathbf{LN}, n, N_c) \rightarrow \mathcal{CH}_M = \underset{\substack{|\mathcal{CH}| \leq k \\ \mathbf{s}(Ch_i) = n}}{\text{argmax}} \left(\sum_{Ch_i \in \mathcal{CH}} \mathbf{e}(Ch_i) \right) \qquad (6)$$

$$\overset{(*)}{=} \underset{\substack{|\mathcal{CH}| \leq k \\ \mathbf{s}(Ch_i) || \mathbf{r}(Ch_i) = n}}{\text{argmax}} (bc_n) \overset{(**)}{=} \text{MBI}(\mathbf{LN}, n, k),$$

which reduces to the MBI problem. Here, the first equality (∗) holds because the summation of the all shortest paths passing from out-going edges is equal to the total number of shortest paths passing through that node. In other words, the summation of edge betweenness centrality of all out-going edges of a node is equal to betweenness centrality of that node. The second equality (∗) follows from the definition of the MBI problem given in Definition 2.

Now, we can prove our theorem by contradiction. Let assume there exists an approximation to MRI problem within a factor greater than $1 - \frac{1}{2\epsilon}$. Then, the same approximation would hold for the subproblem of MRI, MRI_FF with a certain maximal fee, namely 1. However, in Eq. 6, we showed that MRI_FF problem is equivalent to the MBI problem. This contradicts Theorem 2. Therefore, MRI problem cannot be polynomially approximated within a factor greater than $1 - \frac{1}{2\epsilon}$, unless $P = NP$. □

4.2   Channel Selection Function

We present a *greedy* algorithm CSF to approximate the MRI problem. CSF takes the PCN and the requested number of channels as input and outputs the set of nodes to whom channels are created. It internally calls CFF, the algorithm for deciding the fee of a channel. Formally, we have

$$\text{CFF}(\mathcal{CH} \cup Ch) \rightarrow R_{Ch} :$$
$$R_{Ch} = \text{TotalER}(\mathcal{CH} \cup Ch, f) \text{ where } f = \underset{f_i \in [1, f_{max}]}{\text{argmax}} \left(\text{TotalER}(\mathcal{CH} \cup Ch, f_i) \right),$$

$$\text{TotalER}(\mathcal{CH} \cup Ch, f_i) = \text{ER}(Ch)_{\mathbf{f}(Ch) = f_i} + \sum_{Ch_j \in \mathcal{CH}} \text{ER}(Ch_j). \qquad (7)$$

As detailed in Algorithm 1, our greedy algorithm for CSF consists of the following five key steps:

1. Start with an initial PCN of nodes and channels.
2. At each step, try all possible channels between our node and other nodes.
3. Compute the maximum reward of the channel by using CFF.
4. Connect to the node who gives the maximum reward and update the PCN.
5. Go to step (2) until the desired number of channels is established.

Algorithm 1. Channel Selection Function

Input: LN and N_c
Output: $\mathcal{CH}$
1: **function** CSF(**LN**, N_c)
2:     $\mathcal{CH} \leftarrow \emptyset$
3:     **while** $|\mathcal{CH}| < N_c$ **do**
4:         $maxRew \leftarrow 0, selectednode = None$
5:         **for** Each node $n_i \in$ **LN do**
6:             Create a channel between (n, n_i): $\mathbf{LN}_i \leftarrow AddEdges(\mathbf{LN}, [n, n_i])$
7:             Calculate the reward $R_{n_i} \leftarrow$ CFF($\mathbf{LN}_i, \mathcal{CH} \cup [n, n_i]$)
8:             **if** $maxRew \leq R_{n_i}$ **then**
9:                 $maxRew = R_{n_i}$
10:                $selectednode = n_i$
11:            **end if**
12:        **end for**
13:        $\mathcal{CH} \leftarrow \mathcal{CH} \bigcup \{selectednode\}$
14:        $\mathbf{LN} \leftarrow AddEdges(\mathbf{LN}, [n, selectednode])$
15:    **end while**
16:    **return** $\mathcal{CH}$
17: **end function**

Next, we ascertain that channel additions cannot reduce the expected revenue, indicating that nodes should add all channels they can fund. Here, it is important to note that we do not take into account the channel opening cost *ChCost*. Thus, if the marginal reward improvement of a new channel is zero, there is no point in add the channel.

Theorem 4 (Monotonicity). *The objective function of Algorithm 1 is a monotone non-decreasing function.*

Proof A function $\mathcal{F} : \Omega \rightarrow \mathbb{R}$ is a monotone function if it satisfies the following condition:

$$\forall S \subseteq T \subseteq \Omega, \quad \mathcal{F}(S) \leq \mathcal{F}(T). \tag{8}$$

In our case, we have to show that CFF($\mathcal{CH} \cup [n, n_i]$) $\geq$ CFF($\mathcal{CH}$) for any solution $\mathcal{CH}$ and node n_i such that $[n, n_i] \notin \mathcal{CH}$ where $\mathcal{CH}$ is the current channel list of node n.

Note that CFF checks for all possible fee values to maximize the total reward. In that sense, it would be enough to show that for the maximum fee value f_{max}, which can be formulated by using Eq. 7 (with $\mathbf{LN}_0 = \mathbf{LN} \cup \mathcal{CH}$ and $\mathbf{LN}_i = \mathbf{LN} \cup \mathcal{CH} \cup [n, n_i]$):

$$\mathsf{CFF}(\mathbf{LN}, \mathcal{CH} \cup [n, n_i]) \geq \mathsf{TotalER}(\mathbf{LN}, \mathcal{CH} \cup [n, n_i], f = f_{max}) \overset{?}{\geq} \mathsf{CFF}(\mathbf{LN}, \mathcal{CH})$$

$$\Longleftrightarrow \mathsf{ER}(Ch, \mathbf{LN}_i)_{f=f_{max}} + \sum_{\forall Ch_j \in \mathcal{CH}} \mathsf{ER}(Ch_j, \mathbf{LN}_i) \overset{?}{\geq} \sum_{\forall Ch_j \in \mathcal{CH}} \mathsf{ER}(Ch_j, \mathbf{LN}_0)$$

$$\Longleftrightarrow \mathsf{ER}(Ch, \mathbf{LN}_i)_{f=f_{max}} \overset{?}{\geq} \sum_{\forall Ch_j \in \mathcal{CH}} \mathsf{ER}(Ch_j, \mathbf{LN}_0) - \mathsf{ER}(Ch_j, \mathbf{LN}_i)$$

$$\Longleftrightarrow \mathbf{e}([n, n_i], \mathbf{LN}_i) \cdot f_{max} \overset{?}{\geq} \sum_{\forall Ch_j \in \mathcal{CH}} (\mathbf{e}(Ch_j, \mathbf{LN}_0) - \mathbf{e}(Ch_j, \mathbf{LN}_i)) \cdot \mathbf{f}(Ch_j)$$

$$\overset{(*)}{\Longleftarrow} \mathbf{e}([n, n_i], \mathbf{LN}_i) \overset{?}{\geq} \sum_{\forall Ch_j \in \mathcal{CH}} (\mathbf{e}(Ch_j, \mathbf{LN}_0) - \mathbf{e}(Ch_j, \mathbf{LN}_i))$$

$$\Longleftrightarrow \mathbf{e}([n, n_i], \mathbf{LN}_i) + \sum_{\forall Ch_j \in \mathcal{CH}} \mathbf{e}(Ch_j, \mathbf{LN}_i) \overset{?}{\geq} \sum_{\forall Ch_j \in \mathcal{CH}} \mathbf{e}(Ch_j, \mathbf{LN}_0)$$

$$\overset{(**)}{\Longleftrightarrow} \mathbf{bc}(n, \mathbf{LN}_i) \overset{?}{\geq} \mathbf{bc}(n, \mathbf{LN}_0).$$

Here, $(*)$ condition is true since for all channels $\mathbf{f}(Ch_i) \leq f_{max}$ by the definition. Also, each term $\mathbf{e}(Ch_j, \mathbf{LN}_0) - \mathbf{e}(Ch_j, \mathbf{LN}_i)$ is non-negative as new channels of node n cannot increase the number of shortest paths passing through existing channels of the same node. Thus, the multiplication with a positive number preserves the inequality. $(**)$ is satisfied since the summation of edge betweenness centrality of all out-going edges of a node is equal to betweenness centrality of that node. At the end, $\mathbf{bc}(n, \mathbf{LN}_i) \geq \mathbf{bc}(n, \mathbf{LN}_0)$ holds because betweenness centrality is a monotone function, see Theorem 1. □

4.3   Efficient Search Algorithm for the Channel Fee Function

No closed-form formula finds the best fee amount maximizing the expected reward due to the term $\mathbf{e}(Ch)$ for a channel Ch. Here, we analyze Eq. 4 to minimize the computational cost by discarding some parts of the search space. First of all, since $\mathbf{e}(\mathbf{LN})$ is not affected by changes to the fees of channels, the denominator is irrelevant for optimizing the $\mathsf{ER}(Ch)$. Therefore, CFF can be seen as a function of the edge betweenness centrality of the channel $\mathbf{e}(Ch)$ and its fee $\mathbf{f}(Ch)$. Secondly, $\mathbf{e}(Ch)$ is negatively affected by $\mathbf{f}(Ch)$ because increasing the fee means an increase in the weight of the edge that results in a lower chance of being in the shortest paths (see Fig. 3 in Appendix A for an illustrative example).

Two observations give rise to an efficient search algorithm for finding the most suitable fee. The first observation utilizes the fact that edge betweenness centrality is a monotone decreasing function concerning the channel fee. Let the expected reward of a channel for chosen fees $f_3 > f_1$ be $r_1 = e_1 \cdot f_1$ and $r_3 = e_3 \cdot f_3$, respectively. If $r_3 > r_1$, let

$$f_2 = f_1 \cdot \frac{r_3}{r_1} = f_3 \cdot \frac{e_3}{e_1}. \tag{9}$$

It can be seen that the expected reward r_α for any fee f_α where $f_1 < f_\alpha \leq f_2$ is at most r_3:

$$r_\alpha = e_\alpha \cdot f_\alpha \leq e_1 \cdot f_\alpha \leq e_1 \cdot f_2 = e_3 \cdot f_3 = r_3. \tag{10}$$

In other words, there is no need to compute the expected reward values for the fees in between f_1 and f_2 as they cannot be optimal values.

The second observation is that increasing the fee of an out-going channel Ch cannot decrease the edge betweenness of another out-going channel Ch' of the same node. Such an increase can only reduce the edge betweenness of channels that are on a path containing Ch by removing the path from the set of shortest paths. However, as shortest paths cannot have loops, two out-going channels of the same node cannot be on the same shortest path. Now, let $\mathcal{CH}$ be the set of previously selected channels. Let r_1' and r_3' be the sum of the expected fees of all channels $Ch' \in \mathcal{CH}$ for fees f_1 and f_3 with $f_3 > f_1$. By the above observation, we have $r_3' \geq r_1'$.

Our recursive algorithm divides the space of all possible fee values from 1 to f_{max} into d intervals. For each interval i, let $r_i = \mathsf{ER}(Ch, \mathbf{f}(Ch) = f_i)$ be the expected reward of Ch and $r_i' \leftarrow \sum_{Ch' \in \mathcal{CH}} \mathsf{ER}(Ch', \mathbf{f}(Ch'))$ be the total reward of the other channels. By the first observation, the maximal increase in r_i is $\frac{f_{i+1}}{f_i}$ and by the second observation $r_{i+1}' \geq r_i'$ as $f_{i+1} > f_i$. Thus, the maximum possible reward value for interval i is $\widetilde{R}_i = r_i \cdot \frac{f_{i+1}}{f_i} + r_{i+1}'$. If $\widetilde{R}_i$ is greater than the current maximum reward value, the algorithm recursively searches for a maximum in the interval, otherwise discards the interval. We present the pseudocode of the algorithm in Appendix B.

This completes the description of our algorithm, which we evaluate in the following in comparison to other approaches based on common centrality metrics.

5   Evaluation

In this section, we evaluate our proposed fee strategy for a real-world topology. Our evaluation quantifies the total reward gained by **A** when using our greedy algorithm.

To emphasize the high effectiveness of our solution, we compared it with other channel and fee selection algorithm. For the channel selection, we considered random nodes as well as connecting to nodes with a high centrality for three centrality metrics: i) degree, i.e., connecting to the nodes with the most connections, ii) betweenness centrality, and iii) pagerank [18]. For the fee strategy, we compute the results for both cases where the channel fees are the default values and they are determined by CFF.

5.1   Model

In Lightning network, the upcoming transactions and current balances of channels are not known. Thus, we need to model the network and transactions.

Transactions. Like Sect. 4, our evaluation assumes that all source-destination pairs are equally likely. Furthermore, we categorize the transactions into three groups based on the amounts:

- *Micro payments* are the transactions involving a very small amount of coins. To represent this category, we use the transaction amount of 100 Satoshi, which is about one cent[4]. An example of a use case would be the streaming services where you pay small amounts per service.
- *Medium payments*: are the transactions spent for daily living expenses like buying a coffee, which is represented with 10000 Satoshi.
- *Macro payments*: are transactions of high amounts, which is represented with 1000000 Satoshi. The amount of these transactions are in the order of 100 Euros.

From these categories, it is most likely that micro payments are usually restricted to nodes that have a direct channel. Otherwise, the base fee for the payment greatly exceeds the actual payment value. Therefore, our target transactions are medium and macro payments, which are analyzed separately.

Network. Following our system model in Sect. 3, networks are represented as weighted directed graphs. The weights of the edges in the graph model are calculated according to the fee rate and base fees of the channels. Since the fee rate depends on the transaction amount, the weights of the same edges for medium and macro payments will be different. The graph generated for the medium (macro) payments is called medium (macro) graph.

5.2   Setup

We obtained a snapshot of the Lightning Network (LN) data from 1*ml.com* on July 10 2019, which contains 4618 nodes and 68729 edges in total. When we delete the edges with insufficient capacity, the medium graph has 68697 edges and the macro graph has 32193 edges.

As a node requires at least two connections to be contained in any shortest paths, we first connected **A** to the two nodes with the highest degree (, which happen to have the highest pagerank as well). For these two connections, we use the default fee rate and base fee values in both directions of the edges. Based on this initial scenario, we now connect **A** to additional nodes.

The experiments use $ChCost = 8192$ Satoshi, which reflects the fluctuating Bitcoin transaction fee estimates[5]. When establishing a new channel, our simulation added edges in both directions. The base fee and the fee rate of the in-coming edge corresponded to the default value to model that i) most users currently stick to the default values and ii) **A** has no control over the in-coming channel fees as they are determined by the other party. For the outgoing edges, we utilize either CFF to determine the best fee value or use default values. When

---

[4] https://awebanalysis.com/en/convert-satoshi-to-euro-eur/.
[5] https://bitcoinfees.info/.

using CFF, we set $f_{max} = ChCost$. Otherwise, the total fee cost of the transaction in the payment network is higher than the cost in the Bitcoin network and the sender is hence unlikely to proceed with the payment.

5.3 Experimental Results

Figures 1 and 2 show the performance of our greedy algorithm in comparison to the other approaches in terms of the total reward improvement per new channel connections. The x-axis shows the number of connections added and the y-axis represents the total reward of node **A**. Since, for each case, we started with the same two connections, the total reward values have the same offset.

Figure 1 displays the result for the medium graph. When using default values, the reward was consistently lower than for our fee selection algorithm. More precisely, for centrality-based selection of channels, fee optimization increased the reward by a factor of roughly 2. Selecting channels strategically doubled the gain further in comparison to using Pagerank centrality, which was the most beneficial one of the centrality-based selection methods. Figure 2 shows the results of macro graph. The results were similar to the case of medium payments, though the overall gain was slightly higher.

In terms of fee computation efficiency, our experimental results show that the recursive algorithm described in Sect. 4.3 reduced the search space of fees in the magnitude of 10–100.

5.4 Discussion

From the experimental results, it can be seen that our greedy algorithm outperformed other centrality metrics. Furthermore, the beneficial effect of the fee selection function was evident when comparing the results with and without it.

Note that adding new connections to the nodes with the highest centrality metrics did not increase the total reward in comparison to random selection much, in particular for betweenness centrality. The reason here is that connecting to nodes with many shortest path passing them does not imply that the newly added channels offer shorter paths. Instead, directly focusing on the betweenness centrality of **A** results in larger improvements.

Figures 1 and 2 furthermore show few but notable differences between medium and macro payments. First, the overall gain was higher for macro payments as expected due to the higher transaction value and hence increased revenue for a similar fee rate. However, the base rate, which is 1000 Satoshi by default[6] in comparison to a default rate of 0.001, dominates the fee value, so that the 100-fold increase in the transaction value does not translate to a similar increase in gain. Secondly, the differences between various centrality measures are more distinct for macro payments, see Fig. 2.

---

[6] The default fee values may change regarding the imported implementation. Our analysis on dataset shows that 33177 out of 68733 edges use the defaults we adopted.

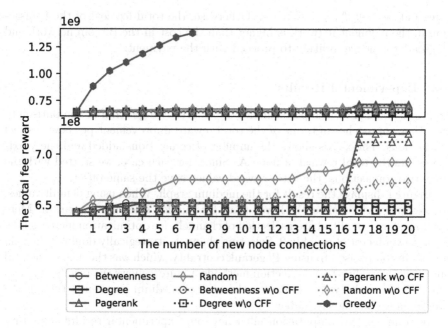

Fig. 1. Total fee reward of our node in medium graph. The bottom figure excludes the greedy results to present a clear comparison of the rest.

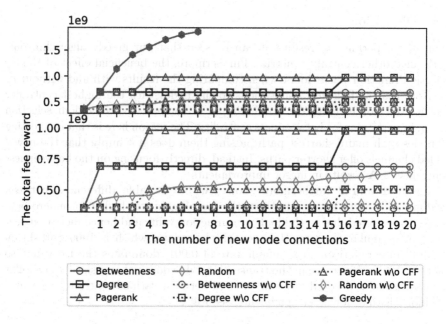

Fig. 2. Total fee reward of our node in macro graph. The bottom figure excludes the greedy results to present a clear comparison of the rest.

Overall, our greedy algorithm promises higher fees for individual nodes. Even if nodes cannot or do not desire to select their channels, they can still gain an advantage by using our more sophisticated fee selection algorithm for already established channels.

One key limitation of our design is that it does not consider channel capacities as such. When all transactions have the same known value, A will only establish channels with sufficient collateral. However, in practice, A does not have such information and routing may fail due to a lack of capacity. Thus, integrating capacity information into both our model and our evaluation is clearly necessary in the future.

6   Conclusion

In this paper, we formalized an optimization problem for maximizing fees in payment channel networks, presented a heuristic algorithm for solving the problem, and evaluated our algorithm on real-world data sets. Our work demonstrates that routing fees can be a strong incentive for locking coins in payment channels. Fees as incentive hence have the potential to motivate rational users to fund payment channel and hence increase the ability of these networks to route payments.

In this work, we focused on one individual node aiming to optimize its profit. Future work should design a game-theoretical framework for networks containing only rational nodes aiming to maximize their profit. For the continued usage of payment channel networks, incentives should ensure that strategies for optimizing profit locally also optimize the overall network health in terms of the availability of cost-effective paths. It remains an open question if the current fee model is a suitable incentive to further collaboration and network health.

Acknowledgments. This work was partially supported by Ripple's University Blockchain Research Initiative.

A   Illustrative Example of the EBC vs. Fee Relationship of a Channel

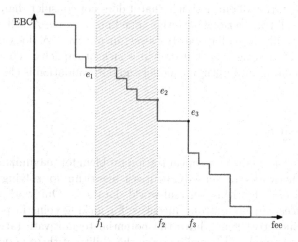

Fig. 3. Illustrative example of the EBC vs. fee relationship of a channel.

B   Pseudocode Channel Fee Function

Algorithm 2 is a recursive algorithm for determining the best fee in one step of the greedy algorithm.

Algorithm 2. Channel Fee Function

Input: LN, $\mathcal{CH}$ and Ch
Output: R_{max} and f_{max}
1: **function** CFF(**LN**, $\mathcal{CH} \cup Ch, f_l, f_h$)
2:    % Initialization: $f_l \leftarrow 1, f_h \leftarrow ChCost, R_{max} \leftarrow 0, f_{max} \leftarrow 1$
3:    % **d** is the division parameter
4:    **if** $f_h - f_l \leq$ **d then** % Anchor step:
5:       **for** $f \in \{f_l, \ldots, f_h\}$ **do**
6:          $[r, r'] \leftarrow$ TotalER($\mathcal{CH} \cup Ch, f$)
7:          Calculate the reward $R \leftarrow r + r'$
8:          **if** $R \geq R_{max}$ **then**
9:             $R_{max} \leftarrow R$
10:            $f_{max} \leftarrow f$
11:         **end if**
12:      **end for**
13:      **return**
14:   **else** % Recursion step:
15:      **for** $i \in \{1, \ldots, \textbf{d}\}$ **do**
16:         $f_i \leftarrow i \cdot \frac{f_h - f_l}{\textbf{d}} + f_l$
17:      **end for**
18:      **for** $i \in \{1, \ldots, \textbf{d}\}$ **do**
19:         $[r_i, r'_i] \leftarrow$ TotalER($\mathcal{CH} \cup Ch, f_i$)
20:         Calculate the reward $R_i = r_i + r'_i$
21:         **if** $R_i \geq R_{max}$ **then**
22:            $R_{max} \leftarrow R_i$
23:            $f_{max} \leftarrow f_i$
24:         **end if**
25:      **end for**
26:      **for** $i \in \{1, \ldots, \textbf{d}\}$ **do**
27:         Calculate the possible maximum reward $\widetilde{R}_i = r_i \cdot \frac{f_{i+1}}{f_i} + r'_{i+1}$
28:         **if** $\widetilde{R}_i > R_{max}$ **then**
29:            $f_l \leftarrow f_i, f_h \leftarrow f_{i+1}$
30:            **return** CFF(**LN**, $\mathcal{CH} \cup Ch, f_l, f_h$)
31:         **else**
32:            % Do nothing - Discard this interval
33:         **end if**
34:      **end for**
35:   **end if**
36: **end function**
37:
38: **function** TotalER($\mathcal{CH} \cup Ch, f$)
39:    $r \leftarrow$ ER($Ch, \textbf{f}(Ch) = f$)
40:    $r' \leftarrow \sum_{\forall Ch_j \in \mathcal{CH}}$ ER($Ch_j, \textbf{f}(Ch_j)$)
41:    **return** $[r, r']$
42: **end function**

References

1. Basis of lightning technology. https://github.com/lightningnetwork/lightning-rfc/blob/master/00-introduction.md
2. AG, B.T.: Raiden network (2019). https://raiden.network/
3. Avarikioti, G., Janssen, G., Wang, Y., Wattenhofer, R.: Payment network design with fees. In: Garcia-Alfaro, J., Herrera-Joancomartí, J., Livraga, G., Rios, R. (eds.) DPM/CBT-2018. LNCS, vol. 11025, pp. 76–84. Springer, Cham (2018). https://doi.org/10.1007/978-3-030-00305-0_6
4. Bergamini, E., Crescenzi, P., D'Angelo, G., Meyerhenke, H., Severini, L., Velaj, Y.: Improving the betweenness centrality of a node by adding links. ACM J. Exp. Algorithmics **23**, 1–32 (2018)
5. Brânzei, S., Segal-Halevi, E., Zohar, A.: How to charge lightning. CoRR abs/1712.10222 (2017). http://arxiv.org/abs/1712.10222
6. Decker, C., Russell, R., Osuntokun, O.: eltoo: a simple layer2 protocol for bitcoin (2018). https://blockstream.com/eltoo.pdf
7. Decker, C., Wattenhofer, R.: A fast and scalable payment network with bitcoin duplex micropayment channels. In: Pelc, A., Schwarzmann, A.A. (eds.) SSS 2015. LNCS, vol. 9212, pp. 3–18. Springer, Cham (2015). https://doi.org/10.1007/978-3-319-21741-3_1
8. Dong, M., Liang, Q., Li, X., Liu, J.: Celer network: bring internet scale to every blockchain. arXiv preprint arXiv:1810.00037 (2018)
9. Dziembowski, S., Eckey, L., Faust, S., Malinowski, D.: PERUN: virtual payment channels over cryptographic currencies. In: Symposium on Security and Privacy (2019)
10. Egger, C., Moreno-Sanchez, P., Maffei, M.: Atomic multi-channel updates with constant collateral in bitcoin-compatible payment-channel networks. In: CCS (2019)
11. Engelmann, F., Kopp, H., Kargl, F., Glaser, F., Weinhardt, C.: Towards an economic analysis of routing in payment channel networks. In: Proceedings of the 1st Workshop on Scalable and Resilient Infrastructures for Distributed Ledgers, SERIAL@Middleware 2017. ACM (2017)
12. Freeman, L.C.: A set of measures of centrality based on betweenness. Sociometry **40**(1), 35–41 (1977). http://www.jstor.org/stable/3033543
13. Girvan, M., Newman, M.E.J.: Community structure in social and biological networks. Proc. Nat. Acad. Sci. **99**(12), 7821–7826 (2002)
14. Gudgeon, L., Moreno-Sanchez, P., Roos, S., McCorry, P., Gervais, A.: SoK: off the chain transactions. IACR Cryptology ePrint Archive 2019/360 (2019)
15. Hearn, M.: Micro-payment channels implementation now in bitcoinj (2013). https://bitcointalk.org/index.php?topic=244656.0
16. Hoenisch, P., Weber, I.: AODV–based routing for payment channel networks. In: Chen, S., Wang, H., Zhang, L.-J. (eds.) ICBC 2018. LNCS, vol. 10974, pp. 107–124. Springer, Cham (2018). https://doi.org/10.1007/978-3-319-94478-4_8
17. Miller, A., Bentov, I., Bakshi, S., Kumaresan, R., McCorry, P.: Sprites and state channels: payment networks that go faster than lightning. In: Goldberg, I., Moore, T. (eds.) FC 2019. LNCS, vol. 11598, pp. 508–526. Springer, Cham (2019). https://doi.org/10.1007/978-3-030-32101-7_30
18. Page, L., Brin, S., Motwani, R., Winograd, T.: The PageRank citation ranking: bringing order to the web. Technical report, Stanford InfoLab (1999)
19. Poon, J., Dryja, T.: The bitcoin lightning network: scalable off-chain instant payments (2016). https://lightning.network/lightning-network-paper.pdf

20. Prihodko, P., Zhigulin, S., Sahno, M., Ostrovskiy, A., Osuntokun, O.: Flare: an approach to routing in lightning network (2016). https://bitfury.com/content/downloads/whitepaper_flare_an_approach_to_routing_in_lightning_network_7_7_2016.pdf
21. Elements Project: Lightning-getroute (2019). https://github.com/ElementsProject/lightning/blob/master/doc/lightning-getroute.7
22. Rohrer, E., Malliaris, J., Tschorsch, F.: Discharged payment channels: quantifying the lightning network's resilience to topology-based attacks. In: Security & Privacy on the Blockchain (2019)
23. Roos, S., Moreno-Sanchez, P., Kate, A., Goldberg, I.: Settling payments fast and private: efficient decentralized routing for path-based transactions. In: Network and Distributed Systems Security (2018)
24. Stasi, G.D., Avallone, S., Canonico, R., Ventre, G.: Routing payments on the lightning network. In: iThings/GreenCom/CPSCom/SmartData 2018 (2018)

Boomerang: Redundancy Improves Latency and Throughput in Payment-Channel Networks

Vivek Bagaria, Joachim Neu$^{(\boxtimes)}$, and David Tse

Stanford University, Stanford, USA
{vbagaria,jneu,dntse}@stanford.edu

Abstract. In multi-path routing schemes for payment-channel networks, Alice transfers funds to Bob by splitting them into partial payments and routing them along multiple paths. Undisclosed channel balances and mismatched transaction fees cause delays and failures on some payment paths. For atomic transfer schemes, these straggling paths stall the whole transfer. We show that the latency of transfers reduces when redundant payment paths are added. This frees up liquidity in payment channels and hence increases the throughput of the network. We devise *Boomerang*, a generic technique to be used on top of multi-path routing schemes to construct redundant payment paths free of counterparty risk. In our experiments, applying Boomerang to a baseline routing scheme leads to 40% latency reduction and 2× throughput increase. We build on ideas from publicly verifiable secret sharing, such that Alice learns a secret of Bob iff Bob overdraws funds from the redundant paths. Funds are forwarded using Boomerang contracts, which allow Alice to revert the transfer iff she has learned Bob's secret. We implement the Boomerang contract in Bitcoin Script.

Keywords: Payment-channel networks · Redundancy · Atomic multi-path · Routing · Throughput · Latency · Adaptor signatures

1 Introduction

1.1 Payment Channels and Networks

Blockchains provide a method for maintaining a distributed ledger in a decentralized and trustless fashion [23]. However, these so called layer-1 (L1) consensus mechanisms suffer from low throughput and high confirmation latency. From a scaling perspective it would be desirable if transactions could be processed 'locally' by only the involved participants.

Payment channels (PCs) [6,7,28] provide this. Once two participants have established a PC on-chain, they can transact through the channel off-chain without involving L1 every time. Briefly, the mechanism underlying the different PC

V. Bagaria and J. Neu—Contributed equally and listed alphabetically.

© International Financial Cryptography Association 2020
J. Bonneau and N. Heninger (Eds.): FC 2020, LNCS 12059, pp. 304–324, 2020.
https://doi.org/10.1007/978-3-030-51280-4_17

implementations is as follows. The participants escrow a pool of funds on-chain which they can spend only jointly. They can perform a transfer through the PC by agreeing on an updated split of the shared funds which reflects the new balances after the transfer and can be enforced on-chain anytime. Special care is taken that participants can only ever execute the most recent agreement on-chain. PCs improve the throughput, latency and privacy of a blockchain system.

Payment networks (PNs) [9,10,16,21,28] can be constructed on top of PCs. PCs can be linked to establish a path between a source and a destination via some intermediaries. Hash- and time-locked contracts (HTLC) are used to perform transfers via intermediaries without counterparty risk, giving rise to so called layer-2 (L2) PNs. To this end, the destination draws a secret (preimage) and reveals a one-way function of the secret (preimage challenge) to the source. The source then initiates a chain of payments to the destination, all conditional on the revelation of a valid preimage. The destination reveals the secret to claim the funds, setting the chain of payments in motion. Net, the destination is paid, the source pays, and the intermediaries are in balance, up to a small service fee earned for forwarding. For recent surveys on PCs and PNs, see [13,15].

1.2   Routing in Payment Networks

Routing algorithms for PNs find paths and forward funds while optimizing objectives such as throughput, latency, or transaction fees. Recently, the routing problem has been studied extensively and various routing algorithms have been proposed [8,14,19,28–30,33,34]. Early on, it has been discovered, also through the Lightning Torch experiment, that single-path routing restricts the maximum transfer size.[1] Multi-path routing [26] allows for a more flexible use of PC liquidity and hence can accommodate larger transfers by splitting transfers into partial payments that are routed along multiple paths. However, while single-path payments are naturally *atomic*, *i.e.*, they either succeed or fail entirely, simply sending multiple partial payments can lead to half-way incomplete transfers. Atomicity is important to keep payment networks manageable from a systems-design perspective, and is achieved by atomic multi-path payments (AMP, [24]), which most state-of-the-art routing algorithms rely on and Lightning developers are actively working towards.[2] Yet, because of its 'everyone-waits-for-the-last' philosophy, atomicity comes at a cost for latency and throughput.

1.3   Main Contributions

Due to the stochastic nature of PNs, *i.e.*, random delays and failures of payment paths, AMP routing often idles while waiting for a few straggling paths. This leads to a long time-to-completion (TTC) of transfers. Furthermore, already successful partial payments are kept pending, seizing liquidity from the PN that

---

[1] https://diar.co/volume-2-issue-25/#1 (Jun 2018), https://www.coindesk.com/its-getting-harder-to-send-bitcoins-lightning-torch-heres-why (Mar 2019).

[2] https://bitcoin.stackexchange.com/q/89475 (Jul 2019).

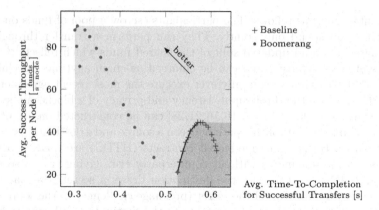

Fig. 1. The blue (resp. red) points mark the tradeoff between latency and throughput of the baseline (resp. Boomerang) AMP routing scheme, obtained by varying an internal parameter. The Pareto fronts (lines) and the achievable regions (shaded) of the tradeoff are shown. Boomerang yields a 2× increase in throughput and a 40 % decrease in latency over the baseline scheme. (Color figure online)

could have served other transfers. As a result, the throughput of the PN reduces. For example, consider a transfer from Alice to Bob of $4 via 4 paths, of which 3 succeed after 1 s and 1 succeeds after 4 s. The transfer has a TTC of 4 s and consumes liquidity $4 · 4 s = $16 · s.

Now suppose instead Alice could send 8 partial payments of $1 each (4 'extra' redundant paths), such that AMP completes once a quorum of 4 out of 8 paths succeeds and Bob cannot steal any extra funds. If 6 paths succeed after 1 s and 2 succeed after 4 s, then the transfer has a TTC of 1 s and consumes liquidity $4 · \$1 · 1\,s + 2 · \$1 · 1\,s + 2 · \$1 · 4\,s = \$14 · s$. Thus, the use of redundant payments reduces the TTC of AMP transfers. As a result, less liquidity is consumed and the PN achieves higher throughput. Similar observations about straggler mitigation using redundancy have been made in large-scale distributed computing [1,5,17].

We devise *Boomerang*, a technique to be used on top of multi-path routing schemes to construct redundant payment paths free of counterparty risk. Building on ideas from publicly verifiable secret sharing, we use a homomorphic one-way function to intertwine the preimage challenges used for HTLC-type payment forwarding, such that Alice learns a secret of Bob iff Bob overdraws funds from the redundant paths. Funds are forwarded using Boomerang contracts, which allow Alice to revert the transfer iff she has learned Bob's secret. We prove the Boomerang construction to be secure, and present an implementation in Bitcoin Script which applies either adaptor signatures based on Schnorr or ECDSA signatures, or elliptic curve scalar multiplication as a one-way function.

We empirically verify the benefits of Boomerang for throughput and latency of AMP routing. For this purpose, we choose a baseline routing scheme which resembles the scheme currently used in Lightning. We enhance this scheme with Boomerang. As can be seen in Fig. 1, redundancy increases the throughput by

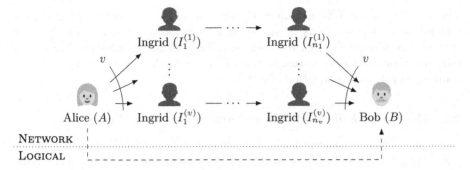

Fig. 2. The TF from A to B (dashed) is implemented by v TXs via intermediaries $(I_1^{(1)}, \dots, I_{n_1}^{(1)}), \dots, (I_1^{(v)}, \dots, I_{n_v}^{(v)})$ (solid).

2x and reduces the TTC (latency) by 40 %. Our results suggest that redundancy is a generic tool to boost the performance of AMP routing algorithms.

1.4 Paper Outline

In Sect. 2, we recall cryptographic preliminaries, introduce the system model, and summarize causes for delay and failure of transfers in payment networks. We devise the Boomerang construction for redundant transactions in Sect. 3, and prove it to be secure. An implementation of Boomerang in Bitcoin Script is presented in Sect. 4. In Sect. 5, we demonstrate the utility of redundancy for improving routing protocols in experiments.

2 Preliminaries

2.1 System Model and Terminology

The topology of a payment network (PN) is given by an undirected graph whose nodes are agents, and whose edges are payment channels (PCs). Each PC endpoint owns a share of the funds in the PC, which we refer to as its liquidity or balance. For privacy reasons it is undesirable to reveal balances to third party nodes. Following Lightning [28, BOLT #7], we assume that nodes have no information about PC balances when taking routing decisions, but know the PN topology. Finally, we assume that PN nodes communicate in a peer-to-peer (P2P) gossiping fashion only along PCs, *i.e.*, PN topology is P2P network topology.

For multi-path routing, we highlight a strict separation between two layers in our terminology (cf. Fig. 2). The 'logical' layer is concerned with *transfers* (TFs) of an amount v of funds from a *source* (Alice, A) to a *destination* (Bob, B). The 'network' layer implements a TF through multiple *transactions* (TXs) from the *sender* to the *receiver* along different paths through multiple intermediaries (Ingrid, I_i). A preimage p_i is used for HTLC-type forwarding of the i-th TX.

The amounts of the TXs add up to the amount of the TF. Routing algorithms schedule a sequence of TXs in an attempt to implement a given TF. Figures of merit are *throughput*, *i.e.*, the average amount of funds transported successfully per time, and *time-to-completion* (TTC), *i.e.*, the average delay between commencement and completion of a TF.

2.2   Delay and Failure of Transactions in Payment Networks

There are various causes for delay and failure of TXs in PNs: *a)* The liquidity of a PC along the desired path is insufficient. *b)* Insufficient fees do not incentivize intermediaries to forward. *c)* Queuing, propagation and processing delay of P2P messages. *d)* PN topology changes, nodes come and go, *e.g.*, due to connectivity or maintenance. *e)* Governments or businesses attempt to censor certain TFs.

2.3   Cryptographic Preliminaries

In this section, we briefly recapitulate the cryptographic tools used throughout the paper. Let $\mathbb{G}$ be a cyclic multiplicative group of prime order q with a generator $g \in \mathbb{G}$. We assume that the discrete logarithm problem (DLP, formally introduced in Sect. A) is hard for g in $\mathbb{G}$, which is commonly assumed to be the case, *e.g.*, in certain elliptic curves (ECs) used in Bitcoin.

Let $H \colon \mathbb{Z}_q \to \mathbb{G}$ with $H(x) \triangleq g^x$, where $\mathbb{Z}_q$ is the finite field of integers modulo q. We require H to be a one-way function, which follows from the DLP hardness assumption. Given a *preimage challenge* $h \triangleq H(x)$, it is difficult to obtain the *preimage* x, but easy to check whether a purported preimage $\hat{x}$ satisfies the challenge (*i.e.*, $H(\hat{x}) = h$).

H has the following homomorphic property which we make extensive use of:

$$\forall n \geq 1 \colon \forall c_1, \dots, c_n \colon \quad H\left(\sum_{i=1}^{n} c_i x_i\right) = \prod_{i=1}^{n} H(x_i)^{c_i} \tag{1}$$

3   The Boomerang Construction

In this section, we show how to add redundant TXs without counterparty risk. To this end, we build up the Boomerang construction in three steps. First, B draws a secret α_0. We use the homomorphic property of H and ideas from publicly verifiable secret sharing [3,12,25,31,32] to construct the preimages p_i and the preimage challenges $H(p_i)$ such that A learns α_0 iff B overdraws funds from the redundant paths. Second, the so called Boomerang contract serves as a building block for contingent transfer of funds, *i.e.*, HTLC-type forwarding with the additional provision that A can revert the TF iff she learns α_0. Finally, the end-to-end procedure of a Boomerang TF is devised from the previously mentioned ingredients. Subsequently, we prove that Boomerang satisfies the relevant notions of security.

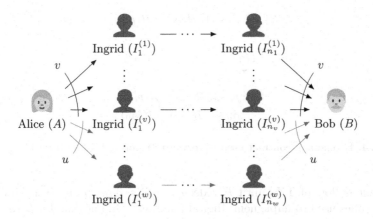

Fig. 3. The TF of amount v from A to B is implemented by the first v out of $w \triangleq v+u$ TXs of unit amount \$1 via $(I_1^{(1)}, \ldots, I_{n_1}^{(1)})$, ..., $(I_1^{(w)}, \ldots, I_{n_w}^{(w)})$.

3.1 Setup of Preimage Challenges

We assume that A and B have agreed out-of-band to partition their TF into v TXs of a unit of funds (\$1) each, without loss of generality (w.l.o.g.). In addition, they use u redundant TXs to improve their TF, so that the total number of TXs is $w \triangleq v+u$ (cf. Fig. 3). First, B chooses a polynomial $P(x)$ of degree $\deg(P) = v$ with coefficients $\alpha_0 \xleftarrow{\text{R}} \mathbb{Z}_q, \ldots, \alpha_v \xleftarrow{\text{R}} \mathbb{Z}_q$ drawn uniformly at random,

$$P(x) = \sum_{j=0}^{v} \alpha_j x^j. \tag{2}$$

Then, B commits to $P(x)$ by providing A with $H(\alpha_0), \ldots, H(\alpha_v)$. Due to the homomorphic property of H, Eq. (1), A can compute

$$\forall i \in \{1, \ldots, v, \ldots, w\}: \quad H(P(i)) = H\left(\sum_{j=0}^{v} \alpha_j i^j\right) = \prod_{j=0}^{v} H(\alpha_j)^{(i^j)}. \tag{3}$$

For the i-th TX, $p_i \triangleq P(i)$ is used as a preimage for HTLC-type forwarding. Hence, A uses $H(p_i) = H(P(i))$ from Eq. (3) as preimage challenge, and informs B out-of-band of which i was used.

To redeem the i-th TX, B reveals $p_i = P(i)$. Should B overdraw by revealing more than v evaluations p_i of $P(x)$, then $\alpha_0, \ldots, \alpha_v$ can be recovered using polynomial interpolation due to $\deg(P) = v$. Recall that α_0 serves as a secret which A can use to revert the TF in this case. As long as B reveals no more than v evaluations of $P(x)$, each α_i remains marginally uniformly distributed. In this case, the TF is final.

Note that A and B do not have to agree on u ahead of time. Instead, A can create virtually infinitely many $H(p_i)$ (as long as $w < q$), and hence send

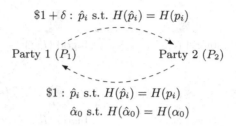

$$\$1 + \delta : \hat{p}_i \text{ s.t. } H(\hat{p}_i) = H(p_i)$$

Party 1 (P_1) Party 2 (P_2)

$$\$1 : \hat{p}_i \text{ s.t. } H(\hat{p}_i) = H(p_i)$$
$$\hat{\alpha}_0 \text{ s.t. } H(\hat{\alpha}_0) = H(\alpha_0)$$

Fig. 4. Boomerang contract used to forward \$1 plus δ TX fees from P_1 to P_2

a continuous flow of TXs until B redeems v TXs. This property is similar to rateless codes used to implement 'digital fountains' [4], and enables B to choose u adaptively during execution of the TF. Furthermore, since there is no risk in 'losing control' over a redundant TX, source routing can be abandoned in favor of the PN taking distributed routing decisions. Conceptually, the use of redundant TXs in PNs is analogous to the use of erasure-correcting codes [11] in communication networks consisting of packet erasure channels [18] and for straggler mitigation in large-scale distributed computing and storage [5,17].

3.2   Boomerang Contract

We devise the Boomerang contract, which implements reversible HTLC-type forwarding as required for Boomerang on top of a PC. Still, w.l.o.g. \$1 funds and δ TX fee are to be forwarded from party P_1 to party P_2.

Conceptually, the desired behavior could be accomplished by two conditional forwardings (cf. Fig. 4), the first of which ('forward', top arrow in Fig. 4) transfers \$1 $+ \delta$ from P_1 to P_2 upon revelation of a preimage $\hat{p}_i$ such that $H(\hat{p}_i) = H(p_i)$, and the second of which ('reverse', bottom arrow in Fig. 4) transfers \$1 back from P_2 to P_1 upon revelation of two preimages $\hat{p}_i$ and $\hat{\alpha}_0$ such that $H(\hat{p}_i) = H(p_i)$ and $H(\hat{\alpha}_0) = H(\alpha_0)$. Note that the two conditions are nested such that if P_1 redeems the second forwarding, then P_2 can redeem the first forwarding. As a result, the Boomerang contract has three possible outcomes. Either, *a)* neither forwarding is redeemed and P_1 retains all funds (*e.g.*, in the case of a timeout or an unused redundant TX), or *b)* only the 'forward' forwarding is redeemed (*i.e.*, B draws funds by revealing $P(i)$ but does not leak α_0), or *c)* both forwardings are redeemed (*i.e.*, B overdraws and reveals both $P(i)$ and α_0). Anyway, P_2 cannot loose funds and thus agrees to deploy the contract on the PC.

Note that Fig. 4 has been simplified for ease of exposition. Indeed, two essential aspects are not captured in Fig. 4 and necessitate the refined final specification of the Boomerang contract in Fig. 5. First, timeouts Δ_{fwd} and Δ_{rev} (relative to current time T_0) need to be chosen such that the source of the TF has time to detect overdraw and reclaim the funds ($\Delta_{\text{fwd}} < \Delta_{\text{rev}}$). Second, having two separate forwardings would requisition twice the liquidity (\$2 $+ \delta$) while the forwardings are pending. Instead, the Boomerang contract as specified by the flow charts in Fig. 5 allows for consistent timeouts with $\Delta_{\text{fwd}} < \Delta_{\text{rev}}$ and requisitions

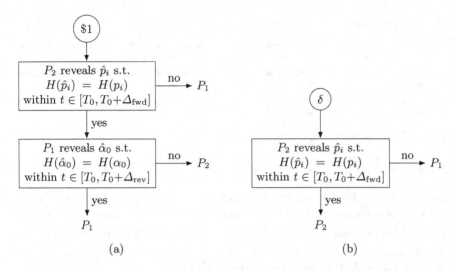

Fig. 5. Flow charts for payout of a Boomerang contract (cf. Fig. 4) concerning (a) \$1 funds and (b) δ TX fees between P_1 and P_2

the TX amount in PC liquidity only once (\$$1 + \delta$). We present an implementation of Fig. 5 in Bitcoin Script on top of Eltoo PCs [6] in Sect. 4. Throughout the paper, we use two circular arrows as in Fig. 4 to visualize a Boomerang contract.

3.3 End-to-End Procedure for Boomerang Transfers

Given the intertwined preimage challenges of Sect. 3.1 and the Boomerang contract of Sect. 3.2, we devise the end-to-end procedure for Boomerang TFs.

To forward a TX along a path from A to B via $I_1, \ldots, I_n$, the timeouts Δ_{fwd} and Δ_{rev} of the Boomerang contracts between A and I_1, I_i and I_{i+1}, and I_n and B need to be chosen in the following way: The forward components' timeouts

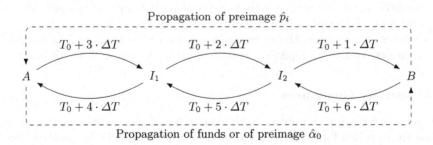

Fig. 6. Staggering of timeouts of Boomerang contracts: The Δ_{fwd} are chosen such that propagation of the preimage $\hat{p}_i$ from B via I_2 and I_1 to A is guaranteed once B reveals $\hat{p}_i$. The Δ_{rev} are chosen such that propagation of the preimage $\hat{\alpha}_0$ from A via I_1 and I_2 to B is guaranteed once A reveals $\hat{\alpha}_0$. (Color figure online)

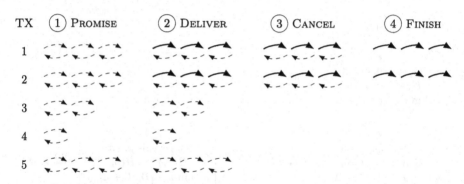

Fig. 7. Stages of a Boomerang TF (here using $w = v + u = 2 + 3$ TXs, each through two I_i): ① A attempts 5 TXs; TXs 1, 2 and 5 reach B, 3 and 4 do not. ② B claims TXs 1 and 2 by revealing $P(1)$ and $P(2)$. ③ The unsuccessful and outstanding TXs 3, 4 and 5 are cancelled upon request from B. ④ A relinquishes the option to retract TXs 1 and 2 as no further funds can be drawn by B.

decrease along the path from A to B. The reverse components' timeouts increase along the path from A to B. Additionally, the earliest reverse component expires later than the latest forward component, to allow A to react to overdraw and activate the reverse components. An example is illustrated in Fig. 6.

A Boomerang TF of v units using $w = v + u$ redundant TXs proceeds, after the setup of preimage challenges out-of-band, in four steps (cf. Fig. 7):

① PROMISE: A attempts $w = v + u$ TXs.
② DELIVER: B claims funds from up to v TXs by revealing the preimages $p_i = P(i)$ to the corresponding preimage challenges $H(p_i)$, activating the forward components of the Boomerang contracts along the respective paths.
③ CANCEL: Upon a request by B which is passed on to the tip of the path of an unsuccessful or surplus TX, outstanding TXs are cancelled. Note that cancellation is counterparty risk-free if it proceeds along the path from B towards A, and honest as well as rational participants have a self-interest in freeing up liquidity that will foreseeably not earn TX fees.
④ FINISH: A renounces the reverse components of the remaining Boomerang contracts to free up liquidity, as there is no more risk of B overdrawing.

3.4 Security Guarantees

We give the following guarantees to the source A and the destination B of a TF, respectively, which formalize security for the outlined Boomerang construction:

Theorem 1 (A-Guarantee). *If more than v of the redundant TXs are drawn from A, then A can recover α_0 and revert all TXs.*

Theorem 2 (B-Guarantee). *As long as B follows the protocol and draws no more than v of the redundant TXs, all TXs are final, except with negligible probability, provided the DLP is hard for $(\mathbb{G}, g)$.*

Corollary 1 (Proofs). *If A knows α_0, this proves that B cheated. If A knows p_i, this proves that B was paid accordingly. A can forge the proofs only with negligible probability, provided the DLP is hard for $(\mathbb{G}, g)$.*

Note that 'drawing' a TX means 'revealing the preimage $p_i = P(i)$ for the challenge $H(p_i)$ of TX i'. Hence, the above guarantees are statements about 'how much preimage information flows' 'into A' and 'out of B', implicitly assuming the worst-case that all intermediary I_i collude with the respective opposing party.

Proof (of Theorem 1: A-Guarantee). Due to the homomorphic property of H, and the fact that A computes the challenges $H(p_i)$ from the commitments $H(\alpha_0), \ldots, H(\alpha_v)$, there exists a unique polynomial of degree v that passes through all $P(i)$. This polynomial can be determined by interpolation, if more than v preimages $p_i = P(i)$ are revealed. Hence, in the case of overdrawing, A can be certain to obtain an α_0, such that A can activate the reverse components of the Boomerang contracts and revert all TXs.   □

Proof (of Theorem 2: B-Guarantee). It suffices to show that one cannot recover α_0 from $H(\alpha_0), \ldots, H(\alpha_v), P(i_1), \ldots, P(i_v)$, with $i_1, \ldots, i_v$ distinct, except with negligible probability, provided that the DLP is hard for $(\mathbb{G}, g)$.

W.l.o.g., assume that all preimages revealed by B have been forwarded to A. Call the task A faces *Alice's problem* (AP), *i.e.*, given an AP instance $(g^{\alpha_0}, \ldots, g^{\alpha_v}, P(i_1), \ldots, P(i_v))$ for known distinct $i_1, \ldots, i_v$, find α_0. We show that AP is computationally infeasible by reducing the DLP to AP.

The reduction proceeds as follows. Assume $\mathcal{B}$ is a blackbox that solves AP instances efficiently. Using $\mathcal{B}$, we construct a DLP solver $\mathcal{A}$. Present $\mathcal{A}$ with a DLP instance (g, g^a). $\mathcal{A}$ samples $P(i_j) \stackrel{R}{\leftarrow} \mathbb{Z}_q$ for $j = 1, \ldots, v$ uniformly at random, such that there exists a unique degree v polynomial interpolating $P(0), P(i_1), \ldots, P(i_v)$, with coefficients $\alpha_0, \ldots, \alpha_v$ chosen uniformly at random. Recall that $P(0) = \alpha_0 = a$ is unknown. By Eq. (2),

$$\underbrace{\begin{bmatrix} P(0) \\ P(i_1) \\ \vdots \\ P(i_v) \end{bmatrix}}_{\triangleq\, p} = \underbrace{\begin{bmatrix} 0^0 & 0^1 & \ldots & 0^v \\ i_1^0 & i_1^1 & \ldots & i_1^v \\ \vdots & \vdots & & \vdots \\ i_v^0 & i_v^1 & \ldots & i_v^v \end{bmatrix}}_{\triangleq\, M} \underbrace{\begin{bmatrix} \alpha_0 \\ \alpha_1 \\ \vdots \\ \alpha_v \end{bmatrix}}_{\triangleq\, \alpha}, \tag{4}$$

where the entries of M are fixed.

As M is a Vandermonde matrix and thus invertible,

$$p = M\alpha \quad \Longleftrightarrow \quad \alpha = M^{-1}p. \tag{5}$$

Let $\tilde{m}_{ij} \triangleq \left\{ M^{-1} \right\}_{ij}$ and $p_j \triangleq \{p\}_j$, where $\{X\}_y$ is the y-th entry of X. Then,

$$\alpha_i = \sum_{j=0}^{v} \tilde{m}_{ij} p_j. \tag{6}$$

Hence, using the homomorphic property of H from Eq. (1), obtain

$$\forall i \in \{0, \ldots, v\}: \quad H(\alpha_i) = H\left(\sum_{j=0}^{v} \tilde{m}_{ij} p_j \right) = \prod_{j=0}^{v} H(p_j)^{\tilde{m}_{ij}}. \tag{7}$$

Now, $\mathcal{A}$ has a tuple $(H(\alpha_0), \ldots, H(\alpha_v), P(i_1), \ldots, P(i_v))$ drawn from the distribution of AP instances implied by the Boomerang protocol. $\mathcal{A}$ invokes the AP oracle $\mathcal{B}$ and obtains $\alpha_0 = a$, which solves the DLP instance.

Thus, an efficient solution to AP implies an efficient solution to DLP. But since DLP is assumed to be hard, AP has to be hard, proving the claim. ☐

Proof (of Corollary 1: Proofs). Theorems 1 and 2 imply that A knows α_0 iff B cheated (except with negligible probability, provided the DLP is hard for $(\mathbb{G}, g)$).

For p_i to serve as proof of payment, it requires that for any $n \leq v$ and known distinct $i_1, \ldots, i_{n+1}$, A cannot obtain $P(i_{n+1})$ from $H(\alpha_0)$, ..., $H(\alpha_v)$, $P(i_1)$, ..., $P(i_n)$ (except with negligible probability, provided the DLP is hard for $(\mathbb{G}, g)$). For $n = v$, this follows from Theorem 2 by contradiction, as α_0 can be computed from $P(i_1), \ldots, P(i_{v+1})$. For $n < v$, the problem is harder than for $n = v$. ☐

4   Implementation in Bitcoin Script

We present an implementation of Boomerang in Bitcoin Script and its deployment on an Eltoo PC. For simplicity, we first present an implementation which hinges on a new opcode for $H(x)$. Subsequently, we refine the implementation to apply adaptor signatures based on Schnorr or ECDSA signatures instead.

4.1   Implementation Using an Opcode for $H(x)$

Assume the addition of a new command ECEXP$\langle g \rangle$ to Bitcoin Script for computing $H(x) = g^x \in \mathbb{G}$. The command would pop x off the stack and push g^x back onto the stack. The necessary cryptographic primitives to do this in ECs are already part of Bitcoin and only need to be exposed to the scripting engine. Then, ECEXP$\langle g \rangle$ can be used as a one-way function in similar situations as the SHA* or HASH* commands, but provides the homomorphic property that can be necessary or useful for applications beyond Boomerang.

We show how the mechanics of the Boomerang contract specified in Fig. 5 can be implemented using Bitcoin Script. To this end, we refer to the settlement transaction of the PC on top of which the Boomerang contract is deployed as TX$_{\text{settle}}$, and to transactions that P_i would use to pay a certain output to

Bitcoin Script implementation of output on $\mathsf{TX}_{\mathrm{settle}}$:

```
1   IF
2       ECEXP⟨g⟩  PUSH⟨H(pᵢ)⟩  EQUALVERIFY
3       2  PUSH⟨pk_{P₁,tmp}⟩  PUSH⟨pk_{P₂,tmp}⟩  2  CHECKMULTISIGVERIFY
4   ELSE
5       PUSH⟨T₀ + Δ_fwd⟩  CHECKLOCKTIMEVERIFY  DROP
6       PUSH⟨pk_{P₁}⟩  CHECKSIGVERIFY
7   ENDIF
```

Redemption for P_1 ('no' branch):

```
1   sig_{P₁}(TX_{payout,P₁})
2   FALSE
```

Redemption for P_2 ('yes' branch):

```
1   sig_{P₁,tmp}(TX_{retaliate})
2   sig_{P₂,tmp}(TX_{retaliate})
3   p̂ᵢ
4   TRUE
```

Bitcoin Script implementation of output on $\mathsf{TX}_{\mathrm{retaliate}}$:

```
1   IF
2       ECEXP⟨g⟩  PUSH⟨H(α₀)⟩  EQUALVERIFY
3       PUSH⟨pk_{P₁}⟩  CHECKSIGVERIFY
4   ELSE
5       PUSH⟨T₀ + Δ_rev⟩  CHECKLOCKTIMEVERIFY  DROP
6       PUSH⟨pk_{P₂}⟩  CHECKSIGVERIFY
7   ENDIF
```

Redemption for P_1 ('yes' branch):

```
1   sig_{P₁}(TX_{payout,P₁})
2   α̂₀
3   TRUE
```

Redemption for P_2 ('no' branch):

```
1   sig_{P₂}(TX_{payout,P₂})
2   FALSE
```

Fig. 8. Implementation of the \$1 outputs (cf. Fig. 5(a)), and witness stacks for redemption, for the two staggered $\mathsf{TX}_{\mathrm{settle}}$ and $\mathsf{TX}_{\mathrm{retaliate}}$ (cf. Fig. 9). For $\mathsf{TX}_{\mathrm{settle}}$: l. 2 enforces revelation of $\hat{p}_i$ s.t. $H(\hat{p}_i) = H(p_i)$, l. 3 requires signatures of the temporary identities $P_{i,\mathrm{tmp}}$ (created separately for each instance of the contract, and used to sign $\mathsf{TX}_{\mathrm{retaliate}}$ as part of the commitment to a forwarding), l. 5 enforces the timelock of $T_0 + \Delta_{\mathrm{fwd}}$, l. 6 requires a signature of P_1. For $\mathsf{TX}_{\mathrm{retaliate}}$: l. 2 enforces revelation of $\hat{\alpha}_0$ s.t. $H(\hat{\alpha}_0) = H(\alpha_0)$, l. 3 requires a signature of P_1, l. 5 enforces the timelock of $T_0 + \Delta_{\mathrm{rev}}$, l. 6 requires a signature of P_2.

themselves as $\mathsf{TX}_{\mathrm{payout},P_i}$. For the signature scheme employed by Bitcoin, an identity P has a public key pk_P and a private (secret) key sk_P. Using sk_P, a signature $\sigma \triangleq \mathsf{sig}_P(x)$ for string x can be created.

The implementation of Fig. 5(a) is provided in Fig. 8. The first condition of the flow chart in Fig. 5(a), which captures the forward component of the Boomerang contract, is implemented as an output of $\mathsf{TX}_{\mathrm{settle}}$. If this condition is met, the distribution of the funds is decided by an additional transaction $\mathsf{TX}_{\mathrm{retaliate}}$ which implements the reverse component of the Boomerang contract. $\mathsf{TX}_{\mathrm{retaliate}}$ is agreed-upon and signed by both parties using temporary one-time identities $P_{i,\mathrm{tmp}}$ as part of the deployment of a Boomerang contract. The implementation of Fig. 5(b) is provided in Fig. 11 of Sect. B.

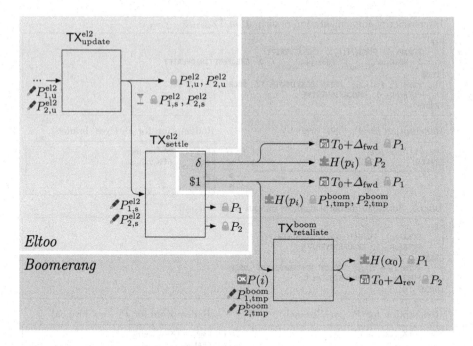

Fig. 9. A Boomerang contract is deployed as outputs and a thereon depending TX on top of the settlement mechanism of an Eltoo PC. (Legend: Boxes are Bitcoin transactions, an arrow leaving/entering a box indicates an output/input, respectively, labels along arrows indicate spending conditions, forks of arrows indicate alternative spending conditions, labels near TX inputs indicate redemption witnesses, 🔒 'requires signature of', ✒ 'signed by', ⚖ 'preimage challenge', ▣ 'preimage solution', 🗓 'absolute time-lock', ⧗ 'relative time-lock'.)

4.2 Implementation Using Adaptor Signatures

The dependency on a new opcode ECEXP$\langle g \rangle$ can be lifted by replacing the hash-lock with adaptor signatures [27] based on Schnorr signatures [20] or ECDSA signatures [22]. A primer on adaptor signatures is given in Sect. C. Rather than one party revealing a preimage x for a challenge $h \triangleq H(x)$ when publishing a TX to claim funds or advance a contract, P_1 and P_2 exchange an adaptor signature σ' for TX which either party can turn into a proper signature σ once they obtain x. Once TX gets published together with σ, the other party can derive x from σ and σ'.

4.3 Deployment of Boomerang on an Eltoo Payment Channel

Figure 9 shows a Boomerang contract for the i-th TX with preimage challenge $H(p_i)$ deployed on top of an Eltoo PC. Transactions and cryptographic identities belonging to Eltoo are marked with $(.)^{el2}$, those belonging to Boomerang are marked with $(.)^{boom}$. Figure 9 also illustrates Figs. 11 and 8.

5   Experimental Evaluation

We evaluate Boomerang in a low-fidelity prototype implementation[3] of the routing components inspired by the testbed of Flash [34]. First, we outline our experimental setup, then we specify the three contending schemes, and finally we present and discuss the observed performance.

5.1   Experimental Setup

The PN topology is drawn from the Watts–Strogatz ensemble where initially $N = 100$ nodes in a regular ring lattice are connected to their 8 nearest neighbors, and subsequently each initial edge is rewired randomly with probability 0.8. For each PC endpoint, its initial liquidity is drawn log-uniformly in $[\log(100), \log(1000)]$. The topology is static and known to all nodes; each PC's balance is only known to the PC's endpoints. 50000 TFs are generated as follows. Source and destination are sampled uniformly from the N nodes. The amounts are drawn from the Ripple dataset used in SpeedyMurmurs [30]. As in previous works, each node has a backlog of TFs it attempts to route one by one. We report sample mean and sample standard deviation of 10 PNs and TF traces.

Our implementation is a low-fidelity prototype of the routing and communications tasks. An abstract PN protocol accommodates different routing schemes (cf. Flash [34]). A TX takes place in two phases: First, in the RESERVE phase, Boomerang contracts are set up along a path from A to B if PC liquidity permits. A is notified whether RESERVE was successful. Second, in the ROLLBACK/EXECUTE phase, the chain of Boomerang contracts is either dismantled (ROLLBACK) or the funds are delivered (EXECUTE). An ABORT message can stop an ongoing RESERVE attempt. Purely informational messages (*e.g.*, outcome of RESERVE) are relayed without delay. Operations on the PC (*e.g.*, deploying a Boomerang contract) are simulated by a uniform delay from 50 ms to 150 ms. Note that PC balances are only discovered implicitly through failed/successful TX attempts, similar to the current state of affairs in Lightning.

The software is written in Golang 1.12.7. Every node is an independent process on a machine with 4× AMD Opteron 6378 processors (total 64 cores). The scenario is chosen such that the CPUs are never fully utilized to avoid distortion from computational limitations. The nodes communicate via 'localhost'.

5.2   Three Simple Routing Protocols

We compare three multi-path routing protocols (pseudo code given in Sect. D). 'Retry' (cf. Algorithm 2) initially attempts v TXs and reattempts up to u of them. 'Redundancy' (cf. Algorithm 3) attempts $v + u$ TXs from the start. 'Redundant-Retry(10)' (cf. Algorithm 4) is a combination of the two, which starts out with $v + \min(u, 10)$ TXs and reattempts up to $u - \min(u, 10)$ of them. The aim is to trade off the lower TTC of 'Redundancy' with the adaptivity of 'Retry'. TXs

---

[3] The source code is available on: https://github.com/tse-group/boomerang

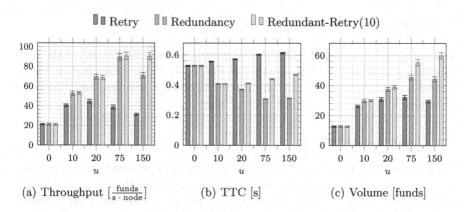

Fig. 10. (a) Average success throughput per node, (b) Average time-to-completion for successful TFs, (c) Average volume for successful TFs.

are routed on paths chosen randomly from a set of precomputed edge-disjoint shortest paths. All three schemes use atomic multi-path (AMP, [24]), *i.e.*, they only EXECUTE once enough successful TX attempts have been made to satisfy the full TF (cf. Algorithm 1). If the TF cannot be fully satisfied, all TXs are ROLLBACKed.

The baseline protocol 'Retry' is rather simplistic compared to recent developments [8,14,19,28–30,33,34]. We choose it because it resembles what currently can and is being done on Lightning. We conjecture that redundancy as a generic technique can boost AMP routing algorithms across the board.

5.3   Simulation Results

Our results are shown in Fig. 10. Supplemental plots can be found in [2, Section E, Fig. 12]. Previous works have gauged the performance of PN routing algorithms in terms of success volume or success count, *i.e.*, for a given trace of TFs, what total amount or number of TFs gets satisfied. However, these metrics are problematic. If TFs are spread out in time then more liquidity is available in the PN. This renders it easier to satisfy a TF and inflates these metrics.

Instead, we consider success throughput, *i.e.*, total amount of successfully transferred funds *per runtime*. The results for $v = 25$ are shown in Fig. 10(a) (cf. [2, Fig. 12(a)]). 'Redundancy' and 'Redundant-Retry(10)' show a 2× increase in throughput compared to 'Retry'.

Another relevant figure of merit is the average time-to-completion (TTC) of a successful TF, *i.e.*, how long is the delay between when the execution of a TF starts and when AMP is finalized. This determines the latency experienced by the user and for how long liquidity is tied up in pending AMP TFs. The results for $v = 25$ in Fig. 10(b) (cf. [2, Fig. 12(b)]) show a 40 % reduction in TTC for 'Redundancy' over 'Retry'. The larger u, the longer 'Retry' takes but the quicker 'Redundancy' completes. This plot also demonstrates how

'Redundant-Retry(10)' trades off between 'Retry' and 'Redundancy'. For $u \leq 10$, 'Redundant-Retry(10)' is identical with 'Redundancy' and hence follows the performance improvement of 'Redundancy'. For $u > 10$, the retry aspect weighs in more and more and 'Redundant-Retry(10)' follows a similar trajectory as 'Retry'.

Finally, Fig. 10(c) (cf. [2, Fig. 12(c)]) shows the average size of a successful TF, where 'Redundant-Retry(10)' outperforms 'Redundancy' by 30 % which in turn outperforms 'Retry' by 40 %. Note that the throughput of 'Redundant-Retry(10)' and 'Redundancy' are comparable. Thus, weighting between adaptively retrying and upfront redundancy trades off TTC and average successful TF volume, at a constant throughput.

Acknowledgments. We thank Giulia Fanti and Lei Yang for fruitful discussions. VB and DT are supported by the Center for Science of Information, an NSF Science and Technology Center, under grant agreement CCF-0939370. JN is supported by the Reed-Hodgson Stanford Graduate Fellowship. Icons from 'Twemoji v12.0' (https:// github.com/twitter/twemoji) by Twitter, Inc and other contributors, licensed under CC BY 4.0.

A   Cryptographic Preliminaries

Let $\mathbb{G}$ be a cyclic multiplicative group of prime order $q \geq 2^{2\lambda}$ with a generator $g \in \mathbb{G}$, where λ is a security parameter. Let $H: \mathbb{Z}_q \to \mathbb{G}$ with $H(x) \triangleq g^x$, where $\mathbb{Z}_q$ is the finite field of size q (i.e., integers modulo q). We require that H be difficult to invert, which is formalized in the following two definitions:

Definition 1 (Negligible Function). *A function $\varepsilon: \mathbb{N} \to \mathbb{R}^+$ is negligible if*

$$\forall c > 0: \exists k_0: \forall k > k_0: \qquad \varepsilon(k) < \frac{1}{k^c}. \tag{8}$$

In other words, negligible is what decays faster than every polynomial.

Definition 2 (Discrete Logarithm (DL) Assumption). *Given a generator g of a group $\mathbb{G}$, and an $x \xleftarrow{\text{R}} \mathbb{Z}_q$ chosen uniformly at random in $\mathbb{Z}_q$, for every probabilistic polynomial time (with respect to λ) algorithm $\mathcal{A}_{\text{DL}}$,*

$$\Pr[\mathcal{A}_{\text{DL}}(g, g^x) = x] = \varepsilon(\lambda). \tag{9}$$

The discrete logarithm problem (DLP) is said to be hard for generator g in group $\mathbb{G}$, if the DL assumption holds for g and $\mathbb{G}$, i.e., no computationally bounded adversary can compute $\log_g(g^x)$ with non-negligible probability. It is commonly assumed that the DLP is hard in certain elliptic curves (ECs), which are hence widely used in cryptographic applications, e.g., in Bitcoin. The DL assumption makes H a one-way function.

B   Implementation of Boomerang Contract in Bitcoin Script via Elliptic Curve Scalar Multiplication

See Figs. 8 and 11 for Bitcoin Script implementations of Fig. 5.

Bitcoin Script implementation of output on $\mathsf{TX}_{\text{settle}}$:

```
1   IF
2       ECEXP⟨g⟩  PUSH⟨H(p_i)⟩  EQUALVERIFY
3       PUSH⟨pk_{P_2}⟩  CHECKSIGVERIFY
4   ELSE
5       PUSH⟨T_0 + Δ_{fwd}⟩  CHECKLOCKTIMEVERIFY  DROP
6       PUSH⟨pk_{P_1}⟩  CHECKSIGVERIFY
7   ENDIF
```

Redemption for P_1 ('no' branch):

```
1   sig_{P_1}(TX_{payout,P_1})
2   FALSE
```

Redemption for P_2 ('yes' branch):

```
1   sig_{P_2}(TX_{payout,P_2})
2   p̂_i
3   TRUE
```

Fig. 11. Bitcoin Script implementation of the output concerning δ TX fee (cf. Fig. 5(b)), and witness stacks for redemption in favor of P_1 and P_2, respectively: l. 2 enforces revelation of $\hat{p}_i$ such that $H(\hat{p}_i) = H(p_i)$, l. 3 requires a signature of P_2, l. 5 enforces the timelock until $T_0 + \Delta_{\text{fwd}}$, l. 6 requires a signature of P_1.

C   Background on Adaptor Signatures

We briefly summarize Schnorr signatures [20]. Let $\tilde{H}$ be a cryptographic hash function (modeled as a random oracle), and $x\|y$ denote the concatenation of x and y. We continue to assume that $\mathbb{G}$ is a multiplicative group with group operation '·'. For Schnorr signatures, every identity is composed of a secret key x and a public key $P \triangleq g^x$. To sign a message m, draw $r \xleftarrow{\text{R}} \mathbb{Z}_q$, then compute $R \triangleq g^r$ and $s = r + \tilde{H}(P\|R\|m)x$. The signature is $\sigma \triangleq (s, R)$. To verify a signature $\sigma \triangleq (s, R)$ for m by P, check

$$g^s \overset{?}{=} R \cdot P^{\tilde{H}(P\|R\|m)}. \tag{10}$$

An adaptor signature σ' has the property that given σ', knowledge of a proper signature σ is equivalent to knowledge of a precommitted value t [27]. Consider parties P_1 and P_2 with secret keys x_i and public keys $P_i \triangleq g^{x_i}$. Both know a commitment $T \triangleq g^t$ to a (potentially unknown) value t. To create an adaptor signature σ' for m, both draw $r_i \xleftarrow{\text{R}} \mathbb{Z}_q$, compute $R_i \triangleq g^{r_i}$, and exchange (P_i, R_i). Then, they compute and exchange

$$s_i' = r_i + \tilde{H}(P_1 \cdot P_2\|R_1 \cdot R_2 \cdot T\|m)x_i. \tag{11}$$

The adaptor signature is $\sigma' = (R_1 \cdot R_2 \cdot T, s_1' + s_2')$. If either P_i gets to know t, they can produce a valid total signature $\sigma = (R_1 \cdot R_2 \cdot T, s_1' + s_2' + t)$. Vice versa, if either P_i learns a valid total signature $\sigma = (R_1 \cdot R_2 \cdot T, s)$, they can compute $t = s - s_1' - s_2'$. For instance, suppose m is a transaction that benefits P_2 and requires a signature from $P_1 \cdot P_2$ with nonce $R_1 \cdot R_2 \cdot T$. Furthermore, suppose P_2 obtains t. Then it can use the adaptor signature σ' to produce a valid total signature σ and claim its funds. In this case, P_1 can recover t from σ and σ'.

D   Pseudo Code of Evaluated Routing Schemes

See Algorithms 1, 2, 3 and 4.

Algorithm 1. Finalize AMP TF

1: **procedure** FINALIZEAMP($\mathcal{O}, \mathcal{P}, v$)   ▷ ABORTs outstanding TX attempts $\mathcal{O}$, EXECUTES/ROLLBACKs successful TXs $\mathcal{P}$ depending on number of required TXs v
2:    SendABORT($\mathcal{O}$)
3:    **if** $|\mathcal{P}| = v$ **then**
4:        SendEXECUTE($\mathcal{P}$)
5:    **else**
6:        SendROLLBACK($\mathcal{P}$)
7:    **end if**
8:    ReceiveRESERVEResponsesAndSendROLLBACK($\mathcal{O}$)
9: **end procedure**

Algorithm 2. 'Retry' routing scheme

1: **procedure** RETRY($\mathcal{T}, v, u$)   ▷ Split each TF $t \in \mathcal{T}$ into v TXs and retry u TXs
2:    **for** $t \in \mathcal{T}$ **do**   ▷ Source $t.s$, destination $t.d$, amount $t.v$
3:        $\mathcal{O}, \mathcal{P}, \mathcal{N} \leftarrow \emptyset, \emptyset, \emptyset$ ▷ TX attempts: outstanding $\mathcal{O}$, successful $\mathcal{P}$, failed $\mathcal{N}$
4:        $u' \leftarrow u$ ▷ Unused TX retries
5:        **for** $i = 1, \ldots, v$ **do**   ▷ Attempt v TXs
6:            $\mathcal{O} \leftarrow \mathcal{O} \cup$ SendRESERVE(RandomPath($t.s, t.d$), $t.v/v$)
7:        **end for**
8:        **while** $|\mathcal{P}| < v \wedge |\mathcal{O}| > 0 \wedge |\mathcal{P}| + |\mathcal{O}| + u' \geq v$ **do**   ▷ TF is contingent
9:            ReceiveAndClassifyRESERVEResponses($\mathcal{O}, \mathcal{P}, \mathcal{N}$)
10:            **for** new elements $r \in \mathcal{N}$ **do**
11:                SendROLLBACK(r)
12:                **if** $u' > 0$ **then**
13:                    $\mathcal{O} \leftarrow \mathcal{O} \cup$ SendRESERVE(RandomPath($t.s, t.d$), $t.v/v$)
14:                    $u' \leftarrow u' - 1$
15:                **end if**
16:            **end for**
17:        **end while**
18:        FINALIZEAMP($\mathcal{O}, \mathcal{P}, v$)
19:    **end for**
20: **end procedure**

Algorithm 3. 'Redundancy' routing scheme

```
1: procedure REDUNDANCY(𝒯, v, u)                    ▷ Split TFs t ∈ 𝒯 into v plus u redundant TXs
2:     for t ∈ 𝒯 do                                  ▷ Source t.s, destination t.d, amount t.v
3:         𝒪, 𝒫, 𝒩 ← ∅, ∅, ∅                        ▷ TX attempts: outstanding 𝒪, successful 𝒫, failed 𝒩
4:         for i = 1, ..., v + u do                              ▷ Attempt v TXs
5:             𝒪 ← 𝒪 ∪ SendRESERVE(RandomPath(t.s, t.d), t.v/v)
6:         end for
7:         while |𝒫| < v ∧ |𝒪| > 0 ∧ |𝒫| + |𝒪| ≥ v do          ▷ TF is contingent
8:             ReceiveAndClassifyRESERVEResponses(𝒪, 𝒫, 𝒩)
9:             for new elements r ∈ 𝒩 do
10:                SendROLLBACK(r)
11:            end for
12:        end while
13:        FINALIZEAMP(𝒪, 𝒫, v)
14:     end for
15: end procedure
```

Algorithm 4. 'Redundant-Retry(10)' routing scheme

```
1: procedure REDUNDANTRETRY(𝒯, v, u, 10)
2:     for t ∈ 𝒯 do                                  ▷ Source t.s, destination t.d, amount t.v
3:         𝒪, 𝒫, 𝒩 ← ∅, ∅, ∅                        ▷ TX attempts: outstanding 𝒪, successful 𝒫, failed 𝒩
4:         u' ← u − min(u, 10)                                  ▷ Unused TX retries
5:         for i = 1, ..., v + min(u, 10) do                    ▷ Attempt v + min(u, 10) TXs
6:             𝒪 ← 𝒪 ∪ SendRESERVE(RandomPath(t.s, t.d), t.v/v)
7:         end for
8:         while |𝒫| < v ∧ |𝒪| > 0 ∧ |𝒫| + |𝒪| + u' ≥ v do      ▷ TF is contingent
9:             ReceiveAndClassifyRESERVEResponses(𝒪, 𝒫, 𝒩)
10:            for new elements r ∈ 𝒩 do
11:                SendROLLBACK(r)
12:                if u' > 0 then
13:                    𝒪 ← 𝒪 ∪ SendRESERVE(RandomPath(t.s, t.d), t.v/v)
14:                    u' ← u' − 1
15:                end if
16:            end for
17:        end while
18:        FINALIZEAMP(𝒪, 𝒫, v)
19:     end for
20: end procedure
```

References

1. Aktas, M.F., Soljanin, E.: Straggler mitigation at scale (2019). http://arxiv.org/abs/1906.10664

2. Bagaria, V., Neu, J., Tse, D.: Boomerang: redundancy improves latency and throughput in payment-channel networks (2019). http://arxiv.org/abs/1910.01834

3. Benaloh, J.C.: Secret sharing homomorphisms: keeping shares of a secret secret (extended abstract). In: Odlyzko, A.M. (ed.) CRYPTO 1986. LNCS, vol. 263, pp. 251–260. Springer, Heidelberg (1987). https://doi.org/10.1007/3-540-47721-7_19

4. Byers, J.W., Luby, M., Mitzenmacher, M., Rege, A.: A digital fountain approach to reliable distribution of bulk data. In: Proceedings of ACM SIGCOMM, Vancouver, B.C., Canada, pp. 56–67 (1998). https://doi.org/10.1145/285237.285258

5. Dean, J., Barroso, L.A.: The tail at scale. Commun. ACM **56**(2), 74–80 (2013). https://doi.org/10.1145/2408776.2408794

6. Decker, C., Russell, R., Osuntokun, O.: eltoo: a simple layer2 protocol for Bitcoin. Technical report (2018). https://blockstream.com/2018/04/30/en-eltoo-next-lightning/

7. Decker, C., Wattenhofer, R.: A fast and scalable payment network with Bitcoin duplex micropayment channels. In: Pelc, A., Schwarzmann, A.A. (eds.) SSS 2015. LNCS, vol. 9212, pp. 3–18. Springer, Cham (2015). https://doi.org/10.1007/978-3-319-21741-3_1

8. Di Stasi, G., Avallone, S., Canonico, R., Ventre, G.: Routing payments on the Lightning network. In: Proceedings of IEEE iThings/GreenCom/CPSCom/SmartData, pp. 1161–1170 (2018). https://doi.org/10.1109/Cybermatics_2018.2018.00209

9. Dziembowski, S., Eckey, L., Faust, S., Malinowski, D.: Perun: virtual payment hubs over cryptocurrencies (2017). https://eprint.iacr.org/2017/635

10. Dziembowski, S., Faust, S., Hostáková, K.: General state channel networks. In: Proceedings of ACM SIGSAC, pp. 949–966, Toronto, Canada (2018). https://doi.org/10.1145/3243734.3243856

11. Elias, P.: Coding for two noisy channels. In: Information Theory, pp. 61–74. Academic Press (1956)

12. Feldman, P.: A practical scheme for non-interactive verifiable secret sharing. In: 28th Annual Symposium on Foundations of Computer Science (SFCS 1987), pp. 427–438, October 1987. https://doi.org/10.1109/SFCS.1987.4

13. Gudgeon, L., Moreno-Sanchez, P., Roos, S., McCorry, P., Gervais, A.: SoK: off the chain transactions (2019). https://eprint.iacr.org/2019/360

14. Hoenisch, P., Weber, I.: AODV–based routing for payment channel networks. In: Chen, S., Wang, H., Zhang, L.-J. (eds.) ICBC 2018. LNCS, vol. 10974, pp. 107–124. Springer, Cham (2018). https://doi.org/10.1007/978-3-319-94478-4_8

15. Jourenko, M., Kurazumi, K., Larangeira, M., Tanaka, K.: SoK: a taxonomy for layer-2 scalability related protocols for cryptocurrencies (2019). https://eprint.iacr.org/2019/352

16. Khalil, R., Gervais, A.: Revive: rebalancing off-blockchain payment networks (2017). https://eprint.iacr.org/2017/823

17. Lee, K., Lam, M., Pedarsani, R., Papailiopoulos, D., Ramchandran, K.: Speeding up distributed machine learning using codes. IEEE Trans. Inf. Theory 64(3), 1514–1529 (2018). https://doi.org/10.1109/TIT.2017.2736066

18. Luby, M., Shokrollahi, A., Watson, M., Stockhammer, T., Minder, L.: RaptorQ forward error correction scheme for object delivery. RFC 6330 (2011). https://doi.org/10.17487/RFC6330

19. Malavolta, G., Moreno-Sanchez, P., Kate, A., Maffei, M.: SilentWhispers: enforcing security and privacy in decentralized credit networks (2016). https://eprint.iacr.org/2016/1054

20. Maxwell, G., Poelstra, A., Seurin, Y., Wuille, P.: Simple Schnorr multi-signatures with applications to Bitcoin (2018). https://eprint.iacr.org/2018/068

21. Miller, A., Bentov, I., Kumaresan, R., Cordi, C., McCorry, P.: Sprites and state channels: payment networks that go faster than Lightning (2017). http://arxiv.org/abs/1702.05812

22. Moreno-Sanchez, P., Kate, A.: Scriptless scripts with ECDSA (2018). https://lists.linuxfoundation.org/pipermail/lightning-dev/2018-April/001221.html

23. Nakamoto, S.: Bitcoin: a peer-to-peer electronic cash system. Technical report (2008). https://bitcoin.org/bitcoin.pdf

24. Osuntokun, O.: AMP: atomic multi-path payments over Lightning (2018). https://lists.linuxfoundation.org/pipermail/lightning-dev/2018-February/000993.html

25. Pedersen, T.P.: Non-interactive and information-theoretic secure verifiable secret sharing. In: Feigenbaum, J. (ed.) CRYPTO 1991. LNCS, vol. 576, pp. 129–140. Springer, Heidelberg (1992). https://doi.org/10.1007/3-540-46766-1_9

26. Piatkivskyi, D., Nowostawski, M.: Split payments in payment networks. In: Garcia-Alfaro, J., Herrera-Joancomartí, J., Livraga, G., Rios, R. (eds.) DPM/CBT -2018. LNCS, vol. 11025, pp. 67–75. Springer, Cham (2018). https://doi.org/10.1007/978-3-030-00305-0_5
27. Poelstra, A.: Scriptless scripts (2018). https://download.wpsoftware.net/bitcoin/wizardry/mw-slides/2018-05-18-12/slides.pdf
28. Poon, J., Dryja, T.: The Bitcoin Lightning network: scalable off-chain instant payments. Technical report (2016). https://lightning.network/docs/
29. Prihodko, P., Zhigulin, S., Sahno, M., Ostrovskiy, A., Osuntokun, O.: Flare: an approach to routing in Lightning network (2016)
30. Roos, S., Moreno-Sanchez, P., Kate, A., Goldberg, I.: Settling payments fast and private: efficient decentralized routing for path-based transactions (2017). http://arxiv.org/abs/1709.05748
31. Schoenmakers, B.: A simple publicly verifiable secret sharing scheme and its application to electronic voting. In: Wiener, M. (ed.) CRYPTO 1999. LNCS, vol. 1666, pp. 148–164. Springer, Heidelberg (1999). https://doi.org/10.1007/3-540-48405-1_10
32. Shamir, A.: How to share a secret. Commun. ACM **22**(11), 612–613 (1979). https://doi.org/10.1145/359168.359176
33. Sivaraman, V., Venkatakrishnan, S.B., Alizadeh, M., Fanti, G., Viswanath, P.: Routing cryptocurrency with the Spider network (2018). http://arxiv.org/abs/1809.05088
34. Wang, P., Xu, H., Jin, X., Wang, T.: Flash: efficient dynamic routing for offchain networks (2019). http://arxiv.org/abs/1902.05260

DLSAG: Non-interactive Refund Transactions for Interoperable Payment Channels in Monero

Pedro Moreno-Sanchez[1]([✉]), Arthur Blue[2], Duc V. Le[3], Sarang Noether[4], Brandon Goodell[4], and Aniket Kate[3]

[1] TU Wien, Vienna, Austria
`pedro.sanchez@tuwien.ac.at`
[2] West Lafayette, USA
[3] Purdue University, West Lafayette, USA
{`le52,aniket`}`@purdue.edu`
[4] Monero Research Lab, Denver, USA
{`sarang,surae`}`@getmonero.org`

Abstract. Monero has emerged as one of the leading cryptocurrencies with privacy by design. However, this comes at the price of reduced expressiveness and interoperability as well as severe scalability issues. First, Monero is restricted to coin exchanges among individual addresses and no further functionality is supported. Second, transactions are authorized by linkable ring signatures, a digital signature scheme used in Monero, hindering thereby the interoperability with virtually all the rest of cryptocurrencies that support different digital signature schemes. Third, Monero transactions require an on-chain footprint larger than other cryptocurrencies, leading to a rapid ledger growth and thus scalability issues.

This work extends Monero expressiveness and interoperability while mitigating its scalability issues. We present *Dual Linkable Spontaneous Anonymous Group Signature for Ad Hoc Groups (DLSAG)*, a linkable ring signature scheme that enables for the first time *non-interactive refund transactions* natively in Monero: DLSAG can seamlessly be implemented along with other cryptographic tools already available in Monero such as commitments and range proofs. We formally prove that DLSAG provides the same security and privacy notions introduced in the original linkable ring signature [29] namely, unforgeability, signer ambiguity, and linkability. We have evaluated DLSAG and showed that it imposes even slightly lower computation and similar communication overhead than the current digital signature scheme in Monero, demonstrating its practicality. We further show how to leverage DLSAG to enable off-chain scalability solutions in Monero such as payment channels and payment-channel networks as well as atomic swaps and interoperable payments with virtually all cryptocurrencies available today. DLSAG is currently being discussed within the Monero community as an option for adoption as a key building block for expressiveness, interoperability, and scalability.

A. Blue—Independent Researcher.

J. Bonneau and N. Heninger (Eds.): FC 2020, LNCS 12059, pp. 325–345, 2020.
https://doi.org/10.1007/978-3-030-51280-4_18

1 Introduction

Bitcoin fails to provide meaningful privacy guarantees as largely demonstrated in the literature [11,12,26,33,42,46]. In this state of affairs, Monero appeared in the cryptocurrency landscape with the distinguishing factor of adopting privacy by a design principle, combining for the first time *stealth address* [44], *linkable ring signatures* [29], *cryptographic commitments* [38] and *range proofs* [16]. As of the time of writing, Monero has been regularly among the top 15 cryptocurrencies in market capitalization, has catered more than 6 million transactions since its creation [8], and is the most popular CryptoNote-style cryptocurrency [1]. Currently, the Monero blockchain processes around 4000 daily transactions and Monero coins are part of a daily trade volume of more than 76M USD [2]. Monero has, however, significant room for improvement. First, Monero suffers from *reduced expressiveness*: While cryptocurrencies like Bitcoin or Ethereum enable somewhat complex policies to spend coins (e.g., a coin can be governed by script-based rules), Monero only supports coins governed with (mostly a single) private key, reducing the functionality to simple transfer of coins with no policy associated with it.

Cryptocurrencies such as Bitcoin and Ethereum overcome this lack of expressiveness by adding a script language at the cost of fungibility [9] (i.e., transaction inputs/outputs can be easily distinguished by their script) and interoperability as those script languages are not compatible with each other. Thus, it is interesting to include new policies to spend Monero coins *cryptographically*, instead of including a scripting language that hampers fungibility and interoperability.

Second, Monero suffers from similar *scalability issues* as Bitcoin [18]: The permissionless nature of the Monero consensus algorithm limits the block rate to one block every two minutes on average. In fact, the scalability problem in Monero is more pressing. The crucial privacy goal in Monero relies on well-established cryptographic constructions to homogenize transactions: linkable ring signatures are used to obfuscate what public key corresponds to the signer of a transaction while commitment schemes and range proofs are leveraged to hide the exchanged amounts, ensure transaction validity and the expected coin supply. These key design choices make Monero transactions require higher on-chain footprint than transactions in other cryptocurrencies. Although used only for less than five years, the Monero blockchain has currently a size of 59.37 GB and grows at around 635 MB per month [4].

Given this trend, it would be interesting to enable payment channels and payment channel networks [6,30,41] in Monero, a scalability solution already adopted in Bitcoin and Ethereum where the transaction rate is no longer limited by the global consensus but rather by the latency among the two users involved in a given payment. However, this is far from trivial as current payment-channel networks are built upon script languages (e.g., hash-time lock contract) or digital signatures schemes such as ECDSA or Schnorr that are not available in Monero. Leveraging these techniques in Monero would hamper its fungibility.

In summary, the current state of affairs in Monero with respect to the reduced expressiveness, lack of interoperability, and severe scalability issues calls for a solution. Adopting solutions provided in other cryptocurrencies like Bitcoin and Ethereum is not seamlessly possible as they are not backwards compatible with Monero. Moreover, as aforementioned, the inclusion of a scripting language would hamper the fungibility and interoperability of Monero.

Our Contributions. In this work, we present *Dual Linkable Spontaneous Anonymous Group Signature for Ad Hoc Groups (DLSAG)*, the linkable ring signature scheme for Monero that improves upon the lack expressiveness, interoperability, and scalability guarantees in Monero. In particular:

- **Expressiveness.** We formalize DLSAG (Sect. 3), a new linkable ring signature scheme that relies only on cryptographic tools already available in Monero and improves its expressiveness. In a bit more detail, DLSAG enables for the first time that Monero coins can be spent with one of two signing keys, depending on the relation between a time flag and the height of the current block in the Monero blockchain.
- **Scalability.** We describe how to leverage the DLSAG signatures to encode for the first time non-interactive refund transactions in Monero, where Alice can pay to Bob a certain amount of coins redeemable by Bob before a certain time in the future. After such time expires, the coins can be refunded to Alice. Refund transactions are the building block that opens the door for the first time to scalability solutions based on payment channels for Monero (Sect. 6). In particular, we describe how to build uni-directional payment channels, payment-channel networks, off-chain conditional payments and atomic swaps.
- **Interoperability.** We further show that it is possible to combine the aforementioned payment channels protocols with the corresponding ones in other cryptocurrencies, making thereby Monero interoperable (Sect. 6).
- **Formal analysis.** We formally prove that DLSAG achieves the security and privacy goals of interest for linkable ring signatures, namely, unforgeability, signer ambiguity, and linkability as introduced in [29] (Sect. 3).
- **Implementation and adoption.** We have implemented DLSAG and evaluated its performance (Sect. 4) showing that it imposes a single bit more of communication overhead and smaller computation overhead as the current digital signature scheme in Monero, demonstrating thus its practicality. In fact, DLSAG is a new result that paves the way in practice towards an expressiveness and scalability solution urgently needed in Monero to improve its integration in the cryptocurrency landscape. DLSAG is actively being discussed within the Monero community as an option for adoption [7,36] and it is compatible with other CryptoNote-style cryptocurrencies [1].

Comparison with Related Work. Poelstra introduced the notion of *Scriptless Scripts* [40] as a means of encoding somewhat limited smart contracts that no longer require the Bitcoin scripting language. Malavolta et al. [31] formalized this notion and extended it to support Schnorr and ECDSA digital signatures. In this work, we instantiate the notion of Scriptless Scripts to realize conditional payments compatible with DLSAG and the current Monero protocol. Bitcoin payment channels [5,19,41] have been presented in the literature as a scalability solution for the Bitcoin blockchain. Bitcoin payment channels have been then leveraged to build payment-channel networks in academia [24,25,30] and in industry [6,39,41]. However, none of these solutions are compatible with the current Monero. They rely on either Bitcoin script [6,30,41], ZCash script [24], Ethereum contracts [25] or Schnorr signature scheme [39], none of which are available in Monero. Similarly, Bitcoin scripts have been leveraged to construct an atomic swap protocol [15]. We, instead, present a payment-channel network and atomic swap protocols that no longer require scripting language, and it is compatible with Monero. Goodell and Noether have proposed threshold signatures [23] for Monero whereas Libert et al. [28] proposed a logarithmic-size ring signature from the DDH assumption; although interesting, they do not address the expressiveness, interoperability and scalability issues considered in this work.

2 Background

Notation. We denote by 1^n the security parameter. We denote by $\mathsf{poly}(\lambda)$ a polynomial function in λ and $\mathsf{negl}(\lambda)$ a negligible function in λ. We denote by $\mathbb{G}$ a cyclic group of prime order q and by g we denote a fixed generator of such group. We denote by $(\mathsf{pk}, \mathsf{sk})$ a pair of public and secret keys. We denote by **pk** an array of public keys. We use letters A to Z to identify users in a protocol. We denote by XMR the Monero coins. Finally, we consider two hash functions: (i) $\mathsf{H_s}$ takes as input a bitstring and outputs a scalar (i.e., $\mathsf{H_s} : \{0,1\}^* \to \mathbb{Z}_q$); (ii) $\mathsf{H_p}$ takes as input a bitstring and outputs an element of $\mathbb{G}$ (i.e., $\mathsf{H_p} : \{0,1\}^* \to \mathbb{G}$).

Transactions. A Monero transaction [44] is divided in *inputs* and *outputs*. They are defined in terms of tuples of the form $(\mathsf{pk}, \mathrm{COM}(\gamma), \Pi\text{-}amt)$ where pk denotes a fresh public key, $\mathrm{COM}(\gamma)$ denotes a *cryptographic commitment* [38] to the amount γ and $\Pi\text{-}amt$ denotes a *range proof* [16] that certifies that the committed amount is within a range $[0, 2^k]$ where k is a system parameter. In particular, each input consists of a set of such tuples while each output consists of a single tuple. The set of public keys included in an input is called a *ring*. Finally, the transaction includes a digital signature σ for each input.

Inputs:

[0] $\{(\mathsf{pk}_1, \mathrm{COM}(v_1), \Pi\text{-}amt_1), \ldots, (\mathsf{pk}_{n-1}, \mathrm{COM}(v_{n-1}), \Pi\text{-}amt_{n-1}),$
$(\mathsf{pk}_A, \mathrm{COM}(5), \Pi\text{-}amt_A)\}$

Outputs:

[0] pk_B, $\mathrm{COM}(4)$, $\Pi\text{-}amt_B$;   [1] pk'_A, $\mathrm{COM}(1)$, $\Pi\text{-}amt'_A$

Authorizations:

[0] σ

Fig. 1. Illustrative example of a (simplified) Monero transaction. Alice (pk_A) contributes 5 XMR to pay 4 XMR to Bob (pk_B) and get 1 XMR back (pk'_A). Finally, the transaction is authorized with a ring signature σ from the input ring.

In the illustrative example shown in Fig. 1, we assume that Alice has previously received 5 XMR in the public key pk_A. We also assume that she wants to pay Bob 4 XMR. For that, Alice first should get Bob's public key (pk_B) and a fresh public key for herself (pk'_A) to keep the change amount. Second, Alice should choose a set of $n - 1$ output tuples $\{(pk_i, COM(v_i), \Pi\text{-}amt_i)\}$ already available in the Monero blockchain to complete the input. Finally, Alice should create a valid signature of the transaction content using the ring $(pk_1, \ldots, pk_{n-1}, pk_A)$ and her private key sk_A. For that, she uses a linkable ring signature scheme.

Linkable Ring Signatures. The signature scheme used in Monero is an instantiation of the *Linkable Spontaneous Anonymous Group Signature for Ad Hoc Groups* (LSAG)[1] signature scheme [29]. We recall the definition of LSAG in Definition 1. Here, we explicitly add a generic definition of the linking algorithm which was briefly mentioned in [29].

Definition 1 (LSAG [29]). *An LSAG signature scheme is a tuple of algorithms (KEYGEN, SIGN, VRFY, LINK) defined as follows:*

- $(sk, pk) \leftarrow \text{KEYGEN}(1^n)$: *The KEYGEN algorithm takes as input the security parameter 1^n and outputs a pair of private key sk and public key pk.*
- $\sigma \leftarrow \text{SIGN}(sk, \mathbf{pk}, m)$: *The SIGN algorithm takes as input a private key sk, a list $\mathbf{pk}$ of n public keys which includes the one corresponding to sk, a message m and outputs a signature σ.*
- $b \leftarrow \text{VRFY}(\mathbf{pk}, m, \sigma)$: *The VRFY algorithm takes as a public key list $\mathbf{pk}$, a message m and a signature σ, and returns 1 if $\exists sk, pk \leftarrow \text{KEYGEN}(1^n)$ s.t. $pk \in \mathbf{pk}$ and $\sigma := \text{SIGN}(sk, \mathbf{pk}, m)$. Otherwise, it returns 0.*
- $b \leftarrow \text{LINK}((\mathbf{pk}_1, m_1, \sigma_1), (\mathbf{pk}_2, m_2, \sigma_2))$: *The LINK algorithm takes as input two triples $(\mathbf{pk}_1, m_1, \sigma_1)$ and $(\mathbf{pk}_2, m_2, \sigma_2)$. The algorithm outputs 1 if $\exists (sk, pk) \leftarrow \text{KEYGEN}(1^n)$ s.t. $pk \in \mathbf{pk}_1$, $pk \in \mathbf{pk}_2$, $\sigma_1 := \text{SIGN}(sk, \mathbf{pk}_1, m_1)$ and $\sigma_2 := \text{SIGN}(sk, \mathbf{pk}_2, m_2)$. Otherwise, the algorithm outputs 0.*

Apart from the straightforward correctness definition, Liu et al. [29] define three security and privacy goals for a LSAG signature scheme. We present them here informally and defer their formal description to Sect. 3.2.

- **Unforgeability**: The adversary without access to the secret key should not be able to compute a valid signature σ on a message m.
- **Signer ambiguity**: Given a valid signature σ on a message m, the adversary should not be able to determine better than guessing what public key within the ring corresponds to the secret key used to create the signature.
- **Linkability**: Given two rings $\mathbf{pk}_1$, $\mathbf{pk}_2$, two valid signatures σ_1, σ_2 in two messages m_1, m_2, there should exist an efficient algorithm that faithfully determines if the same secret key has been used to create both signatures.

---

[1] Monero in fact uses a matrix version of LSAG (MLSAG) [37] to prove balance without revealing spent ring members. We describe here the simplest LSAG version but our constructions can be trivially extended to support matrix version.

Due to the lack of space, we defer to the full version [34] the detailed construction of LSAG used in Monero, and to [37] for its security and privacy analysis.

The current LSAG in Monero only supports transfer of coins authorized by a signature, reducing the expressiveness to payments. Adding a script language (as done in Bitcoin or Ethereum) would harm fungibility (i.e., transaction inputs/outputs can be easily distinguished by their script) and interoperability as those languages are not compatible with each other. Instead, in this work we aim to propose a signature scheme for Monero that cryptographically supports more expressive transaction authorization policies, without hampering the security and privacy guarantees of the current digital signature scheme.

3   Dual-Key LSAG (DLSAG)

3.1   Key Ideas and Construction of DLSAG

Our approach builds upon a *tuple format* defined as $((\mathsf{pk}_{A,0}, \mathsf{pk}_{B,1}), \mathrm{COM}(\gamma),$ $\Pi\text{-}amt, t)$ and that enables to spend it to two different public keys (and potentially two different users) depending on a flag t. A dual-key tuple deviates from the current Monero tuple in two main points (highlighted in blue): (i) it contains two public keys instead of one to identify the two users that can possibly spend the output; and (ii) it includes an additional element t that denotes a switch (e.g., $\mathsf{pk}_{A,0}$ is used if t is smaller than the current block height in the Monero blockchain) between the public keys.

Dual-key tuple format enables the encoding of the logic for a refund transaction. In the sample tuple shown above, assume that t signals that $\mathsf{pk}_{A,0}$ must be used. Then Alice must choose a ring of the form $(\mathbf{pk_0}, \mathbf{pk_1})$, containing $(\mathsf{pk}_{A,0}, \mathsf{pk}_{B,1})$ at some position, and sign with the secret key sk_A, that is, the secret key corresponding to the public key $\mathsf{pk}_{A,0}$. Conversely, if t signals that $\mathsf{pk}_{B,1}$ must be used, Bob can then sign with sk_B instead. Note that if a single user knows both sk_A and sk_B, such an user can always use a dual-key tuple independently of the value t.

The remaining step is to design a linkable ring signature scheme that supports this new tuple format. This, however, requires to address the following challenges.

Key-Image Mechanism. The ring signature scheme currently used in Monero achieves linkability by publishing the key-image constructed from the single public key. For instance, Alice produces a signature with sk_A; the signature will contain the key-image $\mathcal{I} = \mathsf{H}_\mathsf{p}(\mathsf{pk}_A)^{\mathsf{sk}_A}$. If Alice signs again with sk_A, the same key-image would be computed and this can be detected. To mimic this behavior while handling the dual-key tuple format, the challenge is to define a single key-image that uniquely identifies a pair of public keys $(\mathsf{pk}_0, \mathsf{pk}_1)$ and yet can be computed knowing only one of the signing keys sk_b. Similar to the Diffie-Hellman key exchange mechanism [20], our approach redefines the key-image as $\mathcal{J} = g^{\mathsf{sk}_0 \cdot \mathsf{sk}_1}$, fulfilling thereby the expected requirements: (i) knowing sk_b suffices to compute $\mathcal{J} := \mathsf{pk}_{1-b}^{\mathsf{sk}_b}$; (ii) it uniquely identifies $(\mathsf{pk}_0, \mathsf{pk}_1)$ since $\mathsf{pk}_{1-b}^{\mathsf{sk}_b} = \mathsf{pk}_b^{\mathsf{sk}_{1-b}}$.

Hardening Key-Image Linkability. The aforementioned key-image definition allows to link the pair of public keys $(\mathsf{pk}_0, \mathsf{pk}_1)$. However, it is crucial to make the key-image unique not only to the pair of public keys but also to the output that contains them itself. Otherwise, one of the users could create another dual-key tuple with the same pair of public keys, create a signature with it (and thus a key-image), and effectively make the funds in the original tuple unspendable since in Monero every key-image is only allowed to appear once. That can be mitigated by introducing a random unique identifier, m, to each output, and this identifier can be included in the computation of the key-image without violating the security and privacy guarantees of the signature scheme. In Monero, such an unique identifier can be constructed by hashing the transaction that included the output and the output's position in the transaction. Thus, we may view the rings used in DLSAGs as consisting of unique triples, $(\mathsf{pk}_0, \mathsf{pk}_1, m)_{[1,n]}$, and we define the *dual key-image* to be $\mathcal{J} := g^{m_j \cdot \mathsf{sk}_{j,0} \cdot \mathsf{sk}_{j,1}}$, for some $j \in [1, n]$ corresponding to the position of the true signer in the ring.

The rest is to follow the idea of the Monero LSAG modified to support the new linkability tag. Figure 2 introduces the details of the DLSAG construction.

- $(\mathsf{sk}, \mathsf{pk}) \leftarrow \textsc{KeyGen}(1^n)$: Choose $\mathsf{sk}_0, \mathsf{sk}_1$ uniformly at random from $\mathbb{Z}_q$, m as a bitstring chosen uniformly at random from $\{0,1\}^n$. Set both $\mathsf{pk}_b := g^{\mathsf{sk}_b}$ for $b \in \{0,1\}$. Output $\mathsf{sk} = (\mathsf{sk}_0, \mathsf{sk}_1)$, $\mathsf{pk} = (\mathsf{pk}_0, \mathsf{pk}_1, m)$.
- $\sigma \leftarrow \textsc{Sign}(\mathsf{sk}_b, \mathbf{pk}, \mathbf{tx})$: Parse: $((\mathsf{pk}_{1,0}, \mathsf{pk}_{1,1}, m_1), \ldots, (\mathsf{pk}_{n,0}, \mathsf{pk}_{n,1}, m_n)) \leftarrow \mathbf{pk}$. Sample $s_0', s_1, \ldots, s_{n-1}$ from $\mathbb{Z}_q$. Compute:

$$\mathcal{J} := \mathsf{pk}_{n,1-b}^{m_n \cdot \mathsf{sk}_b}; \quad L_0 := g^{s_0'}; \quad R_0 := \mathsf{pk}_{n,1-b}^{s_0' \cdot m_n}; \quad h_0 := \mathsf{H_s}(\mathbf{tx}\|L_0\|R_0);$$

Then, for $i \in \{1, \ldots, n-1\}$, compute the following sequences:
$$L_i := g^{s_i} \cdot \mathsf{pk}_{i,b}^{h_{i-1}}; \quad R_i := \mathsf{pk}_{i,1-b}^{s_i \cdot m_i} \cdot \mathcal{J}^{h_{i-1}}; \quad h_i := \mathsf{H_s}(\mathbf{tx}\|L_i\|R_i)$$

Now, solve for s_0 such that $\mathsf{H_s}(\mathbf{tx}\|g^{s_0} \cdot \mathsf{pk}_{n,b}^{h_{n-1}}\|\mathsf{pk}_{n,1-b}^{s_0 \cdot m_n} \cdot \mathcal{J}^{h_{n-1}}) = h_0$. For that, we get $s_0 = s_0' - h_{n-1} \cdot \mathsf{sk}_b$. Return: $\sigma = (s_0, s_1, \ldots, s_{n-1}, h_0, \mathcal{J}, b)$.
- $b' \leftarrow \textsc{Vrfy}(\mathbf{pk}, \mathbf{tx}, \sigma)$: Parse
  $(s_0, s_1, \ldots, s_{n-1}, h_0, \mathcal{J}, b) \leftarrow \sigma$; $((\mathsf{pk}_{1,0}, \mathsf{pk}_{1,1}, m_1), \ldots, (\mathsf{pk}_{n,0}, \mathsf{pk}_{n,1}, m_n)) \leftarrow \mathbf{pk}$

  For $i \in \{1, \ldots, n\}$, compute the sequences:
  $$L_i := g^{s_i} \cdot \mathsf{pk}_{i,b}^{h_{i-1}}; \quad R_i := \mathsf{pk}_{i,1-b}^{s_i \cdot m_i} \cdot \mathcal{J}^{h_{i-1}}; \quad h_i := \mathsf{H_s}(\mathbf{tx}\|L_i\|R_i)$$

  Return 1 if $h_0 = h_n$. Otherwise, return 0.
- $b \leftarrow \textsc{Link}((\mathbf{pk}_1, \mathbf{tx}_1, \sigma_1), (\mathbf{pk}_2, \mathbf{tx}_2, \sigma_2))$: If $(\textsc{Vrfy}(\mathbf{pk}_1, \mathbf{tx}_1, \sigma_1) \wedge \textsc{Vrfy}(\mathbf{pk}_2, \mathbf{tx}_2, \sigma_2)) = 0$: return 0. Else, parse: $(s_0, s_1, \ldots, s_{n-1}, h_0, \mathcal{J}_1, b_1) \leftarrow \sigma_1$ and $(s_0', s_1', \ldots, s_{n-1}', h_0', \mathcal{J}_2, b_2) \leftarrow \sigma_2$. Return 1 if $\mathcal{J}_1 = \mathcal{J}_2$, and 0 otherwise.

Fig. 2. Construction of DLSAG. For ease of exposition, we assume that the secret key sk_b corresponds with the public key $pk_{n,b}$. As noted before, the position of the true signer's public key is chosen uniformly random.

3.2   Security Analysis

We use the existential unforgeability of ring signatures with respect to insider corruption introduced in [14]. Signer ambiguity and linkability properties are similar to those in LSAG [29], adapted to DLSAG syntax for readability.

Definition 2 (Existential unforgeability of ring signature with respect to insider corruption). *Let λ be a security parameter, let N, q_H, q_S, q_C be natural numbers such that $q_C \leq N \leq \mathsf{poly}(\lambda)$, $1 \leq q_H \leq \mathsf{poly}(\lambda)$, $1 \leq q_S \leq \mathsf{poly}(\lambda)$. Let $(\mathbb{G}, q, g)$ be some group parameters from a Dual LSAG signature scheme* (KeyGen, Sign, Verify, Link). *Let $\mathcal{O}^C$ be a corruption oracle that can be queried up to q_C times which acts as a discrete logarithm oracle. Let $\mathcal{O}^S$ be a signature oracle that can be queried up to q_S times. Presume $\mathcal{O}^S$ takes as input some ring of public keys* **pk**, *message m, signing index ℓ, and parity bit b, and produces as output a valid signature. Let $\mathcal{O}^H$ be a random oracle that can be queried up to q_H times.*

The Dual LSAG signature scheme is said to be existentially unforgeable with respect to insider corruption if any PPT algorithm $\mathcal{A}$ has at most a negligible probability of success in the following game.

1. *The challenger selects a set of N public keys from the Dual LSAG signature scheme key space* $\boldsymbol{PK} \leftarrow \{(\mathsf{pk}_{1,0}, \mathsf{pk}_{1,1}, m_0), \cdots, (\mathsf{pk}_{N,0}, \mathsf{pk}_{N,1}, m_N)\}$ *and sends this set to the player $\mathcal{A}$.*
2. *The player is granted access to oracles $\mathcal{O}^C$, $\mathcal{O}^S$, and $\mathcal{O}^H$.*
3. *The player outputs a message m, a ring of public keys* **pk** $=\{(Y_{1,0}, Y_{1,1}, m_1'), (Y_{2,0}, Y_{2,1}, m_2'), \cdots, (Y_{R,0}, Y_{R,1}, m_R')\} \subseteq \boldsymbol{PK}$ *where $R \geq 1$ and a purported forgery (σ, b).*

The player $\mathcal{A}$ wins if Verify$(\boldsymbol{pk}, m, \sigma) = 1$ *and the following additional success constraints are satisfied:*

- *The keys in* **pk** *are distinct and every key $(Y_{i,0}, Y_{i,1}, m_i') \in$* **pk** *satisfies $(Y_{i,0}, Y_{i,1}, m_i') = (\mathsf{pk}_{j(i),0}, \mathsf{pk}_{j(i),1}, m_{j(i)}) \in \boldsymbol{PK}$ for some $j(i)$;*
- *$\mathcal{O}^C$ has not been queried with any $Y_{i,b}$ for any i;*
- *The purported forgery is not a complete copy of a query to $\mathcal{O}^S$ with its corresponding response.*

Definition 3 (Existential unforgeability with respect to insider corruption [14]). *For a fixed N, q_H, q_S, and q_C, if $\mathcal{A}$ is an algorithm that operates in the game defined Definition 2 in time at most t and succeeds at the above game with probability at least ϵ, we say $\mathcal{A}$ is a $(t, \epsilon, N, q_H, q_S, q_C)$-forger where ϵ is measured over the joint distribution of the random coins of $\mathcal{A}$ and the challenge set $\boldsymbol{PK}$.*

Definition 4 (DLSAG signer ambiguity [29]). *A DLSAG signature scheme with security parameter λ is signer ambiguous if for any PPT algorithm $\mathcal{A}$, on inputs any message m, any list* **pk** *of n public key pairs, any valid signature σ on* **pk** *and m generated by user π, such that $\mathsf{sk}_\pi \notin \mathcal{D}_t$ and any set of t private keys*

$\mathcal{D}_t := \{\mathsf{sk}_1, \ldots, \mathsf{sk}_t\}$ *where* $\{g^{\mathsf{sk}_1}, \ldots, g^{\mathsf{sk}_t}\} \subset \mathbf{pk}_b$, $n - t \geq 2$ *and* b *is extracted from* σ. *There exists a negligible function* $\mathsf{negl}(\cdot)$ *such that:*

$$\left| \Pr[\mathcal{A}(m, \mathbf{pk}, \mathcal{D}_t, \sigma) = \pi] - \frac{1}{n - t} \right| \leq \mathsf{negl}(\lambda)$$

Definition 5 (DLSAG linkability). *A DLSAG signature scheme is linkable if there exists a PPT algorithm* LINK *that takes as input two rings* $\mathbf{pk}_1, \mathbf{pk}_2$, *two messages* $\mathsf{tx}_1, \mathsf{tx}_2$, *their corresponding DLSAG signatures* σ_1, σ_2 *(with respective true signing indices* π_1 *and* π_2 *not provided to* LINK*), and outputs either 0 or 1, such that there exists a negligible function* $\mathsf{negl}(\cdot)$ *with the property that:*

$$\Pr[\mathrm{LINK}((\mathbf{pk}_1, \mathsf{tx}_1, \sigma_1), (\mathbf{pk}_2, \mathsf{tx}_2, \sigma_2)) = 1 | (\mathsf{pk}_{\pi_1}, m_{\pi_1}) \neq (\mathsf{pk}_{\pi_2}, m_{\pi_2})] +$$
$$\Pr[\mathrm{LINK}(\mathbf{pk}_1, \mathsf{tx}_1, \sigma_1), (\mathbf{pk}_2, \mathsf{tx}_2, \sigma_2)) = 0 | (\mathsf{pk}_{\pi_1}, m_{\pi_1}) = (\mathsf{pk}_{\pi_2}, m_{\pi_2})] \leq \mathsf{negl}(\lambda)$$

In this part, we state the theorems for the security of DLSAG. Due to the lack of space, we defer the security proofs to [34].

Theorem 1 (DLSAG unforgeability). *DLSAG signature scheme is existentially unforgeable against adaptive chosen-plaintext attack according to Definition 3 provided that the One-More Discrete Logarithm (OMDL) problem[2] is hard, under the random oracle model.*

Theorem 2 (DLSAG signer ambiguity). *DLSAG achieves signer ambiguity according to Definition 4 provided that the Decisional Diffie-Hellman assumption (DDH) is hard, under the random oracle model.*

Theorem 3 (DLSAG linkability). *DLSAG achieves linkability as defined in Definition 5 provided that the OMDL problem is hard, under the random oracle model.*

Further Security and Privacy Analysis. We have analyzed the security and privacy of the digital signature scheme. Recent privacy studies on Monero [27,35] show that composition of several transactions (and thus signatures) can lead to new threats and leakages. In particular, we observe that DLSAG allows an observer to track when the receiver spends his coin if the sender use the stealth address mechanism used in Monero to generate the one time address for the receiver. Such linkability issue can be mitigated if the receiver spends his coins as soon as he receives it. We defer to the full version [34] the discussion on this and others venues for future work in security and privacy.

4   Implementation and Performance Analysis

Implementation. We developed a prototypical C++ implementation [10] of DLSAG to demonstrate the feasibility of our DLSAG construction in comparison with the Monero LSAG. We have implemented DLSAG and LSAG using the

---

[2] The One-More Discrete Logarithm hardness assumption is defined in [13].

same cryptographic library, libsodium [3], and cryptographic parameters (i.e. the ed25519 curve) as currently used in Monero.

Testbed. We conducted our experiments on a commodity desktop machine, which is equipped with Intel(R) Core(TM) i5-7400 CPU @ 3.00 GHz CPU, 12GB RAM. In these experiments, we focus on evaluating the overhead of DLSAG over LSAG in terms of computation time and signature size.

Computation Time. The results depicted in Table 1 show that the running time of DLSAG is practically the same as the running time of LSAG in both signing and verifying algorithms. Thus, DLSAG could be included in Monero without incurring computation overhead. We estimate that the computation time for DLSAG is systematically a 7% smaller than that of LSAG. One of the main reasons is that in DLSAG, we eliminate the use of hash-to-point evaluations (e.g., as required in the old key-image mechanism). More specifically, for ring of size n, both DLSAG signing and verifying algorithms incur approximately $\approx 4n$ group operations and n hash-to-scalar evaluations while in LSAG, signing and verifying algorithms require additional n hash-to-point evaluations, which we see as the main factor for the differences in running time. Therefore, our evaluation shows that DLSAG does not impose any computation overhead in comparison to current LSAG. In fact, if adopted, DLSAG might even slightly improve the signature creation and verification times.

Signature Size. Here, we studied the overhead in terms of signature size, and thus indirectly the communication overhead imposed by DLSAG. We observed that in comparison to the LSAG signature, the signature of DLSAG has just one extra parity bit to indicate the position of the public key needed for verification (i.e., either pk_0 or pk_1). This short signature size can be achieved at the cost of higher tuple footprint. However, DLSAG enables off-chain payments and thus reducing the number of on-chain tuples required overall. In summary, this evaluation shows that DLSAG can be deployed in practice with almost no communication overhead and yet improves the scalability of Monero since it enables off-chain operations as we discuss later in this paper.

5   DLSAG in Monero

Bootstrapping DLSAG in Monero. DLSAG can be seamlessly added into Monero. First, Monero regularly performs network upgrades for consensus rules

Table 1. Running time (in milliseconds) of DLSAG and LSAG for different ring sizes

	LSAG		DLSAG	
Ring Size	SIGN	VRFY	SIGN	VRFY
5	1.929	1.835	1.771	1.699
10	3.863	3.789	3.665	3.428
15	5.873	5.577	5.625	5.512
20	8.045	7.952	7.516	7.428

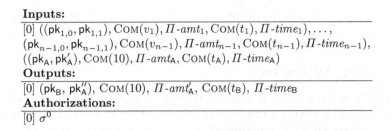

Fig. 3. A simplified Monero transaction using dual-key tuples and hidden timelocks.

and protocol improvements that allows for the integration of new functionality such as DLSAG. Second, it is possible to have transactions that mix LSAG with DLSAG. A mixed transaction will contain a LSAG signature for each single-key input and a DLSAG signature for each input in the dual-key format. In fact, both formats only differ in the number of public keys and the inclusion of an extra field (i.e. flag t). Thus, Monero operations and verifications on the commitment and range proofs remain compatible.

Fungibility. Different tuple formats coexisting on the blockchain may be detrimental to fungibility. For instance, miners might decide to stop mining certain transactions depending on the tuple format chosen. In order to mitigate that, we note that direct transfers using single-key tuples can easily be simulated by setting the two public keys of the dual-key tuples to belong to a single user. Thus, the fungibility of Monero may not be hampered with dual-key tuples only.

Backwards Compatible Timelock Processing. Dual-key tuples contain a flag t in the clear. We envision that this flag is implemented in Monero as a block height, so that given a pair $(\mathsf{pk}_0, \mathsf{pk}_1)$, pk_0 can be used before block t is mined and pk_1 is used afterwards. Although it is unclear and an interesting future research work, it could be possible that the different t values leak enough information for an adversary to break privacy, in the spirit of Monero attacks shown in the recent literature [27,35]. Given that, in this work we proactively propose an alternative timelock processing scheme that allows to have indistinguishable timeouts. This scheme, added as an extension to the dual-key tuple format and DLSAG signature scheme helps to maintain the fungibility of Monero. We note that this timelock processing could be of individual interest as timelocks are part of virtually all cryptocurrencies.

The core idea of the timelock processing scheme is as follows. Instead of including t in the clear, each output contains a Pedersen commitment to that value $\mathrm{COM}(t, r_1)$, where r_1 is the mask value which is included along with a proof (Π-$time$) that t is in the range $[0, 2^k]$. Now, one can prove that t has expired as follows: pick t' such that $t < t'$. If T is a block height such that $t' < T$, that would tell the miner that indeed $t < T$, and such a transaction will be mined only if the appropriate key is being used. In order to convince the miner that the relation $t < t'$ holds, the signer picks a random mask r_2 and forms the Pedersen commitment $\mathrm{COM}(t' - t, r_2)$, and includes this commitment along with the value

t', a range proof Π-*time* to prove that $t' - t$ is in range $[0, 2^k]$ and other ring member information.

5.1   Putting All Together

In this section, we use the illustrative example in Fig. 3 to revisit the processes of spending and verifying a transaction assuming that Monero includes dual-key tuples, supports DLSAG signature scheme and the timelock processing scheme.

Assume that Alice has previously received 10 XMR in the public key $(\mathsf{pk_A}, \mathsf{pk'_A})$ (i.e., input $[0]$). Assume that she wants to pay Bob for a service worth 10 XMR with a certain timeout t_B. Thus, either Bob claims the 10 XMR before t_B or Alice gets them refunded at the address $\mathsf{pk''_A}$. For this, Alice can create the transaction shown in Fig. 3. After this transaction is added to the Monero blockchain, Bob can get his coins by spending the output $[0]$. In the following, we describe the generation of this transaction and how it can be verified by the interested party (e.g., miners).

Transaction Generation. Assume that Alice wants to spend coins held in $(\mathsf{pk_A}, \mathsf{pk'_A})$. First, Alice invokes the SIGN algorithm for DLSAG on input $(\mathsf{sk_A}, ((\mathsf{pk}_{1,0}, \mathsf{pk}_{1,1}), \ldots, (\mathsf{pk}_{n-1,0}, \mathsf{pk}_{n-1,1}), (\mathsf{pk_A}, \mathsf{pk'_A}), \mathsf{tx})$, obtaining thereby a signature σ. Second, she has to use the timelock processing mechanism to prove that t_A has not expired. For that, she creates the tuple $(\mathrm{COM}(t_\mathsf{A}), t'_\mathsf{A}, \mathrm{COM}(t'_\mathsf{A} - t_\mathsf{A}), \Pi\text{-}time_\mathsf{A})$ as mentioned above. Similar to the problem of publishing commitment of amounts, publishing $\mathrm{COM}(t_\mathsf{A})$ would reveal what public key within the ring is being used, hindering thus signer ambiguity. Fortunately, we can adapt the approach in Monero to handle value commitments for $\mathrm{COM}(t_\mathsf{A})$ [34].

Transaction Validation. Every miner can validate the inclusion of Alice's transaction in a block at height T by checking whether $t'_\mathsf{A} < T$. If so, he proceeds to verify the range proofs for the commitment values. Next, he verifies that the DLSAG signature is correct using the corresponding VRFY algorithm. Finally, the miner checks that the dual ring signature is also correct using the VRFY algorithm as defined in DLSAG. We remind that using the extension of DLSAG as defined in the full version [34], the miner would have to verify only one dual signature, using the DLSAG verification algorithm.

6   Applications in Monero Enabled by DLSAG

6.1   Building Blocks

Commitment Scheme. A commitment scheme $\mathrm{COM} = (\mathrm{P_{COM}}, \mathrm{V_{COM}})$ consists of a commitment algorithm $\mathrm{P_{COM}}(m) \rightarrow (\mathsf{com}, \mathsf{decom})$ and a verification algorithm $\mathrm{V_{COM}}(\mathsf{com}, \mathsf{decom}, m) \rightarrow b \in \{0, 1\}$. The commiment scheme allows a prover to commit to a message m without revealing it, and the verficiation algorithm allows a verifiers to be able to verify that message m was committed using the revealed decommitment information decom.

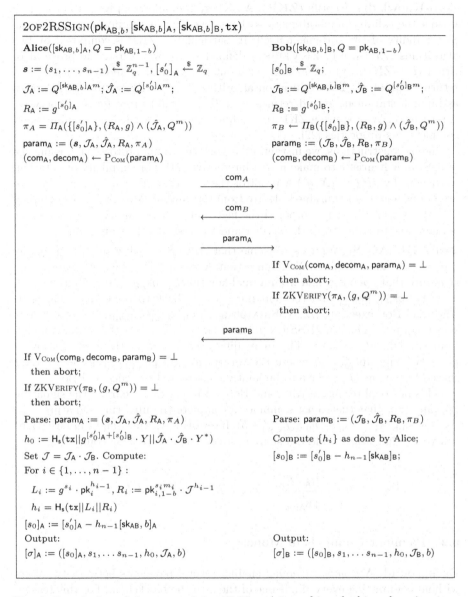

Fig. 4. Description of the protocol $2\text{OF2RSSIGN}(\mathsf{pk}_{\mathsf{AB},b}, [\mathsf{sk}_{\mathsf{AB},b}]_\mathsf{A}, [\mathsf{sk}_{\mathsf{AB},b}]_\mathsf{B}, \mathsf{tx})$, where $\mathsf{pk}_{\mathsf{AB}}$ denotes a one-time address shared between Alice and Bob, $[\mathsf{sk}_{\mathsf{AB},b}]_\mathsf{A}$, $[\mathsf{sk}_{\mathsf{AB},b}]_\mathsf{B}$ denote the Alice and Bob shares of the private key for $\mathsf{pk}_{\mathsf{AB},b}$, and tx denotes the transaction to be signed. The ring used was: $((\mathsf{pk}_{1,0}, \mathsf{pk}_{1,1}, m_1), \ldots, (\mathsf{pk}_{n-1,0}, \mathsf{pk}_{n-1,1}, m_{n-1}), (\mathsf{pk}_{\mathsf{AB},0}, \mathsf{pk}_{\mathsf{AB},1}, m))$ and omitted for readability. The pseudocode in light blue denotes the changes required to implement the $2\text{OF2RSSIGNCOND}(\mathsf{pk}_{\mathsf{AB}}, [\mathsf{sk}_{\mathsf{AB}}]_\mathsf{A}, [\mathsf{sk}_{\mathsf{AB}}]_\mathsf{B}, \mathsf{tx}, Y, Y^*)$ protocol, that additionally takes as input two group elements of the form $Y := g^y$ and $Y^* := \mathsf{pk}_{\mathsf{AB},1-b}^{ym}$. (Color figure online)

Zero-Knowledge Proofs (ZKP). A ZKP system allows a prover to prove to a verifier the validity of a statement without revealing more information than the pure validity of the statement itself. In particular, a ZKP is composed by two algorithms (ZKPROVE, ZKVERIFY) defined as follows. First, the prove algorithm $\Pi \leftarrow \text{ZKPROVE}(st, w)$ takes as input a statement st and a witness w and returns a proof Π. The verification algorithm $\top, \bot \leftarrow \text{ZKVERIFY}(st, \Pi)$ takes as input a statement st and returns $\top$ if Π is a valid proof for st. Otherwise, it returns $\bot$. We require a ZKP that fulfills the zero-knowledge, soundness and completeness properties [22].

In our constructions, we instantiate it with the sigma protocol [45], using the Fiat-Shamir heuristic to make it non-interactive [21]. For simplicity of notation, we denote by $\Pi(\{x\}, (X, g))$ a proof of the fact that $X = g^x$ where X and g are public and x is maintained private from the verifier. Moreover, we denote by $\Pi(\{x\}, (X, g) \wedge (X', g'))$ a proof of the fact that $X = g^x$ and $X' = g'^x$, where x is maintained private from the verifier and the rest of values are public.

2-of-2 DLSAG Signatures. Assume that Alice and Bob want to jointly pay a receiver R for a service. We require that Alice and Bob jointly create a ring signature that spends γ XMR from a dual-key $(\text{pk}_{AB,0}, \text{pk}_{AB,1})$, distributing them as γ' to $(\text{pk}_{R,0}, \text{pk}_{R,1})$ and the remaining $\gamma - \gamma'$ back to themselves. For that, Alice and Bob execute $2\text{OF}2\text{RSSIGN}(\text{pk}_{AB,b}, [\text{sk}_{AB,b}]_A, [\text{sk}_{AB,b}]_B, \text{tx})$ protocol, as shown in Fig. 4. The $2\text{OF}2\text{RSSIGN}$ protocol largely resembles the SIGN algorithm from the DLSAG scheme. The main difference comes in the computation of $h_0 = \text{H}_s(\text{tx} \| g^r \| \text{pk}_{AB,1-b}^{rm})$ where the targets g^r and $\text{pk}_{AB,1-b}^{rm}$, as well as their shared key-image $\mathcal{J}_{AB}$, have to be jointly constructed by Alice and Bob.

This protocol results in Alice and Bob obtaining their share of the signature $[\sigma]_A$ and $[\sigma]_B$ that they must combine to complete the final ring signature $\sigma := ([s_0]_A + [s_0]_B, s_1, \ldots s_{n-1}, h_0, (\mathcal{J}_A \cdot \mathcal{J}_B), b)$. Interestingly, Alice (and similarly Bob) can verify that $[\sigma]_B$ is indeed a share of a valid signature σ by computing

$$g^{([s_0]_A + [s_0]_B)} \stackrel{?}{=} \frac{(R_A \cdot R_B)}{\text{pk}_{AB,b}^{h_{n-1}}}, \text{ where } R_A = g^{[s_0']_A} \text{ and } R_B = g^{[s_0']_B}$$

6.2   Payment Channels in Monero

Background. A *payment channel* enables several payments between two users without committing every single one of them to the blockchain. For this reason, *payment channels* are being widely developed as a scalability solution in cryptocurrencies such as Bitcoin [41]. However, the conceptual differences between Monero and Bitcoin hinder a seamless adoption of Bitcoin payment channels in Monero. We instead leverage the refund transactions described in this work.

The lifecycle of a payment channel between Alice and Bob consists of three steps. First, Alice and Bob must *open* a payment channel by including an on-chain transaction that transfers XMR from Alice into a public key pk_{AB} whose private key sk_{AB} is shared by Alice and Bob, that is, Alice holds $[\text{sk}_{AB}]_A$ and Bob holds $[\mathsf{sk_{AB}}]_B$ such that $[\mathsf{sk_{AB}}]_A + [\mathsf{sk_{AB}}]_B = \mathsf{sk_{AB}}$. Second, they perform *off-chain payments* by locally adjusting how many XMR each of them gets from the shared address. Finally, they must *close* the payment channel by submitting a second on-chain transaction that distributes the XMR from the shared address to Alice and Bob as defined by the last balance agreed off-chain. Thus, payment channels require only two on-chain transactions (open and close) but allow for many off-chain payments to take place during its life time. In the following, we show our design of payments channel using the building blocks explained in Sect. 6.1.

Open a Payment Channel. Assume that Alice holds γ XMR in a dual key $(\mathsf{pk_{A,0}}, \mathsf{pk_{A,1}})$ and she wants to create a payment channel with Bob. First, she transfers γ XMR to a dual key of the form $(\mathsf{pk_{AB}}, \mathsf{pk'_A})$ and sets the timeout to a desired block height t. This way, if Bob never manages to coordinate with Alice to spend from $\mathsf{pk_{AB}}$, she will automatically regain control of her funds after that height, eliminating the need for a separate refund transaction. On the other hand, if Bob has received any off-chain transfers from $\mathsf{pk_{AB}}$, he needs to be sure to put the final balance in a transaction on chain before the block with height t is published.

Off-chain Payments. Assume that Alice wants to pay $\gamma' < \gamma$ XMR to Bob using the aforementioned payment channel. For that, Alice transfers γ' XMR from $(\mathsf{pk_{AB}}, \mathsf{pk_A})$ to a Bob's dual address $(\mathsf{pk_{B,0}}, \mathsf{pk_{B,1}})$ and the change $\gamma - \gamma'$ XMR back to an Alice's dual address $(\mathsf{pk_{A,0}}, \mathsf{pk_{A,1}})$. As the XMR are being spent from the shared address $\mathsf{pk_{AB}}$, the transaction must be signed by both users to be valid. The cornerstone of payment channels, however, is that only Alice signs otx and gives her share of the signature $[\sigma]_A$ to Bob, who can in turn verify it. At this point, Bob publish the transaction and get the γ' XMR before the timelock expires. Instead, Bob locally stores otx and the corresponding signature $[\sigma]_A$ until either Bob receives another off-chain payment for a value higher than γ' XMR or the channel is about to expire.

Close Channel. The channel between Alice and Bob can be closed for two reasons. First, Bob does not wish to receive more off-chain payments from Alice. Then, assume that Bob got a pair $(\mathsf{tx}, [\sigma]_A)$, where tx is the last agreed balance. He can simply complete σ' with his own share $[\sigma']_B$ and publish the transaction. Second, if the timelock included in the deposit transaction expires, and Alice regains control of the original γ XMR deposited.

6.3   Conditional Payments in Monero

A *conditional payment* only becomes valid if the receiver can give the solution to a cryptographic problem such as finding the preimage of a hash value or solving an instance of the discrete logarithm problem. Conditional payments open many new applications such as payment-channel networks as well as atomic swaps and therefore we consider them of independent interest.

We aim to simulate the following *Discrete-log Timelock Contract (DTLC)* contract defined on a group element $Y = g^y$, an amount γ of XMR and a timeout

t. **DTLC (Alice, Bob, Y, γ, t):** (i) If Bob produces a value y such that $g^y = Y$ before t days, Alice pays Bob γ XMR; (ii) If t elapses, Alice gets the γ XMR back.

Here, we describe our implementation of the **DTLC** contract by means of an example. Assume that Alice and Bob got γ XMR in a dual address ($\mathsf{pk_{AB}}$, $\mathsf{pk_A}$) created, for instance, in the opening of a payment channel between Alice and Bob. Further assume that Alice wants to perform a conditional payment (ctx) for $\gamma' < \gamma$ XMR to Bob conditioned on him knowing the discrete logarithm of Y.

Alice and Bob sign ctx using the 2OF2RSSIGNCOND protocol (Fig. 4, light blue pseudocode) on the condition Y. The cornerstone of this protocol is to imagine that there are three users instead of two that jointly execute the protocol: Alice, who contributes $([s_0']_A, [\mathsf{sk_{AB}}]_A)$, Bob, who contributes $([s_0']_B, [\mathsf{sk_{AB}}]_B)$, and a "third user" who contributes (y, y). After running the protocol, Alice and Bob obtain $[\sigma]_A$ and $[\sigma]_B$, but they also require y to complete the signature.

Therefore, after running the 2OF2RSSIGNCOND protocol, Bob gives his signature share $[\sigma]_B$ to Alice who in turn can verify its validity and reply with her signature share $[\sigma]_A$. This exchange, in this order, ensures that ctx is only published if value y is revealed and if the height lock ℓ has not been reached.

Now we note that whenever Bob claims his XMR at the ctx, he should provide the signature σ that contains $[s_0']_A + [s_0']_B + y$, and Bob can do this only if he knows the value y. But as soon as that signature is published, Alice trivially learns y from σ as she already knows $[\sigma]_A$ and $[\sigma]_B$. Additionally, we note that the values y and Y remain invisible, and therefore outside observers cannot use them to link this transaction with any other transactions using the same condition values (e.g. the counterpart transaction in an atomic swap). In fact, this transaction is indistinguishable from those Monero transactions that can be spent unconditionally, contributing thereby to the fungibility (and thus the overall privacy) of the Monero cryptocurrency.

6.4   Payment-Channel Network in Monero

Assume that Alice wants to perform an off-chain payment to Dave using a path of opened payment channels of the form Alice, Bob, Carol, Dave. Such a payment is performed in three phases. First, Dave creates a condition $(Y := g^y, Y^* := \mathsf{pk}_{\mathsf{CD},1}^{ym})$ and communicates the conditions (Y, Y^*) to Alice. Second, Alice creates a conditional payment to Bob under condition (Y, Y^*), who in turn creates a conditional payment to Carol under the same condition, and finally Carol creates the last conditional payment to Dave under condition (Y, Y^*). Finally, in the third phase, Dave reveals y to Carol to pull the coins from her, who in turn, reveals y to Bob and finally Bob to Alice.

We have to overcome a subtle but crucial challenge to make such construction fully compatible with Monero. The problem consists on that the same condition (Y, Y^*) cannot be used by every pair of users in the path: While g is the same for every user, each Y_i^* requires the value y (only known by Dave before the payment is settled) and the dual address ($\mathsf{pk}_{P_i P_{i+1}}$, pk_{P_i}) that defines each of the payment channels (and therefore only known by the two users sharing the channel). To overcome that, we add an extra round of communication where each pair of users forward to the receiver of the payment their shared address' refund address multiplied by their output identifier (i.e., $\mathsf{pk}_A^{m_{AB}}$ where pk_A is the refund address of the pair $(\mathsf{pk}_{AB}, \mathsf{pk}_A)$). Upon reception of these values, the receiver computes the pair (Y, Y_i^*) for each user along with a zero-knowledge proof of the fact that both condition values are constructed as expected. Finally, the receiver sends these conditions and proofs back to each user in the payment path from the receiver to the sender.

Now, before setting the conditional payment, each user must validate the zero-knowledge proof produced by the receiver to ensure that the condition for the incoming payment is built upon the same value y as the condition for the outgoing payment. It is important to note that soundness of the zero-knowledge scheme does not allow Dave to cheat on the proof and still be correctly validated by other users. Otherwise, it could be the situation that an intermediate user loses coins because his outgoing payment goes through but cannot use the same value y for unlocking the incoming payment.

6.5 Atomic Swaps

Monero does not support *Hash Timelock Contract* **HTLC** [43], the building block for atomic swaps in other cryptocurrencies. Instead, we leverage DTLC-based conditional payments (Sect. 6.3) to enable atomic swaps between Monero and other cryptocurrencies. We describe our approach with an example.

Assume that Alice has 1 bitcoin and wants to exchange it by 1 XMR from Bob. For that, Alice first creates a value y and sets $h := \mathsf{H}(y)$, $Y := g^y$, $Y^* := \mathsf{pk}_{AB,1}^y$. She then creates a zero-knowledge proof Π of the fact that the discrete logarithm of Y w.r.t. g and Y^* w.r.t. $\mathsf{pk}_{AB,1}^m$ are the same as the pre-image of h. Second, Alice creates a Bitcoin transaction that transfers her 1 bitcoin to Bob using the **HTLC**(Alice, Bob, h, 1, 1 day). Finally, Alice gives h, Y, Y^* and Π to Bob.

The idea now is that Bob creates a Monero conditional payment conditioned on (Y, Y^*), as described in Sect. 6.3, that transfers his 1 XMR to Alice. However, Bob must first check that indeed the discrete-log of Y and Y^* is also the pre-image of h so that the swap is indeed atomic. Otherwise, Alice could simply claim the 1 XMR from Bob but Bob could not claim the bitcoin from Alice. Bob ensures the atomicity of the swap by checking the validity of the proof Π.

We note that the above protocol requires a zero-knowledge proof protocol such as ZK-Boo [17] or Bulletproofs [16] to prove knowledge of the pre-image of a hash value. We also note that if Schnorr signatures are available in both cryptocurrencies or **HTLC** is substituted by discrete-log based constructions [31], zero-knowledge proofs may not be needed.

7   Concluding Remarks and Outlook

We present DLSAG, a linkable ring signature scheme that serves as a building block to improve expressiveness, interoperability, and scalability in Monero. We have formally proven that DLSAG provides unforgeability, sender ambiguity, and linkability. We also evaluate the performance of DLSAG showing that DLSAG provides a single bit of communication overhead while slightly reducing the computation overhead when compared to current LSAG. Moreover, we contribute additional cryptographic schemes (e.g., timelock processing) to help to maintain the fungibility of Monero. DLSAG enables payment channels, payment channel networks, and atomic swaps for the first time in Monero. DLSAG is currently under consideration by Monero researchers as an option for adoption and it is also compatible with other CryptoNote-style cryptocurrencies [1].

Outlook. In the future, we identify the following future research directions:

– **Bi-directional payment channels:** In this work, we present a construction for uni-directional payment channels. An extension is thus the design and implementation of bi-directional payment channels. In particular, we find interesting to investigate if techniques in other scalability solutions, such as the Lightning Network, are compatible with our payment channels or what are the challenges otherwise.
– **Further expressiveness:** We envision that expressiveness of DLSAG could be expanded with threshold signatures similar to those of Thring [23] and key aggregation similar to that of [32]. A thorough investigation of these approaches constitutes a venue for future research.
– **Extend security and privacy models:** So far, security and privacy definitions for Monero focus on individual signatures. However, recent studies [27,35] show that an adversary that considers several transactions (and thus several signatures) at a time, can create profiling information about the users. Thus, new security and privacy models are required to further characterized the security and privacy notions provided by the complete Monero cryptocurrency. Moreover, we plan to study the privacy guarantees provided by suggested extensions such as the timelock processing scheme.
– **Timelock offset analysis and mitigations:** To prove to the network that a certain timelock t has or has not expired, the signer publishes the timelock offset value t', which leaks information about the position of the real timelock t, which in turn leaks information about whether a certain ring is likely to represent the spend of an output that was controlled by two different parties, or just one. Coming up with heuristics to separate those two cases, on one hand; on the other hand, figuring out the correct timelock distributions to draw t from for transactions where it is not meaningfully being used should become interesting areas of research.
– **New privacy implications:** With the use of DLSAG and the new key image mechanism, we introduce a new privacy implication in the Monero blockchain. In particular, given two rings and their corresponding signatures, the sender can determine whether the two truly spent public keys belong to the same user (i.e., the two public keys where derived from the same stealth address with randomness provided by the sender herself). We refer to the full version [34] for the detailed description of the traceability method and practical countermeasures.

Acknowledgments. This work has been partially supported by the Austrian Science Fund (FWF) through the Lisa Meitner program and by the National Science Foundation under grant CNS-1846316.

References

1. Cryptonote currencies. https://cryptonote.org/coins
2. https://coinmarketcap.com/, https://coinmarketcap.com/
3. Libsodium documentation. https://libsodium.gitbook.io/doc/
4. Monero monthly blockchain growth. https://moneroblocks.info/stats/blockchain-growth
5. Payment channels. https://en.bitcoin.it/wiki/Payment_channels
6. Raiden network. https://raiden.network/
7. Research meeting, 17:00 UTC, 18 March 2019. https://github.com/monero-project/meta/issues/319
8. Understanding the structure of Monero's LMDB and how explore its contents using mdb_stat. https://monero.stackexchange.com/questions/10919/understanding-the-structure-of-moneros-lmdb-and-how-explore-its-contents-using
9. What is Fungibility? https://www.investopedia.com/terms/f/fungibility.asp
10. DLSAG prototype numbers (2019). https://github.com/levduc/DLSAG-prototype-number
11. Androulaki, E., Karame, G.O., Roeschlin, M., Scherer, T., Capkun, S.: Evaluating user privacy in Bitcoin. In: Sadeghi, A.-R. (ed.) FC 2013. LNCS, vol. 7859, pp. 34–51. Springer, Heidelberg (2013). https://doi.org/10.1007/978-3-642-39884-1_4
12. Barber, S., Boyen, X., Shi, E., Uzun, E.: Bitter to better—how to make Bitcoin a better currency. In: Keromytis, A.D. (ed.) FC 2012. LNCS, vol. 7397, pp. 399–414. Springer, Heidelberg (2012). https://doi.org/10.1007/978-3-642-32946-3_29
13. Bellare, Namprempre, Pointcheval, Semanko: The one-more-RSA-inversion problems and the security of Chaum's blind signature scheme. J. Cryptology **16**(3), 185–215 (2003). https://doi.org/10.1007/s00145-002-0120-1
14. Bender, A., Katz, J., Morselli, R.: Ring signatures: stronger definitions, and constructions without random oracles. In: Halevi, S., Rabin, T. (eds.) TCC 2006. LNCS, vol. 3876, pp. 60–79. Springer, Heidelberg (2006). https://doi.org/10.1007/11681878_4
15. Bowe, S., Hopwood, D.: Hashed time-locked contract transactions (2017). https://github.com/bitcoin/bips/blob/master/bip-0199.mediawiki
16. Bünz, B., Bootle, J., Boneh, D., Poelstra, A., Wuille, P., Maxwell, G.: Bulletproofs: short proofs for confidential transactions and more. In: S&P, pp. 315–334 (2018)
17. Chase, M., et al.: Post-quantum zero-knowledge and signatures from symmetric-key primitives (2017). https://eprint.iacr.org/2017/279
18. Croman, K., et al.: On scaling decentralized blockchains. In: Clark, J., Meiklejohn, S., Ryan, P.Y.A., Wallach, D., Brenner, M., Rohloff, K. (eds.) FC 2016. LNCS, vol. 9604, pp. 106–125. Springer, Heidelberg (2016). https://doi.org/10.1007/978-3-662-53357-4_8
19. Decker, C., Wattenhofer, R.: A fast and scalable payment network with Bitcoin duplex micropayment channels. In: Pelc, A., Schwarzmann, A.A. (eds.) SSS 2015. LNCS, vol. 9212, pp. 3–18. Springer, Cham (2015). https://doi.org/10.1007/978-3-319-21741-3_1
20. Diffie, W., Hellman, M.: New directions in cryptography. IEEE Trans. Inf. Theor. **22**(6), 644–654 (2006)

21. Fiat, A., Shamir, A.: How to prove yourself: practical solutions to identification and signature problems. In: Odlyzko, A.M. (ed.) CRYPTO 1986. LNCS, vol. 263, pp. 186–194. Springer, Heidelberg (1987). https://doi.org/10.1007/3-540-47721-7_12

22. Goldreich, O., Micali, S., Wigderson, A.: Proofs that yield nothing but their validity or all languages in NP have zero-knowledge proof systems. JACM **38**(3), 691–729 (1991)

23. Goodell, B., Noether, S.: Thring signatures and their applications to spender-ambiguous digital currencies. Cryptology ePrint Archive, Report 2018/774, 2018. https://eprint.iacr.org/2018/774

24. Green, M., Miers, I.: Bolt: Anonymous payment channels for decentralized currencies. In: CCS, pp. 473–489 (2017)

25. Khalil, R., Gervais, A.: Revive: rebalancing off-blockchain payment networks. In: CCS, pp. 439–453 (2017)

26. Koshy, P., Koshy, D., McDaniel, P.: An analysis of anonymity in Bitcoin using P2P network traffic. In: Christin, N., Safavi-Naini, R. (eds.) FC 2014. LNCS, vol. 8437, pp. 469–485. Springer, Heidelberg (2014). https://doi.org/10.1007/978-3-662-45472-5_30

27. Kumar, A., Fischer, C., Tople, S., Saxena, P.: A traceability analysis of Monero's blockchain. In: Foley, S.N., Gollmann, D., Snekkenes, E. (eds.) ESORICS 2017. LNCS, vol. 10493, pp. 153–173. Springer, Cham (2017). https://doi.org/10.1007/978-3-319-66399-9_9

28. Libert, B., Peters, T., Qian, C.: Logarithmic-size ring signatures with tight security from the DDH assumption. In: Lopez, J., Zhou, J., Soriano, M. (eds.) ESORICS 2018. LNCS, vol. 11099, pp. 288–308. Springer, Cham (2018). https://doi.org/10.1007/978-3-319-98989-1_15

29. Liu, J.K., Wei, V.K., Wong, D.S.: Linkable spontaneous anonymous group signature for Ad Hoc groups. In: Wang, H., Pieprzyk, J., Varadharajan, V. (eds.) ACISP 2004. LNCS, vol. 3108, pp. 325–335. Springer, Heidelberg (2004). https://doi.org/10.1007/978-3-540-27800-9_28

30. Malavolta, G., Moreno-Sanchez, P., Kate, A., Maffei, M., Ravi, S.: Concurrency and privacy with payment-channel networks. In: CCS, pp. 455–471 (2017)

31. Malavolta, G., Moreno-Sanchez, P., Schneidewind, C., Kate, A., Maffei, M.: Anonymous multi-hop locks for blockchain scalability and interoperability. In: NDSS, January 2019

32. Maxwell, G., Poelstra, A., Seurin, Y., Wuille, P.: Simple schnorr multi-signatures with applications to Bitcoin. Cryptology ePrint Archive, Report 2018/068, 2018. https://eprint.iacr.org/2018/068

33. Meiklejohn, S., et al.: A fistful of Bitcoins: characterizing payments among men with no names (IMC 2013). In: IMC, pp. 127–140 (2013)

34. Moreno-Sanchez, P., Randomrun, Le, D.V., Noether, S., Goodell, B., Kate, A.: DLSAG: non-interactive refund transactions for interoperable payment channels in monero. Cryptology ePrint Archive, Report 2019/595, 2019. https://eprint.iacr.org/2019/595

35. Möser, M., et al.: An empirical analysis of traceability in the Monero blockchain. PETS **2018**(3), 143–163 (2018)

36. Noether, S., Goodel, B.: Dual linkable ring signatures. https://ww.getmonero.org/resources/research-lab/pubs/MRL-0008.pdf

37. Noether, S., Mackenzie, A.: Ring confidential transactions. Ledger **1**, 1–18 (2016)

38. Pedersen, T.P.: Non-interactive and information-theoretic secure verifiable secret sharing. In: Feigenbaum, J. (ed.) CRYPTO 1991. LNCS, vol. 576, pp. 129–140. Springer, Heidelberg (1992). https://doi.org/10.1007/3-540-46766-1_9

39. Poelstra, A.: Lightning in scriptless scripts (2017). https://lists.launchpad.net/mimblewimble/msg00086.html

40. Poelstra, A.: Scriptless scripts (2017). https://download.wpsoftware.net/bitcoin/wizardry/mw-slides/2017-03-mit-bitcoin-expo/slides.pdf

41. Poon, J., Dryja, T.: The Bitcoin Lightning Network. Whitepaper (2016). http://lightning.network/

42. Reid, F., Harrigan, M.: An analysis of anonymity in the Bitcoin system. In: Altshuler, Y., Elovici, Y., Cremers, A., Aharony, N., Pentland, A. (eds.) Security and Privacy in Social Networks. Springer, New York (2013)

43. Rusty: Lightning Networks Part II: Hashed Timelock Contracts (HTLCs) (2015). https://rusty.ozlabs.org/?p=462

44. van Saberhagen, N.: Cryptonote v 2.0. Whitepaper (2013). https://cryptonote.org/whitepaper.pdf

45. Schnorr, C.P.: Efficient signature generation by smart cards. J. Cryptology **4**(3), 161–174 (1991). https://doi.org/10.1007/BF00196725

46. Spagnuolo, M., Maggi, F., Zanero, S.: BitIodine: extracting intelligence from the Bitcoin network. In: Christin, N., Safavi-Naini, R. (eds.) FC 2014. LNCS, vol. 8437, pp. 457–468. Springer, Heidelberg (2014). https://doi.org/10.1007/978-3-662-45472-5_29

CERBERUS Channels: Incentivizing Watchtowers for Bitcoin

Zeta Avarikioti[1], Orfeas Stefanos Thyfronitis Litos[2(✉)],
and Roger Wattenhofer[1]

[1] ETH Zürich, Zürich, Switzerland
[2] University of Edinburgh, Edinburgh, Scotland
o.thyfronitis@ed.ac.uk

Abstract. Bitcoin and similar blockchain systems have a limited transaction throughput because each transaction must be processed by all parties, on-chain. Payment channels relieve the blockchain by allowing parties to execute transactions off-chain while maintaining the on-chain security guarantees, *i.e.*, no party can be cheated out of their funds. However, to maintain these guarantees all parties must follow blockchain updates ardently. To alleviate this issue, a channel party can hire a "watchtower" to periodically check the blockchain for fraud on its behalf.

However, watchtowers will only do their job properly if there are financial incentives, fees, and punishments. There are known solutions, but these need complex smart contracts, and as such are not applicable to Bitcoin's simple script language. This raises the natural question of whether incentivized watchtowers are at all possible in a system like Bitcoin.

In this work, we answer this question affirmatively, by introducing CERBERUS channels, an extension of Lightning channels. CERBERUS channels reward watchtowers while remaining secure against bribing and collusion; thus participants can safely go offline for an extended period of time. We show that CERBERUS channels are correct, and provide a proof-of-concept implementation in the Bitcoin script language.

Keywords: Bitcoin · Security · Payment channels · Payment network · Lightning network · Watchtowers · Collateral · Incentives

1 Introduction

1.1 Motivation

Since its inception, Bitcoin [18] is the leading cryptocurrency in terms of market capitalization. Unfortunately, Bitcoin suffers from limited transaction throughput due to its underlying consensus mechanism. Specifically, Bitcoin handles at most 7 transactions/s [7], while other payment systems, such as Visa, handle tens of thousands. This is a major obstacle on the wide adoption of Bitcoin.

© International Financial Cryptography Association 2020
J. Bonneau and N. Heninger (Eds.): FC 2020, LNCS 12059, pp. 346–366, 2020.
https://doi.org/10.1007/978-3-030-51280-4_19

Payment channels are the foremost solution for scaling decentralized blockchain systems such as Bitcoin. They allow transactions between two parties to happen off-chain, while maintaining the security guarantees of the blockchain. Specifically, two parties can open a channel with a single on-chain transaction and then execute multiple transactions privately and off-chain on this channel. The blockchain is only used to close the channel or in case of dispute.

Although payment channels offer a simple and efficient solution to the limited transaction throughput of blockchain systems, they have a major drawback. The correct operation of a payment channel depends on all parties of the channel being active and in sync with the blockchain. Otherwise, a party of the channel can close the channel in a wrong state, *i.e.*, a party can publish an outdated version of the channel's funds distribution. This old state will be considered final, unless the counterparty disputes it within a specific time period. This dispute time is chosen when the channel is initiated on-chain; after t blocks, a fraudulent transaction cannot be disputed anymore. Hence, to maintain the security of the payment channel, both parties must be online at least once every t blocks.

A natural solution to relieve the parties from this necessity is outsourcing the dispute process to third-parties, known as watchtowers [3,10]. Watchtowers on Bitcoin Lightning network [19] mainly focus on maintaining privacy; however, the current design does not provide incentives for watchtower participation. In particular, the party that hires the watchtower pays it only if fraud happens. However, the watchtower knows that rational parties never commit fraud, thus there is little incentive to become a watchtower in the first place. Additionally, a rational watchtower can benefit from unintentional broadcasting of revoked updates and thus may lobby for buggy or misleading channel software. A naive alternative would be for the hiring party to pay the watchtower a small fee regularly, *e.g.*, each time a channel transaction is executed. In this case, however, a rational watchtower would avoid the cost of storing the hiring party's data and monitoring the blockchain and would thus fail to act upon fraud.

In this paper, we introduce CERBERUS channels, where watchtowers are (i) incentivized to participate in the system, and (ii) penalized in case they do not act upon fraud. In particular, each party has the option to employ a watchtower as a service provider. The watchtower is paid for every transaction executed on the channel and locks collateral on-chain as guarantee for its honest behavior. In case the watchtower misbehaves and does not dispute an outdated state, the cheated party can claim the watchtower's collateral. Hence, rational watchtowers are incentivized both to participate and act upon fraud. In our construction, the parties can go offline for an extended period of time and need only be online to penalize the watchtower. This way we weaken the availability requirement for the parties of a payment channel. More importantly, CERBERUS channels build upon and extend Lightning channels and only require timelocks and additional transactions. We also provide a proof-of-concept implementation (https://github.com/OrfeasLitos/cerberus-script).

1.2   Related Work

Payment channels were first introduced by Spilman [20] as unidirectional channels and were later established as bidirectional channels [9,19]. Currently, there exist a variety of bidirectional payment channels constructions, some applicable only on platforms that allow for arbitrary smart contracts such as Ethereum [5,11,13,17], and some applicable also on blockchain systems with limited scripting languages like Bitcoin [6,8,9,19]. This work falls in the second category.

The most famous and active payment network is Lightning [19] currently operating more than 35,900 channels by over 9,900 nodes with a sum of more than 830₿ [4]. However, Lighting as well as most of the other payment networks require channel parties that are frequently online, watching the blockchain. To address this issue, Dryja introduced Monitors [10], also known as Watchtowers [3], a third-party solution that acts as a proxy for a channel's party effectively allowing the party to go offline for a long period of time while maintaining the security of the channel (the other party cannot cheat). Watchtowers mainly focus on privacy preserving techniques to ensure the hired third-party does not learn any information about the off-chain transactions. Thereafter, DCWC [6] was proposed, a distributed protocol for watchtower services, in an attempt to involve all full nodes in the system and consequently enhance security. However, both these works, Watchtowers and DCWC, fail to provide the necessary incentives for participation in the system. In particular, the watchtowers are paid upon fraud. Thus, since no rational party will commit fraud, watchtowers will never be paid. Therefore, assuming rational participants, the existence of watchtowers is not a Nash equilibrium. On the contrary, CERBERUS channels provide the necessary incentives mechanisms for watchtowers (rewards and punishment).

In the same vein, McCorry et al. presented Pisa [16], a protocol that outsources the dispute handling of (state[1]) channels to third-parties. However, Pisa has two shortcomings: First, the main protocol implementation is not secure against bribing since the watchtower's collateral is not linked to the party or the channel on-chain, hence the watchtower can double-spend it. Second, Pisa is not compatible with Bitcoin, because it requires a smart contract not expressible in script. On the contrary, CERBERUS channels are applicable to Bitcoin and furthermore they do not suffer from the security problems of Pisa since the watchtower's collateral is linked to the hiring party with an on-chain transaction.

More recently, Avarikioti et al. introduced Brick [5], an asynchronous off-chain construction that employs a committee of watchtowers. Although Brick manages to remove the synchrony requirements on the network layer and the perfect blockchain assumption while maintaining the security of channels, it is not compatible with Bitcoin-like platforms, as opposed to CERBERUS channels.

In a different line of work, Khabbazian et al. [15] proposed a lightweight watchtower design in which watchtowers do not need to store the signed justice (revocation) transactions, but instead can extract them directly from the commitment transactions that appear on the blockchain. This work is independent

---

[1] State channels generalize payment channels to support smart contracts [17].

and complementary to ours, and can be applied also to CERBERUS channels to improve the storage requirements for the watchtower service.

1.3 Our Contribution

To summarize, the contribution of this paper is the following:

- We introduce CERBERUS payment channels that enable participants on Bitcoin to employ watchtowers and thus go securely offline for an extended period of time.
- We define the desired properties for payment channel solutions and prove CERBERUS channels are secure under our security model. Specifically, we show watchtowers are incentivized to both participate and act upon fraud. Thus, CERBERUS channels are secure against collusion and bribing.
- We provide a proof-of-concept implementation of CERBERUS channels on Bitcoin (Sect. 6).

2 Background and Notation

2.1 Payment Channels

For the rest of the paper, when we refer to payment channels we imply Lightning channels, currently operating on the Bitcoin network. We now provide a brief overview of Lightning channels, on which CERBERUS channels build upon.

To open a payment channel, the parties publish a funding transaction where they lock their funds into a common account, i.e., both parties must sign to spend the output of the funding transaction. Every time the parties execute a transaction, they update the current state of the channel accordingly, meaning they distribute the funding transaction's output as agreed and sign the resulting "commitment" transaction. In addition, each party reveals to the counterparty a secret that allows the counterparty to sign a "revocation" transaction that spends the previous commitment transaction; the revocation transaction awards the cheating party's funds to the cheated party, effectively punishing the party that tried to cheat. The output of the party that published the commitment transaction is locked for a time period, known as the revocation period. The cheated party must publish the revocation transaction during the revocation period, otherwise the cheating party will be able to spend the balance of the revoked state. Thus the security of the channel construction crucially depends on all parties of the channel watching the blockchain and being online at least once during the revocation period.

2.2 Contracts

A contract is an agreement that can be enforced on the blockchain. Enforcing such a contract depends on the operations the programming language allows with respect to transaction outputs. Most recent cryptocurrencies, such as Ethereum, support a Turing-complete language and thus can enforce arbitrary rules with a *smart contract*. However, Bitcoin (as well as other cryptocurrencies) has strict limitations on the scripting language and allows only specific operations. As a result Bitcoin's contracts are simpler and with limited functionality. Next, we discuss the operations allowed in script with respect to transaction outputs, on which CERBERUS channels build upon.

Signatures. A signature is the most basic form of contract and is essentially a proof of ownership of a transaction output. We denote by σ_A the signature that corresponds to the public key A. (We omit the signed message, as it always is the transaction which contains the signature, with a placeholder in the location of the signature). Further, an m-of-n *multisignature* is a contract that demands at least m signatures which correspond to any m of the n predefined public keys. If m valid signatures are provided then the output is immediately spendable. In this work, we will only use 2-of-2 multisignatures, so we introduce the following notation: $\sigma_{A,B}$ expresses that the output of the transaction can only be spent with both the signatures of A and B.

Timelocks. Timelocks are another type of contract. When a transaction or a transaction output is timelocked it cannot be included in the blockchain until the specified time has elapsed. There are two types of timelocks, *absolute* [1] and *relative* [2]. Transactions or transaction outputs with an absolute timelock become valid when the specified timestamp or block height is reached. On the other hand, a relative timelock allows a transaction output to be locked for a time relative to the block that included that output. Relative timelocks are used in the Lightning protocol as well as in our protocols. We denote by Δt a relative timelock that expires t blocks (confirmations) after the transaction is included in the blockchain. After this time the output of the transaction is spendable.

2.3 UTXO Notation

In this section we introduce the necessary notation for our protocol.

We assume the blockchain is UTXO-based (UTXO: Unspent Transaction Output), meaning that transactions consist of inputs and outputs. A transaction connects its inputs to UTXOs (removing the latter from the UTXO set) and creates new UTXOs, its outputs. Each UTXO can only be spent as a whole. A UTXO consists of a monetary value and the conditions under which it can be spent, *e.g.*, a signature corresponding to a public key, a timelock etc.

We denote by $o = (x \mid C)$ the UTXO that holds a monetary value of x coins that can be spent when conditions C are met. For example, $o = (10 \mid \sigma_A)$ means that the signature that matches the public key A can spend the output o which is equivalent to 10 coins.

A transaction in this model is a mapping from a set of UTXOs, called inputs, to a (new) set of UTXOs, called outputs. We define a transaction as follows:

$$TX_i = [o_j, o_k, \dots] \mapsto [o_i^1, o_i^2, \dots]$$

where o_j, o_k, etc. are the inputs of the transaction and $o_i^1, o_i^2, \ldots$ are the first, second, etc. outputs, respectively. If transaction TX_i has a single output we simply write o_i. Moreover, if the specific UTXO that is input to a transaction is irrelevant to the protocol design, we refer to it as #. If we demand the input to belong to a specific public key A and hold a specific value of x coins, but which of the UTXOs owned by A is spent by the input is irrelevant to the protocol design, we refer to it as $(x \mid \#_{\sigma_A})$. For instance,

$$TX_i = \big[(0.8 \mid \#_{\sigma_A}), o_k^2\big] \mapsto \big[(1 \mid h(s)), (0.5 \mid \sigma_B)\big]$$

denotes the transaction TX_i that spends a UTXO from the party A with value 0.8 coins and the second output of transaction TX_k and creates two new UTXOs. The first output holds the value of 1 coin and can be spent with the secret s, while the second holds 0.5 coins and can be spent with B's signature.

3 Protocol Overview

3.1 System Model

Cryptographic Assumptions. We make the typical cryptographic assumptions, *i.e.*, there are secure communication channels between participants, and cryptographically secure hash functions, signatures, and encryption schemes. Additionally, all parties of the protocol (watchtowers, channel parties, external adversaries) are computationally bounded.

Blockchain Assumptions. We assume a perfect blockchain, in the sense that both persistence and liveness hold [12]. In particular, we assume that if a valid transaction is propagated in the blockchain network it cannot be censored and will be included in the "permanent" part of the blockchain immediately[2].

Network Model. We assume that any participant of a channel can go offline (intentionally or due to a Denial-of-Service (DoS) attack) for a (long) period of time up to T. Furthermore, we consider watchtowers that are resilient against DoS attacks. We argue this assumption is realistic since watchtowers are also required to lock high collateral to participate in the system and thus operators will invest in anti-DoS protection.

Threat Model. We assume that the watchtowers as well as the channel participants are rational players. Thus, they will only deviate from the honest protocol execution if they can gain more profit. Moreover, channel participants can collude with the watchtower(s).

---

[2] Note that CERBERUS channels can be made secure for any confirmation time k, but we choose $k = 1$ to simplify the protocol and security analysis.

3.2   CERBERUS Overview

CERBERUS channels aim to alleviate the need for the channel parties to be frequently online watching the blockchain. We propose simple modifications on the Lightning protocol that allow the parties to employ watchtowers while incentives for active participation and thus security of the channels are guaranteed.

In particular, in CERBERUS, the watchtower is rewarded for every update on the channel but also locks collateral as guarantee for the case he does not act upon fraud. The party employing the watchtower can claim the collateral within the penalty period, if the latter misbehaves. The penalty period is however much larger than the revocation period, hence the hiring party can go offline for an extended period of time. On the other hand, on a normal operation of the channel the watchtower can reclaim the collateral when its service is terminated. The watchtower has the option to terminate its service to the party at any point during the protocol execution subject to the penalty period. In such a case, the party can either update the channel and employ a new watchtower, close the channel, or be online more frequently to avoid fraud.

3.3   Payment Channel Properties

We define the desired properties of a payment channel construction below, summarizing the work of [5,14,16,17].

1. **Security:** Any party of the channel can enforce the last agreed state (balance) on-chain at any time.
2. **Privacy:** No third-party, external to the payment channel, can gain information about the state (distribution of funds) of the channel.
3. **Scale-out:** The number of transactions on-chain is constant.

The first two, namely Safety and Privacy, are security properties, while the third is the performance property that is required in a channel to achieve its main purpose – higher transaction throughput.

We note that these properties are also met by Lightning, but under a different network model. Specifically, Lighting requires participants to be frequently online watching the blockchain to guarantee security. In this work, we aim to alleviate this requirement, thus providing security as specified in Sect. 3.1.

4   CERBERUS Design

In this section, we describe in detail the architecture of CERBERUS payment channels. We base our design on Lightning channels, and introduce the necessary modifications and extensions to guarantee the desired properties under the predefined model for our design and the applicability to Bitcoin.

First, we divide the channel lifetime in four phases: *Open, Update, Abort* and *Close*. Then, we describe the necessary transactions and present the protocol design for each phase. To simplify the description, we assume, wlog, that party B has hired watchtower W and the potentially cheating party is A.

We note that CERBERUS can accommodate the usecase where only one party wishes to hire a watchtower, as well as that in which both parties choose to do so. Different watchtowers can be used by the two parties. In the case neither party employs a watchtower, the protocol reverts to Lightning.

4.1 Phase: Open

Similarly to the Lightning protocol, phase *Open* includes a funding transaction and a commitment transaction. The funding transaction creates a common account between the parties and is eventually published on-chain to notarize the committed funds, hence the opening of the channel. The funding transaction of a CERBERUS channel spends the funds of the channel parties and creates a new 2-of-2 multisig output spendable only if the parties collaborate.

The commitment transaction (first of many to follow) distributes the funds between the parties and is signed and held in private by both parties. The commitment transaction, if published, does not allow the publishing party to spend its funds immediately, to ensure there is enough time for punishment in case of fraud (*i.e.*, the commitment transaction is not the last agreed state by the channel parties). This is known as the revocation period, denoted by t. The first commitment transaction should be signed by both parties before signing and publishing the funding transaction to avoid a hostage situation.

Furthermore, we introduce two new transactions in phase *Open*, the *collateral transaction* and *reclaim transaction*, that involve the watchtower service. The collateral transaction is funded by the watchtower, while its output is a joint account between the watchtower and the hiring party. The value of the collateral is slightly higher than the channel funds. The reclaim transaction, on the other hand, allows the watchtower to reclaim the collateral, effectively terminating its service. The output of the reclaim transaction can be spent as follows: either a long "penalty" period T has elapsed since the watchtower signed and published on-chain the reclaim transaction, or both the signatures of the watchtower and the party are present. Intuitively, the penalty period T allows the cheated party to penalize an inactive/malicious watchtower, during phase *Close*. Further, timelock T allows the party employing the watchtower to be notified either in case of fraud or in case the watchtower simply wants to withdraw its service. In the latter case, the party can either be online more frequently (revocation period), close the channel, or collaboratively update the channel to cancel out the previous commitment transactions and employ a new watchtower. Note that the reclaim transaction is signed by both the watchtower and the hiring party before the collateral transaction is put on-chain to avoid a hostage situation.

Further, $T >> t$, and security holds as long as any participant in a CERBERUS channel employing a watchtower is offline for at most T time.

Next, we present in detail the transactions involved in the first phase, *Open*.

– **Funding transaction:** Opens a channel between two parties, A and B. The inputs are the parties' funds and the output is a 2-of-2 multisig of A and B.

- **Commitment transaction:** Updates the state of the channel, *i.e.*, the distribution of the funds between the parties. The input of the commitment transaction spends the output of the funding transaction. The commitment transaction has two outputs, one for each channel party, and distributes the funds of the channel to the two parties as agreed. Each party has its own version of the commitment transaction, signed by the counterparty. Each version has two outputs, one awarded to the party holding the commitment transaction, wlog party A, and one awarded to the counterparty B. Both outputs are timelocked for the revocation period t. Further, each output can be spent before t time elapses in collaboration with the watchtower W, *i.e.*, if both the watchtower and the corresponding party sign a transaction.
- **Collateral transaction:** Commits the watchtower's collateral on-chain. Note that the value of the collateral should be slightly higher than the total funds of the channel. The input of the collateral transaction is funded by the watchtower, while the output is a 2-of-2 multisig of B and W.
- **Reclaim transaction:** Allows the watchtower to reclaim the collateral. The input of the reclaim transaction spends the output of the collateral transaction. The output, on the other hand, requires the signature of the watchtower relatively timelocked by T or both the signatures of W and B.

Protocol: Open

Preconditions: A, B and W own on-chain a, b and c coins respectively. It holds that $c > a + b$ and W is employed by B.
A and B prepare the necessary transactions.

1. A and B create the funding transaction:
   $$TX_f = \left[(a \mid \#_{\sigma_A}), (b \mid \#_{\sigma_B})\right] \mapsto (a + b \mid \sigma_{A,B})$$
2. A and B create the first commitment transaction (version held by A):
   $$TX_{C1A} = o_f \mapsto \left[(a \mid (\sigma_A \wedge \Delta t) \vee \sigma_{A,W}), (b \mid (\sigma_B \wedge \Delta t) \vee \sigma_{B,W})\right]$$

A and B open the channel.

3. B sends the signature of TX_{C1A} to A. Symmetrically, A sends the signature of TX_{C1A} to B.
4. Both A and B sign TX_f and publish it on-chain, as in Lightning.

W locks its collateral for the channel on-chain.

5. W creates the collateral and reclaim transactions and sends both to B:
   $$TX_{Coll} = (c \mid \#_{\sigma_W}) \mapsto (c \mid \sigma_{W,B})$$
   $$TX_{RC} = o_{Coll} \mapsto (c \mid (\sigma_W \wedge \Delta T) \vee (\sigma_{B,W}))$$
6. B verifies, signs and sends to W the signature for the input of TX_{RC}.
7. W signs and publishes on-chain the collateral transaction TX_{Coll}.

Postconditions: Opening of the channel between A and B with total value $a + b$ coins, and employment of W from B with c coins as collateral.

4.2   Phase: Update

The second phase, *Update*, materializes the main functionality of a channel. In this phase, the parties update the current state of the channel (distribution of funds) and consequently transactions are executed off-chain. The *Update* phase in the Lightning protocol consists of a (new) commitment transaction and a revocation transaction. The commitment transaction represents the last, agreed by both parties, state of the channel. On the other hand, the revocation transaction allows a party to claim all the funds of the channel in case the other party publishes the previous commitment transaction (attempts to cheat).

The *Update* phase in Cerberus produces the following transactions: a commitment transaction, a revocation transaction, and two penalty transactions. The revocation transaction spends both outputs of the previous valid commitment transaction and awards them to the cheated party B. The revocation transaction is signed by the potentially cheating party A and is sent to B. Then, both party B and watchtower W sign, exchange and store the revocation transaction. Note that B will not sign the new commitment transaction unless both A and W sign the revocation transaction. Further, A acts as in Lightning.

The penalty transactions allow B to penalize watchtower W during the penalty period in case fraud occurred and W did not publish the revocation transaction in time. Specifically, the penalty transactions both depend on the previous commitment transaction and on the collateral and reclaim transactions, respectively. Hence, the penalty transaction is valid only if fraud occurs and is not revoked. Thus, the revocation transaction has a double functionality; it awards the money of cheater A to the cheated party B and additionally acts as insurance for W, since it invalidates the penalty transactions by spending the outputs of the commitment transaction. Note that B will only sign the new commitment transaction after receiving the signed penalty transactions from W.

Further, we assume that a watchtower is paid regularly on every channel update by the hiring party via a one-way payment channel[3].

To sum up, during the *Update* phase the following transactions are created:

- **Revocation transaction:** In case of fraud, *i.e.*, if party A publishes a revoked commitment transaction, the revocation transaction returns all channel funds to the cheated party B. The inputs of the revocation transaction spend the outputs of the commitment transaction. The output of the revocation transaction is awarded to the cheated party B.
- **Penalty transaction 1:** Allows a party to claim the watchtower's collateral during the penalty period T, in case fraud occurred and the watchtower did not act during the revocation period t. The inputs of penalty transaction 1 are (a) the output that reflects B's channel balance on the corresponding commitment transaction, and (b) the output of the collateral transaction. The output of penalty transaction 1 awards all funds to B.
- **Penalty transaction 2:** Allows a party to claim the watchtower's collateral during the penalty period T, in case fraud occurred and the watchtower did

---

[3] Ideally, this payment should be integrated with Cerberus for efficiency.

not revoke it during time t, but tried to reclaim the collateral. The inputs of penalty transaction 2 are (a) the output that reflects B's channel balance on the corresponding commitment transaction, and (b) the output of the reclaim transaction. The output awards all funds to B.

All described transactions and their dependencies are illustrated in Fig. 1.

Protocol: Update

Preconditions: A and B own a coins and b coins respectively in a channel. W has a locked collateral of c coins. Note that $a' + b' = a + b$.

1. B creates the next commitment transaction:
   $TX_{C,i+1,A} = o_f \mapsto \big[(a' \mid (\sigma_A \wedge \Delta t) \vee \sigma_{A,W}), (b' \mid (\sigma_B \wedge \Delta t) \vee \sigma_{B,W})\big]$.
2. B creates and sends to A the revocation transaction for the previous commitment transaction:
   $TX_{RiA} = \big[o^1_{CiA}, o^2_{CiA}\big] \mapsto (a + b \mid \sigma_B)$.
3. A sends to B its signature for the revocation transaction TX_{RiA}.
4. B sends to W both parties' signatures for the revocation transaction TX_{RiA}, along with the commitment transaction TX_{CiA}.
5. W sends to B its signature for the revocation transaction TX_{RiA}.
6. W creates penalty transactions 1 and 2:
   $TX_{P1iA} = \big[o_{Coll}, o^2_{CiA}\big] \mapsto (b + c \mid \sigma_B)$, $TX_{P2iA} = \big[o_{RC}, o^2_{CiA}\big] \mapsto (b + c \mid \sigma_B)$
7. W sends to B its signatures for o_{Coll} and o_{RC}.
8. B sends to A its signature for $TX_{C,i+1,A}$.

Postconditions: A, B own a', b' coins, resp. W has c coins locked as collateral.

4.3   Phase: Close

The last phase, *Close*, handles the closing of a CERBERUS channel. Similarly to the Lightning protocol, in this phase either the parties close the channel in collaboration or a commitment transaction is published on-chain unilaterally by one of the channel parties. As soon as the commitment transaction is included on-chain the revocation period t begins, allowing the counterparty or the watchtower to supervene to a potential dispute resolution.

Collaborative Closure. The normal closure of the channel (no cheating occurs) is described in Protocol CLOSE (A). Note that in this case, both parties sign the agreed distribution of the channel's funds and the funds are immediately awarded to the parties as soon as the transaction is included in the blockchain, *i.e.*, no timelocks are required.

Non-collaborative Non-cheating Closure. This happens if one party wants to close the channel and the other is unresponsive. Then, the responsive party publishes on-chain the last commitment transaction (already signed by both parties on last update). After time t, the funds of the channel are distributed to the parties according to the published state. As soon as the last commitment is published on-chain, the watchtower can safely put on-chain the reclaim transaction, since no penalty transaction corresponding to the last commitment transaction exists. Consequently, the watchtower can spend the collateral after time T, or immediately if the hiring party agrees to collaborate and sign a transaction that spends the collateral and awards the funds to the watchtower.

Protocol: CLOSE (A) (Non-cheating channel closure)
Preconditions: A owns a coins, B owns b coins, W has a locked collateral of c coins.

1. A and B sign and broadcast $o_f \mapsto \left[(a \mid \sigma_A), (b \mid \sigma_B)\right]$.
2. W publishes on-chain the reclaim transaction TX_{RC} (can spend it after T).

Postconditions: The channel is closed, A owns a' coins, B owns b' coins and the collateral is returned to the watchtower W.

Cheating Closure & Responsive Watchtower. In case A cheats and publishes an old commitment transaction, the watchtower publishes the corresponding revocation transaction during the dispute period, awarding all the funds of the channel to the cheated party B. Then, the watchtower can publish the reclaim transaction and spend its output safely since the corresponding penalty transaction has been invalidated. As described in Protocol CLOSE (B), publishing the revocation and reclaim transaction can be done simultaneously, since the timelock t on the hiring party's output of the published commitment transaction guarantees that the hiring party cannot claim the watchtower's collateral during the revocation period. On the other hand, in case B cheats, A acts exactly as in Lightning.

Protocol: CLOSE (B) (Cheating party & responsive watchtower)
Preconditions: A owns a coins, B owns b coins, W has a locked collateral of c coins. The last commitment transaction is denoted TX_{CnA}.

1. Party A publishes on-chain an old commitment transaction TX_{CiA}, $i < n$.
2. During the revocation period t, W publishes the corresponding revocation transaction TX_{RiA}.
3. W publishes on-chain the reclaim transaction TX_{RC} (can spend it after T).

Postconditions: The channel is closed, the channel funds are awarded to the cheated party B, and the collateral returned to the watchtower W.

Protocol: CLOSE (C) (Cheating party & unresponsive/malicious watchtower)
Preconditions: A owns a coins, B owns b coins, W has a locked collateral of c
coins. The last commitment transaction is denoted TX_{CnA}.

1. Party A publishes on-chain an old commitment transaction TX_{CiA}, $i < n$
   waits for the timelock to expire and spends the $(a \mid \sigma_A \wedge \varDelta t)$ output.
2. B checks the chain periodically every time T and notices TX_{CiA} is on-chain
   and spent. If W has published the reclaim transaction TX_{RC}, B publishes
   Penalty transaction 2 TX_{P2iA}. Else, B publishes Penalty transaction 1
   TX_{P1iA}.

Postconditions: The channel is closed, the channel funds are awarded to the
parties according to the published commitment transaction TX_{CiA}, and the
collateral (c coins) is awarded to party B.

Cheating Closure & Unresponsive Watchtower. If the watchtower does not publish the revocation transaction in time when fraud occurs, the cheated party can
publish a penalty transaction and claim the watchtower's collateral. Specifically,
if the reclaim transaction is not published, the cheated party publishes penalty
transaction 1. Otherwise, if the watchtower has published the reclaim transaction
but not the revocation transaction, the cheated party publishes penalty transaction 2. Both penalty transactions are valid, as long as the cheated party does not
spend its output of the commitment transaction. Further, penalty transaction 2
is valid only if less than time T has elapsed since the reclaim transaction was
put on-chain. Hence, the cheated party must go online within at most T time to
claim the watchtower's collateral. CLOSE (C) describes this case.

4.4 Phase: Abort

In this phase, W withdraws the collateral and thus terminates its employment
by party B. *Abort* is an intermediate phase, that can occur at any time between
phases *Open* and *Close*[4]. To that end, the watchtower publishes on-chain the
reclaim transaction. Consequently, timelock T comes in effect, locking the watchtower's collateral for the penalty period. During this period, an honest hiring
party will check the blockchain once. The party can then close the channel, hire
a new watchtower or monitor the blockchain every t time.

5 Security Analysis

5.1 Security

We show that CERBERUS channels are secure within our system model under
any collusion/bribing scheme involving the channel parties and the watchtower.

---

[4] We assume that a rational watchtower will publish the reclaim transaction at the
latest when the channel is closed.

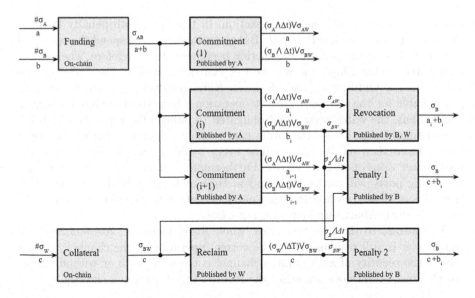

Fig. 1. Cerberus channel transactions. When many spending conditions are available in the output, the one used is explicitly shown emphasized in the input.

Lemma 1. *Phase Abort does not affect the security of a* Cerberus *channel, i.e., no honest party or watchtower can be cheated out of its funds.*

Proof. To prove the lemma, we distinguish three cases:

(a) *Abort* terminates before *Close* initiates.
(b) *Abort* terminates during *Close*.
(c) *Abort* includes *Close* entirely, *i.e.*, *Close* initiates at most $T - t$ after the reclaim transaction is put on-chain.

In the first case, the watchtower withdraws the collateral, and is not liable anymore for the channel operation. Specifically, W publishes on-chain the reclaim transaction. Since no commitment transaction is published on-chain, all penalty transactions that can interfere with the ownership of the collateral are invalid. Hence, the watchtower claims the collateral after time T elapses – before *Close* initiates. From that point on, the security of the channel – the funds of the hiring party – is the same as in a Lightning channel, unless the channel is updated with a new watchtower service.

For the second case, suppose *Abort* initiates at time $t = 0$, and there is a time t', such that $T - t < t' < T$, in which *Close* initiates. If the closing of the channel is collaborative between the parties or the last commitment transaction was published by one of the parties, there are no valid penalty transactions that can interfere with the ownership of the collateral. Hence, the collateral will be owned by the watchtower at time T. Further, the funds of the channel parties will be distributed as last agreed. However, the channel can close with one of the parties publishing an old commitment transaction. In this case, both penalty transactions become valid at time $t'+t > T$. But the watchtower can spend the collateral at time T, before any penalty transaction becomes valid. Therefore, when Abort terminates during *Close*, the watchtower can safely reclaim the collateral, no matter how a CERBERUS channel closes. Note, however, that the watchtower is not liable for the channel's correct operation when Abort terminates during *Close*. Thus, the watchtower is not obligated to publish the revocation transaction in time. Nevertheless, the hiring party comes online once during the *Abort* phase. From then on, it comes online every t time, since it realizes that the watchtower stops offering its service. Furthermore, it holds $t'+t > T$. Therefore, the hiring party will notice the fraud in time and will publish the revocation transaction. Hence, no honest hiring party or watchtower can be cheated out of its funds when Abort terminates during *Close*.

In contrast to the first two cases, when *Abort* includes *Close* entirely, the watchtower is still responsible for the correct operation of the channel. In such a case, the security of a CERBERUS channel is the same with or without phase *Abort*. Thus, *Abort* does not affect the security of a CERBERUS channel. □

Lemma 2. *An honest* CERBERUS *member cannot be cheated out of its funds.*

Proof. Watchtowers are incentivized to participate in CERBERUS channels due to the occasional rewards on every update. Thus, we need only show that under any collusion scheme CERBERUS channels remain secure with respect to the system model of Sect. 3.1. This implies the scheme is also secure if no collusion occurs, *e.g.*, normal channel operation or the watchtower is offline. Note that whenever we assume collusion, it can also be the case that the same person handles both colluding identities. There can be the following collusion schemes:

(i) Both parties of the channel A and B collude. According to the cryptographic assumptions, the signature of the watchtower cannot be forged, hence the parties cannot create a penalty transaction without the collaboration of the watchtower. Moreover, the channel parties only hold the watchtower's signature for revocation and penalty transactions of previous commitment transactions. The reclaim transaction is only held by W and phase *Abort* does not affect the security of the protocol (Lemma 1). Therefore, the only available action for the colluding parties is to publish a previous commitment transaction on purpose. In such a case, an honest hence online watchtower publishes the corresponding revocation transaction. As soon as the revocation transaction is on-chain, one of the inputs of both penalty transactions – which is the same as the one in the revocation transaction – become invalid thus both penalty transaction become invalid. Therefore, the malicious parties cannot claim an honest watchtower's collateral.

(ii) Watchtower W colludes with party A. In this case, the malicious parties try to cheat B's balance out of the channel (equivalent to at most $a + b$ coins), while B is offline. We assume *Abort* has not initiated, since it does not affect the security of the channel[5] (Lemma 1). The colluding parties cannot forge B's signature to close the channel in a new state. Thus, the only available action is to publish a previous and more favorable to A commitment transaction. However, for each previous commitment transaction, party B holds two corresponding penalty transactions that award the collateral of the watchtower to B. Therefore, as soon as B goes online (within the time window T), B will publish the suitable penalty transaction on-chain (type 2 if the reclaim transaction is on-chain, type 1 otherwise) and claim the watchtower's collateral, $c > a + b$ coins. Note that this argument holds because the watchtower's collateral is locked on-chain involving the hiring party and thus cannot be used in parallel for other channels/parties.

(iii) In the last case, B colludes with watchtower W. This is the simplest case, since A is either online or employs its own watchtower. If A is online the security holds similarly to the Lightning protocol, *i.e.*, A publishes the revocation transaction on-chain and receives all the funds of the channel. If A employs a watchtower, then the previous analysis holds. □

Lemma 3. *A* CERBERUS *channel will not close in a state that is not the last state agreed by all the participants of the channel.*

Proof. Any party of a CERBERUS channel cannot gain more profit by deviating from the honest protocol execution, because all parties involved in a CERBERUS channel always maintain (at least) their funds as shown in Lemma 2. Hence, a rational party that aims to maximize its profit will honestly follow the CERBERUS protocol in every phase, and ultimately close the CERBERUS channel in a non-cheating state, as described in Sect. 4. □

Lemma 4. *Any party of a* CERBERUS *channel can close it at any time.*

Proof. Both parties of the CERBERUS channel hold at least one valid commitment transaction (the one created at the last execution of the Update protocol, or if no update has taken place, the unique commitment transaction created during the Open protocol) which allows them to initiate phase *Close*, unilaterally, as described in Sect. 4.3. Hence, a CERBERUS channel will be closed at the latest within time t from publishing a commitment transaction on-chain (given a perfect underlying blockchain protocol and network synchrony). □

Theorem 1. CERBERUS *channels achieve Security (as defined in Sect. 3.3).*

Proof. Lemma 4 states that any party can close a CERBERUS channel at any time. From Lemma 3, it holds that a CERBERUS channel can only close on the last agreed by all parties state. Hence, any party of a CERBERUS channel can enforce the last agreed state on-chain at any time. □

---

[5] To be precise, *Abort* could have initiated but less than $T-t$ time has elapsed between the reclaim transaction was published on-chain and the time *Close* initiated.

5.2   Performance

Next, we show that CERBERUS channels scale well, meaning that the number of on-chain transactions is constant and independent of the number of transactions executed in a channel, similarly to the Lightning protocol. The analysis below considers a single watchtower for each party of the channel. We discuss the scalability of the protocol if we enable multiple watchtowers in Sect. 7.

Theorem 2. CERBERUS *channels achieve Scale-out.*

Proof. In phase *Open*, a CERBERUS channel requires 3 transactions, one funding transaction to open the channel and two collateral transactions for each watchtower to lock the collateral to the corresponding party of the channel. Phase *Update* is executed off-chain, hence no transactions are published on-chain.

During phase *Close*, the number of on-chain transactions can vary, however in the worst case 4 transactions are published. Specifically, in case of a non-cheating closure 3 transactions are published: (i) either a commitment transaction published unilaterally by a party of the channel, or a collaborative closing transaction published by both parties, (ii)-(iii) one reclaim transaction for each of the parties' watchtowers, published by the corresponding watchtowers respectively.

On the contrary, in case of fraud and a responsive watchtower, the following 4 transactions are necessary: (i) an old commitment transaction published by the cheating party (step 1, protocol CLOSE (B)), (ii) the reclaim transaction of the cheating party's watchtower, published by the watchtower, (iii) the revocation transaction from the cheated party's watchtower, published by the watchtower (step 2, protocol CLOSE (B)), and (iv) the reclaim transaction of the cheated party's watchtower, published by the watchtower (step 3, protocol CLOSE (B)).

In case of fraud and an unresponsive watchtower, up to 4 transactions are published on-chain, as illustrated in Protocol CLOSE (C): (i) an old commitment transaction published by the cheating party, (ii) the reclaim transaction of the cheating party's watchtower (published by the watchtower), (iii) the reclaim transaction of the cheated party's watchtower (published by the watchtower), and (iv) the corresponding penalty transaction published by the cheated party.

Phase *Abort* is an optional intermediate phase that allows the watchtower to withdraw its service to the channel party. This phase includes one on-chain transaction – the reclaim transaction – but not additively to phase *Close*. After phase *Abort* the protocol for the party is similar to the Bitcoin Lightning protocol, which requires at most 3 on-chain transactions in total per channel. Thus, the worst case performance analysis does not include phase *Abort*.

Overall, a CERBERUS channel requires at most 7 on-chain transactions.   □

6   Cerberus Transactions Script

Consider a channel between Alice and Bob, where only Bob is using a watchtower. The funding and the collateral transactions both have a 2-of-2 multisig output. Their script is 2 <pubkey1> <pubkey2> 2 OP_CHECKMULTISIG, where pubkey1, pubkey2 are the funding keys of Alice and Bob for the funding transaction and the collateral keys of Bob and the watchtower for the collateral, sorted by ascending order of their DER-encodings[6].

The reclaim transaction has one input that spends the collateral output with script 0 <collateral_pubkey1_sig> <collateral_pubkey2_sig>. It has one output, with the script of Fig. 2. The public keys belong to Bob and the watchtower and are sorted by their DER-encodings.

The commitment transaction has a unique input that spends the funding output with witness script 0 <pubkey1_sig> <pubkey2_sig>. It also has two outputs, the scripts of which are slight variations of each other (replace Alice with Bob and vice-versa). Figure 3 depicts the first output, while the exact scripts of both outputs can be found in the proof-of-concept implementation https://github.com/OrfeasLitos/cerberus-script. For the first output, the two revocation public keys are those of Alice and the watchtower, sorted by ascending order of their DER-encodings. Similarly sorted are the revocation public keys of Bob and the watchtower in the second output.

```
OP_IF # Penalty
   2 <penalty_pubkey1>
   <penalty_pubkey2> 2
   OP_CHECKMULTISIG
OP_ELSE # Normal
   <long_delay>
   OP_CHECKSEQUENCEVERIFY
   OP_DROP
   <watchtower_penalty_pubkey>
   OP_CHECKSIG
OP_ENDIF
```

```
OP_IF # Revocation
   2 <revocation_pubkey1>
   <revocation_pubkey2> 2
   OP_CHECKMULTISIG
OP_ELSE # Normal
   <bob_delay>
   OP_CHECKSEQUENCEVERIFY
   OP_DROP
   <alice_delayed_pubkey>
   OP_CHECKSIG
OP_ENDIF
```

Fig. 2. Reclaim transaction output script.

Fig. 3. Commitment transaction 1st output script.

The revocation transaction spends the outputs of the commitment transaction following the revocation path. The witness script of both inputs is 0 <revocation_pubkey1_sig> <revocation_pubkey2_sig> 1 with the appropriate signatures for each output. It has a P2WPKH[7] output to Bob's public key.

The penalty transaction 1 spends the second output of the commitment transaction and the output of the collateral transaction. It also has a single plain P2WPKH output to Bob's public key. The first input follows the normal path and has a witness script <bob_delayed_pubkey_sig> 0, whereas the second input has a witness script 0 <collateral_pubkey1_sig> <collateral_pubkey2_sig>.

Lastly, the penalty transaction 2 is similar to penalty transaction 1, but it spends the collateral instead of the reclaim transaction. Explicitly, penalty

---

[6] https://github.com/bitcoin/bips/blob/master/bip-0066.mediawiki.

[7] https://wiki.trezor.io/P2WPKH.

transaction 2 spends the 2nd output of the commitment and the output of the
reclaim transaction following the penalty path. It has a single plain P2WPKH
output to Bob's public key. The first input follows the normal path and has a
witness script `<bob_delayed_pubkey_sig> 0`, whereas the second input has a
witness script `0 <penalty_pubkey1_sig> <penalty_pubkey2_sig> 1`.

7   Limitations and Future Work

Privacy. CERBERUS channels maintain the privacy property, as defined in
Sect. 3.3, assuming that the watchtowers are considered internal to the channel
parties. This means that the transactions executed off-chain during the phase
Update are known only to the parties of the channel and the hired watchtowers.
Any other third-party, external to the channel, does not have any knowledge on
the state of the channel. Nevertheless, CERBERUS channels do not guarantee privacy from the watchtowers. Although Lightning watchtowers preserve the privacy
of transactions from watchtowers, they also suffer from inadequate incentives for
participation in the system. On the other hand, CERBERUS channels provide
the necessary incentive mechanisms to guarantee security, but watchtowers are
aware of all transactions executed in the channel. Introducing stronger privacy
mechanisms while maintaining the appropriate incentives is left for future work.

Extension to Multiple Watchtowers. To enhance security against possible
crash failures or withdrawal of watchtower service, parties can employ many
watchtowers. In such a case, every watchtower needs to lock its collateral on-
chain, thus the number of on-chain transactions grows linearly with the number
of watchtowers. However, to guarantee security, the sum of all watchtowers' collateral can remain the same, *i.e.*, at least greater than the total funds locked in
the channel by both parties. This way the counterparty of the channel cannot
bribe all watchtowers since the sum of the required bribes will exceed the party's
potential gain. Therefore, there will be at least one watchtower that will publish
the revocation transaction in case of fraud.

Rewards and Collateral. In the current system, rewards are awarded to the
watchtowers on every update of the channel by the hired party via a one-way
channel. Ideally, these rewards should be returned to the hired party if the watchtower misbehaves. To this end, we can modify the collateral transaction to build
a bidirectional payment channel in which the watchtower locks collateral and the
hirer locks future rewards. Then, during an update of the CERBERUS channel
and upon receiving the signed penalty transaction, the hirer sends some funds in
this channel, paying the watchtower for its service. Note that this process does
not require a fair exchange protocol since the watchtower can simply withdraw
its service in case the hiring party does not pay the reward, similarly to the current protocol. However, this modification implies that the watchtowers' rewards
will be locked during the lifetime of the channel.

Assumptions. In every channel construction that the counterparty is allowed to publish on-chain a valid outdated state, timelocks are necessary to secure the construction. Assuming distrusting parties (including the watchtower), this implies that every party must be online once in a while to verify the correct operation of the construction. Hence, at best we can alleviate the availability assumption, but not abolish it completely. In turn, due to timelocks, the security of CERBERUS channels depends on synchrony assumptions and a perfect blockchain that cannot be censored. Although we enable shorter revocation periods and parties can go offline for an extended period of time, we cannot decouple the dependency of the security of payment channels on Bitcoin from the liveness and synchrony of the underlying blockchain.

References

1. BIP65. https://github.com/bitcoin/bips/blob/master/bip-0065.mediawiki. Accessed 19 Nov 2019
2. BIP68. https://github.com/bitcoin/bips/blob/master/bip-0068.mediawiki. Accessed 19 Nov 2019
3. Bitcoin Lightning fraud? Laolu is building a watchtower to fight it. https://www.coindesk.com/laolu-building-watchtower-fight-bitcoin-lightning-fraud. Accessed 29 Jun 2018
4. Real-time lightning network statistics. https://1ml.com/statistics. Accessed 17 Sept 2019
5. Avarikioti, G., Kogias, E.K., Wattenhofer, R.: Brick: asynchronous state channels. arXiv preprint: 1905.11360 (2019)
6. Avarikioti, G., Laufenberg, F., Sliwinski, J., Wang, Y., Wattenhofer, R.: Towards secure and efficient payment channels (2018)
7. Croman, K., et al.: On scaling decentralized blockchains. In: Clark, J., Meiklejohn, S., Ryan, P.Y.A., Wallach, D., Brenner, M., Rohloff, K. (eds.) FC 2016. LNCS, vol. 9604, pp. 106–125. Springer, Heidelberg (2016). https://doi.org/10.1007/978-3-662-53357-4_8
8. Decker, C., Russell, R., Osuntokun, O.: eltoo: a simple layer2 protocol for Bitcoin (2018)
9. Decker, C., Wattenhofer, R.: A fast and scalable payment network with Bitcoin duplex micropayment channels. In: Pelc, A., Schwarzmann, A.A. (eds.) SSS 2015. LNCS, vol. 9212, pp. 3–18. Springer, Cham (2015). https://doi.org/10.1007/978-3-319-21741-3_1
10. Dryja, T.: Unlinkable outsourced channel monitoring (2016)
11. Dziembowski, S., Eckey, L., Faust, S., Malinowski, D.: Perun: virtual payment hubs over cryptographic currencies. Technical report, IACR Cryptology ePrint Archive 2017, 2017
12. Garay, J., Kiayias, A., Leonardos, N.: The Bitcoin backbone protocol: analysis and applications. In: Oswald, E., Fischlin, M. (eds.) EUROCRYPT 2015. LNCS, vol. 9057, pp. 281–310. Springer, Heidelberg (2015). https://doi.org/10.1007/978-3-662-46803-6_10
13. Green, M., Miers, I.: Bolt: anonymous payment channels for decentralized currencies. In: Proceedings of the 2017 ACM SIGSAC Conference on Computer and Communications Security, pp. 473–489. ACM (2017)

14. Gudgeon, L., Moreno-Sanchez, P., Roos, S., McCorry, P., Gervais, A.: SoK: off the chain transactions. IACR Cryptology ePrint Arch. **2019**, 360 (2019)
15. Khabbazian, M., Nadahalli, T., Wattenhofer, R.: Outpost: a responsive lightweight watchtower. Cryptology ePrint Archive, Report 2019/986, 2019. https://eprint.iacr.org/2019/986
16. McCorry, P., Bakshi, S., Bentov, I., Miller, A., Meiklejohn, S.: Pisa: arbitration outsourcing for state channels. IACR Cryptology ePrint Arch. **2018**, 582 (2018)
17. Miller, A., Bentov, I., Kumaresan, R., McCorry,P.: Sprites: Payment channels that go faster than lightning. CoRR, abs/1702.05812 (2017)
18. Nakamoto, S.: Bitcoin: A peer-to-peer electronic cash system (2008)
19. Poon, J., Dryja, T.: The bitcoin lightning network: Scalable off-chain instant payments (2015)
20. Spilman, J.: Anti dos for tx replacement. https://lists.linuxfoundation.org/pipermail/bitcoin-dev/2013-April/002433.html. Accessed 17 Apr 2019

Secure Computation

Communication-Efficient (Client-Aided) Secure Two-Party Protocols and Its Application

Satsuya Ohata[1](✉) and Koji Nuida[1,2]

[1] National Institute of Advanced Industrial Science and Technology,
Tokyo, Japan
satsuya.ohata@aist.go.jp
[2] The University of Tokyo, Tokyo, Japan
nuida@mist.i.u-tokyo.ac.jp

Abstract. Secure multi-party computation (MPC) allows a set of parties to compute a function jointly while keeping their inputs private. Compared with the MPC based on garbled circuits, some recent research results show that MPC based on secret sharing (SS) works at a very high speed. Moreover, SS-based MPC can be easily vectorized and achieve higher throughput. In SS-based MPC, however, we need many communication rounds for computing concrete protocols like equality check, less-than comparison, etc. This property is not suited for large-latency environments like the Internet (or WAN). In this paper, we construct semi-honest secure communication-efficient two-party protocols. The core technique is *Beaver triple extension*, which is a new tool for treating multi-fan-in gates, and we also show how to use it efficiently. We mainly focus on reducing the number of communication rounds, and our protocols also succeed in reducing the number of communication bits (in most cases). As an example, we propose a less-than comparison protocol (under practical parameters) with *three* communication rounds. Moreover, the number of communication bits is also 38.4% fewer. As a result, total online execution time is 56.1% shorter than the previous work adopting the same settings. Although the computation costs of our protocols are more expensive than those of previous work, we confirm via experiments that such a disadvantage has small effects on the whole online performance in the typical WAN environments.

1 Introduction

Secure multi-party computation (MPC) [13,25] allows a set of parties to compute a function f jointly while keeping their inputs private. More precisely, the $N(\geq 2)$ parties, each holding private input x_i for $i \in [1, N]$, are able to compute the output $f(x_1, \cdots, x_N)$ without revealing their private inputs x_i. Some recent research showed there are many progresses in the research on MPC based on secret sharing (SS) and its performance is dramatically improved. SS-based MPC can be easily vectorized and suitable for parallel executions. We can obtain

J. Bonneau and N. Heninger (Eds.): FC 2020, LNCS 12059, pp. 369–385, 2020.
https://doi.org/10.1007/978-3-030-51280-4_20

large throughput in SS-based MPC since we have no limit on the size of vectors. This is a unique property on SS-based MPC, and it is compatible with the SIMD operations like mini-batch training in privacy-preserving machine learning. We cannot enjoy this advantage in the MPC based on garbled circuits (GC) or homomorphic encryption (HE). The most efficient MPC scheme so far is three-party computation (3PC) based on 2-out-of-3 SS (e.g., [1,7]). In two-party computation (2PC), which is the focus of this paper, we need fewer hardware resources than 3PC. Although it does not work at high speed since we need heavy pre-computation, we can mitigate this problem by adopting slightly new MPC models like client/server-aided models that we denote later.

In addition to the advantage as denoted above, the amount of data transfer in online phase is also small in SS-based MPC than GC/HE-based one. However, the number of communication rounds we need for computation is large in SS-based MPC. We need one interaction between computing parties when we compute an arithmetic multiplication gate or a boolean AND gate, which is time-consuming when processing non-linear functions since it is difficult to make the circuit depth shallow. This is a critical disadvantage in real-world privacy-preserving applications since there are non-linear functions we frequently use in practice like equality check, less-than comparison, max value extraction, activation functions in machine learning, etc. In most of the previous research, however, this problem has not been seriously treated. This is because they assumed there is (high-speed) LAN connection between computing parties. Under such environments, total online execution time we need for processing non-linear functions is small even if we need many interactions between computing parties since the communication latency is usually very short (typically ≤ 0.5 ms). This assumption is somewhat strange in practice, as the use of LAN suggests that MPC is executed on the network that is maintained by the same administrator/organization. In that case, it is not clear if the requirement for SS that parties do not collude is held or not. Hence, it looks more suitable to assume non-local networks like WAN. However, large communication latency in WAN becomes the performance bottleneck in SS-based MPC. We find by our experiments that the time caused by the communication latency occupies more than 99% in some cases for online total execution time. To reduce the effect of the large communication latency, it is important to develop SS-based MPC with fewer communication rounds. In other words, we should put in work to make the circuit shallower to improve the concrete efficiency of SS-based MPC.

1.1   Related Work

MPC Based on Secret Sharing. There are many research results on SS-based MPC. For example, we have results on highly-efficient MPC (e.g., [1,7]), concrete tools or the toolkit (e.g., [4,9,21,22]), mixed-protocol framework [10,18,23], application to privacy-preserving machine learning or data analysis (e.g., [18,20,23]), proposal of another model for speeding up the pre-computation [17,20], etc. As denoted previously, however, we have not been able to obtain good experimental results for computing large circuits over WAN environments. For example, [20] denoted the neural network training on WAN setting is not practical yet.

MPC Based on Garbled Circuit or Homomorphic Encryption. There are also many research results on GC/HE-based MPC. For example, we have results on the toolkit (e.g., [16]), encryption switching protocols [8,15], privacy-preserving machine learning (e.g., [5,11,14]), etc. Recently, we have many research results on GC for more than three parties (e.g., [19,27]). Note that it is difficult to improve the circuit size on standard boolean GC [26], which is a bottleneck on GC-based MPC. Moreover, [3,6] proposed the GC-based MPC for WAN environments and showed the benchmark using AES, etc. Even if we adopt the most efficient GC [26] with 128-bit security, however, we need to send at least 256-bit string per an AND gate. This is two orders of magnitude larger than SS-based MPC. We construct the round-efficient protocol while keeping data traffic small.

1.2 Our Contribution

There are two main contributions in this paper. First, we propose the method for treating multi-fan-in gates in semi-honest secure SS-based 2PC and show how to use them efficiently. Second, we propose many round-efficient protocols and show their performance evaluations via experiments. We explain the details of them as follows:

1. We propose the method for treating multi-fan-in MULT/AND gates over $\mathbb{Z}_{2^n}$ and some techniques for reducing the communication rounds of protocols. Our N-fan-in gates are based on the extension of Beaver triples, which is a technique for computing standard 2-fan-in gates. In our technique, however, we have a disadvantage that the computation costs and the memory costs are exponentially increased by N; that is, we have to limit the size of N in practice. On the other hand, we can improve the costs of communication. More concretely, we can compute arbitrary N-fan-in MULT/AND with one communication round and the amount of data transfer is also improved. Moreover, we show performance evaluation results on above multi-fan-in gates via experiments. More concretely, see Sects. 3 and 5.1.
2. We propose round-efficient protocols using multi-fan-in gates. We need fewer interactions for our protocols between computing parties in online phase than previous ones. When we use shares over $\mathbb{Z}_{2^{32}}$, compared with the previous work [4], we reduce the communication rounds as follows: Equality : $(5 \rightarrow 2)$, Comparison : $(7 \rightarrow 3)$, and Max for 3 elements:$(18 \rightarrow 4)$. Moreover, we show the performance evaluation results on our protocols via experiments. From our experiments, we find the computation costs for multi-fan-in gates and protocols based on them have small effects on the whole online performance in the typical WAN environments. We also implement an application (a privacy-preserving exact edit distance protocol for genome strings) using our protocols. More concretely, see Sects. 4, 5.2, and 5.3.

2   Preliminaries

2.1   Syntax for Secret Sharing

A 2-out-of-2 secret sharing $((2,2)$-SS) scheme over $\mathbb{Z}_{2^n}$ consists of two algorithms: Share and Reconst. Share takes as input $x \in \mathbb{Z}_{2^n}$, and outputs $([\![x]\!]_0, [\![x]\!]_1) \in \mathbb{Z}_{2^n}^2$, where the bracket notation $[\![x]\!]_i$ denotes the share of the i-th party (for $i \in \{0,1\}$). We denote $[\![x]\!] = ([\![x]\!]_0, [\![x]\!]_1)$ as their shorthand. Reconst takes as input $[\![x]\!]$, and outputs x. For arithmetic sharing $[\![x]\!]^{\mathsf{A}} = ([\![x]\!]_0^{\mathsf{A}}, [\![x]\!]_1^{\mathsf{A}})$ and boolean sharing $[\![x]\!]^{\mathsf{B}} = ([\![x]\!]_0^{\mathsf{B}}, [\![x]\!]_1^{\mathsf{B}})$, we consider power-of-two integers n (e.g. $n = 64$) and $n = 1$, respectively.

2.2   Secure Two-Party Computation Based on $(2, 2)$-Additive Secret Sharing

Here, we explain how to compute arithmetic ADD/MULT gates on $(2,2)$-additive SS. We use the standard $(2,2)$-additive SS scheme, defined by

- Share(x): randomly choose $r \in \mathbb{Z}_{2^n}$ and let $[\![x]\!]_0^{\mathsf{A}} = r$ and $[\![x]\!]_1^{\mathsf{A}} = x - r \in \mathbb{Z}_{2^n}$.
- Reconst$([\![x]\!]_0^{\mathsf{A}}, [\![x]\!]_1^{\mathsf{A}})$: output $[\![x]\!]_0^{\mathsf{A}} + [\![x]\!]_1^{\mathsf{A}}$.

We can compute fundamental operations; that is, $\mathsf{ADD}(x,y) := x + y$ and $\mathsf{MULT}(x,y) := xy$. $[\![z]\!] \leftarrow \mathsf{ADD}([\![x]\!], [\![y]\!])$ can be done locally by just adding each party's shares on x and on y. $[\![w]\!] \leftarrow \mathsf{MULT}([\![x]\!], [\![y]\!])$ can be done in various ways. We will use the standard method based on Beaver triples (BT) [2]. Such a triple consists of $\mathsf{bt}_0 = (a_0, b_0, c_0)$ and $\mathsf{bt}_1 = (a_1, b_1, c_1)$ such that $(a_0 + a_1)(b_0 + b_1) = (c_0 + c_1)$. Hereafter, a, b, and c denote $a_0 + a_1$, $b_0 + b_1$, and $c_0 + c_1$, respectively. We can compute these BT in offline phase. In this protocol, each i-th party P_i $(i \in \{0,1\})$ can compute the multiplication share $[\![z]\!]_i = [\![xy]\!]_i$ as follows: (1) P_i first compute $([\![x]\!]_i - a_i)$ and $([\![y]\!]_i - b_i)$. (2) P_i sends them to P_{1-i}. (3) P_i reconstruct $x' = x - a$ and $y' = y - b$. (4) P_0 computes $[\![z]\!]_0 = x'y' + x'b_0 + y'a_0 + c_0$ and P_1 computes $[\![z]\!]_1 = x'b_1 + y'a_1 + c_1$. Here, $[\![z]\!]_0$ and $[\![z]\!]_1$ calculated as above procedures are valid shares of xy; that is, $\mathsf{Reconst}([\![z]\!]_0, [\![z]\!]_1) = xy$. We abuse notations and write the ADD and MULT protocols simply as $[\![x]\!] + [\![y]\!]$ and $[\![x]\!] \cdot [\![y]\!]$, respectively. Note that similarly to the ADD protocol, we can also locally compute multiplication by constant c, denoted by $c \cdot [\![x]\!]$.

We can easily extend above protocols to boolean gates. By converting $+$ and $-$ to $\oplus$ in arithmetic ADD and MULT protocols, we can obtain XOR and AND protocols, respectively. We can construct NOT and OR protocols from the properties of these gates. When we compute $\mathsf{NOT}([\![x]\!]_0^{\mathsf{B}}, [\![x]\!]_1^{\mathsf{B}})$, P_0 and P_1 output $\neg[\![x]\!]_0^{\mathsf{B}}$ and $[\![x]\!]_1^{\mathsf{B}}$, respectively. When we compute $\mathsf{OR}([\![x]\!], [\![y]\!])$, we compute $\neg\mathsf{AND}(\neg[\![x]\!], \neg[\![y]\!])$. We abuse notations and write the XOR, AND, NOT, and OR protocols simply as $[\![x]\!] \oplus [\![y]\!]$, $[\![x]\!] \wedge [\![y]\!]$, $\neg[\![x]\!]$ (or $\overline{[\![x]\!]}$), and $[\![x]\!] \vee [\![y]\!]$, respectively.

2.3   Semi-honest Security and Client-Aided Model

In this paper, we consider simulation-based security notion in the presence of semi-honest adversaries (for 2PC) as in [12]. As described in [12], composition theorem for the semi-honest model holds; that is, any protocol is privately computed as long as its subroutines are privately computed.

In this paper, we adopt client-aided model [20, 21] (or server-aided model [17]) for 2PC. In this model, a client (other than computing parties) generates and distributes shares of secrets. Moreover, the client also generates and distributes some necessary BTs to the computing parties. This improves the efficiency of offline computation dramatically since otherwise computing parties would have to generate BTs by themselves jointly via heavy cryptographic primitives like homomorphic encryption or oblivious transfer. The only downside for this model is the restriction that any computing party is assumed to not collude with the client who generates BTs for keeping the security.

3   Core Tools for Round-Efficient Protocols

In this section, we propose a core tool for round-efficient 2PC that we call "Beaver triple extension (BTE)". Moreover, we explain some techniques for precomputation to reduce the communication rounds in online phase.

3.1 N-fan-in MULT/AND via N-Beaver Triple Extension

N-Beaver Triple Extension. Let N be a positive integer. Let $\mathcal{M} = \mathbb{Z}_M$ for some M (e.g., $M = 2^n$). Write $[1, N] = \{1, 2, \ldots, N\}$. We define a client-aided protocol for generating N-BTE as follows:

1. Client randomly chooses $[\![a_{\{\ell\}}]\!]_0$ and $[\![a_{\{\ell\}}]\!]_1$ from $\mathcal{M}$ ($\ell = 1, \ldots, N$). Let $a_{\{\ell\}} \leftarrow [\![a_{\{\ell\}}]\!]_0 + [\![a_{\{\ell\}}]\!]_1$. For each $I \subseteq [1, N]$ with $|I| \geq 2$, by setting $a_I \leftarrow \prod_{\ell \in I} a_{\{\ell\}}$, client randomly chooses $[\![a_I]\!]_0 \in \mathcal{M}$ and sets $[\![a_I]\!]_1 \leftarrow a_I - [\![a_I]\!]_0$.
2. Client sends all the $[\![a_I]\!]_0$ to P_0 and all the $[\![a_I]\!]_1$ to P_1.

Note that, in the protocol above, the process of randomly choosing $[\![a_I]\!]_0$ and then setting $[\![a_I]\!]_1 \leftarrow a_I - [\![a_I]\!]_0$ is equivalent to randomly choosing $[\![a_I]\!]_1$ and then setting $[\![a_I]\!]_0 \leftarrow a_I - [\![a_I]\!]_1$. Therefore, the roles of P_0 and P_1 are symmetric.

Multiplication Protocol. For $\ell = 1, \ldots, N$, let $([\![x_\ell]\!]_0, [\![x_\ell]\!]_1)$ be given shares of ℓ-th secret input value $x_\ell \in \mathcal{M}$. The protocol for multiplication is constructed as follows:

1. Client generates and distributes N-BTE $([\![a_I]\!]_0)_I$ and $([\![a_I]\!]_1)_I$ to the two parties as described above.
2. For $k = 0, 1$, P_k computes $[\![x'_\ell]\!]_k \leftarrow [\![x_\ell]\!]_k - [\![a_{\{\ell\}}]\!]_k$ for $\ell = 1, \ldots, N$ and sends those $[\![x'_\ell]\!]_k$ to P_{1-k}.
3. For $k = 0, 1$, P_k computes $x'_\ell \leftarrow [\![x'_\ell]\!]_{1-k} + [\![x'_\ell]\!]_k$ for $\ell = 1, \ldots, N$.
4. P_0 outputs $[\![y]\!]_0$ given by

$$[\![y]\!]_0 \leftarrow \prod_{\ell=1}^{N} x'_\ell + \sum_{\emptyset \neq I \subseteq [1,N]} \left(\prod_{\ell \in [1,N] \setminus I} x'_\ell \right) [\![a_I]\!]_0$$

while P_1 outputs $[\![y]\!]_1$ given by

$$[\![y]\!]_1 \leftarrow \sum_{\emptyset \neq I \subseteq [1,N]} \left(\prod_{\ell \in [1,N] \setminus I} x'_\ell \right) [\![a_I]\!]_1 \, .$$

We can prove the correctness and semi-honest security of this protocol. Due to the page limitation, we show the proofs in the full version of this paper.

3.2   Discussion on Beaver Triple Extension

We can achieve the same functionality of N–MULT/AND by using 2–MULT/AND multiple times and there are some trade-offs between these two strategies. In the computation of N-fan-in MULT/AND using N-BTE, the memory consumption and computation cost increase exponentially with N. Therefore, we have to put a restriction on the size of N and concrete settings change optimal N. In this paper, we use N–MULT/AND for $N \leq 9$ to construct round-efficient protocols. On the other hand, N-fan-in MULT/AND using N-BTE needs fewer communication costs. Notably, the number of communication rounds of our protocol does not depend on N and this improvement has significant effects on practical performances in WAN settings. Because of the problems on the memory/computation costs we denoted above, however, there is a limitation for the size of N. When we use L-fan-in MULT/AND ($L \leq N$) gates, we need $\frac{\lceil \log N \rceil}{\lceil \log L \rceil}$ communication rounds for computing N-fan-in MULT/AND.

Damgård et al. [9] also proposed how to compute N-fan-in gates in a round-efficient manner using Lagrange interpolation. Each of their scheme and ours has its merits and demerits. Their scheme has an advantage over memory consumption and computational costs; that is, their N-fan-in gates do not need exponentially large memory and computation costs. On the other hand, their scheme needs two communication rounds to compute N-fan-in gates for any N and requires the share spaces to be $\mathbb{Z}_p$ (p: prime). A 2PC scheme over $\mathbb{Z}_{2^n}$ is sometimes more efficient than one over $\mathbb{Z}_p$ when we implement them using low-level language (e.g., C++) since we do not have to compute remainders modulo 2^n for all arithmetic operations.

3.3   More Techniques for Reducing Communication Rounds

On Weights at Most One. We consider the plain input x that all bits are 0, or only a single bit is 1 and others are 0. In this setting, we can compute the share representing whether all the bits of x are 0 or not without communications between P_0 and P_1. More concretely, we can compute it by locally computing XOR for all bits on each share. This technique is implicitly used in the previous work [4] for constructing an arithmetic overflow detection protocol Overflow, which is an important building block for constructing less-than comparison and more. We show more skillful use of this technique for constructing Overflow to avoid heavy computation in our protocols. More concretely, see Sect. 4.2.

Arithmetic Blinding. We consider the situation that two clients who have secrets also execute computation (i.e., an input party is equal to a computing party), which is the different setting from client-aided 2PC. During the multiplication protocol, both P_0 and P_1 obtain $x - a$ and $y - b$. Here, P_0 finds a and P_1 finds b since P_0 and P_1 know the value of x and y, respectively. Therefore, it does not matter if P_0 and P_1 previously know the corresponding values; that is, P_0 can send b_0 to P_1 and P_1 can send a_1 to P_0 in the pre-computation phase. This operation does not cause security problems. By above pre-processing, P_0 and P_1 can directly send $x - a$ and $y - b$ in the multiplication protocol, respectively. As a result, we can reduce the amount of data transfer in the multiplication protocol. Even in the client-aided 2PC setting, this situation appears in the boolean-to-arithmetic conversion protocol. More concretely, see Sect. 4.3.

Trivial Sharing. We consider the setting that an input party is not equal to a computing party, which is the same one as standard client-aided 2PC. In this situation, we can use the share $[\![b]\!]_i$ ($i \in \{0, 1\}$) itself as a secret value for computations by considering another party has the share $[\![0]\!]_{1-i}$. Although we find this technique in the previous work [4], we can further reduce the communication rounds of two-party protocols by combining this technique and BTE. More concretely, see Sect. 4.3.

4   Communication-Efficient Protocols

In this section, we show round-efficient 2PC protocols using BTE and the techniques in Sect. 3.3. For simplicity, in this section, we set a share space to $\mathbb{Z}_{2^{16}}$ and use N-fan-in gates ($N \leq 5$) to explain our proposed protocols. Although we omit the protocols over $\mathbb{Z}_{2^{32}}/\mathbb{Z}_{2^{64}}$ due to the page limitation, we can obtain the protocols with the same communication rounds with $\mathbb{Z}_{2^{16}}$ by using 7 or less fan-in AND over $\mathbb{Z}_{2^{32}}$ and 9 or less fan-in AND over $\mathbb{Z}_{2^{64}}$. We omit the correctness of the protocols adopting the same strategy in the previous work [4].

4.1   Equality Check Protocol and Its Application

An equality check protocol $\mathsf{Equality}([\![x]\!]^A, [\![y]\!]^A)$ outputs $[\![z]\!]^B$, where $z = 1$ iff $x = y$. We start from the approach by [4] and focus on reducing communication rounds. In $\mathsf{Equality}$, roughly speaking, we first compute $t = x - y$ and then check if all bits of t are 0 or not. If all the bits of t are 0, it means $t = x - y = 0$. We show our two-round $\mathsf{Equality}$ as in Algorithm 1: In our strategy, more generally, we need $\frac{\lceil \log n \rceil}{\lceil \log L \rceil}$ communication rounds for executing $\mathsf{Equality}$ when we set the share space to $\mathbb{Z}_{2^n}$ and use N-OR ($N \leq L$). By using our $\mathsf{Equality}$, we can also obtain a three-round round-efficient table lookup protocol TLU. We show the construction of our TLU in the full version of this paper.

Algorithm 1. Our Proposed Equality

Functionality: $[\![z]\!]^B \leftarrow \mathsf{Equality}([\![x]\!]^A, [\![y]\!]^A)$

Ensure: $[\![z]\!]^B$, where $z = 1$ iff $x = y$.

1: P_0 and P_1 locally compute $[\![t]\!]_0^A = [\![x]\!]_0^A - [\![y]\!]_0^A$ and $[\![t]\!]_1^A = [\![y]\!]_1^A - [\![x]\!]_1^A$, respectively.

2: P_i ($i \in \{0,1\}$) locally extend $[\![t]\!]_i^A$ to binary and see them as boolean shares; that is, P_i obtain $[[\![t[15]\!]]_i^B, \cdots, [\![t[0]\!]]_i^B]$.

3: P_i compute $[\![t'[j]\!]]^B \leftarrow \mathsf{4\text{-}OR}([\![t[4j]\!]]^B, [\![t[4j+1]\!]]^B, [\![t[4j+2]\!]]^B, [\![t[4j+3]\!]]^B)$ for $j \in [0, \cdots, 3]$.

4: P_i compute $[\![t'']\!]^B \leftarrow \mathsf{4\text{-}OR}([\![t'[0]\!]]^B, [\![t'[1]\!]]^B, [\![t'[2]\!]]^B, [\![t'[3]\!]]^B)$.

5: P_i compute $[\![z]\!]^B = \neg[\![t'']\!]^B$.

6: **return** $[\![z]\!]^B$.

Algorithm 2. Our Proposed MSNZB

Functionality: $[\![z]\!]^B \leftarrow \mathsf{MSNZB}([\![x]\!]^B)$

Ensure: $[\![z]\!]^B = [[\![z[15]\!]]^B, \cdots, [\![z[0]\!]]^B]$, where $z[j] = 1$ for the largest value j such that $x[j] = 1$ and $z[k] = 0$ for all $j \neq k$.

1: P_i ($i \in \{0,1\}$) set $[\![t[j]\!]]_i^B = [\![x[j]\!]]_i^B$ for $j \in [3,7,11,15]$. Then P_i parallelly compute
$[\![t[j]\!]]^B \leftarrow \mathsf{2\text{-}OR}([\![x[j]\!]]^B, [\![x[j+1]\!]]^B)$ for $j \in [2,6,10,14]$,
$[\![t[j]\!]]^B \leftarrow \mathsf{3\text{-}OR}([\![x[j]\!]]^B, [\![x[j+1]\!]]^B, [\![x[j+2]\!]]^B)$ for $j \in [1,5,9,13]$, and
$[\![t[j]\!]]^B \leftarrow \mathsf{4\text{-}OR}([\![x[j]\!]]^B, [\![x[j+1]\!]]^B, [\![x[j+2]\!]]^B, [\![x[j+3]\!]]^B)$ for $j \in [0,4,8,12]$.

2: P_i compute $[\![t'[j]\!]]_i^B = [\![t[j]\!]]_i^B$ for $j \in [3,7,11,15]$ and compute
$[\![t'[j]\!]]_i^B = [\![t[j]\!]]_i^B \oplus [\![t[j+1]\!]]_i^B$ for $j \in [0,1,2,4,5,6,8,9,10,12,13,14]$.

3: P_i locally compute $[\![s[j]\!]]_i^B = \bigoplus_{k=4j}^{4j+3} [\![t'[k]\!]]_i^B$ for $j \in [1,2,3]$.

4: P_i compute $[\![z[j]\!]]_i^B = [\![t'[j]\!]]_i^B$ for $j \in [12, \cdots, 15]$. Then P_i parallelly compute
$[\![z[j]\!]]^B \leftarrow \mathsf{2\text{-}AND}([\![t'[j]\!]]^B, \neg[\![s[3]\!]]^B)$ for $j \in [8, \cdots, 11]$,
$[\![z[j]\!]]^B \leftarrow \mathsf{3\text{-}AND}([\![t'[j]\!]]^B, \neg[\![s[2]\!]]^B, \neg[\![s[3]\!]]^B)$ for $j \in [4, \cdots, 7]$, and
$[\![z[j]\!]]^B \leftarrow \mathsf{4\text{-}AND}([\![t'[j]\!]]^B, \neg[\![s[1]\!]]^B, \neg[\![s[2]\!]]^B, \neg[\![s[3]\!]]^B)$ for $j \in [0, \cdots, 3]$.

5: **return** $[\![z]\!]^B = [[\![z[15]\!]]^B, \cdots, [\![z[0]\!]]^B]$.

4.2 Overflow Detection Protocol and Applications

An arithmetic overflow detection protocol Overflow has many applications and is also a core building block of less-than comparison protocol. The same as the approach by [4], we construct Overflow via the most significant non-zero bit extraction protocol MSNZB. We first explain how to construct MSNZB efficiently and then show two-round Overflow.

A protocol for extracting the most significant non-zero bit ($\mathsf{MSNZB}([\![x]\!]^B = [[\![x[15]\!]]^B, \cdots, [\![x[0]\!]]^B])$) finds the position of the first "1" of the x and outputs such a boolean share vector $[\![z]\!]^B = [[\![z[15]\!]]^B, \cdots, [\![z[0]\!]]^B]$. In [4], we used a "prefix-OR" operation for executing MSNZB. On the other hand, in our construction, we first separate a bit string into some blocks and compute in-block MSNZB. Then, we compute correct MSNZB for x via in-block MSNZB. We show our two-round MSNZB as in Algorithm 2. Based on the above MSNZB, we can construct an arithmetic overflow detection protocol $\mathsf{Overflow}([\![x]\!]^A, k)$. This protocol outputs $[\![z]\!]^B$, where $z = 1$ iff the condition $([\![x]\!]_0^A \bmod 2^k + [\![x]\!]_1^A \bmod 2^k) \geq 2^k$ holds. We also start from the approach by [4]. In their Overflow,

---

Algorithm 3. Our Proposed Overflow

Functionality: $[\![z]\!]^{\mathsf{B}} \leftarrow \mathsf{Overflow}([\![x]\!]^{\mathsf{A}}, k)$
Ensure: $[\![z]\!]^{\mathsf{B}}$, where $z = 1$ iff $([\![x]\!]^{\mathsf{A}}_0 \bmod 2^k) + ([\![x]\!]^{\mathsf{A}}_1 \bmod 2^k) \geq 2^k$.

1: P_0 locally extends $([\![x]\!]^{\mathsf{A}}_0 \bmod 2^k)$ to binary and obtains
   $[\![d]\!]^{\mathsf{B}}_0 = [[\![d[15]]\!]^{\mathsf{B}}_0, \cdots, [\![d[0]]\!]^{\mathsf{B}}_0]$. P_1 also locally extends $(-[\![x]\!]^{\mathsf{A}}_1 \bmod 2^k)$ to binary
   and obtains $[\![d]\!]^{\mathsf{B}}_1 = [[\![d[15]]\!]^{\mathsf{B}}_1, \cdots, [\![d[0]]\!]^{\mathsf{B}}_1]$.
2: P_i $(i \in \{0,1\})$ set $[\![t[j]]\!]^{\mathsf{B}}_i = [\![d[j]]\!]^{\mathsf{B}}_i$ for $j \in [3, 7, 11, 15]$. Then P_i parallelly compute
   $[\![t[j]]\!]^{\mathsf{B}} \leftarrow 2\text{-OR}([\![d[j]]\!]^{\mathsf{B}}, [\![d[j+1]]\!]^{\mathsf{B}})$ for $j \in [2, 6, 10, 14]$,
   $[\![t[j]]\!]^{\mathsf{B}} \leftarrow 3\text{-OR}([\![d[j]]\!]^{\mathsf{B}}, [\![d[j+1]]\!]^{\mathsf{B}}, [\![d[j+2]]\!]^{\mathsf{B}})$ for $j \in [1, 5, 9, 13]$, and
   $[\![t[j]]\!]^{\mathsf{B}} \leftarrow 4\text{-OR}([\![d[j]]\!]^{\mathsf{B}}, [\![d[j+1]]\!]^{\mathsf{B}}, [\![d[j+2]]\!]^{\mathsf{B}}, [\![d[j+3]]\!]^{\mathsf{B}})$ for $j \in [0, 4, 8, 12]$.
3: P_i compute $[\![t'[j]]\!]^{\mathsf{B}}_i = [\![t[j]]\!]^{\mathsf{B}}_i$ for $j \in [3, 7, 11, 15]$ and compute
   $[\![t'[j]]\!]^{\mathsf{B}}_i = [\![t[j]]\!]^{\mathsf{B}}_i \oplus [\![t[j+1]]\!]^{\mathsf{B}}_i$ for $j \in [0, 1, 2, 4, 5, 6, 8, 9, 10, 12, 13, 14]$.
4: P_i locally compute $[\![w[j]]\!]^{\mathsf{B}}_i = \bigoplus_{k=4j}^{4j+3} [\![t'[k]]\!]^{\mathsf{B}}_i$ for $j \in [1, 2, 3]$.
5: P_0 sets $[\![u[j]]\!]^{\mathsf{B}}_0 = 0$ for $j \in [0, \cdots, 15]$ and
   P_1 sets $[\![u[j]]\!]^{\mathsf{B}}_1 = [\![d[j]]\!]^{\mathsf{B}}_1$ for $j \in [0, \cdots, 15]$.
6: P_i parallelly compute
   $[\![v[j]]\!]^{\mathsf{B}} \leftarrow 2\text{-AND}([\![t'[j]]\!]^{\mathsf{B}}, [\![u[j]]\!]^{\mathsf{B}})$ for $j \in [12, \cdots, 15]$,
   $[\![v[j]]\!]^{\mathsf{B}} \leftarrow 3\text{-AND}([\![t'[j]]\!]^{\mathsf{B}}, [\![u[j]]\!]^{\mathsf{B}}, \neg[\![w[3]]\!]^{\mathsf{B}})$ for $j \in [8, \cdots, 11]$,
   $[\![v[j]]\!]^{\mathsf{B}} \leftarrow 4\text{-AND}([\![t'[j]]\!]^{\mathsf{B}}, [\![u[j]]\!]^{\mathsf{B}}, \neg[\![w[2]]\!]^{\mathsf{B}}, \neg[\![w[3]]\!]^{\mathsf{B}})$ for $j \in [4, \cdots, 7]$, and
   $[\![v[j]]\!]^{\mathsf{B}} \leftarrow 5\text{-AND}([\![t'[j]]\!]^{\mathsf{B}}, [\![u[j]]\!]^{\mathsf{B}}, \neg[\![w[1]]\!]^{\mathsf{B}}, \neg[\![w[2]]\!]^{\mathsf{B}}, \neg[\![w[3]]\!]^{\mathsf{B}})$ for $j \in [0, \cdots, 3]$.
7: P_i locally compute $[\![z]\!]^{\mathsf{B}}_i = \bigoplus_{\ell=0}^{15} [\![v[\ell]]\!]^{\mathsf{B}}_i$.
8: P_i compute $[\![z]\!]^{\mathsf{B}} = \neg[\![z]\!]^{\mathsf{B}}$.
9: If $[\![x]\!]^{\mathsf{A}}_1 = 0$, then P_1 locally computes $[\![z]\!]^{\mathsf{B}}_1 = [\![z]\!]^{\mathsf{B}}_1 \oplus 1$
10: **return** $[\![z]\!]^{\mathsf{B}}$.

---

we check whether or not there exists 1 in $u = (-[\![x]\!]_1 \bmod 2^k)$ at the same position of MSNZB on $d = (([\![x]\!]_0 \bmod 2^k) \oplus (-[\![x]\!]_1 \bmod 2^k))$. Even if we apply our two-round MSNZB in this section, we need three communication rounds for their Overflow since we need one more round to check the above condition using 2-AND. Here, we consider further improvements by combining MSNZB and 2-AND; that is, we increase the fan-in of AND on the step 4 in Algorithm 2 and push the computation of 2-AND into that step as in Algorithm 3: Moreover, we can construct one-round Overflow for small shares spaces (in practice). We show a concrete construction in the full version of this paper.

We have many applications of Overflow like less-than comparison Comparison, which is a building block of the maximum value extraction protocol. In particular, thanks to the round-efficient Overflow, we can obtain a three-round Comparison. Morita et al. [21] proposed a constant (= five)-round Comparison using multi-fan-in gates that works under the shares over $\mathbb{Z}_p$ [9]. Our Comparison is more round-efficient than theirs under the parameters we consider in this paper.

4.3 Boolean-to-Arithmetic Conversion Protocol and Extensions

A boolean-to-arithmetic conversion protocol B2A($[\![x]\!]^{\mathsf{B}}$) outputs $[\![z]\!]^{\mathsf{A}}$, where $z = x$. In (1-bit) boolean shares, there are four cases; that is, $([\![x]\!]^{\mathsf{B}}_0, [\![x]\!]^{\mathsf{B}}_1) = (0, 0)$, $(0, 1), (1, 0), (1, 1)$. Even if we consider these boolean shares as arithmetic ones,

---

Algorithm 4. Our Proposed B2A

Functionality: $[\![z]\!]^A \leftarrow \mathsf{B2A}([\![x]\!]^B)$

Ensure: $[\![z]\!]^A$, where $z = x$.

1: In pre-computation phase, the client randomly chooses $a, b \in \mathbb{Z}_{2^{16}}$, computes $c = ab$, chooses a randomness $r \in \mathbb{Z}_{2^{16}}$, and sets $(c_0, c_1) = (r, c - r)$. Then the client sends (a, c_0) and (b, c_1) to P_0 and P_1, respectively.

2: P_i $(i \in \{0, 1\})$ set $[\![x]\!]_i^A = [\![x]\!]_i^B$.

3: P_0 computes $x' = [\![x]\!]_0^A - a$ and P_1 computes
   $x'' = [\![x]\!]_1^A - b$. Then they send them to each other.

4: P_0 computes $[\![z]\!]_0^A = [\![x]\!]_0^A - 2(x'x'' + x'' \cdot a + c_0)$ and
   P_1 computes $[\![z]\!]_1^A = [\![x]\!]_1^A - 2(x' \cdot b + c_1)$.

5: **return** $[\![z]\!]^A$

---

it works well in the first three cases; that is, $0 \oplus 0 = 0 + 0$, $0 \oplus 1 = 0 + 1$, and $1 \oplus 0 = 1 + 0$. However, $1 \oplus 1 \neq 1 + 1$ and we have to correct the output of this case. Based on this idea and the technique in Sect. 3.3 (trivial sharing), [4] proposed the construction of B2A. In their protocol, we use a standard arithmetic multiplication protocol and need one communication round. In the setting of client-aided 2PC, however, B2A satisfies the condition that input party is equal to the computing party. Therefore, we can apply the techniques in Sect. 3.3 (arithmetic blinding) and construct more efficient B2A as in Algorithm 4: Although the number of communication rounds is the same as in [4], our protocol is more efficient. First, the data transfer in online phase is reduced from $2n$-bits to n-bits. Moreover, the number of randomnesses we need in pre-computation is reduced from five to three, and the data amount for sending from the client to P_0 and P_1 is reduced from $3n$-bits to $2n$-bits.

We can extend the above idea and obtain protocols like BX2A: $[\![b]\!]^B \times [\![x]\!]^A = [\![bx]\!]^A$, BC2A: $[\![b]\!]^B \times [\![c]\!]^B = [\![bc]\!]^A$, and BCX2A: $[\![b]\!]^B \times [\![c]\!]^B \times [\![x]\!]^A = [\![bcx]\!]^A$. These protocols are useful when we construct a round-efficient maximum value extraction protocol (and its variants) in Sect. 4.4.

BX2A: $[\![b]\!]^B \times [\![x]\!]^A = [\![bx]\!]^A$ We usually need to compute the multiplication of a boolean share $[\![b]\!]^B$ and an arithmetic one $[\![x]\!]^A$ (e.g., TLU, ReLU function in neural networks). We call this protocol BX2A in this paper. [18] proposed one-round BX2A under the $(2, 3)$-replicated SS, such construction in 2PC has not been known. By almost the same idea as B2A, we can construct one-round BX2A in 2PC as follows:

1. P_i $(i \in \{0, 1\})$ set $[\![b]\!]_i^A = [\![b]\!]_i^B$.
2. P_0 sets $[\![b']\!]_0^A = [\![b]\!]_0^B$ and $[\![b'']\!]_0^A = 0$, and P_1 sets $[\![b']\!]_1^A = 0$ and $[\![b'']\!]_1^A = [\![b]\!]_1^B$.
3. P_i compute

$$[\![s]\!]_i^A \leftarrow \text{2-MULT}([\![b]\!]^A, [\![x]\!]^A)$$

$$[\![t]\!]_i^A \leftarrow \text{3-MULT}([\![b']\!]^A, [\![b'']\!]^A, [\![x]\!]^A).$$

4. P_i computes $[\![z]\!]_i^A = [\![s]\!]_i^A - 2[\![t]\!]_i^A$.

Here, we denote this computation as $[\![bx - 2b_0 b_1 x]\!]^A$.

BC2A: $[\![b]\!]^{\mathsf{B}} \times [\![c]\!]^{\mathsf{B}} = [\![bc]\!]^{\mathsf{A}}$ Almost the same idea as BX2A, we can compute $[\![b]\!]^{\mathsf{B}} \times [\![c]\!]^{\mathsf{B}} = [\![bc]\!]^{\mathsf{A}}$ (BC2A) with one communication round. We use this protocol in 3-Argmax/3-Argmin in Sect. 4.4. We can construct one-round BC2A by computing

$$[\![bc - 2b_0 b_1 - 2c_0 c_1 + 2b_0 \overline{c_0} b_1 \overline{c_1} + 2\overline{b_0} c_0 \overline{b_1} c_1]\!]^{\mathsf{A}}.$$

We need 2-MULT and 4-MULT for this protocol.

BCX2A: $[\![b]\!]^{\mathsf{B}} \times [\![c]\!]^{\mathsf{B}} \times [\![x]\!]^{\mathsf{A}} = [\![bcx]\!]^{\mathsf{A}}$ Almost the same idea as the above protocols, we can also compute $[\![b]\!]^{\mathsf{B}} \times [\![c]\!]^{\mathsf{B}} \times [\![x]\!]^{\mathsf{A}} = [\![bc]\!]^{\mathsf{A}}$ (BCX2A) with one communication round. We use this protocol in Max/Min in Sect. 4.4. We can construct one-round BC2A by computing

$$[\![bcx - 2b_0 b_1 x - 2c_0 c_1 x + 2b_0 \overline{c_0} b_1 \overline{c_1} x + 2\overline{b_0} c_0 \overline{b_1} c_1 x]\!]^{\mathsf{A}}.$$

We need 3-MULT and 5-MULT for this protocol.

4.4 The Maximum Value Extraction Protocol and Extensions

The maximum value extraction protocol $\mathsf{Max}([\![x]\!]^{\mathsf{A}})$ outputs $[\![z]\!]^{\mathsf{A}}$, where z is the largest value in x. We first explain the case of Max for three elements (3-Max), which is used for computing edit distance, etc. We denote a j-th element of x as $x[j]$; that is, $x = [x[0], x[1], x[2]]$. We start from a standard tournament-based construction. If the condition $x[0] < x[1]$ holds, $x' = x[1]$. Otherwise, $x' = x[0]$. By repeating the above procedure once more using $[\![x']\!]^{\mathsf{A}}$ and $[\![x[2]]\!]^{\mathsf{A}}$, we can extract the maximum value among x. In this strategy, we need 16 $(= (6 + 1 + 1) \times 2)$ communication rounds, and 8 $(= (3 + 1) \times 2)$ communication rounds even if we apply our three-round Comparison (in Sect. 4.2) and BX2A (in Sect. 4.3). This is mainly because we cannot parallelly execute Comparison. To solve this disadvantage, we first check the magnitude relationship for all elements using Comparison. Then we extract the maximum value. Based on these ideas, we show our 3-Max as in Algorithm 5: Although the computation costs obviously increased, this is four-round 3-Max by applying our Comparison and BCX2A. Based on the above idea, we can also obtain the minimum value extraction protocol, argument of the maximum/minimum extraction protocols, and (argument of) the maximum/minimum value extraction protocols with $N(>3)$ inputs. We show the construction of these protocols in the full version of this paper.

5 Performance Evaluation

We demonstrate the practicality of our arithmetic/boolean gates and protocols. We implemented 2PC simulators and performed all benchmarks on a single laptop computer with Intel Core i7-6700K 4.00 GHz and 64 GB RAM. We implemented simulators using Python 3.7 with Numpy v1.16.2 and vectorized all gates/protocols. We assumed 10 MB/s $(= 80000$ bits/ms) bandwidth and 40 ms RTT latency as typical WAN settings, and calculate the data transfer time

---

Algorithm 5. Our Proposed 3-Max

Functionality: $[\![z]\!]^A \leftarrow \mathsf{Max}([\![x]\!]^A)$
Ensure: $[\![z]\!]^A$, where z is the largest element in x.
1: P_i $(i \in \{0,1\})$ parallelly compute
  $[\![c_{01}]\!]^B \leftarrow \mathsf{Comparison}([\![x[0]]\!]^A, [\![x[1]]\!]^A)$,
  $[\![c_{02}]\!]^B \leftarrow \mathsf{Comparison}([\![x[0]]\!]^A, [\![x[2]]\!]^A)$, and
  $[\![c_{12}]\!]^B \leftarrow \mathsf{Comparison}([\![x[1]]\!]^A, [\![x[2]]\!]^A)$.
2: P_i compute $[\![c_{10}]\!]_i^B = \neg[\![c_{01}]\!]_i^B$, $[\![c_{20}]\!]_i^B = \neg[\![c_{02}]\!]_i^B$, and $[\![c_{21}]\!]_i^B = \neg[\![c_{12}]\!]_i^B$.
3: P_i parallelly compute
  $[\![t[0]]\!]_i^A \leftarrow \mathsf{BCX2A}([\![c_{10}]\!]^B, [\![c_{20}]\!]^B, [\![x[0]]\!]^A)$,
  $[\![t[1]]\!]_i^A \leftarrow \mathsf{BCX2A}([\![c_{01}]\!]^B, [\![c_{21}]\!]^B, [\![x[1]]\!]^A)$, and
  $[\![t[2]]\!]_i^A \leftarrow \mathsf{BCX2A}([\![c_{02}]\!]^B, [\![c_{12}]\!]^B, [\![x[2]]\!]^A)$.
4: P_i compute $[\![z]\!]_i^A = \Sigma_{j=0}^2 [\![t[j]]\!]_i^A$.
5: **return** $[\![z]\!]^A$.

(DTT) and communication latency (CL) using these values. We adopted the client-aided model; that is, we assumed in our experiments that clients generate BTE in their local environment without using HE/OT.

5.1 Performance of Basic Gates

Here we show experimental results on N-AND. We set $N = [2, \cdots, 9]$ and 1 to $10^6 (= 1000000)$ batch in our experiments. Here we mainly show the experimental results on the cases of 1/1000/1000000 batch. The results are as in Table 1 and Fig. 1: We find (1) the pre-computation time, online computation time, and data transfer time are exponentially growing up with respect to N; (2) the dominant part in online total execution time is WAN latency especially in the case of small batch. If we compute $N(>2)$-AND using multiple 2-AND gates, we need two or more communication rounds. Therefore, our scheme is especially suitable for the 2PC with relatively small batch (e.g., $\leq 10^5$) as it yields low WAN latency.

5.2 Performance of Our Protocols

Here we show experimental results on our proposed protocols (Equality, Comparison, and 3-Max). We implemented the baseline protocols [4] and our proposed ones in Sect. 4. Same as the evaluation of N-AND, we mainly show the results of our experiments over $\mathbb{Z}_{2^{32}}$ with 1/1000/1000000 batch in Table 2 and Fig. 2 (relations between batch size and online execution time). Same as the cases with N-AND, WAN latency is the dominant part of the online total execution time. In relatively small batch ($\leq 10^4$), all our protocols are faster than baseline ones in the online total execution time since ours require fewer communication rounds. For example in Comparison with 1 batch, we need more online computation time than the baseline one. However, communication costs are smaller. As a result, our Comparison is 56.1% faster than baseline one (280.6 ms → 122.1 ms) in our WAN settings. As already mentioned, our protocols are not suitable for a (extremely) large batch since the computation cost is larger than baseline ones.

Table 1. Evaluation on N-AND with 1(upper)/1000(middle)/1000000(lower) batch.

	pre-comp. time (ms)	online comp. time (ms)	# of comm. bits (bit)	data trans. time (ms)	# of comm. rounds	comm. latency (ms)	online total exec. time (ms)
	0.015	0.019	2	2.5×10^{-5}	1	40	40.0
2-AND	2.39	0.033	2×10^3	2.5×10^{-2}	1	40	40.1
	2439	19.4	2×10^6	25.0	1	40	84.4
	0.041	0.032	3	3.75×10^{-5}	1	40	40.0
3-AND	4.80	0.053	3×10^3	3.75×10^{-2}	1	40	40.1
	4899	33.1	3×10^6	37.5	1	40	110.6
	0.067	0.055	4	5.0×10^{-5}	1	40	40.1
4-AND	9.04	0.091	4×10^3	5.0×10^{-2}	1	40	40.1
	9383	62.8	4×10^6	50.0	1	40	152.8
	0.11	0.089	5	6.25×10^{-5}	1	40	40.1
5-AND	17.2	0.16	5×10^3	6.25×10^{-2}	1	40	40.2
	17700	111.7	5×10^6	62.5	1	40	214.2
	0.20	0.16	6	7.5×10^{-5}	1	40	40.2
6-AND	33.0	0.28	6×10^3	7.5×10^{-2}	1	40	40.4
	34059	203.0	6×10^6	75.0	1	40	318.0
	0.38	0.32	7	8.75×10^{-5}	1	40	40.3
7-AND	64.3	0.53	7×10^3	8.75×10^{-2}	1	40	40.6
	66123	370.8	7×10^6	87.5	1	40	498.3
	0.76	0.64	8	1.0×10^{-4}	1	40	40.6
8-AND	125.1	1.06	8×10^3	1.0×10^{-1}	1	40	41.2
	129553	700.7	8×10^6	100.0	1	40	840.7
	1.63	1.39	9	1.125×10^{-4}	1	40	41.4
9-AND	245.2	2.25	9×10^3	1.125×10^{-1}	1	40	42.4
	255847	1346	9×10^6	112.5	1	40	1498.5

5.3   Application: Privacy-Preserving (Exact) Edit Distance

We implemented a privacy-preserving edit distance protocol using our protocols (Equality, B2A, and 3-Min). Unlike many previous works on approximate edit distance (e.g., [24]), here we consider the exact edit distance. We computed an edit distance between two length-L genome strings (S_0 and S_1) via standard dynamic programming (DP). It appears four characters in the strings; that is, A, T, G, and C. In DP-matrix, we fill the cell $x[i][j]$ by the following rule:

$$x[i][j] = \text{3-Min}([x[i-1][j]+1, x[i][j-1]+1, x[i-1][j-1]+e])$$

Here, $e = 0$ if the condition $S_0[i] = S_1[j]$ holds, and otherwise $e = 1$. We can compute e using Equality (two rounds) and B2A (one round). To reduce the total online execution time, we calculate the edit distance as follows:

1. We parallelly compute e for all cells and store them in advance. This procedure requires three communication rounds.
2. Diagonal cells in DP-matrix are independent with each other. Therefore, we can parallelly compute these cells $x[d][0], x[d-1][1], \cdots, x[0][d]$ (for each d) to reduce the communication rounds.

By applying the above techniques, we can compute exact edit distance for two length-L strings with $3+4(2L-1) = (8L-1)$ communication rounds. We used the arithmetic shares and protocols over $\mathbb{Z}_{2^{16}}$ in our experiments. The experimental results are as in Table 3: As we can see from the experimental results, most of the online total execution time is occupied by the communication latency.

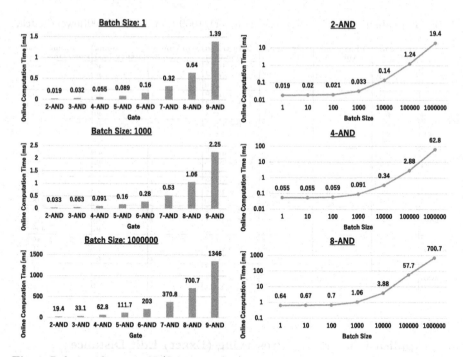

Fig. 1. Relations between N (fan-in number), batch size, and online computation time for N-AND: we show the relations between N and online computation time with 1/1000/1000000 batch (left), and show the relations between batch size and online computation time for 2/4/8-AND (right).

Table 2. Evaluation of our protocols over $\mathbb{Z}_{2^{32}}$ for $1/10^3/10^6$ batches. In each cell, we show our experimental results on the baseline (upper) and ours (lower).

	pre-comp. time (ms)	online comp. time (ms)	# of comm. bits (bit)	data trans. time (ms)	# of comm. rounds	comm. latency (ms)	online total exec. time (ms)
Equality	0.15	0.18	62	7.75×10^{-4}	5	200	200.2
(1 batch)	0.76	0.52	38	4.75×10^{-4}	2	80	80.5
Comparison	1.5	0.54	970	1.21×10^{-2}	7	280	280.6
(1 batch)	3.9	2.1	712	8.9×10^{-3}	3	120	122.1
3-Max	3.1	1.2	2196	2.75×10^{-2}	18	720	721.2
(1 batch)	9.7	2.3	3960	4.95×10^{-2}	4	160	162.3
Equality	74.7	0.61	62×10^3	0.78	5	200	201.4
(10^3 batch)	500.5	1.1	38×10^3	0.48	2	80	80.9
Comparison	1398	8.25	970×10^3	12.1	7	280	300.4
(10^3 batch)	2745	11.6	712×10^3	8.9	3	120	140.5
3-Max	2891	17.5	2196×10^3	27.5	18	720	765.0
(10^3 batch)	8635	36.3	3960×10^3	49.5	4	160	245.8
Equality	77574	761.4	62×10^6	780	5	200	1741
(10^6 batch)	500617	1233	38×10^6	480	2	80	1793
Comparison	1445847	13895	970×10^6	12100	7	280	26275
(10^6 batch)	2799437	20748	712×10^6	8900	3	120	29768
3-Max	2956155	28252	2196×10^6	27500	18	720	56472
(10^6 batch)	8571664	69935	3960×10^6	49500	4	160	119595

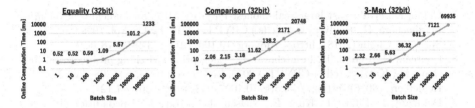

Fig. 2. Relations between batch size and online computation/execution time of the protocols over $\mathbb{Z}_{2^{32}}$.

Table 3. Experimental results of privacy-preserving exact edit distance with 2^ℓ-length two strings ($\ell = [2, \cdots, 10]$).

string length	pre-comp. time (s)	online comp. time (s)	data trans. time (s)	comm. latency (s)	online total exec. time (s)
4	0.04	0.01	4.0×10^{-4}	1.24	1.25
8	0.14	0.02	1.4×10^{-3}	2.52	2.54
16	0.57	0.04	5.7×10^{-3}	5.08	5.13
32	2.2	0.10	2.3×10^{-2}	10.2	10.3
64	8.1	0.22	9.2×10^{-2}	20.4	20.7
128	33.4	0.54	3.7×10^{-1}	40.9	41.8
256	135.7	1.5	1.5	84.9	84.9
512	534.1	4.8	5.9	163.8	174.5
1024	2262	16.0	23.4	327.6	367.0

Acknowledgements. This work was partly supported by JST CREST JPMJCR19F6 and the Ministry of Internal Affairs and Communications Grant Number 182103105.

References

1. Araki, T., Furukawa, J., Lindell, Y., Nof, A., Ohara, K.: High-throughput semi-honest secure three-party computation with an honest majority. In: Proceedings of the 2016 ACM SIGSAC Conference on Computer and Communications Security, Vienna, Austria, 24–28 October 2016, pp. 805–817 (2016)
2. Beaver, D.: Efficient multiparty protocols using circuit randomization. In: Feigenbaum, J. (ed.) CRYPTO 1991. LNCS, vol. 576, pp. 420–432. Springer, Heidelberg (1992). https://doi.org/10.1007/3-540-46766-1_34
3. Ben-Efraim, A., Lindell, Y., Omri, E.: Optimizing semi-honest secure multiparty computation for the internet. In: Proceedings of the 2016 ACM SIGSAC Conference on Computer and Communications Security, Vienna, Austria, 24–28 October 2016, pp. 578–590 (2016)
4. Bogdanov, D., Niitsoo, M., Toft, T., Willemson, J.: High-performance secure multiparty computation for data mining applications. Int. J. Inf. Secur. **11**(6), 403–418 (2012). https://doi.org/10.1007/s10207-012-0177-2
5. Bost, R., Popa, R.A., Tu, S., Goldwasser, S.: Machine learning classification over encrypted data. In: 22nd Annual Network and Distributed System Security Symposium (NDSS 2015), San Diego, California, USA, 8–11 February 2015 (2015)
6. Byali, M., Joseph, A., Patra, A., Ravi, D.: Fast secure computation for small population over the internet. In: Proceedings of the 2018 ACM SIGSAC Conference on Computer and Communications Security (CCS 2018), Toronto, ON, Canada, 15–19 October 2018, pp. 677–694 (2018)

7. Chida, K., et al.: Fast large-scale honest-majority MPC for malicious adversaries. In: Shacham, H., Boldyreva, A. (eds.) CRYPTO 2018. LNCS, vol. 10993, pp. 34–64. Springer, Cham (2018). https://doi.org/10.1007/978-3-319-96878-0_2

8. Couteau, G., Peters, T., Pointcheval, D.: Encryption switching protocols. In: Robshaw, M., Katz, J. (eds.) CRYPTO 2016. LNCS, vol. 9814, pp. 308–338. Springer, Heidelberg (2016). https://doi.org/10.1007/978-3-662-53018-4_12

9. Damgård, I., Fitzi, M., Kiltz, E., Nielsen, J.B., Toft, T.: Unconditionally secure constant-rounds multi-party computation for equality, comparison, bits and exponentiation. In: Halevi, S., Rabin, T. (eds.) TCC 2006. LNCS, vol. 3876, pp. 285–304. Springer, Heidelberg (2006). https://doi.org/10.1007/11681878_15

10. Demmler, D., Schneider, T., Zohner, M.: ABY - a framework for efficient mixed-protocol secure two-party computation. In: 22nd Annual Network and Distributed System Security Symposium (NDSS 2015), San Diego, California, USA, 8–11 February 2015 (2015)

11. Gilad-Bachrach, R., Dowlin, N., Laine, K., Lauter, K.E., Naehrig, M., Wernsing, J.: Cryptonets: applying neural networks to encrypted data with high throughput and accuracy. In: Proceedings of the 33nd International Conference on Machine Learning (ICML 2016), New York City, NY, USA, 19–24 June 2016, pp. 201–210 (2016)

12. Goldreich, O.: The Foundations of Cryptography - Volume 2, Basic Applications. Cambridge University Press, Cambridge (2004)

13. Goldreich, O., Micali, S., Wigderson, A.: How to play any mental game or a completeness theorem for protocols with honest majority. In: Proceedings of the 19th Annual ACM Symposium on Theory of Computing, 1987, New York, New York, USA, pp. 218–229 (1987)

14. Juvekar, C., Vaikuntanathan, V., Chandrakasan, A.: GAZELLE: a low latency framework for secure neural network inference. In: 27th USENIX Security Symposium, USENIX Security 2018, Baltimore, MD, USA, 15–17 August 2018, pp. 1651–1669 (2018)

15. Kolesnikov, V., Sadeghi, A.R., Schneider, T.: How to combine homomorphic encryption and garbled circuits - improved circuits and computing the minimum distance efficiently. In: International Workshop on Signal Processing in the Encrypted Domain (SPEED 2009) (2009)

16. Liu, X., Deng, R.H., Choo, K.R., Weng, J.: An efficient privacy-preserving outsourced calculation toolkit with multiple keys. IEEE Trans. Inf. Forensics Secur. 11(11), 2401–2414 (2016)

17. Mohassel, P., Orobets, O., Riva, B.: Efficient server-aided 2pc for mobile phones. PoPETs 2016(2), 82–99 (2016)

18. Mohassel, P., Rindal, P.: Aby³: a mixed protocol framework for machine learning. In: Proceedings of the 2018 ACM SIGSAC Conference on Computer and Communications Security (CCS 2018), Toronto, ON, Canada, 15–19 October 2018, pp. 35–52 (2018)

19. Mohassel, P., Rosulek, M., Zhang, Y.: Fast and secure three-party computation: the garbled circuit approach. In: Proceedings of the 22nd ACM SIGSAC Conference on Computer and Communications Security, Denver, CO, USA, 12–16 October 2015, pp. 591–602 (2015)

20. Mohassel, P., Zhang, Y.: Secureml: a system for scalable privacy-preserving machine learning. In: 2017 IEEE Symposium on Security and Privacy (SP 2017), San Jose, CA, USA, 22–26 May 2017, pp. 19–38 (2017)

21. Morita, H., Attrapadung, N., Teruya, T., Ohata, S., Nuida, K., Hanaoka, G.: Constant-round client-aided secure comparison protocol. In: Lopez, J., Zhou, J., Soriano, M. (eds.) ESORICS 2018. LNCS, vol. 11099, pp. 395–415. Springer, Cham (2018). https://doi.org/10.1007/978-3-319-98989-1_20

22. Nishide, T., Ohta, K.: Multiparty computation for interval, equality, and comparison without bit-decomposition protocol. In: Okamoto, T., Wang, X. (eds.) PKC 2007. LNCS, vol. 4450, pp. 343–360. Springer, Heidelberg (2007). https://doi.org/10.1007/978-3-540-71677-8_23

23. Riazi, M.S., Weinert, C., Tkachenko, O., Songhori, E.M., Schneider, T., Koushanfar, F.: Chameleon: a hybrid secure computation framework for machine learning applications. In: Proceedings of the 2018 on Asia Conference on Computer and Communications Security (AsiaCCS 2018), Incheon, Republic of Korea, 04–08 June 2018, pp. 707–721 (2018)

24. Schneider, T., Tkachenko, O.: EPISODE: efficient privacy-preserving similar sequence queries on outsourced genomic databases. In: Proceedings of the 2019 ACM Asia Conference on Computer and Communications Security (AsiaCCS 2019), Auckland, New Zealand, 09–12 July 2019, pp. 315–327 (2019)

25. Yao, A.C.: How to generate and exchange secrets (extended abstract). In: 27th Annual Symposium on Foundations of Computer Science, Toronto, Canada, 27–29 October 1986, pp. 162–167 (1986)

26. Zahur, S., Rosulek, M., Evans, D.: Two halves make a whole. In: Oswald, E., Fischlin, M. (eds.) EUROCRYPT 2015. LNCS, vol. 9057, pp. 220–250. Springer, Heidelberg (2015). https://doi.org/10.1007/978-3-662-46803-6_8

27. Zhu, R., Cassel, D., Sabry, A., Huang, Y.: NANOPI: extreme-scale actively-secure multi-party computation. In: Proceedings of the 2018 ACM SIGSAC Conference on Computer and Communications Security (CCS 2018), Toronto, ON, Canada, 15–19 October 2018, pp. 862–879 (2018)

Secure Computation of the kth-Ranked Element in a Star Network

Anselme Tueno[1]([✉]), Florian Kerschbaum[2], Stefan Katzenbeisser[3], Yordan Boev[1], and Mubashir Qureshi[1]

[1] SAP SE, Walldorf, Germany
anselme.kemgne.tueno@sap.com
[2] University of Waterloo, Waterloo, Canada
[3] University of Passau, Passau, Germany

Abstract. We consider the problem of securely computing the kth-ranked element in a sequence of n private integers distributed among n parties. The kth-ranked element (e.g., minimum, maximum, median) is of particular interest in collaborative benchmarking and auctions. Previous secure protocols for the kth-ranked element require a communication channel between each pair of parties. A server model naturally fits with the client-server architecture of Internet applications in which clients are connected to the server and not to other clients. It simplifies secure computation by reducing the number of rounds and improves its performance and scalability. In this paper, we propose different approaches for privately computing the kth-ranked element in the server model, using either garbled circuits or threshold homomorphic encryption. Our schemes have a constant number of rounds and can compute the kth-ranked element within seconds for up to 50 clients in a WAN.

Keywords: k^{th}-ranked element · Garbled circuit · Homomorphic encryption

1 Introduction

Given n parties each holding a private integer, we consider the problem of securely computing the kth-ranked element (KRE) of these n integers. This is a secure multiparty computation (SMC) where several parties wish to compute a function on their private input while revealing only the output of the computation. The computation of the kth-ranked element is of particular interest in settings such as collaborative benchmarking and auctions, where the individual inputs are sensitive, yet the KRE is of mutual interest to all parties [1,22].

Benchmarking. A key performance indicator (KPI) is a statistical quantity measuring the performance of a business process. Benchmarking is a management process where a company compares its KPI to the statistics of the same KPIs of a group of competitors from a peer group. A peer group is a group of similar companies, usually competitors, wanting to compare against each other.

J. Bonneau and N. Heninger (Eds.): FC 2020, LNCS 12059, pp. 386–403, 2020.
https://doi.org/10.1007/978-3-030-51280-4_21

Confidentiality. Confidentiality is of the utmost importance in benchmarking, since KPIs allow the inference of sensitive information. Companies are therefore hesitant to share their business performance data due to the risk of losing a competitive advantage [22]. The confidentiality issue can be addressed using SMC [3,16,32], which guarantees that no party will learn more than the output of the protocol, i.e., the other parties' inputs remain confidential.

Communication Model. Generic SMC protocols [1,3,16,32] can be used to keep KPIs confidential. They require a communication channel between each pair of parties. We will refer to this approach as the *standard model*. Protocols in this model do not scale easily to a large number of parties as they are highly interactive, resulting in high latency. Moreover, they are difficult to deploy as special arrangements are required between each pair of parties to establish a secure connection [10]. A promising approach for overcoming these limitations is to use the help of a small set of untrusted non-colluding servers. We will therefore refer to it as the *server model*. Relying on multiple non-colluding servers requires a different business model for providers of a privacy-preserving service [23]. We therefore use a communication model consisting of clients (with private inputs) and a server. In this model, the server provides no input and does not learn the output, but makes its computational resources available to the clients [20,22]. There are communication channels only between each client and the server resulting in a centralized communication pattern, i.e., a star network. This model naturally fits with the client-server architecture of Internet applications and allows a service provider to play the server's role. It simplifies the secure protocol, and improves its performance and scalability [10,20].

Table 1. Notations and schemes' properties

Symbol	Interpretation
μ	Bitlength of inputs
n	Number of clients
t	Secret sharing threshold, $t \leq n$
κ	Bitlength of asymmetric ciphertext
λ	Security parameter
$x_1, \ldots, x_n$	Client's inputs
$x_i^b = x_{i\mu} \ldots x_{i1}$	Bit representation of x_i with MSB $x_{i\mu}$
$\|y\|$	Bitlength of integer y, e.g., $\|x_i\| = \mu$
$[\![x_i]\!]$	x_i's ciphertext under public key pk
$[\![x_i]\!]_j$	x_i's ciphertext under public key pk_j
$[\![x_i^b]\!]$	Bitwise encryption $([\![x_{i\mu}]\!], \ldots, [\![x_{i1}]\!])$
$i \xleftarrow{\$} \mathbb{S}$	Choose a random element i in set $\mathbb{S}$
$\{i_1, \ldots, i_t\} \xleftarrow{\$} \mathbb{S}$	Choose t random distinct elements in $\mathbb{S}$
$\mathfrak{S}_n$	Set of all permutations of $\{1, \ldots, n\}$

(a) Notations.

	#Rounds	CR	FT
Kre-Ygc	4	$n-1 \mid 0$	0
Kre-Ahe	4	$t-1 \mid t$	$n-t$
Kre-She	2	$t-1 \mid t$	$n-t$
[1]	$O(\mu)$	$t-1 \mid$ n/a	$n-t$

(b) Schemes' properties: Column "#Rounds" is the number of rounds. Column "CR" refers to the number of parties that can collude - server excluded | server included - without breaking the privacy of non-colluding clients. Column "FT" refers to the number of parties that can fail without preventing the protocol to properly compute the intended functionality.

Table 2. Schemes' complexity: rows CC-C/S and BC-C/S denote the computation and communication (bit) complexity for each client and the server, respectively. The columns "sym." and "asym." denote symmetric and asymmetric operations in KRE-YGC.

	KRE-YGC		KRE-AHE	KRE-SHE	[1]
	sym.	asym.			
CC-C	$O(n\mu)$	$O(n)$	$O(n\mu)$	$O(\mu)$	$O(n\mu^2)$
CC-S	$O(n^2\mu)$	$O(n\log n)$	$O(n^2\mu)$	$O(n^2\mu\log\mu)$	n/a
BC-C	$O(n\mu\lambda)$	$O(n\kappa)$	$O(n\mu\kappa)$	$O((\mu+n)\kappa)$	$O(n\mu^2\lambda)$
BC-S	0	$O(n^2\kappa)$	$O(n^2\mu\kappa)$	$O(n\kappa)$	n/a

Contribution. In summary, we propose different approaches for securely computing the kth-ranked element (KRE) in a star network using garbled circuits (GC) or additive homomorphic encryption (AHE) or somewhat homomorphic encryption (SHE). Our schemes are secure against a semi-honest adversary:

- Our first scheme KRE-YGC uses Yao's GC [2,28] to compare clients' inputs.
- Our second scheme KRE-AHE is based on threshold AHE. We perform the comparison using the DGK protocol [12]. We also propose a modified variant of the Lin-Tzeng comparison protocol [27] that can be used instead of DGK, and that is faster at the cost of a small increase of the communication cost.
- The third scheme KRE-SHE is based on SHE and allows the server to non-interactively compute the KRE such that the clients only interact to jointly decrypt the result.

We compare the approaches in Tables 1b and 2 using the following measures:

- Rounds: In contrast to [1], our schemes have a constant number of rounds.
- Collusion-resistance: measures the number of parties that can collude without violating the privacy of the non-colluding ones.
- Fault-tolerance: measures the number of parties that can fail without preventing the protocol to properly compute the intended functionality.
- Complexity: This refers to the computation and communication complexity. A summary is illustrated in Table 2. We provide a detailed analysis in the full paper.

Structure. The remainder of the paper is structured as follows. We begin by presenting related work in Sect. 2 and some preliminaries in Sect. 3. We present our security model in Sect. 4 and a technical overview in Sect. 5. The different approaches are presented in Sects. 6 to 8. We discuss some implementation details and evaluation results in Sect. 9, before concluding our work in Sect. 10. We provide further details in the full paper.

2 Related Work

Our work is related to SMC. There are generic SMC protocols [13,21] that can be used to compute the kth-ranked element (KRE) of the union of n private datasets. Aggarwal et al. [1] introduced the first specialized protocol for the KRE. Their multiparty protocol performs a binary search in the input domain resulting in $O(\mu)$ comparisons and, hence, requiring $O(\mu)$ sequential rounds. Each round requires an SMC that performs two summations with complexity $O(n\mu)$ and two comparisons with complexity $O(\mu)$. As a result each client performs $O(n\mu^2)$ operations and sends $O(n\mu^2)$ bits. Our protocols perform $O(n^2)$ comparisons, that can be executed in parallel, and have either 4 or 2 rounds. We stress that all our $O(n^2)$ comparisons can be executed in parallel while the $O(\mu)$ comparisons of Aggarwal et al. must be executed sequentially one per round. In our 4-round schemes each client is involved in only $O(n)$ comparisons while each comparison in [1] involves all n clients. As a result, a client in our 4-round schemes has a complexity of $O(n)$ per round but must execute only 4 rounds, while a client in [1] has a complexity of $O(n)$ per round as well but must execute up to μ rounds. In the 2-round scheme, all $O(n^2)$ comparisons are performed non-interactively by the server which in our model is allowed to be computationally more powerful. Our communication model allows to reduce the number of rounds from μ to 4 or 2. We note that $\mu = 32$ in our experiments for the 4-rounds schemes and $\mu = 16$ for the 2-round scheme. A summary of the complexity of our schemes is illustrated in Table 2.

The server model for SMC was introduced in [15], used in Kerschbaum [23], and cryptographic studied in [20]. The computation of the kth-ranked element is also addressed in [4,5] where the server is replaced by a blockchain.

3   Preliminaries

Garbled Circuit (GC). A GC [2,14,28,33] can be used for secure 2-party computation. To evaluate a function f on input x_i, x_j, a garbling scheme $(F, e) \leftarrow Gb(1^\lambda, s, f)$ takes a security parameter λ, a random seed s, a Boolean encoding of f and outputs a GC F and an encoding string e that is used to derive garbled inputs $\bar{x}_i, \bar{x}_j$ from x_i, x_j, i.e. there is a function En such that $\bar{x}_i \leftarrow En(e, x_i)$ and $\bar{x}_j \leftarrow En(e, x_j)$. The garbling scheme is correct if $F(\bar{x}_i, \bar{x}_j) = f(x_i, x_j)$.

Homomorphic Encryption (HE). A HE consists of the usual algorithms for key generation $(pk, sk) \leftarrow KeyGen(\lambda)$, encryption $Enc(pk, m)$ (we denote $Enc(pk, m)$ by $[\![m]\!]$), decryption $Dec(sk, c)$. HE has an additional evaluation algorithm $Eval(pk, f, c_1, \ldots, c_n)$ that takes pk, an n-ary function f and ciphertexts $c_1, \ldots c_n$. It outputs a ciphertext c such that if $c_i = [\![m_i]\!]$ then it holds:

$$Dec(sk, Eval(ek, f, [\![m_1]\!], \ldots, [\![m_n]\!])) = Dec(sk, [\![f(m_1, \ldots, m_n)]\!]).$$

We require HE to be IND-CPA secure. If the scheme supports only addition, then it is *additively homomorphic*. Schemes such as [24,30] are additively homomorphic and have the following properties:

- Add/Multiply: $\forall m_1, m_2, [\![m_1]\!] \cdot [\![m_2]\!] = [\![m_1 + m_2]\!]$, and $[\![m_1]\!]^{m_2} = [\![m_1 \cdot m_2]\!]$,
- Xor: $\forall a, b \in \{0, 1\}, \text{XOR}([\![a]\!], b) = [\![a \oplus b]\!] = [\![1]\!]^b \cdot [\![a]\!]^{(-1)^b}$.

Threshold Homomorphic Encryption (THE). A THE [6] allows to share the private key to the parties using a threshold secret sharing scheme such that a subset of parties is required for decryption. Hence, instead of sk as above, the key generation outputs a set of shares $\mathbb{SK} = \{sks_1, \ldots, sks_n\}$ which are distributed to the clients. The decryption algorithm is replaced by the following algorithms:

- $\tilde{m}_i \leftarrow Decp(sks_i, c)$: The probabilistic partial decryption algorithm takes a ciphertext c and a share $sks_i \in \mathbb{SK}$ of the private key and outputs $\tilde{m}_i$.
- $m' \leftarrow Decf(\mathbb{M}_t)$: The deterministic final decryption algorithm takes a subset $\mathbb{M}_t = \{\tilde{m}_{j_1}, \ldots, \tilde{m}_{j_t}\} \subseteq \{\tilde{m}_1, \ldots, \tilde{m}_n\}$ of shares and outputs a message m'.

We refer to it as *threshold decryption*. It is correct if for all $\mathbb{M}_t = \{\tilde{m}_{j_1}, \ldots, \tilde{m}_{j_t}\}$ such that $|\mathbb{M}_t| \geq t$ and $\tilde{m}_{j_i} = Decp(sks_{j_i}, \llbracket m \rrbracket)$, it holds $m = Decf(\mathbb{M}_t)$.

When used in a protocol, we denote by *combiner* the party which executes $Decf()$. It receives a set $\mathbb{M}_t = \{\tilde{m}_{j_1}, \ldots, \tilde{m}_{j_t}\}$ of partial decryption, runs $m' \leftarrow Decf(\mathbb{M}_t)$ and moves to the next step of the protocol specification.

4   Security Definition

This section provides definitions related to our model and security requirements. We start by defining the kth-ranked element of a sequence of integers.

Definition 1. *Let $\mathbb{X} = \{x_1, \ldots, x_n\}$ be a set of n distinct integers and $\tilde{x}_1, \ldots, \tilde{x}_n$ be the corresponding sorted set, i.e., $\tilde{x}_1 < \ldots < \tilde{x}_n$, and $\mathbb{X} = \{\tilde{x}_1, \ldots, \tilde{x}_n\}$. The rank of an element $x_i \in \mathbb{X}$ is j, such that $x_i = \tilde{x}_j$. The kth-ranked element (KRE) is the element $\tilde{x}_k$ with rank k.*

If the rank is $k = \lceil \frac{n}{2} \rceil$ then the element is called *median*. If $k = 1$ (resp. $k = n$) then the element is called *minimum* (resp. *maximum*).

Definition 2. *Let $C_1, \ldots, C_n$ be n clients each holding a private μ-bit integer $x_1, \ldots, x_n$ and S be a server which has no input. Our ideal functionality $\mathcal{F}_{\text{KRE}}$ receives $x_1, \ldots, x_n$ from the clients, computes the KRE $\tilde{x}_k$ and outputs $\tilde{x}_k$ to each client C_i. Moreover, $\mathcal{F}_{\text{KRE}}$ outputs a leakage $\mathcal{L}_i$ to each C_i and $\mathcal{L}_S$ to S.*

The leakage is specific to each protocol and contains information such as n, t, λ, κ, μ (see Table 1a). It can be inferred from the party's view. In case of collusion, additional leakage might include comparison results or the rank of some inputs.

Definition 3. *The view of the i-th party during an execution of the protocol on input $\vec{x} = (x_1, \ldots, x_n)$ is denoted by: $\mathsf{View}_i(\vec{x}) = \{x_i, r_i, m_{i1}, m_{i2}, \ldots\}$, where r_i represents the outcome of the i-th party's internal coin tosses, and m_{ij} represents the j-th message it has received.*

Since the server has no input, x_i in its view will be replaced by the empty string. We say that two distributions $\mathcal{D}_1$ and $\mathcal{D}_2$ are computationally indistinguishable (denoted $\mathcal{D}_1 \overset{c}{\equiv} \mathcal{D}_1$) if no probabilistic polynomial time (PPT) algorithm can distinguish them except with negligible probability. In this paper, we assume a semi-honest adversary. That is, parties follow the protocol, but the adversary tries to infer as much information as possible.

Definition 4. *Let $\mathcal{F}_{\text{KRE}} : (\{0,1\}^\mu)^n \mapsto \{0,1\}^\mu$ be the functionality that takes n μ-bit inputs $x_1, \ldots, x_n$ and returns their KRE. Let $I = \{i_1, \ldots, i_t\} \subset \{1, \ldots, n + 1\}$ be a subset of indexes of corrupted parties (Server's input x_{n+1} is empty), $\vec{x} = (x_1, \ldots, x_n)$ and $\text{View}_I(\vec{x}) = (I, \text{View}_{i_1}(\vec{x}), \ldots, \text{View}_{i_t}(\vec{x}))$. A protocol t-privately computes $\mathcal{F}_{\text{KRE}}$ in the semi-honest model if there exists a PPT simulator SIM such that: $\forall I, |I| = t, \mathcal{L}_I = \bigcup_{i \in I} \mathcal{L}_i : \text{SIM}(I, (x_{i_1}, \ldots, x_{i_t}), \mathcal{F}_{\text{KRE}}(\vec{x}), \mathcal{L}_I) \stackrel{c}{\equiv} \text{View}_I(\vec{x})$.*

5   Technical Overview

In an initialization phase, clients generate and exchange cryptographic keys through the server, i.e., using the help of a non-colluding trusted third party. We stress that the initialization is run once and its complexity does not depend on the functionality $\mathcal{F}_{\text{KRE}}$. We therefore focus on the actual computations.

Definition 5. *Let $x_i, x_j, 1 \le i, j, \le n$, be integer inputs of C_i, C_j. Then the comparison bit b_{ij} of the pair (x_i, x_j) is defined as 1 if $x_i \ge x_j$ and 0 otherwise. The computation of $x_i \ge x_j$ is distributed and involves C_i, C_j, where they play different roles, e.g., generator and evaluator. Similar to the functional programming notation of an ordered pair, we use head and tail to denote C_i and C_j.*

Lemma 1. *Let $x_1, \ldots, x_n$ be n distinct integers, $r_1, \ldots, r_n \in \{1, \ldots, n\}$ their respective ranks and b_{ij} the comparison bit for (x_i, x_j). It holds $r_i = \sum_{j=1}^{n} b_{ij}$.*

To make sure that inputs are indeed distinct before the protocol, one can use the indexes of each C_i as differentiator [1]. Each C_i appends the $\log n$-bit string of i at the end of the bit string of x_i, resulting in a new input of length $\mu + \log n$. Note that, the extended input will be used only for input comparison, to avoid leaking the index of the winning client. For simplicity, we assume in the remainder of the paper, that the x_i's are all distinct μ-bit integers. Therefore, it is not necessary to compare all pairs (x_i, x_j), since $b_{ji} = 1 - b_{ij}$.

We would like to equally distribute the computation tasks among the clients. As example for $n = 3$, we need to compute only 3 (instead of 9) comparisons resulting in three *head* roles and three *tail* roles. Then we would like each of the three clients to play the role *head* as well as *tail* exactly once. We use Definition 6 and Lemma 2 to equally distribute the roles *head* and *tail* between clients.

Definition 6. *Let $\mathbb{X} = \{x_1, \ldots, x_n\}$ be a set of n integers. We define the predicate* PAIRED *as follows*

$$\text{PAIRED}(i, j) := (i \equiv 1 \pmod 2) \wedge i > j \wedge j \equiv 1 \pmod 2)) \vee \tag{1a}$$
$$(i \equiv 1 \pmod 2) \wedge i < j \wedge j \equiv 0 \pmod 2)) \vee \tag{1b}$$
$$(i \equiv 0 \pmod 2) \wedge i > j \wedge j \equiv 0 \pmod 2)) \vee \tag{1c}$$
$$(i \equiv 0 \pmod 2) \wedge i < j \wedge j \equiv 1 \pmod 2)). \tag{1d}$$

Lemma 2. *Let* $\mathbb{X} = \{x_1, \ldots, x_n\}$ *be a set of* n *integers and the predicate* PAIRED *be as above. Then comparing only pairs* (x_i, x_j) *such that* PAIRED(i, j) = *true is enough to compute the rank of all elements in* $\mathbb{X}$.

For example, if $n = 3$, we compute b_{ij} only for (x_1, x_2), (x_2, x_3), (x_3, x_1). If $n = 4$, we compare only (x_1, x_2), (x_1, x_4), (x_2, x_3), (x_3, x_1), (x_3, x_4), (x_4, x_2).

The predicate PAIRED (Eq. 1) is used in our schemes to reduce the number of comparisons and to equally distribute the computation task of the comparisons among the clients. As pointed out by an anonymous reviewer, PAIRED can be simplified as: $(i > j \wedge i \equiv j \pmod 2)) \vee (i < j \wedge i \not\equiv j \pmod 2)$.

Let $\#head_i$ (resp. $\#tail_i$) denote the number of times PAIRED(i, j) = *true* (resp. PAIRED(j, i)=*true*) holds. For example, if $n = 3$, we have $\#head_i = \#tail_i = 1$ for all clients. However, for $n = 4$, we have $\#head_1 = \#head_3 = 2$, $\#tail_1 = \#tail_3 = 1$, $\#head_2 = \#head_4 = 1$ and $\#tail_2 = \#tail_4 = 2$.

Lemma 3. *Let* $\mathbb{X} = \{x_1, \ldots, x_n\} \subset \mathbb{N}$ *and assume the predicate* PAIRED *is used to sort* $\mathbb{X}$. *If* n *is odd then:* $\#head_i = \#tail_i = \frac{n-1}{2}$. *If* n *is even then:*

$$\#head_i = \begin{cases} \frac{n}{2} & \textit{if } i \textit{ odd} \\ \frac{n}{2} - 1 & \textit{if } i \textit{ even} \end{cases} \qquad \#tail_i = \begin{cases} \frac{n}{2} - 1 & \textit{if } i \textit{ odd} \\ \frac{n}{2} & \textit{if } i \textit{ even}. \end{cases}$$

6 Protocol KRE-YGC

KRE-YGC is based on GC and consists of an initialization and a main part. It does not tolerate collision with the server. An AHE ciphertext is denoted by $[\![\cdot]\!]$.

6.1 KRE-YGC Initialization

The initialization consists of public key distribution and Diffie-Hellman (DH) key agreement. Each client C_i sends its public key pk_i of an AHE to the server S. Then S distributes the pk_i to all C_i. In our implementation, we use Paillier's scheme [30] , but any AHE scheme such as [24] will work. Then each pair (C_i, C_j) of clients runs DH key exchange through the server to generate a common secret key $ck_{ij} = ck_{ji}$. The key ck_{ij} is used by C_i and C_j to seed the pseudorandom number generator of the garbling scheme that is used to generate a comparison GC for x_i and x_j, i.e. $Gb(1^\lambda, ck_{ij}, f_>)$, where $f_>$ is a Boolean comparison circuit. For GC comparison, we use the schemes of Kolesnikov et al. [25, 26].

6.2 KRE-YGC Main Protocol

Protocol 1 is a 4-round protocol in which we use GC to compare inputs and to reveal a blinded comparison bit to the server. Then we use AHE to unblind the comparison bits, compute the ranks and the KRE without revealing anything to the parties. Let $f_>$ be defined as: $f_>((a_i, x_i), (a_j, x_j)) = a_i \oplus a_j \oplus b_{ij}$, where $a_i, a_j \in \{0, 1\}$, i.e., $f_>$ computes $b_{ij} = [x_i > x_j]$ and blinds the bits b_{ij} with a_i, a_j.

Comparing Inputs. For each pair (x_i, x_j), if $\text{PAIRED}(i, j) = true$ the parties do the following:

- C_i chooses a masking bit $a_i^{ij} \overset{\$}{\leftarrow} \{0, 1\}$ and extends its input to (a_i^{ij}, x_i). Then using the common key ck_{ij}, it computes $(F_>^{ij}, e) \leftarrow Gb(1^\lambda, ck_{ij}, f_>)$ and $(\bar{a}_i^{ij}, \bar{x}_i^{ij}) \leftarrow En(e, (a_i^{ij}, x_i))$, and sends $F_>^{ij}$, $(\bar{a}_i^{ij}, \bar{x}_i^{ij})$ to S.
- C_j chooses a masking bit $a_j^{ij} \overset{\$}{\leftarrow} \{0, 1\}$ and extends its input x_j to (a_j^{ij}, x_j). Then using the common key $ck_{ji} = ck_{ij}$, it computes $(F_>^{ij}, e) \leftarrow Gb(1^\lambda, ck_{ji}, f_>)$ and $(\bar{a}_j^{ij}, \bar{x}_j^{ij}) \leftarrow En(e, (a_j^{ij}, x_j))$, and sends only $(\bar{a}_j^{ij}, \bar{x}_j^{ij})$ to S.
- We have $b'_{ij} \leftarrow F_>^{ij}((\bar{a}_i^{ij}, \bar{x}_i^{ij}), (\bar{a}_j^{ij}, \bar{x}_j^{ij})) = a_i^{ij} \oplus a_j^{ij} \oplus b_{ij}$ (i.e. b_{ij} is hidden to S). The server then evaluates all GCs (Steps 1 to 5).

Unblinding Comparison Bits. Using AHE, the parties unblind each $b'_{ij} = a_i^{ij} \oplus a_j^{ij} \oplus b_{ij}$, where a_i^{ij} is known to C_i and a_j^{ij} is known to C_j, without learning anything. As a result $[\![b_{ij}]\!]_i$ and $[\![b_{ij}]\!]_j$ are revealed to S encrypted under pk_i and pk_j. This is illustrated in Steps 6 to 16 and works as follows:

- S sends b'_{ij} to C_i and C_j. They reply with $[\![a_j^{ij} \oplus b_{ij}]\!]_i$ and $[\![a_i^{ij} \oplus b_{ij}]\!]_j$.
- S forwards $[\![a_i^{ij} \oplus b_{ij}]\!]_j$, $[\![a_j^{ij} \oplus b_{ij}]\!]_i$ to C_i, C_j. They reply with $[\![b_{ij}]\!]_j$, $[\![b_{ij}]\!]_i$.
- S sets $[\![b_{ji}]\!]_j = [\![1 - b_{ij}]\!]_j$.

Computing the Rank. The computation of the rank is done at the server by homomorphically adding comparison bits. Hence for each i, the server computes $[\![r_i]\!]_i = [\![\sum_{j=1}^n b_{ij}]\!]_i$. Then, it chooses a random number α_i and computes $[\![\beta_i]\!]_i = [\![(r_i - k) \cdot \alpha_i]\!]_i$ (Steps 17 to 19). The ciphertext $[\![\beta_i]\!]_i$ encrypts 0 if $r_i = k$ (i.e., x_i is the kth-ranked element) otherwise it encrypts a random plaintext.

Computing the KRE's Ciphertext. Each client C_i receives $[\![\beta_i]\!]_i$ encrypted under its public key pk_i and decrypts it. Then if $\beta_i = 0$, C_i sets $m_i = x_i$ otherwise $m_i = 0$. Finally, C_i encrypts m_i under each client's public key and sends $[\![m_i]\!]_1, \ldots, [\![m_i]\!]_n$ to the server (Steps 20 to 22).

Revealing the KRE's Ciphertext. In the final steps (Steps 23 to 24), the server adds all $[\![m_j]\!]_i$ encrypted under pk_i and reveals $[\![\sum_{j=1}^n m_j]\!]_i$ to C_i.

KRE-YGC protocol correctly computes the KRE. The proof follows from the correctness of the GC protocol, Lemmas 1 and 2 and the correctness of the AHE scheme. KRE-YGC is not fault-tolerant and a collusion with the server reveals all inputs to the adversary. In the next section, we address this using threshold HE. We stress that using threshold HE in KRE-YGC is not enough as the server has all GCs and each client can decode all GCs involving its input.

Protocol 1. KRE-YGC Protocol

1: **for** $i := 1, j := i + 1$ **to** n **do**	14: $C_i \to S$: $[\![b_{ij}]\!]_j$
2: **if** PAIRED(i,j) **then**	15: $C_j \to S$: $[\![b_{ij}]\!]_i$
3: $C_i \to S$: $F_>^{ij}, (\bar{a}_i^{ij}, \bar{x}_i^{ij})$	16: S: **let** $[\![b_{ji}]\!]_j \leftarrow [\![1 - b_{ij}]\!]_j$
4: $C_j \to S$: $(\bar{a}_j^{ij}, \bar{x}_j^{ij})$	17: **for** $i := 1$ **to** n **do**
5: S: **let** $b_{ij}' \leftarrow F_>^{ij}(\bar{x}_i^{ij}, \bar{x}_j^{ij})$	18: S: $[\![r_i]\!]_i \leftarrow [\![\sum_{j=1}^n b_{ij}]\!]_i$ $\triangleright\ b_{ii} = 1$
6: **for** $i := 1, j := i + 1$ **to** n **do**	19: $S \to C_i$: $[\![\beta_i]\!]_i \leftarrow [\![(r_i - k) \cdot \alpha_i]\!]_i$, for a
7: **if** PAIRED(i,j) **then**	random α_i
8: $S \to C_i$: $b_{ij}' = a_i^{ij} \oplus a_j^{ij} \oplus b_{ij}$	20: **for** $i := 1$ **to** n **do**
9: $S \to C_j$: $b_{ij}' = a_i^{ij} \oplus a_j^{ij} \oplus b_{ij}$	21: C_i: $m_i := \begin{cases} x_i & \text{if } \beta_i = 0 \\ 0 & \text{if } \beta_i \neq 0 \end{cases}$
10: $C_i \to S$: $[\![a_j^{ij} \oplus b_{ij}]\!]_i$	
11: $C_j \to S$: $[\![a_i^{ij} \oplus b_{ij}]\!]_j$	22: $C_i \to S$: $[\![m_i]\!]_1, \ldots, [\![m_i]\!]_n$
12: $S \to C_i$: $[\![a_i^{ij} \oplus b_{ij}]\!]_j$	23: **for** $i := 1$ **to** n **do**
13: $S \to C_j$: $[\![a_j^{ij} \oplus b_{ij}]\!]_i$	24: $S \to C_i$: $[\![\sum_{j=1}^n m_j]\!]_i$

7   Protocol KRE-AHE

In this section, we describe KRE-AHE (Protocol 4) which instantiates the comparison with DGK [12]. We start by describing the initialization.

7.1   KRE-AHE Initialization

We assume threshold key generation. Hence, there is a public/private key pair (pk, sk) for an AHE, where sk is split in n shares $sks_1, \ldots, sks_n$ such that client C_i gets share sks_i and at least t shares are required to reconstruct sk. Additionally, each C_i has its own AHE key pair (pk_i, sk_i) and publishes pk_i. We denote by $[\![x_i]\!], [\![x_i]\!]_j$ encryptions of x_i under pk, pk_j respectively (Table 1a).

7.2   DGK Comparison Protocol

We briefly reviewing DGK [12]. To determine whether $x_i \leq x_j$ or $x_i > x_j$, one computes for each $1 \leq u \leq \mu$ the following numbers z_u: $z_u = s + x_{iu} - x_{ju} + 3\sum_{v=u+1}^{\mu}(x_{iv} \oplus x_{jv})$. Let (pk_i, sk_i) be the key pair of C_i. Client C_i will be called *Generator* and C_j *Evaluator*. Privately evaluating $x_i \geq x_j$ works as follows:

- C_i sends $[\![x_{i\mu}]\!]_i, \ldots, [\![x_{i1}]\!]_i$ (encrypted under pk_i) to client C_j.
- C_j chooses a random bit δ_{ji}, sets $s = 1 - 2 \cdot \delta_{ji}$, computes $[\![z_u]\!]_i$ as defined above, sends $([\![z_\mu]\!]_i, \ldots, [\![z_1]\!]_i)$ to C_i in a random order and outputs δ_{ji}.
- If one $[\![z_u]\!]_i$ decrypts to 0 then C_i sets $\delta_{ij} = 1$ else $\delta_{ij} = 0$. C_i outputs δ_{ij}.

In our server model, clients run the protocol through the server such that after the computation the server learns $[\![\delta_{ij} \oplus \delta_{ji}]\!]$ encrypted under pk. That is, C_j sends $[\![z_{i\mu}]\!]_i, \ldots, [\![z_{i1}]\!]_i, [\![\delta_{ji}]\!]$ to C_i via the server, where each $[\![z_{iu}]\!]_i$ is encrypted under pk_i and $[\![\delta_{ji}]\!]$ is encrypted under pk. Client C_i computes the shared bit δ_{ij} and sends back $[\![\delta_{ij} \oplus \delta_{ji}]\!]$ to the server. In DGK, clients C_i and C_j perform respectively $O(\mu)$ and $O(6\mu)$ asymmetric operations. We will denote a call to the DGK comparison between C_i, C_j as DGKCOMPARE(i,j).

7.3   Modified Lin-Tzeng Comparison Protocol

We now describe our modified version of the Lin-Tzeng comparison protocol [27], which can be used instead of DGK. It is faster at the cost of sending μ more ciphertexts for each comparison. The main idea of Lin and Tzeng's scheme is to reduce the greater-than comparison to the set intersection of prefixes.

Input Encoding. Let INT$(y_\eta \cdots y_1) = y$ be a function that takes a bit string of length η and parses it into the η-bit integer $y = \sum_{l=1}^{\eta} y_l \cdot 2^{l-1}$. The *0-encoding* $V_{x_i}^0$ and *1-encoding* $V_{x_i}^1$ of an integer input x_i are the following vectors: $V_{x_i}^0 = (v_{i\mu}, \cdots, v_{i1}), V_{x_i}^1 = (u_{i\mu}, \cdots, u_{i1})$, such that for each $l, (1 \leq l \leq \mu)$

$$v_{il} = \begin{cases} \text{INT}(x_{i\mu}x_{i\mu-1} \cdots x_{il'}1) & \text{if } x_{il} = 0 \\ r_{il}^{(0)} & \text{if } x_{il} = 1 \end{cases} \qquad u_{il} = \begin{cases} \text{INT}(x_{i\mu}x_{i\mu-1} \cdots x_{il}) & \text{if } x_{il} = 1 \\ r_{il}^{(1)} & \text{if } x_{il} = 0, \end{cases}$$

where $l' = l + 1$, $r_{il}^{(0)}$, $r_{il}^{(1)}$ are random numbers of a fixed bitlength $\nu > \mu$ (e.g. $2^\mu \leq r_{il}^{(0)}, r_{il}^{(1)} < 2^{\mu+1}$) with $LSB(r_{il}^{(0)}) = 0$ and $LSB(r_{il}^{(1)}) = 1$ (LSB is the least significant bit). If the INT function is used the compute the element at position l, then we call it a *proper encoded element* otherwise we call it a *random encoded element*. Note that a random encoded element $r_{il}^{(1)}$ at position l in the 1-encoding of x_i is chosen such that it is guaranteed to be different to a proper or random encoded element at position l in the 0-encoding of x_j, and vice versa. Hence, it is enough if $r_{il}^{(1)}$ and $r_{il}^{(0)}$ are just one or two bits longer than any possible proper encoded element at position l. Also note that the bitstring $x_{i\mu}x_{i\mu-1} \cdots x_{il}$ is interpreted by the function INT as the bitstring $y_{\mu-l+1} \cdots y_1$ with length $\mu-l+1$ where $y_1 = x_{il}, y_2 = x_{i(l+1)}, \ldots, y_{\mu-l+1} = x_{i\mu}$. If we see $V_{x_i}^0, V_{x_i}^1$ as sets, then $x_i > x_j$ iff they have exactly one common element.

Lemma 4. *Let x_i and x_j be two integers, then $x_i > x_j$ iff $V = V_{x_i}^1 - V_{x_j}^0$ has a unique position with 0.*

The Protocol. Let $[\![V_{x_i}^0]\!]_i = ([\![v_{i\mu}]\!]_i, \ldots, [\![v_{i1}]\!]_i), [\![V_{x_i}^1]\!]_i = ([\![u_{i\mu}]\!]_i, \ldots, [\![u_{i1}]\!]_i)$ denote encryption of $V_{x_i}^0$ and $V_{x_i}^1$. Let $[\![V_{x_i}^1 - V_{x_j}^0]\!]_i = ([\![u_{i\mu} - v_{j\mu}]\!]_i, \ldots, [\![u_{i1} - v_{j1}]\!]_i)$. Client C_i sends $[\![V_{x_i}^0]\!]_i, [\![V_{x_i}^1]\!]_i$ to C_j via the server. Client C_j randomly chooses between evaluating either $[\![V_{x_i}^1 - V_{x_j}^0]\!]_i$ or $[\![V_{x_i}^1 - V_{x_j}^0]\!]_i$ and sets $\delta_{ji} \leftarrow 0$ or $\delta_{ji} \leftarrow 1$ accordingly. Then it randomizes each ciphertext and sends them back to C_i in a random order. If one of these ciphertexts decrypts to 0, C_i sets $\delta_{ij} = 1$ else $\delta_{ij} = 0$. This is clearly faster than DGK at the cost of increasing the communication (μ more ciphertexts are sent to C_j). Due to place constraint, we discuss in the full paper the difference of our modification to the original protocol [27].

7.4   KRE-AHE Main Protocol

KRE-AHE is a 4-round protocol in which inputs are compared interactively using DGK. The comparison bits are encrypted under pk and revealed to the server which then computes the ranks of the x_i's and triggers a threshold decryption.

Uploading Ciphertext. Each C_i sends $[\![x_i]\!]$ (encrypted under pk) and $[\![x_i^b]\!]_i = ([\![x_{i\mu}]\!]_i, \ldots, [\![x_{i1}]\!]_i)$ (encrypted under its own public key pk_i) to the server. This is illustrated in Step 2 of protocol 4. The server then initializes a matrix $G = [g_{11}, \ldots, g_{nn}]$, where $g_{ii} = [\![1]\!]$ and $g_{ij}(i \neq j)$ will be computed using DGK as $g_{ij} = [\![b_{ij}]\!]$ if PAIRED(i, j) is true, and an array $X = [[\![x_1]\!], \ldots, [\![x_n]\!]]$ (Step 3).

Comparing Inputs. In this step, pairs of clients run DGKCOMPARE with the server as explained above. If (i, j) satisfies the predicate PAIRED, then C_i runs DGK as generator and C_j is the evaluator. After the computation, C_i and C_j get shares δ_{ij} and δ_{ji} of the comparison bit and the server gets $[\![b_{ij}]\!] = [\![\delta_{ij} \oplus \delta_{ji}]\!]$ which is encrypted under pk (the server cannot decrypt $[\![b_{ij}]\!]$).

Computing the KRE's Ciphertext. After all admissible comparisons have been computed (and the result stored in the matrix G), the server uses Algorithm 2 to compute the rank of each input x_i, i.e., $[\![r_i]\!] = [\![\sum_{j=1}^{n} b_{ij}]\!]$. Now, the server has the encrypted ranks $[\![r_1]\!], \ldots, [\![r_n]\!]$, where exactly one $[\![r_i]\!]$ encrypts k. Since we are looking for the element whose rank is k, the server then computes $y_i = ([\![r_i]\!] \cdot [\![k]\!]^{-1})^{\alpha_i} \cdot [\![x_i]\!] = [\![(r_i - k)\alpha_i + x_i]\!]$ for all i, where α_i is a number chosen randomly in the plaintext space. Therefore, for the ciphertext $[\![r_i]\!]$ encrypting k, y_i is equal to $[\![x_i]\!]$. Otherwise y_i encrypts a random plaintext.

Algorithm 2. Computing the KRE's ciphertext in KRE-AHE

1: **function** COMPUTEKREAHE(G, X, k)	8: $[\![r_i]\!] \leftarrow [\![r_i]\!] \cdot g_{ij}$
2: **parse** G **as** $[g_{11}, \ldots, g_{nn}]$	9: **else**
3: **parse** X **as** $[[\![x_1]\!], \ldots, [\![x_n]\!]]$	10: $[\![r_i]\!] \leftarrow [\![r_i]\!] \cdot [\![1]\!] \cdot g_{ji}^{-1}$
4: **for** $i := 1$ **to** n **do**	11: **for** $i := 1$ **to** n **do**
5: $[\![r_i]\!] \leftarrow g_{ii}$	12: $y_i \leftarrow ([\![r_i]\!] \cdot [\![k]\!]^{-1})^{\alpha_i} \cdot [\![x_i]\!]$
6: **for** $j := 1$ **to** n $(j \neq i)$ **do**	13: **return** $[y_1, \ldots, y_n]$
7: **if** PAIRED(i, j) **then**	

Algorithm 3. Decryption Request in KRE-AHE

1: **function** DECREQ(Y, i, t, π)	7: $u \leftarrow u + n$ ▷ $1 \leq u \leq n$
2: **parse** Y **as** $[y_1, \ldots, y_n]$	8: $I^{(i)} = I^{(i)} \cup \{u\}$
3: **let** $Z^{(i)} = [z_1^{(i)}, \ldots, z_t^{(i)}]$	9: $v \leftarrow \pi(u)$
4: **for** $j := 1$ **to** t **do**	10: $z_j^{(i)} = y_v'$
5: $u \leftarrow i - t + j \bmod n$	11: **return** $(Z^{(i)}, I^{(i)})$
6: **if** $u \leq 0$ **then**	

Decrypting the KRE's Ciphertext. In Step 12, the server distributes the result $Y = [y_1, \ldots, y_n]$ of Algorithm 2 to the clients for threshold decryption. For that, the array Y is passed as $n \times 1$ matrix to Algorithm 3.

Lemma 5 shows that the ciphertexts generated from Algorithm 3 allow to correctly decrypt $Y = [y_1, \ldots, y_n]$. The first part shows that each C_i receives a subset of t elements of Y. The second part shows that each y_i is distributed to exactly t different C_i which allows a correct threshold decryption of each row.

Lemma 5. *Let* $\mathbb{X} = \{x_1, \ldots, x_n\}$ *be a set of* n *elements,* $\mathbb{X}_i = \{x_{i-t+1}, \ldots, x_i\}$, $1 \leq i \leq n$, *where the indexes in* $\mathbb{X}_i$ *are computed modulo* n, *and* $t \leq n$. *Then:*

- *Each subset* $\mathbb{X}_i$ *contains exactly* t *elements of* $\mathbb{X}$ *and*
- *Each* $x \in \mathbb{X}$ *is in exactly* t *subsets* $\mathbb{X}_i$.

In Step 16, the server S receives partial decryptions from the clients, forwards them to the corresponding combiner (Step 18). Each combiner C_j performs a final decryption (Step 21) resulting in a message $\tilde{x}_j$ whose bitlength is less or equal to μ if it is the KRE. Combiner C_j then sets $m^{(j)} = \tilde{x}_j$ if $|\tilde{x}_j| \leq \mu$, otherwise $m^{(j)} = 0$ (Step 22). Then $m^{(j)}$ is encrypted with the public key of all clients and send to S (Step 23). Finally, the server reveals the KRE to each C_i (Step 25).

Protocol 4. KRE-AHE Protocol

1: **for** $i := 1$ **to** n **do**
2:   $C_i \to S$: $[\![x_i]\!], [\![x_i^b]\!]_i$
3: S: **let** $G = [g_{11}, \ldots, g_{nn}]$
   S: **let** $X = [[\![x_1]\!], \ldots, [\![x_n]\!]]$
4: **for** $i := 1, j := i + 1$ **to** n **do**
5:   **if** PAIRED(i, j) **then**
6:     C_i, C_j, S: $g_{ij} \leftarrow$ DGKCOMPARE(i, j)

7: S: $Y \leftarrow$ COMPUTEKREAHE(G, X, k)
8: S: **let** $\pi \xleftarrow{\$} \mathfrak{S}_n$ be a permutation
9: S: **parse** Y **as** $[y_1, \ldots, y_n]$
10: S: **let** $Y' = [y_{\pi(1)}, \ldots, y_{\pi(n)}]$
11: **for** $i := 1$ **to** n **do**
12:   $S \to C_i$: $Q^{(i)} \leftarrow$ DECREQ(Y', i, t, π)
13:   C_i: **parse** $Q^{(i)}$ **as** $(Z^{(i)}, I^{(i)})$
     parse $I^{(i)}$ **as** $[j_1, \ldots, j_t]$

       parse $Z^{(i)}$ as $[z_{j_1}^{(i)}, \ldots, z_{j_t}^{(i)}]$
14: **for** $i := 1$ **to** n **do**
15:   **for each** j in $I^{(i)}$ **do**
16:     $C_i \to S$: $h_j^{(i)} \leftarrow [\![Decp(sks_i, z_j^{(i)})]\!]_j$
17: **for** $j := 1$ **to** n **do**
18:   $S \to C_j$: $(h_j^{(i_1)}, \ldots, h_j^{(i_t)})$
19: **for** $j := 1$ **to** n **do**
20:   C_j: $d_u = Dec(sk_j, h_j^{(i_u)}), u = 1, \ldots, t$
21:   C_j: $\tilde{x}_j \leftarrow Decf(d_1, \ldots, d_t)$
22:   C_j: $m^{(j)} := \begin{cases} \tilde{x}_j & \text{if } |\tilde{x}_j| \leq \mu \\ 0 & \text{if } |\tilde{x}_j| > \mu \end{cases}$
23:   $C_j \to S$: $[\![m^{(j)}]\!]_1, \ldots, [\![m^{(j)}]\!]_n$
24: **for** $i := 1$ **to** n **do**
25:   $S \to C_i$: $[\![\sum_{j=1}^n m^{(j)}]\!]_i$
26:   C_i: $Dec(sk_i, [\![\sum_{j=1}^n m^{(j)}]\!]_i)$

KRE-AHE correctly computes the KRE. This follows from the correctness of DGK [12], Lemmas 1 and 5 and the correctness of AHE. KRE-AHE evaluates comparisons interactively but requires threshold decryption for $O(n)$ elements. In KRE-AHE, we can evaluate either the comparison or the rank at the server, but not both. In the next scheme, we compute the KRE's ciphertext non-interactively at the server. Clients are only required for the threshold decryption.

8 Protocol KRE-SHE

This section describes KRE-SHE based on SHE. Hence, $[\![x]\!]$ now represents an SHE ciphertext of the plaintext x. The initialization and threshold decryption are similar to KRE-AHE.

8.1 SHE Routines

Protocol KRE-SHE is based on the BGV scheme [9] as implemented in HElib [17] and requires binary plaintext space and Smart-Vercauteren ciphertext packing (SVCP) technique [31]. Using SVCP, a ciphertext consists of a fixed number m of slots encrypting bits, i.e. $[\![\cdot | \cdot | \ldots | \cdot]\!]$. The encryption of a bit b replicates b to all slots, i.e., $[\![b]\!] = [\![b|b| \ldots |b]\!]$. However, one can pack the bits of x_i^b in one ciphertext and will denote it by $[\![\vec{x}_i]\!] = [\![x_{i\mu}| \ldots |x_{i1}|0| \ldots |0]\!]$.

Each C_i sends $[\![x_i^b]\!], [\![\vec{x}_i]\!]$ to S as input to Algorithm 5 which uses built-in routines to compute the KRE. We denote addition and multiplication routines by the operators $\oplus$ and $\odot$. Then addition of packed ciphertexts is defined as component-wise addition mod 2: $[\![b_{i1}| \ldots |b_{im}]\!] \oplus [\![b_{j1}| \ldots |b_{jm}]\!] = [\![b_{i1} \oplus b_{j1}| \ldots |b_{im} \oplus b_{jm}]\!]$. The multiplication is defined similarly: $[\![b_{i1}| \ldots |b_{im}]\!] \odot [\![b_{j1}| \ldots |b_{jm}]\!] = [\![b_{i1} \odot b_{j1}| \ldots |b_{im} \odot b_{jm}]\!]$, where $b_{iu} \odot b_{ju}$ is a multiplication mod 2.

Let x_i, x_j be two integers, $b_{ij} = [x_i > x_j]$ and $b_{ji} = [x_j > x_i]$, the routine SHECMP takes $[\![x_i^b]\!], [\![x_j^b]\!]$, compares x_i and x_j and returns $[\![b_{ij}]\!], [\![b_{ji}]\!]$. Note that if the inputs to SHECMP encrypt the same value, then the routine outputs two ciphertexts of 0. The comparison circuit has depth $\log(\mu - 1) + 1$ and requires $O(\mu \log \mu)$ homomorphic multiplications [11].

Let $b_{i1}, \ldots, b_{in}$ be n bits such that $r_i = \sum_{j=1}^{n} b_{ij}$ and let $r_i^b = r_{i\log n}, \ldots, r_{i1}$ be the bit representation of r_i. The routine SHEFADDER implements a full adder on $[\![b_{i1}]\!], \ldots, [\![b_{in}]\!]$ and returns $[\![r_i^b]\!] = ([\![r_{i\log n}]\!], \ldots, [\![r_{i1}]\!])$.

There is no built-in routine for equality check in HElib. We implemented it using SHECMP and addition. Let x_i and x_j be two μ-bit integers. We use SHEEQUAL to denote the equality check routine and implement SHEEQUAL($[\![x_i^b]\!], [\![x_j^b]\!]$) by first computing $([\![b_i']\!], [\![b_i'']\!])$=SHECMP($[\![x_i^b]\!], [\![x_j^b]\!]$) and then $[\![\beta_i]\!] = [\![b_i']\!] \oplus [\![b_i'']\!] \oplus [\![1]\!]$. This results in $\beta_i = 1$ if $x_i = x_j$ and $\beta_i = 0$ otherwise.

8.2 KRE-SHE Main Protocol

In KRE-SHE, the server S receives encrypted inputs from clients. For each client's integer x_i, the encrypted input consists of:

- an encryption $[\![x_i^b]\!] = ([\![x_{i\mu}]\!], \ldots, [\![x_{i1}]\!])$ of the bit representation and
- an encryption $[\![\vec{x}_i]\!] = [\![x_{i\mu}| \ldots |x_{i1}|0| \ldots |0]\!]$ of the packed bit representation.

Then the server runs Algorithm 5 which uses SheCmp to pairwise compare the inputs resulting in encrypted comparison bits $[\![b_{ij}]\!]$. Then SheFAdder is used to compute the rank of each input by adding comparison bits. The result is an encrypted bit representation $[\![r_i^b]\!]$ of the ranks. Using the encrypted bit representations $[\![k^b]\!]$, $[\![r_i^b]\!]$ of k and each rank, SheEqual checks the equality and returns an encrypted bit $[\![\beta_i]\!]$. Recall that because of SVCP the encryption of a bit β_i is automatically replicated in all slots, i.e., $[\![\beta_i]\!] = [\![\beta_i|\beta_i| \ldots |\beta_i]\!]$, such that evaluating $[\![\vec{y_i}]\!] \leftarrow [\![\vec{x_i}]\!] \odot [\![\beta_i]\!]$, $1 \le i \le n$, and $[\![\vec{y_1}]\!] \oplus \ldots \oplus [\![\vec{y_n}]\!]$ returns the KRE's ciphertext. Correctness and security follow from Lemma 1, correctness and security of SHE. The leakage is $\mathcal{L}_S = \mathcal{L}_i = \{n, t, \kappa, \lambda, \mu\}$.

Algorithm 5. Computing the KRE's Ciphertext in Kre-She

1: **function** ComputeKreShe(X, Z, c)
2:   **parse** X as $[\![[\![x_1^b]\!], \ldots, [\![x_n^b]\!]]\!]$
    parse Z as $[\![[\![\vec{x}_1]\!], \ldots, [\![\vec{x}_n]\!]]\!]$
    parse c as $[\![k^b]\!]$
3:   **for** $i := 1$ **to** n **do**
4:     $[\![b_{ii}]\!] \leftarrow [\![1]\!]$
5:     **for** $j := i + 1$ **to** n **do**
6:       $([\![b_{ij}]\!], [\![b_{ji}]\!]) \leftarrow$ SheCmp$([\![x_i^b]\!], [\![x_j^b]\!])$

7: **for** $i := 1$ **to** n **do**
8:   $[\![r_i^b]\!] \leftarrow$ SheFAdder$([\![b_{i1}]\!], \ldots, [\![b_{in}]\!])$
9: **for** $i := 1$ **to** n **do**
10:   $[\![\beta_i]\!] \leftarrow$ SheEqual$([\![r_i^b]\!], [\![k^b]\!])$
11: **for** $i := 1$ **to** n **do**
12:   $[\![\vec{y_i}]\!] \leftarrow [\![\vec{x_i}]\!] \odot [\![\beta_i]\!]$
13: **return** $[\![\vec{y_1}]\!] \oplus \ldots \oplus [\![\vec{y_n}]\!]$

---

9 Evaluation

This section presents our evaluation results. We implemented Kre-Ygc and Kre-Ahe as client-server Java applications while using SCAPI [14]. As Kre-She mostly consists of the homomorphic evaluation by the server, we implemented Algorithm 5 and n-out-of-n threshold decryption using HElib [17,18].

Experimental Setup. For Kre-Ygc and Kre-Ahe, we experimented using for the server a machine with a 6-core Intel(R) Xeon(R) E-2176M CPU @ 2.70 GHz and 32 GB of RAM, and for the clients two machines with each two Intel(R) Xeon(R) CPU E7-4880 v2 @ 2.50 GHz. The client machines were equipped with 8 GB and 4 GB of RAM, and were connected to the server via WAN. Windows 10 Enterprise was installed on all three machines. For each experiment, about 3/5 of the clients were run on the machine with 8 GB RAM while about 2/5 were run on the machine with 4 GB RAM. Since the main computation of Kre-She is done on the server, we evaluate only Algorithm 5 on a Laptop with Intel(R) Core(TM) i5-7300U CPU @ 2.60 GHz running 16.04.1-Ubuntu.

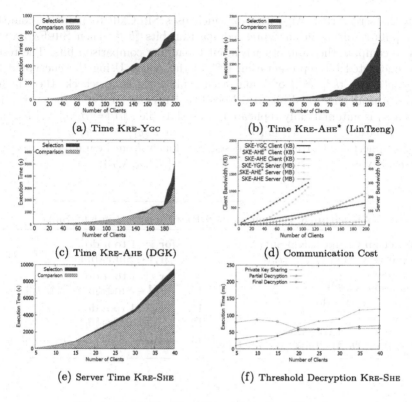

(a) Time KRE-YGC

(b) Time KRE-AHE* (LinTzeng)

(c) Time KRE-AHE (DGK)

(d) Communication Cost

(e) Server Time KRE-SHE

(f) Threshold Decryption KRE-SHE

Fig. 1. Results for KRE-YGC, KRE-AHE, KRE-SHE

Results. We evaluated KRE-YGC, KRE-AHE at security level $\lambda = 128$, bitlength $\mu = 32$ and (minimal) threshold $t = 2$ for threshold decryption. We instantiated KRE-AHE with Elliptic Curve ElGamal using curve `secp256r1`. We implemented ElGamal using CRT-based technique of Hu et al. [19] and pre-computation of the logarithm table [7] for fast threshold decryption [8]. Figure 1 shows our results which are summarized in Table 3 for $n = 100$.

KRE-YGC is the most efficient in both computation and communication and takes 197 s to each client to compute the KRE of 100 clients in a WAN setting. The communication is 0.31 MB for each client and 5.42 MB for the server. However, KRE-YGC is neither collusion-resistant nor fault-tolerant.

KRE-AHE is the second most efficient and is collusion-resistant and fault-tolerant. In KRE-AHE, the comparisons can be evaluated non-interactively using LinTzeng or interactively using both LinTzeng and DGK. The non-interactive variant (denoted by KRE-AHE*) requires $O(n^2)$ threshold decryptions. It computation cost is illustrated in Fig. 1b. The interactive one, whose cost is illustrated in Fig. 1c, requires only $O(n)$ threshold decryptions. In Table 3, we also illustrate the costs when $t = 1$ (i.e., each C_i knows sk) for both KRE-AHE and KRE-AHE* and when $t = n$ (i.e., all C_i run the decryption) for KRE-AHE.

Table 3. Performance Comparison for 100 clients: C-Bits (resp. S-Bits) denotes the number of bits sent by each client (resp. the server). t is the number of clients for the treshold decryption.

	KRE-YGC	KRE-AHE			KRE-AHE*	
t	n/a	1	2	100	1	2
Time (s)	197.00	353.00	336.00	441.00	1024.00	1749.00
C-Bits (MB)	0.31	0.30	0.30	0.32	0.56	1.11
S-Bits (MB)	5.42	56.07	56.12	60.56	111.37	222.67

Table 4. Performance Comparison to [1]: Rows B-C/S is the communication for each client/server.

		n								
		10	11	12	13	14	15	16	17	18
[1]	time (s)	2.09	3.37	3.88	6.26	6.30	13.50	14.48	21.69	23.38
	B-C (MB)	13.50	18.21	20.03	25.69	27.83	50.13	53.71	64.97	69.03
KRE-YGC	time (s)	1.20	1.31	1.59	2.02	2.34	2.43	3.02	3.31	3.76
	B-C (KB)	30.62	33.24	37.02	39.64	43.43	46.05	49.83	52.46	56.23
	B-S (KB)	68.55	81.36	95.24	110.22	126.27	143.40	161.62	180.92	201.28
KRE-AHE	time (s)	3.45	3.96	4.74	4.84	5.31	5.71	5.98	6.70	6.86
	B-C (KB)	28.41	34.66	35.22	41.47	42.02	48.27	48.83	55.08	55.63
	B-S (KB)	575.15	701.25	840.15	991.21	1155.15	1331.14	1520.10	1721.06	1935.05

We evaluated Algorithm 5 of KRE-SHE at security level at least 110. The result is illustrated in Fig. 1e for inputs with bitlength $\mu = 16$. The computation is dominated by the inputs' comparison and takes less than one hour for 25 clients. We also evaluated in Fig. 1f the performance of the threshold decryption with a n-out-of-n secret sharing. For up to 40 clients threshold decryption costs less than 0.15 s. KRE-SHE is practically less efficient than all other schemes, but has the best asymptotic complexity.

As a result KRE-YGC is suitable if the server is non-colluding and clients cannot fail. If collusion and failure are an issue, then either KRE-AHE or KRE-SHE is suitable. KRE-SHE has the best asymptotic complexity, but, requires more efficient SHE.

Comparison to [1]. We implemented the semi-honest scheme of Aggarwal et al. [1] using MP-SPDZ [29] which is the state-of-the-art framework for secret sharing based multiparty computation. We evaluated KRE-YGC, KRE-AHE and [1] on a machine with a 6-core Intel(R) Xeon(R) E-2176M CPU @ 2.70 GHz and 32 GB of RAM. The input bitlength is 32. For evaluating [1], we used MP-SPDZ's option for semi-honest Shamir. A summary of the evaluation in Table 4 shows that our schemes scale better for increasing values of n.

10   Conclusion

In this paper, we considered the problem of computing the KRE (with applications to benchmarking) of n clients' private inputs. We proposed and compare different approaches based on garbled circuits or threshold HE. The computation is supported by the server which coordinates the protocol and undertakes as much computations as possible. The server is oblivious, and does not learn the input of the clients. We also implemented and evaluated our schemes.

Acknowledgments. We thank the anonymous reviewers for their valuable comments, and Andreas Fischer and Jonas Böhler for helpful contribution to some implementations.

References

1. Aggarwal, G., Mishra, N., Pinkas, B.: Secure computation of the kth-ranked element. In: Cachin, C., Camenisch, J.L. (eds.) EUROCRYPT 2004. LNCS, vol. 3027, pp. 40–55. Springer, Heidelberg (2004). https://doi.org/10.1007/978-3-540-24676-3_3
2. Bellare, M., Hoang, V.T., Rogaway, P.: Foundations of garbled circuits. In: CCS (CCS 2012), pp. 784–796 (2012)
3. Ben-Or, M., Goldwasser, S., Wigderson, A.: Completeness theorems for non-cryptographic fault-tolerant distributed computation. In: STOC, pp. 1–10. ACM, New York (1988)
4. Blass, E.-O., Kerschbaum, F.: Strain: a secure auction for blockchains. In: Lopez, J., Zhou, J., Soriano, M. (eds.) ESORICS 2018. LNCS, vol. 11098, pp. 87–110. Springer, Cham (2018). https://doi.org/10.1007/978-3-319-99073-6_5
5. Blass, E., Kerschbaum, F.: Secure computation of the kth-ranked integer on blockchains. IACR Cryptology ePrint Arch. **2019**, 276 (2019)
6. Boneh, D., et al.: Threshold cryptosystems from threshold fully homomorphic encryption. In: Shacham, H., Boldyreva, A. (eds.) CRYPTO 2018. LNCS, vol. 10991, pp. 565–596. Springer, Cham (2018). https://doi.org/10.1007/978-3-319-96884-1_19
7. Boneh, D., Goh, E.-J., Nissim, K.: Evaluating 2-DNF formulas on ciphertexts. In: Kilian, J. (ed.) TCC 2005. LNCS, vol. 3378, pp. 325–341. Springer, Heidelberg (2005). https://doi.org/10.1007/978-3-540-30576-7_18
8. Boneh, D., Shoup, V.: A graduate course in applied cryptography (2017). https://crypto.stanford.edu/~dabo/cryptobook/
9. Brakerski, Z., Gentry, C., Vaikuntanathan, V.: Fully homomorphic encryption without bootstrapping. ECCC **18**, 111 (2011)
10. Catrina, O., Kerschbaum, F.: Fostering the uptake of secure multiparty computation in e-commerce. In: PARES 2008 (ARES 2008), pp. 693–700 (2008)
11. Cheon, J.H., Kim, M., Lauter, K.: Homomorphic computation of edit distance. In: Brenner, M., Christin, N., Johnson, B., Rohloff, K. (eds.) FC 2015. LNCS, vol. 8976, pp. 194–212. Springer, Heidelberg (2015). https://doi.org/10.1007/978-3-662-48051-9_15
12. Damgård, I., Geisler, M., Krøigaard, M.: Efficient and secure comparison for online auctions. In: Pieprzyk, J., Ghodosi, H., Dawson, E. (eds.) ACISP 2007. LNCS, vol. 4586, pp. 416–430. Springer, Heidelberg (2007). https://doi.org/10.1007/978-3-540-73458-1_30
13. Damgård, I., Keller, M., Larraia, E., Pastro, V., Scholl, P., Smart, N.P.: Practical covertly secure MPC for dishonest majority – or: breaking the SPDZ limits. In: Crampton, J., Jajodia, S., Mayes, K. (eds.) ESORICS 2013. LNCS, vol. 8134, pp. 1–18. Springer, Heidelberg (2013). https://doi.org/10.1007/978-3-642-40203-6_1

14. Ejgenberg, Y., Farbstein, M., Levy, M., Lindell, Y.: SCAPI: the secure computation application programming interface. IACR Cryptol. ePrint Arch. **2012**, 629 (2012)
15. Feige, U., Killian, J., Naor, M.: A minimal model for secure computation (extended abstract). In: STOC 1994, pp. 554–563 (1994)
16. Goldreich, O., Micali, S., Wigderson, A.: How to play any mental game. In: STOC, pp. 218–229. ACM, New York (1987)
17. Halevi, S., Shoup, V.: Algorithms in HElib. In: Garay, J.A., Gennaro, R. (eds.) CRYPTO 2014. LNCS, vol. 8616, pp. 554–571. Springer, Heidelberg (2014). https://doi.org/10.1007/978-3-662-44371-2_31
18. Helib. https://github.com/homenc/HElib (2019)
19. Hu, Y., Martin, W., Sunar, B.: Enhanced flexibility for homomorphic encryption schemes via CRT. In: ACNS (2012)
20. Kamara, S., Mohassel, P., Raykova, M.: Outsourcing multi-party computation. IACR Cryptology ePrint Arch. **2011**, 272 (2011)
21. Keller, M., Orsini, E., Scholl, P.: MASCOT: faster malicious arithmetic secure computation with oblivious transfer. In: CCS 2016, pp. 830–842 (2016)
22. Kerschbaum, F.: Building a privacy-preserving benchmarking enterprise system. Enterp. IS **2**(4), 421–441 (2008)
23. Kerschbaum, F.: Adapting privacy-preserving computation to the service provider model. In: CSE, pp. 34–41 (2009)
24. Koblitz, N.: Elliptic curve cryptosystems. Math. Comput. **48**(177), 203–209 (1987)
25. Kolesnikov, V., Sadeghi, A.-R., Schneider, T.: Improved garbled circuit building blocks and applications to auctions and computing minima. In: Garay, J.A., Miyaji, A., Otsuka, A. (eds.) CANS 2009. LNCS, vol. 5888, pp. 1–20. Springer, Heidelberg (2009). https://doi.org/10.1007/978-3-642-10433-6_1
26. Kolesnikov, V., Schneider, T.: Improved garbled circuit: free XOR gates and applications. In: Aceto, L., Damgård, I., Goldberg, L.A., Halldórsson, M.M., Ingólfsdóttir, A., Walukiewicz, I. (eds.) ICALP 2008. LNCS, vol. 5126, pp. 486–498. Springer, Heidelberg (2008). https://doi.org/10.1007/978-3-540-70583-3_40
27. Lin, H., Tzeng, W.: An efficient solution to the millionaires' problem based on homomorphic encryption. In: Ioannidis, J., Keromytis, A., Yung, M. (eds.) ACNS 2005. LNCS, vol. 3531, pp. 456–466. Springer, Heidelberg (2005). https://doi.org/10.1007/11496137_31
28. Lindell, Y., Pinkas, B.: A proof of security of Yao's protocol for two-party computation. J. Cryptology **22**(2), 161–188 (2009)
29. Multi-protocol spdz (2019). https://github.com/data61/MP-SPDZ
30. Paillier, P.: Public-key cryptosystems based on composite degree residuosity classes. In: Stern, J. (ed.) EUROCRYPT 1999. LNCS, vol. 1592, pp. 223–238. Springer, Heidelberg (1999). https://doi.org/10.1007/3-540-48910-X_16
31. Smart, N.P., Vercauteren, F.: Fully homomorphic simd operations. Des. Codes Crypt. **71**(1), 57–81 (2014)
32. Yao, A.C.: Protocols for secure computations. In: SFCS 1982, pp. 160–164. IEEE Computer Society, Washington (1982)
33. Zahur, S., Rosulek, M., Evans, D.: Two halves make a whole. In: Oswald, E., Fischlin, M. (eds.) EUROCRYPT 2015. LNCS, vol. 9057, pp. 220–250. Springer, Heidelberg (2015). https://doi.org/10.1007/978-3-662-46803-6_8

Insured MPC: Efficient Secure Computation with Financial Penalties

Carsten Baum[1(✉)], Bernardo David[2], and Rafael Dowsley[3]

[1] Aarhus University, Aarhus, Denmark
carsten.baum@outlook.com
[2] IT University of Copenhagen, Copenhagen, Denmark
[3] Bar-Ilan University, Ramat Gan, Israel

Abstract. Fairness in Secure Multiparty Computation (MPC) is known to be impossible to achieve in the presence of a dishonest majority. Previous works have proposed combining MPC protocols with cryptocurrencies in order to financially punish aborting adversaries, providing an incentive for parties to honestly follow the protocol. The focus of existing work is on proving that this approach is possible and unfortunately they present monolithic and mostly inefficient constructions. In this work, we put forth the first UC secure modular construction of "Insured MPC", where either the output of the private computation (which describes how to distribute funds) is fairly delivered or a proof that a set of parties has misbehaved is produced, allowing for financial punishments. Moreover, both the output and the proof of cheating are publicly verifiable, allowing third parties to independently validate an execution. We present an efficient compiler that implements Insured MPC from an MPC protocol with certain properties, a standard (non-private) Smart Contract and a publicly verifiable homomorphic commitment scheme. As an intermediate step, we propose the first construction of a publicly verifiable homomorphic commitment scheme with composability guarantees.

1 Introduction

Secure Multiparty Computation (MPC) allows a set of mutually distrusting parties to evaluate an arbitrary function on secret inputs. The participating parties learn nothing beyond the output of the computation, while malicious behavior at runtime does not alter the output. An intuitive and in practice often required feature of MPC is that if a cheating party obtains the output, then all the honest parties should do so as well. Protocols which guarantee this are also called *fair*. In his seminal work, Cleve [18] proved that fair MPC with a dishonest majority is impossible to achieve in the standard communication model. While the result can be circumvented for specific functions [3,4,22] in

---

C. Baum—Part of this work was done while the author was with Bar-Ilan University.
R. Dowsley—Part of this work was done while the author was with Aarhus University.

© International Financial Cryptography Association 2020
J. Bonneau and N. Heninger (Eds.): FC 2020, LNCS 12059, pp. 404–420, 2020.
https://doi.org/10.1007/978-3-030-51280-4_22

the two-party setting, the result of [18] prevents MPC from being applicable in certain interesting scenarios.

With the advent of cryptocurrencies, [2,8] initiated a line of research that avoids the aforementioned drawback by imposing financial penalties on misbehaving parties. Such monetary punishments would then incentivize fair behavior of the protocol participants, assuming that they are rational and that the penalties are high enough. This is achieved by constructing a protocol which interacts with a public ledger and digital currency. The overall structure of their idea is as follows: (i) The parties run the secure computation, but delay the reconstruction of the output; (ii) Each party deposits a collateral on the public ledger; (iii) The parties reconstruct the output. Each party obtains the collateral back if it can prove that it behaved honestly during the reconstruction; and (iv) If some parties have cheated, then their share of the collateral is distributed among the honest participants. Several works [27,29,30] generalized this concept and improved the performance with respect to the amount of interaction with the public ledger as well as the collateral that each party needs to deposit. In particular, Kumaresan et al. [1,2,30] introduced the idea of MPC with cash distribution, in which the inputs and outputs of the parties consist of both data and money. In this latter case, the public ledger is used both to enforce financial penalties as well as to distribute money according to the output of the secure computation.

1.1 Related Works: Fair Computation vs. Fair Output Delivery

Before presenting our techniques and design choices, it is worthwhile to discuss first *which* adversarial behavior should be punishable: it is possible to obtain protocols that punish deviations at any point of their execution or protocols that only punish adversaries who learn the output but prevent the honest parties from learning it. In this second approach, adversaries that abort the protocol but do not learn the output are not punished. One therefore has to distinguish between two types of protocols: those that punish all cheating yield *Fair Computation with Penalties*, while the second approach only allows *Fair Output Delivery with Penalties*. One can roughly classify the state-of-the-art using this distinction.

Fair Computation. [2] follows this line of work, but have high round and communication complexities overheads. As [27] correctly pointed out, care must be taken when choosing the "inner" MPC protocol (which is compiled to obtain financial penalties): to achieve this, the protocol must have a property called *Identifiable Abort* (ID-MPC, [25]). As [2] uses GMW [21], their specific construction achieves this property, but not every MPC protocol is suitable for their approach. On the other hand, [27] requires constant rounds but rely on expensive generic zero knowledge proofs to achieve the necessary properties.

Fair Output Delivery. This line of work has been independently initiated by [1,8] and most of the protocols in this line of work still require several rounds of interaction with the public ledger as well as storing all MPC protocol messages on the ledger. The currently most efficient approach [9] relies on an "inner" MPC protocol that performs the actual computation and then secret shares the result, outputting not the result itself but commitments to each of the shares and privately giving to each party the opening for one of these commitments. The parties subsequently post all (closed) commitments to the public ledger. After the parties agree that the commitments posted on the public ledger correspond to those obtained from the MPC protocol, each party opens its commitment in public. This implicitly has identifiable abort because all parties can publicly agree if another participant has failed to post a valid opening to its commitment on the ledger. In particular, this approach relies on a smart contract that punishes parties that fail to post valid openings for their commitments to shares. However, a caveat, both from a theoretical and practical point of view, is that current protocols compute both the secret sharing of the result and the commitments to each share inside the MPC in a white-box way, which adds significant computational and communication overheads. Moreover, in order to achieve composable security, the expensive preprocessing phase of a composable commitment scheme would have to be executed as part of the circuit computed by the "inner" MPC protocol.

Other Related Work. Recently Choudhuri et al. [17] constructed fair MPC using a Bulletin Board but relying on stronger assumptions (Witness Encryption or Trusted Hardware). MPC on *permissioned* ledgers has been suggested in [7] but requires all messages to be posted on a public ledger for verification and does not support financial penalties. MPC with public verification such as [6] requires high bulletin board storage that is unsuitable for smart contracts. ID-MPC without public verifiability has been constructed in e.g. [25].

Composability and Efficiency. With the exception of [27], none of the previous works have been shown to achieve composability guarantees. However, the approach of [27] incurs very high computational and communication overheads, since it compiles an "inner" MPC protocol to achieve identifiable abort and public verifiability by using expensive generic zero-knowledge proofs. Even the previous works that do not achieve composability [1,2,8,28–31] incur high round and communication complexities overheads, since they require non-constant extra rounds for each round of the MPC protocol in order to implement financial penalties. While the approach of [9] circumvents the need for such extra rounds by relying on a smart contract, it introduces overheads by requiring secret sharing and commitment schemes to be computed as part of the circuit evaluated by the MPC protocol after the actual function that is evaluated.

1.2   Our Contributions

In this work, we give the first universally composable modular construction of MPC achieving fair output delivery with financial penalties that can be instantiated with a concretely efficient protocol. While previous works have focused at obtaining protocols that can be instantiated using the Bitcoin or Ethereum blockchains as a public ledger, we focus instead on the MPC aspects of such constructions. We design a protocol from generic building blocks with security analysed in the Global Universal Composability framework (GUC). This modular approach directly pinpoints the properties that the "inner" MPC protocol and other underlying protocols must have in such constructions, including precise definitions of the necessary public verifiability properties. Besides shedding light on theoretical aspects of MPC with fair output delivery with penalties, our approach also paves the way for concrete implementations, since it uses generic building blocks that have highly efficient instantiations and combines them in a way that yields highly efficient constructions. Moreover, due to its modular nature, our protocol directly benefits from any future efficiency improvements to its building blocks (*i.e.* the more efficient publicly verifiable additively homomorphic commitments recently introduced in [15]).

Linearly Homomorphic Commitments with Delayed Public Verifiability. This primitive acts as the central hub of our construction. Such commitment schemes are additively homomorphic, allowing one to open linear combinations of commitments without revealing the individual commitments themselves. Moreover, they allow for any third party to verify that a message is a valid opening for a given commitment. We remark that existing constructions achieving all of these properties do not have composability guarantees.

Modular Design. Based on a multiparty additively homomorphic commitment scheme with delayed public verifiability and a suitable "inner" MPC, we give a modular approach for constructing "Insured MPC": first, we combine the inner MPC with the commitment scheme to achieve *MPC with publicly verifiable output*. In this step, we leverage a property of the inner MPC output phase to avoid computing secret sharing or commitments inside the MPC itself, instead computing commitments before the actual output is revealed. Given a (non-private) Smart Contract functionality and a global clock we can then construct a cheater identifiable output reconstruction phase in a modular way where the Smart Contract mediates the reconstruction, receiving openings to the commitments obtained in the previous step. In case of disagreement during reconstruction, the Smart Contract can identify the cheaters as the parties who failed to provide commitment openings. This reconstruction phase and posterior public verification of the resulting output are mostly light-weight due to our commitment scheme, which allows for verification of openings using only calls to a Pseudorandom Generator. Our technique adds no overhead to the circuit being computed inside the MPC (differently from [9,31]) and little overhead to the MPC protocol (differently from [27]), since each party only computes and posts to the public ledger a number of commitments linear in the output size.

Efficient Instantiation. We show how to instantiate all sub-protocols efficiently. We modify the constant-round MPC of [23] to work as the "inner" MPC while essentially keeping the same concrete efficiency. Our publicly verifiable additively homomorphic commitment scheme only performs Random Oracle calls after a small number of base Oblivious Transfers (OT) using a publicly verifiable OT scheme, achieving the same concrete efficiency as the non-publicly verifiable scheme of [19]. As we use a restricted programmable and observable global RO [11] we are then still able to prove security of all steps in GUC.

Full Version. In this extended abstract we only provide an overview of our construction, while the complete building blocks, protocols and proofs appear in the full version, which can be found in [10].

2 Preliminaries

Let $y \xleftarrow{\$} F(x)$ denote running the randomized algorithm F on input x yielding output y. Similarly, $y \leftarrow F(x)$ is used if F is deterministic. For a set $\mathcal{X}$, let $x \xleftarrow{\$} \mathcal{X}$ denote x chosen uniformly at random from $\mathcal{X}$. For any $k \in \mathbb{N}$ we write $[k]$ for the set $\{1, \ldots, k\}$. Let n be the number of parties in an MPC scheme, $\mathcal{A}$ be an adversary and $\mathcal{S}$ the ideal-world simulator. $\mathcal{P} = \{\mathcal{P}_1, \ldots, \mathcal{P}_n\}$ denotes the set of parties where $I \subsetneq \mathcal{P}$ are the corrupted and $\overline{I} = \mathcal{P} \setminus I$ the uncorrupted parties. τ denotes the computational and κ the statistical security parameter. As we focus on MPC over $\mathbb{F}_2$ we use $\mathbb{F}$ for conciseness. In this work, the (G)UC framework [12,13] is used to analyze security. We refer interested readers to the aforementioned works for more details. Several functionalities in this work allow *public verifiability*. To model this, we follow the approach of [5] and allow the set of verifiers $\mathcal{V}$ to be dynamic by adding register and de-register instructions as well as instructions that allow $\mathcal{S}$ to obtain the list of registered verifiers. Functionalities with public verifiability include the (de-)registration interfaces, which are omitted in the descriptions for simplicity. Due to space constraints, the mentioned interfaces are fully described in the full version.

We focus on *Secure Multiparty Computation* with security against a static, rushing and malicious adversary $\mathcal{A}$ corrupting up to $n - 1$ of the n parties and introduce the functionality $\mathcal{F}_{\mathsf{Online}}$ which we realize in this work. This functionality, as depicted in Fig. 1, realizes what we call *MPC with Punishable Abort* or *Insured MPC*: $\mathcal{F}_{\mathsf{Online}}$ computes the result $\boldsymbol{y}$ honestly, but will only output it if every party $\mathcal{P}_i$ sent coins $\mathsf{coins}(d)$ to it first. $\mathcal{F}_{\mathsf{Online}}$ hands these coins back if everyone obtains $\boldsymbol{y}$. $\mathcal{A}$ can withhold the output from honest parties, but only at the expense of losing its provided coins. In case of no cheating, $\mathcal{F}_{\mathsf{Online}}$ redistributes additional coins based on $\boldsymbol{y}$ based on a *Cash Distribution Function*.

Definition 1 (Cash Distribution Function). *Let* $g : \mathbb{F}^m \times \mathbb{N}^n \to \mathbb{N}^n$ *be such that* $\forall \boldsymbol{y} \in \mathbb{F}^m, t^{(1)}, \ldots, t^{(n)} \in \mathbb{N}$ *it holds that* $\sum_i t^{(i)} = \sum_i e^{(i)}$ *for* $(e^{(1)}, \ldots, e^{(n)}) \leftarrow g(\boldsymbol{y}, t^{(1)}, \ldots, t^{(n)})$. *Then* g *is called a* Cash Distribution Function.

Observe that our functionality $\mathcal{F}_{\mathsf{Online}}$ allows $\mathcal{A}$ to *delay* the delivery of the correct output by some time, which is necessary for technical reasons. $\mathcal{F}_{\mathsf{Online}}$ is defined in the presence of a GUC functionality $\mathcal{F}_{\mathsf{Clock}}$ which we will not fully specify here (we use the version of [26]). $\mathcal{F}_{\mathsf{Clock}}$ provides a counter readable consistently by all parties which progresses if all honest parties send a tick signal. One would obviously like to get a result in terms of wall-clock time, but this is difficult to specify in UC. We implement $\mathcal{F}_{\mathsf{Online}}$ using a Smart Contract functionality which could emulate wall-clock time to a certain extent. We will furthermore later make use of a coin-flipping functionality $\mathcal{F}_{\mathsf{CT}}$ which outputs unbiased random bits to all parties. Both functionalities are provided in the full version.

3   The Building Blocks

In this section we will introduce the different building blocks for our construction.

Functionality $\mathcal{F}_{\mathsf{Online}}$ interacts with the parties $\mathcal{P}_1, \ldots, \mathcal{P}_n$ as well as the global functionality $\mathcal{F}_{\mathsf{Clock}}$. This functionality is parameterized by a circuit C representing the computation with an output of length m, the compensation amount q, the security deposit $d \geq (n-1)q$ and a cash distribution function g. $\mathcal{S}$ specifies a set $I \subset [n]$ of corrupted parties.

Input: Upon first input ($\textsc{Input}, sid, i, x^{(i)}$) by $\mathcal{P}_i$ and ($\textsc{Input}, sid, i, \cdot$) by all other parties the functionality stores the value $(i, x^{(i)})$ internally. Every further such message with the same sid and i is ignored.

Evaluate: Upon input ($\textsc{Compute}, sid$) by all parties and if the inputs $(i, x^{(i)})_{i \in [n]}$ for all parties have been received, compute $\boldsymbol{y} = C(x^{(1)}, \ldots, x^{(n)})$. If $\mathcal{S}$ sends ($\textsc{Abort}, sid$) during **Input** or **Evaluate** then send ($\textsc{Abort}, sid$) to all parties and stop.

Deposit: Wait for each party $\mathcal{P}_i$ to send ($\textsc{Deposit}, sid, \mathsf{coins}(d + t^{(i)})$) containing the d coins of the security deposit as well as the $t^{(i)} \geq 0$ coins that $\mathcal{P}_i$ wants to use as financial input in the computation. Send ($\textsc{Deposited}, sid, \mathcal{P}_i, d + t^{(i)}$) to $\mathcal{S}$ upon receiving it. If all honest parties sent their deposit then send ($\textsc{Update}, sid$) to $\mathcal{F}_{\mathsf{Clock}}$. Then query $\mathcal{F}_{\mathsf{Clock}}$ until $\nu = 1$. If by $\nu = 1$ some parties $j \in I$ sent $\mathsf{coins}(c^{(j)})$ with $c^{(j)} < d$ then return the collateral to all honest parties and $\mathcal{S}$. Afterwards send ($\textsc{Abort}, sid$) to the honest parties and abort. If all went ok, then activate **Reveal**.

Reveal: Send ($\textsc{Output}, sid, \boldsymbol{y}$) to $\mathcal{S}$, ($\textsc{Update}, sid$) to $\mathcal{F}_{\mathsf{Clock}}$ and wait until $\nu = 2$. $\mathcal{S}$ may now either send ($\textsc{No-Output}, sid$) or ($\textsc{Ok}, sid, \boldsymbol{y}$). Afterwards send ($\textsc{Update}, sid$) to $\mathcal{F}_{\mathsf{Clock}}$ and activate **Resolve**.

Resolve: Query $\mathcal{F}_{\mathsf{Clock}}$ until $\nu = 3$. Then send ($\textsc{Update}, sid$) to $\mathcal{F}_{\mathsf{Clock}}$ and query until $\nu = 4$.

1. Wait for the message ($\textsc{Punish}, sid, \mathsf{punish}$) from $\mathcal{S}$ where $\mathsf{punish} \subseteq I$. If $\mathcal{S}$ sent ($\textsc{No-Output}, sid, \boldsymbol{y}$) in **Reveal** then $\emptyset \neq \mathsf{punish}$.

2. Depending on punish do the following:
   - If $\mathsf{punish} = \emptyset$ then compute $e^{(1)}, \ldots, e^{(n)} \leftarrow g(\boldsymbol{y}, t^{(1)}, \ldots, t^{(n)})$.
   - Otherwise set $e^{(i)} \leftarrow d + t^{(i)} + |\mathsf{punish}| \cdot q$ for each party $\mathcal{P}_i \in \mathcal{P} \setminus \mathsf{punish}$ and $e^{(i)} \leftarrow d - q \cdot (n - |\mathsf{punish}|) + t^{(i)}$ for each $\mathcal{P}_i \in \mathsf{punish}$.

3. For each $\mathcal{P}_i \in \mathcal{P}$ send ($\textsc{Payout}, sid, \mathcal{P}_i, \mathsf{coins}(e^{(i)})$) to $\mathcal{P}_i$ and ($\textsc{Payout}, sid, \mathcal{P}_i, e^{(i)}$) to each other party.

4. If $\mathcal{S}$ sent ($\textsc{Ok}, sid, \boldsymbol{y}$) in **Reveal** then send ($\textsc{Output}, sid, \boldsymbol{y}$) to each honest party, otherwise send ($\textsc{No-Output}, sid$).

Fig. 1. Functionality $\mathcal{F}_{\mathsf{Online}}$ for Secure Multiparty Computation with Punishable Abort and Cash Distribution.

Linearly Homomorphic Commitments with Delayed Public Verifiability.

A crucial building block of our Insured MPC protocol is the multiparty commitment functionality $\mathcal{F}_{\mathsf{HCom}}$ that is additively homomorphic and allows delayed public verifiability (i.e., after the opening phase it is possible for any third party to verify the opening information). This functionality is depicted in

Fig. 3. $\mathcal{F}_{\mathsf{HCom}}$ is GUC-realized with security in the restricted programmable and observable RO model of Camenisch et al. [11] using multiple building blocks as depicted in Fig. 2 and sketched below. The full construction including a proof of security can be found in the full version.

First, we realize a simple (non-homomorphic) commitment functionality with public verifiability $\mathcal{F}_{\mathsf{Com}}$ by observing that the canonical RO based commitment scheme shown to be UC-secure in [11] is trivially publicly verifiable.

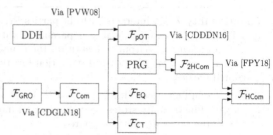

$\mathcal{F}_{\mathsf{Com}}$ is then used to realize a publicly verifiable equality testing functionality $\mathcal{F}_{\mathsf{EQ}}$ and a publicly verifiable coin

Fig. 2. The Building Blocks of the Additively Homomorphic Multiparty Commitment with Public Verifiability.

tossing functionality $\mathcal{F}_{\mathsf{CT}}$. These functionalities are versions of the functionalities in Frederiksen et al. [19] that are augmented to allow public verifiability. We also use an oblivious transfer functionality with delayed public verifiability $\mathcal{F}_{\mathsf{pOT}}$ in which the receiver can activate an interface that allows any party to verify that the receiver used a given choice bit and received a given message. We show that $\mathcal{F}_{\mathsf{pOT}}$ can be realized using $\mathcal{F}_{\mathsf{Com}}$ and the DDH-based OT protocol of Peikert et al. [33]. A two-party homomorphic commitment with delayed public verifiability functionality $\mathcal{F}_{\mathsf{2HCom}}$ is then realized with a construction based on the scheme of Cascudo et al. [16], which we augment to achieve public verifiability by leveraging $\mathcal{F}_{\mathsf{pOT}}$. Finally, $\mathcal{F}_{\mathsf{2HCom}}$, $\mathcal{F}_{\mathsf{EQ}}$ and $\mathcal{F}_{\mathsf{CT}}$ are used to obtain a public verifiable version of the protocol of Frederiksen et al. [19], yielding a protocol that realizes the additively homomorphic multiparty commitment functionality with public verifiability $\mathcal{F}_{\mathsf{HCom}}$.

MPC with Secret-Shared Output. In our construction we depart from a flavor of MPC that provides partial outputs which can be used to reconstruct the final output through linear operations, which is captured precisely in functionality $\mathcal{F}_{\mathsf{MPC-SO}}$ in Fig. 4. This functionality provides a secret-sharing of the output value: given all shares, any party can use it to obtain the output value while even $n-1$ shares do not reveal any information about it. To reconstruct, a special function f for the reconstruction process must be used. We call this function f a *Reconstruction Function*, whose definition and use was already implicit in previous work [24,34].

Definition 2 (Reconstruction Function). *Let* $f : (\mathbb{F}^m)^{n+1} \to \mathbb{F}^m$ *be a function. We call f a reconstruction function if for all $\bar{y} \in \mathbb{F}^m$, for all $i \in [n]$ and for all $s^{(1)}, \ldots s^{(n-1)} \in \mathbb{F}^m$, the induced function $\hat{f}_i : \mathbb{F}^m \to \mathbb{F}^m$ such that $\hat{f}_i(\cdot) = f(\bar{y}, s^{(1)}, \ldots, s^{(i-1)}, \cdot, s^{(i)}, \ldots, s^{(n-1)})$ is a bijection which is poly-time computable in both directions.*

Functionality $\mathcal{F}_{\mathsf{HCom}}$ is parameterized by $k \in \mathbb{N}$ and interacts with a set of parties $\mathcal{P}$, a set of verifiers $\mathcal{V}$ and an adversary $\mathcal{S}$ (who may abort at any time).

Init: Upon receiving (INIT, sid) from parties $\mathcal{P}$, initialize empty lists raw and actual.

Commit: Upon receiving (COMMIT, $sid, \mathcal{I}$) from $\mathcal{P}_i \in \mathcal{P}$ where $\mathcal{I}$ is a set of unused identifiers, for every $cid \in \mathcal{I}$, sample a random $\boldsymbol{x}_{cid} \xleftarrow{\$} \mathbb{F}^k$, set raw$[cid] = \boldsymbol{x}_{cid}$ and send (COMMIT-RECORDED, $sid, \mathcal{I}$) to all parties $\mathcal{P}$ and $\mathcal{S}$.

Input: Upon receiving a message (INPUT, $sid, \mathcal{P}_i, cid, \boldsymbol{y}$) from $\mathcal{P}_i \in \mathcal{P}$ and messages (INPUT, $sid, \mathcal{P}_i, cid$) from every party in $\mathcal{P}$ other than $\mathcal{P}_i$, if a message (COMMIT, $sid, \mathcal{I}$) was previously received from $\mathcal{P}_i$ and raw$[cid] = \boldsymbol{x}_{cid} \neq \perp$, set raw$[cid] = \perp$, set actual$[cid] = \boldsymbol{y}$ and send (INPUT-RECORDED, $sid, \mathcal{P}_i, cid$) to all parties in $\mathcal{P}$ and $\mathcal{S}$. Otherwise broadcast (ABORT, sid) and halt.

Random: Upon receiving (RANDOM, sid, cid) from all parties $\mathcal{P}$, if raw$[cid] = \boldsymbol{x}_{cid} \neq \perp$, set actual$[cid] = \boldsymbol{x}_{cid}$, set raw$[cid] = \perp$ and send (RANDOM-RECORDED, sid, cid) to all parties $\mathcal{P}$ and $\mathcal{S}$. Otherwise broadcast (ABORT, sid) and halt.

Linear Combination: Upon receiving (LINEAR, $sid, \{(cid, \alpha_{cid})\}_{cid \in \mathcal{I}}, \boldsymbol{\beta}, cid'$) where all $\alpha_{cid} \in \mathbb{F}$ and $\boldsymbol{\beta} \in \mathbb{F}^k$ from all parties $\mathcal{P}$, if actual$[cid] = \boldsymbol{x}_{cid} \neq \perp$ for all $cid \in \mathcal{I}$ and raw$[cid'] = $ actual$[cid'] = \perp$, set actual$[cid'] = \boldsymbol{\beta} + \sum_{cid \in \mathcal{I}} \alpha_{cid} \cdot \boldsymbol{x}_{cid}$ and send (LINEAR-RECORDED, $sid, \{(cid, \alpha_{cid})\}_{cid \in \mathcal{I}}, \boldsymbol{\beta}, cid'$) to all parties $\mathcal{P}$ and $\mathcal{S}$. Otherwise broadcast (ABORT, sid) and halt.

Open: Upon receiving (OPEN, sid, cid) from all parties $\mathcal{P}$, if actual$[cid] = \boldsymbol{x}_{cid} \neq \perp$, send (OPEN, $sid, cid, \boldsymbol{x}_{cid}$) to $\mathcal{S}$. If $\mathcal{S}$ does not abort, send (OPEN, $sid, cid, \boldsymbol{x}_{cid}$) to all parties $\mathcal{P}$.

Check Opening: Upon receiving (CHECK-NOT-OPEN, sid, cid) from $\mathcal{P}_i \in \mathcal{P} \cup \mathcal{V}$, if parties $\{\hat{p}_1, \ldots, \hat{p}_k\} \subset \mathcal{P}$ did not send (OPEN, sid, cid), send (CHECK-NOT-OPEN, $sid, \{\hat{p}_1, \ldots, \hat{p}_k\}$) to $\mathcal{P}_i$.

Initialize Verification: Upon receiving a message (VERIFICATION-START, $sid, \mathcal{P}_i$) from a party $\mathcal{P}_i \in \mathcal{P}$, send (VERIFICATION-START, $sid, \mathcal{P}_i$) to all parties $\mathcal{P}$ and $\mathcal{V}$ and ignore all messages with this sid in all other interfaces but messages (CHECK-NOT-OPEN, sid, cid) in the Check Opening interface and messages (VERIFY, $sid, cid, \boldsymbol{x}'_{cid}$) in the Public Verification interface.

Public Verification: Upon receiving (VERIFY, $sid, cid, \boldsymbol{x}'_{cid}$) from a party $\mathcal{V}_j \in \mathcal{V}$, if a set of parties $\{\mathcal{P}'_1, \ldots, \mathcal{P}'_m\} \subseteq \mathcal{P}$ has not sent a message (VERIFICATION-START, sid), send (VERIFY-FAIL, $sid, \{\mathcal{P}'_1, \ldots, \mathcal{P}'_m\}$) to $\mathcal{V}_j$. Otherwise, if a message (OPEN, sid, cid) has been received from all parties $\mathcal{P}$ and actual$[cid] = \boldsymbol{x}_{cid} = \boldsymbol{x}'_{cid}$, set $f = 1$ (otherwise set $f = 0$) and send (VERIFIED, sid, cid, f) to $\mathcal{V}_j$.

Fig. 3. Functionality $\mathcal{F}_{\mathsf{HCom}}$ For Homomorphic Multiparty Commitment With Delayed Public Verifiability

$\mathcal{F}_{\mathsf{MPC-SO}}$ can be efficiently realized, for instance, by a slightly modified version of the constant-round preprocessed BMR protocol of Hazay et al. [23] which we provide in the full version of this work.

The Smart Contract. Central to our solution for financially fair output delivery is the smart contract functionality $\mathcal{F}_{\mathsf{SC}}$ which is described in Fig. 5. This is a Global UC-functionality, meaning that other functionalities can contact it (as

---

Functionality $\mathcal{F}_{\mathsf{MPC-SO}}$ interacts with the parties $\mathcal{P}$ and is parametrized by a circuit C with inputs $x^{(1)}, \ldots, x^{(n)}$ and output $\boldsymbol{y} = (y_1, \ldots, y_m) \in \mathbb{F}^m$. $\mathcal{S}$ provides a set $I \subset [n]$ of corrupt parties and can at any point send (ABORT, sid) to $\mathcal{F}_{\mathsf{MPC-SO}}$, which in turn sends (ABORT, sid, $\perp$) to $\mathcal{P}$ and terminates. Let the reconstruction function f be the XOR over $\mathbb{F}$.

Input: Upon input (INPUT, $sid, i, x^{(i)}$) by $\mathcal{P}_i$ and input (INPUT, $sid, i, \cdot$) by all other parties the functionality stores the value $(sid, i, x^{(i)})$ internally. Every further such message with the same sid and i is ignored.

Evaluate: Upon input (COMPUTE, sid) by all parties in $\mathcal{P}$ and if the inputs $(sid, i, x^{(i)})_{i \in [n]}$ for all parties have been stored internally, compute $\boldsymbol{y} = (y_1, \ldots, y_m) \leftarrow C(x^{(1)}, \ldots, x^{(n)})$ and store $(sid, \boldsymbol{y})$ locally.

Share Output: Upon input (SHARE-OUTPUT, sid) and if **Evaluate** was finished:
1. For each $h \in [m]$, pick an unused cid_h and send (REQUEST-SHARES, $sid, \{cid_h\}_{h \in [m]}$) to $\mathcal{S}$. For each $i \in I$, $\mathcal{S}$ sends (OUTPUT-SHARES, $sid, \{(cid_h, s^{(i)}_{cid_h})\}_{h \in [m]}$). Then for $i \in \overline{I}$ sample $s^{(i)}_{cid_h} \xleftarrow{\$} \mathbb{F}$, store $(sid, cid_h, i, s^{(i)}_{cid_h})$ and send (OUTPUT-SHARES, $sid, \{(cid_h, s^{(i)}_{cid_h})\}_{h \in [m]}$) to $\mathcal{P}_i$.

2. For each $h \in [m]$, sample $\overline{z_{cid_h}} \in \mathbb{F}$ such that $f(\overline{z_{cid_h}}, s^{(1)}_{cid_h}, \ldots, s^{(n)}_{cid_h}) = y_h$ and store $(sid, cid_h, \overline{z_{cid_h}})$. Send (SHARE-ADVICES, $sid, \{(cid_h, \overline{z_{cid_h}})\}_{h \in [m]}$) to $\mathcal{S}$. If $\mathcal{S}$ sends (DELIVER-ADVICES, $sid, \{cid_h\}_{h \in [m]}$), then send (SHARE-ADVICES, sid, $\{(cid_h, \overline{z_{cid_h}})\}_{h \in [m]}$) to all $\mathcal{P}_i \in \overline{I}$.

Share Random Value: Upon input (SHARE-RANDOM, sid), pick $z \xleftarrow{\$} \mathbb{F}$ and an unused cid, set $\overline{z_{cid}} = 0$ and send (REQUEST-SHARES, sid, cid) to $\mathcal{S}$. For each $i \in I$, $\mathcal{S}$ sends (SHARE, $sid, cid, s^{(i)}_{cid}$). Then sample $s^{(i)}_{cid} \xleftarrow{\$} \mathbb{F}$ for $i \in \overline{I}$ such that $z = f(\overline{z_{cid}}, s^{(1)}_{cid}, \ldots, s^{(n)}_{cid})$, store $(sid, cid, i, s^{(i)}_{cid})$ and send (SHARE, $sid, cid, s^{(i)}_{cid}$) to $\mathcal{P}_i$.

Linear Combination: Upon input (LINEAR, $sid, \{(cid, \alpha_{cid})\}_{cid \in \mathcal{I}}, cid'$) from all parties $\mathcal{P}$, if all $\alpha_{cid} \in \mathbb{F}$, all $cid \in \mathcal{I}$ have stored values and cid' is unused, set $s^{(i)}_{cid'} \leftarrow \sum_{cid \in \mathcal{I}} \alpha_{cid} \cdot s^{(i)}_{cid}$ for each $i \in [n]$, $\overline{z_{cid'}} \leftarrow \sum_{cid \in \mathcal{I}} \alpha_{cid} \cdot \overline{z_{cid}}$, record $\{(sid, cid', i, s^{(i)}_{cid'})\}_{i \in [n]}$, $(sid, cid', \overline{z_{cid'}})$, and send (LINEAR-RECORDED, $sid, \{(cid, \alpha_{cid})\}_{cid \in \mathcal{I}}, cid'$) to all parties $\mathcal{P}$ and $\mathcal{S}$.

Reveal: Upon input (REVEAL, sid, cid, i) by $\mathcal{P}_i$, send (REVEAL, $sid, cid, i, s^{(i)}_{cid}$) to $\mathcal{S}$. If $\mathcal{S}$ sends (DELIVER-REVEAL, sid, cid, i), send (REVEAL, $sid, cid, i, s^{(i)}_{cid}$) to all parties.

Private Reveal: Upon input (REVEAL, sid, cid, i, j) by $\mathcal{P}_i$:
- if $\mathcal{P}_i \in I$ or $\mathcal{P}_j \in I$ then send (REVEAL, $sid, cid, i, s^{(i)}_{cid}$) to $\mathcal{S}$. If $\mathcal{S}$ sends (DELIVER-REVEAL, sid, cid, i, j), send (REVEAL, $sid, cid, i, s^{(i)}_{cid}$) to $\mathcal{P}_j$.

- else send (REVEAL, $sid, cid, i, s^{(i)}_{cid}$) to $\mathcal{P}_j$.

Fig. 4. Functionality $\mathcal{F}_{\mathsf{MPC-SO}}$ for MPC with Secret-Shared Output and Linear Secret Share Operations.

we will see later). It is defined with respect to the global clock $\mathcal{F}_{\mathsf{Clock}}$ although it would be possible to include this into $\mathcal{F}_{\mathsf{SC}}$ already.

The main purpose of $\mathcal{F}_{\mathsf{SC}}$ is twofold as it abstracts two necessary properties of certain blockchains such as Ethereum. Namely, it allows parties to contribute coins towards it and upon which $\mathcal{F}_{\mathsf{SC}}$ acts in a deterministic, publicly known

---

Functionality $\mathcal{F}_{SC}$ interacts with the parties $\mathcal{P}$ and global functionalities $\mathcal{F}_{\text{Ident}}, \mathcal{F}_{\text{Clock}}$. It is parameterized by the compensation q, the deposit $d \geq (n-1)q$, the reconstruction function f and the cash distribution function g. $\mathcal{F}_{SC}$ has an initially empty list $\mathcal{M}$ of messages posted to the authenticated public bulletin board.

Lock-in Deposits: Upon receiving (LOCK-IN, sid, coins$(d + t^{(i)})$) from $\mathcal{P}_i$ where d coins are security deposit and $t^{(i)} \geq 0$ coins are used by $\mathcal{P}_i$ as monetary input in the computation: Query $\mathcal{F}_{\text{Clock}}$ with (READ, sid). If $\nu > 0$ return the money, otherwise accept it. If this was the first message (LOCK-IN, sid) send (UPDATE, sid) to $\mathcal{F}_{\text{Clock}}$.

Check Deposits: If (READ, sid) to $\mathcal{F}_{\text{Clock}}$ returns $\nu = 1$ for the first time: If $(\mathcal{P}_i, sid, \text{OUTPUT-SCRAMBLED}, \overline{y}) \in \mathcal{M}$ for each $i \in [n]$ with the same $\overline{y}$ and each $\mathcal{P}_i$ sent (LOCK-IN, sid, coins$(d + t^{(i)})$) then send (UPDATE, sid) to $\mathcal{F}_{\text{Clock}}$. If not then reimburse all parties that sent **coins** and abort.

Check Outputs: If (READ, sid) to $\mathcal{F}_{\text{Clock}}$ returns $\nu = 2$ for the first time: Let J_1 be the maximal set such that $\forall i \in J_1 : (\mathcal{P}_i, sid, \text{OUTPUT-SHARE}, z^{(i)}) \notin \mathcal{M}$. Then send (UPDATE, sid) to $\mathcal{F}_{\text{Clock}}$.

Challenge Outputs: If (READ, sid) to $\mathcal{F}_{\text{Clock}}$ returns $\nu = 3$ for the first time: Let J_2 be the maximal set of parties such that $\forall i \in J_2 : (\mathcal{P}_i, sid, \text{CHALLENGE}, \top) \in \mathcal{M}$. Send (UPDATE, sid) to $\mathcal{F}_{\text{Clock}}$.

Obtain Verification Data: If (READ, sid) to $\mathcal{F}_{\text{Clock}}$ returns $\nu = 4$ for the first time:
1. If $J_1 \neq \emptyset$ then run Punish(J_1) and stop. If $J_2 = \emptyset$ then run CompPay() and stop.
2. If $J_2 \neq \emptyset$ then send (VERIFY, sid, $z^{(1)}, \ldots, z^{(n)}$) to $\mathcal{F}_{\text{Ident}}$.
   - If $\mathcal{F}_{\text{Ident}}$ returns (VERIFY-FAIL, sid, J_3) then run Punish(J_3) and stop.
   - If $\mathcal{F}_{\text{Ident}}$ returns (REVEAL-FAIL, sid, ref$^{(1)}, \ldots,$ ref$^{(n)}$) then set $J_3 \leftarrow \bigcup_{i \in [n]}$ ref$^{(i)}$. Run Punish(J_3) and stop.
   - If $\mathcal{F}_{\text{Ident}}$ returns (OPEN-FAIL, sid, J_3) and $J_3 \neq \emptyset$ then run Punish(J_3) and stop. If $J_3 = \emptyset$ then run CompPay().

Post to Bulletin Board: Upon receiving (POST, sid, OFF, m) from $\mathcal{P}_i \in \mathcal{P}$, if there is no $(\mathcal{P}_i, sid, \text{OFF}, m') \in \mathcal{M}$, append $(\mathcal{P}_i, sid, \text{OFF}, m)$ to the list $\mathcal{M}$ of authenticated messages that were posted in the public bulletin board.

Read from Bulletin Board: Upon receiving (READ, sid) from a party, return $\mathcal{M}$.

Macro Punish(punish): Let punish $\subset [n]$ and reimburse $= [n] \setminus$ punish. Define $e^{(i)}$ as $d - q \cdot |\text{reimburse}| + t^{(i)}$ if $i \in$ punish and $d + q \cdot |\text{punish}| + t^{(i)}$ if $i \in$ reimburse and then run Pay$(e^{(1)}, \ldots, e^{(n)})$.

Macro CompPay: Compute $y \leftarrow f(\overline{y}, z^{(1)}, \ldots, z^{(n)})$ and $(e^{(1)}, \ldots, e^{(n)}) \leftarrow g(y, t^{(1)}, \ldots, t^{(n)})$. Then run Pay$(d + e^{(1)}, \ldots, d + e^{(n)})$.

Macro Pay$(e^{(1)}, \ldots, e^{(n)})$: For each $\mathcal{P}_i \in \mathcal{P}$ send (PAYOUT, sid, $\mathcal{P}_i$, coins$(e^{(i)})$) to $\mathcal{P}_i$ and (PAYOUT, sid, $\mathcal{P}_i$, $e^{(i)}$) to each other party.

Fig. 5. The stateful contract functionality $\mathcal{F}_{SC}$ that is used to enforce penalties on parties that misbehave in the multiparty computation protocol and to distribute money.

manner. This can be realized by a standard Smart Contract, hence the name $\mathcal{F}_{SC}$. Moreover, $\mathcal{F}_{SC}$ also provides a public bulletin board functionality which can also be accessed by third parties. A Bulletin Board is a publicly readable storage for messages which cannot be erased after being posted. We use an *authenticated* Bulletin Board, which means that messages that are posted can be related to specific parties. These can be implemented from a standard Bulletin Board and

414 C. Baum et al.

signatures.[1] As we focus on the MPC aspects rather than compatibility with a blockchain based public ledger, we model the public ledger as an ideal Bulletin Board that allows for parties to immediately write and read messages.

$\mathcal{F}_{SC}$'s remaining interfaces are then tailored towards our application, interact with the information stored on the bulletin board and can, as mentioned before, be realized as a smart contract. Namely, the functionality ensures that first all parties deposit coins, then all parties send output shares and have the possibility to challenge outputs that they deem incorrect. In that case, $\mathcal{F}_{SC}$ identifies the cheaters together with $\mathcal{F}_{Ident}$ (which is defined later) and punishes cheating parties by splitting up their deposits. Conversely, if no party cheated or raises concern then $\mathcal{F}_{SC}$ returns the deposits and redistributes additional coins according to a cash distribution function g that is fixed in advance.

4 Our Construction

We now describe how the aforementioned building blocks can be combined to construct $\mathcal{F}_{Online}$ from $\mathcal{F}_{MPC-SO}$. We will therefore proceed in two steps. First, we realize an intermediate functionality $\mathcal{F}_{Ident}$ which realizes a flavor of Publicly Verifiable MPC, from which we then in a second step construct Insured MPC.

The functionality $\mathcal{F}_{Ident}$ can be found in Fig. 7. It describes MPC with a flavor of publicly verifiable output. Here, the parties can verify that the computation until the output reconstruction was done correctly. If so, then they run a subcomputation which reconstructs the output and which furthermore allows to determine if a party aborted or provided incorrect shares. In particular, $\mathcal{F}_{Ident}$ allows for third parties to verify that either a given output was indeed obtained from the MPC or a given party has misbehaved in the output phase.

Then, using the functionality $\mathcal{F}_{SC}$ we realize $\mathcal{F}_{Online}$, i.e. MPC with fair output delivery with penalties. There, $\mathcal{F}_{SC}$ uses the properties of $\mathcal{F}_{Ident}$ to either determine the distribution of funds according to the output or punish the identified cheaters. The relations among the functionalities are summarized in Fig. 6.

Building Publicly Verifiable MPC. We now sketch a protocol Π_{Ident} which realizes $\mathcal{F}_{Ident}$ in the $\mathcal{F}_{MPC-SO}, \mathcal{F}_{HCom}, \mathcal{F}_{CT}$-hybrid model with the XOR function over $\mathbb{F}^m$ as the reconstruction function. The full protocol together with a proof of security is presented in the full version.

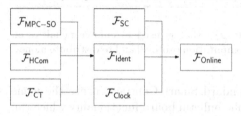

In the protocol, the parties first use $\mathcal{F}_{MPC-SO}$ to securely compute the output $\boldsymbol{y} = C(x^{(1)}, \ldots, x^{(n)})$ inside the MPC functionality. The output is then not immediately reconstructed, but instead all parties learn a vector $\boldsymbol{z} \in \mathbb{F}^m$ and each party $\mathcal{P}_i$ additionally obtains a share vector $\boldsymbol{s}^{(i)} \in \mathbb{F}^m$ such that $\boldsymbol{y} = \boldsymbol{z} \bigoplus \boldsymbol{s}^{(i)}$.

Fig. 6. Steps of the MPC Protocol Compiler.

Each party also generates random blinding values $\boldsymbol{r}^{(i)} \in \mathbb{F}^\kappa$ using $\mathcal{F}_{MPC-SO}$.

---

[1] There exist impossibility results on realizing this primitive [20,32], but we avoid these by allowing for setup, which is also necessary for UC secure MPC [14].

Functionality $\mathcal{F}_{\text{Ident}}$ interacts with the parties $\mathcal{P}$ and also provides an interface to register verifiers $\mathcal{V}$. It is parameterized by a circuit C (with inputs $x^{(1)}, \ldots, x^{(n)}$ and output $y \in \mathbb{F}^m$) and a reconstruction function f. $\mathcal{S}$ provides a set $I \subset [n]$ of corrupt parties. Throughout **Init**, **Input**, **Evaluate** and **Share**, $\mathcal{S}$ can at any point send (ABORT, sid), upon which $\mathcal{F}_{\text{Ident}}$ broadcasts $(\text{ABORT}, sid, \perp)$ and terminates. Throughout **Reveal** and **Verify**, $\mathcal{S}$ at any point is allowed to send (ABORT, sid, J). If $J \subseteq I$ then $\mathcal{F}_{\text{Ident}}$ will send (ABORT, sid, J) to all honest parties and terminate.

Init: Upon first input (INIT, sid) by all $\mathcal{P}_i \in \mathcal{P}$ set $\textbf{rev}, \textbf{ver}, \textbf{ref}^{(1)}, \ldots, \textbf{ref}^{(n)} \leftarrow \emptyset$.

Input: Upon first input $(\text{INPUT}, sid, i, x^{(i)})$ by $\mathcal{P}_i$ and input $(\text{INPUT}, sid, i, \cdot)$ by all other parties the functionality stores the value $(i, x^{(i)})$ internally. Every further such message with the same sid and i is ignored.

Evaluate: Upon first input $(\text{COMPUTE}, sid)$ by all $\mathcal{P}_i \in \mathcal{P}$ and if inputs $(i, x^{(i)})_{i \in [n]}$ for all parties are stored internally, compute $y \leftarrow C(x^{(1)}, \ldots, x^{(n)})$ and store y locally.

Share: Upon first input (SHARE, sid) by $\mathcal{P}_i \in \mathcal{P}$ and if **Evaluate** was finished:

1. For each $\mathcal{P}_i \in \mathcal{P}$ sample $s^{(i)} \xleftarrow{\$} \mathbb{F}^m$ uniformly at random and store it locally. Then send $s^{(i)}$ for each $i \in I$ to $\mathcal{S}$.

2. Upon $(\text{DELIVER-SHARE}, sid, i)$ from $\mathcal{S}$ for $i \in \overline{I}$ send $(\text{OUTPUT}, sid, s^{(i)})$ to $\mathcal{P}_i$.

3. Sample $\bar{y} \in \mathbb{F}^m$ such that $f(\bar{y}, s^{(1)}, \ldots, s^{(n)}) = y$.

4. Send $(\text{OUTPUT}, sid, \bar{y})$ to $\mathcal{S}$. If $\mathcal{S}$ sends $(\text{DELIVER-OUTPUT}, sid, \bar{y})$ then send $(\text{OUTPUT}, sid, \bar{y})$ to all $\mathcal{P}_i \in \overline{I}$.

Reveal: Upon input (REVEAL, sid, i) by $\mathcal{P}_i$, if $i \notin \textbf{rev}$ and $\textbf{ref}^{(i)} = \emptyset$ send $(\text{REVEAL}, sid, i, s^{(i)})$ to $\mathcal{S}$.

- If $\mathcal{S}$ sends $(\text{REVEAL-OK}, sid, i)$ then set $\textbf{rev} \leftarrow \textbf{rev} \cup \{i\}$, send $(\text{REVEAL}, sid, i, s^{(i)})$ to all parties in $\mathcal{P}$.

- If $\mathcal{S}$ sends $(\text{REVEAL-NOT-OK}, sid, i, J)$ with $J \subseteq I$ then send $(\text{REVEAL-FAIL}, sid, i)$ to all parties in $\mathcal{P}$ and set $\textbf{ref}^{(i)} \leftarrow J$.

Test Reveal: Upon input $(\text{TEST-REVEAL}, sid)$ from a party in $\mathcal{P} \cup \mathcal{V}$ define $\overline{\textbf{ref}}^{(i)} = \textbf{ref}^{(i)}$ if $i \in \textbf{rev}$ and $\overline{\textbf{ref}}^{(i)} \leftarrow \textbf{ref}^{(i)} \cup \{i\}$ otherwise. Then send $(\text{REVEAL-FAIL}, sid, \overline{\textbf{ref}}^{(1)}, \ldots, \overline{\textbf{ref}}^{(n)})$ to $\mathcal{P}$ and $\mathcal{V}$.

Allow Verify: Upon input $(\text{START-VERIFY}, sid, i)$ from party $\mathcal{P}_i \in \mathcal{P}$ set $\textbf{ver} \leftarrow \textbf{ver} \cup \{i\}$. If $\textbf{ver} = [n]$ then deactivate all interfaces except **Test Reveal** and **Verify**.

Verify: Upon input $(\text{VERIFY}, sid, z^{(1)}, \ldots, z^{(n)})$ by $\mathcal{V}_i \in \mathcal{V}$ with $z^{(j)} \in \mathbb{F}^m$:
- If $\textbf{ver} \neq [n]$ then return $(\text{VERIFY-FAIL}, sid, [n] \setminus \textbf{ver})$.

- If $\textbf{ver} = [n]$ and $\textbf{rev} \neq [n]$ then send to $\mathcal{V}_i$ what **Test Reveal** sends.

- If $\textbf{ver} = \textbf{rev} = [n]$ then compute the set $\textbf{ws} \leftarrow \{j \in [n] \mid z^{(j)} \neq s^{(j)}\}$ and return $(\text{OPEN-FAIL}, sid, \textbf{ws})$.

Fig. 7. Functionality $\mathcal{F}_{\text{Ident}}$ for an MPC with Publicly Verifiable Output.

Then each $\mathcal{P}_i$ commits to $s^{(i)}, r^{(i)}$ using $\mathcal{F}_{\text{HCom}}$ in order to make the shares $s^{(i)}$ publicly verifiable later. To ensure correctness, the parties use $\mathcal{F}_{\text{CT}}$ to sample a random matrix $\alpha \in \mathbb{F}_2^{\kappa \times m}$, compute and open the output $\alpha \times s^{(i)} + r^{(i)}$ in both $\mathcal{F}_{\text{MPC-SO}}, \mathcal{F}_{\text{HCom}}$ for each $\mathcal{P}_i$ and abort if this value differs for any party.

Otherwise, the parties set $\overline{y} \leftarrow z$ as their public advice and continue the protocol with the committed values $s^{(i)}$.

To implement the **Reveal** and **Verify**-type interfaces of $\mathcal{F}_{\mathsf{Ident}}$ we use the respective interfaces of $\mathcal{F}_{\mathsf{HCom}}$. Namely, the opening commands of $\mathcal{F}_{\mathsf{HCom}}$ can be used to generate the unreliable but identifiable opening of $s^{(i)}$ by each party. These openings are made publicly verifiable and tested by using the **Verification** interfaces of the functionality.

Theorem 1. *The aforementioned Π_{Ident} UC-realizes $\mathcal{F}_{\mathsf{Ident}}$ (with XOR over $\mathbb{F}^m$ as the reconstruction function) against static active adversaries corrupting $< n$ parties in the $\mathcal{F}_{\mathsf{MPC-SO}}, \mathcal{F}_{\mathsf{HCom}}, \mathcal{F}_{\mathsf{CT}}$-hybrid model with broadcast.*

Proof (Sketch). Define a simulator $\mathcal{S}$ where $\mathcal{F}_{\mathsf{CT}}, \mathcal{F}_{\mathsf{HCom}}$ are global and $\mathcal{F}_{\mathsf{MPC-SO}}$ a local functionality and which itself simulates the protocol Π_{Ident} with $\mathcal{A}$ using dummy honest parties. In the full proof we will first show that if a party obtains values $r^{(i)}, s^{(i)}$ from $\mathcal{F}_{\mathsf{MPC-SO}}$ but commits to differing values towards $\mathcal{F}_{\mathsf{HCom}}$, then the opened values $\alpha \times s^{(i)} + r^{(i)}$ from $\mathcal{F}_{\mathsf{MPC-SO}}, \mathcal{F}_{\mathsf{HCom}}$ are identical with probability $O(2^{-\kappa})$ as we are essentially evaluating a universal hash function on these inputs. We then use the fact that we can extract the shares which $\mathcal{A}$ uses for the dishonest parties from our simulated $\mathcal{F}_{\mathsf{MPC-SO}}$ to provide these to $\mathcal{F}_{\mathsf{Ident}}$. The shares of the output of $\mathcal{F}_{\mathsf{MPC-SO}}$ can be altered during the opening of z so that the advice obtained by $\mathcal{A}$ is consistent with the output of $\mathcal{F}_{\mathsf{Ident}}$. That the simulation of the **Reveal, Verify** interfaces using $\mathcal{F}_{\mathsf{HCom}}$ is indistinguishable then follows as the values of the dishonest parties inside $\mathcal{F}_{\mathsf{HCom}}$ coincide with those provided to $\mathcal{F}_{\mathsf{Ident}}$ by $\mathcal{S}$, while the equivocability of $\mathcal{F}_{\mathsf{HCom}}$ allows to simulate the opening and verification of the $s^{(i)}$ values.

From Publicly Verifiable MPC to Insured MPC. We now sketch a protocol Π_{Compiler} that realizes the functionality $\mathcal{F}_{\mathsf{Online}}$ with punishable abort in the $\mathcal{F}_{\mathsf{Ident}}, \mathcal{F}_{\mathsf{SC}}, \mathcal{F}_{\mathsf{Clock}}$-hybrid model. In Π_{Compiler}, $\mathcal{F}_{\mathsf{Ident}}$ will obtain the inputs $x^{(i)}$ from all parties and provide both the advice $\bar{y}$ and shares $s^{(i)}$ that are necessary for the reconstruction of y to the parties. To reliably reconstruct y, each $\mathcal{P}_i$ sends $\bar{y}$ as well as $\mathsf{coins}(d+t^{(i)})$ to the bulletin board $\mathcal{F}_{\mathsf{SC}}$. The coins $\mathsf{coins}(d)$ are used to reimburse other parties in case $\mathcal{P}_i$ aborts, while $\mathsf{coins}(t^{(i)})$ is the input of $\mathcal{P}_i$ into the cash distribution function g. Then, $\mathcal{F}_{\mathsf{Ident}}$ is used by each party $\mathcal{P}_i$ to reveal its share $s^{(i)}$ to all other parties and a value $z^{(i)}$ is posted on $\mathcal{F}_{\mathsf{SC}}$ (where $z^{(i)}$ might be different from $s^{(i)}$ if the adversary cheats). We use $\mathcal{F}_{\mathsf{Clock}}$ to determine if all parties opened/posted their shares $z^{(i)}$ in time and proceed if so. If a party cheats during the opening phase with $\mathcal{F}_{\mathsf{Ident}}$, the protocol instructs all parties to post a complaint on $\mathcal{F}_{\mathsf{SC}}$ within a limited time period (enforced by $\mathcal{F}_{\mathsf{Clock}}$). Once the parties have reacted to complaints by activating verification, $\mathcal{F}_{\mathsf{SC}}$ contacts $\mathcal{F}_{\mathsf{Ident}}$ to verify the correctness of the $z^{(i)}$. An adversary may withhold his share, provide an incorrect share or abort this verification, thus preventing both $\mathcal{F}_{\mathsf{SC}}$ and the honest parties from obtaining the result. In such a case, let $\mathtt{punish} \subseteq I$ be the set of aborting or cheating parties, and $\mathtt{reimburse} = \mathcal{P} \backslash \mathtt{punish}$. Each party from $\mathtt{reimburse}$ will be reimbursed by $\mathsf{coins}(d - q \cdot |\mathtt{reimburse}| + t^{(i)})$ by

$\mathcal{F}_{SC}$, whereas the rest is fairly distributed among the non-cheating parties, which obtain $\mathsf{coins}(d + q \cdot |\mathsf{punish}| + t^{(i)})$. If all parties act honestly, then $\mathcal{F}_{SC}$ uses g to determine the correct payoffs that are then sent to all parties. This also happens if parties cheat by not revealing $s^{(i)}$ via $\mathcal{F}_{\mathsf{Ident}}$, but posting the correct value on $\mathcal{F}_{SC}$, because we cannot distinguish a setting where a dishonest party did not reveal the correct share towards an honest party (which sends a complaint) from a dishonest party framing an honest party.

Theorem 2. *Protocol* Π_{Compiler} *UC-realizes* $\mathcal{F}_{\mathsf{Online}}$ *in the* $\mathcal{F}_{\mathsf{Ident}}, \mathcal{F}_{SC}$-*hybrid model with global* $\mathcal{F}_{\mathsf{Clock}}$ *against static and active adversaries corrupting* $< n$ *parties.*

Proof (Sketch). Define a simulator $\mathcal{S}$ which will interact with the hybrid-world adversary $\mathcal{A}$ in the presence of $\mathcal{F}_{\mathsf{Online}}, \mathcal{F}_{\mathsf{Clock}}, \mathcal{F}_{SC}$. $\mathcal{S}$ simulates an instance of Π_{Compiler} by emulating honest parties and running copies of $\mathcal{F}_{\mathsf{Ident}}, \mathcal{F}_{SC}$ and $\mathcal{F}_{\mathsf{Clock}}$. Both $\mathcal{F}_{\mathsf{Online}}, \mathcal{F}_{\mathsf{Ident}}$ use the same cash distribution function g and reconstruction function f. $\mathcal{S}$ runs Π_{Compiler} with random inputs for the simulated honest parties, extracts the inputs of the dishonest parties from $\mathcal{F}_{\mathsf{Ident}}$ and forwards these to $\mathcal{F}_{\mathsf{Online}}$. $\mathcal{S}$ also inputs coins on behalf of $\mathcal{A}$ into $\mathcal{F}_{\mathsf{Online}}$ (if $\mathcal{A}$ sends these to $\mathcal{F}_{SC}$) and uses the leakage from $\mathcal{F}_{\mathsf{Online}}$ to simulate coins from the emulated parties. $\mathcal{S}$ opens those shares $s^{(i)}$ of honest parties towards $\mathcal{A}$ that it obtained from $\mathcal{F}_{\mathsf{Online}}$ (same for $\overline{\boldsymbol{y}}$) and forwards any aborts of the dishonest parties to $\mathcal{F}_{\mathsf{Online}}$. Depending if $\mathcal{F}_{SC}$ punishes parties or compensates them send the set used by Punish to $\mathcal{F}_{\mathsf{Online}}$ or $\emptyset$. It is easy to see that the output which $\mathcal{A}$ obtains during the simulation is consistent with $\mathcal{F}_{\mathsf{Online}}$, and so are the shares as it does not see $s^{(i)}$ for $i \in \overline{I}$ until the output y is known to $\mathcal{S}$. The coins-values which $\mathcal{S}$ sends are consistent with those from $\mathcal{F}_{SC}$ (and vice versa) and both $\mathcal{F}_{\mathsf{Online}}, \mathcal{F}_{SC}$ abort in the same cases. We see that by construction if $\mathcal{F}_{SC}$ calls Punish then the set given to the macro is non-empty. $\mathcal{F}_{SC}$ either punishes parties that do not send $\boldsymbol{z}^{(i)}$, do not activate verification or where verification of $\boldsymbol{z}^{(i)}$ fails. All of these can only occur for dishonest parties.

Hiding the Output y While Distributing Cash. It is immediate that our protocol Π_{Compiler} leaks the value $\boldsymbol{y}$ to any user of the distributed ledger. By the construction of $\mathcal{F}_{SC}$, we can keep it private if one only wants to obtain MPC with fair output delivery with penalties (without cash distribution). If cash distribution is indeed required, then we can augment the MPC input by $t^{(1)}, \ldots, t^{(n)}$, the output by $e^{(1)}, \ldots, e^{(n)}$ and compute the latter based on $g, \boldsymbol{y}$ inside the MPC. During the output phase we only publish the "public" part of the advice on $\mathcal{F}_{SC}$, which can then perform the cash distribution reliably.

Acknowledgments. This work has been supported by the BIU Center for Research in Applied Cryptography and Cyber Security in conjunction with the Israel National Cyber Bureau in the Prime Minister's Office, the European Research Council (ERC) under the European Unions' Horizon 2020 research and innovation programme under grant agreement No 669255 (MPCPRO) and the DFF under grant agreement number 9040-00399B (*TrA²C*).

References

1. Andrychowicz, M., Dziembowski, S., Malinowski, D., Mazurek, Ł.: Fair two-party computations via bitcoin deposits. In: Böhme, R., Brenner, M., Moore, T., Smith, M. (eds.) FC 2014. LNCS, vol. 8438, pp. 105–121. Springer, Heidelberg (2014). https://doi.org/10.1007/978-3-662-44774-1_8
2. Andrychowicz, M., Dziembowski, S., Malinowski, D., Mazurek, L.: Secure multiparty computations on bitcoin. In: 2014 IEEE Symposium on Security and Privacy, pp. 443–458. IEEE Computer Society Press, May 2014
3. Asharov, G.: Towards characterizing complete fairness in secure two-party computation. In: Lindell, Y. (ed.) TCC 2014. LNCS, vol. 8349, pp. 291–316. Springer, Heidelberg (2014). https://doi.org/10.1007/978-3-642-54242-8_13
4. Asharov, G., Beimel, A., Makriyannis, N., Omri, E.: Complete characterization of fairness in secure two-party computation of boolean functions. In: Dodis, Y., Nielsen, J.B. (eds.) TCC 2015. LNCS, vol. 9014, pp. 199–228. Springer, Heidelberg (2015). https://doi.org/10.1007/978-3-662-46494-6_10
5. Badertscher, C., Maurer, U., Tschudi, D., Zikas, V.: Bitcoin as a transaction ledger: a composable treatment. In: Katz, J., Shacham, H. (eds.) CRYPTO 2017. LNCS, vol. 10401, pp. 324–356. Springer, Cham (2017). https://doi.org/10.1007/978-3-319-63688-7_11
6. Baum, C., Damgård, I., Orlandi, C.: Publicly auditable secure multi-party computation. In: Abdalla, M., De Prisco, R. (eds.) SCN 2014. LNCS, vol. 8642, pp. 175–196. Springer, Cham (2014). https://doi.org/10.1007/978-3-319-10879-7_11
7. Benhamouda, F., Halevi, S., Halevi, T.: Supporting private data on hyperledger fabric with secure multiparty computation. In: 2018 IEEE International Conference on Cloud Engineering (IC2E), pp. 357–363, April 2018
8. Bentov, I., Kumaresan, R.: How to use Bitcoin to design fair protocols. In: Garay, J.A., Gennaro, R. (eds.) CRYPTO 2014. LNCS, vol. 8617, pp. 421–439. Springer, Heidelberg (2014). https://doi.org/10.1007/978-3-662-44381-1_24
9. Bentov, I., Kumaresan, R., Miller, A.: Instantaneous decentralized poker. In: Takagi, T., Peyrin, T. (eds.) ASIACRYPT 2017. LNCS, vol. 10625, pp. 410–440. Springer, Cham (2017). https://doi.org/10.1007/978-3-319-70697-9_15
10. Baum,C., David, B., Dowsley, R.: Insured MPC: Efficient Secure Computation with Financial Penalties (Full Version). Cryptology ePrint Archive, Report 2018/942 (2018). https://eprint.iacr.org/2018/942
11. Camenisch, J., Drijvers, M., Gagliardoni, T., Lehmann, A., Neven, G.: The wonderful world of global random oracles. In: Nielsen, J.B., Rijmen, V. (eds.) EUROCRYPT 2018. LNCS, vol. 10820, pp. 280–312. Springer, Cham (2018). https://doi.org/10.1007/978-3-319-78381-9_11
12. Canetti, R.: Universally composable security: a new paradigm for cryptographic protocols. In: 42nd FOCS, pp. 136–145. IEEE Computer Society Press, October 2001
13. Canetti, R., Dodis, Y., Pass, R., Walfish, S.: Universally composable security with global setup. In: Vadhan, S.P. (ed.) TCC 2007. LNCS, vol. 4392, pp. 61–85. Springer, Heidelberg (2007). https://doi.org/10.1007/978-3-540-70936-7_4
14. Canetti, R., Fischlin, M.: Universally composable commitments. In: Kilian, J. (ed.) CRYPTO 2001. LNCS, vol. 2139, pp. 19–40. Springer, Heidelberg (2001). https://doi.org/10.1007/3-540-44647-8_2

15. Cascudo, I., Damgård, I., David, B., Döttling, N., Dowsley, R., Giacomelli, I.: Efficient UC commitment extension with homomorphism for free (and applications). In: Galbraith, S.D., Moriai, S. (eds.) ASIACRYPT 2019. LNCS, vol. 11922, pp. 606–635. Springer, Cham (2019). https://doi.org/10.1007/978-3-030-34621-8_22

16. Cascudo, I., Damgård, I., David, B., Döttling, N., Nielsen, J.B.: Rate-1, linear time and additively homomorphic UC commitments. In: Robshaw, M., Katz, J. (eds.) CRYPTO 2016. LNCS, vol. 9816, pp. 179–207. Springer, Heidelberg (2016). https://doi.org/10.1007/978-3-662-53015-3_7

17. Choudhuri, A.R., Green, M., Jain, A., Kaptchuk, G., Miers, I.: Fairness in an unfair world: fair multiparty computation from public bulletin boards. In: Thuraisingham, B.M., Evans, D., Malkin, T., Xu, D. (eds.) ACM CCS 17, pp. 719–728. ACM Press, October/November 2017

18. Cleve, R.: Limits on the security of coin flips when half the processors are faulty (extended abstract). In: 18th ACM STOC, pp. 364–369. ACM Press, May 1986

19. Frederiksen, T.K., Pinkas, B., Yanai, A.: Committed MPC. In: Abdalla, M., Dahab, R. (eds.) PKC 2018. LNCS, vol. 10769, pp. 587–619. Springer, Cham (2018). https://doi.org/10.1007/978-3-319-76578-5_20

20. Garay, J.A., Katz, J., Koo, C.-Y., Ostrovsky, R.: Round complexity of authenticated broadcast with a dishonest majority. In: 48th FOCS, pp. 658–668. IEEE Computer Society Press, October 2007

21. Goldreich, O., Micali, S., Wigderson, A.: How to play any mental game or a completeness theorem for protocols with honest majority. In: Aho, A. (ed.) 19th ACM STOC, pp. 218–229. ACM Press, May 1987

22. Gordon, S.D., Hazay, C., Katz, J., Lindell, Y.: Complete fairness in secure two-party computation. In: Ladner, R.E., Dwork, C. (eds.) 40th ACM STOC, pp. 413–422. ACM Press, May 2008

23. Hazay, C., Scholl, P., Soria-Vazquez, E.: Low cost constant round MPC combining BMR and oblivious transfer. In: Takagi, T., Peyrin, T. (eds.) ASIACRYPT 2017. LNCS, vol. 10624, pp. 598–628. Springer, Cham (2017). https://doi.org/10.1007/978-3-319-70694-8_21

24. Ishai, Y., Kushilevitz, E., Lindell, Y., Petrank, E.: On combining privacy with guaranteed output delivery in secure multiparty computation. In: Dwork, C. (ed.) CRYPTO 2006. LNCS, vol. 4117, pp. 483–500. Springer, Heidelberg (2006). https://doi.org/10.1007/11818175_29

25. Ishai, Y., Ostrovsky, R., Zikas, V.: Secure multi-party computation with identifiable abort. In: Garay, J.A., Gennaro, R. (eds.) CRYPTO 2014. LNCS, vol. 8617, pp. 369–386. Springer, Heidelberg (2014). https://doi.org/10.1007/978-3-662-44381-1_21

26. Katz, J., Maurer, U., Tackmann, B., Zikas, V.: Universally composable synchronous computation. In: Sahai, A. (ed.) TCC 2013. LNCS, vol. 7785, pp. 477–498. Springer, Heidelberg (2013). https://doi.org/10.1007/978-3-642-36594-2_27

27. Kiayias, A., Zhou, H.-S., Zikas, V.: Fair and robust multi-party computation using a global transaction ledger. In: Fischlin, M., Coron, J.-S. (eds.) EUROCRYPT 2016. LNCS, vol. 9666, pp. 705–734. Springer, Heidelberg (2016). https://doi.org/10.1007/978-3-662-49896-5_25

28. Kumaresan, R., Bentov, I.: How to use Bitcoin to incentivize correct computations. In: Ahn, G.-J., Yung, M., Li, N. (eds.) ACM CCS 14, pp. 30–41. ACM Press, November 2014

29. Kumaresan, R., Bentov, I.: Amortizing secure computation with penalties. In: Weippl, E.R., Katzenbeisser, S., Kruegel, C., Myers, A.C., Halevi, S. (eds.) ACM CCS 16, pp. 418–429. ACM Press, October 2016

30. Kumaresan, R., Moran, T., Bentov, I.: How to use Bitcoin to play decentralized poker. In: Ray, I., Li, N., Kruegel, C. (eds.) ACM CCS 15, pp. 195–206. ACM Press, October 2015

31. Kumaresan, R., Vaikuntanathan, V., Vasudevan, P.N.: Improvements to secure computation with penalties. In: Weippl, E.R., Katzenbeisser, S., Kruegel, C., Myers, A.C., Halevi, S. (eds.) ACM CCS 16, pp. 406–417. ACM Press, October 2016

32. Lindell, Y., Lysyanskaya, A., Rabin, T.: On the composition of authenticated byzantine agreement. In: 34th ACM STOC, pp. 514–523. ACM Press, May 2002

33. Peikert, C., Vaikuntanathan, V., Waters, B.: A framework for efficient and composable oblivious transfer. In: Wagner, D. (ed.) CRYPTO 2008. LNCS, vol. 5157, pp. 554–571. Springer, Heidelberg (2008). https://doi.org/10.1007/978-3-540-85174-5_31

34. Rabin, T., Ben-Or, M.: Verifiable secret sharing and multiparty protocols with honest majority (extended abstract). In: 21st ACM STOC, pp. 73–85. ACM Press, May 1989

Privacy

Zether: Towards Privacy in a Smart Contract World

Benedikt Bünz[1]([⊠]), Shashank Agrawal[2], Mahdi Zamani[2], and Dan Boneh[1]

[1] Stanford University, Stanford, CA, USA
{benedikt,dabo}@cs.stanford.edu
[2] Visa Research, Palo Alto, CA, USA
{shaagraw,mzamani}@visa.com

Abstract. Smart contract platforms such as Ethereum and Libra provide ways to seamlessly remove trust and add transparency to various distributed applications. Yet, these platforms lack mechanisms to guarantee user privacy, even at the level of simple payments, which are essential for most smart contracts.

In this paper, we propose *Zether*, a trustless mechanism for privacy-preserving payments in smart contract platforms. We take an account-based approach similar to Ethereum and Libra for efficiency and usability. Zether is implemented as a smart contract that keeps account balances encrypted and exposes methods to deposit, transfer, and withdraw funds to/from accounts through cryptographic proofs at only a small cost.

We address several technical challenges to protect Zether against replay attacks and front-running situations and develop a mechanism to enable interoperability with arbitrary smart contracts, making applications like auctions, payment channels, and voting privacy-preserving. To make Zether efficient, we propose Σ-Bullets, a zero-knowledge proof system that is optimized for Σ-protocols. We implement Zether as an Ethereum smart contract and show its practicality by measuring the amount of gas used by the Zether contract. A Zether confidential transaction costs about 0.014 ETH or approximately \$1.51 (as of early 2019), which can be drastically reduced with minor changes to Ethereum that we describe in the paper.

1 Introduction

Smart contracts are computer programs that can directly control digital assets [48], and hence automate the execution of operations that involve digital payments such as digital auctions, lotteries, and crowd-sales. Following the rise of cryptocurrencies, blockchain-based smart contract platforms such as Ethereum [23] enable execution of smart contracts in a decentralized, transparent fashion, removing/reducing the liabilities of trusted intermediaries.

A smart contract is typically written in a powerful programming language, such as Solidity [47], and is executed over a replicated state that is visible to the public. While this allows anyone to automatically verify the correct execution of the contract, it can expose sensitive user data to untrusted entities. One

J. Bonneau and N. Heninger (Eds.): FC 2020, LNCS 12059, pp. 423–443, 2020.
https://doi.org/10.1007/978-3-030-51280-4_23

may choose to simply encrypt all the state data to avoid such exposures. Unfortunately, this makes the verification process significantly expensive, leading to massively-high execution fees.

In contrast, depending on the application, one may choose to encrypt only the information pertaining to the transfer of assets (i.e., payments) happening as part of the contract execution. In fact, in many scenarios, especially those involving competitive risks such as stock trading and auctions, payments information (i.e., amounts and identities of the senders/recipients), are the main source of privacy concerns. Unfortunately, existing techniques for confidential and anonymous payments, such as Monero [38] and Zcash [50], do not easily and efficiently extend to smart contract payments, and popular smart contract platforms such as Ethereum do not provide any privacy mechanism. Furthermore, existing privacy-preserving smart contract mechanisms, such as Hawk [30] and Ekiden [17], are not completely trustless (see Sect. 3 for details).

Most existing payment confidentiality mechanisms (e.g., [2,34,36,38,50]) are in the *unspent-transaction-output (UTXO)* model popularized by Bitcoin. In this model, the inputs to a new transaction are the unspent outputs of previous transactions. UTXOs are not well-suited for applications that need to maintain some state [13], so smart-contract platforms like Ethereum operate in the account-based model. Another drawback of existing UTXO-based mechanisms is that they require major changes to the design of the underlying cryptocurrency (typically Bitcoin), and thus have spun off into separate cryptocurrencies. An immediate benefit of smart contract platforms like Ethereum is that allow deploying new applications without much changes to the underlying blockchain protocol.

Our Contribution. We propose *Zether*, a fully-decentralized, privacy-preserving payment mechanism in the account-based model. Zether requires no changes to the design of the underlying smart contract platform (e.g., Ethereum). As such, the techniques used in Zether can apply to other account-based cryptocurrencies, completely independent of their blockchain/consensus mechanisms.

Our contributions can be summarized as follows:

- *Confidentiality.* Transactions on Zether are confidential by design. Account balances are kept encrypted at all times and users provide cryptographic proofs to spend their money.
- *Anonymity.* Zether allows anonymous transfers, i.e., can hide the sender and the receiver of a transaction among a group of users chosen by the sender. Our protocol neither requires any trusted setup nor any changes to the underlying smart contract platform.
- *Zero-Knowledge Proofs.* To make Zether efficient, we propose a new zero-knowledge (ZK) proof mechanism, called Σ-**Bullets**, which enhances the interoperability of Σ-protocols [21] and Bulletproofs [12] to perform range proofs with ElGamal encryptions efficiently.
- *Implementation.* We implement Zether as an Ethereum smart contract and measure the gas amount required for executing it. We show that Zether is

practical today and with already-planned enhancements to Ethereum will become even more efficient.
- *Interoperability.* Zether allows locking an account to a smart contract, making it easy to "add" privacy to existing applications. We show how Zether can be used to perform sealed-bid auction, confidential payment channel, confidential stake-voting, and private proof-of-stake.

In [11], we describe how Zether can be used in several applications to achieve a strong notion of privacy. These applications include sealed-bid auctions, confidential payment channels, stake voting, and proof-of-stake consensus.

2   Overview of Zether

Our design consists of a smart contract, referred to as the *Zether smart contract (ZSC)* that manages Zether tokens denoted by ZTH. The contract maintains an encrypted account information, referred to as a *Zether account*, for any user who wishes to transact privately using ZTH over the underlying smart contract platform.

To make payment transactions confidential, several proposals (e.g., [34, 38,41]) use homomorphic commitments, such as Pedersen commitments [39]. Though such commitments are simple and efficient, the opening of these commitments must be transferred to the receiver, say Bob, so that he can spend the money later. This randomness could be stored on-chain in some encrypted manner or sent directly to Bob through a separate channel. In the UTXO model, if Bob is unable to recover the randomness (an incorrect value was encrypted/sent, nothing sent at all, etc), then it cannot spend the UTXO later. However, other UTXOs controlled by Bob are not affected at all and could still be spent. On the other hand, with an account-based model, since all the incoming transfers go into the same account, failure to recover the randomness for even a single transfer could render the whole account unusable. One could require senders to encrypt the randomness under receivers' public key, and prove that the commitment indeed uses the randomness encrypted.

Zether uses ElGamal encryption with messages in the exponent [19] to achieve homomorphism and create efficient ZK-proofs of correct encryption. Zether accounts are identified with ElGamal public keys which are stored in the contract's internal state. To fund an account with public key y with b ZTH, the user sends b ETH to ZSC which generates an ElGamal encryption of b with randomness 0 and "adds" it to the encrypted balance associated with y.[1] The user can convert ZTH back to ETH by revealing the current balance $b^\star$ and providing a ZK-proof that y's ciphertext indeed encrypts $b^\star$.

In order to transfer some b amount of ZTH to a public key y' without revealing b itself, one can encrypt b under both y and y'. A ZK-proof is provided to show that the two ciphertexts are well-formed and the remaining balance associated

---

[1] If y has no record on ZSC yet, then a new record is created and initialized with the aforementioned ciphertext.

with y is positive. Zether relies on a new ZK-proof system, called Σ-Bullets, to efficiently prove correctness statements over the encrypted transfer balance and the new sender balance.

While the above design is simple and efficient, it introduces multiple challenges which we briefly discuss in the following.

Front-Running Problem. In Zether, ZK-proofs are generated with respect to a certain state of the contract. For example, the ZK-proof in a transfer transaction needs to show that the remaining balance is positive. A user, Alice, generates this proof with respect to her current account balance, stored in an encrypted form on the contract. Unfortunately, if another user, Bob, transfers some ZTH to Alice, and Bob's transaction gets processed first, then Alice's transaction will be rejected because the proof will not be valid anymore. This can happen even if Bob is totally benign and yet Alice loses the fees she paid to process her transaction. We refer to this situation as the *front-running* problem. Burn transactions have a similar problem, too: a proof that a ciphertext encrypts a certain value becomes invalid if the ciphertext changes.

To solve this problem, one could introduce a new type of transaction that just locks an account to keep away incoming transfers. Alice could wait until this transaction gets into the blockchain before initiating an outgoing transfer (or doing a burn). While this seems to fix the problem (at the cost of making transfer, the primary transaction, a two-step process), it creates new problems for users like Bob who want to send ZTH to Alice. Alice's account may not be locked when Bob publishes a transfer transaction tx, but it could get locked before tx gets in, resulting in tx being rejected.

Pending Transfers. To address the front-running problem, we keep all the incoming transfers in a *pending* state. These transfers are rolled over into the accounts from time to time so that the incoming funds could be spent. This rollover cannot happen at arbitrary times, otherwise the proofs would get invalidated again. To handle this, we divide time into *epochs* each consisting of k consecutive transaction blocks. The choice of k depends on two factors: (1) The gap between the latest state of blockchain and any user's view, and (2) the time it takes to get a transaction into the blockchain. At the end of every epoch, pending transfers are rolled over into the corresponding accounts.

Unfortunately, a smart contract does not do anything unless a transaction is sent to it. One may rollover the pending transfers for *all* accounts on the receipt of the first message in an epoch. This, however, places an unreasonably large burden on the sender of that message: it will have to pay for the cost of rolling over the accounts that it does *not* own, which could be too many. Furthermore, users would have no way to know if their transaction would be the first in an epoch, so they cannot estimate the right amount of gas to supply. To avoid this, Zether rollovers an account in an epoch when the first message from *this* account is received; so, one message rolls over only one account. Note that there could be accounts that do not get rolled over for several consecutive epochs because no transaction is initiated from them.

Replay Protection. Ethereum provides replay protection of its own by associating nonces with every account, which need to be signed into every transaction. Unfortunately, this level of protection is not enough for Zether because: (1) Zether accounts have their own public keys which are not associated with Ethereum addresses, and (2) Zether transactions contain *non-interactive* ZK-proofs. A malicious actor can steal these proofs and reuse them in new transactions. If the state of the account has not changed, then the new transactions will also be processed successfully, leading to loss of funds.

To protect against such issues, we associate a nonce with every Zether account. The nonces are incremented as transactions are processed. A new transaction from an account must sign the latest value of the nonce associated with the account along with the transaction data, which includes any ZK-proof. This approach binds all components of a transaction together and ensures freshness. ZK-proofs cannot be imported into malicious transactions and valid transactions cannot be replayed.

Anonymous Transfers. To allow anonymous transactions in Zether, we require more complex ZK-proofs, a new replay and double-spend protection mechanism, and a new mechanism to lock accounts to smart contracts. An anonymous transaction allows a user, Alice, to send some b ZTH to another user, Bob, while hiding both her and Bob's identity among a larger group of n users. Alice generates n ciphertexts $C_1, \ldots, C_n$, one for each member of the group, respectively and provides a ZK-proof, π, showing that all the ciphertexts encrypt 0 ZTH except two of them which encrypt b ZTH but with difference signs, i.e., b and $-b$. Also, the proof shows that the remaining balance of the account with positive amount is non-negative.

A major challenge in providing anonymity is the size of the new ZK-proof, π, which increases linearly with the size of the anonymity set, n. Zether provides several optimizations to reduce the size of π and its verification overhead. Namely, each ZK-proof contains only two range proofs that are computed using the one-out-of-many proofs of Groth and Kohlweiss [28]. These proofs can be used to give a secondary encryption to one out of n ciphertexts without revealing which original ciphertext was re-encrypted. One-out-of-many proofs can be used to build ring-signatures. Alice uses this proof to create secondary encryptions of b and $-b$, respectively along with a secondary encryption of Alice's balance b^*. Alice then shows the relationship between b and $-b$ and that b and $b^* - b$ are non-negative using a range proof.

Σ-Bullets. Zether uses a custom ZK-proofs system, Σ-Bullets, to certify the correctness of encrypted transactions without revealing any additional information to the public. Σ-Bullets integrate Bulletproofs [12] with Σ-protocols to enable efficient proofs on algebraically-encoded values such as $\exists x : g^x = y \wedge h^x = u \in \mathbb{G}$. Bulletproofs on the other hand is a circuit proof system that is well suited for range proofs and other more complicated arithmetic statements. Bulletproofs does enable proofs on Pedersen committed values if all values use the same commitment key. With Σ-Bullets, we can efficiently prove that a set of ElGamal encrypted values are in some range. Further, we combine one-out-of-many proofs [28], also known as ring signatures, with range proofs to allow anonymous transfers. The one-out-of-many proof is a Σ-protocol that hides which account is being used. Bulletproof is then used to show that the account has sufficient funds for the transfer.

Σ-Bullets inherits from Bulletproofs the trapdoor-free setup and the short, logarithmic-sized, proof lengths. The ability to prove statements on encrypted values further significantly reduces the prover and verifier time compared to a naive implementation using Bulletproofs. We describe Σ-Bullets in detail in [11].

3 Related Work

Confidential transactions for Bitcoin were first proposed by Maxwell [34] who uses Pedersen commitments [39] and OR-proofs to hide transaction amounts while allowing to verify that the sum of outputs of a transaction is no more than the sum of inputs. Monero [38] uses a special type of signature scheme to hide the origins and destinations of transactions among a set of UTXOs chosen by the sender (anonymity set). The size of the signature, however, increases linearly with the size of the anonymity set. Thus, the anonymity properties of the extension to Zether is similar to that Monero.

Zcash [50], based on Zerocash [2], provides anonymity at a sublinear cost using a more sophisticated ZK-proof system called zkSNARKs [26]. Senders and recipients are hidden among the group of people who use shielded addresses. Both Monero and ZCash utilize a set of nullifiers which grows linear in the number of transactions. The downside of using SNARKs is that a large common reference string (CRS) needs to be generated beforehand in a way that no one knows the trapdoor, which is a challenging task [42]. Spenders needs to download the CRS and generate proofs for a large circuit, which is very time consuming [2,51].

CoinJoin [33] provides a way for a set of users to jointly create a Bitcoin transaction. MimbleWimble/Grin [27,41] combines confidential transactions [34] and CoinJoin along with techniques to aggregate transactions non-interactively. CoinShuffle [44] and Mixcoin [8] are mixing protocols for Bitcoin. TumbleBit [29] uses an untrusted intermediary, called a tumbler, to make transactions unlinkable. Möbius [35] replaces the tumbler with an Ethereum smart contract. Zether's approach to anonymity is different from the above: it does not rely on active participation of other users. Zether users can choose their own anonymity set like Monero. On the other hand, if a mixing service is used actively, it may provide better anonymity.[2]

Hawk [30] is a framework for building arbitrary smart contracts in a privacy-preserving way. In particular, it can completely hide the bid values in an auction. This generality, however, comes at a significant cost. In Hawk, the private portion of a contract is converted into a circuit. A manager, who is trusted with the private inputs of participants, generates a zk-SNARK proof on the circuit [3] to show that it has been executed correctly. Apart from the fact that SNARKs

---

[2] One can potentially use Zether in combination with Möbius on Ethereum to get the best of both worlds. We leave this as an interesting open question.

rely on trusted setup, the reference string is also circuit-dependent, so a different string needs to be generated for every contract. Moreover, the circuit model puts a bound on the number of users who can participate.

As a result, though Hawk is quite powerful and could provide better privacy, it is not fully decentralized and would be too expensive to use for simple contracts. Another general-purpose framework, Ekiden [17], addresses both the performance and confidentiality problems with smart contract platforms, but relies on trusted execution environments like Intel SGX, so are not fully decentralized either.

RSCoin, Solidus, zkLedger, etc. [16,22,37] operate in a model that falls somewhere between a fully decentralized setting like that of Bitcoin/Ethereum and a centralized setting like that of modern financial systems. In this model, the banks regulate the monetary supply but use a blockchain to transact. There is some similarity between the techniques used here and zkLedger's, where every bank has an account. A sending bank A in zkLedger creates several commitments to send some money x to a receiving bank B. The commitment corresponding to A is to $-x$, to B is to x, and all other commitments are to zero. Then, there are proofs to show that the commitments are well-formed and A has more than x amount of money. While we use similar ideas in our protocol, Zether needs to deal with issues like front-running, replay, compatibility, etc. that come with building a smart contract on an open platform.

Concurrent Work. Zexe [10] is a recent proposal for a private scripting language for Zerocash-style currencies. It provides similar functionality to Bitcoin script while hiding the inputs to the script and the script itself. It, however, does not support stateful computations in the way a smart contract does.

QuisQuis [25] is a new anonymity system designed to address some of the problems with cryptocurrencies like Monero and Zcash (e.g., the set of unspent outputs keep growing). Their model is an interesting hybrid of UTXO and account models. While the basic unit is an account (consisting of a public key and a commitment), they are only of one-time use: old accounts are destroyed and new accounts created in a transaction. Our Σ-Bullets protocol is similar to the techniques used in QuisQuis [25], where a Pedersen commitment contains the same value as an ElGamal encryption and then execute the Bulletproof on the ElGamal encrypted values. Σ-Bullets more directly incorporates the Σ-protocol with the Bulletproof protocol.

Unfortunately, QuisQuis suffers from front-running attacks (public keys in an anonymity set may get updated just before the transaction is processed) and puts additional burden on clients (they have to go through the list of all updated keys to find out which one belongs to them). More importantly, QuisQuis is a standalone cryptocurrency while Zether is a system that can be deployed on any smart contract platform, and can be used by other smart contracts to achieve privacy.

4   Preliminaries

ElGamal Encryption. ElGamal encryption is a public key encryption scheme secure under the DDH assumption. A random number from $\mathbb{Z}_p^\star$, say x, acts as a private key, and $y = g^x$ is the public key corresponding to that. To encrypt an integer b, it is first mapped to one or more group elements. If $b \in \mathbb{Z}_p$, then a simple mapping would be to just raise g to b. Now, a ciphertext for b is given by $(g^b y^r, g^r)$ where $r \leftarrow_\$ \mathbb{Z}_p^\star$. With knowledge of x, one can divide $g^b y^r$ by $(g^r)^x$ to recover g^b. However, g^b needs to be brute-forced to compute b.

We argue that this is not an issue. First, as we will see, the Zether smart contract does not need to do this, only the users would do it. Second, users will have a good estimate of ZTH in their accounts because, typically, the transfer amount is known to the receiver. Thus, brute-force computation would occur only rarely. Third, one could represent a large range of values in terms of smaller ranges. For instance, if we want to allow amounts up to 64 bits, we could instead have 2 amounts of 32 bits each, and encrypt each one of them separately. In this paper, for simplicity, we will work with a single range, 1 to MAX, and set MAX to be 2^{32} in the implementation.

The primary benefit of putting balances in exponent is that it makes ElGamal encryption additively homomorphic. If b and b' are encrypted under the same public key y to get ciphertexts $(C_L = g^b y^r, C_R = g^r)$ and $(C'_L = g^{b'} y^{r'}, C'_R = g^{r'})$ respectively, then $(C_L C'_L = g^{b+b'} y^{r+r'}, C_R C'_R = g^{r+r'})$ is an encryption of $b + b'$ under y.

Zero-Knowledge Proofs. A zero-knowledge (ZK) proof of a statement does not reveal any information beyond the validity of the statement. For example, one could prove that two ciphertexts encrypt the same message without revealing the message itself. Though any NP statement can be proved in zero-knowledge, the concrete costs depend on a number of factors.

Σ-protocols are honest-verifier public-coin zero-knowledge interactive proofs of a special form. Very efficient Σ protocols exist for proving a wide variety of algebraic statements like knowledge of b and r s.t. an ElGamal ciphertext encrypts b with randomness r. The Fiat-Shamir transform is a way of transforming any public-coin honest-verifier ZK-proof (like Σ protocols) into a *non-interactive* zero-knowledge *proof of knowledge* in the random oracle model.

A ZK-proof for the statement

$$\mathsf{st} : \{(a, b, c, \ldots; x, y, z, \ldots) : f(a, b, c, \ldots, x, y, z, \ldots)\}$$

means that the prover shows knowledge of $x, y, z, \ldots$ such that $f(a, b, c, \ldots, x, y, z, \ldots)$ is true, where $a, b, c, \ldots$ are public variables. We use $\mathsf{st}[a, b, c, \ldots]$ to denote an instance of st where the variables $a, b, c, \ldots$ have some fixed values.

We represent a non-interactive ZK (NIZK) proof system with algorithms $(\mathsf{Setup_{nizk}}, \mathsf{Prove}, \mathsf{Verify_{nizk}})$, where $\mathsf{Setup_{nizk}}$ outputs some public parameters, Prove generates a proof for a statement given a witness, and $\mathsf{Verify_{nizk}}$ checks if the proof is valid w.r.t the statement. Zether uses NIZKs that are a) correct, an honest prover can produce a valid proof b) zero-knowledge, a verifier learns nothing from the proof but the validity of the statement, and c) sound, a computationally bounded prover cannot convince a verifier of a false statement. Σ protocols, with the Fiat-Shamir transform applied, have all these properties.

Digital Signatures. Signature schemes are used to authorize messages by *signing* them. A verifier can check a signature but will be unable to forge a signature on a previously unsigned message. Signatures can be built from Fiat-Shamir transformed NIZK proofs [1].

We represent a signature scheme with algorithms $(\mathsf{Setup_{sig}}, \mathsf{Sign}, \mathsf{Verify_{nizk}})$, where $\mathsf{Setup_{sig}}$ outputs some public parameters, Sign generates a signature on an input message, and $\mathsf{Verify_{nizk}}$ checks if the signature is valid w.r.t. the message. Zether requires a signature scheme that is a) correct, it is possible to create valid signatures on arbitrary messages and b) existentially unforgeable, a computationally bounded adversary cannot create a valid signature on a *new* message, even after seeing signatures on other messages. We omit formal definitions for brevity and refer to [6] for a thorough treatment of the properties.

5   The Zether Protocol

Notations. We use λ to denote the security parameter. Let $\mathsf{GroupGen}$ be a polynomial-time algorithm that on input 1^λ outputs $(p, g, \mathbb{G})$ where $p = \Theta(\lambda)$, p is prime, $\mathbb{G}$ is a group of order p, g is a generator of $\mathbb{G}$, and the decisional Diffie-Hellman (DDH) assumption holds in $\mathbb{G}$. The DDH assumption states that a tuple $(g, g^a, g^b, g^{a \cdot b})$ is computationally indistinguishable from (g, g^a, g^b, g^c) for random a, b, c. It implies the discrete logarithm assumption.

Let $\mathbb{Z}_p$ denote the integers modulo p. $\mathbb{Z}_p^*$ is the set of inverses in $\mathbb{Z}_p$. We use $[a, b]$ for $a, b \in \mathbb{Z}$ to denote the set of integers $\{a, a + 1, \ldots, b - 1, b\}$. We use $x \leftarrow_{\$} S$ to denote that x is sampled uniformly at random from a set S. We use PPT as a shorthand for probabilistic polynomial time and $\mathsf{negl}(\lambda)$ to denote negligible functions.

Zether Components. The Zether consists of three components: a global setup algorithm that is run once to generate the global parameters for the protocol as well as to deploy the Zether smart contract. The second component is the Zether smart contract (ZSC) that handles transactions between users, interoperability with external smart contracts, and keeps the state of the system. The final component of the mechanism are the user algorithms which describe how users can interact with the smart contract and create valid transactions. A user is of course not bound to the behavior described in the user algorithms. Our security proof in [11] shows that even if an adversarial user does not comply with these algorithms, he can't break Zether's correctness, privacy and over-draft protections.

Setup. The setup algorithm calls $\mathsf{Setup_{nizk}}$ and $\mathsf{Setup_{sig}}$ as subroutines which are the setup algorithms for the proof system and the signature scheme, respectively. The former setup could depend on the relations for which proofs are constructed. If these subroutines are trustless, then the whole setup is trustless, meaning that its correctness can be verified publicly. In the implementation (Sect. 6), we use Bulletproofs [12] and Schnorr signatures [45], both of which have a trustless setup. Zether significantly differs from Zcash [50] in this respect because Zcash has a trusted setup and its security is broken if the setup is subverted.

Setup algorithm is formally described in Fig. 2. Apart from setting up the proof system and signature scheme, it initializes account tables acc and pending transfers table pTransfers (recall that incoming transfers are put into a pending state first), a last roll over epoch table lastRollOver to keep track of the last epochs accounts were updated, a lock table lock to keep track of the addresses to which accounts are locked, a counter table ctr to prevent replay attacks, and a variable b_{total} that tracks the total amount of ZTH held by the contract. The setup also specifies an epoch length E and a maximum amount value MAX.

Zero-Knowledge Relations. Each transfer and burn transaction in Zether contains a ZK-proof which ensures that the transfer is valid without revealing the reasons why it is valid.

Burn Transaction. Let us first consider a burn transaction where a user needs to verifiably decrypt his Zether balance. It can certainly do this by revealing its secret key to the smart contract. However, an adversary can use the secret key to decrypt all previous balances and transactions of the user, thus completely breaking its privacy. So, instead of decrypting in the clear, the user creates a ZK-proof for the following statement:

$$\mathsf{st}_{\mathsf{burn}} : \left\{ (y, C_L, C_R, u, b, g, g_{\mathsf{epoch}}; \mathsf{sk}) : y = g^{\mathsf{sk}} \wedge C_L = g^b C_R^{\mathsf{sk}} \right\}. \tag{1}$$

The statement shows that the user knows an sk such that y is indeed the public key corresponding to sk and (C_L, C_R) is a valid encryption of b under y. A simple Σ-protocol can be used to prove the statement.

Transfer Transaction. Let us now consider a transfer transaction. Suppose a user wants to transfer an amount $b^\star$ from a public key y to a public key $\bar{y}$. Let (C_L, C_R) be the encryption of balance associated with y. The smart contract needs to deduct $b^\star$ from y's balance and add the same amount to $\bar{y}$'s balance, which will be put into a pending state. Since we need to hide $b^\star$ in this process, user will encrypt $b^\star$ under both y and $\bar{y}$ to get (C, D) and $(\overline{C}, \overline{D})$, respectively. Now, it must provide a proof to show that:

1. both ciphertexts are well formed and encrypt the same value $b^\star$;
2. $b^\star$ is a positive value; and,
3. the remaining balance of y, say b', is positive too.

More formally, a user proves the following statement:

$$\mathsf{st}_{\mathsf{ConfTransfer}} : \big\{ (y, \bar{y}, C_L, C_R, C, D, \overline{C}, g; \mathsf{sk}, b^\star, b', r) :$$
$$C = g^{b^\star} y^r \wedge \overline{C} = g^{b^\star} \bar{y}^r \wedge D = g^r \wedge$$
$$C_L / C = g^{b'} (C_R / D)^{\mathsf{sk}} \wedge y = g^{\mathsf{sk}} \wedge$$
$$b^\star \in [0, \mathsf{MAX}] \wedge b' \in [0, \mathsf{MAX}] \big\}. \tag{2}$$

Kurosawa [31] first showed that in the ElGamal encryption scheme, randomness can be reused to encrypt to multiple recipients. We use the same idea here to make the zero-knowledge component more efficient: the same random number r is used to encrypt $b^\star$ under both y and $\bar{y}$.

Zether Contract. The Zether contract (ZSC) is defined in Fig. 1. It consists of five public methods Fund, Burn, Transfer, Lock, Unlock and two additional internal helper methods RollOver, CheckLock. The helper methods are used to modularize the contract's logic. We use Solidity syntax at some places in the description of ZSC, instead of introducing new notation. We now discuss ZSC's methods in detail.

Rolling Over. Pending transfers for an account must be rolled over into the account every epoch, or at least in the epochs the account is used. However, no instruction on a smart contract can execute unless triggered by a transaction. As a result, all public methods of ZSC first call RollOver on the input public key(s).

Given a public key y, RollOver checks if the last roll over was in an older epoch. If yes, then it rolls over the pending transfers pTransfers[y] into acc[y] and resets pending transfers as well as the last roll over epoch.

Check Lock. Every transaction to operate on an account is associated with an Ethereum address (returned by msg.sender). If the account is unlocked, then it can be operated from any address. However, if it is locked to a certain address, then it can only be operated from that address. CheckLock is an internal methods to check these two conditions. All the methods call CheckLock before operating on an account.

Locking. Given a public key y, an address addr and a signature σ_{lock}, Lock checks if it is appropriate to operate on the account by calling CheckLock, which will be discussed in more detail shortly, and verifies that σ_{lock} is a valid signature on addr and the current value of counter ctr[y]. It sets lock[y] to be addr and increments the counter, which ensures that this lock transaction cannot be replayed. Unlock method also calls CheckLock first, then sets the pending lock to be $\bot$.

Funding. Anybody can fund an account, even an account that he/she does not own, by simply specifying the public key y and transferring some ETH. The only exception is for locked accounts; they can only be operated from the locking address. (One could have a different rule for funding locked accounts.) Fund converts ETH into ZTH. The ETH gets stored in the smart contract and the ZTH are homomorphically added to y's (pending) balance. If the account does not exist yet, a new one is created. Fund also ensures that the deposit does not exceed the total amount of funds, MAX, that Zether can handle.

Burn. Burn converts ZTH back to ETH. It verifies the proof π_{burn} against $\mathsf{st}_{\mathsf{burn}}$ (see (1)) to ensure that the sender knows the right private key and is claiming the right amount. It also checks a signature on the transaction data and the current value of counter, which prevents replay attacks. Note that a burn operation does not close an account.

Fund
- INPUTS: public key y
1. RollOver(y)
2. Let $b = \text{msg.value}$
3. require:
    - $b + b_{total} \leq \text{MAX}$
    - CheckLock(y,msg.sender) $= 1$
4. If acc$[y] = \perp$:
    - Let $H = \text{block.number}$, $e = \lfloor H/E \rfloor$
    - Set acc$[y] = (1,1)$
    - Set pTransfers$[y] = (g^b,1)$
    - Set lock$[y] = \perp$
    - Set lastRollOver$[y] = e$
    - Set ctr$[y] = 0$
  Else:
    - Set
      pTransfers$[y] = \text{pTransfers}[y] \circ (g^b,1)$
5. Set $b_{total} = b_{total} + b$

Transfer
- INPUTS: sender public key y, recipient public key $\overline{y}$, ciphertexts (C,D), $(\overline{C},D)$ proof π_{Transfer}, signature σ_{transfer}
1. RollOver(y)
2. RollOver($\overline{y}$)
3. Let $(C_L,C_R) = \text{acc}[y]$
4. require:
    - CheckLock(y,msg.sender) $= 1$
    -
      Verify$_{\text{nizk}}$(st$_{\text{ConfTransfer}}[y,\overline{y},C_L,C_R,C,\overline{C},D]$, π_{transfer}) $= 1$
    - Verify$_{\text{nizk}}(y,(\overline{y},C,\overline{C},D,\pi_{\text{transfer}},\text{ctr}[y]),$ $\sigma_{\text{transfer}}) = 1$
5. Set acc$[y] = \text{acc}[y] \circ (C^{-1},D^{-1})$
6. Set pTransfers$[\overline{y}] = \text{pTransfers}[\overline{y}] \circ (\overline{C},D)$
7. Set ctr$[y] = \text{ctr}[y] + 1$

Lock
- INPUTS: public key y, Ethereum address addr, signature σ_{lock}
1. RollOver(y)
2. require:
    - CheckLock(y,msg.sender) $= 1$
    - Verify$_{\text{nizk}}(y,(\text{addr},\text{ctr}[y]),\sigma_{\text{lock}}) = 1$
3. Set lock$[y] = \text{addr}$
4. Set ctr$[y] = \text{ctr}[y] + 1$

Burn
- INPUTS: public key y, balance b, proof π_{burn}, signature σ_{burn}
1. RollOver(y)
2. Let $(C_L,C_R) = \text{acc}[y]$
3. require:
    - CheckLock(y,msg.sender) $= 1$
    - Verify$_{\text{nizk}}(\text{st}_{\text{burn}}[y,C_L,C_R,b,g],\pi_{\text{burn}}) = 1$
    - Verify$_{\text{nizk}}(y,(b,\pi_{\text{burn}},\text{ctr}[y]),\sigma_{\text{burn}}) = 1$
4. Set acc$[y] = \text{acc}[y] \circ (C_L^{-1},C_R^{-1})$
5. Set ctr$[y] = \text{ctr}[y] + 1$
6. Set $b_{total} = b_{total} - b$
7. Do msg.sender.transfer(b)

Unlock
- INPUTS: public key y
1. RollOver(y)
2. require:
    - CheckLock(y,msg.sender) $= 1$
3. Set lock$[y] = \perp$

Internal Helper Methods

RollOver
- INPUTS: public key y
1. Let $H = \text{block.number}$, $e = \lfloor H/E \rfloor$
2. If lastRollOver$[y] < e$:
    - Set acc$[y] = \text{acc}[y] \circ \text{pTransfers}[y]$
    - Set pTransfers$[y] = (1,1)$
    - Set lastRollOver$[y] = e$

CheckLock
- INPUTS: public key y, Ethereum address addr
- OUTPUT: 1 if account y can be operated by addr; 0 otherwise
1. If lock$[y] = \perp$ or lock$[y] = \text{addr}$:
    - Output 1
  Else:
    - Output 0

Fig. 1. ZSC: The Zether smart contract

Setup

INPUT: Security parameter λ (in unary)

1. $(p,g,\mathbb{G}) \leftarrow \mathsf{GroupGen}(1^\lambda)$
2. $\mathsf{pp_{nizk}} \leftarrow \mathsf{Setup_{nizk}}(1^\lambda)$
3. $\mathsf{pp_{sig}} \leftarrow \mathsf{Setup_{sig}}(1^\lambda)$
4. Initialize
   - empty account table, $\mathsf{acc} : \mathbb{G} \rightarrow \mathbb{G}^2$
   - empty pending transfers table, $\mathsf{pTransfers} : \mathbb{G} \rightarrow \mathbb{G}^2$
   - an empty last roll over epoch table, $\mathsf{lastRollOver} : \mathbb{G} \rightarrow \mathbb{Z}$,
   - an empty lock table, $\mathsf{lock} : \mathbb{G} \rightarrow \{0,1\}^*$,
   - an empty counter table, $\mathsf{ctr} : \mathbb{G} \rightarrow \mathbb{Z}$,
   - total balance $b_{\mathsf{total}} \in \mathbb{Z}$ to 0,
5. Deploy smart contract ZSC (Figure 1) with parameters $(p, g, \mathbb{G})$, $\mathsf{pp_{nizk}}$, $\mathsf{pp_{sig}}$, acc, $\mathsf{pTransfers}$, $\mathsf{lastRollOver}$, lock, b_{total}, MAX, E.

Fig. 2. Zether setup

Transfer. Transfer transfers some ZTH from an account to another. The proof π_{transfer} makes sure that the ciphertext has the right form and the sender has enough money (see Eq. (2)). Similar to Burn, there is a signature here to prevent replay attacks.

Note that the transferred amount is added to pTransfers of the recipient, not acc (i.e., it will be rolled over into acc in a later epoch). Thus, outgoing transfers of the recipient in this epoch will not be invalidated.

User Algorithms. User algorithms specify how users can interact with ZSC. CreateTransferTx and CreateBurnTx first do a roll over of the input public keys to ensure that any pending transfers are rolled over. CreateBurnTx uses ReadBalance to recover the amount of ZTH in the account. Using the private key, ReadBalance finds the right b s.t. $C_L/C_R^x = g^b$. In typical cases, a user would *not* have to try all positive integers one by one to recover b. She will already have a good estimate of b (Fig. 3).

5.1 Anonymous Zether

We now describe the anonymous version of Zether. While this version hides both sender and receiver apart from hiding the transfer amount, it also incurs some additional costs. First, the size of ZK-proof for a transfer increases linearly with the size of the anonymity set. Second, as we will see, users would be able to do only one transfer or burn transaction per epoch (not one of each). We discuss some issues pertinent to the design of anonymous Zether below. For a detailed description of anonymous Zether, we refer the reader to the full version of this paper [11].

Replay and Double-Spend Protection. An anonymous transaction published by Alice involves multiple accounts only one of which Alice may own. To preserve anonymity, all the accounts involved in the transaction must be treated in the same way. Thus, the nonces associated with each one of them should be

CreateAddress
- INPUTS: 1^λ
- OUTPUT: $x \in \mathbb{Z}_p, y \in \mathbb{G}$
1. $x \leftarrow_\$ \mathbb{Z}_p$
2. $y = g^x$

CreateTransferTx
- INPUTS: sender public key y, receiver public key $\bar{y}$, sender private key x, sender balance b_{from}, transfer amount $b^\star$, state st_h of ZSC
- OUTPUT:
  $tx_{trans} = (y, \bar{y}, C, \bar{C}, D, \pi_{transfer}, \sigma_{transfer})$
1. Roll over y, $\bar{y}$ in st_h
2. Let $(C_L, C_R) = acc[y]$
3. $r \leftarrow_\$ \mathbb{Z}_p$
4. Set $C = g^{b^\star} y^r$
5. Set $\bar{C} = g^{b^\star} \bar{y}^r$
6. Set $D = g^r$
7. Set $w = (x, b^\star, b_{from}, r)$
8. $\pi_{transfer} =$
   $\mathsf{Prove}(st_{ConfTransfer}[y, \bar{y}, C_L, C_R, C, \bar{C}, D, g], w)$
9. $\sigma_{transfer} =$
   $\mathsf{Sign}(x, (\bar{y}, C, \bar{C}, D, \pi_{transfer}, ctr[y]))$

CreateBurnTx
- INPUTS: private key x, state st_h of ZSC
- OUTPUT: $tx_{burn} = (y, b, \pi_{burn}, \sigma_{burn})$
1. Let $b = \mathsf{ReadBalance}(x, st_h)$
2. $w = (x)$
3. Set $y = g^x$
4. Let $(C_L, C_R) = acc[y]$
5. $\pi_{burn} = \mathsf{Prove}(st'_{burn}[y, C_L, C_R, b, g], w)$
6. $\sigma_{burn} = \mathsf{Sign}(x, (b, \pi_{burn}, ctr[y]))$

CreateLockTx
- INPUTS: private key x, locking Ethereum address addr, state st_h of ZSC
- OUTPUT: $tx_{lock} = (y, addr, \sigma_{lock})$
1. Compute $\sigma_{lock} = \mathsf{Sign}(x, (addr, ctr[y]))$
2. Set $y = g^x$

ReadBalance
- INPUTS: private key y, state st_h of ZSC
- OUTPUT: balance b
1. Set $y = g^x$
2. Roll over y in st_h
3. $(C_L, C_R) = acc[y]$
4. Find b s.t. $C_L / C_R^x = g^b$

Fig. 3. User algorithms of Zether

incremented. Other account holders involved in Alice's transaction may have generated a transaction with the previous value of nonce. Unfortunately, if their transactions get in later, then they will be rejected. If even one of them gets in before, then Alice's transaction will be rejected.

We take a different approach to replay protection, which has some similarities with that of Monero. Every epoch will be associated with a base g_{epoch} derived from hashing some fixed string like 'Zether' and the current epoch number. To initiate a transfer or burn transaction from an account with public key $y = g^{sk}$, g_{epoch}^{sk} must be included in the transaction. More precisely, the proof π described above for a transfer transaction will also show knowledge of sk such that $\bar{g} = g_{epoch}^{sk}$ for $\bar{g}$ included in the transaction. (Burn transactions' proofs will also include this.) Importantly, $\bar{g}$ is computationally unlinkable to y under the DDH assumption. We refer to $\bar{g}$ as a nonce in the sequel.

While in the case of confidential transfers, we subtract the transfer amount from the sender's balance immediately but keep it pending for the receiver, one cannot take the same approach for anonymous transfers. All the transfer amounts, whether positive (for the receiver), negative (for the sender), or zero (for others) have to be kept pending. Thus, an anonymous transaction would not immediately affect the balance of any of the users involved. This opens up the system to double-spending attacks. A user could generate two transactions in an epoch, sending her total balance to two different users. The attached ZK-proofs would both be valid because they will be verified against the same state. Fortunately, the nonce, in addition to preventing replay attacks, also prevents such double-spending attacks.

During every epoch, ZSC will accumulate nonces as they come, rejecting any transaction that reuses a nonce. An important difference from Monero is that the set of nonces does not grow indefinitely; it is reset to null at the beginning of every epoch. Thus, providing anonymity does not lead to a continuous growth in the size of the state of ZSC. A drawback of this approach to replay protection and double-spending is that even honest users can only initiate at most one transfer or burn transaction in a given epoch.

Global Updates. With the new replay protection mechanism in place, a few global updates need to be made in every epoch: set the base for the epoch and empty the nonce set. We will have to make the updates at the receipt of the very first message in an epoch, be it from any account. Thus, users will have to provide a little more gas to cover the possibility that their message could be the very first one in an epoch. In most cases, this extra gas will be reimbursed.

Locking to Smart Contracts. If some accounts involved in an anonymous transfer are locked to a smart contract, then all of the locked accounts must be locked to the same contract. Furthermore, the transfer is processed only if it comes from that contract. Also, locking must not come into effect immediately. Suppose Alice publishes a transaction in a certain epoch to lock her account to a smart contract. Another user Bob may have published a transfer transaction (at about the same time as Alice) with Alice in his anonymity set while her account was still unlocked. If Alice's transaction gets in first, locking her account, then Bob's transaction will be rejected. The same holds for unlocking as well. Therefore, when ZSC is invoked to lock/unlock an account, it just records the request but does not act on it immediately. When the account is rolled over in some later epoch, the request will be executed.

Lock transactions also need replay protection. In fact, using the account secret key, the sender must sign both the nonce and an address (to which the account will be locked) in the case of confidential transfers, and both the epoch base and address in the case of anonymous transfers. As a result, for the latter case, lock transactions must be published at the beginning of an epoch just like transfer and burn transactions.

5.2 Σ-Bullets

Transfer and AnonTransfer are relatively-large relations that involve proofs on encrypted data. We, therefore, want to use a proof system that (1) is efficient, i.e., has short proofs and efficient verification, and (2) allows proofs on encrypted data. Bulletproofs [12] is a generic zero-knowledge proof system that produces short (logarithmic sized) proofs without relying on a trusted setup. Bulletproofs was specifically designed to work with Confidential Transactions (CT) [34] as it directly proves statements containing values committed to as Pedersen commitments. Its short proofs and trustless setup make Bulletproofs an intriguing choice for Zether's underlying proof system. However, unlike the UTXO-based CT, Zether relies on ElGamal encryptions as commitments. We, therefore, aim to use a proof system that can prove statements on ElGamal ciphertexts.

It is not sufficient to simply replace Pedersen commitments with ElGamal encryptions as the latter cannot be "opened" similar to commitments and are also not additively homomorphic if encryptions are under different keys, as is the case in Zether. Also, for AnonTransfer, we need to combine a one-out-of-many proof[3] with range proofs. A one-out-of-many proof is used to select the receiver and sender transfer encryption and the range proof ensures that no overdraft happens. Bulletproofs enables efficient range proofs and there are logarithmic sized efficient Σ-protocols [18] for doing one-out-of-many proofs [9,28].

To efficiently prove these statements and instantiate Zether, we design Σ-Bullets as an extension of Bulletproofs. Given an arithmetic circuit, a Σ-Bullets proof ensures that a public linear combination of the circuit's wires is equal to some witness of a Σ-protocol. This enhancement in turn enables proofs on many different encodings such as ElGamal encryptions, ElGamal commitments, or Pedersen commitments in different groups or using different generators. Further, it allows the combination of different specialized Σ-protocols such as one-out-of-many proofs or accumulator proofs [15] with the generic circuit-base proof system Bulletproofs. This will benefit other systems that want to prove statements on additively-encoded witnesses. We describe Σ-Bullets in detail in [11].

6   Empirical Evaluation

We implemented basic Zether as an Ethereum smart contract showing that Zether is feasible today and can be run on top of the Ethereum virtual machine. We also discuss several optimizations that we made in order to improve the performance of the contract. Further, we will analyze what small improvements to the EVM would significantly benefit Zether. Some of these improvements have been discussed independently and are already part of the Ethereum improvement proposal (EIP) track.

6.1   Solidity Implementation and Optimizations

The Zether smart contract is implemented in Solidity and makes use of several observations. Ethereum recently introduced precompiled contracts for elliptic-curve operations on the curve BN-128 [4]. These precompiled contracts reduce the cost of executing these operations compared to direct implementations. The

---

[3] A non-interactive one-out-of-many proof can be used to instantiate a ring-signature in which a signer reveals that she knows a private key out of.

reason is that miners can use specialized software, i.e., special cryptography libraries, to run these functions more efficiently. The operations were originally introduced to support pairing-based ZK-SNARKs. Σ-Bullets do not require pairings and the curve BN-128 is not an optimal choice in terms of efficiency or security for Bulletproofs/Σ-Bullets. Nevertheless, we chose to implement Zether using this curve because it is natively supported (precompiled contracts are far cheaper than a Solidity implementation of another curve such as secp256k1 [46].) As we explain in Sect. 6.3, this means that we have to rely on the DDH assumption in the $\mathbb{G}_1$ group of BN-128. This assumption is called the external DDH or XDH assumption and is less general than the DDH assumption.

Despite the precompiled contract, a majority of the gas cost lies in the cryptographic operations used, especially curve multiplication. We therefore aimed to reduce the number of exponentiations to an absolute minimum. We did this by implementing the optimizations presented in Sect. 6.2 of [12].

We did not implement multi-exponentiation as this would not be beneficial. Multi-exponentiations reduce the number of curve operations but do this by splitting up the exponentiation. Multi-exponentiation algorithms assume that a k-bit exponentiation use k curve operations. This is not the case for Solidity however. The gas cost for an exponentiation is independent of the exponents length and curve additions are relatively overpriced to curve multiplications. A curve multiplication is only 80 times more expensive than a curve addition even if the exponent has 256 bits. Therefore, multi-exponentiation would not lower but increase the gas cost.

In a further optimization, we rolled out the inner product argument and combined all possible exponentiations into a single large statement. Furthermore, we slightly modified the recursive inner product argument such that it terminates at $n = 4$ instead of $n = 1$. By doing this, the prover has to send 6 more elements in $\mathbb{Z}_p$ but on the other hand saves sending 4 Pedersen hashes which are elements in $\mathbb{G}$. Since Solidity does not support point compression, i.e., points in $\mathbb{G}$ are encoded using 64 bytes and scalars using 32 bytes, this small modification therefore saves 64 bytes in space and also reduces the number of curve exponentiations that need to be done. In total for the ConfTransfer transaction, the elliptic curve operations for the account state manipulations, the Σ-protocol and the 2 32-bit range proofs use 156 curve additions and 154 curve multiplications (Table 1).

A further optimization concerns the common reference string (CRS). Bulletproofs unlike SNARKs do not use a structured reference string which would require a trusted setup. Nevertheless, Bulletproofs still requires a long linear-sized reference string that the verifier needs to access. While the CRS could be generated on the fly, this would add over 3.9 million gas to the cost of the transaction. Storing the CRS in the blockchain storage also creates high additional cost as loading a 32-byte word costs 200 gas. On the other hand, loading a 32-byte code instruction costs only 3 gas which is why we choose to hard-code the generators into the smart contract. While this makes the contract-generation process more expensive, it is a one-time cost which is amortized over the lifetime of a contract.

Table 1. Gas costs of ZSC methods

	Gas Cost	In USD	EC Cost	|tx|
Burn	384k	$0.080	329k	160 bytes
Fund	260k	$0.035	41k	64 bytes
Transfer	7,188k	$1.51	6,455k	1,472 bytes
Lock	223k	$0.049	83k	128 bytes
Unlock	193k	$0.041	83k	96 bytes

6.2   Measurements

We now present several measurements for our implementation of basic Zether. We measure the total gas cost which includes the basic cost for sending a transaction, the storage cost as well as the proof/signature verification. We also present the gas cost in USD using a gas cost price of 2 Gwei per unit of gas [24] and exchange rate of 105 USD per ETH [32]. At the time of writing, a basic Zether transaction costs about 1.5 USD. We also show that a majority of the cost is produced by elliptic-curve operations by factoring out their gas cost. For a transfer transaction, the elliptic-curve operations make up 90% of the total cost. For a fund transaction, the majority of the cost comes from initializing a new account. Adding funds to an existing account is significantly cheaper. Finally, we present the size of the transaction data. Note that this does not include the basic Ethereum transaction data which is roughly 110 bytes.

6.3   Ethereum Limitations and Future Directions

Currently, Ethereum's computation power is very limited. A simplified estimate is that at 3 gas units per arithmetic operation, Ethereum currently supports less than 180 k operations per second for the whole network. There are several efforts to increase the scalability of Ethereum [14,49]. The majority of the cost of a transaction in Zether comes from the cryptographic operations. Despite heavily optimizing them, they make up for almost 90% of the cost. These operations seem overpriced when compared to operations like hashing. This discrepancy has been noted and discussed independently [5]. There currently exists an EIP to reduce the gas cost of elliptic curve multiplications by a factor of 6.66 and additions by a factor of 3.33 [5]. A further EIP reduces the cost of calling a precompiled contract [43] which would reduce the cost for each cryptographic operation by another 700 units of gas. If both of these were implemented, the cost of a Zether transfer would reduce to roughly 1.7 million gas (0.36 USD). At that point, optimizations on the non-cryptographic part of the contract could probably further reduce the cost.

There are further changes that Ethereum could make that would benefit Zether. One of them would be supporting elliptic-curve operations for more efficient curves like secp256k1 [46] or Curve25519-ristretto [20]. Another would be supporting multi-exponentiation techniques that can reduce the number of cryptographic operations needed to verify the range proofs [40].

A simple but significant optimization that can be implemented without changing Ethereum applies to the proof verification: Bulletproofs can be batch verified. This means that verifying k aggregated proofs is significantly faster than verifying k single proofs. If transactions were collected by some service provider, combined to a single transaction and then sent to the Zether contract, it would significantly reduce the verification cost per proof. However, all transactions in a batch must be valid because a single invalid transaction will cause the whole verification to fail. Batch verification requires randomness but this randomness can either be sampled from the block header [7] or generated from a hash of the proofs.

References

1. Abdalla, M., An, J.H., Bellare, M., Namprempre, C.: From identification to signatures via the Fiat-Shamir transform: minimizing assumptions for security and forward-security. In: Knudsen, L.R. (ed.) EUROCRYPT 2002. LNCS, vol. 2332, pp. 418–433. Springer, Heidelberg (2002). https://doi.org/10.1007/3-540-46035-7_28. (April/May 2002)
2. Ben-Sasson, E., et al.: Zerocash: decentralized anonymous payments from Bitcoin. Cryptology ePrint Archive, Report 2014/349 (2014). http://eprint.iacr.org/2014/349
3. Ben-Sasson, E., Chiesa, A., Tromer, E., Virza, M.: Succinct non-interactive zero knowledge for a von Neumann architecture. In: Proceedings of the 23rd USENIX Conference on Security Symposium, pp. 781–796. SEC 2014. USENIX Association (2014). dl.acm.org/citation.cfm?id=2671225.2671275
4. Precompiled contracts for addition and scalar multiplication on the elliptic curve alt bn128. https://eips.ethereum.org/EIPS/eip-196
5. Reduce alt bn128 precompile gas costs. https://eips.ethereum.org/EIPS/eip-1108
6. Boneh, D., Shoup, V.: A Graduate Course in Applied Cryptography, Cambridge (2018). cryptobook.us
7. Bonneau, J., Clark, J., Goldfeder, S.: On bitcoin as a public randomness source. Cryptology ePrint Archive, Report 2015/1015 (2015). http://eprint.iacr.org/2015/1015
8. Bonneau, J., Narayanan, A., Miller, A., Clark, J., Kroll, J.A., Felten, E.W.: Mixcoin: Anonymity for Bitcoin with accountable mixes. Cryptology ePrint Archive, Report 2014/077 (2014). http://eprint.iacr.org/2014/077
9. Bootle, J., Cerulli, A., Chaidos, P., Ghadafi, E., Groth, J., Petit, C.: Short accountable ring signatures based on DDH. Cryptology ePrint Archive, Report 2015/643 (2015). http://eprint.iacr.org/2015/643
10. Bowe, S., Chiesa, A., Green, M., Miers, I., Mishra, P., Wu, H.: Zexe: Enabling decentralized private computation. Cryptology ePrint Archive, Report 2018/962 (2018). https://eprint.iacr.org/2018/962
11. Bünz, B., Agrawal, S., Zamani, M., Boneh, D.: Zether: Towards privacy in a smart contract world. Cryptology ePrint Archive, Report 2019/191 (2019). https://eprint.iacr.org/2019/191

12. Bünz, B., Bootle, J., Boneh, D., Poelstra, A., Wuille, P., Maxwell, G.: Bulletproofs: short proofs for confidential transactions and more. In: 2018 IEEE Symposium on Security and Privacy, pp. 315–334. IEEE Computer Society Press, May 2018
13. Buterin, V.: Thoughts on UTXOs (2016). https://medium.com/@ConsenSys/ thoughts-on-utxo-by-vitalik-buterin-2bb782c67e53
14. Buterin, V., Griffith, V.: Casper the friendly finality gadget. CoRR abs/1710.09437 (2017). arxiv.org/abs/1710.09437
15. Camenisch, J., Lysyanskaya, A.: Dynamic Accumulators and application to efficient revocation of anonymous credentials. In: Yung, M. (ed.) CRYPTO 2002. LNCS, vol. 2442, pp. 61–76. Springer, Heidelberg (2002). https://doi.org/10.1007/3-540-45708-9_5. (August 2002)
16. Cecchetti, E., Zhang, F., Ji, Y., Kosba, A.E., Juels, A., Shi, E.: Solidus: confidential distributed ledger transactions via PVORM. In: Thuraisingham, B.M., Evans, D., Malkin, T., Xu, D. (eds.) ACM CCS 17, pp. 701–717. ACM Press, October/November 2017
17. Cheng, R., et al.: Ekiden: A platform for confidentiality-preserving, trustworthy, and performant smart contract execution. CoRR abs/1804.05141 (2018). arxiv.org/abs/1804.05141
18. Cramer, R., Damgård, I.: Zero-knowledge proofs for finite field arithmetic, or: can zero-knowledge be for free? In: Krawczyk, H. (ed.) CRYPTO 1998. LNCS, vol. 1462, pp. 424–441. Springer, Heidelberg (1998). https://doi.org/10.1007/BFb0055745. (August 1998)
19. Cramer, R., Gennaro, R., Schoenmakers, B.: A secure and optimally efficient multi-authority election scheme. In: Fumy, W. (ed.) EUROCRYPT 1997. LNCS, vol. 1233, pp. 103–118. Springer, Heidelberg (1997). https://doi.org/10.1007/3-540-69053-0_9. (May 1997)
20. Curve25519-ristretto. https://ristretto.group/
21. Dåmgard, I.: On sigma protocols. https://www.cs.au.dk/~ivan/Sigma.pdf
22. Danezis, G., Meiklejohn, S.: Centrally banked cryptocurrencies. In: NDSS 2016. The Internet Society, February 2016
23. Ethereum Project: Blockchain App Platform. https://www.ethereum.org/
24. Ethereum Gasstation. https://ethgasstation.info/calculatorTxV.php
25. Fauzi, P., Meiklejohn, S., Mercer, R., Orlandi, C.: Quisquis: a new design for anonymous cryptocurrencies. Cryptology ePrint Archive, Report 2018/990 (2018). https://eprint.iacr.org/2018/990
26. Gennaro, R., Gentry, C., Parno, B., Raykova, M.: Quadratic span programs and succinct NIZKs without PCPs. In: Johansson, T., Nguyen, P.Q. (eds.) EUROCRYPT 2013. LNCS, vol. 7881, pp. 626–645. Springer, Heidelberg (2013). https:// doi.org/10.1007/978-3-642-38348-9_37. (May 2013)
27. Grin. https://grin-tech.org/
28. Groth, J., Kohlweiss, M.: One-out-of-many proofs: or how to leak a secret and spend a coin. In: Oswald, E., Fischlin, M. (eds.) EUROCRYPT 2015. LNCS, vol. 9057, pp. 253–280. Springer, Heidelberg (2015). https://doi.org/10.1007/978-3-662-46803-6_9. (April 2015)
29. Heilman, E., Alshenibr, L., Baldimtsi, F., Scafuro, A., Goldberg, S.: Tumblebit: an untrusted bitcoin-compatible anonymous payment hub. In: NDSS 2017. The Internet Society, February/March 2017
30. Kosba, A.E., Miller, A., Shi, E., Wen, Z., Papamanthou, C.: Hawk: The blockchain model of cryptography and privacy-preserving smart contracts. In: 2016 IEEE Symposium on Security and Privacy, pp. 839–858. IEEE Computer Society Press, May 2016

31. Kurosawa, K.: Multi-recipient public-key encryption with shortened ciphertext. In: Naccache, D., Paillier, P. (eds.) PKC 2002. LNCS, vol. 2274, pp. 48–63. Springer, Heidelberg (2002). https://doi.org/10.1007/3-540-45664-3_4. (February 2002)
32. Total Market Capitalization. https://coinmarketcap.com/charts
33. Maxwell, G.: Coinjoin: Bitcoin privacy for the real world (2013). https://bitcointalk.org/?topic=279249
34. Maxwell, G.: Confidential transactions (2015). https://people.xiph.org/~greg/confidential_values.txt
35. Meiklejohn, S., Mercer, R.: Möbius: trustless tumbling for transaction privacy. PoPETs **2018**(2), 105–121 (2018)
36. Miers, I., Garman, C., Green, M., Rubin, A.D.: Zerocoin: anonymous distributed E-cash from Bitcoin. In: 2013 IEEE Symposium on Security and Privacy, pp. 397–411. IEEE Computer Society Press, May 2013
37. Narula, N., Vasquez, W., Virza, M.: zkLedger: privacy-preserving auditing for distributed ledgers. In: 15th USENIX Symposium on Networked Systems Design and Implementation, NSDI 2018, Renton, WA, USA, 9–11 April 2018, pp. 65–80 (2018)
38. Noether, S.: Ring signature confidential transactions for Monero. Cryptology ePrint Archive, Report 2015/1098 (2015). http://eprint.iacr.org/2015/1098
39. Pedersen, T.P.: Non-interactive and information-theoretic secure verifiable secret sharing. In: Feigenbaum, J. (ed.) CRYPTO 1991. LNCS, vol. 576, pp. 129–140. Springer, Heidelberg (1992). https://doi.org/10.1007/3-540-46766-1_9. dl.acm.org/citation.cfm?id=646756.705507
40. Pippenger, N.: On the evaluation of powers and monomials. SIAM J. Comput. **9**(2), 230–250 (1980)
41. Poelstra, A.: Mimblewimble (2016). https://scalingbitcoin.org/papers/mimblewimble.pdf
42. Announcing the world's largest multi-party computation ceremony. https://www.zfnd.org/blog/powers-of-tau/
43. PRECOMPILED CALL opcode (Remove CALL costs for precompiled contracts). https://eips.ethereum.org/EIPS/eip-1109
44. Ruffing, T., Moreno-Sanchez, P., Kate, A.: CoinShuffle: practical decentralized coin mixing for bitcoin. In: Kutyłowski, M., Vaidya, J. (eds.) ESORICS 2014. LNCS, vol. 8713, pp. 345–364. Springer, Cham (2014). https://doi.org/10.1007/978-3-319-11212-1_20. (September 2014)
45. Schnorr, C.P.: Efficient identification and signatures for smart cards. In: Quisquater, J.-J., Vandewalle, J. (eds.) EUROCRYPT 1989. LNCS, vol. 434, pp. 688–689. Springer, Heidelberg (1990). https://doi.org/10.1007/3-540-46885-4_68. (abstract) (rump session), (April 1990)
46. Secp256k1. https://en.bitcoin.it/wiki/Secp256k1
47. Solidity webpage. https://solidity.readthedocs.io
48. Szabo, N.: Smart contracts: building blocks for digital markets. EXTROPY: J. Transhumanist Thought **16** (1996)
49. Zamfir, V.: Casper the friendly ghost: a correct by construction blockchain consensus protocol (2017). https://github.com/ethereum/research/blob/master/papers/CasperTFG/CasperTFG.pdf
50. Zcash: Privacy-protecting digital currency. https://z.cash/
51. zcash Documentation. https://media.readthedocs.org/pdf/zcash/english-docs/zcash.pdf

An Airdrop that Preserves Recipient Privacy

Riad S. Wahby[1]([✉]), Dan Boneh[1], Christopher Jeffrey[2], and Joseph Poon[3]

[1] Stanford University, Stanford, USA
rsw@cs.stanford.edu
[2] Purse.io, San Francisco, USA
[3] Pasadena, USA

Abstract. A common approach to bootstrapping a new cryptocurrency is an *airdrop*, an arrangement in which existing users give away currency to entice new users to join. But current airdrops offer no recipient privacy: they leak which recipients have claimed the funds, and this information is easily linked to off-chain identities.

In this work, we address this issue by defining a *private airdrop* and describing concrete schemes for widely-used user credentials, such as those based on ECDSA and RSA. Our private airdrop for RSA builds upon a new zero-knowledge argument of knowledge of the factorization of a committed secret integer, which may be of independent interest. We also design a *private genesis airdrop* that efficiently sends private airdrops to millions of users at once. Finally, we implement and evaluate. Our fastest implementation takes 40–180 ms to generate and 3.7–10 ms to verify an RSA private airdrop signature. Signatures are 1.8–3.3 kiB depending on the security parameter.

Keywords: Cryptocurrency · Airdrop · User privacy · Zero-knowledge proof of knowledge of factorization of an RSA modulus

1 Introduction

Newly-created cryptocurrencies face a chicken-and-egg problem: users appear to prefer currencies that already have a thriving ecosystem [41]. For general-purpose cryptocurrencies, this might entail a healthy transaction volume. For currencies supporting distributed applications, it could mean having a critical mass of clients already using the provided functionality. In both cases, the bottom line is: to attract users, you must already have some.

This problem is well known in practice. One response is an *airdrop*, an arrangement in which the existing users of a cryptocurrency give value in their currency to non-users, at no cost, to entice them to become users. Airdrops have become increasingly popular [2,14,16,51], with recent high-profile examples including Stellar [76] and OmiseGO [63].

Extended abstract. The full paper is available from https://goosig.crypto.fyi.

J. Bonneau and N. Heninger (Eds.): FC 2020, LNCS 12059, pp. 444–463, 2020.
https://doi.org/10.1007/978-3-030-51280-4_24

As the name implies, an airdrop is designed to transfer value to *passive* recipients. To be most effective at recruiting new users, an airdrop should not require recipients to enroll ahead of time—or, in the best case, even to know about the airdrop in advance. This is effected by leveraging existing cryptographic infrastructure. Commonly, recipients claim their airdropped value on a new blockchain by reusing their identities from some other, well-established blockchain.

While airdrops to existing blockchains are convenient, using other cryptographic infrastructure may be more effective at recruiting desirable users. A very interesting example is GitHub, since it has tens of millions of users [44], many of whom use SSH keys to access repositories and PGP keys to sign commits. GitHub publishes users' public keys [45,46], which allows cryptocurrencies to design airdrops intended for developers by allowing them to claim airdropped funds using keys from GitHub. The PGP web of trust [66], Keybase [53], GitLab [47], and the X.509 PKI [30] are interesting for similar reasons.

Yet, no matter the infrastructure they target, airdrops have a serious flaw: they offer no privacy to their recipients. This means that an observer can easily learn whether or not any given recipient has claimed her airdropped value. Even cryptocurrencies that provide anonymity mechanisms for on-chain transactions (e.g., [10,20]; §5) do not prevent this leakage, because a recipient must first use her existing identity to claim the airdropped funds. And using cryptographic infrastructure like GitHub exacerbates this privacy leak since GitHub accounts, PGP keys, etc., are often tied to software projects and professional activities. All told, these issues act as a *disincentive* for privacy-conscious recipients to redeem their awards, which reduces the airdrop's effectiveness in recruiting new users.

Existing solutions fall short of addressing this issue. The simplest possible approach—sending each recipient a fresh secret key for claiming her funds—carries an even stronger disincentive: it requires recipients to trust the sender. Both the sender and recipient know the secret key, so either can take the funds, but neither can prove who did. Meanwhile, a dishonest sender might garner free publicity with an airdrop, only to claw back the funds; or an incompetent one might accidentally disclose the secret keys. To avoid this trust requirement, a workable solution must allow *only* the recipient to withdraw the funds.

A more plausible approach is to have recipients claim airdrop funds by proving their identities in zero knowledge. Concretely, a recipient proves that she knows the secret key for some pre-existing public key (say, the RSA public key of her GitHub credential), and that no prior airdrop claim has used this public key. To preserve her privacy, she must do so without revealing which public key she is using. But proving knowledge of one secret key among a large list of RSA keys using general-purpose zero-knowledge proof systems [3,9,12,21,25,27,43,64,80] is too expensive: infeasible computational cost, enormous proofs, and/or a setup phase whose incorrect execution allows proving false statements (see §5).

Meanwhile, infrastructures like GitHub are primarily based on RSA because it is, anecdotally, the most widely-supported key type for both SSH [75] and PGP [49]. This means that taking advantage of these infrastructures effectively requires support for airdrops to RSA keys.

Our Contributions. This work builds an efficient and practical private airdrop system using special-purpose zero-knowledge proofs designed for this task.

First, we define precisely the required functionality and security properties for a *private airdrop scheme* (§2.1). Second, we exhibit practical private airdrop schemes designed to work with ECDSA (§3) and RSA (§4) credentials. Our ECDSA scheme extends in a straightforward way to Schnorr [73], EdDSA [13], and similar credentials. To construct our RSA scheme, we devise a new succinct zero-knowledge proof of knowledge (ZKPK) of the factorization of a committed secret integer, which we prove secure in the generic group model for groups of unknown order [32,74]. This new ZKPK may be of independent interest.

In the full paper, we carefully describe how to use private airdrops to bootstrap a new cryptocurrency, a scheme we call a *private genesis airdrop* [79, §5]. This scheme is designed to handle millions of recipients, each of whom has hundreds of keys of mixed types (some RSA, some ECDSA, etc.) and who may potentially have lost one or more of their keys. The scheme lets the airdrop's sender prove the total value of the airdrop, while enabling airdrop recipients to prove non-payment in case the sender was dishonest.

We have also implemented and evaluated our schemes [79, §6]. Our evaluation focuses on the private airdrop scheme for RSA (which is more costly than the one for ECDSA) and the private genesis airdrop. Depending on the security parameter, our fastest implementation takes 40–180 ms for an airdrop recipient to generate an RSA-based private airdrop signature comprising 1.8–3.3 kiB. The signature takes miners 3.7–10 ms to verify. The scheme requires a trusted setup to generate one global RSA modulus with an unknown factorization. Eliminating trusted setup, by using class groups of unknown order, increases signing and verifying times by 9–13× in our reference implementation. Compared with a private airdrop to one recipient, a private genesis airdrop to one million users, each with one thousand public keys, increases signature size by less than 1.8× in the worst case. Our implementations are available under open-source licenses [48,50].

2   Background and Definitions

$[\ell]$ denotes the set of integers $\{0, 1, \ldots, \ell - 1\}$. λ is a security parameter (e.g., $\lambda = 128$); we generally leave λ implicit. Primes(2λ) is the set of the smallest $2^{2\lambda}$ odd primes; this is roughly the primes up to $2\lambda + \log(2\lambda)$ bits in length.

Detailed knowledge of blockchains and cryptocurrencies is not required to understand this work. For now, we regard a blockchain simply as an append-only log of transactions. We give slightly more detail in the full paper [79, §5]; curious readers can also consult the survey of Bonneau et al. [19].

2.1   Private Airdrop Scheme

High-Level Description. In a private airdrop, a *sender* S creates a *token* and a *secret* for a *recipient* R whose public key is *pk*. The sender sends the secret to

$\mathcal{R}^1$ and records the token in a blockchain transaction. To claim the airdrop, $\mathcal{R}$ uses the token, the secret, and her secret key sk (i.e., corresponding to pk) to sign a new transaction. Any *verifier* $\mathcal{V}$ (i.e., other blockchain stakeholders) can verify this signature using the token, and *does not* learn the recipient's pk.

Syntax. Let $\mathsf{SIG} := (\mathsf{gen}^{\mathsf{SIG}}, \mathsf{sign}^{\mathsf{SIG}}, \mathsf{verify}^{\mathsf{SIG}})$ be a signature scheme secure against existential forgery under a chosen message attack. The derived private airdrop scheme PAD with implicit security parameter λ is a tuple of four algorithms:

setup$(1^\lambda) \xrightarrow{\text{R}} \mathsf{pp}$: Output pp, which is an implicit input to the other algorithms.

send$(pk) \xrightarrow{\text{R}} (c, s)$: Compute and output token c and secret s for public key pk, where $(pk, sk) \xleftarrow{\text{R}} \mathsf{gen}^{\mathsf{SIG}}()$. Here c is a public airdrop token that can later be claimed by a recipient whose public key is pk. The element s is a secret that the recipient will use, along with sk, to claim the token c.

sign$(sk, (c, s), msg) \xrightarrow{\text{R}} sig$: Sign message $msg \in \{0, 1\}^\star$ under token-secret pair (c, s) using secret key sk, where $(pk, sk) \xleftarrow{\text{R}} \mathsf{gen}^{\mathsf{SIG}}()$ and $(c, s) \xleftarrow{\text{R}} \mathsf{send}(pk)$. An airdrop recipient uses this algorithm to claim the airdrop token c.

verify$(c, msg, sig) \rightarrow \{\mathsf{OK}, \bot\}$: OK if sig is valid for msg and token c, else $\bot$. This algorithm is used to verify a claim for the token c.

PAD may also be *validatable*, in which case it has an additional algorithm:

validate$(pk, (c, s)) \rightarrow \{\mathsf{OK}, \bot\}$: This algorithm outputs OK if token c with secret s granted to public key pk is valid, else it outputs $\bot$.

For schemes that are not validatable, we let $\mathsf{validate}(\cdot, \cdot)$ output OK for all inputs.

Functionality. We require that, for all messages $msg \in \{0, 1\}^\star$,

$$\Pr \left[\begin{array}{c} \mathsf{verify}(c, msg, sig) = \mathsf{OK} \wedge \mathsf{validate}(pk, (c, s)) = \mathsf{OK} \\ \text{where} \quad \mathsf{pp} \xleftarrow{\text{R}} \mathsf{setup}(1^\lambda) \quad (pk, sk) \xleftarrow{\text{R}} \mathsf{gen}^{\mathsf{SIG}}() \\ (c, s) \xleftarrow{\text{R}} \mathsf{send}(pk) \quad\quad sig \xleftarrow{\text{R}} \mathsf{sign}(sk, (c, s), msg) \end{array} \right] \geq 1 - \mathsf{negl}(\lambda)$$

Security. PAD is secure if it is *anonymous*, *unforgeable*, and *orthogonal* to SIG. *Anonymity* means, informally, that c and sig reveal nothing about pk or sk, other than a well-defined leakage given by a function Λ. This ensures that claiming a token c does not reveal the claimant's identity, as required for privacy.

Definition 1. *PAD is Λ-anonymous if there is a leakage function Λ such that for all PPT adversaries $\mathcal{A}$ there exists a simulator Sim such that the following two distributions are statistically indistinguishable, letting $\mathsf{pp} \xleftarrow{\text{R}} \mathsf{setup}(1^\lambda)$:*

$$D_{\mathrm{r}} = \left\{ \begin{array}{c} (pk, sk) \xleftarrow{\text{R}} \mathsf{gen}^{\mathsf{SIG}}() \\ (c, s) \xleftarrow{\text{R}} \mathsf{send}(pk) \\ (msg, \mathsf{st}) \xleftarrow{\text{R}} \mathcal{A}(c) \\ sig \xleftarrow{\text{R}} \mathsf{sign}(sk, (c, s), msg) \\ \text{output } (pk, c, msg, sig, \mathsf{st}) \end{array} \right\} ; \quad D_{\mathrm{s}} = \left\{ \begin{array}{c} (pk, sk) \xleftarrow{\text{R}} \mathsf{gen}^{\mathsf{SIG}}() \\ \mathsf{H} \xleftarrow{\text{R}} \Lambda(pk, sk) \\ (c, msg, sig, \mathsf{st}) \xleftarrow{\text{R}} \mathsf{Sim}(\mathsf{H}) \\ \text{output } (pk, c, msg, sig, \mathsf{st}) \end{array} \right\}$$

---

[1] This is usually accomplished by encrypting the secret to the recipient's pk and publishing the resulting ciphertext, so no explicit private channel is necessary.

Remark 1. Sim sees only H (not pk), yet simulates $(c, msg, sig, \mathsf{st})$. This means that this 4-tuple reveals nothing about the challenge pk except the leakage $H = \Lambda(pk, sk)$. $\mathcal{A}$ does not learn s because in an airdrop only the sender and recipient do, and the goal is to keep *other* parties from learning the recipient's identity.

Remark 2. Sim appears to forge a valid signature (see Definition 2), but this does not result in a real-world attack on our private airdrop schemes (§3, §4). The reason for this is that we instantiate these schemes in the random oracle model [8], and Sim is allowed to program the random oracle.

Remark 3. A slightly stronger definition of anonymity also includes sk in the output of both distributions. Anonymity under this definition implies, roughly speaking, that even knowledge of the key sk corresponding to a token c is not sufficient to connect sig to pk. The schemes in the following sections meet this stronger notion, but it does not appear necessary in practice.

Unforgeability means, roughly speaking, that without sk one cannot generate a valid PAD signature for any message, even given valid PAD signatures for other messages and valid signatures in the underlying SIG for arbitrary messages. Consider Forge, a game between adversary $\mathcal{A}$ and challenger $\mathcal{C}$:

Setup: $\mathcal{C}$ sets $\mathsf{pp} \xleftarrow{\text{R}} \mathsf{setup}(1^\lambda)$, $(pk, sk) \xleftarrow{\text{R}} \mathsf{gen}^{\mathsf{SIG}}()$, and $(c, s) \xleftarrow{\text{R}} \mathsf{send}(pk)$, then sends pk, (c, s) to $\mathcal{A}$.
Query: $\mathcal{A}$ makes any number of queries of type Q1 and Q2, in any interleaving.
   Q1: $\mathcal{A}$ sends msg_i^{SIG} to $\mathcal{C}$, who replies with $sig_i^{\mathsf{SIG}} \xleftarrow{\text{R}} \mathsf{sign}^{\mathsf{SIG}}(sk, msg_i^{\mathsf{SIG}})$.
   Q2: $\mathcal{A}$ sends msg_j to $\mathcal{C}$, who replies with $sig_j \xleftarrow{\text{R}} \mathsf{sign}(sk, (c, s), msg_j)$.
Forge: $\mathcal{A}$ outputs $(\hat{m}, \hat{s})$, winning if $\mathsf{verify}(c, \hat{m}, \hat{s}) = \mathsf{OK} \wedge \bigwedge_j \hat{m} \neq msg_j$.

Definition 2. *Let adversary $\mathcal{A}$'s advantage in* Forge *be* $\mathrm{Adv}_{\mathcal{A}}^{\mathsf{Forge}} = \Pr[\mathcal{A} \text{ wins}]$. PAD *is **unforgeable** if, for any PPT $\mathcal{A}$,* $\mathrm{Adv}_{\mathcal{A}}^{\mathsf{Forge}} \leq \mathsf{negl}(\lambda)$.

Orthogonality means, informally, that PAD signatures do not help to create a SIG forgery. In other words, the airdrop scheme does not weaken the user's credential (e.g., for authenticating to GitHub). Consider Ortho, a game between adversary $\mathcal{A}$ and challenger $\mathcal{C}$:

Setup: $\mathcal{C}$ sets $\mathsf{pp} \xleftarrow{\text{R}} \mathsf{setup}(1^\lambda)$ and $(pk, sk) \xleftarrow{\text{R}} \mathsf{gen}^{\mathsf{SIG}}()$, then sends pk to $\mathcal{A}$, who chooses (c, s) and sends them to $\mathcal{C}$. Finally, $\mathcal{C}$ aborts if $\mathsf{validate}(pk, (c, s)) = \bot$.
Query: $\mathcal{A}$ makes any number of queries of type Q1 and Q2, in any interleaving.
   Q1: $\mathcal{A}$ sends msg_i to $\mathcal{C}$, who replies with $sig_i \xleftarrow{\text{R}} \mathsf{sign}^{\mathsf{SIG}}(sk, msg_i)$.
   Q2: $\mathcal{A}$ sends msg_j^{PAD} to $\mathcal{C}$, who replies with $sig_j^{\mathsf{PAD}} \xleftarrow{\text{R}} \mathsf{sign}(sk, (c, s), msg_j^{\mathsf{PAD}})$.
Forge: $\mathcal{A}$ outputs $(\hat{m}, \hat{s})$, winning if $\mathsf{verify}^{\mathsf{SIG}}(pk, \hat{m}, \hat{s}) = \mathsf{OK} \wedge \bigwedge_i \hat{m} \neq msg_i$.

The game wkOrtho is similar, but further requires $\bigwedge_j \hat{m} \neq msg_j^{\mathsf{PAD}}$ for $\mathcal{A}$ to win.

Definition 3. *Let adversary $\mathcal{A}$'s advantage in* Ortho *be* $\mathrm{Adv}_{\mathcal{A}}^{\mathsf{Ortho}} = \Pr[\mathcal{A} \text{ wins}]$. PAD *is **orthogonal** to SIG if, for any PPT adversary $\mathcal{A}$,* $\mathrm{Adv}_{\mathcal{A}}^{\mathsf{Ortho}} \leq \mathsf{negl}(\lambda)$. PAD *is **weakly orthogonal** if* Ortho *is replaced with* wkOrtho *in this definition.*

Remark 4. The PAD scheme of Sect. 4 gives orthogonality, while the scheme of Sect. 3 gives only weak orthogonality. In practice, weak orthogonality suffices as long as messages signed in the PAD scheme cannot be confused with messages signed in the SIG scheme; this appears to be true in our applications.

2.2 Zero-Knowledge Proofs in Generic Groups

In this section we briefly review the notion of a generic group of unknown order and zero-knowledge proof systems with respect to such groups, following [18].

Generic Groups. We use the generic group model for groups of unknown order as defined by Damgård and Koprowski [32]. The group is parameterized by two integer public parameters A, B. The order of the group is sampled uniformly from $[A, B]$. The group $\mathbb{G}$ is defined by a random injective function $\sigma : \mathbb{Z}_{|\mathbb{G}|} \to \{0, 1\}^\ell$, for some ℓ where $2^\ell \gg |\mathbb{G}|$. The group elements are $\sigma(0), \sigma(1), \ldots, \sigma(|\mathbb{G}| - 1)$. A *generic group algorithm* $\mathcal{A}$ is a probabilistic algorithm. Let $\mathcal{L}$ be a list that is initialized with the encodings given to $\mathcal{A}$ as input. The algorithm can query two generic group oracles:

- $\mathcal{O}_1$ samples a random $r \in \mathbb{Z}_{|\mathbb{G}|}$ and returns $\sigma(r)$, which is appended to the list of encodings $\mathcal{L}$.
- When $\mathcal{L}$ has size q, the second oracle $\mathcal{O}_2(i, j, \pm)$ takes two indices $i, j \in \{1, \ldots, q\}$ and a sign bit, and returns $\sigma(x_i \pm x_j)$, which is appended to $\mathcal{L}$.

Note that unlike Shoup's generic group model [74], the algorithm is not given $|\mathbb{G}|$, the order of the group $\mathbb{G}$.

The Representation Extraction Lemma. Let $\mathcal{A}$ be an algorithm that outputs a generic group element $u \in \mathbb{G}$. The following lemma from [37] shows that there is an extractor that can extract from $\mathcal{A}$ an integer representation of u relative to a supplied set of group generators. Moreover, this integer representation is unique.

Lemma 1 (Unique representation extraction in generic groups). *Let $\mathbb{G}$ be a generic group of unknown order where $|B - A|$ is super-polynomial in λ. Let $\mathcal{A}_1, \mathcal{A}_2$ be two randomized algorithms that interact with group oracles for $\mathbb{G}$ and make at most a polynomial in λ queries to these oracles. Suppose that each algorithm makes at most q type-1 queries and let $g_1, \ldots, g_q \in \mathbb{G}$ be the returned random group elements. Each of $\mathcal{A}_1$ and $\mathcal{A}_2$ eventually outputs some $u_i \in \mathbb{G}$.*

Then there is an extractor $\mathcal{B}$ that emulates the generic group oracles for $\mathcal{A}_i$ $i \in \{1, 2\}$ such that when $\mathcal{B}$ interacts with $\mathcal{A}_i$ the following holds with overwhelming probability: if $\mathcal{A}_i$ outputs $u_i \in \mathbb{G}$ then the extractor $\mathcal{B}_i$ outputs a representation $\alpha_{i,1}, \ldots, \alpha_{i,q} \in \mathbb{Z}$ such that $u_i = g_1^{\alpha_{i,1}} \cdots g_q^{\alpha_{i,q}}$. Moreover, if $u_1 = u_2$ then the two representations are the same, namely $\alpha_{1,j} = \alpha_{2,j}$ for $j = 1, \ldots, q$.

Argument Systems. An argument system for a relation $\mathfrak{R} \subset \mathcal{X} \times \mathcal{W}$ is a triple of randomized polynomial time algorithms $(Pgen, \mathcal{P}, \mathcal{V})$, where $Pgen$ takes an implicit security parameter λ and outputs a common reference string (crs) pp. If the setup algorithm uses only public randomness we say that the setup is transparent and that the crs is unstructured. The prover $\mathcal{P}$ takes as input a statement $x \in \mathcal{X}$, a witness $w \in \mathcal{W}$, and the crs pp. The verifier $\mathcal{V}$ takes as input pp and x and after interaction with $\mathcal{P}$ outputs 0 or 1. We denote the transcript between the prover and verifier by $\langle \mathcal{V}(\mathsf{pp}, x), \mathcal{P}(\mathsf{pp}, x, w) \rangle$ and write $\langle \mathcal{V}(\mathsf{pp}, x), \mathcal{P}(\mathsf{pp}, x, w) \rangle = 1$ to indicate that the verifier accepted the transcript. If $\mathcal{V}$ uses only public randomness we say that the protocol is public coin.

Definition 4 (Completeness). *An argument system $(Pgen, \mathcal{P}, \mathcal{V})$ for a relation $\mathfrak{R}$ is **complete** if for all $(x, w) \in \mathfrak{R}$:*

$$\Pr\left[\langle \mathcal{V}(\mathsf{pp}, x), \mathcal{P}(\mathsf{pp}, x, w) \rangle = 1 : \mathsf{pp} \xleftarrow{\text{R}} Pgen(1^\lambda) \right] = 1.$$

We now define soundness and knowledge extraction for our protocols. The adversary is modeled as two algorithms $\mathcal{A}_0$ and $\mathcal{A}_1$, where $\mathcal{A}_0$ outputs the instance $x \in \mathcal{X}$ *after* $Pgen$ is run, and $\mathcal{A}_1$ runs the interactive protocol with the verifier using a state output by $\mathcal{A}_0$. In slight deviation from the soundness definition used in statistically sound proof systems, we do not universally quantify over the instance x (i.e. we do not require security to hold for all input instances x). This is due to the fact that in the computationally-sound setting the instance itself may encode a trapdoor of the crs pp (e.g. the order of a group of unknown order), which can enable the adversary to fool a verifier. Requiring that an efficient adversary $\mathcal{A}_0$ outputs the instance x prevents this. For soundness, no efficient adversary $\mathcal{A}_1$ can make the verifier accept when no witness for x exists. For an argument of knowledge, there should be an extractor that can extract a valid witness whenever $\mathcal{A}_1$ is convincing.

Definition 5 (Arguments (of Knowledge)). *An argument system $(Pgen, \mathcal{P}, \mathcal{V})$ is **sound** if for all PPT adversaries $\mathcal{A} = (\mathcal{A}_0, \mathcal{A}_1)$:*

$$\Pr\left[\begin{array}{l} \langle \mathcal{V}(\mathsf{pp}, x), \mathcal{A}_1(\mathsf{pp}, x, \mathsf{state}) \rangle = 1 \wedge \nexists w \; (x, w) \in \mathfrak{R} \\ \textit{where } \mathsf{pp} \xleftarrow{\text{R}} Pgen(1^\lambda), (x, \mathsf{state}) \xleftarrow{\text{R}} \mathcal{A}_0(\mathsf{pp}) \end{array} \right] \leq \mathsf{negl}.$$

*Additionally, the argument system is an **argument of knowledge** if for all PPT adversaries $\mathcal{A}_1$ there exists a PPT extractor Ext such that for all PPT adversaries $\mathcal{A}_0$:*

$$\Pr\left[\begin{array}{l} \langle \mathcal{V}(\mathsf{pp}, x), \mathcal{A}_1(\mathsf{pp}, x, \mathsf{state}) \rangle = 1 \wedge (x, w') \notin \mathfrak{R} \\ \textit{where} \qquad \mathsf{pp} \xleftarrow{\text{R}} Pgen(1^\lambda) \\ \qquad\qquad (x, \mathsf{state}) \xleftarrow{\text{R}} \mathcal{A}_0(\mathsf{pp}) \\ \qquad\qquad w' \xleftarrow{\text{R}} \mathsf{Ext}(\mathsf{pp}, x, \mathsf{state}) \end{array} \right] \leq \mathsf{negl}.$$

Any argument of knowledge is also sound. In some cases we may further restrict $\mathcal{A}$ in the security analysis, in which case we would say the system is an argument of knowledge for a restricted class of adversaries. For example, in this work we construct argument systems for relations that depend on a group $\mathbb{G}$ of unknown order. In the analysis we replace $\mathbb{G}$ with a generic group and restrict $\mathcal{A}$ to a generic group algorithm that interacts with the oracles for this group. We say that the protocol is an *argument of knowledge in the generic group model*.

Definition 6 (Zero Knowledge). *We say an argument system* $(Pgen, \mathcal{P}, \mathcal{V})$ *for* $\mathfrak{R}$ *has* **statistical zero-knowledge** *if there exists a PPT simulator* Sim *such that for* $(x, w) \in \mathfrak{R}$ *the following distribution are statistically indistinguishable:*

$$D_{\text{real}} = \left\{ \begin{array}{c} \langle \mathcal{P}(\text{pp}, x, w), \mathcal{V}(\text{pp}, x) \rangle \\ \text{where pp} \xleftarrow{\text{R}} Pgen(1^\lambda) \end{array} \right\} \; ; \; D_{\text{Sim}} = \left\{ \begin{array}{c} \text{Sim}(\text{pp}, x, \mathcal{V}(\text{pp}, x)) \\ \text{where pp} \xleftarrow{\text{R}} Pgen(1^\lambda) \end{array} \right\}$$

Definition 7 (Non interactive arguments). *A* **non-interactive argument system** *is an argument system where the interaction between* $\mathcal{P}$ *and* $\mathcal{V}$ *consists of only a single round. We write the prover* $\mathcal{P}$ *as* $\mathcal{P}(\text{pp}, x, w) \rightarrow \pi$ *and the verifier as* $\mathcal{V}(\text{pp}, x, \pi) \rightarrow \{0, 1\}$.

The Fiat-Shamir heuristic [35] and its multi-round generalization [11] transform public coin arguments into non-interactive ones, in the random oracle model [8].

3   Warm-Up: A Private Airdrop to ECDSA Keys

Let $\mathbb{H}$ with generator $\hat{g}$ be a cyclic group of prime order $\hat{q}$. Let the ECDSA signature scheme in $\mathbb{H}$ be the triple $(\text{gen}_{\mathbb{H}}^{\text{DSA}}() \xrightarrow{\text{R}} (pk, sk), \text{sign}_{\mathbb{H}}^{\text{DSA}}(sk, msg) \xrightarrow{\text{R}} sig,$ $\text{verify}_{\mathbb{H}}^{\text{DSA}}(pk, msg, sig) \rightarrow \{\text{OK}, \bot\}); (pk, sk) = (\hat{g}^x, x)$ is an ECDSA key pair.

We now define PAD-DSA, a private airdrop scheme to ECDSA keys. Intuitively, the token c in this scheme is a fresh ECDSA public key derived from an existing key, such that only that key's owner can compute the corresponding secret. In particular, PAD-DSA leverages the fact that $c = pk^s = \hat{g}^{x \cdot s} \in \mathbb{H}$ is an ECDSA public key whose corresponding secret key is $sk \cdot s = x \cdot s \in \mathbb{Z}_{\hat{q}}$. Further, if s is chosen at random, pk^s is independent of pk, so c reveals nothing about pk.

Thus, PAD-DSA is the validatable private airdrop scheme given by:

setup$(1^\lambda) \rightarrow$ pp: Output $\bot$; this scheme uses no public parameters.
send$(pk) \xrightarrow{\text{R}} (c, s)$: Choose $s \xleftarrow{\text{R}} [\hat{q}] \setminus \{0\}$, set $c \leftarrow pk^s \in \mathbb{H}$, and output (c, s).
sign$(sk, (c, s), msg) \xrightarrow{\text{R}} sig$: Output $\text{sign}_{\mathbb{H}}^{\text{DSA}}(sk \cdot s \in \mathbb{Z}_{\hat{q}}, (c, msg))$.
verify$(c, msg, sig) \rightarrow \{\text{OK}, \bot\}$: Output $\text{verify}_{\mathbb{H}}^{\text{DSA}}(c, (c, msg), sig)$.
validate$(pk, (c, s)) \rightarrow \{\text{OK}, \bot\}$: OK if $s \in [\hat{q}] \setminus \{0\} \wedge c = pk^s \in \mathbb{H}$, else $\bot$.

Theorem 1. *PAD-DSA is anonymous (Definition 1), with no leakage.*

We prove Theorem 1 in the full paper [79, §3].

Definition 8 (Idealized ECDSA [23,33]). *The triple* $(\text{gen}_{\mathbb{H}}^{DSA}, \text{sign}_{\mathbb{H}}^{DSA}, \text{verify}_{\mathbb{H}}^{DSA})$ *is the* **idealized ECDSA** *algorithm if the two hash functions called as subroutines by* $\text{sign}_{\mathbb{H}}^{DSA}$ *and* $\text{verify}_{\mathbb{H}}^{DSA}$ *are modeled as random oracles.*

Theorem 2. PAD-DSA *is unforgeable (Definition 2) when* $(\text{gen}_\mathbb{H}^{DSA}, \text{sign}_\mathbb{H}^{DSA},$ $\text{verify}_\mathbb{H}^{DSA})$ *is modeled as the idealized ECDSA algorithm.*

Theorem 3. PAD-DSA *is weakly orthogonal to ECDSA in* $\mathbb{H}$ *(Definition 3) when* $(\text{gen}_\mathbb{H}^{DSA}, \text{sign}_\mathbb{H}^{DSA}, \text{verify}_\mathbb{H}^{DSA})$ *is modeled as the idealized ECDSA algorithm.*

Dauterman et al. [33, Theorem 5, Appendix C] prove a statement equivalent to Theorem 2. PAD-DSA is, in effect, a signature under a related key; Theorem 3 captures the required security against related-key attacks. Morita et al. [59, Theorem 2] prove a statement equivalent to this theorem, and also suggest a tweak to DSA whose use would give full (rather than weak) orthogonality for PAD-DSA.

An alternative to the above scheme is to use $c = pk \cdot \hat{g}^s = \hat{g}^{x+s}$, with signing key $x + s \in \mathbb{Z}_{\hat{q}}$, similarly to hierarchical deterministic wallets [81]. PAD-DSA also extends naturally to Schnorr [73], EdDSA [13], and related schemes.

4   A Private Airdrop to RSA Keys

Let $\mathbb{G}$ be a group of unknown order (§2.2) with generators g, h having unknown discrete-log relation. Let $\mathbb{H}$ be an auxiliary cyclic group of known prime order $\hat{q}$ with generators $\hat{g}$, $\hat{h}$ having unknown discrete-log relation. Let $n \in [N]$ be a secret integer where N is a public upper bound on n and $N > |\mathbb{G}| \cdot 2^\lambda$. Let $c := g^n \cdot h^s \in \mathbb{G}$ be a Pedersen commitment [65] to n with opening $s \xleftarrow{\text{R}} [N]$.

In this section we construct a private airdrop to RSA keys. We proceed in two steps: we first construct an interactive zero-knowledge proof of knowledge (ZKPK) of the factorization of an RSA modulus $n \in \mathbb{Z}$ given a public Pedersen commitment [65] to this n (see §4.1 and §4.2). We then make this protocol non-interactive via the Fiat-Shamir heuristic [35], yielding a private airdrop (§4.3).

One way to prove knowledge of the factorization of a committed n is for the prover to commit to integers p and q, and then prove that they are nontrivial factors of n. We instantiate this approach in Sect. 4.1, but verifying the proof is costly: it requires an exponentiation by a several thousand-bit exponent.

To address this, in Sect. 4.2 we describe a second ZKPK that reduces the verifier's work by roughly $5\times$ and gives $\approx$13–49% shorter proofs. The resulting protocol leaks a small amount of information about n: at most two bits, This can be reduced to just one leaked bit under a mild assumption (Corollary 1, §4.3).

Remark 5. The protocols of this section are insecure if the group $\mathbb{G}$ contains a non-identity element of known order. In the group $\mathbb{Z}_m^\times$ the element -1 has order 2, and hence this group is unsuitable for our protocols. Instead, we work in the quotient group $\mathbb{G} := \mathbb{Z}_m^\times/\{\pm 1\}$, where elements are represented as integers in the interval $[1, m/2]$ and the product of x and y is defined as $x \cdot y = \min(z, m - z)$ where $z = (x \cdot y \bmod m)$. In this group -1 is the same as 1, and presumably there are no other known elements of known order other than the identity. We discuss the group $\mathbb{G}$ further in the full paper [79, §7].

4.1   PoKF$_1$: ZKPK of Factorization of a Committed Integer

To prove knowledge of the factorization of n, the prover establishes the relation

$$\mathfrak{R}'_{g,h} := \left\{ \begin{array}{cc} \left(c \in \mathbb{G}, \quad (n,p,q,s) \in [N] \times \mathbb{Z}^3 \right), & \text{where} \\ c = g^n \cdot h^s, \qquad p \cdot q = n, \qquad p \notin \{\pm 1, \pm n\} \end{array} \right\} \qquad (1)$$

where c is the statement and (n,p,q,s) is the witness. At a high level, the proof works as follows: the prover $\mathcal{P}$ sends the verifier $\mathcal{V}$ two Pedersen commitments c_p and c_q to p and q, respectively, then proves that $p \cdot q = n$ and $p \notin \{\pm 1, \pm n\}$. For this purpose, we combine folklore sigma protocols [6,28,31,54,62,73] with recent work extending such protocols to generic groups of unknown order [18].

To efficiently prove that $p \notin \{\pm 1, \pm n\}$ we make use of the auxiliary group $\mathbb{H}$. Recall that $\mathcal{V}$ has commitments to p and n, and could therefore prove that $p \notin \{\pm 1, \pm n\}$ by proving that $(p^2 - 1)(p^2 - n^2) \neq 0$ as integers. However, this requires a relatively large proof containing multiple elements of $\mathbb{G}$.

To sidestep this issue, we take a different approach: rather than execute the proof in $\mathbb{G}$, our $\mathcal{P}$ and $\mathcal{V}$ execute it in a much smaller group $\mathbb{H}$ of known prime order (say, an elliptic curve group). For RSA moduli at practical security levels the order of $\mathbb{H}$ is all but certainly coprime to p, $p \pm 1$, and $p \pm n$, so this suffices to convince $\mathcal{V}$ that $p \notin \{\pm 1, \pm n\}$ in $\mathbb{Z}$ for essentially any n.

The prover $\mathcal{P}$ provides a commitment $\hat{c}_{p^2} \in \mathbb{H}$ to p^2, from which $\mathcal{V}$ can compute a commitment to $p^2 - 1$ as $\hat{c}_{p^2}/\hat{g} \in \mathbb{H}$. To do the same for $p^2 - n^2$ the verifier $\mathcal{V}$ needs a commitment $\hat{c}_{n^2} \in \mathbb{H}$ to n^2. Fortunately, in the airdrop context this is easy to arrange, by requiring the sender $\mathcal{S}$ to compute the token as $(c, \hat{c}_{n^2})$ with corresponding secret (s, s_2). This gives the modified relation

$$\mathfrak{R}''_{g,h,\hat{g},\hat{h}} := \left\{ \begin{array}{cc} \left((c, \hat{c}_{n^2}) \in \mathbb{G} \times \mathbb{H}, \quad (n,p,q,s,s_2) \in [N] \times \mathbb{Z}^3 \times [\hat{q}] \right), \\ \text{where} \quad c = g^n \cdot h^s, \qquad \hat{c}_{n^2} = \hat{g}^{(n^2)} \cdot \hat{h}^{s_2}, \\ p \cdot q = n, \qquad p \notin \{\pm 1, \pm n\} \mod \hat{q} \end{array} \right\} \qquad (2)$$

for statement $(c, \hat{c}_{n^2})$ and witness (n,p,q,s,s_2).

We leave details of PoKF$_1$ to the full paper [79, §4.1, Appxendix B].

4.2   PoKF$_2$: Reducing Costs by Allowing (1-bit) Leakage

As mentioned previously, PoKF$_1$ suffers from high verification cost [79, §4.1, Appendix B.4]. In this section, we give a protocol that reduces both verification and communication cost compared to PoKF$_1$, but leaks one bit about n. This leakage appears to be acceptable in private airdrop applications.

To prove knowledge of factorization of n, the prover establishes the following relation for $w \in [N]$ where $w^2 \equiv t \pmod{n}$ and $t \in \mathbb{Z}$ is prime, $2 \leq t < \lambda$. (Recall that computing square roots modulo n is equivalent to factoring n.)

$$\mathfrak{R}_{g,h} := \left\{ \begin{array}{cc} \left((c,t) \in \mathbb{G} \times [\lambda], \quad (n,s,w,a) \in [N]^4 \right), & \text{where} \\ c = g^n \cdot h^s \in \mathbb{G}, \quad w^2 = t + a \cdot n \in \mathbb{Z}, \quad 2 \leq t < \lambda \text{ a prime} \end{array} \right\} \qquad (3)$$

454   R. S. Wahby et al.

Here (c, t) is the statement and (n, s, w, a) is the witness. The integer relation $w^2 = t + a \cdot n$ proves that $w^2 \equiv t \pmod{n}$, as required.

Remark 6. Common hardware security tokens for RSA keys (e.g., [82]) implement a signing oracle abstraction. This means that the device's owner has access to (at best) an eth root in $\mathbb{Z}_n$ for $(n, e) = pk$—and *not* to the factorization of n. Furthermore, these security tokens often fix $e = 65537$. In principle, it is possible to adapt our ZKPK to a relation analogous to (3) for w^* a 65537th root of t. This proof would be an order of magnitude longer, but would eliminate the leakage about n, and support security tokens. We leave to future work the problem of devising a concretely small ZKPK supporting these security tokens.

We now give an interactive ZKPK for Relation (3), building on the results of Boneh et al. [18]. This relation leaks that $t \in \mathbb{Z}$ is a quadratic residue modulo the committed n. As discussed below (Corollary 1, §4.3), this leakage amounts to one bit under a standard cryptographic assumption.

Protocol PoKF$_2$ for relation (3) between prover $\mathcal{P}$ and verifier $\mathcal{V}$ works as follows. $\mathcal{V}$'s input is $(c, t) \in \mathbb{G} \times [\lambda]$ with t prime, and $\mathcal{P}$'s input is $(c, t, n, s, w, a) \in \mathbb{G} \times [N]^5$. To start, $\mathcal{P}$ chooses two random integers $s_1, s_2 \xleftarrow{\text{R}} [N]$ and computes $c_1 \leftarrow g^w \cdot h^{s_1} \in \mathbb{G}$ and $c_2 \leftarrow g^a \cdot h^{s_2} \in \mathbb{G}$. Next, define a homomorphism $\phi : \mathbb{Z}^8 \rightarrow \mathbb{G}^4 \times \mathbb{Z}$ parameterized by g, h, c, c_1, c_2:

$$\phi \begin{pmatrix} w, w2, s1, a, \\ na, s1w, sa, s2 \end{pmatrix} := \begin{pmatrix} g^w \cdot h^{s1}, & g^a \cdot h^{s2}, & g^{w2} \cdot h^{s1w}/c_1^w, \\ g^{na} \cdot h^{sa}/c^a, & w2 - na \end{pmatrix} \quad (4)$$

It is easy to see that ϕ is a group homomorphism whose range is the group $\mathbb{G}^4 \times \mathbb{Z}$. We will write the group operation in this group multiplicatively. That is, if $(a_i, b_i, c_i, d_i, e_i) \in \mathbb{G}^4 \times \mathbb{Z}$ for $i \in \{1, 2\}$, then

$$(a_1, b_1, c_1, d_1, e_1) \cdot (a_2, b_2, c_2, d_2, e_2) := (a_1 a_2, \ b_1 b_2, \ c_1 c_2, \ d_1 d_2, \ e_1 + e_2).$$

To prove knowledge of a witness for relation (3), it suffices for $\mathcal{P}$ to prove that it knows a ϕ-preimage of $T := (c_1, c_2, 1, 1, t) \in \mathbb{G}^4 \times \mathbb{Z}$. In other words, we need a ZKPK for a vector $\mathbf{v}' = (w', w2', s1', a', na', s1w', sa', s2') \in \mathbb{Z}^8$ such that

$$\phi(\mathbf{v}') = T = (c_1, c_2, 1, 1, t) \in \mathbb{G}^4 \times \mathbb{Z}. \quad (5)$$

This proves that c_1 is a commitment to $w' \in \mathbb{Z}$, c_2 is a commitment to $a' \in \mathbb{Z}$, $w2' = (w')^2$, and $na' = a' \cdot n$ for some integer a'. The fifth term in (5) proves that $(w')^2 - a' \cdot n = t \in \mathbb{Z}$, as required.

We design a ZKPK for a ϕ-preimage using a zero-knowledge protocol due to Boneh et al. [18, Appxendix A]. Here, the verifier $\mathcal{V}$ is given $T \in \mathbb{G}^4 \times \mathbb{Z}$ and the prover $\mathcal{P}$ is given T and $\mathbf{v} \in \mathbb{Z}^8$ where $\phi(\mathbf{v}) = T$. The protocol works as follows:

(1) $\mathcal{P}$ sets $\mathbf{r} := (r_w, r_{w2}, r_{s1}, r_a, r_{na}, r_{s1w}, r_{sa}, r_{s2}) \in \mathbb{Z}^8$ where $r_w, r_{w2}, r_{na}, r_a \xleftarrow{\text{R}} [2^{2\lambda + \log(2\lambda)} \cdot 2^\lambda]$ and $r_{s1}, r_{s1w}, r_{sa}, r_{s2} \xleftarrow{\text{R}} [N \cdot 2^{2\lambda + \log(2\lambda)}]$. $\mathcal{P}$ then computes $\mathbf{R} \leftarrow \phi(\mathbf{r}) \in \mathbb{G}^4 \times \mathbb{Z}$ and sends $(c_1, c_2, \mathbf{R})$ to $\mathcal{V}$.

(2) $\mathcal{V}$ chooses challenges $ch \xleftarrow{\text{R}} [2^\lambda]$ and $\ell \xleftarrow{\text{R}} \mathsf{Primes}(2\lambda)$,[2] and sends them to $\mathcal{P}$.

(3) $\mathcal{P}$ computes $\mathbf{z} \leftarrow (ch \cdot \mathbf{v} + \mathbf{r}) \in \mathbb{Z}^8$, $\mathbf{z}_\ell \leftarrow (\mathbf{z} \bmod \ell) \in [\ell]^8$, $\mathbf{z}_q \leftarrow \lfloor \mathbf{z}/\ell \rfloor \in \mathbb{Z}^8$, and $\mathbf{Z}_q \leftarrow \phi(\mathbf{z}_q)$; and sends $(\mathbf{Z}_q, \mathbf{z}_\ell) \in (\mathbb{G}^4 \times \mathbb{Z}) \times [\ell]^8$ to $\mathcal{V}$.

(4) $\mathcal{V}$ accepts if $\mathbf{Z}_q^\ell \cdot \phi(\mathbf{z}_\ell) = T^{ch} \cdot \mathbf{R}$ in $\mathbb{G}^4 \times \mathbb{Z}$.

Verification cost is dominated by evaluation of $\mathbf{Z}_q^\ell \cdot \phi(\mathbf{z}_\ell)$, which entails four multi-exponentiations with exponents of size at most $2\lambda + \log(2\lambda)$ bits (i.e., the bit length of ℓ; §2). For $\lambda = 128$ and $N \approx 2^{4096}$, this is roughly 5× less expensive than the verification cost of protocol PoKF_1 from the prior section. As we discuss in the full paper [79, Appxendix B.4], PoKF_2 also gives $\approx$13–49% smaller proofs.

Remark 7. The commitment c_2 to the integer a is necessary for soundness, and in particular to ensure that a is an integer. If c_2 along with s_2 and the second coordinate of ϕ are eliminated then there is an attack where an adversarial prover can prove knowledge of $(\sqrt{3} \bmod n)$ using $a = 1/n$ and $w = 2$.

Theorem 4. *Protocol PoKF_2 is a zero-knowledge protocol for $\mathfrak{R}_{g,h}$ from (3).*

Definition 9. *Algorithm $\mathcal{G}$ is an **honest instance generator** for $\mathfrak{R}_{g,h}$ (Eq. (3)) if it chooses integers n, s, t, and outputs (c, t) where $c := g^n \cdot h^s \in \mathbb{G}$ and $t \in [\lambda]$.*

Theorem 5. *Protocol PoKF_2 is an argument of knowledge for the relation $\mathfrak{R}_{g,h}$ in (3) for instances (c, t) generated by an honest instance generator $\mathcal{G}$, when the group $\mathbb{G}$ is a modeled as a generic group of unknown order.*

We prove Theorems 4 and 5 in the full paper [79, Appxendix C].

4.3 PAD-RSA: A Private Airdrop for RSA Keys

We construct PAD-RSA by applying the Fiat-Shamir heuristic [35] to the interactive ZKPK PoKF_2 from Sect. 4.2. We optimize further in [79, §4.4].

Let $(\mathsf{gen}^{\mathsf{RSA}}() \xrightarrow{\text{R}} (pk, sk), \mathsf{sign}^{\mathsf{RSA}}(sk, msg) \xrightarrow{\text{R}} sig, \mathsf{verify}^{\mathsf{RSA}}(pk, msg, sig) \rightarrow \{\mathsf{OK}, \bot\})$ be an RSA signature scheme, e.g., RSA-FDH [8]. Then PAD-RSA is given by:

setup$(1^\lambda) \xrightarrow{\text{R}} \mathsf{pp}$: Select a group of unknown order $\mathbb{G}$ generated by g and h, and $N > |\mathbb{G}| \cdot 2^\lambda$ an upper bound on the size of RSA moduli that can be used with these parameters. Output $\mathsf{pp} = (\mathbb{G}, g, h, N, \lambda)$. We discuss $\mathbb{G}$ candidates below.

send$(pk) \xrightarrow{\text{R}} (c, s)$: For $(n, e) = pk$, $s \xleftarrow{\text{R}} [N]$, $c \leftarrow g^n \cdot h^s \in \mathbb{G}$, output (c, s).

sign$(sk, (c, s), msg) \xrightarrow{\text{R}} sig$: For $(n, p, q) = sk$, do:

(1) choose a random prime $2 \leq t < \lambda$ such that t is a quadratic residue in $\mathbb{Z}_n$,

(2) find integers (w, a) such that $w^2 = t + an$ in $\mathbb{Z}$ (i.e. $w^2 \equiv t \bmod n$),

---

(3) choose a random $s_1 \xleftarrow{\text{R}} [N]$ and compute $c_1 \leftarrow g^w \cdot h^{s_1} \in \mathbb{G}$,

(4) choose a random $s_2 \xleftarrow{\text{R}} [N]$ and compute $c_2 \leftarrow g^a \cdot h^{s_2} \in \mathbb{G}$,

(5) compute $\mathbf{v} \leftarrow (w, w^2, s_1, a, n \cdot a, s_1 \cdot w, s \cdot a, s_2)$,

(6) set $\mathbf{r} := (r_w, r_{w2}, r_{s1}, r_a, r_{na}, r_{s1w}, r_{sa}, r_{s2}) \in \mathbb{Z}^8$ where
$r_w, r_{w2}, r_{na}, r_a \xleftarrow{\text{R}} [2^{2\lambda + \log(2\lambda)} \cdot 2^\lambda]$ and $r_{s1}, r_{s1w}, r_{sa}, r_{s2} \xleftarrow{\text{R}} [N \cdot 2^{2\lambda + \log(2\lambda)}]$,

(7) compute $\mathbf{R} \leftarrow \phi(\mathbf{r}) \in \mathbb{G}^4 \times \mathbb{Z}$, where ϕ is the homomorphism defined in (4),

(8) compute $(ch, \ell) \leftarrow \text{Hash}(msg, \mathbb{G}, g, h, c, c_1, c_2, t, \mathbf{R})$, where $ch \in [2^\lambda]$ and $\ell \in \text{Primes}(2\lambda)$ (e.g., by treating the hash output as a PRG seed),

(9) compute $\mathbf{z} \leftarrow (ch \cdot \mathbf{v} + \mathbf{r}) \in \mathbb{Z}^8$, $\mathbf{z}_\ell \leftarrow (\mathbf{z} \bmod \ell) \in [\ell]^8$, $\mathbf{z}_q \leftarrow \lfloor \mathbf{z}/\ell \rfloor \in \mathbb{Z}^8$, $\mathbf{Z}_q \leftarrow \phi(\mathbf{z}_q) \in \mathbb{G}^4 \times \mathbb{Z}$,

(10) output the signature $sig = (c_1, c_2, t, ch, \ell, \mathbf{Z}_q, \mathbf{z}_\ell)$.

verify$(c, msg, sig) \rightarrow \{\text{OK}, \bot\}$: For $(c_1, c_2, t, ch, \ell, \mathbf{Z}_q, \mathbf{z}_\ell) = sig$,

(1) output $\bot$ if $t \notin [\lambda]$ or not prime, $c1, c2 \notin \mathbb{G}$, $\mathbf{Z}_q \notin \mathbb{G}^4 \times \mathbb{Z}$, or $\mathbf{z}_\ell \notin [\ell]^8$.

(2) with $T := (c_1, c_2, 1, 1, t) \in \mathbb{G}^4 \times \mathbb{Z}$, compute $\mathbf{R}' \leftarrow \mathbf{Z}_q^\ell \cdot \phi(\mathbf{z}_\ell)/T^{ch} \in \mathbb{G}^4 \times \mathbb{Z}$.

(3) compute $(ch', \ell') \leftarrow \text{Hash}(msg, \mathbb{G}, g, h, c, c_1, c_2, t, \mathbf{R}')$, where $ch' \in [2^\lambda]$ and $\ell' \in \text{Primes}(2\lambda)$,

(4) output OK if $ch' = ch$ and $\ell' = \ell$, else output $\bot$.

validate$(pk, (c, s)) \rightarrow \{\text{OK}, \bot\}$: Output OK if $s \in [N] \wedge c = g^n \cdot h^s \in \mathbb{G}$, else $\bot$.

As discussed in Remark 5, the security of PAD-RSA relies crucially on $\mathbb{G}$ containing no elements of known order other than the identity. $\mathbb{Z}_m^\times/\{\pm 1\}$ for m an RSA modulus with unknown factorization is a convenient choice, but it requires a trusted setup (to generate m without leaking its factorization). A candidate $\mathbb{G}$ that does not require trusted setup is the class group of imaginary quadratic order [24]. We discuss further in the full paper [79, §7].

Since the ZKPK of Sect. 4.2 is complete, PAD-RSA is a valid scheme. The following theorems establish the security properties of PAD-RSA. Corollary 1 and Theorem 8 rely on the quadratic residuosity assumption (QRA) [15]: informally, for RSA modulus m with unknown factorization, distinguishing between a square modulo m and a non-square with Jacobi symbol $+1$ is infeasible.

Theorem 6. *PAD − RSA is Λ^{RSA}-anonymous (Definition 1) in the ROM. Λ^{RSA} reveals two bits about $(n, e) = (pk, sk)$, namely, a small prime quadratic residue mod n.*

Corollary 1. *Under QRA, $\Lambda^{\text{RSA}}(pk, sk)$ leaks one bit about pk with respect to any RSA modulus of unknown factorization, to any PPT observer.*

Theorem 7. *PAD − RSA is unforgeable in the random oracle model if computing $\sqrt{t} \in \mathbb{Z}_n$ from RSA public key $(n, e) = pk$ is hard, $2 \leq t < \lambda$ a prime.*

Theorem 8. *PAD − RSA is orthogonal to RSA under QRA in the ROM.*

We prove Theorems 6–8 and Corollary 1 in the full paper [79, §4.3].

5   Related Work

Anonymity and Privacy for Cryptocurrencies. Our work relates broadly to privacy for cryptocurrency users, but it attacks a different problem than prior work. We very briefly rehearse that work for context. Following Bünz et al. [25], we separate prior work into anonymity, hiding associations between identities and transactions, and confidentiality, hiding contents of transactions.

While Bitcoin was intended to provide anonymity [60], in practice it does not [4,57]. Early responses to this issue hide transaction history by shuffling together unrelated transactions [55,71]. More recent work uses cryptographic machinery to give stronger guarantees [10,61,72]. CryptoNote stealth addresses [72] are similar to a PAD in that they allow a sender to derive an anonymous identity from a recipient's public key. But this scheme requires a special public key format, is incompatible with RSA keys, and has no formal security statement.

A related line of work deals with confidentiality. Maxwell showed how to construct transactions whose inputs and outputs are hidden in cryptographic commitments, and which include zero-knowledge proofs attesting to validity [56]. Later work built upon and refined this approach [38,52,67,68]. Most recently, Bünz et al. [25] showed how to significantly improve the costs of the zero-knowledge proofs on which confidential transactions are built.

Efficient Airdrops. MerkleMine [58] and pooled payments [69] are methods for compressing airdrops using Merkle trees. These are similar to our private genesis airdrop (described in the full paper [79, §5]), but our design entails more complexity because it aims to preserve the privacy of recipients, supports multiple keys per recipient, and allows recipients to accuse the sender of dishonesty.

A recent survey of airdrops [36] discusses the cost of these and other methods.

General-Purpose Zero-Knowledge Proofs and Private Smart Contracts. Several lines of work have produced frameworks for constructing zero-knowledge proofs for general NP statements; other work has applied these ideas to constructing smart contracts. For space reasons we defer this discussion to the full paper [79, §8]. In sum, these works pay a high cost for their generality, and are far more expensive than the special-purpose ZKPK of Sect. 4.

Group Signatures, Ring Signatures, etc. In a group signature scheme [7,29], users join a group by registering with an administrator; thereafter, any user can sign for the group. This signature does not reveal which user signed, just that one member of the group did. Private airdrops are vaguely similar to group signatures, but they disconnect the anonymity set (*all* users who own a certain key type) from the signing set (exactly one user, designated by the sender). Our private genesis airdrop (described in the full paper [79, §5]) is roughly a "one-time-per-user" group signature with extra properties tailored to our application.

Ad-hoc anonymous identification schemes [34] and ring signatures [70], unlike group signatures, have no administrator. Instead, users create ad-hoc anonymity sets out of existing keys, then create signatures which reveal only that one user in the anonymity set was the signer. Private airdrops are similar to ring signatures in that they do not require users to register with an administrator, but an administrator (the sender) is nevertheless required.

The ring signature scheme of Abe et al. [1] admits signatures whose ad-hoc anonymity sets mix keys of different types. In this scheme, signing and verifying time and signature size are all linear in the size of the anonymity set. Our private genesis airdrop scheme also allows signatures with anonymity sets having mixed key types; it has logarithmic and concretely small cost in the size of the anonymity set, but requires a sender to set up the scheme.

Anonymous proxy signatures [39] let a delegator give signing privileges to a proxy. The delegator's role is faintly reminiscent of the sender's in a private airdrop; and like the recipient, the proxy's identity is kept secret. But the delegator retains signing privileges after designating a proxy, whereas the private airdrop sender permanently transfers signing privileges for a given token to its recipient.

Proving Knowledge of Factorization of an RSA Modulus. A large body of work deals with proving knowledge of factorization of RSA moduli. Much of this is in the setting where the modulus n is public (e.g., [22,40,42,78]) and is thus unsuitable for our application, since revealing n would violate anonymity.

Camenisch and Michels [26] give a protocol for proving that $a \cdot b \equiv d \bmod n$ for committed values a, b, d, and n, that is secure under the discrete log assumption. This is considerably milder than our modeling $\mathbb{G}$ as a generic group of unknown order (§4.2; [79, §7]). On the other hand, as a consequence of impossibility results for Σ-protocols in groups of unknown order [5,77], the protocol requires k repetitions for soundness 2^{-k}, wherein each repetition requires five range proofs and five proofs of knowledge of a commitment's opening. This means that proofs are orders of magnitude larger and costlier to verify than in our scheme.

6   Conclusion

We have defined private airdrops, which allow users to create signatures using their cryptographic credentials *without* revealing those credentials, and we have described concrete private airdrop schemes for ECDSA and RSA keys. To construct private airdrops for RSA, we defined a new zero-knowledge argument of knowledge of the factorization of a committed integer, in generic groups of unknown order.

In the full paper [79, §5] we describe how to use these private airdrops to bootstrap a new cryptocurrency, using a design we call a private genesis airdrop. Private genesis airdrops handle millions of recipients, each having hundreds of public keys, potentially of different types. The creator of a private genesis airdrop can prove the total value he has airdropped; if he created the airdrop dishonestly, recipients can prove that they did not receive the promised funds.

Finally, we have implemented and evaluated our schemes [79, §6]. In our fastest implementation, private airdrop signatures for RSA keys take tens to hundreds of milliseconds to create and milliseconds to verify, and they comprise at most a few kilobytes. The private genesis airdrop scheme increases signature size by about a kilobyte for an airdrop to millions of users, each having hundreds of keys; its computational overhead is negligible. While these costs are expensive compared to plain RSA signatures, we believe that may be justified, in the airdrop setting, by the improvement in recipient privacy.

Our implementations are available under open-source licenses [48,50].

Acknowledgments. This work was supported in part by the NSF, the ONR, the Simons Foundation, the Stanford Center for Blockchain Research, and the Ripple Foundation. The authors thank Fraser Brown, Henry Corrigan-Gibbs, and Dmitry Kogan for helpful conversations, and David Mazières for pointing out the need for the orthogonality property.

References

1. Abe, M., Ohkubo, M., Suzuki, K.: 1-out-of-n signatures from a variety of keys. In: Zheng, Y. (ed.) ASIACRYPT 2002. LNCS, vol. 2501, pp. 415–432. Springer, Heidelberg (2002). https://doi.org/10.1007/3-540-36178-2_26. (December 2002)
2. Airdrop Alert. https://airdropalert.com/
3. Ames, S., Hazay, C., Ishai, Y., Venkitasubramaniam, M.: Ligero: lightweight sublinear arguments without a trusted setup. In: ACM CCS, October/November 2017
4. Androulaki, E., Karame, G.O., Roeschlin, M., Scherer, T., Capkun, S.: Evaluating user privacy in bitcoin. In: Sadeghi, A.-R. (ed.) FC 2013. LNCS, vol. 7859, pp. 34–51. Springer, Heidelberg (2013). https://doi.org/10.1007/978-3-642-39884-1_4. (April 2013)
5. Bangerter, E., Camenisch, J., Krenn, S.: Efficiency limitations for Σ-protocols for group homomorphisms. In: Micciancio, D. (ed.) TCC 2010. LNCS, vol. 5978, pp. 553–571. Springer, Heidelberg (2010). https://doi.org/10.1007/978-3-642-11799-2_33. (February 2010)
6. Bangerter, E., Camenisch, J., Maurer, U.: Efficient proofs of knowledge of discrete logarithms and representations in groups with hidden order. In: Vaudenay, S. (ed.) PKC 2005. LNCS, vol. 3386, pp. 154–171. Springer, Heidelberg (2005). https://doi.org/10.1007/978-3-540-30580-4_11. (January 2005)
7. Bellare, M., Micciancio, D., Warinschi, B.: Foundations of group signatures: formal definitions, simplified requirements, and a construction based on general assumptions. In: Biham, E. (ed.) EUROCRYPT 2003. LNCS, vol. 2656, pp. 614–629. Springer, Heidelberg (2003). https://doi.org/10.1007/3-540-39200-9_38. (May 2003)
8. Bellare, M., Rogaway, P.: Random oracles are practical: A paradigm for designing efficient protocols. In: ACM CCS, November 1993
9. Ben-Sasson, E., Bentov, I., Horesh, Y., Riabzev, M.: Scalable zero knowledge with no trusted setup. In: Boldyreva, A., Micciancio, D. (eds.) CRYPTO 2019. LNCS, vol. 11694, pp. 701–732. Springer, Cham (2019). https://doi.org/10.1007/978-3-030-26954-8_23. (August 2019)
10. Ben-Sasson, E., et al.: Zerocash: decentralized anonymous payments from bitcoin. In: IEEE S&P, May 2014

11. Ben-Sasson, E., Chiesa, A., Spooner, N.: Interactive oracle proofs. In: Hirt, M., Smith, A. (eds.) TCC 2016. LNCS, vol. 9986, pp. 31–60. Springer, Heidelberg (2016). https://doi.org/10.1007/978-3-662-53644-5_2. (October/November 2016)

12. Ben-Sasson, E., Chiesa, A., Tromer, E., Virza, M.: Succinct non-interactive zero knowledge for a von Neumann architecture. In: USENIX Security, August 2014

13. Bernstein, D.J., Duif, N., Lange, T., Schwabe, P., Yang, B.-Y.: High-speed high-security signatures. In: Preneel, B., Takagi, T. (eds.) CHES 2011. LNCS, vol. 6917, pp. 124–142. Springer, Heidelberg (2011). https://doi.org/10.1007/978-3-642-23951-9_9. (September/October 2011)

14. Bjorøy, T.V.: The latest crypto PR craze: 'airdropping' free coins into your wallet. VentureBeat, September 2017

15. Blum, L., Blum, M., Shub, M.: Comparison of two pseudo-random number generators. In: Chaum, D., Rivest, R.L., Sherman, A.T. (eds.) Advances in Cryptology, pp. 61–78. Springer, Boston, MA (1983). https://doi.org/10.1007/978-1-4757-0602-4_6

16. Bogart, S.: The trend that is increasing the urgency of owning Bitcoin and Etherium. Forbes (Oct 2017)

17. Boneh, D., Bünz, B., Fisch, B.: A survey of two verifiable delay functions. Cryptology ePrint Archive, Report 2018/712 (2018). https://eprint.iacr.org/2018/712

18. Boneh, D., Bünz, B., Fisch, B.: Batching techniques for accumulators with applications to IOPs and stateless blockchains. In: Boldyreva, A., Micciancio, D. (eds.) CRYPTO 2019. LNCS, vol. 11692, pp. 561–586. Springer, Cham (2019). https://doi.org/10.1007/978-3-030-26948-7_20. (August 2019)

19. Bonneau, J., Miller, A., Clark, J., Narayanan, A., Kroll, J.A., Felten, E.W.: SoK: research perspectives and challenges for bitcoin and cryptocurrencies. In: IEEE S&P, May 2015

20. Bonneau, J., Narayanan, A., Miller, A., Clark, J., Kroll, J.A., Felten, E.W.: Mixcoin: anonymity for bitcoin with accountable mixes. In: Christin, N., Safavi-Naini, R. (eds.) FC 2014. LNCS, vol. 8437, pp. 486–504. Springer, Heidelberg (2014). https://doi.org/10.1007/978-3-662-45472-5_31. (March 2014)

21. Bootle, J., Cerulli, A., Chaidos, P., Groth, J., Petit, C.: Efficient zero-knowledge arguments for arithmetic circuits in the discrete log setting. In: Fischlin, M., Coron, J.-S. (eds.) EUROCRYPT 2016. LNCS, vol. 9666, pp. 327–357. Springer, Heidelberg (2016). https://doi.org/10.1007/978-3-662-49896-5_12. (May 2016)

22. Boyar, J., Friedl, K., Lund, C.: Practical zero-knowledge proofs: giving hints and using deficiencies. In: Quisquater, J.-J., Vandewalle, J. (eds.) EUROCRYPT 1989. LNCS, vol. 434, pp. 155–172. Springer, Heidelberg (1990). https://doi.org/10.1007/3-540-46885-4_18. (April 1990)

23. Brickell, E., Pointcheval, D., Vaudenay, S., Yung, M.: Design validations for discrete logarithm based signature schemes. In: Imai, H., Zheng, Y. (eds.) PKC 2000. LNCS, vol. 1751, pp. 276–292. Springer, Heidelberg (2000). https://doi.org/10.1007/978-3-540-46588-1_19. (January 2000)

24. Buchmann, J., Hamdy, S.: A survey on IQ cryptography. In: Public-Key Cryptography and Computational Number Theory, September 2000

25. Bünz, B., Bootle, J., Boneh, D., Poelstra, A., Wuille, P., Maxwell, G.: Bulletproofs: short proofs for confidential transactions and more. In: IEEE S&P, May 2018

26. Camenisch, J., Michels, M.: Proving in zero-knowledge that a number is the product of two safe primes. In: Stern, J. (ed.) EUROCRYPT 1999. LNCS, vol. 1592, pp. 107–122. Springer, Heidelberg (1999). https://doi.org/10.1007/3-540-48910-X_8. (May 1999)

27. Chase, M., et al.: Post-quantum zero-knowledge and signatures from symmetric-key primitives. In: ACM CCS, October/November 2017
28. Chaum, D., Pedersen, T.P.: Wallet databases with observers. In: Brickell, E.F. (ed.) CRYPTO 1992. LNCS, vol. 740, pp. 89–105. Springer, Heidelberg (1993). https://doi.org/10.1007/3-540-48071-4_7. (August 1993)
29. Chaum, D., van Heyst, E.: Group signatures. In: EUROCRYPT, April 1991
30. Cooper, D., Santesson, S., Farrell, S., Boeyen, S., Housley, R., Polk, W.: Internet X.509 Public Key Infrastructure Certificate and Certificate Revocation List (CRL) Profile. Technical Report RFC5280, IETF, May 2008
31. Cramer, R.J.F.: Modular design of secure yet practical cryptographic protocols. Ph.D. thesis, Universiteit van Amsterdam, January 1997
32. Damgård, I., Koprowski, M.: Generic lower bounds for root extraction and signature schemes in general groups. In: Knudsen, L.R. (ed.) EUROCRYPT 2002. LNCS, vol. 2332, pp. 256–271. Springer, Heidelberg (2002). https://doi.org/10.1007/3-540-46035-7_17. (April/May 2002)
33. Dauterman, E., Corrigan-Gibbs, H., Mazières, D., Boneh, D., Rizzo, D.: True2F: backdoor-resistant authentication tokens. In: IEEE S&P, May 2019
34. Dodis, Y., Kiayias, A., Nicolosi, A., Shoup, V.: Anonymous identification in Ad Hoc groups. In: Cachin, C., Camenisch, J.L. (eds.) EUROCRYPT 2004. LNCS, vol. 3027, pp. 609–626. Springer, Heidelberg (2004). https://doi.org/10.1007/978-3-540-24676-3_36. (May 2004)
35. Fiat, A., Shamir, A.: How to prove yourself: practical solutions to identification and signature problems. In: Odlyzko, A.M. (ed.) CRYPTO 1986. LNCS, vol. 263, pp. 186–194. Springer, Heidelberg (1987). https://doi.org/10.1007/3-540-47721-7_12. (August 1987)
36. Fröwis, M., Böhme, R.: The operational cost of Ethereum airdrops (2019). arXiv:1907.12383, https://arxiv.org/abs/1907.12383
37. Fuchsbauer, G., Kiltz, E., Loss, J.: The algebraic group model and its applications. In: Shacham, H., Boldyreva, A. (eds.) CRYPTO 2018. LNCS, vol. 10992, pp. 33–62. Springer, Cham (2018). https://doi.org/10.1007/978-3-319-96881-0_2. (August 2018)
38. Fuchsbauer, G., Orrù, M., Seurin, Y.: Aggregate cash systems: a cryptographic investigation of mimblewimble. In: Ishai, Y., Rijmen, V. (eds.) EUROCRYPT 2019. LNCS, vol. 11476, pp. 657–689. Springer, Cham (2019). https://doi.org/10.1007/978-3-030-17653-2_22. (May 2019)
39. Fuchsbauer, G., Pointcheval, D.: Anonymous proxy signatures. In: Ostrovsky, R., De Prisco, R., Visconti, I. (eds.) SCN 2008. LNCS, vol. 5229, pp. 201–217. Springer, Heidelberg (2008). https://doi.org/10.1007/978-3-540-85855-3_14. (September 2008)
40. Fujisaki, E., Okamoto, T.: Statistical zero knowledge protocols to prove modular polynomial relations. In: Kaliski, B.S. (ed.) CRYPTO 1997. LNCS, vol. 1294, pp. 16–30. Springer, Heidelberg (1997). https://doi.org/10.1007/BFb0052225. (August 1997)
41. Gandal, N., Halaburda, H.: Competition in the cryptocurrency market. Technical Report DP10157, Center for Economic Policy Research, September 2014
42. Gennaro, R., Micciancio, D., Rabin, T.: An efficient non-interactive statistical zero-knowledge proof system for quasi-safe prime products. In: ACM CCS, November 1998
43. Giacomelli, I., Madsen, J., Orlandi, C.: ZKBoo: Faster zero-knowledge for Boolean circuits. In: USENIX Security, August 2016

44. GitHub: About. https://github.com/about
45. GitHub: User public keys. https://developer.github.com/v3/users/keys/
46. GitHub: User GPG keys. https://developer.github.com/v3/users/gpg_keys/
47. GitLab: Users API. https://docs.gitlab.com/ce/api/users.html
48. GooSig: short signatures from RSA that hide the signer's public key. https://github.com/kwantam/GooSig
49. GnuPG frequently asked questions. https://www.gnupg.org/faq/gnupg-faq.html#default_rsa2048
50. handshake-org/goosig: Anonymous RSA signatures. https://github.com/handshake-org/goosig/
51. ICO Drops. https://icodrops.com/
52. Jedusor, T.E.: Mimblewimble. Technical report, July 2016. https://github.com/mimblewimble/docs/wiki/MimbleWimble-Origin
53. Keybase.io. https://keybase.io/
54. Maurer, U.M.: Unifying zero-knowledge proofs of knowledge. In: AFRICACRYPT, June 2009
55. Maxwell, G.: CoinJoin: Bitcoin privacy for the real world, August 2013. https://bitcointalk.org/index.php?topic=279249
56. Maxwell, G.: Confidential transactions. Technical report (2016). https://people.xiph.org/~greg/confidential_values.txt
57. Meiklejohn, S., et al.: A fistful of bitcoins: characterizing payments among men with no names. In: IMC, October 2013
58. MerkleMine specification. https://github.com/livepeer/merkle-mine/blob/master/SPEC.md
59. Morita, H., Schuldt, J.C.N., Matsuda, T., Hanaoka, G., Iwata, T.: On the security of the schnorr signature scheme and DSA against related-key attacks. In: Kwon, S., Yun, A. (eds.) ICISC 2015. LNCS, vol. 9558, pp. 20–35. Springer, Cham (2016). https://doi.org/10.1007/978-3-319-30840-1_2
60. Nakamoto, S.: Bitcoin: A peer-to-peer electronic cash system (2008)
61. Noether, S., Mackenzie, A.: Ring confidential transactions. Ledger 1, 1–18 (2016)
62. Okamoto, T.: Provably secure and practical identification schemes and corresponding signature schemes. In: Brickell, E.F. (ed.) CRYPTO 1992. LNCS, vol. 740, pp. 31–53. Springer, Heidelberg (1993). https://doi.org/10.1007/3-540-48071-4_3. (August 1993)
63. OmiseGO airdrop update, August 2017. https://www.omise.co/omisego-airdrop-update
64. Parno, B., Howell, J., Gentry, C., Raykova, M.: Pinocchio: nearly practical verifiable computation. In: IEEE S&P, May 2013
65. Pedersen, T.P.: Non-interactive and information-theoretic secure verifiable secret sharing. In: Feigenbaum, J. (ed.) CRYPTO 1991. LNCS, vol. 576, pp. 129–140. Springer, Heidelberg (1992). https://doi.org/10.1007/3-540-46766-1_9. (August 1992)
66. Penning, H.P.: Analysis of the strong set in the PGP web of trust, December 2018. https://pgp.cs.uu.nl/plot/
67. Poelstra, A.: Mimblewimble. Technical report, October 2016. https://scalingbitcoin.org/papers/mimblewimble.pdf
68. Poelstra, A., Back, A., Friedenbach, M., Maxwell, G., Wuille, P.: Confidential assets. Technical report, April 2017. https://blockstream.com/bitcoin17-final41.pdf

69. Pooled payments (scaling solution for one-to-many transactions). https://ethre
    sear.ch/t/pooled-payments-scaling-solution-for-one-to-many-transactions/590
70. Rivest, R.L., Shamir, A., Tauman, Y.: How to leak a secret. In: Boyd, C. (ed.)
    ASIACRYPT 2001. LNCS, vol. 2248, pp. 552–565. Springer, Heidelberg (2001).
    https://doi.org/10.1007/3-540-45682-1_32. (December 2001)
71. Ruffing, T., Moreno-Sanchez, P., Kate, A.: CoinShuffle: practical decentralized coin
    mixing for bitcoin. In: Kutyłowski, M., Vaidya, J. (eds.) ESORICS 2014. LNCS,
    vol. 8713, pp. 345–364. Springer, Cham (2014). https://doi.org/10.1007/978-3-319-
    11212-1_20. (September 2014)
72. van Saberhagen, N.: CryptoNote v 2.0. Technical report, October 2013
73. Schnorr, C.P.: Efficient identification and signatures for smart cards. In: Brassard,
    G. (ed.) CRYPTO 1989. LNCS, vol. 435, pp. 239–252. Springer, New York (1990).
    https://doi.org/10.1007/0-387-34805-0_22. (August 1990)
74. Shoup, V.: Lower bounds for discrete logarithms and related problems. In: Fumy,
    W. (ed.) EUROCRYPT 1997. LNCS, vol. 1233, pp. 256–266. Springer, Heidelberg
    (1997). https://doi.org/10.1007/3-540-69053-0_18. (May 1997)
75. ssh-keygen(1): OpenBSD manual pages. https://man.openbsd.org/ssh-keygen
76. We're distributing 16 billion Lumens to Bitcoin holders, March 2017. https://www.
    stellar.org/blog/bitcoin-claim-lumens-2/
77. Terelius, B., Wikström, D.: Efficiency limitations of Σ-protocols for group homo-
    morphisms revisited. In: Visconti, I., De Prisco, R. (eds.) SCN 2012. LNCS, vol.
    7485, pp. 461–476. Springer, Heidelberg (2012). https://doi.org/10.1007/978-3-
    642-32928-9_26. (September 2012)
78. van de Graaf, J., Peralta, R.: A simple and secure way to show the validity of your
    public key. In: Pomerance, C. (ed.) CRYPTO 1987. LNCS, vol. 293, pp. 128–134.
    Springer, Heidelberg (1988). https://doi.org/10.1007/3-540-48184-2_9. (August
    1988)
79. Wahby, R.S., Boneh, D., Jeffrey, C., Poon, J.: An airdrop that preserves recipient
    privacy, January 2020. https://goosig.crypto.fyi
80. Wahby, R.S., Tzialla, I., shelat, A., Thaler, J., Walfish, M.: Doubly-efficient
    zkSNARKs without trusted setup. In: IEEE S&P, May 2018
81. Wuille, P.: BIP 32: Hierarchical deterministic wallets, February 2012. https://
    github.com/bitcoin/bips/blob/master/bip-0032.mediawiki
82. The YubiKey. https://www.yubico.com/products/yubikey-hardware/

RingCT 3.0 for Blockchain Confidential Transaction: Shorter Size and Stronger Security

Tsz Hon Yuen[1](✉), Shi-Feng Sun[2,3], Joseph K. Liu[2], Man Ho Au[1],
Muhammed F. Esgin[2,3], Qingzhao Zhang[4], and Dawu Gu[4]

[1] The Univeristy of Hong Kong, Pok Fu Lam, Hong Kong
{thyuen,allenau}@cs.hku.hk
[2] Monash University, Melbourne, Australia
{shifeng.sun,joseph.liu,muhammed.esgin}@monash.edu
[3] Data61, CSIRO, Canberra, Australia
[4] Shanghai Jiao Tong University, Shanghai, China
{fszqz001,dwgu}@sjtu.edu.cn

Abstract. In this paper, we propose the most efficient blockchain ring confidential transaction protocol (RingCT3.0) for protecting the privacy of the sender's identity, the recipient's identity and the confidentiality of the transaction amount. For a typical 2-input transaction with a ring size of 1024, the ring signature size of our RingCT3.0 protocol is 98% less than the ring signature size of the original RingCT1.0 protocol used in Monero. Taking the advantage of our compact RingCT3.0 transcript size, privacy-preserving cryptocurrencies can enjoy a much lower transaction fee which will have a significant impact on the crypto-economy.

In addition to the significant improvement in terms of efficiency, our scheme is proven secure in a stronger security model. We remove the trusted setup assumption used in RingCT2.0. Our scheme is anonymous against non-signing users who are included in the ring, while we show that the RingCT1.0 is not secure in this improved model. Our implementation result shows that our protocol outperforms existing solutions, in terms of efficiency and security.

1 Introduction

Monero, Dash and Zcash are three popular privacy-preserving cryptocurrencies having total market capitalization of USD 1.5 billion. They are ranked at 16, 26 and 32 of all cryptocurrencies as of December 2019. They use different cryptographic techniques: Monero [15] uses linkable ring signatures, Pedersen commitment and Diffie-Hellman key agreement; Dash uses coin shuffling; Zcash [1] uses general zero-knowledge proof (zk-SNARK). These cryptographic techniques mainly suffer from two drawbacks: inefficient signature generation/verification, or large signature size. The latter is more concerned in public blockchains, since it is directly related to the transaction fee.

© International Financial Cryptography Association 2020
J. Bonneau and N. Heninger (Eds.): FC 2020, LNCS 12059, pp. 464–483, 2020.
https://doi.org/10.1007/978-3-030-51280-4_25

Transaction Fee. In public blockchain, the *miners* are motivated for bookkeeping because they earn rewards in terms of new cryptocurrency mined and the transaction fee from each transaction they recorded. The transaction fee is determined by the size of the transaction data. Different cryptocurrencies have their own *fee rate*, i.e., the price per kB of transaction data. During Nov 2017 to Feb 2018, Bitcoin's fee rate reaches 0.008 BTC/kB (which is over USD 100/kB at that time); since then, Bitcoin's fee rate is relatively stable at 0.0002 BTC/kB (which is about USD 1.6/kB). Monero has a stable fee rate of about 0.0008 XMR/kB (which is about USD 0.2/kB).

Transaction fee depends on the length of the transaction data, which is dominated by the signature length of the senders. In Bitcoin, a *typical* transaction of 2-input-2-output contains 2 ECDSA signatures, the length of which is 1kB. As of December 2019, the average transaction fee of Bitcoin is USD 0.25 and the monthly transaction fee of the whole Bitcoin system is USD 2.5 M. In Monero, the total signature size for a typical confidential transaction is 13.2 kB. Therefore, any effort to reduce the signature size will have a significant impact. The improvement in signature size is relatively more important than the improvement in computation efficiency for public blockchains.

Ring Signatures in Blockchain. In this paper, we will focus on the ring signature [17], which allows a user to dynamically choose a set of public keys (including his own) and to sign messages on behalf of the set, without revealing his identity. In anonymous e-cash or cryptocurrency system, linkable-anonymity is more suitable than perfect anonymity since a double-spent payment can be detected. In a linkable ring signature [11], given any two signatures, the verifier knows that whether they are generated by the same signer (even though the verifier still does not know who the actual signer is).

RingCT. The first blockchain Confidential Transaction (CT) [12] is a proposed enhancement to the Bitcoin protocol for hiding payment values in the blockchain. In cryptocurrency Monero, linkable ring signature is used with CT to give a *Ring Confidential Transaction* (RingCT) protocol [15]. For M transaction inputs, they correspond to M ring signatures of ring size $O(n)$ each, where n is the number of possible signer. In addition the net transaction amount (which should be equal to a commitment of zero) also corresponds to a ring signature of ring size $O(n)$. Therefore, Monero's RingCT1.0 [15] has $(M + 1)$ signatures of size $O(n)$ each. Since the large signature size limits the number n of possible signers, the value of n in Monero's official wallet software ranges from 5 to 20 only. As a result, the sender anonymity for RingCT1.0 is at most 1-out-of-20. Due to the small ring size, there are some attacks to the anonymity of Monero users such as [9,14,21].

The RingCT1.0 paper [15] does not give any notion and security model of RingCT, which are then later formalized in [18] and they give a RingCT2.0 protocol with $(M+1)$ signatures of size $O(1)$ by using trusted public parameters. However, the use of trusted public parameters is not desirable in the setting of public blockchain. Note that the above comparison ignores the computation of range proof (e.g., an efficient range proof can be adopted from [4]), the M

key images for linking double-spending transactions, and the computation of N committed output transaction amount.

There are also some post-quantum secure constructions for RingCT. Lattice RingCT v1.0 [20] is the first RingCT protocol that provides post-quantum security. However, it only supports single-input-single-output. That is, "no change" can be given for any transaction. A multi-input-multi-output veresion has been proposed as Lattice RingCT v2.0 [19]. These two schemes are not practical, as the size of the transaction is linear and is about 1 million times larger than the RingCT 1.0 used in Monero. A more practical solution has been proposed as MatRiCT [6] which enjoys the log-size efficiency for transactions. It is still a thousand times larger than the RingCT1.0 for most of the smaller ring size (e.g. less than 1000 user). Therefore it may be only suitable for those applications that require post-quantum security.

1.1   Our Contributions

Our goal is to construct a cost-efficient blockchain RingCT protocol by using an efficient ring signature scheme without trusted setup, and to prove the security in a stronger security model. Specifically, the contributions of this paper include:

1. We build a novel efficient ring signature scheme to construct RingCT3.0 protocol with the shortest RingCT transcript size, without using trusted setup. As shown in Table 1, our RingCT3.0 has ring signature size of $O(M + \log n)$ and the original RingCT1.0 [15] has ring signature size of $O(Mn)$. Consider a typical transaction (i.e., number of inputs $M = 2$) with a ring size of 1024, our ring signature size (1.3 kB) is 98.6% less than the ring signature size of [15] (98 kB). It provides significant savings of the transaction fee for privacy-preserving cryptocurrencies. In addition, it becomes practical to include a larger ring size (e.g., to include 10^5 users with less than 1800 bytes for the signature size) and therefore (having a large ring size) makes it extremely difficult to launch an anonymity attack based on blockchain data analysis.
2. We give a strong security model for RingCT. In particular, we give a clearer security model for the balance property, and give a stronger security model for anonymity by considering insider attack. We will show that the original RingCT1.0 protocol in [15] is not secure in this anonymity model for insider attack. Then we will show that our RingCT3.0 is secure in this improved model.
3. Our significant improvements in the RingCT3.0 protocol rely on our proposed brand new ring signature scheme. It is the shortest ring signature without trusted setup in the literature (refer to Table 2). The idea comes from an innovative technique to construct an efficient set membership proof of n public keys in the base group, instead of in the exponent. We believe these two primitives are of independent interest and contributions.

2   Background

Vector Notations. For a scalar $c \in \mathbb{Z}_p$ and a vector $\vec{a} = (a_1, \ldots, a_n) \in \mathbb{Z}_p^n$, we denote by $\vec{b} = c\vec{a}$ the vector of $b_i = c \cdot a_i$ for $i \in [1, n]$. Let $\langle \vec{a}, \vec{b} \rangle = \sum_{i=1}^{n} a_i b_i$ denote the inner product between two vectors $\vec{a}, \vec{b}$, and $\vec{a} \circ \vec{b} = (a_1 \cdot b_1, \ldots, a_n \cdot b_n)$ denote the Hadamard product.

Table 1. Size of RingCT without trusted setup for a set of M transaction inputs and each input generates a ring signature of ring size n (excluding the range proof, the key images and the input/output accounts), for 128-bit security.

RingCT	Communication		Actual Size for $M = 2$ (Bytes)				
	$\mathbb{G}$	$\mathbb{Z}_p$	$n = 16$	$n = 64$	$n = 256$	$n = 1024$	$n = 4096$
RingCT1.0	$M + 1$	$(M+1)(n+1)$	1731	6339	24771	98499	393411
This paper	$2 \log nM + 9$	$M+8$	947	1079	1211	1343	1475

Table 2. Summary of $O(\log n)$-size DL-based ring signatures for n public keys.

Ring Signatures	Signature Size		Actual Size (Bytes)				
	$\mathbb{G}$	$\mathbb{Z}_p$	$n = 16$	$n = 64$	$n = 256$	$n = 1024$	$n = 4096$
[8]	$4 \log n$	$3 \log n + 1$	944	1400	1856	2312	2768
[2]	$\log n + 12$	$\frac{3}{2} \log n + 6$	912	1074	1236	1398	1560
This paper	$2 \log n + 7$	7	719	1079	1211	1343	1475

We use $\vec{k}^n$ to denote the vector containing the first n-th powers of $k \in \mathbb{Z}_p$. That is $\vec{k}^n = (1, k, k^2, \ldots, k^{n-1}) \in \mathbb{Z}_p^n$. We use the vector notation to Pedersen vector commitment. Let $\vec{g} = (g_1, \ldots, g_n) \in \mathbb{G}^n$ be a vector of generators and $\vec{a} = (a_1, \ldots, a_n) \in \mathbb{Z}_p^n$, then $C = \vec{g}^{\vec{a}} = \prod_{i=1}^{n} g_i^{a_i}$.

3   Overview of RingCT3.0

We give a brief overview on how to improve the efficiency and the security of the RingCT protocol using a step-by-step approach.

3.1   Efficient RingCT3.0 Protocol

We give a new design of ring signature scheme to build an efficient RingCT without using trusted setup. This construction is composed of a number of new primitives and techniques.

Set Membership Proof. Our basic idea is to start with a set membership proof of a set of public keys, without trusted setup. We give the first set membership proof without trusted setup for public keys in the base group. The intuition is that we can have a set of public keys $\vec{Y} = (Y_1, \ldots, Y_n)$ and a binary vector $\vec{b}_L = (b_1, \ldots, b_n)$. Denote $\vec{Y}^{\vec{b}_L} = \prod_{i=1}^{n} Y_i^{b_i}$. For a public key $Y_i \in \vec{Y}$, we set $C = h^\beta Y_i$ for some public group element h and randomness β. We observe that C is a Pedersen commitment of the secret key $x_i = \log_g Y_i$. Also, when $\vec{b}_L$ only has the bit at position i equal to 1, we have:

$$C = h^\beta Y_i = h^\beta \vec{Y}^{\vec{b}_L}.$$

Define $\vec{b}_R$ as $\vec{b}_R = \vec{b}_L - \vec{1}^n$, where $\vec{1}^n = (1, \ldots, 1)$ of length n. We give a zero-knowledge proof for the above condition of $\vec{b}_L$ by showing that:

$$\vec{b}_L \circ \vec{b}_R = \vec{0}^n, \quad \vec{b}_L - \vec{b}_R = \vec{1}^n, \quad \langle \vec{b}_L, \vec{1}^n \rangle = 1,$$

where $\circ$ denotes the Hadamard product. Since the zero-knowledge proof hides the knowledge of $\vec{b}_L$, the position index i of the committed public key is hidden.

In order to give an efficient set membership proof of $\vec{b}_L$ with length n, we use the inner product argument in [4] to reduce the proof size to $\log n$. One non-trivial tweak of our construction is to ensure the security of the Pedersen commitment C on the public key Y_i. We have to set $h = \text{Hash}(\vec{Y})$ (Hash denotes a cryptographic hash function), such that the discrete logarithm (DL) between the public key Y_i and h is not known.

Our set membership proof is fundamentally different from the existing approaches. [2,3,8] prove that for a set of commitments, one of them is committed to 0. They use n polynomials of degree $\log n$ to hide the prover index and run a zero-knowledge proof for the polynomials. Our scheme uses a zero-knowledge proof to prove that $\vec{b}_L$ is a binary vector with Hamming weight 1 and uses the inner product argument in [4] to reduce the proof size to $\log n$. Details of the set membership proof is given in the appendix.

Linkable Ring Signatures. We propose the use of set membership proof for constructing ring signatures directly. The signer can directly give a zero-knowledge proof of knowing: (1) a committed public key ($C = h^\beta Y_i$) which is in the set of n public keys, and (2) the secret key which corresponds to the committed public key. Details of the ring signature is given in the full version of the paper [22]. However, turning it into linkable ring signature is a non-trivial task.

Firstly, we convert our ring signature into a linkable ring signature by giving an extra linkability tag (also called key image in Monero) for each signer. The security proof of our ring signature scheme requires that the DL between different users' public key should be unknown to the adversary. However, in the security model of balance and non-slanderability for RingCT, the adversary is allowed to have more than one secret key. If we simply use the users' public keys as the representation of users in the ring, the scheme is not secure since the adversary knows the DL between public keys.

The classical representation of user i in DL-setting is the public key $Y_i = g^{x_i}$ where x_i is the user's secret key. Hence, we give a new proposal of using $Y_i g_i^d$ as the *user representation* in the set $\vec{Y}$, where Y_i is the public key, g_i is the system parameter and d is the hash of all public keys in the ring. For each user representation $Y_i g_i^d$, the g_i component cannot be canceled out by Y_i due to the exponent d added. Now consider the DL between user representations. Even though the adversary knows the secret keys x_i of other users (which is allowed in the security model), the DL relation between different users' representation is still unknown guaranteed by the DL between g and g_i.

Compressing Multiple Inputs for RingCT3.0. A trivial construction of RingCT with M multiple input is to include M linkable ring signatures and then proves that the sum of input amount is equal to the sum of output amount. As a result, we can obtain a RingCT with signature size $O(M \log n)$. In this paper, we follow the technique of proving multiple range proof in [4] to further compress our RingCT 3.0. In short, we use the first n bit of $\vec{b_L}$ to represent the first linkable ring signature, the second n bit of $\vec{b_L}$ to represent the second linkable ring signature and so on. As a result, we have a nM bit of $\vec{b_L}$ for M inputs. By applying the inner product argument, the correctness of $\vec{b_L}$ is proven with a proof of size $O(\log nM)$. However, we still need M group elements to show the correctness of M key images. Therefore, our final RingCT 3.0 has a proof size of $O(M + \log n)$.

3.2 Strong Security Model for RingCT3.0

As compared to the formal security model of RingCT proposed in [18], we propose a few improvements:

- We remove the use of trapdoor in system parameters. Therefore, this model is more suitable for public blockchain, as compared with RingCT2.0 [18].
- We give a clearer definition of the balance property. We observe that the balance property requires that any malicious user cannot (1) spend any account of an honest user, (2) spend her own accounts with the sum of input amount being different from that of output amount, and (3) double spend any of her accounts. Therefore, we break down the balance property into unforgeability, equivalency and linkability. As a result, the security of each property can be evaluated easily.
- We give a stronger security model of anonymity than the model in [18]. We consider the anonymity against insider attacks. Note that the original RingCT [15] is not secure in this improved model.

Anonymity Against Insider Attacks. We observe that anonymity for RingCT protocol is more complicated than the anonymity of linkable ring signatures. Given the knowledge of the input and output amount, the level of anonymity of RingCT protocol may be lowered. For a transaction with multiple input accounts, multiple linkable ring signatures are generated. Yet, they are correlated when validating the balance of input and output amount. This extra relationship may lower the level of anonymity.

The previous model of anonymity [18] only considered outsider security (i.e., not against the recipient and other members of the ring). In this paper, we define two improved models for anonymity: anonymity against recipient (who knows all the output account secret keys and their amounts) and anonymity against ring insiders (who knows some input account secret keys and their amounts). The collusion of recipient and ring insiders will inevitably lower the level of anonymity. Therefore, we do not capture it in our security model.[1]

Anonymity of RingCT1.0. We first review the original RingCT1.0 [15]. Denote $\mathbb{A}_{in}$ as the set of all input accounts and $\mathbb{A}_S$ as the set of real signers. Arrange $\mathbb{A}_{in}$ as an $M \times n$ matrix with each row containing only one account in $\mathbb{A}_S$. [15] requires that all signing accounts are in the same column in $\mathbb{A}_{in}$. One ring signature is generated for each row. The graphical representation is shown in the following figure.

The real signers must be located in the same column. It is because RingCT1.0 [15] includes an extra ring signature, where each "ring public key" is computed by the product of all coins in each column, divided by all output coins. It is used to guarantee the balance of the input and output amount.

We observe that if the adversary knows one of the secret key in the first column, he can check if any of the key images is generated from this secret key. If not, the adversary can rule out the possibility that the real signer is from the first column. The level of anonymity is already lowered. By knowing $n-1$ secret keys in different columns, the adversary can find out which M input accounts are the real signer. Therefore, the original RingCT1.0 [15] is not secure against our model of anonymity against ring insiders.

Anonymity of RingCT3.0. In order to provide anonymity against ring insiders, we have to break the distribution of real signer in $\mathbb{A}_{in}$ in RingCT1.0 [15]. We achieve this by three steps: (1) for the k-th row, we change the user representation of our RingCT3.0 as:

$$\vec{Y}_k = \{(\mathsf{pk}_{in,k}^{(1)})^{d_0^{k-1}}(C_{in,k}^{(1)})^{d_1}g_1^{d_2}, \ldots, (\mathsf{pk}_{in,k}^{(n)})^{d_0^{k-1}}(C_{in,k}^{(n)})^{d_1}g_n^{d_2}\},$$

for some hash values d_0, d_1, d_2, and system parameters $g_1, \ldots, g_n$; (2) compute a batch inner product argument for the set $\vec{Y} = \vec{Y}_1||\ldots||\vec{Y}_M$, such that one element from each $\vec{Y}_k$ is committed in a commitment B_1; (3) prove the sum of amounts committed in B_1 is equal to the sum of amounts for all the output coins $C_{out,j}$. The second step is done by computing B_1 as the commitment of the multiplication of one element in each $\vec{Y}_k$ for all k. The third step is done via showing that the coins committed in B_1 divides by $\prod_j C_{out,j}^{d_1}$ is a commitment to zero. It can be done without the need of using ring signatures.

---

[1] This property is different from the simple ring signature setting [16] or the tumbler setting [13], since we also consider different transaction amount in different UTXO.

4   Security Model for RingCT

We give the security definitions and models for RingCT which is modified from [18]. A RingCT protocol consists of a tuple of polynomial time algorithms (**Setup, KeyGen, Mint, AccountGen, Spend, Verify**), the syntax of which are described as follows:

- $pp \leftarrow$ **Setup**(1^λ): it takes a security parameter $\lambda \in \mathbb{N}$, and outputs the system parameters pp. All algorithms below have implicitly pp as part of their inputs.
- $(\mathsf{sk}, \mathsf{pk}) \leftarrow$ **KeyGen**(): In order to provide anonymity to the recipient, the concept of *stealth address* was used in RingCT1.0 [15]. It can be viewed as dividing the algorithm into two parts: generating a long-term key pairs for each user, and generating a one-time key pairs for each transaction.
    - **LongTermKeyGen.** It outputs a long term secret key ltsk and a long term public key ltpk.
    - **OneTimePKGen.** On input a long term public key ltpk, it outputs pk and the auxiliary information R_{ot}.
    - **OneTimeSKGen.** On input a one-time public key pk, an auxiliary information R_{ot} and a long term secret key ltsk, it outputs the one-time secret key sk.
- $(cn, \mathsf{ck}) \leftarrow$ **Mint**$(\mathsf{pk}, \mathsf{a})$: it takes as input a public key pk and an amount a, outputs a coin cn for pk as well as the associated coin key ck.
- $(act, \mathsf{ask})/\bot \leftarrow$ **AccountGen**$(\mathsf{sk}, \mathsf{pk}, cn, \mathsf{ck}, \mathsf{a})$: it takes as input a user key pair $(\mathsf{sk}, \mathsf{pk})$, a coin cn, a coin key ck and an amount a. It returns $\bot$ if ck is not the coin key of cn with amount a. Otherwise, it outputs the account $act \doteq (\mathsf{pk}, cn)$ and the corresponding account secret key is $\mathsf{ask} \doteq (\mathsf{sk}, \mathsf{ck}, \mathsf{a})$.
- $(\mathbb{A}_{\mathsf{out}}, \pi, \mathbb{S}, \mathbb{C}k_{\mathsf{out}})/\bot \leftarrow$ **Spend**$(\mathsf{m}, \mathbb{K}_S, \mathbb{A}_S, \mathbb{A}_{\mathsf{in}}, \mathbb{O})$: it takes as input a group $\mathbb{A}_S$ of accounts together with the corresponding account secret keys $\mathbb{K}_S$, an arbitrary set $\mathbb{A}_{\mathsf{in}}$ of groups of input accounts containing $\mathbb{A}_S$, a set $\mathbb{O}$ of output public keys with the corresponding output amounts, and some transaction string $\mathsf{m} \in \{0, 1\}^*$, it outputs $\bot$ if the sum of output amount in $\mathbb{O}$ is different from the sum of input amount in $\mathbb{K}_S$. Otherwise, it outputs a set of output accounts $\mathbb{A}_{\mathsf{out}}$, a proof π, a set $\mathbb{S}$ of serial numbers and a set of output coin keys $\mathbb{C}k_{\mathsf{out}}$. Each serial number $S_i \in \mathbb{S}$ corresponds to one account secret key $\mathsf{ask}_i \in \mathbb{K}_S$.
- $1/0/-1 \leftarrow$ **Verify**$(\mathsf{m}, \mathbb{A}_{\mathsf{in}}, \mathbb{A}_{\mathsf{out}}, \pi, \mathbb{S})$: it takes as input a message m, a set of input accounts $\mathbb{A}_{\mathsf{in}}$, a set of output accounts $\mathbb{A}_{\mathsf{out}}$, a proof π and a set of serial numbers $\mathbb{S}$, the algorithm outputs -1 if the serial numbers in $\mathbb{S}$ is spent previously. Otherwise, it checks if the proof π is valid for the transaction tx, and outputs 1 or 0, meaning a `valid` or `invalid` spending respectively.

The formal security model is given in the full version of the paper [22]. We give a high level description as follows.

Perfect Correctness. The perfect correctness property requires that a user can spend any group of her accounts w.r.t. an arbitrary set of groups of input accounts, each group containing the same number of accounts as the group she intends to spend.

Anonymity. The anonymity of RingCT is more complicated than the anonymity of linkable ring signatures, due to the extra knowledge of transaction amount. The previous model of anonymity in RingCT1.0 only considered outsider security only (i.e., not against the recipient and other members of the ring). As introduced in §3.2, we define two stronger models for anonymity: anonymity against recipients (who know all the output amounts) and anonymity against ring insiders (who know some input account secret keys and their amounts).

Anonymity Against Recipients. The anonymity against recipients property requires that without the knowledge of any input account secret key and input amount (which are within a valid *Range*: from 0 to a maximum value), the spender's accounts are successfully hidden among all the honestly generated accounts, even when the output accounts and the output amounts are known.

Anonymity Against Ring Insiders. The anonymity against ring insiders property requires that without the knowledge of output account secret key and output amount (which are within a valid *Range*), the spender's accounts are successfully hidden among all uncorrupted accounts.

Balance. The balance property requires that any malicious user cannot (1) spend any account of an honest user, (2) spend her own accounts with the sum of input amount being different from that of output amount, and (3) double spend any of her accounts. Therefore, the balance property can be modeled by three security models: unforgeability, equivalence and linkability.

Non-slanderability. The non-slanderability property requires that a malicious user cannot prevent any honest user from spending. It is infeasible for any malicious user to produce a valid spending that shares at least one serial number with a honestly generated spending.

5   RingCT 3.0

For the ease of presentation, we first present a basic construction of RingCT3.0 with linkable ring signature. Then we optimize our construction to $\log(n)$-size by using the inner-product argument in [4], where n is the size of the ring.

5.1   Our Basic Construction

We give our basic construction in this section. Our scheme uses a zero-knowledge range proof of a value committed in a Pederson commitment. Denote $\mathsf{RP} = (\mathsf{RSetup}, \mathsf{RProof}, \mathsf{RVerify})$ as a zero-knowledge range proof for the statement:

$$PoK : \{(\mathsf{a}, \kappa) : C = h_c^{\mathsf{a}} g_c^{\kappa} \wedge \mathsf{a} \in [R_{\min}, R_{\max}]\}.$$

The range proof can be instantiated by the Bulletproof [4].

Our basic construction is as follows.

Setup. On input security parameter λ and the maximum size of ring $n_{\max}$, it picks a group $\mathbb{G}$ of prime order p and some generators $g_c, h_c, g, u \in \mathbb{G}$, $\vec{g} = (g_1, \ldots, g_{n_{\max}})$, $\vec{h} = (h_1, \ldots, h_{n_{\max}}) \in \mathbb{G}^{n_{\max}}$. Suppose that $H_j : \{0,1\}^* \to \mathbb{Z}_p$ for $j = 1, 2, 4, 5$, $H_3 : \{0,1\}^* \to \mathbb{G}$ and $H_6 : \mathbb{G} \to \mathbb{Z}_p$ are collision resistant hash functions. It also runs RSetup of the range proof. Assume these parameters are known in the system.

KeyGen. The algorithm is divided as follows.

- **LongTermKeyGen.** The user picks his long term secret key $\mathsf{ltsk} \doteq (x_1, x_2) \in \mathbb{Z}_p^2$ and computes his long term public key $\mathsf{ltpk} \doteq (g^{x_1}, g^{x_2})$.
- **OneTimePKGen.** On input a long term public key $\mathsf{ltpk} = (g^{x_1}, g^{x_2})$, it picks a random $r_{\mathsf{ot}} \in \mathbb{Z}_p$ and computes a one-time public key $\mathsf{pk} = g^{x_1} \cdot g^{H_6((g^{x_2})^{r_{\mathsf{ot}}})}$. It outputs pk and the auxiliary information $R_{\mathsf{ot}} \doteq g^{r_{\mathsf{ot}}}$.
- **OneTimeSKGen.** On input a one-time public key pk, an auxiliary information R_{ot} and a long term secret key $\mathsf{ltsk} = (x_1, x_2)$, it checks if $\mathsf{pk} = g^{x_1} \cdot g^{H_6(R_{\mathsf{ot}}^{x_2})}$. If it is correct, then it outputs the one-time secret key $\mathsf{sk} = x_1 + H_6(R_{\mathsf{ot}}^{x_2})$.

Mint. On input a public key pk, an amount $\mathsf{a} \in \mathbb{Z}_p$, the algorithm chooses $\kappa \in \mathbb{Z}_p$ uniformly at random and computes the coin $C = g_c^\kappa h_c^{\mathsf{a}}$. It returns the coin C and the coin key $\mathsf{ck} = \kappa$.

AccountGen. On input a user key pair $(\mathsf{sk}, \mathsf{pk})$, a coin C and a coin key $\mathsf{ck} = \kappa$ (where the pair (pk, C) is listed as the output of a transaction) and an amount a, it checks if $C = g_c^\kappa h_c^{\mathsf{a}}$. If it is true, then it outputs the account $act \doteq (\mathsf{pk}, C)$ and the corresponding account secret key is $ask \doteq (\mathsf{sk}, \mathsf{ck}, \mathsf{a})$.

Spend. On input a set of M signer's input accounts $\mathbb{A}_S$ with a set of account secret keys $\{ask_k = (\mathsf{sk}_k, \kappa_{\mathsf{in},k}, \mathsf{a}_{\mathsf{in},k})\}_{k \in [1,M]}$, a set of nM input accounts $\mathbb{A}_{\mathsf{in}}$ which contains $\mathbb{A}_S$ (where $n < n_{\max}$ is the size of the ring), a set of N output amount $\{\mathsf{a}_{\mathsf{out},j}\}_{j \in [1,N]}$ corresponding to N recipient's public keys $\{\mathsf{pk}_{\mathsf{out},j}\}_{j \in [1,N]}$, and a transaction message m, it first checks the amount balance. If $\sum_{k=1}^{M} \mathsf{a}_{\mathsf{in},k} \neq \sum_{j=1}^{N} \mathsf{a}_{\mathsf{out},j}$, the transaction amount is not correct and it returns $\bot$.

Arrange $\mathbb{A}_{\mathsf{in}}$ as an $M \times n$ matrix with each row containing only one account in $\mathbb{A}_S$. Denote the column index ind_k as the position of the k-th element in $\mathbb{A}_S$ appearing in row k, column ind_k of $\mathbb{A}_{\mathsf{in}}$. The graphical representation is as follows:

$$
\mathbb{A}_{\mathsf{in}} = \begin{vmatrix} act_1^{(1)} & \cdots & \cdots & act_1^{(n)} \\ \vdots & & & \vdots \\ act_k^{(1)} & & & act_k^{(n)} \\ \vdots & & & \vdots \\ act_M^{(1)} & & & act_M^{(n)} \end{vmatrix}, \quad \mathbb{A}_S = \begin{vmatrix} act_1^{(\mathsf{ind}_1)} \\ \vdots \\ act_k^{(\mathsf{ind}_k)} \\ \vdots \\ act_M^{(\mathsf{ind}_M)} \end{vmatrix}
$$

The spend protocol can be roughly separated into two parts. The first part is mainly about the balance of the input and output amount. The second part is mainly about the ring signature providing anonymity of the sender.

We first give some sub-protocols for the *balance* property as follows.

1. Generate One-Time Public Key: The sender converts all recipient's long term public keys to one-time public keys by **OneTimePKGen**. The auxiliary information is appended to the transaction message m.
2. Generate Output Coins. It first runs $(C_{\text{out},j}, \kappa_{\text{out},j}) \leftarrow \textbf{Mint}(a_{\text{out},j})$, for all $j \in [1, N]$. It sets $\mathbb{A}_{\text{out}} = \{(\text{pk}_{\text{out},j}, C_{\text{out},j})\}_{j \in [1,N]}$ as the set of N output accounts.
   The sender can later privately send the amount $a_{\text{out},j}$ and coin key $\kappa_{\text{out},j}$ to each secret key owner of $\text{pk}_{\text{out},j}$. Denote $\mathbb{C}k_{\text{out}}$ as the set of all coin keys.
3. Generate Range Proof. It runs the RProof of the range proof for all $a_{\text{out},j}$ where $j \in [1, N]$. Denote π_{range} as the set of output of RProof for all j.
4. Prepare Balance Proof. Denote the coin for $act_k^{(\text{ind}_k)}$ as $C_{\text{in},k}^{(\text{ind}_k)}$. Recall that the coin key of $C_{\text{in},k}^{(\text{ind}_k)}$ is $(a_{\text{in},k}, \kappa_{\text{in},k})$. If sum of input amount is equal to the sum of output amount, we have $\prod_{k=1}^{M} C_{\text{in},k}^{(\text{ind}_k)} / \prod_{j=1}^{N} C_{\text{out},j} = g_c^{\sum_{k=1}^{M} \kappa_{\text{in},k} - \sum_{j=1}^{N} \kappa_{\text{out},j}}$.
   Denote $\Delta \doteq \sum_{k=1}^{M} \kappa_{\text{in},k} - \sum_{j=1}^{N} \kappa_{\text{out},j}$.

Next, we give some sub-protocols for the *ring signature* part. Denote $act_k^{(i)} = (\text{pk}_{\text{in},k}^{(i)}, C_{\text{in},k}^{(i)})$ for $i \in [1, n]$ and the signer index is ind_k. The sender runs as follows.

1. Generate One-Time Secret Key: The sender converts his long term secret key to one-time secret keys by **OneTimeSKGen**.
2. Generate Key Images. Denote $(\text{sk}_k, \cdot, \cdot)$ as the account secret key for $act_k^{(\text{ind}_k)}$. It computes the key image $U_k = u^{\frac{1}{\text{sk}_k}}$.
3. Ring Formation. Denote the concatenated string str as the concatenation of $\{act_k^{(1)} || \ldots || act_k^{(n)}\}_{k \in [1,M]}$. The prover computes $d_0 = H_2(0, \text{str})$, $d_1 = H_2(1, \text{str})$ and $d_2 = H_2(2, \text{str})$. The prover sets $\vec{Y} = \vec{Y}_1 || \ldots || \vec{Y}_M$, where:

$$\vec{Y}_k = ((\text{pk}_{\text{in},k}^{(1)})^{d_0^{k-1}} (C_{\text{in},k}^{(1)})^{d_1} g_1^{d_2}, \ldots, (\text{pk}_{\text{in},k}^{(n)})^{d_0^{k-1}} (C_{\text{in},k}^{(n)})^{d_1} g_n^{d_2}) \quad \text{for } k \in [1, M].$$

4. Prepare Signer Index. For $k \in [1, M]$, the sender generates a binary vector $\vec{b}_{L,k} = (b_{k,1}, \ldots, b_{k,n})$, where $b_{k,i} = 1$ when $i = \text{ind}_k$ and $b_{k,i} = 0$ otherwise. Define $\vec{b}_L = \vec{b}_{L,1} || \ldots || \vec{b}_{L,M}$ and $\vec{b}_R = \vec{b}_L - \vec{1}^n$. We will prove in zero knowledge that $\vec{b}_{L,k}$ is a binary vector with only one bit equal to 1. It is equivalent to showing: $\vec{b}_L \circ \vec{b}_R = \vec{0}^n$, $\vec{b}_L - \vec{b}_R = \vec{1}^n$, $\langle \vec{b}_{L,k}, \vec{1}^n \rangle = 1$ for $k \in [1, M]$.
5. Signature Generation. It consists of the following steps.
   - *Commit 1.* It sets $h = H_3(\vec{Y})$, picks random $\alpha_1, \alpha_2, \beta, \rho, r_{\alpha_1}, r_{\alpha_2}, r_{\text{sk}_1}, \ldots,$ $r_{\text{sk}_M}, r_\delta \in \mathbb{Z}_p, \vec{s}_L, \vec{s}_R \in \mathbb{Z}_p^{nM}$ and computes:

$$B_1 = h^{\alpha_1} \prod_{k=1}^{M} (\text{pk}_{\text{in},k}^{(\text{ind}_k)})^{d_0^{k-1}} (C_{\text{in},k}^{(\text{ind}_k)})^{d_1} g_{\text{ind}_k}^{d_2}, \quad B_2 = h^{\alpha_2} \prod_{k=1}^{M} g_{\text{ind}_k}, \quad A = h^\beta \vec{h}^{\vec{b}_R},$$

$$S_1 = h^{r_{\alpha_1} - d_2 r_{\alpha_2}} g^{\sum_{k=1}^{M} r_{\text{sk}_k} d_0^{k-1}} g_c^{d_1 r_\Delta}, \quad S_2 = h^\rho \vec{Y}^{\vec{s}_L} \vec{h}^{\vec{s}_R}, \quad S_3 = \prod_{k=1}^{M} U_k^{r_{\text{sk}_k} d_0^{k-1}}.$$

Observe that $B_1 = h^{\alpha_1} \vec{Y}^{\vec{b}_L}$.

- *Challenge 1.* Denote the concatenated string $\mathsf{str}' = \vec{Y}||B_1||B_2||A||S_1||S_2||$ $S_3||U_1||\ldots||U_M$. It computes $y = H_4(1, \mathsf{str})$, $z = H_4(2, \mathsf{str})$ and $w = H_4(3, \mathsf{str})$.
- *Commit 2.* It can construct two degree 1 polynomials of variable X:

$$l(X) = \vec{b_L} - z\vec{1}^{nM} + \vec{s_L} \cdot X,$$

$$r(X) = \vec{y}^{nM} \circ (w\vec{b_R} + wz\vec{1}^{nM} + \vec{s_R} \cdot X) + \sum_{k=1}^{M} z^{1+k} \cdot (\vec{0}^{(k-1)n}||\vec{1}^n||\vec{0}^{(M-k)n}).$$

Denote $t(X) = \langle l(X), r(X) \rangle$, which is a degree 2 polynomial. We can write $t(X) = t_0 + t_1 X + t_2 X^2$, and t_0, t_1, t_2 can be computed by using $(\vec{b_L}, \vec{b_R}, \vec{s_L}, \vec{s_R}, w, y, z)$. In particular, observe that

$$t_0 = w\langle\vec{b_L}, \vec{b_R} \circ \vec{y}^{nM}\rangle + zw\langle\vec{b_L} - \vec{b_R}, \vec{y}^{nM}\rangle + \sum_{k=1}^{M} z^{1+k}\langle\vec{b_L}, \vec{0}^{(k-1)n}||\vec{1}^n||$$

$$\vec{0}^{(M-k)n}\rangle - wz^2\langle\vec{1}^{nM}, \vec{y}^{nM}\rangle - \sum_{k=1}^{M} z^{2+k}\langle\vec{1}^{nM}, \vec{0}^{(k-1)n}||\vec{1}^n||\vec{0}^{(M-k)n}\rangle,$$

$$= \sum_{k=1}^{M} z^{1+k} + w(z - z^2)\langle\vec{1}^{nM}, \vec{y}^{nM}\rangle - \sum_{k=1}^{M} nz^{2+k}.$$

It picks random $\tau_1, \tau_2 \in \mathbb{Z}_p$, and computes: $T_1 = g^{t_1}h^{\tau_1}, T_2 = g^{t_2}h^{\tau_2}$.
- *Challenge 2.* It computes $x = H_5(w, y, z, T_1, T_2, \mathtt{m})$.
- *Response.* It computes:

$$\tau_x = \tau_1 \cdot x + \tau_2 \cdot x^2, \quad \mu = \alpha_1 + \beta \cdot w + \rho \cdot x, \quad z_{\alpha_1} = r_{\alpha_1} + \alpha_1 \cdot x,$$

$$z_{\alpha_2} = r_{\alpha_2} + \alpha_2 \cdot x, \quad z_\Delta = r_\Delta + \Delta \cdot x, \quad z_{\mathsf{sk},k} = r_{\mathsf{sk},k} + \mathsf{sk}_k \cdot x \text{ for } k \in [1, M],$$

$$\vec{r} = \vec{y}^{nM} \circ (w\vec{b_R} + wz\vec{1}^{nM} + \vec{s_R} \cdot x) + \sum_{k=1}^{M} z^{1+k} \cdot (\vec{0}^{(k-1)n}||\vec{1}^n||\vec{0}^{(M-k)n}),$$

$$\vec{l} = \vec{b_L} - z \cdot \vec{1}^{nM} + \vec{s_L} \cdot x, \quad t = \langle\vec{l}, \vec{r}\rangle.$$

It outputs $\sigma_{\mathsf{ring}} = (B_1, B_2, A, S_1, S_2, S_3, T_1, T_2, \tau_x, \mu, z_{\alpha_1}, z_{\alpha_2}, z_{\mathsf{sk},1}, \ldots, z_{\mathsf{sk},M}, z_\Delta, \vec{l}, \vec{r}, t)$ and the key image $(U_1, \ldots, U_M)$.

Output. Denote $\mathbb{S}$ as a set of serial number $\{U_1, \ldots, U_M\}$. Then the output of the spend algorithm is $(\mathbb{A}_{\mathsf{out}}, \pi = (\pi_{\mathsf{range}}, \sigma_{\mathsf{ring}}), \mathbb{S}, \mathbb{C}k_{\mathsf{out}})$.

Verify. On input a message $\mathtt{m}$, a set of input accounts $\mathbb{A}_{\mathsf{in}}$, a set of output accounts $\mathbb{A}_{\mathsf{out}}$, a proof π and a set $\mathbb{S}$ of serial numbers and a set $\mathbb{U}$ of serial numbers in the past, then it checks:

1. If there exists any U in both $\mathbb{S}$ and $\mathbb{U}$, returns -1 and exits since it is a double spending of the previous transaction. We can use Bloom filter on $\mathbb{U}$ to speed up the detection of double spending.
2. It runs the RVerify algorithm of the range proof with input from π_{range} and the output coins in $\mathbb{A}_{\mathsf{out}}$.
3. It checks the ring signature σ_{ring} and key images $U_k \in \mathbb{S}$ for $k \in [1, M]$. It computes d_0, d_1, d_2 and $\vec{Y}$ as in the Ring Formation of the **Spend** protocol,

using $\mathbb{A}_{in}$. Denote the concatenated string $\mathsf{str} = \vec{Y}||B_1||B_2||A||S_1||S_2||S_3||U_1||\ldots||U_M$. It computes $h = H_3(\vec{Y})$, $y = H_4(1, \mathsf{str})$, $z = H_4(2, \mathsf{str})$, $w = H_4(3, \mathsf{str})$ and $x = H_5(w, y, z, T_1, T_2, \mathtt{m})$. Define $\vec{h}' = (h'_1, \ldots, h'_{nM}) \in \mathbb{G}^{nM}$ such that $h'_i = h_i^{y^{-i+1}}$ for $i \in [1, nM]$. It returns 1 if all of the following hold and returns 0 otherwise:

$$t = \langle \vec{l}, \vec{r} \rangle, \tag{1}$$

$$g^t h^{\tau_x} = g^{\sum_{k=1}^{M} z^{1+k}(1-nz)+w(z-z^2)\langle \vec{1}^{nM}, \vec{y}^{nM} \rangle} \cdot T_1^x \cdot T_2^{x^2}, \tag{2}$$

$$h^{\mu} \vec{Y}^{\vec{l}} \vec{h}'^{\vec{r}} = B_1 A^w S_2^x \vec{Y}^{-z \cdot \vec{1}^{nM}} \vec{h}'^{wz \cdot \vec{y}^{nM} + \sum_{k=1}^{M} z^{1+k} \cdot (\vec{0}^{(k-1)n}||\vec{1}^n||\vec{0}^{(M-k)n})}, \tag{3}$$

$$h^{z_{\alpha_1} - d_2 z_{\alpha_2}} g^{\sum_{k=1}^{M} z_{\mathsf{sk},k} d_0^{k-1}} g_c^{d_1 z_\Delta} = S_1(B_1 \cdot \prod_{j=1}^{N} C_{\mathsf{out},j}^{d_1} \cdot B_2^{-d_2})^x, \tag{4}$$

$$\prod_{k=1}^{N} U_k^{z_{\mathsf{sk},k} d_0^{k-1}} = S_3 \cdot u^{x \sum_{k=1}^{N} d_0^{k-1}}. \tag{5}$$

Security Analysis. The security proofs of the following theorems are given in the full version of the paper [22].

Theorem 1 (Balance). *Our scheme is unforgeable if the DL assumption holds in $\mathbb{G}$ in the random oracle model (ROM). Our scheme is equivalent w.r.t. insider corruption if the DL assumption holds in $\mathbb{G}$ in the ROM and RP is a secure zero-knowledge range proof. Our scheme is linkable w.r.t. insider corruption if the DL assumption holds in $\mathbb{G}$ in the ROM.*

Theorem 2 (Anonymity). *Our scheme is anonymous against recipients if the q-DDHI assumption holds in $\mathbb{G}$ in the ROM, where q is the number of Spend oracle query. Our scheme is anonymous against ring insiders if the q-DDHI assumption holds in $\mathbb{G}$ in the ROM and RP is a secure zero-knowledge range proof.*

Theorem 3 (Non-slander). *Our scheme is non-slanderable w.r.t. insider corruption if the DL assumption holds in $\mathbb{G}$ in the random oracle model.*

5.2 Our Efficient Construction

The last step towards our final construction is to use the improved inner product argument in [4] to compress the $O(n)$-size vector $\vec{l}, \vec{r}$ in the ring signature part to a $O(\log n)$-size proof. Denote **IPProve**, **IPVerify** as the inner product argument. Details of the algorithm can be found in [4]. We give the modified **Spend'** and **Verify'** algorithms as follows.

- **Spend'**. On input $(\mathtt{m}, \mathbb{K}_S, \mathbb{A}_S, \mathbb{A}_{in}, \mathbb{O})$, it runs $(\mathbb{A}_{out}, \pi = (\pi_{\mathsf{range}}, \sigma_{\mathsf{ring}}), \mathbb{S}, \mathbb{C}k_{out})$
  $\leftarrow$ **Spend**$(\mathtt{m}, \mathbb{K}_S, \mathbb{A}_S, \mathbb{A}_{in}, \mathbb{O})$). For each $\sigma_{\mathsf{ring}} = (B_1, B_2, A, S_1, S_2, S_3, T_1, T_2, \tau_x, \mu, z_{\alpha_1}, z_{\alpha_2}, z_{\mathsf{sk},1}, \ldots, z_{\mathsf{sk},M}, z_\Delta, \vec{l}, \vec{r}, t)$, it computes $P = \vec{Y}^{\vec{l}} \vec{h}'^{\vec{r}}$, where $\vec{Y}$ and $\vec{h}'$ are defined in **Spend**. it runs $(\vec{L}, \vec{R}, a, b) \leftarrow$ **IPProve**$(\vec{Y}, \vec{h}', t, P, \vec{l}, \vec{r})$.

Note that $\vec{L}, \vec{R}$ are vectors of $\mathbb{G}$ with size $\log n$. It sets $\sigma'_{\text{ring}} = (B_1, B_2, A, S_1, S_2, S_3, T_1, T_2, \tau_x, \mu, z_{\alpha_1}, z_{\alpha_2}, z_{\text{sk},1}, \ldots, z_{\text{sk},M}, z_\Delta, t, P, \vec{L}, \vec{R}, a, b)$. The algorithm outputs $(\mathbb{A}_{\text{out}}, \pi = (\pi_{\text{range}}, \sigma'_{\text{ring}}), \mathbb{S}, \mathbb{C}k_{\text{out}})$.

- **Verify'.** On input $(\mathbb{m}, \mathbb{A}_{\text{in}}, \mathbb{A}_{\text{out}}, \pi = (\pi_{\text{range}}, \sigma'_{\text{ring}}), \mathbb{S})$, denote $\sigma'_{\text{ring}} = (B_1, B_2, A, S_1, S_2, S_3, T_1, T_2, \tau_x, \mu, z_{\alpha_1}, z_{\alpha_2}, z_{\text{sk},1}, \ldots, z_{\text{sk},M}, z_\Delta, t, P, \vec{L}, \vec{R}, a, b)$. It runs $0/1 \leftarrow \textbf{IPVerify}(\vec{Y}, \vec{h}', t, P, (\vec{L}, \vec{R}, a, b))$, where $\vec{Y}$ and $\vec{h}'$ are defined in **Verify**. It outputs 0 if **IPVerify** outputs 0. Otherwise, it runs as the **Verify** algorithm, except that equation (3) is modified to:

$$h^\mu P = B_1 \cdot A^w \cdot S_2^x \cdot \vec{Y}^{-z \cdot \vec{1}^{nM}} \cdot \vec{h}'^{wz \cdot \vec{y}^{nM} + \sum_{k=1}^M z^{1+k} \cdot (\vec{0}^{(k-1)n} || \vec{1}^n || \vec{0}^{(M-k)n})}.$$

The security of our final construction follows from the security of the improved inner product argument in [4], which is based on the DL assumption in the random oracle model.

6 Efficiency Analysis

Proof Size of RingCT. RingCT3.0 has size of $O(M + \log n)$ excluding the key images and committed outputs, where n is the size of the ring and M is the number of transaction input. As shown in Fig. 1a, RingCT3.0 is significantly shorter than Monero's RingCT1.0 even for small ring size (ring size ≥ 16) and hence RingCT3.0 can reduce the transaction fee by more than 90%. Since the proof size increases logarithmically, the sender can increase the anonymity level by increasing the ring size without increasing the cost drastically. Increasing the ring size of 1000 only increases the transaction fee by 45%.

Consider a typical transaction (i.e., number of inputs $M = 2$) with a ring size of 1024, our ring signature size (1.3 kB) is 98.6% less than the ring signature size of [15] (98 kB). For the ring size of 1024, the cost of the ring signature part for RingCT1.0 is already about USD 20, which is not practical. On the other hand, the cost of the ring signature part for RingCT3.0 is only about USD 0.27.

Running Time of RingCT. We implemented the RingCT3.0 in Ubuntu 16.04, Intel Core i5-6200U 2.3GHz, 8GB RAM. We used the BouncyCastle's Java library for Curve 25519 in our implementation. Each element in $\mathbb{G}$ is represented by 33 bytes and each element in $\mathbb{Z}_p$ is represented by 32 bytes.

We compare the running time of the Spend protocol of RingCT3.0 in Fig. 2a and RingCT1.0 in Fig. 2c. Our RingCT3.0 outperforms RingCT1.0 when the ring size exceeds 64. Our RingCT3.0 is better for larger ring size and more user input. When the ring size is 1024 and the input size is 20, RingCT3.0 is about 2 times faster than RingCT1.0.

We compare the running time of the Verify protocol of RingCT3.0 in Fig. 2b and RingCT1.0 in Fig. 2d. Our RingCT3.0 outperforms RingCT1.0 when the ring size exceeds 32. When the ring size reaches 1024 and the input size is 20, RingCT3.0 is more than 2 times faster than RingCT1.0.

In general, the running time of RingCT3.0 is comparatively shorter than the time of generating a block of transactions, which is 2 min in Monero and 10 min

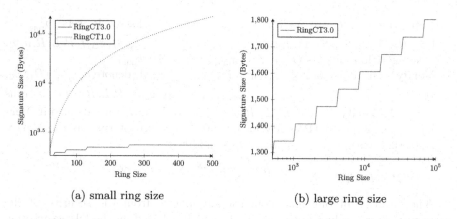

(a) small ring size   (b) large ring size

Fig. 1. Comparison of RingCT and RingCT3.0 for a transaction with 2 inputs.

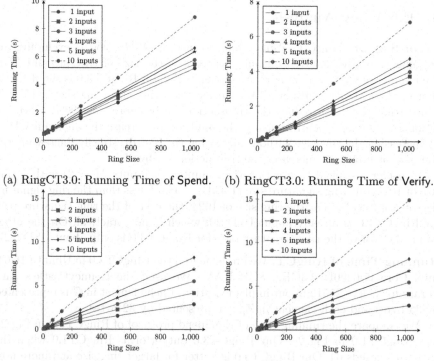

(a) RingCT3.0: Running Time of Spend.   (b) RingCT3.0: Running Time of Verify.

(c) RingCT1.0: Running Time of Spend.   (d) RingCT1.0: Running Time of Verify.

Fig. 2. Performance of RingCT3.0 and RingCT1.0.

in Bitcoin. Therefore, RingCT3.0 will not be the bottleneck of the blockchain system.

7 Comparison with Omniring

Recently, a parallel and independent work on RingCT, called *Omniring*, is proposed [10]. They also used the inner product argument as a building block. However, they used a different ring formation, especially for the case of multiple input. Even for M inputs, the total ring size is still n (rather than the total ring size of nM in our RingCT3.0). The signature size of Omniring is $2\log(3+2n+4M)+9$ $\mathbb{G}$ or $\mathbb{Z}_p$ elements. Our scheme is $2\log(nM)+M+17$ $\mathbb{G}$ or $\mathbb{Z}_p$ elements. In practice n is much larger than M (e.g., $n \geq 1024$ and $M < 5$).

Another major difference between our paper and [10] is the modeling on privacy. They use a single model on privacy to capture the indistinguishability of all possible combinations of transaction input. We use two different models to capture the anonymity against ring insiders and recipients. We illustrate the differences with a simple example. Consider the Omniring [10] with a transaction of two inputs, one output and ring size 8:

Input 1	Input 2	Input 3	Input 4	Input 5	Input 6	Input 7	Input 8	→	Output
$2	$8	$3	$7	$4	$6	$12	$13		$10

Since their anonymity model allows the adversary to know the account balance for all parties, their security proof guarantees that no PPT adversary can distinguish between the case of "Input 1 and 2 are real signers", "Input 3 and 4 are real signers" and "Input 5 and 6 are real signers". The level of anonymity is only limited to the number of possible combinations of transaction input, which is 1/3 in this case. In practice, a signer does not know the transaction amount of other UTXOs in RingCT. The chances of having many possible combinations of transaction input is relatively low, if the signer forms the ring by randomly picking UTXOs in the blockchain. It is possible that there is only 1 legitimate combination. In this case, the honest signer has no security guarantees according to the anonymity model in [10].

On the other hand, our RingCT 3.0 have a structure as follows:

	Input 1	Input 2	Input 3	Input 4	Input 5	Input 6	Input 7	Input 8	→	Output
Ring 1	$2	$8	$3	$7	$4	$6	$12	$13		$10
Ring 2	$7	$11	$6	$12	$4	$7	$5	$2		

Our anonymity against ring insiders shows that the real signer in ring 1 (resp. ring 2) is hidden between input 1 to 8 of ring 1 (resp. ring 2), since the output amount is hidden from the adversary. Our anonymity against recipients shows that the real signer in ring 1 (resp. ring 2) is also hidden between input 1 to 8 of ring 1 (resp. ring 2), since the input amount are hidden from the adversary. The level of anonymity is 1/8 in both cases.

8 Conclusion

We propose the RingCT3.0 protocol, which is more efficient and more secure than the existing RingCT1.0 used in Monero. For a typical 2-input transaction with a ring size of 1024, the ring signature size of our RingCT3.0 protocol is 98% less than the ring signature size of the RingCT1.0 protocol.

A   Set Membership Proof without Trusted Setup

We first review the definition of set membership proof in [5] and then we give our new construction without using trusted setup.

Definition 1. [5] *Let $C = (Gen, Com, Open)$ be the generation, the commit and the open algorithm of a commitment scheme. For an instance c, a proof of set membership with respect to commitment scheme C and set Φ is a proof of knowledge for the following statement:*

$$PK\{(\mu, \rho) : c \leftarrow Com(\mu; \rho) \wedge \mu \in \Phi\}.$$

The security model for set membership proof follows the standard definitions of zero-knowledge proof: perfect completeness, computational soundness and perfect zero-knowledge.

In this section, we consider the following modified set membership proof for a set Φ of base group elements :

$$PK\{(\mu, \rho) : c = g^\mu h^\rho \wedge g^\mu \in \Phi\}.$$

A.1   Our Basic Construction

Our construction is essentially a set membership proof for group elements which is the domain of public keys. It is the first set membership proof for public keys in the base group, instead of in the exponent. The intuition of our scheme is introduced in the previous section. Our construction is as follows.

- **Setup.** On input security parameter 1^λ and the maximum size of the set of membership public key N, it picks a group $\mathbb{G}$ of prime order p and some generators $g \in \mathbb{G}, \vec{h} = (h_1, \ldots, h_N) \in \mathbb{G}^N$. Suppose that $H_j : \{0,1\}^* \to \mathbb{Z}_p$ for $j = 1, 2, 3, 4$, $H_6 : \{0,1\}^* \to \mathbb{G}$ are collision resistant hash functions. Let $C = (Gen, Com, Open)$ be the Pedersen commitment scheme. Assume these parameters are known in the system.
- **PKGen.** It randomly picks $x \in \mathbb{Z}_p$ and outputs a public key $Y = g^x$.
- **Prove.** On input the set of $n \le N$ public keys as $\vec{Y} = (Y_1, Y_2, \ldots, Y_n)$ and denote the set member $\sigma = Y_{i^*} \in \vec{Y}$, with corresponding secret key x_{sk,i^*}. The prover runs as follows.
  1. *Prepare Index.* The prover generates a binary vector $\vec{b_L} = (b_1, \ldots, b_n)$, where $b_i = 1$ when $i = i^*$ and $b_i = 0$ otherwise. Define $\vec{b_R} = \vec{b_L} - \vec{1^n}$. It proves in zero knowledge that $\vec{b_L}$ is a binary vector with only one bit equal to 1. It is equivalent to showing:

  $$\vec{b_L} \circ \vec{b_R} = \vec{0^n}, \quad \vec{b_L} - \vec{b_R} = \vec{1^n}, \quad \langle \vec{b_L}, \vec{1^n} \rangle = 1.$$

  2. *Commit 1.* It computes $h = H_6(\vec{Y})$. It picks random $\alpha, \beta, \rho, r_\alpha, r_{sk} \in \mathbb{Z}_p$, $\vec{s_L}, \vec{s_R} \in \mathbb{Z}_p^n$ and computes:

  $$A_1 = h^\alpha \vec{Y}^{\vec{b_L}} = h^\alpha Y_{i^*}, \quad A_2 = h^\beta \vec{h}^{\vec{b_R}}, \quad S_1 = h^{r_\alpha} g^{r_{sk}}, \quad S_2 = h^\rho \vec{Y}^{\vec{s_L}} \vec{h}^{\vec{s_R}}.$$

Note that A_1 is the Pedersen commitment of the secret key of Y_{i*} for randomness α.

3. *Challenge 1.* Denote the concatenated string $\mathsf{str} = \vec{Y}||A_1||A_2||\ S_1||S_2$. It computes $y = H_2(\mathsf{str})$, $z = H_3(\mathsf{str})$ and $w = H_4(\mathsf{str})$.

4. *Commit 2.* It can construct two degree 1 polynomials of variable X:

$$l(X) = \vec{b_L} - z \cdot \vec{1}^n + \vec{s_L} \cdot X,$$
$$r(X) = \vec{y}^n \circ (w \cdot \vec{b_R} + wz \cdot \vec{1}^n + \vec{s_R} \cdot X) + z^2 \cdot \vec{1}^n.$$

Denote $t(X) = \langle l(X), r(X) \rangle$, which is a degree 2 polynomial. We can write $t(X) = t_0 + t_1 X + t_2 X^2$, and t_0, t_1, t_2 can be computed by using $(\vec{b_L}, \vec{b_R}, \vec{s_L}, \vec{s_R}, w, y, z)$. In particular, observe that

$$t_0 = w \langle \vec{b_L}, \vec{b_R} \circ \vec{y}^n \rangle + zw \langle \vec{b_L} - \vec{b_R}, \vec{y}^n \rangle$$
$$+ z^2 \langle \vec{b_L}, \vec{1}^n \rangle - wz^2 \langle \vec{1}^n, \vec{y}^n \rangle - z^3 \langle \vec{1}^n, \vec{1}^n \rangle,$$
$$= z^2 + w(z - z^2)\langle \vec{1}^n, \vec{y}^n \rangle - z^3 \langle \vec{1}^n, \vec{1}^n \rangle.$$

It picks random $\tau_1, \tau_2 \in \mathbb{Z}_p$, and computes:

$$T_1 = g^{t_1} h^{\tau_1}, \quad T_2 = g^{t_2} h^{\tau_2}.$$

5. *Challenge 2.* It computes $x = H_1(w, y, z, T_1, T_2)$.

6. *Response.* It computes:

$$\tau_x = \tau_1 \cdot x + \tau_2 \cdot x^2,$$
$$\mu = \alpha + \beta \cdot w + \rho \cdot x,$$
$$z_\alpha = r_\alpha + \alpha \cdot x,$$
$$z_{sk} = r_{sk} + x_{sk,i*} \cdot x,$$
$$\vec{l} = l(x) = \vec{b_L} - z \cdot \vec{1}^n + \vec{s_L} \cdot x,$$
$$\vec{r} = r(x) = \vec{y}^n \circ (w \cdot \vec{b_R} + wz \cdot \vec{1}^n + \vec{s_R} \cdot x) + z^2 \cdot \vec{1}^n,$$
$$t = \langle \vec{l}, \vec{r} \rangle.$$

It outputs A_1 and $\sigma = (A_2, S_1, S_2, T_1, T_2, \tau_x, \mu, z_\alpha, z_{sk}, \vec{l}, \vec{r}, t)$.

- **Verify.** On input a set of public keys $\vec{Y}$, A_1 and the proof $\sigma = (A_2, S_1, S_2, T_1, T_2, \tau_x, \mu, z_\alpha, z_{sk}, \vec{l}, \vec{r}, t)$, denote the concatenated string $\mathsf{str} = \vec{Y}||A_1||A_2||S_1||S_2$. It computes $h = H_6(\vec{Y})$, $y = H_2(\mathsf{str})$, $z = H_3(\mathsf{str})$, $w = H_4(\mathsf{str})$ and $x = H_1(w, y, z, T_1, T_2)$. Define $\vec{h'} = (h'_1, \ldots, h'_n) \in \mathbb{G}^n$ such that $h'_i = h_i^{y^{-i+1}}$ for $i \in [1, n]$. It checks if all of the following hold:

$$t = \langle \vec{l}, \vec{r} \rangle, \tag{6}$$

$$g^t h^{\tau_x} = g^{z^2 + w(z - z^2)\langle \vec{1}^n, \vec{y}^n \rangle - z^3 \langle \vec{1}^n, \vec{1}^n \rangle} \cdot T_1^x \cdot T_2^{x^2}, \tag{7}$$

$$h^\mu \vec{Y}^{\vec{l}} \vec{h'}^{\vec{r}} = A_1 \cdot A_2^w \cdot S_2^x \cdot \vec{Y}^{-z \cdot \vec{1}^n} \cdot \vec{h'}^{wz \cdot \vec{y}^n + z^2 \cdot \vec{1}^n}, \tag{8}$$

$$h^{z_\alpha} g^{z_{sk}} = S_1 A_1^x. \tag{9}$$

Theorem 4. *The set membership proof is secure if the discrete logarithm assumption holds in $\mathbb{G}$ in the random oracle model.*

The proof is given in the full version of the paper [22].

A.2   Set Membership Proof with Logarithm Size

Our scheme in the last section is linear size of n for the part of $\vec{l}$ and $\vec{r}$. Observe that the verifier can compute $A_1 \cdot A_2^w \cdot S_2^x \cdot \vec{Y}^{-z \cdot \vec{1}^n} \cdot \vec{h'}^{wz \cdot \vec{y}^n + z^2 \cdot \vec{1}^n}$. We note that verifying both equations (6) and (8) is equivalent to verifying the witness $\vec{l}$ and $\vec{r}$ satisfying the inner-product relation. Therefore, it can be fitted into the improved inner-product argument framework from [4] to give a zero knowledge proof π of $\vec{l}, \vec{r}$ such that:

$$P = \vec{Y'}^{\vec{l}} \vec{h'}^{\vec{r}} \quad \wedge \quad t = \langle \vec{l}, \vec{r} \rangle.$$

The size of π is $2 \cdot \lceil \log_2(n) \rceil$ elements in $\mathbb{G}$ and 2 elements in $\mathbb{Z}_p$. The signer's work is dominated by $\log n + 1$ multi-exponentiations in $\mathbb{G}$ of size $2n, n, n/2, \ldots, 1$ respectively. The verifier's work is dominated by a single multi-exponentiations in $\mathbb{G}$ of size $2n + 2 \log_2 n + 1$.

To sum up, the set membership proof output is $\sigma = (A_1, A_2, S_1, S_2, T_1, T_2, \tau_x, \mu, z_\alpha, z_{sk}, t, \pi)$, which has size $2 \cdot \lceil \log_2(n) \rceil + 6$ elements in $\mathbb{G}$ and 7 elements in $\mathbb{Z}_p$. The signer's work is dominated by three multi-exponentiations in $\mathbb{G}$ of size $2n + 1$, $2n$ and $n + 1$ respectively. The verifier's work is dominated by two multi-exponentiations in $\mathbb{G}$ of size $2n + 2 \log_2 n + 1$ and $n + 4$ respectively.

References

1. Ben-Sasson, E., et al.: Zerocash: decentralized anonymous payments from bitcoin. In: IEEE SP 2014, pp. 459–474. IEEE Computer Society (2014)
2. Bootle, J., Cerulli, A., Chaidos, P., Ghadafi, E., Groth, J., Petit, C.: Short accountable ring signatures based on DDH. In: Pernul, G., Ryan, P.Y.A., Weippl, E. (eds.) ESORICS 2015. LNCS, vol. 9326, pp. 243–265. Springer, Cham (2015). https://doi.org/10.1007/978-3-319-24174-6_13
3. Bootle, J., Groth, J.: Efficient batch zero-knowledge arguments for low degree polynomials. In: Abdalla, M., Dahab, R. (eds.) PKC 2018. LNCS, vol. 10770, pp. 561–588. Springer, Cham (2018). https://doi.org/10.1007/978-3-319-76581-5_19
4. Bünz, B., Bootle, J., Boneh, D., Poelstra, A., Wuille, P., Maxwell, G.: Bulletproofs: short proofs for confidential transactions and more. In: IEEE S&P 2018, pp. 315–334. IEEE (2018)
5. Camenisch, J., Chaabouni, R., Shelat, A.: Efficient protocols for set membership and range proofs. In: Pieprzyk, J. (ed.) ASIACRYPT 2008. LNCS, vol. 5350, pp. 234–252. Springer, Heidelberg (2008). https://doi.org/10.1007/978-3-540-89255-7_15
6. Esgin, M.F., Zhao, R.K., Steinfeld, R., Liu, J.K., Liu, D.: Matrict: efficient, scalable and post-quantum blockchain confidential transactions protocol. In: Cavallaro, L., Kinder, J., Wang, X., Katz, J. (eds.) CCS 2019, pp. 567–584. ACM (2019)

7. Foley, S.N., Gollmann, D., Snekkenes, E. (eds.): ESORICS 2017, LNCS, vol.10493. Springer (2017)

8. Groth, J., Kohlweiss, M.: One-out-of-many proofs: or how to leak a secret and spend a coin. In: Oswald, E., Fischlin, M. (eds.) EUROCRYPT 2015. LNCS, vol. 9057, pp. 253–280. Springer, Heidelberg (2015). https://doi.org/10.1007/978-3-662-46803-6_9

9. Kumar, A., Fischer, C., Tople, S., Saxena, P.: A traceability analysis of monero's blockchain. In: Foley, S., et al. [7], pp. 153–173. https://doi.org/10.1007/978-3-319-66399-9_9

10. Lai, R.W.F., Ronge, V., Ruffing, T., Schröder, D., Thyagarajan, S.A.K., Wang, J.: Omniring: scaling private payments without trusted setup. In: Cavallaro, L., Kinder, J., Wang, X., Katz, J. (eds.) CCS 2019, pp. 31–48. ACM (2019)

11. Liu, J.K., Wei, V.K., Wong, D.S.: Linkable spontaneous anonymous group signature for Ad Hoc groups. In: Wang, H., Pieprzyk, J., Varadharajan, V. (eds.) ACISP 2004. LNCS, vol. 3108, pp. 325–335. Springer, Heidelberg (2004). https://doi.org/10.1007/978-3-540-27800-9_28. (extended abstract)

12. Maxwell, G.: Confidential transactions (2015). https://people.xiph.org/~greg/confidential_values.txt

13. Meiklejohn, S., Mercer, R.: Möbius: trustless tumbling for transaction privacy. PoPETs 2018(2), 105–121 (2018)

14. Möser, M., et al.: An empirical analysis of traceability in the monero blockchain. PoPETs 2018(3), 143–163 (2018)

15. Noether, S.: Ring Signature Confidential Transactions for Monero. Cryptology ePrint Archive, Report 2015/1098 (2015). http://eprint.iacr.org/

16. Park, S., Sealfon, A.: It wasn't me! - repudiability and claimability of ring signatures. In: Boldyreva, A., Micciancio, D. (eds.) CRYPTO 2019. LNCS, vol. 11694, pp. 159–190. Springer, Cham (2019). https://doi.org/10.1007/978-3-030-26954-8_6

17. Rivest, R.L., Shamir, A., Tauman, Y.: How to leak a secret. In: Boyd, C. (ed.) ASIACRYPT 2001. LNCS, vol. 2248, pp. 552–565. Springer, Heidelberg (2001). https://doi.org/10.1007/3-540-45682-1_32

18. Sun, S., Au, M.H., Liu, J.K., Yuen, T.H.: RingCT 2.0: a compact accumulator-based (linkable ring signature) protocol for blockchain cryptocurrency monero. In: Foley, S.N. et al. [7], pp. 456–474

19. Torres, W.A.A., Kuchta, V., Steinfeld, R., Sakzad, A., Liu, J.K., Cheng, J.: Lattice RingCT V2.0 with multiple input and multiple output wallets. In: Jang-Jaccard, J., Guo, F. (eds.) ACISP 2019. LNCS, vol. 11547, pp. 156–175. Springer, Cham (2019). https://doi.org/10.1007/978-3-030-21548-4_9

20. Torres, W.A.A., et al.: Post-quantum one-time linkable ring signature and application to ring confidential transactions in blockchain (Lattice RingCT v1.0). In: Susilo, W., Yang, G. (eds.) ACISP 2018. LNCS, vol. 10946, pp. 558–576. Springer, Cham (2018). https://doi.org/10.1007/978-3-319-93638-3_32

21. Wijaya, D.A., Liu, J.K., Steinfeld, R., Liu, D.: Monero ring attack: recreating zero mixin transaction effect. In: IEEE TrustCom, pp. 1196–1201. IEEE (2018)

22. Yuen, T.H., et al.: Ringct 3.0 for blockchain confidential transaction: Shorter size and stronger security. Cryptology ePrint Archive, Report 2019/508 (2019). https://eprint.iacr.org/2019/508

BLAZE: Practical Lattice-Based Blind Signatures for Privacy-Preserving Applications

Nabil Alkeilani Alkadri[1]([✉]), Rachid El Bansarkhani[2],
and Johannes Buchmann[1]

[1] Technische Universität Darmstadt, Darmstadt, Germany
nabil.alkadri@tu-darmstadt.de, buchmann@cdc.informatik.tu-darmstadt.de
[2] QuantiCor Security GmbH, Darmstadt, Germany
rachid.elbansarkhani@quanticor-security.de

Abstract. Blind signatures constitute basic cryptographic ingredients for privacy-preserving applications such as anonymous credentials, e-voting, and Bitcoin. Despite the great variety of cryptographic applications blind signatures also found their way in real-world scenarios. Due to the expected progress in cryptanalysis using quantum computers, it remains an important research question to find practical and secure alternatives to current systems based on the hardness of classical security assumptions such as factoring and computing discrete logarithms. In this work we present BLAZE: a new practical blind signature scheme from lattice assumptions. With respect to all relevant efficiency metrics BLAZE is more efficient than all previous blind signature schemes based on assumptions conjectured to withstand quantum computer attacks. For instance, at approximately 128 bits of security signatures are as small as 6.6 KB, which represents an improvement factor of 2.7 compared to all previous candidates, and an expansion factor of 2.5 compared to the NIST PQC submission Dilithium. Our software implementation demonstrates the efficiency of BLAZE to be deployed in practical applications. In particular, generating a blind signature takes just 18 ms. The running time of both key generation and verification is in the same order as state-of-the-art ordinary signature schemes.

Keywords: Blind signatures · Lattices · Post-quantum · Privacy

1 Introduction

Blind signature schemes allow users while interacting with a signer to generate signatures on messages such that the signer gets no information about the message being signed (*blindness*). The user in turn is not able to produce any valid signature without interacting with the signer (*one-more unforgeability*). Blind signatures were proposed by Chaum [12] and have become fundamental building blocks in privacy-oriented cryptography. One of the main applications of blind

© International Financial Cryptography Association 2020
J. Bonneau and N. Heninger (Eds.): FC 2020, LNCS 12059, pp. 484–502, 2020.
https://doi.org/10.1007/978-3-030-51280-4_26

signatures is anonymous credentials [6], which allow users to privately obtain and prove possession of credentials while revealing as little about themselves as possible. This complies with the European privacy standards [32,33] and the National Strategy for Trusted Identities in Cyberspace [16]. An established real-life use case of blind signatures in anonymous credentials is the U-Prove technology [31] designed by Microsoft. U-Prove is one of the technologies, to which the Microsoft's Open Specification Promise [30] applies and is integrated for example by Gemalto - a leading digital security company - in its smart card technology in order to enhance privacy [21]. Another application of blind signatures is e-voting [25], where authorities can blindly sign public keys used by voters to anonymously cast their votes. Further applications of blind signatures include e-cash systems utilizing the Bitcoin blockchain [22], where entities blindly sign digital coins withdrawn by users for selling and buying products and services over the Internet and open networks.

Currently, the real-world applications mentioned above rely on classical blind signature schemes, where the security is based on the hardness of number-theoretic assumptions such as factoring large integers and computing discrete logarithms. For instance, the U-Prove protocol implemented by Gemalto employs blind signature constructions, which are secure as long as computing discrete logarithms is hard [31]. As it is meanwhile known, number-theoretic assumptions are not secure for the long-term, especially when taking into account the developments of quantum computers. Consequently, these constructions have to be replaced with blind signature schemes that are comparable in terms of efficiency and are secure or at least conjectured to be secure under quantum computer attacks. More concretely, we need post-quantum candidates of blind signature schemes in order to further preserve privacy standards and anonymity considerations. While such proposals do exist [9,34,36], they cannot be deployed in practical applications due to their poor performance as well as large keys and signatures (see Table 1).

Our Contributions. In this work we present a new and practical lattice-based blind signature scheme that we call BLAZE. It provides statistical blindness and strong one-more unforgeability in the random oracle model (ROM) assuming the hardness of the ring short integer solution (RSIS) problem. We provide a software implementation of BLAZE attesting its practicality and propose parameters targeting approximately 128 bits of security. Our implementation and parameters show that BLAZE is more efficient than the previous blind signature schemes [9,34,36] based on assumptions believed to withstand quantum computer attacks. More precisely, at approximately the same security level BLAZE achieves significant improvement factors with respect to all efficiency metrics including key generation, signing, verification, and sizes of keys and signatures (see Table 1). The parameters used in our implementation are in the order of current state-of-the-art ordinary signature schemes such as the recent lattice-based NIST submission Dilithium [17]. For instance, a blind signature produced by BLAZE occupies only 6.6 KB of memory, which is larger by a factor of 2.5 compared to Dilithium. Furthermore, the fact that BLAZE is *strongly* one-more unforgeable (i.e., the same message may be signed arbitrary many times, which

Table 1. Comparison of the existing blind signature schemes that are conjectured to be secure under quantum computer attacks. The table contents are adopted from Sect. 4, [36, Table 3], [34, Table 1,2], and [9, Table 1]. We note that only the size of public keys and signatures are given in [9]. Sizes are given in kilo bytes (KB), timings in milliseconds (ms) and cycles (in parentheses). Benchmarking our parameters were carried out on an Intel Core i7-6500U, operating at 2.3 GHz and 8GB of RAM. The timings given in [36] were obtained on an AMD Opteron CPU, running at 2.3 GHz, while those given in [34] were obtained on a 3.3 GHz Intel Quadcore.

Scheme	Bit security	Sizes			Performance		
		Secret key	Public key	Signature	Key generation	Signing	Verification
BLAZE (this work)	113	0.8	3.9	6.6	0.1 (204, 671)	17.8 (35, 547, 397)	0.1 (276, 210)
[36]	102	23.6	23.6	89.4	52	283	57
[34]	102	36.6	54.6	17.6	9392	3662	2656
[9]	100	-	15	200	-	-	-

is an important feature for schemes deployed in practice), allows us to prove BLAZE in the new security model *honest-user unforgeability* recently proposed by Schröder and Unruh [37, Lemma 10]. It has been shown to be more convenient for blind signature schemes as it removes certain types of attacks not captured in the traditional security model of blind signatures due to Pointcheval and Stern [35].

Our Techniques. In order to give an overview of our techniques, it is instructive to sketch the signing protocol of the blind signature scheme introduced by Rückert [36] at ASIACRYPT 2010 (RBS), since it is also lattice-based. RBS is one-more unforgeable in the ROM assuming the hardness of RSIS. Its complete description can be found in the full version of this paper [4]. A signature generated by RBS has the form $(\mathbf{r}, \hat{c}, \hat{\mathbf{z}})$, where $\mathbf{r}$ is a bit string, $\hat{c}$ is output by a random oracle H, and $\hat{\mathbf{z}}$ is a vector of polynomials with bounded coefficients. The signing protocol works as follows: Upon receiving a "commitment" from the signer $\mathcal{S}$, the user $\mathcal{U}$ computes and blinds $\hat{c}$. This is accomplished by computing $\hat{c}^* = \hat{c} - \hat{u}$ for some random secret element $\hat{u}$ and applying rejection sampling on $\hat{c}^*$ to make sure that it masks $\hat{c}$. If this is not the case, $\mathcal{U}$ selects a new $\hat{u}$ and repeats until success and then proceeds by sending $\hat{c}^*$ to $\mathcal{S}$. Subsequently, $\mathcal{S}$ responds with a vector $\hat{\mathbf{z}}^*$ only after carrying out rejection sampling on this vector and making sure that it does not leak information about the secret key, otherwise $\mathcal{S}$ restarts the protocol. Then, $\mathcal{U}$ transforms this response into the vector $\hat{\mathbf{z}}$. Here, $\mathcal{U}$ applies rejection sampling in order to further maintain blindness. More precisely, the vector $\hat{\mathbf{z}}^*$ must be concealed within $\hat{\mathbf{z}} = \hat{\mathbf{z}}^* - \hat{\mathbf{v}}$, where $\hat{\mathbf{v}}$ is a uniform random masking vector chosen by $\mathcal{U}$. Finally, $\mathcal{U}$ sends a signal to $\mathcal{S}$. This signal is either an ok message or it includes a proof of failure, which allows $\mathcal{S}$ to verify that no valid signature has been obtained by $\mathcal{U}$ in case the last rejection sampling step has been failed and it further indicates that a protocol restart is required. In addition, the protocol employs statistically hiding and computationally binding commitments to ensure blindness and one-more unforgeability over restarts. In other words, $\mathcal{U}$ signs a commitment to the message, using a randomness $\mathbf{r}$, instead of the message itself and reveals its opening along with the signature.

The goal of our new design in BLAZE is to improve all relevant sizes and running times as well as security. Our observation is that removing the first rejection sampling procedure carried out by $\mathcal{U}$ constitutes the main measure towards achieving this goal. This is established in BLAZE via a new kind of *partitioning and permutation* technique, which may be of independent interest. It works as follows: Rather than subtracting the masking term $\hat{u}$ from $\hat{c}$, we use signed rotation polynomials for masking. The resulting elements still lie in the range of H and are randomized by rotation. Here, it is crucial for H to output elements with exactly κ entries from $\{\pm 1\}$ and $n - \kappa$ entries equal to zero, where n is the number of entries. A random element with entries in other sets may still leak information even after rotation. More formally, let $R = \mathbb{Z}[x]/\langle x^n + 1 \rangle$ and $\hat{p}_j \in R$ (for $j = 1, \ldots, \kappa$) be signed rotation polynomials, i.e., they have the form $\pm x^i$ for some $i \in \mathbb{Z}$. We split the output $\hat{c}$ of H into κ signed rotation polynomials $\hat{c}_1, \ldots, \hat{c}_\kappa$. These polynomials have each a coefficient from $\{\pm 1\}$ and degree at most $n - 1$. Then, we "permute" each part $\hat{c}_j$ using one of the secret polynomials $\hat{p}_j^{-1}$. The resulting elements $\hat{c}_j^*$ will then be signed by $\mathcal{S}$ to $\hat{z}^*$. In order for the final signature (output by $\mathcal{U}$) to be successfully verified, we must account for the partitioning and rotation. That is, multiplying the entries of $\hat{z}^*$ each with $\hat{p}_j$ and summing them up with secret masking terms yields the signature part $\hat{z}$. This technique does not only remove one rejection sampling step, it also ensures shorter signatures and speeds up the remaining two rejection sampling procedures. This is because the norm bound of $\hat{z}^*$ and consequently $\hat{z}$ becomes significantly smaller. In RBS, the element $\hat{c}^*$ has entries bounded by $n - 1$ and hence, the masking term used to compute $\hat{z}^*$ must be large enough to hide the secret term. Consequently, the same must apply to the masking term used to compute $\hat{z}$ and hide $\hat{z}^*$. In BLAZE, however, smaller masking terms can be used to compute $\hat{z}^*$ and $\hat{z}$, since each $\hat{c}_j^*$ has the norm 1, for $j = 1, \ldots, \kappa$. We note that κ is much smaller than n and selected such that H provides enough security.

In case the last rejection sampling procedure fails, we take a similar approach to RBS and design a proof of failure allowing $\mathcal{U}$ to convince $\mathcal{S}$ that no valid signature has been obtained and hence letting $\mathcal{S}$ restart the protocol. This proof includes all secret elements generated by $\mathcal{U}$ during signing. In order to still ensure statistical blindness, $\mathcal{U}$ signs a commitment τ to the message rather than the message itself and includes its opening in the final signature. The binding property of τ preserves the strong one-more unforgeability.

Related Work. In addition to RBS, there are other lattice-based constructions of blind signatures found in literature. However, we show in the full version of this paper [4] that they are insecure. More precisely, we show for the proposal in [40] how the secret key can simply be recovered already after two executions of its signing protocol. For the remaining schemes [13,19,20,38,39] we show that any user is able to solve the underlying lattice problem in just one execution of the signing protocol. Concerning lattice-based constructions, this leaves us with the scheme RBS. Other post-quantum blind signature schemes that we are aware of is the multivariate-based one from [34] and the code-based one proposed in [9].

Table 1 shows that BLAZE is more efficient than those schemes in terms of all efficiency metrics.

Outline. In Sect. 2 we give the background required throughout this work. Then, we present in Sect. 3 our new blind signature scheme BLAZE. Afterwards, we propose in Sect. 4 concrete parameters and compare BLAZE with the schemes [9, 34,36]. Finally, we give a conclusion and discuss possible future directions in Sect. 5.

2   Preliminaries

Notation. We let $\mathbb{N}, \mathbb{Z}, \mathbb{R}$ denote the set of natural numbers, integers, and real numbers, respectively. For a positive integer k, we let $[k]$ denote the set $\{1, 2, \ldots, k\}$. We denote column vectors with bold lower-case letters and matrices with bold upper-case letters. For any positive integer q, we write $\mathbb{Z}_q$ to denote the set of integers in the range $[-\frac{q}{2}, \frac{q}{2}) \cap \mathbb{Z}$. The Euclidean norm ($\ell_2$-norm) of a vector $\mathbf{v}$ with entries v_i is defined as $\|\mathbf{v}\| = (\sum_i |v_i|^2)^{1/2}$, and its ℓ_∞-norm as $\|\mathbf{v}\|_\infty = \max_i |v_i|$. We define the ring $R = \mathbb{Z}[x]/\langle x^n + 1 \rangle$ and its quotient $R_q = R/qR$, where n is power of 2. A ring element $a_0 + a_1 x + \ldots + a_{n-1}x^{n-1} \in R_q$ is denoted by $\hat{a}$ and it corresponds to a vector $\mathbf{a} \in \mathbb{Z}_q^n$ via coefficient embedding. Hence, $\|\hat{a}\| = \|\mathbf{a}\|$ and $\|\hat{a}\|_\infty = \|\mathbf{a}\|_\infty$. We write $\hat{\mathbf{a}} = (\hat{a}_1, \ldots, \hat{a}_k) \in R_q^k$ to denote a vector of ring elements. The norms of $\hat{\mathbf{a}}$ are defined by $\|\hat{\mathbf{a}}\| = (\sum_{i=1}^k \|\hat{a}_i\|^2)^{1/2}$ and $\|\hat{\mathbf{a}}\|_\infty = \max_i \|\hat{a}_i\|_\infty$. We let $\mathbb{T}_\kappa^n$ denote the set of all $(n-1)$-degree polynomials with coefficients from $\{-1, 0, 1\}$ and Hamming Weight κ. All logarithms in this work are to base 2, and we always denote the security parameter by $\lambda \in \mathbb{N}$. A function $f : \mathbb{N} \to \mathbb{R}$ is called *negligible* if there exists an $n_0 \in \mathbb{N}$ such that for all $n > n_0$, it holds $f(n) < \frac{1}{p(n)}$ for any polynomial p. With $\mathrm{negl}(\lambda)$ we denote a negligible function in λ. A probability is called overwhelming if it is at least $1 - \mathrm{negl}(\lambda)$. The *statistical distance* between two distributions X, Y over a countable domain D is defined by $\frac{1}{2}\sum_n |X(n) - Y(n)|$. We write $x \leftarrow D$ to denote that x is sampled according to a distribution D. By $x \leftarrow_\$ S$ we denote that x is assigned a uniform random element from a finite set S. For two algorithms $\mathcal{A}, \mathcal{B}$ we write $(x, y) \leftarrow \langle \mathcal{A}(a), \mathcal{B}(b) \rangle$ to describe the joint execution of $\mathcal{A}$ and $\mathcal{B}$ in an interactive protocol with private inputs a for $\mathcal{A}$ and b for $\mathcal{B}$ as well as private outputs x for $\mathcal{A}$ and y for $\mathcal{B}$. Accordingly, we write $\mathcal{A}^{\langle \cdot, \mathcal{B}(b) \rangle^k}(a)$ if $\mathcal{A}$ can invoke up to k executions of the protocol with $\mathcal{B}$.

2.1   Blind Signatures and Their Security

Definition 1 (Blind Signature Scheme). *A blind signature scheme BS is a tuple of polynomial-time algorithms BS=(BS.KGen,BS.Sign,BS.Verify) such that:*

- *BS.KGen(1^λ) is a key generation algorithm that outputs a pair of keys (pk,sk), where pk is a public key and sk is a secret key.*
- *BS.Sign(sk, pk, μ) is an interactive protocol between a signer $\mathcal{S}$ and a user $\mathcal{U}$. The input of $\mathcal{S}$ is a secret key sk, whereas the input of $\mathcal{U}$ is a public key pk*

Game $\mathsf{Blind}_{\mathsf{BS},\mathcal{S}^*}(\lambda)$	Game $\mathsf{Forge}_{\mathsf{BS},\mathcal{U}^*}(\lambda)$
1: $(\mathsf{pk}, \mu_0, \mu_1, \mathsf{st}_{\mathsf{fin}}) \leftarrow \mathcal{S}^*(\mathsf{fin}, 1^\lambda)$	1: $(\mathsf{pk}, \mathsf{sk}) \leftarrow \mathsf{BS.KGen}(1^\lambda)$
2: $b \leftarrow_\$ \{0,1\}$	2: $\mathsf{H} \leftarrow \mathcal{H}(1^\lambda)$
3: $\mathsf{st}_{\mathsf{iss}} \leftarrow \mathcal{S}^{*\langle \cdot, \mathcal{U}(\mathsf{pk},\mu_b)\rangle^1, \langle \cdot, \mathcal{U}(\mathsf{pk},\mu_{1-b})\rangle^1}(\mathsf{iss}, \mathsf{st}_{\mathsf{fin}})$	3: $((\mu_1, \sigma_1), \cdots, (\mu_l, \sigma_l)) \leftarrow \mathcal{U}^{*\mathsf{H}(\cdot), \langle \mathcal{S}(\mathsf{sk}), \cdot\rangle^\infty}(\mathsf{pk})$
4: $\sigma_b := \mathcal{U}(\mathsf{pk}, \mu_b), \sigma_{1-b} := \mathcal{U}(\mathsf{pk}, \mu_{1-b})$	4: $k := \#$ successful signing invocations
5: if $(\sigma_0 = \bot \lor \sigma_1 = \bot)$ then	5: if $\Big(\mu_i \neq \mu_j$ for all $1 \leq i < j \leq l \land$
6: $(\bot, \bot) \leftarrow (\sigma_0, \sigma_1)$	$\quad$ $\mathsf{BS.Verify}(\mathsf{pk}, \mu_i, \sigma_i) = 1, \forall i \in [l] \land$
7: $b^* \leftarrow \mathcal{S}^*(\mathsf{gue}, \sigma_0, \sigma_1, \mathsf{st}_{\mathsf{iss}})$	$\quad$ $k + 1 = l\Big)$ then
8: if $b^* = b$ then	6: return 1
9: return 1	7: return 0
10: return 0	

Fig. 1. Security games of blindness and one-more unforgeability. In the blindness game the modes find, issue, guess are shortened to fin, iss, gue, respectively.

and a message $\mu \in \mathcal{M}$, where $\mathcal{M}$ is the message space. The output of $\mathcal{S}$ is a view $\mathcal{V}$ (interpreted as a random variable) and the output of $\mathcal{U}$ is a signature σ, i.e., $(\mathcal{V}, \sigma) \leftarrow \langle \mathcal{S}(\mathsf{sk}), \mathcal{U}(\mathsf{pk}, \mu)\rangle$. We write $\sigma = \bot$ to denote failure.

- $\mathsf{BS.Verify}(\mathsf{pk}, \mu, \sigma)$ is a verification algorithm that outputs 1 if the signature σ is valid and 0 otherwise.

Blind signature schemes require the completeness property, i.e., $\mathsf{BS.Verify}$ always (or with overwhelming probability) validates honestly signed messages under honestly created keys. Security of blind signatures is captured by two security notions: blindness and one-more unforgeability [23,35].

Definition 2 (Blindness). A blind signature scheme BS is called (t, ε)-blind if for any adversarial signer $\mathcal{S}^*$ running in time at most t and working in modes find, issue, and guess, the game $\mathsf{Blind}_{\mathsf{BS},\mathcal{S}^*}(\lambda)$ depicted in Fig. 1 outputs 1 with probability $\Pr[\mathsf{Blind}_{\mathsf{BS},\mathcal{S}^*}(\lambda) = 1] \leq \frac{1}{2} + \varepsilon$, i.e., the advantage of $\mathcal{S}^*$ in the game is given by $\varepsilon = \mathrm{Adv}_{\mathsf{BS},\mathcal{S}^*}(\lambda) = \big|\Pr[b^* = b] - \frac{1}{2}\big|$. The scheme is statistically blind if it is $(t = \infty, \varepsilon = \mathrm{negl}(\lambda))$-blind.

Definition 3 (One-more Unforgeability). Let $\mathcal{H}$ be a family of random oracles. A blind signature scheme BS is called $(t, q_{\mathsf{Sign}}, q_{\mathsf{H}}, \varepsilon)$-one-more unforgeable in the random oracle model if for any adversarial user $\mathcal{U}^*$ running in time at most t and making at most $q_{\mathsf{Sign}}, q_{\mathsf{H}}$ signing and hash queries, the game $\mathsf{Forge}_{\mathsf{BS},\mathcal{U}^*}(\lambda)$ depicted in Fig. 1 outputs 1 with probability $\Pr[\mathsf{Forge}_{\mathsf{BS},\mathcal{U}^*}(\lambda) = 1] \leq \varepsilon$. The scheme is strongly $(t, q_{\mathsf{Sign}}, q_{\mathsf{H}}, \varepsilon)$-one-more unforgeable if the condition $\mu_i \neq \mu_j$ in the game changes to $(\mu_i, \sigma_i) \neq (\mu_j, \sigma_j)$ for all $1 \leq i < j \leq l$.

2.2 Lattices and Gaussians

Let $\mathbf{B} = \{\mathbf{b}_1, \ldots, \mathbf{b}_k\} \in \mathbb{R}^{m \times k}$ be a set of linearly independent vectors, where $k \leq m$. The m-dimensional lattice $\mathcal{L}$ of rank k generated by $\mathbf{B}$ is given by $\mathcal{L}(\mathbf{B}) = \{\mathbf{B}\mathbf{x} \mid \mathbf{x} \in \mathbb{Z}^k\} \subset \mathbb{R}^m$. If $m = k$, then $\mathcal{L}$ is full-rank. The determinant of $\mathcal{L}$, denoted by $\det(\mathcal{L})$, is given by $\sqrt{\det(\mathbf{B}^\top \cdot \mathbf{B})}$, where $\mathbf{B}$ is any basis of $\mathcal{L}$. The discrete Gaussian distribution $D_{\mathcal{L}, \sigma, \mathbf{c}}$ over a lattice $\mathcal{L}$ with standard deviation $\sigma > 0$ and center $\mathbf{c} \in \mathbb{R}^n$ is defined as follows: The probability of any $\mathbf{x} \in \mathcal{L}$ is given by $D_{\mathcal{L},\sigma,\mathbf{c}}(\mathbf{x}) = \rho_{\sigma,\mathbf{c}}(\mathbf{x})/\rho_{\sigma,\mathbf{c}}(\mathcal{L})$, where $\rho_{\sigma,\mathbf{c}}(\mathbf{x}) = \exp(\frac{-\|\mathbf{x}-\mathbf{c}\|^2}{2\sigma^2})$ and $\rho_{\sigma,\mathbf{c}}(\mathcal{L}) = \sum_{\mathbf{x}\in\mathcal{L}} \rho_{\sigma,\mathbf{c}}(\mathbf{x})$. The subscript $\mathbf{c}$ is taken to be $\mathbf{0}$ when omitted. Sampling from $D_{\mathcal{L},\sigma}$ using a specified randomness ρ is denoted by $D_{\mathcal{L},\sigma}(\rho)$. The following two lemmas are used throughout this work.

Lemma 1 ([27, **Lemma 4.4**]). *For any $t, \eta > 0$ we have*

1. $\Pr_{x \leftarrow D_{\mathbb{Z},\sigma}}[|x| > t \cdot \sigma] \leq 2\exp(-t^2/2)$.
2. $\Pr_{\mathbf{x} \leftarrow D_{\mathbb{Z}^m,\sigma}}[\|\mathbf{x}\| > \eta\sigma\sqrt{m}] \leq \eta^m \exp(\frac{m}{2}(1 - \eta^2))$.

Lemma 2 ([27, **Theorem 4.6, Lemma 4.7**]). *Let $V \subseteq \mathbb{Z}^m$ with elements having norms bounded by T, $\sigma = \omega(T\sqrt{\log m})$, and $h : V \to \mathbb{R}$ be a probability distribution. Then there exists a constant $M = O(1)$ such that $\forall \mathbf{v} \in V$: $\Pr[D_{\mathbb{Z}^m,\sigma}(\mathbf{z}) \leq M \cdot D_{\mathbb{Z}^m,\sigma,\mathbf{v}}(\mathbf{z}); \ \mathbf{z} \leftarrow D_{\mathbb{Z}^m,\sigma}] \geq 1 - \varepsilon$, where $\varepsilon = 2^{-\omega(\log m)}$. Furthermore, the following two algorithms are within statistical distance $\delta = \varepsilon/M$.*

1. $\mathbf{v} \leftarrow h$, $\mathbf{z} \leftarrow D_{\mathbb{Z}^m,\sigma,\mathbf{v}}$, *output* $(\mathbf{z}, \mathbf{v})$ *with probability* $\frac{D_{\mathbb{Z}^m,\sigma}(\mathbf{z})}{M \cdot D_{\mathbb{Z}^m,\sigma,\mathbf{v}}(\mathbf{z})}$.
2. $\mathbf{v} \leftarrow h$, $\mathbf{z} \leftarrow D_{\mathbb{Z}^m,\sigma}$, *output* $(\mathbf{z}, \mathbf{v})$ *with probability* $1/M$.

Moreover, the probability that the first algorithm outputs something is at least $(1-\varepsilon)/M$. If $\sigma = \alpha T$ for any positive α, then $M = \exp(\frac{12}{\alpha} + \frac{1}{2\alpha^2})$ with $\varepsilon = 2^{-100}$.

We let $\mathsf{RejSamp}(x)$ denote an algorithm that carries out rejection sampling on input x. It outputs 1 if it accepts and 0 otherwise. We write $\mathsf{RejSamp}(x; r)$ to specify the randomness r used within the algorithm. In the following we define the related lattice problem.

Definition 4 (Ring Short Integer Solution (RSIS) Problem). *Let n, q, m be positive integers and β a positive real. Given a vector $\hat{\mathbf{a}} = (\hat{a}_1, \ldots, \hat{a}_m)$ chosen uniformly random from R_q^m, the Hermite Normal Form of the RSIS problem asks to find a non-zero vector $\hat{\mathbf{x}} = (\hat{\mathbf{x}}', \hat{x}_{m+1}) = (\hat{x}_1, \ldots, \hat{x}_m, \hat{x}_{m+1}) \in R^{m+1}$ such that $\|\hat{\mathbf{x}}\| \leq \beta$ and $[\hat{\mathbf{a}} \ 1] \cdot \hat{\mathbf{x}} = \hat{\mathbf{a}}\hat{\mathbf{x}}' + \hat{x}_{m+1} = \sum_{i=1}^m \hat{a}_i \hat{x}_i + \hat{x}_{m+1} = 0 \pmod{q}$.*

Any instance I of RSIS is called (t, ε)-hard if any algorithm $\mathcal{A}$ running in time at most t can solve I with probability ε.

3   BLAZE: The New Blind Signature Scheme

In this section we present BLAZE: our new and practical blind signature scheme. It is statistically blind and strongly one-more unforgeable in the ROM. As opposed to RBS, BLAZE has to pass 2 rejection sampling procedures rather than 3; one is performed by the signer to conceal the secret key and one by the user to achieve blindness. That is, we remove one rejection sampling step from the user side by splitting the output of the random oracle generated by the user into monomials with entries from $\{-1, 1\}$ and permuting them using secret monomials with entries from $\{-1, 1\}$ as well.

We first introduce new tools and technical lemmas employed within BLAZE. The proofs are provided in the full version of this paper [4].

Definition 5. *Define by* $\hat{\mathbb{T}} = \{(-1)^s \cdot x^i \mid \text{for } s \in \mathbb{N} \text{ and } i \in \mathbb{Z}\}$ *the set of signed permutation polynomials which represent a rotation multiplied by a sign.*

Lemma 3. *Let* $\hat{p} \in \hat{\mathbb{T}}$ *with* $\hat{p} = (-1)^s \cdot x^i$ *for some* $i \in \mathbb{Z}$ *and* $s \in \{0,1\}$*. Then,* $\hat{\mathbb{T}}$ *is a group with respect to multiplication in* R *and the inverse of* $\hat{p}$ *is given by* $\hat{p}^{-1} = (-1)^{1-s} \cdot x^{n-i} \in \hat{\mathbb{T}}$.

Lemma 4. *Let* $\hat{c} \in \mathbb{T}^n_\kappa$ *and* $\hat{c}_1, \ldots, \hat{c}_\kappa$ *be a partition of* $\hat{c}$ *such that* $\hat{c} = \sum_{j=1}^\kappa \hat{c}_j$ *and each* $\hat{c}_j$ *contains exactly the* j^{th} *non-zero entry of* $\hat{c}$ *at exactly the same position. Furthermore, let* $\hat{c}_j^* = \hat{p}_j^{-1}\hat{c}_j$ *for random signed rotations* $\hat{p}_1, \ldots, \hat{p}_\kappa \in \hat{\mathbb{T}}$*. Then,* $\hat{c}_j^*, \hat{c}_j \in \hat{\mathbb{T}}$ *and we have*

$$\Pr_{\hat{p}_j \leftarrow_s \hat{\mathbb{T}}}[(\hat{c}_1^*, \ldots, \hat{c}_\kappa^*) = (\hat{p}_1^{-1}\hat{c}_1, \ldots, \hat{p}_\kappa^{-1}\hat{c}_\kappa) \mid \hat{c}] = \qquad (1a)$$

$$\Pr_{\hat{p}_j \leftarrow_s \hat{\mathbb{T}}, \hat{c} \leftarrow_s \mathbb{T}^n_\kappa}[(\hat{c}_1^*, \ldots, \hat{c}_\kappa^*) = (\hat{p}_1^{-1}\hat{c}_1, \ldots, \hat{p}_\kappa^{-1}\hat{c}_\kappa)] = (2n)^{-\kappa} \qquad (1b)$$

In the following we give a detailed description of our new blind signature scheme BLAZE. We let Expand be a public random function on λ-bit strings (e.g., a pseudorandom number generator). It takes a uniform random seed from $\{0,1\}^\lambda$ as input and expands it to any desired length. This function is solely used for saving bandwidth as it is deterministic, i.e., given some input it always generates the same output. We let $H : \{0,1\}^* \to \mathbb{T}^n_\kappa$ be a public hash function modeled as a random oracle. We further let Com $: \{0,1\}^* \times \{0,1\}^\lambda \to \{0,1\}^\lambda$ be a statistically hiding and computationally binding commitment function. Finally, we let Compress and Decompress be functions for (de)compressing Gaussian elements (see the full version [4] for description). The respective algorithms of BLAZE are formally described in Fig. 2.

Key Generation. Given 1^λ the algorithm chooses a uniform random seed from $\{0,1\}^\lambda$ and expands it to a vector $\hat{\mathbf{a}} \in R_q^m$ using Expand. The secret key is given by sk $= (\hat{\mathbf{s}}_1, \hat{s}_2)$, which is sampled from $D^m_{\mathbb{Z}^n, \sigma} \times D_{\mathbb{Z}^n, \sigma}$. The public key is set to pk $= (\text{seed}, \hat{b} = \hat{\mathbf{a}}\hat{\mathbf{s}}_1 + \hat{s}_2 \pmod{q})$.

Signing. Given sk, seed, and a message μ the signer $\mathcal{S}$ samples the masking terms $(\hat{\mathbf{y}}_{j,1}^*, \hat{y}_{j,2}^*)$ from $D^m_{\mathbb{Z}^n, s^*} \times D_{\mathbb{Z}^n, s^*}$ for $j \in [\kappa]$ and sends the polynomials $\hat{y}_j = \hat{\mathbf{a}}\hat{\mathbf{y}}_{j,1}^* + \hat{y}_{j,2}^* \pmod{q}$ to the user $\mathcal{U}$.

Upon receiving $\hat{y}_1, \ldots, \hat{y}_\kappa$, $\mathcal{U}$ computes $\tau = \text{Com}(\mu; \mathbf{r})$, $\tau' = \text{Com}(\rho'; \mathbf{r}')$, where $\mathbf{r}, \mathbf{r}', \rho'$ are selected uniformly random from $\{0,1\}^\lambda$. Then, it expands seed to the vector $\hat{\mathbf{a}}$ using the function Expand and selects uniformly random elements $\hat{p}_1, \ldots, \hat{p}_\kappa \in \hat{\mathbb{T}}$. Furthermore, $\mathcal{U}$ samples a pair $(\hat{\mathbf{e}}_1, \hat{e}_2)$ from $D^m_{\mathbb{Z}^n, s} \times D_{\mathbb{Z}^n, s}$ using a randomness $\rho \in \{0,1\}^\lambda$, which is used to reduce the communication complexity, i.e., a proof of failure sent by $\mathcal{U}$ (see below) includes only ρ rather than the pair $(\hat{\mathbf{e}}_1, \hat{e}_2)$. Then, $\mathcal{U}$ generates $\hat{c} = H(\hat{\mathbf{a}}\hat{\mathbf{e}}_1 + \hat{e}_2 + \sum_{j=1}^\kappa \hat{p}_j\hat{y}_j \pmod{q}, \tau', \tau) \in \mathbb{T}^n_\kappa$. Subsequently, $\mathcal{U}$ splits $\hat{c}$ into partitions $\hat{c}_1, \ldots, \hat{c}_\kappa \in \hat{\mathbb{T}}$ such that $\hat{c} = \sum_{j=1}^\kappa \hat{c}_j$ and the jth partition $\hat{c}_j$ contains the jth non-zero entry of $\hat{c}$ at exactly the same

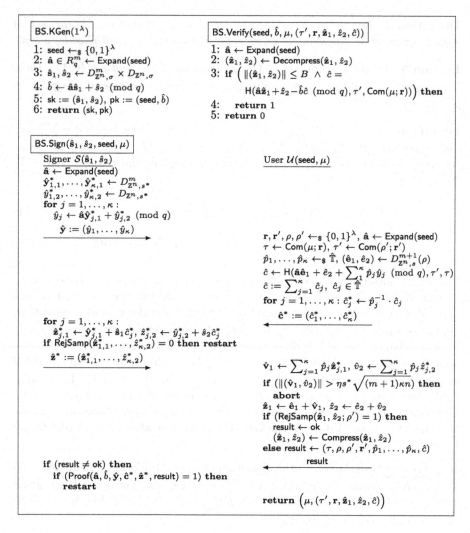

Fig. 2. A formal description of the new blind signature scheme BLAZE.

position. Afterwards, $\mathcal{U}$ masks each partition $\hat{c}_j$ by computing $\hat{c}_j^* = \hat{p}_j^{-1} \cdot \hat{c}_j$ for all $j \in [\kappa]$. Then, $\mathcal{U}$ sends $\hat{c}_1^*, \ldots, \hat{c}_\kappa^*$ to $\mathcal{S}$.

Using the partitions $\hat{c}_j^*$, $\mathcal{S}$ computes $\hat{\mathbf{z}}_{j,1}^* = \hat{\mathbf{y}}_{j,1}^* + \hat{s}_1 \hat{c}_j^*$ and $\hat{z}_{j,2}^* = \hat{y}_{j,2}^* + \hat{s}_2 \hat{c}_j^*$. Subsequently, $\mathcal{S}$ applies rejection sampling on $(\hat{\mathbf{z}}_{j,1}^*, \hat{z}_{j,2}^*)$ to make sure that they do not leak information about sk. If RejSamp outputs 1, $\mathcal{S}$ sends $(\hat{\mathbf{z}}_{j,1}^*, \hat{z}_{j,2}^*)$ to $\mathcal{U}$, otherwise $\mathcal{S}$ restarts the protocol.

Upon receiving $(\hat{\mathbf{z}}_{j,1}^*, \hat{z}_{j,2}^*)$, $\mathcal{U}$ computes $\hat{\mathbf{v}}_1 = \sum_{j=1}^{\kappa} \hat{p}_j \hat{\mathbf{z}}_{j,1}^*$, $\hat{v}_2 = \sum_{j=1}^{\kappa} \hat{p}_j \hat{z}_{j,2}^*$ and checks that $\|(\hat{\mathbf{v}}_1, \hat{v}_2)\|$ is bounded by $\eta s^* \sqrt{(m+1)\kappa n}$. This check rules out malicious signers and ensures that the generated signatures are valid and blind. This check can be skipped in applications with trustworthy signers. In order for

---

Proof($\hat{\mathbf{a}}, \hat{b}, \hat{\mathbf{y}}, \hat{\mathbf{c}}^*, \hat{\mathbf{z}}^*,$ result)

1: $\hat{\mathbf{y}} := (\hat{y}_1, \ldots, \hat{y}_\kappa)$, $\hat{\mathbf{c}}^* := (\hat{c}_1^*, \ldots, \hat{c}_\kappa^*)$, $\hat{\mathbf{z}}^* := (\hat{\mathbf{z}}_{1,1}^*, \ldots, \hat{\mathbf{z}}_{\kappa,1}^*, \hat{z}_{1,2}^*, \ldots, \hat{z}_{\kappa,2}^*)$

2: result $:= (\tau, \rho, \rho', \mathbf{r}', \hat{p}_1, \ldots, \hat{p}_\kappa, \hat{c})$

3: $\tau' \leftarrow \mathsf{Com}(\rho'; \mathbf{r}')$, $(\hat{\mathbf{e}}_1, \hat{e}_2) \leftarrow D_{\mathbb{Z}^n,s}^{m+1}(\rho)$

4: $\hat{\mathbf{z}}_1 \leftarrow \hat{\mathbf{e}}_1 + \sum_{j=1}^\kappa \hat{p}_j \hat{\mathbf{z}}_{j,1}^*$, $\hat{z}_2 \leftarrow \hat{e}_2 + \sum_{j=1}^\kappa \hat{p}_j \hat{z}_{j,2}^*$

5: **if** $\Big(\sum_{j=1}^\kappa \hat{p}_j \hat{c}_j^* = \hat{c} = \mathsf{H}(\hat{\mathbf{a}}\hat{\mathbf{e}}_1 + \hat{e}_2 + \sum_{j=1}^\kappa \hat{p}_j \hat{y}_j \pmod{q}, \tau', \tau) \wedge$

   $\hat{c} = \mathsf{H}(\hat{\mathbf{a}}\hat{\mathbf{z}}_1 + \hat{z}_2 - \hat{b}\hat{c} \pmod{q}, \tau', \tau) \wedge \mathsf{RejSamp}(\hat{\mathbf{z}}_1, \hat{z}_2; \rho') = 0 \Big)$ **then**

6:   **return 1**

7: **return 0**

Fig. 3. The algorithm carried out by the signer in order to verify the proof of failure (see Fig. 2).

the verification to succeed, the pair $(\hat{\mathbf{z}}_1, \hat{z}_2)$ that will be output by $\mathcal{U}$ must be brought into the form $\hat{\mathbf{z}}_1 = \hat{\mathbf{y}}_1^* + \hat{\mathbf{s}}_1 \hat{c}, \hat{z}_2 = \hat{y}_2^* + \hat{s}_2 \hat{c}$, for some $\hat{\mathbf{y}}_1^*, \hat{y}_2^*$. This is attained by multiplying $\hat{\mathbf{z}}_{j,1}^*, \hat{z}_{j,2}^*$ with $\hat{p}_j$, summing them up together with the masking terms $\hat{\mathbf{e}}_1, \hat{e}_2$, and applying $\mathsf{RejSamp}(\hat{\mathbf{z}}_1, \hat{z}_2; \rho')$ to ensure that $\hat{\mathbf{z}}_{j,1}^*, \hat{z}_{j,2}^*$ are concealed. Thus, $\mathcal{U}$ must already have taken this into account via the input to H. In fact, we must have $\hat{\mathbf{a}}\hat{\mathbf{y}}_1^* + \hat{y}_2^* = \hat{\mathbf{a}}\hat{\mathbf{e}}_1 + \hat{e}_2 + \sum_{j=1}^\kappa \hat{p}_j \hat{y}_j \pmod{q}$. Therefore, $\mathcal{U}$ sets $\hat{\mathbf{z}}_1 = \hat{\mathbf{e}}_1 + \sum_{j=1}^\kappa \hat{p}_j \hat{\mathbf{z}}_{j,1}^*$ and $\hat{z}_2 = \hat{e}_2 + \sum_{j=1}^\kappa \hat{p}_j \hat{z}_{j,2}^*$. Finally, $\mathcal{U}$ compresses $(\hat{\mathbf{z}}_1, \hat{z}_2)$ using the function $\mathsf{Compress}$ and sends result $= \mathsf{ok}$ to $\mathcal{S}$. The signature is given by $(\tau', \mathbf{r}, \hat{\mathbf{z}}_1, \hat{z}_2, \hat{c})$. If $\mathsf{RejSamp}$ outputs 0, $\mathcal{U}$ sends $\mathcal{S}$ a proof of failure by setting result $= (\tau, \rho, \rho', \mathbf{r}', \hat{p}_1, \ldots, \hat{p}_\kappa, \hat{c})$. In this case $\mathcal{S}$ verifies that $\mathcal{U}$ has indeed not obtained a valid signature (see Fig. 3), and restarts the protocol.

Note that in order to verify that the rejection sampling process applied on $(\hat{\mathbf{z}}_1, \hat{z}_2)$ does not accept using some randomness, $\mathcal{S}$ requires the randomness ρ' used by $\mathcal{U}$ for which $\mathsf{RejSamp}(\hat{\mathbf{z}}_1, \hat{z}_2; \rho') = 0$. Therefore, ρ' must be part of the proof of failure. However, it cannot be part of the signature, since it may leak information about the secret terms involved in computing $\hat{\mathbf{z}}_1, \hat{z}_2$. This is why $\mathcal{U}$ computes a commitment τ' to ρ' and involves τ' in the computation of $\hat{c}$ in order to preserve security, hence τ' is included in the signature to allow verification.

Verification. On input (seed, $\hat{b}, \mu, (\tau', \mathbf{r}, \hat{\mathbf{z}}_1, \hat{z}_2, \hat{c})$) the verifier uses Expand to compute $\hat{\mathbf{a}}$ out of seed, decompresses $(\hat{\mathbf{z}}_1, \hat{z}_2)$ using $\mathsf{Decompress}$. It accepts if and only if $\|(\hat{\mathbf{z}}_1, \hat{z}_2)\|$ is smaller than some predefined bound B and the output of H on $(\hat{\mathbf{a}}\hat{\mathbf{z}}_1 + \hat{z}_2 - \hat{b}\hat{c} \pmod{q}, \tau', \mathsf{Com}(\mu; \mathbf{r}))$ is equal to $\hat{c}$.

The following states the completeness, blindness, and strong one-more unforgeability of BLAZE.

Theorem 1 (Completeness). *Let Com be a statistically hiding and computationally binding commitment function. Let $\alpha^*, \alpha, \eta > 0$, $s^* = \alpha^* \sqrt{\kappa} \cdot \|(\hat{\mathbf{s}}_1, \hat{s}_2)\|$, $s = \eta \alpha \sqrt{(m+1)\kappa n} s^*$, and $B = \eta s \sqrt{(m+1)n}$. After at most $M = M_\mathcal{S} \cdot M_\mathcal{U}$ repetitions, any blind signature produced by BLAZE is validated with probability at least $1 - 2^{-\lambda}$, where $M_\mathcal{S} = \exp(\frac{12}{\alpha^*} + \frac{1}{2\alpha^{*2}})$ and $M_\mathcal{U} = \exp(\frac{12}{\alpha} + \frac{1}{2\alpha^2})$ are the expected number of repetitions by the signer and user, respectively.*

Proof. For an honestly generated signature $(\tau', \mathbf{r}, \hat{\mathbf{z}}_1, \hat{z}_2, \hat{c})$, the pair $(\hat{\mathbf{z}}_1, \hat{z}_2)$ is distributed according to $D_{\mathbb{Z}^n, s}^{m+1}$ and bounded by $\eta s \sqrt{(m+1)n} = B$ with probability $1 - \eta^{(m+1)n} \exp(\frac{(m+1)n}{2}(1 - \eta^2))$ (see Lemma 1). By a suitable choice of η we obtain $\|(\hat{\mathbf{z}}_1, \hat{z}_2)\| \leq B$ with probability $1 - 2^{-\lambda}$.

The condition $\mathsf{H}(\hat{\mathbf{a}}\hat{\mathbf{z}}_1 + \hat{z}_2 - \hat{b}\hat{c} \pmod q), \tau', \tau) = \hat{c}$ is satisfied due to the correctness of Com and the following:

$$\hat{\mathbf{a}}\hat{\mathbf{z}}_1 + \hat{z}_2 - \hat{b}\hat{c} = \hat{\mathbf{a}}\Big(\hat{\mathbf{e}}_1 + \sum_{j=1}^{\kappa} \hat{p}_j \hat{\mathbf{z}}_{j,1}^*\Big) + \Big(\hat{e}_2 + \sum_{j=1}^{\kappa} \hat{p}_j \hat{z}_{j,2}^*\Big) - \hat{b}\hat{c}$$

$$= \hat{\mathbf{a}}\Big(\hat{\mathbf{e}}_1 + \sum_{j=1}^{\kappa}(\hat{\mathbf{s}}_1 \hat{c}_j + \hat{p}_j \hat{\mathbf{y}}_{j,1}^*)\Big) + \hat{e}_2 + \sum_{j=1}^{\kappa}(\hat{s}_2 \hat{c}_j + \hat{p}_j \hat{y}_{j,2}^*) - \hat{b}\hat{c}$$

$$= \hat{\mathbf{a}}\hat{\mathbf{e}}_1 + \hat{e}_2 + \sum_{j=1}^{\kappa} \hat{p}_j \left(\hat{\mathbf{a}}\hat{\mathbf{y}}_{j,1}^* + \hat{y}_{j,2}^*\right) + (\hat{\mathbf{a}}\hat{\mathbf{s}}_1 + \hat{s}_2)\,\hat{c} - \hat{b}\hat{c}$$

$$= \hat{\mathbf{a}}\hat{\mathbf{e}}_1 + \hat{e}_2 + \sum_{j=1}^{\kappa} \hat{p}_j \hat{y}_j \pmod q$$

By Lemma 2, the rejection sampling procedure carried out by the signer accepts with probability

$$D_{\mathbb{Z}^{(m+1)\kappa n}, s^*}(\mathbf{z}^*)/(M_{\mathcal{S}} \cdot D_{\mathbb{Z}^{(m+1)\kappa n}, s^*, \mathbf{v}^*}(\mathbf{z}^*)),$$

where $\mathbf{z}^*, \mathbf{v}^*$ are the vector representations of

$$(\hat{z}_{1,1}^*, \ldots, \hat{z}_{\kappa,2}^*), \ (\hat{s}_1 \hat{c}_1^*, \ldots, \hat{s}_1 \hat{c}_\kappa^*, \hat{s}_2 \hat{c}_1^*, \ldots, \hat{s}_2 \hat{c}_\kappa^*)$$

and the expected number of repetitions is given by $M_{\mathcal{S}} = \exp(\frac{12}{\alpha^*} + \frac{1}{2\alpha^{*2}})$ for $s^* = \alpha^* \|\mathbf{v}^*\| = \alpha^* \sqrt{\kappa} \|(\hat{s}_1, \hat{s}_2)\|$.

The rejection sampling step performed by $\mathcal{U}$ accepts with probability

$$D_{\mathbb{Z}^{(m+1)n}, s}(\mathbf{z})/(M_{\mathcal{U}} \cdot D_{\mathbb{Z}^{(m+1)n}, s, \mathbf{v}}(\mathbf{z})),$$

where $\mathbf{z}, \mathbf{v}$ are the vector representations of $(\hat{\mathbf{z}}_1, \hat{z}_2)$, $(\sum_{j=1}^{\kappa} \hat{p}_j \hat{\mathbf{z}}_{j,1}^*, \sum_{j=1}^{\kappa} \hat{p}_j \hat{z}_{j,2}^*)$ and the expected number of repetitions is $M_{\mathcal{U}} = \exp(\frac{12}{\alpha} + \frac{1}{2\alpha^2})$ for $s = \alpha \|\mathbf{v}\|$. The polynomials in $\mathbf{v}$ are distributed according to $D_{\mathbb{Z}^n, \sqrt{\kappa} s^*}$ (see [10, Theorem 9]). Hence, $\|\mathbf{v}\| \leq \eta \sqrt{(m+1)\kappa n} s^*$ and $s = \eta \alpha \sqrt{(m+1)\kappa n} s^*$. Therefore, the total expected number of repetitions is $M = M_{\mathcal{S}} \cdot M_{\mathcal{U}}$.

Finally, we note that when choosing η as described above, the condition $\|(\hat{v}_1, \hat{v}_2)\| \leq \eta s^* \sqrt{(m+1)\kappa n}$ carried out by $\mathcal{U}$ (see Fig. 2) is satisfied with probability at least $1 - 2^{-\lambda}$. □

Theorem 2 (Blindness). *Let* Com *be a statistically hiding and computationally binding commitment function. The scheme* BLAZE *is* $(t = \infty, \varepsilon = \frac{2^{-100}}{M_{\mathcal{U}}})$-*blind.*

Proof. In the game $\mathsf{Blind}_{\mathsf{BS},\mathcal{S}^*}(\lambda)$ given in Definition 2 the adversarial signer $\mathcal{S}^*$ selects two messages μ_0, μ_1 and interacts with the user $\mathcal{U}$ twice, i.e., $\mathcal{U}(\mathsf{seed}, \mu_b)$ in the first run and subsequently $\mathcal{U}(\mathsf{seed}, \mu_{1-b})$ for a random bit b chosen by $\mathcal{U}$. We show that after each interaction, $\mathcal{U}$ does not leak any information about the respective message being signed. More precisely, the exchanged messages during protocol execution together with the user's output (interpreted as random variables) are independently distributed, especially also from the message being signed. This requires analyzing only the pair $(\hat{\mathbf{z}}_1, \hat{z}_2)$, since τ' is a statistically hiding commitment, $\mathbf{r}$ is uniformly random, $\hat{c} \in \mathbb{T}_\kappa^n$ and $\hat{c}_1^*, \dots, \hat{c}_\kappa^* \in \hat{\mathbb{T}}$ are uniformly random and independently distributed from $\hat{c}$ (see Lemma 4).

Let $(\hat{\mathbf{z}}_1, \hat{z}_2)_b$ and $(\hat{\mathbf{z}}_1, \hat{z}_2)_{1-b}$ be the pairs output by $\mathcal{U}(\mathsf{seed}, \mu_b)$, $\mathcal{U}(\mathsf{seed}, \mu_{1-b})$, respectively. They have the form $(\hat{\mathbf{z}}_1, \hat{z}_2) = (\hat{\mathbf{e}}_1 + \sum_{j=1}^\kappa \hat{p}_j \hat{\mathbf{z}}_{j,1}^*, \hat{e}_2 + \sum_{j=1}^\kappa \hat{p}_j \hat{z}_{j,2}^*)$, where $\hat{p}_1, \dots, \hat{p}_\kappa$ are uniform random elements from $\hat{\mathbb{T}}$, the elements $\hat{\mathbf{z}}_{1,1}^*, \dots, \hat{z}_{\kappa,2}^*$ have entries distributed as $D_{\mathbb{Z},s^*}$, and $\hat{\mathbf{e}}_1, \hat{e}_2$ have entries distributed according to $D_{\mathbb{Z},s}$. When applying rejection sampling (Lemma 2) on $(\hat{\mathbf{z}}_1, \hat{z}_2)_b, (\hat{\mathbf{z}}_1, \hat{z}_2)_{1-b}$, they completely hide $(\hat{\mathbf{z}}_{1,1}^*, \dots, \hat{z}_{\kappa,2}^*)_b, (\hat{\mathbf{z}}_{1,1}^*, \dots, \hat{z}_{\kappa,2}^*)_{1-b}$, respectively, and become independently distributed within statistical distance of $\frac{2^{-100}}{M_\mathcal{U}}$ from $D_{\mathbb{Z},s}^{(m+1)n}$.

Furthermore, if the protocol needs to be restarted, then the user generates fresh $\mathbf{r}, \mathbf{r}', \rho, \rho', \hat{p}_1, \dots, \hat{p}_\kappa$. Therefore, protocol executions are independent of each other and hence the signer does not get information about the message being signed. Moreover, the proof of failure also maintains blindness due to the statistical hiding property of Com.

Finally, we note that checking the length of $(\hat{\mathbf{v}}_1, \hat{v}_2)$ made by the user (see Fig. 2) maintains blindness by preventing a malicious signer from choosing $(\hat{\mathbf{z}}_{1,1}^*, \dots, \hat{z}_{\kappa,2}^*)$ according to some distribution that makes the protocol fail. $\qquad\square$

Remark 1. Similar to RBS, we note that BLAZE remains blind under the stronger blindness definition given in [1], i.e., even if pk is chosen maliciously by $\mathcal{S}^*$. This is because the above proof does not exploit any special features of the key. Furthermore, selective failure blindness [11] is already achieved since a commitment to the message is being signed using a statistically hiding commitment scheme [18].

Theorem 3 (Unforgeability). *Let* Com *be a statistically hiding and computationally binding commitment function.* BLAZE *is strongly* $(t_\mathcal{A}, q_{\mathsf{Sign}}, q_H, \varepsilon_\mathcal{A})$*-one-more unforgeable if* RSIS *is* $(t_\mathcal{D}, \varepsilon_\mathcal{D})$*-hard. That is, if it is hard to find* $\hat{\mathbf{x}} \neq \mathbf{0}$ *satisfying* $[\hat{\mathbf{a}}\ 1] \cdot \hat{\mathbf{x}} = 0 \pmod{q}$ *and* $\|\hat{\mathbf{x}}\| \leq 2B + s/\alpha$*, where* $t_\mathcal{D} \leq t_\mathcal{A} + q_H^{q_{\mathsf{Sign}}}(q_{\mathsf{Sign}} + q_H)$ *and* $\varepsilon_\mathcal{D} \geq \min\{\varepsilon_1, \varepsilon_2\}$*. The probabilities* $\varepsilon_1, \varepsilon_2$ *are given in the proof.*

Proof. We assume that there exists a forger $\mathcal{A}$ that wins the one-more unforgeability game given in Definition 3 with probability $\varepsilon_\mathcal{A}$. We construct a reduction algorithm $\mathcal{D}$ that solves RSIS as described in the theorem statement with probability $\varepsilon_\mathcal{D}$.

Setup. The input of $\mathcal{D}$ is a uniform random vector $\hat{\mathbf{a}} \in R_q^m$. The reduction $\mathcal{D}$ samples $(\hat{\mathbf{s}}_1, \hat{s}_2)$ from $D_{\mathbb{Z}^n,\sigma}^m \times D_{\mathbb{Z}^n,\sigma}$ and computes $\hat{b} = \hat{\mathbf{a}}\hat{\mathbf{s}}_1 + \hat{s}_2 \pmod{q}$. Then,

$\mathcal{D}$ randomly selects answers for random oracle queries $\{\hat{h}_1, \ldots, \hat{h}_{q_H}\}$, and runs the forger $\mathcal{A}$ with public key $(\hat{a}, \hat{b})$.

Random Oracle Query. The reduction $\mathcal{D}$ maintains a list L_H, which includes pairs of random oracle queries and their answers. If H was previously queried on some input, then $\mathcal{D}$ looks up its entry in L_H and returns its answer $\hat{c} \in \mathbb{T}_\kappa^n$. Otherwise, it returns the first unused $\hat{c}$ and updates the list.

Blind Signature Query. Upon receiving signature queries from the forger $\mathcal{A}$ as a user, $\mathcal{D}$ interacts as a signer with $\mathcal{A}$ according to the signing protocol (see Fig. 2).

Output. After $k \leq q_{\mathsf{Sign}}$ successful executions of the signing protocol, $\mathcal{A}$ outputs $k+1$ distinct messages and their valid signatures $(\mu_1, \mathsf{sig}_1), \ldots, (\mu_{k+1}, \mathsf{sig}_{k+1})$. Then, one of the following two cases applies:

Case 1. $\mathcal{D}$ finds two signatures of messages $\mu, \mu' \in \{\mu_1, \ldots, \mu_{k+1}\}$ with the same random oracle answer $\hat{c}$. In this case the verification algorithm yields

$$\mathsf{H}(\hat{a}\hat{z}_1 + \hat{z}_2 - \hat{b}\hat{c} \pmod{q}, \tau', \tau) = \mathsf{H}(\hat{a}\hat{z}_1' + \hat{z}_2' - \hat{b}\hat{c} \pmod{q}, \nu', \nu) .$$

This implies that $\mu = \mu'$ and $\hat{a}\hat{z}_1 + \hat{z}_2 = \hat{a}\hat{z}_1' + \hat{z}_2' \pmod{q}$ with overwhelming probability (otherwise, $\mathcal{A}$ would have found a second preimage of $\hat{c}$ or the binding property of Com does not hold). Since $\mu = \mu'$, this implies that $(\hat{z}_1, \hat{z}_2) \neq (\hat{z}_1', \hat{z}_2')$. This yields $\hat{a}(\hat{z}_1 - \hat{z}_1') + (\hat{z}_2 - \hat{z}_2') = 0 \pmod{q}$. Since the signatures are valid, we have $\|(\hat{z}_1, \hat{z}_2)\| \leq B$ and $\|(\hat{z}_1', \hat{z}_2')\| \leq B$. Hence, $\|(\hat{z}_1 - \hat{z}_1', \hat{z}_2 - \hat{z}_2')\| \leq 2B$.

Case 2. If all signatures output by $\mathcal{A}$ have distinct random oracle answers, then $\mathcal{D}$ guesses an index $i \in [k+1]$ such that $\hat{c}_i = \hat{h}_j$ for some $j \in [q_H]$. Then, it records the pair $(\mu_i, (\tau', \mathbf{r}, \hat{z}_1, \hat{z}_2, \hat{c}_i))$ and invokes $\mathcal{A}$ again with the same random tape and random oracle queries $\{\hat{h}_1, \ldots, \hat{h}_{j-1}, \hat{h}_j', \ldots, \hat{h}_{q_H}'\}$, where $\{\hat{h}_j', \ldots, \hat{h}_{q_H}'\}$ are fresh random elements. The output of $\mathcal{A}$ includes a pair $(\mu_i', (\tau'', \mathbf{r}'', \hat{z}_1', \hat{z}_2', \hat{c}_i'))$, and $\mathcal{D}$ returns $(\hat{z}_1 - \hat{z}_1' - \hat{s}_1(\hat{c}_i - \hat{c}_i'), \hat{z}_2 - \hat{z}_2' - \hat{s}_2(\hat{c}_i - \hat{c}_i'))$. The reduction $\mathcal{D}$ retries at most q_H^{k+1} times with different random tape and random oracle queries.

Analysis. First, we note that the environment of $\mathcal{A}$ is perfectly simulated by $\mathcal{D}$ and signatures are generated with the same probability as in the real execution of BS.Sign. If the first case (**Case 1.**) applies, $\mathcal{D}$ solves RSIS with norm bound $2B$. Next, we analyze the second case (**Case 2.**). In this case one of the $k + 1$ pairs output by $\mathcal{A}$ is by assumption not generated during the execution of the signing protocol. The probability of correctly guessing the index i corresponding to this pair is $1/(k+1)$, where there are q_H^{k+1} index pairs (i, j) such that $\hat{c}_i = \hat{h}_j$. Therefore, one of the q_H^{k+1} reruns of $\mathcal{A}$ yields the correct index pair (i, j). The probability that $\hat{c}_i$ was a random oracle query made by $\mathcal{A}$ is at least $1 - 1/|\mathbb{T}_\kappa^n|$. Thus, the probability that $\hat{c}_i = \hat{h}_j$ is at least $\varepsilon_\mathcal{A} - 1/|\mathbb{T}_\kappa^n|$. By the General Forking Lemma [8], the probability that $\hat{c}_i'$ is used by $\mathcal{A}$ in the forgery such that $\hat{c}_i \neq \hat{c}_i'$ and $\hat{a}\hat{z}_1 + \hat{z}_2 - \hat{b}\hat{c}_i = \hat{a}\hat{z}_1' + \hat{z}_2' - \hat{b}\hat{c}_i' \pmod{q}$ is at least

$$\varepsilon_{\mathsf{fork}} \geq \left(\varepsilon_\mathcal{A} - \frac{1}{|\mathbb{T}_\kappa^n|} \right) \cdot \left(\frac{\varepsilon_\mathcal{A} - 1/|\mathbb{T}_\kappa^n|}{q_{\mathsf{Sign}} + q_H} - \frac{1}{|\mathbb{T}_\kappa^n|} \right) .$$

Therefore, by setting $\hat{b} = \hat{a}\hat{s}_1 + \hat{s}_2 \pmod{q}$ we obtain $\hat{a}\hat{\mathbf{v}}_1 + \hat{v}_2 = 0 \pmod{q}$, where $\hat{\mathbf{v}}_1 = \hat{\mathbf{z}}_1 - \hat{\mathbf{z}}_1' - \hat{\mathbf{s}}_1(\hat{c}_i - \hat{c}_i')$ and $\hat{v}_2 = \hat{z}_2 - \hat{z}_2' - \hat{s}_2(\hat{c}_i - \hat{c}_i')$. Since $(\hat{\mathbf{s}}_1, \hat{s}_2)$ are not uniquely defining $\hat{b}$ when $(m+1)\log(d) > \log(q)$ and d is an integer bound on the coefficients of $(\hat{\mathbf{s}}_1, \hat{s}_2)$, $\mathcal{A}$ does not know which $(\hat{\mathbf{s}}_1, \hat{s}_2)$ is being used to construct $(\hat{\mathbf{v}}_1, \hat{v}_2)$. Hence, $(\hat{\mathbf{v}}_1, \hat{v}_2) \neq \mathbf{0}$ with probability at least $1/2$. Since both signatures are valid, we have $\|(\hat{\mathbf{z}}_1, \hat{z}_2)\| \leq B$ and $\|(\hat{\mathbf{z}}_1', \hat{z}_2')\| \leq B$. Moreover we have $\|(\hat{\mathbf{s}}_1, \hat{s}_2) \cdot (\hat{c}_i - \hat{c}_i')\| \leq 2\eta\sigma\sqrt{(m+1)\kappa n}$. This implies that

$$\|(\hat{\mathbf{v}}_1, \hat{v}_2)\| \leq 2(B + \eta\sigma\sqrt{(m+1)\kappa n}) < 2B + s/\alpha \ .$$

The success probability of $\mathcal{D}$ is given by $\varepsilon_1 \geq \dfrac{\varepsilon_{\text{fork}}}{2(k+1)}$, which is non-negligible if $\varepsilon_{\mathcal{A}}$ is non-negligible.

Finally, we analyze the case that users can generate a valid signature after an aborted interaction with $\mathcal{S}$. The proof of failure $\text{result} = (\tau, \rho, \rho', \mathbf{r}', \hat{p}_1, \ldots, \hat{p}_\kappa, \hat{c})$ satisfies the 3 checks carried out by $\mathcal{S}$ (see step 5 in Fig. 3). In the following we denote these checks by C1, C2, and C3, respectively. Now, assume that a user $\mathcal{U}$ obtains a valid signature $(\tau'', \mathbf{r}'', \hat{\mathbf{z}}_1', \hat{z}_2', \hat{c}')$ after an aborted interaction. If $\hat{c}' = \hat{c}$, then by C2 we obtain $\hat{a}(\hat{\mathbf{z}}_1 - \hat{\mathbf{z}}_1') + \hat{z}_2 - \hat{z}_2' = 0 \pmod{q}$. The case $(\hat{\mathbf{z}}_1, \hat{z}_2) = (\hat{\mathbf{z}}_1', \hat{z}_2')$ contradicts C3, hence w.l.o.g. $\hat{\mathbf{z}}_1 \neq \hat{\mathbf{z}}_1'$. Note that the norm of $(\hat{\mathbf{z}}_1, \hat{z}_2)$ is bounded by $B + \eta s^*\sqrt{(m+1)\kappa n} = B + s/\alpha$. Hence, $\|(\hat{\mathbf{z}}_1 - \hat{\mathbf{z}}_1', \hat{z}_2 - \hat{z}_2')\| \leq 2B + s/\alpha$. If $\hat{c}' \neq \hat{c}$, then by C1 we must have $\hat{c}_j^* = \hat{p}_j^{-1}\hat{c}_j = (\hat{p}_j')^{-1}\hat{c}_j'$, where $\hat{p}_j' \neq \hat{p}_j$ for all $j \in [\kappa]$. Otherwise, the signature $(\tau'', \mathbf{r}'', \hat{\mathbf{z}}_1', \hat{z}_2', \hat{c}')$ was not obtained from the aborted interaction. Hence, we have $\hat{p}_j^{-1} = (\hat{p}_j')^{-1}\hat{c}_j'\hat{c}_j^{-1}$. Therefore, $\mathcal{U}$ must have predicted the output of H in order to determine $\hat{p}_j^{-1}$. The success probability of $\mathcal{D}$ by an aborted interaction is at least $\varepsilon_2 \geq \varepsilon_{\mathcal{A}}(1 - 1/|\mathbb{T}_\kappa^n|)$, which is non-negligible if $\varepsilon_{\mathcal{A}}$ is non-negligible. Therefore, the overall success probability of $\mathcal{D}$ is $\varepsilon_{\mathcal{D}} \geq \min\{\varepsilon_1, \varepsilon_2\}$. $\square$

Remark 2. As mentioned in Sect. 1, strong one-more unforgeability already implies strong honest-user unforgeability [37, Lemma 10]. Furthermore, the above proof assumes that the vector $\hat{\mathbf{a}}$ is given, while in practical applications it can be generated from a seed in order to save bandwidth by only storing the seed instead of the whole vector. Security under this assumption can be proven by the following simple reduction: Assuming the existence of an adversary $\mathcal{A}$ against BLAZE, we construct an adversary $\mathcal{B}$ against a variant of BLAZE with public key $(\hat{\mathbf{a}}, \hat{b})$. By modeling the function Expand as a programmable random oracle, $\mathcal{B}$ chooses a random seed$'$, reprograms Expand(seed$'$) = $\hat{\mathbf{a}}$, and invokes $\mathcal{A}$ on input (seed$'$, $\hat{b}$). The output of $\mathcal{B}$ is then the same forgery as the one generated by $\mathcal{A}$.

4 Concrete Parameters and Comparison

In this section we propose concrete parameters for BLAZE and compare our results with the previous blind signature schemes [9,34,36]. We review the parameter description of BLAZE in Table 2. We then describe our parameter

Table 2. A review of parameters and sizes of keys and signatures of BLAZE.

Parameter	Description	Bounds
λ	security parameter	
n	dimension	power of 2
$m+1$	number of polynomials (secret key)	$m \in \mathbb{Z}_{\geq 1}$
q	modulus	prime, $q = 1 \pmod{2n}$
σ	standard deviation (secret key)	$\sigma > 0$, $(m+1)\log(t\sigma) > \log(q)$
κ	Hamming weight of H's output	$2^\kappa \binom{n}{\kappa} \geq 2^\lambda$
s^*	standard deviation (signer)	$s^* = \alpha^* \sqrt{\kappa} \,\|(\hat{s}_1, \hat{s}_2)\|$, $\alpha^* > 0$
s	standard deviation (signatures)	$s = \eta\alpha\sqrt{(m+1)\kappa n}s^*$, $\alpha, \eta > 0$,
		$\eta^{(m+1)n} \exp(\frac{(m+1)n}{2}(1-\eta^2)) \leq 2^{-\lambda}$
M	number of repetitions	$M = M_{\mathcal{S}} \cdot M_{\mathcal{U}}$, $M_{\mathcal{S}} = \exp(\frac{12}{\alpha^*} + \frac{1}{2\alpha^{*2}})$,
		$M_{\mathcal{U}} = \exp(\frac{12}{\alpha} + \frac{1}{2\alpha^2})$
secret key size (bit)		$(m+1)n\lceil\log(t\sigma+1)\rceil$, $2e^{-t^2/2} \leq 2^{-\lambda}$
public key size (bit)		$n\lceil\log q\rceil + \lambda$
signature size without compression (bit)		$\kappa(1 + \lceil\log n\rceil) + (m+1)n\lceil\log(ts+1)\rceil + 2\lambda$

selection and the methodology to estimate the security. We note that parameters for the scheme [9] and [34,36] were selected targeting 100 and 102 bits of security, respectively. Therefore, we select our parameters targeting approximately the same security level. A description of our software implementation can be found in the full version of this paper [4].

Parameters. Table 3 shows the parameters selected for BLAZE. We give some insights of how these parameters were selected. A detailed description of selecting parameters in lattice-based cryptography can be found in [3]. We set $n = 1024$, which is a typical choice for lattice-based schemes targeting medium or high security levels. The choice of $m = 1$ changes the hardness of recovering the secret key given the public key from RSIS to the ring learning with errors problem [28]. By setting $m = 3$ and $\sigma = 9.6$, key recovery is based on RSIS and the existence of at least two secret keys given the public key is ensured following Theorem 3. For optimal efficiency, the performance of BLAZE was evaluated using the first parameter set. The modulus q is chosen large enough such that the underlying RSIS instance provides the desired security level. We set κ such that the cardinality of $\mathbb{T}_\kappa^n$ is large enough for security. The parameters $\alpha^*, \alpha, M_{\mathcal{S}}$, and $M_{\mathcal{U}}$ are selected such that the total average number of restarts is given by 2.9.

Security. We describe the methodology used to estimate the security of the proposed parameters. We considered the asymptotically best algorithms known to solve the underlying lattice problems with no memory restrictions. More precisely, we used the well known and widely used LWE estimator [2] (with commit-id 62b5edc on 2019-09-11) to measure the hardness of recovering the secret key. Furthermore, we considered the lattice reduction algorithm BKZ [15] to estimate the hardness of forging signatures. BKZ uses a solver for the shortest vector problem (SVP) in lattices of dimension b, where b is called the block size. The best known SVP solver [7] runs in time $\approx 2^{0.292b}$. Running BKZ with block size b on a k-dimensional lattice $\mathcal{L}$ takes time $8k2^{0.292b+16.4}$ [7]. Due to [14], after calling BKZ we obtain a vector of length $\delta^k \cdot \det(\mathcal{L})^{1/k}$, where

Table 3. Concrete parameters for BLAZE and sizes (in KB) of keys and signatures.

λ	n	m	q	σ	κ	α^*	α	s^*	s	M_S	M_U	M	sk size	pk size	signature size
113	1024	1	$\approx 2^{31}$	0.5	16	20	25	2172.2	11796306	1.8	1.6	2.9	0.8	3.9	6.6
122	1024	3	$\approx 2^{31}$	9.6	16	20	25	54067.2	380633088	1.8	1.6	2.9	3.5	3.9	15.6

$\delta = \left(b \cdot (\pi b)^{\frac{1}{b}} / (2\pi e) \right)^{\frac{1}{2(b-1)}}$. According to Theorem 3, forging a signature implies solving RSIS for the matrix $[\hat{a}\ 1]$ with norm bound $\beta = 2B + s/\alpha$. Given β we determined δ by setting $\beta = \delta^k \cdot \det(\mathcal{L})^{1/k}$. Then, we used the formula of δ given above to deduce the minimum block size b required for BKZ to achieve δ. Then, we computed the cost of BKZ.

Comparison. Table 1 shows that our scheme BLAZE improves upon the previous blind signature schemes [9,34,36] with respect to all relevant efficiency metrics. We note that we considered only the best parameter set proposed for RBS in [36, Table 3] for the target security level of 102 bits.

5 Conclusion

We highlight few notable conclusions from our results and possible future work. We presented BLAZE, a new practical lattice-based blind signature scheme providing statistical blindness under adversely-chosen keys [1] and the strongest version of unforgeability [37] in the ROM. We have shown that BLAZE improves upon all previous works on blind signatures based on assumptions conjectured to withstand quantum computer attacks.

Similar to [36], the unforgeability proof of BLAZE requires the signing queries q_{Sign} to be limited to $o(\lambda)$. As mentioned in [36] and originally by Pointcheval and Stern [35], this constraint is an artifact of the proof and is not unusual for efficient blind signatures. It was left open to achieve a polynomial-time reduction in both q_{Sign} and key size. We extend this research question to investigating the security of BLAZE in the quantum random oracle model (QROM). A possible direction towards this goal may involve the results of Kiltz et al. [24] on the security of Fiat-Shamir signatures in QROM. Further improvements that can be made on BLAZE's design are the following:

- Utilize the compression technique of Bai and Galbraith [5] to obtain shorter signatures. This approach requires further analysis regarding correctness and security. In particular, the *strong* one-more unforgeability is then not directly preserved. Consequently, the security of the resulting scheme under the new security model by Schröder and Unruh [37] cannot be established in a straightforward way.
- Reduce the communication complexity of the signing protocol by compressing the Gaussian vector $\hat{\mathbf{z}}^*$ using the algorithm Compress before sending them to the user (see Fig. 2).
- Generalize BLAZE so that it is based on lattices over modules [26]. This allows for more flexibility when selecting parameters.

– Finally, we note that BLAZE can directly be transformed into an identity-based blind signature scheme. Secret keys can be extracted from the master secret key using any preimage sampleable trapdoor function, e.g., due to [29].

Acknowledgements. The authors are grateful to the anonymous reviewers of FC20 for their comments and suggestions. This work has been partially supported by the German Research Foundation (DFG) as part of project P1 within the CRC 1119 CROSS-ING.

References

1. Abdalla, M., Namprempre, C., Neven, G.: On the (im)possibility of blind message authentication codes. In: Pointcheval, D. (ed.) CT-RSA 2006. LNCS, vol. 3860, pp. 262–279. Springer, Heidelberg (2006). https://doi.org/10.1007/11605805_17
2. Albrecht, M., Player, R., Scott, S.: On the concrete hardness of learning with errors. J. Math. Cryptol. **9**(3), 169–203 (2015). https://bitbucket.org/malb/lwe-estimator/src
3. Alkeilani Alkadri, N., Buchmann, J., El Bansarkhani, R., Krämer, J.: A framework to select parameters for lattice-based cryptography. Cryptology ePrint Archive, Report 2017/615 (2017). http://eprint.iacr.org/2017/615
4. Alkeilani Alkadri, N., El Bansarkhani, R., Buchmann, J.: BLAZE: Practical lattice-based blind signatures for privacy-preserving applications. Cryptology ePrint Archive, Report 2019/1167 (2019). http://eprint.iacr.org/2019/1167, Full version of this paper
5. Bai, S., Galbraith, S.D.: An improved compression technique for signatures based on learning with errors. In: Benaloh, J. (ed.) CT-RSA 2014. LNCS, vol. 8366, pp. 28–47. Springer, Cham (2014). https://doi.org/10.1007/978-3-319-04852-9_2
6. Baldimtsi, F., Lysyanskaya, A.: Anonymous credentials light. In: ACM Conference on Computer and Communications Security - CCS 13, pp. 1087–1098. ACM (2013)
7. Becker, A., Ducas, L., Gama, N., Laarhoven, T.: New directions in nearest neighbor searching with applications to lattice sieving. In: ACM-SIAM Symposium on Discrete Algorithms, SODA 2016, pp. 10–24. SIAM (2016)
8. Bellare, M., Neven, G.: Multi-signatures in the plain public-key model and a general forking lemma. In: ACM Conference on Computer and Communications Security, pp. 390–399. ACM (2006)
9. Blazy, O., Gaborit, P., Schrek, J., Sendrier, N.: A code-based blind signature. In: IEEE International Symposium on Information Theory, ISIT 2017, pp. 2718–2722. IEEE (2017)
10. Boneh, D., Freeman, D.M.: Linearly homomorphic signatures over binary fields and new tools for lattice-based signatures. In: Catalano, D., Fazio, N., Gennaro, R., Nicolosi, A. (eds.) PKC 2011. LNCS, vol. 6571, pp. 1–16. Springer, Heidelberg (2011). https://doi.org/10.1007/978-3-642-19379-8_1
11. Camenisch, J., Neven, G., Shelat, A.: Simulatable adaptive oblivious transfer. In: Naor, M. (ed.) EUROCRYPT 2007. LNCS, vol. 4515, pp. 573–590. Springer, Heidelberg (2007). https://doi.org/10.1007/978-3-540-72540-4_33
12. Chaum, D.: Blind signatures for untraceable payments. Adv. Cryptol.-CRYPTO **82**, 199–203 (1982)
13. Chen, L., Cui, Y., Tang, X., Hu, D., Wan, X.: Hierarchical id-based blind signature from lattices. In: International Conference on Computational Intelligence and Security, CIS 2011, pp. 803–807. IEEE Computer Society (2011)

14. Chen, Y.: Réduction de réseau et sécurité concrete du chiffrement completement homomorphe. Ph.D. thesis, ENS-Lyon, France (2013)
15. Chen, Y., Nguyen, P.Q.: BKZ 2.0: Better lattice security estimates. In: Lee, D.H., Wang, X. (eds.) ASIACRYPT 2011. LNCS, vol. 7073, pp. 1–20. Springer, Heidelberg (2011). https://doi.org/10.1007/978-3-642-25385-0_1
16. HASNC Coordinator: National strategy for trusted identities in cyberspace. Cyberwar Resources Guide, Item #163 (2010), http://www.projectcyw-d.org/resources/items/show/163, Accessed 11 Sep 2019
17. Ducas, L., Kiltz, E., Lepoint, T., Lyubashevsky, V., Schwabe, P., Seiler, G., Stehlé, D.: CRYSTALS-Dilithium: a lattice-based digital signature scheme. Trans. Crypt. Hardw. Embed. Syst. - TCHES **2018**(1), 238–268 (2018)
18. Fischlin, M., Schröder, D.: Security of blind signatures under aborts. In: Jarecki, S., Tsudik, G. (eds.) PKC 2009. LNCS, vol. 5443, pp. 297–316. Springer, Heidelberg (2009). https://doi.org/10.1007/978-3-642-00468-1_17
19. Gao, W., Hu, Y., Wang, B., Xie, J.: Identity-based blind signature from lattices in standard model. In: Chen, K., Lin, D., Yung, M. (eds.) Inscrypt 2016. LNCS, vol. 10143, pp. 205–218. Springer, Cham (2017). https://doi.org/10.1007/978-3-319-54705-3_13
20. Gao, W., Hu, Y., Wang, B., Xie, J., Liu, M.: Identity-based blind signature from lattices. Wuhan Univ. J. Nat. Sci. **22**(4), 355–360 (2017). https://doi.org/10.1007/s11859-017-1258-x
21. Gemalto: Integration of gemalto's smart card security with microsoft u-prove (2011). https://www.securetechalliance.org/gemalto-integrates-smart-card-security-with-microsoft-u-prove. Accessed 11 Sep 2019
22. Heilman, E., Baldimtsi, F., Goldberg, S.: Blindly signed contracts: anonymous on-blockchain and off-blockchain bitcoin transactions. In: Clark, J., Meiklejohn, S., Ryan, P.Y.A., Wallach, D., Brenner, M., Rohloff, K. (eds.) FC 2016. LNCS, vol. 9604, pp. 43–60. Springer, Heidelberg (2016). https://doi.org/10.1007/978-3-662-53357-4_4
23. Juels, A., Luby, M., Ostrovsky, R.: Security of blind digital signatures. In: Kaliski, B.S. (ed.) CRYPTO 1997. LNCS, vol. 1294, pp. 150–164. Springer, Heidelberg (1997). https://doi.org/10.1007/BFb0052233
24. Kiltz, E., Lyubashevsky, V., Schaffner, C.: A concrete treatment of Fiat-Shamir signatures in the quantum random-oracle model. In: Nielsen, J.B., Rijmen, V. (eds.) EUROCRYPT 2018. LNCS, vol. 10822, pp. 552–586. Springer, Cham (2018). https://doi.org/10.1007/978-3-319-78372-7_18
25. Kumar, M., Katti, C.P., Saxena, P.C.: A secure anonymous e-voting system using identity-based blind signature scheme. In: Shyamasundar, R.K., Singh, V., Vaidya, J. (eds.) ICISS 2017. LNCS, vol. 10717, pp. 29–49. Springer, Cham (2017). https://doi.org/10.1007/978-3-319-72598-7_3
26. Langlois, A., Stehlé, D.: Worst-case to average-case reductions for module lattices. Des. Codes Crypt. **75**(3), 565–599 (2014). https://doi.org/10.1007/s10623-014-9938-4
27. Lyubashevsky, V.: Lattice signatures without trapdoors. In: Pointcheval, D., Johansson, T. (eds.) EUROCRYPT 2012. LNCS, vol. 7237, pp. 738–755. Springer, Heidelberg (2012). https://doi.org/10.1007/978-3-642-29011-4_43
28. Lyubashevsky, V., Peikert, C., Regev, O.: On ideal lattices and learning with errors over rings. In: Gilbert, H. (ed.) EUROCRYPT 2010. LNCS, vol. 6110, pp. 1–23. Springer, Heidelberg (2010). https://doi.org/10.1007/978-3-642-13190-5_1

29. Micciancio, D., Peikert, C.: Trapdoors for lattices: simpler, tighter, faster, smaller. In: Pointcheval, D., Johansson, T. (eds.) EUROCRYPT 2012. LNCS, vol. 7237, pp. 700–718. Springer, Heidelberg (2012). https://doi.org/10.1007/978-3-642-29011-4_41

30. Microsoft: Microsoft's open specification promise (2007). https://docs.microsoft.com/en-us/openspecs/dev_center/ms-devcentlp/1c24c7c8-28b0-4ce1-a47d-95fe1ff504bc. Accessed 11 Sept 2019

31. Paquin, C.: U-Prove technology overview v1.1 (revision 2) (2013). https://www.microsoft.com/en-us/research/publication/u-prove-technology-overview-v1-1-revision-2/

32. European Parliament Council of the European Union: Regulation (ec) no 45/2001. Official Journal of the European Union (2001)

33. European Parliament of the Council European Union: Directive 2009/136/ec. Official Journal of the European Union (2009)

34. Petzoldt, A., Szepieniec, A., Mohamed, M.S.E.: A practical multivariate blind signature scheme. In: Kiayias, A. (ed.) FC 2017. LNCS, vol. 10322, pp. 437–454. Springer, Cham (2017). https://doi.org/10.1007/978-3-319-70972-7_25

35. Pointcheval, D., Stern, J.: Security arguments for digital signatures and blind signatures. J. Cryptol. 13(3), 361–396 (2000)

36. Rückert, M.: Lattice-based blind signatures. In: Abe, M. (ed.) ASIACRYPT 2010. LNCS, vol. 6477, pp. 413–430. Springer, Heidelberg (2010). https://doi.org/10.1007/978-3-642-17373-8_24

37. Schröder, D., Unruh, D.: Security of blind signatures revisited. J. Cryptol. 30(2), 470–494 (2017)

38. Zhang, L., Ma, Y.: A lattice-based identity-based proxy blind signature scheme in the standard model. Math. Probl. Eng. 2014 (2014)

39. Zhang, Y., Hu, Y.: Forward-secure identity-based shorter blind signature from lattices. Am. J. Netw. Commun. 5(2), 17–26 (2016)

40. Zhu, H., Tan, Y., Zhang, X., Zhu, L., Zhang, C., Zheng, J.: A round-optimal lattice-based blind signature scheme for cloud services. Future Gener. Comput. Syst. 73, 106–114 (2017)

Crypto Foundations

Non-interactive Proofs of Proof-of-Work

Aggelos Kiayias[1], Andrew Miller[2], and Dionysis Zindros[3(✉)]

[1] University of Edinburgh, IOHK, Edinburgh, Scotland
`akiayias@inf.ed.ac.uk`
[2] University of Illinois at Urbana-Champaign,
Initiative for Cryptocurrencies and Contracts, Urbana, USA
`amiller@cs.umd.edu`
[3] National and Kapodistrian University of Athens, IOHK, Athens, Greece
`dionyziz@di.uoa.gr`

Abstract. Decentralized consensus protocols based on proof-of-work (PoW) mining require nodes to download data linear in the size of the blockchain even if they make use of Simplified Payment Verification (SPV). In this work, we put forth a new formalization of proof-of-work verification by introducing a primitive called Non-Interactive Proofs of Proof-of-Work (NIPoPoWs). We improve upon the previously known SPV NIPoPoW by proposing a novel NIPoPoW construction using super-blocks, blocks that are much heavier than usual blocks, which capture the fact that proof-of-work took place without sending all of it. Unlike a traditional blockchain client which must verify the entire linearly-growing chain of PoWs, clients based on superblock NIPoPoWs require resources only logarithmic in the length of the chain, instead downloading a compressed form of the chain. Superblock NIPoPoWs are thus *succinct* proofs and, due to their non-interactivity, require only a single message between the prover and the verifier of the transaction. Our construction allows the creation of *superlight* clients which can synchronize with the network quickly even if they remain offline for large periods of time. Our scheme is provably secure in the Bitcoin Backbone model. From a theoretical point of view, we are the first to propose a cryptographic prover–verifier definition for decentralized consensus protocols and the first to give a construction which can synchronize non-interactively using only a logarithmically-sized message.

1 Introduction

Proof-of-work blockchain clients such as mobile wallets today are based on the Simplified Payment Verifications (SPV) protocol, which was described in the original Bitcoin paper [14], and allows them to synchronize with the network by downloading only block headers and not the entire blockchain with transactions. However, such initial synchronization still requires receiving all the block headers. In this work, we study the question of whether better protocols exist and in particular if downloading fewer block headers is sufficient to securely synchronize with the rest of the blockchain network. Our requirement is that the

J. Bonneau and N. Heninger (Eds.): FC 2020, LNCS 12059, pp. 505–522, 2020.
https://doi.org/10.1007/978-3-030-51280-4_27

system remains decentralized and that useful facts about the blockchain (such as the Merkle root of current account balances in Ethereum [5,19]) can be deduced from the downloaded data.

Our Contributions. We put forth a cryptographic security definition for Non-Interactive Proofs of Proof-of-Work protocols which describes what such a synchronization protocol must achieve (Sect. 2). We then construct a protocol which solves the problem and requires sending only a logarithmic number of blocks from the chain. We construct a protocol which can synchronize recent blocks, the *suffix proofs* protocol (Sect. 4). We analyze the security and succinctness of our protocol in Sect. 5. In Sect. 6, we show a simple addition to the suffix proofs protocol which allows synchronizing any part of the blockchain that the client may be interested in, the *infix proofs* protocol.

Previous Work. The need for succinct clients was first identified by Nakamoto in his original paper [14]. Predicates pertaining to events occurring in the blockchain have been explored in the setting of sidechains [2]. It has also been implemented for simple classes of predicates such as atomic swaps [10,15], which do not allow full synchronization. Non-succinct certificates about proof-of-*stake* blockchains have been proposed in [8], but their scheme is not applicable to proof-of-*work*. Superblocks were first described in the Bitcoin Forum [13] and later formalized [11] to describe their *Proofs of Proof-of-Work* which have limited applications due to interactivity, lack of security, and inability to prove facts buried deep within the blockchain. We improve upon their work with a security definition, an interactive construction, and an attack against their scheme which works with overwhelming probability.

2 Model and Definitions

Our model is based on the "backbone" model for proof-of-work cryptocurrencies [7], extended with SPV. Following their model, we assume *synchrony* (*partial synchrony* with *bounded delay* [16] is left for future work) and constant difficulty.

Backbone Model. The entities on the blockchain network are of 3 kinds: (1) Miners, who try to mine new blocks on top of the longest known blockchain and broadcast them as soon as they are discovered. Miners commit new transactions they receive from clients. (2) Full nodes, who maintain the longest blockchain without mining and also act as the provers in the network. (3) Verifiers or stateless clients, who do not store the entire blockchain, but instead connect to provers and ask for proofs in regards to which blockchain is the largest. The verifiers attempt to determine the value of a predicate on these chains, for example whether a particular payment has been finalized.

Our main challenge is to design a protocol so that clients can sieve through the responses they receive from the network and reach a conclusion that should never disagree with the conclusion of a full node who is faced with the same objective and infers it from its local blockchain state.

We model proof-of-work discovery attempts by using a random oracle [3]. The random oracle produces κ-bit strings, where κ is the system's security parameter. The network is synchronized into numbered rounds, which correspond to moments in time. n denotes the total number of miners in the game, while t denotes the total number of adversarial miners. Each miner is assumed to have equal mining power captured by the number of queries q available per player to the random oracle per round, each query of which succeeds independently with probability p (a successful query produces a block with valid proof-of-work). Mining pools and miners of different computing power can be captured by assuming multiple players combine their computing power. This is made explicit for the adversary, as they do not incur any network overhead to achieve communication between adversarial miners. On the contrary, honest players discovering a block must *diffuse* it (broadcast it) to the network at a given round and wait for it to be received by the rest of the honest players at the beginning of the next round. A round during which an honest block is diffused is called a *successful round*; if the number of honest blocks diffused is one, it is called a *uniquely successful round*. We assume there is an honest majority, i.e., that $t/n < 0.5$ with a constant minimum gap [7]. We further assume the network is adversarial, but there is no eclipsing attacks [9]. More specifically, we allow the adversary to reorder messages transmitted at a particular round, to inject new messages thereby capturing Sybil attacks [6], but not to drop messages. Each honest miner maintains a local chain $\mathcal{C}$ which they consider the current active blockchain. Upon receiving a different blockchain from the network, the current active blockchain is changed if the received blockchain is longer than the currently adopted one. Receiving a different blockchain of the same length as the currently adopted one does not change the adopted blockchain.

Blockchain blocks are generated by including the following data in them: ctr, the nonce used to achieve the proof-of-work; x the Merkle tree [12] root of the transactions confirmed in this block; and *interlink* [11], a vector containing pointers to previous blocks, including the id of the previous block. The *interlink* data structure contains pointers to more blocks than just the previous block. We will explain this further in Sect. 3. Given two hash functions H and G modelled as random oracles, the id of a block is defined as $\mathsf{id} = H(ctr, G(x, \mathsf{interlink}))$. In bitcoin's case, both H and G would be SHA256.

The Prover and Verifier Model. In our protocol, the nodes include a *proof* along with their responses to clients. We need to assume that clients are able to connect to at least one correctly functioning node (i.e., that they cannot be eclipsed from the network [1,9]). Each client makes the same request to every node, and by verifying the proofs the client identifies the correct response. Henceforth we will call clients *verifiers* and nodes *provers*.

The prover-verifier interaction is parameterized by a predicate (e.g. "the transaction tx is committed in the blockchain"). The predicates of interest in our context are predicates on the active blockchain. Some of the predicates are more suitable for succinct proofs than others. We focus our attention in *stable* predicates having the property that all honest miners share their view of them in a way that is updated in a predictable manner, with a truth-value that persists as the blockchain grows (an example of an unstable predicate is e.g., the least significant bit of the hash of last block). Following the work of [7], we wait for k blocks to bury a block before we consider it *confirmed* and thereby the predicates depending on it stable. k is the *common prefix* security parameter, which in Bitcoin folklore is often taken to be $k = 6$.

In our setting, for a given predicate Q, several provers (including adversarial ones) will generate proofs claiming potentially different truth values for Q based on their claimed local longest chains. The verifier receives these proofs and accepts one of the proofs, determining the truth value of the predicate. We denote a *blockchain proof protocol* for a predicate Q as a pair (P, V) where P is the *prover* and V is the *verifier*. P is a PPT algorithm that is spawned by a full node when they wish to produce a proof, accepts as input a full chain C and produces a proof π as its output. V is a PPT algorithm which is spawned at some round (having only Genesis), receives a pair of proofs (π_A, π_B) from both an honest party and the adversary and returns its decision $d \in \{T, F\}$ before the next round and terminates. The honest miners produce proofs for V using P, while the adversary produces proofs following some arbitrary strategy. Before we introduce the security properties for blockchain proof protocols we introduce some necessary notation for blockchains.

Notation. Blockchains are finite block sequences obeying the *blockchain property*: that in every block in the chain there exists a pointer to its previous block. A chain is *anchored* if its first block is *genesis*, denoted *Gen*. For chain addressing we use Python brackets $C[\cdot]$ as in [17]. A zero-based positive number in a bracket indicates the indexed block in the chain. A negative index indicates a block from the end, e.g., $C[-1]$ is the tip of the blockchain. A range $C[i : j]$ is a subarray starting from i (inclusive) to j (exclusive). Given chains C_1, C_2 and blocks A, Z we concatenate them as $C_1 C_2$ or $C_1 A$. $C_2[0]$ must point to $C_1[-1]$ and A must point to $C_1[-1]$. We denote $C\{A : Z\}$ the subarray of the chain from A (inclusive) to Z (exclusive). We can omit blocks or indices from either side of the range to take the chain to the beginning or end respectively. The *id* function returns the id of a block given its data, i.e., $\mathsf{id} = H(ctr, G(x, \mathsf{interlink}))$.

2.1 Provable Chain Predicates

Our aim is to prove statements about the blockchain, such as "The transaction tx is included in the current blockchain" without transmitting all block headers. We consider a general class of predicates that take on values *true* or *false*. Since a Bitcoin-like blockchain can experience delays and intermittent forks, not all honest parties will be in exact agreement about the entire chain. However, when all honest parties are in agreement about the truth value of the predicate, we require that the verifier also arrives at the same truth value.

To aid the construction of our proofs, we focus on predicates that are *monotonic*; they start with the value *false* and, as the blockchain grows, can change their value to *true* but not back.

Definition 1 *(Monotonicity).* *A chain predicate* $Q(\mathcal{C})$ *is* monotonic *if for all chains* $\mathcal{C}$ *and for all blocks* B *we have that* $Q(\mathcal{C}) \Rightarrow Q(\mathcal{C}B)$.

Additionally, we require that our predicates only depend on the *stable* portion of the blockchain, blocks that are buried under k subsequent blocks. This ensures that the value of the predicate will not change due to a blockchain reorganization.

Definition 2 *(Stability).* *Parameterized by* $k \in \mathbb{N}$, *a chain predicate* Q *is* k-stable *if its value only depends on the prefix* $\mathcal{C}[: -k]$.

2.2   Desired Properties

We now define two desired properties of a non-interactive blockchain proof protocol, *succinctness* and *security*.

Definition 3 *(Security).* *A blockchain proof protocol* (P, V) *about a predicate* Q *is* secure *if for all environments and for all PPT adversaries* $\mathcal{A}$ *and for all rounds* $r \geq \eta k$, *if* V *receives a set of proofs* $\mathcal{P}$ *at the beginning of round* r, *at least one of which has been generated by the honest prover* P, *then the output of* V *at the end of round* r *has the following constraints:*

- *If the output of* V *is* false, *then the evaluation of* $Q(\mathcal{C})$ *for* all *honest parties must be* false *at the end of round* $r - \eta k$.
- *If the output of* V *is* true, *then the evaluation of* $Q(\mathcal{C})$ *for* all *honest parties must be* true *at the end of round* $r + \eta k$.

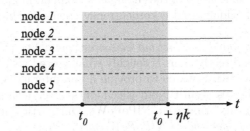

Fig. 1. The truth value of a fixed predicate Q about the blockchain, as seen from the point of view of 5 honest nodes, drawn on the vertical axis, over time, drawn as the horizontal axis. The truth value evolves over time starting as *false* at the beginning, indicated by a dashed red line. At some point in time t_0, the predicate is ready to be evaluated as *true*, indicated by the solid blue line. The various honest nodes each realize this independently over a period of ηk duration, shaded in gray. The predicate remains *false* for everyone before t_0 and *true* for everyone after $t_0 + \eta k$. (Color figure online)

Some explanation is needed for the rationale of the above definition. The parameter η is borrowed from the Backbone [7] work and indicates the rate at which new blocks are produced, i.e., the number of rounds needed on average to produce a block. If the scheme is secure, this means that the output of the verifier should match the output of a *potential honest full node*. However, in various executions, not all potential honest full node behaviors will be instantiated. Therefore, we require that, if the output of the proof verifier is *true* then, consistently with honest behavior, all other honest full nodes will converge to the value *true*. Conversely, if the output of the proof verifier is *false* then, consistently with honest behavior, all honest full nodes must have indicated *false* sufficiently long in the past. The period ηk is the period needed for obtaining sufficient confirmations (k) in a blockchain system. A predicate's value has the potential of being *true* as seen by an honest party starting at time t_0. Before time t_0, all honest parties agree that the predicate is *false*. It takes ηk time for all parties to agree that the predicate is *true*, which is certain after time $t_0 + \eta k$. The adversary may be able to convince the verifier that the predicate has any value during the period from t_0 to $t_0 + \eta k$. However, our security definition mandates that before time t_0 the verifier will necessarily output *false* and after time $t_0 + \eta k$ the verifier will necessarily output *true* (Fig. 1).

Definition 4 *(Succinctness)*. *A blockchain proof protocol (P, V) about a predicate Q is* succinct *if for all PPT provers $\mathcal{A}$, any proof π produced by $\mathcal{A}$ at some round r, the verifier V only reads a $O(polylog(r))$-sized portion of π.*

It is easy to construct a *secure but not succinct* protocol for any computable predicate Q: The prover provides the entire chain $\mathcal{C}$ as a proof and the verifier simply selects the longest chain: by the *common-prefix property* of the backbone protocol (c.f. [7]), this is consistent with the view of every honest party (as long as Q depends only on a *prefix* of the chain, as we explain in more detail shortly). In fact this is how widely-used cryptocurrency clients (including SPV clients) operate today.

It is also easy to build *succinct but insecure* clients: The prover simply sends the predicate value directly. This is roughly what hosted wallets do [4].

The challenge we will solve is to provide a non-interactive protocol that at the same time achieves security and succinctness over a large class of useful predicates. We call this primitive a NIPoPoWs. Our particular instantiation for NIPoPoWs is a *superblock-based NIPoPoW construction*.

3   Consensus Layer Support

3.1   The Interlink Pointers Data Structure

In order to construct our protocol, we rely on the *interlink data structure* [11]. This is an additional hash-based data structure that is proposed to be included in the header of each block. The interlink data structure is a skip-list [18] that makes it efficient for a verifier to process a sparse subset of the blockchain, rather than only consecutive blocks.

Valid blocks satisfy the proof-of-work condition: $id \leq T$, where T is the mining target. Throughout this work, we make the simplifying assumption that

T is constant. Some blocks will achieve a lower id. If $id \leq \frac{T}{2^\mu}$ we say that the block is of level μ. All blocks are level 0. Blocks with level μ are called μ-*superblocks*. μ-superblocks for $\mu > 0$ are also $(\mu - 1)$-superblocks. The level of a block is given as $\mu = \lfloor \log(T) - \log(\mathsf{id}(\mathsf{B})) \rfloor$ and denoted *level*(B). By convention, for *Gen* we set $id = 0$ and $\mu = \infty$.

Observe that in a blockchain protocol execution it is expected $1/2$ of the blocks will be of level 1; $1/4$ of the blocks will be of level 2; $1/8$ will be of level 3; and $1/2^\mu$ blocks will be of level μ. In expectation, the number of superblock levels of a chain $\mathcal{C}$ will be $\Theta(\log(\mathcal{C}))$ [11]. Figure 2 illustrates the blockchain superblocks starting from level 0 and going up to level 3 in case these blocks are distributed exactly according to expectation. Here, each level contains half the blocks of the level below.

We wish to connect the blocks at each level with a *previous block* pointer pointing to the most recent block of the same level. These pointers must be included in the data of the block so that proof-of-work commits to them. As the level of a block cannot be prediced before its proof-of-work is calculated, we extend the *previous block id* structure of classical blockchains to be a vector, the *interlink vector*. The interlink vector points to the most recent preceding block of every level μ. Genesis is of infinite level and hence a pointer to it is included in every block. The number of pointers that need to be included per block is in expectation $\log(|\mathcal{C}|)$.

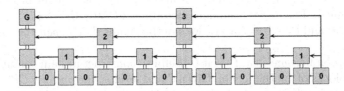

Fig. 2. The hierarchical blockchain. Higher levels have achieved a lower target (higher difficulty) during mining. All blocks are connected to the genesis block G.

The algorithm for this construction is shown in Algorithm 1 and is borrowed from [11]. The interlink data structure turns the blockchain into a skiplist-like [18] data structure.

The updateInterlink algorithm accepts a block B', which already has an interlink data structure defined on it. The function evaluates the interlink data structure which needs to be included as part of the next block. It copies the existing interlink data structure and then modifies its entries from level 0 to level(B') to point to the block B'.

Algorithm 1. updateInterlink

1: **function** updateInterlink(B')
2:      interlink ← B'.interlink
3:      **for** $\mu = 0$ to $level(B')$ **do**
4:          interlink[μ] ← id(B')
5:      **end for**
6:      **return** interlink
7: **end function**

Traversing the Blockchain. As we have now extended blocks to contain multiple pointers to previous blocks, if certain blocks are omitted from the middle of a chain we will obtain a subchain, as long as the *blockchain property* is maintained (i.e., that each block must contain an interlink pointer to its previous block in the sequence).

Blockchains are sequences, but it is more convenient to use set notation for some operations. Specifically, $B \in \mathcal{C}$ and $\emptyset$ have the obvious meaning. $\mathcal{C}_1 \subseteq \mathcal{C}_2$ means that all blocks in $\mathcal{C}_1$ exist in $\mathcal{C}_2$, perhaps with additional blocks intertwined. $\mathcal{C}_1 \cup \mathcal{C}_2$ is the chain obtained by sorting the blocks contained in both $\mathcal{C}_1$ and $\mathcal{C}_2$ into a sequence (this may be not always defined, as pointers may be missing). We will freely use set builder notation $\{B \in \mathcal{C} : p(B)\}$. $\mathcal{C}_1 \cap \mathcal{C}_2$ is the chain $\{B : B \in \mathcal{C}_1 \wedge B \in \mathcal{C}_2\}$. In all cases, the blockchain property must be maintained. The lowest common ancestor is $\mathsf{LCA}(\mathcal{C}_1, \mathcal{C}_2) = (\mathcal{C}_1 \cap \mathcal{C}_2)[-1]$. If $\mathcal{C}_1[0] = \mathcal{C}_2[0]$ and $\mathcal{C}_1[-1] = \mathcal{C}_2[-1]$, we say the chains $\mathcal{C}_1, \mathcal{C}_2$ *span* the same block range.

It will soon become clear that it is useful to construct a chain containing only the superblocks of another chain. Given $\mathcal{C}$ and level μ, the *upchain* $\mathcal{C}\uparrow^\mu$ is defined as $\{B \in \mathcal{C} : level(B) \geq \mu\}$. A chain containing only μ-superblocks is called a *μ-superchain*. It is also useful, given a μ-superchain $\mathcal{C}'$ to go back to the regular chain $\mathcal{C}$. Given chains $\mathcal{C}' \subseteq \mathcal{C}$, the *downchain* $\mathcal{C}'\downarrow_\mathcal{C}$ is defined as $\mathcal{C}\{\mathcal{C}'[0] : \mathcal{C}'[-1]\}$. $\mathcal{C}$ is the *underlying chain* of $\mathcal{C}'$. The underlying chain is often implied by context, so we will simply write $\mathcal{C}'\downarrow$. By the above definition, the $\mathcal{C}\uparrow$ operator is absolute: $(\mathcal{C}\uparrow^\mu)\uparrow^{\mu+i} = \mathcal{C}\uparrow^{\mu+i}$. Given a set of consecutive rounds $S = \{r, r+1, \cdots, r+j\} \subseteq \mathbb{N}$, we define $\mathcal{C}^S = \{B \in \mathcal{C} : B$ was generated during $S\}$.

4   Non-interactive Blockchain *suffix* proofs

In this section, we introduce our non-interactive suffix proofs. With foresight, we caution the reader that the non-interactive construction we present in this section is *insecure*. A small patch will later allow us to modify our construction to achieve security.

We allow provers to prove general predicates Q about the chain $\mathcal{C}$. Among the predicates which are stable, in this section, we will limit ourselves to *suffix sensitive* predicates. We extend the protocol to support more flexible predicates (such as transaction inclusion, as needed for our applications) which are not limited to the suffix in Sect. 6.

Definition 5 (Suffix sensitivity). *A chain predicate Q is called k-suffix sensitive if its value can be efficiently computed given the last k blocks of the chain.*

Example. In general our applications will require predicates that are not suffix-sensitive. However, as an example, consider the predicate "an Ethereum contract at address C has been initialized with code h at least k blocks ago" where h does not invoke the `selfdestruct` opcode. This can be implemented in a suffix-sensitive way because, in Ethereum, each block includes a Merkle Trie over all of the contract codes [5,19], which cannot be changed after initialization. This predicate is thus also monotonic and k-stable. Any predicate which is both *suffix-sensitive* and k-*stable* must solely depend on data at block $C[-k]$.

4.1 Construction

We next present a generic form of the verifier first and the prover afterwards. The generic form of the verifier works with any practical suffix proof protocol. Therefore, we describe the generic verifier first before we talk about the specific instantiation of our protocol. The generic verifier is given access to call a protocol-specific proof comparison operator $\leq_m$ that we define. We begin the description of our protocol by first illustrating the generic verifier. Next, we describe the prover specific to our protocol. Finally, we show the instantiation of the $\leq_m$ operator, which plugs into the generic verifier to make a concrete verifier for our protocol.

The Generic Verifier. The Verify function of our NIPoPoW construction for suffix predicates is described in Algorithm 2. The verifier algorithm is parameterized by a chain predicate Q and security parameters k, m; k pertains to the amount of proof-of-work needed to bury a block so that it is believed to remain stable (e.g., $k = 6$); m is a security parameter pertaining to the prefix of the proof, which connects the genesis block to the k-sized suffix. The verifier receives several proofs by different provers in a collection of proofs $\mathcal{P}$ at least one of which will be honest. Iterating over these proofs, it extracts the best.

    Each proof is a chain. For honest provers, these are subchains of the adopted chain. Proofs consist of two parts, π and χ; $\pi\chi$ must be a valid chain; χ is the proof suffix; π is the prefix. We require $|\chi| = k$. For honest provers, χ is the last k blocks of the adopted chain, while π consists of a selected subset of blocks from the rest of their chain preceding χ. The method of choice of this subset will become clear soon.

Algorithm 2. The Verify algorithm for the NIPoPoW protocol

1: **function** Verify$_{m,k}^{Q}(\mathcal{P})$
2:     $\tilde{\pi} \leftarrow (\text{Gen})$ ▷ Trivial anchored blockchain
3:     **for** $(\pi, \chi) \in \mathcal{P}$ **do**   ▷ Examine each proof (π, χ) in $\mathcal{P}$
4:         **if** validChain$(\pi\chi) \wedge |\chi| = k \wedge \pi \geq_m \tilde{\pi}$ **then**
5:             $\tilde{\pi} \leftarrow \pi$
6:             $\tilde{\chi} \leftarrow \chi$ ▷ Update current best
7:         **end if**
8:     **end for**
9:     **return** $\tilde{Q}(\tilde{\chi})$
10: **end function**

The verifier compares the proof prefixes provided to it by calling the $\geq_m$ operator. We will get to the operator's definition shortly. Proofs are checked for validity before comparison by ensuring $|\chi| = k$ and calling validChain which checks if $\pi\chi$ is an anchored blockchain.

At each loop iteration, the verifier compares the next candidate proof prefix π against the currently best known proof prefix $\tilde{\pi}$ by calling $\pi \geq_m \tilde{\pi}$. If the candidate prefix is better than the currently best known proof prefix, then the currently known best prefix is updated by setting $\tilde{\pi} \leftarrow \pi$. When the best known prefix is updated, the suffix $\tilde{\chi}$ associated with the best known prefix is also updated to match the suffix χ of the candidate proof by setting $\tilde{\chi} \leftarrow \chi$. While $\tilde{\chi}$ is needed for the final predicate evaluation, it is not used as part of any comparison, as it has the same size k for all proofs. The best known proof prefix is initially set to (Gen), the trivial anchored chain containing only the genesis block. Any well-formed proof compares favourably against the trivial chain.

After the end of the **for** loop, the verifier will have determined the best proof $(\tilde{\pi}, \tilde{\chi})$. We will later prove that this proof will necessarily belong to an honest prover with overwhelming probability. Since the proof has been generated by an honest prover, it is associated with an underlying honestly adopted chain $\mathcal{C}$. The verifier then extracts the value of the predicate Q on the underlying chain. Note that, because the full chain is not available to the verifier, the verifier here must evaluate the predicate on the suffix. Because the predicate is suffix-sensitive, it is possible to do so. As a technical detail, we denote $\tilde{Q}$ the predicate which accepts only a k-suffix of a blockchain and outputs the same value that Q would have output if it had been evaluated on a chain with that suffix.

Algorithm 3. The Prove algorithm for the NIPoPoW protocol

```
 1: function Prove_{m,k}(C)
 2:     B ← C[0]                                              ▷ Genesis
 3:     for μ = |C[−k − 1].interlink| down to 0 do
 4:         α ← C[: −k]{B :}↑^μ
 5:         π ← π ∪ α
 6:         if m < |α| then
 7:             B ← α[−m]
 8:         end if
 9:     end for
10:     χ ← C[−k :]
11:     return πχ
12: end function
```

The Concrete Prover. The NIPoPoW prover construction is shown in Algorithm 3. The honest prover is supplied with an honestly adopted chain C and security parameters m, k and returns proof $\pi\chi$, which is a chain. The suffix χ is the last k blocks of C. The prefix π is constructed by selecting various blocks from $C[: -k]$ and adding them to π, which consists of a number of blocks for every level μ from the highest level $|C[-k].\text{interlink}|$ down to 0. At the highest possible level at which at least m blocks exist, all these blocks are included. Then, inductively, for every superchain of level μ that is included in the proof, the suffix of length m is taken. Then the underlying superchain of level $\mu - 1$ spanning from this suffix until the end of the blockchain is also included. All the μ-superblocks which are within this range of m blocks will also be $(\mu - 1)$-superblocks and so we do not want to keep them in the proof twice (we use the union set notation to indicate this). Each underlying superchain will have $2m$ blocks in expectation and always at least m blocks. This is repeated until level $\mu = 0$ is reached. Note that no check is necessary to make sure the top-most level has at least m blocks, even though the verifier requires this. The reason is the following: Assume the blockchain has at least m blocks in total. Then, when a superchain of level μ has less than m blocks in total, these blocks will all be necessarily included into the proof by a lower-level superchain $\mu - i$ for some $i > 0$. Therefore, it does not hurt to add them to π earlier.

Figure 3 contains an example proof constructed for parameters $m = k = 3$. The top superchain level which contains at least m blocks is level $\mu = 2$. For the m-sized suffix of that level, 6 blocks of superblock level 1 are included to span the same range ($2m$ blocks at this level). For the last 3 blocks of the 1-superchain, blocks of level 0 spanning the same range are included (again $2m$ blocks at this level). Note that the superchain at a lower levels may reach closer to the end of the blockchain than a higher level. Level 3 was not used, as it does not yet have a sufficient number of blocks.

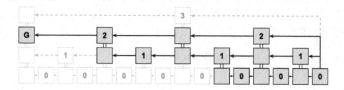

Fig. 3. NIPoPoW *prefix* π for $m = 3$. It includes the Genesis block G, three 2-superblocks, six 1-superblocks, and six 0-blocks.

Algorithm 4. The algorithm implementation for the $\geq_m$ operator to compare two proofs in the NIPoPoW protocol parameterized with security parameter m. Returns *true* if the underlying chain of player A is deemed longer than the underlying chain of player B.

1: **function** best-arg$_m$$(\pi, b)$
2:     $M \leftarrow \{\mu : |\pi\!\uparrow^\mu \{b :\}| \geq m\} \cup \{0\}$ ▷ Valid levels
3:         **return** $\max_{\mu \in M}\{2^\mu \cdot |\pi\!\uparrow^\mu \{b :\}|\}$ ▷ Score for level
4: **end function**
5: **operator** $\pi_A \geq_m \pi_B$
6:     $b \leftarrow (\pi_A \cap \pi_B)[-1]$ ▷ LCA
7:         **return** best-arg$_m$$(\pi_A, b) \geq$ best-arg$_m$$(\pi_B, b)$
8: **end operator**

The Concrete Verifier. The $\geq_m$ operator which performs the comparison of proofs is presented in Algorithm 4. It takes proofs π_A and π_B and returns *true* if the first proof is winning, or *false* if the second is winning. It first computes the LCA block b between the proofs. As parties A and B agree that the blockchain is the same up to block b, arguments will then be taken for the diverging chains after b. An *argument* is a subchain of a proof provided by a prover such that its blocks are after the LCA block b and they are all at the same level μ. The best possible argument from each player's proof is extracted by calling the best-arg$_m$ function. To find the best argument of a proof π given b, best-arg$_m$ collects all the indices μ which point to superblock levels that contain valid arguments after block b. Argument validity requires that there are at least m μ-superblocks following block b, which is captured by the comparison $|\pi\!\uparrow^\mu \{b :\}| \geq m$. 0 is always considered a valid level, regardless of how many blocks are present there. These level indices are collected into set M. For each of these levels, the score of their respective argument is evaluated by weighting the number of blocks by the level as $2^\mu|\pi\!\uparrow^\mu \{b :\}|$. The highest possible score across all levels is returned. Once the score of the best argument of both A and B is known, they are directly compared and the winner returned. An advantage is given to the first proof in case of a tie by making the $\geq_m$ operator favour the adversary $\mathcal{A}$.

Looking ahead, the core of the security argument will be that, given a block b, it will be difficult for a mining minority adversary to produce blocks descending from b faster than the honest party. This holds for blocks of any level.

5 Analysis

We now give a sketch indicating why our construction is secure. The fully formal security proof, together with a detail in the construction which ensures statistical *goodness* and is necessary for withstanding full $1/2$ adversaries, appears in the appendix.

Theorem 1 (Security). *Assuming honest majority, the Non-interactive Proofs of Proof-of-Work construction for computable k-stable monotonic suffix-sensitive predicates is secure with overwhelming probability in κ.*

Proof (Sketch). Suppose an adversary produces a proof $\pi_\mathcal{A}$ and an honest party produces a proof π_B such that the two proofs cause the predicate Q to evaluate to different values, while at the same time all honest parties have agreed that the correct value is the one obtained by π_B. Because of Bitcoin's security, $\mathcal{A}$ will be unable to make these claims for an actual underlying 0-level chain.

We now argue that the operator $\leq_m$ will signal in favour of the honest parties. Suppose b is the LCA block between $\pi_\mathcal{A}$ and π_B. If the chain forks at b, there can be no more adversarial blocks after b than honest blocks after b, provided there are at least k honest blocks (due to the Common Prefix property). We will now argue that, further, there can be no more disjoint $\mu_\mathcal{A}$-level superblocks than honest μ_B-level superblocks after b.

To see this, let b be an honest block generated at some round r_1 and let the honest proof be generated at some round r_3. Then take the sequence of consecutive rounds $S = (r_1, \cdots, r_3)$. Because the verifier requires at least m blocks from each of the provers, the adversary must have m $\mu_\mathcal{A}$-superblocks in $\pi_\mathcal{A}\{b :\}$ which are not in $\pi_B\{b :\}$. Therefore, using a negative binomial tail bound argument, we see that $|S|$ must be long; intuitively, it takes a long time to produce a lot of blocks $|\pi_\mathcal{A}\{b :\}|$. Given that $|S|$ is long and that the honest parties have more mining power, they must have been able to produce a longer $\pi_B\{b :\}$ argument (of course, this comparison will have the superchain lengths weighted by $2^{\mu_\mathcal{A}}, 2^{\mu_B}$ respectively). To prove this, we use a binomial tail bound argument; intuitively, given a long time $|S|$, a lot of μ_B-superblocks $|\pi_B\{b :\}|$ will have been honestly produced.

We therefore have a fixed value for the length of the adversarial argument, a negative binomial random variable for the number of rounds, and a binomial random variable for the length of the honest argument. By taking the expectations of the above random variables and applying a Chernoff bound, we see that the actual values will be close to their means with overwhelming probability, completing the proof. □

We formalize the above proof sketch in the full version of this paper.

Lastly, the following theorem illustrates that our proofs are succinct. Intuitively, the number of levels exchanged is logarithmic in the length of the chain, and the number of blocks in each level is constant. The formal proofs are included in the Appendix.

Theorem 2 (Optimistic succinctness). *In an optimistic execution, Non-Interactive Proofs of Proof-of-Work produced by honest provers are succinct with the number of blocks bounded by $4m \log(|\mathcal{C}|)$, with overwhelming probability in m.*

6   Non-interactive Blockchain *infix* proofs

In the main body we have seen how to construct proofs for suffix predicates. As mentioned, the main purpose of that construction is to serve as a stepping stone for the construction of this section that presents a more useful class of proofs. This class of proofs allows proving more general predicates that can depend on multiple blocks even buried deep within the blockchain.

More specifically, the generalized prover for *infix proofs* allows proving any predicate $Q(\mathcal{C})$ that depends on a number of blocks that can appear anywhere within the chain (except the k suffix for stability). These blocks constitute a *subset* $\mathcal{C}'$ of blocks, the *witness*, which may not necessarily form a chain. This allows proving useful statements such as, for example, whether a transaction is confirmed. We next formally define the class of predicates that will be of interest.

Definition 6 (Infix sensitivity). *A chain predicate $Q_{d,k}$ is infix sensitive if it can be written in the form*

$$Q_{d,k}(\mathcal{C}) = \begin{cases} \text{true}, & \textit{if } \exists \mathcal{C}' \subseteq \mathcal{C}[:-k] : |\mathcal{C}'| \leq d \wedge D(\mathcal{C}') \\ \text{false}, & \textit{otherwise} \end{cases}$$

where D is an arbitrary efficiently computable predicate such that, for any block sets $\mathcal{C}_1 \subseteq \mathcal{C}_2$ we have that $D(\mathcal{C}_1) \to D(\mathcal{C}_2)$.

Note that $\mathcal{C}'$ is a blockset and may not necessarily be a blockchain. Furthermore, observe that for all blocksets $\mathcal{C}' \subseteq \mathcal{C}$ we have that $Q(\mathcal{C}') \to Q(\mathcal{C})$. This will allow us to later argue that adding more blocks to a blockchain cannot invalidate its witness.

Similarly to suffix-sensitive predicates, infix-sensitive predicates Q can be evaluated very efficiently. Intuitively this is possible because of their localized nature and dependency on the $D(\cdot)$ predicate which requires only a small number of blocks to conclude whether the predicate should be true.

Example. We next show how to express the predicate that asks whether a certain transaction with id $txid$ has been confirmed as an infix sensitive predicate. We define the predicate D^{txid} that receives a single block and tests whether a transaction with id $txid$ is included. The predicate $Q_{1,k}^{txid}$ is defined as in Definition 6 using the predicate D^{txid} and the parameter k which in this case determines the desired stability of the assertion that $txid$ is included (e.g., $k = 6$). Q

alone proves that a particular block is included in the blockchain. Some auxiliary data is supplied by the prover to aid the provability of transaction inclusion: the Merkle Tree proof-of-inclusion path to the transactions Merkle Tree root, similar to an SPV proof. This data is logarithmic in the number of transactions in the block and, hence, constant with respect to blockchain size. In case of a vendor awaiting transaction confirmation to ship a product, the proof that a certain transaction paid into a designated address for the particular order is sufficient. In this scheme it is impossible to determine whether the money has subsequently been spent in a future block, and so must only be used by the vendor holding the respective secret keys.

In the above example, note that if the verifier outputs *false*, this behavior will generally be inconclusive in the sense that the verifier could be outputting *false* either because the payment has not yet been confirmed or because the payment was never made.

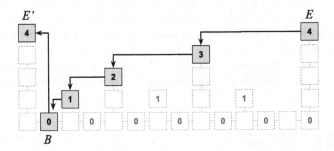

Fig. 4. An infix proof descend. Only blue blocks are included in the proof. Blue blocks of level 4 are part of π, while the blue blocks of level 1 through 3 are produced by followDown to get to the block of level 0 which is part of $\mathcal{C}'$. (Color figure online)

Algorithm 5. The Prove algorithm for infix proofs

```
 1: function ProveInfix_{m,k}(C, C', height)
 2:     aux ← ∅
 3:     (π, χ) ← Prove_{m,k}(C)                        ▷ Start with a suffix proof
 4:     for B ∈ C' do
 5:         for E ∈ π do
 6:             if height[E] ≥ height[B] then
 7:                 aux ← aux ∪ followDown(E, B, height)
 8:                 break
 9:             end if
10:         end for
11:     end for
12:     return (aux ∪ π, χ)
13: end function
```

The construction of these proofs is shown in Algorithm 5. The infix prover accepts two parameters: The chain C which is the full blockchain and C' which is a sub-blockset of the blockchain and whose blocks are of interest for the predicate in question. The prover calls the previous suffix prover to produce a proof as usual. Then, having the prefix π and suffix χ of the suffix proof in hand, the infix prover adds a few auxiliary blocks to the prefix π. The prover ensures that these auxiliary blocks form a chain with the rest of the proof π. Such auxiliary blocks are collected as follows: For every block B of the subset C', the immediate previous (E') and next (E) blocks in π are found. Then, a chain of blocks R which connects E back to B is found by the algorithm followDown. If E' is of level μ, there can be no other μ-superblock between B and E', otherwise it would have been included in π. Therefore, B already contains a pointer to E' in its interlink, completing the chain.

The way to connect a superblock to a previous lower-level block is implemented in Algorithm 6. Block B' cannot be of higher or equal level than E, otherwise it would be equal to E and the followDown algorithm would return. The algorithm proceeds as follows: Starting at block E, it tries to follow a pointer to as far as possible. If following the pointer surpasses B, then the procedure at this level is aborted and a lower level is tried, which will cause a smaller step within the skiplist. If a pointer was followed without surpassing B, the operation continues from the new block, until eventually B is reached, which concludes the algorithm.

Algorithm 6. The followDown function which produces the necessary blocks to connect a superblock E to a preceeding regular block B.

```
 1: function followDown(E, B, height)
 2:     aux ← ∅; μ ← level(E)
 3:     while E ≠ B do
 4:         B' ← blockById[E.interlink[μ]]
 5:         if height[B'] < height[B] then
 6:             μ ← μ − 1
 7:         else
 8:             aux ← aux ∪ {E}
 9:             E ← B'
10:         end if
11:     end while
12:     return aux
13: end function
```

An example of the output of followDown is shown in Fig. 4. This is a portion of the proof shown at the point where the superblock levels are at level 4. A descend to level 0 was necessary so that a regular block would be included in the chain. The level 0 block can jump immediately back up to level 4 because it has a high-level pointer.

The verification algorithm must then be modified as in Algorithm 7.

The algorithm works by calling the suffix verifier. It also maintains a blockDAG collecting blocks from all proofs (it is a DAG because *interlink* can be adversarially defined in adversarially mined blocks). This DAG is maintained in the blockById hashmap. Using it, ancestors uses simple graph search to extract the set of ancestor blocks of a block. In the final predicate evaluation, the set of ancestors of the best blockchain tip is passed to the predicate. The ancestors are included to avoid an adversary who presents an honest chain but skips the blocks of interest. In particular, such an adversary would work by including a complete suffix proof, but "forgetting" to include the blocks generated by followDown for the infix proof pertaining to blocks in $\mathcal{C}'$.

Algorithm 7. The verify algorithm for the NIPoPoW infix protocol

---

1: **function** ancestors(B, blockById)
2:     **if** $B = $ Gen **then**
3:         **return** $\{B\}$
4:     **end if**
5:     $\mathcal{C} \leftarrow \emptyset$
6:     **for** id $\in B$.interlink **do**
7:         **if** id $\in$ blockById **then**
8:             $B' \leftarrow$ blockById[id]
9:             $\mathcal{C} \leftarrow \mathcal{C} \cup$ ancestors(B', blockById)   ▷ Collect into DAG
10:         **end if**
11:     **end for**
12:     **return** $\mathcal{C} \cup \{B\}$
13: **end function**
14: **function** verify-infx$_{\ell,m,k}^{D}(\mathcal{P})$
15:     blockById $\leftarrow \emptyset$
16:     **for** $(\pi, \chi) \in \mathcal{P}$ **do**
17:         **for** $B \in \pi$ **do**
18:             blockById[id(B)] $\leftarrow B$
19:         **end for**
20:     **end for**
21:     $\tilde{\pi} \leftarrow$ best $\pi \in \mathcal{P}$ according to suffix verifier
22:     **return** $D($ancestors($\tilde{\pi}[-1]$, blockById)$)$
23: **end function**

Acknowledgements. The authors wish to thank Giorgos Panagiotakos at the University of Edinburgh, Peter Gaži at IOHK, and Nikos Leonardos at the University of Athens for their insights regarding the attack against the interactive Proofs of Proof-of-Work scheme. We also wish to thank Giorgos Christoglou at Imperial College London and Kostis Karantias at the University of Ioannina for their insights and comments while they implemented the schemes described in this paper as part of their master theses, as well as Sebastien Guillemot at Emurgo R&D who provided valuable feedback. All three of them read many versions of this paper in detail and their contributions helped significantly shape and improve it.

522   A. Kiayias et al.

References

1. Apostolaki, M., Zohar, A., Vanbever, L.: Hijacking bitcoin: routing attacks on cryptocurrencies. In: 2017 IEEE Symposium on Security and Privacy (SP), pp. 375–392. IEEE (2017)
2. Back, A., et al.: Enabling blockchain innovations with pegged sidechains (2014). http://www.opensciencereview.com/papers/123/enablingblockchain-innovations-with-pegged-sidechains
3. Bellare, M., Rogaway, P.: Random oracles are practical: a paradigm for designing efficient protocols. In Proceedings of the 1st ACM Conference on Computer and communications security, pp. 62–73. ACM (1993)
4. Bonneau, J., Miller, A., Clark, J., Narayanan, A., Kroll, J.A., Felten, E.W.: Sok: research perspectives and challenges for bitcoin and cryptocurrencies. In: 2015 IEEE Symposium on Security and Privacy (SP), pp. 104–121. IEEE (2015)
5. Buterin, V., et al.: A next-generation smart contract and decentralized application platform. white paper (2014)
6. Douceur, J.R.: The sybil attack. In: Druschel, P., Kaashoek, F., Rowstron, A. (eds.) IPTPS 2002. LNCS, vol. 2429, pp. 251–260. Springer, Heidelberg (2002). https://doi.org/10.1007/3-540-45748-8_24
7. Garay, J., Kiayias, A., Leonardos, N.: The bitcoin backbone protocol: analysis and applications. In: Oswald, E., Fischlin, M. (eds.) EUROCRYPT 2015. LNCS, vol. 9057, pp. 281–310. Springer, Heidelberg (2015). https://doi.org/10.1007/978-3-662-46803-6_10
8. Gazi, P., Kiayias, A., Zindros, D.: Proof-of-stake sidechains. In: IEEE Symposium on Security & Privacy (2019)
9. Heilman, E., Kendler, A., Zohar, A., Goldberg, S.: Eclipse attacks on bitcoin's peer-to-peer network. In: USENIX Security Symposium, pp. 129–144 (2015)
10. Maurice Herlihy. Atomic cross-chain swaps. arXiv preprint arXiv:1801.09515 (2018)
11. Kiayias, A., Lamprou, N., Stouka, A.-P.: Proofs of proofs of work with sublinear complexity. In: Clark, J., Meiklejohn, S., Ryan, P.Y.A., Wallach, D., Brenner, M., Rohloff, K. (eds.) FC 2016. LNCS, vol. 9604, pp. 61–78. Springer, Heidelberg (2016). https://doi.org/10.1007/978-3-662-53357-4_5
12. Merkle, R.C.: A digital signature based on a conventional encryption function. In: Pomerance, C. (ed.) CRYPTO 1987. LNCS, vol. 293, pp. 369–378. Springer, Heidelberg (1988). https://doi.org/10.1007/3-540-48184-2_32
13. Miller, A.: The high-value-hash highway, bitcoin forum post (2012)
14. Nakamoto, S.: Bitcoin: A peer-to-peer electronic cash system (2008)
15. Nolan, T.: Alt chains and atomic transfers, May 2013. bitcointalk.org
16. Pass, R., Seeman, L., Shelat, A.: Analysis of the blockchain protocol in asynchronous networks. In: Coron, J.-S., Nielsen, J.B. (eds.) EUROCRYPT 2017. LNCS, vol. 10211, pp. 643–673. Springer, Cham (2017). https://doi.org/10.1007/978-3-319-56614-6_22
17. Pass, R., Shi, E.: Fruitchains: a fair blockchain. In: Proceedings of the ACM Symposium on Principles of Distributed Computing, pp. 315–324. ACM (2017)
18. Pugh, W.: Skip lists: a probabilistic alternative to balanced trees. Commun. ACM 33(6), 668–676 (1990)
19. Wood, G.: Ethereum: A secure decentralised generalised transaction ledger. Ethereum Project Yellow Paper 151, 1–32 (2014)

Proof-of-Burn

Kostis Karantias[1]([✉]), Aggelos Kiayias[3,4], and Dionysis Zindros[1,2]

[1] IOHK, Athens, Greece
kostis.karantias@iohk.io, dionyziz@di.uoa.gr
[2] University of Athens, Athens, Greece
[3] University of Edinburgh, Edinburgh, Scotland
[4] IOHK, Edinburgh, UK
akiayias@inf.ed.ac.uk

Abstract. *Proof-of-burn* has been used as a mechanism to destroy cryptocurrency in a verifiable manner. Despite its well known use, the mechanism has not been previously formally studied as a primitive. In this paper, we put forth the first cryptographic definition of what a proof-of-burn protocol is. It consists of two functions: First, a function which generates a cryptocurrency address. When a user sends money to this address, the money is irrevocably destroyed. Second, a verification function which checks that an address is really unspendable. We propose the following properties for burn protocols. *Unspendability*, which mandates that an address which verifies correctly as a burn address cannot be used for spending; *binding*, which allows associating metadata with a particular burn; and *uncensorability*, which mandates that a burn address is indistinguishable from a regular cryptocurrency address. Our definition captures all previously known proof-of-burn protocols. Next, we design a novel construction for burning which is simple and flexible, making it compatible with all existing popular cryptocurrencies. We prove our scheme is secure in the Random Oracle model. We explore the application of destroying value in a legacy cryptocurrency to bootstrap a new one. The user burns coins in the source blockchain and subsequently creates a proof-of-burn, a short string proving that the burn took place, which she then submits to the destination blockchain to be rewarded with a corresponding amount. The user can use a standard wallet to conduct the burn without requiring specialized software, making our scheme user friendly. We propose burn verification mechanisms with different security guarantees, noting that the target blockchain miners do not necessarily need to monitor the source blockchain. Finally, we implement the verification of Bitcoin burns as an Ethereum smart contract and experimentally measure that the gas costs needed for verification are as low as standard Bitcoin transaction fees, illustrating that our scheme is practical.

1 Introduction

Since the dawn of history, humans have entertained the defiant thought of money burning, sometimes literally, for purposes ranging from artistic effect [8] to protest [21], or to prevent it from falling into the hands of pirates [11,20].

© International Financial Cryptography Association 2020
J. Bonneau and N. Heninger (Eds.): FC 2020, LNCS 12059, pp. 523–540, 2020.
https://doi.org/10.1007/978-3-030-51280-4_28

People did not shy away from the practice in the era of cryptocurrencies. Acts of money burning immediately followed the inception of Bitcoin [22] in 2009, with the first recorded instance of intentional cryptocurrency destruction taking place on August 2010 [27], a short three months after the first real-world transaction involving cryptocurrency in May 2010 [7]. For the first time, however, cryptocurrencies exhibit the unique ability for money burning to be provable retroactively in a so-called *proof-of-burn*.

First proposed by Iain Stewart in 2012 [26], proof-of-burn constitutes a mechanism for the destruction of cryptocurrency irrevocably and provably. The ability to create convincing proofs changed the practice of money burning from a fringe act to a rational and potentially useful endeavour. It has since been discovered that metadata of the user's choice—a so-called *tag*—can be uniquely ascribed to an act of burning, allowing each burn to become tailored to a particular purpose. Such protocols have been used as a consensus mechanism similar to proof-of-stake (Slimcoin [23]), as a mechanism for establishing identity (OpenBazaar [24,32]), and for notarization (Carbon dating [12] and OpenTimestamps [28]). A particularly apt use case is the destruction of one type of cryptocurrency to create another. In one prolific case, users destroyed more than 2,130.87 BTC ($1.7M at the time, $21.6M in today's prices) for the bootstrapping of the Counterparty cryptocurrency [1].

While its adoption is undeniable, there has not been a formal treatment for proof-of-burn. This is the gap this work aims to fill.

Our Contributions. A summary of our contributions is as follows:

(i) **Primitive definition.** Our definitional contribution introduces proof-of-burn as a cryptographic primitive for the first time. We define it as a protocol which consists of two algorithms, a burn address *generator* and a burn address *verifier*. We put forth the foundational properties which make for secure burn protocols, namely *unspendability*, *binding*, and *uncensorability*. One of the critical features of our formalization is that a tag has to be bound cryptographically with any proof-of-burn operation.

(ii) **Novel construction.** We propose a novel and simple construction which is flexible and can be adapted for use in existing cryptocurrencies, as long as they use public key hashes for address generation. To our knowledge, all popular cryptocurrencies are compatible with our scheme. We prove our construction secure in the Random Oracle model [6].

(iii) **Bootstrapping mechanism.** We propose a cryptocurrency proof-of-burn bootstrapping mechanism which for the first time does not require target blockchain miners to connect to external blockchain networks. Our mechanism in principle allows burning from any proof-of-work-based cryptocurrency.

(iv) **Experimental results.** We provide a comprehensively tested production grade implementation of the bootstrapping mechanism in Ethereum written in Solidity, which we release as open source software. Our implementation can be used to consume proofs of burn of a source blockchain within a target blockchain. We provide experimental measurements for the cost of burn verification and find that, in current Ethereum prices, burn verification costs $0.28

per transaction. This allows coins burned on one blockchain to be consumed on another for the purposes of, for example, ERC-20 tokens creation [30].

Workflow. A user who wishes to burn her coins generates an address which we call a *burn address*. This address encodes some user-chosen metadata called the *tag*. She then proceeds to send any amount of cryptocurrency to the burn address. After burning her cryptocurrency, she proves to any interested party that she irrevocably destroyed the cryptocurrency in question.

Properties. We define the following properties for a proof-of-burn protocol:

- **Unspendability.** No one can spend the burned cryptocurrency.
- **Binding.** The burn commits only to a single tag.
- **Uncensorability.** Miners who do not agree with the scheme cannot censor burn transactions.

Finally, we consider the *usability* of a proof-of-burn protocol important: whether a user is able to create a burn transaction using her regular cryptocurrency wallet.

Notation. We use $\mathcal{U}(S)$ to denote the uniform distribution obtained by sampling any item of the finite set S with probability $\frac{1}{|S|}$. We denote the support of a distribution $\mathcal{D}$ by $[\mathcal{D}]$. We also use $[n]$ to denote the set of integers from 1 to n. We denote the empty string by ϵ and string concatenation by $\|$.

2   Defining Proof-of-Burn

We now formally define what a proof-of-burn protocol is. Let κ be the security parameter. The protocol consists of two functions GenBurnAddr and BurnVerify and works as follows. Alice first generates an address burnAddr to which she sends some cryptocurrency. The address is generated by invoking GenBurnAddr($1^\kappa, t$) and encodes information contained in a tag t, a string of Alice's choice. When the transaction is completed, she gives the transaction and tag to Bob who invokes BurnVerify($1^\kappa, t$, burnAddr) to verify she irrevocably destroyed the cryptocurrency while committing to the provided tag.

Definition 1 (Burn protocol). *A burn protocol Π consists of two functions* GenBurnAddr($1^\kappa, t$) *and* BurnVerify($1^\kappa, t$, burnAddr) *which work as follows:*

- GenBurnAddr($1^\kappa, t$): *Given a tag $t \in \{0,1\}^*$, generate a burn address.*
- BurnVerify($1^\kappa, t$, burnAddr): *Given a tag $t \in \{0,1\}^*$ and an address* burnAddr, *return* true *if and only if* burnAddr *is a burn address and correctly encodes t.*

We require that the burn scheme is *correct*.

Definition 2 (Correctness). *A burn protocol Π is* correct *if for all $t \in \{0,1\}^*$ and for all $\kappa \in \mathbb{N}$ it holds that* BurnVerify($1^\kappa, t$, GenBurnAddr($1^\kappa, t$)) = true.

With foresight, we remark that the implementation of GenBurnAddr and BurnVerify will typically be deterministic, which alleviates the need for a probabilistic correctness definition.

Naturally, for GenBurnAddr to generate addresses that "look" valid but are unspendable according to the blockchain protocol requires that the burn protocol respects its format. We abstract the address generation and spending verification of the given system into a *blockchain address protocol*:

Definition 3 (Blockchain address protocol). *A blockchain address protocol Π_α consists of two functions* GenAddr *and* SpendVerify*:*

- GenAddr(1^κ): *Returns a tuple* (pk, sk)*, denoting the cryptocurrency address* pk *(a public key) used to receive money and its respective secret key* sk *which allows spending from that address.*
- SpendVerify(m, σ, pk): *Returns* true *if the transaction m spending from receiving address pk has been authorized by the signature σ (by being signed by the respective private key).*

We note that, while the blockchain address protocol is not part of the burn protocol, the *security* properties of a burn protocol Π will be defined *with respect to* a blockchain address protocol Π_α.

These two functionalities are typically implemented using a public key signature scheme and accompanied by a respective signing algorithm. The signing algorithm is irrelevant for our burn purposes, as burning entails the inability to spend. As the format of m is cryptocurrency-specific, we intentionally leave it undefined. In both Bitcoin and Ethereum, m corresponds to transaction data. When a new candidate transaction is received from the network, the blockchain node calls SpendVerify, passing the public key pk, which is the address spending money incoming to the new transaction m, together with a signature σ, which signs m and should be produced using the respective secret key.

To state that the protocol generates addresses which cannot be spent from, we introduce a game-based security definition. The unspendability game SPEND-ATTACK is illustrated in Algorithm 1.

Algorithm 1. The challenger for the burn protocol game-based security.

1: **function** SPEND-ATTACK$_{\mathcal{A},\Pi}(\kappa)$
2:     $(t, m, \sigma, pk) \leftarrow \mathcal{A}(1^\kappa)$
3:     **return** (BurnVerify($1^\kappa, t, pk$) $\wedge$ SpendVerify(m, σ, pk))
4: **end function**

Definition 4 (Unspendability). *A burn protocol Π is* unspendable *with respect to a blockchain address protocol Π_α if for all probabilistic polynomial-time adversaries $\mathcal{A}$ there exists a negligible function* negl(κ) *such that* Pr[SPEND-ATTACK$_{\mathcal{A},\Pi}(\kappa)$ = true] $\leq$ negl(κ).

Algorithm 2. The challenger for the burn protocol game-based security.

```
1: function BIND-ATTACK_{A,Π}(κ)
2:     (t, t', burnAddr) ← A(1^κ)
3:     return (t ≠ t' ∧ BurnVerify(1^κ, t, burnAddr) ∧ BurnVerify(1^κ, t', burnAddr))
4: end function
```

It is desired that a burn address encodes one and only one tag. Concretely, given a burn address burnAddr, BurnVerify($1^κ$, t, burnAddr) should only evaluate to true for a single tag t. The game BIND-ATTACK in Algorithm 2 captures this property.

Definition 5 (Binding). *A burn protocol Π is binding if for all probabilistic polynomial-time adversaries A there is a negligible function negl($κ$) such that* $\Pr[\text{BIND-ATTACK}_{A,Π}(κ)] \leq negl(κ)$.

We note here that the correctness and binding properties of a burn protocol are irrespective of the blockchain address protocol it was designed for.

We are now ready to define what constitutes a *secure proof-of-burn protocol*.

Definition 6 (Security). *Let Π be a correct burn protocol. We say Π is secure with respect to a blockchain address protocol $Π_α$ if it is* unspendable *and* binding *with respect to $Π_α$.*

The aforementioned properties form a good basis for a burn protocol. We observe that it may be possible to detect whether an address is a burn address. While this is desirable in certain circumstances, it allows miners to censor burn transactions. To mitigate this, we propose *uncensorability*, a property which mandates that a burn address is indistinguishable from a regular address if its tag is not known. During the execution of protocols which satisfy this property, when the burn transaction appears on the network, only the user who performed the burn knows that it constitutes a burn transaction prior to revealing the tag. Naturally, as soon as the tag is revealed, *correctness* mandates that the burn transaction becomes verifiable.

Definition 7 (Uncensorability). *Let T be a distribution of tags. A burn protocol Π is* uncensorable *if the distribution ensembles* $\{(pk, sk) ←$ GenAddr($1^κ$); $pk\}_κ$ *and* $\{t ← T; pk ←$ GenBurnAddr($1^κ$, t); $pk\}_κ$ *are computationally indistinguishable.*

3 Construction

We now present our construction for an uncensorable proof-of-burn protocol. To generate a burn address, the tag t is hashed and a perturbation is performed on the hash by toggling the last bit. Verifying a burn address burnAddr encodes a certain tag t is achieved by invoking GenBurnAddr with tag t and checking whether the result matches burnAddr. If it matches, the burnAddr correctly encodes t. Our construction is illustrated in Algorithm 3.

Algorithm 3. Our uncensorable proof-of-burn protocol for Bitcoin P2PKH.

```
1: function GenBurnAddr_H(1^κ, t)
2:     th ← H(t)
3:     th' ← th ⊕ 1                              ▷ Key perturbation
4:     return th'
5: end function
6: function BurnVerify_H(1^κ, t, th')
7:     return (GenBurnAddr_H(1^κ, t) = th')
8: end function
```

We outline the blockchain address protocol for Bitcoin Pay to Public Key Hash (P2PKH) [2], with respect to which we prove our construction secure and uncensorable in Sect. 5. It is parametrized by a secure signature scheme S and a hash function H. GenAddr uses S to generate a keypair and hashes the public key to generate the public key hash. A tuple consisting of the public key hash and the secret key is returned. SpendVerify takes a spending transaction m, a scriptSig σ and a public key hash pkh. The scriptSig should contain the public key pk corresponding to pkh such that $H(pk) = pkh$ and a valid signature σ' for the spending transaction m [2]. If these conditions are met, the function returns true, otherwise it returns false. The blockchain address protocol is illustrated in Algorithm 4.

Algorithm 4. The Bitcoin P2PKH algorithm, parameterized by a signature scheme $S = (\mathsf{Gen}, \mathsf{Sig}, \mathsf{Ver})$.

```
1: function GenAddr_{S,H}(1^κ)
2:     (pk, sk) ← Gen(1^κ)
3:     pkh ← H(pk)
4:     return (pkh, sk)
5: end function
6: function SpendVerify_{S,H}(m, σ, pkh)
7:     (pk, σ') ← σ
8:     return (H(pk) = pkh ∧ Ver(m, σ', pk))
9: end function
```

---

4 Comparison

We now compare three alternatives for proof-of-burn proposed in previous work against our scheme: OP_RETURN, P2SH OP_RETURN and nothing-up-my-sleeve. These schemes are instances of our burn primitive.

We study whether the aforementioned schemes satisfy binding, unspendability and uncensorability. Additionally, we compare them on how easily they translate to multiple cryptocurrencies, a property we call *flexibility*, as well as whether a standard *user friendly* wallet can be used to burn money. A summary of our comparison is illustrated on Table 1.

Table 1. Comparison between proof-of-burn schemes.

	Binding	Flexible	Unspendable	Uncensorable	User friendly
OP_RETURN	•		•		
P2SH OP_RETURN	•		•	•	•
Nothing-up-my-sleeve		•	•	•	•
$a \oplus 1$ (this work)	•	•	•	•	•

OP_RETURN. Bitcoin supplies a native OP_RETURN [5] opcode. The Bitcoin Script interpreter deems an output **unspendable** when this opcode is encountered. The tag is included directly in the Bitcoin Script, hence the scheme is **binding** by definition. This Bitcoin-specific opcode is **inflexible** and does not translate to other cryptocurrencies such as Monero [29]. It is trivially **censorable**. However, the output is prunable, benefiting the network. Standard wallets **do not provide a user friendly interface** for such transactions. Any provably failing [26] Bitcoin Script can be used in OP_RETURN's stead.

P2SH OP_RETURN. An OP_RETURN can be used as the redeemScript for a Pay to Script Hash (P2SH) [4] address. **Binding** and **unspendability** are accomplished by the collision resistance of the hash function RIPEMD160 ∘ SHA256. Similarly to OP_RETURN this scheme is **inflexible**. From the one-wayness of the hash function it is **uncensorable**. Finally, the scheme is **user friendly** since any wallet can create a burn transaction.

Nothing-up-My-Sleeve. An address is manually crafted so that it is clear it was not generated from a regular keypair. For example, the all-zeros address is considered nothing-up-my-sleeve[1]. The scheme is **not binding**, as no tag can be associated with such a burn, and **flexible** because such an address can be generated for any cryptocurrency. It is hard to obtain a public key hashing to this address, thus funds sent to it are **unspendable**. On the other hand, because a widely known address is used, the scheme is **censorable**. Finally, the address is a regular recipient and any wallet can be used to fund it, making it **user friendly**.

---

[1] The Bitcoin address 1111111111111111111114oLvT2 encodes the all-zeros string and has received more than 50,000 transactions dating back to Aug 2010.

5 Analysis

We now move on to the analysis of our scheme. As the scheme is deterministic, its correctness is straightforward to show.

Theorem 1 (Correctness). *The proof-of-burn protocol Π of Sect. 3 is correct.*

Proof. Based on Algorithm 3, $\mathsf{BurnVerify}(1^\kappa, t, \mathsf{GenBurnAddr}(1^\kappa, t)) = \mathsf{true}$ if and only if $\mathsf{GenBurnAddr}(1^\kappa, t) = \mathsf{GenBurnAddr}(1^\kappa, t)$, which always holds as GenBurnAddr is deterministic. □

We now state a simple lemma pertaining to the distribution of Random Oracle outputs.

Lemma 1 (Perturbation). *Let $p(\kappa)$ be a polynomial and $F : \{0,1\}^\kappa \longrightarrow \{0,1\}^\kappa$ be a permutation. Consider the process which samples $p(\kappa)$ strings $s_1, s_2, \ldots, s_{p(\kappa)}$ uniformly at random from the set $\{0,1\}^\kappa$. The probability that there exists $i \neq j$ such that $s_i = F(s_j)$ is negligible in κ.*

We will now apply the above lemma to show that our scheme is unspenable.

Theorem 2 (Unspendability). *If H is a Random Oracle, then the protocol Π of Sect. 3 is unspendable.*

Proof. Let $\mathcal{A}$ be an arbitrary probabilistic polynomial time SPEND-ATTACK adversary. $\mathcal{A}$ makes at most a polynomial number of queries $p(\kappa)$ to the Random Oracle. Let MATCH denote the event that there exist $i \neq j$ with $s_i = F(s_j)$ where $F(s) = s \oplus 1$.

If the adversary is successful then it has presented t, pk, pkh such that $H(pk) = pkh$ and $H(t) \oplus 1 = pkh$. Observe that $\text{SPEND-ATTACK}_{\mathcal{A},\Pi}(\kappa) = \mathsf{true} \Rightarrow$ MATCH. Therefore $Pr[\text{SPEND-ATTACK}_{\mathcal{A},\Pi}(\kappa)] \leq Pr[\text{MATCH}]$. Apply Lemma 1 on F to obtain $Pr[\text{SPEND-ATTACK}_{\mathcal{A},\Pi}(\kappa)] \leq \mathsf{negl}(\kappa)$. □

We note that the security of the signature scheme is not needed to prove unspendability. Were the signature scheme of the underlying cryptocurrency ever found to be *forgeable*, the coins burned through our scheme would remain unspendable. We additionally remark that the choice of the permutation $F(x) = x \oplus 1$ is arbitrary. Any one-to-one function beyond the identity function would work equally well.

Preventing Proof-of-Burn. It is possible for a cryptocurrency to prevent proof-of-burn by requiring every address to be accompanied by a proof of possession [25]. To the best of our knowledge, no cryptocurrency features this.

Next, our binding theorem only requires that the hash function used is collision resistant and is in the standard model.

Theorem 3 (Binding). *If H is a collision resistant hash function then the protocol of Sect. 3 is binding.*

Algorithm 5. The collision adversary $\mathcal{A}^*$ against H using a proof-of-burn BIND-
-ATTACK adversary $\mathcal{A}$.

1: **function** $\mathcal{A}^*_\mathcal{A}(1^\kappa)$
2:     $(t, t', \_) \leftarrow \mathcal{A}(1^\kappa)$
3:     **return** (t, t')
4: **end function**

Proof. Let $\mathcal{A}$ be an arbitrary adversary against Π. We will construct the Collision Resistance adversary $\mathcal{A}^*$ against H.

The collision resistance adversary, illustrated in Algorithm 5, calls $\mathcal{A}$ and
obtains two outputs, t and t'. If $\mathcal{A}$ is successful then $t \neq t'$ and $H(t) \oplus 1 =
H(t') \oplus 1$. Therefore $H(t) = H(t')$.

We thus conclude that $\mathcal{A}^*$ is successful in the COLLISION game if and only if
$\mathcal{A}$ is successful in the BIND-ATTACK game.

$$\Pr[\text{BIND-ATTACK}_{\mathcal{A},\Pi}(\kappa) = \mathsf{true}] = \Pr[\text{COLLISION}_{\mathcal{A}^*,H}(\kappa) = \mathsf{true}]$$

From the collision resistance of H it follows that $\Pr[\text{COLLISION}_{\mathcal{A}^*,H} = \mathsf{true}] <
\mathsf{negl}(\kappa)$. Therefore, $\Pr[\text{BIND-ATTACK}_{\mathcal{A},\Pi} = \mathsf{true}] < \mathsf{negl}(\kappa)$, so the protocol Π is
binding.   □

We now posit that no adversary can predict the public key of a secure signature scheme, except with negligible probability. We call a distribution *unpredictable* if no probabilistic polynomial-time adversary can predict its sampling.

Lemma 2 (Public key unpredictability). *Let $S = (\mathsf{Gen}, \mathsf{Sig}, \mathsf{Ver})$ be a secure signature scheme. Then the distribution ensemble $X_\kappa = \{(sk, pk) \leftarrow \mathsf{Gen}(1^\kappa); pk\}$
is unpredictable.*

The following lemma shows that the output of the random oracle is indistinguishable from random if the input is unpredictable (for the complete proofs see
the Appendix).

Lemma 3 (Random Oracle unpredictability). *Let $\mathcal{T}$ be an unpredictable distribution ensemble and H be a Random Oracle. The distribution ensemble
$X = \{t \leftarrow \mathcal{T}; H(t)\}$ is indistinguishable from the uniform distribution ensemble
$\mathcal{U}(\{0,1\}^\kappa)$.*

Theorem 4 (Uncensorability). *Let $S = (\mathsf{Gen}, \mathsf{Sig}, \mathsf{Ver})$ be a secure signature
scheme, H be a Random Oracle, and $\mathcal{T}$ be an unpredictable tag distribution.
Then the protocol of Sect. 3 instantiated with $H, S, \mathcal{T}$ is uncensorable.*

Proof. Let X be the distribution ensemble of public keys generated using
GenAddr and Y that of keys generated using GenBurnAddr.

From Lemma 2 the distribution of public keys generated from S is unpredictable. The function GenAddr samples a public key from S and applies the
random oracle H to it. Applying Lemma 3, we obtain that $X \approx_c \mathcal{U}(\{0,1\}^\kappa)$.

The function $H'(x) = H(x) \oplus 1$ is a random oracle (despite not being independent from the random oracle H). Since $\mathcal{T}$ is unpredictable, and applying Lemma 3 with random oracle H', we obtain that $Y \approx_c \mathcal{U}(\{0,1\}^\kappa)$.

By transitivity, X and Y are computationally indistinguishable.   □

From the above, we conclude that the tags used during the burn process must be unpredictable. If the tag is chosen to contain a randomly generated public key from a secure signature scheme, or its hash, Lemmas 2 and 3 show that sufficient entropy exists to ensure uncensorability. Our cross-chain application makes use of this fact.

6   Consumption

Over the last 5 years there has been an explosion of new cryptocurrencies. Unfortunately, it is hard for a new cryptocurrency to gain traction. Without traction, no market depth ensues and a cryptocurrency has difficulty getting listed in exchanges. But without being listed in exchanges, a cryptocurrency cannot gain traction.

This chicken-and-egg situation presents the need for a solution that circumvents exchanges and allows users to acquire the cryptocurrency directly. We propose utilizing proof-of-burn to allow users to obtain capital on a new *target* cryptocurrency by burning a legacy *source* cryptocurrency. The target blockchain may support burning from multiple sources.

Workflow. A user wishes to acquire a target cryptocurrency. She uses her target address as a tag to generate a source burn address. She then sends an amount of source cryptocurrency to that address. She submits a proof of this burn to a smart contract [10] on the target chain, where it is verified and she is credited an equivalent amount of currency. Proof-of-burn verification happens in either a centralized manner which is lighter on computation, or in a decentralized manner using Non-Interactive Proofs of Proof-of-Work (NIPoPoWs) [9,15–18]. Target miners need not be connected to every other source blockchain network. We call this property *miner-isolation* and propose methods to achieve it.

We now describe how a target smart contract verifies a burn took place on the source chain. We make use of the Proof-of-Work Sidechains mechanism [19] in which they propose a generic information transfer construction. We tailor it towards our purposes for proof-of-burn transfers. We call the user the *prover* and the smart contract the *verifier*. The prover wishes to convince the verifier that an event occurred on the source chain. We define an event as a simple value transfer described by a transaction id txid, a receiving address addr and an amount. Simple value transfers are supported by all cryptocurrencies, allowing a verifier to process burns from a wide range of source blockchains. Note that this event type does not yet distinguish between burn and non-burn addresses.

A verifier checks an event occurred on the source chain by ensuring its transaction is contained in a stable block [13,14] in the best source chain. Specifically, the following data are supplied to the smart contract as a proof:

- tx: The transaction which contains the burn on the source chain.
- b: The block header for the block which contains tx.
- τ_{tx}: An inclusion proof showing tx $\in b$.
- τ_b: A proof that b is contained in the best (i.e., most proof-of-work) source chain and is stable.

We assume the source blockchain provides a function verify-tx(addr, amount, b, tx, τ_{tx}) which can be written in the smart contract language of the target blockchain and verifies the validity of a source transaction. It takes a source address addr, an amount, a block b, a transaction tx and a proof τ_{tx} for the inclusion of tx in b. It returns true if tx contains a transfer of amount to addr and the proof τ_{tx} is valid.

The proof τ_{tx} is usually a Merkle Tree inclusion proof. More concretely, in Bitcoin, each block header contains a commitment to the set of transaction ids in the block in the form of a Merkle Tree root. Ethereum stores a similar commitment in its header—the root of a Merkle–Patricia Trie [31].

For verifying that a provided block b belongs to the best source blockchain and is stable, we assume the existence of a function in-best-chain(b). We explore how it can be implemented in the "Verifying block connection" paragraph below.

Bootstraping Mechanism. Being able to verify events, we can grant target cryptocurrency to users who burn source cryptocurrency. After burning on the source blockchain, the user calls the claim function with the aforementioned event and a proof for it. This function ensures that the event provided is valid and has not been claimed before (i.e. no one has been granted target cryptocurrency for this specific event in the past), that it corresponds to the transaction tx and that the block b is stable, belongs to the best source chain and contains tx. Then, after verifying by invoking BurnVerify that the receiving address of the event is a burn address where the tag is the function caller's address, it releases the amount of coins burned in the form of an ERC-20 token. We present the contract burn-verifier with this capability in Algorithm 6.

Algorithm 6. A contract for verifying burns from the source chain. This smart contract runs within the target blockchain.

```
1: contract burn-verifier extends crosschain; ERC20
2:     mapping(address ⇒ uint256) balances
3:     claimed-events ← ∅
4:     function claim(e, b, τtx)
5:         block-ok ← in-best-chain(b)
6:         tx-ok ← verify-tx(e.addr, e.amount, b, e.tx, τtx)
7:         event-ok ← e ∉ claimed-events
8:         if block-ok ∧ tx-ok ∧ event-ok ∧ BurnVerify(msg.sender, e.addr) then
9:             claimed-events ← claimed-events ∪ {e}
10:            balances[msg.sender] += e.amount
11:        end if
12:    end function
13: end contract
```

In the interest of keeping this implementation generic we assume that the user receives a token in return for his burn. However, instead of minting a token, the target cryptocurrency could allow the burn verifier contract to mint native cryptocurrency for any user who successfully claims an event. This would allow the target cryptocurrency to be bootstrapped entirely though burning as desired.

Verifying Block Connection. We now shift our attention to the problem of verifying a block belongs in the best source chain. We provide multiple ways of implementing the aforementioned in-best-chain method.

Direct Observation. Miners connect to the source blockchain network and have access to the best source chain. A miner can thus evaluate if a block is included in that chain and is stable. This mechanism does not provide miner-isolation. It is adopted by Counterparty.

NIPoPoWs. Verifying block connection can be achieved through NIPoPoWs, as in [19]. We remark that with this setup a block connection proof may be considered valid provisionally, but there needs to be a period in which the proof can be disputed for the smart contract to be certain for the validity of the proof. Specifically, when a user performs a claim, they have to put down some collateral. If they have provided a valid NIPoPoW, a contestation period begins. Within that period a challenger can dispute the provided proof which – provided that the dispute is successful – would turn the result of in-best-chain to false, abort the claim and grant the challenger the user's collateral. If the contestation period ends with the proof undisputed, then in-best-chain evaluates to true, the collateral gets returned to the user and the claim is performed successfully.

Federation. A simpler approach is to allow a federation of n nodes monitoring the source chain to vote for their view of the best source chain. This construction works under the assumption that the majority of the federation is honest.

The best source chain is expressed as the root $\mathcal{M}$ of a Merkle Tree containing the chain's stable blocks as leaves. Each federation node connects to both blockchain networks, calculates $\mathcal{M}$ and submits their vote for it every time a new source chain block is found. When a majority of $\lfloor \frac{n}{2} \rfloor + 1$ nodes agrees on the same $\mathcal{M}$, it is considered valid.

Having a valid $\mathcal{M}$, a verifier verifies a Merkle Tree inclusion proof π_b for $b \in \mathcal{M}$ and is certain the block provided is part of the best source chain and is stable. This approach is illustrated in Algorithm 7. The more suitable Merkle Mountain Range [9] data structure can be used to store $\mathcal{M}$ in place of regular Merkle Trees, as they constitute a more efficient append-only structure.

7   Empirical Results

In order to evaluate our consumption mechanisms, we implement the federated consumption mechanism in Solidity. We provide a concrete implementation of the burn-verifier contract described in Algorithm 6. We implement the crosschain parent contract from [19]. We verify transaction data by making use of the open

Algorithm 7. A in-best-chain implementation which verifies that a block b is included in the best source chain using the federation mechanism. $\mathcal{M}$ denotes the latest MMR approved by the federation majority.

```
1:  votes ← ∅
2:  best-idx ← 0
3:  𝓜 ← ε
4:  function vote_FED(m, σ, pk)
5:      if pk ∈ FED ∧ Ver(m, σ, pk) then    ▷ Check that pk is a valid federation member
6:          (𝓜*, idx) ← m
7:          votes[m] ← votes[m] ∪ {pk}
8:          if |votes[m]| ≥ ⌊|FED|/2⌋ + 1 ∧ idx > best-idx then
9:              𝓜 ← 𝓜*                                    ▷ Update accepted MMR
10:             best-idx ← idx
11:         end if
12:     end if
13: end function
14: function in-best-chain_𝓜(b, τ_b)
15:     return Ver_MT(𝓜, b, τ_b)
16: end function
```

source bitcoin-spv library [3]. Finally, the federation mechanism for verifying block connection is employed. The members of the federation can vote on their computed checkpoints using the vote function.

We release our implementation as open source software under the MIT license[2]. The implementation is production-ready and fully tested with 100% code coverage.

At the time of writing we obtain the median gas price of 6.9 gwei and the price of Ethereum in US Dollars at \$170.07. The cost of gas in USD is calculated by the formula $gas * 1.173483 * 10^{-6}$ rounded to two decimal places.

Method	Gas cost	Equivalent in USD
vote	50103 gas	\$0.06
submit-event-proof	157932 gas	\$0.19
claim	78267 gas	\$0.09
Total claim cost	262817 gas	\$0.28

For the end user to prove an event and claim her burn, the cost is thus \$0.28. Comparatively, for a Bitcoin transaction to be included in the next block at the time of writing a user has to spend \$0.77.

---

[2] https://github.com/decrypto-org/burn-paper/tree/master/experiment.

Appendix: Full Proofs

Applying an efficiently computable function to indistinguishable distributions preserves indistinguishability.

Lemma 4 (Indistinguishability preservation). *Given two computationally indistinguishable distribution ensembles $\{X_\kappa\}_{\kappa\in\mathbb{N}}$ and $\{Y_\kappa\}_{\kappa\in\mathbb{N}}$, let $\{f_\kappa\}_{\kappa\in\mathbb{N}}$ be a family of efficiently computable functions. Then the distribution ensembles $X' = \{f_\kappa(X_\kappa)\}_{\kappa\in\mathbb{N}}$ and $Y' = \{f_\kappa(Y_\kappa)\}_{\kappa\in\mathbb{N}}$ are computationally indistinguishable.*

We call a distribution ensemble *unpredictable* if no polynomial-time adversary can guess its output. We observe that, if each element of a distribution appears with negligible probability, then the distribution must be unpredictable. Public keys generated from secure signature schemes must be unpredictable.

Algorithm 8. The existential forgery $\mathcal{A}$ which tries to guess the secret key through sampling.

```
1: function A_S(1^κ, pk)
2:     (pk, sk) ← Gen(1^κ)
3:     return (ε, Sig(sk, ε))
4: end function
```

Lemma 2 (Public key unpredictability). *Let $S = (\mathsf{Gen}, \mathsf{Sig}, \mathsf{Ver})$ be a secure signature scheme. Then the distribution ensemble $X_\kappa = \{(sk, pk) \leftarrow \mathsf{Gen}(1^\kappa); pk\}$ is unpredictable.*

Proof. Let $p = \max_{\widehat{pk}\in[X_\kappa]} \Pr_{pk \leftarrow X_\kappa}[pk = \widehat{pk}]$. Consider the existential forgery adversary $\mathcal{A}$ illustrated in Algorithm 8 which works as follows. It receives pk as its input from the challenger, but ignores it and generates a new key pair $(pk', sk') \leftarrow \mathsf{Gen}(1^\kappa)$. Since the two invocations of Gen are independent,

$$\Pr[pk = pk'] \geq \max_{\widehat{pk}\in[X_\kappa]} \Pr[pk = \widehat{pk} \wedge pk' = \widehat{pk}]$$

$$= \max_{\widehat{pk}\in[X_\kappa]} \Pr[pk = \widehat{pk}]\Pr[pk' = \widehat{pk}]$$

$$= \max_{\widehat{pk}\in[X_\kappa]} \left(\Pr[pk = \widehat{pk}]\right)^2 = p^2.$$

The adversary checks whether $pk = pk'$. If not, it aborts. Otherwise, it uses sk' to sign the message $m = \epsilon$ and returns the forgery $\sigma = \mathsf{Sig}(sk, m)$. From the correctness of the signature scheme, if $pk = pk'$, then $\mathsf{Ver}(pk, \mathsf{Sig}(sk, m)) = \mathsf{true}$ and the adversary is successful. Since the signature scheme is secure, $\Pr[\mathsf{Sig\text{-}forge}^{cma}_{\mathcal{A},S}] = \mathsf{negl}(\kappa)$. But $\Pr[pk = pk'] \leq \Pr[\mathsf{Sig\text{-}forge}^{cma}_{\mathcal{A},S}]$ and therefore $p \leq \sqrt{\Pr[pk = pk']} \leq \mathsf{negl}(\kappa)$. From this, we deduce that the distribution ensemble X_κ is unpredictable. $\square$

Algorithm 9. The predictor $\mathcal{A}^*$ of the distribution X which makes use of a distinguisher $\mathcal{A}$ between X and $U(\{0,1\}^\kappa)$.

1: $i \leftarrow 0$
2: $Q \leftarrow \emptyset$ ▷ Record of all random oracle queries
3: **function** $H'_H(x)$
4:     $i \leftarrow i + 1$
5:     $Q[i] \leftarrow H(x)$
6:     **return** $Q[i]$
7: **end function**
8: **function** $\mathcal{A}^*_{X,\mathcal{A}}(1^\kappa)$
9:     $b \xleftarrow{\$} \{0,1\}$
10:     **if** $b = 0$ **then**
11:         $z \leftarrow X$
12:         $j \xleftarrow{\$} [r]$
13:     **else**
14:         $z \leftarrow U(\{0,1\}^\kappa)$
15:     **end if**
16:     $b^* \leftarrow \mathcal{A}^{H'}(z)$
17:     **if** $b = 1 \vee j > i$ **then**
18:         **return** FAILURE
19:     **end if**
20:     **return** Q[j]
21: **end function**

Lemma 3 (Random Oracle unpredictability). *Let $\mathcal{T}$ be an unpredictable distribution ensemble and H be a Random Oracle. The distribution ensemble $X = \{t \leftarrow \mathcal{T}; H(t)\}$ is indistinguishable from the uniform distribution ensemble $\mathcal{U}(\{0,1\}^\kappa)$.*

Proof. Let $\mathcal{A}$ be an arbitrary polynomial distinguisher between X and $\mathcal{U}(\{0,1\}^\kappa)$. We construct an adversary $\mathcal{A}^*$ against PREDICT$_{\mathcal{T}}$. Let r denote the (polynomial) maximum number of random oracle queries of $\mathcal{A}$. The adversary $\mathcal{A}^*$ is illustrated in Algorithm 9 and works as follows. Initially, it chooses a random bit $b \xleftarrow{\$} \{0,1\}$ and sets $Z = X$ if $b = 0$, otherwise sets $Z = \mathcal{U}(\{0,1\}^\kappa)$. It samples $z \leftarrow Z$. If $b = 0$, then z is chosen by applying GenAddr which involves calling the random oracle H with some input pk. It then chooses one of $\mathcal{A}$'s queries $j \xleftarrow{\$} [r]$ uniformly at random. Finally, it outputs the input received by the random oracle during the jth query of $\mathcal{A}$.

We will consider two cases. Either $\mathcal{A}$ makes a random oracle query containing pk, or it does not. We will argue that, if $\mathcal{A}$ makes a random oracle query containing pk with non-negligible probability, then $\mathcal{A}^*$ will be successful with non-negligible probability. However, we will argue that, if $\mathcal{A}$ does not make the particular random oracle query, it will be unable to distinguish X from $\mathcal{U}(\{0,1\}^\kappa)$.

Let QRY denote the event that $b = 0$ and $\mathcal{A}$ asks a random oracle query with input pk. Let x denote the random variable sampled by the challenger in the predictability game of $\mathcal{A}^*$. Let EXQRY denote the event that $b = 0$ and $\mathcal{A}$ asks a random oracle query with input equal to x. Observe that, since the input to $\mathcal{A}$ does not depend on x, we have that $\Pr[\text{EXQRY}] = \Pr[\text{QRY}]$. As j is chosen independently of the execution of $\mathcal{A}$, conditioned on EXQRY the probability that $\mathcal{A}^*$ is able to correctly guess which query caused EXQRY will be $\frac{1}{r}$. Therefore we obtain that $\Pr[\text{PREDICT}_{\mathcal{A}^*, \mathcal{T}}(\kappa) = \text{true}] = \frac{1}{r}\Pr[\text{EXQRY}] = \frac{1}{r}\Pr[\text{QRY}]$. As $\Pr[\text{PREDICT}_{\mathcal{A}^*, \mathcal{T}}(\kappa) = \text{true}] \leq \text{negl}(\kappa)$ and r is polynomial in κ, we deduce that $\Pr[\text{QRY}] \leq \text{negl}(\kappa)$.

Consider the computational indistinguishability game in which the distinguisher gives a guess b^* attempting to identify the origin b of its input (with $b = 0$ indicating that the first distribution was sampled, and $b = 1$ indicating that the second distribution was sampled). If $b = 0$, then the distinguisher $\mathcal{A}$ receives a truly random input $pkh = H(pk)$. If the distinguisher does not query the random oracle with input pk, the input of the distinguisher is truly random and therefore $\Pr[b^* = 0 | b = 0 | \neg \text{QRY}] = \Pr[b^* = 0 | b = 1]$.

Consider the case where $b = 0$ and apply total probability to obtain

$$
\begin{aligned}
&\Pr[b^* = 0 | b = 0] = \\
&\Pr[b^* = 0 | \text{QRY}]\Pr[\text{QRY}] + \Pr[b^* = 0 | b = 0 | \neg \text{QRY}]\Pr[\neg \text{QRY}] \\
&\leq \Pr[b^* = 0 | \text{QRY}]\Pr[\text{QRY}] + \Pr[b^* = 0 | b = 0 | \neg \text{QRY}] \\
&\leq \Pr[\text{QRY}] + \Pr[b^* = 0 | b = 0 | \neg \text{QRY}]
\end{aligned}
$$

Then $\Pr[\text{DIST-GAME}_{\mathcal{A}, X, \mathcal{U}(\{0,1\}^\kappa)} = \text{true}] = \Pr[b = b^*]$ is the probability of success of the distinguisher. Applying total probability we obtain

$$
\begin{aligned}
\Pr[b = b^*] &= \Pr[b = b^* | b = 0]\Pr[b = 0] + \Pr[b = b^* | b = 1]\Pr[b = 1] \\
&= \frac{1}{2}(\Pr[b^* = 0 | b = 0] + \Pr[b^* = 1 | b = 1]) \\
&\leq \frac{1}{2}(\Pr[\text{QRY}] + \Pr[b^* = 0 | b = 0 | \neg \text{QRY}] + \Pr[b^* = 1 | b = 1]) \\
&= \frac{1}{2}(\Pr[\text{QRY}] + \Pr[b^* = 0 | b = 1] + \Pr[b^* = 1 | b = 1]) \\
&= \frac{1}{2}(\Pr[\text{QRY}] + \Pr[b^* = 0 | b = 1] + (1 - \Pr[b^* = 0 | b = 1])) \\
&= \frac{1}{2}(1 + \Pr[\text{QRY}]) \leq \frac{1}{2} + \text{negl}(\kappa)
\end{aligned}
$$

$\square$

References

1. Counterparty. https://counterparty.io/
2. Developer guide - bitcoin. https://bitcoin.org/en/developer-guide
3. summa-tx/bitcoin-spv: utilities for Bitcoin SPV proof verification on other chains. https://github.com/summa-tx/bitcoin-spv/

4. Andresen, G.: BIP 0016: Pay to Script Hash, January 2012. https://github.com/bitcoin/bips/blob/master/bip-0016.mediawiki
5. Bartoletti, M., Pompianu, L.: An analysis of bitcoin OP_RETURN metadata. In: Brenner, M., et al. (eds.) FC 2017. LNCS, vol. 10323, pp. 218–230. Springer, Cham (2017). https://doi.org/10.1007/978-3-319-70278-0_14
6. Bellare, M., Rogaway, P.: Random oracles are practical: a paradigm for designing efficient protocols. In: Ashby, V. (ed.) ACM CCS 1993, pp. 62–73. ACM Press, November 1993
7. Bonneau, J., Miller, A., Clark, J., Narayanan, A., Kroll, J.A., Felten, E.W.: SoK: research perspectives and challenges for bitcoin and cryptocurrencies. In: 2015 IEEE Symposium on Security and Privacy, pp. 104–121. IEEE Computer Society Press, May 2015
8. Brook, C.: K Foundation Burn a Million Quid. Ellipsis Books, London (1997)
9. Bünz, B., Kiffer, L., Luu, L., Zamani, M.: Flyclient: super-light clients for cryptocurrencies. IACR Cryptology ePrint Archive, 2019:226 (2019)
10. Buterin, V., et al.: A next-generation smart contract and decentralized application platform. White paper (2014)
11. Cicero, M.T.: De Inventione (85 BC)
12. Clark, J., Essex, A.: CommitCoin: carbon dating commitments with bitcoin. In: Keromytis, A.D. (ed.) FC 2012. LNCS, vol. 7397, pp. 390–398. Springer, Heidelberg (2012). https://doi.org/10.1007/978-3-642-32946-3_28
13. Garay, J.A., Kiayias, A., Leonardos, N.: The bitcoin backbone protocol: analysis and applications. In: Oswald, E., Fischlin, M. (eds.) EUROCRYPT 2015. Part II. LNCS, vol. 9057, pp. 281–310. Springer, Heidelberg (2015). https://doi.org/10.1007/978-3-662-46803-6_10
14. Garay, J., Kiayias, A., Leonardos, N.: The bitcoin backbone protocol with chains of variable difficulty. In: Katz, J., Shacham, H. (eds.) CRYPTO 2017. Part I. LNCS, vol. 10401, pp. 291–323. Springer, Cham (2017). https://doi.org/10.1007/978-3-319-63688-7_10
15. Karantias, K.: Enabling NIPoPoW applications on bitcoin cash. Master's thesis, University of Ioannina, Ioannina, Greece (2019)
16. Karantias, K., Kiayias, A., Zindros, D.: Compact storage of superblocks for NIPoPoW applications. In: Pardalos, P., Kotsireas, I., Guo, Y., Knottenbelt, W. (eds.) Mathematical Research for Blockchain Economy. SPBE, pp. 77–91. Springer, Cham (2020). https://doi.org/10.1007/978-3-030-37110-4_6
17. Kiayias, A., Lamprou, N., Stouka, A.-P.: Proofs of proofs of work with sublinear complexity. In: Clark, J., Meiklejohn, S., Ryan, P.Y.A., Wallach, D.S., Brenner, M., Rohloff, K. (eds.) FC 2016. LNCS, vol. 9604, pp. 61–78. Springer, Heidelberg (2016). https://doi.org/10.1007/978-3-662-53357-4_5
18. Kiayias, A., Miller, A., Zindros, D.: Non-interactive proofs of proof-of-work (2017)
19. Kiayias, A., Zindros, D.: Proof-of-work sidechains. In: Bracciali, A., Clark, J., Pintore, F., Rønne, P.B., Sala, M. (eds.) FC 2019. LNCS, vol. 11599, pp. 21–34. Springer, Cham (2020). https://doi.org/10.1007/978-3-030-43725-1_3
20. Laertius, D.: Lives of the Eminent Philosophers, Book II (chap. 8), p. 100. Oxford University Press, Oxford (2018)
21. Landsburg, S.E.: The Armchair Economist (revised and updated May 2012): Economics & Everyday Life. Simon and Schuster, New York (2007)
22. Nakamoto, S.: Bitcoin: a peer-to-peer electronic cash system (2008). https://bitcoin.org/bitcoin.pdf

23. P4Titan. Slimcoin a peer-to-peer crypto-currency with proof-of-burn, May 2014. https://www.doc.ic.ac.uk/~ids/realdotdot/crypto_papers_etc_worth_reading/ proof_of_burn/slimcoin_whitepaper.pdf

24. Patterson, S.: Proof-of-burn and reputation pledges, August 2014. https://www. openbazaar.org/blog/proof-of-burn-and-reputation-pledges/

25. Ristenpart, T., Yilek, S.: The power of proofs-of-possession: securing multiparty signatures against rogue-key attacks. Cryptology ePrint Archive, Report 2007/264 (2007). http://eprint.iacr.org/2007/264

26. Stewart, I.: Proof of burn - bitcoin wiki, December 2012. https://en.bitcoin.it/ wiki/Proof_of_burn

27. suppp. Interesting bitcoin address, bitcoin forum post (2013). https://bitcointalk. org/index.php?topic=237143.0

28. Todd, P.: OpenTimestamps: scalable, trustless, distributed timestamping with bitcoin (2016). https://petertodd.org/2016/opentimestamps-announcement

29. Van Saberhagen, N.: Cryptonote v2.0 (2013). https://cryptonote.org/whitepaper. pdf

30. Vogelsteller, F., Buterin, V.: ERC 20 token standard (2015). https://github.com/ ethereum/EIPs/blob/master/EIPS/eip-20.md

31. Wood, G.: Ethereum: a secure decentralised generalised transaction ledger. Ethereum Proj. Yellow Pap. **151**, 1–32 (2014)

32. Zindros, D.: Trust in decentralized anonymous marketplaces. Master's thesis, National Technical University of Athens, Athens, Greece (2016)

Non-interactive Cryptographic Timestamping Based on Verifiable Delay Functions

Esteban Landerreche[1]($\boxtimes$), Marc Stevens[1], and Christian Schaffner[2,3]

[1] Centrum Wiskunde & Informatica (CWI), Amsterdam, The Netherlands
esteban@cwi.nl
[2] Institute of Logic, Language and Computation, University of Amsterdam, Amsterdam, The Netherlands
[3] QuSoft, Amsterdam, The Netherlands

Abstract. We present the first treatment of non-interactive publicly-verifiable timestamping schemes in the Universal Composability framework. Inspired by the timestamping properties of Bitcoin, we use non-parallelizable computational work that relates to elapsed time to avoid previous impossibility results on non-interactive timestamping. We introduce models of verifiable delay functions (VDF) related to a clock and non-interactive timestamping in the UC-framework. These are used to present a secure construction that provides improvements over previous concrete constructions. Namely, timestamps forged by the adversary are now limited to a certain time-window that depends only on the adversary's ability to compute VDFs more quickly and on the length of corruption. Finally, we discuss how our construction can be added to non-PoW blockchain protocols to prevent costless simulation attacks.

Keywords: Non-interactive cryptographic timestamping · Universal composability · Verifiable delay functions · Time-lock cryptography

1 Introduction

In the digital domain, giving evidence that a certain amount of time has passed is more challenging than in the physical world. Exploring how to reliably create digital timestamps has been an active research area for the last thirty years. The first paper to deal with digital timestamping by Haber and Stornetta [9] presented solutions which utilized cryptography to limit the trust deposited on the party doing the timestamping. Their solution is based on a hashchain: a sequence of documents linked through a collision-resistant hash function.

In the literature, almost every timestamping service requires interaction with a group of validators and provides security guarantees only for the ordering of events, timestamping relative to other events. Non-interactive timestamping has been explored previously in [12], where the authors present a generic impossibility result. Because there is no interaction between prover and verifier, an

J. Bonneau and N. Heninger (Eds.): FC 2020, LNCS 12059, pp. 541–558, 2020.
https://doi.org/10.1007/978-3-030-51280-4_29

adversarial prover could simply simulate the execution of an honest prover 'in the past' to generate a fake timestamp. They sidestep this result by working in the bounded-storage model where they construct a secure protocol, where the adversary is unable to simulate an honest prover due to lack of storage. Another approach to sidestep this result is to relate computational work to elapsed time. This was mentioned in [11] as a possible application for their proof-of-sequential-work construction. The same idea is what allows Bitcoin to act as a decentralized timestamping service.

Haber and Stornetta's timestamping hashchain served as the inspiration for the blockchain that underlies Bitcoin [13]. Even when it was not its stated goal, Bitcoin achieved timestamps that are more trustworthy than those of the original construction. Proofs of work were introduced to prevent malicious adversaries from overwhelming honest parties through false identities. Each block of the Bitcoin blockchain contains a certificate that, on average, a certain amount of work has been invested in its creation. Given an idea of how much computational power is available to the network, it is possible to assert the age of any piece of data on the blockchain, with higher certainty than previous non-centralized systems. One can assume the age of a record approximately corresponds to its depth in the blockchain, unless an adversary's computational power exceeds the honest Bitcoin miners' computational power. Under non-standard yet realistic assumptions, Bitcoin provides long-term proofs of the age of its blocks.

While timestamping is mentioned as a goal of Bitcoin in the original whitepaper its security properties were only recently formalized in [1]. There, the authors study which timestamping guarantees can be achieved through interaction with an existing ledger. While there is a level of public verifiability in ledger-based timestamping, they require accepting the assumptions of the underlying blockchain protocol. Bitcoin was able to sidestep impossibility results about non-interactive timestamping by connecting time with work, but at a high price.

Unfortunately proof of work is incredibly wasteful, which is why there has been a search for more sustainable replacements. While there are many proposals for different Sybil-resistance mechanisms, none of them provide these additional timestamping guarantees. In fact, all of these solutions explicitly avoid the computational investment that allows for timestamping in Bitcoin. However, the large computational work is the mechanism behind Bitcoin's resilience to costless-simulation and long-range attacks. Non-proof-of-work solutions require additional cryptographic assumptions, like secure erasures [8], in order to maintain the same level of robustness as Bitcoin.

The main goal of this paper is to find another solution to base the security of timestamping on computational work in a manner that is not wasteful while being easy to apply. We take ideas from the same timestamping protocol that influenced Bitcoin to construct a hashchain-based protocol using verifiable delay functions (VDFs). Using non-parallelizable work allows us to have assumptions that are realistic, as adversaries only gain a computational advantage with faster processors, not with more processors. We quantify the advantage of the adversary in terms of the factor that she is able to compute VDFs faster compared to an honest prover. Our scheme offers similar timestamping guarantees of proofs of work for distributed ledgers that do not rely on proof of work, as we briefly discuss in the last section of this paper.

1.1 Our Contributions

We study non-interactive cryptographic timestamping based on Verifiable Delay Functions (VDFs) in the Universal-Composability (UC) framework and the Random-Oracle Model (ROM). This is the first treatment of non-interactive timestamping in the UC model by introducing non-interactive computational proofs-of-age which act as a lower bound on the age of a record.

We define an ideal timestamping functionality $\mathcal{F}_{ts}^{\alpha}$ that maintains a time-stamped record of messages. It can be queried to generate a non-interactive proof for the record's age at the time of proof-generation. We parametrize the adversary's advantage with a *time-diluting* factor α.

For a record of age *TrueAge*, the ideal functionality allows timestamps of age *StampAge* that are correct (*StampAge* $\leq$ *TrueAge*) or forged timestamps with a claimed age bounded as *StampAge* $\leq \alpha \cdot \min(t_{\text{corr}}, \textit{TrueAge})$, where t_{corr} is the time since corruption (or $-\infty$ if uncorrupted).

In particular this implies that she cannot create any forged timestamps with age larger than $T \cdot \alpha$, which is possible in a similar construction by Mahmoody et al. [11], where for any record of any age the adversary can craft forged timestamps that are at most α times older than the record's true age. In the full version of this paper we provide a treatment of Mahmoody et al.'s construction in the UC-framework for easy comparison with our work.

Our main contribution is presented in Sect. 4. We define the functionality $\mathcal{F}_{ts}^{\alpha}$ and present our hashchain-based protocol. We show our construction securely realizes the timestamping functionality in the random-oracle model and universal-composability framework against an adversary that can compute verifiable delay functions faster than the prover by the time-diluting factor α.

2   Model and Definitions

We construct our protocol in the universal-composability framework [5,6] where two PPT algorithms $\mathcal{Z}$ and $\mathcal{A}$ interact with parties executing a protocol. We assume a hybrid model where parties have access to a global clock, random oracles, an unforgeable signature scheme and the $\mathcal{F}_{\text{VDF}}^{\Gamma}$ functionality that represents our verifiable delay function.

Time. We will work in the synchronous model presented in [10] where parties have access to a clock functionality $\mathcal{F}_{\text{clock}}$ (as seen in [2]). For the clock to advance, each party must input an instruction to the clock that they have done all their computations for the current round. Once every party and the adversary have finished their computations for the round, the clock ticks and the next round begins. The clock allows us to give meaningful statements about the passage of time, but our protocol does not make any assumption on the synchronicity of communication between the parties. We will refer to the encoding of the round number as a **time receipt** with constant length θ.

Cryptographic Hash Function. Let $\mathsf{H} : \{0,1\}^* \to \{0,1\}^\lambda$ be a collision-resistant cryptographic hash function, which we model as a random oracle.

Sequences. We denote a sequence of ℓ elements from a set X as $S = \langle x_i \mid x_i \in X \rangle_\ell$, where the elements of the sequence are indexed by $i \in \{0, \dots, \ell - 1\}$. When it is more practical or clear from context, we may denote a sequence as $S = \langle x_0 \dots, x_{\ell-1} \rangle_\ell$ or simply $\langle x_i \rangle_\ell$. We also avoid writing the subscript ℓ when the length of the sequence is not relevant. When we wish to append an element x to the end of a sequence S we write $\langle S, x \rangle$.

Public-Key Signatures. We assume a EU-CMA signature scheme with security parameter κ. For consistency, we represent the computations related to this scheme as interaction with a signature oracle Σ in the following way:

- Each participant has a public/secret key pair (pk, sk) known to Σ.
- On query $\Sigma.\mathsf{sign}(sk, msg)$:
  A signature $sig \in \{0,1\}^\kappa$ is generated and the tuple (sk, msg, sig) is stored in memory. Return sig.
- On query $\Sigma.\mathsf{verify}(pk, msg, sig)$:
  If (sk, msg, sig) is in the memory of Σ and (pk, sk) is a valid keypair, return 1. Otherwise, return 0.

We assume the probability that any PPT adversary forges a signature without knowledge of the corresponding secret key is negligible in κ.

3 Verifiable Delay Functions

Informally, verifiable delay functions are functions that require inherently sequential computation and can be efficiently verified.

Definition 3.1. *A **verifiable delay function** (VDF) is a triple of algorithms* $(\mathsf{init_{VDF}}, \mathsf{eval_{VDF}}, \mathsf{verify_{VDF}})$ *with security parameter μ and parameters $g, v \in \mathbb{N}$*

$\mathsf{init_{VDF}}(\mu) \to pp$ *A probabilistic algorithm which, given a security parameter μ outputs public parameters pp.*

$\mathsf{eval_{VDF}}(pp, x, s) \to (y, p)$ *is a slow cryptographic algorithm that given public parameters pp, input $x \in \{0,1\}^*$ and a strength parameter s computes an output y and a proof p.*

$\mathsf{verify_{VDF}}(pp, x, s, y, p)$ *is a fast cryptographic algorithm that for public parameters pp, input x, strength parameter s, output y and proof $p \in \{0,1\}^\mu$ outputs 1 if y is the correct output of the VDF on input x given pp and s.*

For clarity, we avoid writing pp as inputs to $\mathsf{eval}_{\mathsf{VDF}}$ and $\mathsf{verify}_{\mathsf{VDF}}$. As verifiable delay functions are a recent invention, the current definitions differ slightly from each other. Our definition is closer to the definitions in [14,15] where both the solving and verification algorithms get as input a parameter s that represents the number of sequential work necessary to execute $\mathsf{eval}_{\mathsf{VDF}}$. In other constructions, this parameter is input only to the initialization algorithm [3,4]. Choosing to use it as an input at the time of execution allows us to run VDFs for different strengths given the same initial parameters. While generally VDFs are computed with the strength determined in advance, it is possible to execute some of them [14,15] and halting them at some unknown point in the future.

A VDF must satisfy the following security properties:

Correctness $\mathsf{verify}_{\mathsf{VDF}}(x, s, \mathsf{eval}_{\mathsf{VDF}}(x,s)) = 1$ for all $x \in \{0,1\}^*$ and $s \in \mathbb{N}$.

Soundness The probability that $\mathsf{verify}_{\mathsf{VDF}}(x, s, y, p) = 1$ when $y \neq \mathsf{eval}_{\mathsf{VDF}}(x,s)$ is negligible.

Sequentiality No efficient algorithm $\mathcal{A}$ that executes less than s sequential steps can compute values (y, p) for an input x (with sufficient min-entropy) such that $\mathsf{verify}_{\mathsf{VDF}}(x, s, y, p) = 1$ with non-negligible probability.

Uniqueness For each x there an unique y such that $\mathsf{verify}_{\mathsf{VDF}}(x, s, y, p) = 1$.

Additionally, we expect verification of the VDF to be efficient. The algorithm $\mathsf{verify}_{\mathsf{VDF}}$ must not take more than $O(\log(s))$ sequential computational steps.

Wesolowski presents a simple VDF in [15] based on iterated squaring in groups of unknown order. His construction is particularly practical because of its succinctness, as the proof consists of a single group element. Additionally, it does not require to choose the **strength** s before starting the computation. Computing the function consists of repeated squarings, which can be stopped at any moment to get an output of strength s after s squarings. Continuous execution has only a linear cost on space, in order to save enough values to efficiently compute the proof p.

Wesolowski's VDF fulfills all the security properties expected from a VDF and is the model from which we construct our functionality $\mathcal{F}_{\mathsf{VDF}}^{\Gamma}$. Additionally, the security of our scheme is based on assumptions on the possibility of computing the VDF quickly enough to ensure that the adversary's advantage through faster hardware is minimal. Research on optimized algorithms and specialized hardware for computing [15] is an active research topic[1, 2] meaning that our assumptions should not be too far from reality.

3.1 The VDF Functionality

The primary goal of our construction is to generate non-interactive proofs that a certain amount of time has passed since a message was recorded by the prover. The first step to do that is representing our VDF in the UC framework.

---

[1] https://vdfresearch.org/.
[2] https://medium.com/@chia_network/chia-vdf-competition-guide-5382e1f4bd39.

Oracle $\mathcal{F}_{\mathsf{VDF}}^{\Gamma}$

The functionality is parametrized by a set Γ and a parameter ψ and has access to the clock $\mathcal{F}_{\mathsf{clock}}$ and the random oracle $\mathsf{VDF} : \{0,1\}^* \times \mathbb{N} \rightarrow \{0,1\}^{\mu} \times \{0,1\}^{\mu}$. The functionality manages a set $\mathcal{P}$ of parties P_i. For every party, it manages a query set Q_i and a rate $\gamma_i \in \Gamma$. The functionality holds corresponding parameters $Q_{\mathcal{A}}$ and $\gamma_{\mathcal{A}}$ for the adversary. All Q_i as well as $\mathcal{P}$ are initialized as $\varnothing$.
Whenever $\mathcal{F}_{\mathsf{VDF}}^{\Gamma}$ is activated, it sets $t^* \leftarrow \mathcal{F}_{\mathsf{clock}}.\mathtt{clock\text{-}read}$.

Computing the function

- On input $(\mathtt{start}, x)$ from any party P_i or the adversary $\mathcal{A}$, the functionality adds (x, t^*) to Q_i. It then sends $\mathtt{started}$ back.
- On input $(\mathtt{output}, x)$ from any party P_i or the adversary $\mathcal{A}$, the functionality checks if the party started the computation, that is $(x, t_s) \in Q_i$. If it did not, output $\bot$. If it did, compute the strength s by taking the time elapsed since the start and letting $s \leftarrow \lfloor t^* - t_s/\gamma_i \rfloor$. Let $(y, p) \leftarrow \mathsf{VDF}(x, s)$ and return (s, y).
- On input $(\mathtt{proof}, x, s, y)$ from a party P_i or the adversary $\mathcal{A}$, check whether $(x, t') \in Q_i$ with $t^* - t' \leq \gamma_i s + \lceil \psi/\gamma_i \rceil$. If they did not, return $\bot$. Otherwise, let $(y, p) \leftarrow \mathsf{VDF}(x, s)$ and return p. Otherwise, return $\bot$.

Verification

- On input $(\mathtt{verify}, x, y, s, p)$ from any party P_i or $\mathcal{A}$, checks whether $(y, p) = \mathsf{VDF}(x, s)$. If so, outputs 1. Otherwise, output 0.

Corruption

- Whenever $\mathcal{A}$ corrupts a party P_i, additionally update the adversarial query list: $Q_{\mathcal{A}}^* \leftarrow Q_{\mathcal{A}}^* \cup \{(x, t^* - \gamma_{\mathcal{A}}/\gamma_i(t^* - t)) \mid (x, t) \in Q_i\}$. Then send Q_i to $\mathcal{A}$;

Fig. 1. The functionality $\mathcal{F}_{\mathsf{VDF}}^{\Gamma}$ is the only way to query the random oracle VDF.

The universal composability framework is very powerful but requires multiple simplifying assumptions. In order to avoid explicitly dealing with simulation overheads and fine-grained complexity in general, UC deals with closed complexity classes. Any time an ITM is activated, it can perform arbitrary polytime computations. Without additional tools, it is impossible to quantify the amount of computation executed by any party. Moderately-hard functions, like VDFs as well as proofs-of-resource (work, space, replication etc.) are functions that will eventually be computed at a cost of time or some other resource. Universal composability is not natively equipped to handle such functions, as there is no natural way to represent this cost.

A way to utilize these functions in UC is through functionality wrappers, as exemplified in [2] where parties can only query the random oracle a certain number of times per timestep We follow a similar approach, where our VDF functionality is the only way parties can access an underlying random oracle. It is a natural question whether the VDF presented in [15] can actually UC-realize our functionality. This question goes beyond the scope of our paper, but further work is ongoing to understand whether it is possible to prove this within the constraints of the UC framework. On the other hand, the functionality fulfills the expected security properties of a VDF.

Our functionality $\mathcal{F}_{\mathsf{VDF}}^{\Gamma}$ is described in Fig. 1 and simulates the continuous execution of the VDF. When the execution of the VDF is finished, the party gets back the output of the VDF after a certain number of iterations, which we call *strength*. Whenever an execution of the VDF is completed, the strength is also output to the party, so they receive the pair (s, y). In order to calculate the appropriate strength of an execution after a certain amount of time we introduce the parameter γ_P which represents the time needed for an iteration of the underlying function for party P. We call this parameter the **rate of party** P. In this setting with only one party, we assume the adversary has rate $\gamma_{\mathcal{A}} = \gamma/\alpha$ where her advantage $\alpha \geq 1$ is not too large (≤ 2). While we cannot ensure the physical reality of this assumption, the impossibility of parallelization greatly limits this possible advantage, in contrast to generic (parallelizable) computation.

The functionality has access to the random oracle VDF which has an output of size 2μ which we parse as two distinct outputs: the result of the VDF (y) and its proof (p), which allows for verification. On occassion we will refer to the pair (y, p) as Y. Parties can only access this random oracle through $\mathcal{F}_{\mathsf{VDF}}^{\Gamma}$. Given an **output** query, they get the function output y, which constitutes the first half of the random oracle, as well as the strength. A **proof** query, requires the output y and returns p. This functionality depends on the clock functionality $\mathcal{F}_{\mathsf{clock}}$ presented in [2], our version of which can be found on the full version of this paper.

The functionality $\mathcal{F}_{\mathsf{VDF}}^{\Gamma}$ captures the desirable properties of a verifiable delay function. Correctness, soundness and uniqueness follow from the use of a random oracle for VDF. The functionality models sequentiality because a certain amount of time must pass before a party can get certain output. The functionality extends the standard corruption mechanism [6, §7.1] of an adversary corrupting a party and allows not only the adversary taking over that party's existing VDF computations, but also to continue them with its faster rate. To do so, the functionality checks the current strength of the computed function $(t^* {-} t/\gamma)$ and multiplies it by the adversary's rate to compute the hypothetical time in which the adversary would have started the computation to reach the strength at corruption. It then saves that time in the adversary's query log $Q_{\mathcal{A}}$.

Participants are able to input any string to the functionality, as a full-domain hash is applied to any inputs in our choice of VDF to prevent trivially re-using previously computed proofs. We require a canonical unambiguous encoding of integers $s \in \mathbb{N}$ as bitstrings, so (s, y, p) has a natural description as a bitstring $s||y||p \in \{0,1\}^*$.

4   Creating a Timestamping Scheme

In this section we will first present the timestamping functionality $\mathcal{F}_{\mathsf{ts}}^{\alpha}$ and then a protocol that realizes it through our VDF functionality.

4.1   A Timestamping Functionality

The goal of the timestamping functionality $\mathcal{F}_{ts}^{\alpha}$ is to generate proofs of *age* and prevent dishonest parties from claiming that something is older than it really is. Because we want to reflect the realities of an adversary having access to faster computational rates, the functionality allows for timestamps to be forged under certain circumstances. The adversary will be able to dilute the proven age by at most a time-dilution factor $\alpha \geq 1$. We then show that we can efficiently and securely instantiate this functionality with the use of VDFs. What our functionality does not do is prevent an attacker from post-dating a record, that is, pretending the record is "younger" and was first recorded later than it was. A simpler functionality, based on the construction from [11] can be found in the full version of this paper. The main difference between the two is that the following functionality does not allow the adversary to take advantage of already existing timestamps. That is, an adversary must start from scratch whenever she tries to forge a timestamp and cannot take advantage of honestly-computed work. We present our functionality in Fig. 2.

The functionality accepts three inputs from the parties and manages the corruption of the prover. When the prover is corrupted, the adversary can start forging timestamps by a factor α. The functionality receives records through the `record` query and stores them when this happens. It generates a timestamp whenever it receives a `stamp` input with the appropriate record. The adversary can choose how the timestamp looks like but can only modify the age if she has corrupted the prover. She is limited by the `checkstamp` procedure, which checks whether the presented age of the timestamp is correct. If the prover is honest, it simply checks whether the age in the timestamp does not exceed the time elapsed since the record was originally queried. When the prover has been corrupted, the adversary can stretch a timestamp by a factor α but only if enough time has elapsed since corruption of the prover. An adversary can only modify a timestamp if she has been in control of the functionality for at least the age of the timestamp divided by α. This implies that any accepted timestamp produced by the adversary with claimed age older than $\alpha \cdot (\mathcal{F}_{clock}.\texttt{clock-read} - t_{corr})$ is truthful. Such a assertion cannot be established for the scheme in [11]. The procedure additionally checks whether the triple of record, timestamp and age has been registered before. Then, the triple is registered with a validity bit v which states whether the timestamp is valid. The `verify` query simply checks whether a triple is in the list of generated timestamps and outputs the associated validity bit. If the timestamp was not previously generated but is within acceptable parameters, it queries the adversary whether it is a valid timestamp or not and outputs the adversary's answer.

4.2   Random Oracle Sequences

In order to construct a protocol that realizes our functionality, we need to introduce some additional concepts. Exclusively using verifiable delay functions for timestamping is not practical, as it requires continuous execution of the function

Timestamping functionality $\mathcal{F}_{ts}^{\alpha}$

The functionality is parametrized with an adversarial time-diluting factor $\alpha \geq 1$. It answers queries for a dummy prover $\mathcal{P}$ and a set $\mathcal{V}$ of dummy verifiers V_i and interacts with an adversary $\mathcal{A}$.

Let $t_{\text{corr}} \leftarrow \infty$ represent the time the adversary sends a corrupt message to the functionality. It maintains two internal lists: $R \subset \{0,1\}^* \times \{0,1\}^\theta$ for (record,time)-tuples and $C \subset \{0,1\}^* \times \{0,1\}^\theta \times \{0,1\}^* \times \{0,1\}$ for (record, age, proof, valid)-tuples. Whenever $\mathcal{F}_{ts}^{\alpha}$ is activated, it sets $t^* \leftarrow \mathcal{F}_{\text{clock}}.\texttt{clock-read}$.

Creating a timestamp
- On input (**record**, c), the functionality records (c, t^*) in R and sends a message (**record**, c) to the adversary. After she responds with **ok**, it sends **ok** back to the prover.
- On input (**stamp**, c), the functionality relays (**stamp**, c) to the adversary. After she responds with (c, a, u, v), the functionality runs the procedure checkstamp(c, a, u, v) and returns (c, a, u) to the prover, where u is the timestamp string certifying age a.

Verifying a timestamp
- On input (**verify**, c, a, u), if a tuple of the form $(c, a, u, \hat{v})$ exists in C then it outputs $\hat{v}$. If no such tuple is found then it inputs (**cnewstamp**, c, a, u) to the adversary and gets back (v') and runs checkstamp(c, a, u, v'). After that, a unique tuple $(c, a, u, \hat{v})$ will exist in C and it outputs $\hat{v}$.

Party Corruption
- On input (**corrupt**) to $\mathcal{P}$, set $t_{\text{corr}} \leftarrow t$, beyond standard corruption management [6, §7.2].

Procedure checkstamp(c, a, u, v)
Let $\hat{t} = \min(\{t \mid (c,t) \in R\} \cup \{\infty\})$.
If $a > (t^* - \hat{t})$: /* Claimed age a larger than true age */
  If $a > \alpha \cdot \min(t^* - t_{\text{corr}}, t^* - \hat{t})$ then $v \leftarrow 0$;
If $\exists (c, a, u, \hat{v}) \in C$ then $v \leftarrow \hat{v}$; /* For consistency. */
Let $C \leftarrow C \cup (c, a, u, v)$.

Fig. 2. Timestamping functionality $\mathcal{F}_{ts}^{\alpha}$

in order to have an up-to-date timestamp. Additionally, each record would need a different instance of the VDF, making it impractical to timestamp multiple records. Instead, our construction is based on the hashchain originally presented in [9]. Instead of simply providing an ordering of events, the VDFs allow for a proof of age. Our timestamps consist of sequences of VDF-proofs that are linked to each other through cryptographic hash functions, modelled as random-oracle sequences as originally presented in [7]. We enhance these constructions by adding VDFs to the sequences, maintaining the property that dictates that such sequences can only be built in a sequential manner, allowing us to realize our timestamping functionality.

First we introduce Merkle trees, which will allow us to construct our desired sequences. Merkle trees are balanced binary trees, where the ordered leaf nodes are each labeled with a bitstring, and where each non-leaf node has two child nodes and is labeled by the hash of its children's labels. The root hash of a Merkle tree equals the label of the root node. Merkle trees allow for short set membership proofs of length $O(log(N))$ for a set of size N. For convenience we define some interface functions that deal with Merkle trees in a canonical deterministic way.

MT.root(T) computes the root hash h of the Merkle Tree for some finite ordered
  sequence $T = \langle x_i \mid x_i \in \{0,1\}^* \rangle$ of bit strings and outputs $h \in \{0,1\}^\lambda$.
MT.path(T, v) outputs the Merkle path described as a sequence of strings $\langle x_i \mid$
  $x_i \in \{0,1\}^\lambda \rangle_\ell$ where $x_0 = v$, $x_{\ell-1} = \mathsf{MT.root}(T)$, $x_i \in \{0,1\}^\lambda$ and either
  $x_{i+1} = \mathsf{H}(x_i \| \mathsf{H}(x_{i-1}))$ or $x_{i+1} = \mathsf{H}(\mathsf{H}(x_{i-1}) \| x_i)$ for all $i > 0$.
MT.verify(P) given an input sequence $P = \langle x_i \mid x_i \in \{0,1\}^\lambda \rangle_\ell$ outputs 1 if P is
  a valid Merkle path. It outputs 0 otherwise.

With a slight abuse of notation we also use MT.root(T) recursively, *i.e.*, if one of the elements S of T is not a bitstring but a set or sequence, we use MT.root(S) as the bitstring representing S. For example, if $T = (a, b, S)$ with bitstrings $a, b \in \{0,1\}^*$ and a set of bitstrings $S = \{c, d, e\}$, then MT.root(T) = MT.root($(a, b, \mathsf{MT.root}(S))$). This similarly extends to MT.path(T, v), *e.g.*, where $v \in S$ in the previous example.

Our timestamps are based on random-oracle sequences, originally presented in [7]. In contrast with that work, our sequences are generated by two distinct random oracles, H and VDF, which is why we call them $H2$-sequences:

Definition 4.1 (H2-sequence). *Given functions* $\mathsf{H} : \{0,1\}^* \to \{0,1\}^\lambda$ *and* $\mathsf{VDF} : \{0,1\}^* \times \mathbb{N} \to \{0,1\}^\mu$, *an H2-sequence of length ℓ is defined as a sequence* $S = \langle (s_i, x_i) \mid s_i \in \mathbb{N} \cup \{\bot\}, x_i \in \{0,1\}^* \rangle_\ell$, *where the following holds for each* $0 \le i < \ell$: *if $s_i = \bot$ then $\mathsf{H}(x_i)$ is contained in x_{i+1} as continuous substring[3]; otherwise $s_i \in \mathbb{N}$ and $\mathsf{VDF}(s_i, x_i)$ is contained in x_{i+1} as a continuous substring. We let I_{VDF} be the index set of all elements $(s_i, x_i) \in S$ such that $s_i \ne \bot$ and call it the VDF-index set of S and we call $S[I_{\mathsf{VDF}}] = \langle (s_i, x_i) \in S \mid i \in I_{\mathsf{VDF}} \rangle$ the VDF-subsequence of S. We refer to $\mathsf{str}(S) = \sum_{i \in I_{\mathsf{VDF}}} s_i$ as the strength of the H2-sequence S.*

Additionally, our sequences must contain time receipts, which we need to ensure that adversaries cannot take advantage of existing timestamps in order to forge new timestamps, forcing them to start from scratch.

Definition 4.2 (H2T-sequence). *Let* $S = \langle (s_i, x_i) \rangle_\ell$ *be an H2-sequence of length ℓ with I_{VDF} the VDF-index set of S and $I_{\mathsf{VDF}}^{-1} = \{i-1 \mid i \in I_{\mathsf{VDF}}, s_{i-1} = \bot\}$. We call S an H2T-sequence if the following properties hold:*

---

[3] That is, $x_{i+1} = a \| \mathsf{H}(x_i) \| b$ for some $a, b \in \{0,1\}^*$.

1. For $i \in I_{\mathsf{VDF}}^{-1} \cup I_{\mathsf{VDF}}$: $x_i = t_i \| r_i$ where $t_i \in \{0,1\}^\theta$ is a time receipt and r_i is an arbitrary string.
2. For all $i, j \in I_{\mathsf{VDF}}^{-1} \cup I_{\mathsf{VDF}}$: if $i < j$ then $t_i \leq t_j$.
3. For all $i, j \in I_{\mathsf{VDF}}$: if $i < j$ then $t_i < t_j$.

We say S has ε **delay** if for all $i \in I_{\mathsf{VDF}}$, if $i - 1 \in I_{\mathsf{VDF}}^{-1}$ then we have that $t_i - t_{i-1} \leq \varepsilon$. If $I \neq \varnothing$ then we call the first element of $S[I_{\mathsf{VDF}}^{-1}]$ the root of S (root(S)) and the time receipt $t_{\min}$ in root(S) the root time of S and we call age(S) $= t_{\max} - t_{\min}$ the age of the sequence, where $t_{\max} = \max\{t_i \mid i \in I_{\mathsf{VDF}}\}$ is the last time receipt.

It is important to make sure that these sequences can only be constructed sequentially, one element at a time. When she has access to a faster rate, the adversary will be able to *forge* a sequence's age up to a certain point. We can bound the ability of the adversary to create a sequence which seems τ time steps older than it really is.

Lemma 4.3 (Unforgeable $H2T$-sequences). If $t_1 - t_0 < \tau \cdot \frac{\gamma}{\gamma_A - \gamma}$ then an adversary can create an $H2T$-sequence S of age age(S) $= t_1 - (t_0 - \tau)$ within $t_1 - t_0$ time steps with probability at most $2 \cdot (q_1 \cdot 2^{-\lambda} + q_2 \cdot 2^{-\mu}) \cdot (Q_1 + Q_2 + |S|)$, where $\mathcal{A}$ made q_1 queries of total bitlength Q_1 to H and q_2 queries of total bitlength Q_2 to $\mathcal{F}_{\mathsf{VDF}}^\Gamma$.

Proof. The proof can be found in the full version.

Additionally, we use signatures to prevent the adversary to output valid sequences without corrupting the prover.

Definition 4.4 ($H2TS$-sequence). Let pk be a public key for a signature scheme Σ and $S = \langle (s_i, x_i) \rangle_\ell$ be an $H2T$-sequence of length ℓ with I_{VDF} and I_{VDF}^{-1} defined the same way as Definition 4.2. We call S an $H2TS$-**sequence for** pk if for $i \in I_{\mathsf{VDF}}^{-1}$: $x_i = t_i \| r_i \| \sigma_i$ where $t_i \in \{0,1\}^\theta$ is a time receipt and $\sigma_i \in \{0,1\}^\kappa$ is such that $\Sigma.\mathsf{verify}(pk, t_i \| r_i, \sigma_i) = 1$.

The aforementioned sequences provide the security properties that we expect our timestamps to have. Instead of dealing with them directly, our prover maintains a list of blocks, each containing the VDF proof and the record to be timestamped as well as additional information. These blocks are chained through the use of hash functions, each block containing a hash of the previous block, similar to a blockchain.

Definition 4.5 (Block). We define a block for a party $\mathcal{P}$ with public key $pk \in \{0,1\}^*$ as a tuple $B = (rnd, prev, vi, vo, t, c)$ and

1. $rnd \in \mathbb{N}$ is the sequence number of the block;
2. $prev \in \{0,1\}^*$ is the root hash $\mathsf{MT.root}(B_{rnd-1})$ of the previous block B_{rnd-1}, or $prev = \mathsf{H}(pk)$ when $rnd = 0$;
3. $vi = (t^u, sig) \in \{0,1\}^\theta \times \{0,1\}^\kappa$ is a (time receipt, signature)-pair such that $\Sigma.\mathsf{verify}(pk, t^u \| prev, sig) = 1$;

4. $vo = (s, Y)$ is a VDF output: $Y = \mathsf{VDF}(t^u||prev||sig, s)$
5. $t \in \{0, 1\}^\theta$ is a time receipt of the creation of the block;
6. $c \in \{0, 1\}^*$ is the entry to be timestamped;

For convenience we use the notation $B.pk$, $B.rnd$, $B.prev$, $B.vi$, $B.vo$, $B.t^u$, $B.sig$, $B.t$, $B.s$, $B.Y$ and $B.c$ to refer to these elements in block B. Note that $B.Y$ is the pair (y, p) which is an output of VDF.

We assume that there is a canonical construction for the Merkle tree of a block such that $B.t||B.Y$ is a leaf of the tree. This choice comes from the fact that elements of $S[I_{\mathsf{VDF}}]$ look like this, where each element of the sequence consists of the output of a VDF (Y) preceded by a time receipt (t).

Additionally, we have that $prev$ and c must also be leaves, for similar reasons. These assumptions allow for an easy characterization of the link between these instances and the next VDF input.

Definition 4.6 (Chain). *We define a* chain *for a party* $\mathcal{P}$ *with public key* $pk \in \{0, 1\}^*$ *as a sequence of blocks* $C = (B_0, \ldots, B_k)$ *where for all* $0 \le i \le k$:

1. $B_i.rnd = i$;
2. $B_0.prev = \mathsf{H}(pk)$ *and* $B_i.prev = \mathsf{MT.root}(B_{i-1})$ *for* $i > 0$;
3. $B_i.Y = \mathsf{VDF}(B_i.t^u||B_i.prev||B_i.sig, B_i.s)$ *for* $i \ge 0$;
4. $\Sigma.\mathsf{verify}(pk, B_i.t^u||B_i.prev, B_i.sig) = 1$;
5. $B_i.t < B_j.t$ *for all* $i < j \le k$;

Let $\mathsf{len}(C) = k$ be the **length** of C. We define the notations $C[i] = B_i$ for block indexing, $\mathsf{last}(C) = B_k$ for the last block of C and $C[i : r) = (B_i, \ldots, B_{r-1})$ for subchains (in particular $C[i :) = (B_i, \ldots, \mathsf{last}(C))$).

Having $B_i.prev = \mathsf{MT.root}(B_{i-1})$ (and $prev$ being a leaf of the canonical Merkle tree) allows us to generate a Merkle tree for the entire chain by concatenating Merkle trees through $prev$. This construction allows us to create an *H2TS*-sequence starting from any element in a block (in particular c) and ending at the end of the chain, passing through every VDF proof and including every time receipt t and t^u. This allows a party to attest an age of c. A detailed explanation of this construction can be found in the full version. Given a chain C we refer to the *H2TS*-sequence starting from $B_i.c$ and going through the entire subchain $C[i :)$ as $\mathsf{h2ts}(C, i)$. Note that if we want to keep the timestamped records secret, we can ensure that $B.c$ is simply a hash of the record. The first element of the *H2TS*-sequence would simply be the record, followed by its hash.

4.3 Realizing the Functionality

In Fig. 3 we present a timestamping protocol based on the chains presented in Definition 4.6 and *H2TS*-sequences. We then show that this protocol realizes the functionality $\mathcal{F}_{ts}^\alpha$ from Fig. 2. Each time that the prover gets a new **record** query, they stop their current execution of $\mathcal{F}_{\mathsf{VDF}}^\Gamma$, then create a block containing the input from the **record** query and the output of $\mathcal{F}_{\mathsf{VDF}}^\Gamma$. Finally, they query the

┌─ **$H2TS$-based prover $\mathcal{P}^{\gamma,\varepsilon}_{\text{H2TS}}$** ─────────────────────────

Given parameter VDF rate γ, interrupt time ϵ. It answers queries from the environment $\mathcal{Z}$ and interacts with its oracle $\mathcal{F}^{\Gamma}_{\text{VDF}}$ and executes a digital signature scheme Σ with keypair (pk, sk). It maintains a chain C initialized by a block $((0, \mathsf{H}(pk), (\bot, 0), (0^\theta, 0^\kappa), 0^\theta, \bot))$ and a variable triple $(t^u, prev, sig)$. Upon initialization, it sets $t^u \leftarrow \mathcal{F}_{\text{clock}}.\mathtt{clock\text{-}read}$, $prev \leftarrow \mathsf{MT.root}(B_0)$ and $sig \leftarrow \Sigma.\mathsf{sign}(sk, t^u||prev)$ and inputs $(\mathtt{start}, t^u||prev||sig)$ to $\mathcal{F}^{\Gamma}_{\text{VDF}}$. The block creation process takes at most ε time steps. That is, for any consecutive blocks in the chain B_i and B_{i+1}, we have that $B_{i+1}.t^u - B_i.t \leq \varepsilon$. Whenever $\mathcal{P}^{\gamma,\varepsilon}_{\text{H2TS}}$ is activated, it sets $t^* \leftarrow \mathcal{F}_{\text{clock}}.\mathtt{clock\text{-}read}$.

- On input $(\mathtt{record}, c)$, the prover stops its current instance of $\mathcal{F}^{\Gamma}_{\text{VDF}}$ by querying $\mathtt{output}(t^u||prev||sig)$ and gets back (s, y) returns $\mathtt{ok}$. UIf it has a backlog of $\mathtt{record}$ queries, then it it at the end.
- When the prover is active $\lceil \psi/\gamma \rceil$ timesteps after the $\mathtt{record}$, query, it queries for the VDF proof with $\mathtt{proof}(t^u||prev||sig, s, y)$, getting back p. The prover then constructs a block in the following manner and then appends it at the end of C: $block \leftarrow (\mathsf{len}(C) + 1, prev, (t^u, sig), (s, (y, p)), t^*, c)$. The prover saves new values for its variables $t^u \leftarrow \mathcal{F}_{\text{clock}}.\mathtt{clock\text{-}read}$, $prev \leftarrow \mathsf{MT.root}(C)$ and $sig \leftarrow \Sigma.\mathsf{sign}(sk, t^u||prev)$. Finally, it starts the VDF computation again by inputting $(\mathtt{start}, t^u||prev||sig)$ to $\mathcal{F}^{\Gamma}_{\text{VDF}}$. If the prover has a backlog of $\mathtt{record}$ queries, it acts as if it just received the one at the top of the list.
- On input $(\mathtt{stamp}, c)$, the prover checks whether there is a block B_i in C that contains c in $B_i.c$. If there is no such i^*, it returns $(c, 0, \bot)$. If such block exists, it takes the smallest such i^*. It then constructs u by computing $\mathsf{h2ts}(C, i)$. The prover then outputs (c, a^*, u).

└───

┌─ **$H2TS$-based verifier $\mathcal{V}^{\gamma,\varepsilon}_{\text{H2TS}}$** ─────────────────────

Given parameter VDF rate γ and interrupt time ϵ. It answers queries from the environment $\mathcal{Z}$ and interacts with its oracle $\mathcal{F}^{\Gamma}_{\text{VDF}}$ and can make queries of the form $\Sigma.\mathsf{verify}(pk, msg, sig)$ for a given pk. Whenever $\mathcal{V}^{\gamma,\varepsilon}_{\text{H2TS}}$ is activated, it sets $t^* \leftarrow \mathcal{F}_{\text{clock}}.\mathtt{clock\text{-}read}$.

- On input $(\mathtt{verify}, c, a, u)$, the verifier parses u as an $H2TS$-sequence $S := \langle (s_i, x_i) \rangle_l$ with VDF-index set I_{VDF} and time receipt index I^{-1}_{VDF} and first element $(\bot, c)$. If it can't, it returns 0. Then, it verifies all signatures in the elements of $S[I^{-1}_{\text{VDF}}]$, the correctness of the $H2TS$-structure with $\mathsf{h2tsverify}(S, \gamma, \varepsilon)$ and the additional information through $\neg\mathsf{verchain}(C)$. If all these checks are successful, it outputs 1, else it outputs 0.

└───

Fig. 3. $H2TS$-based timestamping protocol

VDF functionality again with this block as an input. When creating a timestamp, the prover finds the block with the expected record and extracts the $H2TS$-sequence from it up to the end of the chain.

It is important to ensure the correct structure of the timestamp sequences to meaningfully realize $\mathcal{F}^{\alpha}_{\text{ts}}$. Timestamps can be split and recombined, creating new timestamps without interacting with the functionality. While this is a desirable feature in general, it introduces complications in UC. Our functionality can deal with cases of timestamps that are merged to create a longer timestamp for a certain value. In these cases, the functionality asks the adversary whether the new proof is valid. The adversary is still not able to make the functionality accept a proof that is longer than it should be (the timestamp must pass checkstamp).

However, our functionality is not equipped to deal with other cases that would occur naturally. For example, take the following $H2TS$-sequence, where $z = \mathsf{H}(x) || \mathsf{H}(y)$:

$$\langle (\bot, x), (\bot, \mathsf{H}(x) || \mathsf{H}(y)), (\bot, t || \mathsf{H}(z) || sig), (s, t^* || \mathsf{VDF}(x_2, s)) \rangle.$$

It is clear that substituting the first element of the sequence with $(\bot, y)$ results in a valid $H2TS$-sequence of strength s for y. In order to properly construct a protocol that realizes this functionality we must either give the functionality understanding of the structure of Merkle trees or "artificially" require additional parameters for verification. We choose to do the latter. The verifier can check whether an $H2TS$-sequence corresponds to the canonical Merkle tree of a chain. This makes cases like the previous example invalid (assuming that x was the content c of the block). We call this verification function verchain.

We constructed our $H2TS$-sequences with an ε-delay, representing the time between VDF executions. Such a delay is required as we need to take into account the time spent creating a new block. For simplicity, we assume that the adversary also has an advantage constructing the chain. Instead of taking ε time steps, the adversary takes $\varepsilon_A = \lceil \varepsilon/\alpha \rceil$. In this setting, we consider that $\lceil \psi/\gamma \rceil < \varepsilon$ as it is necessary to add the proof of the VDF for quick verification. In practice, the proof may be presented in a different place, allowing us to make ε smaller.

Theorem 4.7. *Let $\mu \in \mathbb{N}^+$ be the security parameter. For any real-world PPT adversary $\mathcal{A}$ with oracle access to $\mathcal{F}_{\mathsf{VDF}}^{\Gamma}$, there exists a black-box PPT simulator $\mathcal{A}_{id}$ such that for any PPT environment $\mathcal{Z}$ the probability that $\mathcal{Z}$ can distinguish between the ideal world with $\mathcal{F}_{ts}^{\alpha}$ and $\mathcal{A}_{id}$ (cf. Fig. 2, 4) and the real world with $\mathcal{A}$, $\mathcal{P}_{H2TS}^{\gamma,\varepsilon}$ and $\mathcal{V}_{H2TS}^{\gamma,\varepsilon}$ (cf. Fig. 3) is negligible in μ, λ and κ.*

Proof. Let $\mathcal{S}_{H2TS}^{\mathcal{A}}$ be as defined in Fig. 4. We consider the distribution of the joint views of all parties in the execution

$$(\Pi_{ideal}, \Pi_{real}) \leftarrow \mathrm{EXEC}(\mathcal{Z}^{\mathrm{IDEAL}(\mathcal{F}_{ts}^{\alpha}, \mathcal{S}_{H2TS}^{\mathcal{A}})}, \mathcal{Z}^{\mathrm{REAL}(\mathcal{P}_{H2TS}^{\gamma,\varepsilon}, \mathcal{V}_{H2TS}^{\gamma,\varepsilon}, \mathcal{A})}),$$

where all $ITMs$ receive the same starting input tape and randomness tape in the real and ideal worlds.

In order to prove the theorem we only have to bound the probability that the two views of $\mathcal{Z}$ diverge:

$$|\Pr[\mathcal{Z}^{\mathrm{IDEAL}} = 1] - \Pr[\mathcal{Z}^{\mathrm{REAL}} = 1]| \leq \Pr[\mathrm{VIEW}(\mathrm{IDEAL}) \neq \mathrm{VIEW}(\mathrm{REAL})].$$

One can verify that in the ideal world all queries by $\mathcal{Z}$ and their answers by $\mathcal{P}_{H2TS}^{\gamma,\varepsilon}$ are perfectly forwarded by the functionality and the simulator. Actually the only way for $\mathcal{Z}$'s view to be different is when a verify query by $\mathcal{Z}$ results in a different outcome between the ideal world and real world. We now bound the probability that this event occurs. Let $(t_{\text{bad}}, \mathcal{Z}, (\text{verify}, c, a, u))$ be the first query for which the answer o_i in the ideal world differs from the output $o_r \neq o_i$ in the real world. Let q_{verify}, and q_{VDF} be the maximum of the amount of verify and VDF queries, respectively, made in Π_{real} or Π_{ideal}. Below we only consider what happened up to time t_{bad} and disregard anything afterwards.

Assume $o_i = 1$, this is only possible if $\mathcal{S}^{\mathcal{A}}_{\text{H2TS}}$ has output $(c, a, u, 1)$ (as answer to a stamp query or as a stamped query). That can only happen when $\mathcal{V}^{\gamma,\varepsilon}_{\text{H2TS}}(\text{verify}, c, a, u) = 1$ and thus that $o_r = 1$, which is a contradiction. It follows that $o_i = 0$ and $o_r = 1$ and u is of the form

$$\langle((s_i, p_i), t_i, c_i, \sigma_i) | s_i \in \mathbb{N}^+, p_i \in \{0,1\}^\mu, t_i \in \{0,1\}^\theta, \sigma_i \in \{0,1\}^\kappa \rangle_l$$

where:

$$\Sigma.\text{verify}((s_i, p_i)||t_i||c_i, \sigma_i, pk_\mathcal{P}) = 1 \qquad\qquad a = \sum s_i / \gamma$$
$$\text{VDF}((s_i, p_i)||t_i||c_i||\sigma_i, s_{i+1}) = p_{i+1} \qquad\qquad a \leq (t_{\text{bad}} - t_0)$$

Now consider the case when (c, a, u) was not legitimately constructed through the functionality in the ideal world. Then, the simulator has to more actively deal with proofs that were not generated through stamp but constructed by the adversary/environment. If u was constructed by truncating and recombining previous proof chains in a valid way, they would have been accepted through the checknewstamp query to $\mathcal{S}^{\mathcal{A}}_{\text{H2TS}}$. Additionally, proofs legitimately computed by the adversary would be accepted through this mechanism, as the simulator ensures that the appropriate record query is created whenever a start query is input into $\mathcal{F}^{\Gamma}_{\text{VDF}}$.

To continue, we bound the probability that the adversary has constructed the proof in a non-sequential manner by Lemma 4.3 as at most $2 \cdot (q_{\text{H}} \cdot 2^{-\lambda} + q_{\text{VDF}} \cdot 2^{-\mu}) \cdot (Q_{\text{H}} + Q_{\text{VDF}} + |S|)$. Thus in the remainder of the proof we can assume the adversary has constructed the proof sequentially.

Since $o_i = 0$, it must be caused by one of the rules in **Procedure checkstamp** resulting in $v = 0$ for (c, a, u):

1. The case that c was not recorded by $\mathcal{F}^{\alpha}_{\text{ts}}$:
   Whenever $\mathcal{A}$ wants to construct a valid timestamp for a record c, they must take a particular hash r as part of the input to $\mathcal{F}^{\Gamma}_{\text{VDF}}$ such that it fulfills verchain. Any other sequence of hashes will not be accepted by $\mathcal{V}^{\gamma,\varepsilon}_{\text{H2TS}}$. As $\mathcal{S}^{\mathcal{A}}_{\text{H2TS}}$ has access to all random oracle calls, it can check the c used to construct a particular r that is input to $\mathcal{F}^{\Gamma}_{\text{VDF}}$ and generate the respective record to $\mathcal{F}^{\alpha}_{\text{ts}}$. Therefore, $\mathcal{A}$ can only construct a timestamp without triggering a record query through a collision in H, which has probability at most $q_{\text{H}} \cdot 2^{-\lambda} \cdot Q_{\text{H}}$.
2. The case that the claimed age a is older than the real age a_r times α:
   As $\mathcal{A}$ only has access to $\mathcal{F}^{\Gamma}_{\text{VDF}}$ then they can only create $H2TS$-sequences diluted by a factor α. As the time-dilution factor acts the same over

---

Simulator $\mathcal{S}_{\text{H2TS}}^{\mathcal{A}}$

The simulator $\mathcal{S}_{\text{H2TS}}^{\mathcal{A}}$ simulates an instance of prover $\mathcal{P}'$ who runs $\mathcal{P}_{\text{H2TS}}^{\gamma,\varepsilon}$ and verifiers $\mathcal{V}'$ which run $\mathcal{V}_{\text{H2TS}}^{\gamma,\varepsilon}$. It maintains a list R of all stamp queries and responses from $\mathcal{F}_{\text{ts}}^{\alpha}$. It simulates $\mathcal{F}_{\text{VDF}}^{\Gamma}$ through lazy sampling of VDF.

Creating a timestamp

- On input (record, c) from $\mathcal{F}_{\text{ts}}^{\alpha}$, the simulator inputs (record, c) into $\mathcal{P}$ and then sends back ok.
- On input (stamp, c) from $\mathcal{F}_{\text{ts}}^{\alpha}$, the simulator queries the relevant proof from $\mathcal{P}'$ with a (stamp, c) query. Then it checks the validity of such a proof through $\mathcal{V}_{\text{H2TS}}^{\gamma,\varepsilon}$.verify$(c,a,u)$ to get a validity bit v. Then it returns (c,a,u,v) to $\mathcal{F}_{\text{ts}}^{\alpha}$.
- If the prover has been corrupted, whenever the adversary $\mathcal{A}$ inputs (start, $t||\text{MT.root}(B_i)||\sigma$) to $\mathcal{F}_{\text{VDF}}^{\Gamma}$, if $\Sigma.\text{verify}(t||\text{MT.root}(B_i),\sigma,pk_{\mathcal{P}}) = 1$ then input (record, $B_i.c$) to $\mathcal{F}_{\text{ts}}^{\alpha}$ through the backdoor tape.

Getting a new timestamp

- On input from (cnewstamp, c,a,u) from $\mathcal{F}_{\text{ts}}^{\alpha}$. The simulator checks the validity of such a proof through $\mathcal{V}_{\text{H2TS}}^{\gamma,\varepsilon}$.verify$(c,a,u)$ and returns the response.

Fig. 4. Simulator $\mathcal{S}_{\text{H2TS}}^{\mathcal{A}}$

γ and ε, the adversary gains no additional advantage by changing the spacing of the time receipts in the sequence. Hence, it is impossible for the adversary to have created this proof in a sequential manner.

3. The case that the claimed age a is older than the time a_{corr} since corruption times α:

   The adversary cannot stretch VDF strengths of an honest chain in order to make it seem older because of the honest time receipts. Hence, if the adversary created this proof in a sequential manner and it started with a VDF of the form $\text{VDF}(t||x||\sigma)$ with a valid signature then it is clear the adversary succeeded in forging a digital signature before corruption. The probability of this event is negligible in κ.

4. The case that $(c,a,u,0) \in R$:

   The same analysis holds, but then for the first time checkstamp(c,a,u) was called.

As the number to all queries are polynomially bounded by μ, λ or κ, the probability of distinguishing is negligible in μ, λ and κ. $\square$

We have shown that we can create secure timestamps through random-oracle sequences. This result also allows for an efficient way to create timestamps for a large number of records through Merkle trees. Our analysis naturally extends to that context, as we only require the existence of an *H2TS*-sequence.

5   Beyond Timestamping

We have constructed a timestamping protocol based on verifiable delay functions. Our motivation, however, was to replicate the robustness of proof-of-work blockchains with respect to costless-simulation and long-range attacks. Our timestamping protocol adds a sequential-computation cost that does not have the associated economic and environmental costs of proof-of-work. Fortunately, our construction already looks like a blockchain where the entries of the ledger are encoded in c as defined in Definition 4.5. As long as a blockchain contains the outputs of verifiable delay functions over the block hashes it will be possible to extract the necessary $H2TS$-sequences. We leave it to further work to find the best way to implement this while allowing for network delays and forks.

References

1. Abadi, A., Ciampi, M., Kiayias, A., Zikas, V.: Timed signatures and zero-knowledge proofs -timestamping in the blockchain era-. Cryptology ePrint Archive, Report 2019/644 (2019). https://eprint.iacr.org/2019/644
2. Badertscher, C., Maurer, U., Tschudi, D., Zikas, V.: Bitcoin as a transaction ledger: a composable treatment. In: Katz, J., Shacham, H. (eds.) CRYPTO 2017. LNCS, vol. 10401, pp. 324–356. Springer, Cham (2017). https://doi.org/10.1007/978-3-319-63688-7_11
3. Boneh, D., Bonneau, J., Bünz, B., Fisch, B.: Verifiable delay functions. In: Shacham, H., Boldyreva, A. (eds.) CRYPTO 2018. LNCS, vol. 10991, pp. 757–788. Springer, Cham (2018). https://doi.org/10.1007/978-3-319-96884-1_25
4. Boneh, D., Bünz, B., Fisch, B.: A survey of two verifiable delay functions. Cryptology ePrint Archive, Report 2018/712 (2018). http://eprint.iacr.org/2018/712
5. Canetti, R.: Universally composable security: a new paradigm for cryptographic protocols. In: 2001 Proceedings of the 42nd IEEE Symposium on Foundations of Computer Science, pp. 136–145. IEEE (2001)
6. Canetti, R.: Universally composable security: a new paradigm for cryptographic protocols. Cryptology ePrint Archive, Report 2000/067 (2019). v.20190826:041954 https://eprint.iacr.org/eprint-bin/getfile.pl?entry=2000/067&version=20190826:041954&file=067.pdf
7. Cohen, B., Pietrzak, K.: Simple proofs of sequential work. In: Nielsen, J.B., Rijmen, V. (eds.) EUROCRYPT 2018. LNCS, vol. 10821, pp. 451–467. Springer, Cham (2018). https://doi.org/10.1007/978-3-319-78375-8_15
8. David, B., Gaži, P., Kiayias, A., Russell, A.: Ouroboros praos: an adaptively-secure, semi-synchronous proof-of-stake blockchain. In: Nielsen, J.B., Rijmen, V. (eds.) EUROCRYPT 2018. LNCS, vol. 10821, pp. 66–98. Springer, Cham (2018). https://doi.org/10.1007/978-3-319-78375-8_3
9. Haber, S., Stornetta, W.S.: How to time-stamp a digital document. J. Cryptol. **3**(2), 99–111 (1991). https://doi.org/10.1007/BF00196791
10. Katz, J., Maurer, U., Tackmann, B., Zikas, V.: Universally composable synchronous computation. In: Sahai, A. (ed.) TCC 2013. LNCS, vol. 7785, pp. 477–498. Springer, Heidelberg (2013). https://doi.org/10.1007/978-3-642-36594-2_27
11. Mahmoody, M., Moran, T., Vadhan, S.: Publicly verifiable proofs of sequential work. In: ICTS, pp. 373–388. ACM (2013)

12. Moran, T., Shaltiel, R., Ta-Shma, A.: Non-interactive timestamping in the bounded storage model. In: Franklin, M. (ed.) CRYPTO 2004. LNCS, vol. 3152, pp. 460–476. Springer, Heidelberg (2004). https://doi.org/10.1007/978-3-540-28628-8_28
13. Nakamoto, S.: Bitcoin: A peer-to-peer electronic cash system (2008)
14. Pietrzak, K.: Simple verifiable delay functions. In: 10th Innovations in Theoretical Computer Science Conference (ITCS 2019). Schloss Dagstuhl-Leibniz-Zentrum fuer Informatik (2018)
15. Wesolowski, B.: Efficient verifiable delay functions. In: Ishai, Y., Rijmen, V. (eds.) EUROCRYPT 2019. LNCS, vol. 11478, pp. 379–407. Springer, Cham (2019). https://doi.org/10.1007/978-3-030-17659-4_13

Empirical Studies

Open Market or Ghost Town? The Curious Case of OpenBazaar

James E. Arps and Nicolas Christin(✉)

CyLab, Carnegie Mellon University, Pittsburgh, USA
{jarps,nicolasc}@cmu.edu

Abstract. OpenBazaar, a decentralized electronic commerce marketplace, has received significant attention since its development was first
announced in early 2014. Using multiple daily crawls of the OpenBazaar
network over approximately 14 months (June 25, 2018–September 3,
2019), we measure its evolution over time. We observed 6,651 unique
participants overall, including 980 who used Tor at one point or another.
More than half of all users (3,521) were only observed on a single day
or less, and, on average, only approximately 80 users are simultaneously
active on a given day. As a result, economic activity is, unsurprisingly,
much smaller than on centralized anonymous marketplaces. Furthermore,
while a majority of the 24,379 distinct items listed seem to be legal
offerings, a majority of the measurable economic activity appears to be
related to illicit products. We also discover that vendors are not always
using prudent security practices, which makes a strong case for imposing
secure defaults. We conclude that OpenBazaar, so far, has not gained
much traction to usher in the new era of decentralized, private, and
legitimate electronic commerce it was promising. This could be due to a
lack of user demand for decentralized marketplaces, lack of integration
of private features, or other factors, such as a higher learning curve for
users compared to centralized alternatives.

Keywords: Measurement · Peer-to-peer systems · Electronic
commerce

1 Introduction

OpenBazaar, originally called DarkMarket, is a peer-to-peer electronic commerce
platform that has attracted significant media attention [10,13,14]. It was first
envisioned in 2014 as a response to the government takedown of the Silk Road
[6] online anonymous ("darknet") marketplace [10]. However, OpenBazaar developers quickly pivoted away from the darknet marketplace space and toward a
decentralized e-commerce platform. The project raised several million dollars in
seed funding through a startup called OB1 [13,14].

While the default OpenBazaar *search engine* is developed by OB1 and filters
undesirable items such as narcotics [15], the OpenBazaar project itself is open-
source and the developers cannot prevent vendors from listing such items using
the platform.

J. Bonneau and N. Heninger (Eds.): FC 2020, LNCS 12059, pp. 561–577, 2020.
https://doi.org/10.1007/978-3-030-51280-4_30

Interestingly, the takedown of the Silk Road marketplace failed to curb illicit activity on centralized anonymous marketplaces. On the contrary, Silk Road's successors have been thriving [9,18,21,30]: As of 2017, the leading marketplaces were grossing hundreds of millions of dollars per year [9], with no decline in sight, despite adversarial events such as law enforcement operations and "exit scams," in which some marketplace operators abruptly shut down their servers, taking with them any money left in escrow on the platform.

Given that OpenBazaar, thanks to its decentralized architecture, could prevent or mitigate most of these adversarial events, and given the clear economic demand for such services, we would expect thriving economic activity on a peer-to-peer platform such as OpenBazaar. This is what we measure in this paper.

For approximately 14 months (June 25, 2018–September 3, 2019), we have been crawling the OpenBazaar network on a near-daily basis to get a sense of the number of participants and the size of the overall network. By scraping listings offered by each vendor and the associated feedback left by buyers (similar to techniques used in related work, e.g., [6,18,30]), we also estimate the economic activity taking place on OpenBazaar. Finally, we can examine the extent of users' mindfulness about operational security when trading in illicit or illegal products.

Our findings are rather sobering. While there is undeniable network activity, and a reasonably large number of items available on the OpenBazaar network (at least 24,379 distinct listings observed during our measurement period), economic activity remains modest, and appears to be mostly generated by illicit product sales. Furthermore, many vendors appear to misunderstand the security guarantees offered by OpenBazaar or fall prey to some configuration defaults, and publicly reveal some potentially compromising information about themselves: Nearly a fifth of the vendors that use OpenBazaar over the Tor network [8] have accidentally revealed their IP address at some point in time.

The remainder of this paper is organized as follows. We discuss relevant background on OpenBazaar in Sect. 2, describe our collection methodology in Sect. 3, and present our results in Sect. 4. We explain how our work differs from related efforts in Sect. 5, and conclude in Sect. 6.

2   The OpenBazaar System

Imagine Alice wishes to join the OpenBazaar network and purchase an item. First, she downloads the OpenBazaar client from https://openbazaar.org, where she is presented with a "Get Started" page which allows her to edit her profile. Since all users on the platform can act as both buyers and vendors, she may also begin creating item listings if she were so inclined. Crucially, if Alice proceeds with the default setup process *even once*, her public IP address will be leaked to the network. Indeed, using Tor with OpenBazaar requires an extra configuration step, which is not immediately evident to first-time users. While the OpenBazaar client prompts the user if it detects that Tor is already running on the user's machine, we do not expect this to be common for most users.

Once Alice creates her account, she can explore the listings on the platform. OpenBazaar's peer-to-peer backbone is the InterPlanetary File System (IPFS), an open-source protocol which allows content storage and addressing across a network of distributed nodes [3]. IPFS can be used as an alternative to a traditional client/server architecture – instead of clients requesting data from a server, here, a node provides a hash of the content it is requesting to its peers, who are either able to provide the requested content or query their own peers for its location.

Since IPFS does not support a centralized repository of item listings, search is implemented through a third-party search engine. At the time of writing, the only search engine enabled by default in the OpenBazaar GUI is created by the OB1 developers – other known search engines, such as SearchBizarre and a service operated by BlockStamp, require a manual addition to the client which may not be intuitive for new users. These search engines operate their own crawlers which travel the network to index users and listings, where their results can then be queried by users who have added their search engine to the OpenBazaar client. Existing third-party search engines exist mainly to provide an uncensored view of listings on the platform, as OB1's search engine does not include listings for illicit products.

Listings are stored over IPFS using a Distributed Hash Table (DHT), where nodes store the hash of a given user, item, or feedback along with their location on the network. If a node visits a vendor page or views one of its listings, it also stores the information it receives locally for a certain period of time, allowing for an added level of redundancy across the network. This enables vendors not to be perpetually logged in. The system has been designed with the intention that individual listings will be re-seeded for about a week after their owner was last seen online [22].

When Alice clicks on a listing she is interested in, her client attempts to fetch the relevant information from her peers by querying the DHT for the item hash. If Bob, the store owner, is online, Alice will often be able to receive the listing directly from Bob – otherwise, Bob's data is typically seeded by other IPFS peers for a set period of time. If Alice can retrieve the item hash, she is brought to a listing page which contains information about the item such as its price, description, shipping details, preferred cryptocurrency payment method, and pictures of the item. Currently, OpenBazaar supports payment in Bitcoin, Bitcoin Cash, Litecoin, and Zcash [2]. Zcash required a full installation of its binary for more than half of the duration of our study, which raises usability concerns; Litecoin was added only in the second half of our measurement interval.

When purchasing an item through OpenBazaar, Alice may opt to directly send cryptocurrency to Bob to pay him, or to use a moderator service to hold the funds in escrow until the item is received. Moderators are OpenBazaar users who volunteer to mediate disputes between other users and decide the eventual distribution of funds using multisignature transactions, and usually do so in exchange for a small fixed-percentage fee. Moderators receive community feedback, but individual moderators are chosen by the vendor at the time of listing creation. Regardless, Alice sends her payment details and shipping information to Bob through the platform and the sale proceeds as it would on existing services such as eBay.

3   Data Collection Methodology

We turn now to our data collection methodology, outlining our objectives first, before discussing the mechanisms we use and their limitations.

3.1   Objectives

Contrary to traditional dark-web marketplaces [30], data collection on Open-Bazaar is encouraged rather than discouraged, which eschews most of the constraints one faces when attempting to scrape a network stealthily. In fact, since OpenBazaar is not regulated by any central authority, our node cannot be easily banned from the network. While it could be blocked by individual nodes, we received no indication that this happened at any point during the study. Therefore, our primary focuses were on data completeness and collection speed.

We elected to scrape data ourselves, despite the existence of several search providers for OpenBazaar. Some OpenBazaar search providers service the OpenBazaar GUI (i.e., they return JSON parseable by the OpenBazaar client GUI), while others simply serve their results on public-facing webpages. Regardless of the method used, we noticed some search engines – in particular, the most popular search engine, run by OB1 at http://openbazaar.com – do not display results for illicit products. As a result, we needed to build our own OpenBazaar crawling infrastructure to obtain uncensored data.

Ethics of Data Collection. The data we collect are volunteered by OpenBazaar participants. In particular, listings, descriptions, and user feedback are all made publicly available for everyone to see. We previously referred to our Institutional Review Board (IRB) to determine whether data collected in related work [6,30] could be publicly reshared. Our IRB had opined this line of work was not human-subject research. The only difference with previous research is that here, we do collect IP addresses of other clients. But, in doing so, our crawler does not collect any information a regular OpenBazaar node would not collect for operational purposes. In short, like most peer-to-peer network measurement research (see e.g., [7]), our measurements do not put users at additional risk compared to participating in the peer-to-peer network in the first place.

3.2   Crawler Design

Our crawler runs over Tor and leverages the OpenBazaar API [24], which is a modified version of the IPFS API. First, our crawler queries a list of its connected peers (GET http://localhost:4002/ob/peers/). For each of those peers, we retrieve their closest connected peers (GET http://localhost:4002/ob/closestpeers/[peer_ID]), and add them to a list, recursively continuing until we no longer find any new peers (in our testing, this usually took between five and seven rounds). Using each peer's unique user ID, we can then make separate API calls to retrieve all of their current listings (GET http://localhost:4002/ob/listings/[peer_ID]) as well as all reviews left for those listings. Users, items, and reviews are all uniquely identified within OpenBazaar by a 46-character alphanumeric hash, which allows us to reliably track them across different scrapes. We log the approximate geographic location of peers with public IP addresses with FreeGeoIP (now called ipstack, [1]).

The crawler makes use of Python's Requests library [26], and the relatively small size of the network means that it is very fast (often completing in an hour or less). However, to avoid too much redundancy and to reduce strain on the Tor network, we chose to scrape the network once every two to four hours. This provided sufficient coverage on a daily basis, and by leaving our OpenBazaar node running while the scraper was not in use, we also contributed to the overall health of the network.

3.3   Potential Limitations

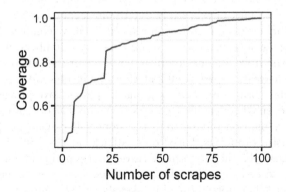

Fig. 1. Estimated coverage as a function of the number of scrapes.

Network Coverage. One risk of measuring a decentralized marketplace is that our node could lack a complete view of the network, and it was not uncommon for our scraper's requests to the DHT to time out for certain items or users. Figure 1 depicts the relative coverage percentage of items seen on the network during April 2019. We observed 6,292 items on the network during this time, and saw 85% of them during the first two days (i.e., the first 24 scrapes), encountering the rest over the following seven. The large number of scrapes required to observe this proportion of the network is indicative of the high levels of churn we discuss in Sect. 4.1. Non-seller nodes (which make up the majority of network participants) also have little incentive to leave their OpenBazaar clients open for long periods of time, as they do not need their listings to be seeded by other network participants. The diminishing returns shown by the curve suggest that there are few items remaining to be found by the crawler.

While the number of items we observe is less than the number reported by the OB1 developers [5], we often found through manual inspection that many items returned in the later pages of a given search result performed through their service failed to load in our client. This is likely because the OpenBazaar protocol attempts to cache data from inactive nodes for approximately a week [22] before they are "forgotten" by the network. For example, if Alice owns a store and do not log on for a few days, other nodes should still be able to access Alice's store for approximately a week because it will be cached collectively by the other nodes in the network. Since OB1's search engine returns results indexed by its crawlers and then stored on its own servers, it is likely that its results contain stale listings that are no longer reachable on the network.

We therefore believe that our view of the network is typical of that seen by an average node; this motivates the need for our crawler to frequently scrape the entire network to increase coverage.

Economic Coverage. Unlike many other marketplaces, leaving a review is not mandatory after a purchase on OpenBazaar. We were unable to purchase any items ourselves as a part of this study due to our legal counsel's concerns about inadvertently participating in money laundering, but we confirmed this with one of the OpenBazaar developers. As a result, our sales numbers in Sect. 4.2 are a lower bound, even if we assume complete coverage of the network.

Despite this caveat, we are confident that our results are useful for two reasons. First, social norms on anonymous marketplaces have proven quite strong over the years: even when leaving feedback is not mandatory, buyers often do so, especially if they plan on buying from the same seller again in the future [30]. Soska and Christin's analysis, based on feedback ratings [30], showed numbers very close to those obtained externally through criminal complaints, when vendors were arrested or through marketplace takedowns, even when leaving feedback was not actively enforced by all marketplaces. The importance of feedback on those marketplaces was also evident when the original Silk Road changed the way feedback was tallied (shifting from per-item feedback, to aggregate, per-vendor feedback) and quickly reversed course in the face of customer complaints [6].

Furthermore, our reported distribution of sales by category is likely valid. One could think that users purchasing illicit items on OpenBazaar would be less likely to leave a public review than users purchasing legal products. As we will see, our results do not support this hypothesis.

4   Results

We next turn to our measurement results. We first describe network-level metrics such as the size of the peer-to-peer network, or the underlying churn in IP addresses we see participating in the network, before turning to discussing the economic activity that appears to take place on OpenBazaar. We then examine the security and privacy precautions vendors take.

4.1 Network-Level Metrics

The OpenBazaar Peer-to-Peer Network. Over our entire measurement interval, we have observed 6,651 distinct network participants, using 6,116 distinct IP addresses.

Table 1. OpenBazaar demographics. Users do not have any product listings; sellers have at least one active listing; active sellers have realized at least one documented sale.

	With Tor	Without Tor	Total
Users	743	4,487	5,230
Sellers	197	1,057	1,254
Active sellers	40	127	167
Total	980	5,670	6,651

Table 1 breaks down these participants into finer-grained demographics, distinguishing between *users*, who do not list any product, and are therefore assumed to be solely browsing or buying items; *sellers*, who list at least one product, but do not have any documented sale – that is no one left any feedback for them; and *active sellers*, who have received at least one piece of feedback. We also break down these participants between those who use Tor and those who do not.

Figure 2 shows, for each day, the number of OpenBazaar hosts we have encountered during our multiple scrapes on that day. The lighter curve denotes the fraction of hosts that are using the Tor network. We observe that the population has been relatively steady, at approximately 80 users simultaneously online on any given day throughout our measurement interval. The few downward spikes denote measurement issues rather than network instability.

The gaps in the plot denote times during which our measurement infrastructure was disabled, or otherwise unable to properly collect data.

The seemingly decreasing number of Tor users toward the end of the measurement interval might be a slight undercount. Through experimentation with our own test nodes, we discovered that OpenBazaar nodes in version 2.3.1 and higher running over Tor, sometimes failed to appear in our crawls, despite being online and reachable (that is, if one knew their node ID). This coincides, and may be due to the backwards-incompatible [23] software upgrade on March 19, 2019 (OpenBazaar 2.3.1), which may have affected some long-term participants over Tor. Overall, compared to Table 1, this plot seems to indicate that the vast majority of OpenBazaar users are actually rarely online. To better understand

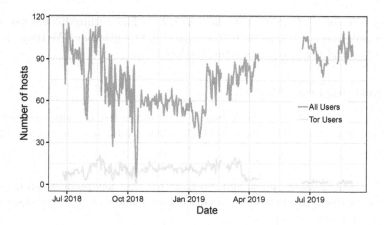

Fig. 2. Number of hosts on the OpenBazaar peer-to-peer network. Each point is the cumulative number of different hosts seen over all measurements taken on a specific day.

the dynamics of the OpenBazaar network, we next turn to a survivability analysis. Similar to Christin [6], we estimate vendor "lifespan" by recording the time we first saw a vendor, and the time we saw them last. They may have left and rejoined in the meantime—here we are looking at the vendor lifetime, regardless of their transient activity. To account for measurement effects (e.g., vendors still being present on the last day of measurement), Fig. 3 depicts a Kaplan-Meier estimator [16] that shows the probability a given user seen on day 0 will be seen again after x days, broken down by the categories defined in Table 1.

Churn is high among regular users: more than two thirds of them stay less than a day. Vendors, on the other hand tend to stay longer, especially vendors that have documented sales (i.e., that have received feedback). Roughly three quarters of all participants do not stay more than a week; a few users remain on the network throughout our measurement interval. Log-rank tests confirm that visually striking differences between the survival curves for all of these user categories are statistically significant ($p < 0.0001$). In short: vendors tend to be long-lived, while regular users are not, and usage of Tor is positively correlated with longer presence on the network.

Geographical Considerations. Figure 4 shows the geolocation of the IP addresses of participants that are not using Tor. OpenBazaar seems to be fairly international, with the usually observed concentration of users in North America and Europe. A couple of points with strange locations (e.g., Easter Island) suggest certain participants use VPNs, some of which are known to advertise implausible locations that fool geolocation databases [32]. We generally do not observe meaningful differences between different types of users, even though Western Africa,

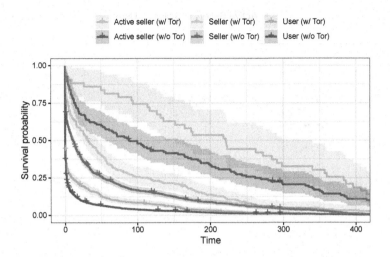

Fig. 3. Survivability analysis of OpenBazaar users. Kaplan-Meier estimator that shows the probability a given user seen on day 0 will be seen again after x days, broken down for different types of users. Shaded areas indicate 95% C.I. (Color figure online)

India and Thailand/Malaysia feature a larger proportion than we expected of active sellers – again, it is hard to tell whether this could be due to VPN usage.

4.2   Economic Activity

We next turn to a study of economic activity on OpenBazaar. We observed 24,379 distinct item listings during our measurement intervals. The apparent high average ratio of listings per seller ($\approx$40) is due to the ease of creating listings (including test listings) and to a few "power users" who have thousands of listed items on the platform.

Item Listing Survivability. We start with a survival plot in Fig. 5 shows the probability an item seen at time zero will still be available on the network x days later. The median item stays online for approximately three weeks. One quarter of all items disappears (i.e., are delisted) within a day, which further motivates the need to repeatedly crawl the network for completeness. A handful of items were present throughout our measurement interval. The "jumps" observed in the graph correspond to a large number of items belonging to a given vendor being all delisted on the same day, presumably because the vendor node had been offline for long enough to have its listings cleared from the IPFS cache.[1]

---

[1] Item listings do *not* automatically disappear when an item is sold out. The seller needs to either delete the listing, or be offline for a long enough period of time for the listing to stop being seeded by the network. We differentiate between the two cases by only counting visible reviews for an item as a sale and not considering disappearing listings as possible sales.

• Active Seller   Seller   User

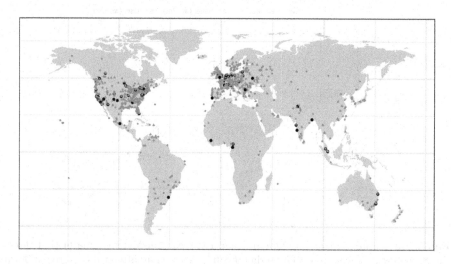

Fig. 4. Geolocation of OpenBazaar users. Users are network participants; Sellers are users with at least one listing; Active sellers are sellers with at least one feedback.

Overall, the survivability analysis paints a picture eerily similar to that of the early days of online anonymous marketplaces [6]: most items are very short-lived. As discussed in prior work [6,30], short-lived items are usually indicative of vendors holding low stocks, which in turn suggests that vendors operates primarily in the retail space, with small product quantities, and (usually) low sales volumes.

Preliminary Economic Analysis. We next examine economic activity on Open-Bazaar, across item categories. We initially attempted to feed each of the 24,379 item listings we observed into the 16-category item classifier proposed by Soska and Christin [30], who trained their item classification with listings from the Agora and Evolution marketplaces and showed very high (>98%) accuracy when evaluating *a priori* unknown listings.

We realized, however, that items classified in the "Miscellaneous" category represented a disproportionately high fraction of all listings, which led us to further break this category down into additional categories: Adult Toys, Art, Clothing, Jewelry, Print Media, and Souvenirs. We took 200 new items from our OpenBazaar corpus, hand-labeled them,[2] and added them five times (i.e., an extra 1,000 items) to the original training set consisting of 62,989 labeled items from Evolution and Agora. Our resulting classifier operates on 22 categories. Table 2 shows very good performance metrics, with precision and recall,

---

[2] A single researcher was tasked with this labeling, hence we do not report agreement numbers.

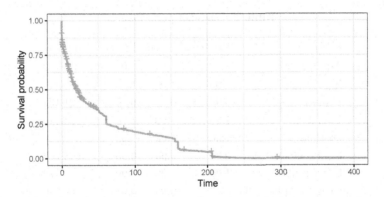

Fig. 5. Survivability analysis of OpenBazaar items. The plot is a Kaplan-Meier estimator that shows the probability a given item seen on day 0 will be seen again after x days. The median lifetime of an item is approximately 22 days. The curve fully overlaps the very narrow 95% confidence interval.

overall, being over 0.96. This is unsurprising, given that the modified classifier is very close to the original classifier from Soska and Christin – we merely added $1,000/63,989 \approx 1.6\%$ of new training data to the original classifier. The support, here, is much larger than the number of items we observed in OpenBazaar, since we are evaluating with 10-fold cross-validation on the original dataset provided by Soska and Christin[3] [30] *and* the OpenBazaar data. Certain categories (e.g., Adult Toys) do appear very rarely, though. The overall support for the new categories is fairly small (240 items); this again is unsurprising, as the imbalance in training sets means that an item needs to closely resemble a training example to be classified as one of the new sub-categories. In other words, our modified classifier closely mimics what Soska and Christin used; in a few "obvious" cases, it will manage to further identify a subcategory, but will do so very conservatively.

Next, we present the category breakdown for these 24,379 listings in Table 3. Simply looking at listing counts (columns 2 and 3), close to half of the listings are in the "Misc.," "Print Media," and "Souvenirs" categories, which generally denote legitimate items. The third largest category, "Digital goods," contains a mix of legitimate (e.g., e-books and other guides) and illegitimate (pornographic website account passwords) items. In short, a majority of items *listed* on OpenBazaar shops appear to be for legal products.

However, looking at actual sales (columns 4 through 6) paints a very different picture. To compute sales for a given item listing, using the same technique as in related efforts [6,30], we add up the price of the item to its total sales at each time a feedback for a sale of that item is recorded. Feedback that were recorded prior to our monitoring the OpenBazaar network are counted if the corresponding item was still listed when we scraped the network, and feedback

---

[3] The dataset is available from IMPACT, https://www.impactcybertrust.org.

Table 2. Classifier performance.

Category	Precision	Recall	F1-score	Support
Adult Toys	1.00	1.00	1.00	3
Art	1.00	1.00	1.00	24
Benzos	0.97	0.98	0.97	21,132
Cannabis	1.00	1.00	1.00	113,516
Clothing	1.00	1.00	1.00	38
Digital Goods	0.94	0.96	0.95	158,162
Dissociatives	1.00	0.99	0.99	7,172
Drug Paraphernalia	0.97	0.98	0.97	15,740
Ecstasy	1.00	0.99	0.99	49,184
Electronics	0.96	0.94	0.95	5,379
Jewelry	0.76	1.00	0.87	13
Misc	0.87	0.80	0.83	47,651
Opioids	0.98	0.98	0.98	25,511
Prescription	0.95	0.93	0.94	23,023
Print Media	1.00	0.96	0.98	113
Psychedelics	1.00	1.00	1.00	31,023
Sildenafil	0.98	0.97	0.97	31,22
Souvenirs	1.00	0.90	0.95	49
Steroids	0.99	1.00	0.99	17,044
Stimulants	0.98	0.99	0.99	55,555
Tobacco	1.00	1.00	1.00	3,966
Weapons	0.99	0.97	0.98	5,341
Total	0.96	0.96	0.96	582,761

was still accessible. As noted before, reviews are not mandatory in OpenBazaar, so that the sales numbers presented are a lower bound. Even with this caveat, sales volumes appear to be very modest. We only count around $217,000 in total sales over our measurement interval. By comparison, sales on Silk Road [6,30] and AlphaBay [21], two of the largest online anonymous marketplaces, reached hundreds of *millions* of dollars in revenue.

Looking a bit more carefully at the data revealed an interesting outlier: one vendor, *P...A*, appeared to be single-handedly responsible for 60% of all sales on OpenBazaar. In particular, that vendor had three pieces of feedback for a $36,000+ listing for a kilogram of cocaine, which should have accounted for more than $100,000 in sales by itself. When we manually inspected this specific vendor, we discovered that for most of their items, the feedback appeared to be fake: very closely clustered timestamps, all with highly positive ratings and uninformative messages for highly priced items. This strongly suggested an attempt at manip-

Table 3. Sales observed during our measurement interval. The values in columns 4–6 exclude vendor $P...A$, whose feedback seems highly questionable, and likely fake.

Category	Listings (count)	Listings (%)	Sales (count, corrected)	Sales (USD, corrected)	Sales (%, corrected)
Adult Toys	182	0.747	0	0	0.0
Art	331	1.358	10	975	1.13
Benzos	155	0.636	8	1,650	1.92
Cannabis	1,910	7.835	318	22,450	26.1
Clothing	1,881	7.72	30	375	0.437
Digital Goods	2,701	11.079	139	1,312	1.53
Dissociatives	21	0.086	2	1,050	1.22
Drug Paraphernalia	829	3.4	13	224	0.261
Ecstasy	243	0.997	10	4,895	5.69
Electronics	1,906	7.818	23	2,389	2.78
Jewelry	354	1.452	9	208	0.243
Misc	6,796	27.876	333	4,028	4.69
Opioids	223	0.915	17	2,207	2.57
Prescription	289	1.185	23	808	0.941
Print Media	4,902	20.107	6	123	0.144
Psychedelics	242	0.993	125	17,653	20.5
Sildenafil	45	0.185	41	792	0.921
Souvenirs	791	3.245	60	3,587	4.17
Steroids	69	0.283	2	11	0.0128
Stimulants	242	0.993	24	20,835	24.2
Tobacco	34	0.139	1	5	0.005
Weapons	233	0.956	8	374	0.436
Total	24,379	100	1,202	85,954	100

ulation by the vendor.[4] While in centralized marketplaces, padding feedback with misleading information is prohibited, and frequently results in banning the vendors engaging in such deceptive practices, the decentralized nature of OpenBazaar makes this kind of enforcement difficult. We do note, though, that OpenBazaar supports moderators that can assist in ensuring transactions are conducted satisfactorily (see Sect. 2); unsurprisingly, all of $P...A$'s listings were unmoderated. We removed this vendor, and the 33 associated sales, from further consideration in columns 4–6, to obtain an hopefully more accurate picture of

---

[4] Interestingly, *one* of their items seemed to have legitimate feedback, which pre-dated all of the seemingly deceptive feedback discussed here.

sales on OpenBazaar – excluding *P...A*, the total amount of sales is actually around $86,000.

As Table 3 shows, the category distribution of items that do sell is very different from the category distribution of items that are merely listed. Over 25% of all recorded sales are for cannabis-related products (including seeds), and more than three quarters of all recorded sales are for drugs – prescription drugs or narcotics.[5] This higher economic activity occurs despite the fact that the OpenBazaar developers have taken active measures to try to make illicit items harder to find, by excluding them from their built-in search engine search results, which suggests that the demand for illicit offerings far outpaces that for legitimate goods available on OpenBazaar.

Table 4. Distribution of feedback ratings. 5 is best, 1 is worst.

Score	Count	Percent
5	1,302	85.32%
4	28	1.83%
3	34	2.22%
2	29	1.90%
1	133	8.71%

Feedback Ratings. An alternative hypothesis would be that buyers of legitimate products are somehow less likely to leave feedback than buyers of illicit goods. We found no evidence to support that hypothesis. Specifically, we present the feedback ratings we observed in Table 4. OpenBazaar uses a 5-point rating scale, where higher scores are better, i.e., vendor strive to obtain 5-star feedback. The ratings we see heavily skew positive, as has been observed in general (legitimate) e-commerce platforms [27], and feedback distribution presents striking similarities with with that obtained for feedback left by Silk Road patrons [6, Table 3]: 5's dominate, followed by 1's, and other ratings are less frequently used.

4.3 Operational Security

While much of the core OpenBazaar vendor base tends to connect over Tor, not all of these users are truly anonymous. Indeed, user IDs are persistent across sessions. By comparing the unique user IDs of the 980 nodes seen connecting over Tor with those seen connecting over public IP addresses, we found that 173 users (17.7%) had revealed an IP address at some point in time. Not all of these users may have wished to remain anonymous during the entire collection cycle, but we did observe some obvious lapses in operational security, such as US vendors selling marijuana offering global shipping. It appears a version of

---

[5] The disproportionate volume of Psychedelics sales seems to be mostly influenced by one specific vendor, who has been highly successful on various online anonymous markets, and also operates their own vendor shop, and has presence on OpenBazaar.

the OpenBazaar client which is pre-bundled with Tor is in development, which should alleviate this problem over time [25].

At the beginning of our measurement timeframe, OpenBazaar nodes were tied to a single cryptocurrency – if a vendor wished to, for example, sell the same items both with Bitcoin and Bitcoin Cash, they were required to maintain two distinct nodes with identical listings. Furthermore, for some time using Zcash on the platform also required running a full Zcash node. As a result, activity on the platform was conducted almost entirely in Bitcoin until the release of a multiwallet feature on January 17, 2019, which added native support for the three currencies mentioned plus Litecoin. Previous studies (e.g., [20]) have shown that Bitcoin is highly traceable, meaning that early purchases on the platform may be able to de-anonymize certain vendors. Since the introduction of the multiwallet, however, there has been large growth in Zcash usage, with at least[6] 12,441 observed listings accepting payment in the currency.

5   Related Work

This work follows a long lineage of peer-to-peer network measurements, which can be traced back to studies of file-sharing networks such as Napster [29], or Gnutella [28]; or, beyond file-sharing, of Skype [11]. Later papers focused on specific metrics to better understand user behavior. For instance, Gummadi et al. studied peer churn on Kazaa [12], while others investigated overall peer availability [4,31], or resilience to poisoning attacks [7,19]. A number of papers looked into the economics of online anonymous marketplaces and have documented their rise in popularity [6,9,30]. In comparison, our analysis of OpenBazaar shows fairly modest revenues. Finally, also related to the operational security aspects we outline in this paper are attempts to quantify cryptocurrency traceability – notably efforts to trace Bitcoin [20], Monero [21], and Zcash [17].

6   Conclusion

We conducted multiple daily crawls of the OpenBazaar distributed marketplace over approximately 14 months (June 25, 2018–September 3, 2019). More than half of the 6,651 participants we observed were present only for less than a day, but users relying on Tor tended to be much longer lived, particularly if they were actively selling items. Economic activity is orders of magnitude smaller than on centralized anonymous marketplaces, and while most listed items are for legitimate products, the majority of items that do result in sales are for narcotics. Finally, vendors are not always using prudent security practices, leaking for instance their IP address despite generally connecting over Tor, which makes a strong case for imposing secure defaults—fortunately, the OpenBazaar developers are already reportedly working on this [25].

---

[6] A bug in our parser code for items with multiple currencies prevented us from precisely computing the number of such listings, but we could recover this lower bound.

We conclude that OpenBazaar, so far, has not gained much traction to usher in the new era of decentralized, private, and legitimate electronic commerce it was promising.[7] This could be due to a lack of user demand for decentralized marketplaces, lack of integration of private features, or other factors, such as a higher learning curve for users compared to centralized alternatives.

Acknowledgments. We thank our shepherd, Ben Edwards, and the anonymous reviewers for numerous comments that greatly improved this paper. We are also grateful to Kyle Soska for extensive discussions about this work. This research was partially supported by DHS Office of Science and Technology under agreement number FA8750-17-2-0188.

References

1. Apilayer: ipstack (2019). https://ipstack.com/. Accessed 20 June 2020
2. Ben-Sasson, E., et al.: Zerocash: Decentralized anonymous payments from bitcoin. In: IEEE Symposium on Security and Privacy, pp. 459–474. IEEE Computer Society, May 2014
3. Benet, J.: IPFS - content addressed, versioned, P2P file system. Technical report, June 2014, draft 3. https://arxiv.org/abs/1407.3561
4. Bhagwan, R., Savage, S., Voelker, G.M.: Understanding availability. In: Kaashoek, M.F., Stoica, I. (eds.) IPTPS 2003. LNCS, vol. 2735, pp. 256–267. Springer, Heidelberg (2003). https://doi.org/10.1007/978-3-540-45172-3_24
5. CC_EF_JTF: Did OpenBazaar ever take off? OpenBazaar developer comments on total number of listings, April 2019. https://www.reddit.com/r/Bitcoin/comments/bad0nh/did_openbazaar_ever_take_off/ekbd2k6/
6. Christin, N.: Traveling the silk road: a measurement analysis of a large anonymous online marketplace. In: Proceedings of the 22nd World Wide Web Conference (WWW 2013), Rio de Janeiro, Brazil, pp. 213–224, May 2013
7. Christin, N., Weigend, A., Chuang, J.: Content availability, pollution and poisoning in peer-to-peer file sharing networks. In: Proceedings of ACM EC 2005, Vancouver, BC, Canada, pp. 68–77, June 2005
8. Dingledine, R., Mathewson, N., Syverson, P.: Tor: the second-generation onion router. In: Proceedings of the 13th USENIX Security Symposium, August 2004
9. European Monitoring Centre for Drugs and Drug Addition and Europol: Drugs and the darknet: perspectives for enforcement, research and policy, November 2017. http://www.emcdda.europa.eu/system/files/publications/6585/TD0417834ENN.pdf
10. Greenberg, A.: Inside the 'darkmarket' prototype, a Silk Road the FBI can never seize, April 2014. https://www.wired.com/2014/04/darkmarket/
11. Guha, S., Daswani, N.: An experimental study of the skype peer-to-peer VoIP system. Technical report, Cornell University (2005)
12. Gummadi, K., Dunn, R., Saroiu, S., Gribble, S., Levy, H., Zahorjan, J.: Measurement, modeling, and analysis of a peer-to-peer file-sharing workload. In: Proceedings of ACM SOSP 2003, Bolton Landing, NY, pp. 314–329, October 2003

---

[7] We sent an earlier preprint of this paper to the OpenBazaar developers, but did not receive any feedback.

13. Higgins, S.: OpenBazaar raises $1 million for decentralised marketplace, June 2015. https://www.coindesk.com/openbazaar-raises-1-million-from-silicon-valley-giants
14. Higgins, S.: Bitcoin-powered marketplace OpenBazaar raises $3 million, December 2016. https://www.coindesk.com/bitcoin-powered-marketplace-openbazaar-raises-3-million
15. Jeffryes, J.: Remove BlockBooth from search providers. OpenBazaar developer comments on OB1 censorship policy, April 2019. https://github.com/OpenBazaar/openbazaar-desktop/issues/1569
16. Kaplan, E., Meier, P.: Nonparametric estimation from incomplete observations. J. Am. Stat. Assoc. **53**, 457–481 (1958)
17. Kappos, G., Yousaf, H., Maller, M., Meiklejohn, S.: An empirical analysis of anonymity in Zcash. In: Proceedings of the USENIX Security, August 2018
18. Kruithof, K., Aldridge, J., Décary Hétu, D., Sim, M., Dujso, E., Hoorens, S.: Internet-facilitated drugs trade: an analysis of the size, scope and the role of the Netherlands. Technical report RR1607 (2016). https://www.rand.org/pubs/research_reports/RR1607.html
19. Liang, J., Kumar, R., Xi, Y., Ross, K.: Pollution in P2P file sharing systems. In: Proceedings of IEEE INFOCOM 2005, Miami, FL, March 2005
20. Meiklejohn, S., et al.: A fistful of bitcoins: characterizing payments among men with no names. In: Proceedings of the ACM/USENIX Internet Measurement Conference, Barcelona, Spain, pp. 127–140, October 2013
21. Möser, M., et al.: An empirical analysis of traceability in the Monero blockchain. In: Proceedings of PETS, Barcelona, Spain, vol. 3, July 2018
22. OB1 Team: OpenBazaar seller guide - what to expect in this decentralized marketplace, October 2017. https://openbazaar.org/blog/openbazaar-seller-guide-what-to-expect-in-this-decentralized-marketplace/
23. OpenBazaar: OpenBazaar 2.3.1 is released with IPFS rebase, March 2019. https://www.openbazaar.org/blog/openbazaar-2-3-1-release-ipfs-rebase/
24. OpenBazaar Team: Openbazaar API. https://api.docs.openbazaar.org/
25. Patt, S.: Create "OpenBazaar-Private" installer, March 2019. https://github.com/OpenBazaar/openbazaar-desktop/issues/1735
26. Reitz, K.: Requests: Http for humans, May 2019. https://requests.readthedocs.io
27. Resnick, P., Zeckhauser, R.: Trust among strangers in internet transactions: empirical analysis of eBay's reputation system. Advances in Applied Microeconomics, vol. 11, pp. 127–157 (2002)
28. Ripeanu, M., Foster, I.: Mapping the gnutella network: macroscopic properties of large-scale peer-to-peer systems. In: Druschel, P., Kaashoek, F., Rowstron, A. (eds.) IPTPS 2002. LNCS, vol. 2429, pp. 85–93. Springer, Heidelberg (2002). https://doi.org/10.1007/3-540-45748-8_8
29. Saroiu, S., Gummadi, K., Gribble, S.: A measurement study of peer-to-peer file sharing systems. In: Proceedings of SPIE/ACM MMCN 2002, San Jose, CA, pp. 156–170, January 2002
30. Soska, K., Christin, N.: Measuring the longitudinal evolution of the online anonymous marketplace ecosystem. In: Proceedings of the 24th USENIX Security Symposium (USENIX Security 2015), Washington, DC, pp. 33–48, August 2015
31. Stutzbach, D., Rejaie, R.: Understanding churn in peer-to-peer networks. In: Proceedings of the 6th ACM SIGCOMM Conference on Internet Measurement, pp. 189–202. ACM (2006)
32. Weinberg, Z., Cho, S., Christin, N., Sekar, V., Gill, P.: How to catch when proxies lie: verifying the physical locations of network proxies with active geolocation. In: Proceedings of the 17th ACM Internet Measurement Conference (IMC 2017), Boston, MA, October 2018

Exploring the Monero Peer-to-Peer Network

Tong Cao[1], Jiangshan Yu[2(✉)], Jérémie Decouchant[1], Xiapu Luo[3], and Paulo Verissimo[1]

[1] SnT, University of Luxembourg, Luxembourg City, Luxembourg
[2] Monash University, Melbourne, Australia
`j.yu.research@gmail.com`
[3] The Hong Kong Polytechnic University, Kowloon, Hong Kong

Abstract. As of September 2019, Monero is the most capitalized privacy-preserving cryptocurrency, and is ranked tenth among all cryptocurrencies. Monero's on-chain data privacy guarantees, i.e., how mixins are selected in each transaction, have been extensively studied. However, despite Monero's prominence, the network of peers running Monero clients has not been analyzed. Such analysis is of prime importance, since potential vulnerabilities in the peer-to-peer network may lead to attacks on the blockchain's safety (e.g., by isolating a set of nodes) and on users' privacy (e.g., tracing transactions flow in the network).

This paper provides the first step study on understanding Monero's peer-to-peer (P2P) network. In particular, we deconstruct Monero's P2P protocol based on its source code, and develop a toolset to explore Monero's network, which allows us to infer its topology, size, node distribution, and node connectivity. During our experiments, we collected 510 GB of raw data, from which we extracted 21,678 IP addresses of Monero nodes distributed in 970 autonomous systems. We show that Monero's network is highly centralized—13.2% of the nodes collectively maintain 82.86% of the network connections. We have identified approximately 2,758 active nodes per day, which is 68.7% higher than the number reported by the MoneroHash mining pool. We also identified all concurrent outgoing connections maintained by Monero nodes with very high probability (on average 97.98% for nodes with less than 250 outgoing connections, and 93.79% for nodes with more connections).

1 Introduction

As blockchains aim at implementing decentralized and trustworthy systems, they often rely on peer-to-peer (P2P) protocols for membership management and information dissemination. This makes the P2P network a critical element of blockchains, as the security of the underlying consensus protocols and the privacy of transactions are all tightly related to its implementation [1–7].

J. Yu and J. Decouchant—These authors contributed equally.

J. Bonneau and N. Heninger (Eds.): FC 2020, LNCS 12059, pp. 578–594, 2020.
https://doi.org/10.1007/978-3-030-51280-4_31

Monero is a privacy-centric cryptocurrency, and is currently ranked the first among privacy-preserving cryptocurrencies with a market capitalization of 1.248 Billion USD, and the 10th among all cryptocurrencies[1]. Much research has been done on analysing the privacy of Monero [8–12], with a focus on on-chain data analysis, i.e., how the mixins (a.k.a. decoy inputs) are selected in each transaction and how they provide privacy guarantees. However, little research has been done to investigate Monero's P2P network, even though network level attacks have been studied on the specific networks of Bitcoin and Ethereum [1–3,13–15].

Analysing the resilience of a blockchain to network level attacks is challenging, as it requires a deep understanding on the underlying network. In this paper, we present a first step of work towards analysing Monero's security and privacy against network level attacks. In particular, we perform an analysis of Monero's network protocol, and identify possible ways to infer the network topology. We develop a toolset to implement our findings. Our tool set includes *NodeScanner* and *NeighborFinder*. *NodeScanner* automatically discovers peers in the Monero network, no matter whether they are currently online or not. We classify the discovered peers in three categories, namely active and reachable nodes, active and unreachable nodes, and inactive nodes. A node is active if it is currently online, and is reachable if *NodeScanner* can successfully connect to it. Compared to previous works [6,16–18], *NeighborFinder* is able to identify the unreachable active nodes in the network, which are the active direct neighbors of nodes that could be reached, for the network topology inference.

Our experimental results show that Monero's network is highly centralized— 0.7% of the active nodes maintain more than 250 outgoing connections, and 86.8% of the nodes do not maintain more than 8 outgoing connections. These 86.8% nodes collectively maintain only 17.14% of the overall connections in the network. Our toolset is also very effective in observing the network – after a single week of data collection, our toolset already discovered 68.7% more active peers than Monerohash [19] – a Monero mining pool that is the only known pool providing data on the Monero node distribution. On average, our toolset identified approximately 2,758 active nodes per day, while Monerohash only showed about 1,635 active nodes. Furthermore, we report our analysis of the collected data regarding an estimation of our network coverage, the network connectivity, and the node distribution in the Monero P2P network.

Our contributions are summarized as follows:

- to the best of our knowledge, our work is the first to describe how to infer Monero's peer-to-peer network, which would enable further studies on the network level security analysis of Monero;
- we provide the first toolset to implement our findings on exploring the Monero peer-to-peer network. In particular, *NodeScanner* explores existing and historical nodes in the Monero network, and *NeighborFinder* identifies neighbors of the Monero nodes. We plan to release our toolset as an open source project shortly; and

---

[1] https://coinmarketcap.com. Data fetched on Sept. 12, 2019.

- we conduct an experiment to evaluate Monero's network, and show the effectiveness of our methods. We provide insights and a security analysis of its network size, distribution, and connectivity.

Disclosure. We have disclosed our research findings to the Monero team, which has been working on patching the peer-to-peer protocol, and publicly acknowledged our findings in their git commit[2].

The remaining of this paper is organized as follows. Section 2 provides a high level overview on the different designs of P2P protocol in different major cryptocurrencies, and highlights the particularities of Monero's P2P membership protocol. Section 3 provides an overview of our analysis pipeline, and the algorithms we used to implement the discovery of the nodes and the inference of their connections. Section 4 details the results obtained after analyzing the data collected during one week, and provides a discussion on the privacy and security issues that can arise after a P2P network exposure. Section 5 reviews related works, and we conclude this paper in Sect. 6.

2   Monero's P2P Membership Protocol

Peer-to-peer (P2P) networks have been designed and extensively studied to allow decentralized message exchanges. They have been getting a renewed attention since Satoshi Nakamoto described Bitcoin in 2008. Indeed, inspired by Bitcoin, thousands of cryptocurrencies serving different purposes have been created. However, no standard P2P protocol has been proposed for blockchains. Instead, different P2P protocols have been designed and adapted by different cryptocurrencies [20–22].

Monero relies on its peer-to-peer network to disseminate transactions and blocks. Unfortunately, a proper presentation of Monero's peer-to-peer protocol has been missing from the literature. This section describes Monero's peer-to-peer membership protocol based on its source code, which is available from Monero's official working repository[3].

2.1   Initialization

Monero hardcodes a set of hostnames, which can be translated to IP addresses through the DNS service, and IP addresses of seed nodes that new participants can contact to be bootstrapped into the peer-to-peer network. Those seed nodes are operated by the Monero core team.

New joiners can obtain a limited number of active peers' IP addresses from the seed nodes to initialize their peer lists. They can then start initiating connections with peers, exchange membership lists and discover other peers, until they have established their desired number of connections.

---

[2] https://github.com/monero-project/monero/blob/960c2158010d30a375207310a36a
7a942b9285d2/src/p2p/net_peerlist.h.

[3] Commit hash   14a5c2068f53cfe1af3056375fed2587bc07d320,   https://github.com/
monero-project/monero.

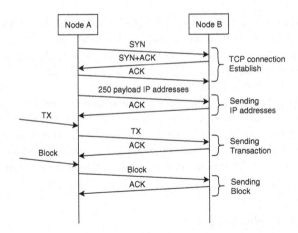

Fig. 1. Message exchange in the Monero network

2.2 Peer List

In Monero, each node maintains a peer list consisting of two parts, i.e., a *white_list*, and a *gray_list*. In the peer list of a peer A, the information of each recorded peer not only contains its identity, its IP address, and the TCP port number it uses, but also a special *last_seen* data field, which is the time at which the peer has interacted with peer A for the last time. All the peers in the lists are ordered chronologically according to their *last_seen* data, i.e., the most recently seen peers are at the top of the list.

Each time a node receives information about a set of peers, this information is inserted into its *gray_list*. Nodes update their *white_list* and *gray_list* through a mechanism called "graylist housekeeping", which periodically pings randomly selected peers in the *gray_list*. If a peer from the *gray_list* is responsive, then its information will be promoted to the *white_list* with an updated *last_seen* field, otherwise it will be removed from the *gray_list*. To handle idle connections, nodes check their connections through the *IDLE_HANDSHAKE* protocol, and update the *last_seen* fields if they successfully connected to the corresponding neighbors, otherwise they drop the associated connection. Nodes also periodically handshake their current connections, and update the *last_seen* field of the associated responsive peers. If a peer does not respond to the handshake request, then the requesting node will disconnect from this neighbor, and connect to a new neighbor chosen from the *white_list*. The disconnected peers will stay in the *white_list*. The maximum sizes of the *white_list*, and of the *gray_list*, are equal to 1,000 and 5,000, respectively. If the number of peers in these lists grow over the maximum allowed size, then the peers with the oldest *last_seen* fields will be removed from the list.

Nodes broadcast messages (e.g., transactions and blocks) to their neighbors through TCP connections. Nodes choose their neighbors from the *white_list*. If not enough peers from the *white_list* are currently online, then a node will choose its neighbors from the *gray_list*. Nodes to which previous connections were established are classified as anchor nodes, and stored in the *white_list*. Monero ensures that every node is connected to at least two anchor nodes to prevent a node from being isolated by an attacker. To discover other participants, nodes exchange membership messages by sending a TCP *SYN* message to their neighbors. Upon receiving a *SYN* message, the neighbors create a message whose payload contains detailed information of its top 250 peers in the *white_list*, and send it back to the requester. The requester inserts the received peer data into its *gray_list*, and runs the graylist housekeeping protocol to update the lists. More details about the TCP connection and data transmission will be presented in Sect. 2.3.

2.3   Information Propagation

By default, each peer maintains 8 outgoing connections and accepts 1 incoming connection. A peer residing behind a firewall or a NAT does not accept incoming connections, and only maintains 8 outgoing connections. Peers are allowed to define their maximum number of outgoing and incoming connections. Monero recommends peers to increase the number of their connections according to their capacity, for an improved network connectivity.

Three types of messages are propagated in Monero, respectively containing peers information, transactions, and blocks. A node establishes connections with others through a TCP handshake (SYN-SYN-ACK) as illustrated in Fig. 1, and can subsequently exchange peer information through the established connection.

3   Analysis Pipeline Overview

In this section, we introduce the different data structures and the processes we implemented, along with the associated network tools they rely on. We also detail our algorithmic approaches to monitor the active Monero nodes and to infer their neighbors. The analysis pipeline is illustrated in Fig. 2.

3.1   Construction

We deploy full Monero nodes to collect data in the Monero network. These nodes establish connections with peers in the network, and store packets into their local storage. We adapt two network measurement tools, i.e., *tcpflow*[4] and *nmap*[5], to collect data and analyze the Monero network. As mentioned in Sect. 2, each received TCP packet contains the most recent 250 IP addresses of the sender's *white_list*. Thus, all received IP addresses are recent out-bound peers of the sender. We then use our first tool, *NodeScanner*, to collect the IP addresses of discovered Monero nodes and store them in the *NodePool*.

---

[4] https://www.tecmint.com/tcpflow-analyze-debug-network-traffic-in-linux/.
[5] https://nmap.org/.

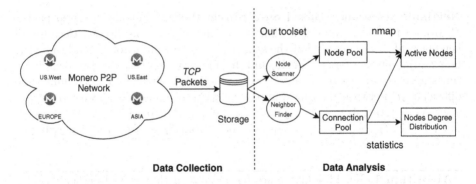

Fig. 2. Analysis pipeline overview

We use our second tool *NeighborFinder* to infer the neighbors of reached nodes that sent the TCP packets to collectors, and store them in the *ConnectionPool*. Each connection consists of a node we reached and of its neighbor, which are both active. We introduce in greater details our developed tools in Sect. 3.3.

3.2 Neighbor Inference Based on Membership Messages

As introduced in Sect. 2.2, Monero clients execute a gray list housekeeping protocol and an idle connections prevention protocol to evict inactive nodes from their peer list. As a consequence, the outbound neighbors of a node are often associated with the freshest *last_seen* in its peer list, which enables the identification of a node's neighbors from the membership messages it sends.

3.3 Nodes Discovery and Connections Inference

Our deployed nodes accept incoming connections and initiate outgoing connections to receive TCP packets from other nodes. Let $P = \{P_1, P_2, P_3, ..., P_j\}$ be the set of j TCP packets a collector receives from a reached node, such that each packet P_k ($k \in [1, j]$) contains a set $A_k = \{A_{k,1}, A_{k,2}, A_{k,3}, ..., A_{k,250}\}$ of IP addresses and a set $T_k = \{T_{k,1}, T_{k,2}, T_{k,3}, ..., T_{k,250}\}$ of *last_seen* timestamps.

NodeScanner. After having received a set P of packets from node $\mathcal{N}$, *NodeScanner* identifies the set $A = \{A_1, A_2, A_3, ..., A_j\}$ of included IP addresses, extracts the set $U = A_1 \cup A_2 \cup A_3 \cup ... \cup A_j$ of unique IP addresses from A, and inserts all unique IP addresses into the *NodePool*.

NeighborFinder. Our second tool aims at identifying a set N_k of neighbors from each P_k ($k \in [1, j]$). Over the various packets P_1 to P_j, it identifies the overall set of neighbors $N = N_1 \cup N_2 \cup N_3 \cup ... \cup N_j$. In the following, we first indicate our neighbors inference approach based on the time difference of the nodes' *last_seen* timestamps in a single packet, and then refine this approach by relying on several received packets.

Neighbors Inference Based on a Single Packet. For any received packet P_k from a node $\mathcal{N}$, we assume that it contains $r < 250$ neighbors. Because all neighbors of $\mathcal{N}$ are updated at the same time, the neighbors of $\mathcal{N}$ tend to be the first r adjacent IP addresses of A_k, and the difference between any two neighbors' timestamps tends to be small. If we assume that there is a maximum time difference μ^6 between the timestamps of any two neighbors, then we can extract a set $N_k' = \{A_{k,i}, A_{k,i+1}, A_{k,i+2}, ..., A_{k,i+r-1} | r \in [1, 250], i \in [1, 251 - r], \forall x \in [i, i + r - 1], T_{k,x} - T_{k,x+1} \le \mu\}$ of neighbors from P_k as shown in Algorithm 1.

Algorithm 1. Neighbors inference based on a single received packet

---

Input : P_k: Packets;
   μ: The maximum time difference between the *last_seen* timestamps of a node's neighbors;
   A_k: the IP addresses of P_k;
   T_k: the *last_seen* timestamps of P_k;
Output: Neighbors set N_k';

1 **for** $(y = 1, y < 250, y{+}{+})$ **do**
2 | **if** $T_{k,y} - T_{k,(y+1)} \le \mu$ **then**
3 | | $N_k' \longleftarrow A_{k,y}$
4 | **end**
5 | **if** $T_{k,(y+1)} - T_{k,(y+2)} > \mu$ **then**
6 | | $N_k' \longleftarrow A_{k,(y+1)}$; **break**
7 | **end**
8 **end**

Each node iteratively checks its connections through the *IDLE_HANDSHAKE* procedure, which makes a node send SYN packets to all of its neighbors. Following this procedure, the *last_seen* timestamps of handshaked neighbors are updated with the current time if nodes can be contacted, otherwise connections are dropped. This mechanism prevents idle connections to be maintained. However, the answers to the SYN packet can be received at a different time, which leads to different answer delays. It is therefore necessary to set μ to a value that is large enough to discover all neighbors, but small enough to limit false positives. This problem only exists when we rely on a single packet to infer the neighbors of a target node, and disappears when multiple packets are used.

Improved Neighbors Inference Based on Multiple Packets. During a connection with a node, it frequently happens that our monitoring nodes successively receive multiple packets from a node. If an IP address appears in successive packets, and its *last_seen* has been updated, then we can conclude that the node corresponding to this IP address is a neighbor of the sender. We use the set $N'' = \{A_{k,y} \mid , A_{k,y} = A_{(k+1),z}, T_{k,y} \ne T_{(k+1),z}, A_{k,y} \in P_k, T_{k,y} \in P_k,$

---

[6] We set μ to the value of the *IDLE_HANDSHAKE* interval, i.e., 60 seconds.

Algorithm 2. Neighbors inference based on two received packets

---

Input   : Packets P_k and $P_{(k+1)}$;

A_k, $A_{(k+1)}$: the IP addresses in P_k, resp. P_{k+1};

T_k, $T_{(k+1)}$: the *last_seen* timestamps in P_k, resp. P_{k+1};

Output: Neighbors set N_k'';

1 **foreach** $A_{k,y} = A_{(k+1),z}$ **do**

2   **if** $T_{k,y} \neq T_{(k+1),z}$ **then**

3        $N_k'' \longleftarrow A_{k,y}$

4   **end**

5 **end**

$A_{(k+1),z} \in P_{(k+1)}, T_{(k+1),z} \in P_{(k+1)}\}$ to denote the IP addresses that have been updated between packets P_k and $P_{(k+1)}$. We then extract the neighbors of node $\mathcal{N}$ following Algorithm 2.

4   Experiments

This section describes our experimental settings, validation approach, data analysis methods and results. We also discuss the potential threats of a network topology exposure.

4.1   Settings

We deployed four full nodes in the Monero network: two in the U.S. (California and Virginia), one in Europe (Luxembourg), and one in Asia (Japan). Each node ran on an Ubuntu 16.04 machine with an Intel Xeon Platinum 8000 series processor. We make use of the four nodes not only to collect data, but also to have access to a ground truth and verify our neighbor inference algorithms.

We manually modified the settings on our Monero nodes so that they could establish the largest number of connections with other nodes. First, we set the maximum number of incoming and outgoing connections to 99,999 to force our nodes to actively search for new neighbors. Second, we modified the number of opened files, socket receive buffer, and socket send buffer of used machines to the maximum number (1,048,576, 33,554,432, 33,554,432 respectively) in order to simultaneously maintain a large amount of TCP connections.

We collected 510 GB of raw data containing 12,563,962 peer list messages (as shown in Table 1). We extracted 21,678 IP addresses, which belong to 970 ASs[7]. Out of these collected IP addresses, our nodes established connections with 3,626 peers, and identified 703 peers to which no connection could not be established, but that were active and connected to reached nodes. We say that peers are active and reachable if our nodes can establish connections with them. We say

---

[7] We use the whois (https://www.ultratools.com/tools/ipWhoisLookup) database to find the ASN for each IP address.

Table 1. Data collected from Tokyo (T), Luxembourg (L), California (C), and Virginia (V)

#Received Peer List Messages	Node		Connection	
T: 1,971,514; L: 2,308,968 C: 3,892,225; V: 4,391,255	**IP Addresses**	**ASN**	**Host Level**	**AS Level**
	21,678	970	338,023	87,013

peers are active but unreachable if they are connected to nodes we connected to and if a connection could not be established with them. We say a peer is inactive if it is neither connected to our nodes, nor connected to responsive peers. If our nodes were not able to connect to a peer, then it either meant that the peer was already fully connected during the data collection, or that it was offline. To reduce the number of possible false negatives, we consider that a peer is offline if the peer is not connected to our nodes or to the neighbors of our nodes, and if their *last_seen* has not been updated during the data collection process.

4.2 Validation

We used the node in Luxembourg to establish three connections with the nodes in California, Virgina, and Tokyo respectively. We compared the identities of the nodes identified by *NeighborFinder* as neighbors with the ground truth of our deployed nodes. Since the payload data of membership messages can contain at most 250 IP addresses, a part of a node's neighbors could not be observed in a single message when it maintained more than 250 outgoing connections. Therefore, we specifically set up a node maintaining more than 250 outgoing neighbors in Tokyo to verify our algorithms. The validation reported a precision of 100% with 97.98% recall (i.e., all inferred neighbors were real neighbors, and 2.12% of the nodes identified as Non-neighbors were false negatives) when the number of neighbors is smaller than 250, and a precision of 100% with 93.79% recall for the node in Tokyo.

4.3 Measuring the Network Coverage

Previous tools [23–26] relied on the number of reached nodes to estimate their network coverage in Bitcoin and Ethereum. However, unreachable active nodes, which are also a part of the nework, have been overlooked by these tools. In this section, we introduce our method, which takes unreachable nodes into account, to estimate the network coverage. We show the effectiveness of our tools by comparing our results with the data provided by the MoneroHash mining pool [19].

NeighborFinder determined the neighbors of reached nodes even when it was not possible to contact them. This allowed us to:

- **identify the fully connected nodes.** When a node has reached its maximum number of incoming connections, it does not accept any new inbound

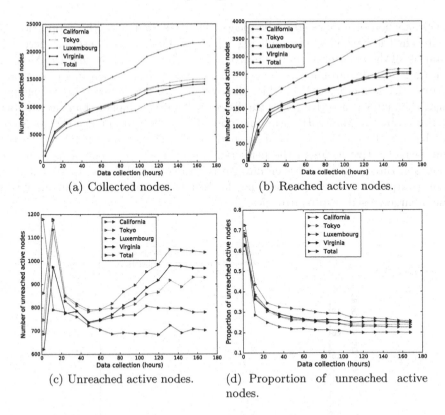

(a) Collected nodes.

(b) Reached active nodes.

(c) Unreached active nodes.

(d) Proportion of unreached active nodes.

Fig. 3. Analysis of the collected IP addresses during the data collection process.

neighbor. In this case, previous approaches cannot identify these fully connected active nodes. However, *NeighborFinder* can discover them through the connections they have established with reached nodes.

- **estimate the network size by observing the proportion of unreached active nodes.** Unfortunately, there is no ground truth to validate the network size in permissionless blockchains. We use $\frac{num.\ unreached\ active\ nodes}{num.\ collected\ nodes} \in [0,1]$ as a metric to estimate the proportion of the Monero network that has been reached. In practice, our tools have discovered almost all long-term running nodes in the network when the new reached nodes cannot present information about any new nodes. The overall proportion of unreached active nodes is illustrated in Fig. 3(d).

We present the data collection statistics in Fig. 3, where we respectively show the data collected by the node in California in red, Virginia in black, Japan in yellow, and Luxembourg in green. The total number of reached nodes is represented in blue. Figure 3(a) shows the number of discovered peers. Figure 3(b) shows the number of active nodes connected to our servers. Figure 3(c) shows the number of active but unreachable peers. Figure 3(d) shows the evolution of proportion of unreached active peers. After the first 80 h, the proportion of unreached active nodes are stabilizing, which means that our toolset has detected almost all the long-term running active nodes. Thus, it is likely that the Monero network contains around 2,758 active nodes per day as shown in Fig. 4. Compared with Monerohash [19], which discovered 1,635 active nodes in average per day, the number of active nodes we discovered is 68.7% higher than the number reported by the MoneroHash mining pool. To the best of our knowledge, Monerohash is the only Monero mining pool providing information related to the number of active nodes in the network. Moreover, the number of daily active nodes in Bitcoin [23] and Ethereum [24] is estimated to be close to 10,000. It is not a surprise to see that Monero has far less daily active nodes than those two more largely used cryptocurrencies.

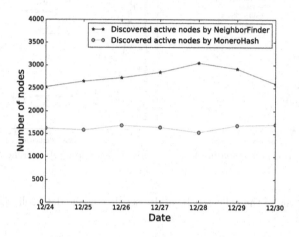

Fig. 4. Active nodes discovered daily by *NeighborFinder* and MoneroHash.

4.4   Node Distribution

In a cryptocurrency P2P overlay, different nodes play different roles and exhibit various connectivities in a real world implementation. It is essential to analyze how nodes are connected and located in the network to measure the resilience of the blockchain systems to network level attacks, which are surveyed in Sect. 5. In this section, we present the experiment results regarding to peer freshness, connectivity, and node distributions alongside with their implications.

Peer Freshness. Our approach shows that only about 20% (i.e., 4,329) of the discovered nodes were active, and the remaining nodes were offline during the data collection period. This indicates that a majority of the exchanged IP addresses are inactive in Monero's network, and might decrease the network connectivity.

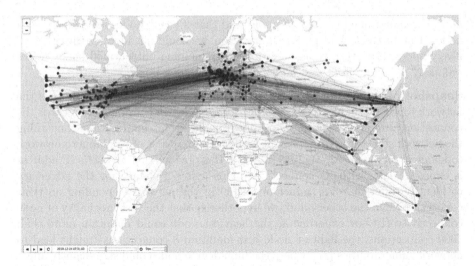

Fig. 5. Snapshot of the Monero network obtained after one hour. Each dot represents a Monero node, whose darkness is proportional to the number of connections it maintains. The lightness of lines denotes their uptimes.

Connectivity. We say that a node is of degree N if it maintains at most N outgoing connections. We classify active nodes into three categories based on their degree: *light node (degree ≤ 8), medium node ($8 < degree \leq 250$),* and *heavy node (degree > 250).* As shown in Table 2, most of the nodes (86.8%) collectively maintain only 17.14% of the connections, while the remaining 13.2% of the nodes maintain 82.86% of the connections. On the other hand, Monero has hardcoded 8 seed nodes in the system, and we initially suspected that all of them would be heavy nodes. Our experiments showed that only 3 of the seed nodes were active, and that two of them were heavy nodes, while another one was a medium node. Later on, we contacted the Monero team for clarification, and they confirmed that 5 seed nodes were not available[8]. By comparing the discovered heavy nodes with public Monero mining pools[9] and seed nodes[10], we found that 9 heavy

Table 2. Number of active nodes in the ConnectionPool.

	Light nodes	Medium nodes	Heavy nodes	Total
Reached	3146 (86.8%)	452 (12.5%)	28 (0.7%)	3626
Unreached	-	-	-	703
Total	3146	452	28	4329

---

[8] https://github.com/monero-project/monero/issues/5314.

[9] http://moneropools.com/.

[10] https://github.com/monero-project/monero/blob/577a8f5c8431d385bf9d11c30b5e3 e8855c16cca/src/p2p/net_node.inl.

nodes are maintained by mining pools, and that 2 heavy nodes are Monero seed nodes. Due to the lack of public information, we could not identify the other 17 heavy nodes. However, we assume that the remaining unidentified heavy nodes are likely to be the front-end nodes of private mining pools.

Snapshot of the Monero Network Topology. We collected snapshots of the network topology thanks to the *ConnectionPool*, which continuously records the connections' updates. Those snapshots provide useful information concerning the network structure. We represent a one hour snapshot of the Monero network topology observed on 12/24/2018 in Fig. 5. It is obvious that an user's IP address is exposed along with its connections. This leaves a chance for the adversary to identify different roles (miner or client) in the network depending on their connectivity. On the other hand, we hypothesize that the vast inequality of node connectivity (In our experiment, the heaviest node could maintain more than 1000 connections, the lightest node just maintain 8 connections) might lead to network vulnerabilities [27], where the high degree node could significantly affect low degree node to select neighbors.

Geographic Distribution. We present in Fig. 6 the location of the Monero nodes depending on their classification. Approximately 50% of the heavy nodes, which are likely the mining pools, are located in the US, while the light nodes, which are likely clients, are more evenly distributed around the world.

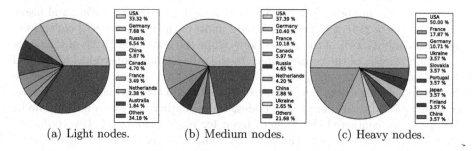

(a) Light nodes.   (b) Medium nodes.   (c) Heavy nodes.

Fig. 6. Nodes location distribution

Degree Distribution. Monero's peer-to-peer network is unstructured, permissionless and very dynamic. In particular, a node is allowed to change its neighbors as we analyzed in Sect. 2. To further analyze how nodes are connected over time, we counted the numbers of neighbors of active nodes during one week, and plot their distribution in Fig. 7. The blue dots represent the distribution of outgoing neighbors of the nodes. The results indicate that a small fraction of the nodes have more than 1000 outgoing neighbors, while a large fraction of nodes have less than 100 outgoing neighbors. The red dots represent the distributions of both incoming and outgoing neighbors. Comparing with the blue dots, one can see that the node with a large number of outgoing neighbors are likely to maintain a

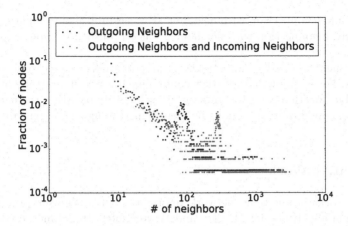

Fig. 7. Number of outgoing neighbors of heavy, medium, and light nodes. (Color figure online)

large number of incoming neighbors as well. More importantly, the small jumps in both blue and red dots indicate that a number of nodes have not kept the number of connections fixed by default in order to gain a better connectivity. We point out that this is an unique feature of Monero, which implies a high network dynamism.

4.5   Potential Threats

Using our tools, one can identify Monero's network topology and the connectivity of nodes. An example is shown in Fig. 8, which illustrates the neighbors of a *light node (5.X.X.X)*[11] during the 9-h monitoring process. Each color represents a neighbor of the node. It shows that neighbor 1–6 stayed connected with the node for the entire 9 h, whereas the connection with neighbor 7 is dropped around the

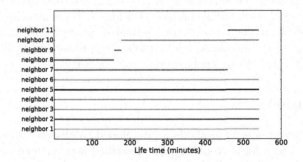

Fig. 8. Dynamic neighbor tracking of a light node in 9 h.

---

[11] Hidden IP address to protect the privacy of this light node.

8th hour, and a connection with neighbor 11 was established to replace neighbor 7. Similarly, a connection with neighbor 9 was established to replace neighbor 8 after 3 h.

With such knowledge, an attacker can potentially launch different types of attacks. For example, an attacker could launch a targeted attack by monopolizing all connections of a victim node [1], selectively partition the network [3], or even deanonymize transactions by identifying the first node relaying a transaction [5,6].

5   Related Work

Previous works studied the network information of leading cryptocurrencies, e.g., Bitcoin and Ethereum. Decker and Wattenhofer [16,28] measured the rate of information propagation between reached nodes in Bitcoin. Relying on the received messages from reached nodes, interconnections of reached nodes were inferred in Bitcoin [18,29] to evaluate network properties. To infer whether two reached nodes are connected in Bitcoin, Grundmann et al. [30] suggested to use double spent transactions as probing messages, and S. D. Segura et al. [31] suggested to use orphan transactions. Kim et al. [26] deployed 30 nodes on one machine to collect network messages to measure the Ethereum network. However, the node interconnections are difficult to infer in Ethereum, and unreachable nodes cannot be observed.

Network level attacks have been studied in Bitcoin and Ethereum. Routing attacks [3,15] are facilitated by the fact that Bitcoin's protocol makes nodes exchange messages in plain text during the peer-to-peer communications. This allows an adversary to partition the network, and delay the dissemination of messages among nodes. Eclipse attacks, in Bitcoin [1,13] and in Ethereum [2], pointed out that unsolicited incoming connections can be leveraged by an adversary to continuously send large amount of fake packets to a given node, and fill the table of its stored IP addresses, forcing it to restart. These attacks demonstrated that an attacker can monopolize all connections of a targeted node with high probability. Deanonymization attacks [5,6,32] have been introduced to track transactions and discover the generator's IP address. These attacks aim at linking the IP address of a node with the transactions it created, with the requirement of monitoring interconnections. Such attacks require, or are facilitated, by an understanding of the peer-to-peer overlay and topology.

6   Conclusion

In this work, we presented methods we developed to observe Monero's peer-to-peer network, and infer its topology. We described how one can deploy Monero nodes to discover all the nodes participating in the protocol, and their interconnections, using the *last_seen* timestamps in the peer lists that nodes exchange. For accuracy, we compared our methods' results with the ground truth of our deployed nodes. Our experiments show that even though Monero is a privacy-preserving cryptocurrency, it is still possible to accurately discover the nodes in the network and their interconnections. Our analysis provides insights about Monero's degree of centralization, and about the privacy and security issues potentially caused by a network topology exposure. As future work, we will conduct a deeper network-based security and privacy analysis of Monero, based on the tools provided in this paper.

Acknowledgments. This work is partially supported by the Fonds National de la Recherche Luxembourg (FNR) through PEARL grant FNR/P14/8149128.

References

1. Heilman, E., Kendler, A., Zohar, A., Goldberg, S.: Eclipse attacks on bitcoin's peer-to-peer network. In: USENIX Security Symposium (2015)
2. Marcus, Y., Heilman, E., Goldberg, S.: Low-resource eclipse attacks on Ethereum's peer-to-peer network. IACR Cryptology ePrint Archive 2018/236 (2018)
3. Apostolaki, M., Zohar, A., Vanbever, L.: Hijacking bitcoin: routing attacks on cryptocurrencies. In: IEEE Security and Privacy (SP) (2017)
4. Bonneau, J., Miller, A., Clark, J., Narayanan, A., Kroll, J.A., Felten, E.W.: SoK: research perspectives and challenges for bitcoin and cryptocurrencies. In: 2015 IEEE Symposium on Security and Privacy (SP), May 2015
5. Biryukov, A., Khovratovich, D., Pustogarov, I.: Deanonymisation of clients in bitcoin P2P network. In: ACM CCS (2014)
6. Biryukov, A., Tikhomirov, S.: Deanonymization and linkability of cryptocurrency transactions based on network analysis. In: EuroS&P (2019)
7. Natoli, C., Yu, J., Gramoli, V., Veríssimo, P.J.E.: Deconstructing blockchains: a comprehensive survey on consensus, membership and structure. CoRR (2019)
8. Möser, M., et al.: An empirical analysis of traceability in the monero blockchain. PoPETs **2018**(3), 143–163 (2018)
9. Kumar, A., Fischer, C., Tople, S., Saxena, P.: A traceability analysis of Monero's blockchain. In: Foley, S.N., Gollmann, D., Snekkenes, E. (eds.) ESORICS 2017. LNCS, vol. 10493, pp. 153–173. Springer, Cham (2017). https://doi.org/10.1007/978-3-319-66399-9_9
10. Yu, Z., Au, M.H., Yu, J., Yang, R., Xu, Q., Lau, W.F.: New empirical traceability analysis of cryptonote-style blockchains. In: Goldberg, I., Moore, T. (eds.) FC 2019. LNCS, vol. 11598, pp. 133–149. Springer, Cham (2019). https://doi.org/10.1007/978-3-030-32101-7_9
11. Yu, J., Au, M.H.A., Veríssimo, P.: Re-thinking untraceability in the cryptonote-style blockchain. In: IEEE Computer Security Foundations Symposium (CSF) (2019)
12. Wijaya, D.A., Liu, J., Steinfeld, R., Liu, D., Yu, J.: On the unforkability of Monero. In: ACM Asia Conference on Information, Computer and Communications Security (ASIACCS) (2019)
13. Nayak, K., Kumar, S., Miller, A., Shi, E.: Stubborn mining: generalizing selfish mining and combining with an eclipse attack (2016)
14. Natoli, C., Gramoli, V.: The balance attack or why forkable blockchains are ill-suited for consortium. In: DSN (2017)
15. Ekparinya, P., Gramoli, V., Jourjon, G.: Impact of man-in-the-middle attacks on Ethereum. In: SRDS (2018)

16. Decker, C., Wattenhofer, R.: Information propagation in the bitcoin network. In: IEEE P2P (2013)
17. Koshy, D.: An Analysis of Anonymity in Bitcoin Using P2P Network Traffic. Pennsylvania State University (2013)
18. Neudecker, T., Andelfinger, P., Hartenstein, H.: Timing analysis for inferring the topology of the bitcoin peer-to-peer network. In: IEEE UIC (2016)
19. MoneroHash: Monerohash - monero mining pool (2018). https://monerohash.com/nodes-distribution.html. Accessed 23 Dec 2018–30 Dec 2018
20. Nakamoto, S.: Bitcoin: a peer-to-peer electronic cash system (2008)
21. Wood, G.: Ethereum: a secure decentralised generalised transaction ledger. Ethereum Proj. Yellow Pap. **151**, 1–32 (2014)
22. Van Saberhagen, N.: Cryptonote v 2.0 (2013)
23. Bitnodes: Bitnodes (2018). https://bitnodes.earn.com/nodes/. Accessed 23 Dec 2018–30 Dec 2018
24. Ethernodes: Ethernodes (2018). https://www.ethernodes.org/network/1. Accessed 23 Dec 2018–30 Dec 2018
25. Neudecker, T.: Characterization of the bitcoin peer-to-peer network (2015–2018) (2019). http://dsn.tm.kit.edu/bitcoin/publications/bitcoin_network_characterization.pdf
26. Kim, S.K., Ma, Z., Murali, S., Mason, J., Miller, A., Bailey, M.: Measuring ethereum network peers. In: ACM IMC (2018)
27. Singh, A., Castro, M., Druschel, P., Rowstron, A.: Defending against eclipse attacks on overlay networks. In: Proceedings of the 11th Workshop on ACM SIGOPS European Workshop. EW 11 (2004)
28. Croman, K., et al.: On scaling decentralized blockchains - (A position paper). In: Clark, J., Meiklejohn, S., Ryan, P.Y.A., Wallach, D., Brenner, M., Rohloff, K. (eds.) FC 2016. LNCS, vol. 9604, pp. 106–125. Springer, Heidelberg (2016). https://doi.org/10.1007/978-3-662-53357-4_8
29. Miller, A., et al.: Discovering bitcoin's public topology and influential nodes (2015)
30. Grundmann, M., Neudecker, T., Hartenstein, H.: Exploiting transaction accumulation and double spends for topology inference in bitcoin. In: Zohar, A., et al. (eds.) FC 2018. LNCS, vol. 10958, pp. 113–126. Springer, Heidelberg (2019). https://doi.org/10.1007/978-3-662-58820-8_9
31. Delgado-Segura, S., et al.: TxProbe: discovering bitcoin's network topology using orphan transactions. CoRR (2018)
32. Fanti, G., Viswanath, P.: Deanonymization in the bitcoin P2P network. In: NIPS (2017)

Surviving the Cryptojungle: Perception and Management of Risk Among North American Cryptocurrency (Non)Users

Artemij Voskobojnikov$^{(\boxtimes)}$, Borke Obada-Obieh, Yue Huang,
and Konstantin Beznosov

University of British Columbia, Vancouver, Canada
{voskart,borke,huang13i,beznosov}@ece.ubc.ca

Abstract. With the massive growth of cryptocurrency markets in recent years has come an influx of new users and investors, pushing the overall number of owners into the millions. At the same time, the number of distinct cryptocurrencies has exploded to over 4,900. In this burgeoning and chaotic "cryptojungle," new and unexplored incentives and risks drive the behavior of users and non-users of cryptocurrencies. While previous research has focused almost exclusively on Bitcoin, other cryptocurrencies and utility tokens have been ignored. This paper presents findings from an interview study of cryptocurrency users and non-users ($N = 20$). We specifically focus on their perceptions and management of cryptocurrency risks as well as their reasons for or against involvement with cryptocurrencies. Our results suggest that associated risks and mitigation strategies (among other factors) might be specific to a particular crypto-asset and its application area. Further, we identify misunderstandings of both users and non-users that might lead to skewed risk perceptions or dangerous errors. Lastly, we discuss ways of aiding users with managing risks, as well as design implications for coin management tools.

1 Introduction

Cryptocurrencies have come a long way since the introduction of Bitcoin in 2009 [24]. Emerging technologies, such as Ethereum or EOS, allow the issuance of tokens, and this was one of the reasons for the rapid expansion of the domain. Nowadays, the resulting "cryptojungle" entails close to 5,000 different cryptocurrencies and tokens [12] with wide-ranging application areas.

Despite prior research on security risks in the blockchain domain, little is known about users' perception and management of risk. The main focus in the literature has been on identifying potential attack vectors and risk scenarios [18,20], without taking the respective end-users into account. While Sas et al. [25] present some risks experienced by Bitcoin users, risk management has not been investigated any further. Addressing this knowledge gap will inform the development of more effective technology support for the users of cryptocurrencies and tokens.

© International Financial Cryptography Association 2020
J. Bonneau and N. Heninger (Eds.): FC 2020, LNCS 12059, pp. 595–614, 2020.
https://doi.org/10.1007/978-3-030-51280-4_32

It is also vital to understand informed non-users' perceptions of the risks associated with cryptocurrencies. Gao et al. [16] were the first to study non-users of Bitcoin and identified *lack of perceived usefulness* and *lack of understanding* as two reasons for non-involvement. Unlike Gao et al., who interviewed participants with very limited knowledge about cryptocurrencies, our goal was to recruit *informed non-users* who had considered involvement with cryptocurrencies but had decided against it. Potential findings could then be leveraged by industry to ease the onboarding process and eventually facilitate adoption.

To investigate how cryptocurrency users and non-users perceive and manage risks, we conducted semi-structured interviews. We recruited 20 participants from the metropolitan area of Vancouver, Canada, comprising 11 users and 9 non-users. Some interviews were in person and others via telephone. An iterative coding approach based on Grounded Theory [14] was applied by three researchers, and data was collected until theoretical saturation was reached.

Several themes emerged when we probed our participants more deeply about risks in the cryptocurrency domain. User participants identified a variety of risks, such as scam coins and questionable exchanges, but only a few of those risks resulted in actual losses. Further, *risk acceptance* turned out to be a prominent risk-management technique employed by users. Non-users, on the other hand, were concerned with the potential implications of involvement with cryptocurrency. Amongst other concerns, our participants mentioned the possibility of being judged by their social circle, as well as the poor usability of exchanges and tools. Our findings suggest that perceived risks depend on the particular asset as well as the individual's reasons and motivations for using it. The perceived risk severity appears to be linked to the amount invested.

Lastly, we identified our participants' misunderstandings. Most were not knowledgeable about the underlying cryptography, including private and public keys, while some non-users had a skewed risk perception. For example, the latter were concerned with governments tracing potential cryptocurrency transactions back to them. While the implications of misperceptions differ, both users and non-users are affected. For users, misunderstandings can lead to monetary losses, and non-users might decide against any involvement at all because they have assessed the risks incorrectly.

One of the main issues to emerge was the usability of coin management tools (CMTs). In our study, both users and non-users reported having faced challenges when looking into purchasing or using cryptocurrencies, with some participants saying that the usability of current CMTs posed a significant risk and barrier to entry. Some users had addressed transactions incorrectly or failed to make them in the first place, and non-users reported being overwhelmed by the onboarding process of exchanges and the overall number of available CMTs.

To summarize, our contributions are as follows:

- We conducted the first investigation of risks perceived by users and informed non-users of cryptocurrencies.
- We identified factors linked to risk perception and mitigation in the cryptocurrency domain.

– We identified misunderstandings in both users and non-users that can lead to monetary losses or non-involvement, respectively.

2   Background

2.1   Cryptocurrencies and Utility Tokens

Bitcoin and cryptocurrencies in general make use of public-key cryptography and consequently force users to deal with this in one way or another. Traditionally, cryptocurrency wallets can be seen as means for storing one or more private and public cryptographic key pairs. Wallet addresses consist of hashes of the respective public cryptographic keys, and transactions are cryptographically signed transfers of funds from one public key to another. Unlike in centralized payment systems, however, the responsibility is shifted onto the user, and payments can only be successfully concluded by using a private key.

Besides private keys, wallets can also be accessed by using mnemonics. These consist of 12 to 24 words in the case of the BIP-39 standard [1], which are used to deterministically create key pairs for a cryptocurrency wallet. To further enhance the security, a passphrase can be used as a salt, thus guaranteeing that adversaries who know the mnemonic will still be denied access to the funds. This option is supported by many wallet providers [7].

Nowadays, the application areas of cryptocurrencies are wide-ranging and go beyond the initial vision of an alternative payment system. Emerging technologies, such as Ethereum, allow the issuance of tokens, which exist on the respective blockchain and are used within applications. Examples of such applications are social networks and games. Some participants in our study used the terms *cryptocurrencies* and *tokens* interchangeably. In the following sections, we make distinctions where applicable and otherwise use the term *crypto-assets* when referring to both of them.

2.2   Coin Management Tools

A wide range of options exist when it comes to storing crypto-assets. Such wallets, or coin management tools, as Krombholz et al. [21] defined them, emerged. In the case of hosted wallets, the responsibility is shifted from the users to the CMT providers. To use hosted wallets, users are often asked by providers to verify their identities in a so-called know-your-customer (KYC) process to combat money laundering and fraud. Prominent examples of hosted wallets are major exchanges, such as Binance, which do not give users access to the private keys. This abstraction, while arguably making the exchange more usable, poses a risk for users, as they might lose assets in the case of shutdowns or hacks, which has indeed happened (Mt.Gox [10], QuadrigaCX [11]).

Besides transferring funds to third parties, users also can choose to be solely responsible for the management of their crypto-assets. Here, two options exist: *hot wallets* and *cold wallets*. Hot wallets are connected to the internet and can be mobile applications, desktop wallets, online wallets, or utility platforms run by blockchain start-ups. Compared to hot wallets, cold wallets can provide a better level of protection. Hardware wallets, which are specialized cold wallets, often store private keys in the secure key storage provided by microcontrollers. However, cold wallets are kept offline. Paper wallets with printed private and public keys, as well as USB sticks with key files, also fall under this category.

3   Related Work

3.1   Risks in the Cryptocurrency Domain

When users interact with blockchain-based technologies, they are directly or indirectly exposed to a significant number of risks. Bonneau et al. [9] survey the underlying security concerns in Bitcoin and possible attack vectors that might compromise the distributed ledger. Most of these attack vectors, however, only indirectly affect the users of crypto-assets.

To understand users' perception, one has to determine what risks affect them. Bitcoin's pseudonymity, for example, is considered one of its key features, but as research has shown, this pseudonymity can be used to track and identify users [5,23]. Third-party sites can also pose a risk to users. Goldfeder et al. [17] showed that payment gateways may leak personally identifiable information, including the names, emails, and addresses of crypto-asset users.

Risks associated with the usage of Bitcoin are well documented. However, other crypto-assets have not yet been investigated. Both Böhme et al. [8] and Grant et al. [18] provide comprehensive overviews of Bitcoin risks, and Kiran et al. [20] further propose a grouping of these into *social risks, legal risks, economic risks, technological risks,* and *security risks.*

Besides identifying potential risks, qualitative investigations have been conducted providing insights into user experiences and perceptions. Here, Sas et al. [25] were the first to uncover some reasons for monetary losses.

Perception of risks associated with Bitcoin can be found in the literature [4,21]. While users were asked to assess the severity of risk scenarios in [21], Abramova et al. [4] investigated factors influencing risk perception among Bitcoin users. Results suggest that Bitcoin users are concerned with potential monetary losses, regulatory restrictions imposed by governments, and a general lack of adoption. However, it has yet to be determined how well aware users are of these risks and what controls they personally apply for mitigation. We further believe that perceived risks and mitigation techniques depend on the crypto-asset and are influenced by factors unidentified in previous studies.

3.2   Concerns Regarding Usable Security and Privacy

In addition to crypto-assets being lost due to technological vulnerabilities, user-induced errors are very common. Bitcoins are theft resistant by design, and assets can only be compromised by private key leakages [13]. Eskandari et al. [15]

conducted a cognitive walkthrough for various Bitcoin key management systems. Their findings suggest that the metaphors being used can often be unclear for end-users, leading them to make dangerous errors.

Empirical evidence of users experiencing such dangerous errors was first offered by Krombholz et al. [21]. Out of the 990 participants in an online survey, almost 23% indicated they had lost bitcoins. Of those who had, 43% indicated the loss had been their own fault.

Gao et al. [16] conducted the first purely qualitative study investigating the mental models of both users and non-users of Bitcoin. The main contributions of the study were to identify misconceptions about privacy and security properties, as well as a general lack of understanding in both users and non-users about the underlying technology.

Investigating the mental models of risk should make it possible to address inconsistencies that could lead to dangerous errors. Such errors pose a risk and can lead to the loss of bitcoins, as reported by Sas et al. [25]. It is therefore of interest to understand the behavior of users when it comes to the protection of their crypto-assets. By expanding the study beyond Bitcoin, and investigating security behaviors regarding crypto-assets in general, it should be possible to understand what factors influence users in their decision making.

4   Methodology

In this section we describe our recruitment process, the interview procedure itself, as well as the coding methodology and process.

4.1   Recruitment and Participants

We recruited participants aged 19 and older from the metropolitan region around our university. Users of crypto-assets were recruited through professional blockchain LinkedIn groups, our department's graduate reading seminar, a mailing list, and the community Slack channel of a blockchain club at our university, as well as a meetup group focused on decentralization. Non-users were recruited with the help of community managers of a local cryptocurrency exchange platform and through personal contacts. There was no formal screening process; instead, we were in direct contact with all potential participants. This was especially necessary for non-users, whom we wanted to ensure had some prior familiarity with crypto-assets.

4.2   Interview Procedure

We conducted semi-structured interviews both in person and via telephone. The researchers followed an interview guide (Appendix A), ensuring consistency across participants. The following broad research questions were investigated.

- **RQ1:** What are the current usages of cryptocurrencies?
- **RQ2:** How do owners manage their cryptocurrencies?
- **RQ3:** What is the perception of cryptocurrency-related risks?
- **RQ4:** How do owners manage the risks?
- **RQ5:** What factors influence users' security behavior?

Naturally, non-users could not answer some of these questions. We therefore focused on their perception of risks and how that influenced their decisions about crypto-assets. For both users and non-users, we validated the questions by conducting two pilot interviews and altered the questions, if needed. All interviews were recorded, transcribed, and anonymized. Each participant was compensated $15. The study was approved by our university's research ethics board.

4.3   Coding Procedure

An iterative coding approach based on Grounded Theory [14] was applied. Three researchers independently performed open coding of the interview transcripts, and the results were discussed and added to a shared codebook once the researchers' codes converged. Axial coding followed, whereby themes and concepts between codes emerged. During the selective coding process, the raw data was analyzed again to further enrich the results of the previous coding stages.

We do not report on inter-coder reliability, as codes are only an interim product in Grounded Theory and change throughout the data analysis [14]. We stopped recruiting once it became clear that we had reached code saturation. Throughout the study, the interviews were recoded several times after our codes converged, and the interview guide was adjusted based on our intermediate findings [14].

4.4   Limitations

As with all qualitative investigations, the results of this study are not necessarily generalizable to the whole population of cryptocurrency users and informed non-users. Our aim, however, was to interview a diverse sample. We ensured its diversity by recruiting through multiple channels and including participants from diverse backgrounds, including investors, miners, consultants, and blockchain developers. Since we investigated users' security and privacy behaviors, it is possible that some participants decided against disclosing sensitive information such as monetary losses. Some potential participants might have chosen not to participate in our study because of privacy concerns.

All of our participants were in North America. While this geographical restriction might have impacted our results, we strove to recruit a diverse sample. Compared to previous qualitative studies [16,19,25], our sample was more diverse in terms of gender, education, occupation, and age.

5   Results

5.1   Participants

We interviewed 20 participants, 11 of whom were users (age: max. = 43, mean = 28.8, median = 28, min. = 19) and 9 non-users (age: max. 57, mean = 32.4, median = 30, min. = 19). Seven of the 11 users had a technical background and 5 were active members of blockchain-related meetup groups. Detailed demographics can be found in Appendix B.

5.2   Motivation for Using Crypto-Assets (RQ1)

A prevalent underlying theme in users' involvement with crypto-assets is investment. While potential monetary gains are regarded as one of the main reasons for involvement [16,21], participants in our study broke this down into short-term and long-term investments. PU6[1] considered crypto-assets, and bitcoins in particular, as a personal retirement plan: *"For me, I think [...] that's my retirement plan [...]. I don't see it necessarily as a store of value."* PU2, PU3, PU4, PU5, PU6, and PU9 referred to the investment strategy as "holding" crypto-assets, with PU9 explaining: *"I feel like I'm holding a lot of bags still [...] I own bitcoins, I own Ethereum, EOS, MakerDao [...] and Power Ledger."*

Participants also indicated having used cryptocurrencies to purchase goods. Some of these goods were physical and others digital. PU1 bought a ticket for a cryptocurrency convention, and PU6 mentioned a partial asset value transfer: *"I like to buy precious metals, so I get bullion with my bitcoins."* None of the participants indicated they had purchased illicit goods. One user described having gotten into the cryptocurrency space through a friend who was a drug dealer at the time and was using cryptocurrencies.

Everyday items were also purchased, as explained by PU10: *"I have a friend who has a yoga studio who accepts [cryptocurrencies] as payment and another friend who has a restaurant that used to accept [cryptocurrencies as] payment."* Digital goods bought with cryptocurrencies included video games. PU7 explained: *"So [I purchased video games from] Steam for example [...] not drugs."*

Unlike speculators, who deal mostly with exchanges, participants who use cryptocurrencies as a medium of exchange interact with various parties, such as merchants. Therefore, the risks also differ. Some respondents used cryptocurrencies as alternatives to banks. PU1, PU4, and PU6 all reported instances where banks fell short in their eyes, with PU6 saying: *"the one thing that intrigues me about cryptocurrencies is that you're your own bank."*

A desire to learn more about crypto-assets was another motivation for some users. PU1, PU2, and PU7 cited curiosity as one of the main reasons for looking into the domain, with PU1 stating: *"Curiosity and learning. I'm in a time in my life where learning is very important. So I just want to learn more."*

---

[1] We use the prefix "PU" when referring to those participants who used crypto-assets at the time of the interview.

Lastly, user participants reported owning utility tokens. The application areas of these tokens were wide ranging and included browsers, social media, betting platforms, and games. PU1, PU4, PU7, and PU8 all mentioned having used various platforms, with PU1 recalling placing a bet with Augur: *"I would scroll through a bunch of different markets, like sports, politics, and I clicked on things that were interesting and I said, 'Okay, Golden State is winning this year.'"*

For all the above-mentioned application areas of crypto-assets, the interaction partners appeared to differ depending on the area. PU1, PU7, and PU10 purchased goods and interacted with merchants that accepted cryptocurrency, whereas others only interacted with exchanges (PU6 and PU8). Therefore, it is possible that the users would have been exposed to different risks, based on which crypto-assets they owned and how they used them.

5.3   Reasons for Not Using Crypto-Assets (RQ1)

During interviews with non-users, several reasons for their non-involvement emerged. Negative views about cryptocurrencies were prevalent among non-users. PN1,[2] PN2, PN3, PN5, PN6, and PN8 associated cryptocurrencies with the drug trade and other illegal activities, with PN3 saying: *"Somebody told me about the dark net [...] you know, selling drugs and guns and all kinds of illegal [stuff]."*

Non-users believed that some cryptocurrencies, bitcoin in particular, had reached their peak values and that this was a reason for not purchasing any. PN1, PN3, PN5, PN6, and PN8 expressed their concerns about investment in cryptocurrencies not making sense from a financial standpoint, with PN5 stating the belief that the *"Bitcoin price was about $20,000 and there was not much room for an increase."*

The ability of the government to trace all cryptocurrency transactions was another stumbling block. PN3 stated they would consider getting cryptocurrencies *"if you actually had privacy and the government couldn't track it [back to me]."* This belief was not shared by all non-users, though, as PN8 trusted Bitcoin's anonymity: *"I feel like [Bitcoin] would be extremely private. I don't think it has been hacked at this point, like, there's no way to trace a payment."* Interestingly, although expressing opposing views, both of these statements hint at PN3's and PN8's inadequate mental models about cryptocurrencies.

On the other hand, the lack of government involvement in the domain was a deterrent for some non-users. PN2, PN4, PN5, PN6, and PN9 stated that regulations could potentially lead to more transparency, which could result in wider adoption. Such regulations could also reduce undesirable volatility, as PN4 explained: *"Well, if it's not regulated, I just feel like it could be just so volatile."*

When trying to enter the cryptocurrency domain, non-users had experienced barriers to entry. PN1 expressed displeasure with the verification processes of exchanges, saying, *"I think it takes a few weeks to get verified for the ID. And*

---

[2] We use the prefix "PN" to refer to those participants who did not use crypto-assets at the time of the interview.

then, when you make a purchase, you have to do another type of verification."
This non-user had also considered getting cryptocurrencies through mining but
faced challenges: *"I tried [mining] but I realized that all [...] the computers [are]
specifically made for mining bitcoins. So maybe my personal computer is really
good [but for mining] it doesn't really work."*

5.4   Handling of Crypto-Assets (RQ2)

The following sections highlight how participants were storing their crypto-
assets, what CMTs they were using, and why they were doing so. We also discuss
the usability concerns about existing tools that many of the users brought up.

Storage. Hosted wallets were one of the most popular CMTs among our participants. All 11 users had used a cryptocurrency exchange at some point. Coinbase,
Binance, Bittrex, and QuadrigaCX were some of the exchanges they mentioned.

While all of the users interacted with an exchange, the nature of their interactions varied. PU1 only purchased Ethereum on Coinbase, just to transfer it over
to his personal software wallet, whereas others kept most of their crypto-assets on
exchanges. PU7, for example, said: *"I actually put a lot of funds on exchanges,
as I think [keeping them in your own wallet is] the equivalent of keeping cash
under your mattress [...]."*

Their method for storing crypto-assets appeared to be linked to the amount
owned. PU1, PU2, PU10, and PU3 were all willing to consider different storing
options, with PU2 summing it up thus: *"If I store more, I'll think about storing
it in a safer place."*

Software wallets were also a popular type of CMT. All of our user participants
had used software wallets, such as Exodus, Parity, MetaMask, or Jaxx. PU4,
PU6, PU7, and PU11 reported having used paper wallets, whereas hardware
wallets were the least reported, used only by PU4, PU6, and PU11.

Options for storing crypto-assets also appeared to depend on the way they
were used. PU4, PU5, and PU6 all reported storing bitcoins more securely than
other crypto-assets. PU4 and PU6 stored bitcoins in hardware wallets, with
PU4 breaking down investments into two categories: *"Long-term holdings like
bitcoins—I store offline. Small investments—I'm not necessarily super concerned
about. A lot of them are utility tokens, and I'm not necessarily interested in a
return."* Although using a software wallet, PU5 had additional tactics for increasing its security: *"I have a software wallet and then I hide my files on something
else and then I encrypt."* Further, PU5 and PU6 reported having certain cryptocurrencies solely to trade them on exchanges to gather more bitcoins. For this
purpose, PU5 used Litecoin, which has faster confirmation times ($\sim$2 min) than
Bitcoin (10 min). PU6 reported storing so-called "shitcoins"[3] on exchanges, stating: *"Only my bitcoins [are stored in a hardware wallet]; shitcoins all stay on the
exchanges till they make me bitcoins and then [bitcoins] get sent back [to my
hardware wallet]."*

---

[3] A pejorative term for crypto-assets that have no intrinsic value.

Users Experience Issues with Existing CMTs. Several users reported usability concerns about existing CMTs. PU1, PU5, PU7, PU9, and PU11 all mentioned usability issues with current software. PU11 explained specific troubles with MetaMask: *"You have to enter a gas amount in some other currency that you have never heard called Gwei and then a lot of the times the recommended amount isn't enough."* PU7 described a long learning curve: *"I consider myself [...] decently tech-savvy, [but] it took me a while to kind of get used to it. [...] It's not difficult but it's not intuitive."* PU1, talking about Augur, mentioned: *"I would scroll through a bunch of different markets [...] but I wasn't able to post [the] transaction."* PN1, although interested in purchasing cryptocurrencies, had not been able to do so: *"I had a really hard time learning [Ethereum]. [...] I spent a few days [...] and I just gave up, cause it is kind of too hard."*

Several users had encountered too much friction in the onboarding phase at exchanges. PU1, PU2, PU4, PU5, PU7, and PU8 expressed dissatisfaction with the verification processes, with PU2 saying: *"Just too bothersome to get the KYC. At the beginning of the year, I KYCed Bitstamp; it took me 2 months to get approved."*

When it came to ownership and the underlying technology, participants appeared to have misunderstandings. PU1 claimed to own the private key on Coinbase, which is not possible. PU2 stated that she did not understand the cryptographic principles: *"I haven't figured out how they have the private key on the phone wallet [...] I still don't understand the private and public key."*

5.5 Risks

Besides commonly known risks, such as volatility or lack of regulatory involvement, our participants also discussed risks that, to the best of our knowledge, have not yet been reported in the academic literature.

Perceived Risks (RQ3). Non-users were afraid of being judged by their social circle if they purchased cryptocurrency. PN6 explained: *"Cryptocurrency was initially used on the black markets, right, and if you tell people that you have some bitcoins or other cryptocurrencies, people will think that maybe you are buying something illegal."*

Personal safety associated with cryptocurrency ownership was also considered a risk. PU6 stated: *"somebody could literally take a gun and put it against your head and say 'give me your private key.' It's not like [they] can take you to the bank and say 'give me all your money'."*

The risk of inheritors not being able to access cryptocurrency after the purchaser's death was also brought up. PU11 explained: *"I think one risk that a lot of people don't think about is what happens when you die—so making sure that there's a way for whoever is going to be inheriting your cryptocurrency to actually access it."*

While some users spoke favorably about cryptocurrency adoption, others had concerns about what effects it might bring. PU11 explained how decentralization could be jeopardized by corporations: *"we're starting to see that with Facebook talking about doing a stable coin, or Microsoft and Google and Amazon all kind of launching blockchain as a service type product, so potentially the benefits of decentralized systems could be lost."* PU9 believed that rapid cryptocurrency adoption might undermine governments: *"governments now have power that's underpinned by their ability to control currency, and if they lost that, I'm concerned about how they would allocate capital and value to underpin some of the public needs of society [...]."* This user further explained how early adopters would have an unfair monetary advantage compared to the general public: *"if you own, say, 1 to 10 bitcoins now, you will be the 0.01% or 0.001% of the world's wealthiest people in 20 years potentially [...] and I think in that sense [one] risk is a massive redistribution of wealth."*

Risk perception appeared to be linked to the amount of money invested. PU1, PU2, PU10, and PU3 said that the severity of the risks would grow if they invested more, with PU1 saying: *"If I had multiple thousands, I'd consider it more, but I haven't given [the risk of storing cryptocurrency on exchanges] too much thought."*

Experienced Losses (RQ3). Losses were attributed to only a few risks, despite our participants mentioning many more. However, none of the participants reported having had their cryptocurrencies compromised. PU4, PU5, PU6, PU9, and PU11 had all experienced losses, each for different reasons. PU4 said that he had been phished after exposing and explaining a scam to others: *"I see an email request, you can tell the URL is wrong. Then, I close that MyEther-Wallet. [...] Then I opened it up the next day, they happened to leave the scam tab open [and I used the phishing website to import my wallet file]."*

PU11 and PU5 had lost cryptocurrency due to their own errors. PU11 explained: *"I definitely have one wallet with a small amount of bitcoins that I can't access—I lost the key."* PU9 also had lost a key, when using an ATM: *"[I] went to an ATM years ago [and] bought one bitcoin for like $100 or $200 like that, uh, and it stopped in a wallet I don't have the secret, I don't have a private key."* PU6 experienced an exchange shutdown, resulting in the loss of a substantial amount of cryptocurrency: *"I ended up losing a third of my portfolio that was on that exchange [...] it was over 100 Litecoins or something."*

Risk Management (RQ4 & RQ5). The risk-management techniques of our participants can be grouped into three categories: avoidance, reduction, and acceptance. Risk avoidance was most prevalent in non-users.

Volatility was a major concern for both user and non-user participants. The former reduced this risk through portfolio diversification. PU3 and PU4 reported counteracting volatility by purchasing multiple coin types instead of a single one, with PU3 saying: *"We like sort of started [...] dividing our assets. [...] so maybe we made sure we are safe from all sides in case the value falls."* Unlike the rest of the participants, PU6 enjoyed the volatility, explaining: *"it's very volatile [...]*

and that's when you gonna make the most money [...] So I personally love the volatility."

When it came to securing assets, some participants emphasized the importance of having a private key. This technique was mentioned by PU3, PU4, PU7, PU9, PU10, and PU11, with PU7 saying: *"Keep your own private key [...] When I say that, I know it's so difficult because it's not easy to operate."* PU2 and PU4 said that using multiple wallets and multiple devices prevents a single point of failure: *"In general, being across multiple devices, multiple wallets just helps protect [against] all those one-off dramas."*

The choice of wallets was influenced by whether or not users were able to access their private key. PU3, PU4, PU7, PU9, PU10, and PU11 preferred wallets with private key access, with PU7 equating key and ownership the following way: *"If you don't have the private key, it's not yours. It's that easy [...]."*

Fully insured storages were viewed as ultimate solutions. Both PU6 and PU9 explained how these solutions would provide the best security, with PU9 saying: *"it's these underground vaults in Switzerland—they're all over the world, you don't really know where they are, and it's a fully insured cold storage solution, but the thing is it's like multi-sig so [...] if they want to move your coins or your assets, they need your signature."*

One user considered seed phrases superior to key-based CMTs. PU1 argued that the seed phrase was a good alternative to the concept of private keys: *"The memorization of a seed phrase seems very plausible. I think people can memorize 12 words and then you could take it totally offline."*

Education was considered a possible mitigation technique by both users and non-users. PU4 stated that education is important and can be used as a way to prevent losses in the context of pyramid schemes: *"Education is very important. If there is a mining rig and you are getting paid day by day and everything works fine until one day it is not."* Similarly, PN4 stressed the importance of research for non-users, saying: *"I would have to do the research to understand it to be comfortable putting my money into something."*

One common theme among users was the acceptance of potential risks. PU4, PU5, PU6, and PU7 reported that when using exchanges, they knew they did not own the private key and everything would be gone in the case of an exchange shutdown. PU6 summarized this sentiment well: *"It's just part of the game."* When talking about "shitcoins," the same user expressed a willingness to operate on questionable exchanges, stating that *"especially with a lot of these real shitcoins, they're on really [questionable] exchanges right? So [...] you kind of have to play in there, in the mud and get dirty."*

An overview of risks and mitigation techniques can be found in Appendix C.

6 Discussion

Participants' three major reasons for using crypto-assets were speculation, exchange, and utility. Each particular application area exposes the respective user to new CMTs, such as software wallets, hardware wallets, payment processors, and utility platforms. User interfaces as well as underlying technological features differ according to the CMT and consequently expose users to different risks. Hosted wallets, such as exchanges, do not allow users to access their private keys, which in the case of a shutdown results in monetary loss. Cold wallets, on the other hand, while not affected by shutdowns are often more complex to use, as reported by our participants. Our findings suggest that usage scenarios were important factors linked to the user experience (UX), as well as risk perception and management.

All user participants had used exchanges at some point during their involvement. One voiced a willingness to accept the risk of losing crypto-assets in order to make gains on questionable exchanges with so-called "shitcoins." Four users accepted the risk of storing their crypto-assets on exchanges without having direct access to their private key.

Risk perception also seemed to depend on how much participants valued the respective crypto-asset. Here, we consider the amount invested in the particular asset. Our user participants stored their long-term holdings in the form of bitcoins in more secure ways and said they did not consider risks associated with short-term holdings a major concern. Similarly, four other users with smaller amounts said they would consider more secure storage options, but only if they had purchased more.

6.1   Misconceptions and Usability Barriers

Users had dangerous knowledge gaps and misconceptions when it came to the key building blocks of cryptocurrencies. Some users did not know the difference between public and private keys, and one incorrectly believed that they had access to their private key while using an exchange. Such a misconception could lead to a false sense of security and control over wallets, particularly nowadays when the crypto markets (and the exchanges that operate on them) are so volatile.

Non-users had their own set of misconceptions. Some believed that cryptocurrencies are mainly used to purchase illicit drugs. While this was one of the main uses of bitcoin in its early days [6], the applications nowadays are wide ranging. Non-users also discussed the notion of cryptocurrency privacy. While some believed that transactions could be traced back to them by the government, others believed in their anonymity.

Current CMTs have usability problems. Combined with misconceptions about cryptocurrencies' building blocks, these UX problems result in barriers that are hard to overcome. Participants' usability concerns also seemed dependent on the respective crypto-asset. One participant explained having failed to use Augur, as they were not able to make a transaction using their application's interface. Another found Monero harder to use than other cryptocurrencies because of the two pairs of keys: private and public. We therefore believe that findings on usability issues with Bitcoin key management tools [15] and the identified risks affecting Bitcoin usability [13] are not necessarily applicable to other crypto-assets and their applications.

6.2 Risks

Our results suggest that risk perception and management among crypto-asset (non)users goes beyond Bitcoin, as it depends on such factors as the application area, storage method, and amount invested. Further investigation is needed to reveal other factors related to risk perception and to further our understanding of the risk-management practices among users and informed non-users.

New crypto-assets bring new risks for users. The vast majority of our user participants owned multiple crypto-assets, with PU7 owning as many as 50. Such variety can be dangerous, as different crypto-assets pose different risks and challenges for their respective users. For example, initial coin offerings (ICOs) are not always created in good faith [2], and utility tokens can end up being pyramid schemes [3], as reported by PU4, PU5, and PU6. While risks associated with Bitcoin are fairly well documented [8,15,18,20], other crypto-assets have thus far been ignored by the research community.

Design recommendations to combat some of the risks can be found in the literature. Authorized exchanges were proposed by Sas et al. [25] to combat dishonest traders through verification processes for buyers and sellers. Our data, however, suggests that both users and non-users consider such procedures bothersome and a significant barrier to entry. Since verification is mandatory, it should be in the interest of exchanges to optimize this process.

Public key cryptography appeared to still be a hindrance for many. Some participants considered keeping the private key private to avoid losses in potential shutdowns of exchanges. This, however, can only be done if the respective user understands the value of the private key. Some of our participants reported having accidentally deleted wallet files, while others did not understand what private and public keys were in the first place. One possible reason for this finding is that CMT providers do not convey the importance of keys clearly enough. While hosted wallets, such as exchanges, do not allow users access to private keys, others such as software wallets do. Therefore, depending on the CMT, users require a different level of understanding to ensure correct and secure handling. Sandboxes allowing newcomers to first get familiar with the terms and technology, as well as more guidance from CMT providers could especially help new users overcome existing fears of the unknown, as reported by many of our informed non-users.

Personalization would be another way to support users [22]. Perhaps wallet providers could create separate user profiles for beginners and experts, allowing users to select a level of abstraction. For example, advanced transaction settings would only be displayed for experienced users, whereas new users would only see the bare minimum. Simpler terms—e.g., "transaction fees" instead of "gas price"—could further improve the user experience for newcomers, making involvement in the domain less foreign.

6.3   Implications for Theory and Practice

Our investigation of crypto-assets other than Bitcoin has revealed risks and usability concerns previously undocumented in the literature. Usability research on blockchain-based technologies has been Bitcoin-centric [16,20,21,25]. While bitcoin is still the most popular cryptocurrency, our results suggest that associated risks do depend on the application area and crypto-asset. Pyramid schemes in the form of mining pools, unregulated ICOs, "shitcoins," and tokens all pose new risks to both existing and new users and can lead to monetary losses.

When looking at crypto-assets, one also has to consider CMTs, as they are vital to UX. Our participants reported owning as many as 50 different currencies, and while exchanges support a variety of tokens, not all software wallets do. Such wallets support different subsets of crypto-assets, and the included features are also wide ranging. Newcomers looking into purchasing cryptocurrency can easily be overwhelmed by the number of different wallets, as was the case for PN1.

Monetary losses due to self-induced errors were reported by multiple user participants. By creating more usable and intuitive software wallets, possibly employing terms from payment platforms already familiar to users, one might be able to decrease the chances of losing crypto-assets due to self-induced errors. By also adding two-factor authentication, similar to some online banking platforms, it would be possible to reduce the risk of users sending crypto-assets to an incorrect address, which some participants reported having done.

Some informed non-users seemed to hold negative beliefs about cryptocurrency use. Educating potential new users about other application areas for blockchain-based technologies could help reduce the negative views and social risks associated with cryptocurrency involvement.

7   Conclusion

We conducted semi-structured interviews to further an understanding of how users and non-users perceive and manage risks related to crypto-assets. We identified that perceived risks and mitigation techniques are dependent on the specific crypto-asset, its storage options, and the amount being invested. Further, misunderstandings seemed to be prevalent in both users and non-users and could lead to dangerous errors, potentially resulting in monetary losses.

To truly understand risk perception and management in the domain, one therefore needs to study crypto-assets beyond bitcoin, as they expose users to new risks and challenges. We believe that to reduce risks, further public education is necessary, and government involvement is needed to combat pyramid schemes and unregulated ICOs.

Acknowledgements. This research has been supported in part by a gift from Scotiabank to UBC and by an NSERC Engage Grant (with Symetria), #EGP538930-19. We would like to thank members of the Laboratory for Education and Research in Secure Systems Engineering (LERSSE), who provided their feedback on the reported research and earlier versions of the paper. We thank our anonymous reviewers for all the feedback and suggestions they provided to improve the paper.

Appendices

A Interview Questions

Interview guides for both users and non-users of cryptocurrencies follow. Research questions that were addressed are in bold.

A.1 Users of Cryptocurrencies

RQ1: What are the current usages of cryptocurrencies?
Q1. Please tell me about how you got into cryptocurrencies.
Q2. How much money have you spent?
Q3. What do you use cryptocurrencies for?
Q3.1 How many transactions do you perform?
Q4. How has this usage changed over time? If it did, why?
Q5. How many different currencies do you own?
Q5.1 What three currencies have you invested the most money in? Why?
Q5.2 Do you use these currencies for different use cases? Why?
Q6. What factors influence you when making a decision to invest in a currency?
Q6.1 How well do you research the currency prior to an investment?
Q6.2 How knowledgeable are you about currencies that you have invested in?
Q6.3 Can you explain the concept behind blockchain to me?

RQ2: How do holders manage their cryptocurrency?
Q.7 How do you store your cryptocurrencies?
Q7.1 Please name the wallets you personally use the most.
Q7.2 Why did you choose these wallets?
Q7.3 How many different wallets do you use?
Q7.4 For how many of these wallets do you own the private key?
Q7.5 Can you explain to me what a private key is?
Q7.6 What do you need the private key for?
Q7.8 How is a private key different from a public key?
Q7.9 Do you store different currencies in different wallets?

RQ3: What is the perception of cryptocurrency-related security risk?
Q8 Have you ever lost cryptocurrency?
Q8.1 How much money did you lose?
Q8.2 Were you able to recover the key(s)?
Q9 What risks are you personally aware of when it comes to cryptocurrencies?
Q9.1 What is the most severe one according to you? Why?
Q10 What measures do you use to mitigate those risks? (**RQ4**)
Q10.1 What measures worked and which ones did not? Why?
Q11. In what ways do you protect different cryptocurrencies? (**RQ5**)
Q11.1 What factors influence your decisions?

A.2   Non-Users of Cryptocurrencies

RQ1: What are the current usages of cryptocurrencies?
Q1. What payment systems do you use in your daily life?
Q2. How did you hear about cryptocurrencies for the first time?
Q3. What cryptocurrencies have you heard of?
Q4. How do you view your understanding of cryptocurrencies?
Q4.1 And of the underlying technological background?
Q5. What do you think cryptocurrencies are used for?
Q6. Why do you believe people purchase cryptocurrencies?
Q7. Why did you choose not to purchase cryptocurrencies?
Q7.1 What would have to happen for you to reconsider?

RQ3: What is the perception of cryptocurrency-related security risk?
Q8. What risks come with the usage of cryptocurrencies?
Q8.1 What is the most severe one? Why?
Q9. Can you think of ways users can protect themselves? (RQ4)

B   Participant Demographics

The following two tables display the participants' demographics. The number
of owned crypto-assets was self-reported and the ownership was not validated
(Tables 1 and 2).

Table 1. User demographics

Participant	Age	Gender	Degree Achieved	Occupation	User Since	Number of Owned Crypto-Assets
PU1	21	M	Bachelor's	Looking for work	2016	2
PU2	28	F	Master's	News editor (blockchain domain)	2017	4
PU3	23	F	Bachelor's	Student	2016	1
PU4	22	M	Bachelor's	Entrepreneur (blockchain domain)	2016	12
PU5	40	-	College	Systems analyst (web technologies)	2013	3
PU6	30	M	No degree	Small business owner	2012	4
PU7	19	M	High school	Blockchain advisor	2014	50
PU8	21	M	High school	Student	2014	12
PU9	31	M	Bachelor's	Sales	2013	6
PU10	43	M	Master's	Software developer (energy)	2013	4
PU11	39	M	JD	Blockchain advisor (law)	2015	5

Table 2. Non-user demographics

Participant	Age	Gender	Degree Achieved	Occupation
PN1	23	F	Bachelor's	Student
PN2	53	F	No high school diploma	Asst. manager (money exchange)
PN3	57	M	College	Driver
PN4	30	F	ND	Naturopathic doctor
PN5	30	M	PhD	Research assistant
PN6	30	F	PhD	Financial advisor
PN7	25	M	Bachelor's	Teaching assistant
PN8	25	M	Bachelor's	Student
PN9	19	M	High school	Student

C   Schematic Overview of the Results

The following figure depicts the findings of the interview study. Based on our research questions we created five groups, *use cases, reasons against an involvement, perceived risks, reasons for losses,* and *risk management.* We use distinct colors for users and non-users and show relationships where appropriate (Fig. 1).

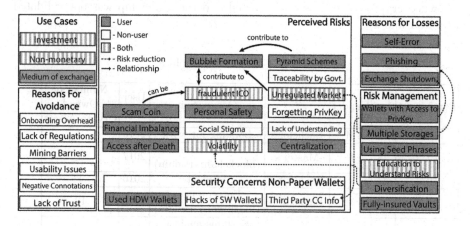

Fig. 1. Findings overview

References

1. BIP 39 Standard. https://github.com/bitcoinbook/bitcoinbook/blob/
2. Cointelegraph: ICO Scams (2018). https://cointelegraph.com/news/new-study-says-80-percent-of-icos-conducted-in-2017-were-scams. Accessed 23 Sept 2019
3. Cointelegraph: Ponzi Schemes (2019). https://cointelegraph.com/news/from-ponzi-schemes-to-ico-exits-ethereums-blockchain-has-been-the-platform-of-choice-for-scammers. Accessed 23 Sept 2019

4. Abramova, S., Böhme, R.: Perceived benefit and risk as multidimensional determinants of bitcoin use: a quantitative exploratory study. In: Proceedings of the Thirty Seventh International Conference on Information Systems (ICIS), Dublin, Ireland (2016)
5. Androulaki, E., Karame, G.O., Roeschlin, M., Scherer, T., Capkun, S.: Evaluating user privacy in bitcoin. In: Sadeghi, A.-R. (ed.) FC 2013. LNCS, vol. 7859, pp. 34–51. Springer, Heidelberg (2013). https://doi.org/10.1007/978-3-642-39884-1_4
6. Bitcoin.com: Illegal Activity No Longer Dominant Use of Bitcoin: DEA Agent. https://news.bitcoin.com/illegal-activity-use-bitcoin-dea-agent/. Accessed 28 Feb 2019
7. Blockplate: The BIP39 (Mnemonic Seed) Wallet List (2019). https://www.blockplate.com/blogs/blockplate/list-of-bip39-wallets-mnemonic-seed. Accessed 20 July 2019
8. Böhme, R., Christin, N., Edelman, B., Moore, T.: Bitcoin: economics, technology, and governance. J. Econ. Perspect. **29**(2), 213–38 (2015)
9. Bonneau, J., Miller, A., Clark, J., Narayanan, A., Kroll, J.A., Felten, E.W.: SoK: research perspectives and challenges for bitcoin and cryptocurrencies. In: 2015 IEEE Symposium on Security and Privacy, pp. 104–121, May 2015. https://doi.org/10.1109/SP.2015.14
10. CoinDesk: Mt. Gox Allegedly Loses $350 Million in Bitcoin (744,400 BTC), Rumoured to be Insolvent (2014). https://www.coindesk.com/mt-gox-loses-340-million-bitcoin-rumoured-insolvent. Accessed 27 Apr 2019
11. CoinDesk: From Law to Lawlessness: Bits of the Untold QuadrigaCX Story (2019). https://www.coindesk.com/from-law-to-lawlessness-bits-of-the-untold-quadrigacx-story. Accessed 27 Apr 2019
12. CoinMarketCap: Distinct Cryptocurrencies (2019). https://coinmarketcap.com/all/views/all/. Accessed 15 Sept 2019
13. Conti, M., Sandeep Kumar, E., Lal, C., Ruj, S.: A survey on security and privacy issues of bitcoin. IEEE Commun. Surv. Tutorials **20**(4), 3416–3452 (2018)
14. Corbin, J., Strauss, A.: Basics of Qualitative Research: Techniques and Procedures for Developing Grounded Theory. SAGE Publications (2014). https://books.google.ca/books?id=hZ6kBQAAQBAJ
15. Eskandari, S., Barrera, D., Stobert, E., Clark, J.: A first look at the usability of bitcoin key management. In: NDSS Symposium 2015. Internet Society (2015)
16. Gao, X., Clark, G.D., Lindqvist, J.: Of two minds, multiple addresses, and one ledger: characterizing opinions, knowledge, and perceptions of bitcoin across users and non-users. In: Proceedings of the 2016 CHI Conference on Human Factors in Computing Systems. CHI 2016, pp. 1656–1668. ACM, New York (2016). https://doi.org/10.1145/2858036.2858049
17. Goldfeder, S., Kalodner, H., Reisman, D., Narayanan, A.: When the cookie meets the blockchain: privacy risks of web payments via cryptocurrencies. Proc. Priv. Enhancing Technol. **4**, 179–199 (2018)
18. Grant, G., Hogan, R.: Bitcoin: risks and controls. J. Corp. Account. Finance **26**(5), 29–35 (2015)
19. Khairuddin, I.E., Sas, C., Clinch, S., Davies, N.: Exploring motivations for bitcoin technology usage. In: Proceedings of the 2016 CHI Conference Extended Abstracts on Human Factors in Computing Systems, pp. 2872–2878. ACM (2016)
20. Kiran, M., Stanett, M.: Bitcoin Risk Analysis. NEMODE Policy Paper (2015)

21. Krombholz, K., Judmayer, A., Gusenbauer, M., Weippl, E.: The other side of the coin: user experiences with bitcoin security and privacy. In: Grossklags, J., Preneel, B. (eds.) FC 2016. LNCS, vol. 9603, pp. 555–580. Springer, Heidelberg (2017). https://doi.org/10.1007/978-3-662-54970-4_33
22. Kumar, R.L., Smith, M.A., Bannerjee, S.: User interface features influencing overall ease of use and personalization. Inf. Manag. **41**(3), 289–302 (2004)
23. Meiklejohn, S., et al.: A fistful of bitcoins: characterizing payments among men with no names. In: Proceedings of the 2013 Conference on Internet Measurement Conference. IMC 2013, pp. 127–140. ACM, New York (2013). https://doi.org/10.1145/2504730.2504747
24. Nakamoto, S.: Bitcoin: A Peer-to-Peer Electronic Cash System (2008). http://bitcoin.org/bitcoin.pdf. Accessed 28 Feb 2019
25. Sas, C., Khairuddin, I.E.: Design for trust: an exploration of the challenges and opportunities of bitcoin users. In: Proceedings of the 2017 CHI Conference on Human Factors in Computing Systems. CHI 2017, pp. 6499–6510. ACM, New York (2017). https://doi.org/10.1145/3025453.3025886

Smart Contracts

Address Clustering Heuristics
for Ethereum

Friedhelm Victor(✉) ⓘD

Technical University of Berlin, Straße des 17. Juni 135, 10623 Berlin, Germany
friedhelm.victor@tu-berlin.de

Abstract. For many years, address clustering for the identification of
entities has been the basis for a variety of graph-based investigations
of the Bitcoin blockchain and its derivatives. Especially in the field of
fraud detection it has proven to be useful. With the popularization and
increasing use of alternative blockchains, the question arises how to recognize entities in these new systems. Currently, there are no heuristics
that can directly be applied to Ethereum's account balance model. This
drawback also applies to other smart contract platforms like EOS or
NEO, for which previous transaction network analyses have been limited to address graphs. In this paper, we show how addresses can be
clustered in Ethereum, yielding entities that are likely in control of multiple addresses. We propose heuristics that exploit patterns related to
deposit addresses, multiple participation in airdrops and token authorization mechanisms. We quantify the applicability of each individual
heuristic over the first 4 years of the Ethereum blockchain and illustrate
identified entities in a sample token network. Our results show that we
can cluster 17.9% of all active externally owned account addresses, indicating that there are more than 340,000 entities that are likely in control
of multiple addresses. Comparing the heuristics, we conclude that the
deposit address heuristic is currently the most effective approach.

Keywords: Blockchain · Accounts · Ethereum · Network analysis

1 Introduction

Since the introduction and popularization of Bitcoin [22] in 2009, blockchain and
cryptocurrency analysis has gained a foothold in science as well as in business. A
number of established companies and startups are investigating blockchain data
for purposes related to cryptoasset assessment, insights for financial institutions
and the support of law enforcement [7]. In most of these networks, an individual
can participate with several pseudonymous addresses, the creation of which is
virtually cost-free. For outsiders, it is not necessarily obvious that they belong
to the same entity. Cryptocurrencies are also used for criminal activities where
the perpetrators hope to cover up their traces. To hide their identity, extortion-
ists do not use the same address for every victim [25], and money laundering

© International Financial Cryptography Association 2020
J. Bonneau and N. Heninger (Eds.): FC 2020, LNCS 12059, pp. 617–633, 2020.
https://doi.org/10.1007/978-3-030-51280-4_33

is carried out using a large number of addresses [21]. In blockchain-based voting systems, where currency balance determines voting power, equality could be faked when a user distributes their assets to multiple addresses. Therefore, a core component of many investigations is the detection of single entities that interact through multiple addresses. To detect such entities, a number of address clustering heuristics have been proposed for Bitcoin, that have also been reused in derivatives like Litecoin and ZCash [11,14]. Most of the existing heuristics are based on Bitcoin's UTXO model which allows a single transaction to have multiple inputs and outputs. However, a growing number of blockchain implementations have not adopted this model. A prominent example is Ethereum, which instead employs an account model where a regular transaction has one source and one destination account address. Apart from Ethereum, this account model is also present in other popular smart contract platforms such as EOS or NEO. Existing address clustering heuristics based on multiple inputs or outputs cannot be used for transactions with single inputs and outputs.

However, performing entity identification on account model blockchains such as Ethereum is of great interest, as it forms the basis for entity graph analysis, which allows for better assessment of network properties related to usage, wealth distribution and fraudulent activity. For example, Ether payments are also accepted in darknet marketplaces [15], and ponzi schemes exist through smart contracts [2,6]. It is likely that money laundering also exist on Ethereum, and the emergence of decentralized finance services like on-chain derivatives, loans and the use of decentralized exchanges are likely targets for manipulation. The underlying schemes may rely on the idea of creating the illusion of interaction between supposedly distinct participants.

Our Contribution. In this work, we propose several novel address clustering heuristics for Ethereum's account model, derived from the analysis of phenomena surrounding deposit addresses, multiple participation in airdrops and self-authorization. We explore each heuristic in detail and quantify their applicability over time. Our results show that we can cluster 17.9% of all active externally owned account addresses, indicating that there are more than 340,000 entities likely in control of multiple addresses. Comparing the heuristics, we conclude that the deposit address heuristic is currently the most effective approach. To allow for the heuristics to be used in practice, we published an implementation of them on GitHub[1].

The remainder of this paper is structured as follows: In Sects. 2 and 3, we provide an overview of the background on Ethereum, Tokens and Airdrops, as well as existing research results on address clustering for entity identification. In Sect. 4, we describe the data that forms the basis of our analyses and provide a set of high-level statistics of our data set. In Sect. 5 we study the heuristics of exchange deposit address reuse, airdrop multi-participation and token transfer authorization. We analyze the heuristics over time in Sect. 6, before discussing (Sect. 7) and summarizing the results of our paper in Sect. 8.

---

[1] https://github.com/etherclust/etherclust.

2   Background

After the creation of Bitcoin in 2009 [22], many alternative blockchains and associated cryptocurrencies have been proposed. By market capitalization in 2019, Ethereum [33] is the second most popular blockchain after Bitcoin. Both systems are open-source, public, distributed and rely on a Proof-of-Work-based consensus algorithm. To interact with the transaction network, users typically use a wallet software. They can create and manage multiple public/private key pairs, which can be used to sign transactions. For each key pair, an address is derived from the public key, serving as a pseudonymous identifier.

While both Bitcoin and Ethereum share the basic notion of an address, they differ in their abstraction of currency transfer. In Bitcoin, each transaction on the ledger must have one or multiple Unspent Transaction Output (UTXO) as input, which may be used by the corresponding holders of the private keys. Each UTXO contains a certain amount of Bitcoin. With each transaction, the inputs are spent, and the outputs are new UTXO.

In Ethereum, each regular transaction has one sender and one receiver account address. An account can either be an Externally Owned Account (EOA), where the private key is owned by an external user, or a smart contract account. Smart contract accounts contain executable code and don't have a private key. Their address is determined by the deployer's address and nonce, and the code can be executed by sending transactions to them, optionally with parameters.

2.1   Tokens

Smart contracts are frequently used to create token systems. A token can represent a variety of transferable and countable goods such as votes, memberships, loyalty points, shares or other utility [3]. To create a new token that is compatible with popular wallet software, developers can follow implementation standards such as ERC20[2] for fungible tokens, or ERC721[3] for non-fungible tokens. Similar standards exist on other smart contract platforms.

2.2   ICOs, Bounties and Airdrops

Startups have embraced the idea of tokens in order to raise funds in an Initial Coin Offering (ICO), and distribute tokens in return for investment. Apart from distributing tokens only for investment, some token creators also offer so-called bounties, in which social-media engagement, translation and other activities are rewarded with tokens. This idea can also be found in several so-called Airdrops, in which a large number of participants can obtain tokens either for free or for similar online activities such as re-tweeting or following an online presence. By giving out tokens to a large number of addresses, the airdrop operators hope to kickstart their project. If the value of the tokens increases at a later stage, the founders can sell some of their retained tokens.

---

[2] https://eips.ethereum.org/EIPS/eip-20.

[3] https://eips.ethereum.org/EIPS/eip-721.

3   Related Work

In the context of distributed ledgers, address clustering heuristics determine a one-to-many mapping of entities to addresses [9]. While the addresses are likely to be controlled by the same entity, some addresses could be clustered incorrectly. Due to a lack of ground truth, quantifying the error rate is very difficult.

Notwithstanding, a long line of research has examined the anonymity properties of Bitcoin [1,18,24,27,31], frequently using address clustering to identify entities. Therefore, they can study transaction graphs between entities. This is in contrast to Ethereum, where the existing studies focus on the address graph [5,8, 30,32], as no entity identification heuristics have been proposed so far.

3.1   Address Clustering Methods

The most frequently used approaches to cluster addresses in Bitcoin and other UTXO based ledgers are the multiple input heuristic, and the change heuristic. The multiple input heuristic is based on the idea that multiple UTXOs which are used as input for a transaction are most likely controlled by the same entity [18,26]. Similarly, the change heuristic assumes that a previously unused one-time change address created by a transaction is likely controlled by the same entity that created the transaction [1,18,31]. The effectiveness of these heuristics has been studied [9] and are implemented in open source analysis software like BlockSci [13] and GraphSense [11], which enable a range of features, including the tagging of entire address clusters given a label of one of its members.

By exploiting Airdrops based on existing wallets on Bitcoin, the reuse of addresses in newly created blockchains has enabled cross-ledger address clustering [10]. Related, and as an example of heuristics proposed for an alternative blockchain, Moreno-Sanchez et al. have developed clustering heuristics for the Ripple platform [20]. They exploit exchange gateways that allow exchanging Ripple with Bitcoins and other altcoins and are thus able to link wallets across cryptocurrencies. However, the approach it is not based on deposit address reuse, which is introduced in this paper.

Considering network-level information, Neudecker and Hartenstein associate IP addresses to transactions and exploit correlations with clusters [23]. Apart from these heuristics, Bitcoin users have been identified based on features derived from their transaction behavior [19]. By similar means, Jourdan et al. have characterized Bitcoin entities [12]. To the best of our knowledge, no clustering heuristics have been proposed for Ethereum's account model so far.

3.2   Address Clustering Countermeasures

To complicate the analysis of currency flows and disguise existing entities, a number of coin mixing services have been developed. These include CoinJoin [16] which lets separate entities create transactions jointly, causing the standard multiple-input heuristic to produce false results, as well as XIM [4] and Coin-Shuffle [28]. Coin mixing services have also been proposed for Ethereum, through smart contract-based solutions like Möbius [17] and Mixeth [29].

4   Data Collection

To perform our analyses, we have collected all blocks, transactions and event data up until block number 8,500,000 on the Ethereum blockchain, which appeared on September 7th, 2019. The following fundamental data was used:

- **Transaction** data consists of a source and a target account address, as well as the amount of Ether transferred or smart contract function called. This data also includes *internal* transactions, that originate from smart contracts but are originally triggered by an EOA.
- **Event** data consists of a list of topics, that characterize the event, and a data field carries some value. This lets us extract any type of event a smart contract has triggered. Therefore, we extract all token `Transfer` events and the token minting events `Mint`, `Distr`, `Airdrop` and `Tokendrop`, that are sometimes used for initial token distributions. Finally, we retrieve `Approval` events, which state that an owner approves another address to spend some of his tokens. The type and number of extracted events are listed in Table 1.

4.1   Account Types

For the following heuristics and analyses, we make extensive use of knowledge about the characteristics of addresses on the Ethereum blockchain. We categorize each address into whether it is an EOA or a smart contract, if it has mined blocks, and whether any transactions originate from it. If an address was never source of a transaction, we define it as inactive. One such inactive address is 0x0000000000000000000000000000000000000000, which is commonly used to *burn* cryptoassets. Ether or tokens that are sent to this address become inaccessible because in all likelihood no one has the private key to this account.

Finally, we also obtained a list of addresses that are known to belong to exchanges. To do so, we have extracted all exchange addresses as listed by Etherscan[4], adding additional addresses manually, which we identified through our own exchange deposits and research on public discussion forums. Table 2 shows the number and type of accounts in our dataset.

Table 1. Event types and counts

Event type	Count
Transfer	255,931,124
Mint	3,528,933
Distr	7,978,077
Airdrop	156,131
Tokendrop	19,036
Approval	7,325,925

Table 2. Account address types and counts

Account characteristic	Count
EOA, active	53,291,969
EOA, inactive	22,641,698
Smart contract	17,970,742
Miner address	4,922
EOA, exchange	186
Smart contract, exchange	28

---

[4] https://etherscan.io/accounts/label/exchange.

5   Heuristics

In the following subsections, we illustrate three entity identification heuristics: deposit address reuse, airdrop multi-participation and self-authorization. Each of the heuristics are based on usage patterns that can be observed on the Ethereum ledger. This means they are not inherent to the protocol, so that their effectiveness could change over time.

5.1   Deposit Address Reuse

The fact that the reuse of exchange deposit addresses provides a way to link addresses to each other is practically known, but has not yet been systematically exploited. In order to sell Ether or other cryptoassets, a user has to send them to an exchange. To credit the assets to the correct account, exchanges typically create so-called deposit addresses, which will then forward received funds to a main address. As these deposit addresses are created per customer, multiple addresses that send funds to the same deposit address are highly likely to be controlled by the same entity. This concept is illustrated in Fig. 1. The key challenge lies in identifying these deposit addresses. Their characteristic property is that they forward received amounts to a major exchange account. The forwarded amount is often slightly less than what was received, as the exchange has to pay for the transaction costs. In most cases, deposit addresses are EOAs, but they can also be smart contracts. When depositing tokens on the cryptocurrency exchange Kraken for example, users are instructed to send them to a given smart contract address, identical versions of which have been mass deployed in advance. This makes it trivial to identify all identical token deposit contracts deployed by Kraken. They are designed to forward received tokens automatically, thereby passing on the transaction costs to the user. Here, we focus on the forwarding principle.

Identifying deposit addresses relies on two parameters: the maximum amount difference between what was received and forwarded: a_{max} and the maximum

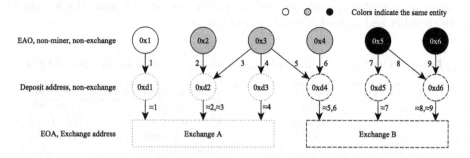

Fig. 1. Deposit address reuse: if 0xd1 to 0xd6 are exchange controlled deposit addresses that forward what is received, we cluster addresses that use the same deposit address. We can see 5 entities: 2 exchanges (dotted/dashed) and 3 potential users (colored).

time difference between receiving and forwarding: t_{max}. While the timing restriction ensures the forwarding characteristic, avoiding coincidental matches, a_{max} frequently corresponds to the transaction fees that are paid in the forwarding process. However, if a deposit address is a smart contract, the fee can be 0, as the EOA initiating the transaction pays for the fee. Secondly, if a sufficiently small amount of Ether is transferred to a forwarding deposit address, the exchange may wait for more deposits to make it worth the transaction fees. In the case of tokens, a_{max} is typically 0, as transaction fees cannot be paid with tokens.

Sometimes exchanges send funds to one another. As these could accidentally appear as a deposit address in a forwarding trace, we exclude known exchange addresses. We also require that the deposit address only forwards to a single exchange address. In practice however, an exchange may change their main wallet address. By imposing this restriction, we avoid accidentally linking major exchanges to the same entity. Finally, we exclude addresses using a deposit address that are either a known exchange address or have mined blocks. The former case appears frequently when users send funds directly between exchanges, the latter is frequent in mining pools, where participants request their share to be sent to a deposit address directly. For the full process see Algorithm 1.

Algorithm 1: Deposit address reuse heuristic

Input : $G(V, E)$, $V_{exch} \subset V$, $V_{miner} \subset V$, a_{max}, t_{max}
  V: addresses, E: Ether transactions and token transfers
Output: Mappings M_e and M_u of addresses for each entity

1 **foreach** path $v_u \to v_d \to v_e$,
2   where $v_u \notin V_{exch} \cup V_{miner}$, $v_d \notin V_{exch}$, $v_e \in V_{exch}$ **do**
3 | $e_1 = v_u v_d$; $e_2 = v_d v_e$;
4 | **if** $e_1.type = e_2.type$ **and**
5 | $e_1.amount - e_2.amount \in [0, a_{max}]$ **and**
6 | $e_2.blockNumber - e_1.blockNumber \in [0, t_{max}]$ **then**
7 | | depositAddresses.add(v_d);
8 | | exchangeEntities.addPath($v_d \to v_e$);   // builds a graph
9 | | userEntities.addPath($v_u \to v_d$);   // builds a graph

10 // find weakly connected components as address clusters
11 M_e = getWCC(exchangeEntities) ;   // for exchanges
12 // remove deposit addresses as they belong to exchanges
13 M_u = getWCC(userEntities) \ depositAddresses ;   // for users

---

Parameter Estimation. We initially identify Ether and token forwarding traces in a time window t_{max} of 10,000 blocks, and an amount difference a_{max} of 1 Ether. In the result, the empirical a_{max} in non-contract forwards is 0.0083 Ether at the 95th percentile, and t_{max} at the 95th percentile is 3,185 blocks, corresponding to approximately 13 h. Hence we rerun the extraction with thresholds $a_{max} = 0.01$ Ether and $t_{max} = 3,200$ blocks. As a result, we identify 13,104,448 traces that forward Ether or tokens to an EOA exchange address.

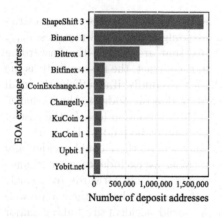

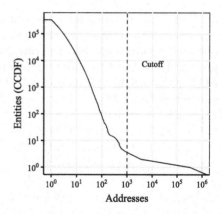

Fig. 2. Top 10 EOA exchange addresses by number of deposit addresses that only forward Ether and tokens to them. About 1.7 million belong to Shapeshift.

Fig. 3. CCDF showing how many entities each map to a minimum number of addresses. For example, about 10,000 entities consist of 10 or more addresses.

Results. Clustering the deposit addresses with the exchanges provides insight into how large the exchange clusters are. Figure 2 illustrates the top 10 exchange addresses by cluster size. We can see that Shapeshift and Binance form some of the largest clusters, with the former covering more than 1.7 million deposit addresses. In total, we can associate 6,670,392 deposit addresses to 186 EOA exchange addresses. Out of these, 5,671,405 are EOA, which means relative to all active EOA accounts, exchange deposit addresses account for 10.6%.

With respect to the accounts that have sent transactions or tokens to deposit addresses, we can make the following statements: Out of the 3,261,091 addresses that have used a deposit address, 1,446,715 (44.3%) have reused a deposit address with more than one account. In total, there are 333,107 entities that consist of more than one address. We can explore the full distribution with a complementary cumulative distribution function (CCDF), which is illustrated in Fig. 3. There, we can also see that we find 4 entities with each more than 1,000 addresses (indicated by the cutoff). While not impossible, we believe such large address clusters are unlikely, and therefore ignore them.

Limitations. To consider how this heuristic could lead to false positives, we assume the role of an adversary. As soon as we receive a transaction from an arbitrary address, we send the same amount to one of the known Exchange wallets. This would result in our account being considered a forwarding deposit address. In this way, the sending address cluster could be extended to include our own address. Furthermore, we've only investigated one layer of forwarding. With this approach, we also can't capture which major exchange addresses belong to each other, as we've limited deposit addresses to only have one target.

5.2   Airdrop Multi-participation

Airdrops are a popular mechanism to distribute tokens. On the Ethereum blockchain, they are performed through smart contracts. The owners of the smart contract may choose recipients randomly, based on past activity, or ask users to sign up through online forms. Some of these registration processes require users to perform certain actions on social media, such as posting articles or becoming a follower. The amount of tokens given to each user is either fixed, or based on existing account balances. If the amount is fixed, there is an incentive to cheat the system. A single user could sign up with multiple email addresses and perform actions with multiple social media accounts. Once the airdrop is performed, the user will receive the tokens on all of his registered addresses. Since it is impractical to manage the tokens on all of them, they are usually collected and aggregated to one address.

We can exploit this pattern to identify single entities that receive tokens multiple times. The concept is illustrated in Fig. 4. We identify Airdrops where a fixed amount of tokens is distributed to many recipients. Then we search for addresses that have been forwarded the same amount from the initial recipients. It is important to ensure that these second hop recipients are not exchange wallets or DEX contracts, as several honest recipients may transfer their tokens there directly. Furthermore, they must not be inactive accounts, as this could indicate many recipients burning the token.

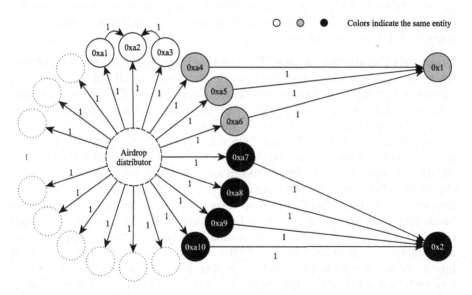

Fig. 4. In a token airdrop, where a large number of addresses (0xa1, ..., 0xan) receive the same token amount (in this case 1), we cluster addresses that forward the exact received amount to a single address. Receiving addresses should be active EOAs, and should not be an exchange or a smart contract, such as a DEX.

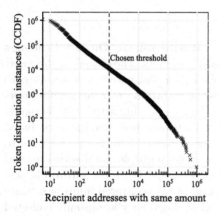
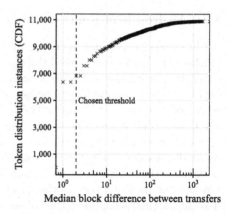

Fig. 5. CCDF illustrating fixed amount token distribution sizes. At the threshold, there are about 10,000 distribution events with at least 1,000 recipients.

Fig. 6. CDF illustrating median block difference between airdrop distribution transactions. At a difference of less than 2, there are 6,819 distribution events.

The heuristic depends on two inputs. First, a set of airdrops with equal amounts, characterized by a signature of a distributing address, a token network and an amount. Second, the minimum number of token aggregations agg_{min} into a single address. The second parameter is trivial to choose, as multi-participation in its smallest form consists of two airdrop recipient addresses forwarding their tokens to a third address ($agg_{min} = 2$). In this case a single entity would be in control of at least 3 addresses.

Input and Parameter Choice. The main challenge lies in identifying airdrops. As we have no ground truth on airdrops, we first examine all same-source, fixed amount token distribution events. Figure 5 shows the CCDF of same amount token distributions. We can observe that there are about 10,000 distribution events with at least 1,000 recipients. Manual inspection reveals that this also includes token transfers within the EOS token network, which was an ICO, not an airdrop. Therefore we must further filter the set of token distribution events. As airdrops are frequently distributed in an automated fashion, we can inspect the temporal domain of such a distribution event. We calculate the block difference between the individual airdrop token transfers and calculate the median block difference. If it is very low, a large number of addresses received their tokens in a short time frame, so we assume it to be an airdrop. Figure 6 shows a cumulative distribution function (CDF) of how many distribution events fall into a maximum median block difference. The fastest same-amount EOS transfers with at least 1,000 recipients occur with a median block difference of 4. Therefore, we only select distributions where this difference is less than 2. This means at least 500 recipients have received their tokens in consecutive time steps of at most one block, corresponding to about 15 s on average.

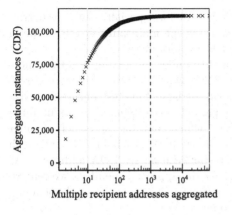

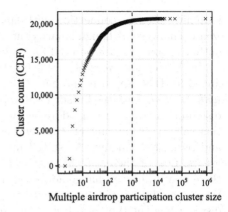

Fig. 7. CDF illustrating recipient aggregation instances. For example, there are 111,174 instances where between 2 and 1,000 recipients are aggregated.

Fig. 8. CDF illustrating the final cluster sizes after joining. At the chosen threshold, there are 20,453 clusters containing between 2 and 1000 addresses.

Secondly, we need to determine what constitutes a suspicious aggregation process. Figure 7 shows the CDF of aggregation instances by maximum number of addresses collected from. Already two airdrop recipients forwarding their tokens to a single address can constitute multi-participation. Visible in the plot, the CDF reaches a plateau from about 1,000 token receiver aggregations. There are aggregations with more addresses participating, but only very few of them.

Results. Retrieving all aggregations results in 4,880,118 traces from airdrop source to final collecting address. The median time between airdrop and collection is 10 days, with the lower quartile at 40 h. One user likely participates in multiple airdrops, where each multi-participation may slightly differ. Depending on the requirements for airdrop participation, users may add additional addresses, or not use all of them. As such, address clusters can merge. Once the joining is performed, we obtain our final entity clusters. The corresponding distribution is illustrated in Fig. 8. Due to the merging, the number of entities we can extract is lower than the number of aggregation instances depicted in Fig. 7. Some very large clusters have formed, which are unlikely to exist. This could be due to a collecting address that is actually a service used by many users. Secondly, some token transfers may have been falsely identified as airdrops. To reduce such issues, we only consider entities consisting of at most 1,000 addresses. Using this threshold, we count 675,512 addresses, likely controlled by 20,453 entities.

5.3 Self-authorization

The ERC20 token standard requires an `approve` function to allow another address to spend tokens on behalf of the actual owner. Through the execution, a spender address gains access to a limited amount of tokens. This functionality is mainly used in connection with smart contracts, especially with decentralized exchanges. Although smart contract use is the main purpose, this type of authorization can also be used for regular EOA addresses.

In this section, we exploit this functionality under the assumption that there are users that approve another address they own. We call this process *selfauthorization*. Reasons for such self approval might include test purposes or risk distribution over several addresses with partial accessibility. Successful function calls typically emit an `Approval` event, which contains the owner, spender and permitted amount. As stated in Sect. 4, we have obtained 7,325,925 such events. Out of these, 338,510 ($\approx$4.6%) are between active EOA addresses. As there may still be exchange addresses among the approved spenders, we remove them accordingly. Finally, we extract all unique pairs of owners and spenders, disregarding the type of token or the amount.

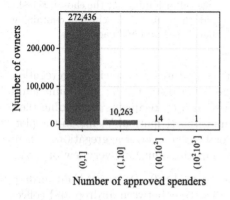

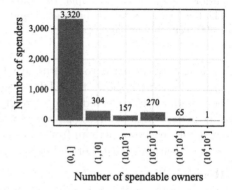

Fig. 9. Most EOA owners approve exactly one EOA spender. More than 100 approved spenders appears once.

Fig. 10. Most spenders have been approved by one owner, one spender is approved by more than 10,000 owners.

We can then study the relationship between these owners and spenders. Figure 9 illustrates that the vast majority of owner addresses only approve one spender address. However, it appears that this single spender address is frequently the same across many owner addresses: On the far right side of Fig. 10, we can observe that there is one spender address, that has been approved by more than 10,000 owners, and 65 addresses with more than 1,000 owners. For these, it is unlikely that they belong to the same entity. To extract entities, we believe a limit of up to 10 owners approving the same spender and up to 10 spenders approved by the same owner is a plausible. Doing so, lets us extract 4,599 entities from 7,107 addresses.

6   Analysis

In this section, we study the applicability of each clustering heuristic over time. Secondly, we apply the heuristics on a sample token network which highlights how the results allow for an interpretation of the interactions in the network.

Figure 11 illustrates how many newly seen addresses are clustered with an existing entity per block range of 100,000 blocks. It clearly illustrates that the deposit address clustering heuristic is the most effective by number of captured addresses. Most of these however, are the exchange deposit addresses themselves. Both deposit address reuse and multiple airdrop participation decrease in number of captured addresses. Even though the number of addresses captured by multi-airdrop participation is much lower, they appear consistently relative to the total number of addresses captured by all heuristics. The self-authorization heuristic however, only captures a very small number of addresses. In fact, there are so few of them, that they are not visible in the chart. With all clustering heuristics combined, we can cluster 10,561,143 addresses into 343,467 entities. The majority of these addresses belong to the exchange entities, which include smart contract deposit addresses. The number of EOA addresses we were able to cluster is 9,562,153, which equates to a share of 17.9% relative to all active EOAs.

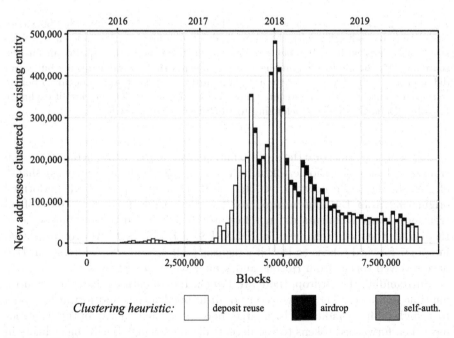

Fig. 11. Newly seen addresses that are clustered with previously seen addresses. The exchange deposit address clustering heuristic is responsible for most address clusters.

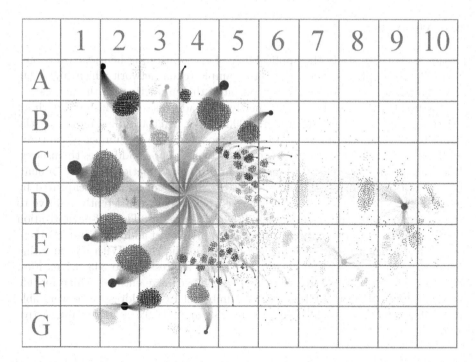

Fig. 12. The Bionic token network (0xef51c9377feb29856e61625caf9390bd0b67ea18). Nodes close to each other with the same shade of gray indicate the same entity. Node size corresponds with their indegree. The Bionic token network contains an airdrop source at D4, the circle surrounding it are recipients that received tokens, but never did anything with them. But there are many airdrop recipients that appear to belong to the same entity, as they aggregate their received tokens. At D9, the HotBit exchange is visible. Deposit addresses belonging to HotBit are visible in C8.

In Fig. 12, we illustrate the airdrop and deposit heuristics applied to the token transfers of only the Bionic token network, and highlight entities with shades of gray. In the token network, we can see that an airdrop has been performed originating from D4. The airdrop itself is responsible for a large part of all transfers. Many recipients did not forward their received tokens, but some of them trade them on exchanges like IDEX (E8) or Hotbit (D9). Airdrop recipients in C7-D7 forward tokens to Hotbit's deposit addresses in D8. Addresses in D10 have received tokens from Hotbit, and some have been sent back.

Surrounding the airdrop, there are 170 clusters of entities that likely control multiple addresses. They have received airdropped tokens and forwarded them to a single address, indicated by a larger node size. The majority of these entities have then forwarded tokens to the decentralized exchange IDEX, most likely in order to sell them. Due to the many transfers involved in collecting from multiple addresses, the token network appears to have significant activity, when in reality, a large portion of this activity originates from a few entities.

7 Discussion

Due to a lack of ground-truth labels on which addresses actually belong to the same entity, it is very difficult to assess the quality of the clustering heuristics. This same issue is prevalent in existing UTXO-based clustering heuristics. In comparison to them, the proposed approaches in this paper have the drawback that they are not parameter-free. They require lists of previously known addresses or thresholds. Nevertheless, in the case of deposit address reuse, the advantage lies in the fact that the usefulness can be improved when provided with more labels of major exchange addresses. Some of the very large cluster formations could be due to unknown exchange addresses. In the case of airdrop multi-participation, the main challenge is identifying airdrops correctly. We have chosen the path of counting same amount recipients, as well as considering the temporal domain. As a result, some very large clusters have formed which we had to exclude. The quality of the results would benefit from more sophisticated airdrop detection methods. With respect to the utility of each of the heuristics, we can state the following: whereas deposit address reuse and self-authorization may provide insightful links for future analysis surrounding fraudulent behavior, we expect that the clusters around airdrop multi-participation are mostly limited to the particular use case of multi-participation.

8 Conclusion and Future Work

This paper is the first to propose clustering heuristics for Ethereum's account model, including an analysis of their applicability. We have explored deposit address reuse, airdrop multi-participation and self-authorization. For each heuristic, we have analyzed and selected parameters as inputs. We have shown that the exchange deposit address reuse heuristic captures the majority of addresses, whereas the airdrop multi-participation heuristic can provide fewer but additional address clusters. The self-authorization heuristic however, has only provided very few results. Overall, we are able to cluster 17.9% of active addresses on the Ethereum blockchain, which may form the foundation of future entity graph analyses related to usage assessments or fraud detection.

8.1 Future Work

As part of future work, we believe the detection of exchange wallets is important to improve the clustering results. Further usage patterns on the Ethereum blockchain can be studied. They may provide insight into how entities use them, which in turn allows for clustering heuristics. Examples include online wallets, identity management solutions like ERC 725, smart contracts related to games, gambling or services in the realm of decentralized finance.

Another challenge is the question of how to treat smart contract accounts when identifying entities. A smart contract could act as a regular wallet, in which case the owner is likely the creator. But it is also possible that the smart contract merely forwards currency, in which case an owner is not important.

References

1. Androulaki, E., Karame, G.O., Roeschlin, M., Scherer, T., Capkun, S.: Evaluating user privacy in bitcoin. In: Sadeghi, A.-R. (ed.) FC 2013. LNCS, vol. 7859, pp. 34–51. Springer, Heidelberg (2013). https://doi.org/10.1007/978-3-642-39884-1_4
2. Bartoletti, M., Pes, B., Serusi, S.: Data mining for detecting bitcoin ponzi schemes. In: 2018 Crypto Valley Conference on Blockchain Technology (CVCBT), pp. 75–84. IEEE (2018)
3. Bartoletti, M., Pompianu, L.: An empirical analysis of smart contracts: platforms, applications, and design patterns. In: Brenner, M., et al. (eds.) FC 2017. LNCS, vol. 10323, pp. 494–509. Springer, Cham (2017). https://doi.org/10.1007/978-3-319-70278-0_31
4. Bissias, G., Ozisik, A.P., Levine, B.N., Liberatore, M.: Sybil-resistant mixing for bitcoin. In: Proceedings of the 13th Workshop on Privacy in the Electronic Society, pp. 149–158. ACM (2014)
5. Chen, T., et al.: Understanding ethereum via graph analysis. In: IEEE International Conference on Computer Communications, pp. 1484–1492. IEEE (2018)
6. Chen, W., Zheng, Z., Cui, J., Ngai, E., Zheng, P., Zhou, Y.: Detecting ponzi schemes on ethereum: towards healthier blockchain technology. In: Proceedings of the 2018 World Wide Web Conference, pp. 1409–1418. International World Wide Web Conferences Steering Committee (2018)
7. Fanusie, Y.J., Robinson, T.: Bitcoin laundering: an analysis of illicit flows into digital currency services. A memorandum by the Center on Sanctions and Illicit Finance and Elliptic, January 2018
8. Ferretti, S., D'Angelo, G.: On the ethereum blockchain structure: a complex networks theory perspective. Concurr. Comput.: Pract. Exp. 32, e5493 (2020)
9. Harrigan, M., Fretter, C.: The unreasonable effectiveness of address clustering. In: 2016 International IEEE Conferences on Ubiquitous Intelligence & Computing, Advanced and Trusted Computing, Scalable Computing and Communications, Cloud and Big Data Computing, Internet of People, and Smart World Congress (UIC/ATC/ScalCom/CBDCom/IoP/SmartWorld), pp. 368–373. IEEE (2016)
10. Harrigan, M., Shi, L., Illum, J.: Airdrops and privacy: a case study in cross-blockchain analysis. In: 2018 IEEE International Conference on Data Mining Workshops (ICDMW), pp. 63–70. IEEE (2018)
11. Haslhofer, B., Karl, R., Filtz, E.: O bitcoin where art thou? Insight into large-scale transaction graphs. In: SEMANTiCS (Posters, Demos) (2016)
12. Jourdan, M., Blandin, S., Wynter, L., Deshpande, P.: Characterizing entities in the bitcoin blockchain. In: 2018 IEEE International Conference on Data Mining Workshops (ICDMW), pp. 55–62. IEEE (2018)
13. Kalodner, H., Goldfeder, S., Chator, A., Möser, M., Narayanan, A.: BlockSci: design and applications of a blockchain analysis platform. arXiv preprint arXiv:1709.02489 (2017)
14. Kappos, G., Yousaf, H., Maller, M., Meiklejohn, S.: An empirical analysis of anonymity in Zcash. In: 27th USENIX Security Symposium, USENIX Security 2018, pp. 463–477 (2018)
15. Madore, P.H.: Crypto Market OpenBazaar Confirms Upcoming Support for Ethereum (2019). https://www.ccn.com/openbazaar-adding-support-ethereum-soon/. Accessed 12 Sept 2019
16. Maxwell, G.: CoinJoin: Bitcoin privacy for the real world (2013). bitcointalk. org/index.php?topic=279249. Accessed 12 Sept 2019

17. Meiklejohn, S., Mercer, R.: Möbius: trustless tumbling for transaction privacy. In: Proceedings on Privacy Enhancing Technologies, pp. 105–121 (2018)
18. Meiklejohn, S., et al.: A fistful of bitcoins: characterizing payments among men with no names. In: Proceedings of the Internet Measurement Conference - IMC 2013, no. 6, pp. 127–140 (2013)
19. Monaco, J.V.: Identifying bitcoin users by transaction behavior. In: Biometric and Surveillance Technology for Human and Activity Identification XII, vol. 9457, p. 945704. International Society for Optics and Photonics (2015)
20. Moreno-Sanchez, P., Zafar, M.B., Kate, A.: Listening to whispers of ripple: linking wallets and deanonymizing transactions in the ripple network. In: Proceedings on Privacy Enhancing Technologies, no. 4, pp. 436–453 (2016)
21. Möser, M., Böhme, R., Breuker, D.: An inquiry into money laundering tools in the bitcoin ecosystem. In: 2013 APWG eCrime Researchers Summit, pp. 1–14. IEEE (2013)
22. Nakamoto, S.: Bitcoin: a peer-to-peer electronic cash system (2008)
23. Neudecker, T., Hartenstein, H.: Could network information facilitate address clustering in bitcoin? In: Brenner, M., et al. (eds.) FC 2017. LNCS, vol. 10323, pp. 155–169. Springer, Cham (2017). https://doi.org/10.1007/978-3-319-70278-0_9
24. Ober, M., Katzenbeisser, S., Hamacher, K.: Structure and anonymity of the bitcoin transaction graph. Future Internet 2, 237–250 (2013)
25. Paquet-Clouston, M., Haslhofer, B., Dupont, B.: Ransomware payments in the bitcoin ecosystem. J. Cybersecur. 5(1), 1–11 (2019). tyz003
26. Reid, F., Harrigan, M.: An analysis of anonymity in the bitcoin system. In: Altshuler, Y., Elovici, Y., Cremers, A., Aharony, N., Pentland, A. (eds.) Security and Privacy in Social Networks, pp. 197–223. Springer, New York (2013). https://doi.org/10.1007/978-1-4614-4139-7_10
27. Ron, D., Shamir, A.: Quantitative analysis of the full bitcoin transaction graph. In: Sadeghi, A.-R. (ed.) FC 2013. LNCS, vol. 7859, pp. 6–24. Springer, Heidelberg (2013). https://doi.org/10.1007/978-3-642-39884-1_2
28. Ruffing, T., Moreno-Sanchez, P., Kate, A.: CoinShuffle: practical decentralized coin mixing for bitcoin. In: Kutyłowski, M., Vaidya, J. (eds.) ESORICS 2014. LNCS, vol. 8713, pp. 345–364. Springer, Cham (2014). https://doi.org/10.1007/978-3-319-11212-1_20
29. Seres, I.A., Nagy, D.A., Buckland, C., Burcsi, P.: MixEth: efficient, trustless coin mixing service for ethereum. IACR Cryptology ePrint Archive, p. 341 (2019)
30. Somin, S., Gordon, G., Altshuler, Y.: Network analysis of ERC20 tokens trading on ethereum blockchain. In: Morales, A.J., Gershenson, C., Braha, D., Minai, A.A., Bar-Yam, Y. (eds.) ICCS 2018. SPC, pp. 439–450. Springer, Cham (2018). https://doi.org/10.1007/978-3-319-96661-8_45
31. Spagnuolo, M., Maggi, F., Zanero, S.: BitIodine: extracting intelligence from the bitcoin network. In: Christin, N., Safavi-Naini, R. (eds.) FC 2014. LNCS, vol. 8437, pp. 457–468. Springer, Heidelberg (2014). https://doi.org/10.1007/978-3-662-45472-5_29
32. Victor, F., Lüders, B.K.: Measuring ethereum-based ERC20 token networks. In: Goldberg, I., Moore, T. (eds.) FC 2019. LNCS, vol. 11598, pp. 113–129. Springer, Cham (2019). https://doi.org/10.1007/978-3-030-32101-7_8
33. Wood, G.: Ethereum: a secure decentralised generalised transaction ledger. https://github.com/ethereum/yellowpaper

What are the Actual Flaws in Important Smart Contracts (And How Can We Find Them)?

Alex Groce[1]([☒]), Josselin Feist[2], Gustavo Grieco[2], and Michael Colburn[2]

[1] Northern Arizona University, Flagstaff, AZ 86011, USA
alex.groce@nau.edu
[2] Trail of Bits, New York, NY 10003, USA

Abstract. An important problem in smart contract security is under-standing the likelihood and criticality of discovered, or potential, weak-nesses in contracts. In this paper we provide a summary of Ethereum smart contract audits performed for 23 professional stakeholders, avoid-ing the common problem of reporting issues mostly prevalent in low-quality contracts. These audits were performed at a leading company in blockchain security, using both open-source and proprietary tools, as well as human code analysis performed by professional security engineers. We categorize 246 individual defects, making it possible to compare the severity and frequency of different vulnerability types, compare smart contract and non-smart contract flaws, and to estimate the efficacy of automated vulnerability detection approaches.

1 Introduction

Smart contracts are versatile instruments that can not only facilitate and verify transactions in financial services, but also track the movement of physical goods and intellectual property. Security and correctness are essential for smart con-tract technology, because contracts possess the authority to allocate high-value resources between complex systems and are, for the most part, autonomous.

Security researchers have worked to describe vulnerabilities and produce tools that find flaws in smart contracts, but most of the discussions of such flaws concentrate on a small number of actual exploits [20,24]. Moreover, many studies examine *all* the contracts on a blockchain or focus on "popular" [2] contracts, but these contracts often are produced by development efforts where security and correctness are not prioritized. While informative, these analyses do not represent the contracts that are likely to become the infrastructure of a smart-contract future.

A better alternative for understanding smart contract flaws is to analyze bugs discovered during professional security audits. Early investors in smart contracts expose themselves to risks that could be devastating if the code is insecure or incorrect. Given these consequences, it is more likely that an initial effort is made to produce correct code. Therefore, flaws discovered during paid security

© International Financial Cryptography Association 2020
J. Bonneau and N. Heninger (Eds.): FC 2020, LNCS 12059, pp. 634–653, 2020.
https://doi.org/10.1007/978-3-030-51280-4_34

audits provide a better ground truth for recommending ways to improve smart contract security. This paper presents an analysis of the types of flaws detected in 23 Solidity/Ethereum [4,32] smart contract audits performed by Trail of Bits (https://trailofbits.com), a leading company in the field.

2   Related Work

To our knowledge, *no* previous work reports flaws detected in paid security audits of important smart contracts. We have not even found any manual examination of large numbers of smart contracts with reasonable criteria for removing uninteresting contracts (which would ensure quality analysis). However, there are other important efforts to classify or describe smart contract flaws. Atzei, Bartoletti, and Cimoli produced a taxonomy of possible *attacks* on smart contracts, with examples of actual exploit code [1]. Their categories have some overlap with those used in this paper, but are more focused on specific-exploit patterns and exclude some types of flaws that are not tied to a specific attack. We believe that every category present in their taxonomy is also represented by at least one finding in our set. Their purpose is largely orthogonal to ours and presents a useful alternative view of the topic, but one based more on speculation about exploits than on concrete data about the prevalence and seriousness of flaws in real contracts. Mense and Flatscher [16] combine a summary of known vulnerability types with a simple comparison of then-available tools, while Saad et al. [23] expand the scope of analysis to general blockchain attack surfaces, but provide a similar categorization of smart contract vulnerabilities. Dika's thesis also [7] provides another, earlier, summary of vulnerability types, analyses, and tools. In general, the types of flaws discussed in these works are a subset of those we discuss below.

Perez and Livshits provide a (provocatively titled) analysis of actual executed exploits on 21K contracts reported in various academic papers, which provides a useful additional perspective, but they use a very different data set with purposes almost completely unrelated to ours [19]. They find that, while reentrancy is the most dangerous category of problem (over 65% of actual exploits in the wild), even reentrancy exploits have resulted in loss of less than 10K Ether to date. The relatively small size of exploits to date vs. potential future losses affirms that information about undetected flaws in audited high-value, high-visibility contracts is important to the community.

Smart contract analysis/verification research often touches on the topic of expected vulnerabilities [3,6,8–10,10,11,13,14,18,22,30], but this research is, to our knowledge, always based on author perceptions of threats, not statistical inference from close examinations of high-quality/critical contracts.

3   Summary of Findings

The results below are based on 23 audits performed by Trail of Bits. Of these, all but five are public, and the reports are available online [29]. The number of findings per audit ranged from 2–22, with a median and mean of 10 findings. Reports ranged in size from just under 2K words to nearly 13K words, with a total size of over 180K words. It is also worth mentioning that each audit focused on a code-base that has between one to a few dozen of contracts that Trail of Bits reviewed manually and using automated tools. The total number of audited contracts is thus considerably more than 23 (some individual audits covered more than 23 contracts).

The time allotted for audits ranged from one person-week to twelve person-weeks, with a mean of six person-weeks and a median of four person-weeks. The audits were prepared by a total of 24 different auditors, with most audits prepared by multiple individuals (up to five). The mean number of authors was 2.6, and the median was three. The most audits in which a single author participated was 12, the mean was 3.2; the median was only two audits. In general, while these audits are all the product of a single company, there is considerable diversity in the set of experts involved.

Most of these assessments used static and dynamic analysis tools in addition to manual analysis of code, but the primary source of findings was manual. In particular, a version of the Slither static analyzer [9] which included a number of detectors not available in the public version, was applied to many of the contracts. In some cases, property-based testing with Echidna [26] and symbolic analysis with Manticore [17,25] were also applied to detect some problems. Only five audits did not use automated tools. Fifteen of the audits made use of Slither, ten made use of Manticore, and eight made use of Echidna. However, when Slither was used in audits, it was usually used much more extensively than Manticore or Echidna, which were typically restricted to a few chosen properties of high interest. Only four findings are explicitly noted in the findings as produced by a tool, all by Slither. However, other findings may have resulted from automated analyses in a less explicit fashion.

3.1 Smart Contract Findings

Our analysis is based on 246 total findings. Tables 1 and 2 summarize information on these findings (Table 2). Each flaw is classified according to its severity, considering the potential impact of the exploit to be:

- *High* if it affects a large numbers of users, or has serious legal and financial implications;
- *Medium* if it affects individual users' information, or has possible legal implications for clients and moderate financial impact;
- *Low* if the risk is relatively small or is not a risk the customer has indicated is important;
- *Informational* if the issue does not pose an immediate risk, but is relevant to security best practices.

Another important property of each finding is how difficult it is to exploit:

- *Low* for commonly exploited flaws where public tools exist or exploitation can be easily automated;

- *Medium* for flaws that require in-depth knowledge of a complex system;
- *High* for flaws where an attacker must have privileged insider access to the system, or must discover other weaknesses, for exploitation.

The findings categories are sorted by the frequency of severity counts; ties in the high-severity findings count are broken by counting medium-severity findings, and further ties are broken by low-severity findings. Appendix A shows exact counts for categories and severities/difficulties. Raw data is also available [28].

The categories in these tables are generally the categories used in the audit reports submitted to clients, but in some cases we have corrected obviously incorrect categories given the continuous evolution of the security landscape for smart contracts. Additionally, we have introduced a few new categories in cases where findings were clearly placed in a category of dubious relevance due to the lack of a suitable category. The most significant systematic change is that we separated *race conditions* and *front-running* from all other timing issues, due to 1) the large number of race conditions relative to other timing issues; 2) the general qualitative difference between race conditions and other timing-based exploits (e.g., there is a large literature addressing detection and mitigation of race conditions specifically); and 3) the specific relevance of front-running to smart contracts. Our analysis calls special attention to findings classified as **high-low**, that is **high severity** and **low difficulty**. These offer attackers an easy way to inflict potentially severe harm. There were 27 high-low findings, all classified as one of eight categories: data validation, access controls, numerics, undefined behavior, patching, denial of service, authentication, or timing.

Data Validation. Data validation covers the large class of findings in which the core problem is that input received from an untrusted source (e.g., arguments to a `public` function of a contract) is not properly vetted, with potentially harmful consequences (the type of harm varies widely). Not only is this a frequently appearing problem, with more than three times as many findings as the next most common category, it is a *serious* issue in many cases, with the largest absolute number of high-low findings (10), and a fairly high percent of high-low findings (11%). Data validation can sometimes be detected statically, by using taint to track unchecked user input to a dangerous operation (e.g., an array de-reference), but in many cases the consequences are not obviously problematic unless one understands a contract's purpose. Ironically, the safer execution semantics of Solidity/EVM make some problems that would clearly be security flaws in C or C++ harder to automatically detect. In Solidity, it is not always incorrect to allow a user to provide an array index: If the index is wrong, in many cases, the call will simply revert, and there is no rule that contract code should never revert. From the point of view of a fuzzer or static analysis tool, distinguishing bad reverts from intended ones is difficult without guidance. Automated static or dynamic analysis to detect many of the instances of missing/incorrect data validation identified in the audits would require some user annotations, either in the form of properties or at least annotating some functions or statements as not expected to revert, but given that information, would likely prove effective.

Table 1. Severity and difficulty distributions for finding categories. The second column shows what percent of all findings that category represents; the remaining columns are percentages *within-category*.

Category	%	High-Low	Severity					Difficulty			
			High	Med.	Low	Info.	Und.	High	Med.	Low	Und.
data validation	36%	11%	21%	36%	24%	13%	6%	27%	16%	55%	2%
access controls	10%	25%	42%	25%	12%	21%	0%	33%	12%	54%	0%
race condition	7%	0%	41%	41%	6%	12%	0%	100%	0%	0%	0%
numerics	5%	23%	31%	23%	38%	8%	0%	31%	8%	62%	0%
undefined behavior	5%	23%	31%	15%	31%	8%	15%	15%	8%	77%	0%
patching	7%	11%	17%	11%	39%	28%	6%	6%	11%	61%	22%
denial of service	4%	10%	20%	30%	30%	20%	0%	50%	0%	40%	10%
authentication	2%	25%	50%	25%	25%	0%	0%	50%	0%	50%	0%
reentrancy	2%	0%	50%	25%	25%	0%	0%	50%	25%	0%	25%
error reporting	3%	0%	29%	14%	0%	57%	0%	43%	29%	29%	0%
configuration	2%	0%	40%	0%	20%	20%	20%	60%	20%	20%	0%
logic	1%	0%	33%	33%	33%	0%	0%	100%	0%	0%	0%
data exposure	1%	0%	33%	33%	0%	33%	0%	33%	33%	33%	0%
timing	2%	25%	25%	0%	75%	0%	0%	75%	0%	25%	0%
coding-bug	2%	0%	0%	67%	33%	0%	0%	17%	0%	83%	0%
front-running	2%	0%	0%	80%	0%	20%	0%	100%	0%	0%	0%
auditing and logging	4%	0%	0%	0%	33%	44%	22%	33%	0%	56%	11%
missing-logic	1%	0%	0%	0%	67%	33%	0%	0%	0%	100%	0%
cryptography	0%	0%	0%	0%	100%	0%	0%	100%	0%	0%	0%
documentation	2%	0%	0%	0%	25%	50%	25%	0%	0%	75%	25%
API inconsistency	1%	0%	0%	0%	0%	100%	0%	0%	0%	100%	0%
code-quality	1%	0%	0%	0%	0%	100%	0%	0%	0%	100%	0%

Access Controls. Access control findings describe cases where use of a legitimate operation of a contract should be restricted to certain callers (the owner, minters, etc.), but access control is either faulty or not implemented at all. Most often, access control findings are cases where access control is too permissive, but nearly a third of these findings involve overly restrictive access control. While there are three times as many data validation findings as access control findings, there are nearly as many high-low findings for access control as for data validation. One in four access control findings is high-low, and 42% of access control findings are high severity. In general, automatic detection of access control problems without additional specification is often plausible. In four of our findings, it would suffice to check standard ERC20 token semantics, enforce the **paused** state for a contract, or assume that only certain users should be able to cause self-destruction. Cases where access controls are too restrictive would require additional specification but, but, given that effort, are also often likely to be handled well by property-based testing.

Table 2. Optimistic percentages of each category detectable by automated methods.

Category	% Dynamic	% Static	Category	% Dynamic	% Static
data validation	57%	22%	logic	0%	0%
access controls	50%	4%	data exposure	0%	0%
race condition	6%	59%	timing	50%	25%
numerics	46%	69%	coding-bug	67%	50%
undefined behavior	0%	31%	front-running	0%	0%
patching	17%	33%	auditing and logging	0%	38%
denial of service	40%	0%	missing-logic	67%	0%
authentication	25%	0%	cryptography	0%	100%
reentrancy	75%	100%	documentation	0%	0%
error reporting	29%	14%	API inconsistency	0%	0%
configuration	0%	0%	code-quality	0%	67%

Race Condition. Race conditions are cases in which the behavior of a contract depends (in an unintended way) on an improperly restricted ordering of operations or events. Often, the consequence of one particular unexpected ordering is clearly incorrect. The race condition category had zero high-low findings, but was responsible for seven of the 60 total high-severity findings across all audits. The top three categories (data validation, access controls, and race conditions) made up over half of all high-severity findings. A full 41% of race conditions are high severity. Nearly half (nine) of the race condition findings concern a known ERC20 issue [31], and could certainly be identified automatically by a static analysis tool. Due to the nature of many blockchain race conditions, understanding the impact of the race would often be hard for a dynamic analysis.

Numerics. Numerics findings involve the semantics of Solidity arithmetic: Most are overflow errors, some are underflow errors, and a few involve precision losses. These findings also include cases where a "safe math" library or function is used, so there is no actual overflow/underflow resulting in an incorrect value, but the resulting revert causes problems. Three numerics findings are high-low (23%), and 31% are high severity. Rounding or precision (six findings) and overflow (three findings) are the most common numerics errors. Many rounding and overflow problems can likely be flagged using static analysis, but to determine whether the behavior is problematic would require custom properties.

Undefined Behavior. The undefined behavior category includes cases where a contract relies on unspecified or under-specified semantics of the Solidity language or the EVM, so the actual semantic intent of the contract is either currently unclear or may become so in the future. For instance, in Solidity, the evaluation order of expressions in the same statement is not specified. Instead, it is only guaranteed that statements are executed in order. Three (23%) of the undefined behavior findings are high-low, and 31% of undefined behavior findings are high severity. Undefined behavior is often easy to statically detect.

Patching. Patching findings concern flaws in the process to upgrade or change contract behavior. The immutability of code on the blockchain requires the use of complex, hard-to-get-right methods to allow changes. Two (11%) of the patching findings are high-low, and 17% are high severity. Many patching issues are complex environmental problems that likely require human expertise, but some common patterns of bad upgrade logic might be amenable to static detection, and a dynamic analysis can detect that a contract is broken after a faulty update.

Denial of Service. Denial of service covers findings that are not well described by another class (e.g., if lack of data validation causes denial of service, we still classify it as data validation), and where the consequence of a flaw is either complete shut-down of a contract or significant operational inefficiency. If we included all cases where denial of service is an important potential consequence of a flaw, or even the only important consequence, the category would be larger. One denial of service finding was high-low, and 20% of findings were high severity. Most denial of service findings would require fairly complex custom properties specifying system behavior, in part because "simple" denial of service due to some less complex cause falls under another category.

Authentication. Authentication findings specifically concern cases where the mechanism used to determine identity or authorization is flawed, as opposed to cases where the access rules are incorrect. That is, in authentication problems, the logic of who is allowed to do what is correct, but the determination of "who" is flawed. While only one authentication finding is high-low, fully half of all authentication problems are high severity; in fact, authentication is tied with the infamous reentrancy problem in terms having the greatest percentage of high severity issues. Three of the observed authentication problems are highly idiosyncratic, and may not even be automatically detectable with complex custom properties. However, the remaining problem should be dynamically detectable using "off-the-shelf" ERC20 token semantics properties.

Reentrancy. Reentrancy is a widely discussed and investigated flaw in Ethereum smart contracts [1]. In a reentrancy attack, a contract calls an external contract, before "internal work" (primarily state changes) is finished. Through some route, the external contract *re-enters* code that expected the internal work to be complete. No reentrancy problems detected in audits were high-low, but 50% of the findings were high severity. Reentrancy is a serious problem, but, due to its well-defined structure, is usually amenable to static and dynamic detection. In particular, static detection with relatively few false positives is probably already possible using Slither, for most important reentrancies.

Error Reporting. Error reporting findings involve cases in which a contract does not properly report, propagate, or handle error conditions. There are no high-low error reporting findings in the audits, but 29% of error reporting find-ings are high severity. In some cases error reporting is a difficulty category to cap-ture without further specification, and specifying that errors should be reported or handled in a certain way generally requires the same understanding that would have produced correct code in the first place. However, ERC20 seman-tics make some error reporting problems easy to automatically detect. Incorrect error *propagation* is also usually statically detectable [21]; however, this was not the type of error reporting problem discovered in audits.

Configuration. Configuration findings generally describe cases in which a bad configuration may lead to bad behavior even when the contract itself is correct. In smart contracts, this is often related to financial effects, e.g., bad market/pricing parameters. There are no high-low findings in this category, but 40% of findings are high priority. Configuration problems are usually fairly subtle, or even eco-nomic/financial in nature, and detection is likely to rely on manual analysis.

Logic. Logic findings describe incorrect protocols or business logic, where the implementation is as intended, but the reasoning behind the intention is incor-rect. Somewhat surprisingly, this category has no high-low findings, and only three fundamental logic flaws were described in the audits. One of the three logic flaws described was high severity, however. Based on the small number of findings it is hard to guess how often custom properties might allow dynamic detection of logic flaws. If the bad logic often leads to a violation of the expected invariants of a contract, then it can be detected, but if the fault is in the under-standing of desirable invariants (which may often be the case), manual inspection by another set of expert eyes may be the only plausible detection method.

Data Exposure. Data exposure findings are those in which information that should not be public is made public. For instance, some smart contracts offer guarantees to users regarding the information about them stored on the blockchain. If an attacker can infer data about users by observing confirmed or unconfirmed transactions, then that is classified as a data exposure issue. There are no high-low data exposure findings, but 33% are high severity. Most data exposure problems are not likely to be amenable to automatic detection.

Timing. Timing findings concern cases (that are neither race conditions nor front-running) where manipulation of timing has negative consequences. For the most part, these findings involved assuming intervals between events (especially blocks) that may not hold in practice. One of the four timing findings (the only high severity one) was high-low. Timing problems can be amenable to automated detection in that static or dynamic analysis can certainly recognize when code depends on, for instance, the block timestamp.

Coding-Bug. Coding-bug is a catch-all category for problems that, whatever their consequences, amount to a "typo" in code, rather than a likely intentional error on a developer's part. Off-by-one loop bounds that do not traverse an entire array are a simple example. There were no high-low or high-severity coding bugs in the smart contracts audited, which suggests that the worst simple coding problems may be detected by existing unit tests or human inspection of code, in the relatively small code bases of even larger smart contracts. On the other hand, 67% of coding bugs were medium severity, the second-highest rate for that severity; only one other class exceeded 41% medium-severity findings.

Front-Running. Front-running generalizes the financial market concept of front-running, where a trader uses advance non-public knowledge of a pending transaction to "predict" future prices and/or buy or sell before the pending state change. In smart contracts, this means that a contract 1) exposes information about future state changes (especially to a "market") and 2) allows transactions that exploit this knowledge. It is both a timing and data exposure problem, but is assigned its own category because the remedy is often different. Front-running is a well-known concern in smart contracts, but in fact no high-low or even high-severity front-running problems were detected in our audits. On the other hand, front-running had the largest percent of medium-severity findings (80%), so it is not an insignificant problem. Front-running, by its nature, is probably hard to detect dynamically, and very hard to detect statically.

Auditing and Logging. Auditing and logging findings describe inadequate or incorrect logging; in most cases incorrect or missing contract events. There were no high-low, high-severity, or medium-severity auditing or logging findings. If explicit checks for events are included in (automated) testing, such problems can easily be detected, but if such checks are included, the important events are also likely to be present and correct, so this is not a great fit for dynamic analysis. On the other hand, it is often easy to statically note when an important state change is made but no event is associated with it.

Missing-Logic. Missing-logic findings are cases in which—rather than incorrect logic for handling a particular set of inputs, or missing validation to exclude those inputs—there is a correct way to handle inputs, but it is missing. Structurally, missing-logic means that code should add another branch to handle a special case. Interestingly, while this seems like a potentially serious issue, there were no high-low or even medium-severity missing-logic findings. The ease of detecting missing logic with custom properties depends on the consequences of the omission; static analysis seems unlikely find most missing logic.

Cryptography. Cryptography findings concern cases where incorrect or insufficient cryptography is used. In our smart contract audits, the one (low severity, high difficulty) cryptography finding concerned use of an improper pseudo-

Table 3. Most common finding categories in other audits.

Category	#	%	Change	Category	#	%	Change
data validation	41	53%	-17%	patching	6	8%	-1%
denial of service	23	30%	-26%	authentication	5	6%	-4%
configuration	20	26%	-24%	timing	4	5%	-3%
data exposure	18	23%	-22%	numerics	2	3%	+3%
access controls	14	18%	-8%	auditing and logging	2	3%	+1%
cryptography	12	16%	-16%	race condition	1	1%	+6%
undefined behavior	7	9%	-4%	error reporting	1	1%	+2%

random number generator, something a static analysis tool can often flag in the blockchain context, where bad sources of randomness are fairly limited.

Documentation. Documentation findings describe cases where the contract code is not incorrect, but there is missing or erroneous documentation. As you would expect, this is never a high- or even medium-severity issue, and is not amenable to automated detection.

API Inconsistency. API inconsistencies are cases in which a contract's individual functions are correct, but the calling pattern or semantics of related functionalities differs in a way likely to mislead a user and produce incorrect code calling the contract. All of these issues were informational, and while it is conceivable that machine learning approaches could identify API inconsistencies, it is not a low-hanging fruit for automated detection.

Code-Quality. Finally, code quality issues have no semantic impact, but involve code that is hard to read or maintain. As expected, such issues are purely informational. Code quality problems in general would seem to be highly amenable to static analysis, but not to dynamic analysis.

3.2   Comparison to Non-Smart-Contract Audits

It is interesting to compare the distribution of finding types for smart contract audits to other security audits [29] performed by the same company. Table 3 compares smart contract audit frequencies with those for a random sample of 15 non-smart contract audits, with categories never present in smart contract audits or only present in smart contract audits removed.

The largest changes are categories of findings that are common in other audits, but not common in smart contracts. One of these, denial of service, may be primarily due to the re-categorization of denial of service findings with a clear relevance to another category in the smart contract findings. Changing the five findings whose type was clarified back to denial of service still leaves a significant gap, however. This is likely due to the different nature of interactions with the network in non-smart-contract code; in a sense, many denial of service problems and solutions are delegated to the general Ethereum blockchain, so individual contracts have less responsibility and thus fewer problems.

A more general version of the same difference likely explains why configuration problems are far less prevalent in smart contract code. At heart, smart contracts are more specialized and focused, and live in a simple environment (e.g., no OS/network interactions), so the footprint of configurations, and thus possible mis-configurations, is smaller. Similarly, the temptation to roll your own cryptography in a smart contract is much smaller. For one thing, implementing any custom cryptography in Solidity would be impractical enough to daunt even those unwise enough to attempt it, and gas costs would be prohibitive. Data validation is also easier in a world where, for the most part, transactions are the only inputs. Data exposure problems are probably less common because it is well understood that information on the blockchain is public, so the amount of data that is presumed unexposed is much smaller, or, in many cases, non-existent.

3.3   Threats to Validity

Contracts submitted for audit varied in their level of maturity; some assessments were performed on contracts essentially ready for release (or already released) that reflected the final stage of internal quality control processes. Others were performed on much more preliminary implementations and designs. This does not invalidate the findings, but some flaw types may be more prevalent in less polished contracts. Of course, the primary threat to validity is that the data is all drawn from a set of 23 audits performed by one company over a period of about two years. We address this concern in Sect. 5.

4   Discussion: How to Find Flaws in Smart Contracts

4.1   Property-Based Testing and Symbolic Execution

Property-based testing [5,12,15] involves 1) a user defining custom properties (usually, in practice, reachability properties declaring certain system states or function return values as "bad"), and then 2) using either fuzzing or symbolic execution to attempt to find inputs or call sequences violating the properties. Some variant of property-based testing is a popular approach to smart contract analysis. Automated testing with custom properties is both a significant low-hanging fruit and anything but a panacea. Of the 246 findings, only 91 could be possibly labeled as detectable with user-defined properties, or with automated testing for standard semantics of ERC20 tokens and other off-the-shelf dynamic checks. On the other hand, 17 of the 27 most important, high severity, low difficulty, findings, were plausibly detectable using such properties. While not effective for some classes of problems, analysis using custom properties (and thus, likely, dynamic rather than static analysis), might have detected over 60% of the most important findings. This mismatch in overall (37%) and high-low

(63%) percent of findings amenable to property-based testing is likely due to the fact that categories almost never detectable by automated testing—code quality, documentation, auditing and logging—are seldom high-low, and those where it is most effective—data validation, access controls, and numerics—constitute a large portion of the total set of high-low findings. Also, intuition tells us that if a finding has major detrimental consequences (high severity) but is not extremely hard to exploit (low difficulty) this is precisely the class of problems a set of key invariants plus effective fuzzing or symbolic execution is suited to find.

4.2 Static Analysis

The full potential of static analysis is harder to estimate. Four of the issues in these findings were definitely detected using the Slither static analysis tool, which has continued to add new detectors and fix bugs since the majority of the audits were performed. Of these four issues, one was high severity, undetermined difficulty, a classic reentrancy. An additional four issues are certainly detectable using Slither (these involve deletion of mappings, which is also the root issue in one of the findings that was definitely detected by Slither). Some of the overflow/underflow problems, as noted above, might also be statically detectable if false positives are allowed. There are likely other individual findings amenable to static analysis, but determining the practicality of such detection is in some ways more difficult than with dynamic analysis using a property-based specification. The low-hanging fruit for static analysis is general patterns of bad code, not reachability of a complex bad state. While some cases in which we speculate that a finding is describable by a reachability property may not, in fact, prove practical—current tools may have too much trouble generating a transaction sequence demonstrating the problem—it is fairly easy to determine that there is indeed an actual state of the contract that can be identified with the finding. Whether a finding falls into a more general pattern not currently captured by, for instance, a Slither detector, is harder to say, since the rate of false positives and scalability of precision needed to identify a problem is very hard to estimate. Our conservative guess is that perhaps 65 of the 246 findings (26%), and 9 of the high-low findings (33%), are plausibly detectable by static analysis. While these are lower percentages than for dynamic approaches, the effort required is much, much lower: The dynamic analysis usually depends on a user actually thinking of, and correctly implementing, the right property, as well as a tool reaching the bad state. For the statically detectable problems, issues like those in these findings would almost always be found just by running the static analysis tool.

4.3 Unit Testing

There was no additional unit testing as part of the security audits performed. It is therefore impossible to say how effective adding unit tests would be in discovering flaws during audits, based on this data. However, it is possible to examine the relationship between pre-existing unit tests and the audit results. Fourteen of the contracts audited had what appeared to be considerable unit tests; it is impossible to determine the quality of these tests, but there was certainly quantity, and significant development effort. Two of the contracts had moderate unit tests; not as good as the 14 contracts in the first category, but still representing a serious effort to use unit testing. Two contracts had modest unit tests: non-trivial, but clearly far from complete tests. Three had weak unit tests; technically there were unit tests, but they are practically of almost no value in checking the correctness of the contract. Finally, two contracts appeared to have no unit tests at all. Did the quantity of unit tests have an impact on audit results? If so, the impact was far from clear. The contracts that appeared to lack unit tests had nine and four findings, respectively: fewer than most other contracts. The largest mean number of issues (11.5) was for contracts with modest unit tests, but essentially the mean finding counts for considerable (11.1), moderate (10.5), modest (11.5), and weak (11) unit tests were indistinguishable. Furthermore, restricting the analysis to counting only high-severity findings also produces no significant correlation. For total findings, Kendall τ correlation is an extremely weak 0.09 ($p = 0.61$) indicating even this correlation is likely to be pure chance. For high-severity findings, the τ correlation drops to 0.5 ($p = 0.78$). Note further that these weak/unsupported correlations are *in the "wrong" direction*. It seems fair to say that even extensive unit tests are not the most effective way to avoid the kind of problems found in high-quality security audits.

4.4 Manual Analysis

With few exceptions, these findings demonstrate the effectiveness of manual analysis. Expert attention from experienced auditors can reveal serious problems even in well-tested code bases. While four of the audits produced no high-severity findings, 11 audits found three or more. As far as we can tell, all of the high-low severity issues were the result of manual analysis alone, though there were recommendations for how to use tools to detect/confirm correction in some cases.

4.5 Recommendations

The set of findings that could possibly be detected by *either* dynamic *or* static analysis is slightly more than 50%, and, most importantly, includes 21 of the 27 high-low findings. That is, making generous assumptions about scalability, property-writing, and willingness to wade through false positives, a skilled user of both static and dynamic tools could detect more than three out of four high-low issues. Note that the use of both approaches is key: 61 findings overall and 12 high-low findings are likely to only be detectable dynamically, while 35 findings, four of them high-low, are likely to only by found using static analysis.

While static analysis alone is less powerful than manual audits or dynamic analysis, the low effort, and thus high cost-benefit ratio, makes the use of all available high-quality static analysis tools an obvious recommendation. (Also, printers and code understanding tools often provided by static analyzers make manual audits more effective [9].) Some of the findings in these audits could have been easily detected by developers using then-current versions of the best tools.

When 35% of high-severity findings are not likely to be detected even with considerable tool improvement and manual effort to write correctness properties, it is implausible to claim that tools will be a "silver bullet" for smart contract security. It is difficult, at best, to imagine that nearly half of the total findings and almost 25% of the high-low findings would be detected even with high-effort, high-expertise construction of custom properties and the use of better-than-state-of-the-art dynamic and static analysis. Therefore, manual audits by external experts will remain a key part of serious security and correctness efforts for smart contracts for the foreseeable future.

On the other hand, the gap between current tool-based detection rates (very low) and our estimated upper limit on detection rates (50% of all issues, and over 75% of the most important issues) suggests that there is a large potential payoff from improving state-of-the-art standards for analysis tools and putting more effort into property-based testing. The experience of the security community using AFL, libFuzzer, and other tools also suggests that there are "missing" findings. The relatively immature state of analysis tools when most of these audits were performed likely means that *bugs unlikely to be detected by human reasoning were probably not detected.* The effectiveness of fuzzing in general suggests that such bugs likely exist in smart contracts as well, especially since the most important target category of findings for dynamic analyses, data validation, remains a major source of smart contract findings. In fact, a possible additional explanation for the difference of 36% data validation findings for smart contract audits and 51% for non-smart-contract audits could be that non-smart-contract audits have access to more powerful fuzzers. Eliminating the low-hanging fruit for automated tools will give auditors more time to focus on the vulnerabilities that require humans-in-the-loop and specialized skills. Moreover, effort spent writing custom properties is likely to pay off, even if dynamic analysis tools are not yet good enough to produce a failing test. Just understanding what invariants *should* hold is often enough to alert a human to a flaw.

Finally, while it is impossible to make strong claims based on a set of only 23 audits, it seems likely that unit tests, even quite substantial ones, do not provide an effective strategy for avoiding the kinds of problems detected during audits. Unit tests, of course, have other important uses, and should be considered an essential part of high-quality code development, but developer-constructed manual unit tests may not really help detect high-severity security issues. It does seem likely that the effort involved in writing high-quality unit tests would be very helpful in dynamic analysis: Generalizing from unit tests to invariants and properties for property-based testing seems likely to be an effective way to detect some of what the audits exposed.

5   Audits from Other Companies

In order to partially validate our findings, we also performed an analysis of audits prepared by two other leading companies in the field [27], ChainSecurity and ConsenSys Diligence. While differences in reporting standards and categorizations, and the fact that we do not have access to unpublished reports (which could bias statistics), make it difficult to analyze these results with the same confidence as our own reports, the overall picture that emerged was broadly compatible with our conclusions. The assignment of findings to semantically equivalent difficulties and severities, and the assessment of potential for automated analysis methods, was performed by a completely independent team. The results summarized here are for 225 findings in public reports for ChainSecurity and 168 from ConsenSys Diligence, over 19 and 18 audits, respectively. Appendix B provides detailed results on these findings.

First, the potential of automated methods is similar. For ChainSecurity, 39% of all issues were plausibly detectable by dynamic analysis (e.g., property-based testing, possibly with a custom property), and 22% by automated static analysis. For ConsenSys Diligence, those numbers were 41% and 24%. Restricting our interest to **high-low** findings, the percentages were 67% and 63% for dynamic analysis and 11% and 38% for static analysis, respectively. Combining both methods, the potential detection rates were 51% and 52% for all findings, and 67% and 75% for high-low findings. The extreme similarity of these results to ours affirms that our results concerning detection methods are unlikely to be an artifact of our audit methods or the specific set of contracts we audited.

Second, while the category frequencies were quite different than those in our audits (e.g., more numerics and access controls, fewer data validation findings), there were no new categories, and all of our categories were present (though ChainSecurity found no race conditions). Reentrancy was not, as previous literature might lead one to suspect, a prominent source of high-low problems, or even a very common problem, and there was only one high-low reentrancy.

6   Conclusions

Understanding how best to protect high-value smart contracts against attackers (and against serious errors by non-malicious users or the creators of the contract) is difficult in the absence of information about the actual problems found in high-value smart contracts by experienced auditors using state-of-the-art technologies. This paper presents a wealth of empirical evidence to help smart-contract developers, security researchers, and security auditors improve their understanding of the types of faults found in contracts, and the potential for various methods to detect those faults. Based on an in-depth examination of 23 paid smart contract audits performed by Trail of Bits, validated by a more limited examination of public audits performed by ChainSecurity and ConsenSys Diligence, we conclude that 1) the literature is somewhat misleading with respect to the most important kinds of smart contract flaws, which are more like flaws in other critical code than one might think; 2) there is likely a large potential payoff in making more effective use of automatic static and dynamic analyses to detect the worst problems in smart contracts; 3) nonetheless, many key issues will never be amenable to purely-automated or formal approaches, and 4) high-quality unit tests alone do not provide effective protection against serious contract flaws. As future work, we plan to extend our analysis of other companies' audits to include unit test quality, and examine issues that cut across findings categories, such as the power of ERC20 standards to help find flaws.

Appendix A: Raw Counts for Finding Categories

This table provides exact counts for categories, and severities within categories.

Category	#	High-Low	Severity					Difficulty			
			High	Med.	Low	Info.	Und.	High	Med.	Low	Und.
data validation	89	10	19	32	21	12	5	24	14	49	2
access controls	24	6	10	6	3	5	0	8	3	13	0
race condition	17	0	7	7	1	2	0	17	0	0	0
numerics	13	3	4	3	5	1	0	4	1	8	0
undefined behavior	13	3	4	2	4	1	2	2	1	10	0
patching	18	2	3	2	7	5	1	1	2	11	4
denial of service	10	1	2	3	3	2	0	5	0	4	1
authentication	4	1	2	1	1	0	0	2	0	2	0
reentrancy	4	0	2	1	1	0	0	2	1	0	1
error reporting	7	0	2	1	0	4	0	3	2	2	0
configuration	5	0	2	0	1	1	1	3	1	1	0
logic	3	0	1	1	1	0	0	3	0	0	0
data exposure	3	0	1	1	0	1	0	1	1	1	0
timing	4	1	1	0	3	0	0	3	0	1	0
coding-bug	6	0	0	4	2	0	0	1	0	5	0
front-running	5	0	0	4	0	1	0	5	0	0	0
auditing and logging	9	0	0	0	3	4	2	3	0	5	1
missing-logic	3	0	0	0	2	1	0	0	0	3	0
cryptography	1	0	0	0	1	0	0	1	0	0	0
documentation	4	0	0	0	1	2	1	0	0	3	1
API inconsistency	2	0	0	0	0	2	0	0	0	2	0
code-quality	2	0	0	0	0	2	0	0	0	2	0
Total	246	27	60	68	60	46	12	88	26	122	10

Appendix B: ChainSecurity and ConsenSys Audits

The process for analyzing findings in other companies' audits involved 1) mapping the category of the finding to our set, and 2) translating a different formulation of worst-case impact and probability estimation into our high-low severity and difficulty classes. For more details see the full data set [27]. The first two tables show severity and difficulty distributions. The first table in each pair of tables is for ChainSecurity, and the second is for ConsenSys Diligence.

Category	%	High-Low	Severity					Difficulty			
			High	Med.	Low	Info.	Und.	High	Med.	Low	Und.
access controls	24%	8%	28%	21%	45%	6%	0%	40%	26%	34%	0%
data validation	14%	3%	19%	28%	47%	6%	0%	47%	9%	44%	0%
logic	6%	7%	36%	50%	14%	0%	0%	29%	50%	21%	0%
numerics	9%	0%	10%	15%	75%	0%	0%	40%	20%	40%	0%
denial of service	5%	0%	17%	25%	58%	0%	0%	67%	33%	0%	0%
configuration	3%	14%	29%	29%	43%	0%	0%	71%	0%	29%	0%
authentication	2%	0%	50%	25%	25%	0%	0%	0%	75%	25%	0%
coding-bug	2%	20%	40%	0%	60%	0%	0%	20%	0%	80%	0%
missing-logic	4%	0%	13%	13%	63%	13%	0%	25%	0%	75%	0%
cryptography	1%	50%	50%	50%	0%	0%	0%	50%	0%	50%	0%
patching	7%	0%	7%	0%	73%	20%	0%	87%	13%	0%	0%
reentrancy	2%	0%	20%	0%	80%	0%	0%	80%	0%	20%	0%
documentation	4%	0%	13%	0%	50%	38%	0%	13%	13%	63%	0%
data exposure	0%	0%	100%	0%	0%	0%	0%	100%	0%	0%	0%
timing	5%	0%	0%	27%	64%	9%	0%	45%	27%	27%	0%
front-running	2%	0%	0%	25%	75%	0%	0%	75%	25%	0%	0%
auditing and logging	3%	0%	0%	14%	29%	57%	0%	14%	0%	86%	0%
error reporting	2%	0%	0%	25%	50%	25%	0%	0%	25%	75%	0%
undefined behavior	1%	0%	0%	50%	50%	0%	0%	50%	50%	0%	0%
API-inconsistency	2%	0%	0%	0%	100%	0%	0%	40%	0%	60%	0%
code-quality	3%	0%	0%	0%	50%	50%	0%	0%	0%	83%	0%
race condition	0%	N/A	N/A	N/A	N/A	N/A	N/A	N/A	N/A	N/A	N/A

Category	%	High-Low	Severity					Difficulty			
			High	Med.	Low	Info.	Und.	High	Med.	Low	Und.
access controls	10%	0%	35%	12%	47%	6%	0%	29%	29%	41%	0%
configuration	10%	6%	25%	13%	56%	0%	0%	56%	6%	31%	6%
front-running	4%	14%	57%	14%	29%	0%	0%	71%	14%	14%	0%
reentrancy	4%	14%	43%	43%	14%	0%	0%	57%	14%	29%	0%
coding-bug	6%	10%	30%	10%	50%	10%	0%	20%	10%	70%	0%
logic	8%	8%	15%	31%	54%	0%	0%	15%	23%	62%	0%
numerics	13%	5%	10%	14%	71%	5%	0%	52%	24%	24%	0%
data validation	6%	0%	10%	20%	70%	0%	0%	50%	20%	30%	0%
API inconsistency	2%	0%	25%	25%	50%	0%	0%	25%	0%	75%	0%
cryptography	1%	50%	50%	50%	0%	0%	0%	50%	0%	50%	0%
error reporting	3%	20%	20%	0%	80%	0%	0%	20%	0%	80%	0%
timing	2%	0%	25%	0%	75%	0%	0%	50%	0%	50%	0%
race condition	1%	0%	100%	0%	0%	0%	0%	100%	0%	0%	0%
missing-logic	11%	0%	0%	26%	68%	5%	0%	0%	11%	84%	0%
authentication	1%	0%	0%	100%	0%	0%	0%	50%	50%	0%	0%
denial of service	2%	0%	0%	67%	0%	0%	0%	0%	33%	33%	0%
documentation	2%	0%	0%	33%	33%	33%	0%	67%	0%	33%	0%
data exposure	1%	0%	0%	100%	0%	0%	0%	0%	0%	100%	0%
code-quality	7%	0%	0%	0%	82%	9%	0%	45%	9%	36%	0%
patching	3%	0%	0%	0%	80%	20%	0%	80%	0%	20%	0%
undefined behavior	1%	0%	0%	0%	50%	50%	0%	0%	0%	0%	100%
auditing and logging	3%	0%	0%	0%	0%	100%	0%	0%	0%	100%	0%

The next two tables show absolute severity and difficulty counts for finding categories for other company audits, as in Appendix A.

Category	#	High-Low	Severity					Difficulty			
			High	Med.	Low	Info.	Und.	High	Med.	Low	Und.
access controls	53	4	15	11	24	3	0	21	14	18	0
data validation	32	1	6	9	15	2	0	15	3	14	0
logic	14	1	5	7	2	0	0	4	7	3	0
numerics	20	0	2	3	15	0	0	8	4	8	0
denial of service	12	0	2	3	7	0	0	8	4	0	0
configuration	7	1	2	2	3	0	0	5	0	2	0
authentication	4	0	2	1	1	0	0	0	3	1	0
coding-bug	5	1	2	0	3	0	0	1	0	4	0
missing-logic	8	0	1	1	5	1	0	2	0	6	0
cryptography	2	1	1	1	0	0	0	1	0	1	0
patching	15	0	1	0	11	3	0	13	2	0	0
reentrancy	5	0	1	0	4	0	0	4	0	1	0
documentation	8	0	1	0	4	3	0	1	1	5	0
data exposure	1	0	1	0	0	0	0	1	0	0	0
timing	11	0	0	3	7	1	0	5	3	3	0
front-running	4	0	0	1	3	0	0	3	1	0	0
auditing and logging	7	0	0	1	2	4	0	1	0	6	0
error reporting	4	0	0	1	2	1	0	0	1	3	0
undefined behavior	2	0	0	1	1	0	0	1	1	0	0
API inconsistency	5	0	0	0	5	0	0	2	0	3	0
code-quality	6	0	0	0	3	3	0	0	0	5	0
Total	225	9	42	45	117	21	0	96	44	83	0

Category	#	High-Low	Severity					Difficulty			
			High	Med.	Low	Info.	Und.	High	Med.	Low	Und.
access controls	17	0	6	2	8	1	0	5	5	7	0
configuration	16	1	4	2	9	0	0	9	1	5	1
front-running	7	1	4	1	2	0	0	5	1	1	0
reentrancy	7	1	3	3	1	0	0	4	1	2	0
coding-bug	10	1	3	1	5	1	0	2	1	7	0
logic	13	1	2	4	7	0	0	2	3	8	0
numerics	21	1	2	3	15	1	0	11	5	5	0
data validation	10	0	1	2	7	0	0	5	2	3	0
API inconsistency	4	0	1	1	2	0	0	1	0	3	0
cryptography	2	1	1	1	0	0	0	1	0	1	0
error reporting	5	1	1	0	4	0	0	1	0	4	0
timing	4	0	1	0	3	0	0	2	0	2	0
race condition	1	0	1	0	0	0	0	1	0	0	0
missing-logic	19	0	0	5	13	1	0	0	2	16	0
authentication	2	0	0	2	0	0	0	1	1	0	0
denial of service	3	0	0	2	0	0	0	0	1	1	0
documentation	3	0	0	1	1	1	0	2	0	1	0
data exposure	1	0	0	1	0	0	0	0	0	1	0
code-quality	11	0	0	0	9	1	0	5	1	4	0
patching	5	0	0	0	4	1	0	4	0	1	0
undefined behavior	2	0	0	0	1	1	0	0	0	0	2
auditing and logging	5	0	0	0	0	5	0	0	0	5	0
Total	168	8	30	31	91	13	0	61	24	77	3

The final two tables report the estimated automated dynamic and static analysis detection potential for the categories in the other companies' audits.

Category	% Dynamic	% Static	Category	% Dynamic	% Static
access controls	43%	6%	reentrancy	60%	100%
data validation	31%	13%	documentation	0%	0%
logic	50%	7%	data exposure	0%	0%
numerics	80%	55%	timing	36%	36%
denial of service	33%	25%	front-running	0%	0%
configuration	29%	0%	auditing and logging	0%	0%
authentication	50%	25%	error reporting	100%	25%
coding-bug	100%	40%	undefined behavior	0%	50%
missing-logic	63%	0%	API-inconsistency	20%	20%
cryptography	50%	0%	code-quality	0%	17%
patching	7%	73%	race condition	N/A	N/A

Category	% Dynamic	% Static	Category	% Dynamic	% Static
access controls	18%	12%	timing	25%	0%
configuration	31%	25%	race condition	0%	0%
front-running	0%	0%	missing-logic	47%	0%
reentrancy	100%	71%	authentication	50%	0%
coding-bug	50%	10%	denial of service	67%	0%
logic	62%	8%	documentation	0%	0%
numerics	95%	71%	data exposure	0%	0%
data validation	20%	10%	code-quality	9%	45%
API inconsistency	50%	25%	patching	0%	60%
cryptography	100%	0%	undefined behavior	0%	50%
error reporting	20%	40%	auditing and logging	0%	0%

References

1. Atzei, N., Bartoletti, M., Cimoli, T.: A survey of attacks on ethereum smart contracts (SoK). In: Maffei, M., Ryan, M. (eds.) POST 2017. LNCS, vol. 10204, pp. 164–186. Springer, Heidelberg (2017). https://doi.org/10.1007/978-3-662-54455-6_8

2. Bragagnolo, S.: On contract popularity analysis. https://github.com/smartanvil/smartanvil.github.io/blob/master/_posts/2018-03-14-on-contract-popularity-analysis.md

3. Brent, L., et al.: Vandal: a scalable security analysis framework for smart contracts. CoRR, abs/1809.03981 (2018)

4. Buterin, V.: Ethereum: a next-generation smart contract and decentralized application platform (2013). https://github.com/ethereum/wiki/wiki/White-Paper

5. Claessen, K., Hughes, J.: QuickCheck: a lightweight tool for random testing of Haskell programs. In: International Conference on Functional Programming (ICFP), pp. 268–279 (2000)

6. ConsenSys. Mythril: a security analysis tool for Ethereum smart contracts (2017). https://github.com/ConsenSys/mythril-classic

7. Dika, A.: Ethereum smart contracts: security vulnerabilities and security tools. Master's thesis, NTNU (2017)

8. Ducasse, S., Rocha, H., Bragagnolo, S., Denker, M., Francomme, C.: Smartanvil: open-source tool suite for smart contract analysis. Technical report hal-01940287, HAL (2019)

9. Feist, J., Greico, G., Groce, A.: Slither: a static analysis framework for smart contracts. In: International Workshop on Emerging Trends in Software Engineering for Blockchain (2019)

10. Grishchenko, I., Maffei, M., Schneidewind, C.: Ethertrust: sound static analysis of Ethereum bytecode (2018)

11. Grishchenko, I., Maffei, M., Schneidewind, C.: A semantic framework for the security analysis of Ethereum smart contracts (2018). arXiv:1802.08660. Accessed 12 Mar 2018

12. Holmes, J., et al.: TSTL: the template scripting testing language. Int. J. Softw. Tools Technol. Transfer **20**(1), 57–78 (2016). https://doi.org/10.1007/s10009-016-0445-y

13. Krupp, J., Rossow, C.: teEther: gnawing at Ethereum to automatically exploit smart contracts. In: USENIX Security (2018)

14. Luu, L., Chu, D.-H., Olickel, H., Saxena, P., Hobor, A.: Making smart contracts smarter. In: CCS 2016 (2016)

15. MacIver, D.R.: Hypothesis: test faster, fix more, March 2013. http://hypothesis.works/

16. Mense, A., Flatscher, M.: Security vulnerabilities in Ethereum smart contracts. In: Proceedings of the 20th International Conference on Information Integration and Web-Based Applications & Services, iiWAS2018, pp. 375–380. ACM, New York (2018)
17. Mossberg, M., et al.: Manticore: a user-friendly symbolic execution framework for binaries and smart contracts. In: IEEE/ACM International Conference on Automated Software Engineering, accepted for publication
18. Nikolic, I., Kolluri, A., Sergey, I., Saxena, P., Hobor, A.: Finding the greedy, prodigal, and suicidal contracts at scale. In: ACSAC (2018)
19. Perez, D., Livshits, B.: Smart contract vulnerabilities: does anyone care? (2019)
20. Daian, P.: Analysis of the DAO exploit, 18 June 2016. http://hackingdistributed. com/2016/06/18/analysis-of-the-dao-exploit/. Acceded 10 Jan 2019
21. Rubio-González, C., Gunawi, H.S., Liblit, B., Arpaci-Dusseau, R.H., Arpaci-Dusseau, A.C.: Error propagation analysis for file systems. In: ACM SIGPLAN Conference on Programming Language Design and Implementation (PLDI), pp. 270–280 (2009)
22. Tikhomirov, S., et al.: Smartcheck: static analysis of Ethereum smart contracts. In: WETSEB (2018)
23. Saad, M., et al.: Exploring the attack surface of blockchain: a systematic overview. arXiv preprint arXiv:1904.03487 (2019)
24. SpankChain. We got spanked: What we know so far, 8 October 2018. https:// medium.com/spankchain/we-got-spanked-what-we-know-so-far-d5ed3a0f38fe. Acceded 10 Jan 2019
25. Trail of Bits. Manticore: Symbolic execution for humans (2017). https://github. com/trailofbits/manticore
26. Trail of Bits. Echidna: Ethereum fuzz testing framework (2018). https://github. com/trailofbits/echidna
27. Trail of Bits. Analysis of external audits (2019). https://github.com/trailofbits/ publications/tree/master/datasets/smart_contract_audit_findings/other_audit_ sources
28. Trail of Bits. Smart contract audit findings (2019). https://github.com/trailofbits/ publications/tree/master/datasets/smart_contract_audit_findings
29. Trail of Bits. Trail of bits security reviews (2019). https://github.com/trailofbits/ publications#security-reviews
30. Tsankov, P., Dan, A., Drachsler-Cohen, D., Gervais, A., Bünzli, F., Vechev, M.: Securify: practical security analysis of smart contracts. In: CCS 2018 (2018)
31. GitHub user: 3sGgpQ8H. Attack vector on ERC20 API. https://github.com/ ethereum/EIPs/issues/20#issuecomment-263524729
32. Wood, G.: Ethereum: a secure decentralised generalised transaction ledger (2014). http://gavwood.com/paper.pdf

Characterizing Code Clones in the Ethereum Smart Contract Ecosystem

Ningyu He[1], Lei Wu[2], Haoyu Wang[3(✉)], Yao Guo[1(✉)], and Xuxian Jiang[4]

[1] MOE Key Lab of HCST, School of EECS, Peking University, Beijing, China
yaoguo@ptu.edu.cn
[2] School of Cyber Science and Technology, Zhejiang University, Hangzhou, China
[3] Beijing University of Posts and Telecommunications, Beijing, China
haoyuwang@bupt.edu.cn
[4] PeckShield, Inc., Hangzhou, China

Abstract. In this paper, we present the first large-scale and systematic study to characterize the code reuse practice in the Ethereum smart contract ecosystem. We first performed a detailed similarity comparison study on a dataset of 10 million contracts we had harvested, and then we further conducted a qualitative analysis to characterize the diversity of the ecosystem, understand the correlation between code reuse and vulnerabilities, and detect the plagiarized DApps. Our analysis revealed that over 96% of the contracts had duplicates, while a large number of them were similar, which suggests that the ecosystem is highly homogeneous. Our results also suggested that roughly 9.7% of the similar contract pairs have exactly the same vulnerabilities, which we assume were introduced by code clones. In addition, we identified 41 DApps clusters, involving 73 plagiarized DApps which had caused huge financial loss to the original creators, accounting for 1/3 of the original market volume.

Keywords: Code clone · Smart contract · Ethereum · Vulnerability

1 Introduction

Smart contracts, the most important innovation of Ethereum, provide the ability to "digitally facilitate, verify, and enforce the negotiation or performance of a contract" [45], while the correctness of its execution is ensured by the consensus protocol of Ethereum. Such a courageous attempt has been approved by the market, *i.e.*, Ethereum's market cap was around $14.5B on February 26th, 2019 [2], the largest volume besides Bitcoin. As of this writing, roughly 10 million smart contracts have been deployed on the Ethereum Mainnet.

Smart contracts are typically written in higher level languages, *e.g.*, Solidity [39] (a language similar to JavaScript and C++), then compiled to Ethereum Virtual Machine (EVM) bytecode. As one of the most important rules on Ethereum, "Code is Law", means all executions and transactions are final and immutable.

© International Financial Cryptography Association 2020
J. Bonneau and N. Heninger (Eds.): FC 2020, LNCS 12059, pp. 654–675, 2020.
https://doi.org/10.1007/978-3-030-51280-4_35

```
DiviesInterface constant private Divies = \
    DiviesInterface(0xc7029...);
JIincForwarderInterface constant private Jekyll_Island_Inc = \
    JIincForwarderInterface(0xdd49...);
PlayerBookInterface constant private PlayerBook = \
    PlayerBookInterface(0xD60d...);
F3DexternalSettingsInterface constant private extSettings = \
    F3DexternalSettingsInterface(0x3296...);

string constant public name = "FoMo3D Long Official";
string constant public symbol = "F3D";
uint256 private rndExtra_ = extSettings.getLongExtra();
uint256 private rndGap_ = extSettings.getLongGap();
uint256 constant private rndInit_ = 1 hours;
uint256 constant private rndInc_ = 30 seconds;
uint256 constant private rndMax_ = 24 hours;
```

```
PlayerBookInterface constant private PlayerBook = \
    PlayerBookInterface(0x8676...);

string constant public name = "imfomo Long Official";
string constant public symbol = "imfomo";
uint256 private rndExtra_ = 30;
uint256 private rndGap_ = 30;
uint256 constant private rndInit_ = 10 minutes;
uint256 constant private rndInc_ = 60 seconds;
uint256 constant private rndMax_ = 10 minutes;
```

(a) Original Fomo3D   (b) Modified Fomo3D

Fig. 1. The original Fomo3D and a plagiarized contract from it.

As a result, one main characteristic of smart contracts is that a considerable number of them published source code to gain the users' trust and prove the security of their code, especially for the popular ones [22]. This feature is more noticeable for Decentralized Applications (DApps for short, which consist of one or more contracts). In general, their code base should be available for scrutiny and governed by autonomy, distinguished from the traditional closed-source applications that require the end users to trust the developers in terms of decentralization as they cannot directly access data via any central source.

However, the open-source nature of smart contracts has provided convenience for plagiarists to create **contract clones**, *i.e.*, copying code from other available contracts. The impact of contract clones is two-fold. On one hand, the plagiarists could insert arbitrary/malicious code into the normal contracts. A typical example is the so-called `honeypot smart contracts` [26–28], which are scam contracts that try to fool users with stealthy tricks. On the other hand, as many smart contracts are suffering from serious vulnerabilities, the copy-paste vulnerabilities would be inherited by the plagiarized contracts.

Here, we use Fomo3D [36] as a motivating example, which is a popular and phenomenal Ponzi-like game. At its peak in 2018, Fomo3D had over 10,000 daily active users with a volume of over 40,000 ETHs [35]. As a result, numerous Fomo3D-like games sprang up with plagiarism behaviors by simply reusing the source code of the original one. Unfortunately, some hackers had figured out the design flaw of the airdrop mechanism in the original Fomo3D [25]. Consequently, almost all the awkward imitators were exposed to those attackers. *LastWinner*, one of the most successful followers of Fomo3D, was attacked and lost more than 5,000 ETHs within 4 days [31]. Figure 1 shows a plagiarized contract example originated from Fomo3D [35]. Interestingly, the vulnerable part was kept wholly intact by the plagiarist, but all the dependent contracts, and some arguments like round timer and round increment, were modified to make it appear as a brand new game as shown in Fig. 1.

This Paper. We present a large scale systematic study to characterize the code clone behaviors of Ethereum smart contracts in a comprehensive manner. To this end, we have collected by far the largest Ethereum smart contract dataset with nearly 10 million smart contracts deployed between July 2015 to December 2018. To address the scalability issues introduced by the large scale dataset, we first seek to identify the duplicate contracts by removing code from unrelated functions (*e.g.*, creation code and Swarm code), and tokenizing the code to keep opcodes only. After the pre-processing step to remove duplicate contracts, the dataset has been shrunk to less than 1% of the original size. For the remaining 78, 611 distinct contracts, we take advantage of a customized fuzzy hashing approach to generate the fingerprints and then conduct a pair-wise similarity comparison. Specifically, we adopt a pruning strategy to discard "very different" contracts by comparing the meta features (*e.g.*, length of opcode), to accelerate the comparison procedure. Based on a similarity threshold of 70, we are able to identify 472, 663 similar smart contract pairs (with 47, 242 contracts involved) for user-created contracts, which suggested that over 63.29% of the distinct user-created contracts have at least one similar contract in our dataset.

Then, we further seek to understand the reasons leading to contract clones and characterize their security impacts.

(1) The Reasons Leading to Contract Clones. Over 60% of the distinct contracts were grouped into roughly 10 K clusters, while the cluster distribution follows a typical Pareto principle. Top 20% of the clusters occupied over 60% of the distinct contracts. With regard to the whole dataset including all the duplicates, the top 1% of the clusters account for 95% of the contracts. ERC20 token contracts, ICO and AirDrop, and Game contracts are the most popular clusters. A large number of similar contracts were created based on the same template (*i.e.*, ERC20 template). We have manually summarized a list of 53 common templates used in the Ethereum smart contract ecosystem. **This result reveals the homogeneity nature of the smart contract ecosystem.**

(2) Vulnerability Provenance. Copy-paste vulnerabilities were prevalent in most popular software systems. Here, we study the relationship between contract clones and the presence of vulnerabilities, from two aspects. First, we scanned all the unique contracts using a state-of-the-art vulnerability scanner [37]. Over 20, 346 distinct smart contracts (27.26%) contain at least one vulnerability. **Considering the large number of duplicates, we were able to identify tenfold vulnerable contracts (205, 010).** Then, for the distinct contracts, as a number of them have similar code, we further compare whether they were exposed to similar vulnerabilities. **Overall, our results suggest that roughly 9.7% of the similar contract pairs have exactly the same vulnerabilities, which we assume were introduced by code clones.**

(3) Plagiarized DApps. As a DApp is more complicated than a smart contract, *i.e.*, one DApp could include one or more contracts, thus we further study the similarity between DApps, seeking to identify the plagiarized ones. Using a bipartite graph matching approach, we identified 41 DApp clusters, involving 73 plagiarized DApps. **The plagiarized ones have caused huge financial loss to the original creators, accounting for 1/3 of the original volume.**

To the best of our knowledge, this is the first systematic study of code clones in the Ethereum smart contract ecosystem *at scale*. Our results revealed the highly homogeneous nature of the ecosystem, *i.e.*, code clones are prevalent, which helps spread vulnerabilities and makes it easier for plagiarists. Our results motivated the need for research efforts to identify security issues introduced by copy-paste behaviors. Our efforts can positively contribute to the smart contract ecosystem, and promote the best operational practices for developers.

2   Background

2.1   Ethereum

External Owned Account vs. Contract Account. The basic unit of Ethereum is an *account* and there are two types of accounts [21]: External Owned Account (EOA) and Contract Account. An EOA is controlled by private keys that are externally owned by a user. More importantly, there is no code associated with it. One can send messages from an EOA by creating and signing a transaction. On the contrary, a contract account is controlled by its associated contract code, which might be activated on receiving a message.

User-Created Contract vs. Contract-Created Contract. Smart contract can be created either by users, or by existing contracts. In this paper, we follow the terminology "user-created contract" and "contract-created contract" adopted by Kiffer et al. [60] to distinguish these two types of creations.

Decentralized Applications (DApps). Ethereum aims to create an alternative protocol to build DApps [34], which are stored on and executed by the Ethereum system. Specifically, a DApp is *a contract or a collection of contracts that have an interface on the Internet, typically a website or a browser game, which could be interacted by players or users directly.* A number of websites emerged to host DApps lists [15–17].

2.2   Ethereum Virtual Machine (EVM)

EVM is the runtime environment for smart contracts. Specifically, a sandboxed virtual stack machine is embedded within each full Ethereum node, responsible for executing contract bytecode with a 256-bit register stack [20]. Its operators and operands are all pushed onto the stack indistinguishably, except for data that require persistent storage space. Therefore, all the immediate numbers and data to be used by the operation code will be *pushed* onto the stack.

Generally, developers implement their smart contracts with the Solidity language, then build the source code using the Solidity compiler, a.k.a. *solc*, to generate the EVM bytecode. A typical EVM bytecode is composed of three parts: *creation code*, *runtime code* and *swarm code*, as shown in Fig. 2.

Creation code is only executed by EVM once during the transaction of the contract deployment. It determines the initial states of the smart contract

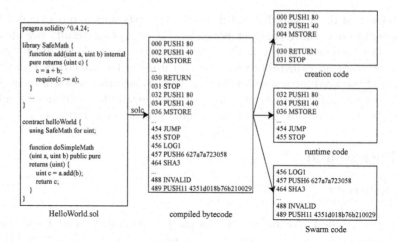

Fig. 2. An example of Helloworld.sol and its corresponding bytecode.

being deployed and returns a copy of the runtime code. It usually end with the sequence: `PUSH 0x00, RETURN, STOP`, corresponding to `0x6000f300` (cf. Fig. 2).

Runtime code is the most crucial part, including function selector, function wrapper, function body and exception handling. Based on the corresponding operations, EVM will execute runtime code accordingly. Besides, in order to label jumping destinations of the function selector, solc sorts functions by their signatures, *i.e.*, the leading 4 bytes of the SHA-3 hashes of function declarations with a well-defined format [38]. Accordingly, adding new functions or deleting existing ones will not affect the relative order of the remaining functions.

Swarm code is not served for execution purpose. Solc uses the metadata of a contract, including compiler version, source code and the located block number, to calculate the so-called Swarm hash, which can be used to query on *Swarm*, a decentralized storage system, to prove the consistency between the contract you see and the contract being deployed, namely *what you see is what you get*. As a result, re-deploying a smart contract would result in a different swarm code, even with the same creation code and runtime code. Swarm code always begins with `0xa165`, *i.e.*, `LOG1 PUSH 6`. The following six bytes are `0x627a7a723058`, whose leading four bytes can be decoded as "bzzr", the Swarm's URL scheme. Furthermore, Swarm code always ends with `0x0029`, which means the hash part length between `0xa165` and `0x0029` is 41 bytes long. In short, we are able to identify the swarm code quickly and precisely based on those hard-coded bytes.

3   Methodology

Overall Process. We summarize our approach in Fig. 3. The pipeline starts with the dataset with nearly 10 million smart contracts we have collected. We first seek to remove duplicate smart contracts to reduce the computational workload in two steps: 1) removing the creation and Swarm code parts, which are not

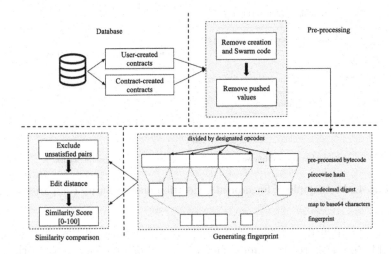

Fig. 3. An overview of our approach on smart contract similarity comparison.

useful for analyzing; 2) removing all assigned values in assignment statements and function calls. To this end, the smart contracts were scanned for tokenization by generating token hashes, which allow us to capture subtle differences of the clones. After that, for the remaining contracts with distinct token hashes, we take advantage of a customized fuzzy hashing approach to generate the fingerprints. Lastly, we enforce a pair-wise comparison strategy with pruning to achieve scalability. The output of the whole analysis pipeline is a set of contract clone pairs with the corresponding similarity scores. Note that the output results will be further correlated with our in-depth analysis in Sect. 5, including contract clustering, vulnerability provenance and DApps plagiarism detection.

In this paper, we did not rely on heavy-weight methods such as comparing the control-flow graph (CFG) and program dependency graph (PDG), mainly due to two reasons. First, our approach should be scalable. Second, the simplicity of smart contracts and EVM bytecode, *i.e.*, the relatively simple logic and function invocations, makes it unnecessary to adopt those heavy approaches. To the best of our knowledge, we did not even identify smart contracts with heavy obfuscation. We evaluate the effectiveness of our approach in Sect. 4.

3.1 Pre-processing

The purpose of pre-processing is two-fold: first identifying the duplicate contracts, and then tokenizing contracts for further comparison.

As we mentioned, creation code and Swarm code have nothing to do with similarity calculation. Fortunately, they can be easily identified and removed from the bytecode. Afterwards, we use a hash set to guarantee the uniqueness of the remaining contracts in terms of runtime code. Secondly, to enable fast and accurate fingerprint generation, we further remove all the immediate numbers

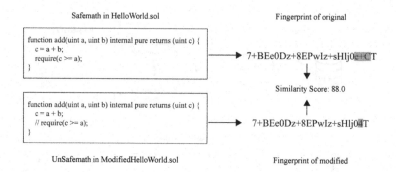

Fig. 4. An example of fingerprint generation and similarity comparison.

after opcode `PUSH` to eliminate the interference of operands. Again, we use a hash table to guarantee the uniqueness of the remaining contracts. In this way, we obtain a minimized database with little feature lost for similarity detection.

3.2 Generating Fingerprint

Calculating the edit distance between two given sequences is a well-known way to measure their similarity. In this work, we use a *fuzzy hashing* technique [61] to condense the original bytecode to a much shorter fingerprint and then calculate the edit distance between two fingerprints. Unlike traditional hash functions, fuzzy hashing first divides the bytecode sequence into smaller pieces, then uses a piece-wise hash function to perform the calculation for each piece and finally concatenates those generated piece-wise hashes to form a fingerprint. Suppose someone modifies one particular function, all the related pieces would generate different piece-wise hashes with the original ones, but the other pieces were not affected at all. In short, fuzzy hashing has advantages of accurate representation and less computing-time consumption.

However, there still exists challenges to determine the boundary of each piece. Previous work chooses a boundary randomly or simply divides the sequence by a pre-defined step (*e.g.*, seven bytes) [40]. Nevertheless, a smart contract is not just a piece of plain-text. It has semantic meaning. To address the challenge, we propose a customized fuzzy hashing algorithm, which is capable of segmenting smart contracts precisely to generate feasible piece-wise hashes.

Customized Fuzzy Hashing. After investigating the bytecode and its execution procedure in EVM, we identify the runtime code that can be further divided into several sub-sequences to perform a basic block level analysis. In Solidity, opcodes `JUMP`, `JUMPI`, `REVERT`, `STOP`, `RETURN` are the indicators of the interruption of logical relationship, and these opcodes often mean that the current block should be terminated in building the control flow graph (CFG). Furthermore, as we mentioned in Sect. 2, runtime code always keeps the order of function selector, function wrapper, *etc.*, and maintains the relative order between functions. After dividing, the piece-wise hash function will be applied on each of the blocks to generate a four byte hexadecimal digest and then mapped to a base-64 character after modulo 64. Finally, a fingerprint is generated by concatenating these characters (cf. Algorithm 1 in Appendix and Fig. 4).

3.3 Similarity Comparison

At this stage, we are able to perform pair-wise comparison to characterize the similarity between contracts. Since pair-wise comparisons are computationally expensive (billions of comparisons), we propose a pruning strategy here to tackle the problem. Intuitively, similar contracts should share similar attributes with minor modifications (opcode length in particular). If two contracts are "very different" in the opcode length, we will stop comparing the fingerprints and mark them as dissimilar. In our implementation, if more than 30% attributes of two smart contracts are different, the comparison process will stop.

For each contract pair, we calculate the edit distance between the fingerprints, and then map it to a similarity score in the range of 0 to 100, as follows:

$$similarityScore = \left[1 - \frac{distance}{\max(len(fp1), len(fp2))} \right] * 100 \qquad (1)$$

Figure 4 shows an example of the fingerprints we generated for HelloWorld.sol and its modified version, respectively. In the modified version, we have removed the *require* statement of the *SafeMath* library, which may lead to an overflow vulnerability. The difference between these two fingerprints is highlighted. Obviously, only a few characters within the fingerprint have changed, and the similarity score calculated by our approach is 88.0.

4   Quantitative Analysis

In this section, we focus exclusively on quantitative analysis, which provides some straightforward but interesting findings we observed before we perform more detailed analysis in Sect. 5.

4.1   Dataset

We have collected by far the largest smart contract dataset at the time of writing, covering almost 10 million smart contracts deployed on the Ethereum Mainnet from July 30th, 2015 to December 31st, 2018. As shown in Table 1, only 2.1 million contracts are user-created, and the number of contract-created contracts is four times greater than user-created ones. They were owned by 124,015 accounts, including 94,307 for the user-created contracts and 29,708 for the contract-created contracts.

Table 1. An overview of the dataset before and after pre-processing.

Contract type	# Contracts (# Owned Accounts)	After Swarm code removing	After push arguments removing
user-created	2,121,745 (94,307)	105,258	74,647
contract-created	7,729,012 (29,708)	4,539	3,964

4.2 Pre-processing

The pre-processing step is helpful in removing duplicates. It turns out that the proportion of contracts to be analyzed has been shrunk dramatically to $0.798\%(78,611/9,850,757)$ of the original dataset we collected. Especially for the contract-created contracts, only $3,964$ distinct contracts remained.

To figure out the reason for the huge number of duplicates, we first grouped the duplicated contracts into clusters, and then analyzed the distribution of those clusters (cf. Figure 8 in Appendix.) We list the top 10 contracts with the most duplicates in Table 2. It shows that the top 10 clusters represent the majority of the user-created contracts (62.37%) and the contract-created contracts (82.26%).

After further investigation, we found that most of the user-created contracts belonged to `transfer wallets`. The transfer wallet can be used in different ways, e.g., avoiding regulation by initiating multiple and multilevel small transfers, which splits a large balance from one account to several seemingly irrelevant accounts. Some contracts are regarded as `forwarders` (the contract name), which are not wallets but might be functionally similar to those transfer wallets in some way, such as transferring ETHs or tokens. Note that there are forwarders in contract-created contracts as well. Besides, some of the other duplicated contracts are controlled by exchanges, e.g., Poloniex [24], to manage issued tokens, such as Golem [44] and Storj [41].

As for the contract-created contracts, some clusters are owned by the Bittrex exchange [23]. More interestingly, the second largest cluster is a token issued by Gastoken [43], which allows users to make profits by tokenizing gas based on the refund mechanism on storage in Ethereum. We also found lots of `Proxy` contracts, which were used to redirect all incoming message calls to other deployed contracts. In addition, many contracts belong to ENS [19] (Ethereum Name Service), a naming system based on the Ethereum Blockchain. Finally, there are two interesting groups related to CryptoMidwives [4], which are a kind of contracts aiming to get profit from 'CryptoServices' (i.e., CryptoKitties-like games).

4.3 Similarity Comparison

For all the original 10 million smart contracts, it would be unfeasible for us to perform pair-wise comparison. Taking advantage of our pruning strategies, we are able to narrow down the contract pairs by almost four orders of magnitude, which greatly reduces the burden on similarity comparison.

The Distribution of Similarity Score. With our pruning strategies, over 308 million user-created contract pairs and 1.2 million contract-created pairs

Table 2. Top 10 contracts with the most number of duplicates.

User-created contracts		Contract-created contracts	
# Duplicates	Use	# Duplicates	Use
390,020	Transfer wallet	1,619,511	Bittrex wallet
306,600	Transfer wallet	1,284,440	Gastoken
125,929	Transfer wallet	776,441	Bittrex wallet
123,787	Transfer wallet	544,834	Proxy
89,134	Transfer wallet	540,094	Proxy
85,782	Transfer wallet	511,894	Forwarder
68,297	Token manager of Poloniex	420,822	ENS
59,543	Token-only forwarder	277,380	CryptoMidwives
37,628	Transfer wallet	196,260	CryptoMidwives
36,625	Token manager of Poloniex	185,889	Forwarder

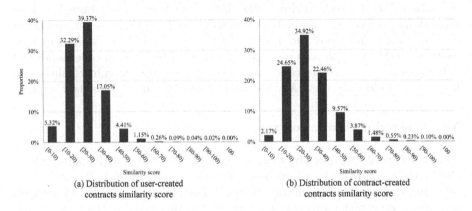

(a) Distribution of user-created
contracts similarity score

(b) Distribution of contract-created
contracts similarity score

Fig. 5. The distribution of similarity scores for smart contract pairs.

were compared, and Fig. 5 shows the distribution of similarity scores. Roughly 90% of the contract pairs have similarity scores less than 40, while only a small percentage of contract pairs have similarity scores higher than 70, among them are 0.153% of user-created contracts and 0.879% of contract-created contracts. In addition, 300 contract pairs have the highest similarity score, *i.e.*, 100.

Determining the Threshold. First, for smart contract pairs with similarity score at different ranges (e.g., [50, 60) and [60, 70)), we randomly samples 100 pairs each range (1,100 pairs in total). Note that, to better get the ground truth, we select only the smart contract pairs with source code available. The first two authors performed manually comparison of the source code to label the ground truth. In this way, we could measure the accuracy of our approach at different thresholds. It is interesting to observe that, with a threshold of 80, our approach could achieve a precision of 100%, while with only 66% of recall. With a threshold of 60, our approach could achieve a recall rate of 96%, while with only 86% of precision. As a result, we empirically found that 70 is a good indicator to achieve the balance, with 97.5% of precision and 88% of recall at this threshold. It is also the reason why we propose a prune strategy (cf. Section 3.3) to discard the different smart contract pairs. Note that, this threshold is inline with other fuzzy hashing based code clone detection studies [56,75].

In the end, 472,663 user-created contracts pairs (with 47,242 contracts involved) and 11,161 contract-created contracts pairs (with 2,409 contracts involved) were considered to be similar.

5   Qualitative Analysis

Our previous observations suggest that over 96.07% of user-created contracts and 99.97% of contract-created contracts have duplicates, and a large number of contract pairs were similar. In this section, we delve deeper into qualitative evaluation. We first seek to cluster the distinct contracts into groups based on their similarity scores, for which we try to understand the reasons leading to contract clones and study the diversity of the ecosystem (*e.g.*, what are these contracts?). Then we propose to explore the correlation between code clones and vulnerabilities, *i.e.*, whether code clones lead to the spread of vulnerabilities. At last, we try to identify the DApp Clones in the wild and measure their impact.

5.1   Clustering Smart Contracts

The Clustering Approach. Here, we use a simple but effective approach to cluster these contracts based on their similarity scores. Specifically, we cluster any contract pair whose similarity score is 70 or higher. Therefore, we are able to build a `weighted undirected graph` by treating each contract as a node. There will be an edge between two nodes if their similarity score (*i.e.*, weight) is larger than or equal to 70. Then, we traverse the graph and consider each `connected component` as a cluster. To sum up, only unique contracts are used to construct the graph, and only contracts with edges whose weights are higher than 70 can be regarded as a connected component to form a cluster.

Clustering Result. We apply the clustering approach on user-created contracts and contract-created contracts, respectively. The results are presented in Fig. 6, which follows a long-tail distribution. For user-created contracts, over 63.29% of them were clustered into 9,971 clusters, with 27,405 isolated nodes. For contract-created contracts, 60.77% of them were clustered into 2,409 clusters.

We further investigate whether these clusters follow the `Pareto principle` (*i.e.*, the 80/20 rule). The results suggest that the distribution of clusters follows a typical `Pareto Effect` after cluster size based normalization, as shown in Fig. 7. For the distinct contracts, the top 20% of the clusters account for 60% of the contracts. With regards to all the contracts, including all the duplicates, the top 1% of the clusters account for over 95% of the contracts (95.24% and 95.30% for the user-created and contract-created contracts, respectively).

What are These Smart Contract Clusters? Table 3 lists the top 10 clusters for user-created contracts and contract-created contracts. We manually went

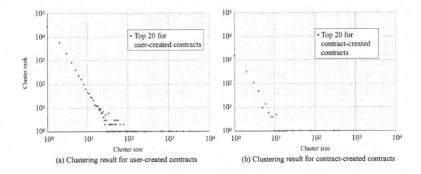

(a) Clustering result for user-created contracts   (b) Clustering result for contract-created contracts

Fig. 6. The distribution of clusters.

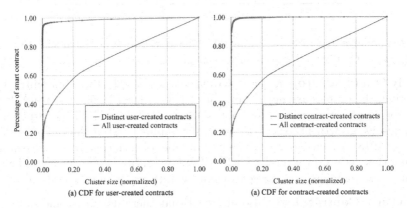

(a) CDF for user-created contracts   (a) CDF for contract-created contracts

Fig. 7. CDF of smart contracts according to cluster sizes.

through these clusters and labelled them according to their functionalities. Each type of contracts has its own characteristic functions, *e.g.*, refund and deposit, airdrop and distribution, transfer and so on. Our exploration suggests that the largest clusters mainly fall into the following categories:

(1) ERC-20 Clusters. ERC-20 related contracts take the majority of popular clusters. We successfully identified a number of ERC-20 clusters, which might derive from different solc versions, as new versions of solc may bring in new opcodes; or more importantly, from different ERC-20 templates, as a result of different implementations of revisions of ERC-20 standard (*e.g.*, OpenZeppelin [42] libraries). By manually analyzing the top 100 clusters, we have compiled a list of 53 different templates that were widely used in smart contracts. Note that the similar contracts created by these templates were not necessarily plagiarized.

(2) Game Contracts. Many popular clusters are game contracts. The largest game cluster is `Fomo3D-like contracts`. Due to the popularity of Fomo3D, numerous developers just copied and pasted the original open-source contracts to

Table 3. Top 10 clusters for both user-created and contract-created contracts.

User-created contracts		Contract-created contracts	
Size (with dup)	Usage	Size (with dup)	Usage
3,338 (15,713)	ERC-20 token	382 (1,799)	ERC-20 token
2,293 (19,263)	ERC-20 token	295 (1,983)	ERC-20 token
1,596 (11,737)	ERC-20 token	76 (1,210)	ERC-20 token
1,155 (6,174)	ERC-20 token	43 (209)	ICO
1,022 (6,466)	ERC-20 token	28 (223)	ICO
724 (4,494)	ERC-20 token	20 (571)	Airdrop Exploit
662 (2,418)	ERC-20 token	18 (39)	ERC-20 token
343 (1,054)	Other contract	16 (30)	ITO
278 (972)	ERC-20 Token	15 (922)	Airdrop Exploit
253 (509)	Fomo3D-like game	13 (20)	Exchange wallet

create similar games. Besides Fomo3D, other popular games such as `PoWH3D` [12] and `CryptoKitties` [3], have contract clones as well.

(3) ICO and Airdrop Exploit Contracts. ICO [29] stands for Initial Coin Offering, the cryptocurrency equivalent of IPO (Initial Public Offering). It is a way for crypto startups to raise money by selling tokens. ICO has experienced an explosive growth since 2017 [32] (and the bubble burst at the end of the third quarter 2018), which explains why a vast number of such contracts were deployed during this period. In terms of Airdrop Exploit contracts [18], attackers have to create large numbers of these contracts to win the 'race of exploitation'.

(4) Other Contracts. We also observed that there do exist some short contracts with extremely simple operations, *e.g.*, a pair of getter and setter, fetching data from storage, *etc.*. Such contracts were grouped into clusters as well.

> *Observation-1: Although millions of contracts were deployed on Ethereum, most of them were duplicates and share same/similar code and functionalities, which suggested the homogeneous nature of the ecosystem.*

5.2 Vulnerability Provenance

We then seek to explore the correlation between code clones and security vulnerabilities in two ways. First, we want to measure the vulnerability introduced by duplicate contracts, *i.e.*, the original contracts are suffering from vulnerabilities, and other duplicate contracts (with same hash values) would inherit the vulnerabilities. Then, for the distinct contracts that were very similar, we seek to measure whether they have the same vulnerabilities introduced by code clones.

Vulnerability Detection. To identify security vulnerabilities, we take advantage of a state-of-the-art tool [37] developed by PeckShield. It is a bytecode level static analysis framework composed of multiple program analysis techniques, including control flow analysis, data flow analysis and symbolic execution. We focus on 7 types of vulnerabilities that might cause damages with real impact,

Table 4. Distribution of vulnerability similarity across similar contract pairs.

	Same Vul behaviors		Different Vul Behaviors		
	Neither is vulnerable	Both are vulnerable	One is vulnerable	Both are vul & overlapped	Both are vul & not overlapped
Same author	26,570	3,813	6,368	1,678	247
Different author	180,101	42,368	143,146	58,338	10,034
Total	206,671	46,181	149,514	60,016	10,281

including (1) reentrancy, (2) overflow, (3) cross-function race condition, (4) mismatched constructor, (5) ownership takeover, (6) manipulable suicide address and (7) ERC-20 related vulnerabilities. As it is not the emphasis of this paper, we will use the results directly without giving technical details of the tool.

Vulnerable Duplicate Smart Contracts. We have scanned all the distinct contracts, including 74, 647 user-created and 3, 964 contract-created contracts. It is interesting to see that, although only 25 K distinct user-created contracts were vulnerable, considering all the duplicate contracts, we have identified over 1.2 million vulnerable contracts. As for the contract-created contracts, the result is more striking. Only 51 unique contract-created contracts were vulnerable, but we have identified over 2.2 million vulnerable contracts when we consider all the duplicates. This result suggests that a large number of duplicate contracts would suffer from the vulnerability issues inherited from the original contracts.

Copy-Paste Vulnerabilities. Then, we try to measure the copy-paste vulnerabilities from those similar contract pairs (with different hash values). For the 472 K similar pairs we identified (with scores over 70), we measure the similarity in vulnerabilities between them, *i.e.*, whether they share the same types of vulnerabilities and the same number of vulnerabilities. *For contracts that share both the same types and same number of vulnerabilities, we will mark them as having exactly the same vulnerability behaviors.* Note that, we further differentiate the authors of the contracts to determine whether the contract pairs are code clones between different authors or the re-deployment from the same author. As shown in Table 4, we have classified the results into two general categories.

Same Vulnerability Behaviors. Over 53% of similar contract pairs have the same vulnerability behaviors. Over 46 K contract pairs share the same vulnerabilities, and over 90% of them were created by different authors. This indicates that when someone copied the code, he/she did not know that the original contracts were vulnerable, and thus inherited the same vulnerabilities.

Different Vulnerability Behaviors. Over 46% of the similar contract pairs have different vulnerability behaviors. For over 149 K contract pairs where only one contract is vulnerable, roughly 96% of them were created by different authors. It indicates that when the authors copy and paste the code, they may have identified the vulnerabilities and thus patched them. Another scenario to explain this is that their modification of the original contracts may introduce new security vulnerabilities. Besides, over 12% of the similar contract pairs were found sharing vulnerabilities, which could also be introduced by code reuse.

Case Study. Here, we use the Fomo3D-like game contracts as a case study. We have identified 253 distinct contracts belonging to this cluster. As the original Fomo3d game suffers from the "Airdrop Vulnerability [1]", over 80% (213 out of 253) of its contract clones also share the same vulnerability.

> *Observation-2: Copy-paste vulnerabilities were prevalent in the smart contract ecosystem, duplicate contracts and similar contract would inherit security issues from the original vulnerable ones.*

5.3   Clone Detection of DApps

As Ethereum DApps are usually open-source, the plagiaristic behaviors could also be widespread. Different from the normal smart contracts, a DApp may consist of one or more smart contracts. To measure the extent of similarity between DApps, we proposed an advanced similarity detection method.

Definition. Here, we use the term *DApp Clones* to describe the scenario where two DApps deployed by different authors share the similar core functionalities. We use the accounts to differentiate the authorship. As a large number of smart contracts were created on top of templates, thus we will first eliminate the impact introduced by the templates based on the list we labelled in Sect. 5.1.

Approach. For a given DApp pair, we first construct a weighted bipartite graph for them, and conduct bipartite graph matching on the graph. A bipartite graph is a graph whose vertices (contracts) can be divided into two disjoint sets U and V, such that every edge connects a vertex in U to one in V, *i.e.*, U and V are independent sets. Here, we will calculate the similarity score between contracts and take the score as the weight of the corresponding edge. Specifically, we take advantage of the *Kuhn–Munkres algorithm* [30] to identify the maximum matching - a set of the most edges with the following two properties: 1) no two edges share an endpoint; 2) the weight of edges must be guaranteed to be the highest. Therefore, we are able to calculate the similarity between DApps with more than one contract. As the calculation is not commutative, *i.e.*, $Sim(DApp1, DApp2) \neq Sim(DApp2, DApp1)$, we keep the higher one as the final score.

Result. We have made our best efforts to collect 2,533 DApps from well-known DApp browsers [15–17]. We also crawled related metadata, *e.g.*, category, volume, and the deployed time. Based on the definition of DApp clones, we have successfully identified 127 DApp clone pairs with 114 distinct DApps in total. We further grouped them into 41 clusters by leveraging the approach mentioned in Sect. 5.1. The results are shown in Fig. 9 (cf. Appendices).

Impact. To measure the impact of DApp Clones, we decided to take the historical volume as the indicator to identify the potential financial losses. Even worse, the high volume often means an active market which might attract more capital inflows, thus it would cause more damage to the original authors.

In particular, we first analyzed all these 41 clusters and treated the earliest deployed DApp as the original one. Thus, we have 41 original DApps, and 73 plagiarized DApp clones in our dataset. Then we calculated the differences between the original volume and the plagiarized volumes.

The overall volume of the 41 original DApps is 304, 797.344 ETH, while the volume of the 73 DApp clones reaches 89, 565.321 ETH (more than USD 19 million on Sep 21, 2019, around 30% of the original market. The figures are diverse across the clusters by examining those clusters individually. For 18 out of the 41 clusters, the volumes of the clones are higher than those of the corresponding original DApps, with some clones attracting two to three times more volumes than the original. In Table 5 (cf. Appendices), we summarized the statistics for the top 10 clusters in Fig. 9.

> *Observation-3: DApp clones caused great financial losses to the original DApps, which exposed a contradiction between copyright protection and the open-source nature of the Ethereum ecosystem.*

6 Related Work

Characterizing the Blockchain Ecosystem. Several work have already been published to measure the Blockchain ecosystem [50,57,67,68,73]. For example, Chen *et al.* characterized money transfer, contract creation and contract invocation of Ethereum based on graph analysis [50]. Some researchers focused on financial activities, including the Ponzi scheme [51] and ICO behavior [55] These studies may have a correlation with part of our work, however, our work is the first systematic attempt to study contract clone phenomenon and its impact.

Program Analysis of the Smart contracts. Based on program analysis techniques (*e.g.*, symbolic execution and formal verification), several frameworks have been proposed to detect vulnerabilities in contracts [33,58,66,71]. Some other studies were focused on topics including reverse engineering [76], detecting gas-costly patterns [49], automatically creating exploits [62], etc. However, none of them performed a comprehensive study on the vulnerability provenance.

Code Clone Detection. Code clone detection techniques have been studied extensively for dozens of years, including text-based techniques [63,69], token-based techniques [46,47,59,64], counting-based techniques [74], and syntactic approaches [48,52,70], etc. These techniques were also widely explored in related domains, such as mobile app repackaging detection [53,54,72,75]. In this work, we take advantage of a customized fuzzy hashing technique [61], which is both light-weight and effective. A limited number of studies have explored code cloning in smart contracts. For example, Kiffer *et al.* identified substantial code reuse in Ethereum [60]. Furthermore, Liu *et al.* proposed ECLONE [65], which is able to detect semantic clones for smart contracts. However, none of them have measured the ecosystem in large-scale, and characterized their security impacts.

7   Concluding Remarks and Future Work

We present the first systematic attempt to characterize the code clone phenomenon in the Ethereum ecosystem. By analyzing the 10 million contracts, we have revealed the homogeneity nature of the ecosystem. We discovered and measured the security impacts of contract clones, e.g., helping spread the security vulnerabilities and causing financial losses to the original DApps authors, etc.

There are a number of future lines of work we will explore. First, the threshold used to identify contract clones can be improved by adopting adaptive approaches. Second, we may have coverage issues on manually labelling the contract templates, which can be alleviated by exploring some advanced techniques. Lastly, part of our findings, such as those economic intensive phenomena in the Ethereum ecosystem, deserve more focused studies. Nonetheless, we believe our efforts and observations could positively contribute to the community and promote the best operational practices for smart contract developers.

Acknowledgment. This work is supported by the National Key Research and Development Program (2017YFB1001904) and the National Natural Science Foundation of China (61702045, 61772042). Haoyu Wang and Yao Guo are co-corresponding authors.

8   Appendices

8.1   Fingerprint Generation Algorithm

The detailed fingerprint generation algorithm is shown in Algorithm 1.

Algorithm 1. Generating the fingerprint for smart contract.

Input: *bytecode* of arbitrary contract
Output: Fingerprint *fp*
Description: *pc* - character representing current piece, *ph* - the piece hash, *tv* - trigger value, *b64map* - mapping integer to base64 character

```
 1: procedure GENERATEFP(bytecode)
 2:     InitTriggerValue(tv)
 3:     InitBase64Map(b64map)
 4:     InitPieceCharacter(pc)
 5:     InitPieceHash(ph)
 6:     pieces ← CutOff(bytecode, tv)
 7:     for all piece from pieces do
 8:         UpdatePieceHash(ph, piece)
 9:         MapToPieceCharacter(pc, ph, b64map)
10:         fp ← Concatenate(fp, pc)
11:         InitPieceHash(ph)
12:     return fp
```

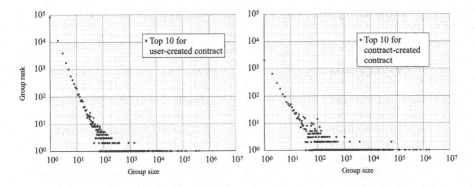

Fig. 8. The distribution of contract clusters grouped by opcode hash values.

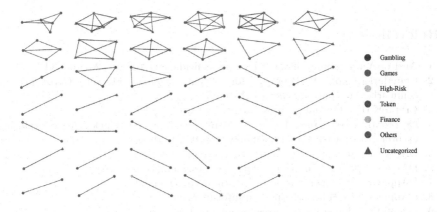

Fig. 9. Clustering results of 127 DApp clone pairs (114 unique DApps).

8.2 The Distribution of Contract Clusters Grouped by Opcode Hash Values

Figure 8 shows the distribution of contract clusters grouped by opcode hash values.

8.3 Clustering Results of the 127 Dapp Clone Pairs

Figure 9 shows the result of the clustering results of the 127 Dapp clone pairs we identified.

8.4 Top Dapp Clone Clusters and Their Volumes

Table 5 lists the statistics of the top 10 Dapp clone clusters.

Table 5. Top 10 Dapp Clone clusters and their volumes (ETH).

Original DApp	# Clones	Original volume	Plagiarized volume	Ratio
CryptoCountries [5]	4	67,885.244	2.355	<0.01%
PoWTF [13]	4	331.074	1,012.649	305.87%
Po50 [10]	4	76.801	213.058	277.42%
Pepe Farm [9]	4	25.428	33.577	132.05%
Crypto Miner [7]	4	17,312.026	155.437	0.90%
PoWH 3D [12]	4	187,950.872	1,778.146	0.95%
CryptoTubers [8]	3	95.378	470.967	493.79%
PoHD [11]	3	242.607	5,867.961	2418.71%
Proof Of Craig Grant Coin [14]	3	642.056	94.315	14.69%
Crypto Gaming Coin [6]	3	4.711	555.142	11783.95%

References

1. Airdrop Vulnerability. https://blog.peckshield.com/2018/07/24/fomo3d/
2. CoinMarketCap, a Browser for Cryptocurrency Market Cap. https://coinmarketcap.com/currencies/ethereum/
3. CryptoKitties Official Website. https://www.cryptokitties.co/
4. CryptoMidwives Introduction. https://medium.com/block-science/exploring-cryptokitties-part-2-the-cryptomidwives-a0df37eb35a6
5. DApp, Crypto Countries. https://cryptocountries.io/
6. DApp, Crypto Gaming Coin. https://cyptogamingcoin.surge.sh/
7. DApp, Crypto Miner Token. https://minertoken.cloud/
8. DApp, Crypto Tubers. https://cryptotubers.co/
9. DApp, Pepe Farm. http://www.pepefarm.club
10. DApp, Po50. http://po50.surge.sh/exchange/
11. DApp, PoHD. https://pohd.io/
12. DApp, PoWH 3D. https://powh.io/
13. DApp, PoWTF. https://powtf.com/
14. DApp, Proof Of Craig Grant Coin. http://www.pocg.site
15. DAppRadar, a DApp Browser. https://dappradar.com/
16. DAppReview, a DApp Browser. https://dapp.review/
17. DAppTotal, a DApp Browser. https://dapptotal.com/
18. Definition of Airdrop Mechanism. https://coinsutra.com/what-is-airdrop/
19. Ethereum Name Service. https://ens.domains/
20. Ethereum Virtual Machine. http://ethdocs.org/en/latest/introduction/what-is-ethereum.html#ethereum-virtual-machine
21. Ethereum Whitepaper. https://github.com/ethereum/wiki/wiki/White-Paper
22. Etherscan, a Ethereum Smart Contract Browser. https://etherscan.io/
23. Exchange, Bittrex. https://international.bittrex.com/
24. Exchange, Poloniex. https://poloniex.com/
25. Fomo3D Attack Event. https://blog.peckshield.com/2018/07/24/fomo3d/
26. Honeypot Smart Contract. https://medium.com/coinmonks/dissecting-an-ethereum-honey-pot-7102d7def5e0
27. Honeypot Smart Contract. https://medium.com/coinmonks/an-analysis-of-a-couple-ethereum-honeypot-contracts-5c07c95b0a8d

28. Honeypot Smart Contract. https://medium.com/coinmonks/the-phenomena-of-smart-contract-honeypots-755c1f943f7b
29. Initial Coin Offering. https://bitcoinmagazine.com/guides/what-ico
30. KM Algorithm. https://brilliant.org/wiki/hungarian-matching/
31. Last Winner Attack Event. https://medium.com/@anchain.ai/largest-smart-contract-attacks-in-blockchain-history-exposed-part-1-93b975a374d0
32. List of ICO Resources. http://startupmanagement.org/2017/03/13/the-ultimate-list-of-ico-resources-18-websites-that-track-initial-cryptocurrency-offerings/
33. Mythril, Smart Contract Analyzer. https://github.com/ConsenSys/mythril-classic
34. Official Explanation of DApp. https://github.com/ethereum/wiki/wiki/White-Paper#ethereum
35. Official Fomo3D Contract. https://etherscan.io/address/0xa62142888aba8370742be823c1782d17a0389da1
36. Official Fomo3D Website. https://exitscam.me/
37. PeckShield, Inc., Scanner. https://peckshield.com/securityrating/scan.html
38. Smart Contract Function Signature. https://solidity.readthedocs.io/en/v0.5.3/abi-spec.html#function-selector
39. Solidity. https://solidity.readthedocs.io/en/v0.6.0/
40. Spamsum Algorithm. https://www.samba.org/ftp/unpacked/junkcode/spamsum/README
41. Storj Token. https://storj.io/
42. Template Library, OpenZeppelin. https://github.com/OpenZeppelin/openzeppelin-solidity
43. Token, GasToken. https://gastoken.io/
44. Token, Golem. https://golem.network/
45. Wikipedia of Ethereum. https://en.wikipedia.org/wiki/Ethereum
46. Baker, B.S.: On finding duplication and near-duplication in large software systems. In: Proceedings of 2nd Working Conference on Reverse Engineering, pp. 86–95. IEEE (1995)
47. Baker, B.S.: Parameterized pattern matching: algorithms and applications. J. Comput. Syst. Sci. **52**(1), 28–42 (1996)
48. Baxter, I.D., Yahin, A., Moura, L., Sant'Anna, M., Bier, L.: Clone detection using abstract syntax trees. In: Proceedings. International Conference on Software Maintenance (Cat. No. 98CB36272), pp. 368–377. IEEE (1998)
49. Chen, T., Li, X., Luo, X., Zhang, X.: Under-optimized smart contracts devour your money. In: 2017 IEEE 24th International Conference on Software Analysis, Evolution and Reengineering (SANER), pp. 442–446. IEEE (2017)
50. Chen, T., et al.: Understanding ethereum via graph analysis. In: IEEE INFOCOM 2018-IEEE Conference on Computer Communications, pp. 1484–1492. IEEE (2018)
51. Chen, W., Zheng, Z., Cui, J., Ngai, E., Zheng, P., Zhou, Y.: Detecting ponzi schemes on ethereum: towards healthier blockchain technology. In: Proceedings of the 2018 World Wide Web Conference on World Wide Web, pp. 1409–1418. International World Wide Web Conferences Steering Committee (2018)
52. Corazza, A., Di Martino, S., Maggio, V., Scanniello, G.: A tree kernel based approach for clone detection. In: 2010 IEEE International Conference on Software Maintenance, pp. 1–5. IEEE (2010)
53. Crussell, J., Gibler, C., Chen, H.: Attack of the clones: detecting cloned applications on android markets. In: Foresti, S., Yung, M., Martinelli, F. (eds.) ESORICS 2012. LNCS, vol. 7459, pp. 37–54. Springer, Heidelberg (2012). https://doi.org/10.1007/978-3-642-33167-1_3

54. Crussell, J., Gibler, C., Chen, H.: Scalable semantics-based detection of similar android applications. In: European Symposium on Research in Computer Security (ESORICS), vol. 13 (2013)
55. Fenu, G., Marchesi, L., Marchesi, M., Tonelli, R.: The ICO phenomenon and its relationships with ethereum smart contract environment. In: 2018 International Workshop on Blockchain Oriented Software Engineering (IWBOSE), pp. 26–32. IEEE (2018)
56. Glanz, L., et al.: Codematch: obfuscation won't conceal your repackaged app. In: Proceedings of the 2017 11th Joint Meeting on Foundations of Software Engineering, pp. 638–648. ACM (2017)
57. Huang, Y., et al.: Characterizing eosio blockchain. arXiv preprint arXiv:2002.05369 (2020)
58. Kalra, S., Goel, S., Dhawan, M., Sharma, S.: Zeus: analyzing safety of smart contracts. In: 25th Annual Network and Distributed System Security Symposium, NDSS, pp. 18–21 (2018)
59. Kamiya, T., Kusumoto, S., Inoue, K.: CCFinder: a multilinguistic token-based code clone detection system for large scale source code. IEEE Trans. Softw. Eng. 28(7), 654–670 (2002)
60. Kiffer, L., Levin, D., Mislove, A.: Analyzing ethereum's contract topology. In: Proceedings of the Internet Measurement Conference 2018, pp. 494–499. ACM (2018)
61. Kornblum, J.: Identifying almost identical files using context triggered piecewise hashing. Digital Invest. 3, 91–97 (2006)
62. Krupp, J., Rossow, C.: teether: Gnawing at ethereum to automatically exploit smart contracts. In: 27th USENIX Security Symposium (USENIX Security 18), pp. 1317–1333 (2018)
63. Lee, S., Jeong, I.: SDD: high performance code clone detection system for large scale source code. In: Companion to the 20th annual ACM SIGPLAN Conference on Object-Oriented Programming, Systems, Languages, and Applications, pp. 140–141. ACM (2005)
64. Li, Z., Lu, S., Myagmar, S., Zhou, Y.: CP-miner: finding copy-paste and related bugs in large-scale software code. IEEE Trans. Softw. Eng. 32(3), 176–192 (2006)
65. Liu, H., Yang, Z., Liu, C., Jiang, Y., Zhao, W., Sun, J.: Eclone: detect semantic clones in ethereum via symbolic transaction sketch. In: Proceedings of the 2018 26th ACM Joint Meeting on European Software Engineering Conference and Symposium on the Foundations of Software Engineering, pp. 900–903. ACM (2018)
66. Luu, L., Chu, D.H., Olickel, H., Saxena, P., Hobor, A.: Making smart contracts smarter. In: Proceedings of the 2016 ACM SIGSAC Conference on Computer and Communications Security, pp. 254–269. ACM (2016)
67. Norvill, R., Pontiveros, B.B.F., State, R., Awan, I., Cullen, A.: Automated labeling of unknown contracts in ethereum. In: 2017 26th International Conference on Computer Communication and Networks (ICCCN). pp. 1–6. IEEE (2017)
68. Payette, J., Schwager, S., Murphy, J.: Characterizing the ethereum address space (2017)
69. Roy, C.K., Cordy, J.R.: NICAD: Accurate detection of near-miss intentional clones using flexible pretty-printing and code normalization. In: 2008 16th IEEE International Conference on Program Comprehension, pp. 172–181. IEEE (2008)
70. Selim, G.M., Foo, K.C., Zou, Y.: Enhancing source-based clone detection using intermediate representation. In: 2010 17th Working Conference on Reverse Engineering, pp. 227–236. IEEE (2010)

71. Tsankov, P., Dan, A., Drachsler-Cohen, D., Gervais, A., Buenzli, F., Vechev, M.: Securify: practical security analysis of smart contracts. In: Proceedings of the 2018 ACM SIGSAC Conference on Computer and Communications Security, pp. 67–82. ACM (2018)

72. Wang, H., Guo, Y., Ma, Z., Chen, X.: Wukong: a scalable and accurate two-phase approach to android app clone detection. In: Proceedings of the 2015 International Symposium on Software Testing and Analysis, pp. 71–82. ACM (2015)

73. Xia, P., et al.: Characterizing cryptocurrency exchange scams. arXiv preprint arXiv:2003.07314 (2020)

74. Yuan, Y., Guo, Y.: Boreas: an accurate and scalable token-based approach to code clone detection. In: Proceedings of the 27th IEEE/ACM International Conference on Automated Software Engineering, pp. 286–289. ACM (2012)

75. Zhou, W., Zhou, Y., Jiang, X., Ning, P.: Detecting repackaged smartphone applications in third-party android marketplaces. In: Proceedings of the Second ACM Conference on Data and Application Security and Privacy, pp. 317–326. ACM (2012)

76. Zhou, Y., Kumar, D., Bakshi, S., Mason, J., Miller, A., Bailey, M.: Erays: reverse engineering ethereum's opaque smart contracts. In: 27th USENIX Security Symposium (USENIX Security 18), pp. 1371–1385 (2018)

Smart Contracts for Government Processes: Case Study and Prototype Implementation (Short Paper)

Magnus Krogsbøll[1], Liv Hartoft Borre[1], Tijs Slaats[2], and Søren Debois[1(✉)]

[1] IT University of Copenhagen, Copenhagen, Denmark
{magkr,livb,debois}@itu.dk
[2] University of Copenhagen, Copenhagen, Denmark
slaats@di.ku.dk

Abstract. We study blockchain-based integrity-protected smart contracts as an implementation mechanism for municipal government processes. To this end, we attempted a prototype implementation of such a process in collaboration with a Danish Municipality. We find that such an implementation is possible, despite the obvious confidentiality requirements, and that it does provide benefits: integrity guarantees, verifiability, direct collaboration and payments between the parties. These benefits come at the cost of latency, pr. transactions charges, immutability of errors, and a very concerning single point of failure the municipal government: losing blockchain private keys means losing control over municipal government casework, *with no recourse*. Our municipal government partner felt that altogether no immediately pressing problem was solved by the implementation, and that the latter risk clearly outweighed any benefits. We note that smart contract implementations of government processes needs to be immutable and outside of the government's control when running; however, they also need to be updatable when laws change, and provide an "out" for the rare case when errors in the contract implementation result in unlawful behaviour. We propose these conflicting requirements as a foundational research challenge for blockchain to be applicable to governmental processes.

Keywords: Applications of blockchain · Electronic government · Smart contracts · Ethereum · Governmental processes

1 Introduction

Municipal governments in modern democracies exercise *power* over their citizens: they decide who is or is not entitled to receive welfare benefits; which sports clubs receive financial support, which parents are unfit for their role. This power is checked by national or federal laws defining exactly how these decisions are made, and appeals institutions providing redress to citizens who can prove that these laws were violated. Even so, for society to function, the public must *trust* that

J. Bonneau and N. Heninger (Eds.): FC 2020, LNCS 12059, pp. 676–684, 2020.
https://doi.org/10.1007/978-3-030-51280-4_36

municipal governments mostly do right; that decisions are fair and in accordance with law; that appeals are mostly unnecessary, and that the successful appeal is the rare exception.

In this paper, we investigate to what extent we can supplant trust in municipal government with the integrity guarantees provided by smart contracts [3,18] running on a blockchain [14,17]. We do so by experiment: In collaboration with the Danish Syddjurs Municipality, we have constructed a prototype implementation of a specific social benefits process as an Ethereum smart contract. The implementation is available online [2].

The process is defined by §42 in the Danish Law on Social Service [7], which describes the circumstances under which parents are entitled to compensation for earnings lost due to the caring for a child with a long-term illness. The implementation revolves around an Ethereum smart contract which serves as an intermediary between the citizen, the municipal government caseworker, and the Appeals Board. This contract encodes (to an extent) the law: the caseworker records in the contract that necessary steps, like procuring documentation or conducting public hearings, has been taken; the contract does not allow decisions until all such steps require by law have been concluded.

We conducted this case study in collaboration with the Danish Syddjurs Municipality, who assisted us in both understanding the §42 process and in evaluating the eventual prototype.

Our key findings are that it *is* possible to replace part of the trust in municipal government with a smart contract while preserving the necessary confidentiality requirements. Doing so provides transparency to both the citizen, incontrovertible history for the appeals institution, and reduces the possibility for procedural errors by the municipal government, such as deciding upon a case without having procured all law-mandated documentation. It allows for streamlining of the process through semi-automated intervention by an appeals institution, and potentially removes the possibility for the municipality to ignore a reversal on appeal (which would otherwise have to be remedied in court).

Syddjurs Municipality expressed severe concerns that (a) the additional integrity guarantees provide no real-world benefit; (b) it remains unresolved who defines the smart contract and how it will be updated when the law changes; and, most severely, (c) the contract introduces a single-point of failure: should the municipal government leak the keys to the smart contract, they will have lost control of their processes (and payouts) *with no possible recourse*. We conclude that addressing this dichotomy between on the one hand providing trustworthy immutable contracts, on the other requiring the ability to support (1) constantly changing laws and (2) the reversal of outlier cases which were handled in an unlawful manner is a significant research challenge for blockchain to be applicable to governmental processes.

Related Work. Ours is not the first to study applications of blockchain technology to governmental processes. Most notably, [23] considers such applications in the abstract, proposing a number of possible applications and their trade-offs. However, that paper does not consider the question of who controls the eventual update of smart contracts and treats the subject purely in theory, whereas in the current paper we take an experimental approach. In [5] a case study of applying blockchain technologies to governmental processes is presented. Along similar lines, [6] provides an overview of a large set of ongoing governmental projects that include the application of blockchain technologies. This paper provides an analysis and discussion of the potential consequences of such projects for society at large. The paper [15] provides a brief overview of existing academic literature related to blockchain technologies and discusses potential applications in e-government, going in more detail on one proposed case study. Unlike the current paper, this study is however hypothetical, with no actual implementation to underpin it. For process management in general, opportunities and challenges for blockchain was discussed in [12], and implementation of generic "process engines" on Ethereum is well-studied [4, 8, 9].

Process. Our explorative case study proceeded as follows. Staff from the Syddjurs Municipality Digitalisation Office proposed the §42 process to us; then kindly provided both a presentation of their §42 workflows, an interview, and subsequent e-mail clarifications. Based on this information, we independently designed and implemented a smart-contract–based prototype system supporting this workflow. Finally, we evaluated this prototype jointly with Syddjurs Municipality Digitalisation Office staff and management. The present paper mirrors this structure: we first present the §42 process (Sect. 2); then present the prototype design and implementation (Sect. 3); and finally present findings based on the joint evaluation (Sect. 4).

2   The §42 Process

The process implemented in our experiment is defined in §42 of the Social Services Act [7], which describes how parents of children with disabilities or long-term illness may, under certain conditions, be compensated by the municipality for their loss of earnings due to the necessity of caring for the child at home. Citizens may appeal decisions, in which case the process includes the Appeals Board, a Danish public institution that may overrule municipal governments.

A recent study by the Appeals Board [1] found across-the-board issues in municipalities' execution of these processes, especially (1) failure to obtain sufficient information for lawful processing of a case, and (2) failure to sufficiently justify decisions. Note that while a smart contract may alleviate (1)—by requiring that documents are uploaded before a decision is made—it seems unlikely that (2) can be detected by automated methods, as we cannot (yet) automatically decide if the *contents* of those documents warrants a particular decision.

The process proceeds through 3 phases depicted in Fig. 1; *decisions* are made along the way, and the process terminates on unfavourable decisions.

In **Phase 1** (Fig. 2), the municipal government calls the parents for a guidance meeting. The caseworker may at this point decide that the parents' situation is out of scope for §42. Otherwise, the caseworker collects documentation to

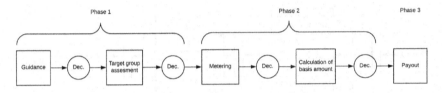

Fig. 1. The full §42 process

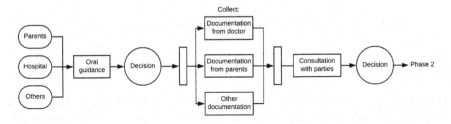

Fig. 2. Phase 1 of the §42 process

establish that care at home is (a) necessary and (b) most expedient. Again, the caseworker may at this point decide that (a) and (b) are not the case, and the parents not eligible. In **Phase 2**, the caseworker collects additional documentation to calculate lost earnings, and any possible offsetting absent of expenses (e.g., gasoline not used when not driving to work). In **Phase 3**, decisions are made regards to payouts. Each month the parents document their lost earnings, and the caseworker then issues a payout. Every six months the municipality must review the case from (repeat Phase 1), and every year the government updates their rate and the compensation has to be recalculated from Phase 2.

The citizen may appeal any decisions made (Fig. 3). The appealed decision is then either ratifies or amended by the caseworker. A ratified decision is immediately forwarded to the appeals board, which eventually either ratifies, changes, disbands, or returns the decision; in the latter case requiring the municipal government to re-process the case from the *previous* decision onwards.

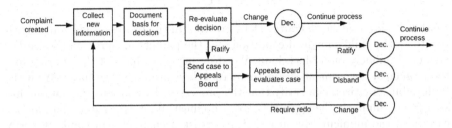

Fig. 3. The appeal process

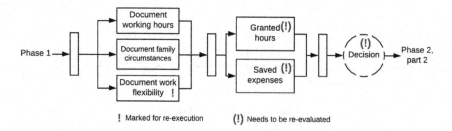

Fig. 4. Illustration of the Appeals Board marking a data in the process

3   Prototype

The prototype system comprises a smart contract (enforcing the process), web-interfaces for each of the actors (citizen, municipal caseworker, appeals board), and a local database each for the municipality and the appeals board.

Each task in the is classified as either a decision; the acquisition or processing of data in the form of documents or numbers (say, a number of hours or the claimed amount); or payments. The smart contract accordingly implements a simple process engine along the lines of [8,9]. The process itself is specified as a dependency graph over tasks; a task is only available for execution if all of its dependencies have been executed. A task can be marked as requiring re-execution (used in appeals, see below). The process model assigns roles to tasks (citizen, municipal caseworker, or appeals board), and implements role-based access control via Ethereum addresses.

An appeal of a decision interrupts the process and forces the municipality to review the case by marking the tasks after the previous decision as requiring re-execution. If the municipality changes its decision, the case continues (although the citizen may again appeal the changed decision). If the decision is re-executed with the same data (the same decision), the appeal and case is sent to the Appeals Board. Via the smart contract, the Appeals Board manifests its decision by marking tasks for re-execution, thereby forcing the municipality to re-evaluate the case; or by setting the process state outright, thereby overruling the decision. We illustrate the process state after an appeals decision in Fig. 4.

Confidentiality and Verifiability. Data involved in the process is generally sensitive (e.g., the child's medical condition and the parents income), and so cannot be stored publicly on a blockchain. We store instead a hash of the information; the municipal government stores the actual data in a local database. With the hash public, a citizen can verify that the process really contains the data he has submitted. Similarly the appeals board, who must receive the actual data for the case from the municipality on a distinct, trusted channel, can similarly verify that the municipal government is forwarding the correct data.

In contrast to, e.g., [22], we do not decentralise *storage* of data: The municipal government and possibly the Appeals Board both retain—and have responsibil-

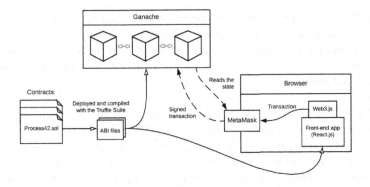

Fig. 5. Overview of communication with a local blockchain

ity for—full local copies of the data involved in the case. The privacy of the citizen towards the municipal government is not an issue here: he has none[1].

Implementation. The system (Fig. 5) comprises *front-end* "React" webapps [16] for the citizen and the municipal caseworker, back-end smart contracts on the blockchain, and a local database for the municipal government. Each of actor (citizen, municipal caseworker, appeals board) interacts with the system through a web interface resembling contemporary case management systems in use at Syddjurs such as Acadre or the Open Case Manager. The *backend* consists of Ethereum contracts written in Solidity 0.5.0, deployed with Truffle [19]. The front-end application React [16] webapps uses the MetaMask [13] library to communicate with the blockchain. The prototype was deployed only on a local test chain. We expect deployment on the "real" Ethereum blockchain to be straightforward, even under the concomitant increased latency and cost.

4 Findings

So what have we learned from our implementation of the §42 process? First of all: *it is possible.* It was, at the outset, not obvious that confidentiality requirements could be met, nor that the complex mechanics of appeals and process rollbacks could be (easily) implemented; nor was it obvious that the formalisation of process execution rules in a smart contract would be helpful.

Pros. The implementation realises both the main envisioned benefits of (1) process transparency and verifiability by citizens and Appeals Board alike; and (2) that process execution is guaranteed to follows the steps set out in the law. This key benefit was identified both by our municipal government partner and, implicitly, by the Appeals Board [1]. Moreover, (3) the implementation allows the

---

[1] It is an interesting question whether government institutions ought to process cases *anonymously,* and how that might be arranged. We leave this for future work.

Appeals Board to impose directions directly on the process rather than relying on a possibly intransigent municipal government to act against its own convictions. Finally, (4) assuming a generally accepted blockchain based currency accessible to the smart contract, direct payout from the contract may significantly decrease the municipal governments banking costs.

Cons. In societies like the Scandinavian countries, where government motivation (but perhaps not ability) is generally trusted by the public, correct process execution (2) could just as well be enforced by an ordinary (non-blockchain) computer system, operated by some central government authority.

Moreover, several additional concerns are apparent or were raised by our municipal government partner in the final evaluation. (A) On the blockchain, immutability cuts both ways [10,11]: once deployed, there is no mechanism for the municipal government to alter or fix a smart contract; and there is similarly no mechanism for the municipal government to fix its own (non-decision) processual mistakes. This point is especially acute if the contract has access to municipal government funds, and may disburse these independently. Moreover, (B) transaction latency and (C) transaction cost remain considerable concerns [21].

It is the estimation of our municipal government partner that because there is public trust in government institutions, (2) does not apply, and it is sufficient to implement better traditional IT systems; that savings from on-chain payouts are not realisable in the foreseeable future (4); and that latency costs (B) and transaction costs (C) already outweigh the remaining benefits of verifiability (1) and direct Appeals Board interventions (3).

Moreover, the loss of control of the parts of the process *for which it has responsibility* implicit in (A) is completely unacceptable. While concerns regarding latency and transaction costs can be addressed by permissioned blockchains [20], such blockchains also place control of the processes firmly back in the governments hands, obviating any reduction in trust. In addition, challenges regarding the updateability of running processes would remain. These challenges are general to the application of blockchain technologies in government: government institutions are in general responsible for both administering particular laws, and organising transitions when the law changes.

Thus we conclude this paper with a challenge to the community: It seems smart contract implementations of government processes needs on the one hand to be immutable and outside the governments control when running; however, they also need to be updatable when laws change, and have an "out" for the rare case when errors in the contract implementation result in unlawful behaviour. We propose these conflicting requirements as a foundational research challenge for blockchain to be applicable to governmental processes.

Acknowledgments. We are indebted to Syddjurs Municipality, Denmark, for volunteering time and information without which this paper would not be. We are particularly grateful to Nicklas Pape Healy and Sofie Lykke Sørensen.

Work supported by the Innovation Fund Denmark project *EcoKnow* (7050-00034A). We gratefully acknowledge Syddjurs Municipality for their contributions to the case study and insightful comments.

References

1. Ankestyrelsens praksisundersøgelse om tabt arbejdsfortjeneste efter servicelovens §42. Investigation 978–87-7811-322-0, Ankestyrelsen, June 2017
2. Borre, L.H., Krogsbøll, M.: Prototype implementation. https://github.com/ magkr/Smart-Contracts-for-Government-Processes-Implementation
3. Buterin, V., et al.: A next-generation smart contract and decentralized application platform. White paper (2014)
4. García-Bañuelos, L., Ponomarev, A., Dumas, M., Weber, I.: Optimized execution of business processes on blockchain. In: Carmona, J., Engels, G., Kumar, A. (eds.) BPM 2017. LNCS, vol. 10445, pp. 130–146. Springer, Cham (2017). https://doi. org/10.1007/978-3-319-65000-5_8
5. Hou, H.: The application of blockchain technology in e-government in China. In: ICCCN 2017, pp. 1–4, July 2017
6. Jun, M.S.: Blockchain government - a next form of infrastructure for the twenty-first century. J. Open Innov. Technol. Market Complex. 4(1), 1–12 (2018). https:// doi.org/10.1186/s40852-018-0086-3
7. Bekendtgørelse af lov om social service, Børne- og Socialministeriet, August 2017
8. López-Pintado, O., García-Bañuelos, L., Dumas, M., Weber, I.: Caterpillar: a blockchain-based business process management system. In: BPM Demo Track and BPM Dissertation Award (BPM 2017), 13 September 2017 (2017)
9. Madsen, M.F., Gaub, M., Høgnason, T., Kirkbro, M.E., Slaats, T., Debois, S.: Collaboration among adversaries: distributed workflow execution on a blockchain. In: 2018 Symposium on Foundations and Applications of Blockchain (2018)
10. Mavridou, A., Laszka, A.: Designing secure ethereum smart contracts: A finite state machine based approach. arXiv preprint arXiv:1711.09327 (2017)
11. Mavridou, A., Laszka, A., Stachtiari, E., Dubey, A.: Verisolid: Correct-by-design smart contracts for ethereum. arXiv preprint arXiv:1901.01292 (2019)
12. Mendling, J., Weber, I., Aalst, W.V.D., et al.: Blockchains for business process management challenges and opportunities. ACM Trans. Manage. Inf. Syst. 9, 4:1–4:16 (2018)
13. MetaMask. https://metamask.io/
14. Nakamoto, S., et al.: Bitcoin: A peer-to-peer electronic cash system (2008)
15. Ølnes, S.: Beyond Bitcoin enabling smart government using blockchain technology. In: Scholl, H.J., et al. (eds.) EGOVIS 2016. LNCS, vol. 9820, pp. 253–264. Springer, Cham (2016). https://doi.org/10.1007/978-3-319-44421-5_20
16. React - A JavaScript library for building user interfaces. https://reactjs.org/index. html
17. Swan, M.: Blockchain: Blueprint for a New Economy. O'Reilly Media Inc., Newton (2015)
18. Szabo, N.: Formalizing and securing relationships on public networks. First Monday 2(9) (1997)

19. Truffle Suite—Sweet Tools for Smart Contracts. https://truffleframework.com/
20. Wüst, K., Gervais, A.: Do you need a blockchain? In: 2018 Crypto Valley Conference on Blockchain Technology (CVCBT), pp. 45–54. IEEE (2018)
21. Wüst, K., Kostiainen, K., Capkun, V., Capkun, S.: Prcash: fast, private and regulated transactions for digital currencies. In: International Conference on Financial Cryptography and Data Security (2019)
22. Zyskind, G., Nathan, O., et al.: Decentralizing privacy: using blockchain to protect personal data. In: Security and Privacy Workshops, pp. 180–184. IEEE (2015)
23. Ølnes, S., Ubacht, J., Janssen, M.: Blockchain in government: benefits and implications of distributed ledger technology for information sharing. Gov. Inf. Q. **34**(3), 355–364 (2017)

Author Index

Printed in the United States
By Bookmasters